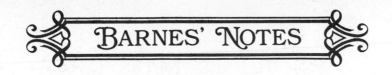

Notes on the New Testament

Albert Barnes

Edited by

Robert Frew

HEBREWS

BAKER BOOK HOUSE

Grand Rapids, Michigan 49506

BARNES' NOTES

Heritage Edition Fourteen Volumes 0834-4

When ordering by ISBN (International Standard Book Number), numbers listed above should be preceded by 0-8010-.

Reprinted from the 1884-85 edition published by Blackie & Son,
London, edited by Robert Frew

ISBN: 0-8010-0848-4

Printed and bound in the United States of America

PUBLISHERS' PREFACE

THE Epistle to the Hebrews forms a most important part of the New Testament. It exhibits the connection between the Old and New Dispensations of Religion, throws a flood of light on the Old Testament Scripture, and illustrates the Harmony of the Scheme of Redemption, in the midst of changing ages and economies. It contains the most sublime descriptions of the dignity and glory of Christ's person, the excellence of his sacrifice, and the superiority of his gospel; intermingled with hortatory matter, wherever the grand argument can admit of a pause, full of solemnity and pathos.

The Author's Commentary will be regarded by many as even superior, either to that on Romans or Corinthians. Indeed, it may be fairly questioned if there be any English Commentary on the Hebrews which combines, to so great an extent, the advantages both of a critical and practical exposition. Two classes of readers, therefore, seldom both pleased with the same work, will, it is believed, here find equal satisfaction. The critic may have his difficulties resolved, and the Christian his heart improved. In the "Introduction," various important questions, which have long interested the learned, but which in many commentaries are either passed in silence, or dismissed with a word, are here ably handled, if not in every case satisfactorily solved. The points alluded to are those regarding the Pauline origin of the Epistle, the parties to whom it was addressed, the language in which it was written, with its date, occasion, scope, and character. At the same time the critical and doctrinal difficulties throughout the Epistle are fairly met, and treated with ability, scholarship, and candour. In this department of his labours, the Author is fully up to the modern mark, and never leaves the reader to complain that a judgment has been formed in ignorance of what the more recent authorities have alleged, while his independence is everywhere manifest. His criticisms and doctrinal discussions are frequently relieved by the most beautiful and pertinent illustrations. The poets furnish him with apposite quotations. The beauties of Spenser and Shakspere occasionally adorn his pages. It would be difficult to find a more beautiful exposition than that on angelic ministry, at chap. i. 14, or that on sympathy with the slave, chap. xiii. 3. On this last subject, the Author scorns to maintain a prudential yet criminal silence, and far as his voice goes—and that is throughout America—vindicates the cause of the oppressed.

The peculiarity of this Edition lies in the careful revision to which the text of the Author has been subjected, and the addition, as in the Volumes already published, of supplementary Notes in smaller type, wherever such were deemed necessary. In a few instances where the importance of the subject demanded it, these have extended to considerable length, and will, it is hoped, enhance the value of the work among Scotch Theologians. The Publishers, therefore, send out this Edition of Barnes' Notes on the Hebrews, in the confident expectation that it will prove extremely useful and popular.

INTRODUCTION

§ 1. *Preliminary Remarks.*

I⊤ need not be said that this epistle has given rise to much discussion among writers on the New Testament. Indeed there is probably no part of the Bible in regard to which so many conflicting views have been entertained. The name of the author ; the time and place where the epistle was written ; the character of the book ; its canonical authority ; the language in which it was composed ; and the persons to whom it was addressed, all have given rise to great difference of opinion. Among the causes of this are the following :—The name of the author is not mentioned. The church to which it was sent, if sent to any particular church, is not designated. There are no certain marks of time in the epistle, as there often are in the writings of Paul, by which we can determine the time when it was written.

It is not the design of these Notes to go into an extended examination of these questions. Those who are disposed to pursue these inquiries, and to examine the questions which have been started in regard to the epistle, can find ample means in the larger works that have treated of it ; and especially in Lardner ; in Michaelis' Introduction ; in the Prolegomena of Kuinoel ; in Hug's Introduction ; and PARTICULARLY in Professor Stuart's invaluable Commentary on the Epistle to the Hebrews. No other work on this portion of the New Testament is so complete as his, and in the Introduction he has left nothing to be desired in regard to the literature of the Epistle.

Controversies early arose in the church in regard to a great variety of questions pertaining to this epistle, which are not yet fully settled. Most of those questions, however, pertain to the *literature* of the epistle, and however they may be decided, are not such as to affect the respect which a Christian ought to have for it as a part of the word of God. They pertain to the inquiries, to whom it was written ; in what language, and at what time it was composed ; questions which in whatever way they may be settled, do not affect its canonical authority, and should not shake the confidence of Christians in it as a part of divine revelation. The only inquiry on these points which it is proper to institute in these Notes is, whether the claims of the epistle to a place in the canon of Scripture are of such a kind as to allow Christians to read it as a part of the oracles of God ? May we sit down to it feeling that we are perusing that which has been given by inspiration of the Holy Ghost as a part of revealed truth ? Other questions are interesting in their places, and the solution of them is worth all which it has cost ; but they need not embarrass us here, nor claim our attention as preliminary to the exposition of the epistle. All that will be attempted, therefore, in this Introduction, will be such a *condensation* of the evidence collected by others, as shall show that this epistle has of right a place in the volume of revealed truth, and is of authority to regulate the faith and practice of mankind.

§ 2. To whom was the Epistle written?

It purports to have been written to the " Hebrews." This is not found, indeed, in the body of the epistle, though it occurs in the subscription at the end. It differs from *all* the other epistles of Paul in this respect, and from most of the others in the New Testament. In all of the other epistles of Paul, the church or person to whom the letter was sent is specified in the commencement. This, however, commences in the form of an essay or homily ; nor is there anywhere *in* the epistle any direct intimation to what church it was sent. The subscription at the end is of no authority, as it cannot be supposed that the author himself would affix it to the epistle, and as it is known that many of those subscriptions are false. See the remarks at the close of the Notes on Romans, and 1. Corinthians. Several questions present themselves here which we may briefly investigate.

(1.) *What is the evidence that it was written to the Hebrews?* In reply to this we may observe (1.) That the inscription at the commencement, " The Epistle of Paul the Apostle to the Hebrews," though not affixed by the author, may be allowed to express the current sense of the church in ancient times in reference to a question on which they had the best means of judging. These inscriptions at the commencement of the epistles have hitherto in general escaped the suspicion of spuriousness, to which the subscriptions at the close are justly exposed. *Michaelis.* They should not in any case be called in question, unless there is good reason from the epistle itself, or from some other source. This inscription is found in all our present Greek manuscripts, and in nearly all the ancient versions. It is found in the Peshito, the old Syriac version, which was made in the first or in the early part of the second century. It is the title given to the epistle by the Fathers of the second century, and onward. *Stuart.* (2.) The testimony of the Fathers. Their testimony is unbroken and uniform. With one accord they declare this, and this should be regarded as testimony of great value. Unless there is some good reason to depart from such evidence, it should be regarded as decisive. In this case there is no good reason for calling it in question, but every reason to suppose it to be correct ; nor so far as I have found is there any one who has doubted it. (3.) The internal evidence is of the highest character that it was written to Hebrew converts. It treats of Hebrew institutions. It explains their nature. It makes no allusion to Gentile customs or laws. It all along supposes that those to whom it was sent were familiar with the Jewish history ; with the nature of the temple service ; with the functions of the priestly office ; and with the whole structure of their religion. No other person than those who had been Jews are addressed throughout the epistle. There is no attempt to explain the nature or design of any customs except those with which they were familiar. At the same time it is equally clear that they were *Jewish converts*—converts trom Judaism to Christianity—who are addressed. The writer addresses them as Christians, not as those who were *to be* converted to Christianity ; he explains to them the Jewish customs as one would do to those who had been converted from Judaism ; he endeavours to guard them from apostasy, as if there were danger that they would *relapse* again into the system from which they were converted. These considerations seem to be decisive ; and in the view of all who have written on the epistle, as well as of the Christian world at large, they settle the question. It has never been held that the epistle was directed to *Gentiles ;* and in all the opinions and questions which have been started on the subject, it has been admitted that, wherever they resided, the persons to whom the epistle was addressed were originally Hebrews who had never been converted to the Christian religion.

(II.) *To what particular church of the Hebrews was it written ?* Very different opinions have been held on this question. The celebrated Storr held that it was written to the Hebrew part of the churches in Galatia ; and that the epistle to the Galatians was addressed to the Gentile part of those churches. Semler and Noessett maintained that it was written to the churches in Macedonia, and particularly to the church of Thessalonica. Bolten maintains that it was addressed to the Jewish Christians who fled from Palestine in a time of persecution. about the year 60, and who were scattered through Asia Minor. Michael Weber supposed that it was addressed to the church at Corinth. Ludwig conjectured that it was addressed to a church in Spain. Wetstein supposes that it was written to the church at Rome. Most of these opinions are mere conjectures, and all of them depend on circumstances which furnish only slight evidence of probability. Those who are disposed to examine these, and to see them confuted, may consult Stuart's Commentary on the Hebrews, Intro. § 5—9. The common, and the almost universally received opinion is that the epistle was addressed to the Hebrew Christians in Palestine. The reasons for this opinion, briefly, are the following. (1.) The testimony of the ancient church was uniform on this point—that the epistle was not only written to the Hebrew Christians, but to those who were in Palestine. Lardner affirms this to be the testimony of Clement of Alexandria, Jerome, Euthalius, Chrysostom, Theodoret, and Theophylact; and adds that this was the general opinion of the ancients. Works, vol. vi. pp. 80, 81. ed. Lond. 1829. (2.) The *inscription* at the commencement of the epistle leads to this supposition. That inscription, though not appended by the hand of the author, was early affixed to it. It is found not only in the Greek manuscripts, but in all the early versions, as the Syriac and the Itala ; and was doubtless affixed at a very early period, and by whomsoever affixed, expressed the current sense at the time. It is hardly possible that a mistake would be made on this point ; and unless there is good evidence to the contrary, this ought to be allowed to determine the question. That inscription is, " The Epistle of Paul the Apostle to the Hebrews." But who are the Hebrews—the 'Εβϱᾱιοι ? Professor Stuart has endeavoured to show that this was a term that was employed exclusively to denote the *Jews in Palestine*, in contradistinction from foreign Jews, who were called *Hellenists*. Comp. my Notes on Acts vi. 1. Bertholdt declares that there is not a single example which can be found in early times of Jewish Christians out of Palestine being called Hebrews. See a Dissertation on the Greek Language in Palestine, and of the meaning of the word *Hellenists*, by Hug, in the Bib. Repository, vol. i. 547, 548. Comp. also Robinson's Lex. on the word 'Εβϱᾱιος. If this be so, and if the inscription be of any authority, then it goes far to settle the question. The word *Hebrews* occurs but three times in the New Testament, (Acts vi. 1 ; 2 Cor. xi. 22 ; Phil. iii. 5,) in the first of which it is certain that it is used in this sense, and in both the others of which it is probable. There can be no doubt, it seems to me, that an ancient writer acquainted with the usual sense of the word *Hebrew*, would understand an inscription of this kind—"written to the Hebrews"—as designed for the inhabitants of Palestine, and not for the Jews of other countries. (3.) There are some passages in the epistle itself which Lardner supposes indicate that this epistle was written to the Hebrews in Palestine, or to those there who had been converted from Judaism to Christianity. As those passages are not conclusive, and as their force has been called in question, and with much propriety, by Professor Stuart (pp. 32—34), I shall merely refer to them. They can be examined at leisure by those who are disposed, and though they do not *prove* that the epistle was addressed to the Hebrew Christians in Palestine, yet they can be best interpreted on that supposition, and a peculiar significancy would be attached to them on this supposition. They are the following : ch. i. 2 ; iv. 2 ; ii. 1—4 ; v. 12 ; iv. 4—6 ; x. 26—29, 32—34 ; xiii. 13, 14. The argument of Lardner is that these would be more applicable to their condition than to others ; a position which I think cannot be doubted. Some of them are of so general character, indeed, as to be applicable to Christians elsewhere ; and in regard to some of them it cannot be certainly demonstrated that the state of things referred to existed in Judea, but taken together they would be more applicable *by far* to them than to the circumstances of any others of which we have knowledge ; and this may be allowed to have *some* weight at least in determining to whom the epistle was sent. (4.) The internal evidence of the epistle corresponds with the supposition that it was written to the Hebrew Christians in Palestine. The passages referred to in the previous remarks (3) might be adduced here as proof. But there is other proof. It *might* have been otherwise. There might be such strong internal proof that an epistle was not addressed to a supposed people, as completely to neutralize all the evidence derived from an inscription like that prefixed to this epistle, and all the evidence derived from tradition. But it is not so here. All the circumstances referred to in the epistle ; the general strain of remark ; the argument; the allusions, are just such as would be likely to be found in an epistle addressed to the Hebrew Christians in Palestine, and such as would *not* be likely to occur in an epistle addressed to any other place or people. They are such as the following : (*a.*) The familiar acquaintance with the Jewish institutions supposed by the writer to exist among those to whom it was sent—a familiarity hardly to be expected even of Jews who lived in other countries. (*b.*) The danger so frequently adverted to of their relapsing into their former state ; of apostatizing from Christianity, and of embracing again the Jewish rites and ceremonies—a danger that would exist nowhere else in so great a degree as in Judea. Comp. ch. ii. 1—3 ; iii. 7—11, 15 ; iv. 1 ; vi. 1—8 ; x. 26—35. (*c.*) The nature of the discussion in 'the epistle — not turning upon the obligation of circumcision, and the distinction of meats and drinks, which occupied so much of the attention of the apostles and early Christians in other places—but a discussion relating to the whole structure of the Mosaic economy, the pre-eminence of Moses or Christ, the meaning of the rites of the temple, &c. These great questions would be more likely to arise in Judea than elsewhere, and it was important to discuss them fully, as it is done in this epistle. In other places they would be of less interest, and would excite less difficulty. (*d.*) The allusion to local places and events ; to facts in their history ; and to the circumstances of public worship, which would be better understood there than elsewhere. There are no allusions—or if there are they are very brief and infrequent—to heathen customs, games, races, and philosophical opinions, as there are often in the other epistles of the New Testament. Those to whom the epistle was sent, are presumed to have an intimate and minute knowledge of the Hebrew history, and such a knowledge as could be hardly supposed elsewhere. Comp. ch. xi., particularly vs. 32—39. Thus it is implied that they so well understood the subjects referred to relating to the Jewish rites, that it was not necessary that the writer should specify them particularly. See ch. ix. 5. Of what other persons could this be so appropriately said as of the dwellers in Palestine? (*e.*) The circumstances of trial and persecution so often referred to in the epistle, agree well with the known condition of the church in Palestine. That it was subjected to great trials we know ; and though this was extensively true of other churches, yet it is probable that there were more vexatious and grievous exactions ; that there was more spite and malice ; that there were more of the trials arising from the separation of families and the losses of property attending a profession of Christianity in Palestine than elsewhere in the early Christian church. These considerations—though not so conclusive as to furnish absolute demonstration—go far to settle the question. They seem to me so strong as to preclude any reasonable doubt, and are such as the mind can repose on with a great degree of confidence in regard to the original destination of the epistle.

(3.) *Was it addressed to a particular church in Palestine, or to the Hebrew Christians there in general?*
Whether it was addressed to the churches in general in Palestine, or to some particular church there, it is now impossible to determine. Prof. Stuart inclines to the opinion that it was addressed to the church in Cesarea. The ancients in general supposed it was addressed to the church in Jerusalem. There are some *local* references in the epistle which look as though it was directed to some particular church. But the means of determining this question are put beyond our reach, and it is of little importance to settle the question. From the allusions to the temple, the priesthood, the sacrifices, and the whole train of peculiar institutions there, it would seem probable that it was directed to the church in Jerusalem. As that was the capital of the nation, and the centre of religious influence ; and as there was a large and flourishing church there, this opinion would seem to have great probability ; but it is impossible now to determine it. If we suppose that the author sent the epistle, in the first instance, to some local church, near the central seat of the great influence which he intended to reach by it — addressing to that church the particular communications in the last verses—we shall make a supposition which, so far as can now be ascertained, will accord with the truth in the case.

§ 3. *The Author of the Epistle.*

To those who are familiar with the investigations which have taken place in regard to this epistle, it need not be said that the question of its authorship has given rise to much discussion. The design of these Notes does not permit me to go at length into this inquiry. Those who are disposed to see the investigation pursued at length, and to see the objections to the Pauline origin examined in a most satisfactory manner, can find it done in the Introduction to the Epistle to the Hebrews, by Prof. Stuart, pp. 77—260. All that my purpose requires is to state, in a very brief manner, the evidence on which it is ascribed to the apostle Paul. That evidence is, briefly, the following :
(1.) That derived from the church at Alexandria. Clement of Alexandria says, that Paul wrote to the Hebrews, and that this was the opinion of Pantaenus, who was at the head of the celebrated Christian school at Alexandria, and who flourished about A. D. 180. Pantaenus lived near Palestine. He must have been acquainted with the prevailing opinions on the subject, and his testimony must be regarded as proof that the epistle was regarded as Paul's by the churches in that region. Origen, also of Alexandria, ascribes the epistle to Paul ; though he says that the *sentiments* are those of Paul, but that the words and phrases belong to some one relating the apostle's sentiments, and as it were commenting on the words of his master. The testimony of the church at Alexandria was uniform after the time of Origen, that it was the production of Paul. Indeed there seems never to have been any doubt in regard to it there, and from the commencement it was admitted as his production. The testimony of that church and school is particularly valuable, because (*a*) it was near to Palestine, where the epistle was probably sent; (*b*) Clement particularly had travelled much, and would be likely to understand the prevailing sentiments of the East; (*c*) Alexandria was the seat of the most celebrated theological school of the early Christian ages, and those who were at the head of this school would be likely to have correct information on a point like this; and (*d*) Origen is admitted to have been the most learned of the Greek Fathers, and his testimony that the "sentiments" were those of Paul may be regarded as of peculiar value.
(2.) It was inserted in the translation into the Syriac, made very early in the second century, and in the old Italic version, and was hence believed to be of apostolic origin, and is by the inscription ascribed to Paul. This may be allowed to express the general sense of the churches at that time, as this

would not have been done unless there had been a general impression that the epistle was written by him. The fact that it was *early* regarded as an inspired book is also conclusively shown by the fact that the second epistle of Peter, and the second and third epistles of John, are not found in that version. They came later into circulation than the other epistles, and were not possessed, or regarded as genuine, by the author of that version. The epistle to the Hebrews *is* found in these versions, and was, therefore, regarded as one of the inspired books. In those versions it bears the inscription, " To the Hebrews."

(3) This epistle was received as the production of Paul by the Eastern churches. Justin Martyr, who was born at Samaria, quotes it, about the year 140. It was found, as has been already remarked, in the Peshito—the old Syriac version, made in the early part of the second century. Jacob, bishop of Nisibis, also (about A.D. 325) repeatedly quotes it as the production of an apostle. Ephrem Syrus, or the Syrian, abundantly ascribes this epistle to Paul. He was the disciple of Jacob of Nisibis, and no man was better qualified to inform himself on this point than Ephrem. No man stands deservedly higher in the memory of the Eastern churches. After him, all the Syrian churches acknowledged the canonical authority of the epistle to the Hebrews. But the most important testimony of the Eastern church is that of Eusebius, bishop of Cesarea, in Palestine. He is the well-known historian of the church, and he took pains from all quarters to collect testimony in regard to the Books of Scripture. He says, " There are fourteen epistles of Paul, manifest and well known : but yet there are some who reject that to the Hebrews, alleging in behalf of their opinion, that it was not received by the church of Rome as a writing of Paul." The testimony of Eusebius is particularly important. He had heard of the objection to its canonical authority. He had weighed that objection. Yet in view of the testimony in the case, he regarded it as the undoubted production of Paul. As such it was received in the churches in the East ; and the fact which he mentions, that its genuineness had been disputed by the church of Rome, and that he specifies no other church, proves that it had *not* been called in question in the East. This seems to me to be sufficient testimony to settle this inquiry. The writers here referred to lived in the very country to which the epistle was evidently written, and their testimony is uniform. Justin Martyr was born in Samaria; Ephrem passed his life in Syria; Eusebius lived in Cesarea, and Origen passed the last twenty years of his life in Palestine. The churches there were unanimous in the opinion that this epistle was written by Paul, and their united testimony should settle the question. Indeed when their testimony is considered, it seems remarkable that the subject should have been regarded as doubtful by critics, or that it should have given rise to so much protracted investigation. I might add to the testimonies above referred to, the fact that the epistle was declared to be Paul's by the following persons : Archelaus, bishop of Mesopotamia, about A. D. 300; Adamantius, about 330 ; Cyril, of Jerusalem, about 348; the Council of Laodicea, about 363; Epiphanius, about 368 ; Basil, 370; Gregory Nazianzen, 370 ; Chrysostom, 398, &c. &c. Why should not the testimony of such men and churches be admitted? What more clear or decided evidence could we wish in regard to any fact of ancient history? Would not such testimony be ample in regard to an anonymous oration of Cicero, or poem of Virgil or Horace? Are we not constantly acting on far feebler evidence in regard to the authorship of many productions of celebrated English writers?

(4.) In regard to the Western churches, it is to be admitted that, like the second epistle of Peter, and the second and third epistles of John, the canonical authority was for some time doubted, or was even called in question. But this may be accounted for. The epistle had not the name of the author. All the other epistles of Paul had. As the epistle was addressed to the

Hebrews in Palestine, it may not have been soon known to the Western churches. As there were spurious epistles and gospels at an early age, much caution would be used in admitting any anonymous production to a place in the sacred canon. Yet it was not *long* before all these doubts were removed, and the epistle to the Hebrews was allowed to take its place among the other acknowledged writings of Paul. It was received as the epistle of Paul by Hilary, bishop of Poictiers, about A. D. 354; by Lucifer, bishop of Cagliari, 354; by Victorinus, 360; by Ambrose, bishop of Milan, 360; by Rufinus, 397, &c. &c. Jerome, the well-known Latin Father, uses in regard to it the following language : "This is to be maintained, that this epistle, which is inscribed to the Hebrews, is not only received by the churches at the East as the apostle Paul's, but has been in past times by all ecclesiastical writers in the Greek language ; although most [Latins] think that Barnabas or Clement was the author." Still, it was not rejected by *all* the Latins. Some received it in the time of Jerome as the production of Paul. See Stuart, pp. 114, 115, for the full testimony of Jerome. Augustine admitted that the epistle was written by Paul. He mentions that Paul wrote fourteen epistles, and specifies particularly the epistle to the Hebrews. He often cites it as a part of Scripture, and quotes it as the production of an apostle. *Stuart*, p. 115. From the time of Augustine it was undisputed. By the council of Hippo, A. D. 393, the third council of Carthage, 397, and the fifth council of Carthage, 419, it was declared to be the epistle of Paul, and was as such commended to the churches.

(5.) As another proof that it is the writing of Paul, we may appeal to the internal evidence. (*a*) The author of the epistle was the companion and friend of Timothy. "Know ye that our brother Timothy is set at liberty"— or is sent away—ἀπολελυμένον—"with whom if he come speedily, I will make you a visit." ch. xiii. 23. Sent away, perhaps, on a journey, to visit some of the churches, and expected soon to return. In Phil. ii. 19, Paul speaks of sending Timothy to them "so soon as he should see how it would go with him," at the same time expressing a hope that he should himself see them shortly. What is more natural than to suppose that he *had* now sent Timothy to Philippi ; that during his absence he wrote this epistle ; that he was waiting for his return ; and that he proposed, if Timothy should return soon, to visit Palestine with him ? And who would more naturally say this than the apostle Paul—the companion and friend of Timothy; by whom he had been accompanied in his travels ; and by whom he was regarded with special interest as a minister of the gospel ? (*b*) In ch. xiii. 18, 19, he asks their prayers that he might be restored to them ; and in ver. 23, he expresses a confident expectation of being able soon to come and see them. From this it is evident that he was then imprisoned, but had hope of speedy release—a state of things in exact accordance with what existed at Rome. Phil. ii. 17— 24. (*c*) He was in bonds when he wrote this epistle. Heb. x. 34, "Ye had compassion of me *in my bonds ;*" an expression that will exactly apply to the case of Paul. He was in "bonds" in Palestine ; he was two whole years in Cesarea a prisoner (Acts xxiv. 27); and what was more natural than that the Christians in Palestine should have had compassion on him, and ministered to his wants? To what other person would these circumstances so certainly be applicable ? (*d*) The salutation (ch. xiii. 24,) "they of Italy salute you," agrees with the supposition that it was written by Paul when a prisoner at Rome. Paul writing from Rome, and acquainted with Christians from other parts of Italy, would be likely to send such a salutation. In regard to the *objections* which may be made to this use of the passage, the reader may consult Stuart's Intro. to the Hebrews, p. 127, *seq.* (*e*) The *doctrines* of the epistle are the same as those which are taught by Paul in his undisputed writings. It is true that this consideration is not conclusive, but the want of it would be conclusive evidence *against* the position that Paul wrote it. But the resemblance is not *general.* It is not such as any man would exhibit who held to the same general system of truth. It relates to *peculiarities* of doctrine, and is such as would be manifested by a man who had been reared and trained as Paul had. (1.) No one can doubt that the author was formerly a Jew—and a Jew who had been familiar to an uncommon degree with the institutions of the Jewish religion. Every rite and ceremony ; every form of opinion ; every fact in their history, is perfectly familiar to him. And though the other apostles were Jews, yet we can hardly suppose that they had the familiarity with the minute rites and ceremonies so accurately referred to in this epistle, and so fully illustrated. With Paul all this was perfectly natural. He had been brought up at the feet of Gamaliel, and had spent the early part of his life at Jerusalem in the careful study of the Old Testament, in the examination of the prevalent opinions, and in the attentive observance of the rites of religion. The other apostles had been born and trained, apparently, on the banks of Gennesareth, and certainly with few of the opportunities which Paul had had for becoming acquainted with the institutions of the temple service. This consideration is fatal, in my view, to the claim which has been set up for Clement as the author of the epistle. It is wholly incredible that a foreigner should be so familiar with the Jewish opinions, laws, institutions, and history, as the author of this epistle manifestly was. (2.) There is the same preference for Christianity over Judaism in this epistle which is shown by Paul in his other epistles, and exhibited in the same form. Among these points are the following— *The gospel imparts superior light.* Comp. Gal. iv. 3, 9 ; 1 Cor. xiv. 20 ; Eph. iv. 11—13 ; 2 Cor. iii. 18; with Heb. i. 1, 2 ; ii. 2—4 ; viii. 9—11 ; x. 1 ; xi. 39, 40. *The gospel holds out superior motives and encouragements to piety.* Comp. Gal. iii. 23 ; iv. 2, 3 ; Rom. viii. 15—17 ; Gal. iv. 4 ; v. 13 ; 1 Cor. vii. 19 ; Gal. vi. 15 ; with Heb. ix. 9, 14 ; xii. 18—24, 28 ; viii. 6—13. *The gospel is superior in promoting the real and permanent happiness of mankind.* Comp. Gal. iii. 13 ; 2 Cor. iii. 7, 9 ; Rom. iii. 20; Rom. iv. 24, 25 ; Eph. i. 7; Rom. v. 1, 2 ; Gal. ii. 16 ; and the same views in Heb. xii. 18—21 ; ix. 9; x. 4, 11 ; vi. 18—20 ; vii. 25; ix. 24. *The Jewish dispensation was a type and shadow of the Christian.* See Col. ii. 16, 17 ; 1 Cor. x. 1—6 ; Rom. v. 14 ; 1 Cor. xv. 45—47 ; 2 Cor. iii 13—18 ; Gal. iv. 22—31 ; iv. 1—5 ; and for the same or similar views, see Hebrews ix. 9—14 ; x. 1 ; viii. 1—9 ; ix. 22—24. *The Christian religion was designed to be perpetual, while the Jewish was intended to be abolished.* See 2 Cor. iii. 10, 11, 13, 18; iv. 14—16 ; Rom. vii. 4—6 ; Gal. iii. 21— 25 ; iv. 1—7 ; v. 1 ; and for similar views compare Heb. viii. 6—8, 13 ; vii. 17—19 ; x. 1—14. *The person of the Mediator is presented in the same light by the writer of the epistle to the Hebrews and by Paul.* See Phil. ii. 6—11 ; Col. i. 15—20 ; 2 Cor. viii. 9 ; Eph. iii. 9 ; 1 Cor. viii. 6 ; xv. 25—27 ; and for the same and similar views, see Heb. i. 2, 3 ; ii. 9, 14 ; xii. 2 ; ii. 8; x. 13. *The death of Christ is the propitiatory sacrifice for sin.* See 1 Tim. i. 15 ; 1 Cor. xv. 3 ; Rom. viii. 32 ; iii. 24 ; Gal. i. 4 ; ii. 20 ; 1 Cor. v. 7 ; Eph. i. 7 ; Col. i. 14 ; 1 Tim. ii. 6 ; 1 Cor. vi. 20 ; vii. 23 ; Rom. v. 12—21 ; iii. 20, 28 ; viii. 3 ; 1 Tim. ii. 5, 6. For similar views see Heb. i. 3 ; ii. 9 ; v. 8, 9 ; vii., viii., ix., x. *The general method and arrangement of this epistle and the acknowledged epistles of Paul are the same.* It resembles particularly the epistles to the Romans and the Galatians, where we have first a doctrinal and then a practical part. The same is true also to some extent of the epistles to the Ephesians, Colossians, and Philippians. The epistle to the Hebrews is on the same plan. As far as ch. x. 19. it is principally doctrinal ; the remainder is mainly practical. *The manner of appealing to, and applying the Jewish Scriptures, is the same in this epistle as in those of Paul.* The general structure of the epistle, and the slightest comparison between them, will show this with sufficient clearness. The general remark to be made in view of this comparison is, that the epistle to the Hebrews is just such an one as Paul might be expected to write ; that it agrees with what we know to have been his early training, his views, his manner of life, his opinions, and his habit in writing ; that it accords better with his views than with those of any other known writer of antiquity ; and that it falls in with the circumstances in which he was known to be placed, and the general object which he had in view. So satisfactory are these views to my mind, that they seem to have all the force of demonstration which can be had in regard to any anonymous publication, and it is a matter of wonder that so much doubt has been experienced in reference to the question who was the author.

It is difficult to account for the fact that the name of the author was omitted. It is found in every other epistle of Paul, and in general it is appended to the epistles in the New Testament. It is omitted, however, in the three epistles of John, for reasons which are now unknown. And there may have been similar reasons also unknown for omitting it in this case. The simple *fact* is, that it is anonymous ; and whoever was the author, the same difficulty will exist in accounting for it. If this fact will prove that Paul was not the author, it would prove the same thing in regard to any other person, and would thus be ultimately conclusive evidence that it *had* no author. What were the reasons for omitting the name can be only matter of conjecture. The most probable opinion, as it seems to me, is this. The name of Paul was odious to the Jews. He was regarded by the nation as an apostate from their religion, and everywhere they showed peculiar malignity against him. See the Acts of the Apostles. The fact that he was so regarded by them might indirectly influence even those who had been converted from Judaism to Christianity. They lived in Palestine. They were near the temple, and were engaged in its ceremonies and sacrifices—for there is no evidence that they broke off from those observances on their conversion to Christianity. Paul was abroad. It might have been reported that he was preaching against the temple and its sacrifices, and even the Jewish Christians in Palestine might have supposed that he was carrying matters too far. In these circumstances it might have been *imprudent* for him to have announced his name at the outset, for it might have aroused prejudices which a wise man would wish to allay. But if he could present an argument, somewhat in the form of an essay, showing that he believed that the Jewish institutions were appointed by God, and that he was not an apostate and an infidel ; if he could conduct a demonstration that would accord in the main with the prevailing views of the Christians in Palestine, and that was adapted to strengthen them in the faith of the gospel, and explain to them the true nature of the Jewish rites, then the object could be gained without difficulty, and then they would be prepared to learn that Paul was the author, without prejudice or alarm. Accordingly he thus conducts the argument ; and at the close gives them such *intimations* that they would understand who wrote it without much difficulty. If this was the motive, it was an instance of *tact* such as was certainly characteristic of Paul, and such as was not unworthy any man. I have no doubt that this was the true motive. It would be soon known who wrote it ; and accordingly we have seen it was never disputed in the Eastern churches.

§ 4. *The time when written.*

In regard to the time when this epistle was written, and the place where, critics have been better agreed than on most of the questions which have been started in regard to it. Mill was of opinion that it was written by Paul in the year 63, in some part of Italy, soon after he had been released from imprisonment at Rome. Wetstein was of the same opinion. Tillemont also places this epistle in the year 63, and supposes that it was written while Paul was at Rome, or at least in Italy, and soon after he was released from imprisonment. Basnage supposes it was written about the year 61, and during the imprisonment of the apostle. Lardner supposes also that it was written in the beginning of the year 63, and soon after the apostle was released from his confinement. This also is the opinion of Calmet. The circumstances in the epistle which will enable us to form an opinion on the question about the time and the place are the following :—

(1.) It was written while the temple was still standing, and before Jerusalem was destroyed. This is evident from the whole structure of the epistle. There is no allusion to the destruction of the temple or the city, which there certainly would have been if they had been destroyed. Such an event would have contributed much to the object in view, and would have furnished an irrefragable argument that the institutions of the Jews were intended to be superseded by another and a more perfect system. Moreover, there are allusions in the epistle which suppose that the temple service was then performed. See Heb. ix. 9; viii. 4, 5. But the city and temple were destroyed in the year 70, and of course the epistle was written before that year.

(2.) It was evidently written before the civil wars and commotions in Judea, which terminated in the destruction of the city and nation. This is clear, because there are no allusions to any such disorders or troubles in Palestine, and there is no intimation that they were suffering the evils incident to a state of war. Comp. ch. xii. 4. But those wars commenced A.D. 66, and evidently the epistle was written before that time.

(3.) They were not suffering the evils of violent persecution. They had indeed formerly suffered (comp. ch. x. 32, 34); James and Stephen had been put to death (Acts vii., xii.); but there was no violent and bloody persecution then raging in which they were called to defend their religion at the expense of blood and life. Ch. x. 32, 33. But the persecution under Nero began in the year 64, and though it began at Rome, and was confined to a considerable degree to Italy, yet it is not improbable that it extended to other places, and it is to be presumed that if such a persecution were raging at the time when the epistle was written there would be some allusion to this fact. It may be set down, therefore, that it was written before the year 64.

(4.) It is equally true that the epistle was written during the latter part of the apostolic age. The author speaks of the *former* days in which after they were illuminated they had endured a great fight of afflictions, and when they were made a gazing-stock, and were plundered by their oppressors (ch. x. 32—34); and he speaks of them as having been so long converted that they ought to have been qualified to teach others (ch. v. 12); and hence it is fairly to be inferred that they were not *recent* converts, but that the church there had been established for a considerable period. It may be added, that it was *after* the writer had been imprisoned—as I suppose in Cesarea (see § 3) —when they had ministered to him; ch. x. 34. But this was as late as the year 60.

(5.) At the time when Paul wrote the epistles to the Ephesians, Philippians, and Colossians, he had hopes of deliverance. Timothy was evidently with him. But now he was absent; ch. xiii. 23. In the epistle to the Philippians (ch. ii. 19—23) he says, "But I trust in the Lord Jesus to send Timotheus shortly unto you, that I may be also of good comfort, when I know your state." He expected, therefore, that Timothy would come back to him at Rome. It is probable that Timothy was sent soon after this. The apostle had a fair prospect of being set at liberty, and sent him to them. *During his absence* at this time, it would seem probable, this epistle was written. Thus the writer says (ch. xiii. 23), "Know ye that our brother Timothy is *set at liberty*"—or rather, SENT AWAY, or SENT ABROAD (see note in that place) ; " with whom if he come shortly, I will see you." That is, if he returns soon, as I expect him, I will pay you a visit. It is probable that the epistle was written while Timothy was thus absent at Philippi, and when he returned, Paul and he went to Palestine, and thence to Ephesus. If so it was written somewhere about the year 63, as this was the time when Paul was set at liberty.

(6.) The epistle was written evidently in Italy. Thus in ch. xiii. 24, the writer says, " They of Italy salute you." This would be the natural form of salutation on the supposition that it was written there. He mentions none by name, as he does in his other epistles, for it is probable that none of those who were at Rome would be known by name in Palestine. But there was a *general* salutation, showing the interest which they had in the Christians in Judea, and expressive of regard for their welfare. This expression is, to my mind, conclusive evidence that the epistle was written in Italy; and *in* Italy there was no place where this would be so likely to occur as at Rome.

§ 5. *The language in which it was written.*

This is a vexed and still unsettled question, and it does not seem to be possible to determine it with any considerable degree of certainty. Critics of the ablest name have been divided on it, and what is remarkable, have appealed to the same arguments to prove exactly opposite opinions—one class arguing that the style of the epistle is such as to prove that it was written in Hebrew, and the other appealing to the same proofs to demonstrate that it was written in Greek. Among those who have supposed that it was written in Hebrew are the following, viz.:—Some of the Fathers—as Clement of Alexandria, Theodoret, John Damascenus, Theophylact; and among the moderns, Michaelis has been the most strenuous defender of this opinion. This opinion was also held by the late Dr. James P. Wilson, who says, " It was probably written in the vulgar language of the Jews;" that is, in that mixture of Hebrew, Syriac, and Chaldee, which was usually spoken in the time of the Saviour, and which was known as the Syro-Chaldaic.

On the other hand, the great body of critics have supposed it was written in the Greek language. This was the opinion of Fabricius, Lightfoot, Whitby, Beausobre, Capellus, Basnage, Mill, and others, and is also the opinion of Lardner, Hug, Stuart, and perhaps of most modern critics. These opinions may be seen examined at length in Michaelis' Introduction, Hug, Stuart, and Lardner.

The arguments in support of the opinion that it was written in Hebrew are, briefly, the following: (1.) The testimony of the Fathers. Thus Clement of Alexandria says, " Paul wrote to the Hebrews in the Hebrew language, and Luke carefully translated it into Greek." Jerome says, "Paul as a Hebrew wrote to the Hebrews in Hebrew—Scripserat ut Hebræus Hebraice;" and then he adds, "this epistle was translated into Greek, so that the colouring of the style was made diverse in this way from that of Paul's." (2.) The fact that it was written for the use of the Hebrews, who spoke the Hebrew, or the *Talmudic* language, is alleged as a reason for supposing that it must have been written in that language. (3.) It is alleged by Michaelis, that the style of the Greek, as we now have it, is far more pure and classical than Paul elsewhere employs, and that hence it is to be inferred that it was translated by some one who was master of the Greek language. On this, however, the most eminent critics disagree. (4.) It is alleged by Michaelis, that the quotations in the epistle, as we have it, are made from the Septuagint, and that they are foreign to the purpose which the writer had in view as they are now quoted, whereas they are exactly in point as they stand in the Hebrew. Hence he infers that the original Hebrew was quoted by the author, and that the translator used the common version at hand instead of making an exact translation for himself. Of the fact alleged here, however, there may be good ground to raise a question ; and if it were so, it would not *prove* that the writer might not have used the common and accredited translation, though *less* to his purpose than the original. Of the fact, moreover, to which Michaelis here refers, Prof. Stuart says, "He has not adduced a single instance of what he calls a *wrong translation* which wears the appearance of any considerable probability." The only instance urged by Michaelis which seems to me to be plausible is Heb. i. 7. These are the principal arguments which have been urged in favour of the opinion that this epistle was written in the Hebrew language. They are evidently not conclusive. The only argument of any considerable weight is the testimony of some of the Fathers, and it may be doubted whether they gave this as a matter of historic fact or only as a matter of opinion. See Hug's Introduction, § 144. It is morally certain that in one respect their statement cannot be true. They state that it was translated by Luke ; but it is capable of the clearest proof that it was not translated by Luke, the author of the Gospel and the Acts of the Apostles, since there is the most remarkable dissimilarity in the style.

On the other hand there are alleged in favour of the opinion that it was written in Greek the following considerations, viz. :—

(1.) The fact that we have no Hebrew original. If it was written in Hebrew, the original was early lost. None of the Fathers say that they had seen it ; none quote it. All the copies that we have are in Greek. If it was written in Hebrew, and the original was destroyed, it must have been at a very early period, and it is remarkable that no one should have mentioned the fact or alluded to it. Besides, it is scarcely conceivable that the original should have so soon perished, and that the translation should have altogether taken its place. If it was addressed to the Hebrews in Palestine, the same reason which made it proper that it should have been *written* in Hebrew would have led them to *retain* it in that language, and we might have supposed that Origen, or Eusebius, or Jerome, who lived there, or Ephrem the Syrian, would have adverted to the fact that there was there a Hebrew original. The Jews were remarkable for retaining their sacred books in the language in which they were written, and if this were written in Hebrew it is difficult to account for the fact that it was so soon suffered to perish.

(2.) The presumption—a presumption amounting to almost a moral certainty—is, that an apostle writing to the Christians in Palestine would write in Greek. This presumption is based on the following circumstances : (*a*) The fact that all the other books of the New Testament were written in Greek, unless the Gospel by Matthew be an exception. (*b*) This occurred in cases where it would seem to have been as improbable as it was that one writing to the Hebrews should use that language. For instance, Paul wrote to the church in Rome in the Greek language, though the *Latin* language was that which is in universal use there. (*c*) The Greek was a common language in the East. It seems to have been familiarly spoken, and to have been commonly understood. (*d*) Like the other books of the New Testament, this epistle does not appear to have been intended to be confined to the Hebrews only. The writings of the apostles were regarded as the property of the church at large. Those writings would be copied and spread abroad. The Greek was a far better language for such a purpose than the Hebrew. It was polished and elegant ; was adapted to the purpose of discoursing on moral subjects ; was fitted to express delicate shades of thought, and was the language which was best understood by the world at large. (*e*) It was the language which Paul would naturally use unless there was a strong reason for his employing the Hebrew. Though he was able to speak in Hebrew (Acts xxi. 40), yet he had spent his early days in Tarsus, where the Greek was the vernacular tongue, and it was probably that which he had first learned. Besides this, when this epistle was written he had been absent from Palestine about twenty-five years, and in all that time he had been there but a few days. He had been where the Greek language was universally spoken. He had been among Jews who spoke that language. It was the language used in their synagogues, and Paul had addressed them in it. After thus preaching, conversing, and writing in that language for twenty-five years, is it any wonder that he should prefer writing in it; that he should naturally do it; and is it not to be presumed that he would do it in this case? These presumptions are so strong that they ought to be allowed to settle a question of this kind unless there is positive proof to the contrary.

(3.) There is *internal* proof that it was written in the Greek language. The evidence of this kind consists in the fact that the writer bases an *argument* on the meaning and force of Greek words, which could not have occurred had he written in Hebrew. Instances of this kind are such as these. (*a*) In ch. ii. he applies a passage from Ps. viii. to prove that the Son of God must have had a human nature, which was to be exalted above the angels, and placed at the head of the creation. The passage is, " Thou hast made him a little while inferior to the angels." Ch. ii. 7, *margin.* In the Hebrew, in Ps. viii. 5, the word rendered *angels,* is אלהים—*Elohim—God ;* and the sense of *angels* attached to that word, though it may sometimes occur, is so unusual, that an argument would not have been built on the Hebrew. (*b*) In ch. vii. 1, the writer has explained the name *Melchizedek,* and translated it *king of Salem*—telling what it is *in Greek*—a thing which would not have been done had he written in Hebrew, where the word was well understood. It is *possible,* indeed, that a translator might have done this, but the explanation seems to be interwoven with the discourse itself, and to constitute a part of the argument. (*c.*) In ch. ix 16, 17, there is an argument on the meaning of the word *covenant*—διαθήκη—which could not have occurred had the epistle been in Hebrew. It is founded on the double meaning of that word—denoting both a *covenant* and a *testament,* or *will.* The Hebrew word—ברית—*Berith*—has no such double signification. It means *covenant* only, and is never used in the sense of the word *will,* or testament. The proper translation of that word would be συνθήκη—*syntheke*—but the translators of the Septuagint uniformly used the former—διαθήκη—*diatheke*—and on this word the argument of the apostle is based. This could not have been done by a translator; it must have been by the original author, for it is incorporated into the argument. (*d*) In ch. x. 3—9, the author shows that Christ came to make an atonement for sin, and that in order to this it was necessary that he should have a human body. This he shows was not only necessary, but was predicted. In doing this, he appeals to Ps. xl. 6—"A body hast thou prepared for me." But the Hebrew here is, "Mine ears hast thou opened." This passage would have been much less pertinent than the other form—"a body hast thou prepared me ;"—and indeed it is not easy to see how it would bear at all on the object in view. See ver. 10. But in the Septuagint the phrase stands as he quotes it—" a body hast thou prepared for me ;" a fact which demonstrates, whatever difficulties there may be about the *principle* on which he makes the quotation, that the epistle was written in Greek. It may be added, that it has nothing of the appearance of a translation. It is not stiff, forced, or constrained in style, as translations usually are. It is impassioned, free, flowing, full of animation, life, and colouring, and has all the appearance of being an original composition. So clear have these considerations appeared, that the great body of critics now concur in the opinion that the epistle was originally written in Greek.

§ 6. *The design and general argument of the Epistle.*

The general purpose of this epistle is, to preserve those to whom it was sent from the danger of apostasy. Their danger on this subject did not arise so much from persecution, as from the circumstances that were fitted to attract them again to the Jewish religion. The temple, it is supposed, and indeed it is evident, was still standing. The morning and evening sacrifice was still offered. The splendid rites of that imposing religion were still observed. The authority of the law was undisputed. Moses was a lawgiver, sent from God, and no one doubted that the Jewish form of religion had been instituted by their fathers in conformity with the direction of God. Their religion had been founded amidst remarkable manifestations of the Deity—in flames, and smoke. and thunder ; it had been communicated by the ministration of angels ; it had on its side and in its favour all the venerableness and sanction of a remote antiquity ; and it commended itself by the pomp of its ritual, and by the splendour of its ceremonies. On the other hand, the new form of religion had little or nothing of this to commend it. It was of recent origin. It was founded by the Man of Nazareth, who had been trained up in their own land, and who had been a carpenter, and who had had no extraordinary advantages of education. Its rites were few and simple. It had no splendid temple service ; none of the pomp and pageantry, the music and the magnificence of the ancient religion. It had no splendid array of priests in magnificent vestments, and it had not been imparted by the ministry of angels. Fishermen were its ministers ; and by the body of the nation it was regarded as a schism, or heresy, that enlisted in its favour only the most humble and lowly of the people.

In these circumstances, how natural was it for the enemies of the gospel in Judea to contrast the two forms of religion, and how keenly would Christians there feel it ! All that was said of the antiquity and the divine origin of the Jewish religion they knew and admitted ; all that was said of its splendour and magnificence they saw ; and all that was said of the humble origin of their own religion they were constrained to admit also. *Their* danger was not that arising from persecution. It was that of being affected by considerations like these, and of relapsing again into the religion of their fathers, and of apostatizing from the gospel ; and it was a danger which beset no other part of the Christian world.

To meet and counteract this danger was the design of this epistle. Accordingly the writer contrasts the two religions in all the great points on which the minds of Christians in Judea would be likely to be affected, and shows the superiority of the Christian religion over the Jewish in every respect, and especially in the points that had so much attracted their attention, and affected their hearts. He begins by showing that the *Author* of the Christian religion was superior in rank to any and all who had ever delivered the word of God to man. He was superior to the prophets, and even to the angels. He was over all things, and all things were subject to him. There was, therefore, a special reason why they should listen to him, and obey his commands ; ch. i., ii. He was superior to Moses, the great Jewish lawgiver, whom they venerated so much, and on whom they so much prided themselves ; ch. iii. Having shown that the Great Founder of the Christian religion was superior to the prophets, to Moses, and to the angels, the writer proceeds to show that the Christian religion was characterized by having a High Priest superior to that of the Jews, and of whom the Jewish high priest was but a type and emblem. He shows that all the rites of the ancient religion, splendid as they were, were also but types, and were to vanish away—for they had had their fulfilment in the realities of the Christian faith He shows that the Christian's High Priest derived his origin and his rank from a more venerable antiquity than the Jewish high priest did—for he went back to Melchizedek, who lived long before Aaron, and that he had far superior dignity from the fact that he had entered into the Holy of Holies in heaven. The Jewish high priest entered once a year into the most holy place in the temple ; the Great High Priest of the Christian faith had entered into the Most Holy place—of which that was but the type and emblem—into heaven.

In short, whatever there was of dignity and honour in the Jewish faith had more than its counterpart in the Christian religion; and while the Christian religion was permanent, that was fading. The rites of the Jewish system, magnificent as they were, were designed to be temporary. They were mere types and shadows of things to come. They had their fulfilment in Christianity That had an Author more exalted in rank by far than the author of the Jewish system; it had a High Priest more elevated and enduring; it had rites which brought men nearer to God; it was the substance of what in the temple service was type and shadow. By considerations such as these the author of this epistle endeavours to preserve them from apostasy. Why should they go back? Why should they return to a less perfect system? Why go back from the substance to the shadow? Why turn away from the true sacrifice to the type and emblem? Why linger around the earthly tabernacle, and contemplate the high priest there, while they had a more perfect and glorious High Priest, who had entered into the heavens? And why should they turn away from the only perfect sacrifice—the great offering made for transgression—and go back to the bloody rites which were to be renewed every day? And why forsake the perfect system—the system that was to endure for ever —for that which was soon to vanish away? The author of this epistle is very careful to assure them that *if* they thus apostatized, there could be no hope for them. If they now rejected the sacrifice of the Son of God, there was no other sacrifice for sin. That was the last great sacrifice for the sins of men. It was designed to close all bloody offerings. It was not to be repeated. If that was rejected, there was no other. The Jewish rites were soon to pass away; and even if they were not, they could not cleanse the conscience from sin. Persecuted then though they might be; reviled, ridiculed, opposed, yet they should not abandon their Christian hope, for it was their all; they should not neglect him who spake to them from heaven, for in dignity, rank, and authority, he far surpassed all who in former times had made known the will of God to men.

This epistle, therefore, occupies a most important place in the book of revelation, and without it that book would be incomplete. It is the most full explanation which we have of the meaning of the Jewish institutions. In the epistle to the Romans we have a system of religious doctrine, and particularly a defence of the great doctrine of justification by faith. Important doctrines are discussed in the other epistles; but there was something wanted that would show the meaning of the Jewish rites and ceremonies, and their connection with the Christian scheme; something which would show us how the one was preparatory to the other; and I may add, something that would restrain the *imagination* in endeavouring to show how the one was designed to introduce the other. The one was a system of *types* and *shadows*. But on nothing is the human mind more prone to wander than on the subject of emblems and analogies. This has been shown abundantly in the experience of the Christian church, from the time of Origen to the present. Systems of divinity, commentaries, and sermons, have shown everywhere how prone men of ardent imaginations have been to find types in everything pertaining to the ancient economy; to discover hidden meanings in every ceremony; and to regard every pin and hook and instrument of the tabernacle as designed to inculcate some *truth*, and to shadow forth some fact or doctrine of the Christian revelation. It was desirable to have *one* book that should tell how that is; to fetter down the imagination and bind it by severe rules, and to restrain the vagaries of honest but credulous devotion. Such a book we have in the epistle to the Hebrews. The ancient system is there explained by one who had been brought up in the midst of it, and who understood it thoroughly; by one who had a clear insight into the relation which it bore to the Christian economy; by one who was under the influence of divine inspiration, and who could not err. The Bible would have been incomplete without this book : and when I think of the relation between the Jewish and the Christian systems ; when I look on the splendid rites of the ancient economy, and ask their meaning ; when I wish a full guide to heaven, and ask for that which gives completeness to the whole, I turn instinctively to the Epistle to the Hebrews. When I wish also that which shall give me the most elevated view of the Great Author of Christianity and of his work, and the most clear conceptions of the sacrifice which he made for sin : and when I look for considerations that shall be most effectual in restraining the soul from apostasy, and for considerations to enable it to bear trials with patience and with hope, my mind recurs to this book, and I feel that the book of revelation, and the hopes of man, would be incomplete without it.

PAUL THE APOSTLE TO THE HEBREWS.

CHAPTER I.

ANALYSIS OF THE CHAPTER.

The main object of the epistle is to commend the Christian religion to those who were addressed in it in such a way as to prevent defection from it. This is done, principally, by showing its superiority to the Mosaic system. The great danger of Christians in Palestine was of relapsing into the Jewish system. The imposing nature of its rites; the public sentiment in its favour ; the fact of its antiquity, and its undisputed divine origin, would all tend to that. To counteract this, the writer of this epistle shows that the gospel had higher claims on their attention, and that if that was rejected ruin was inevitable. In doing this, he begins, in this chapter, by showing the superiority of the Author of Christianity to prophets and to the angels; that is, that he had a rank that entitled him to the profoundest regard. The drift of this chapter, therefore, is to show the dignity and exalted nature of the Author of the Christian system—the Son of God. The chapter comprises the following points :—

I. The announcement of the fact that God, who had formerly spoken by the prophets, had in this last dispensation spoken by his Son; vers. 1, 2.

II. The statement respecting his rank and dignity. He was (1) the heir of all things; (2) the creator of the worlds; (3) the brightness of the divine glory and the proper expression of his nature; (4) he upheld all things; vers. 2, 3.

III. The work and exaltation of the Author of the Christian system. (1.)

He, by his own unassisted agency, purified us from our sins. (2.) He is seated at the right hand of God. (3.) He has a more exalted and valuable inheritance than the angels, in proportion as his name is more exalted than theirs ; vers. 3, 4.

IV. Proofs that what is here ascribed to him belongs to him, particularly that he is declared to be superior to the angels; vers. 5—14.

(1.) The angels have never been addressed with the title of Son : ver. 5.

(2.) He is declared to be the object of worship by the angels, while they are employed merely as the messengers of God; vers. 6, 7.

(3.) He is addressed as God, and his throne is said to be for ever and ever; vers. 8, 9.

(4.) He is addressed as immutable. He is declared to have laid the foundations of heaven and earth; and though they would perish, yet he would remain the same; vers. 10—12.

(5.) None of the angels had been addressed in this manner, but they were employed in the subordinate work of ministering to the heirs of salvation; vers. 13, 14.

From this train of reasoning, the inference is drawn in ch. ii. 1—4, that we ought to give diligent heed to what had been spoken. The Great Author of the Christian scheme had peculiar claims to be heard, and there was peculiar danger in disregarding his message. The *object* of this chapter is, to impress those to whom the epistle was addressed with the high claims of the Founder of Christianity, and to show that it was superior in this respect to any other system.

CHAPTER I.

GOD, who[a] at sundry times and in divers manners spake

a Nu. 12. 6, 8.

1. *God who at sundry times.* The commencement of this epistle varies from all the others which Paul wrote. In every other instance he at first announces his name, and the name of the church or of the individual to whom he wrote. In regard to the reason why he here varies from that custom, see the Introduction, § 3. This commences with the full acknowledgment of his belief that God had made important revelations in past times, but that now he had communicated his will in a manner that more especially claimed their attention. This announcement was of particular importance here. He was writing to those who had been trained up in the full belief of the truths taught by the prophets. As the object of the apostle was to show the superior claims of the gospel, and to lead them from putting confidence in the rites instituted in accordance with the directions of the Old Testament, it was of essential importance that he should admit that their belief of the inspiration of the prophets was well founded. He was not an infidel. He was not disposed to call in question the divine origin of the books which were regarded as given by inspiration. He fully admitted all that had been held by the Hebrews on that head, and yet showed that the *new* revelation had more important claims to their attention. The word rendered "at sundry times"—πολυμερῶς—means *in many parts.* It refers here to the fact that the former revelation had been given in various parts. It had not all been given at once. It had been communicated from time to time as the exigencies of the people required, and as God chose to communicate it. At one time it was by history, then by prophecy, by poetry, by proverbs, by some solemn and special message, &c. The ancient revelation was a *collection* of various writings, on different subjects, and given at different times;

in time past unto the fathers by the prophets,

2 Hath in these last days

but *now* God had addressed us by *his Son*—the one great Messenger who had come to finish the divine communications, and to give a uniform and connected revelation to mankind. The contrast here is between the numerous separate *parts* of the revelation given by the prophets, and the oneness of that given by his Son. The word does not elsewhere occur in the New Testament. ¶ *And in divers manners*—πολυτρόπως. In many ways. It was not all in one mode. He had employed various methods in communicating his will. At one time it was by direct communication, at another by dreams, at another by visions, &c. In regard to the various methods which God employed to communicate his will, see Introduction to Isaiah, § 7. In contradistinction from these, God had now spoken by his Son. He had addressed us in one uniform manner. It was not by dreams, or visions; it was a direct communication from him. The word used here, also, occurs nowhere else in the New Testament. ¶ *In times past.* Formerly; in ancient times. The series of revelations began, as recorded by Moses, with Adam (Gen. iii.), and terminated with Malachi—a period of more than three thousand five hundred years. From Malachi to the time of the Saviour there were no recorded divine communications, and the whole period of *written* revelation, or when the divine communications were recorded from Moses to Malachi, was about a thousand years. ¶ *Unto the fathers.* To our ancestors; to the people of ancient times. ¶ *By the prophets.* The word *prophet* in the Scriptures is used in a wide signification. It means not only those who predict future events, but those who communicate the divine will on any subject. See Notes on Rom. xii. 6; 1 Cor. xiv. 1. It is used here in that large sense—as denoting all those by whom God had made communications to the Jews in former times.

spoken *a* unto us by *his* Son, whom he hath appointed heir *b*

a De.18.15.		*b* Ps.2.8.

2. *Hath in these last days.* In this the final dispensation; or in this dispensation under which the affairs of the world will be wound up. Phrases similar to this occur frequently in the Scriptures. They do not imply that the world was soon coming to an end, but that that was the *last* dispensation, the *last* period of the world. There had been the patriarchal period, the period under the law, the prophets, &c., and *this* was the period during which God's *last* method of communication would be enjoyed, and under which the world would close. It might be a *very long* period, but it would be the *last* one; and so far as the meaning of the phrase is concerned, it might be the longest period, or longer than all the others put together, but still it would be the *last* one. See Notes on Acts ii. 17; Isa. ii. 2. ¶ *Spoken unto us.* The word "*us*" here does not of necessity imply that the writer of the epistle had actually heard him, or that they had heard him to whom the epistle was written. It means that God had now communicated his will to man by his Son. It may be said with entire propriety that God has spoken to *us* by his Son, though *we* have not personally heard or seen him. We have what he spoke and caused to be recorded for our direction. ¶ *By his Son.* The title commonly given to the Lord Jesus, as denoting his peculiar relation to God. It was understood by the Jews to denote equality with God (Notes, John v. 18; comp. John x. 33, 36), and is used with such a reference here. See Notes on Rom. i. 4, where the meaning of the phrase "Son of God" is fully considered. It is implied here that the fact that the Son of God has spoken to us imposes the highest obligations to attend to what he has said; that he has an authority superior to all those who have spoken in past times; and that there will be peculiar guilt in refusing to attend to what he has spoken. See ch. ii. 1—4; comp. ch. xii. 25.

of all things, by whom also he made the worlds;

c John1.3.

The *reasons* for the superior respect which should be shown to the revelations of the Son of God may be such as these:—(1.) His rank and dignity. He is the equal with God (John i. 1), and is himself called God in this chapter; ver. 8. He has a right, therefore, to command, and when he speaks men should obey (2.) The clearness of the truths which he communicated to man on a great variety of subjects that are of the highest moment to the world. Revelation has been gradual—like the breaking of the day in the east. At first there is a little light; it increases and expands till objects become more and more visible, and then the sun rises in full-orbed glory. At first we discern only the *existence* of some object—obscure and undefined; then we can trace its outline; then its colour, its size, its proportions, its drapery—till it stands before us fully revealed. So it has been with revelation. There is a great variety of subjects which we now see clearly, which were very imperfectly understood by the teaching of the prophets, and would be now if we had only the Old Testament. Among them are the following:—(*a*) The character of God. Christ came to make him known as a *merciful* being, and to show *how* he could be merciful as well as just. The views given of God by the Lord Jesus are far more clear than any given by the ancient prophets; compared with those entertained by the ancient philosophers, they are like the sun compared with the darkest midnight. (*b*) The way in which man may be reconciled to God. The New Testament—which may be considered as that which God "has spoken to us by his Son"—has told us how the great work of being reconciled to God can be effected. The Lord Jesus told us that he came to "give his life a ransom for many;" that he laid down his life for his friends; that he was about to die for man; that he would draw all men to him. The prophets indeed—particularly Isaiah—threw much light on these points. But the mass of the people did not understand their revelations. They pertained to future events—always difficult to be understood. But Christ has told us the way of salvation, and he has made it so plain that he who runs may read. (c) The *moral* precepts of the Redeemer are superior to those of any and all that had gone before him. They are elevated, pure, expansive, benevolent—such as became the Son of God to proclaim. Indeed this is admitted on all hands. Infidels are constrained to acknowledge that all the moral precepts of the Saviour are eminently pure and benignant. If they were obeyed, the world would be filled with justice, truth, purity, and benevolence. Error, fraud, hypocrisy, ambition, wars, licentiousness, and intemperance, would cease; and the opposite virtues would diffuse happiness over the face of the world. Prophets had indeed delivered many moral precepts of great importance, but the purest and most extensive body of just principles of good morals on earth are to be found in the teachings of the Saviour. (d) He has given to us the clearest view which man has had of the future state; and he has disclosed in regard to that future state a class of truths of the deepest interest to mankind, which were before wholly unknown or only partially revealed. 1. He has revealed the certainty of a state of future existence—in opposition to the Sadducees of all ages. This was denied before he came by multitudes, and where it was not, the arguments by which it was supported were often of the feeblest kind. The *truth* was held by some—like Plato and his followers—but the *arguments* on which they relied were feeble, and such as were unfitted to give rest to the soul. The *truth* they had obtained by TRADITION; the *arguments* were THEIR OWN. 2. He revealed the doctrine of the resurrection of the body. This before was doubted or denied by nearly all the world. It was held to be absurd and impossible. The Sa-

viour taught its certainty; he raised up more than one to show that it was possible; he was himself raised, to put the whole matter beyond debate. 3. He revealed the certainty of future judgment—the judgment of all mankind. 4. He disclosed great and momentous truths respecting the future state. Before he came, all was dark. The Greeks spoke of Elysian fields, but they were dreams of the imagination; the Hebrews had some faint notion of a future state where all was dark and gloomy, with perhaps an occasional glimpse of the truth that there is a holy and blessed heaven; but to the mass of mind all was obscure. Christ revealed a heaven, and told us of a hell. He showed us that the one might be gained and the other avoided. He presented important motives for doing it; and had he done nothing more, his communications were worthy the profound attention of mankind. I may add, (3.) That the Son of God has claims on our attention from the MANNER in which he spoke. He spoke as one having "authority;" Matt vii. 29. He spoke as a *witness* of what he saw and knew; John iii. 11. He spoke without doubt or ambiguity of God, and heaven, and hell. His is the language of one who is familiar with all that he describes; who saw all, who knew all. There is no hesitancy or doubt in his mind of the truth of what he speaks; and he speaks as if his whole soul were impressed with its unspeakable importance. Never were so momentous communications made to men of *hell* as fell from the lips of the Lord Jesus (see Notes on Matt. xxiii. 33); never were announcements made so fitted to awe and appal a sinful world. ¶ *Whom he hath appointed heir of all things;* see Ps. ii. 8; comp. Notes Rom. viii. 17. This is language taken from the fact that he is "*the* SON of God." If a son, then he is an heir—for so it is usually among men. This is not to be taken *literally*, as if he inherits anything as a man does. An heir is one who inherits anything after the death of its possessor—usually his father. But this

3 Who [a] being the brightness of *his* glory, and the express

a John i. 14.

cannot be applied in this sense to the Lord Jesus. The language is used to denote his rank and dignity as the Son of God. As such all things are his, as the property of a father descends to his son at his death. The word rendered *heir* — κληρονόμος — means properly (1) one who acquires any thing by lot; and (2) an *heir* in the sense in which we usually understand the word. It may also denote a *possessor* of anything received as a portion, or of property of any kind; see Rom. iv. 13, 14. It is in every instance rendered *heir* in the New Testament. Applied to Christ, it means that as the Son of God he is possessor or lord of all things, or that all things are his; comp. Acts ii. 36; x. 36; John xvii. 10; xvi. 15. "All things that the Father hath are mine." The sense is, that all things belong to the Son of God. Who is so *rich* then as Christ? Who so able to endow his friends with enduring and abundant wealth? ¶ *By whom.* By whose agency; or who was the actual agent in the creation. Grotius supposes that this means, "on account of whom;" and that the meaning is, that the universe was formed with reference to the Messiah, in accordance with an ancient Jewish maxim. But the more common and classical usage of the word rendered *by* (διὰ), when it governs a genitive, as here, is to denote the instrumental cause; the agent by which anything is done; see Matt. i. 22; ii. 5, 15, 23; Luke xviii. 31; John ii. 17; Acts, ii. 22, 43; iv. 16; xii. 9; Rom. ii. 16; v. 5. It *may be true* that the universe was formed with reference to the glory of the Son of God, and that this world was brought into being in order to show his glory; but it would not do to establish that doctrine on a passage like this. Its obvious and proper meaning is, that he was the agent of the creation—a truth that is elsewhere abundantly taught; see John i. 3, 10; Col. i. 16; Eph. iii. 9; 1 Cor. viii. 6. This sense, also, better agrees with the design of the

apostle in this place. His object is to set forth the dignity of the Son of God. This is better shown by the consideration that he was the *creator* of all things, than that all things were made *for* him. ¶ *The worlds.* The universe, or creation. So the word here—αἰών—is undoubtedly used in ch. xi. 3. The word properly means *age* — an indefinitely long period of time; then perpetuity, ever, eternity—*always being.* For an extended investigation of the meaning of the word, the reader may consult an essay by Prof. Stuart, in the Spirit of the Pilgrims, for 1829, pp. 406—452. From the sense of *age*, or *duration*, the word comes to denote the present and future age; the present world and the world to come; the present world, with all its cares, anxieties, and evils; the men of this world—a wicked generation, &c. Then it means the world—the material universe – creation as it is. The only perfectly clear use of the word in this sense in the New Testament is in Heb. xi. 3, and there there can be no doubt. "Through faith we understand that the *worlds* were made by the word of God, so that things which are seen were not made of things which do appear." The passage before us will bear the same interpretation, and this is the most obvious and intelligible. What would be the meaning of saying that the *ages* or *dispensations* were made by the Son of God? The Hebrews used the word—צוֹלם—*Olâm*—in the same sense. It properly means *age, duration*; and thence it came to be used by them to denote the world—made up of *ages* or generations; and then the world itself. This is the fair, and, as it seems to me, the only intelligible interpretation of this passage — an interpretation amply sustained by texts referred to above as demonstrating that the universe was made by the agency of the Son of God. Comp. Notes on vers. 10, and on John i. 3.

3. *Who being the brightness of hi-*

image of his person, and upholding all things by the word of his power, when *a* he had by him-

a ch.7.27;9.12-14.

self purged our sins, sat down *b* on the right hand of the Majesty on high.

b Ps.110.

glory. This verse is designed to state the dignity and exalted rank of the Son of God, and is exceedingly important with reference to a correct view of the Redeemer. Every word which is employed is of great importance, and should be clearly understood in order to a correct apprehension of the passage. First, in what manner does it refer to the Redeemer? To his divine nature? To the mode of his existence before he was incarnate? Or to him as he appeared on earth? Most of the ancient commentators supposed that it referred to his divine dignity before he became incarnate, and proceed to argue on that supposition on the mode of the divine existence. The true solution seems to me to be, that it refers to him as incarnate, but still has reference to him *as* the incarnate *Son of God.* It refers to him as Mediator, but not simply or mainly as a man. It is rather to him as divine—thus, in his incarnation, being the brightness of the divine glory, and the express image of God. That this is the correct view is apparent, I think, from the whole scope of the passage. The drift of the argument is, to show his dignity *as he has spoken to us* (ver. 1), and not in the period antecedent to his incarnation. It is to show his claims to our reverence as sent from God—the last and greatest of the messengers which God has sent to man. But then it is a description of him *as he actually is*—the incarnate Son of God; the equal of the Father in human flesh; and this leads the writer to dwell on his divine character, and to argue from that; vers. 8, 10—12. I have no doubt, therefore, that this description refers to his divine nature, but it is the divine nature as it appears in human flesh. An examination of the words used will prepare us for a more clear comprehension of the sense. The word *glory—δόξα—*means properly a *seeming, an appearance;* and then (1) praise, applause, honour; (2) dig-

nity, splendour, glory; (3) brightness, dazzling light; and (4) excellence perfection, such as belongs to God and such as there is in heaven. It is probably used here, as the word—רבכ—*Kábhodh—*is often among the Hebrews, to denote splendour, brightness, and refers to the divine perfections as resembling a bright light, or the sun. The word is applied to the sun and stars, 1 Cor. xv. 40, 41; to the light which Paul saw on the way to Damascus, Acts xxii. 11; to the shining of Moses' face, 2 Cor. iii. 7; to the celestial light which surrounds the angels, Rev. xviii. 1; and to glorified saints, Luke ix. 31, 32; and to the dazzling splendour or majesty in which God is enthroned; 2 Thess i. 9; 2 Pet. i. 17; Rev. xv. 8; xxi. 11, 23. Here there is a comparison of God with the sun; he is encompassed with splendour and majesty; he is a being of light and of infinite perfection. It refers to *all in God* that is bright, splendid, glorious; and the idea is, that the Son of God is the *brightness* of it all. The word rendered *brightness — ἀπαύγασμα —* occurs nowhere else in the New Testament. It means properly *reflected splendour,* or the light which emanates from a luminous body. The rays or beams of the sun are its "brightness," or that by which the sun is seen and known. The sun itself we do not see; the beams which flow from it we do see. The meaning here is, that if God be represented under the image of a luminous body, as he is in the Scriptures (see Ps. lxxxiv. 11; Mal. iv. 2), then Christ is the radiance of that light, the brightness of that luminary. *Stuart.* He is that by which we perceive God, or by which God is made known to us in his real perfections; comp. John i. 18; xiv. 9.—It is by him only that the true character and glory of God is known to men. This is true in regard to the great system of revelation but it is especially true in regard to the views which men have of God

Matt. xi. 27. "No man knoweth the Son but the Father; neither knoweth any man the Father save the Son, and he to whomsoever the Son will reveal him.' The human soul is dark respecting the divine character until it is enlightened by Christ. It sees no beauty, no glory in his nature—nothing that excites wonder, or that wins the affections, until it is disclosed by the Redeemer. *Somehow* it happens, account for it as men may, that there are no elevating practical views of God in the world; no views that engage and hold the affections of the soul; no views that are transforming and purifying, but those which are derived from the Lord Jesus. A man becomes a Christian, and at once he has elevated, practical views of God. He is to him the most glorious of all beings. He finds supreme delight in contemplating his perfections. But he may be a philosopher or an infidel, and though he may profess to believe in the existence of God, yet the belief excites no practical influence on him; he sees nothing to admire; nothing which leads him to worship him; comp. Rom. i. 21. ¶ *And the express image.* The word here used— χαρακτηρ—likewise occurs nowhere else in the New Testament. It is that from which our word *character* is derived. It properly means *a graving-tool;* and then something engraved, or stamped—*a character*–as a letter, mark, sign. The image stamped on coins, seals, wax, expresses the idea: and the sense here is, that if God be represented under the idea of a substance, or being, then Christ is the exact resemblance of that—as an image is of the stamp or die. The resemblance between a stamp and the figure which is impressed is exact; and so is the resemblance between the Redeemer and God; see Col. i. 15. "Who is the image of the invisible God." ¶ *Of his person.* The word *person* with us denotes an individual being, and is applied to human beings, consisting of body and soul. We do not apply it to anything dead—not using it with reference to the body when the spirit is gone. It is applied to man—with individual and separate

consciousness and will; with body and soul; with an existence separate from others. It is evident that it cannot be used in this sense when applied to God, and that this word does not express the true idea of the passage here. Tindal renders it, more accurately, *substance.* The word in the original —ὑποστασις—whence our word *hypostasis,* means, literally, *a foundation,* or *substructure.* Then it means a well-founded trust, firm expectation, confidence, firmness, boldness; and then *reality, substance, essential nature.* In the New Testament, it is rendered *confident,* or *confidence* (2 Cor. ix. 4; xi. 17; Heb. iii. 14); *substance* (Heb. xi. 1); and *person* in the passage before us. It is not elsewhere used. Here it properly refers to the essential nature of God—that which distinguishes him from all other beings, and which, if I may so say, *constitutes him God;* and the idea is, that the Redeemer is the exact resemblance of *that.* This resemblance consists, probably, in the following things—though perhaps the enumeration does not include all—but in these he certainly resembles God, or is his exact image. (1.) In his original mode of being, or before the incarnation. Of this we know little. But he had a "glory with the Father before the world was;" John xvii. 5. He was "in the beginning with God, and was God;" John i. 1. He was in intimate union with the Father, and was one with Him, in certain respects; though in certain other respects, there was a distinction. I do not see any evidence in the Scriptures of the doctrine of "eternal generation," and it is certain that that doctrine militates against the *proper eternity* of the Son of God. The natural and fair meaning of that doctrine would be, that there was a time when he had not an existence, and when he began to be, or was begotten. But the Scripture doctrine is, that he had a strict and proper eternity. I see no evidence that he was in any sense *a derived being*—deriving his existence and his divinity from the Father. The Fathers of the Christian church, it is believed, held that the Son of God as to his divine, as well as his human nature. was *derived* from the Father. Hence the Nicene creed speaks of him as "begotten of the Father before all worlds; God of God, Light of Light, very God of very God, begotten not made"—language implying derivation in his divine nature. They held, with one voice, that he was God; but it was in this manner; see Stuart, Excursus III. on the Epistle to the Hebrews. But this is incredible and impossible. A *derived* being cannot in any proper sense be God; and if there is any attribute which the Scriptures have ascribed to the Saviour with peculiar clearness, it is that of proper eternity; Rev.i.11,17; John i.1.

[Perhaps the doctrine of Christ's natural or eternal Sonship had been as well understood without the help of the term "generation," which adds nothing to our stock of ideas on the subject, and gives rise, as the above remarks prove, to objections which attach altogether to the *word*, and from which the *doctrine* itself is free. In fairness, however, it should be remembered that, like many other theological terms, the term in question, when applied to Christ's Sonship, is not to be understood in the ordinary acceptation, as implying derivation or extraction. It is used as making some approach to a proper term only, and in this case, as in others of like nature, it is but just to respect the acknowledged rule, that when human phraseology is employed concerning the divine nature, all that is imperfect, all that belongs to the creature, is to be rejected, and that only retained which comports with the majesty of the Creator. It is on this very principle that Professor Stuart, in his first excursus, and Trinitarians generally, have so successfully defended the use of the word "person" to designate a distinction in the Godhead. Overlooking this principle, our author deduces consequences from the doctrine of eternal generation, which do not properly belong to it, and which its advocates distinctly repudiate. That doctrine cannot militate against the proper eternity of the Son, since, while it uses the term generation, not *more humano*, but with every thing of human infirmity separated from it, it supplies also the adjunct "eternal." Whatever some indiscreet advocates of the eternal Sonship may have affirmed, it should never be forgotten, that the ablest friends equally with the author, contend that there is NO DERIVATION OR COMMUNICATION OF ESSENCE FROM THE FATHER TO THE SON. "Although the terms Father and Son indicate a relation analogous to that among men, yet, as in the latter case, it is a relation between two ma-

terial and separate beings, and in the former, is a relation in the same spiritual essence, the one can throw no light upon the other; and to attempt to illustrate the one by the other is equally illogical and presumptuous. We can conceive the communication of a material essence by one material being to another, because it takes place in the generation of animals; but the communication of a spiritual, indivisible, immutable essence is altogether inconceivable, especially when we add, that the supposed communication does not constitute a different being, but takes place in the essences communicating." Dick's Theol. vol. ii page 71. It is readily allowed that the Fathers, and many since their times, have written unguardedly on this mysterious subject; but their errors, instead of leading us to reject the doctrine entirely, should lead us only to examine the Scriptures more fully, and form our opinions on them alone. The excellent author already quoted has well remarked: "I cannot conceive what object they have in view who admit the Divinity, but deny the natural Sonship of our Saviour, unless it be to get rid of the strange notions about communication of essence and subordination which have prevailed so much; and in this case, like too many disputants, in avoiding one extreme, they run into the other."]

It *may* have been that it was by him that the perfections of God were made known before the incarnation to the angelic world, but on that point the Scriptures are silent. (2.) On earth he was the brightness of the divine glory, and the express image of his person. (*a*) It was by him, eminently, that God was made known to men—as it is by the beams of the sun that that is made known. (*b*) He bore an exact resemblance to God. He was just such a being as we should suppose God to be were he to become incarnate, and to act as a man. He was the embodied representation of the Deity. He was pure—like God. He was benevolent—like God. He spake to the winds and storms—like God. He healed diseases—like God. He raised the dead—like God. He wielded the power which God only can wield, and he manifested a character in all respects like that which we should suppose God would evince if he appeared in human flesh, and dwelt among men. And this is saying much. It is in fact saying that the account in the Gospels is real, and that the

Christian religion is true. Uninspired men could never have drawn such a character as that of Jesus Christ, unless that character had actually existed. The attempt has often been made to describe God, or to show how he would speak and act if he came down to earth. Thus the Hindoos speak of the incarnations of Vishnu; and thus Homer, and Virgil, and most of the ancient poets, speak of the appearance of the gods, and describe them as they were supposed to appear. But how different from the character of the Lord Jesus! *They* are full of passion, and lust, and anger, and contention, and strife; they come to mingle in battles, and to take part with contending armies, and they evince the same spirit as *men*, and are merely *men of great power, and more gigantic passions;* but Christ is GOD IN HUMAN NATURE. The form is that of man; the spirit is that of God. He walks, and eats, and sleeps as a man; he thinks, and speaks, and acts like God. He was born as a man—but the angels adored him as God. As a man he ate; yet by a word he created food for thousands, as if he were God. Like a man he slept on a pillow while the vessel was tossed by the waves; like God he rose, and rebuked the winds and they were still. As a man he went, with affectionate interest, to the house of Martha and Mary. As a man he sympathized with them in their affliction, and wept at the grave of their brother; like God he spoke, and the dead came forth to the land of the living. As a man he travelled through the land of Judea. He was without a home. Yet everywhere the sick were laid at his feet, and health came from his touch, and strength from the words of his lips — as if he were God. As a man he prayed in the garden of Gethsemane; he bore his cross to Calvary; he was nailed to the tree: yet then the heavens grew dark, and the earth shook, and the dead arose—as if he were God. As a man he slept in the cold tomb—like God he rose, and brought life and immortality to light. He lived on earth as a man—he ascended to heaven like God. And in all the

life of the Redeemer, in all the variety of trying situations in which he was placed, there was not a word or action which was inconsistent with the supposition that he was the incarnate God. There was no failure of any effort to heal the sick or to raise the dead; no look, no word, no deed that is not perfectly consistent with this supposition; but on the contrary, his life is full of events which can be explained on no other supposition than that he was the appropriate shining forth of the divine glory, and the exact resemblance of the essence of God. There are not two Gods—as there are not two suns when the sun shines. It is *the one* God, in a mysterious and incomprehensible manner shining into the world in the face of Jesus Christ. See Note on 2 Cor. iv. 6. As the wax bears the perfect image of the seal—perfect not only in the outline, but in the filling up—in all the lines, and features, and letters, so is it with the Redeemer. There is not one of the divine perfections which has not the counterpart in him, and if the glory of the divine character is seen at all by men, it will be seen in and through him. ¶ *And upholding all things by the word of his power.* That is, by his powerful word, or command. The phrase "word of his power" is a Hebraism, and means his efficient command. There could not be a more distinct ascription of divinity to the Son of God than this. He upholds or sustains all things —*i. e.* the universe. It is not merely the earth; not only its rocks, mountains, seas, animals and men, but it is the universe—all distant worlds. How can he do this who is not God? He does it by his word—his command. What a conception! That a simple *command* should do all this! So the world was made when God "spake and it was done; he commanded and it stood fast;" Ps. xxxiii. 9. So the Lord Jesus *commanded* the waves and the winds, and they were still (Matt. viii. 26, 27); so he spoke to diseases and they departed, and to the dead and they arose; comp. Gen. i. 3. I know not how men can *explain away* this ascription of infinite power to the Redeemer. There can be no higher

4 Being made so much better than the angels, as he hath by inheritance obtained a more excellent name than they.

5 For unto which of the angels said he at any time, *a* Thou art my Son, this day have I begotten

a Ps.2.7.

idea of omnipotence than to say that he upholds all things by his word; and assuredly he who can *hold up* this vast universe so that it does not sink into anarchy or into nothing, must be God. The same power Jesus claimed for himself; see Matt. xxviii. 18. ¶ *When he had by himself purged our sins.* "*By himself*"—not by the blood of bulls and lambs, but by his own blood. This is designed to bring in the grand feature of the Christian scheme, that the purification made for sin was by *his* blood, instead of the blood which was shed in the temple-service. The word here rendered "purged" means *purified* or *expiated*; see Notes on John xv. 2. The literal rendering is, "having made purification for our sins." The purification or cleansing which he effected was by his blood; see 1 John i. 7. "The blood of Jesus Christ cleanseth from all sin." This the apostle here states to have been the great object for which he came, and having done this, he sat down on the right hand of God; see ch. vii. 27; ix. 12—14. It was not merely to *teach* that he came; it was to purify the hearts of men, to remove their sins, and to put an end to sacrifice by the sacrifice of himself. ¶ *Sat down on the right hand of the Majesty on high.* Of God; see Notes on Mark xvi. 19; Eph. i. 20—23.

4. *Being made so much better.* Being exalted so much above the angels. The word "better" here does not refer to moral character, but to exaltation of rank. As Mediator; as the Son of God in our nature, he is exalted far above the angels. ¶ *Than the angels.* Than all angels of every rank; see Notes on Eph. i. 21; comp. 1 Pet. iii. 22. "Angels, and authorities, and powers being made subject unto him." He is exalted to his mediatorial throne, and all things are placed beneath his feet. ¶ *As he hath by inheritance.* Or in virtue of his name—the Son of God; an exaltation such as is implied in that name. As

a son has a rank in a family above servants; as he has a control over the property above that which servants have, so it is with the Mediator. He is the *Son* of God: angels are the *servants* of God, and the servants of the church. They occupy a place in the universe compared with that which he occupies, similar to the place which servants in a family occupy compared with that which a son has. To illustrate and prove this is the design of the remainder of this chapter. The argument which the apostle insists on is, that the title "THE Son of God" is to be given to him alone. It has been conferred on no others. Though the angels, and though saints are called in general "*sons* of God," yet the title "THE *Son of God*" has been given to him only. As the apostle was writing to Hebrews, he makes his appeal to the Hebrew Scriptures alone for the confirmation of this opinion. ¶ *A more excellent name.* To wit, the name *Son.* It is a more honourable and exalted name than has ever been bestowed on them. It involves more exalted privileges, and entitles him on whom it is bestowed to higher respect and honour than any name ever bestowed on them.

5. *For unto which of the angels,* &c. The object of this is, to prove that the Son of God, who has spoken to men in these last days, is superior to the angels. As the apostle was writing to those who had been trained in the Jewish religion, and who admitted the authority of the Old Testament, of course he made his appeal to that, and undoubtedly referred for proof to those places which were generally admitted to relate to the Messiah. Abarbanel says, that it was the common opinion of the Jewish doctors that the Messiah would be exalted above Abraham, Moses, and the angels. *Stuart.* There is a difficulty, as we shall see, in applying the passages which follow to the Messiah—a difficulty which we may find it not easy to explain

thee? And again, [a] I will be to | him a Father, and he shall be to
a 2Sa.7.14. | me a Son?

Some remarks will be made on the particular passages as we go along. In general it may be observed here, (1.) That it is to be presumed that those passages were in the time of Paul applied to the Messiah. He seems to argue from them as though this was commonly understood, and is at no pains to prove it. (2.) It is to be presumed that those to whom he wrote would at once admit this to be so. If this were not so, we cannot suppose that he would regard this mode of reasoning as at all efficacious, or adapted to convince those to whom he wrote. (3.) He did not apprehend that the application which he made of these texts would be called in question by the countrymen of those to whom he wrote. It is to be presumed, therefore, that the application was made in accordance with the received opinions, and the common interpretation. (4.) Paul had been instructed in early life in the doctrines of the Jewish religion, and made fully acquainted with all their principles of interpretation. It is to be presumed, therefore, that he made these quotations in accordance with the prevalent belief, and with principles which were well understood and admitted. (5.) Every age and people have their own modes of reasoning. They may differ from others, and others may regard them as unsound, and yet to that age and people they are satisfactory and conclusive. The ancient philosophers employed modes of reasoning which would not strike us as the most forcible, and which perhaps we should not regard as tenable. So it is with the Chinese, the Hindoos, the Mohammedans now. So it was with the writers of the dark ages who lived under the influence of the scholastic philosophy. They argue from admitted principles in their country and time—just as we do in ours. Their reasoning was as satisfactory to them as ours is to us. (6.) In a writer of any particular age we are to expect to find the prevailing mode of reasoning, and appeals to the usual arguments on any subject. We are not to look for

methods of argument founded on the inductive philosophy in the writings of the schoolmen, or in the writings of the Chinese or the Hindoos. It would be unreasonable to expect it. We are to expect that they will be found to reason in accordance with the customs of their time; to appeal to such arguments as were commonly alleged; and if they are reasoning with an adversary, *to make use of the points which he concedes*, and to urge them as fitted to convince *him*. And this is not wrong. It may strike him with more force than it does us; it may be that we can see that is not the most solid mode of reasoning, but still it may not be in itself an improper method. That the writers of the New Testament should have used that mode of reasoning sometimes, is no more surprising than that we find writers in China reasoning from acknowledged principles, and in the usual manner there, or than that men in our own land reason on the principles of the inductive philosophy. These remarks may not explain *all* the difficulties in regard to the proof-texts adduced by Paul in this chapter, but they may remove *some* of them, and may so prepare the way that we may be able to dispose of them all as we advance. In the passage which is quoted in this verse, there is not much difficulty in regard to the propriety of its being thus used. The difficulty lies in the subsequent quotations in the chapter. [It is, doubtless, of very great importance in conducting an argument, to select such proofs as are likely to weigh most with those whom we wish to convince. To argue from *admitted* principles saves both time and labour, and more readily secures success than any other method. To vindicate the Apostle, however, on the ground alleged here, under the fifth and sixth particulars, will, by many, be regarded as scarcely consistent with that respect, which the high *authority of inspiration* claims. Ordinary writers *may* employ arguments in themselves inadmissible, but which pass current in their time and country, and therefore serve the *immediate* design equally well with more solid reasoning. The Chinese, Hindoos, &c., may do all this, without any reflection on their honesty, and with little perhaps on their wisdom, it being quite unreasonable to look for the inductive philosophy among them. But men will expect something more from an inspired apostle. *He* must use no argument merely because it will pass, or is commonly employed. He must be wise enough to understand what is the true mode of reasoning on any point, whatever the prevalent fashion may be, and honest enough to employ that mode alone; otherwise the inductive philosophy should enable us now-a-days to detect flaws in the reasoning of inspiration. Admitting, for a moment, that the apostle may possibly have condescended, when reasoning with his Jewish adversary, "to make use of the points which he conceded, and to urge them as fitted to convince *him*," even while he knew that this was not the most solid mode of reasoning, what is to become of those who in course of time acquire sufficient philosophy to discover the real unsoundness of the argument? What are we to do? Dismiss the whole, the infidel might sneeringly tell us, as suited to ignorant "Hebrews or Hindoos." Besides, once admitting this principle, there is room for jealousy in regard to the length to which it might be carried. How much of the reasoning in this epistle might be affected by it! The truth is, that the passages quoted must have been *acknowledged by the Jews* properly to belong to the subject, or the apostle would not so confidently have adduced them as proof. At the same time, they must in *reality* have belonged to it, or he never could have used them at all. "This was not enough," says Owen, "that those with whom he dealt acknowledged these words to be spoken concerning the Messiah, unless they were so really, that so his arguments might proceed *ex veris* as well as *ex concessis*, from what was true, as on what was granted." To the same purpose Mr. Scott remarks, "that the compositions of inspired apostles are of equal authority with the passages they adduce—and if they were sufficient proofs to the persons immediately concerned, they must be sufficient for all who consider the writer as fully knowing, by divine *inspiration*, both the doctrine of Christ and the true meaning of the Scriptures." It is this fact, the fact of inspiration, that renders such vindication of the apostle's reasoning as that attempted above, not only needless, but injurious. Besides, when we come to examine the passages in question, the difficulty regarding their application is, after all, not very great, as our author himself, in his able exposition of them, abundantly shows.

¶ *Said he at any time.* He never used language respecting the angels like that which he employs respecting his Son. He never applied to any

one of them the name *Son.* ¶ *Thou art my Son.* The name "*sons* of God," is applied in the Scriptures to saints, and may have been given to the angels. But the argument here is, that the name, my "Son" has never been given to any one of them particularly and by eminence. In a large, general sense, they are the sons of God, or the children of God, but the name is given to the Lord Jesus, the Messiah, in a peculiar sense, implying a peculiar relation to him, and a peculiar dominion over all things. This passage is quoted from Psalm ii.—a Psalm that is usually believed to pertain particularly to the Messiah, and one of the few Psalms that have undisputed reference to him; see Notes on Acts iv. 25; xiii. 33. ¶ *This day;* see Notes on Acts xiii. 33, where this passage is applied to the resurrection of Christ from the dead;—proving that the phrase "this day" does not refer to the doctrine of eternal generation, but to the resurrection of the Redeemer—"the FIRST-BEGOTTEN of the dead;" Rev. i. 5. Thus Theodoret says of the phrase "this day," "it does not express his eternal generation, but that which is connected with time." The argument of the apostle here does not turn on the *time* when this was said, but on the fact that this *was* said to him and not to any one of the angels, and this argument will have equal force whether the phrase be understood as referring to the fact of his resurrection, or to his previous existence. The structure and scope of the second Psalm refers to his exaltation *after* the kings of the earth set themselves against him, and endeavoured to cast off his government from them. In spite of that, and subsequent to that, he would set his king, which they had rejected, on his holy hill of Zion; see Ps. ii. 2—6. ¶ *Have I begotten thee.* See this place explained in the Notes on Acts xiii. 33. It *must*, from the necessity of the case, be understood figuratively; and must mean, substantially, "I have *constituted*, or *appointed* thee." If it refers to his resurrection, it means that that resurrection was a kind of *begetting* to life, or, a beginning of life; see Rev. i. 5.

And yet though Paul (Acts xiii. 33) has applied it to the resurrection of the Redeemer, and though the name "Son of God" is applied to him on account of his resurrection (see Notes on Rom. i. 4), yet I confess this does not seem to me to come up to all that the writer here intended. The phrase, "THE Son of God," I suppose, properly denotes that the Lord Jesus sustained a relation to God, designated by that name, corresponding to the relations which he sustained to man, designated by the name "the Son of man." The one implied that he had a peculiar relation to God, as the other implied that he had a peculiar relation to man. This is indisputable. But on what particular account the name was given him, or how he was manifested to be the Son of God, has been the great question. Whether the name refers to the mode of his existence before the incarnation, and to his "being begotten from eternity," or to the incarnation and the resurrection, has long been a point on which men have been divided in opinion. The natural idea conveyed by the title "THE Son of God" is, that he sustained a relation to God which implied more than was human or angelic; and this is certainly the drift of the argument of the apostle here. I do not see, however, that he refers to the doctrine of "eternal generation," or that he means to teach that. His point is, that God had declared and treated him as a Son—as superior to the angels and to men, and that this was shown in what had been said of him in the Old Testament. This would be equally clear, whether there is reference to the doctrine of eternal generation or not. The sense is, "he is more than human. He is more than angelic. He has been addressed and treated as a Son—which none of the angels have. They are regarded simply as ministering spirits. They sustain subordinate stations, and are treated accordingly. He, on the contrary, is the brightness of the divine glory. He is treated and addressed as a Son. In his original existence this was so. In his incarnation this was so. When on earth this was so; and in his resurrection, ascension, and session at the right hand of God, he was treated in all respects as a Son—as superior to all servants, and to all ministering spirits." The exact reference, then, of the phrase "this day have I begotten thee," in the Psalm, is to the act of constituting him in a public manner the Son of God—and refers to God's setting him as king on the "holy hill of Zion"—or making him king over the church and the world as Messiah; and this was done, eminently, as Paul shows (Acts xiii.), by the resurrection. It was based, however, on what was fit and proper. It was not arbitrary. There was a reason why he should thus be exalted rather than a man or an angel; and this was, that he was the God incarnate, and had a nature that qualified him for universal empire, and he was thus appropriately called "THE Son of God."

[No doctrine is advanced, by pressing into its service, such texts as sound criticism declares not strictly to belong to it. Yet, without doubt, many advocates of the eternal Sonship have done violence to this passage, with the design of upholding their views. That doctrine, however, happily is not dependent on a single text; and ample ground will remain for its friends, even if we admit, as in candour we must, that our author has fully made out his case against this text as a proof one. It seems clear, that neither σήμερον nor its corresponding הַיּוֹם can denote eternity; of such signification there is no example. The sense is uniformly confined to limited duration, Ps. xcv. 7; Heb iv 7 The order of the second Psalm, too, certainly does prove that the "begetting" took place after the opposition which the kings and rulers made to Christ, and not prior to it. Accordingly the text is elsewhere quoted in reference to the resurrection of Christ, Rom i 4; Acts xiii. 33. Besides, the chief design of the apostle in the place is not so much to show why Christ is called the Son of God, as simply to direct attention to the fact that he has this name, on the possession of which the whole argument is founded. He inherits a name which is never given to angels, and that of itself is proof of his superiority to them, whether we suppose the ground of the title to lie in his previous existence, or, with our author, in his incarnate Deity. But on this question, it must be admitted, that the passage determines nothing.

All this is substantially allowed by Owen, than whom a more stanch supporter of the doctrine of eternal Sonship cannot be named,

'The apostle, in this place," says he, "does not treat of the eternal generation of the Son, but of his exaltation and pre-eminence above angels. The word also, הַיּוֹם, constantly in the Scripture denotes some signal time, one day, or more. And that expression, ' this day have I begotten thee,' following immediately upon that other typical one, ' I have set my King upon my holy hill of Zion,' seems to be of the same import, and in like manner to be interpreted." On the general doctrine of the Sonship, the author has stated his views both here and elsewhere. That it is eternal or has its origin in the previous existence of Christ, he will not allow. It is given to the second person of the Trinity because he became " God *incarnate*," so that but for the incarnation and the economy of redemption, he would not have had this name. But the eternal Sonship of Christ rests on a body of evidence, that will not soon or easily be set aside. See that evidence adduced in a supplementary Note under Rom. i. 4. Meanwhile we would simply ask the reader, if it do not raise our idea of the love of God, in the mission of Christ, to suppose that he held the *dear* relation of Son *previous* to his coming—that BEING THE SON, he was sent to prove what a sacrifice the FATHER could make, in yielding up one so near, and so dear. But this astonishing evidence of love, if not destroyed, is greatly weakened, by the supposition that there was no Sonship until the sending of Christ. See also supplementary Note under verse 3.]

¶ *And again, I will be to him a Father.* This passage is evidently quoted from 2 Sam. vii. 14. A *sentiment* similar to this is found in Ps. lxxxix. 20—27. As these words were originally spoken, they referred to Solomon. They occur in a promise to David that he should not fail to have an heir to sit on his throne, or that his throne should be perpetual. The promise was particularly designed to comfort him in view of the fact that God would not suffer *him* to build the temple because his hands had been defiled with blood. To console him in reference to that, God promises him far greater honour than that would be. He promises that the house should be built by one of his own family, and that his family and kingdom should be established for ever. That in this series of promises the *Messiah* was included as a descendant of David, was the common opinion of the Jews, of the early Christians, and has been of the great body of interpreters. It was

certainly from such passages as this, that the Jews derived the notion which prevailed so universally in the time of the Saviour that the Messiah was to be the son or the descendant of David; see Matt. xxii. 42—45 ; ix. 27 ; xv. 22 ; xx. 30, 31; Mark x. 47, 48 ; Luke xviii. 38, 39; Matt. xii. 23 ; xxi. 9 ; John vii. 42 ; Rom.i.3 ; Rev.v.5 ; xxii.16. That opinion was universal. No one doubted it ; and it must have been common for the Jews to apply such texts as this to the Messiah. Paul would not have done it in this instance unless it had been usual. Nor was it improper. If the Messiah was to be a descendant of David, then it was natural to apply these promises in regard to his posterity in an eminent and peculiar sense to the Messiah. They were a part of the promises which included him, and which terminated in him. The promise, therefore, which is here made is, that God would be to him, in a peculiar sense, a Father, and he should be a Son. It does not, as I suppose, pertain originally exclusively to the Messiah, but *included* him as a descendant of David. To him it would be applicable in an eminent sense ; and if applicable to him *at all*, it proved all that the passage here is adduced to prove—that the name *Son* is given to the Messiah —a *name* not given to angels. That is just the point on which the argument turns. What is *implied* in the bestowment of that name is another point on which the apostle discourses in the other parts of the argument, I have no doubt, therefore, that while these words originally might have been applicable to Solomon, or to any of the other descendants of David who succeeded him on the throne, yet they at last terminated in the Messiah—to whom pre-eminently God would be a Father ; comp. Introduction to Isaiah, § 7, iii. (3), and Notes on Isa. vii. 16.

[The promise, doubtless, had a special reference to the Messiah. Nay, we may safely assert, that the *chief* reference was to him, for in the case of typical persons and things that which they adumbrate is principally to be regarded. So here, though the original application of the passage be to Solomon, the type of Christ, yet it finds its great and ulti-

6 ¹ And again, when he bring- | eth in the first-begotten into the
1 or, *when he bringeth again*.

mate application in the person of the glorious
antitype. However strange this double application may seem to us, it is quite in accordance with the whole system of things under
the Jewish dispensation. Almost every thing
connected with it was constructed on this
typical principle. This the apostles understood so well, that they were never stumbled
by it, and what is remarkable, and of the last
importance on this subject, *never for a moment
drawn from the ultimate and chief design of
a promise or prophecy* by its primary reference
to the type. They saw *Christ* in it, and made
the application *solely* to him, passing over entirely the literal sense, and seizing at once
the ultimate and superior import. The very
passage in question (2 Sam. vii. 11—17), is thus
directly applied not only here, but throughout
the New Testament; Luke i. 32, 33; Acts ii.
30, 37 ; xiii. 22, 23. Now certainly the apos-
)les are the best judges in matters of this
kind. Their authority, in regard to the sense
of passages quoted by them from the Old Testament, is just as great as in the case of the
original matter of the New Testament. That
Christ was indeed principally intended is farther evident from the fact, that *when the
kingdom had passed from the house of David*,
succeeding prophets repeat the promise in
2 Sam. vii. as yet to be fulfilled. See Jer.
xxxiii. 14, 26. Now connecting this fact
with the direct assertion of the writer of the
New Testament above referred to, every
doubt must be removed.

It will be alleged, however, that while the
direct application to the Messiah, of this and
other prophecies, is obvious and authoritative,
it is yet desirable, and they who deny inspiration will insist on it as essential, to prove
that there is at least nothing in the original
places, whence such citations are made, inconsistent with such application. Such proof
seems to be especially requisite here; for immediately after the words, " I will be his
Father and he shall be my Son," there follows : " if he commit iniquity, I will chasten
him with the rod of men, and with the stripes
of the children of men," 2 Sam. vii. 14; which
last sentence, it is affirmed, cannot, in any
sense, be applicable to the Messiah. It has
been said in reply, that though such language
cannot be applied to Christ *personally*, it may
yet refer to him as the *covenant head* of his
people. Though there be no iniquity in him,
" such failings and transgressions as disannul
not the covenant, often fall out on their part
for whom he undertaketh therein." In accordance with this view, it has been observed
by Mr. Pierce, and others after him, that the
Hebrew relative אשר should be translated
whosoever; in which case, the sense is, whoso-

ever of *his children*, i. e. the Messiah's, shall
commit iniquity, &c. And to this effect indeed is the alteration of the words in the 89th
Psalm, where the original covenant is repeated, " if HIS CHILDREN forsake my law—
then will I visit their transgression with the
rod, and their iniquity with stripes."

Perhaps, however, the better solution of
the difficulty is that which at once admits,
that the words in question cannot apply to
the Antitype but to the type only. It is a
mistake to suppose, that in a typical passage
every thing must necessarily have its antity
pical reference. The reader will find some
excellent and apposite remarks on this subject in Dr. Owen's commentary on the place.
" No type," says that judicious writer, " was in
all things a type of Christ, but only in that
particular wherein he was designed of God so
to be. David was a type of Christ, but not
in all things that he was and did. In his
conquests of the enemies of the church, in his
throne and kingdom, he was so; but in his
private actions, whether as a man, or as a
king, or captain, he was not so. Nay, not all
things spoken of him that was a type, even in
those respects wherein he was a type, are
spoken of him as a type, or have any respect
unto the thing signified, but some of them
may belong to him in his personal capacity
only. And the reason is, that he who was a
type by God's institution, might morally fail
in the performance of his duty, even then
and in those things wherein he was a type.
And this wholly removes the difficulty connected with the words 'if he sin against me ;'
for those words relating to the moral duty of
Solomon, in that wherein he was a type of
Christ, namely, the rule and administration of
his kingdom, may not at all belong to Christ,
who was prefigured by God's institution of
things, and not in any moral deportment in
the observance of them." These observations
seem to contain the true principles of expli-
cation in this and similar cases. The solution of Professor Stuart is not materially different. " Did not God," says he, " engage,
that David should have successors on his
earthly throne, and also that he *should* have
a son who would sit on a *spiritual* throne, and
have a kingdom of which David's own was
but a mere type ? Admitting this, our difficulty is diminished if not removed. *The iniquity committed is predicated of that part of
David's seed, who might commit it*, i. e. his
successors on the *national* throne, while the
more exalted condition predicated of his successor, belongs to Him to whom was given a
kingdom over all."

6. *And again.* Marg. *When he
bringeth in aga'n.* The proper con-

world, he saith, And *a* let all | the angels of God worship

a Ps.97.7 | him.

struction of this sentence probably is, "But when, moreover, he brings in," &c. The word "*again*" refers not to the fact that the Son of God is brought *again* into the world, implying that he had been introduced before; but it refers to the course of the apostle's argument, or to the declaration which is made about the Messiah in another place. "The name *Son* is not only given to him as above, but *also* in another place, or on another occasion when he brings in the first-begotten into the world." ¶ *When he bringeth in.* When he introduces. So far as the *language* here is concerned this might refer to the *birth* of the Messiah, but it is evident from the whole connection that the writer means to refer to something that is *said* in the Old Testament. This is plain because the passage occurs among quotations designed to prove a specific point—that the Son of God, the Author of the Christian system, was superior to the angels. A *declaration of the writer* here, however true and solemn, would not have answered the purpose. A *proof-text* was wanting; a text which would be admitted by those to whom he wrote to bear on the point under consideration. The meaning then is, "that on another occasion different from those to which he had referred, God, when speaking of the Messiah, or when introducing him to mankind, had used language showing that he was superior to the angels." The meaning of the phrase, "when he bringeth in," therefore, I take to be, when he *introduces* him to men; when he makes him known to the world—to wit, by the declaration which he proceeds immediately to quote. ¶ *The first-begotten.* Christ is called the "*first-begotten*," with reference to his resurrection from the dead, in Rev. i. 5, and Col. i. 18. It is probable here, however, that the word is used, like the word *first-born*, or *first-begotten* among the Hebrews, by way of eminence. As the first-born was the principal heir, and had peculiar privileges, so the Lord Jesus Christ sustains a

similar rank in the universe of which God is the Head and Father; see Notes on John i. 14, where the word "only-begotten" is used to denote the dignity and honour of the Lord Jesus. ¶ *Into the world.* When he introduces him to mankind, or declares what he is to be. ¶ *He saith, And let all the angels of God worship him.* Much difficulty has been experienced in regard to this quotation, for it cannot be denied that it is intended to be a quotation. In the Septuagint these very words occur in Deut. xxxii. 43, where they are inserted in the Song of Moses. But they are not in the Hebrew, nor are they in all the copies of the Septuagint. The Hebrew is, "Rejoice, O ye nations with his people; for he will avenge the blood of his servants, and will render vengeance to his adversaries." The Septuagint is, "Rejoice ye heavens with him; and let all the angels of God worship him. Let the nations rejoice with his people, and let all the sons of God be strong in him, for he has avenged the blood of his sons." But there are objections to our supposing that the apostle had this place in his view, which seem to me to settle the matter. (1.) One is, that the passage is not in the Hebrew; and it seems hardly credible that in writing to Hebrews, and to those residing in the very country where the Hebrew Scriptures were constantly used, he should adduce as a proof-text on an important doctrine what was not in their Scriptures. (2.) A second is, that it is omitted in all the ancient versions except the Septuagint. (3.) A third is, that it is impossible to believe that the passage in question in Deuteronomy had any reference to the Messiah. It does not relate to his "introduction" to the world. It would not occur to any reader that it had any such reference. The context celebrates the victory over the enemies of Israel which God will achieve. After saying that "his arrows would be drunk with blood, and that his sword would devour flesh with the blood of the slain and of captives, from the time when he begans to take vengeance on an enemy," the Septuagint (not the Hebrew) immediately asserts, "let the heavens rejoice at the same time with him, and let all the angels of God worship him." That is, "Let the inhabitants of the heavenly world rejoice in the victory of God over the enemies of his people, and let them pay their adoration to him." But the Messiah does not appear to be alluded to anywhere in the context; much less described as "*introduced into the world*." There is, moreover, not the slightest evidence that it was ever supposed by the Jews to have any such reference; and though it *might* be said that the apostle merely quoted *language* that expressed his meaning—as we often do when we are familiar with any well-known phrase that will exactly suit our purpose and convey an idea—yet it should be remarked that this is not the way in which this passage is quoted. It is *a proof-text*, and Paul evidently meant to be understood as saying that that passage had a *fair* reference to the Messiah. It is evident, moreover, that it would be admitted to have such a reference by those to whom he wrote. It is morally certain, therefore, that this was *not* the passage which the writer intended to quote. The probability is, that the writer here referred to Psalm xcvii. 7, (in the Sept. Ps. xcvi. 7). In that place, the Hebrew is, "worship him, all *ye* gods"—אֱלֹהִים־כָּל—*all ye Elohim*. In the Septuagint it is, "Let all his angels worship him;" where the translation is literal, except that the word *God*—"*angels of God*" —is used by the apostle instead of *his* —"all *his* angels"—as it is in the Septuagint. The word "gods"—*Elohim*—is rendered by the word *angels* —but the word may have that sense. Thus it is rendered by the LXX.; in Job xx. 15; and in Psalm viii. 6; cxxxvii. 1. It is well known that the word *Elohim* may denote kings and magistrates, because of their rank and dignity; and is there anything improbable in the supposition that, for a similar reason, the word may be given also to angels? The fair interpretation of the passage then would be, to refer it to *angelic beings*—and

the command in Ps. xcvii. is for them to do homage to the being there referred to. The only question then is, whether the Psalm can be regarded properly as having any reference to the Messiah? Did the apostle fairly and properly use this language as referring to him? On this we may remark, (1.) That the *fact* that he uses it thus may be regarded as proof that it would be admitted to be proper by the Jews in his time, and renders it probable that it was in fact so used. (2.) Two Jewish Rabbins of distinction —Raschi and Kimchi—affirm that all the Psalms from xciii. to ci. are to be regarded as referring to the Messiah. Such was, and is, the opinion of the Jews. (3.) There is nothing *in* the Psalm which forbids such a reference, or which can be shown to be inconsistent with it. Indeed the whole Psalm *might* be taken as beautifully descriptive of the "*introduction*" of the Son of God into the world, or as a sublime and glorious description of his advent. Thus in ver. 1, the earth is called on to rejoice that the Lord reigns. In vers. 2—5, he is introduced or described as coming in the most magnificent manner—clouds and darkness attend him; a fire goes before him; the lightnings play; and the hills melt like wax —a sublime description of his coming, with appropriate symbols, to reign, or to judge the world. In ver. 6, it is said that all people shall see his glory; in ver. 7, that all who worship graven images shall be confounded, and *all the angels are required to do him homage;* and in vers. 8—12, the effect of his advent is described as filling Zion with rejoicing, and the hearts of the people of God with gladness. It can · not be *proved*, therefore, that this Psalm had no reference to the Messiah; but the presumption is that it had, and that the apostle has quoted it not only as it was *usually* regarded in his time, but as it was designed by the Holy Ghost. If so, then it *proves*, what the writer intended, that the Son of God should be adored by the angels; and of course that he was superior to them. It proves also more. Whom would God require the angels to adore? A creature? A man? A fellow-angel?

7 And [1] of the angels he saith, [a] | Who maketh his angels spirits, and his ministers a flame of fire.

1 *unto*.   a Ps.104.4.

To ask these questions is to answer them. He could require them to worship none but God, and the passage proves that the Son of God is divine. 7. *And of the angels he saith, Who maketh his angels spirits.* He gives to them an inferior name, and assigns to them a more humble office. They are mere ministers, and have not ascribed to them the name of *Son.* They have a name which implies a more humble rank and office—the name "spirit," and the appellation of a "flame of fire." They obey his will as the winds and the lightnings do. The *object* of the apostle in this passage is to show that the angels serve God in a ministerial capacity—as the winds do; while the Son is Lord of all. The one serves him passively, as being wholly under his control; the other acts as a Sovereign, as Lord over all, and is addressed and regarded as the equal with God. This quotation is made from Ps. civ. 4. The passage *might* be translated, " Who maketh his angels *winds,* and his ministers a flame of fire ;" that is, "who makes his angels *like* the winds, or as swift as the winds, and his ministers as rapid, as terrible, and as resistless as the lightning." So Doddridge renders it ; and so did the late Rev. Dr. J. P. Wilson. *MS. Notes.* The passage in the Psalm is susceptible, I think, of another interpretation, and *might* be regarded as meaning, " who makes the winds his messengers, and the flaming fire his ministers ;" and perhaps this is the sense which would most naturally occur to a reader of the Hebrew. The Hebrew, however, will admit of the construction here put upon it, and it cannot be proved that it was the original intention of the passage to show that the angels were the mere servants of God, rapid, quick, and prompt to do his will —like the winds. The Chaldee Paraphrase renders the passage in the Psalm, " Who makes his messengers swift as the wind ; his ministers strong like a flame of fire." Prof. Stuart maintains that the passage in the

Psalms cannot mean " who makes the winds his messengers," but that the intention of the Psalmist is to describe the *invisible* as well as the *visible* majesty of God, and that he refers to the angels as a part of the retinue which goes to make up his glory. This does not seem to me to be perfectly certain ; but still it cannot be demonstrated that Paul has made an improper use of the passage. It is to be presumed that *he*, who had been trained in the knowledge of the Hebrew language, would have had a better opportunity of knowing its fair construction than we can ; and it is morally certain that he would employ the passage *in an argument* as it was commonly understood by those to whom he wrote—that is, to those who were familiar with the Hebrew language and literature. If he has so used the passage ; if he has—as no one can disprove—put the fair construction on it, then it is just in point. It proves that the angels are the *attendant servants* of God ; employed to grace his train, to do his will, to accompany him as the clouds and winds and lightnings do, and to occupy a subordinate rank in his creation. ¶ *Flame of fire.* This probably refers to lightning—which is often the meaning of the phrase. The word "*ministers*" here, means the same as angels, and the sense of the whole is, that the attending retinue of God, when he manifests himself with great power and glory, is like the winds and the lightning. His angels are like them. They are prompt to do his will—rapid, quick, obedient in his service ; they are in all respects subordinate to him, and occupy, as the winds and the lightnings do, the place of servants. They are not addressed in language like that which is applied to the Son of God, and they must all be far inferior to him.

8. *But unto the Son* he saith. In Psalm xlv. 6, 7. The fact that the writer of this epistle makes this application of the Psalm to the Messiah, proves that it was so applied in his

8 But unto the Son *he saith,* | *a* Thy throne, O God, *is* for ever

a Ps.45.6,7.

time, or that it would be readily admitted to be applicable to him. It has been generally admitted, by both Jewish and Christian interpreters, to have such a reference. Even those who have doubted its primary applicability to the Messiah, have regarded it as referring to him in a secondary sense. Many have supposed that it referred to Solomon in the primary sense, and that it has a secondary reference to the Messiah. To me it seems most probable that it had an original and exclusive reference to the Messiah. It is to be remembered that the hope of the Messiah was the peculiar hope of the Jewish people. The coming of the future king, so early promised, was the great event to which they all looked forward with the deepest interest. That hope inspired their prophets and their bards, and cheered the hearts of the nation in the time of despondency. The Messiah, if I may so express it, was the *hero* of the Old Testament—more so than Achilles is of the Iliad, and Æneas of the Ænead. The sacred poets were accustomed to employ all their most magnificent imagery in describing him, and to present him in every form that was beautiful in their conception, and that would be gratifying to the pride and hopes of the nation. Every thing that is gorgeous and splendid in description is lavished on him, and they were never under any apprehension of attributing to him too great magnificence in his personal reign ; too great beauty of moral character ; or too great an extent of dominion. That which would be regarded by them as a magnificent description of a monarch, they freely applied to him ; and this is evidently the case in this Psalm. That the description may have been in part derived from the view of Solomon in the magnificence of his court, is possible, but no more probable than that it was derived from the general view of the splendour of any Oriental monarch, or than that it might have been the description of a monarch

which was the pure creation of inspired poetry. Indeed, I see not why this Psalm should ever have been supposed to be applicable to Solomon. His *name* is not mentioned. It has no *peculiar* applicability to him. There is nothing that would apply to him which would not also apply to many an Oriental prince. There are some things in it which are much less applicable to him than to many others. The king here described is *a conqueror.* He girds his sword on his thigh, and his arrows are sharp in the hearts of his foes, and the people are subdued under him. This was not true of Solomon. His was a reign of peace and tranquillity, nor was he ever distinguished for war. On the whole, it seems clear to me, that this Psalm is designed to be a beautiful poetic description of the Messiah *as king.* The images are drawn from the usual characteristics of an Oriental prince, and there are many things in the poem—as there are in parables—for the sake of *keeping,* or *verisimilitude,* and which are not, in the interpretation, to be cut *to the quick.* The writer imagined to himself a magnificent and beautiful prince ;—a prince riding prosperously in his conquests ; swaying a permanent and wide dominion ; clothed in rich and splendid vestments ; eminently upright and pure ; and scattering blessings everywhere—and that prince was the Messiah. The Psalm, therefore, I regard as relating originally and exclusively to Christ ; and though in the interpretation, the *circumstances* should not be unduly pressed, nor an attempt be made to *spiritualize* them, yet the *whole* is a glowing and most beautiful description of Christ as a King. The same principles of interpretation should be applied to it which are applied to parables, and the same allowance be made for the introduction of circumstances for the sake of *keeping,* or for finishing the story. If this be the correct view, then Paul has quoted the Psalm in conformity exactly with its original intention, as he undoubt-

and ever : a sceptre of righteous- 1 *rightness, or straitness.* ness [1] *is* the sceptre of thy kingdom :

edly quoted it as it was understood in his time. ¶ *Thy throne.* A throne is the seat on which a monarch sits, and is here the symbol of dominion, because kings when acting as rulers sit on thrones. Thus a throne becomes the emblem of authority or empire. Here it means, that his *rule* or *dominion* would be perpetual— "*for ever and ever*"—which assuredly could not be applied to Solomon. ¶ *O God.* This certainly could not be applied to Solomon ; but applied to the Messiah it proves what the apostle is aiming to prove—that he is above the angels. The argument is, that a name is given to *him* which is never given to *them*. They are not called *God* in any strict and proper sense. The *argument* here requires us to understand this word, as used in a sense more exalted than any name which is ever given to angels, and though it may be maintained that the name אלהים *Elohim,* is given to magistrates or to angels, yet *here* the argument requires us to understand :t as used in a sense *superior* to what it ever is when applied to an angel— or of course to any creature, since it was the express design of the argument to prove that the Messiah was superior to the angels. The word *God* should be taken in its natural and obvious sense, unless there is some necessary reason for limiting it. If applied to magistrates (Ps. lxxxii. 6), it *must* be so limited. If applied to the Messiah, there is no such necessity, (John i. 1 ; Isa. ix. 6 ; 1 John v. 20 ; Phil. ii. 6), and it should be taken in its natural and proper sense. The *form* here — ὁ Θεὸς—is in the vocative case and not the nominative. It is the usual form of the vocative in the Septuagint, and nearly the only form of it. *Stuart.* This then is a direct address to the Messiah, calling him God ; and I see not why it is not to be used in the usual and proper sense of the word. Unitarians proposed to translate this, " God is thy throne ;" but how can God be *a throne* of a creature ? What is the meaning

of such an expression ? Where is there one parallel ? And what must be the nature of that cause which renders such an argument necessary ? —This refers, as it seems to me, to the Messiah *as king.* It does not relate to his mode of existence *before* the incarnation, but to him as the magnificent monarch of his people. Still, the ground or reason why this name is given to him is that he is *divine.* It is language which properly expresses his nature. He must have a divine nature, or such language would be improper. I regard this passage, therefore, as full proof that the Lord Jesus is divine ; nor is it possible to evade this conclusion by any fair interpretation of it. It cannot be wrong to address him as God ; nor addressing him as such, not to regard him as divine. ¶ *Is for ever and ever.* This could not in any proper sense apply to Solomon. As applied to the Messiah, it means that his essential kingdom will be perpetual, Luke i. 33. As Mediator his kingdom will be given up to the Father, or to God without reference to a mediatorial work, (1 Cor. xv. 24, 28—see Notes on these verses), but his reign over his people will be perpetual. There never will come a time when they shall not obey and serve him, though the peculiar form of his kingdom, as connected with the work of *mediation,* will be changed. The form of the organized church, for example, will be changed, for there shall be no necessity for it in heaven, but the essential dominion and power of the Son of God will not cease. He shall have the same dominion which he had before he entered on the work of mediation ; and that will be eternal. It is also true that, compared with earthly monarchs, his kingdom shall be perpetual. They soon die. Dynasties pass away. But *his* empire extends from age to age, and is properly a *perpetual* dominion. The fair and obvious interpretation of this passage would satisfy me, were there nothing else, that this Psalm had no reference

9 Thou hast loved righteous- | ness, and hated iniquity; there-

to Solomon, but was designed originally as a description of the Messiah
as the expected King and Prince of
his people. ¶ *A sceptre of righteousness.* That is, a right or just sceptre.
The phrase is a Hebraism. The former expression described the *perpetuity* of his kingdom; this describes its
equable nature. It would be just and
equal; see Notes on Isa. xi. 5. A
sceptre is a staff or wand usually made
of wood, five or six feet long, and
commonly overlaid with gold, or ornamented with golden rings. Sometimes, however, the sceptre was made
of ivory, or wholly of gold. It was
borne in the hands of kings as an emblem of authority and power. Probably it had its origin in the staff or
crook of the shepherd—as kings were
at first regarded as the *shepherds* of
their people. Thus Agamemnon is
commonly called by Homer the *shepherd* of the people. The *sceptre* thus
becomes the emblem of kingly office
and power—as when we speak of
swaying a sceptre;—and the idea
here is, that the Messiah would be a
king, and that the authority which he
would wield would be equitable and
just. He would not be governed, as
monarchs often are, by mere caprice,
or by the wishes of courtiers and flatterers; he would not be controlled by
mere *will* and the love of arbitrary
power; but the execution of his laws
would be in accordance with the principles of equity and justice.—How
well this accords with the character
of the Lord Jesus we need not pause
to show; comp. Notes on Isa. xi. 2—5.
9. *Thou hast loved righteousness.*
Thou hast been obedient to the law
of God, or holy and upright. Nothing
can be more truly adapted to express
the character of any one than this is
to describe the Lord Jesus, who was
"holy, harmless, undefiled," who "did
no sin, and in whose mouth no guile
was found;" but it is with difficulty
that this can be applied to Solomon.
Assuredly, for a considerable part of
his life, this declaration could not well
be appropriate to him; and it seems
to me that it is not to be regarded as

descriptive of him at all. It is language prompted by the warm and
pious imagination of the Psalmist describing the future Messiah—and, as
applied to him, is true to the letter.
¶ *Therefore God, even thy God*
The word *even* inserted here by the
translators, weakens the force of the
expression. This *might* be translated,
"O God, thy God hath anointed thee."
So it is rendered by Doddridge,
Clarke, Stuart, and others. The
Greek will bear this construction, as
well the Hebrew in Ps. xlv. 7. In the
margin in the Psalm it is rendered
"O God." This is the most natural
construction, as it accords with what
is just said before. "Thy throne, O
God, is for ever. Thou art just and
holy, therefore, O God, thy God hath
anointed thee," &c. It is not material,
however, which construction is adopted. ¶ *Hath anointed thee.* An-
ciently kings and priests were consecrated to their office by pouring oil
on their heads; see Lev. viii. 12;
Num. iii. 3; 1 Sam. x. 1; 2 Sam. ii.
7; Ps. ii. 2; Isa. lxi. 1; Acts iv. 27;
x. 38; Note, Matt. i. 1. The expression "*to anoint,*" therefore, comes to
mean to consecrate to office, or to set
apart to some public work. This is
evidently the meaning in the Psalm,
where the whole language refers to
the appointment of the personage
there referred to to the kingly office.
¶ *The oil of gladness.* This probably means the perfumed oil that was
poured on the head, attended with
many expressions of joy and rejoicing.
The inauguration of the Messiah as
king would be an occasion of rejoicing
and triumph. Thousands would exult
at it—as in the coronation of a king;
and thousands would be made glad by
such a consecration to the office of
Messiah. ¶ *Above thy fellows.* Above
thine associates; that is, above all
who sustain the kingly office. He
would be more exalted than all other
kings. Doddridge supposes that it
refers to angels, who might have been
associated with the Messiah in the government of the world. But the more
natural construction is to suppose

fore God, *even* thy God, hath anointed thee with the oil of gladness above thy fellows.

10 And ^a Thou, Lord, in the be-

that it refers to kings, and to mean that he was the most exalted of all. 10. *And.* That is, "To add another instance;" or, "to the Son he saith in another place, or in the following language.' This is connected with ver. 8. "Unto the Son he saith (ver. 8), Thy throne," &c.—*and* (ver. 10) he *also* saith, "Thou Lord," &c. That this is the meaning is apparent, because (1) the *object* of the whole quotation is to show the exalted character of the Son of God, and (2) an address here to JEHOVAH would be wholly irrelevant. Why, in an argument designed to prove that the Son of God was superior to the angels, should the writer break out in an address to JEHOVAH in view of the fact that he had laid the foundations of the world, and that he himself would continue to live when the heavens should be rolled up and pass away? Such is not the manner of Paul or of any other good writer, and it is clear that the writer here designed to adduce this as applicable to the Messiah. Whatever difficulties there may be about the principles on which it is done, and the reason why *this* passage was selected for the purpose, there can be no doubt about the *design* of the writer. He *meant* to be understood as applying it to the Messiah beyond all question, or the quotation is wholly irrelevant, and it is inconceivable why it should have been made. ¶ *Thou Lord.* This is taken from Ps. cii. 25—27. The quotation is made from the Septuagint with only a slight variation, and is an accurate translation of the Hebrew. In the Psalm, there can be no doubt that JEHOVAH is intended. This is apparent on the face of the Psalm, and particularly because the *name* JEHOVAH is introduced in ver. 1, 12, and because he is addressed as the Creator of all things, and as immutable. No one, on reading the Psalm, ever would doubt that it referred to God, and if the apostle

ginning hast laid the foundation of the earth ; and the heavens are the works of thine hands ;

^a Ps. 102. 25.

meant to apply it to the Lord Jesus it proves most conclusively that he is divine. In regard to the difficult inquiry *why* he applied this to the Messiah, or on what principle such an application can be vindicated, we may perhaps throw some light by the following remarks. It must be admitted that probably few persons, if any, on reading the *Psalm*, would suppose that it referred to the Messiah; but (1.) the fact that the apostle thus employs it, proves that it was understood in his time to have such a reference, or at least that those to whom he wrote would admit that it had such a reference. On no other principle would he have used it in an argument. This is at least of some consequence in showing what the prevailing interpretation was. (2.) It cannot be demonstrated that it had no such reference, for such was the habit of the sacred writers in making the future Messiah the theme of their poetry, that no one can *prove* that the writer of this Psalm did not design that the Messiah should be the subject of his praise here. (3.) There is nothing in the Psalm which *may* not be applied to the Messiah; but there is much in it that is peculiarly applicable to him. Suppose, for example, that the Psalmist (vers. 1—11), in his complaints, represents the people of God before the Redeemer appeared—as lowly, sad, dejected, and afflicted—speaking of himself as *one* of them, and as a *fair representative* of that people, the remainder of the Psalm will well agree with the promised redemption. Thus having described the sadness and sorrow of the people of God, he speaks of the fact that God would arise and have mercy upon Zion (vers. 13, 14), that the heathen would fear the name of the Lord, and all the kings of the earth would see his glory (ver. 15), and that when the Lord should build up Zion, he would appear in his glory; ver. 16. To whom else could this be so well applied as to the Messiah? To what time so well as to his time? Thus too in ver. 20, it is said that the Lord would look down from heaven "to hear the groaning of the prisoner, and to loose them that are appointed to death"—language remarkably resembling that used by Isaiah, ch. lxi. 1, which the Saviour applies to himself, in Luke iv. 17—21. The passage then quoted by the apostle (vers. 25—27 of the Psalm) is designed to denote the *immutability* of the Messiah, and the fact that in him all the interests of the church were safe. He would not change. He had formed all things, and he would remain the same. His kingdom would be permanent amidst all the changes occurring on earth, and his people had no cause of apprehension or alarm; ver. 28. (4). Paul applies this language to the Messiah in accordance with the doctrine which he had stated (ver. 2), that it was by him that God "made the worlds." Having stated that, he seems to have felt that it was not improper to apply to him the passages occurring in the Old Testament that speak of the work of creation. The argument is this, "He was in fact the creator of all things." But to the Creator there is applied language in the Scriptures which shows that he was far exalted above the angels. He would remain the same, while the heavens and the earth should fade away. His years are enduring and eternal. *Such* a being must be superior to the angels; such a being must be divine. The words "Thou Lord"—σὺ Κύριε—are not in the Hebrew of the Psalm, though they are in the Septuagint. In the Hebrew, in the Psalm (ver. 24), it is an address to God—"I said, O my God"—אלי—but there can be no doubt that the Psalmist meant to address JEHOVAH, and that the word *God* is used in its proper sense, denoting divinity; see vers. 1, 12, of the Psalm. ¶ *In the beginning;* see Gen. i. 1. When the world was made; comp. Notes on John i. 1, where the same phrase is applied to the Messiah—" In the beginning was the word." ¶ *Hast laid the foundation of the earth.* Hast

made the earth. This language is such as is common in the Scriptures, where the earth is represented as laid on a foundation, or as supported. It is figurative language, derived from the act of rearing an edifice. The meaning here is, that the Son of God was the *original* creator or founder of the universe. He did not merely arrange it out of pre-existing materials, but he was properly its creator or founder. ¶ *And the heavens are the works of thine hands.* This *must* demonstrate the Lord Jesus to be divine. He that made the vast heavens must be God. No creature could perform a work like that; nor can we conceive that power to create the vast array of distant worlds could possibly be delegated. If that power could be delegated, there is not an attribute of Deity which may not be, and thus all our notions of what constitutes divinity would be utterly confounded. The word "heavens" here, must mean all parts of the universe except the earth; see Gen. i. 1. The word *hands* is used, because it is by the hands that we usually perform any work.

11. *They shall perish.* That is, the heavens and the earth. They shall pass away; or they shall be destroyed. Probably no more is meant by the phrase here, than that important changes will take place in them, or than that they will change their form. Still it is not possible to foresee what changes may yet take place in the heavenly bodies, or to say that the present universe may not at some period be destroyed, and be succeeded by another creation still more magnificent. He that created the universe by a word, can destroy it by a word; and he that formed the present frame of nature can cause it to be succeeded by another not less wonderful and glorious. The Scriptures seem to hold out the idea that the present frame of the universe shall be destroyed; see 2 Pet. iii. 10—13; Matt. xxiv. 35. ¶ *But thou remainest.* Thou shalt not die or be destroyed. What a sublime thought! The idea is, that though the heavens and earth should suddenly disappear, or though they should gradually wear out and

11 They shall perish, but thou remainest : and they all shall wax old as doth a garment ;

12 And as a vesture shalt thou fold them up, and they shall be changed : but thou art the same, and thy years shall not fail.

13 But to which of the angels

become extinct, yet there is one infinite being who remains unaffected and unchanged. Nothing can reach or disturb him. All these changes shall take place under his direction, and by his command ; see Rev. xx. 11. Let us not be alarmed then at any revolution. Let us not fear though we should see the heavens rolled up as a scroll, and the stars falling from their places. God, the Creator and the Redeemer, presides over all. He is unchanged. He ever lives ; and though the universe should pass away, it will be only at his bidding, and under his direction. ¶ *And they all shall wax old.* Shall *grow* or become old. The word *wax* is an old Saxon word, meaning to grow, or increase, or become. The heavens here are compared to a garment, meaning that as that grows old and decays, so it will be with the heavens and the earth. The language is evidently figurative ; and yet who can tell how much literal truth there may be couched under it ? Is it absurd to suppose that that sun which daily sends forth so many countless millions of beams of light over the universe, may in a course of ages become diminished in its splendour, and shine with feeble lustre ? Can there be constant exhaustion, a constant burning like that, and yet no tendency to decay at some far distant period ? Not unless the material for its splendour shall be supplied from the boundless resources of the Great Source of Light—God ;—and when he shall choose to withhold it, even that glorious sun must be dimmed of its splendour, and shine with enfeebled beams.

12. *And as a vesture.* A garment ; —literally something thrown around —περιβόλαιον—and denoting properly the outer garment, the cloak or mantle ; see Notes, Matt. v. 40. ¶ *Shalt thou fold them up.* That is, the heavens. They are represented in the Scriptures as *an expanse.* or some-

thing spread out (Heb. in Gen. i. 7): as a *curtain,* or *tent* (Isa. xl. 22), auû as a *scroll* that might be spread out or rolled up like a book or volume, Isa. xxxiv. 4 ; Rev. vi. 14. Here they are represented as a garment or mantle that might be folded up— language borrowed from folding up and laying aside garments that are no longer fit for use. ¶ *And they shall be changed.* That is, they shall be exchanged for others, or they shall give place to the new heavens and the new earth; 2 Pet. iii. 13. The meaning is, that the present form of the heavens and the earth is not to be permanent, but is to be succeeded by others, or to pass away, but that the Creator is to remain the same. ¶ *Thou art the same.* Thou wilt not change. ¶ *And thy years shall not fail.* Thou wilt exist for ever unchanged. What could more clearly prove that he of whom this is spoken is immutable ? Yet it is indubitably spoken of the Messiah, and must demonstrate that he is divine. These attributes cannot be conferred on a creature ; and nothing can be clearer than that he who penned the epistle believed that the Son of God was divine.

13. *But to which of the angels.* The apostle adduces one other proof of the exaltation of the Son of God above the angels. He asks where there is an instance in which God had addressed any one of the angels, and asked him to sit at his right hand until he should subdue his enemies under him? Yet that high honour had been conferred on the Son of God ; and he was therefore far exalted above them. ¶ *Sit on my right hand*; see Notes on ver. 3. This passage is taken from Ps. cx. 1,—a Psalm that is repeatedly quoted in this epistle as referring to the Messiah, and the very passage before is applied by the Saviour to himself, in Matt. xxii. 43, 44, and by Peter it is

said he at any time, *a* Sit on my right hand, until I make thine enemies thy footstool?

a Ps.110.1. *b* Ps.103.21;Da.7.10.
c Ge.19.15,16;Ps.34.7. *d* Ro.8 17.

applied to him in Acts ii. 34, 35. There can be no doubt, therefore, of its applicability to the Messiah. ¶ *Until I make thine enemies thy footstool.* Until I reduce them to entire subjection. A footstool is what is placed under the feet when we sit on a chair, and the phrase here means that an enemy is entirely subdued; comp. Notes on 1 Cor. xv. 25. The phrase *to make an enemy a footstool,* is borrowed from the custom of ancient warriors who stood on the necks of vanquished kings on the occasion of celebrating a triumph over them as a token of their complete prostration and subjection; see Notes on Isa. x. 6. —The enemies here referred to are the foes of God and of his religion, and the meaning is, that the Messiah is to be exalted *until* all those foes are subdued. Then he will give up the kingdom to the Father; see Notes on 1 Cor. xv. 24—28. The exaltation of the Redeemer, to which the apostle refers here, is to the *mediatorial* throne. In this he is exalted far above the angels. His foes are to be subdued to him, but angels are to be employed as mere instruments in that great work.

14. *Are they not all.* There is not one of them that is elevated to the high rank of the Redeemer. Even the most exalted angel is employed in the comparatively humble office of a ministering spirit appointed to aid the heirs of salvation. ¶ *Ministering spirits.* A *ministering spirit* is one that is employed to execute the will of God. The proper meaning of the word here—λειτουργικὰ—(whence our word *liturgy*) is, *pertaining to public service,* or *the service of the people* (λαός); and is applied particularly to those who were engaged in the public service of the temple. They were those who rendered aid to others; who were helpers, or servants. Such is the meaning as used here. They are employed to render *aid* or *assist-*

14 Are they not all ministering *b* spirits, sent forth *c* to minister for them who shall be heirs *d* of salvation?

ance to others—to wit, to Christians. ¶ *Sent forth.* Appointed by God for this. They are *sent;* are under his control; are in a subordinate capacity. Thus *Gabriel* was *sent* forth to convey an important message to Daniel; Dan. ix. 21—23. ¶ *To minister.* For the aid, or succour of such They come to render them assistance —and, if employed in this humble office, how much inferior to the dignity of the Son of God—the Creator and Ruler of the worlds! ¶ *Who shall be heirs of salvation.* To the saints; to Christians. They are called *"heirs* of salvation" because they are adopted into the family of God, and are treated as his sons; see Notes on Rom. viii. 14—17. The main point here is, that the angels are employed in a much more humble capacity than the Son of God; and, therefore, that he sustains a far more elevated rank. But while the apostle has proved that, he has incidentally stated an exceedingly interesting and important doctrine, that the angels are employed to further the salvation of the people of God, and to aid them in their journey to heaven.—In this doctrine there is nothing absurd. It is no more improbable that angels should be employed to aid man, than that one man should aid another; certainly not as improbable as that the Son of God should come down "not to be ministered unto but to minister," (Matt. xx. 28), and that he performed on earth the office of a servant; John xiii. 1—15. Indeed it is a great principle of the divine administration that one class of God's creatures are to minister to others; that one is to aid another—to assist him in trouble, to provide for him when poor, and to counsel him in perplexity. We are constantly deriving benefit from others, and are dependent on their counsel and help. Thus God has appointed parents to aid their children; neighbours to aid their neighbours; the rich to aid the poor; and all over the world the principle is seen, that one is to derive benefit from the aid of others. Why may not the angels be employed in this service? They are pure, benevolent, powerful; and as man was ruined in the fall by the temptation offered by one of an angelic, though fallen nature, why should not others of angelic, unfallen holiness come to assist in repairing the evils which their fallen, guilty brethren have inflicted on the race? To me there seems to be a beautiful propriety in bringing *aid* from another race, as *ruin* came from another race; and that as those endowed with angelic might, though with fiendish malignity, ruined man, those with angelic might, but heavenly benevolence, should aid in his recovery and salvation. Farther, it is, from the necessity of the case, a great principle, that the weak shall be aided by the strong; the ignorant by the enlightened; the impure by the pure; the tempted by those who have not fallen by temptation. All over the world we see this in operation; and it constitutes the beauty of the moral arrangements on the earth; and why shall not this be extended to the inhabitants of other abodes? Why shall not angels, with their superior intelligence, benevolence, and power, come in to perfect this system, and show how much adapted it is to glorify God?—In regard to the *ways* in which angels become ministering spirits to the heirs of salvation, the Scriptures have not fully informed us, but facts are mentioned which will furnish some light on this inquiry. What they do *now* may be learned from the Scripture account of what they *have* done—as it seems to be a fair principle of interpretation that they are engaged in substantially the same employment in which they have ever been. The following methods of angelic interposition in behalf of man are noted in the Scriptures. (1.) They feel a deep interest in man. Thus the Saviour says, "there is joy in the presence of the angels of God over one sinner that repenteth;" Luke xv. 10. Thus also

he says, when speaking of the "little ones" that compose his church, "in heaven their angels do always behold the face of my Father who is in heaven;" Matt. xviii. 10. (2.) They feel a special interest in all that relates to the redemption of man. Thus Peter says of the things pertaining to redemption, "which things the angels desire to look into;" 1 Pet. i. 12. In accordance with this they are represented as praising God over the fields of Bethlehem, where the shepherds were to whom it was announced that a Saviour was born (Luke ii. 13); an angel announced to Mary that she would be the mother of the Messiah (Luke i. 26); an angel declared to the shepherds that he was born (Luke ii. 10); the angels came and ministered to him in his temptation (Matt. iv. 11); an angel strengthened him in the garden of Gethsemane (Luke xxii. 43); angels were present in the sepulchre where the Lord Jesus had been laid, to announce his resurrection to his disciples (John xx. 12); and they reappeared to his disciples on Mount Olivet to assure them that he would return and receive his people to himself, Acts i. 10. (3.) They appear for the defence and protection of the people of God. Thus it is said (Ps. xxxiv. 7), "The angel of the Lord encampeth round about them that fear him, and delivereth them." Thus two angels came to hasten Lot from the cities of the plain, and to rescue him from the impending destruction; Gen. xix. 1, 15. Thus an angel opened the prison doors of the apostles, and delivered them when they had been confined by the Jews; Acts v. 19. Thus the angel of the Lord delivered Peter from prison when he had been confined by Herod; Acts xii. 7, 8. (4.) Angels are sent to give us strength to resist temptation. Aid was thus furnished to the Redeemer in the garden of Gethsemane, when there "appeared an angel from heaven strengthening him;" Luke xxii. 43. The great trial there seems to have been somehow connected with temptation; some influence of the power of darkness, or of the Prince of evil; Luke xxii. 53; comp. John

xiv. 30. In this aid which they rendered to the tempted Redeemer, and in the assistance which they render to us when tempted, there is a special fitness and propriety. Man was at first tempted by a fallen angel. No small part—if not all the temptations in the world—are under the direction now of fallen angels. They roam at large "seeking whom they may devour;" 1 Pet. v. 8. The temptations which occur in life, the numerous allurements which beset our path, all have the marks of being under the control of dark and malignant spirits. What, therefore, can be more appropriate than for the pure angels of God to interpose and aid man against the skill and wiles of their fallen and malignant fellow-spirits? Fallen angelic power and skill—power and skill far above the capability and the strength of man—are employed to ruin us, and how desirable is it for like power and skill, under the guidance of benevolence, to come in to aid us! (5.) They support us in affliction. Thus an angel brought a cheering message to Daniel; the angels were present to give comfort to the disciples of the Saviour when he had been taken from them by death, and when he ascended to heaven. Why may it not be so now, that important consolations, in some way, are imparted to us by angelic influence? And (6.) they attend dying saints, and conduct them to glory. Thus the Saviour says of Lazarus that when he died he was "carried by the angels into Abraham's bosom;" Luke xvi. 22. Is there any impropriety in supposing that the same thing may be done still? Assuredly if anywhere heavenly aid is needed, it is when the spirit leaves the body. If anywhere a guide is needed, it is when the ransomed soul goes up the unknown path to God. And if angels are employed on any messages of mercy to mankind, it is proper that it should be when life is closing, and the spirit is about to ascend to heaven. Should it be said that they are invisible, and that it is difficult to conceive how we can be aided by beings whom we never see, I answer, I know that they are unseen. They no longer appear as they once did to be the visible protectors and defenders of the people of God. But no small part of the aid which we receive from others comes from sources unseen by us. We owe more to *unseen* benefactors than to those whom we see, and the most grateful of all aid, perhaps, is that which is furnished by a hand which we do not see, and from quarters which we cannot trace. How many an orphan is benefited by some unseen and unknown benefactor! So it may be a part of the great arrangements of divine Providence that many of the most needed and acceptable interpositions for our welfare should come to us from invisible sources, and be conveyed to us from God by unseen hands.

REMARKS.

1. The Christian religion has a claim on the attention of man. God has spoken to us in the Gospel by his Son; vers. 1, 2. This fact constitutes a *claim* on us to attend to what is spoken in the New Testament. When God sent prophets to address men, endowing them with more than human wisdom and eloquence, and commanding them to deliver solemn messages to mankind, *that* was a reason why men should hear. But how much more important is the message which is brought by his own Son! How much more exalted is the Messenger! How much higher his claim to our attention and regard! comp. Matt. xxi. 37. Yet it is lamentable to reflect how few attended to him when he lived on the earth, and how few comparatively regard him now. The great mass of men feel no interest in the fact that the Son of God has come and spoken to the human race. Few take the pains to *read* what he said, though all the records of the discourses of the Saviour could be read in a few hours. A newspaper is read; a poem; a novel; a play; a history of battles and sieges; but the New Testament is neglected, and there are thousands even in Christian lands who have not even read through the Sermon on the Mount! Few also listen to the truths which the Re-

deemer taught when they are proclaimed in the sanctuary. Multitudes never go to the place where the gospel is preached; multitudes when there are engaged in thinking of other things, or are wholly inattentive to the truths which are proclaimed. Such a reception has the Son of God met with in our world! The most wonderful of all events is, that he should have come from heaven to be the teacher of mankind; next to that, the most wonderful event is that, when he has come, men feel no interest in the fact, and refuse to listen to what he says of the unseen and eternal world. What a man will say about the *possibility* of making a fortune by some wild speculation will be listened to with the deepest interest; but what the Redeemer says about the *certainty* of heaven and eternal riches there, excites no emotion : what one from the dead might say about the unseen world would excite the profoundest attention; what he has said who has always dwelt in the unseen world, and who knows all that has occurred there, and all that is yet to occur, awakens no interest, and excites no inquiry. Such is man. The visit, too, of an illustrious stranger—like Lafayette to America—will rouse a nation, and spread enthusiasm everywhere; the visit of the Son of God to the earth on a great errand of mercy is regarded as an event of no importance, and excites no interest in the great mass of human hearts.

2. Christ is divine. In the view of the writer of this epistle he was undoubtedly regarded as equal with God. This is so clear that it seems wonderful that it should ever have been called in question. He who made the worlds; who is to be worshipped by the angels; who is addressed as God; who is said to have laid the foundation of the earth, and to have made the heavens, and to be unchanged when all these things shall pass away, must be divine. These are the attributes of God, and belong to him alone. These things *could not* be spoken of a man, an angel, an archangel. It is impossible to conceive that attributes like these

could belong to a creature. If they could, then all our notions of what constitutes the distinction between God and his creatures are confounded, and we can have no intelligible idea of God.

3. It is not improbable that Christ is the medium of communicating the knowledge of the divine essence and perfections to all worlds. He is the brightness of the divine glory—the showing forth—the manifestation of God; ver. 3. The body of the sun is not seen—certainly not by the naked eye. We cannot look upon it But there is a shining, a brightness, a glory, a manifestation which *is* seen! It is in the sun-beams, the manifestation of the glory and the existence of the sun. By his shining the sun is known. So the Son of God —incarnate or not—may be the manifestation of the divine essence. And from this illustration, may we not without irreverence derive an illustration of the doctrine of the glorious Trinity? There is the body of the sun—to us invisible—yet great and glorious, and the source of all light, and heat, and life. The vast body of the sun is the source of all this radiance, the fountain of all that warms and enlivens. All light and heat and life depend on him, and should he be extinct all would die. Thus may it not be with God the Father; God the eternal and unchanging essence—the fountain of all light, and life in the universe.—In the sun there is also the *manifestation*—the shining—the glorious light. The brightness which we see emanates from that—emanates at once, continually, always. While the sun exists, that exists, and cannot be separated from it. By that brightness the sun is seen ; by that the world is enlightened. Without these beams there would be no light, but all would be involved in darkness. What a beautiful representation of the Son of God—the brightness of the divine glory; the medium by which God is made known; the source of light to man, and for aught we know, to the universe! When he shines on men, there is light when he does not shine, there

is as certain moral darkness as there is night when the sun sinks in the west. And for aught we can see, the manifestation which the Son of God makes may be as necessary in all worlds to a proper contemplation of the divine essence, as the beams of the sun are to understand its nature. Then there are the warmth and heat and vivifying influences of the sun—an influence which is the source of life and beauty to the material world. It is not the mere shining—it is the attendant warmth and vivifying power. All nature is dependent on it. Each seed, and bud, and leaf, and flower; each spire of grass, and each animal on earth, and each bird on the wing, is dependent on it. Without that, vegetation would decay at once, and animal life would be extinct, and universal death would reign. What a beautiful illustration of the Holy Spirit, and of his influences on the moral world! " The LORD God is *a Sun*" (Ps. lxxxiv. 11); and I do not see that it is improper thus to derive from the sun an illustration of the doctrine of the Trinity. I am certain we should know nothing of the sun but for the beams that reveal him, and that enlighten the world; and I am certain that all animal and vegetable life would die if it were not for his vivifying and quickening rays. I do not see that it may not be equally probable that the nature—the essence of God would be unknown were it not manifested by the Son of God; and I am certain that all moral and spiritual life would die were it not for the quickening and vivifying influences of the Holy Spirit on the human soul.

4. Christ has made an atonement for sin; ver. 3. He has done it by *himself*." It was not by the blood of bulls and of goats; it was by his own blood. Let us rejoice that we have not now to come before God with a bloody offering; that we need not come leading up a lamb to be slain, but that we may come confiding in that blood which has been shed for the sins of mankind. The great sacrifice has been made. The victim is slain. The blood has been offered which expiates the sin of the world. We may now come at once to the throne of grace, and plead the merits of that blood. How different is our condition from that of the ancient Jewish worshippers! They were required to come leading the victim that was to be slain for sin, and to do this every year and every day. We may come with the feeling that the one great sacrifice has been made for us ; that it is never to be repeated, and that in that sacrifice there is merit sufficient to cancel all our sins. —How different our condition from that of the heathen! They too lead up sacrifices to be slain on bloody altars. They offer lambs, and goats, and bullocks, and captives taken in war, and slaves, and even their own children! But amidst these horrid offerings, while they show their deep conviction that *some* sacrifice is necessary, they have no promise—no evidence whatever, that the sacrifice will be accepted. They go away unpardoned. They repeat the offering with no evidence that their sins are forgiven, and at last they die in despair! We come assured that the " blood of Jesus Christ cleanseth from all sin,"—and the soul rejoices in the evidence that all past sins are forgiven, and is at peace with God.

5. Let us rejoice that the Lord Jesus is thus exalted to the right hand of God; vers. 3, 4. He has gone into heaven. He is seated on the throne of glory. He has suffered the last pang, and shed the last drop of blood that will ever be necessary to be shed for the sins of the world. No cold tomb is again to hold him; and no spear of a soldier is again to enter his side. He is now happy and glorious in heaven. The angels there render him homage (ver. 6), and the universe is placed under his control.

6. It is right to *worship* the Lord Jesus. When he came into the world the *angels* were required to do it (ver. 6), and it cannot be wrong for *us* to do it now. If the angels in heaven might properly worship him, we may. If they worshipped him, he is divine.

Assuredly God would not require them to worship a fellow-angel or a man!—I feel safe in adoring where angels adore ; I do not feel that I have a right to withhold my homage where they have been required to render theirs.

7. It is right to address the Lord Jesus as God ; ver. 8. If he is so addressed in the language of inspiration, it is not improper for us so to address him. We do not err when we adhere closely to the language of the Bible; nor can we have a stronger evidence that we are right than that we express our sentiments and our devotions in the very language of the sacred Scriptures.

8. The kingdom of the Redeemer is a righteous kingdom. It is founded in equity ; vers. 8, 9. Other kingdoms have been kingdoms of cruelty, oppression, and blood. Tyrants have swayed an iron sceptre over men. But not thus with the Redeemer in his kingdom. There is not a law there which is not equal and mild ; not a statute which it would not promote the temporal and eternal welfare of man to obey. Happy is the man that is wholly under his sceptre ; happy the kingdom that yields entire obedience to his laws !

9. The heavens shall perish; the earth shall decay; vers. 10, 11. Great changes have already taken place in the earth—as the researches of geologists show; and we have no reason to doubt that similar changes may have occurred in distant worlds. Still greater changes may be expected to occur in future times, and some of them we may be called to witness. Our souls are to exist for ever; and far on in future ages—far beyond the utmost period which we can now compute—we may witness most important changes in these heavens and this earth. God may display his power in a manner which has never been seen yet; and safe near his throne his people may be permitted to behold the exhibition of power of which the mind has never yet had the remotest conception.

10. Yet amidst these changes, the Saviour will be the same ; ver. 12.

He changes not. In all past revolutions, he has been the same. In all the changes which *have* occurred in the physical world, he has been unchanged ; in all the revolutions which have occurred among kingdoms, he has been unmoved. One change succeeds another ; kingdoms rise and fall and empires waste away; one generation goes off to be succeeded by another, but he remains the same. No matter what tempests howl, or how wars rage, or how the pestilence spreads abroad, or how the earth is shaken by earthquakes, still the Redeemer is the same. And no matter what are *our* external changes, he is the same. We pass from childhood to youth, to manhood, to old age, but he changes not. We are in prosperity or adversity; we may pass from affluence to poverty, from honour to dishonour, from health to sickness, but he is the same. We may go and lie down in the cold tomb, and our mortal frames may decay, but he is the same during our long sleep, and he will remain the same till he shall return and summon us to renovated life. I rejoice that in all the circumstances of life I have the same Saviour. I know what he is. I know, if the expression may be allowed, "where he may be found." Man may change by caprice, or whim, or by some new suggestion of interest, of passion, or ambition. I go to my friend to-day, and find him kind and true—but I have no absolute certainty that I shall find him such to-morrow. His feelings, from some unknown cause, may have become cold towards me. Some enemy may have breathed suspicion into his ear about me, or he may have formed some stronger attachment, or he may be sick, or dead. But nothing like this can happen in regard to the Redeemer. He changes not. I am sure that he is always the same. No one can influence him by slander; no new friendship can weaken the old ; no sickness or death can occur to him to change him; and though the heavens be on fire, and the earth be convulsed, he is THE SAME. In such a Saviour I may confide; in such a friend why should not all confide? Of earthly attachments it has been too truly said,

"And what is friendship but a name,
A charm that lulls to sleep;
A shade that follows wealth or fame,
But leaves the wretch to weep?"

But this can never be said of the attachment formed between the Christian and their gracious Redeemer. That is unaffected by all external changes; that shall live in all the revolutions of material things, and when all earthly ties shall be severed; that shall survive the dissolution of all things.

11. We see the dignity of man; vers. 13, 14. Angels are sent to be his attendants. They come to minister to him here, and to conduct him home "to glory." Kings and princes are surrounded by armed men, or by sages called to be their counsellors; but the most humble saint *may be* encompassed by a retinue of beings of far greater power and more elevated rank. The angels of light and glory feel a deep interest in the salvation of men. They come to attend the redeemed; they wait on their steps; they sustain them in trial; they accompany them when departing to heaven. It is a higher honour to be attended by one of those pure intelligences than by the most elevated monarch that ever swayed a sceptre or wore a crown; and the humblest and obscurest Christian shall soon be himself conducted to a throne in heaven, compared with which the most splendid seat of royalty on earth loses its lustre and fades away.

"And is there care in heaven? and is there love
In heavenly spirits to these creatures base,
That may compassion of their evils move?
There is:—else much more wretched were the case
Of men than beasts; But O! th' exceeding grace
Of Highest God that loves his creatures so,
And all his works of mercy doth embrace,
That blessed angels he sends to and fro,
To serve to wicked man, to serve his wicked foe!

"How oft do they their silver bowers leave,
To come to succour us that succour want!
How do they with golden pinions cleave
The yielding skies, like flying pursuivant,
Against foul fiends to aid us militant!
They for us fight, they watch and duly ward,
And their bright squadrons round about us plant;
And all for love and nothing for reward;
O why should Heavenly God to men have such regard!"
Spenser's Faery Queen, B. II. Canto viii. 1, 2.

12. What has God done for the salvation of man! He formed an eternal plan. He sent his prophets to communicate his will. He sent his Son to bear a message of mercy, and to die the just for the unjust. He exalted him to heaven, and placed the universe under his control that man may be saved. He sent his Holy Spirit; his ministers and messengers for this. And last, to complete the work, he sends his angels to be ministering spirits; to sustain his people; to comfort them in dying; to attend them to the realms of glory. What an interest is felt in the salvation of a single Christian! What a value he has in the universe! And how important it is that he should be holy! A man who has been redeemed by the blood of the Son of God should be pure. He who is an heir of life should be holy. He who is attended by celestial beings, and who is soon — he knows not *how* soon—to be translated to heaven, should be holy. Are angels my attendants? Then I should walk worthy of my companionship. Am I soon to go and dwell with angels? Then I should be pure. Are these feet soon to tread the courts of heaven? Is this tongue soon to unite with heavenly beings in praising God? Are these eyes soon to look on the throne of eternal glory, and on the ascended Redeemer? Then these feet, and eyes, and lips should be pure and holy, and I should be dead to the world, and should live only for heaven.

CHAPTER II.

ANALYSIS OF THE CHAPTER.

The main object of this chapter is, to show that we should attend dili-

CHAPTER II.

I HEREFORE we ought to give the more earnest heed to

the things which we have heard, lest at any time we should [1] let *them* slip.

1 *run out, as leaking vessels.*

gently to the things which were spoken by the Lord Jesus, and not suffer them to glide away from us. The apostle seems to have supposed that some might be inclined to disregard what was spoken by one of so humble appearance as the Lord Jesus; and that they would urge that the Old Testament had been given by the interposition of angels, and was therefore more worthy of attention. To meet this, he shows that important objects were accomplished by his becoming a man; and that even as a man, power and dignity had been conferred on him superior to that of the angels. In illustration of these points, the chapter contains the following subjects:—(1.) An exhortation not to suffer the things which had been spoken to slip from the mind,—or in other words, to attend to them diligently and carefully. The *argument* is, that if what was spoken by the angels under the old dispensation claimed attention, much more should that be regarded which was spoken by the Son of God; vers. 1—4. (2.) Jesus had been honoured, as incarnate, in such a way as to show that he had a right to be heard, and that what he said should receive the profound attention of men; vers. 5—9. The world to come had not been put under the angels as it had been under him (ver. 5); the general principle had been stated in the Scriptures that all things were put under man (vers. 7, 8), but this was fulfilled only in the Lord Jesus, who had been made a little lower than the angels, and when so made crowned with glory and honour; ver. 9. His appearance as a man, therefore, was in no way inconsistent with what had been said of his dignity, or his claim to be heard. (3.) The apostle then proceeds to show why he became a man, and why, though he was so exalted, he was subjected to so severe sufferings: and with this the chapter closes; vers. 10—18. It was because this was

proper from the relation which he sustained to man. The argument is, that the Redeemer and his people were identified; that he did not come to save *angels*, and that, therefore, there was a propriety in his assuming the nature of man, and being subjected to trials like those whom he came to save. In all things it behoved him to be made like his brethren, in order to redeem them, and in order to set them an example, and show them how to suffer. The humiliation, therefore, of the Redeemer; the fact that he appeared as a man, and that he was a sufferer, so far from being a reason why he should not be *heard*, was rather an additional reason why we should attend to what he said. He had a claim to the right of being heard not only from his original dignity, but from the friendship which he has evinced for us in taking upon himself our nature, and suffering in our behalf.

1. *Therefore.* Gr. " On account of this"—Διὰ τοῦτο—that is, on account of the exalted dignity and rank of the Messiah as stated in the previous chapter. The sense is, " Since Christ, the author of the new dispensation, is so far exalted above the prophets, and even the angels, we ought to give the more earnest attention to all that has been spoken." ¶ *We ought.* It is *fit* or *proper* (Gr. δεῖ) that we should attend to those things. When the Son of God speaks to men, every consideration makes it appropriate that we should attend to what is spoken. ¶ *To give the more earnest heed.* To give the more strict attention. ¶ *To the things which we have heard.* Whether directly from the Lord Jesus, or from his apostles. It is possible that some of those to whom the apostle was writing had heard the Lord Jesus himself preach the gospel: others had heard the same truths declared by the apostles. ¶ *Lest at any time.* We ought to attend to those things at all times. We ought

never to forget them; never to be indifferent to them. We are sometimes interested in them, and then we feel indifferent to them; sometimes at leisure to attend to them, and then the cares of the world, or a heaviness and dullness of mind, or a cold and languid state of the affections, renders us indifferent to them, and they are suffered to pass out of the mind without concern. Paul says, that this ought *never* to be done. At no time should we be indifferent to those things. They are always important to us, and we should never be in a state of mind when they would be uninteresting. At all times; in all places; and in every situation of life, we should feel that the truths of religion are of more importance to us than all other truths, and nothing should be suffered to efface their image from the heart. ¶ *We should let them slip.* Marg. *Run out as leaking vessels.* Tindal renders this, "lest we be spilt." The expression here has given rise to much discussion as to its meaning; and has been very differently translated. Doddridge renders it, "lest we let them flow out of our minds." Prof. Stuart, "lest at any time we should slight them." Whitby, "that they may not entirely slip out of our memories." The word here used—παραρρέω—occurs nowhere else in the New Testament. The Septuagint translators have used the word but once. Prov. iii. 21. "Son, do not pass by (μὴ παραρρύῆς) but keep my counsel;" that is, do not pass by my advice by neglect, or suffer it to be disregarded. The word means, according to Passow, to flow by, to flow over; and then to go by, to fall, to go away. It is used to mean to flow near, to flow by—as of a river; to glide away, to escape—as from the mind, *i. e.* to forget; and to glide along—as a thief does by stealth. See *Robinson's Lex.* The Syriac and Arabic translators have rendered it, *that we may not fall.* After all that has been said on the meaning of the word here (*comp. Stuart in loc.*), it seems to me that the true sense of the expression is that of flowing, or gliding by—as a river; and that the meaning here is, that we

should be very cautious that the important truths spoken by the Redeemer and his apostles should not be suffered *to glide by* us without attention, or without profit. We should not allow them to be like a stream that glides on by us without benefiting us; that is, we should endeavour to secure and retain them as our own. The truth taught, is that there is great danger, now that the true system of religion has been revealed, that it will not profit us, but that we shall lose all the benefit of it. This danger may arise from many sources—some of which are the following :—(1.) We may not feel that the truths revealed are important—and before their importance is felt, they may be beyond our reach. So we are often deceived in regard to the importance of objects —and before we perceive their value —they are irrecoverably gone. So it is often with time, and with the opportunities of obtaining an education, or of accomplishing any object which is of value. The opportunity is gone before we perceive its importance. So the young suffer the most important period of life to glide away before they perceive its value, and the opportunity of making much of their talents is lost because they did not embrace the suitable opportunities. (2.) By being engrossed in business. We feel that *that* is now the most important thing. That claims all our attention. We have no time to pray, to read the Bible, to think of religion, for the cares of the world engross all the time—and the opportunities of salvation glide insensibly away, until it is too late. (3.) By being attracted by the pleasures of life. We attend to them now, and are drawn along from one to another, until religion is suffered to glide away with all its hopes and consolations, and we perceive, too late, that we have let the opportunity of salvation slip for ever. Allured by those pleasures, the young neglect it; and new pleasures starting up in future life carry on the delusion, until every favourable opportunity for salvation has passed away. (4.) We suffer favourable *opportunities* to pass by without improving

2 For if the word spoken by angels *a* was steadfast, and *b* every transgression and disobedience received a just recompense of reward;

3 How *c* shall we escape, if wo

a Ac.7.53.   *b* Nu.15,31.   *c* ch.4.1,11.

them. Youth is by far the best time, as it is the most appropriate time, to become a Christian—and yet how easy is it to allow that period to slip away without becoming interested in the Saviour! One day glides on after another, and one week, and one month, one year passes away after another— like a gently-flowing stream—until all the precious time of youth has gone, and we are not Christians. So a revival of religion is a favourable time—and yet many suffer this to pass by without becoming interested in it. Others are converted, and the heavenly influences descend all round us, but we are unaffected, and the season so full of happy and heavenly influences is gone—to return no more. (5.) We let the favourable season slip, because we design to attend to it at some future period of life. So youth defers it to manhood—manhood to old age—old age to a death-bed—and then neglects it—until the whole of life has glided away, and the soul is not saved. Paul knew man. He knew how prone he was to let the things of religion slip out of the mind ---and hence the earnestness of his caution that we should give heed to the subject now—lest the opportunity of salvation should soon glide away. When once passed, it can never be recalled. Learn hence (1.) the truths of religion will not benefit us unless we give heed to them. It will not save us that the Lord Jesus has come and spoken to men, unless we are disposed to listen. It will not benefit us that the sun shines, unless we open our eyes. Books will not benefit us, unless we read them; medicine, unless we take it; nor will the fruits of the earth sustain our lives, however rich and abundant they may be, if we disregard and neglect them. So with the truths of religion. There is truth enough to save the world—but the world disregards and despises it. (2.) It needs not great sins to destroy the soul. Simple *neglect* will do it as

certainly as atrocious crimes. Every man has a sinful heart that will destroy him unless he makes an effort to be saved; and it is not merely the great sinner, therefore, who is in danger. It is the man who *neglects* his soul—whether a moral or an immoral man—a daughter of amiableness, or a daughter of vanity and vice.

2. *For if the word spoken by angels.* The revelation in the Old Testament. It was indeed given by *Jehovah,* but it was the common opinion of the Hebrews that it was by the ministry of angels; see Notes on Acts vii. 38, 53, and Gal. iii. 19,—where this point is fully considered. As Paul was discoursing here of the superiority of the Redeemer to the angels, it was to the point to refer to the fact that the law had been given by the ministry of angels. ¶ *Was steadfast.* Was *firm—* βέβαιος—settled—established. It was not vacillating and fluctuating. It determined what crime was, and it was firm in its punishment. It did not yield to circumstances; but if not obeyed in all respects, it denounced punishment. The idea here is not that everything was *fulfilled,* but it is, that the law so given could not be violated with impunity. It was not *safe* to violate it, but it took notice of the slightest failure to yield perfect obedience to its demands. ¶ *And every transgression.* Literally, *going beyond, passing by.* It means every instance of *disregarding* the law. ¶ *And disobedience.* Every instance of *not hearing* the law—παρακαὴ—and hence every instance of disobeying it. The word here stands opposite to *hearing* it, or attending to it—and the sense of the whole is, that the slightest infraction of the law was sure to be punished. It made no provision for indulgence in sin; it demanded prompt, implicit, and entire obedience. ¶ *Received a just recompense of reward.* Was strictly punished. Subjected to equal retribution. This was the character of the law.

neglect so great salvation ; which [a] at the first began to be spoken

by the Lord, *and* was confirmed unto us by them that heard *him;*

a Mar.1.14.

It threatened punishment for each and every offence, and made no allowance for transgression in any form; comp. Num. xv. 30, 31.

3. *How shall we escape.* How shall we escape the just recompense due to transgressors? What way is there of being saved from punishment, if we suffer the great salvation to be neglected, and do not embrace its offers? The sense is, that there is no other way of salvation, and the neglect of this will be followed by certain destruction. *Why* it will, the apostle proceeds to show, by stating that this plan of salvation was proclaimed first by the Lord himself, and had been confirmed by the most decided and amazing miracles. ¶ *If we neglect.* It is not merely if we commit great sins. Not, if we are murderers, adulterers, thieves, infidels, atheists, scoffers. It is, if we merely *neglect* this salvation—if we do not embrace it—if we suffer it to pass unimproved.—*Neglect* is enough to ruin a man. A man who is in business need not commit forgery or robbery, to ruin himself; he has only to *neglect* his business, and his ruin is certain. A man who is lying on a bed of sickness, need not cut his throat to destroy himself; he has only to *neglect* the means of restoration, and he will be ruined. A man floating in a skiff above Niagara, need not move an oar or make an effort to destroy himself; he has only to *neglect* using the oar at the proper time, and he will certainly be carried over the cataract. Most of the calamities of life are caused by simple *neglect.* By neglect of education children grow up in ignorance ; by neglect a farm grows up to weeds and briars; by neglect a house goes to decay; by neglect of sowing, a man will have no harvest; by neglect of reaping, the harvest would rot in the fields. No worldly interest can prosper where there is neglect; and why may it not be so in religion? There is nothing in earthly affairs that is valuable

that will not be ruined if it is not attended to—and why may it not be so with the concerns of the soul? Let no one infer, therefore, that because he is not a drunkard, or an adulterer, or a murderer, that, therefore, he will be saved. Such an inference would be as irrational as it would be for a man to infer that *because* he is not a murderer his farm will produce a harvest, or that *because* he is not an adulterer *therefore* his merchandise will take care of itself. Salvation would be worth nothing if it cost no effort—and there will be *no* salvation where no effort is put forth. ¶ *So great salvation.* Salvation from sin and from hell. It is called *great* because (1.) its author is great. This is perhaps the main idea in this passage. It "began to be spoken by the Lord;" it had for its author the Son of God, who is so much superior to the angels; whom the angels were required to worship (ch. i. 6); who is expressly called God (ch. i. 8); who made all things, and who is eternal; ch. i. 10 —12. A system of salvation promulgated by him *must* be of infinite importance, and have a claim to the attention of man. (2.) It is *great* because it saves from great sins. It is adapted to deliver from *all* sins, no matter how aggravated. No one is saved who feels that his sins are small, or that they are of no consequence. Each one sees his sins to be black and aggravated, and each one who enters heaven, will go there feeling and confessing that it is a great salvation which has brought such a sinner there. Besides, this salvation delivers from all sin—no matter how gross and aggravated. The adulterer, the murderer, the blasphemer, may come and be saved, and the salvation which redeems such sinners from eternal ruin is *great.* (3.) It is great because it saves from great dangers. The danger of an eternal hell besets the path of each one. All do not see it; and all will not *believe* it when told of it.

4 God *a* also bearing *them* wit-

a Ac.14.3.

ness, both with signs and wonders, and with divers miracles, and

---

But this danger hovers over the path of every mortal. The danger of an eternal hell! Salvation from everlasting burnings! Deliverance from unending ruin! Surely that salvation must be great which shall save from such a doom! If that salvation is neglected, that danger still hangs over each and every man. The gospel did not *create* that danger—it came to deliver from it. Whether the gospel be true or false, each man is by nature exposed to eternal death—just as each one is exposed to temporal death whether the doctrine of the immortality of the soul and of the resurrection be true or false. The gospel comes to provide a remedy for dangers and woes—it does not create them; it comes to deliver men from great dangers—not to plunge them into them. *Back of the gospel*, and before it was preached at all, men were in danger of everlasting punishment, and that system which came to proclaim deliverance from such a danger, is great. (4.) The salvation itself is great in heaven. It exalts men to infinite honours, and places on their heads an eternal crown. Heaven with all its glories is offered to us; and *such* a deliverance, and such an elevation to eternal honours, deserves to be called GREAT. If that is neglected, there is no other salvation; and man must be inevitably destroyed. (5.) It is great because it was effected by infinite displays of power, and wisdom, and love. It was procured by the incarnation and humiliation of the Son of God. It was accomplished amidst great sufferings and self-denials. It was attended with great miracles. The tempest was stilled, and the deaf were made to hear, and the blind to see, and the dead were raised, and the sun was darkened, and the rocks were rent. The whole series of wonders connected with the incarnation and death of the Lord Jesus, was such as the world had not elsewhere seen, and such as was fitted to hold the race in mute admiration and astonishment. If this be so, then re-

ligion is no trifle. It is not a matter of little importance whether we embrace it or not. It is the most momentous of all the concerns that pertain to man; and has a claim on his attention which nothing else can have. Yet the mass of men live in the *neglect* of it. It is not that they are professedly Atheists, or Deists, or that they are immoral or profane; it is not that they oppose it, and ridicule it, and despise it; it is that they simply *neglect* it. They pass it by. They attend to other things. They are busy with their pleasures, or in their counting-houses, in their workshops, or on their farms; they are engaged in politics, or in bookmaking, and they *neglect* religion NOW as a thing of small importance—proposing to attend to it hereafter, as if they acted on the principle that everything else was to be attended to *before* religion. ¶ *Which at the first*. Gr. *Which received the beginning of being spoken*. The meaning is correctly expressed in our translation. Christ *began* to preach the gospel; the apostles followed him. John prepared the way; but the Saviour was properly the first preacher of the gospel. ¶ *By the Lord*. By the Lord Jesus; see Notes on Acts i. 24. ¶ *And was confirmed unto us*, &c. They who heard him preach, that is, the apostles, were witnesses of what he said, and certified us of its truth. When the apostle here says "*us*," he means the church at large. Christians were assured of the truth of what the Lord Jesus spake by the testimony of the apostles; or the apostles communicated it to those who had not heard him in such a manner as to leave no room for doubt.

4. *God also bearing them witness.* By miracles. Giving them the sanction of his authority, or showing that they were sent by him. No man can work a miracle by his own power. When the dead are raised, the deaf made to hear and the blind to see by a word, it is the power of God alone that does it. He thus becomes a

gifts [1] of the Holy Ghost, according to his own will.

1 or, *distributions.*

witness to the divine appointment of him by whose instrumentality the miracle is wrought; or furnishes an attestation that what he *says* is true; see Notes on Acts xiv. 3. ¶ *With signs and wonders.* These words are usually connected in the New Testament. The word rendered *signs*— σημεῖον—means any miraculous event that is fitted to show that what had been predicted by a prophet would certainly take place; see Matt. xii. 38; comp. Note on Isa. vii. 11. A *wonder* — τέρας — denotes a portent, or prodigy—something that is fitted to excite wonder or amazement—and hence a miracle. The words together refer to the various miracles which were performed by the Lord Jesus and his apostles, designed to confirm the truth of the Christian religion. ¶ *And with divers miracles.* Various miracles, such as healing the sick, raising the dead, &c. The miracles were not of one class merely, but were various, so that all pretence of deception should be taken away. ¶ *And gifts of the Holy Ghost.* Marg. *Distributions.* The various influences of the Holy Spirit enabling them to speak different languages, and to perform works beyond the power of man; see Notes on 1 Cor. xii. 4—11. ¶ *According to his will.* As he chose. He acted as a sovereign in this. He gave them where he pleased, and imparted them in such measure as he chose. The sense of this whole passage is, "The gospel has been promulgated to man in a solemn manner. It was first published by the Lord of glory himself. It was confirmed by the most impressive and solemn miracles. It is undoubtedly a revelation from heaven; was given in more solemn circumstances than the law of Moses, and its threatenings are more to be dreaded than those of the law. Beware, therefore, how you trifle with it, or disregard it. It cannot be neglected with safety; its neglect or rejection *must* be attended with condemnation."

5 For unto the angels hath he not put in subjection the world to come, whereof we speak.

5. *For unto the angels hath he not put in subjection.* In this verse the apostle returns to the subject which he had been discussing in ch. i.—the superiority of the Messiah to the angels. From that subject he had been diverted (ch. ii. 1—4), by showing them what must be the consequences of defection from Christianity, and the danger of neglecting it. Having shown that, he now proceeds with the discussion, and shows that an honour had been conferred on the Lord Jesus which had never been bestowed on the angels—to wit, *the supremacy over this world.* This he does by proving from the Old Testament that such a dominion was given to *man* (vers. 6—8), and that this dominion was *in fact* exercised by the Lord Jesus; ver. 9. At the same time, he meets an objection which a Jew would be likely to make. It is, that Jesus appeared to be far inferior to the angels. He was a man of a humble condition. He was poor, and despised. He had none of the external honour which was shown to Moses—the founder of the Jewish economy; none of the apparent honour which belonged to angelic beings. This implied objection he removes by showing the reason why he became so. It was proper, since he came to redeem man, that he should be a man, and not take on himself the nature of angels; and for the same reason it was proper that he should be subjected to sufferings, and be made a man of sorrows; vers. 10—17. The remark of the apostle in the verse before us is, that God had never put the world in subjection to the angels as he had to the Lord Jesus. They had no jurisdiction over it; they were mere ministering spirits; but the world had been put under the dominion of the Lord Jesus. ¶ *The world to come.* The word here rendered *world*—οἰκουμένη—means properly *the inhabited,* or *inhabitable* world; see Matt. xxiv. 14; Luke ii. 1; iv. 5; xxi. 26. (Gr.) Acts

56 HEBREWS. [A. D. 64

6 But one in a certain place testified, saying, *a* What is man,

a Ps.8.4,&c.

that thou art mindful of him? or the son of man, that thou visitest him?

xi. 28; xvii. 6. 31; xix. 27; xxiv. 5; Rom. x. 18; Heb. i. 6; Rev. iii. 10; xii. 9; xvi. 14—in all which places, but one, it is rendered *world.* It occurs nowhere else in the New Testament. The proper meaning is the world or earth considered as inhabitable—and here the jurisdiction refers to the control over man, or the dwellers on the earth. The phrase "the world *to come,*" occurs not unfrequently in the New Testament; comp. Eph. ii. 7; 1 Cor. x. 11; Heb. vi. 5. The same phrase "the world to come,"—עוֹלָם הַבָּא—occurs often in the Jewish writings. According to Buxtorf (Lex. Ch. Talm. Rab.) it means, as some suppose, "the world which is to exist after this world is destroyed, and after the resurrection of the dead, when souls shall be again united to their bodies." By others it is supposed to mean "the days of the Messiah, when he shall reign on the earth." To me it seems to be clear that the phrase here means, *the world under the Messiah*—the world, age, or dispensation which was to succeed the Jewish, and which was familiarly known to them as "the world to come;" and the idea is, that that world, or age, was placed under the jurisdiction of the Christ, and not of the angels. This point the apostle proceeds to make out; comp. Notes on Isa. ii. 2. ¶ *Whereof we speak.* "Of which I am writing;" that is, of the Christian religion, or the reign of the Messiah.

6. *But one in a certain place testified.* The apostle was writing to those who were supposed to be familiar with the Hebrew Scriptures, and where it would be necessary only to make a reference in general without mentioning the name. The place which is quoted here is Ps. viii. 4—6. The *argument* of the apostle is this, that there stood in the sacred Scriptures a declaration that "all things were placed under the control and jurisdiction of MAN," but that that had not yet been accomplished. It was not

true (ver. 8) that all things were subject to him, and the complete truth of that declaration would be found only in the jurisdiction conferred on the Messiah—THE MAN by way of eminence—the incarnate Son of God. It would not occur to any one probably in reading the Psalm that the verse here quoted had any reference to the Messiah. It seems to relate to the dominion which God had given *man* over his works in this lower world, or to the fact that he was made lord over all things. That dominion is apparent, to a considerable extent, everywhere, and is a standing proof of the truth of what is recorded in Gen. i. 26, that God originally gave dominion to man over the creatures on earth, since it is only by this supposition that it can be accounted for that the horse, and the elephant, and the ox, and even the panther and the lion, are subject to the control of man. The argument of Paul seems to be this. " Originally this control was given to man. It was absolute and entire. All things were subject to him, and all obeyed. Man was made a little lower than the angels, and was the undisputed lord of this lower world. He was in a state of innocence. But he rebelled, and this dominion has been in some measure lost. It is found complete only in the *second man, the Lord from heaven* (1 Cor. xv. 47), the Lord Jesus to whom this control is absolutely given. He comes up to the complete idea of man—man as he was in innocence, and man as he was described by the Psalmist, as having been made a little lower than the angels, and having entire dominion over the world." Much difficulty has been felt by commentators in regard to this passage, and to the principle on which it is quoted. The above seems to me to be that which is most probably true. There are two other methods by which an attempt has been made to explain it. One is, that Paul uses the words here by way of *allusion*, or *accommodation* (Doddridge), as words that will express his meaning, without designing to say that the Psalm originally had any reference to the Messiah. Most of the later commentators accord with this opinion. The other opinion is, that David originally referred to the Messiah—that he was deeply and gratefully affected in view of the honour that God had conferred on him; and that in looking down by faith on the posterity that God had promised him (see 2 Sam. vii. 16), he saw one among his own descendants to whom God would give this wide dominion, and expresses himself in the elevated language of praise. This opinion is defended by Prof. Stuart; see his Com. on the Hebrews, Excursus IX.

[That the grand and ultimate reference, in the eighth Psalm, is to the person of the Messiah, none can reasonably doubt. Both our Lord and his apostles have affirmed it ; Matt. xxi. 15, 16 ; 1 Cor. xv. 27 ; Eph. i. 22. Add to these, the place before us, where—as the quotation is introduced *in the midst of an argument, and by way of proof*—the idea of *accommodation* is inconsistent with the wisdom and honesty of the apostles, and therefore inadmissible. The opposite extreme, however, of *sole and original* reference to the Messiah is not so certain. There is a more obvious and primary reference, which at once strikes the reader of the Psalm, and which, therefore, should not be rejected, till disproved. The conjecture, which a learned author mentioned above, has made, regarding the course of thought in the Psalmist's mind, supposing him to have been occupied with the contemplation of the covenant, as recorded in 2 Sam. vii. and of that illustrious descendant, who should be the Son of God, and on whom should be conferred universal empire—at the very time in which he composed the Psalm—is ingenious, but not satisfactory. The least objectionable view is that of *primary* and *secondary*, or *prophetic* reference. This relieves us from the necessity of setting aside the obvious sense of the original place, and, at the same time, preserves the more exalted sense, which our Lord and his apostles have attached to it, and the Spirit of course intended to convey. And in order to preserve this last sense, it is not necessary to ascertain what was the course of feeling in the Psalmist's mind, or whether *he* really had the Messiah in view, since the prophets, on many occa-

sions, might be ignorant of the full import of the words which the Holy Ghost dictated to them. This view, moreover, is all that the necessity of the case demands. It suits the apostle's argument, since the great and prophetic reference is to the Messiah. It presents, also, a complete πληρωσις of the eighth Psalm, which it is allowed on all hands the primary reference alone could not do. It is sufficiently clear that such universal dominion belongs not to man, in his present fallen state. Even if it be allowed that the contemplation of David regarded *man as innocent, as he was when created*, yet absolutely universal dominion did not belong to Adam. Christ alone is Lord of all. Creation animate and inanimate is subject to him.

Here then we have what has been well styled, "the safe middle point, the μεσον αριστον, between the two extremes of supposing this, and such like passages, to belong only to the Messiah, or only to him concerning whom they were first spoken." This middle point has been ably defended by Bishop Middleton. "Indeed," says he, "on no other hypothesis can we avoid one of two great difficulties ; for else we must assert that the multitudes of applications made by Christ and his apostles are fanciful and unauthorised, and wholly inadequate to prove the points for which they are cited ; or, on the other hand, we must believe that the obvious and natural sense of such passages was never intended, and that it is a mere illusion. Of the eighth Psalm the primary import is so certain that it could not be mistaken." The only objection to this double reference, worthy of being noticed, is connected with the clause, Ἡλαττωσας αυτον βραχυ τι παρ' αγγελους, which, it is affirmed, must possess two senses, not only different, but opposite and contradictory. In its primary application to *man*, the idea is plainly that of exaltation and honour. Such was the dignity of man that he was made *but a little* lower than the angels ; on the other hand, the secondary, or prophetic application, gives to the language the sense of humiliation or depression. For, considering the original dignity of Christ, the being made lower than the angels, cannot otherwise be regarded. But may not the clause, in both applications, have the idea of exaltation attached to it ? If so, the objection is at once met. And that this is the case has, we think, been satisfactorily made out "What," asks Prof. Stuart, "is his (Paul's) design ? To prove that Christ in his human nature is exalted above angels How does he undertake to prove this ? First by showing that this nature is made but little inferior to that of the angels, and next that it has been exalted to the empire of the world." This note has been extended to such length, because it involves a *principle* applicable to a multitude of passages. On the whole, it may be observed in reference to all these cases of quotation, that the mind of the pious and humble reader will not be greatly distressed by any difficulties connected with their application, but will ever rest satisfied with the assertion and authority of men, who spake as they were moved by the Holy Ghost.]

¶ *What is man*, &c. What is there in man that entitles him to so much notice? Why has God conferred on him so signal honours? Why has he placed him over the works of his hands? He seems so insignificant; his life is so much like a vapour; he so soon disappears, that the question may well be asked why this extraordinary dominion is given him? He is so sinful also, and so unworthy; so much unlike God, and so passionate and revengeful; is so prone to *abuse* his dominion, that it may well be asked why God has given it to him? Who would suppose that God would give such a dominion over his creatures to one who was so prone to abuse it as man has shown himself to be? He is so *feeble*, also, compared with other creatures—even of those which are made subject to him—that the question may well be asked why God has conceded it to him? Such question may be asked when we contemplate man *as he is.* But similar questions may be asked, if, as was probably the case, the Psalm here be supposed to have had reference to man *as he was created.* Why was one so feeble, and so comparatively without strength, placed over this lower world, and the earth made subject to his control? Why is it that when the heavens are so vast and glorious (Ps. viii. 3), God has taken such notice of man? Of what consequence can *he* be amidst works so wonderful? "When I look on the heavens and survey their greatness and their glory," is the sentiment of David, "why is it that *man* has attracted so much notice, and that he has not been wholly overlooked in the vastness of the works of the Almighty? Why is it that instead of this he has been exalted to so much dignity and honour?" This question,

thus considered, strikes us with more force now than it could have struck David. Let any one sit down and contemplate the heavens as they are disclosed by the discoveries of modern astronomy, and he may well ask the question, "What is *man* that he should have attracted the attention of God, and been the object of so much care?" The same question would not have been inappropriate to David if the Psalm be supposed to have had reference originally to the Messiah, and if he was speaking of himself particularly as the ancestor of the Messiah. "What is man; what am I; what can any of my descendants be, who must be of mortal frame, that this dominion should be given him? Why should any one of a race so feeble, so ignorant, so imperfect, be exalted to such honour?" *We* may ask the question here, and it may be asked in heaven with pertinency and with power, 'Why was *man* so honoured as to be united to the Godhead? Why did the Deity appear in the human form? What was there *in man* that should entitle him to this honour of being united to the Divinity, and of being thus exalted above the angels?' The wonder is not yet solved; and we may well suppose that the angelic ranks look with amazement—but without envy—on the fact that *man*, by his union with the Deity in the person of the Lord Jesus, has been raised above them in rank and in glory. ¶ *Or the son of man.* This phrase means the same as *man*, and is used merely to give *variety* to the mode of expression. Such a change or variety in words and phrases, when the same thing is intended, occurs constantly in Hebrew poetry. The name "son of man" is often given to Christ to denote his intimate connection with our race, and the interest which he felt in us, and is the *common* term which the Saviour uses when speaking of himself. Here it means *man*, and may be applied to human nature everywhere—and therefore to human nature in the person of the Messiah. ¶ *That thou visitest him.* That thou shouldst regard him or treat him with so much honour. Why is he the ob-

7 Thou madest him [1] a little lower than the angels ; thou crownedst him with glory and ho-

1 *a little while inferior to.*

ject of so much interest to the divine mind ?

7. *Thou madest him a little lower than the angels.* Marg. *A little while inferior to.* The Greek may here mean a little inferior in rank, or inferior for a little time. But the probable meaning is, that it refers to inferiority of rank. Such is its obvious sense in Ps. viii., from which this is quoted. The meaning is, that God had made man but little inferior to the angels in rank. He *was* inferior, but still God had exalted him almost to their rank. Feeble, and weak, and dying as he was, God had exalted him, and had given him a dominion and a rank almost like that of the angels. The wonder of the Psalmist is, that God had given to human nature so much honour—a wonder that is not at all diminished when we think of the honour done to man by his connection with the divine nature in the person of the Lord Jesus. If in contemplating the race as it appears ; if when we look at the dominion of man over the lower world, we are amazed that God has bestowed so much honour on our nature, how much more should we wonder that he has honoured man by his connection with the divinity. Paul applies this to the Lord Jesus. His object is to show that he is superior to the angels. In doing this he shows that he had a nature given him in itself but little inferior to the angels, and then that that had been exalted to a rank and dominion far above theirs. That such honour should be put on *man* is what is fitted to excite amazement, and well may one continue to ask *why* it has been done ? When we survey the heavens, and contemplate their glories, and think of the exalted rank of other beings, we may well inquire why has such honour been conferred on man ? ¶ *Thou crownedst him with glory and honour.* That is, with exalted honour. Glory and honour here are nearly synonymous. The meaning is,

nour, and didst set him over the works of thy hands :

8 Thou hast put all things in subjection under his feet. For

that elevated honour had been conferred on human nature. A most exalted and extended dominion had been given to *man,* which showed that God had greatly honoured him. This appeared eminently in the person of the Lord Jesus, "the exalted Man," to whom this dominion was given in the widest extent. ¶ *And didst set him over,* &c. *Man* has been placed over the other works of God (1) by the original appointment (Gen. i. 26) ; (2) man at large—though fallen, sinful, feeble, dying ; (3) man, eminently in the person of the Lord Jesus, in whom human nature has received its chief exaltation. This is what is particularly in the eye of the apostle—and the language of the Psalm will accurately express this exaltation.

8. *Thou hast put all things in subjection,* &c. ; Ps. viii. 6. That is, all things are put under the control of man, or thou hast given him dominion over all things. ¶ *For in that he put all in subjection.* The meaning of this is, that "the *fair interpretation* of the passage in the Psalm is, that the dominion of *man,* or of human nature over the earth, was to be absolute and total. Nothing was to be excepted. But this is not now the fact in regard to man in general, and can be true only of human nature in the person of the Lord Jesus. There the dominion is absolute and universal." The point of the argument of the apostle may be this. "It was the original appointment (Gen. i. 26) that man should have dominion over this lower world, and be its absolute lord and sovereign. Had he continued in innocence, this dominion would have been entire and perpetual. But he fell, and we do not now see him exerting this dominion. What is said of the dominion of *man* can be true only of human nature in the person of the Lord Jesus, and there it *is* completely fulfilled." ¶ *But now we see not yet all things put under him.* That is, "It is not now true that all

in that he put all in subjection under him, he left nothing *that is* not put under him. But ^{a} now

a 1Cor.15.24.

we see not yet all things put under him.

9 But we see Jesus, who ^{b} was

b Ph.2s ·.

things are subject to the control of man. There is indeed a *general* dominion over the works of God, and over the inferior creation. But the control is not universal. A large part of the animal creation rebels, and is brought into subjection only with difficulty. The elements are not entirely under his control ; the tempest and the ocean rage ; the pestilence conveys death through city and hamlet ; the dominion of man is a broken dominion. His government is an imperfect government. The world is not *yet* put wholly under his dominion, but enough has been done to constitute a pledge that it will yet be done. It will be fully accomplished only in him who sustains our nature, and to whom dominion is given over the worlds.''

9. *But we see Jesus.* " We do not see that man elsewhere has the extended dominion of which the Psalmist speaks. But we see the fulfilment of it in Jesus, who was crowned with glory and honour, and who has received a dominion that is superior to that of the angels.'' The *point* of this is, not that he suffered, and not that he tasted death for every man ; but that *on account of this*, or as a *reward* for thus suffering, he was crowned with glory and honour, and that he thus fulfilled all that David (Ps. viii.) had said of the dignity and honour of man. The object of the apostle is, to show that he was *exalted*, and in order to this he shows *why* it was—to wit, because he had suffered death to redeem man ; comp. Phil. ii. 8, 9. ¶ *Who was made a little lower than the angels.* That is, as a man, or when on earth. His assumed rank was inferior to that of the angels. He took upon himself not the nature of angels (ver. 16), but the nature of man. The apostle is probably here answering some implied objections to the rank which it was claimed that the Lord Jesus had, or which *might* be urged to the views which he was defending.

These objections were mainly two. First, that Jesus was a man ; and secondly, that he suffered and died. If that was the fact, it was natural to ask *how* he could be superior to the angels? How could he have had the rank which was claimed for him? This he answers by showing first, that his condition as a man was *voluntarily* assumed—" he was *made* lower than the angels ;" and secondly, by showing that as a consequence of his sufferings and death, he was immediately crowned with glory and honour. This state of humiliation became him in the great work which he had undertaken, and he was immediately exalted to universal dominion, and as Mediator was raised to a rank far above the angels. ¶ *For the suffering of death.* Marg. *By.* The meaning of the preposition here rendered "for" ($\delta\iota\grave{\alpha}$, here governing the accusative) is, "on account of;" that is, Jesus on account of the sufferings of death, or in virtue of that, was crowned with glory and honour. His crowning was the result of his condescension and sufferings; see Notes Phil. ii. 8, 9. It does not here mean, as our translation would seem ·to imply, that he was made a little lower than the angels *in order* to suffer death, but that as a reward for having suffered death he was raised up to the right hand of God. ¶ *Crowned with glory and honour.* That is, at the right hand of God. He was raised up to heaven ; Acts ii. 33; Mark xvi. 19. The meaning is, that he was crowned with the highest honour on account of his sufferings ; comp. Phil. ii. 8, 9 ; Heb. xii. 2 ; v. 7—9 ; Eph. i. 20—23. ¶ *That he.* Or rather, "*since* he by the grace of God tasted death for every man." The sense is, that *after* he had thus tasted death, and as a consequence of it, he was thus exalted. The word here rendered " *that* "— $\H{o}\pi\omega\varsigma$—means usually and properly *that, so that, in order that, to the end that, &c.* But it *may* also mean

made a little lower than the angels, [1] for the suffering of death, crowned *a* with glory and hon-

1 or, *by*.   *a* Acts 2.33.

when, after that, after; see Notes on Acts iii. 19. This is the interpretation which is given by Prof. Stuart (*in loc.*), and this interpretation seems to be demanded by the connection. The general interpretation of the passage has been different. According to that, the sense is, " We see Jesus, for the suffering of death, crowned with glory and honour, so as that, by the grace of God, he might taste of death for every man ;" see Robinson's Lex. on the word ὅπως, and Doddridge on the place. But it is natural to ask *when* Jesus was thus crowned with glory and honour ? It was not *before* the crucifixion—for he was then poor and despised. The connection seems to require us to understand this of the glory to which he was exalted in heaven, and this was *after* his death, and could not be *in order* that he might taste of death. I am disposed, therefore, to regard this as teaching that the Lord Jesus was exalted to heaven in virtue of the atonement which he had made, and this accords with Phil. ii. 8, 9, and Heb. xii. 2. It accords both with *the fact* in the case, and with the design of the apostle in the argument before us. ¶ *By the grace of God.* By the favour of God, or by his benevolent purpose towards men. It was not by any *claim* which man had, but was by his special favour. ¶ *Should taste death.* Should die ; or should experience death ; see Matt. xvi. 28. Death seems to be represented as something bitter and unpalatable — something unpleasant —as an object may be to the taste. Or the language may be taken from *a cup*—since to experience calamity and sorrow is often represented as drinking a cup of woes ; Ps. xi. 6 ; lxxiii. 10 ; lxxv. 8; Isa. li. 17; Matt. xx. 22 ; xxvi. 39. ¶ *For every man.* For all—ὑπὲρ παντὸς—for each and all —whether Jew or Gentile, bond or free, high or low, elect or non-elect. How could words affirm more clearly that the atonement made by the Lord

our ; that he *b* by the grace of God should taste death for every man.

b John 3.16.

Jesus was unlimited in its nature and design ? How can we express that idea in more clear or intelligible language ? That this refers to the atonement is evident—for it says that he "tasted death" for them. The friends of the doctrine of general atonement do not desire any other than Scripture language in which to express their belief. It expresses it exactly—without any need of modification or explanation. The advocates of the doctrine of limited atonement *cannot* thus use Scripture language to express their belief. They cannot incorporate it with their creeds that the Lord Jesus " tasted death FOR EVERY MAN." They are compelled to modify it, to limit it, to explain it, in order to prevent error and misconception. But that system *cannot* be true which requires men to shape and modify the plain language of the Bible in order to keep men from error ! comp. Notes on 2 Cor. v. 14, where this point is considered at length.

[With the author's views on the doctrine of atonement we accord in the main ; yet are here tempted to ask if the advocates of universal atonement would not be under the like necessity, of explaining, modifying, or *extending*, such passages as limit, or seem to limit, the atonement of Christ ; and if in framing a creed, the advantage would not lie about equal on either side ? Neither party would be contented to set down in it those scriptures which seemed least favourable to themselves, without note or explanation. If this remark appear unjust, in as much as the universalist could admit into his creed, that " Christ laid down his life for the sheep," though at the same time he believed farther, that he laid it down not for them only, nay, not for them in any special sense *more than for others ;* let it be observed that the limitarian could just as well admit into his, that " Christ tasted death for every man," or for all men, (Ὑπὲρ παντὸς) though he might believe farther, not for all specially, not for all efficaciously, or with Prof. Stuart on the place, not for all universally, but " for all without distinction, that is, both Jew and Gentile. It is indeed difficult to say on which side explanation would be most needed. In the case of the limited passage it would require to be observed first, that the atonement extended farther than *it* intimated, and besides, that there was no special reference to the parties specified, the sheep, namely. There would be required, in truth, both extension and limitation, that is, if a creed were to be made, or a full view of opinion given. They seem to come nearest the truth on this subject, who deny neither the general nor special aspect of the atonement. On the one hand there is a large class of *universal passages,* which cannot be satisfactorily explained on any other principle than that which regards the atonement as a great remedial plan, that rendered it consistent with the divine honour, to extend mercy to guilty men at large, and which would have been equally requisite had there been an intention to save one, or millions; numbers indeed not forming any part of the question. On the other hand, there is a large class of *special* texts, which cannot be explained without admitting, that while this atonement has reference to all, *yet God in providing it had a special design to save his people by it;* see the whole subject fully discussed, on the author's Note referred to above, and in the supplementary Note, on the same passages, which contains a digest of the more recent controversies on the point.]

Learn hence (vers. 6—9), from the incarnation of the Son of God, and his exaltation to heaven, what an honour has been conferred on human nature. When we look on the weakness and sinfulness of our race, we may well ask, what is man that God should honour him or regard him? He is the creature of a day. He is feeble and dying. He is lost and degraded. Compared with the universe at large, he is a speck, an atom. He has done nothing to deserve the divine favour or notice, and when we look at the race at large we can do it only with sentiments of the deepest humiliation and mortification. But when we look at human nature in the person of the Lord Jesus, we see it honoured there to a degree that is commensurate with all our desires, and that fills us with wonder. We feel that it is an honour to human nature—that it has done much to elevate man—when we look on such a man as Howard or Washington. But how much more has that nature been honoured in the person of the Lord Jesus! (1.) What an honour to us it was that he should take our nature into intimate union with himself—passing by the angelic hosts, and be-

coming a man! (2.) What an honour it was that human nature there was so pure and holy; that *man*—everywhere else so degraded and vile—*could* be seen to be noble, and pure, and godlike! (3.) What an honour it was that the divinity should speak to men in connection with human nature, and perform such wonderful works—that the pure precepts of religion should come forth from human lips—the great doctrines of eternal life be uttered by *a man,* and that from human hands should go forth power to heal the sick and to raise the dead! (4.) What an honour to man it was that the atonement for sin should be made in his own nature, and that the universe should be attracted to that scene where one in our form, and with flesh and blood like our own, should perform that great work. (5.) What an honour it is to man that his own nature is exalted far above all heavens! That one in our form sits on the throne of the universe! That adoring angels fall prostrate before him! That to him is intrusted all power in heaven and on earth! (6.) What an honour to man that one in his nature should be appointed to judge the worlds! That one in our own form, and with a nature like ours, shall sit on the throne of judgment and pronounce the final doom on angels and men! That assembled millions shall be constrained to bow before him, and receive their eternal doom from his hands! That prince and potentate—the illustrious dead of all past times, and the mighty men who are yet to live, shall all appear before him, and all receive from him there the sentence of their final destiny! I see, therefore, the most honour done to my nature as a man, not in the deeds of proud conquerors; not in the lives of sages and philanthropists; not in those who have carried their investigations farthest into the obscurities of matter and of mind; not in the splendid orators, poets, and historians of other times, or that now live — much as I may admire them, or feel it an honour to belong to a race which has produced such illustrious men—but in the fact that the

10 For it became *a* him, for *b*

a Luke 24.26,46.

whom *are* all things, and by whom

b Rom.11.36.

Son of God has chosen a body like my own in which to dwell ; in the inexpressible loveliness evinced in his pure morals, his benevolence, his blameless life ; in the great deeds that he performed on earth ; in the fact that it was this form that was chosen in which to make atonement for sin ; in the honours that now cluster around him in heaven, and the glories that shall attend him when he shall come to judge the world.

" Princes to his imperial name
Bend their bright sceptres down ;
Dominions, thrones, and powers rejoice,
To see him wear the crown.

" Archangels sound his lofty praise
Through every heavenly street,
And lay their highest honours down,
Submissive at his feet.

" Those soft, those blessed feet of his,
That once rude iron tore—
High on a throne of light they stand,
And all the saints adore.

" His head, the dear, majestic head,
That cruel thorns did wound—
See—what immortal glories shine,
And circle it around!

" This is the Man, th' exalted Man,
Whom we, unseen, adore ;
But when our eyes behold his face,
Our hearts shall love him more."

10. *For it became him.* There was a fitness or propriety in it ; it was such an arrangement as became God to make, in redeeming many, that the great agent by whom it was accomplished, should be made complete in all respects by sufferings. The apostle evidently means by this to meet an objection that might be offered by a Jew to the doctrine which he had been stating — an objection drawn from the fact that Jesus was a man of sorrows, and that his life was a life of affliction. This he meets by stating that there was a *fitness* and *propriety* in that fact. There was a reason for it—a reason drawn from the plan and character of God. It was fit, in the nature of the case, that he should be qualified to be *a complete* or *perfect Saviour*—a Saviour just

adapted to the purpose undertaken, by sufferings. The *reasons* of this fitness, the apostle does not state. The amount of it probably was, that it became him as a Being of infinite benevolence ; as one who wished to provide a perfect system of redemption, to subject his Son to such sufferings as should completely qualify him to be a Saviour for all men. This subjection to his humble condition, and to his many woes, made him such a Saviour as man needed, and qualified him fully for his work. There was a propriety that he who should redeem the suffering and the lost should partake of their nature ; identify himself with them ; and share their woes, and the consequences of their sins. ¶ *For whom are all things.* With respect to whose glory the whole universe was made ; and with respect to whom the whole arrangement for salvation has been formed. The phrase is synonymous with " the Supreme Ruler ;" and the idea is, that it became the Sovereign of the universe to provide a *perfect* scheme of salvation—even though it involved the humiliation and death of his own Son. ¶ *And by whom are all things.* By whose agency everything is made. As it was by his agency, therefore, that the plan of salvation was entered into, there was a *fitness* that it should be perfect. It was not the work of fate or chance, and there was a propriety that the whole plan should bear the mark of the infinite wisdom of its Author. ¶ *In bringing many sons unto glory.* To heaven. This was the plan—it was to bring many to heaven who should be regarded and treated as his *sons.* It was not a plan to save a *few*—but to save *many.* Learn hence, (1.) that the plan was full of benevolence. (2.) No representation of the gospel should ever be made which will leave the impression that a few only, or a small part of the whole race, will be saved. There is no such representation in the Bible, and it should not be made. God intends, taking

are all things, in bringing many sons unto glory, to make the cap-

a Isa. 55. 4.

the whole race together, to save a large part of the human family. Few in ages that are past, it is true, may have been saved; few now are his friends and are travelling to heaven; but there are to be brighter days on earth. The period is to arrive when the gospel shall spread over all lands, and during that long period of the millennium, innumerable millions will be brought under its saving power, and be admitted to heaven. All exhibitions of the gospel are wrong which represent it as narrow in its design; narrow in its offer; and narrow in its result. ¶ *To make the captain of their salvation.* The Lord Jesus, who is represented as the leader or commander of the army of the redeemed—"the sacramental host of God's elect." The word "captain" we apply now to an inferior officer—the commander of a "company" of soldiers. The Greek word—ἀρχηγὸς—is a more general term, and denotes, properly, the author or source of anything; then a leader, chief prince. In Acts iii. 15, it is rendered *prince* —"and killed *the prince* of life." So in Acts v. 31. "Him hath God exalted to be *a prince* and a Saviour." In Heb. xii. 2, it is rendered *author.* "Jesus, *the author* and finisher of our faith;" comp. Notes on that place. ¶ *Perfect through sufferings.* Complete by means of sufferings; that is, to render him wholly qualified for his work, so that he should be a Saviour just adapted to redeem man. This does not mean that he was *sinful* before and was made *holy* by his sufferings; nor that he was not in all respects a perfect man before;—but it means, that by his sufferings he was made *wholly fitted* to be a Saviour of men; and that, therefore, the fact of his being a suffering man was no evidence, as a Jew might have urged, that he was not the Son of God. There was a *completeness,* a *filling up,* of all which was necessary to his character as a Saviour, by the sufferings which he endured. We are

tain *a* of their salvation *b* perfect through sufferings.

b Luke 13. 32.

made morally *better* by afflictions, if we receive them in a right manner—for we are sinful, and need to be purified in the furnace of affliction; Christ was not made *better,* for he was before perfectly holy, but he was completely endowed for the work which he came to do, by his sorrows. Nor does this mean here precisely that he was exalted to heaven *as a reward* for his sufferings, or that he was raised up to glory as a consequence of them—which was true in itself—but that he was rendered complete, or fully qualified to be a Saviour by his sorrows. He was rendered thus complete, (1.) Because his suffering in all the forms that flesh is liable to, made him an example to all his people who shall pass through trials. They have before them a perfect model to show them how to bear afflictions. Had this not occurred, he could not have been regarded as a *complete* or *perfect* Saviour—that is, such a Saviour as we need. (2.) He is able to sympathize with them, and to succour them in their temptations, ver. 18. (3.) By his sufferings an atonement was made for sin. He would have been an *imperfect* Saviour—if the name *Saviour* could have been given to him at all—if he had not died to make an atonement for transgression. To render him *complete* as a Saviour, it was necessary that he should suffer and die; and when he hung on the cross in the agonies of death, he could appropriately say, "it is *finished.* The work is complete. All has been done that could be required to be done; and man may now have the assurance that he has a perfect Saviour—perfect not only in moral character, but perfect in his work, and in his adaptedness to the condition of men;" comp. ch. v. 8, 9. Note on Luke xiii. 32. 11. *For both he that sanctifieth.* This refers, evidently, to the Lord Jesus. The *object* is to show that there was such a union between him and those for whom he died, as to

11 For both he that sanctifieth and they who are sanctified *are* all *a* of one : for which cause he is not ashamed to call them brethren ; 12 Saying, *b* I will declare thy name unto my brethren ; in the

a John 17.21.

b Ps.22.22.

make it necessary that he should partake of the same nature, or that he should be a suffering man ; ver. 14. He undertook to redeem and sanctify them. He called them brethren. He identified them with himself. There was, in the great work of redemption, a *oneness* between him and them, and hence it was necessary that he should *assume* their nature— and the fact, therefore, that he appeared as a suffering *man*, does not at all militate with the doctrine that he had a more exalted nature, and was even above the angels. Prof. Stuart endeavours to prove that the word *sanctify* here is used in the sense of, *to make expiation* or *atonement,* and that the meaning is, " he who maketh expiation, and they for whom expiation is made." Bloomfield gives the same sense to the word, as also does Rosenmüller. That the word *may* have such a signification it would be presumptuous in any one to doubt, after the view which such men have taken of it ; but it may be doubted whether this idea is necessary here. The word *sanctify* is a general term, meaning to make holy or pure ; to consecrate, set apart, devote to God ; to regard as holy, or to hallow. Applied to the Saviour here, it may be used in this general sense—that he consecrated, or devoted himself to God—as eminently *the consecrated* or *holy one*— the Messiah (comp. Note on John xvii. 19) ; applied to his people, it may mean that *they* in like manner were *the* consecrated, the holy, the pure, on earth. There is a richness and fulness in the word when so understood. which there is not when it is limited to the idea of expiation ; and it seems to me that it is to be taken in its richest and fullest sense, and that the meaning is, " the great consecrated Messiah—the Holy One of God—and his consecrated and holy followers, are all of one." ¶ *All of one.* Of one family; spirit; Father;

nature. Either of these significations will suit the connection, and some such idea must be understood. The meaning is, that they were united, or partook of *something* in common, so as to constitute a *oneness*, or a brotherhood ; and that since this was the case, there was a propriety in his taking their nature. It does not mean that they were *originally* of one nature or family ; but that it was understood in the writings of the prophets that the Messiah should partake of the nature of his people, and that, *therefore*, though he was more exalted than the angels, there was a propriety that he should appear in the human form ; comp. John xvii. 21. ¶ *For which cause.* That is, because he is thus united with them, or has undertaken their redemption. ¶ *He is not ashamed.* As it might be supposed that one so exalted and pure would be. It might have been anticipated that the Son of God would refuse to give the name *brethren* to those who were so humble, and sunken and degraded as those whom he came to redeem. But he is willing to be ranked with them, and to be regarded as one of their family. ¶ *To call them brethren.* To acknowledge himself as of the same family, and to speak of them as his brothers. That is, *he is so represented as speaking of them in the prophecies respecting the Messiah*—for this interpretation the argument of the apostle demands. It was material for him to show that he was so represented in the Old Testament. This he does in the following verses.

12. *Saying.* This passage is found in Ps. xxii. 22. The whole of that Psalm has been commonly referred to the Messiah ; and in regard to such a reference there is less difficulty than attends most of the other portions of the Old Testament that are usually supposed to relate to him. The following verses of the Psalm are applied to him, or to transactions

midst of the church will I sing praise unto thee.

13 And again, *a* I will put my

a Ps.18.2.   *b* Isa.8.18.

connected with him, in the New Testament, vers. 1, 8, 18 ; and the whole Psalm is so strikingly descriptive of his condition and sufferings, that there can be no reasonable doubt that it had an original reference to him. There is much in the Psalm that cannot be well applied to David; there is nothing which cannot be applied to the Messiah ; and the proof seems to be clear that Paul quoted this passage in accordance with the original sense of the Psalm. The *point* of the quotation here is not that he would " declare the name" of God —but that he gave the name *brethren* to those whom he addressed. ¶ *I will declare thy name*. I will make thee known. The word " name " is used, as it often is, to denote God himself. The meaning is, that it would be a part of the Messiah's work to make known to his disciples the character and perfections of God—or to make them acquainted with God. He performed this. In his parting prayer (John xvii. 6), he says, " I have manifested thy name unto the men whom thou gavest me out of the world." And again, ver. 26, " And I have declared unto them thy name, and will declare it." ¶ *Unto my brethren*. The point of the quotation is in this. He spoke of them as *brethren*. Paul is showing that he was not ashamed to call them such. As he was reasoning with those who had been *Jews*, and as it was necessary as a part of his argument to show that what he maintained respecting the Messiah was found in the Old Testament, he makes his appeal to that, and shows that the Redeemer is represented as addressing his people as *brethren*. It would have been easy to appeal to *facts*, and to have shown that the Redeemer used that term familiarly in addressing his disciples, (comp. Matt. xii. 48, 49 ; xxv. 40 ; xxviii. 10 ; Luke viii. 21 ; John xx. 17), but that would not have been pertinent to his

trust in him. And again, *b* Behold I and the children *c* which God hath given me.

c John 17.6—12.

object. It is full proof to *us*, however, that the prediction in the Psalm was literally fulfilled. ¶ *In the midst of the church*. That is, in the assembly of my brethren. The *point* of the proof urged by the apostle lies in the first part of the quotation. This latter part seems to have been adduced because it might assist their memory to have the whole verse quoted ; or because it contained an interesting truth respecting the Redeemer—though not precisely a *proof* of what he was urging ; or because it *implied* substantially the same truth as the former member. It shows that he was *united* with his church ; that he was one of them ; and that he mingled with them as among brethren. ¶ *Will I sing praise*. That the Redeemer united with his disciples in singing praise, we may suppose to have been in the highest degree probable—though, I believe, but a single case is mentioned—that at the close of the Supper which he instituted to commemorate his death ; Matt. xxvi. 30. This, therefore, proves what the apostle intended— that the Messiah was among them as his brethren—that he spoke to them as such—and mingled in their devotions as one of their number.

13. *And again.* That is, it is said in another place, or language is used of the Messiah in another place, indicating the confidence which he put in God, and showing that he partook of the feelings of the children of God, and regarded himself as one of them. ¶ *I will put my trust in him.* I will confide in God ; implying (1) a sense of dependence on God; and (2) confidence in him. It is with reference to the former idea that the apostle seems to use it here—as denoting a condition where there was felt to be need of divine aid. His object is to show that he took part with his people, and regarded them as brethren —and the purpose of this quotation seems to be to show that he was in

such a situation as to make an expression of *dependence* proper. He was one with his people, and shared their dependence and their piety — using language which showed that he was identified with them, and could mingle with the tenderest sympathy in all their feelings. It is not certain from what place this passage is quoted. In Psalm xviii. 2, and the corresponding passage in 2 Sam. xxii. 3, the Hebrew is אֶחֱסֶה־בֹּן — "I will trust in him;" but this Psalm has never been regarded as having any reference to the Messiah, even by the Jews, and it is difficult to see how it could be considered as having any relation to him. Most critics, therefore, as Rosenmüller, Calvin, Koppe, Bloomfield, Stuart, &c., regard the passage as taken from Isa. viii. 17. The reasons for this are (1.) that the words are the same in the Septuagint as in the epistle to the Hebrews; (2) the apostle quotes the next verse immediately as applicable to the Messiah; (3) no other place occurs where the same expression is found. The Hebrew in Isa. viii. 17, is רִקְדִּית־לֹן — "I will wait for him," or I will trust in him — rendered by the Septuagint πεποιθὼς ἔσομαι ἐπ' αὐτῷ — the same phrase precisely as is used by Paul — and there can be no doubt that he meant to quote it here. The *sense* in Isaiah is, that he had closed his message to the people; he had been directed to seal up the testimony; he had exhorted the nation to repent, but he had done it in vain; — and he had now nothing to do but to put his trust in the Lord, and commit the whole cause to him. His only hope was in God; and he calmly and confidently committed his cause to him. Paul evidently designs to refer this to the Messiah ; and the sense as applied to him is, " The Messiah in using this language expresses himself *as a man*. It is *men* who exercise dependence on God; and by the use of this language he speaks as one who had the nature of man, and who expressed the feelings of the pious, and showed that he was one of them, and that he regarded them as brethren." There is not much difficulty in the *argument* of the pas-

sage; for it is seen that in such language he must speak as *a man*, or as one having human nature; but the main difficulty is on the question how this and the verse following can be applied to the Messiah? In the prophecy, they seem to refer solely to Isaiah, and to be expressive of his feelings alone—the feelings of a man who saw little encouragement in his work, and who having done all that he could do, at last put his sole trust in God. In regard to this difficult, and yet unsettled question, the reader may consult my Introduction to Isaiah, § 7. The following remarks may serve in part to remove the difficulty. (1.) The passage in Isaiah (viii. 17, 18), occurs *in the midst* of a number of predictions relating to the Messiah —preceded and followed by passages that had an ultimate reference undoubtedly to him ; see Isa. vii. 14 ; viii. 8 ; ix. 1—7, and Notes on those passages. (2.) The language, if used of Isaiah, would as accurately and fitly express the feelings and the condition of the Redeemer. There was such a remarkable similarity in the circumstances that the same language would express the condition of both. Both had delivered a solemn message to men ; both had come to exhort them to turn to God, and to put their trust in him — and both with the same result. The nation had disregarded them alike, and now their only hope was to confide in God, and the language here used would express the feelings of both—" I will *trust in God*. I will put confidence in him, and look to him." (3.) There can be little doubt that in the time of Paul this passage was regarded by the Jews as applicable to the Messiah. This is evident, because (a) Paul would not have so quoted it as a *proof text* unless it would be admitted to have such a reference by those to whom he wrote ; and (b) because in Rom. ix. 32, 33, it is evident that the passage in Isa. viii. 14, is regarded as having reference to the Messiah, and as being so admitted by the Jews. It is true that this may be considered merely as an argument *ad hominem*—or an argument from what was admitted by those with whom he was reasoning, without vouching for the precise accuracy of the manner in which the passage was applied—but that method of argument is admitted elsewhere, and why should we not expect to find the sacred writers reasoning as other men do, and especially as was common in their own times?

[Yet the integrity of the apostle would seem to demand, that he argue, not only *ex concessis*, but *ex veris*. We cannot suppose for a moment, that the sacred writers (whatever others might do), would take advantage of erroneous admissions. We would rather expect them to correct these. Proceed upon them, they could not; see the supplementary Note on chap. i. 5. Without the help of this defence, what the author has otherwise alleged here, is enough to vindicate the use the apostle has made of the passage; see also the Note on chap. ii. 6.]

The apostle is showing them that according to *their own Scriptures*, and in accordance with principles which they themselves admitted, it was necessary that the Messiah should be a man and a sufferer; that he should be identified with his people, and be able to use language which would express that condition. In doing this, it is not remarkable that he should apply to him language which *they* admitted to belong to him, and which would accurately describe his condition. (4.) It is not necessary to suppose that the passage in Isaiah had an *original* and *primary* reference to the Messiah. It is evident from the whole passage that it had not. There was a *primary* reference to Isaiah himself, and to his children as being emblems of certain truths. But still, there was a strong *resemblance*, in certain respects, between his feelings and condition and those of the Messiah. There was such a resemblance that the one would not unaptly symbolise the other. There was such a resemblance that the mind—probably of the prophet himself, and of the people— would look forward to the more remote but similar event — the coming and the circumstances of the Messiah. So strong was this resemblance, and so much did the expressions of the prophet here accord with his declarations elsewhere pertaining to the Messiah, that in the course of time they

came to be regarded as relating to him in a very important sense, and as destined to have their complete fulfilment when he should come. As such they seem to have been used in the time of Paul; and no one can PROVE that the application was improper. Who can demonstrate that God did not *intend* that those transactions referred to by Isaiah should be designed as symbols of what would occur in the time of the Redeemer? They were certainly symbolical actions — for they are expressly so said to have been by Isaiah himself (Isa. viii. 18), and none can demonstrate that they might not have had an ultimate reference to the Redeemer. ¶ *And again.* In another verse, or in another declaration; to wit, Isa. viii. 18. ¶ *Behold I and the children which God hath given me.* This is only a part of the passage in Isaiah, and seems to have been partially quoted because the *point* of the quotation consisted in the fact that he sustained to them somewhat of the relation of a parent towards his children—as having the same *nature*, and being identified with them in interest and feeling. As it is used by Isaiah, it means that he and his children were "for signs and emblems" to the people of his time—to communicate and confirm the will of God, and to be *pledges* of the divine favour and protection; see Notes on the passage in Isaiah. As applied to the Messiah, it means that he sustained to his people a relation so intimate that they could be addressed and regarded as his children. They were of one family; one nature. He became one of them, and had in them all the interest which a father has in his sons. He had, therefore, a nature like ours; and though he was exalted above the angels, yet his relation to man was like the most tender and intimate earthly connections, showing that he took part in the same nature with them. The *point* is, that he was a man; that since those who were to be redeemed partook of flesh and blood, *he* also took part of the same (ver. 14), and thus identified himself with them.

14. *Forasmuch then.* Since; or

14 Forasmuch then as the chil- | dren are partakers of flesh and blood

because. ¶ *As the children.* Those who were to become the adopted children of God; or who were to sustain that relation to him. ¶ *Are partakers of flesh and blood.* Have a human and not an angelic nature. Since they are men, he became a man. There was a fitness or propriety that he should partake of their nature; see Notes 1 Cor. xv. 50; Matt. xvi. 17. ¶ *He also himself,* &c. He also became a man, or partook of the same nature with them; see Notes on John i. 14. ¶ *That through death.* By dying. It is implied here (1) that the work which he undertook of destroying him that had the power of death, was to be accomplished by *his own dying;* and (2) that in order to this, it was necessary that he should be a man. An angel does not die, and therefore he did not take on him the nature of angels; and the Son of God in his divine nature could not die, and therefore he assumed a form in which he *could* die—that of a man. In that nature the Son of God could taste of death; and thus he could destroy him that had the power of death. ¶ *He might destroy.* That he might *subdue,* or that he might overcome him, and destroy his dominion. The word *destroy* here is not used in the sense of *closing life,* or of *killing,* but in the sense of bringing into subjection, or crushing his power. This is the work which the Lord Jesus came to perform—to destroy the kingdom of Satan in the world, and to set up another kingdom in its place. This was understood by Satan to be his object : see Notes on Matt. viii. 29 ; Mark i. 24. ¶ *That had the power of death.* I understand this as meaning that the devil was the *cause* of death in this world. He was the means of its introduction, and of its long and melancholy reign. This does not *affirm* anything of his power of inflicting death in particular instances —whatever may be true on that point —but that *death* was a part of his dominion ; that he introduced it; that he seduced man from God, and led on the train of woes which result in death.

He also made it terrible. Instead of being regarded as falling asleep, or being looked on without alarm, it becomes under him the means of terror and distress. What *power* Satan may have in inflicting death in particular instances no one can tell. The Jewish Rabbins speak much of Sammael, "the angel of death"—מלאך המית—מית מ—who they supposed had the control of life, and was the great messenger employed in closing it. The Scriptures, it is believed, are silent on that point. But that Satan was the means of introducing "death into the world, and all our wo," no one can doubt; and over the whole subject, therefore, he may be said to have had *power.* To *destroy* that dominion : to rescue man ; to restore him to life ; to place him in a world where death is unknown ; to introduce a state of things where *not another one would ever die,* was the great purpose for which the Redeemer came. What a noble object ! What enterprise in the universe has been so grand and noble as this ! Surely an undertaking that contemplates the annihilation of DEATH; that designs to bring this dark dominion to an end, is full of benevolence, and commends itself to every man as worthy of his profound attention and gratitude. What woes are caused by death in this world ! They are seen everywhere. The earth is "arched with graves." In almost every dwelling death has been doing his work of misery. The palace cannot exclude him; and he comes unbidden into the cottage. He finds his way to the dwelling of ice in which the Esquimaux and the Greenlander live; to the tent of the Bedouin Arab, and the wandering Tartar; to the wigwam of the Indian, and to the harem of the Turk; to the splendid mansion of the rich, as well as to the abode of the poor. That reign of death has now extended near six thousand years, and will travel on to future times—meeting each generation, and consigning the young, the vigorous, the lovely, and the pure, to dust. Shall that gloomy reign con-he *a* also himself likewise took part of the same; that through death *b* he might destroy him that

a John 1.14.

tinue for ever? Is there no way to arrest it? Is there no place where death can be excluded? Yes: *heaven* —and the object of the Redeemer is to bring us there.

15. And deliver them. Not all of them *in fact*, though the way is open for all. This deliverance relates (1.) to the *dread* of death. He came to free them from that. (2.) From death itself—that is, ultimately to bring them to a world where death shall be unknown. The *dread* of death may be removed by the work of Christ, and they who had been subject to constant alarms on account of it may be brought to look on it with calmness and peace; and ultimately they will be brought to a world where it will be wholly unknown. The *dread* of death is taken away, or they are delivered from that, because (*a*) the *cause* of that dread— to wit, sin, is removed; Notes 1 Cor. xv. 54, 55. (*b*) Because they are enabled to look to the world beyond with triumphant joy. Death conducts them to heaven. A Christian has nothing to fear in death; nothing beyond the grave. In no part of the universe has he any thing to dread, for God is his friend, and he will be his Protector everywhere. On the dying bed; in the grave; on the way up to the judgment; at the solemn tribunal; and in the eternal world, he is under the eye and the protection of his Saviour — and of what should he be afraid? ¶ *Who through fear of death.* From the dread of dying—that is, whenever they think of it, and they think of it *so often* as to make them slaves of that fear. This obviously means the natural dread of dying, and not particularly the fear of punishment beyond. It is *that* indeed which often gives its principal terror to the dread of death, but still the apostle refers here evidently to natural death—as an object which men fear. All men have, by nature, this dread of dying— and perhaps some of the inferior cre-

had the power of death, that is, the devil; 15 And deliver them who

b 1Cor.15.54.

ation have it also. It is certain that it exists in the heart of every *man,* and that God has implanted it there for some wise purpose. There is the dread (1.) of the dying pang, or pain. (2.) Of the darkness and gloom of mind that attends it. (3.) Of the unknown world beyond— the "evil that we know not of." (4.) Of the chilliness, and loneliness, and darkness of the grave. (5.) Of the solemn trial at the bar of God. (6.) Of the condemnation which awaits the guilty— the apprehension of future wo. There is no other evil that we fear so much as we do DEATH—and there is nothing more clear than that God *intended* that we should have a dread of dying. The REASONS why he designed this are equally clear. (1.) One may have been to lead men to *prepare* for it— which otherwise they would neglect. (2.) Another, to *deter them from committing self-murder*—where nothing else would deter them. Facts have shown that it was necessary that there should be some strong principle in the human bosom to prevent this crime—and even the dread of death does not *always* do it. So sick do men become of the life that God gave them; so weary of the world; so overwhelmed with calamity; so oppressed with disappointment and cares, that they lay violent hands on themselves, and rush unbidden into the awful presence of their Creator. This would occur more frequently by far than it now does, if it were not for the salutary fear of death which God has implanted in every bosom. The feelings of the human heart on this subject were never more accurately or graphically drawn than in the celebrated Soliloquy of Hamlet—

——to die ;—to sleep—
No more ;—and by a sleep, to say we end
The heart-ache, and the thousand natural shocks
That flesh is heir to,—'tis a consummation
Devoutly to be wished. To die—to sleep—.
To sleep :—perchance to dream;—ay, there's
the rub;

through ^a fear of death were all their life-time subject to bondage.

a Luke 1.74.

For in that sleep of death what dreams may come,
When we have shuffled off this mortal coil,
Must give us pause :—there's the respect
That makes calamity of so long a life :
For who would bear the whips and scorns of time,
The oppressor's wrong, the proud man's contumely,
The pangs of despised love, the law's delay,
The insolence of office, and the spurns
That patient merit of the unworthy takes,
When he himself might his quietus make
With a bare bodkin? Who would fardels bear,
To grunt and sweat under a weary life ;
But that the dread of something after death,—
The undiscovered country from whose bourne
No traveller returns,—puzzles the will ;
And makes us rather bear those ills we have,
Than fly to others that we know not of ?
Thus conscience does make cowards of us all,
And thus the native hue of resolution
Is sicklied o'er with the pale cast of thought ;
And enterprises of great pith and moment
With this regard their currents turn awry,
And lose the name of action.

God *designed* that man should be deterred from rushing uncalled into his awful presence, by this salutary dread of death — and his implanting this feeling in the human heart is one of the most striking and conclusive proofs of a moral government over the world. This instinctive dread of death can be overcome *only* by religion—and *then* man does not NEED it to reconcile him to life. He becomes submissive to trials. He is willing to bear all that is laid on him. He resigns himself to the dispensations of Providence, and feels that life, even in affliction, is the gift of God, and is a valuable endowment. He now dreads *self-murder* as a crime of deep dye, and religion restrains him and keeps him by a more mild and salutary restraint than the dread of death. The man who has true religion is willing to live or to die ; he feels that life is the gift of God, and that he

16 For verily ¹ he took not on *him the nature of* angels ; but

1 he taketh not hold of angels, but of the seed of Abraham he taketh hold.

will take it away in the best time and manner ; and feeling this, he is willing to leave all in his hands. We may remark (1.) How much do we owe to religion ! It is the only thing that will effectually take away the dread of death, and yet secure this point—to make man willing to live in all the circumstances where God may place him. It is *possible* that philosophy or stoicism may remove to a great extent the dread of death —but then it will be likely to make a man *willing* to take his life if he is placed in trying circumstances. Such an effect it had on Cato in Utica ; and such an effect it had on Hume, who maintained that suicide was lawful, and that to turn a current of blood from its accustomed channel was of no more consequence than to change the course of any other fluid ! (2.) In what a sad condition is the sinner ! Thousands there are who never think of death with composure, and who all their life long are subject to bondage through the fear of it. They never think of it if they can avoid it ; and when it is forced upon them, it fills them with alarm. They attempt to drive the thought away. They travel ; they plunge into business ; they occupy the mind with trifles ; they drown their fears in the intoxicating bowl : but all this tends only to make death more terrific and awful when the reality comes. If man were wise, he would seek an interest in that religion which, if it did nothing else, would deliver him from the dread of death ; and the influence of the gospel in this respect, if it exerted no other, is worth to a man all the sacrifices and self-denials which it would ever require. ¶ *All their life-time subject to bondage.* Slaves of fear ; in a depressed and miserable condition, like slaves under a master. They have no freedom ; no comfort ; no peace. From this miserable state Christ comes to deliver man. Religion enables him to look calmly on

he took on *him* the seed of Abraham.

death and the judgment, and to feel
that all will be well.
16. *For verily.* Truly. ¶ *He took
not on* him the nature of *angels.*
Marg. *He taketh not hold of angels,
but of the seed of Abraham he taketh
hold.* The word here used—ἐπιλαμ-
βάνεται—means, to take hold upon ;
to seize ; to surprise ; to take hold
with a view to detain for one's self.
Robinson. Then it means to take
hold of one as by the hand—with a
view to aid, conduct, or succour ;
Mark viii. 23 ; Acts xxiii. 19. It is
rendered *took,* Mark viii. 23 ; Luke
ix. 47 ; xiv. 4 ; Acts ix. 27 ; xvii. 19;
xviii. 17 ; xxi. 30, 33 ; xxiii. 19 ; Heb.
viii. 9 ; *caught,* Matt. xiv. 31 ; Acts
xvi. 19 ; *take hold,* Luke xx. 20, 26 ;
lay hold, and *laid hold,* Luke xxiii.
26 ; 1 Tim. vi. 12. The general idea
is that of seizing upon, or laying hold
of any one—no matter what the object is—whether to aid, or to drag to
punishment, or simply to conduct.
Here it means to lay hold with reference to *aid,* or *help ;* and the meaning is, that he did not seize the nature of angels, or take it to himself
with reference to rendering *them* aid,
but he assumed the nature of man—
in order to aid *him.* He undertook
the work of human redemption, and
consequently it was necessary for
him to be a man. ¶ *But he took on*
him *the seed of Abraham.* He came
to help the descendants of Abraham,
and consequently as they were men,
he became a man. Writing to Jews,
it was not unnatural for the apostle
to refer particularly to them as the
descendants of Abraham, though this
does not exclude the idea that he died
for the whole human race. It was
true that he came to render aid to the
descendants of Abraham, but it was
also true that he died for all. The
fact that I love one of my children,
and that I make provision for his
education, and *tell* him so, does not
exclude the idea that I love the
others also—and that I may make to
them a similar appeal when it shall be
proper.

17 Wherefore in all things it
behoved him to be made like unto

17. *Wherefore in all things.* In
respect to his body ; his soul ; his
rank and character. There was a
propriety that he should be like them,
and should partake of their nature.
The meaning is, that there was a fitness that nothing should be wanting
in him in reference to the innocent
propensities and sympathies of human nature. ¶ *It behoved him.* It
became him ; or there was a fitness
and propriety in it. The reason why
it was proper, the apostle proceeds to
state. ¶ *Like unto* his *brethren.*
Like unto those who sustained to him
the relation of brethren ; particularly
as he undertook to redeem the descendants of Abraham, and as he was
a descendant of Abraham himself,
there was a propriety that he should
be like them. He calls them brethren ; and it was proper that he should
show that he regarded them as such
by assuming their nature. ¶ *That
he might be a merciful and faithful
high priest.* (1.) That he might be
merciful ; that is, compassionate.
That he might know how to pity us
in our infirmities and trials, by having
a nature like our own. (2.) That he
might be *faithful ;* that is, perform
with fidelity all the functions pertaining to the office of high priest. The
idea is, that it was needful that he
should become a man ; that he should
experience as we do the infirmities
and trials of life, and that by being a
man, and partaking of all that pertained to man except his sins, he
might feel how necessary it was that
there should be *fidelity* in the office
of high priest. Here was a race of
sinners and sufferers. They were
exposed to the wrath of God. They
were liable to everlasting punishment.
The judgment impended over the
race, and the day of vengeance hastened on. *All now depended on the
great high priest.* All their hope
was in his *fidelity* to the great office
which he had undertaken. If he were
faithful, all would be safe ; if he were
unfaithful, all would be lost. Hence
the necessity that he should enter

his brethren, that he might be a merciful *a* and faithful high priest

a Gen.19.15,16.

fully into the feelings, fears, and dangers of man ; that he should become one of the race and be identified with them, so that he might be qualified to perform with faithfulness the great trust committed to him. ¶ *High priest.* The Jewish high priest was the successor of Aaron, and was at the head of the ministers of religion among the Jews. He was set apart with solemn ceremonies — clad in his sacred vestments—and anointed with oil ; Ex. xxix. 5—9 ; Lev. viii. 2. He was by his office the general judge of all that pertained to religion, and even of the judicial affairs of the Jewish nation ; Deut. xvii. 8—12 ; xix. 17 ; xxi. 5 ; xxxiii. 9, 10. He only had the privilege of entering the most holy place once a year, on the great day of expiation, to make atonement for the sins of the whole people ; Lev. xvi. 2, &c. He was the oracle of truth—so that when clothed in his proper vestments, and having on the Urim and Thummim, he made known the will of God in regard to future events. The Lord Jesus became in the Christian dispensation what the Jewish high priest was in the old ; and an important object of this epistle is to show that he far surpassed the Jewish high priest, and in what respects the Jewish high priest was designed to typify the Redeemer. Paul, therefore, early introduces the subject, and shows that the Lord Jesus came to perform the functions of that sacred office, and that he was eminently endowed for it. ¶ *In things pertaining to God.* In offering sacrifice ; or in services of a religious nature. The *great* purpose was to offer sacrifice, and make intercession ; and the idea is, that Jesus took on himself our nature that he might sympathize with us ; that thus he might be faithful to the great trust committed to him—the redemption of the world. Had *he* been unfaithful, all would have been lost, and the world would have sunk down to wo. ¶ *To make reconciliation.* By his

in things *pertaining* to God, to make reconciliation for the sins of the people :

death as a sacrifice. The word here used—*ἱλάσκομαι*—occurs but in one other place in the New Testament (Luke xviii. 13), where it is rendered " God *be merciful* to me a sinner ;" that is, reconciled to me. The *noun* (*ἱλασμός — propitiation*) is used in 1 John ii. 2 ; iv. 10. The word here means properly to *appease*, to reconcile, to conciliate ; and hence to *propitiate* AS TO *sins ;* that is, to propitiate God in reference to sins, or to render him propitious. The Son of God became a man, that he might so fully enter into the feelings of the people as to be faithful, and that he might be qualified as a high priest to perform the great work of rendering God propitious in regard to sins. How he did this, is fully shown in the subsequent parts of the epistle.

18. *For in that he himself,* &c. *Because* he has suffered, he is able to sympathize with sufferers. ¶ *Being tempted.* Or, being *tried.* The Greek word here used is more general in its meaning than the English word *tempted.* It means to *put to the proof ;* to try the nature or character of ; and this may be done either (1.) by subjecting a person to *afflictions* or *sufferings* that his true character may be tried—that it may be seen whether he has sincere piety and love to God ; or (2.) by allowing one to fall into *temptation,* properly so called— where some strong inducement to evil is presented to the mind, and where it becomes thus a *trial* of virtue. The Saviour was subjected to both these in as severe a form as was ever presented to men. His sufferings surpassed all others ; and the temptations of Satan (see Matt. iv.) were presented in the most alluring form in which he could exhibit them. Being *proved* or *tried* in both these respects, he showed that he had a strength of virtue which could bear all that could ever occur to seduce him from attachment to God ; and at the same time to make him a perfect model for those who should be tried

18 For in that he himself hath suffered, being tempted, he is able to succour them that are tempted.

in the same manner. ¶ *He is able to succour*, &c. This does not mean that he would not have had *power* to assist others if he had not gone through these sufferings, but that he is now qualified to sympathize with them from the fact that he has endured like trials. "He knows what sore temptations mean, For he has felt the same." The idea is, that one who has himself been called to suffer is able to sympathize with those who suffer ; one who has been tempted, is able to sympathize with those who are tempted in like manner. One who has been sick is qualified to sympathize with the sick ; one who has lost a child, can sympathize with him who follows his beloved son or daughter to the grave ; one who has had some strong temptation to sin urged upon himself can sympathize with those who are now tempted ; one who has never been sick, or who has never buried a friend, or been tempted, is poorly qualified to impart consolation in such scenes. Hence it is, that ministers of the gospel are often—like their Master—much persecuted and afflicted, that they may be able to assist others. Hence they are called to part with the children of their love ; or to endure long and painful sicknesses, or to pass through scenes of poverty and want, that they may sympathize with the most humble and afflicted of their flock. And they should be willing to endure all this ; for (1.) thus they are like their Master (comp. Col. i. 24 ; Phil. iii. 10) ; and (2.) they are thus enabled to be far more extensively useful. Many a minister owes a large part of his usefulness to the fact that he has been much afflicted ; and for those afflictions, therefore, he should unfeignedly thank God. The idea which is here expressed by the apostle—that one is enabled to sympathize with others from having himself suffered, was long since beautifully expressed by Virgil:

Me quoque per multos similis fortuna labores, Jactatam, hac demum voluit consistere terra. Non ignara mali, miseris succurrere disco
Æn. I. 628.

For I myself like you have been distressed, Till heaven afforded me this place of rest : Like you, an alien in a land unknown, I learn to pity woes so like my own.
Dryden.

Jesus is thus able to alleviate the sufferer. In all our temptations and trials let us remember (1.) that he suffered more—infinitely more—than we can do, and that in all our sorrows we shall never reach what he endured. We enter no region of trial where he has not gone beyond us ; we tread no dark and gloomy way where he has not gone before us. (2.) Let us remember that he is to us *a brother*, for he "is not ashamed to call us brethren." He had a nature like ours ; he condescended to appear as one of our race, with all the innocent propensities and passions of a man. What matchless condescension ! And what an honour for *us* to be permitted to address him as an "elder brother," and to know that he feels a deep sympathy in our woes ! (3.) Let us then, in all times of affliction, look to him. Go not, suffering Christian, to philosophy ; attempt not to deaden your feelings by the art of the Stoic ; but go at once to the Saviour—the great, sympathizing High Priest, who is able to succour you—and rest your burdens on him.

" His heart is made of tenderness, His soul is filled with love.
" Touch'd with a sympathy within, He knows our feeble frame; He knows what sore temptations mean, For he has felt the same.
" Then let our humble faith address His mercy and his power; We shall obtain delivering grace, In every trying hour."

CHAPTER III.

ANALYSIS OF THE CHAPTER.

The Jews valued their religion on many accounts. One was that it had been given by the instrumentality of

CHAPTER III.

WHEREFORE, holy brethren, partakers of the heavenly

distinguished prophets sent from God, and by the medium of angels. The apostle, in the previous chapters, had shown that in these respects the Christian religion had the advantage over theirs, for it had been communicated by one who was superior to any of the prophets, and who had a rank above the angels. Next to this, they valued their religion because it had been imparted by a law-giver so eminent as Moses—a man more distinguished than any other one on earth as a legislator. To him they looked with pride as the founder of their economy, and the medium through whom God had given them their peculiar laws. Next to him, their high priest was the most important functionary in the nation. He was at the head of their religion, and served to distinguish it from all others, for they had no conception of any form of true religion unless the office of high priest was recognised. The apostle, therefore, proceeds to show that in these respects the Christian religion had lost nothing, but had the advantage altogether—that it was founded by one superior to Moses, and that Christ as high priest was superior by far to the high priest of the Jews.

This chapter, and to ver. 13 of ch. iv., relates to the first of these points, and is occupied with showing the superiority of the Redeemer to Moses, and the consequences which result from the admission of that fact. It consists, therefore, of two parts.

I. The first is employed in showing that if the Author of the Christian religion is compared with Moses, he has the preference; vers. 1—6. Moses was indeed faithful, but it was *as a servant*. Christ was faithful, *as a son*. He had a rank as much above that of Moses as one who builds a house has over the house itself.

II. The consequences that resulted from that; ch. iii. vers. 7—19, and ch. iv. 1—13. The general doctrine

calling, consider the apostle and High Priest *a* of our profession, Christ Jesus;

a ch.4.14

here is, that there would be special danger in apostatising from the Christian religion—danger far superior to that which was threatened to the Israelites if they were disobedient to Moses. In illustrating this, the apostle is naturally led to a statement of the warnings against defection under Moses, and of the consequences of unbelief and rebellion there. He entreats them, therefore, (1.) not to harden their hearts against God, as the Israelites did, who were excluded from Canaan; vers. 7—11. (2.) To be on their guard against unbelief; ver. 12. (3.) To exhort one another constantly, and to stimulate one another, that they might not fall away; ver. 13. (4.) To hold the beginning of their confidence steadfast unto the end, and not to provoke God as they did who came out of Egypt; vers. 14—19. In the following chapter (vers. 1—13) he completes the exhortation by showing them that many who came out of Egypt were excluded from the promised land, and that there was equal danger now; and then proceeds with the comparison of Christ with the Jewish high priest, and extends that comparison through the remainder of the doctrinal part of the epistle.

1. *Wherefore.* That is, since Christ sustains such a character as has been stated in the previous chapter; since he is so able to succour those who need assistance; since he assumed our nature that he might be a merciful and faithful high priest, his character ought to be attentively considered, and we ought to endeavour fully to understand it. ¶ *Holy brethren.* The name *brethren* is often given to Christians to denote that they are of one family. It is *possible*, also, that the apostle may have used the word here in a double sense—denoting that they were his brethren as *Christians*, and as *Jews*. The word *holy* is applied to them to denote that they were set apart to God, or that they were sanctified. The

2 Who was faithful to him that [1] appointed him, as also Mo-

1 *made.*

ses [a] *was faithful* in all his house.

a Nu.12.7.

Jews were often called a "holy people," as being consecrated to God; and Christians are holy, not only as consecrated to God, but as sanctified. ¶ *Partakers of the heavenly calling.* On the meaning of the word *calling,* see Notes on Eph. iv. 1. The "*heavenly* calling" denotes the calling which was given to them from heaven, or which was of a heavenly nature. It pertained to heaven, not to earth; it came from heaven, not from earth; it was a calling *to* the reward and happiness of heaven, and not to the pleasures and honours of the world. ¶ *Consider.* Attentively ponder all that is said of the Messiah. Think of his rank; his dignity; his holiness; his sufferings; his death; his resurrection, ascension, intercession. Think of him that you may see the claims to a holy life; that you may learn to bear trials; that you may be kept from apostasy. The character and work of the Son of God are worthy of the profound and prayerful consideration of every man; and especially every Christian should reflect much on him. Of the friend that we love we think much; but what friend have we like the Lord Jesus? ¶ *The apostle.* The word *apostle* is nowhere else applied to the Lord Jesus. The word means one who *is sent*—and in this sense it might be applied to the Redeemer as one *sent* by God, or as by way of eminence THE one sent by him. But the connection seems to demand that there should be some allusion here to one who sustained a similar rank among the Jews; and it is probable that the allusion is to *Moses,* as having been the great apostle of God to the Jewish people, and that Paul here means to say, that the Lord Jesus, under the new dispensation, filled the place of Moses *and* of the high priest under the old, and that the office of "apostle" and "high priest," instead of being now separated, as it was between Moses and Aaron under the old dispensation, was now blended in

the Messiah. The name *apostle* is not indeed given to Moses directly in the Old Testament, but the verb from which the Hebrew word for apostle is derived is frequently given him. Thus in Ex. iii. 10, it is said, "Come now, therefore, and *I will send thee* unto Pharaoh." And in ver. 13, "The God of your fathers *hath sent me unto* you." So also in vers. 14, 15, of the same chapter. From the word there used—שלח—*to send.* the word denoting *apostle*—שליח—is derived; and it is not improbable that Moses would be regarded as being by way of eminence THE one *sent* by God. Further, the Jews applied the word שליח—*apostle,* to the minister of the synagogue; to him who presided over its affairs, and who had the general charge of the services there; and in this sense it might be applied by way of eminence to Moses as being the general director and controller of the religious affairs of the nation, and as *sent* for that purpose. The object of Paul is to show that the Lord Jesus in the Christian system—as the great apostle sent from God—sustained a rank and office similar to this, but superior in dignity and authority. ¶ *And High Priest.* One great object of this epistle is to compare the Lord Jesus with the high priest of the Jews, and to show that he was in all respects superior. This was important, because the office of high priest was that which eminently distinguished the Jewish religion, and because the Christian religion proposed to abolish that. It became necessary, therefore, to show that all that was dignified and valuable in that office was to be found in the Christian system. This was done by showing that in the Lord Jesus was found all the characteristics of a high priest, and that all the functions which had been performed in the Jewish ritual were performed by him, and that all which had been prefigured by the Jewish high priest was fulfilled in him. The apostle here merely alludes to him, or names him as the

3 For this *man* was counted worthy of more glory than Moses, inasmuch as he who hath

high priest, and then postpones the consideration of his character in that respect till after he had compared him with Moses. ¶ *Of our profession.* Of our religion ; of that religion which we profess. The apostle and high priest whom we confessed as ours when we embraced the Christian religion. 2. *Who was faithful;* see Note, ch. ii. 17. He performed with fidelity all the functions entrusted to him. ¶ *To him that appointed him.* Marg. *Made.* The word *made,* however, is used in the sense of constituted, or appointed. The meaning is, that he was faithful to God. Perhaps Paul urges on them the necessity of considering *his fidelity* in order to keep *them* from the danger of apostasy. A leading object of this epistle was to preserve those whom he had addressed from apostatizing from God amidst the temptations and trials to which they were exposed. In doing this, what could be a more powerful argument than to direct their attention to the unwavering constancy and fidelity of the Lord Jesus? The *importance* of such a virtue in the Saviour is manifest. It is seen everywhere ; and all the great interests of the world depend on it. A husband should maintain inviolate fidelity towards a wife, and a wife towards her husband ; a child should be faithful to a parent, a clerk and apprentice to his employer, a lawyer to his client, a physician to his patient, an ambassador to the government that commissions him. No matter what may be the temptations in the way, in all these, and in all other relations, there should be inviolate fidelity. The welfare of the world depended on the faithfulness of the Lord Jesus. Had *he* failed in that, all would have been lost. His fidelity was worthy of the more attentive consideration from the numerous temptations which beset his path, and the attempts which were made to turn him aside from his devotedness to God. Amidst all the temptations of the adversary, and all the

builded *a* the house hath more honour than the house.

a Zec.6.12,13.

trials through which he passed, he never for a moment swerved from fidelity to the great trust which had been committed to his hands. What better example to preserve them from the temptations to apostasy could the apostle propose to the Christians whom he addressed? What, in these temptations and trials, could be more appropriate than for them to *"consider"* the example of the great apostle and high priest of their profession? What more proper for us now in the trials and temptations of *our* lives, than to keep that great and glorious example continually before our eyes? ¶ *As also Moses* was faithful. Fidelity to God was remarkable in Moses. In all the provocations and rebellions of the Jews, he was firm and unwavering. This is affirmed of him in Num. xii. 7, to which place the apostle here alludes, " My servant, Moses, is not so, who is faithful in all his house." The word *house,* as applied to Moses, is used probably in the sense of *family,* as it often is, and refers to the *family* over which he presided—that is, the Jewish nation. The whole Jewish people were *a household,* or the family of God, and Moses was appointed to preside over it, and was faithful in the functions of his office there.

3. *For this* man. The Lord Jesus. The word *"man"* is understood, but there can be no doubt that he is referred to. ¶ *Was counted more worthy.* Was more worthy; or *is* more worthy. The word here used does not refer to anything that had been *said* of him, or to any estimate which had been made of him. It means simply that he was worthy of more honour than Moses. *How* he was so, Paul proceeds to show. ¶ *Of more glory—δόξης.* Honour, dignity, regard. He really had a higher rank, and was worthy of more respect. This was saying much for the Messiah, and that it was proper to say this, Paul proceeds to show. He did not attempt in any way to undervalue Moses and

4 For every house is builded by some *man;* but he that built all things *is* God.

a Num.12.7.

5 And Moses *a* verily *was* faithful in all his house, as a servant *b* for a testimony of *c* those

b Jos.1.2.   c De.18.15—19.

his institutions. He gave him all the honour which the Jews were themselves disposed to render him. He admitted that he had been eminently faithful in the station where God had placed him; and he then proceeds to show that the Lord Jesus was entitled to honour superior to that, and that hence the Christian religion had more to attach its friends to it than the Jewish had. ¶ *Inasmuch as he who hath builded the house.* The idea here is, either that he who is the maker of a house—the architect—is worthy of more respect than the house itself; or that he who is the founder of a family is worthy of more honour than the family of which he is the founder. It seems to me that the former is the meaning—for the latter is not always true. The founder of a family may be really deserving of much less respect than some of his descendants. But it is *always* true that the architect is worthy of more respect than the house which he makes. He exhibits intellect and skill. The house, however splendid, has neither. The plan of the house was drawn by him; its beauty, its proportions, its ornaments, are what he made them, and but for him they would not have existed. Michael Angelo was worthy of more honour than "St. Peter's" at Rome; and Sir Christopher Wren worthy of more than "St. Paul's" at London. Galileo is worthy of more praise than the telescope, and Fulton more than a steam-engine. All the evidence of skill and adaptedness that there is in the invention had its origin in the inventor; all the beauty of the statue or the temple had its origin in the mind of him that designed it. An author is worthy of more honour than a book; and he that forms a work of art is worthy of more respect than the work itself. This is the idea here. Paul assumes that *all* things owed their origin to the Son of God; ch. i. 2, 8, 10. He was the author of the

universe; the source of all wise and well-founded systems; the originator of the Jewish dispensation over which Moses presided. Whatever beauty or excellence there might have been, therefore, in that system, was to be traced to him; and whatever ability even Moses displayed was imparted by him. Christ is really the head of the family over which Moses presided, and has claims, therefore, to higher honour as such.

4. *For every house is builded by some man.* The words in this verse are plain, and the sentiment in it clear. The only difficulty is in seeing the connection, and in understanding how it is intended to bear on what precedes, or on what follows. It is clear that every house must have a builder, and equally clear that God is the Creator of all things. But what is the meaning of this passage in this connection? What is its bearing on the argument? If the verse was entirely omitted, and the fifth verse read in connection with the third, there would be apparently nothing wanting to complete the sense of the writer, or to finish the comparison which he had commenced. Various ways have been adopted to explain the difficulty. Perhaps the following observations may remove it, and express the true sense. (1.) Every family must have a founder; every dispensation an author; every house a builder. There must be some one, therefore, over *all* dispensations— the old and the new—the Jewish and the Christian. (2.) Paul *assumes* that the Lord Jesus was divine. He had demonstrated this in chap. i.; and he argues *as if* this were so, without now stopping to prove it, or even to affirm it expressly. (3.) God must be over *all things.* He is Creator of all, and he must, therefore, be over all. As the Lord Jesus, therefore, is divine, he must be over the Jewish dispensation as well as the Christian—or he must, as God, have

things which were to be spoken after ;

a Ps.2.7,12.

6 But Christ as a Son *a* over his own house ; whose house *b* are we,

b 1 Pet.2.5.

been at the head of that—or over his own family or household. (4.) As such, he must have a glory and honour which could not belong to Moses. He, in his divine character, was the Author of both the Jewish and the Christian dispensations, and he must, therefore, have a rank far superior to that of Moses—which was the point which the apostle designed to illustrate. The meaning of the whole may be thus expressed. " The Lord Jesus is worthy of more honour than Moses. He is so, as the maker of a house deserves more honour than the house. He is divine. In the beginning he laid the foundation of the earth, and was the agent in the creation of all things ; ch. i. 2, 10. He presides, therefore, over everything ; and was over the Jewish and the Christian dispensations—for there must have been some one over them, or the author of them, as really as it must be true that every house is built by some person. Being, therefore, over all things, and at the head of all dispensations, he MUST be more exalted than Moses." This seems to me to be the argument—an argument which is based on the supposition that he is at the head of all things, and that he was the agent in the creation of all worlds. This view will make all consistent. The Lord Jesus will be seen to have a claim to a far higher honour than Moses, and Moses will be seen to have derived his honour, as a servant of the Mediator, in the economy which he had appointed.

5. *Moses* was *faithful—as a servant.* Not as the head of the dispensation ; not as having originated it ; but as in the employ and under the direction of its great Founder and Author—the Messiah. As such a servant he deserves all the honour for fidelity which has ever been claimed for him, but it cannot be the honour which is due to him who is at the head of the family or house. Paul *assumed* that Moses was a *servant,* and argued on that supposition, without attempting

to prove it, because it was so often affirmed in the Old Testament, and must have been conceded by all the Jews. In numerous instances he is spoken of as " THE servant of the Lord ;" see Josh. i. 1, 2 ; ix. 24 ; 1 Chron. vi. 49 ; 2 Chron. xxiv. 9 ; Neh. x. 29 ; Dan. ix. 11 ; Ex. xiv. 31 ; 1 Kings viii. 56 ; Ps. cv. 26. As this point was undisputed, it was only necessary to show that the Messiah was superior to *a servant,* in order to make the argument clear. ¶ *For a testimony.* To bear witness to those truths which were to be revealed ; that is, he was the instrument of the divine communications to the people, or the medium by which God made his will known. He did not *originate* the truths himself ; but he was the mere medium by which God made known his truth to his people—a servant whom He employed to make his will known. The word *" after"* here is not necessary in order to a just translation of this passage, and obscures the sense. It does not mean that he was a witness of those truths which were to be spoken *subsequently* to his time under another dispensation, nor those truths which the apostle proposed to consider in another part of the epistle, as Doddridge supposes ; but it means merely that Moses stood forth as a public witness of the truths which God designed to reveal, or which were to be spoken. God did not speak to his people *directly,* and face to face, but he spoke through Moses as an organ, or medium. The sense is, Moses was a mere *servant* of God to communicate his will to man.

3. *But Christ as a Son over his own house.* He is not a servant. To the whole household or family of God he sustains the same relation which a son and heir in a family does to the household. That relation is far different from that of a servant. Moses was the latter ; Christ was the former. To God he sustained the relation of a Son, and recognised Him

if *a* we hold fast the confidence and the rejoicing of the hope firm unto the end.

a Matt.10.22; ch.10.38,39.

as his Father, and sought in all things to do his will; but over the whole family of God—the entire Church of all dispensations—he was like a son over the affairs of a family. Compared with the condition of a servant, Christ is as much superior to Moses as a son and heir is to the condition of a servant. A servant owns nothing; is heir to nothing; has no authority, and no right to control anything, and is himself wholly at the will of another. A son is the heir of all; has a prospective right to all; and is looked up to by all with respect. But the idea here is not merely that Christ is *a son;* it is that *as* a son he is placed over the whole arrangements of the household, and is one to whom all is entrusted as if it were his own. ¶ *Whose house we are.* Of whose family we are a part, or to which we belong. That is, we belong to the family over which Christ is placed, and not to that which was subject to Moses. ¶ *If we hold fast.* A leading bject of this epistle is to guard those to whom it was addressed against the danger of apostasy. Hence this is introduced on all suitable occasions, and the apostle here says, that the only evidence which they could have that they belonged to the family of Christ, would be that they held fast the confidence which they had unto the end. If they did not do that, it would demonstrate that they never belonged to his family, for evidence of having belonged to his household was to be furnished only by perseverance to the end. ¶ *The confidence.* The word here used originally means *the liberty of speaking boldly and without restraint;* then it means boldness or confidence in general. ¶ *And the rejoicing.* The word here used means properly *glorying, boasting,* and then rejoicing. These words are used here in an adverbial signification, and the meaning is, that the Christian has a confident and a rejoicing hope. It

7 Wherefore, (as the Holy Ghost saith, To-day, *b* if ye will hear his voice,

b Ps.95.7

is (1.) confident—bold—firm. It is not like the timid hope of the Pagan, and the dreams and conjectures of the philosopher; it is not that which gives way at every breath of opposition; it is bold, firm, and manly. It is (2.) *rejoicing*—triumphant, exulting. Why should not the hope of heaven fill with joy? Why should not he exult who has the prospect of everlasting happiness? ¶ *Unto the end.* To the end of life. Our religion, our hope, our confidence in God must be persevered in to the end of life, if we would have evidence that we are his children. If hope is cherished for a while and then abandoned; if men profess religion and then fall away, no matter what were their raptures and triumphs, it proves that they never had any real piety. No evidence can be strong enough to prove that a man is a Christian, unless it leads him to persevere to the end of life.

7. *Wherefore.* In view of the fact that the Author of the Christian dispensation has a rank far superior to that of Moses. Because Christ has claims on us far greater than those which Moses had, let us hearken to his voice, and dread his displeasure. ¶ *As the Holy Ghost saith.* In Ps. xcv. 7—11. This is full proof that in the estimation of the author of this epistle the writer of this Psalm was inspired. The Holy Ghost speaks through the word which he has revealed. The apostle quotes this passage and applies it to those whom he addressed, because the admonition was as pertinent and important under the Christian dispensation, as it was under the Jewish. The danger of hardening the heart by neglecting to hear his voice was as great, and the consequences would be as fearful and alarming. — We should regard the solemn warnings in the Old Testament against sin, and against the danger of apostasy, as addressed by the Holy Ghost to *us*. They are as

8 Harden not your hearts, as in the provocation, in the day of temptation in the wilderness ;

9 When your fathers tempted me, proved me, and saw my works forty years.

applicable to us as they were to those to whom they were at first addressed; and we need all the influence of such appeals, to keep us from apostasy as much as they did. ¶ *To day.* Now; at present. At the very time when the command is addressed to you. It is not to be put off till to-morrow. All God's commands relate to *the present*—to this day—to the passing moment. He gives us no commands *about the future.* He does not require us to repent and to turn to him *to-morrow,* or ten years hence. The reasons are obvious. (1.) Duty pertains to the present. It is our duty to turn from sin, and to love him NOW. (2.) We know not that we shall live to another day. A command, therefore, could not extend to that time unless it were accompanied with a *revelation* that we should live till then—and such a revelation God does not choose to give. Every one, therefore, should feel that whatever commands God addresses to him are addressed to him *now.* Whatever guilt he incurs by neglecting those commands is incurred *now.* For the *present* neglect and disobedience each one is to answer—and each one must give account to God for what he does TO-DAY. ¶ *If ye will hear.* In case you are willing to hearken to God, listen now, and do not defer it to a future period. There is much in a *willingness* to hear the voice of God. A *willingness* to learn is usually the precursor of great attainments in knowledge. A *willingness* to reform, is usually the precursor of reformation. Get a man *willing* to break off his habits of profaneness or intemperance, and usually all the rest is easy. The great difficulty in the mind of a sinner is in his *will.* He is unwilling to hear the voice of God ; unwilling that he should reign over him ; unwilling now to attend to religion. While this unwillingness lasts he will make no efforts, and he sees, or creates a thousand difficulties in the way of his becoming a Christian. But

when that unwillingness is overcome, and he is disposed to engage in the work of religion, difficulties vanish, and the work of salvation becomes easy. ¶ *His voice.* The voice of God speaking to us (1.) in his written word ; (2.) in the preached gospel ; (3.) in our own consciences ; (4.) in the events of his Providence ; (5.) in the admonitions of our relatives and friends. Whatever conveys to us the truth of God, or is adapted to impress that on us, may be regarded as *his voice* speaking to us. He thus speaks to us *every day* in some of these ways ; and every day, therefore, he may entreat us not to harden our hearts.

8. *Harden not your hearts.* Do not render the heart insensible to the divine voice and admonition. A hard heart is that where the conscience is seared and insensible ; where truth makes no impression ; where no religious effect is produced by afflictions ; where preaching is listened to without interest ; and where the mind is unaffected by the appeals of friends. The idea here is, that a refusal to listen to the voice of God is connected with a hardening of the heart. It is in two ways. (1.) The very refusal to do this tends to harden it. And (2.) in order to resist the appeals of God, men must resort to the means of *voluntarily* hardening the heart. This they do by setting themselves against the truth ; by the excuses which they offer for not becoming Christians ; by plunging into sin in order to avoid serious impressions ; and by direct resistance of the Holy Ghost. No inconsiderable part of the efforts of sinners consists in endeavouring to produce insensibility in their minds to the truth and the appeals of God. ¶ *As in the provocation.* Literally, *in the embittering—* ἐν τῷ παραπικρασμῷ. Then it means that which embitters or provokes the mind—as disobedience. Here it refers to what they did to *embitter* the mind of God against them ; that is

10 Wherefore I was grieved
with that generation, and said,
They do always err in *their*

heart ; and they have not known
my ways.
11 So I sware in my wrath,

to the course of conduct which was
adopted to provoke him to wrath.
¶ *In the day of temptation.* In the
time of temptation — the word *day*
being used here, as it is often, to denote an indefinite period, or *time* in
general. The word *temptation* here
refers to the various provocations by
which they *tried* the patience of God.
They rebelled against him ; they did
that which put the divine patience
and forbearance to a trial. It does
not mean that they tempted God to
do evil, but that his long-suffering
was *tried* by their sins. ¶ *In the
wilderness.* The desert through
which they passed. The word *wilderness* in the Scriptures commonly
means a *desert ;* see Notes Matt. iii.
1. " One provocation was in demanding bread at Sin ; a second for
want of water at Massah or Meribah ;
a third time at Sinai with the golden
calf ; a fourth time at Taberah for
want of flesh ; a fifth time at Kadesh
when they refused to go up into
Canaan, and the oath came that they
should die in the wilderness. A like
refusal may prevent us from entering
into rest."—*Dr. J. P. Wilson, MS.
Notes.*
9. *Proved me.* " As if they would
have made an experiment how much
it was possible for me to bear." *Doddridge.* The meaning is, they put
my patience to a thorough trial.
¶ *And saw my works.* That is, my
miracles, or my interpositions in their
behalf. They saw the wonders at the
Red Sea, the descent on Mount Sinai,
the supply of manna, &c., and yet
while seeing those works they rebelled.
Even while sinners look on the doings
of God, and are surrounded by the
proofs of his power and goodness, they
rebel, and provoke him to anger. Men
sin when God is filling their houses
with plenty ; when he opens his hand
daily to supply their wants ; when they
behold the manifestations of his goodness on the sea and on the land ; and
even in the midst of all the blessings

of redemption, they provoke him to
wrath. ¶ *Forty years.* The whole
time during which they were passing
from Egypt to the promised land.
This may mean either that they saw
his works forty years, or that they
tempted him forty years. The sense
is not materially affected whichever
interpretation is preferred.
10. *Wherefore I was grieved.* On
the word *grieved,* see Notes on Eph.
iv. 30. The word here means that he
was offended with, or that he was in-
dignant at them. ¶ *They do always
err in* their *heart.* Their long trial
of forty years had been sufficient to
show that it was a characteristic of
the people that they were disposed to
wander from God. Forty years are
enough to show what the character is.
They had seen his works ; they had
been called to obey him ; they had
received his law ; and yet their conduct
during that time had shown that they
were not disposed to obey him. So
of an individual. A man who has
lived in sin forty years ; who during
all that time has rebelled against God,
and disregarded all his appeals ; who
has lived for himself and not for his
Maker, has shown what his character
is. Longer time is unnecessary ; and
if God should then cut him down and
consign him to hell, he could not be
blamed for doing it. A man who
during forty years will live in sin, and
resist all the appeals of God, shows
what is in his heart, and no injustice
is done if *then* he is summoned before
God, and he swears that he shall not
enter into his rest. ¶ *And they have
not known my ways.* They have been
rebellious. They have not been acquainted with the true God ; or they
have not *approved* my doings. The
word *know* is often used in the Scriptures in the sense of *approving,* or
loving ; see Notes Matt. vii. 23.
11. *So I sware in my wrath.* God
is often represented in the Scriptures
as *swearing*—and usually as swearing
by himself, or by his own existence.

They shall not enter[1] into my rest.)

12 Take heed, brethren, lest there

[1] *if they shall enter. a* Mar. 7.21, 23.

be in any of you an evil *a* heart of unbelief, in *b* departing from the living God.

b Je.2.13.

Of course this is figurative, and denotes a strong affirmation, or a settled and determined purpose. An oath with us implies the strongest affirmation, or the expression of the most settled and determined purpose of mind. The meaning here is, that so refractory and perverse had they showed themselves, that he solemnly resolved that they should never enter into the land of Canaan. ¶ *They shall not enter into my rest.* Marg. As in the original, *if they shall enter.* That is, they shall not enter. The word (□□) *if* has this negative meaning in Hebrew, and this meaning is transferred to the Greek word *if;* comp. 1 Sam. iii. 17; 2 Sam. iii. 35; 2 Kings vi. 31. It is called "my rest" here, meaning that it was such rest as God had provided, or such as he enjoyed. The particular *rest* referred to here was that of the land of Canaan, but which was undoubtedly regarded as emblematic of the "*rest*" in heaven. Into that rest God solemnly said they should never enter. They had been rebellious. All the means of reclaiming them had failed. God had warned and entreated them; he had caused his mercies to pass before them, and had visited them with judgments in vain; and he now declares that for all their rebellion they should be excluded from the promised land. God speaks here in the manner of men. Men are affected with feelings of indignation in such circumstances, and God makes use of such language as expresses such feelings. But we are to understand it in a manner consistent with his character, and we are not to suppose that he is affected with the same emotions which agitate the bosoms of men. The meaning is, that he formed and expressed a deliberate and solemn purpose that they should never enter into the promised land. Whether this *rest* refers here to heaven, and whether the meaning is that God would exclude them from that blessed

world, will be more appropriately considered in the next chapter. The particular idea is, that they were to be excluded from the promised land, and that they should fall in the wilderness. No one can doubt, also, that their conduct had been such as to show that the great body of them were unfit to enter into heaven.

12. *Take heed, brethren.* In view of the conduct of the rebellious Jews, and of their fearful doom, be on your guard lest you also be found to have had the same feelings of rebellion and unbelief. See to it, that under the new dispensation, and in the enjoyment of the privileges of the gospel, you be not found to manifest such feelings as shall exclude you from the heavenly world. The *principle* has been settled by their unbelief that they who oppose God will be excluded from his rest. That may be shown under all dispensations, and in all circumstances, and there is not less danger of it under the gospel than there was when the fathers were conducted to the promised land. You are travelling through a wilderness — the barren wilderness of this world. You are exposed to trials and temptations. You meet with many a deadly and mighty foe. You have hearts prone to apostasy and sin. You are seeking a land of promise; a land of rest. You are surrounded by the wonders of Almighty power, and by the proofs of infinite beneficence. Disobedience and rebellion in you will as certainly exclude you from heaven as their rebellion did them from the promised land; and as their great sin was unbelief, be on your guard lest *you* manifest the same ¶ *An evil heart of unbelief.* An evil, unbelieving heart. The word *unbelief* is used to qualify the word *heart,* by a Hebraism — a mode of speech that is common in the New Testament. An unbelieving heart was the cause of their apostasy, and what worked *their* ruin will produce ours.

13 But exhort *a* one another daily, while it is called To-day; lest

a ch.10.25.

any of you be hardened through the deceitfulness of sin.

The root of their evil was *a want of confidence in God*—and this is what is meant here by a heart of unbelief. The great difficulty on earth everywhere is *a want of confidence in God*—and this has produced all the ills that man has ever suffered. It led to the first apostasy; and it has led to every other apostasy—and will continue to produce the same effects to the end of the world. The apostle says that this heart of unbelief is "*evil*." Men often feel that it is a matter of little consequence whether they have faith or not, provided their *conduct* is right; and hence they do not see or admit the propriety of what is said about the consequences of unbelief in the Scriptures. But what do they say about a want of confidence between a husband and wife? Are there no evils in that? What husband can sleep with quietness on his pillow, if he has no confidence in the virtue of his wife? What child can have peace who has no confidence in a parent? How can there be prosperity in a community where there is no confidence in a bank, or an insurance office, or where one merchant has no confidence in another; where a neighbour has no confidence in his neighbour; where the sick have no confidence in a physician, and where in general all confidence is broken up between man and man? If I wished to produce the deepest distress in any community, and had the power, I would produce the same want of confidence between man and man which there is now between man and his Maker. I would thus take away sleep from the pillow of every husband and wife; every parent and child; and make every man wretched with the feeling that all the property which he had was insecure. Among men, nothing is seen to be productive of greater evil than a want of confidence or faith—and why should not the same evil exist in the divine administration? And if want of confidence produces such results between man and man,

why should it not produce similar, or greater, miseries where it occurs in relation to God? There is not an evil that man endures which might not be alleviated or removed by *confidence* in God; and hence one great object of the Christian religion is, to restore to man his lost confidence in the God that made him. ¶ *In departing from the living God.* Manifested in departing from him; or leading to a departure from him. The idea is, that such a heart of unbelief would be connected with apostasy from God. All apostasy first exists in the heart, and then is manifested in the life. They who indulge in unbelief in any form, or in regard to any subject, should remember that this is the great source of all alienation from God, and that if indulged it will lead to complete apostasy. They who wish to live a life of piety should keep *the heart* right. He that lives "by the faith of the Son of God' is safe; and none is safe but he.

13. *But exhort one another daily.* This is addressed to the members of the churches; and it follows, therefore, (1.) that it is their duty to exhort their brethren; and (2.) that it is their duty to do it *daily;* that is, constantly; see ch. x. 25; 1 Thess. iv. 18; v. 11; Note Rom. xii. 8. While this is the special duty of the ministers of the gospel (1 Tim. vi. 2; 2 Tim. iv. 2; Titus ii. 6, 15), it is also the duty of all the members of the churches, and a most important, but much-neglected duty. This does not refer to *public* exhortation, which more appropriately pertains to the ministers of the gospel, but to that private watch and care which the individual members of the church should have over one another. But in what cases is such exhortation proper? What rules should regulate it? I answer, it may be regarded as a duty, or is to be performed in such cases as the following (1.) Intimate friends in the church should exhort and counsel one another; should admonish each other of their faults; and should aid one another in the divine

life. (2.) Parents should do the same thing to their children. They are placed particularly under their watch and care. A pastor cannot often see the members of his flock in private; and a parent may greatly aid him in his work by watching over the members of their families who are connected with the church. (3.) Sabbath-school teachers may aid much in this duty. They are to be assistants to parents and to pastors. They often have under their care youthful members of the churches. They have an opportunity of knowing their state of mind, their temptations, and their dangers better than the pastor can have. It should be theirs, therefore, to exhort them to a holy life. (4.) The aged should exhort the young. Every aged Christian may thus do much for the promotion of religion. His experience is the property of the church; and he is bound so to employ it as to be useful in aiding the feeble, reclaiming the wandering, recovering the backslider, and directing the inquiring. There is a vast amount of *spiritual capital* of this kind in the church that is unemployed, and that might be made eminently useful in helping others to heaven. (5.) Church members should exhort one another. There may not be the intimacy of personal friendship among all the members of a large church, but still the connection between them should be regarded as sufficiently tender and confidential to make it proper for any one to admonish a brother who goes astray. They belong to the same communion. They sit down at the same supper of the Lord. They express their assent to the same articles of faith. They are regarded by the community as united. Each member sustains a portion of the honour and the responsibility of the whole; and each member should feel that he has a right, and that it is his duty to admonish a brother if he goes astray. Yet this duty is greatly neglected. In what church is it performed? How often do church members see a fellow member go astray without any exhortation or admonition! How often do they hear reports of the inconsistent lives of

other members and perhaps contribute to the circulation of those reports themselves, without any pains taken to inquire whether they are true! How often do the poor fear the rich members of the church, or the rich despise the poor, and see one another live in sin, without any attempt to entreat or save them! I would not have the courtesies of life violated. I would not have any assume a dogmatical or dictatorial air. I would have no one step out of his proper sphere of life. But the principle which I would lay down is, that the fact of church membership should inspire such confidence as to make it proper for one member to exhort another whom he sees going astray. Belonging to the same family; having the same interest in religion; and all suffering when one suffers, why should they not be allowed tenderly and kindly to exhort one another to a holy life? ¶ *While it is called To-day.* While life lasts; or while you may be permitted to use the language "To-day hear the voice of God." The idea is, that the exhortation is not to be intermitted. It is to be our daily business to admonish and exhort one another. Christians are liable every day to go astray; every day they need aid in the divine life; and they who are fellow-heirs with them of salvation should be ever ready to counsel and advise them. ¶ *Lest any of you be hardened;* Notes on ver. 8. It is *possible* for Christians to become in a sense *hardened.* Their minds become less sensitive than they were to the claims of duty, and their consciences become less tender. Hence the propriety of mutual exhortation, that they may always have the right feeling, and may always listen to the commands of God. ¶ *The deceitfulness of sin;* Notes on Eph. iv. 22. Sin is always deceitful. It promises more than it performs. It assures us of pleasure which it never imparts. It leads us on beyond what was supposed when we began to indulge in it. The man who commits sin is always under a delusion; and sin, if he indulges it, will lead him on from one step to another until the heart

14 For we are made partakers of Christ, if *a* we hold the beginning

a ver.6

of our confidence steadfast unto the end ;

becomes entirely hardened. Sin puts on plausible appearances and pretences ; it assumes the name of virtue ; it offers excuses and palliations, until the victim is snared, and then spell-bound he is hurried on to every excess. If sin was always seen in its true aspect when man is tempted to commit it, it would be so hateful that he would flee from it with the utmost abhorrence. What young man would become a drunkard if he saw when he began exactly the career which he would run ? What young man, now vigorous and healthful, and with fair prospects of usefulness and happiness would ever touch the intoxicating bowl, if he saw what he *would be* when he became a sot ? What man would ever enter the room of the gambler if he saw just where indulgence would soon lead him, and if at the commencement he saw exactly the wo and despair which would inevitably ensue ? Who would become a voluptuary and a sensualist, if he saw exactly the close of such a career ? Sin deceives, deludes, blinds. Men do not, or will not, see the fearful results of indulgence. They are deluded by the hope of happiness or of gain ; they are drawn along by the fascinations and allurements of pleasure until the heart beomes hard and the conscience seared—and then they give way without remorse. From such a course, the apostle would have Christians guarded by kind and affectionate exhortation. Each one should feel that he has an interest in keeping his brother from such a doom ; and each Christian thus in danger should be willing to listen to the kind exhortation of a Christian brother.

14. *For we are made partakers of Christ.* We are spiritually united to the Saviour. We become one with him. We partake of his spirit and his allotments. The sacred writers are accustomed to describe the Christian as being closely united to the Saviour, and as being *one* with him ;

see Notes on John xv. 1—7; xvii. 21, 23 ; Eph. v. 30; 1 Cor. xii. 27. The idea is, that we participate in all that pertains to him. It is a union of feeling and affection ; a union of principle and of congeniality ; a union of dependence as well as love ; a union where nothing is to be imparted by us, but everything gained ; and a union, therefore, on the part of the Redeemer of great condescension. It is the union of the branch to the vine, where the branch is supported and nourished *by* the vine, and not the union of the ivy and the oak, where the ivy has its own roots, and merely clings around the oak and climbs up upon it. What else can be said so honourable of man as that he is a "partaker of Christ;" that he shares his feelings here, and that he is to share his honours in a brighter world? Compared with this, what is it to participate with the rich and the gay in their pleasures ; what would it be to share in the honours of conquerors and kings ?

[μετοχοι του Χριστου cannot signify, as some explain, participation *merely* in the blessings of Christ's death, but must be referred, as our author here affirms, to the spiritual union which subsists between Christ and his people. That union doubtless involves, as necessary consequents, "a union of feeling and affection, a union of principle and congeniality, a union of dependence and love." Yet, we think, it is something more. It is a *real* and *vital* union, formed by the one Spirit of Christ, pervading the head and the members of the mystical body. And *this* is the *foundation* of all union of affection, &c. For a condensed view of the subject, see the supplementary Note on Rom. viii. 10.]

¶ *If we hold the beginning of our confidence steadfast ;* see Note ver. 6. If we continue to maintain the same confidence which we had in the beginning, or which we showed at the commencement of our Christian life. At first, they had been firm in the Christian hope. They evinced true and strong attachment to the Redeemer. They were ardent and devoted to his cause. If they continued to maintain that to the end, that is, the end of life ; if in the midst of all temptations and trials they adhered inflexibly to the cause of the Saviour, they would show that they were true Christians, and would partake of the blessedness of the heavenly world with the Redeemer. The idea is, that it is only perseverance in the ways of religion that constitutes certain evidence of piety. Where piety is manifested through life, or where there is an untiring devotion to the cause of God, there the evidence is clear and undoubted. But where there is at first great ardour, zeal, and confidence, which soon dies away, then it is clear that they never had any real attachment to him and his cause. It may be remarked here, that the " beginning of the confidence" of those who are deceived, and who know nothing about religion at heart, is often as bold as where there is true piety. The hypocrite makes up in ardour what he lacks in sincerity ; and he who is really deceived, is usually deceived under the influence of some strong and vivid emotion, which he mistakes for true religion. Often the sincere convert is calm, though decided, and sometimes is even timorous and doubting ; while the self-deceiver is noisy in profession, and clamorous in his zeal, and much disposed to blame the lukewarmness of others. Evidence of piety, therefore, should not be built on that early zeal ; nor should it be concluded that because there is ardour, there is of necessity genuine religion. Ardour is valuable, and true religion is ardent ; but there *is* other ardour than that which the gospel inspires. The evidence of genuine piety is to be found in that which will bear us up under trials, and endure amidst persecution and opposition. The doctrine here is, that it is necessary to persevere if we would have the evidence of true piety. This doctrine is taught everywhere in the Scriptures. Persevere in what? I answer, not (1.) merely in a profession of religion. A man may do that and have no piety. (2.) Not in zeal for party, or sect. The Pharisees had that to

the end of their lives. (3.) Not in mere honesty, and correctness of external deportment. A man may do that *in* the church, as well as *out* of it, and yet have no religion. But we should persevere (1.) in the love of God and of Christ—in conscious, ardent, steady attachment to Him to whom our lives are professedly devoted. (2.) In the secret duties of religion. In that watchfulness over the heart; that communion with God; that careful study of the Bible ; that guardianship over the temper ; and in that habitual intercourse with God in secret prayer which is appropriate to a Christian, and which marks the Christian character. (3.) In the performance of the public duties of religion ; in leading a *Christian* life—as distinguished from a life of worldliness and vanity ; a life of mere morality, and honesty ; a life such as thousands lead who are out of the church. There is something which distinguishes a Christian from one who is not a Christian ; a religious from an irreligious man. There is *something* in religion ; *something* which serves to characterize a Christian, and unless that something is manifested, there can be no evidence of true piety. The Christian is to be distinguished in temper, feeling, deportment, aims, plans, from the men of this world—and unless those characteristics are shown in the life and deportment, there can be no well-founded evidence of religion. Learn (1.) that it is not mere *feeling* that furnishes evidence of religion. (2.) That it is not mere *excitement* that constitutes religion. (3.) That it is not mere ardour. (4.) That it is not mere zeal. All these may be temporary. Religion is something that lasts through life. It goes with a man everywhere. It is with him in trial. It forms his plans ; regulates his temper ; suggests his words ; prompts to his actions. It lives with him in all his external changes, and goes with him through the dark valley of death, and accompanies him up to the bar of God, and is with him for ever.

15. *While it is said, To-day, &c.* That is, persevere as long as life lasts,

15 While it is said, *a* To-day if ye will hear his voice, harden

a ver.7. *b* Num.14.2,&c.

or as long as it can be said "to-day;" and by persevering in this manner you will have evidence that you are the friends of the Redeemer. This is a quotation from Ps. xcv. 7. Paul means, undoubtedly, to make use of this language himself as a direct exhortation to the Christians to whom he was writing. He entreats them, therefore, as long as it could be said " to-day," or as long as life lasted, to take care lest they should harden their hearts as had been done in the temptation in the wilderness.

16. *For some.* Some of the Hebrews who came out of Egypt. The truth was that a large proportion of them rebelled against God, and provoked him to indignation. It is somewhat remarkable that though *all* the Hebrews seem to have joined in the provocation — except a very small number—Paul should have used language which would seem to imply that the number which rebelled was comparatively small. Another version, therefore, has been given to this passage by some of the most eminent critics, consisting merely in a change in the punctuation, by which a different view is given of the whole sentence. According to this it would be a question, and would mean, " But who were they who when they had heard did provoke? Were they not all indeed who came out of Egypt under Moses? And with whom was he angry forty years? Was it not with those who sinned, whose carcasses fell in the wilderness?" This version was adopted by Chrysostom, Theodoret, and others of the Fathers; and is adopted by Rosenmüller, Clarke, Stuart, Pyle, and some others. In favour of it, it may be alleged, (1.) that the Greek will bear it, all the change required being in the punctuation; (2.) that it avoids the difficulty which exists in the other interpretation of supposing the apostle to imply that but few of them rebelled, when the truth was that it was nearly all; (3.) it thus accords with the remainder

not your hearts, as in the provocation.

16 For *b* some, when they had of the exhortation, which consists in a series of questions; and (4.) it agrees with the scope and design of the whole. The object was not to state that it was not *all* who came out of Egypt that rebelled, or that the number was small, but that the great body of them rebelled and fell in the wilderness, and that Christians should be admonished by their example. These reasons seem to be so strong as to make it probable that this is the true construction, and the sense then will be, " For who were they that having heard did provoke? Were they not all who came out of Egypt under Moses?" ¶ *When they had heard.* Had heard God speaking to them, and giving them his commands. ¶ *Did provoke.* Provoked him to anger; or their conduct was such as was fitted to produce indignation; see Note on ver. 8. ¶ *Howbeit.* Αλλά. *But.* This particle " in a series of questions, and standing at the head of a question, means *but, further.* It serves to connect, and give intensity to the interrogation." *Stuart.* Paul means to ask with emphasis whether the great mass of those who came out of Egypt did not apostatize? At the same time he means to intimate that there is no security that they who have witnessed remarkable manifestations of the greatness of God, and who have partaken of extraordinary mercies, will not apostatize and perish. As the Hebrews, who heard God speak from Mount Sinai, revolted and perished, so it is possible that they who witness the mercies of God in redemption, may be in danger of abusing all those mercies, and of perishing. By the example, therefore, of the disobedient Israelites, he would admonish professed Christians of their danger. ¶ *Not all,* &c. According to the interpretation proposed above, " Were they not all who came out of Egypt?" Or " did not all who came out of Egypt?" The word *all* here is not to be taken in the strict sense, It is often used to denote the great

heard, did provoke : howbeit not all that came out of Egypt by Moses.

17 But with whom was he

a Num.26.64,65; Jude 5.

body; a large proportion ; or vast multitudes. Thus it is used in Matt. iii. 5, " Then went out to him Jerusalem, and all Judea, and all the region round about Jordan." So in John iii. 26, " The same baptizeth, and all men came to him." So Phil. ii. 21, " For all seek their own ;" 2 Cor. iii. 2, " Ye are our epistle, known and read of all men." *In fact* there were two exceptions—and but two—of the adults who came out of Egypt — Caleb and Joshua ; Num. xiv. 30. All the others murmured against the Lord, and were prohibited from entering the promised land. Of the great multitudes who came out of Egypt, and who murmured, the exception was so small that the apostle had no scruple in saying in general that they were all rebellious.

17. *But with whom was he grieved forty years ?* With whom was he *angry ;* see Notes on ver. 10. ¶ Was it *not with them that had sinned.* That had sinned in various ways—by rebellion, murmuring, unbelief. As God was angry with them for their sins, we have the same reason to apprehend that he will be angry with *us* if we sin ; and we should, therefore, be on our guard against that unbelief which would lead us to depart from him ; ver. 12. ¶ *Whose carcasses fell,* &c. ; Num. xiv. 29. That is, they all died, and were left on the sands of the desert. The whole generation was strewed along in the way to Canaan. All of those who had seen the wonders that God had done " in the land of Ham ;" who had been rescued in so remarkable a manner from oppression, were thus cut down, and died in the deserts through which they were passing ; Num. xxvi. 64, 65. Such an example of the effects of revolt against God, and of unbelief, was well fitted to admonish Christians in the time of the apostle, and is fitted to admonish us now, of the danger of the sin of unbelief.

grieved forty years ? *was it* not with them that had sinned, whose carcases a fell in the wilderness?

18 And to whom sware b he

b Deut.1.34,35.

We are not to suppose that all of those who thus died were excluded from heaven. Moses and Aaron were among the number of those who were not permitted to enter the promised land, but of their piety there can be no doubt. Beyond all question, also, there were many others of that generation who were truly pious. But at different times they seem all to have partaken of the prevalent feelings of discontent, and were all involved in the sweeping condemnation that they should die in the wilderness.

18. *And to whom sware he ;* Note ver. 11. ¶ *But to them that believed not.* That did not confide in God ; Deut. i. 32. " Yet in this thing *ye did not believe* the Lord your God." In consequence of this want of faith, God solemnly sware unto them that they should not enter into the promised land ; Deut. i. 34, 35. " And the Lord heard the voice of your words, and was wroth, and sware, saying, Surely there shall not one of these men of this evil generation see that good land which I sware to give unto your fathers, save Caleb," &c. The distinct reason, therefore, assigned by Moses why they did not enter the promised land, was a want of faith, and this accords directly with the design of the apostle here. He is exhorting those whom he addressed to beware of an evil heart of unbelief; ver. 12. He says that it was such a heart that excluded the Hebrews from the promised land. The same thing, says he, must exclude you from heaven—the promised home of the believer ; and if that firm confidence in God and his promises which he requires is wanting, you will be excluded from the world of eternal rest.

19. *So we see,* &c. We see from the direct testimony of the Old Testament that unbelief was the reason why they were excluded from the promised land. Let us learn in view of the reasoning and exhortations here,

that they should not enter into his rest, but to them that believed not?

19 So *a* we see that they could not enter in because of unbelief.

a ch.4.6.

(1.) The evil of unbelief. It excluded that whole generation, consisting of many hundred thousand souls, from the land of promise—the land to which they had looked with ardent hopes, and with warm desires. It will exclude countless millions from heaven. A *want of confidence in God* is the great source of evil in this world, and will be the cause of wretchedness to all eternity of unnumbered hosts. But surely that was not a small or unimportant thing which strewed the desert with the bones of that whole generation whom God had in so remarkable a manner rescued from Egyptian servitude. And that cannot be a small matter which will cause multitudes to sink down to infinite wretchedness and despair.

(2.) Let us who are professed Christians be cautious against indulging unbelief in our hearts. Our difficulties all begin there. We lose confidence in God. We doubt his promises, his oaths, his threatenings. In dark and trying times we begin to have doubts about the wisdom of his dealings, and about his goodness. Unbelief once admitted into the heart is the beginning of many woes. When a man loses confidence in God, he is on a shoreless ocean that is full of whirlpools, and rocks, and quicksands, and where it is *impossible* to find a secure anchorage. There is nothing to which he may moor his driven bark; and he will never find safety or peace till he comes back to God.

(3.) Let us live a life of faith. Let us so live that we may say with Paul, " The life that I now live in the flesh I live by the faith of the Son of God, who loved me and gave himself for me." So living, we shall have peace. The mind will be at rest. Storms and tempests may blow, but we shall be secure. Others may be troubled in the vicissitudes of life, but *our* minds will be at peace.

(4.) Let us live expecting the fu-

ture "*rest*" that remains for us. Let us keep our eye fixed upon it. To us there is a rest promised, as there was to the Hebrews whom God had delivered from the land of oppression; and we may by faith attain to that "rest" as they might have reached the land of Canaan.

(5.) Let us persevere to the end. He that draws back must be lost. He that does not endure to the end of life in the ways of religion can never have been a Christian. There is nothing which will furnish certain evidence of religion unless our piety is such as to lead us to persevere till death. The man who enters on the professed Christian life expecting to fall away, or who can look upon the possibility of falling away without concern, has never known anything of the nature of true religion. He cannot be a Christian. He may have had raptures and visions; he may be a loud professor and a noisy and zealous partisan, but he has no evidence that he has ever known anything about religion. That religion which is not connected with a firm and determined purpose by the grace of God to persevere to the end of life, is no true religion; and a man who *expects* to fall away and go back again to the world, or who can look at such an idea without alarm, should regard it as a settled matter that he has no true knowledge of God.

(6.) No man should delay the work of salvation to a future time. *To-day* is the accepted time; to-day the only time of which we have any security. God speaks *to-day*, and to-day his voice should be heard. No man on any subject should defer till to-morrow what ought to be done to-day. He who defers religion till a future time neglects his own best interest; violates most solemn obligations; and endangers his immortal soul. What security *can* any one have that he will live to see another day? What evidence has he that he will be any more disposed to attend to his salva

CHAPTER IV.

L ET us ^a therefore fear, lest a promise being left *us* of enter-

tion then than he is now? What evidence can he have that he will not provoke God by this course, and bring condemnation on his soul? Of all delusions, that is the most wonderful by which dying men are led to defer attention to the concerns of the soul to a future period of life. Nowhere has Satan such advantage as in keeping this delusion before the mind; and if in respect to anything the voice of warning and alarm should be lifted loud and long, it is in reference to this. O why will not men be wise *to-day*? Why will they not embrace the offer of salvation *now*? Why will they not *at once* make sure of eternal happiness? And why, amidst the changes and trials of this life, will they not so secure the everlasting inheritance as to feel that *that* is safe—that there is one thing at least that cannot be shaken and disturbed by commercial embarrassment and distress; one thing secure though friends and kindred are torn away from them; one thing safe when their own health fails, and they lie down on the bed where they will bid adieu to all earthly comforts, and from which they will never rise?

CHAPTER IV.

ANALYSIS OF THE CHAPTER.

This chapter comprises two parts. In the first (vers. 1—13), the apostle pursues and completes the exhortation which he had commenced in the previous chapter, drawn from the comparison of the Saviour with Moses (see the analysis of ch. iii.); and in the second part (vers. 14—16), he enters on the consideration of the character of Christ as a high priest, which is pursued to the end of the doctrinal part of the epistle.

In the first part (vers. 1—13), he describes more at length the character of the "*rest*" to which he had referred in the previous chapter. He shows (ver. 1), that the promise of a "*rest*" yet remains, and that there is still danger, as there was formerly, of coming short of it, or of losing it.

ing into his rest, any of you should seem to come short of it.

^a ch. 12. 15.

He affirms that such was the nature of that promise, that it is applicable to us as well as to those to whom it was first made, and that the promise of rest as really pertains to Christians now as it did to the Hebrews of old; ver. 2. The reason, he adds, (ver. 2.) why *they* did not enter into that rest was, that they had not faith. This he had established in the previous chapter, ver. 18. In vers. 3—6, he proceeds to demonstrate more at length that there is a "rest" remaining for those who believe. The great object in this part of the chapter is to prove that a "rest" remains for believers now; a rest of a spiritual character, and much more desirable than that of the land of Canaan; a rest to which Christians may look forward, and which there may be danger of losing. Addressing Hebrew Christians, he, of course, appeals to the Old Testament, and refers to several places where the word "*rest*" occurs, and argues that those expressions are of such a character as to show that there remains a "rest" for Christians yet. It would have been easy to have *affirmed* this as a part of the Christian revelation, but throughout the epistle he is bringing his illustrations from the Old Testament, and showing to the Hebrew Christians to whom he wrote that there were abundant considerations *in the Old Testament itself* to constitute an argument why they should adhere inviolably to the Christian religion. He says, therefore, ver. 4, that God himself had spoken of *his own rest* from his works; that when he had finished the work of creation he had instituted a *rest* which was characterized by the peace, and beauty, and order of the first Sabbath after the work of creation, when all was new, and lovely, and pure. That might be called the *rest of God*—a beautiful emblem of that which dwells around his throne in heaven. The meaning of this verse (ver. 4) is, that the Bible spoke early of a *rest* which appertained to God himself. In ver. 5, he goes on to say that the prospect of entering into *his* rest was spoken of as a possible thing; that some were excluded, but that there was a place deserved to be called " the rest of God"—" My rest"—to which all may come. Of course, that rest must be of a spiritual nature, and must be different from that of the promised land. That *"rest"* the apostle *implies* it was possible to attain. He does not argue this point at length, but he assumes that God would not create a place of rest in vain ; that it was made to be enjoyed ; and that since those to whom it was at first offered were excluded, it must follow that it remained still ; and as they were excluded by the want of *faith*, it would follow also that it was reserved for those who *had* faith. Of course, therefore, it is offered to Christians now ; ver. 6.

This view, he proceeds to confirm by another consideration ; vers. 7, 8. It is that David, who lived nearly five hundred years after the land of promise had been occupied by the Israelites, spoke *then* of the possibility of entering into such a "rest." He says (Ps. xcv. 7), that, in his time, the people were called to hear the voice of God ; that he warned them against the guilt and danger of hardening their hearts ; that he reminded them that it was by that that the Israelites were excluded from the promised land, and that he said that the same thing would occur if those in his own time should harden their hearts. It followed, therefore, that even in the time of David there was a hope and promise of "rest ;" and that there was something more intended for the true people of God than merely entering into the promised land. There must be something in advance of that ; something that existed to the time of David—and it must be, therefore, a spiritual rest. This, the apostle adds, ver. 8, is conclusive ; for if Joshua had given them all the "rest" that was contemplated, then David would not have spoken as he did of the danger of being excluded from it in his time. He, therefore, (ver. 9), comes to the

conclusion that there must *still* remain a " rest" for the people of God, a *"rest"* to which they were invited, and which they were in danger of losing by unbelief. He adds (ver. 10), that he who enters into that " rest" ceases from toil, as God did from his when he had finished the work of creation. Since, therefore, there is such a "rest," and since there is danger of coming short of it, the apostle urges them (ver. 11), to make every effort to enter into it. He adds (vers. 12, 13), as a consideration to quicken them to earnest effort and to anxious care lest they should be deceived, and should fail of it, the fact that God cannot be deceived ; that his word penetrates the heart, and that everything is naked and open before him. There should, therefore, be the most faithful investigation of the heart, lest they should fail of the grace of God, and lose the hoped-for rest.

In the second portion of the chapter (vers. 14—16), he enters on the consideration of the character of Christ as High Priest, and says that since we have such an High Priest as he is, we should be encouraged to come boldly to the throne of grace. We have encouragement to persevere from the fact that we have such a High Priest, and in all our conscious weakness and helplesness we may look to him for aid.

1. *Let us therefore fear.* Let us be apprehensive that we may possibly fail of that rest. The kind of *fear* which is recommended here is that which leads to caution and care. A man who is in danger of losing his life or health should be watchful ; a seaman that is in danger of running on a lee-shore should be on his guard. So we who have the offer of heaven, and who yet are in danger of losing it, should take all possible precautions lest we fail of it. ¶ *Lest a promise being left* us. Paul assumes here that there *is* such a promise. In the subsequent part of the chapter, he goes more into the subject, and proves from the Old Testament that there is such a promise made to us It is to be remembered that Paul had not the New Testament then to appeal to, as

2 For unto us was the gospel preached, as well as unto them: but the word preached ¹ did

1 *of hearing.*

not profit them, ² not being mixed with faith in them that heard *it.*

2 or, *because they were not united by faith to*

we have, which is perfectly clear on the subject, but that he was obliged to appeal to the Old Testament. This he did not only because the New Testament was not then written, but because he was reasoning with those who had been Hebrews, and who re-ɣarded the authority of the Old Testament as decisive. If his reasoning to us appears somewhat obscure, we should put ourselves in his place, and should remember that the converts then had not the full light which we have now in the New Testament. ¶ *Of entering into his rest.* The rest of God—the rest of the world where he dwells. It is called *his* rest, because it is that which he enjoys, and which he alone can confer. There can be no doubt that Paul refers here to heaven, and means to say that there is a promise left to Christians of being admitted to the enjoyment of that blessed world where God dwells. ¶ *Any of you should seem to come short of it.* The word *"seem"* here is used as a form of gentle and mild address, implying the possibility of thus coming short. The word here—δοκέω—is often used so as to appear to give no essential addition to the sense of a passage, though it is probable that it always gave a shading to the meaning. Thus the phrase *esse videatur* is often used by Cicero at the end of a period, to denote merely that a thing *was*—though he expressed it as though it merely *seemed* to be. Such language is often used in argument or in conversation as a *modest* expression, as when we say a thing *seems* to be so and so, instead of saying "it *is.*" In some such sense Paul probably used the phrase here—perhaps as expressing what we would by this language—" lest it should *appear* at last that any of you had come short of it." The phrase "come short of it" is probably used with reference to the journey to the promised land, where they who came out of Egypt *came short* of that

land, and fell in the wilderness. They did not reach it.—This verse teaches the important truth that, though hea ven is offered to us, and that a "rest" is promised to us if we seek it, yet that there is reason to think that many may fail of reaching it who had expected to obtain it. Among those will be the following classes :— (1.) Those who are professors of religion but who have never known anything of true piety. (2.) Those who are expecting to be saved by their own works, and are looking forward to a world of rest on the ground of what their own hands can do. (3.) Those who defer attention to the subject from time to time until it becomes too late. They expect to reach heaven, but they are not ready to give their hearts to God *now,* and the subject is deferred from one period to another, until death arrests them unprepared. (4.) Those who have been awakened to see their guilt and danger, and who have been almost but not quite ready to give up their hearts to God. Such were Agrippa, Felix, the young ruler (Mark x. 21), and such are all those who are *almost* but not *quite* prepared to give up the world and to devote themselves to the Redeemer. To all these the promise of " rest" is made, if they will accept of salvation as it is offered in the gospel; all of them cherish a hope that they will be saved ; and all of them are destined alike to be disappointed. With what earnestness, therefore, should we strive that we may not fail of the grace of God !

2. *For unto us was the gospel preached as well as unto them.* This translation by no means conveys the sense of the original. According to this it would seem that the *gospel,* as we understand it, or the whole plan of salvation, was communicated to *them,* as well as to *us.* But this is by no means the idea. The discussion has reference only to *the promise of rest,* and the assertion of the apostle

is that this *good news* of a promise of rest is made to *us* as really as it was made to *them*. "Rest" was promised to them in the land of Canaan —an emblem of the eternal rest of the people of God. That was unquestioned, and Paul took it for granted. His object now is, to show that a promise of "rest" is as really made to us as it was to them, and that there is the same danger of failing to secure it as there was then. It was important for him to show that there was such a promise made to the people of God in his time, and as he was discoursing of those who were Hebrews, he of course made his appeal to the Old Testament. The literal translation would be, "For we are *evangelized*—ἐσμὲν εὐηγγελισμένοι —as well as they." The word *evangelize* means to communicate good news, or glad tidings; and the idea here is, that the good news, or glad tidings of "rest" is announced to us as really as it was to them. This the apostle proves in the following verses. ¶ *But the word preached.* Marg. *Of hearing.* The word *preach* we also use now in a technical sense as denoting a formal proclamation of the gospel by the ministers of religion. But this is not the idea here. It means, simply, the word *which they heard;* and refers particularly to the promise of "rest" which was made to them. That message was communicated to them by Moses. ¶ *Did not profit them.* They derived no advantage from it. They rejected and despised it, and were, therefore, excluded from the promised land. It exerted no influence over their hearts and lives, and they lived and died as though no such promise had been made. Thus many persons live and die now. The offer of salvation is made to them. They are invited to come and be saved. They are assured that God is willing to save them, and that the Redeemer stands with open arms to welcome them to heaven. They are trained up under the gospel; are led early in life to the sanctuary; are in the habit of attending on the preaching of the gospel all their days, but still what they hear

exerts no saving influence on their hearts. At the close of life all that could be truly said of them is, that they have not been *profited;* it has been no real advantage to them in regard to their final destiny that they have enjoyed so many privileges. ¶ *Not being mixed with faith in them that heard it.* Marg. "Or, *because they were not united by faith to.*" There are some various readings on this text, and one of these has given occasion to the version in the margin. Many MSS. instead of the common reading—συγκεκραμένος —by which the word *mixed* would be united to ὁ λόγος—"*the word,*" have another reading — συγκεκραμένους — according to which the word *mixed* would refer to "*them,*" and would mean that they who heard the word and rejected it were not *mixed,* or united with those who believed it. The former reading makes the best sense, and is the best sustained; and the idea is, that the message which was preached was not received into the heart by faith. They were destitute of faith, and the message did not profit them. The word *mixed* is supposed by many of the best critics to refer to the process by which *food* is made nutritive, by being properly *mixed* with the saliva and the gastric juice, and thus converted into chyme, and chyle, and then changed into blood. If suitably *mixed* in this manner, it contributes to the life and health of the bodily frame; if not, it is the means of disease and death. So it is supposed the apostle meant to say of the message which God sends to man. If properly received; if mixed or united with faith, it becomes the means of spiritual support and life. If not, it furnishes no aliment to the soul, and will be of no advantage. As food when properly digested incorporates itself with the body, and gives it support, so those critics suppose it to be of the word of God, that it incorporates itself with the internal and spiritual man, and gives it support and life. It may be doubted, however, whether the apostle had any such allusion as this, and whether it is not rather a refinement of the

3 For we which have believed do enter into rest; as he said, *a* As I have sworn in my wrath,

a Ps.95.11.

if they shall enter into my rest; although the works were finished from the foundation of the world.

---

critics than of Paul. The *word* used here properly denotes a mixing or mingling together, like water and wine, 2 Mac. xv. 39; a uniting together in proper proportions and order, as of the body, 1 Cor. xii. 24; and it may refer here merely to a proper *union* of faith with the word, in order that it might be profitable. The idea is, that merely to *hear* the message of life with the outward ear will be of no advantage. It must be *believed*, or it will be of no benefit. The message is sent to mankind at large. God declares his readiness to save all. But this message is of no advantage to multitudes — for such reasons as these. (1.) Many do not attend to it at all. They do not even *listen* respectfully to it. Multitudes go not near the place where the gospel is proclaimed; and many, when there, and when they *seem* to attend, have their minds and hearts on other things. (2.) Many do not *believe* it. They have doubts about the whole subject of religion, or about the particular doctrines of the gospel — and while they do not believe it, how can they be benefited by it? How can a man be profited by the records of *history* if he does not believe them? How can one be benefited by the truths of *science* if he does not believe them? And if a man was assured that by going to a certain place he might close a bargain that would be a great advantage to him, of what use would this information be to him if he did not believe a word of it? So of the knowledge of salvation; the facts of the history recorded in the Bible; the offer of eternal life. (3.) Men do not allow the message of life to influence their conduct, and of course it is of no advantage to them. Of what use can it be if they steadily resist all the influence which it would have, and ought to have, on their lives? They live as though it were ascertained that there is no truth in the Bible; no reason for being in-

fluenced by the offered hope of eternal life, or alarmed by the threatened danger of eternal death. Resolved to pursue a course of life that is at variance with the commands of God, they cannot be profited by the message of salvation. Having no faith which influences and controls the heart, they are not in the least benefited by the offer of heaven. When they die, their condition is in no wise made better by the fact that they were trained up in a pious family; that they were instructed in the Sabbath-school; that they had the Bible in their dwellings, and that they sat regularly under a preached gospel. For any *advantage* to be derived from all this in the future world, they might as well have never heard the message of life. Nay it would have been better for them. The only effect of these privileges is to harden them in guilt, and to sink them deeper in hell; Notes, 2 Cor. ii. 16.

3. *For we which have believed do enter into rest.* That is, it is a certain fact that believers *will* enter into rest. That promise is made to "believers;" and as we have evidence that *we* come under the denomination of believers, it will follow that *we* have the offer of rest as well as they. That this is so, the apostle proceeds to prove; that is, he proceeds to show from the Old Testament that there was a promise to "believers" that they would enter into rest. Since there was such a promise, and since there was danger that by unbelief that "rest" might be lost, he proceeds to show them the danger, and to warn them of it. ¶ *As he said,* &c.; see ch. iii. 11. The meaning of this passage is this. "God made a promise of rest to those who believe. They to whom the offer was first made failed, and did not enter in. It must follow, therefore, that the offer extended to others, since God designed that *some* should enter in, or that it should not be provided in vain. To them it was

a solemn declaration that *unbelievers* should not enter in, and this implied that *believers* would. As we now," says he, "sustain the character of *believers*, it follows that to *us* the promise of rest is now made and we may partake of it." ¶ *If they shall enter*, &c. That is, they shall *not* enter in; see ch. iii. 11. The "rest" here spoken of as reserved for Christians must be different from that of the promised land. It is something that pertains to Christians now, and it must, therefore, refer to the "rest" that remains in heaven. ¶ *Although the works were finished*, &c. This is a difficult expression. What works are referred to? it may be asked. How does this bear on the subject under discussion? How can it be a proof that there remains a "rest" to those who believe now? This was the point to be demonstrated; and this passage was designed clearly to bear on that point. As it is in our translation, the passage seems to make no sense whatever. Tindal renders it, "And that spake he verily long after that the works were made from the foundation of the world laid;" which makes much better sense than our translation. Doddridge explains it as meaning, "And this may lead us further to reflect on what is elsewhere said concerning his works as they were finished from the foundation of the world." But it is difficult to see why they should reflect on his works just then, and how this would bear on the case in hand. Prof. Stuart supposes that the word "rest" must be understood here before "*works*," and translates it, "Shall not enter into my rest, to wit, rest from the works which were performed when the world was founded." Prof. Robinson (*Lex.*) explains it as meaning, "The rest here spoken of, 'MY rest,' could not have been God's resting from his works (Gen. ii. 2), for this rest, the Sabbath, had already existed from the creation of the world." Dr. J. P. Wilson (MS. Notes) renders it, "For we who have believed, do enter into rest (or a cessation) indeed (*καίτοι*) of the works done (among men) from the beginning of the world." Amidst

this variety of interpretation it is difficult to determine the true sense. But perhaps the main thought may be collected from the following remarks. (1.) The Jews as the people of God had a rest promised them in the land of Canaan. Of that they failed by their unbelief. (2.) The purpose of the apostle was to prove that there was a similar promise made to the people of God long subsequent to that, and to which *all* his people were invited. (3.) *That* rest was not that of the promised land, it was such as *God had himself* when he had finished the work of creation. That was peculiarly *his rest*—the rest of God, without toil, or weariness, and after his whole *work* was finished. (4.) His people were invited to the same *rest*— the rest of God— to partake of his felicity; to enter into that bliss which *he* enjoyed when he had finished the work of creation. The happiness of the saints was to be *like* that. It was to be *in their case* also a rest from toil—to be enjoyed at the end of all that *they* had to do. To prove that Christians were to attain to *such* a rest, was the purpose which the apostle had in view—showing that it was a general doctrine pertaining to believers in every age, that there was a promise of rest for them. I would then regard the middle clause of this verse as a parenthesis, and render the whole, "For we who are believers shall enter into rest —[the rest] indeed which occurred when the works were finished at the foundation of the world—as he said [in one place] as I have sworn in my wrath they shall not enter into *my* rest." That was the true rest—such rest or repose as *God* had when he finished the work of creation—such as he has now in heaven This gives the highest possible idea of the dignity and desirableness of that "rest" to which we look forward—for it is to be such as God enjoys, and is to elevate us more and more to him. What more exalted idea can there be of happiness than to participate in the calmness, the peace, the repose, the freedom from raging passions, from wearisome toil, and from agitating

4 For he spake in a certain place of the seventh *day* on this wise, *a* And God did rest the seventh day from all his works.

a Ge 2.2.

5 And in this *place* again, if they shall enter into my rest.

6 Seeing therefore it remaineth that some must enter therein,

cares, which God enjoys? Who, torn with conflicting passions here, wearied with toil, and distracted with care, ought not to feel it a privilege to look forward to that rest? Of this rest the Sabbath and the promised land were emblems. They to whom the promise was made did not enter in, but some *shall* enter in, and the promise therefore pertains to us.

4. *For he spake;* Gen. ii. 2. ¶ *And God did rest.* "At the close of the work of creation he rested. The work was done. *That was the rest of God.* He was happy in the contemplation of his own works; and he instituted that day to be observed as a memorial of *his* resting from his works, and as a *type* of the eternal rest which remained for man." The idea is this, that the notion of *rest* of some kind runs through all dispensations. It was seen in the finishing of the work of creation; seen in the appointment of the Sabbath; seen in the offer of the promised land, and is seen now in the promise of heaven. All dispensations contemplate *rest*, and there must be such a prospect before man now. When it is said that "God did *rest*," of course it does not mean that he was wearied with his toil, but merely that he *ceased* from the stupendous work of creation. He no more put forth creative energy, but calmly contemplated his own works in their beauty and grandeur; Gen. i. 31. In carrying forward the great affairs of the universe, he always has been actively employed (John v. 17), but he is not employed in the work of *creation* properly so called. That is done; and the sublime cessation from that constitutes the "rest of God."

5. *And in this place again;* Ps. xcv. 11. ¶ *If they shall enter.* That is, they shall *not* enter; see Notes ch. iii. 11. The object of quoting this here seems to be two-fold. (1.) To show that even in this Psalm God

spoke of *his* rest, and said that they should not enter into it; and (2.) it is connected with ver. 6, and is designed to show that it was implied that a rest yet remained. "That which deserves to be called *the divine rest* is spoken of in the Scriptures, and as *they* did not enter into it, it follows that it must be in reserve for some others, and that the promise must still remain."

6. *Seeing therefore it remaineth that some must enter therein.* That is, "Since there is a rest spoken of in the Scriptures, implying that it is to be enjoyed by some, and since they to whom it was first promised did not inherit it, it follows that it must still be in reserve." This is the conclusion which the apostle draws from the argument in the previous verses, and is connected with ver. 9, where he says that "there remaineth a rest to the people of God"—the point to which the whole argument tended. The statement in vs. 7, 8, is to be regarded as an *interruption* in stating the conclusion, or as the suggestion of a new thought or a new argument bearing on the subject, which he sets down even while stating the conclusion from his argument. It has the appearance of being *suggested* to him as a new thought of importance, and which he preferred to place even in the midst of the summing up of the argument rather than omit it altogether. It denotes a state of mind full of the subject, and where one idea came hastening after another, and which it was deemed important to notice, even though it should seem to be out of place. The *position* in this verse (6) is, that it was a settled or indisputable matter that some would enter into rest. The implied *argument* to prove this is, (1.) that there was a "rest" spoken of which deserved to be called a *divine rest*, or the "rest of God;" (2.) it could not be supposed that God would prepare such a rest

and they *a* to whom 1 it was first preached entered not in because of unbelief.

7 Again, he limiteth a certain

a ch.3.19.   1 *the gospel.*

in vain, for it would follow that if he had fitted up a world of rest, he designed that it should be occupied. As he knew, therefore, that they to whom it was first offered would not enter in, it must be that he designed it for some others, and that it *remained* to be occupied by us now. ¶ *And they to whom it was first preached.* Marg. *The Gospel.* Gr. *Evangelized;* that is, to whom the good news of the rest was first announced—the Israelites. ¶ *Entered not in because of unbelief;* see Notes ch. iii. 19.

7. *Again, he limiteth.* He designates, or definitely mentions. The word rendered *limiteth*—*ὁρίζει*—means to *bound,* to set a boundary—as of a field or farm ; and then to determine or fix definitely, to designate, appoint. Here it means, that he specifies particularly, or mentions expressly. ¶ *A certain day.* A particular time; he mentions TO-DAY particularly. That is, in the time of David, he uses the word "*to-day,*" as if there was *then* an offer of rest, and as if it were then possible to enter into it. The object of the additional thought was to show that the offer of rest was not confined to the Israelites to whom it was first made; that David regarded it as existing in his day; and that man might even then be invited to come and partake of the rest that was promised. "Nearly five hundred years after the time when the Israelites were going to the promised land, and when the offer of rest was made to them, we hear David speaking of *rest* still; rest which was offered in his time, and which might then be lost by hardening the heart. It could not be, therefore, that the offer of rest pertained *merely* to the promised land. It must be something in advance of that. It must be something existing in the time of David. It must be an offer of heaven." A Jew might feel the force of this argument more than we do; still it is conclusive to prove the point un-

day, saying in David, To-day, after so long a time; (as it is said) To-day, *b* if ye will hear his voice, harden not your hearts.

b Ps.95.7.

der consideration, that there was a rest spoken of long after the offer of the promised land, and that all the promises could not have pertained to that. ¶ *Saying in David.* In a Psalm composed by David, or rather perhaps, saying *by* David; that is, God spake by him. ¶ *To-day.* Now :— that is, even in the time of David. ¶ *After so long a time.* That is, so long after the first promise was made ; to wit, about five hundred years. These are the words of Paul calling attention to the fact that so long a time after the entrance into the promised land there was still a speaking of "*to-day,*" as if even then they were called to partake of the rest. ¶ *As it is said.* To quote it exactly; or to bring the express authority of the Scriptures. It is expressly said even after that long time, "to-day—or NOW, if you will hear his voice." All this is to prove that even in that time there was an offer of rest.

8. *For if Jesus.* Marg. "That is, *Joshua.*" The Syriac renders it, "Joshua the son of Nun." *Jesus* is the Greek mode of writing *Joshua,* and there can be no doubt that Joshua is here intended. The object is to prove that Joshua did *not* give the people of God such a rest as to make it improper to speak of a "rest" after that time. "If Joshua had given them a complete and final rest; if by his conducting them to the promised land all had been done which had been contemplated by the promise, then it would not have been alluded to again, as it was in the time of David." Joshua *did* give them a *rest* in the promised land; but it was not all which was intended, and it did not exclude the promise of another and more important rest. ¶ *Then would he not.* Then *God* would not have spoken of another time when that rest could be obtained. The "*other day*" here referred to is that which is mentioned before by the phrase "*to-*

8 For if [1] Jesus had given them rest, then would he not afterward have spoken of another day.

1 That is, Joshua.

day," and refers to the time in which it is spoken of long after Joshua, to wit, in the time of David.

9. *There remaineth, therefore, a rest.* This is the conclusion to which the apostle comes. The meaning is this, that according to the Scriptures there is *now* a promise of rest made to the people of God. It did not pertain merely to those who were called to go to the promised land, nor to those who lived in the time of David, but it is *still* true that the promise of rest pertains to *all* the people of God of every generation. The *reasoning* by which the apostle comes to this conclusion is briefly this. (1.) That there was a *rest*—called "the rest of God"—spoken of in the earliest period of the world—implying that God meant that it should be enjoyed. (2.) That the Israelites, to whom the promise was made, failed of obtaining that which was promised by their unbelief. (3.) That God intended that *some* should enter into his rest—since it would not be provided in vain. (4.) That long after the Israelites had fallen in the wilderness, we find the same reference to a *rest* which David in his time exhorts those whom he addressed to endeavour to obtain. (5.) That if all that had been meant by the word *rest*, and by the promise, had been accomplished when Joshua conducted the Israelites to the land of Canaan, we should not have heard another day spoken of when it was possible to forfeit that rest by unbelief. It followed, therefore, that there was something besides that; something that pertained to all the people of God to which the name *rest* might still be given, and which they were exhorted still to obtain. The word *rest* in this verse—σαββατισμὸς—*Sabbatism*, in the margin is rendered *keeping of a Sabbath.* It is a different word from σάββατον—*the Sabbath ;* and it occurs nowhere else in the New Testament, and is not found in the Septuagint. It properly means a *keeping Sabbath*

9 There remaineth therefore a [2] rest to the people of God.

10 For he that is entered into his

2 or, *keeping of a Sabbath.*

—from σαββατίζω — to *keep Sabbath.* This word, not used in the New Testament, occurs frequently in the Septuagint; Ex. xvi. 30; Lev. xxiii. 32; xxvi. 35; 2 Chron. xxxvi. 21; and in 3 Esdr. i. 58; 2 Macca. vi. 6. It differs from the word *Sabbath.* That denotes *the time—the day ;* this, *the keeping*, or *observance* of it ; *the festival.* It means here a *resting*, or an observance of sacred repose—and refers undoubtedly to heaven, as a place of eternal rest with God. It cannot mean the rest in the land of Canaan—for the drift of the writer is to prove that that is *not* intended. It cannot mean the *Sabbath*, properly so called—for then the writer would have employed the usual word σάββατον— *Sabbath.* It cannot mean the Christian Sabbath—for the object is not to prove that there is such a day to be observed, and his reasoning about being excluded from it by unbelief and by hardening the heart would be irrelevant. It must mean, therefore, *heaven*—the world of spiritual and eternal rest ; and the assertion is, that there *is* such a *resting*, or *keeping of a Sabbath* in heaven for the people of God. Learn hence, (1.) that heaven is a place of cessation from wearisome toil. It is to be like the "rest" which God had after the work of creation (ver. 4, Note), and of which that was the type and emblem. There will be *employment* there, but it will be without fatigue ; there will be the occupation of the mind, and of whatever powers we may possess, but without weariness. Here we are often worn down and exhausted. The body sinks under continued toil, and falls into the grave. There the slave will rest from his toil ; the man here oppressed and broken down by anxious care will cease from his labours. We know but little of heaven ; but we know that a large part of what now oppresses and crushes the frame will not exist there. Slavery will be un-known ; the anxious care for sup-rest, he also hath ceased from his own works, as God *did* from his.

11 Let *a* us labour therefore to enter into that rest, lest any man

a 2 Pe.1.10.

port will be unknown, and all the exhaustion which proceeds from the love of gain, and from ambition, will be unknown. In the wearisome toils of life, then, let us look forward to the *rest* that remains in heaven, and as the labourer looks to the shades of the evening, or to the Sabbath as a period of rest, so let us look to heaven as the place of eternal repose. (2.) Heaven will be like a Sabbath. The best description of it is to say it is *an eternal Sabbath.* Take the Sabbath on earth when best observed, and extend the idea to eternity, and let there be separated all idea of imperfection from its observance, and that would be heaven. The Sabbath is holy; so is heaven. It is a period of worship; so is heaven. It is for praise and for the contemplation of heavenly truth; so is heaven. The Sabbath is appointed that we may lay aside worldly cares and anxieties for a little season here; heaven that we may lay them aside for ever. (3.) The Sabbath here should be like heaven. It is designed to be its type and emblem. So far as the circumstances of the case will allow, it should be just like heaven. There should be the same employments; the same joys; the same communion with God. One of the best rules for employing the Sabbath aright is, to think what heaven will be, and then to endeavour to spend it in the same way. One day in seven at least should remind us of what heaven is to be; and that day may be, and should be, the most happy of the seven. (4.) They who do not love the Sabbath on earth, are not prepared for heaven. If it is to them a day of tediousness; if its hours move heavily; if they have no delight in its sacred employments, what would an eternity of such days be? How would *they* be passed? Nothing can be clearer than that if we have no such happiness in a season of holy rest, and in holy employments here, we are wholly unprepared for heaven. To the Christian it is the subject of

the highest joy in anticipation that heaven is to be *one long unbroken* SABBATH—an eternity of successive Sabbath hours. But what to a sinner could be a more repulsive and gloomy prospect than such an eternal Sabbath? (5.) If this be so, then what a melancholy view is furnished as to the actual preparation of the great mass of men for heaven! How is the Sabbath now spent? In idleness; in business; in travelling; in hunting and fishing; in light reading and conversation; in sleep; in visiting; in riding, walking, lounging, *ennui;*—in revelry and dissipation; in any and every way *except the right way;* in every way except in holy communion with God. What would the race be if once translated to heaven as they are! What a prospect would it be to this multitude to have to spend *an eternity* which would be but a prolongation of the Sabbath of holiness! (6.) Let those who love the Sabbath rejoice in the prospect of eternal rest in heaven. In our labour let us look to that world where wearisome toil is unknown; in our afflictions, let us look to that world where tears never fall; and when our hearts are pained by the violation of the Sabbath all around us, let us look to that blessed world where such violation will cease for ever. It is not far distant. A few steps will bring us there. Of any Christian it may be said that perhaps his next Sabbath will be spent in heaven—near the throne of God.

10. *For he that is entered into rest.* That is, the man who is so happy as to reach heaven, will enjoy a rest similar to that which God had when he finished the work of creation. It will be (1.) a cessation from toil; and (2.) it will be a rest similar to that of God—the same kind of enjoyment, the same freedom from care, anxiety, and labour. How happy then are they who have entered into heaven! Their toils are over. Their labours are done. Never again will they know fatigue. Never more will they feel

fall after the same example of [1] unbelief.

12 For the word [a] of God is

1 or, *disobedience.*

a Isa. 49.2.	b Rev.1.16.

anxious care. Let us learn then (1.) not to mourn improperly for those who have left us and gone to heaven. Happy in the rest of God, why should not we rejoice? Why wish them back again in a world of toil! (2.) Let us in our toils look forward to the world of rest. Our labours will all be over. The weary man will lay down his burden; the exhausted frame will know fatigue no more. Rest is sweet at night after the toils of day; how much more sweet will it be in heaven after the toils of life! Let us (3.) labour while is is called to-day. Soon we shall cease from *our* work. All that we have to do is to be done soon. We shall soon cease from *our* work as God did from his. What we have to do for the salvation of children, brothers, sisters, friends, and for the world, is to be done soon. From the abodes of bliss we shall not be sent forth to speak to our kindred of the blessedness of that world, or to admonish our friends to escape from the place of despair. The pastor will not come again to warn and invite his people; the parent will not come again to tell his children of the Saviour and of heaven; the neighbour will not come to admonish his neighbour; comp. Luke xvi. 24—29. We shall ALL have ceased from *our* work as God did from *his;* and never again shall we speak to a living friend to invite him to heaven.

11. *Let us therefore labour.* Let us earnestly strive. Since there *is* a rest whose attainment is worth all our efforts ; since so many have failed of reaching it by their unbelief, and since there is so much danger that we may fail of it also, let us give all diligence that we may enter into it. Heaven is never obtained but by diligence ; and no one enters there who does not earnestly desire it, and who does not make a sincere effort to reach it. ¶ *Of unbelief.* Marg. *disobedience.* The word *unbelief* best expresses the sense, as the

quick, and powerful, and sharper than any two-edged sword, [b] piercing even to the dividing asunder of

apostle was showing that this was the principal thing that prevented men from entering into heaven ; see Notes ch. iii. 12.

12. *For the word of God.* The design of this and the following verse is obvious. It is to show that we cannot escape the notice of God; that all insincerity, unbelief, hypocrisy, will be detected by him ; and that since our hearts are perfectly open before him, we should be sincere and should not attempt to deceive him. The sense is, that the truth of God is all-penetrating and searching, and that the real thoughts and intents of the heart will be brought to light, and that if there is insincerity and self-deception there can be no hope of escape. There has been a great variety of opinion here about the meaning of the phrase " the word of God." Some have supposed that it means the Lord Jesus ; others, the whole of the divine revelation ; others the gospel ; others the particular threatening referred to here. The " word of God" is *that which God speaks*—whether it be a promise or a threatening ; whether it be law or gospel; whether it be a simple declaration or a statement of a doctrine. The idea here is, that what *God had said* is fitted to detect hypocrisy and to lay open the true nature of the feelings of the soul, so that there can be no escape for the guilty. His *truth* is adapted to bring out the real feelings, and to show man exactly what he is. Truth always has this power—whether preached, or read, or communicated by conversation, or impressed upon the memory and conscience by the Holy Spirit. There can be no escape from the penetrating, searching application of the word of God. That truth has power to show what man is, and is like a penetrating sword that lays open the whole man ; comp. Isa. xlix. 2. The phrase " the word of God " here may be applied, therefore, to the *truth* of

soul and spirit, and of the joints and marrow, and *is* a discerner of

a the thoughts and intents of the heart.

a Ps.139.2; Jer.17.10; Rev.2.23.

God, however made known to the mind. In some way it will bring out the real feelings, and show what man is. ¶ *Is quick.* Gr. *ζῶν—living.* It is not dead, inert, and powerless. It has a *living* power, and is energetic and active. It is *adapted* to produce this effect. ¶ *And powerful.* Mighty. Its power is seen in awakening the conscience ; alarming the fears ; laying bare the secret feelings of the heart, and causing the sinner to tremble with the apprehension of the coming judgment. All the great changes in the moral world for the better, have been caused by the power of truth. They are such as the truth in its own nature is fitted to effect, and if we may judge of its power by the greatness of the revolutions produced, no words can over-estimate the might of the truth which God has revealed. ¶ *Sharper than any two-edged sword.* Literally, *two-mouthed* sword — *δίστομον.* The word *mouth* was given to the sword because it seemed to *devour* all before it It consumed or destroyed as a wild beast does. The comparison of the word of God to a sword or to an arrow, is designed to show its power of penetrating the heart ; Eccl. xii. 11, " The words of the wise are as goads, and as nails fastened by the masters of assemblies ;" comp. Isa. xlix. 2. " And he hath made my mouth like a sharp sword ;" Rev. i. 16, " And out of his mouth went a sharp two-edged sword;" ii. 12, 16 ; xix. 15. The comparison is common in the classics, and in Arabic poetry ; see Gesenius, on Isa. xlix. 2. The idea is that of piercing, or penetrating ; and the meaning here is, that the word of God reaches the *heart*—the very centre of action, and lays open the motives and feelings of the man. It was common among the ancients to have a sword with two edges. The Roman sword was commonly made in this manner. The fact that it had two edges made it more easy to penetrate, as well as to cut with every way.

¶ *Piercing even to the dividing asunder.* Penetrating so as to divide. ¶ *Soul and spirit.* The animal life from the immortal soul. The former word here—*ψυχή—soul*—is evidently used to denote the *animal life,* as distinguished from the mind or soul. The latter word— *πνεῦμα*—*spirit*— means the soul ; the immaterial and immortal part ; that which lives when the animal life is extinct. This distinction occurs in 1 Thess. v. 23, " your whole spirit, and soul, and body ;" and it is a distinction which we are constantly in the habit of making. There is the body in man— the animal life — and the immortal part that leaves the body when life is extinct. Mysteriously united, they constitute one man. When the animal life is separated from the soul, or when the soul leaves the animated body, the body dies, and life is extinct. To separate the one from the other is, therefore, the same as to take life —and this is the idea here, that the word of God is like a sharp sword that inflicts deadly wounds. The sinner " *dies ;*"—that is, he becomes dead to his former hopes, or is "slain" by the law ; Rom. vii. 9, " I was alive without the law once, but when the commandment came, sin revived, and I died." This is the power referred to here—the power of destroying the hopes of the sinner ; cutting him down under conviction ; and prostrating him as if a sword had pierced his heart. ¶ *And of the joints and marrow.* The figure is still continued of the sword that takes life. Such a sword would seem to penetrate even the joints and marrow of the body. It would separate the joints, and pierce through the very bones to the marrow. A similar effect, Paul says, is produced by truth. It seems to penetrate the very essence of the soul, and lay it all open to the view. ¶ *And is a discerner of the thoughts.* It shows what the thoughts and intentions are. Prof. Stuart, Bloomfield, and some others, suppose that the reference here is to *God* speaking by his word. But the more natural construction certainly is, to refer it to the word or truth of God. It is true that God searches the heart, and knows the thoughts, but that is not the truth which is prominent here. It is, that the thoughts and intents of the heart are brought out to view by the word of God. And can any one doubt this? see Rom. vii. 7 Is it not true that men are made to see their real character under the exhibition of the truth of God? That in the light of the law they see their past lives to be sinful? That the exhibition of truth calls to their recollection many long-forgotten sins? And that their real feelings are brought out when the truth of God is proclaimed? Men then are made to look upon their motives as they had never done before, and to see in their hearts feelings whose existence they would not have suspected if it had not been for the exhibition of the truth. The exhibition of the truth is like pouring down the beams of the sun at midnight on a dark world; and the truth lays open the real feelings of the sinner as that sun would disclose the clouds of wickedness that are now performed under cover of the night. Many a man has a deep and fixed hostility to God and to his gospel who might never be sensible of it if the truth was not faithfully proclaimed. The particular idea here is, that the truth of God will detect the feelings of the hypocrite and self-deceiver. They cannot always conceal their emotions, and the time will come when truth, like light poured into the soul, will reveal their unbelief and their secret sins. They who are cherishing a hope of salvation, therefore, should be on their guard lest they mistake the name for the reality. Let us learn from this verse, (1.) The power of truth. It is *fitted* to lay open the secret feelings of the soul. There is not an effect produced in awakening a sinner; or in his conviction, conversion, and sanctification, which the truth is not *adapted* to produce. The truth of God is not dead; nor fitted to make men *worse;* nor

designed merely to show its own *weakness,* and to be a mere *occasion* on which the Holy Spirit acts on the mind;—it is in its own nature FITTED to produce just the effects which are produced when it awakens, convicts, converts, and sanctifies the soul. (2.) The truth should be preached with the feeling that it is adapted to this end. Men who preach should endeavour to understand the nature of the mind and of the moral feelings, as really as he who would inflict a deadly wound should endeavour to understand enough about anatomy to know where the heart is, or he who administers medicine should endeavour to know what is adapted to remove certain diseases. And he who has no belief in the efficacy of truth to produce any effect, resembles one who should suppose that all knowledge of the human system was needless to him who wished to perform a surgical operation, and who should cut at random—piously leaving it with God to direct the knife; or he who should go into a hospital of patients and administer medicines indiscriminately —devoutly saying that all healing must come from God, and that the use of medicine was only to show its own weakness! Thus many men seem to preach. Yet for aught that appears, truth is just as wisely adapted to save the soul as medicine is to heal the sick; and why then should not a preacher be as careful to study the nature of truth and its adaptedness to a particular end, as a student of the healing art is to understand the adaptedness of medicine to cure disease? The true way of preaching is, to feel that truth is adapted to the end in view; to select that which is best fitted for that end; to preach as if the whole result depended on getting that truth before the mind and into the heart — and *then* to leave the whole result with God—as a physician with right feelings will exert all his skill to save his patient, and then commit the whole question of life and health to God. He will be more likely to praise God intelligently who believes that he has wisely adapted a plan to the end

13 Neither is there any creature that is not manifest in his sight: but all things *are* naked *a* and

opened unto the eyes of him with whom we have to do.

a Pr.15.11.

in view, than he who believes that God works only at random.

13. *Neither is there any creature that is not manifest in his sight.* There is no being who is not wholly known to God. All his thoughts, feelings, plans, are distinctly understood. Of the truth of this there can be no doubt. The *design* of the remark here is, to guard those to whom the apostle was writing from self-deception—since they could conceal nothing from God. ¶ *All things are naked.* Exposed; uncovered. There is nothing that can be concealed from God; Ps. cxxxix. 11, 12.

"The veil of night is no disguise,
No screen from thy all-searching eyes ;
Thy hands can seize thy foes as soon
Thro' midnight shades as blazing noon."

¶ *And opened.*—τιτραχηλισμένα. The word here used—Τραχηλίζω—properly means (1.) To lay bare the neck, or to bend it back, so as to expose the throat to being cut. (2.) To expose; to lay open in any way. *Why* the word is used here has been a matter of inquiry. Some have supposed that the phrase is derived from offering sacrifice, and from the fact that the priest carefully examined the victim to see whether it was sound, before it was offered. But this is manifestly a forced exposition. Others have supposed that it is derived from the custom of bending back the head of a criminal so as to look full in his face, and recognise him so as not to be mistaken ; but this is equally forced and unnatural. This opinion was first proposed by Erasmus, and has been adopted by Clarke and others. Bloomfield, following, as he says, the interpretation of Chrysostom, Grotius (though this is not the sentiment of Grotius), Beza, Atling, Hammond, and others, supposes the allusion to be to the custom of cutting the animal down the back bone through the spinal marrow, and thus of laying it open entirely. This sense would well suit the connection. Gro-

tius supposes that it means to strip off the skin by dividing it at the neck, and then removing it. This view is also adopted substantially by Doddridge. These explanations are forced, and imply a departure more or less from the proper meaning of the Greek word. The most simple and obvious meaning is usually the best in explaining the Bible. The word which the apostle employs relates to the neck—τράχηλος—and not to the spinal marrow, or the skin. The proper meaning of the verb is *to bend the neck back* so as to expose it in front when an animal is slain. *Passow.* Then it means to make bare ; to remove everything like covering ; to expose a thing entirely—as the naked neck is for the knife. The allusion here is undoubtedly to the *sword* which Paul had referred to in the previous verse, as dividing the soul and spirit, and the joints and marrow ; and the meaning is, that in the hand of God, who held that sword, everything was exposed. We are in relation to that, like an animal whose neck is bent back, and laid bare, and ready for the slaughter. Nothing *hinders* God from striking ; there is nothing that can prevent that sword from penetrating the heart— any more than when the neck of the animal is bent back and laid bare, there is anything that can hinder the sacrificing priest from thrusting the knife into the throat of the victim. If this be the true interpretation, then what an affecting view does it give of the power of God, and of the exposedness of man to destruction ! All is bare, naked, open. There is no concealment ; no hindrance ; no power of resistance. In a moment God can strike, and his dreadful sentence shall fall on the sinner like the knife on the exposed throat of the victim. What emotions should the sinner have who feels that he is exposed each moment to the sentence of eternal justice—to the sword of God —as the animal with bent-back neck

14 Seeing then that we have a great high priest, that is passed *a* into the heavens, Jesus the Son of

God, let us hold *b* fast *our* profession.

a ch.9.12,24.   *b* ch.10.23.

is exposed to the knife! And what solemn feelings should all have who remember that all is naked and open before God! Were we *transparent* so that the world could see all we are, who would dare go abroad? Who would wish the world to read all his thoughts and feelings for a single day? Who would wish his best friends to look in upon his naked soul as we can look into a room through a window? O what blushes and confusion; what a hanging down of the head, and what an effort to escape from the gaze of men would there be, if every one knew that all his secret feelings were seen by every person whom he met! Social enjoyment would end; and the now gay and blithe multitudes in the streets would become processions of downcast and blushing convicts. And yet all these are known to God. He reads every thought; sees every feeling; looks through the whole soul. How careful should we be to keep our hearts pure; how anxious that there should be nothing in the soul that we are not *willing* to have known! ¶ *With whom we have to do.* Literally, *with whom is our account.* Our account; our reckoning is to be with him before whom all is naked and open. We cannot, therefore, impose on him. We cannot pass off hypocrisy for sincerity. He will judge us according to truth, not according to appearances; and his sentence, therefore, will be just. A man who is to be tried by one who *knows all about him*, should be a pure and holy man.

14. *Seeing then that we have a great high priest.* The apostle here resumes the subject which had been slightly hinted at in ch. ii. 17; iii. 1, and pursues it to the end of ch. x. The *object* is to show that Christians have a great High Priest as really as the Jews had; to show wherein he surpassed the Levitical priesthood; to show how all that was said of the Aaronic priesthood, and all the types pertaining to that priesthood, were

fulfilled in the Lord Jesus; and to state and illustrate the nature of the consolations which Christians might derive from the fact that they had such an High Priest. One of the things on which the Jews most valued their religion, was the fact that it had such a minister of religion as their high priest—the most elevated functionary of that dispensation. It came therefore to be of the utmost importance to show that Christianity was not inferior to the Jewish religion in this respect, and that the High Priest of the Christian profession would not suffer in point of dignity, and in the value of the blood with which he would approach God, and in the efficacy of his intercession, when compared with the Jewish high priest. Moreover, it was a doctrine of Christianity that the Jewish ritual was to pass away; and its temple services cease to be observed. It was, therefore, of vast importance to show *why* they passed away, and how they were superseded. To do this, the apostle is led into this long discussion respecting their nature. He shows that they were designed to be typical. He proves that they could not purify the heart, and give peace to the conscience. He proves that they were all intended to point to something future, and to introduce the Messiah to the world; and that when this object was accomplished, their great end was secured, and they were thus all fulfilled. In no part of the Bible can there be found so full an account of the design of the Mosaic institutions, as in ch. v.—x. of this epistle; and were it not for this, the volume of inspiration would be incomplete. We should be left in the dark on some of the most important subjects in revelation; we should ask questions for which we could find no certain answer. The phrase "*great* high priest" here is used with reference to a known usage among the Jews. In the time of the apostle the name high priest pertained not only to him who

15 For we have not an high
priest which cannot be touched
^a with the feeling of our infir-

a Ho.11.8.

mities; but was in all points tempted like as *we are, yet* without ^b
sin.

b 1 Pet.2.22; 1 John 3.5.

actually held the office, and who had
the right to enter into the holy of
holies, but to his deputy, and to those
who had held the office but who had
retired from it, and perhaps also the
name was given to the head of each
one of the twenty-four courses or
classes into which the priests were
divided ; comp. Notes, Luke i. 5 ;
Matt. xxvi. 3. The name "great
high priest" would designate him who
actually held the office, and was at
the head of all the other priests; and
the idea here is, not merely that the
Lord Jesus was *a priest*, but that he
was at the head of all ; in the Christian economy he sustained a rank
that corresponded with that of the
great high priest in the Jewish.
¶ *That is passed into the heavens ;*
ch. ix. 12, 24. The Jewish high
priest went once a year into the most
holy place in the temple, to offer the
blood of the atonement ; Notes on
ch. ix. 7. Paul says that the Christian High Priest has gone into heaven. He has gone there also to make
intercession, and to sprinkle the blood
of the atonement on the mercy-seat;
Notes ch. ix. 24, 25. ¶ *Jesus the Son
of God.* Not a descendant of Aaron,
but one much greater—the Son of
God ; Notes ch. i. 2. ¶ *Let us hold
fast our profession ;* see Notes ch. x.
23 ; iii. 14 ; Note, ch. iii. 1. This is
the drift and scope of the epistle—to
show that Christians should hold fast
their profession, and not apostatize.
The object of the apostle now is to
show why the fact that we have such
a High Priest, is a reason why we
should hold fast our professed attachment to him. These reasons—which
are drawn out in the succeeding chapters—are such as the following. (1.)
We may look to him for assistance—
since he can be touched with the feeling of our infirmities ; ch. iv. 15, 16.
(2.) The impossibility of being renewed again if we should fall away
from him, since there is but *one* such
High Priest, and since the sacrifice

for sin can never be repeated; ch. vi.
(3.) The fact that all the ancient
types were fulfilled in him, and that
everything which there was in the
Jewish dispensation to keep men from
apostasy, exists much more powerfully
in the Christian scheme. (4.) The
fact that they who rejected the laws
of Moses died without mercy, and
much more any one who should reject the Son of God must expect more
certain and fearful severity ; ch. x.
27—30. By considerations such as
these, the apostle aims to show them
the danger of apostasy, and to urge
them to a faithful adherence to their
Christian profession.

15. *For we have not an high priest
which cannot be touched.* Our High
Priest is not cold and unfeeling.
That is, we have one who is abundantly qualified to sympathize with
us in our afflictions, and to whom,
therefore, we may look for aid and
support in trials. Had we a high
priest who was cold and heartless;
who simply performed the external
duties of his office without entering
into the sympathies of those who
came to seek for pardon ; who had
never experienced any trials, and who
felt himself above those who sought
his aid, we should necessarily feel
disheartened in attempting to overcome our sins, and to live to God.
His coldness would repel us; his
stateliness would awe us ; his distance and reserve would keep us
away, and perhaps render us indifferent to all desire to be saved. But
tenderness and sympathy attract those
who are feeble, and kindness does
more than anything else to encourage
those who have to encounter difficulties and dangers ; see Notes ch. ii.
16—18. Such tenderness and sympathy has *our* Great High Priest.
¶ *But was in all points tempted like*
as we are. *Tried* as we are ; see
Notes ch. ii. 18. He was subjected
to all the kinds of trial to which we
can be, and he is, therefore, able to

16 Let us therefore come boldly *a* unto the throne of grace, that we may obtain mercy, and find grace to help in time of need.

a Eph.3.12; ch.10.19—22.

sympathize with us and to aid us. He was tempted—in the literal sense; he was persecuted ; he was poor ; he was despised ; he suffered bodily pain; he endured the sorrows of a lingering and most cruel death. ¶ Yet *without sin ;* 1 Pet. ii. 22. *"* Who did no sin ;" Isa. liii. 9, " He had done no violence, neither was there any deceit in his mouth ;" Heb. vii. 26, " Who is holy, harmless, undefiled, separate from sinners." The importance of this fact—that the Great High Priest of the Christian profession was "without sin," the apostle illustrates at length in ch. vii.— ix. He here merely alludes to it, and says that one who was " without sin" was able to assist those who were sinners, and who put their trust in him.

16. *Let us therefore come boldly unto the throne of grace.* " The throne of grace!" What a beautiful expression. A throne is the seat of a sovereign ; a throne of grace is designed to represent a sovereign seated to dispense mercy and pardon. The illustration or comparison here may have been derived from the temple service. In that service God is represented as seated in the most holy place on the mercy seat. The high priest approaches that seat or throne of the divine majesty with the blood of the atonement to make intercession for the people, and to plead for pardon ; see Notes on ch. ix. 7, 8. That scene was emblematic of heaven. God is seated on a throne of mercy. The great High Priest of the Christian calling, having shed his own blood to make expiation, is represented as approaching God and pleading for the pardon of men. To a God willing to show mercy he comes with the merits of a sacrifice sufficient for all, and pleads for their salvation. We may, therefore, come with boldness and look for pardon. We come not depending on our own merits, but we come where a sufficient sacrifice has been offered for human guilt ; and where we are assured that God is mer-

ciful. We may, therefore, come without hesitancy, or trembling, and ask for all the mercy that we need. ¶ *That we may obtain mercy.* This is what we want *first.* We need pardon—as the first thing when we come to God. We are guilty and self-condemned — and our first cry should be for *mercy—mercy.* A man who comes to God not feeling his need of mercy must fail of obtaining the divine favour ; and he will be best prepared to obtain that favour who has the deepest sense of his need of forgiveness. ¶ *And find grace.* Favour—strength, help, counsel, direction, support, for the various duties and trials of life. This is what we *next* need—we all need—we always need. Even when pardoned, we need grace to keep us from sin, to aid us in duty, to preserve us in the day of temptation. And feeling our need of this, we may come and ask of God *all* that we want for this purpose. Such is the assurance given us ; and to this bold approach to the throne of grace all are freely invited. In view of it, let us, (1.) Rejoice that there *is* a throne of grace. What a world would this be if God sat on a throne of *justice* only, and if no mercy were ever to be shown to men ! Who is there who would not be overwhelmed with despair ? But it is not so. He is on A THRONE OF GRACE. By day and by night ; from year to year ; from generation to generation ; he is on such a throne. In every land he may be approached, and in as many different languages as men speak, may they plead for mercy. In all times of our trial and temptation we may be assured that he is seated on that throne, and wherever we are, we may approach him with acceptance. (2.) We *need* the privilege of coming before such a throne. We are sinful —and need mercy ; we are feeble, and need grace to help us. There is not a day of our lives in which we do not need pardon ; not an hour in which we do not need grace. (3.) How

CHAPTER V.

FOR every high priest taken from among men is ordained *a*

a ch.8.3.

obvious are the propriety and necessity of prayer! Every man is a sinner— and should pray for pardon; every man is weak, feeble, dependent, and should pray for grace. Not till a man can prove that he has never done any sin, should he maintain that he has no need of pardon; not till 'he can show that he is able alone to meet the storms and temptations of life, should he feel that he has no need to ask for grace. Yet who can feel this? And how strange it is that all men do not pray! (4.) It is easy to be forgiven. All that needs to be done is to plead the merits of our Great High Priest, and God is ready to pardon. Who would not be glad to be able to pay a debt in a manner so easy? Yet how few there are who are willing to pay the debt to justice thus! (5.) It is easy to obtain all the grace that we need. We have only to *ask for it*— and it is done. How easy then to meet temptation if we would! How strange that any should rely on their own strength, when they may lean on the arm of God! (6.) If men are not pardoned, and if they fall into sin and ruin, they alone are to blame. There IS A THRONE OF GRACE. It is always accessible. There IS A GOD. He is always ready to pardon. There IS A REDEEMER. He is the Great High Priest of men. He is always interceding. His merits may *always* be pleaded as the ground of our salvation. Why then, O why, should any remain unforgiven and perish? On them alone the blame must lie. In their own bosoms is the reason why they are not saved.

CHAPTER V.

ANALYSIS OF THE CHAPTER.

In this chapter the subject of the priestly office of Christ is continued and further illustrated. It had been introduced ch. ii. 16, 18; ch. iii. 1; ch. iv. 14—17. The Jews regarded the office of high priest as an essential feature in the true religion; and it became, therefore, of the highest

for men in things *pertaining* to God, that he may offer both gifts and sacrifices for sins:

importance to show that in the Christian system there was a High Priest every way equal to that of the Jews. In his rank; in his character; and in the sacrifice which he offered, he was more than equal to the Jewish high priest, and they who had forsaken Judaism and embraced Christianity had lost nothing in this respect by the change, and had gained much. It became necessary, therefore, in making out this point, to institute a comparison between the Jewish high priest and the Great Author of the Christian religion; and this comparison is pursued in this and the following chapters. The comparison in this chapter turns mainly on the *qualifications* for the office, and the question whether the Lord Jesus had those qualifications. The chapter embraces the following points :—

I. The qualifications of a Jewish high priest; vers. 1—4. They are these. (1.) He must have been ordained or appointed by God for the purpose of offering gifts and sacrifices for sins; ver. 1. (2.) He must be tender and compassionate in his feelings, so that he can *sympathize* with those for whom he ministers; ver. 2. (3.) He must have an offering to bring to God, and be able to present a sacrifice alike for himself and for the people; ver. 3. (4.) He could not take this honour on himself, but must have evidence that he was called of God, as was Aaron; ver. 4.

II. An inquiry whether these qualifications were found in the Lord Jesus, the great High priest of the Christian dispensation; vers. 5—10. In considering this, the apostle specifies the following qualifications in him, corresponding to those which he had said were required by the Jewish high priest. (1.) He did not take this honour on himself, but was called directly by God, and after an order superior to the Aaronic priesthood—the order of Melchisedek ; vers. 5, 6, 9, 10. (2.) He was kind, tender, and compassionate, and showed that he was able to sympathize with those for whom he had undertaken the office. When on the earth he had evinced all the tenderness which could be desired in one who had come to pity and save mankind. He had a tender, sensitive, human nature. He felt deeply as a man, under the pressure of the great sufferings which he endured, and thus showed that he was abundantly qualified to sympathize with his people ; vers. 7, 8.

III. In verse 10 the apostle had introduced, incidentally, a topic of great difficulty; and he adds (vers. 11 —14), that he had much to say on that subject, but that those whom he addressed were not qualified then to understand it. They ought to have been so far advanced in knowledge as to have been able to embrace the more abstruse and difficult points connected with the doctrines of Christianity. But they needed, he says, instruction even yet in the more simple elements of religion, and he feared that what he had to say of Melchisedek would be far above their comprehension. This point, therefore, he drops for the present, and in ch. vi. states again, and at greater length, the danger of apostasy, and the importance of perseverance in endeavouring to comprehend the sublime mysteries of the Christian religion; and then (ch. vii.) he resumes the subject of the comparison between Christ and Melchisedek.

1. *For every high priest.* That is, among the Jews, for the remarks relate to the Jewish system. The Jews had one high priest who was regarded as the successor of Aaron. The word "*high* priest" means *chief priest;* that is, a priest of higher rank and office than others. By the original regulation the Jewish high priest was to be of the family of Aaron (Ex. xxix. 9), though in later times the office was frequently conferred on others. In the time of the Romans it had become venal, and the Mosaic regulation was disregarded; 2 Mac. iv. 7; Jos. Ant. xv. 3. 1. It was no longer held for

life, so that there were several persons at one time to whom was given the title of high priest. The high priest was at the head of religious affairs, and was the ordinary judge of all that pertained to religion, and even of the general justice of the Hebrew commonwealth ; Deut. xvii. 8—12; xix. 17; xxi. 5; xxvii. 9, 10. He only had the privilege of entering the most holy place once a year, on the great day of atonement, to make expiation for the sins of the people; Lev. xvi. He was to be the son of one who had married a virgin, and was to be free from any corporeal defect; Lev. xxi. 13. The *dress* of the high priest was much more costly and magnificent than that of the inferior order of priests; Ex. xxxix. 1—7. He wore a mantle or robe—*meil*—מעיל—of blue, with the borders embroidered with pomegranates in purple and scarlet; an *ephod*—אפוד—made of cotton, with crimson, purple, and blue, and ornamented with gold worn over the robe or mantle, without sleeves, and divided below the arm-pits into two parts or halves, of which one was in front covering the breast, and the other behind covering the back. In the ephod was a breastplate of curious workmanship, and on the head a mitre. The breastplate was a piece of broidered work about ten inches square, and was made double, so as to answer the purpose of a pouch or bag. It was adorned with twelve precious stones, each one having the name of one of the tribes of Israel. The two upper corners of the breastplate were fastened to the ephod, and the two lower to the girdle.

¶ *Taken from among men.* There may be an allusion here to the fact that the great High Priest of the Christian dispensation had a higher than human origin, and was selected from a rank far above men. Or it may be that the meaning is, that every high priest on earth—including all under the old dispensation and the great high priest of the new—is ordained with reference to the welfare of men, and to bring some valuable offering for man to God. ¶ *Is ordained for men.* Is set apart or consecrated for the welfare of men.

2 Who can [1] have compassion on the ignorant, and on them that are out of the way; for that he

1 *reasonably bear with.*

himself also is compassed with infirmity. *a*

3 And by reason hereof he ought

a ch. 7.28.

The Jewish high priest was set apart to his office with great solemnity; see Ex. xxix. ¶ *In things* pertaining *to God.* In religious matters, or with reference to the worship and service of God. He was not to be a civil ruler, nor a teacher of science, nor a military leader, but his business was to superintend the affairs of religion. ¶ *That he may offer both gifts.* That is, thank-offerings, or oblations which would be the expressions of gratitude. Many such offerings were made by the Jews under the laws of Moses, and the high priest was the medium by whom they were to be presented to God. ¶ *And sacrifices for sin.* Bloody offerings; offerings made of slain beasts. The blood of expiation was sprinkled by him on the mercy-seat, and he was the appointed medium by which such sacrifices were to be presented to God; Notes ch. ix. 6 —10. We may remark here (1.) that the proper office of a *priest* is to present a *sacrifice* for sin. (2.) It is *improper* to give the name *priest* to a minister of the gospel. The reason is, that he offers no sacrifice; he sprinkles no blood. He is appointed to " preach the word," and to lead the devotions of the church, but not to offer sacrifice. Accordingly the New Testament preserves entire consistency on this point, for the name *priest* is never once given to the apostles, or to any other minister of the gospel. Among the Papists there is *consistency*—though gross and dangerous error—in the use of the word *priest.* They believe that the minister of religion offers up " the real body and blood of our Lord ;" that the bread and wine are changed by the words of consecration into the "body and blood, the soul and divinity, of the Lord Jesus " (Decrees of the Council of Trent), and that *this* is really offered by him as a sacrifice. Accordingly they "elevate the host ;" that is, lift up, or offer the sacrifice, and require all to bow before it and

worship, and with this view they are *consistent* in retaining the word *priest.* But why should this name be applied to a *Protestant* minister, who believes that all this is blasphemy, and who claims to have no *sacrifice* to offer when he comes to minister before God? The great sacrifice; the one sufficient atonement, has been offered —and the ministers of the gospel are appointed to proclaim that truth to men, not to offer sacrifices for sin.

2. *Who can have compassion.* Marg. *Reasonably bear with.* The idea is that of *sympathizing with.* The high priest is taken from among men, in order that he may have a fellow-feeling for those on whose behalf he officiates. Sensible of his own ignorance, he is able to sympathize with those who are ignorant; and compassed about with infirmity, he is able to succour those who have like infirmities. ¶ *And on them that are out of the way.* The erring, and the guilty. If he were taken from an order of beings superior to men, he would be less qualified to sympathize with those who felt that they were sinners, and who needed pardon. ¶ *For that he himself also is compassed with infirmity;* see chap. vii. 28. He is liable to err; he is subject to temptation; he must die, and appear before God;—and encompassed with these infirmities, he is better qualified to minister in behalf of guilty and dying men. For the same reason it is, that the ministers of the gospel are chosen from among men. They are of like passions with others. They are sinners; they are dying men. They can enter into the feelings of those who are conscious of guilt; they can sympathize with those who tremble in dread of death; they can partake of the emotions of those who expect soon to appear before God.

3. *And by reason hereof.* Because he is a sinner; an imperfect man. ¶ *As for the people, so also for himself, to offer for sins.* To make an expiation for sins. He needs the

as for the people, so *a* also for himself, to offer for sins.

4 And *b* no man taketh this honour unto himself, but he

a Le.9.7.　　　　　　b 2 Ch.26.18.

same atonement; ho offers the sacrifice for himself which he does for others; Lev. ix. 7. The same thing is true of the ministers of religion now. They come before God feeling that they have need of the benefit of the same atonement which they preach to others; they plead the merits of the same blood for their own salvation which they show to be indispensable for the salvation of others.

4. *And no man taketh this honour to himself.* No one has a right to enter on this office unless he has the qualifications which God has prescribed. There were fixed and definite laws in regard to the succession in the office of the high priest, and to the qualifications of him who should hold the office. ¶ *But he that is called of God as* was *Aaron.* Aaron was designated by name. It was necessary that his successors should have as clear evidence that they were called of God to the office, as though they had been mentioned by name. The manner in which the high priest was to succeed to the office was designated in the law of Moses, but in the time of Paul these rules were little regarded. The office had become venal, and was conferred at pleasure by the Roman rulers. Still it was true that according to the law, to which alone Paul here refers, no one might hold this office but he who had the qualifications which Moses prescribed, and which showed that he was called of God. · We may remark here, (1.) that this does not refer so much to an *internal*, as to an *external* call. He was to have the qualifications prescribed in the law—but it is not specified that he should be conscious of an internal call to the office, or be influenced by the Holy Spirit to it. Such a call was, doubtless, in the highest degree desirable, but it was not prescribed as an essential qualification. (2.) This has no reference to the call to the work of the Christian ministry,

that is called of God, as *was* Aaron.*c*

5 So also Christ *d* glorified not himself to be made an high priest; c Ex.28.1.Nu.16.40.　　d John 8.54.

and should not be applied to it. It should not be urged as a proof-text to show that a minister of the gospel should have a "call" directly from God, or that he should be called according to a certain order of succession. The object of Paul is not to state this—whatever may be the truth on this point. His object is, to show that the Jewish high priest was called of God to *his* office in a certain way, showing that he held the appointment from God, and that *therefore* it was necessary that the Great High Priest of the Christian profession should be called in a similar manner. To this alone the comparison should be understood as applicable.

5. *So also Christ glorified not himself;* see Notes John viii. 54. The meaning is, that Jesus was not ambitious; that he did not obtrude himself into the great office of high priest; he did not enter upon its duties without being regularly called to it. Paul claimed that Christ held that office; but, as he was not descended from Aaron, and as no one might perform its duties without being regularly called to it, it was incumbent on him to show that Jesus was not an intruder, but had a regular vocation to that work. This he shows by a reference to two passages of the Old Testament. ¶ *But he that said unto him.* That is, he who said to him " Thou art my Son," exalted him to that office. He received his appointment from him. This was decisive in the case, and this was sufficient, if it could be made out, for the only claim which Aaron and his successors could have to the office, was the fact that they had received their appointment from God. ¶ *Thou art my Son; Ps.ii.7.* See this passage explained in the Notes on Acts xiii. 33. It is here used with reference to the designation to the priestly office, though in the Psalm more particularly to the anointing to the office of king. The propriety of this applica-

but he that said unto him, ^a Thou art my Son, to-day have I begotten thee.

6 As he saith also in another place, Thou ^b art a priest for ever after the order of Melchisedek.

a Ps.2.7.

b Ps.110.4.

tion is founded on the fact that the language in the Psalm is of so general a character, that it may be applied to *any* exaltation of the Redeemer, or to any honour conferred on him. It is here used with strict propriety, for Paul is saying that Jesus did not exalt *himself*, and in proof of that he refers to the fact that *God* had exalted him by calling him his " Son."
6. *As he saith also in another* place ; Ps. cx. 4. ¶ *Thou* art *a priest for ever.* It is evident here that the apostle means to be understood as saying that the Psalm referred to Christ, and this is one of the instances of quotation from the Old Testament respecting which there can be no doubt. Paul makes much of this argument in a subsequent part of this epistle, (ch. vii.) and reasons as if no one would deny that the Psalm had a reference to the Messiah. ,It is clear from this that the Psalm was understood by the Jews at that time to have such a reference, and that it was so universally admitted that no one would call it in question. That the Psalm refers to the Messiah has been the opinion of nearly all Christian commentators, and has been admitted by the Jewish Rabbins in general also. The *evidence* that it refers to the Messiah is such as the following. (1.) It is a Psalm of David, and yet is spoken of one who was superior to him, and whom he calls his "Lord;" ver. 1. (2.) It cannot be referred to Jehovah himself, for he is expressly (ver. 1.) distinguished from him who is here addressed. (3.) It cannot be referred to any one in the time of David, for there was no one to whom he would attribute this character of superiority but God. (4.) For the same reason there was no one among his posterity, except the Messiah, to whom he would apply this language. (5.) It is expressly ascribed by the Lord Jesus to himself; Matt. xxii. 43, 44. (6.) The scope of the Psalm is such as to be applicable to

the Messiah, and there is no part of it which would be inconsistent with such a reference. Indeed, there is no passage of the Old Testament of which it would be more universally conceded that there was a reference to the Messiah, than this Psalm. ¶ *Thou* art *a priest.* He is not here called a *high priest*, for Melchisedek did not bear that title, nor was the Lord Jesus to be a high priest exactly in the sense in which the name was given to Aaron and his successors. A word is used, therefore, in a general sense to denote that he would be a *priest* simply, or would sustain the priestly office. This was all that was needful to the present argument which was, that he was *designated by God* to the priestly office, and that he had not intruded himself into it. ¶ *For ever.* This was an important circumstance, of which the apostle makes much use in another part of the epistle ; see Notes ch. vii. 8, 23, 24. The priesthood of the Messiah was not to change from hand to hand; it was not to be laid down at death; it was to remain unchangeably the same. ¶ *After the order.* The word rendered *order*— τάξις—means "a setting in order"— hence arrangement or disposition. It may be applied to ranks of soldiers ; to the gradations of office ; or to any rank which men sustain in society. To say that he was of the same *order* with Melchisedek, was to say that he was of the same *rank* or *station.* He was like him in his designation to the office. In what respects he was like him the apostle shows more fully in ch. vii. *One* particular in which there was a striking resemblance, which did not exist between Christ and any other high priest, was, that Melchisedek was both a *priest* and a *king.* None of the kings of the Jews were priests ; nor were any of the priests ever elevated to the office of king. But in Melchisedek these offices were united, and this fact constituted a striking resemblance between him

7 Who in the days of his flesh, | when he had offered up prayers [a]

a Matt.26.39-44

and the Lord Jesus. It was on this principle that there was such pertinency in quoting here the passage from the second Psalm ; see ver. 5. The meaning is, that Melchisedek was of a peculiar rank or order ; that he was not numbered with the Levitical priests, and that there were important features in his office which differed from theirs. In those features it was distinctly predicted that the Messiah would resemble him. ¶ *Melchisedek;* see Notes on ch. vii. 1, *seq.* 7. *Who.* That is, the Lord Jesus— for so the connection demands. The *object* of this verse and the two following is, to show that the Lord Jesus had that qualification for the office of priest to which he had referred in ver. 2. It was one important qualification for that office that he who sustained it should be able to show compassion, to aid those that were out of the way, and to sympathize with sufferers ; in other words, they were themselves encompassed with infirmity, and thus were able to succour those who were subjected to trials. The apostle shows now that the Lord Jesus had those qualifications, as far as it was possible for one to have them who had no sin. In the days of his flesh he suffered intensely ; he prayed with fervour ; he placed himself in a situation where he learned subjection and obedience by his trials ; and in all this he went far beyond what had been evinced by the priests under the ancient dispensation. ¶ *In the days of his flesh.* When he appeared on earth as a man. Flesh is used to denote human nature, and especially human nature as susceptible of suffering. The Son of God still is united to human nature, but it is human nature glorified, for in his case, as in all others, "flesh and blood cannot inherit the kingdom of God," 1 Cor. xv. 50. He has now a glorified body (Phil. iii. 21), such as the redeemed will have in the future world ; comp. Rev. i. 13—17. The phrase "*days* of his flesh," means the *time* when he was incarnate, or when

he lived on earth in human form. The particular time here referred to, evidently, was the agony in the garden of Gethsemane. ¶ *Prayers and supplications.* These words are often used to denote the same thing. If there is a difference, the former— δέησις—means petitions which arise *from a sense of need*—from δέομαι— *to want, to need ;* the latter refers usually to supplication *for protection,* and is applicable to one who under a sense of guilt flees to an altar with the symbols of supplication in his hand. Suppliants in such cases often carried an olive-branch as an emblem of the peace which they sought. A fact is mentioned by Livy respecting the Locrians that may illustrate this passage. " Ten delegates from the Locrians, squalid and covered with rags, came into the hall where the consuls were sitting, extending the badges of suppliants—olive-branches — according to the custom of the Greeks ; and prostrated themselves on the ground before the tribunal, with a lamentable cry ;" Lib. xxix. c. 16. The particular idea in the word here used—ίκιτηρία—is petition for *protection, help,* or *shelter* (*Passow*), and this idea accords well with the design of the passage. The Lord Jesus prayed as one who had *need,* and as one who desired *protection, shelter,* or *help.* The words here, therefore, do not mean the same thing, and are not merely intensive, but they refer to distinct purposes which the Redeemer had in his prayers. He was about to die, and as a man needed the divine *help;* he was, probably, tempted in that dark hour (Note John xii. 31), and he fled to God for *protection.* ¶ *With strong crying.* This word does not mean *weeping,* as the word "crying" does familiarly with us. It rather means an outcry, the voice of wailing and lamentation. It is the cry for help of one who is deeply distressed, or in danger ; and refers here to the *earnest petition* of the Saviour when in the agony of Gethsemane, or when on the cross. It is the *in-*

and supplications, with strong crying and tears, unto him that was

a Matt.26.53.

able *a* to save him from death, and
was heard ¹ in that he feared :

1 *for his piety.*

tensity of the voice which is referred
to when it is raised by an agony of
suffering ; comp. Luke xxii. 44, " He
prayed more earnestly;" Matt. xxvii.
46, " And about the ninth hour Jesus cried with a loud voice—My God,
my God, why hast thou forsaken me?"
see also Matt. xxvi. 38, 39 ; xxvii. 50.
¶ *And tears.* Jesus wept at the grave
of Lazarus (John xi. 35), and over
Jerusalem ; Luke xix. 41. It is not
expressly stated by the Evangelists
that he *wept* in the garden of Gethsemane, but there is no reason to
doubt that he did. In such an intense agony as to cause a bloody
sweat, there is every probability that
it would be accompanied with tears.
We may remark then, (1.) That there
is nothing *dishonourable* in tears,
and that man should not be ashamed
on proper occasions to weep. The
fact that the Son of God wept is a
full demonstration that it is not dis-
graceful to weep. God has so made
us as to express sympathy for others
by tears. Religion does not make
the heart insensible and hard as stoi-
cal philosophy does ; it makes it tender and susceptible to impression.
(2.) It is not *improper* to weep. The
Son of God wept—and if he poured
forth tears it cannot be wrong for
us. Besides, it is a great law of our
nature that in suffering we should
find relief by tears. God would not
have so made us if it had been wrong.
(3.) The fact that the Son of God
thus wept should be allowed deeply to
affect our hearts.

" He wept that we might weep ;
  Each sin demands a tear."

He wept that he might redeem us ;
we should weep that our sins were so
great as to demand such bitter woes
for our salvation. That we had sinned ; that our sins caused him such
anguish ; that he endured for us this
bitter conflict, should make us weep.
Tear should answer to tear, and sigh
respond to sigh, and groan to groan,
when we contemplate the sorrows of

the Son of God in accomplishing our
redemption. That man must have a
hard heart who has never had an
emotion when he has reflected that
the Son of God wept, and bled, and
died for him. ¶ *Unto him that was
able.* To God. He alone was able
then to save. In such a conflict man
could not aid, and the help of angels,
ready as they were to assist him,
could not sustain him. We may derive aid from man in trial ; we may
be comforted by sympathy and counsel ; but there are sorrows where God
only can uphold the sufferer. That
God was *able* to uphold him in his
severe conflict, the Redeemer could
not doubt ; nor need *we* doubt it in
reference to ourselves when deep sorrows come over our souls. ¶ *To save
him from death.* It would seem from
this, that what constituted the agony
of the Redeemer was the dread of
death, and that he prayed that he
might be saved from that. This might
be, so far as the language is concerned, either the dread of death on the
spot by the intensity of his sufferings
and by the power of the tempter, or
it might be the dread of the approaching death on the cross. As the Redeemer, however, knew that he was
to die on the cross, it can hardly be
supposed that he apprehended death
in the garden of Gethsemane. What
he prayed for was, that, if it were
possible, he might be spared from a
death so painful as he apprehended;
Matt. xxvi. 39. Feeling that God
had *power* to save him from that mode
of dying, the burden of his petition
was, that, if human redemption could
be accomplished without such sufferings, it might please his Father to
remove that cup from him. ¶ *And
was heard.* In John xi. 42, the Saviour says, " I know that thou hearest
me always." In the garden of Gethsemane, he was heard. His prayer
was not disregarded, though it was
not *literally* answered. The cup of
death was not taken away; but his
prayer was not disregarded. What

answer was given; what assurance or support was imparted to his soul, we are not informed. The case, however, shows us, (1.) That prayer may be heard even when the sufferings which are dreaded, and from which we prayed to be delivered, may come upon us. They may come with such assurances of divine favour, and such supports, as will be full proof that the prayer was not disregarded. (2.) That prayer offered in faith may not be always *literally* answered. No one can doubt that Jesus offered the prayer of faith; and it is as little to be doubted, if he referred in the prayer to the death on the cross, that it was not *literally* answered; comp. Matt. xxvi. 39. In like manner, it may occur now, that prayer shall be offered with every right feeling, and with an earnest desire for the object, which may not be literally answered. Christians, even in the highest exercise of faith, are not inspired to know what is best for them, and as long as this is the case, it is possible that they may ask for things which it would not be best to have granted. They who maintain that the prayer of faith is always literally answered, must hold that the Christian is under such a guidance of the Spirit of God that he cannot ask anything amiss; see Notes on 2 Cor. xii. 9. ¶ *In that he feared.* Marg. *For his piety.* Coverdale, "Because he had God in honour." Tindal, "Because he had God in reverence." Prof. Stuart renders it, "And was delivered from that which he feared." So also Doddridge. Whitby, "Was delivered from his fear." Luther renders it, "And was heard for that he had God in reverence"—*dass er Gott in Ehren hatte.* Beza renders it, "His prayers being heard, he was delivered from fear." From this variety in translating the passage, it will be seen at once that it is attended with difficulty. The Greek is literally "from fear or reverence"—ἀπὸ της εὐλαβείας The word occurs in the New Testament only in one other place, (Heb. xii. 28), where it is rendered "*fear.*" "Let us serve him with reverence and godly *fear.*" The word properly means *caution, circum-*

spection; then timidity, fear; then the fear of God, reverence, piety. Where the most distinguished scholars have differed as to the meaning of a Greek phrase, it would be presumption in me to attempt to determine its sense. The most natural and obvious interpretation, however, as it seems to me, is, that it means that he was heard on account of his reverence for God; his profound veneration; his submission. Such was his piety that the prayer was *heard,* though it was not literally answered. A prayer may be *heard* and yet not literally answered; it may be acceptable to God, though it may not consist with his arrangements to bestow the very blessing that is sought. The posture of the mind of the Redeemer perhaps was something like this. He knew that he was about to be put to death in a most cruel manner. His tender and sensitive nature as a man shrank from such a death. As a man he went under the pressure of his great sorrows and pleaded that the cup might be removed, and that man might be redeemed by a less fearful scene of suffering. That arrangement, however, could not be made. Yet the spirit which he evinced; the desire to do the will of God; the resignation, and the confidence in his Father which he evinced, were such as were acceptable in his sight. They showed that he had unconquerable virtue; that no power of temptation, and no prospect of the intensest woes which human nature could endure, could alienate him from piety. To show this was an object of inestimable value, and much as it cost the Saviour was worth it all. So now it is worth much to see what Christian piety can endure; what strong temptations it can resist; and what strength it has to bear up under accumulated woes;—and even though the prayer of the pious sufferer is not directly answered, yet that prayer is acceptable to God, and the result of such a trial is worth all that it costs.

8. *Though he were a Son.* Though the Son of God. Though he sustained this exalted rank, and was conscious of it, yet he was willing to

8 Though he were a Son, yet learned he obedience *a* by the things which he suffered :
9 And being made *b* perfect, he became the author of eternal sal-

a Ph.2.8.   *b* ch.2.10.

vation unto all them that obey him ;
10 Called of God an high priest *c*, after the order of Melchisedek.
11 Of whom we have many

c ver.6.

learn experimentally what is meant by obedience in the midst of sufferings. ¶ *Yet learned he obedience.* That is, he learned experimentally and practically. It cannot be supposed that he did not *know* what obedience was ; or that he was *indisposed* to obey God before he suffered ; or that he had, as we have, perversities of nature leading to rebellion which required to be subdued by suffering, but that he was willing to *test* the power of obedience in sufferings ; to become personally and practically acquainted with the nature of such obedience in the midst of protracted woes ; comp. Note on Phil. ii. 8. The *object* here is, to show how well fitted the Lord Jesus was to be a Saviour for mankind ; and the argument is, that he has set us an example, and has shown that the most perfect obedience may be manifested in the deepest sorrows of the body and the soul. Learn hence, that one of the objects of affliction is to lead us *to obey God.* In prosperity we forget it. We become self-confident and rebellious. *Then* God lays his hand upon us ; breaks up our plans ; crushes our hopes ; takes away our health, and teaches us that we *must* be submissive to his will. Some of the most valuable lessons of obedience are learned in the furnace of affliction ; and many of the most submissive children of the Almighty have been made so as the result of protracted woes.
9. *And being made perfect.* That is, being made a *complete* Saviour – a Saviour fitted in all respects to redeem men. Sufferings were necessary to the *completeness* or the *finish* of his character as a Saviour, not to his moral perfection, for he was always without sin ; see this explained in the Notes on ch. ii. 10. ¶ *He became the author.* That is, he was the procuring cause (*αἴτιος*) of salvation. It is to be traced wholly to his sufferings

and death ; see Note ch. ii. 10. ¶ *Unto all them that obey him.* It is not to save those who live in sin. Only those who *obey* him have any evidence that they will be saved ; see Note John xiv. 15.
10. *Called of God.* Addressed by him, or greeted by him. The word here used does not mean that he was *appointed* by God, or *"called"* to the office, in the sense in which we often use the word, but simply that he was *addressed* as such, to wit, in Psalm cx. ¶ *An high priest.* In the Septuagint (Ps. cx. 4), and in ver. 6, above, it is rendered *priest*—*ἱερεύς*—but the Hebrew word—כהן—*kohen*—is often used to denote the high priest, and may mean either ; see Sept. in Lev. iv. 3. Whether the word *priest*, or *high priest*, be used here, does not affect the argument of the apostle. ¶ *After the order of Melchisedek.* Notes ver. 6.
11. *Of whom we have many things to say.* There are many things which seem strange in regard to him ; many things which are hard to be understood. Paul knew that what he had to say of this man as a type of the Redeemer would excite wonder, and that many might be disposed to call it in question. He knew that in order to be understood, what he was about to say required a familiar acquaintance with the Scriptures, and a strong and elevated faith. A young convert ; one who had just commenced the Christian life, could hardly expect to be able to understand it. The same thing is true now. One of the first questions which a young convert often asks, is, Who was Melchisedek ? And one of the things which most uniformly perplex those who begin to study the Bible, is, the statement which is made about this remarkable man. ¶ *Hard to be uttered.* Rather, hard to be *interpreted*, or *explained*. So the Greek word means. ¶ *Seeing*

things to say, and hard to be uttered, seeing ye are dull of hearing.

12 For when for the time ye

ought to be teachers, ye have need that one teach you again which *be* the first principles of the oracles

ye are dull of hearing. That is, when they ought to have been acquainted with the higher truths of religion, they had shown that they received them slowly, and were dull of apprehension. On what particular *fact* Paul grounded this charge respecting them is unknown; nor could we know, unless we were better acquainted with the persons to whom he wrote, and their circumstances, than we now are. But he had doubtless in his eye some fact which showed that they were slow to understand the great principles of the gospel. 12. *For when for the time.* Considering the time which has elapsed since you were converted. You have been Christians long enough to be expected to understand such doctrines. This verse proves that those to whom he wrote were not recent converts. ¶ *Ye ought to be teachers.* You ought to be able to instruct others. He does not mean to say, evidently, that they ought all to become public teachers, or preachers of the gospel, but that they ought to be able to explain to others the truths of the Christian religion. As parents they ought to be able to explain them to their children; as neighbours, to their neighbours; or as friends, to those who were inquiring the way to life. ¶ *Ye have need.* That is, probably, the mass of them had need. As a people, or a church, they had shown that they were ignorant of some of the very elements of the gospel. ¶ *Again.* This shows that they *had been* taught on some former occasion what were the first principles of religion, but they had not followed up the teaching as they ought to have done. ¶ *The first principles.* The very elements; the rudiments; the first lessons—such as children learn before they advance to higher studies. See the word here used explained in the Notes on Gal. iv. 3, under the word "*elements.*" The Greek word is the same. ¶ *Of the oracles of God.* Of the Scriptures, or what God has spoken; see Notes on

Rom. iii. 2. The phrase here may refer to the writings of the Old Testament, and particularly to those parts which relate to the Messiah; or it may include all that God had at that time revealed in whatever way it was preserved; in 1 Pet. iv. 11, it is used with reference to the Christian religion, and to the doctrines which God had revealed in the gospel. In the passage before us, it may mean *the divine oracles or communications,* in whatever way they had been made known. They had shown that they were ignorant of the very rudiments of the divine teaching. ¶ *And are become such.* There is more meant in this phrase than that they simply *were* such persons. The word rendered "are become"—γίνομαι—sometimes implies *a change of state,* or a passing from one state to another—well expressed by the phrase "are become;" see Matt. v. 45; iv. 3; xiii. 32; vi. 16; x. 25; Mark i. 17; Rom. vii. 3, 4. The idea here is, that they had passed from the hopeful condition in which they were when they showed that they had an acquaintance with the great principles of the gospel, and that they had become such as to need again the most simple form of instruction. This agrees well with the general strain of the epistle, which is to preserve them from the danger of apostasy. They were verging towards it, and had come to that state where if they were recovered it must be by being again taught the elements of religion. ¶ *Have need of milk.* Like little children. You can bear only the most simple nourishment. The meaning is, that they were incapable of receiving the higher doctrines of the gospel as much as little children are incapable of digesting solid food. They were in fact in a state of spiritual infancy. ¶ *And not of strong meat.* Greek. "Strong food." The word *meat* with us is used now to denote only animal food. Formerly it meant food in general. The Greek word here means *nourishment.*

of God ; and are become such as have need of milk, *a* and not of strong meat.

13 For every one that useth

a 1Cor.3.1-3.

13. *For every one that useth milk.* Referring to the food of children. The apostle has in view here those Christians who resemble children in this respect, that they are not capable of receiving the stronger food adapted to those of mature age. ¶ Is *unskilful.* Inexperienced ; who has not skill to perform anything. The word is properly applied to one who has not experience or skill, or who is ignorant. Here it does not mean that they were not true Christians—but that they had not the experience or skill requisite to enable them to understand the higher mysteries of the Christian religion. ¶ *In the word of righteousness.* The doctrine respecting the way in which men become righteous, or the way of salvation by the Redeemer ; see Notes on Rom. i. 17. ¶ *For he is a babe.* That is, in religious matters. He understands the great system only as a child may. It is common to speak of " babes in knowledge," as denoting a state of ignorance.

14. *Strong meat.* Solid food pertains to those of maturer years. So it is with the higher doctrines of Christianity. They can be understood and appreciated only by those who are advanced in Christian experience. ¶ *Of full age.* Marg. *Perfect.* The expression refers to those who are grown up. ¶ *Who by reason of use.* Marg. Or, *an habit,* or, *perfection.* Coverdale and Tindal render it, "through custom." The Greek word means *habit, practice.* The meaning is, that by long use and habit they had arrived to that state in which they could appreciate the more elevated doctrines of Christianity. The reference in the use of this word is not to those who *eat food*—meaning that by long use they are able to distinguish good from bad—but it is to experienced Christians, who by long experience are able to distinguish that which is useful in pretended re-

milk *is* unskilful [1] in the word of righteousness : for he is a babe.

14 But strong meat belongeth to them that are of full age, *even*

1 *hath no experience.*   2 or, *perfect.*

ligious instruction from that which is injurious. It refers to the delicate taste which an experienced Christian has in regard to those doctrines which impart most light and consolation. Experience will thus enable one to discern what is fitted to the soul of man ; what elevates and purifies the affections, and what tends to draw the heart near to God. ¶ *Have their senses.* The word here used means properly *the senses*—as we use the term ; the seat of sensation, the smell, taste, &c. Then it means *the internal sense,* the faculty of perceiving truth ; and this is the idea here. The meaning is, that by long experience Christians come to be able to understand the more elevated doctrines of Christianity ; they see their beauty and value, and they are able carefully and accurately to distinguish them from error ; comp. Notes John vii. 17. ¶ *To discern both good and evil.* That is, in doctrine. They will appreciate and understand that which is true ; they will reject that which is false.

1. Let us rejoice that we have a High Priest who is duly called to take upon himself the functions of that great office, and who lives for ever ; vers. 1—6. True, he was not of the tribe of Levi ; he was not a descendant of Aaron ; but he had a more noble elevation, and a more exalted rank. He was the Son of God, and was called to his office by special divine designation. He did not obtrude himself into the work ; he did not unduly exalt himself, but he was directly called to it by the appointment of God. When, moreover, the Jewish high priests could look back on the long line of their ancestors, and trace the succession up to Aaron, it was in the power of the great High Priest of the Christian faith to look farther back still, and to be associated in the office with one of higher antiquity than Aaron,

those who by reason of [1] use have
1 or, *an habit;* or, *perfection.*

and of higher rank—one of the most
remarkable men of all ancient times—
he whom Abraham acknowledged as
his superior, and from whom Abraham
received the benediction.

2. It is not unmanly to weep; ver.
7. The Son of God poured out prayers
and supplications with strong crying
and tears. He wept at the grave of
Lazarus, and he wept over Jerusalem.
If the Redeemer wept, it is not unmanly to weep; and we should not be
ashamed to have tears seen streaming
down our cheeks. Tears are appointed by God to be the natural expression of sorrow, and often to furnish a
relief to a burdened soul. We instinctively honour the man whom we see
weeping when there is occasion for
grief. We sympathize with him in
his sorrow, and we love him the more.
When we see a father who could face
the cannon's mouth without shrinking, yet weeping over the open grave
of a daughter, we honour him **more**
than we could otherwise do. He
shows that he has a heart that can
love and feel, as well as courage that
can meet danger without alarm.
Washington wept whon he signed the
death-warrant of Major Andre; and
who ever read the affecting account
without feeling that his character was
the more worthy of our love? There
is enough in the world to make us weep.
Sickness, calamity, death, are around
us. They come into our dwellings,
and our dearest objects of affection
are taken away, and *God intends* that
we shall deeply feel. Tears here will
make heaven more sweet; and our
sorrows on earth are intended to prepare us for the joy of that day when it
shall be announced to us that "all tears
shall be wiped away from every face."

3. We see the propriety of prayer
in view of approaching death; ver. 7.
The Redeemer prayed when he felt
that he must die. We know, also,
that we must die. True, we shall
not suffer as he did. He had pangs
on the cross which no other dying
man ever bore. But death to us is an
object of dread. The hour of death

their senses exercised to discern
both good and evil.

is a fearful hour. The scene when a
man dies is a gloomy scene. The
sunken eye, the pallid cheek, the
clammy sweat, the stiffened corse, the
coffin, the shroud, the grave, are all
sad and gloomy things. We know
not, too, what severe pangs we may
have when we die. Death may come
to us in some peculiarly fearful form;
and in view of his approach in *any*
way, we should pray. Pray, dying
man, that you may be prepared for
that sad hour; pray, that you may
not be left to complain, and rebel, and
murmur then ; pray that you may lie
down in calmness and peace; pray
that you may be enabled *to honour*
God even in death.

4. It is not sinful to dread death;
ver. 7. The Redeemer dreaded it.
His human nature, though perfectly
holy, shrank back from the fearful
agonies of dying. The fear of death,
therefore, in itself is not sinful. Christians are often troubled because they
have not that calmness in the prospect of death which they suppose they
ought to have, and because their nature shrinks back from the dying pang.
They suppose that such feelings are
inconsistent with religion, and that
they who have them cannot be true
Christians. But they forget their
Redeemer and his sorrows ; they forget the earnestness with which he
pleaded that the cup might be removed. Death is in itself fearful, and it
is a part of our nature to dread it, and
even in the best of minds sometimes
the fear of it is not wholly taken away
until the hour comes, and God gives
them *"dying grace."* There are probably two reasons why God made
death so fearful to man. (1.) One is,
to impress him with the importance
of being prepared for it. Death is to
him the entrance on an endless being,
and it is an object of God to keep the
attention fixed on that as a most
momentous and solemn event. The
ox, the lamb, the robin, the dove,
have no immortal nature; no conscience; no responsibility, and no need
of making preparation for death—

and hence—except in a very slight degree—they seem to have no dread of dying. But not so with man. He has an undying soul. His main business here is to prepare for death and for the world beyond, and hence, by all the fear of the dying pang, and by all the horror of the grave, God would fix the attention of man on his own death as a most momentous event, and lead him to seek that hope of immortality which alone can lay the foundation for any proper removal of the fear of dying. (2.) The other reason is, to deter man from taking his own life. To keep him from this, he is made so as to start back from death. He fears it; it is to him an object of deepest dread, and even when pressed down by calamity and sadness, as a general law, he "had rather bear the ills he has, than fly to others that he knows not of." Man is the only creature in reference to whom this danger exists. There is no one of the brute creation, unless it be the scorpion, that will take its own life, and hence they have not such a dread of dying. But we know how it is with man. Weary of life; goaded by a guilty conscience; disappointed and heart-broken, he is under strong temptation to commit the enormous crime of self-murder, and to rush uncalled to the bar of God. As one of the means of deterring from this, God has so made us that we fear to die; and thousands are kept from this enormous crime by this fear, when nothing else would save them. It is benevolence, therefore, to the world, that man is afraid to die —and in every pang of the dying struggle, and every thing about death that makes us turn pale and tremble at its approach, there is in some way the manifestation of goodness to mankind.

5. We may be comforted in the prospect of death by looking to the example of the Redeemer ; ver. 7. Much as we may fear to die, and much as we may be left to suffer then, of one thing we may be sure. It is, that he has gone beyond us in suffering. The sorrows of our dying will never equal his. We shall never go through such scenes as occurred

in the garden of Gethsemane and on the cross. It may be some consolation that human nature has endured greater pangs than we shall, and that there is one who has surpassed us even in our keenest sufferings. It *should* be to us a source of consolation, also of the highest kind, that he did it that he might alleviate our sorrows, and that he might drive away the horrors of death from us by "bringing life and immortality to light," and that as the result of *his* sufferings our dying moments may be calm and peaceful.

6. It often occurs that men are true Christians, and yet are ignorant of some of the elementary principles of religion ; ver. 12. This is owing to such things as the following ;—a want of early religious instruction ; the faults of preachers who fail to teach their people ; a want of inquiry on the part of Christians, and the interest which they feel in other things above that which they feel in religion. It is often surprising what vague and unsettled opinions many professed Christians have on some of the most important points of Christianity, and how little qualified they are to defend their opinions when they are attacked. Of multitudes in the Church even now it might be said, that they "need some one to teach them what are the very first principles of true religion." To some of the *elementary* doctrines of Christianity about deadness to the world, about self-denial, about prayer, about doing good, and about spirituality, they are utter strangers. So of forgiveness of injuries, and charity, and love for a dying world. These are the *elements* of Christianity—rudiments which children in righteousness should learn ; and yet they are *not* learned by multitudes who bear the Christian name.

7. All Christians ought to be *teachers ;* ver. 12. I do not mean that they should all be *preachers ;* but they should all so live as to *teach* others the true nature of religion. This they should do by their example, and by their daily conversation. Any Christian is qualified to impart useful instruction to others. The servant of

CHAPTER VI.

THEREFORE, *a* leaving the principles [1] of the doctrine

of Christ, let us go on unto perfection ; not laying again the
a Ph.3.12-14.
1 or, *the word of the beginning of Christ.*

lowest rank may teach his master how a Christian should live. A child may thus teach a parent how he should live, and his daily walk may furnish to the parent lessons of inestimable value. Neighbours may thus teach neighbours; and strangers may learn of strangers. Every Christian has a knowledge of the way to be saved which it would be of the highest value to others to know, and is qualified to tell the rich, and proud, and learned sinner, that about himself and of the final destiny of man of which he is now wholly ignorant. Let it be remembered, also, that the world derives its views of the nature of religion from the lives and conduct of its professed friends. It is not from the Bible, or from the pulpit, or from books, that men learn what Christianity is ; it is from the daily walk of those who profess to be its friends ; and every day we live, a wife, a child, a neighbour, or a stranger, is forming *some* view of the nature of religion from what they see in us. How important, therefore, it is that we so live as to communicate to them just views of what constitutes religion !

CHAPTER VI.
ANALYSIS OF THE CHAPTER.

In ch. v. 10, 11, the apostle had said that the Lord Jesus was called to the office of high priest after the order of Melchisedek, and that there were many things to be said of him which were not easy to be understood. They had not, he says, advanced as far in the knowledge of the true religion as might have been reasonably expected, but had rather gone back ; ch. v. 12—14. The design of this chapter seems to be to warn them against the danger of going back *entirely*, and to encourage them to make the highest attainments possible in the knowledge of Christianity, and in the divine life. The apostle would keep them from entire apostasy, and would excite them to make all the advances which they possibly could

make, and particularly he designs to prepare them to receive what he had yet to say about the higher doctrines of the Christian religion. In doing this he presents the following considerations.

(1.) An exhortation to leave the elements or rudiments of the Christian religion, and to go on to the contemplation of the higher doctrines. The elements were the doctrines of repentance, faith, laying on of hands, the resurrection of the dead, and eternal judgment. These entered into the very nature of Christianity. They were its first principles, and were indispensable. The higher doctrines related to other matters, which the apostle called them now to contemplate ; vers. 1—3.

(2.) He warns them, in the most solemn manner, against apostasy. He assures them that *if* they should apostatize, it would be impossible to renew them again. They could not fall away from grace and again be renewed ; they could not, after having been Christians and then apostatizing, be recovered. Their fall in that case would be final and irrecoverable, for there was no other way by which they could be saved ; and by rejecting the Christian scheme, they would reject the only plan by which they could ever be brought to heaven. By this solemn consideration, therefore, he warns them of the danger of going back from their exalted hopes, or of neglecting the opportunities which they had to advance to the knowledge of the higher truths of religion ; vers. 4—6.

(3.) This sentiment is illustrated (vers. 7, 8) by a striking and beautiful figure drawn from agriculture. The sentiment was, that they who did not improve their advantage, and grow in the knowledge of the gospel, but who should go back and apostatize, would inevitably be destroyed. They *could not* be renewed and saved. It will be says the apostle, as it is

foundation of repentance from
a ch.9. 14.   b ch.11.6.

dead ^a words, and of faith ^b toward
God,

with the earth. That which receives the rain that falls, and that bears its proper increase for the use of man, partakes of the divine blessing. That which does not — which bears only thorns and briers—is rejected, and is nigh to cursing, and will be burned with fire.

(4.) Yet the apostle says, he hoped better things of them. They had, indeed, receded from what they had been. They had not made the advances which he says they might have done. But still, there was reason to hope that they would not wholly apostatize, and be cast off by God. They *had* shown that they had true religion, and he believed that God would not forget the evidence which they had furnished that they loved him ; vers. 9, 10.

(5.) He expresses his earnest wish that they *all* would show the same diligence until they attained the full assurance of hope ; vers. 11, 12.

(6.) To encourage them in this, he refers them to the solemn oath which God had taken, and his sacred covenant with them confirmed by an oath, in order that they might have true consolation, and be sustained in the temptations and trials of life. That hope was theirs. It was sure and steadfast. It entered into that within the veil; it had been confirmed by him who had entered heaven as the great High Priest after the order of Melchisedek; vers. 13—20. By such considerations he would guard them from the danger of apostasy ; he would encourage them to diligence in the divine life; and he would seek to prepare them to welcome the more high and difficult doctrines of the Christian religion.

1. *Therefore.* "Since, as was stated in the previous chapter, you *ought* to be capable of comprehending the higher doctrines of religion ; since those doctrines are adapted to those who have been for a considerable time professors of Christianity, and have had opportunities of growing in knowledge and grace—as much as strong

meat is for those of mature years— leave now the elements of Christian doctrine, and go on to understand its higher mysteries." The idea is, that to those who had so long been acquainted with the way of salvation, the elements of Christianity were no more adapted than milk was for grown persons. ¶ *Leaving.* Dismissing ; intermitting ; passing by the consideration of with a view to advance to something higher. The apostle refers to his discussion of the subject, and also to their condition. He wished to go on to the contemplation of higher doctrines, and he desired that they should no longer linger around the mere elements. "Let us advance to a higher state of knowledge than the mere elements of the subject." On the sense of the word "leaving," or quitting with a view to engage in something else, see Matt. iv. 20, 22 ; v. 24. ¶ *The principles.* Marg. *The word of the beginning of Christ.* Tindal renders it, "let us leave the doctrine pertaining to the beginning of a Christian man." Coverdale, "let us leave the doctrine pertaining to the beginning of a Christian life." On the word "principles" see Note ch. v. 12. The Greek there, indeed, is not the same as in this place, but the idea is evidently the same. The reference is to what he regarded as the very elements of the Christian doctrine; and the meaning is, "let us no longer linger here. We should go on to higher attainments. We should wholly understand the system. We should discuss and receive its great principles. You have been long enough converted to have understood these ; but you linger among the very elementary truths of religion. But you cannot remain here. You must either advance or recede; and if you do not go forward, you will go back into entire apostasy, when it will be *impossible* to be renewed." The apostle here, therefore, does not refer to his *discussion* of the points under consideration as the main thing, but to *their state* as one of danger; and in writing to them he was not content to discuss the elements of religion as being alone fitted to their condition, but would have them make higher attainments, and advance to the more elevated principles of the gospel. ¶ *Of the doctrine.* Literally, "*the word*" —λόγον—"reason, or doctrine of the beginning of Christ." That is, the word or reason that pertains to the elements of his system; the first principles of Christian doctrine. ¶ *Of Christ.* Which pertain to the Messiah. Either that which he taught, or that which is taught of him and his religion. Most probably it is the latter —that which pertains to the Messiah, or to the Christian revelation. The idea is, that there is a set of truths which may be regarded as lying at the foundation of Christian doctrine, and those truths they had embraced, but had not advanced beyond them. ¶ *Let us go on.* Let us advance to a higher state of knowledge and holiness. The reference is alike to his discussion of the subject, and to their advancement in piety and in knowledge. He would not linger around these elements in the discussion, nor would he have tnem linger at the threshold of the Christian doctrines. ¶ *Unto perfection;* comp. Notes ch. ii. 10. The word here is used, evidently, to denote an advanced state of Christian knowledge and piety; or the more elevated Christian doctrines, and the holier living to which it was their duty to attain. It does not refer solely to the intention of the apostle to *discuss* the more elevated doctrines of Christianity, but *to such an advance as would secure them from the danger of apostasy.* If it should be said, however, that the word "*perfection*" is to be understood in the most absolute and unqualified sense, as denoting entire freedom from sin, it may be remarked, (1.) that this does not prove that they ever attained to it, nor should this be adduced as a text to show that such an attainment is ever made. To exhort a man to do a thing— however reasonable— is no proof in itself that it is ever done. (2.) It *is* proper to exhort Christians to aim at entire perfection. Even if none have ever reached that

point on earth, that fact does not make it any the less desirable or proper to aim at it. (3.) There is much in making an honest attempt to be perfectly holy, even though we should not attain to it in this life. No man accomplishes much who does not aim high. ¶ *Not laying again the foundation.* Not laying down—as one does a foundation for an edifice. The idea is, that they were not to begin and build all this over again. They were not to make it necessary to lay down again the very cornerstones, and the foundations of the edifice, but since these *were* laid already, they were to go on and build the superstructure and complete the edifice. ¶ *Of repentance from dead works.* From works that *cause* death or condemnation; or that have no vitality or life. The reference may be either to those actions which were sinful in their nature, or to those which related to the *forms* of religion, where there was no spiritual life. This was the character of much of the religion of the Jews; and conversion to the true religion consisted greatly in repentance for having relied on those heartless and hollow forms. It is possible that the apostle referred mainly to these, as he was writing to those who had been Hebrews. When formalists are converted, one of the first and the main exercises of their minds in conversion, consists in deep and genuine sorrow for their dependence on those forms. Religion is life; and irreligion is a state of spiritual death, (comp. Notes on Eph. ii. 1), whether it be in open transgression, or in false and hollow forms of religion. The apostle has here stated what is the first element of the Christian religion. It consists in genuine sorrow for sin, and a purpose to turn from it; see Note Matt. iii. 2. ¶ *And of faith toward God;* see Note on Mark xvi. 16. This is the *second* element in the Christian system. Faith is everywhere required in order to salvation, but it is usually faith *in the Lord Jesus* that is spoken of; see Acts xx. 21. Here, however, faith *in God* is particularly referred to. But there is no essential difference. It is faith in God in regard to

2 Of the doctrine of baptisms, [a] and of laying on [b] of hands, and of [c]

a Ac.19.4,5.   b Ac.8.17.

his existence and perfections, and to his plan of saving men. It includes, therefore, faith in his message and messenger, and thus embraces the plan of salvation by the Redeemer. There is but one God—"the God and Father of our Lord Jesus Christ;" and he who believes in the true God believes in him as Father, Son, and Holy Ghost; the Author of the plan of redemption, and the Saviour of lost men. No one can believe *in the true God* who does not believe in the Saviour; comp. John v. 23; xvii. 3. He who supposes that he confides *in any other* God than the Author of the Christian religion, worships a being of the imagination as really as though he bowed down to a block of wood or stone. If Christianity is true, there is no such God as the infidel professes to believe in, any more than the God of the Brahmin has an existence. To believe *in God*, therefore, is to believe in him as he *actually exists*— as the true God—the Author of the great plan of salvation by the Redeemer. It is needless to attempt to show that faith in the true God is essential to salvation. How can he be saved who has no *confidence* in the God that made him?

2. *Of the doctrine of baptisms.* This is mentioned as the *third* element or principle of the Christian religion. The Jews made much of various kinds of *washings,* which were called *baptisms;* see Note Mark vii. 4. It is supposed also, that they were in the practice of baptizing proselytes to their religion; Note Matt. iii. 6. Since they made so much of various kinds of ablution, it was important that the true doctrine on the subject should be stated as one of the elements of the Christian religion, that they might be recalled from superstition, and that they might enjoy the benefits of what was designed to be an important aid to piety—the true doctrine of baptisms. It will be observed that the plural form is used here— *baptisms.* There are two baptisms

resurrection of the dead, and of eternal judgment.

c Ac.17.31; 26.8.

whose necessity is taught by the Christian religion—baptism by water, and by the Holy Ghost; the first of which is an emblem of the second. These are stated to be among the *elements* of Christianity, or the things which Christian converts would first learn. The necessity of both is taught. He that believeth and is *baptized* shall be saved; Mark xvi. 16. "Except a man be born of water and of the Spirit, he cannot enter into the kingdom of God," John iii. 5. On the baptism of the Holy Ghost, see Notes on Matt. iii. 11; Acts i. 5; comp. Acts xix. 1—6. To understand the true doctrine respecting baptism was one of the first principles to be learned then as it is now, as baptism is the rite by which we are *initiated* into the Church. This was supposed to be so simple that young converts could understand it as one of the elements of the true religion, and the teaching on that subject now should be made so plain that the humblest disciple may comprehend it. If it was an element or first principle of religion; if it was presumed that any one who entered the Church could understand it, can it be believed that it was then so perplexing and embarrassing as it is often made now? Can it be believed that a vast array of learning, and a knowledge of languages and a careful inquiry into the customs of ancient times, was needful in order that a candidate for baptism should understand it? The truth is, that it was probably regarded as among the most simple and plain matters of religion; and every convert was supposed to understand that the application of water to the body in this ordinance, in any mode, was designed to be merely emblematic of the influences of the Holy Ghost. ¶ *And of laying on of hands.* This is the *fourth* element or principle of religion. The Jews practised the laying on of hands on a great variety of occasions. It was done when a blessing was imparted to any one; when prayer was made for one; and when they offered sacrifice they laid their hands on the head of the victim, confessing their sins; Lev. xvi. 21; xxiv. 14; Num. viii. 12. It was done on occasions of solemn consecration to office, and when friend supplicated the divine favour on friend. In like manner, it was often done by the Saviour and the apostles. The Redeemer laid his hands on children to bless them, and on the sick when he healed them; Matt. xix. 13; Mark v. 23; Matt. ix. 18. In like manner the apostles laid hands on others in the following circumstances. (1.) In healing the sick; Acts xxviii. 8. (2.) In ordination to office; 1 Tim. v. 22; Acts vi. 6. (3.) In imparting the miraculous influences of the Holy Spirit; Acts viii. 17, 19; xix. 6. The true doctrine respecting the design of laying on the hands, is said here to be one of the elements of the Christian religion. That the custom of laying on the hands as symbolical of imparting spiritual gifts, prevailed in the Church in the time of the apostles, no one can doubt. But on the question whether it is to be regarded as of perpetual obligation in the Church, we are to remember, (1.) That the apostles were endowed with the power of imparting the influences of the Holy Ghost in a miraculous or extraordinary manner. It was with reference to such an imparting of the Holy Spirit that the expression is used in each of the cases where it occurs in the New Testament. (2.) The Saviour did not appoint the imposition of the hands of a "bishop" to be one of the rites or ceremonies to be observed perpetually in the Church. The injunction to be baptized and to observe his supper is positive, and is universal in its obligation. But there is no such command respecting the imposition of hands. (3.) No one now is intrusted with the power of imparting the Holy Spirit in that manner. There is no class of officers in the Church, that can make good their claim to any such power. What evidence is there that the Holy Spirit is imparted at the rite of "confirmation?" (4.) It is liable to be abused, or to lead persons to substitute the

form for the thing; or to think that because they have been "confirmed," that therefore they are sure of the mercy and favour of God. Still, if it be regarded as a *simple form of admission to a church*, without claiming that it is enjoined by God, or that it is connected with any authority to impart the Holy Spirit, no objection can be made to it any more than there need be to any other form of recognising Church membership. Every pastor has a right, if he chooses, to lay his hands on the members of his flock, and to implore a blessing on them; and such an act on making a profession of religion would have much in it that would be appropriate and solemn. ¶ *And of resurrection of the dead.* This is mentioned as the *fifth* element or principle of the Christian religion. This doctrine was denied by the Sadducees, (Mark xii. 18; Acts xxiii. 8), and was ridiculed by philosophers; Acts xvii. 32. It was, however, clearly taught by the Saviour, (John v. 28, 29), and became one of the cardinal doctrines of his religion. By the resurrection of the dead, however, in the New Testament, there is more intended than the resurrection of the *body*. The question about the resurrection included the whole inquiry about the future state, or whether man would *live at all* in the future world; comp. Notes on Matt. xxii. 23; Acts xxiii. 6. This is one of the most important subjects that can come before the human mind, and one on which man has felt more perplexity than any other. The belief of the resurrection of the dead is an elementary article in the system of Christianity. It lies at the foundation of all our hopes. Christianity is designed to prepare us for a future state; and one of the first things, therefore, in the preparation, is to *assure* us there *is* a future state, and to tell us what it is. It is, moreover, a *peculiar* doctrine of Christianity. The belief of the resurrection is found in no other system of religion, nor is there a ray of light shed upon the future condition of man by any other scheme of philosophy or religion. ¶ *And of eternal judgment.* This is the *sixth* element or principle

3 And this will we do, if *a* God permit.

4 For *it is* impossible *b* for those

a Ja.4.15.   *b* Matt.5.13; 12.31,32; John 15.6; ch.10.26; 2Pe.2.20,21; 1John 5.16.

who were once enlightened, and have tasted of the heavenly gift, and were made partakers of the Holy Ghost.

of religion. It is, that there will be a judgment whose consequences will be eternal. It does not mean, of course, that the *process* of the judgment will be eternal, or that the judgment-day will continue for ever; but that the *results* or *consequents* of the decision of that day will continue for ever. There will be no appeal from the sentence, nor will there be any reversal of the judgment then pronounced. What is decided then will be determined for ever. The approval of the righteous will fix their state eternally in heaven, and in like manner the condemnation of the wicked will fix their doom for ever in hell. This doctrine was one of the earliest that was taught by the Saviour and his apostles, and is inculcated in the New Testament perhaps with more frequency than any other; see Matt. xxv.; Acts xvii. 31. That the consequences or results of the judgment will be *eternal*, is abundantly affirmed; see Matt. xxv. 46; John v. 29; 2 Thess. i. 9; Mark ix. 45, 48.

3. *And this will we do.* We will make these advances towards a higher state of knowledge and piety. Paul had confidence that they would do it (see vers. 9, 10), and though they had lingered long around the elements of Christian knowledge, he believed that they would yet go on to make higher attainments. ¶ *If God permit.* This is not to be interpreted as if God was *unwilling* that they should make such advances, or as if it were *doubtful* whether he would allow it if they made an honest effort, and their lives were spared; but it is a phrase used to denote their *dependence* on him. It is equivalent to saying, "if he would spare their lives, their health, and their reason; if he would continue the means of grace, and would impart his Holy Spirit; if he would favour their efforts and crown them with success, they would make these advances." In reference to *anything*

that we undertake, however pleasing to God in itself, it is proper to recognise our entire dependence on God; see James iv. 13—15; comp. Notes on John xv. 5.

4. *For it is impossible.* It is needless to say that the passage here (vers. 4 – 6), has given occasion to much controversy, and that the opinions of commentators and of the Christian world are yet greatly divided in regard to its meaning. On the one hand, it is held that the passage is not intended to describe those who are true Christians, but only those who have been awakened and enlightened, and who then fall back; and on the other it is maintained that it refers to those who *are* true Christians, and who then apostatize. The contending parties have been Calvinists and Arminians; each party, in general, interpreting it according to the views which are held on the question about falling from grace. I shall endeavour, as well as I may be able, to state the true meaning of the passage by an examination of the words and phrases in detail, observing here, in general, that it seems to me that it refers to true Christians: that the object is to keep them from apostasy, and that it teaches that if they should apostatize, it would be impossible to renew them again or to save them. That it refers to true Christians will be apparent from these considerations. (1.) Such is the sense which would strike the great mass of readers. Unless there were some theory to defend, the great body of readers of the New Testament would consider the expression here used as describing true Christians. (2.) The connection demands such an interpretation. The apostle was addressing Christians. He was endeavouring to keep them from apostasy. The object was not to keep those who were awakened and enlightened from apostasy, but it was to preserve those who were already in the Church of

Christ, from going back to perdition. The kind of exhortation appropriate to those who were awakened and convicted, but who were not truly converted, would be *to become converted;* not to warn them of the danger of *falling away.* Besides, the apostle would not have said of such persons that they *could not* be converted and saved. But of sincere Christians it might be said with the utmost propriety, that they *could not* be renewed again and be saved if they should fall away—because they rejected the only plan of salvation after they had tried it, and renounced the only scheme of redemption after they had tasted its benefits. If that plan could not save them, what could? If they neglected that, by what other means could they be brought to God? (3.) This interpretation accords, as I suppose, with the exact meaning of the phrases which the apostle uses. An examination of those phrases will show that he refers to those who are sincere believers. The phrase "it is impossible" obviously and properly denotes absolute impossibility. It has been contended, by Storr and others, that it denotes only great difficulty. But the meaning which would at first strike all readers would be that *the thing could not be done;* that it was not merely very difficult, but absolutely impracticable. The word — *'αδύνατον* —occurs only in the New Testament in the following places, in all which it denotes that the thing could not be done; Matt. xix. 26; Mark x. 27, "With men this is impossible;" that is, men could not save one who was rich, implying that the thing was wholly beyond human power. Luke xviii. 27, "The things which are impossible with men are possible with God"—referring to the same case; Acts xiv. 8, "A man of Lystra, *impotent* in his feet;" that is, who was wholly *unable* to walk; Rom. viii. 3, "For what the law could not do;" what was absolutely *impossible* for the law to accomplish; that is, to save men; Heb. vi. 18, "In which it was *impossible* for God to lie; Heb. x. 4, "It is not *possible* for the blood of bulls and of goats to take away sin;"

and Heb. xi. 6, "Without faith it is *impossible* to please God;" in all of these instances denoting absolute impossibility. These passages show that it is not merely a great difficulty to which the apostle refers, but that he meant to say that the thing was wholly impracticable; that it could not be done. And if this be the meaning, then it proves that *if* those referred to should fall away, they could never be renewed. Their case was hopeless, and they must perish:—that is, if a true Christian should apostatize, or fall from grace, *he never could be renewed again,* and could not be saved. Paul did not teach that he might fall away and be renewed again as often as he pleased. He had other views of the grace of God than this; and he meant to teach, that if a man should once cast off true religion, his case was hopeless, and he must perish; and by this solemn consideration—the only one that would be effectual in such a case—he meant to guard them against the danger of apostasy. ¶ *For those who were once enlightened.* The phrase "to be enlightened" is one that is often used in the Scriptures, and may be applied either to one whose understanding has been enlightened to discern his duty, though he is not converted (comp. Note John i. 9); or more commonly to one who is truly converted; see Note on Eph. i. 18. It does not of necessity refer to true Christians, though it cannot be denied that it more obviously suggests the idea that the heart is truly changed, and that it is more commonly used in that sense; comp. Ps. xix. 8. Light, in the Scriptures, is the emblem of knowledge, holiness, and happiness, and there is no impropriety here in understanding it in accordance with the more decisive phrases which follow, as referring to true Christians. ¶ *And have tasted.* To *taste* of a thing means, according to the usage in the Scriptures, to *experience,* or to *understand* it. The expression is derived from the fact that the *taste* is one of the means by which we ascertain the nature or quality of an object; comp. Matt. xvi. 28; John viii. 51; Heb. ii. 9. The proper idea here is,

5 And have tasted the good word
a ch.2.5.

of God, and the powers of *a* the
world to come,

that they had *experienced* the heavenly gift, or had learned its nature. ¶ *The heavenly gift.* The gift from heaven, or which pertains to heaven; comp. Note John iv. 10. The expression properly means some favour or gift which has descended from heaven, and may refer to any of the benefits which God has conferred on man in the work of redemption. It might include the plan of salvation; the forgiveness of sins; the enlightening, renewing, and sanctifying influences of the Holy Spirit, or any one of the graces which that Spirit imparts. The use of the article, however—" *the* heavenly gift,"—limits it to something special, as being conferred directly from heaven, and the connection would seem to demand that we understand it of some *peculiar* favour which could be conferred only on the children of God. It is an expression which *may* be applied to sincere Christians; it is at least doubtful whether it can with propriety be applied to any other. ¶ *And were made partakers of the Holy Ghost.* Partakers of the influences of the Holy Ghost—for it is only in this sense that we can partake of the Holy Spirit. We *partake* of food when we share it with others; we *partake* of pleasure when we enjoy it with others; we *partake* of spoils in war when they are divided between us and others. So we partake of the influences of the Holy Spirit when we share these influences conferred on his people. This is not language which can properly be applied to any one but a true Christian; and though it is true that an unpardoned sinner may be enlightened and awakened by the Holy Spirit, yet the language here used is not such as would be likely to be employed to describe his state. It is too clearly expressive of those influences which renew and sanctify the soul. It is as elevated language as can be used to describe the joy of the Christian, and is undoubtedly used in that sense here. If it is not, it would be difficult to find any language which would properly

express the condition of a renewed heart. Grotius, Bloomfield, and some others, understood this of the miraculous gifts of the Holy Spirit. But this is not necessary, and does not accord well with the general description here, which evidently pertains to the mass of those whom the apostle addressed.

5. *And have tasted the good word of God.* That is, either the doctrines which he teaches, and which are good, or pleasant to the soul; or the word of God which is connected with *good*, that is, which promises good. The former seems to me to be the correct meaning—that the word of God, or the truth which he taught, was itself a good. It was that which the soul desired, and in which it found comfort and peace; comp. Ps. cxix. 103; cxli. 6. The meaning here is, that they had experienced the excellency of the truth of God; they had seen and enjoyed its beauty. This is language which cannot be applied to an impenitent sinner. He has no *relish* for the truth of God; sees no beauty in it; derives no comfort from it. It is only the true Christian who has pleasure in its contemplation, and who can be said to "taste" and enjoy it. This language describes a state of mind of which every sincere Christian is conscious. It is that of pleasure in the word of God. He loves the Bible; he loves the truth of God that is preache He sees an exquisite beauty in that truth. It is not merely in its poetry; in its sublimity; in its argument; but he has now a *taste* or *relish* for the truth itself, which he had not before his conversion. Then he might have admired the Bible for its beauty of language or for its poetry; he might have been interested in preaching for its eloquence or power of argument; but now his love is for *the truth*; comp. Ps. xix. 10. There is no book that he so much delights in as the Bible; and no pleasure is so pure as that which he has in contemplating the truth; comp. Josh. xxi. 45; xxiii. 15. ¶ *And the powers of the world to come.*

6 If *a* they shall fall away, to renew them again unto repent-

a Is.1.28.

Or of the "coming age." "The age to come" was a phrase in common use among the Hebrews, to denote the future dispensation, the times of the Messiah. The same idea was expressed by the phrases "the last times," "the end of the world," &c. which are of so frequent occurrence in the Scriptures. They all denoted an age which was to succeed the old dispensation; the time of the Messiah; or the period in which the affairs of the world would be wound up; see Notes on Isa. ii. 2. Here it evidently refers to that period, and the meaning is, that they had participated in the peculiar blessings to be expected in that dispensation—to wit, in the clear views of the way of salvation, and the influences of the Holy Spirit on the soul. The word "powers" here implies that in that time there would be some extraordinary manifestation of the *power* of God. An unusual energy would be put forth to save men, particularly as evinced by the agency of the Holy Spirit on the heart. Of this "power" the apostle here says they of whom he spake had partaken. They had been brought under the awakening and renewing energy which God put forth under the Messiah, in saving the soul. They had experienced the promised blessings of the new and last dispensation; and the language here is such as appropriately describes Christians, and as indeed can be applicable to no other. It may be remarked respecting the various expressions used here (vers. 4, 5), (1.) that they are such as properly denote a renewed state. They obviously describe the condition of a Christian; and though it may be not certain that any *one* of them if taken by itself would *prove* that the person to whom it was applied was truly converted, yet taken together it is clear that they are designed to describe such a state. If they are not, it would be difficult to find any language which would be properly descriptive of the character of a sincere Christian. I

ance; seeing they crucify to themselves the Son of God afresh, and put *him* to an open shame.

regard the description here, therefore, as that which is clearly designed to denote the state of those who were born again, and were the true children of God; and it seems plain to me that no other interpretation would have ever been thought of if this view had not seemed to conflict with the doctrine of the "perseverance of the saints." (2.) There is a regular gradation here from the first elements of piety in the soul to its highest developements; and, whether the apostle so designed it or not, the language describes the successive steps by which a true Christian advances to the highest stage of Christian experience. The mind is (*a*) enlightened; then (*b*) *tastes* the gift of heaven, or has some experience of it; then (*c*) it is made to partake of the influences of the Holy Ghost; then (*d*) there is experience of the excellence and loveliness of the word of God; and (*e*) finally there is a participation of the full "powers" of the new dispensation; of the extraordinary energy which God puts forth in the gospel to sanctify and save the soul.

6. *If they shall fall away.* Literally, "and having fallen away." "There is no *if* in the Greek in this place— "having fallen away." *Dr. J. P. Wilson.* It is not an affirmation that any *had* actually fallen away, or that in fact they *would* do it; but the statement is, that *on the supposition that they had fallen away*, it would be impossible to renew them again. It is the same as supposing a case which in fact might never occur:— as if we should say, "had a man fallen down a precipice it would be impossible to save him," or " had the child fallen into the stream he would certainly have been drowned." But though this literally means, "having fallen away," yet the sense in the connection in which it stands is not improperly expressed by our common translation. The Syriac has given a version which is remarkable, not as a correct translation, but as showing

what was the prevailing belief in the
time in which it was made, (probably.
the first or second century), in regard
to the doctrine of the perseverance of
the saints. "For it is impossible that
they who have been baptized, and who
have tasted the gift which is from
heaven, and have received the spirit
of holiness, and have tasted the good
word of God, and the power of the
coming age, should again sin, so that
they should be renewed again to repentance, and again crucify the Son
of God and put him to ignominy."
The word rendered "fall away" means
properly "to fall near by any one ;"
"to fall in with or meet ;" and thus
to fall aside from, to swerve or deviate
from ; and here means undoubtedly to
apostatize from, and implies an entire
renunciation of Christianity, or a
going back to a state of Judaism,
heathenism, or sin. The Greek word
occurs nowhere else in the New Testament. It is material to remark
here that the apostle does not say
that any true Christian ever had fallen
away. He makes a statement of
what would occur on the supposition
that such a thing should happen—but
a statement may be made of what
would occur on the supposition that a
certain thing should take place, and
yet it be morally certain that the
event never would happen. It would
be easy to suppose what would happen if the ocean should overflow a
continent, or if the sun should cease
to rise, and still there be entire certainty that such an event never would
occur. ¶ To renew them again. Implying that they had been before renewed, or had been true Christians.
The word "again"—πάλιν—supposes
this; and this passage, therefore, con-
firms the considerations suggested
above, showing that they were true
Christians who were referred to.
They had once repented, but it would
be impossible to bring them to this
state again. This declaration of
course is to be read in connection
with the first clause of ver. 4, "It is
impossible to renew again to repentance those who once were true Christians should they fall away." I know
of no declaration more unambiguous

than this. It is a positive declaration.
It is not that it would be very difficult
to do it ; or that it would be impossible for man to do it, though it might
be done by God ; it is an unequivocal
and absolute declaration that it would
be utterly impracticable that it should
be done by any one, or by any means ;
and this, I have no doubt, is the meaning of the apostle. Should a Christian fall from grace, he must perish.
He never could be saved. The reason of this the apostle immediately
adds. ¶ Seeing. This word is not
in the Greek, though the sense is expressed. The Greek literally is, "having again crucified to themselves the
Son of God." The reason here given
is, that the crime would be so great,
and they would so effectually exclude
themselves from the only plan of salvation, that they could not be saved.
There is but one way of salvation.
Having tried that, and then renounced it, how could they then be saved ?
The case is like that of a drowning
man. If there was but one plank by
which he could be saved, and he
should get on that and then push it
away and plunge into the deep, he
must die. Or if there was but one
rope by which the shore could be
reached from a wreck, and he should
cut that and cast it off, he must die.
Or if a man were sick, and there was
but one kind of medicine that could
possibly restore him, and he should
deliberately dash that away, he must
die. So in religion. There is but one
way of salvation. If a man deliberately rejects that, he must perish.
¶ They crucify to themselves the Son
of God afresh. Our translators have
rendered this as if the Greek were
—ἀνασταυροῦντας πάλιν—crucify again,
and so it is rendered by Chrysostom,
by Tindal, Coverdale, Beza, Luther,
and others. But this is not properly
the meaning of the Greek. The word
ἀνασταυρόω – is an intensive word, and
is employed instead of the usual word
"to crucify" only to denote emphasis.
It means that such an act of apostasy
would be equivalent to crucifying him
in an aggravated manner. Of course
this is to be taken figuratively. It
could not be literally true that they

would thus crucify the Redeemer. The meaning is, that their conduct would be *as if* they had crucified him; it would bear a strong resemblance to the act by which the Lord Jesus was publicly rejected and condemned to die. The act of crucifying the Son of God was the great crime which outpeers any other deed of human guilt. Yet the apostle says that should they who had been true Christians fall away and reject him, they would be guilty of a similar crime. It would be a public and solemn act of rejecting him. It would show that if they had been there they would have joined in the cry "crucify him, crucify him." The *intensity* and *aggravation* of such a crime perhaps the apostle meant to indicate by the intensive or emphatic ἀνὰ in the word ἀνασταυροῦντας. Such an act would render their salvation impossible, because (1.) the crime would be aggravated beyond that of those who rejected him and put him to death — for they knew not what they did; and (2.) because it would be a rejection of the only possible plan of salvation after they had had experience of its power and known its efficacy. The phrase "to themselves," Tindal renders, "as concerning themselves." Others, "as far as in them lies," or as far as they have ability to do. Others, "to their own heart." Probably Grotius has suggested the true sense. "They do it *for themselves.* They make the act their own. It is as if they did it themselves ; and they are to be regarded as having done the deed." So we make the act of another our own when we authorize it beforehand, or approve of it after it is done. ¶ *And* put him *to an open shame.* Make him a public example; or hold him up as worthy of death on the cross ; see the same word explained in the Notes on Matt. i. 19, in the phrase "make her a public example." The word occurs nowhere else in the New Testament. Their apostasy and rejection of the Saviour would be like holding him up publicly as deserving the infamy and ignominy of the cross. A great part of the crime attending the crucifixion of the

Lord Jesus, consisted in exhibiting him to the passing multitude as deserving the death of a malefactor. Of that sin they would partake who should reject him, for they would thus show that they regarded his religion as an imposture, and would in a public manner hold him up as worthy only of rejection and contempt. Such, it seems to me, is the fair meaning of this much-disputed passage—a passage which would never have given so much perplexity if it had not been supposed that the obvious interpretation would interfere with some prevalent articles of theology. The passage *proves* that if true Christians should apostatize, it would be impossible to renew and save them. If then it should be asked whether I believe that any true Christian ever did, or ever will fall from grace, and wholly lose his religion, I would answer unhesitatingly, *no ;* comp. Notes on John x. 27, 28; Rom. viii. 38, 39 ; Gal. vi. 4. If then it be asked what was the *use* of a warning like this, I answer, (1.) it would show the great *sin* of apostasy from God if it were to occur. It is proper to state the greatness of an act of sin, though it might never occur, in order to show how it would be regarded by God. (2.) Such a statement might be one of the most effectual means of preserving from apostasy. To state that a fall from a precipice would cause certain death, would be one of the most certain means of preserving one from falling ; to affirm that arsenic would be certainly fatal, is one of the most effectual means of preventing its being taken ; to know that fire certainly destroys, is one of the most sure checks from the danger. Thousands have been preserved from going over the Falls of Niagara by knowing that there would be no possibility of escape ; and so effectual has been this knowledge that it has preserved all from such a catastrophe, except the very few who have gone over by accident. So in religion. The knowledge that apostasy would be fatal, and there could be no hope of being saved should it once occur would be a more effectual preventive

7 For the earth which drinketh in the rain that cometh oft upon it, and bringeth forth herbs meet for

of the danger than all the other means that could be used. If a man believed that it would be an easy matter to be restored again should he apostatize, he would feel little solicitude in regard to it ; and it has occurred in fact, that they who suppose that this may occur, have manifested little of the care to walk in the paths of strict religion, which should have been evinced. (3.) It may be added, that the means used by God to preserve his people from apostasy, have been entirely effectual. There is no evidence that one has ever fallen away who was a true Christian, (comp. John x. 27, 28, and 1 John ii. 19) ; and to the end of the world it will be true that the means which he uses to keep his people from apostasy will not in a single instance fail.

[This view seems not opposed to the doctrine of the saint's perseverance. It professes indeed, to meet the objection usually raised from the passage, if not in a new mode, yet in a mode different from that commonly adopted by orthodox expositors. Admitting that *true* Christians are intended, it is asserted only, that if they *should* fall, their recovery would be impossible. It is not said that they ever *have* fallen or *will* fall. " The apostle .n thus giving judgment on the case, if it should happen, does not declare that it actually does." And as to the use of supposing a case which never can occur, it is argued that *means* are constantly used to bring about that which the decree or determination of God had before rendered certain. These exhortations are the means by which perseverance is secured.

Yet it may be doubted, whether there be any thing in the passage to convince us, that the apostle has introduced an *impossible* case. He seems rather to speak of that which *might* happen, of which there was *danger*. If the reader incline to this view, he will apply the description to professors, and learn from it how far these may go, and yet fall short of the mark But how would this suit the apostle's design ? Well. If *professors* may go *so far*, how much is this fact fitted to arouse ALL to vigilance and inquiry. We, notwithstanding our gifts and *apparent* graces, may not be *true* Christians, may, therefore, not be *secure*, may fall away and sink, under the doom of him whom it is im-

them 1 by whom it is dressed, receiveth blessing *a* from God :

1 or, *for*.   *a* Ps.65.10.

possible to renew. And he must be a very exalted Christian indeed, who does not occasionally find need of inquiry, and examination of evidences. Certainly, the whole passage may be explained in perfect consistency with this application of it. Men may be enlightened, *i. e.* well acquainted with the doctrines and duties of the Christian faith ; may have tasted of the heavenly gift, and been made partakers of the Holy Ghost in his miraculous influences, which many in primitive times enjoyed, without any sanctifying virtue ; may have tasted the good word of God, or experienced impressions of affection and joy under it, as in the case of the stony ground hearers ; may have tasted the powers of the world to come, or been influenced by the doctrine of a future state, with its accompanying rewards and punishments, —and yet not be *true* Christians. " All these things, except miraculous gifts, often take place in the hearts and consciences of men in these days, who yet continue unregenerate. They have knowledge, convictions, fears, hope, joys, and seasons of apparent earnestness, and deep concern about eternal things ; and they are endued with such gifts, as often make them acceptable and useful to others, but they are not truly *humbled ;* they are not *spiritually minded ;* religion is not their element and delight."— *Scott.*

It should be observed, moreover, that while there are many *infallible* marks of the true Christian, none of these are mentioned in this place. The persons described are not said to have been elected, to have been regenerated, to have believed, or to have been sanctified. The apostle writes very differently when describing the character and privileges of the saints, Rom. viii. 27, 30. The succeeding context, too, is supposed to favour this opinion. " They (the characters in question) are, in the following verses, compared to the ground on which the rain often falls, and beareth nothing but thorns and briars. But this is not so with true believers, for faith itself is an herb peculiar to the inclosed garden of Christ. And the apostle afterwards, discoursing of true believers, doth in many particulars distinguish them from such as may be apostates, which is supposed of the persons here intended. He ascribeth to them, in general, better things. and such as accompany salvation. He ascribes a work and labour of love, asserts their preservation, &c."— *Owen.* Our author, however, fortifies himself against the objection in the first part of this quotation, by repeating and applying at verse 7. his *principle* of exposition. "The design," says he, "is to show, that if Christians should become like the barren earth, they would be cast away and lost." Yet the attentive reader of this very ingenious exposition will observe, that the author has difficulty in carrying out his principles, and finds it necessary to introduce the *mere professor* ere he has done with the passage. "It is not supposed," says he, commenting on the 8th verse, "that a true Christian will fall away and be lost, but we may remark, that there are many *professed* Christians who seem to be in danger of such ruin. Corrupt desires are as certainly seen in their lives, as thorns on a bad soil Such are nigh unto cursing. *Unsanctified*, &c., there is nothing else which can be done for them, and they must be lost. What a thought!" Yet that the case of the professor in danger cannot very consistently be introduced by him, appears from the fact, that such ruin as is here described is suspended on a condition which never occurs. It happens *only if* the *Christian* should fall. According to the author, it is not *here* denounced *on any other supposition.* As then true Christians cannot fall, the ruin never can occur *in any case whatever.* From these premises we *dare not* draw the conclusion, that any class of professors will be given over *to* final impenitence.

As to what may be alleged concerning the *apparent* sense of the passage, or the sense which would strike "the mass of readers;" every one will judge according to the sense which himself thinks most obvious. Few perhaps would imagine that the apostle was introducing an impossible case. Nor does the "connection" stand much in the way of the application to professors. In addition to what has already been stated, let it be farther observed, that although the appropriate exhortation to awakened, yet unconverted persons would be, "to become converted; not to warn them of the danger of falling away;" yet the apostle is writing to the Hebrews at large, is addressing a body of professing Christians, concerning whom he could have no infallible assurance that *all of them* were true Christians. Therefore, it was right that they should be warned in the way the apostle has adopted. The objection leaves out of sight the important fact that *the exhortations and warnings addressed to the saints in Scripture are addressed to mixed societies, in which there may be hypocrites as well as believers.* Those who profess the faith, and associate with the church, are addressed without any decision regarding *state.* But the very existence of the warnings implies a fear that there may be some whose state is not safe. And *all*, therefore, have need to inquire whether this be their condition. How appropriate then

such warnings. This consideration, too, will furnish an answer to what has been alleged by another celebrated transatlantic writer, viz. "that whatever may be true in the divine purposes as to the final salvation of all those who are once truly regenerated. and this doctrine I feel constrained to admit, yet nothing can be plainer, than that the sacred writers have every where addressed saints in the same manner as they would ad dress those whom they considered as con stantly exposed to fall away and to perish for ever." Lastly. The phraseology of the passage does not appear to remove it out of all possible application to *mere* professors It has already been briefly explained in con sistency with such application. There is a difficulty, indeed, connected with the phrase, παλιν ανακαινιζειν εις μετανοιαν, *again* to re new to repentance; implying, as is said, that they, to whom reference is made, had been renewed *before.* But what should hinder this being understood of *reinstating in former condition*, or in possession of former privilege? Bloomfield supposes, there may be an allu sion to the non-reiteration of baptism, and Owen explains the phrase of bringing them again into a state of profession by a second renovation, and a second baptism, as a pledge thereof. The renewing he understands here *externally* of a solemn confession of faith and repentance, followed by baptism. This, says he, was their ανακαινισμος, their renovation. It would seem then that there is nothing in the phrase to prevent its interpretation on the same principle that anakainisis has been ap plied to the passage generally.]

7. *For the earth.* The design of the apostle by this comparison is apparent. It is to show the consequences of not making a proper use of all the privileges which Christians have, and the effect which would follow should those privileges fail to be improved. He says, it is like the earth. If that absorbs the rain, and produces an abundant harvest, it receives the divine blessing. If not, it is cursed, or is worthless. The design is to show that *if* Christians should become like the barren earth they would be cast away and lost. ¶ *Which drinketh in the rain.* A comparison of the earth *as if* it were "thirsty"— a comparison that is common in all languages. ¶ *That cometh oft upon it.* The frequent showers that fall. The object is to describe fertile land which is often watered with the rains of heaven. The comparison of "drink-

8 But that which beareth thorns [a] and briars is rejected, and is nigh

a Is.5.6.

unto cursing ; whose end is to be burned.

ing in" the rain is designed to distinguish a mellow soil which receives the rain, from hard or rocky land where it runs off. ¶ And bringeth forth herbs. The word herbs we now limit in common discourse to the small vegetables which die every year, and which are used as articles of food, or to such in general as have not ligneous or hard woody stems. The word here means any thing which is cultivated in the earth as an article of food, and includes all kinds of grains. ¶ Meet for them. Useful or appropriate to them. ¶ By whom it is dressed. Marg. "for whom." The meaning is, on account of whom it is cultivated. The word "dressed" here means cultivated ; comp. Gen. ii. 15. ¶ Receiveth blessing from God. Receives the divine approbation. It is in accordance with his wishes and plans, and he smiles upon it and blesses it. He does not curse it as he does the desolate and barren soil. The language is figurative, and must be used to denote that which is an object of the divine favour. God delights in the harvests which the earth brings forth ; in the effects of dews and rains and suns in causing beauty and abundance ; and on such fields of beauty and plenty he looks down with pleasure. This does not mean, as I suppose, that he renders it more fertile and abundant, for (1.) it cannot be shown that it is true that God thus rewards the earth for its fertility ; and (2.) such an interpretation would not accord well with the scope of the passage. The design is to show that a Christian who makes proper use of the means of growing in grace which God bestows upon him, and who does not apostatize, meets with the divine favour and approbation. His course accords with the divine intention and wishes, and he is a man on whom God will smile—as he seems to do on the fertile earth.

¶ But that which beareth thorns and briars is rejected. That is, by the farmer or owner. It is abandoned

as worthless. The force of the comparison here is, that God would thus deal with those who professed to be renewed if they should be like such a worthless field. ¶ And is nigh unto cursing. Is given over to execration, or is abandoned as useless. The word cursing means devoting to destruction. The sense is not that the owner would curse it in words, or imprecate a curse on it, as a man does who uses profane language, but the language is taken here from the more common use of the word curse—as meaning to devote to destruction. So the land would be regarded by the farmer. It would be valueless, and would be given up to be overrun with fire. ¶ Whose end is to be burned. Referring to the land. The allusion here is to the common practice among the Oriental and Roman agriculturists of burning bad and barren lands. An illustration of this is afforded by Pliny. " There are some who burn the stubble on the field, chiefly upon the authority of Virgil ; the principal reason for which is, that they may burn the seeds of weeds ;" Nat. Hist. xviii. 30. The authority of Virgil, to which Pliny refers, may be found in Georg. i. 84.

" Sæpe etiam steriles incendere profuit agros,

Atque levem stipulam crepitantibus urere flammis."

" It is often useful to set fire to barren lands, and burn the light stubble in crackling flames." The object of burning land in this way was to render it available for useful purposes ; or to destroy noxious weeds, and thorns, and underbrush. But the object of the apostle requires him to refer merely to the fact of the burning, and to make use of it as an illustration of an act of punishment. So, Paul says, it would be in the dealings of God with his people. If after all attempts to secure holy living, and to keep them in the paths of salvation, they should evince none of the spirit of piety, all that could be done would be

9 But, beloved, we are persuaded better things of you, and things that accompany salvation, though we thus speak.

10 For *a* God *is* not unright-

a Matt. 25. 40.

eous to forget your work and labour of love, which ye have showed toward his name, in that ye have ministered to the saints, and do minister.

to abandon them to destruction as such a field is overrun with fire. It is not supposed that a true Christian will fall away and be lost, but we may remark (1.) that there are many professed Christians who seem to be in danger of such ruin. They resist all attempts to produce in them the fruits of good living as really as some pieces of ground do to secure a harvest. Corrupt desires, pride, envy, uncharitableness, covetousness, and vanity are as certainly seen in their lives as thorns and briars are on a bad soil. Such briars and thorns you may cut down again and again; you may strike the plough deep and seem to tear away all their roots; you may sow the ground with the choicest grain, but soon the briars and the thorns will again appear, and be as troublesome as ever. No pains will subdue them, or secure a harvest. So with many a professed Christian. He may be taught, admonished, rebuked, and afflicted, but all will not do. There is essential and unsubdued perverseness in his soul, and despite all the attempts to make him a holy man, the same bad passions are continually breaking out anew. (2.) Such professing Christians are "nigh unto cursing." They are about to be abandoned for ever. Unsanctified and wicked in their hearts, there is nothing else which can be done for them, and they must be lost. What a thought! A professing Christian "nigh unto cursing!" A man, the efforts for whose salvation are about to cease for ever, and who is to be given over as incorrigible and hopeless! For such a man—in the church or out of it—we should have compassion. We have some compassion for an ox which is so stubborn that he will not work—and which is to be put to death; for a horse which is so fractious that he cannot be broken, and which is to be killed; for cattle which

are so unruly that they cannot be restrained, and which are only to be fattened for the slaughter; and even for a field which is desolate and barren, and which is given up to be overrun with briars and thorns; but how much more should we pity a man all the efforts for whose salvation fail, and who is soon to be abandoned to everlasting destruction!

9. *But, beloved, we are persuaded better things.* We confidently hope for better things respecting you. We trust that you are true Christians; that you will produce the proper fruits of holiness; that you will be saved. ¶ *Things that accompany salvation.* Things that pertain to salvation. The Greek phrase here means, "near to salvation," or things that are conjoined with salvation. So Coverdale renders it, "and that salvation is nigher." The form of expression seems to refer to what was said in ver. 8. The land overrun with briars was *nigh* to cursing; the things which Paul saw in them were *nigh* to salvation. From this verse it is evident (1.) that the apostle regarded them as sincere Christians; and (2.) that he believed they would not fall away. Though he had stated what must be the inevitable consequence if Christians *should* apostatize, yet he says that in their case he had a firm conviction that it would not occur. There is no inconsistency in this. We may be certain that if a man should take arsenic it would kill him; and yet we may have the fullest conviction that he will *not* do it. Is not this verse a clear proof that Paul felt that it was certain that true Christians would never fall away and be lost? If he supposed that they might, how could he be persuaded that it would not happen to them? Why not to them as well as to others? Learn hence, that while we assure men that *if* they should fall away

11 And we desire that every one of you do show the same diligence to the *a* full assurance of hope unto the end:

a ch.3.6,14.

they would certainly perish, we may nevertheless address them with the full persuasion that they will be saved. 10. *For God is not unrighteous.* God will do no wrong. He will not forget or fail to reward the endeavours of his people to promote his glory, and to do good. The meaning here is, that by their kindness in ministering to the wants of the saints, they had given full evidence of true piety. If God should forget that, it would be " unrighteous," (1.) because there was a propriety that it should be remembered ; and (2.) because it is expressly promised that it shall not fail of reward; Matt. x. 42. ¶ *Your work.* Particularly in ministering to the wants of the saints. ¶ *Labour of love.* Deeds of benevolence when there was no hope of recompense, or when love was the motive in doing it. ¶ *Which ye have showed toward his name.* Toward him—for the word *name* is often used to denote the person himself. They had showed that they loved God by their kindness to his people ; Matt. xxv. 40, "Inasmuch as ye have done it unto one of the least of these my brethren, ye have done it unto me." ¶ *In that ye have ministered to the saints.* You have supplied their wants. This may refer either to the fact that they contributed to supply the wants of the poor members of the church (comp. Note Gal. ii. 10), or it may refer to some special acts of kindness which they had shown to suffering and persecuted Christians. It is not possible now to know to what particular acts the apostle refers. We may learn (1.) that to show kindness to Christians, because they are Christians, is an important evidence of piety. (2.) It will in no case be unrewarded. God is not " unjust ;" and he will remember an act of kindness shown to his people—even though it be nothing but giving a cup of cold water. 11. *And we desire that every one of you.* We wish that every member of the church should exhibit the same

endeavour to do good until they attain to the full assurance of hope. It is implied here that the full assurance of hope is to be obtained by a persevering effort to lead a holy life. ¶ *The same diligence.* The same strenuous endeavour, the same ardour and zeal. ¶ *To the full assurance of hope.* In order to obtain the full assurance of hope. The word rendered "full assurance," means firm persuasion, and refers to a state of mind where there is the fullest conviction, or where there is no doubt ; see Col. ii. 2 ; 1 Thess. i. 5 ; Heb. x. 22 ; comp. Luke i. 1 ; Rom. iv. 21 ; xiv. 5 ; 2 Tim. iv. 5, 17, where the same word, in different forms, occurs. Hope is a compound emotion (Notes Eph. ii. 12), made up of an earnest *desire* for an object, and a corresponding *expectation* of obtaining it. The hope of heaven is made up of an earnest *wish* to reach heaven, and a corresponding *expectation* of it, or *reason to believe* that it will be ours. The full assurance of that hope exists where there is the highest desire of heaven, and such corresponding evidence of personal piety as to leave no doubt that it will be ours. ¶ *To the end.* To the end of life. The apostle wished that they would persevere in such acts of piety to the end of their course, as to have their hope of heaven fully established, and to leave no doubt on the mind that they were sincere Christians. Learn hence (1.) that full assurance of hope is to be obtained only by holy living. (2.) It is only when that is persevered in that it can be obtained. (3.) It is not by visions and raptures ; by dreams and revelations that it can now be acquired, for God imparts no such direct revelation now. (4.) It is usually only as the result of a life of consistent piety that such an assurance is to be obtained. No man can have it who does not persevere in holy living, and they who do obtain it usually secure it only near the end of a life of eminent devotedness to God. God *could* impart it at once when the soul

12 That ye be not slothful ^a but followers of them who through faith and patience inherit the promises.

13 For when God made promise to Abraham, because he could swear by no greater, he sware by himself,

a Pr.15.19; 2Pe.1.10.

14 Saying, ^b Surely blessing I will bless thee, and multiplying I will multiply thee.

15 And so, after he had patiently endured, he obtained the promise.

b Ge.22.16,17.

is converted, but such is the tendency of man to indolence and sloth that even good men would then relax their efforts, and sit down contented, feeling that they had now the undoubted prospect of heaven. As it is, it is held out as a prize to be won—as that whose acquisition is to cheer us in our old age, when the warfare is over, and when amidst the infirmities of years, and the near prospect of death, we need special consolation; comp. 2 Tim. iv. 6, 7. 12. *That ye be not slothful.* Indolent; inactive. This was what he was especially desirous of guarding them against. By diligent and strenuous effort only could they secure themselves from the danger of apostasy. ¶ *But followers.* Imitators—that you may live as they lived. ¶ *Of them who through faith and patience.* By faith, or confidence in God, and by patience in suffering—referring to those who in times of trial had remained faithful to God, and had been admitted to heaven. In ch. xi. the apostle has given a long list of such persevering and faithful friends of God; see Notes on that chapter. ¶ *The promise.* The promise of heaven. 13. *For when God made promise to Abraham.* That he would bless him, and multiply his seed as the stars of heaven; Gen. xxii. 16, 17. The object of introducing this example here is, to encourage those to whom the apostle was writing to persevere in the Christian life. This he does by showing that God had given the highest possible assurance of his purpose to bless his people, by an oath. Reference is made to Abraham in this argument, probably, for two reasons. (1.) To show the nature of the evidence which Christians have that they will be saved, or the ground of encouragement —being the same as that made to Abraham, and depending, as in his

case, on the promise of God; and (2.) because the *example* of Abraham was just in point. He had persevered. He had relied firmly and solely on the promise of God. He did this when appearances were much against the fulfilment of the promise, and he thus showed the advantage of perseverance and fidelity in the cause of God. ¶ *Because he could swear by no greater.* There is no being greater than God. In taking an oath among men it is always implied that the appeal is to one of superior power, who is able to punish for its infraction. But this could not occur in the case of God himself. There was no greater being than himself, and the oath, therefore, was by his own existence. ¶ *He sware by himself;* Gen. xxii.16. "By myself have I sworn;" comp. Isa. xlv. 23. In an oath of this kind God pledges his veracity; declares that the event shall be as certain as his existence; and secures it by all the perfections of his nature. The usual form of the oath is, "As I live, saith the Lord;" see Num. xiv. 21, 28; Ezek. xxxiii. 11. 14. *Saying, Surely blessing I will bless thee.* That is, I will certainly bless thee. The phrase is a Hebrew mode of expression, to denote emphasis or certainty—indicated by the repetition of a word; comp. Gen. xiv. 23; Ex. viii. 10; Joel iii. 14; Judges v. 30; xv. 16. ¶ *Multiplying I will multiply thee.* I will greatly increase thee—I will grant thee an exceedingly numerous posterity. 15. *And so, after he had patiently endured.* After he had waited for a long time. He did not faint or grow weary, but he persevered in a confident expectation of the fulfilment of what God had so solemnly promised. ¶ *He obtained the promise.* Evidently the promise referred to in the oath— that he would have a numerous pos-

16 For men verily swear by the greater : and an oath *a* for confirmation *is* to them an end of all strife.

17 Wherein God, willing more

a Ex.22.11.   b Ro.8.17.ch.11.9.

terity. The apostle intimates that he had waited for that a long time ; that his faith did not waver, and that in due season the object of his wishes was granted. To see the force of this, we are to remember (1.) that when he was called by God from Haran, and when the promise of a numerous posterity was made to him, he was seventy-five years old ; Gen. xii. 1—5. (2.) Twenty-four years elapsed after this, during which he was a sojourner in a strange land, before the manner in which this promise would be fulfilled was made known to him ; Gen. xvii. 1—16. (3.) It was only when he was an hundred years old, and when he had persevered in the belief of the truth of the promise against all the natural improbabilities of its accomplishment, that he received the pledge of its fulfilment in the birth of his son Isaac ; Gen. xxi. 1—5. (4.) The birth of that son was a pledge that the other blessings implied in the promise would be granted, and in that pledge Abraham may be said to have "received the promise." He did not actually *see* the numerous posterity of which he was to be the honoured ancestor, nor the Messiah who was to descend from him, nor the happy influences which would result to mankind from the fulfilment of the promise. But he saw the certainty that all this would occur; he saw by faith the Messiah in the distance (John viii. 56), and the numerous blessings which would result from his coming. It was a remarkable instance of faith, and one well fitted to the purpose of the apostle. It would furnish ample encouragement to the Christians to whom he wrote, to persevere in their course, and to avoid the dangers of apostasy. If Abraham persevered when *appearances* were so much against the fulfilment of what had been promised, then Christians should persevere under the clearer light and with the more distinct promises of the gospel.

abundantly to show unto the heirs *b* of promise the immutability *c* of his counsel, confirmed [1] *it* by an oath ;

c Ro.11.29.   1 interposed himself.

16. *For men verily swear by the greater.* That is, they appeal to God. They never swear by one who is inferior to themselves. The object of the apostle in this declaration is to show that as far as this could be done it had been by God. He could not indeed swear by one greater than himself, but he could make his promise as certain as an oath taken by men was when they solemnly appealed to Him. He could appeal to his own existence and veracity, which was at any time the most solemn form of an oath, and thus put the mind to rest in regard to the hope of heaven. ¶ *And an oath for confirmation.* An oath taken to confirm or establish anything. ¶ Is *to them an end of all strife.* That is, when two parties are at variance, or have a cause at issue, an oath binds them to adhere to the terms of agreement concluded on, or contracting parties bind themselves by a solemn oath to adhere to the conditions of an agreement, and this puts an end to all strife. They rest satisfied when a solemn oath has been taken, and they feel assured that the agreement will be complied with. Or it may refer to cases where a man was accused of wrong before a court, and where he took a solemn oath that the thing had not been done, and his oath was admitted to be sufficient to put an end to the controversy. The general meaning is clear, that in disputes between man and man, an appeal was made to an oath, and that was allowed to settle it. The connection here is, that as far as the case would admit of, the same thing was done by God. His oath by himself made his promise firm.

17. *Wherein God.* On account of which ; or since an oath had this effect, God was willing to appeal to it in order to assure his people of salvation. ¶ *Willing more abundantly.* In the most abundant manner, or to make the case as sure as possible. It does not mean more abundantly than in

18 That by two immutable things, in which *it was* impossible for God to *a* lie, we might have a

a Tit.1.2.

strong consolation, who have fled for refuge to lay hold *b* upon the hope set before us :

b 1 Tim.6.12.

the case of Abraham, but that he was willing to give the most ample assurance possible. Coverdale renders it correctly, " very abundantly." ¶ *The heirs of promise*. The heirs to whom the promise of life pertained ; that is, all who were interested in the promises made to Abraham — thus embracing the heirs of salvation now. ¶ *The immutability of his counsel*. His fixed purpose. He meant to show in the most solemn manner that his purpose would not change. The plans of God never change ; and all the hope which we can have of heaven is founded on the fact that his purpose is immutable. If he changed his plans ; if he was controlled by caprice ; if he willed one thing to-day and another thing to-morrow, who could confide in him, or who would have any hope of heaven ? No one would know what to expect ; and no one could put confidence in him. The farmer ploughs and sows because he believes that the laws of nature are settled and fixed ; the mariner ventures into unknown seas because the needle points in one direction ; we plant an apple-tree because we believe it will produce apples, a peach because it will produce peaches, a pear because it will produce a pear. But suppose there were no settled laws, that all was governed by caprice ; who would know what to plant ? Who then would plant anything ? So in religion. If there were nothing fixed and settled, who would know what to do ? If God should change his plans by caprice, and save one man by faith to-day and condemn another for the same faith to-morrow ; or if he should pardon a man to-day and withdraw the pardon to-morrow, what security could we have of salvation ? How grateful, therefore, should we be that God has an *immutable counsel*, and that this is confirmed by a solemn oath ! No one could honour a God that had *not* such an immutability of purpose ; and all the hope which man *can* have of heaven

is in the fact that He is unchanging. ¶ *Confirmed* it *by an oath.* Marg. *Interposed himself*. Tindal and Coverdale, " added an oath." The Greek is, " interposed with an oath "—ἐμεσί- τευσεν ὅρκῳ. The word here used — μεσιτεύω—means to mediate or intercede for one ; and then to intervene or interpose. The meaning here is, that *he interposed an oath* between himself and the other party by way of a confirmation or pledge.

18. *That by two immutable things*. What the "two immutable things" here referred to are, has been made a matter of question among commentators. Most expositors, as Doddridge, Whitby, Rosenmüller, Koppe, and Calvin, suppose that the reference is to the *promise* and the *oath* of God, each of which would be a firm ground of the assurance of salvation, and in each of which it would be impossible for God to lie. Prof. Stuart supposes that the reference is to *two oaths*—the oath made to Abraham, and that by which the Messiah was made High Priest according to the order of Melchisedek ; Ps. cx. 4 ; Heb. v. 6, 10. He supposes that thus the salvation of believers would be amply secured, by the promise that Abraham should have a Son, the Messiah, in whom all the families of the earth would be blessed, and in the oath that this Son should be High Priest for ever. But to this interpretation it may be objected that the apostle seems to refer to two things distinct from each other in their nature, and not to two acts of the same kind. There are two kinds of security referred to, whereas the security furnished according to this interpretation would be the same — that arising from an oath. However numerous the oaths might be, still it would be security of the same kind, and if one of them were broken no certainty could be derived from the other. On the supposition, however, that he refers to the *promise* and the *oath*, there would be two kinds of as-

19 Which *hope* we have as an anchor of the soul, both sure and steadfast, and which entereth into that within *a* the veil;

a Le.16.15.

20 Whither *b* the forerunner is for us entered, *even* Jesus, made an high priest for ever after the order of Melchisedek.*c*

b ch.4.14.   c ch.7.17.

surance of different kinds. On the supposition that the *promise* was disregarded—if such a supposition may be made still there would be the security of the *oath*—and thus the assurance of salvation was two-fold. It seems to me, therefore, that the apostle refers to the *promise* and to the *oath* of God, as constituting the two grounds of security for the salvation of his people. Those things were both unchangeable, and when his word and oath are once passed, what he promises is secure. ¶ *In which* it was *impossible for God to lie.* That is, it would be contrary to his nature; it is not for a moment to be supposed; comp. Tit. i. 2, "God—that cannot lie." The impossibility is a *moral* impossibility, and the use of the word here explains the sense in which the words *impossible, cannot,* &c., are often used in the Scriptures. The meaning here is, that such was the love of God for truth; such his holiness of character, that he *could* not speak falsely. ¶ *We might have a strong consolation.* The strongest of which the mind can conceive. The consolation of a Christian is not in his own strength; his hope of heaven is not in any reliance on his own powers. His comfort is, that God has *promised* eternal life to his people, and that He cannot prove false to his word; Titus i. 2. ¶ *Who have fled for refuge.* Referring to the fact that one charged with murder fled to the city of refuge, or laid hold on an altar for security. So we guilty and deserving of death have fled to the hopes of the gospel in the Redeemer. ¶ *To lay hold upon.* To seize and hold fast—as one does an altar when he is pursued by the avenger of blood. ¶ *The hope set before us.* The hope of eternal life offered in the gospel. This is set before us as our refuge, and to this we flee when we feel that we are in danger of death. On the nature of *hope*, see Notes on Eph. ii. 12.

19. *Which* hope *we have as an anchor of the soul.* Hope accomplishes for the soul the same thing which an anchor does for a ship. It makes it fast and secure. An anchor preserves a ship when the waves beat and the wind blows, and as long as the anchor holds, so long the ship is safe, and the mariner apprehends no danger. So with the soul of the Christian. In the tempests and trials of life, his mind is calm as long as his hope of heaven is firm. If that gives way, he feels that all is lost. Among the heathen writers, *hope* is often compared with an anchor. So Socrates said, "To ground hope on a false supposition, is like trusting to a weak anchor." Again—"A ship ought not to trust to one anchor, nor life to one hope." *Both sure and steadfast.* Firm and secure. This refers to the *anchor.* That is fixed in the sand, and the vessel is secure. ¶ *And which entereth into that within the veil.* The allusion to the *anchor* here is dropped, and the apostle speaks simply of *hope.* The "*veil*" here refers to that which in the temple divided the holy from the most holy place; see Notes on Matt. xxi. 12. The place "within the veil"—the most holy place—was regarded as God's peculiar abode—where he dwelt by the visible symbol of his presence. That holy place was emblematic of heaven; and the idea here is, that the hope of the Christian enters into heaven itself; it takes hold on the throne of God; it is made firm by being fastened there. It is not the hope of future riches, honours, or pleasures in this life—for such a hope would not keep the soul steady; it is the hope of immortal blessedness and purity in the world beyond.

20. *Whither.* To which most holy place—heaven. ¶ *The forerunner.* The word here used occurs nowhere else in the New Testament. A *forerunner*—προδρομος—is one who goes before others to prepare the way. The

word is applied to light troops sent forward as scouts; Diod. Sic. 17. 17; comp. " Wisdom of Solomon" (*apoc.*) xii. 8. " Thou didst send wasps, forerunners of thy host, to destroy them by little and little." The meaning here is, that Jesus went *first* into the heavenly sanctuary. He led the way. He has gone there on our account, to prepare a place for us; John xiv. 3. Having such a friend and advocate there, we should be firm in the hope of eternal life, and amidst the storms and tempests around us, we should be calm. ¶ *Made an high priest for ever*; see Notes ch. v. 6, 10. To illustrate this fact, was the object for which this discussion was introduced, and which had been interrupted by the remarks occurring in this chapter on the danger of apostasy. Having warned them of this danger, and exhorted them to go on to make the highest attainments possible in the divine life, the apostle resumes the discussion respecting Melchisedek, and makes the remarks which he intended to make respecting this remarkable man; see ch. v. 11.

REMARKS.

1. We should *aim* at perfection in order that we may have evidence of piety; ver. 1. No man can be a Christian who does *not* do this, or who does not desire to be perfect as God is perfect. No one can be a Christian who is *satisfied* or *contented* to remain in sin; or who would not *prefer* to be made at once as holy as an angel—as the Lord Jesus—as God.

2. We should aim at perfection in order to make great attainments; ver. 1. No man makes any great advance in anything, who does not set his standard high. Men usually accomplish about what they expect to accomplish. If a man expects to be a quack physician, he becomes such; if he is satisfied to be a fourth-rate lawyer, he becomes such; if he is willing to be an indifferent mechanic, he advances no higher; if he has no intention or expectation of being a first-rate farmer, he will never become one. If he sincerely aims, however, to excel, he usually accomplishes his object. And it is so in religion. If

a man does not intend to be an eminent Christian, he may be certain he never will be. Religion is not produced by chance—any more than fine fruit is, or than a good harvest is. One of the principal reasons why President Edwards became so eminent a Christian, was, that in early life he adopted the following resolution, to which he appears always to have adhered, that " on the supposition that there never was to be but one individual in the world, at any one time, who was properly a complete Christian, in all respects of a right stamp, having Christianity always shining in its true lustre, and appearing excellent and lovely, from whatever part, and under whatever character viewed : *Resolved*, To act just as I would do, if I strove with all my might to be that one, who should live in my time." *Life, by S. E. Dwight, D.D.,* p. 72.

3. We should aim to acquire as much *knowledge* of religious truth as we possibly can; vers. 1, 2. True piety is *principle*. It is not fancy, or dreaming, or visions, or enthusiasm. It is based on knowledge, and does not go *beyond* that. No man has any more religion than he has *knowledge* of the way of salvation. He cannot force his religion to overstep the bounds of his knowledge; for *ignorance* contributes nothing to devotion. There may be knowledge where there is no piety; but there can be no true religion where there is no knowledge. If, therefore, a Christian wishes to make advances, he must gain a knowledge of the truth. He must understand the great doctrines of his religion. And in like manner, if we wish the next generation to be intelligent and solid Christians, we must train them up to *understand* the Bible.

4. The consequences of the judgment will be eternal; ver. 2. No truth is more solemn than this. It is this which makes the prospect of the judgment so awful. If the consequences of the sentence were to continue for a few years, or ages, or centuries only, it would be of much less importance. But who can abide

the thought of "*eternal judgment?*" Of an *eternal sentence?* . Here the most fearful and solemn sentence is for a short period. The sentence will soon expire ; or it is mitigated by the hope of a change. Pain here is brief. Disgrace, and sorrow, and heaviness of heart, and all the woes that man can inflict, soon come to an end. There is an outer limit of suffering, and no severity of a sentence, no ingenuity of man, can prolong it far. The man disgraced, and whose life is a burden, will soon die. On the cheeks of the solitary prisoner, doomed to the dungeon for life, a "mortal paleness" will soon settle down, and the comforts of an approaching release by death may soothe the anguish of his sad heart. The rack of torture cheats itself of its own purpose, and the exhausted sufferer is released. " The excess [of grief,] makes it soon mortal." But in the world of future wo the sentence will never expire ; and death will never come to relieve the sufferer. I may ask, then, of my reader, Are you prepared for the " eternal" sentence ? Are you ready to hear a doom pronounced which can never be changed ? Would you be willing to have God judge you just as you are, and pronounce such a sentence as ought to be pronounced now, and have the assurance that it would be eternal ? You seek worldly honour. Would you be willing to be doomed *always* to seek that? You aspire after wealth. Would you be willing to be doomed to aspire after that *always?* You seek pleasure— in the gay and giddy world. Would you be willing to be doomed *always* to seek after that ? You have no religion ; perhaps desire to have none. Yet would you be willing to be doomed to be *always* without religion ? You are a stranger to the God that made you. Would you be willing to be sentenced to be *always* a stranger to God? You indulge in passion, pride, envy, sensuality. Would you be willing to be sentenced *always* to the raging of these passions and lusts ? How few are they who would be willing to have an *eternal* sentence passed on them, or to be

doomed to pursue their present employments, or to cherish their present opinions for ever ! How few who would *dare* to meet a sentence which should be in strict accordance with what was *just*, and which was never to change !

5. With the righteous it should be matter of rejoicing that the judgment is to be eternal ; ver. 2. They can desire no change of the sentence which will assign them to heaven ; and it will be no small part of the joy of the heavenly world, that the results of the judgment will be everlasting. There will be no further trial ; no reversing of the sentence ; no withdrawing of the crown of glory. The righteous are the only ones who have not reason to dread a "just eternal sentence ;" and *they* will rejoice when the time shall come which will fix their doom for ever.

6. We should dread apostasy from the true religion ; ver. 4. We should habitually feel that if we should deny our Lord, and reject his religion, there would be no hope. The die would be cast ; and we must then perish for ever. By this solemn consideration God intends to preserve his people, and it is a consideration which has been so effectual that there is not the least reason to suppose that any one who has ever had any true religion, has fallen away and perished. Many have been *almost* Christians, and have then turned back to perdition (Matt. vii. 22, 23 ; Acts xxvi. 28), but there is no reason to suppose that any who have been true Christians have thus apostatized and been lost. Yet Christians are not kept without watchfulness ; they cannot be kept without the most sincere and constant endeavours to preserve themselves from falling.

7. If the sin of apostasy is so great, then every approach to it is dangerous ; and then every sin should be avoided. He that habitually indulges in sin *cannot* be a Christian ; and every sin which a sincere Christian commits should be measured by the guilt which *would* exist should it become final, and should he wholly fall away. No man can indulge in sin

nd be safe ; and no professed Christian who finds himself *disposed* to indulge in sin, should cherish the expectation of reaching heaven; vers. 4—6.

8. It is a matter of devout gratitude that God *has* kept all his true people from apostasy ; vers. 4—6. If it is true that no one who has been regenerated has ever fallen away; if the means which God has used have been effectual in a world so full of temptations, and when we have hearts so prone to evil ; and if it is the intention of God to keep all to eternal salvation who are truly converted, then it should be to us a subject of devout thankfulness and of encouragement. In view of this, we should admire the wisdom of the plan which thus secures salvation ; we should look to him with the firm assurance that he *will keep* what we have committed to him to the final day.

9. We should improve the privileges which we enjoy so as to receive a blessing from God; vers. 7, 8. It is desirable that a farm should be well cultivated so as not to be overrun with briars and thorns ; desirable that it should produce an abundant harvest, and not exhibit mere barrenness and desolation. Yet, alas, there are many professing Christians who resemble such a field of thorns, and such a scene of desolation. They produce no fruits of righteousness ; they do nothing to extend the kingdom of the Redeemer ! What can such expect but the "curse" of God? What can the end of such be but to be " burned ?"

10. God will not fail to reward his faithful people ; ver. 10. What we have done in his service, and with a sincere desire to promote his glory, unworthy of his notice as it may seem to us to be, he will not fail to reward. It may be unobserved or forgotten by the world ; nay, it may pass out of our own recollection, but it will never fail from the mind of God. Whether it be "two mites" contributed to his cause, or a "cup of cold water given to a disciple," or a life consecrated to his service, it will be alike remembered. What encouragement there is, therefore, to labour in the promotion of his glory, and to do all we can for the advancement of his kingdom !

11. Let us follow those who have inherited the promises ; ver. 12. They are worthy examples. When from their lofty seats in heaven they look back on the journey of life, though to them attended with many trials, they never regret the " faith and patience" by which they were enabled to persevere. We have most illustrious examples to imitate. They are numerous as the drops of dew, and bright as the star of the morning. It is an honour to tread in the footsteps of the holy men who have inherited the promises ; an honour to feel that we are walking in the same path, and are reaching out the hand to the same crown.

12. It is the privilege of those who are truly the children of God to enjoy strong consolation ; vers. 13 — 18. Their hope is based on that which cannot fail. God cannot lie. And when we have evidence that he has promised *us* eternal life, we may open our hearts to the full influence of Christian consolation. It may be asked, perhaps, how we may have that evidence ? Will God speak to us from heaven and assure us that we are his children ? Will he reveal our names as written in his book? Will he come to us in the night-watches and address us by name as his ? I answer, No. None of these things are we to expect. But if we have evidence that we have true repentance, and sincere faith in the Redeemer; if we love holiness and desire to lead a pure life ; if we delight in the Bible and in the people of God, then we may regard him as addressing us in the promises and oaths of his word, and assuring us of salvation. These promises belong to us, and we may apply them to ourselves. And if we have evidence that God *promises* us eternal life, why should we doubt ? We may feel that we are unworthy ; our consciences may reproach us for the errors and follies of our past lives ; but on the unchanging word and oath of God we may rely, and there we may feel secure.

CHAPTER VII.

FOR this Melchisedek, *a* king of Salem, priest of the most high

a Gen.14.18,&c.

God, who met Abraham returning from the slaughter of the kings, and blessed him ;

---

13. How invaluable is the Christian hope ! ver. 19. To us it is like the anchor to a vessel in a storm. We are sailing along the voyage of life. We are exposed to breakers, and tempests. Our bark is liable to be tossed about, or to be shipwrecked. In the agitations and troubles of life, how much we need some anchor of the soul ; something that shall make us calm and serene ! Such an anchor is found in the hope of the gospel. While that hope is firm we need fear nothing. All is then safe, and we may look calmly on, assured that we shall ride out the storm, and come at last safely into the haven of peace. Happy they who have fled for refuge to the faith of the gospel ; whose hope like a steady anchor has entered into heaven and binds the soul to the throne of God ; whose confidence in the Redeemer is unshaken in all the storms of life, and who have the assurance that when the tempest shall have beaten upon them a little longer they will be admitted to a haven of rest, where storms and tempests are for ever unknown. With such a hope we may well bear the trials of this life for the few days appointed to us on earth — for what are the longest trials here compared with that eternal rest which remains for all who love God in a brighter world ?

CHAPTER VII.

ANALYSIS OF THE CHAPTER.

In ch. v. 10, 11, the apostle had introduced the name of Melchisedek, and said that Christ was made an high priest after the same order as he. He added, that he had much to say of him, but that they were not in a state of mind then to receive or understand it. He then (ch. v. 12—14) rebukes them for the little progress which they had made in Christian knowledge ; exhorts them to go on and make higher attainments (ch. vi. 1—3) ; warns them against the danger of apostasy (ch. vi. 4—8) ; and

encourages them to hold fast their faith and hope to the end, in view of the covenant faithfulness of God (ch. vi. 9—20) ; and now returns to the subject under discussion — *the high priesthood of Christ.* His object is to show that he was superior to the Jewish high priest, and for this purpose he institutes the comparison between him and Melchisedek. The *argument* is the following :—

I. That which is drawn from the exalted rank of Melchisedek, and the fact that the ancestor of the whole Jewish priesthood and community— Abraham—acknowledged him as his superior, and rendered tribute to him. But Christ was of the order of Melchisedek, and the apostle, therefore, infers his superiority to the Jewish priesthood ; vers. 1—10. In the prosecution of this argument, the apostle dwells on the import of the name *Melchisedek* (vers. 1, 2) ; states the fact that he was without any known ancestry or descent, and that he stood alone on the pages of the sacred record, and was therefore worthy to be compared with the Son of God, who had a similar pre-eminence (ver. 3) ; urges the consideration that even Abraham, the ancestor of the whole Jewish community and priesthood, paid tithes to him, and thus confessed his inferiority (ver. 4) ; shows that he of whom a blessing was received must be superior to the one who receives it (vers. 6, 7) ; and that even Levi, the ancestor of the whole Levitical priesthood, might be said to have paid tithes in Abraham, and thus to have acknowledged his inferiority to Melchisedek, and consequently to the Son of God, who was of his " order ;" vers. 9, 10.

II. The apostle shows that *"perfection"* could not arise out of the Levitical priesthood, and that a priesthood that introduced a perfect state must be superior ; vers. 11—19. In the prosecution of this argument, he states that perfection could not be arrived at under the Hebrew economy, and that there was need that a priesthood of another order should be formed (ver. 11); that a change of the priesthood involved of necessity a change in the law or administration (ver. 12); that the necessity of change of the law also followed from the fact that the great high priest was now of another tribe than that of Levi (vers. 13, 14); that the Christian High Priest was constituted not after a commandment pertaining to the flesh and liable to change, but "after the power of an endless life"—adapted to a life that was never to change or to end (vers. 15—17); that consequently there was a disannulling of the commandment going before, because it was weak and unprofitable (ver. 18); and that the old law made *nothing* perfect, but that by the new arrangement a system of entire and eternal perfection was introduced; ver. 19.

III. The apostle shows the superiority of the priesthood of Christ to that of the Jewish system from the fact that the great High Priest of the Christian system was constituted with the solemnity of an oath; the Jewish priesthood was not; vers. 20 — 22. His priesthood, therefore, was as much more important and solemn as an oath is superior to a command; and his suretyship became as much more certain as an oath is superior to a simple promise; ver. 22.

IV. The superiority of the priesthood of Christ is further shown from the fact that under the former dispensation there were *many* priests; but here there was but *one*. There, they lived but a brief period, and then gave way to their successors; but here there was no removal by death, there was no succession, there was an unchangeable priesthood; vers. 23, 24. He infers, therefore (ver. 25), that the Christian High Priest was able to save to the uttermost all that came to the Father by him, since he ever lived to make intercession.

V. The last argument is, that under the Levitical priesthood it was necessary for the priest to offer sacrifice for his own sins as well as for

those of the people. No such necessity, however, existed in regard to the High Priest of the Christian system. He was holy, harmless, and undefiled; he had no need to offer sacrifices for his own sins; and in this respect there was a vast superiority of the Christian priesthood over the Jewish; vers. 26 — 28. The force of these several arguments we shall be able to estimate as we advance in the exposition.

1. *For this Melchisedek;* comp. Notes ch. v. 6. The name Melchisedek, from which the apostle derives a portion of his argument here, is Hebrew, צֶדֶק־מַלְכִּי, and is correctly explained as meaning *king of righteousness*—being compounded of two words —*king* and *righteousness*. *Why* this name was given to this man is unknown. Names, however, were frequently given on account of some quality or characteristic of the man; Notes on Isa. viii. 18. This name may have been given on account of his eminent integrity. The apostle calls attention to it (ver. 2,) as a circumstance worthy of notice, that his name, and the name of the city where he reigned, were so appropriate to one who, as a priest, was the predecessor of the Messiah. The account of Melchisedek, which is very brief, occurs in Gen. xiv. 18—20. The name occurs in the Bible only in Gen. xiv., Ps. cx. 4, and in this epistle. Nothing else is certainly known of him. Grotius supposes that he is the same man who in the history of Sanchoniathon is called Συδύκ—*Sydyc.* It has indeed been made a question by some whether such a person ever actually existed, and consequently whether this be a proper name. But the account in Genesis is as simple a historical record as any other in the Bible. In that account there is no difficulty whatever. It is said simply that when Abraham was returning from a successful military expedition, this man, who it seems was well known, and who was respected as a priest of God, came out to express his approbation of what he had done, and to refresh him with bread and wine. As a tribute of gratitude to him, and as a

thank-offering to God, Abraham gave nim a tenth part of the spoils which he had taken. Such an occurrence was by no means improbable, nor would it have been attended with any special difficulty if it had not been for the use which the apostle makes of it in this epistle. Yet on no subject has there been a greater variety of opinion than in regard to this man. The bare recital of the opinions which have been entertained of him would fill a volume. But in a case which *seems* to be plain from the Scripture narrative, it is not necessary even to enumerate these opinions. They only serve to show how easy it is for men to mystify a clear statement of history, and how fond they are of finding what is mysterious and marvellous in the plainest narrative of facts. That he was Shem, as the Jews suppose, or that he was the Son of God himself, as many Christian expositors have maintained, there is not the slightest evidence. That the latter opinion is false is perfectly clear—for if he were the Son of God, with what propriety could the apostle say that he "was made *like* the Son of God" (ver. 3); that is, like himself; or that Christ was constituted a priest "*after the order* of Melchisedek;" that is, that he was a type of himself? The most simple and probable opinion is that given by Josephus, that he was a pious Canaanitish prince; a personage eminently endowed by God, and who acted as the priest of his people. That he combined in himself the offices of priest and king, furnished to the apostle a beautiful illustration of the offices sustained by the Redeemer, and was in this respect, perhaps, the only one whose history is recorded in the Old Testament, who would furnish such an illustration. That his genealogy was not recorded, while that of every other priest mentioned was so carefully traced and preserved, furnished another striking illustration. In this respect, like the Son of God, he stood alone. He was not in *a line* of priests; he was preceded by no one in the sacerdotal office, nor was he followed by any. That he was superior to Abraham, and consequently to all who

descended from Abraham; that a tribute was rendered to him by the great Ancestor of all the fraternity of Jewish priests, was just an illustration which suited the purpose of Paul. His name, therefore, the place where he reigned, his solitariness, his lone conspicuity in all the past, his dignity, and perhaps the air of mystery thrown over him in the brief history in Genesis, furnished a beautiful and striking illustration of the solitary grandeur, and the inapproachable eminence of the priesthood of the Son of God. There is no evidence that Melchisedek was *designed* to be a type of the Messiah, or that Abraham so understood it. Nothing of this kind is affirmed; and how shall *we* affirm it when the sacred oracles are silent?

[Doubtless great care and sobriety are requisite in the interpretation of types, and we admire the caution that, in every instance, demands the authority of Scripture, expressed or distinctly implied. From want of this caution, the greatest extravagancies have been committed, the most fanciful analogies established, where none were intended, and every minute circumstance in the Old Testament exalted into a type of something in the New. The very boards and nails of the tabernacle of Moses have been thus exalted.

Yet in our just aversion to one extreme, it is possible we may run into another. Of the typical character of Melchisedek, we had thought no doubt could be entertained. The canon of typical interpretation, indeed, demands, that in order to constitute the relation between type and antitype, there be, in addition to mere resemblance, *previous design*, and *pre-ordained connection*. And the commentary affirms, that "there is no evidence, that Melchisedek was *designed* to be a type of the Messiah, or that Abraham so understood it." Let it be observed in reply, that in the 110th Psalm the typical character of Melchisedek *seems* expressly acknowledged. It may be alleged, that the prophet simply states resemblance, without affirming that such resemblance was designed or intended. But that a prophet should be commissioned to declare, that Christ's priesthood should be *after such an order*, and yet that in the institution of that exalted order there should have been no designed reference to Christ, is improbable. The prediction seems to involve the original design. And this order of priesthood, too, is far superior to that of Aaron, the typical character of which is admitted. Moreover, the last clause of verse third, in this chapter, according to our

English translation asse a designed connection. Melchisedek was "*made like unto the Son of God.*" The translation is accurate. Αφομοιωμενος, according to Parkhurst, is "*made very like.*" So also Scott: "The composition is probably intended to add energy; *made very like.*" And Bloomfield adopts, "*being made by the divine decree* a type of that great High Priest, who, &c. ;" see Notes in Greek Testament. Lastly, on any other principle than that of *designed* typical relation, it is difficult, if not impossible, to give any just account of the remarkable omissions, the apparently studied silence, in the history of Melchisedek, in regard to those things that are commonly related in notices of lives, however brief. He is introduced to us with an air of impenetrable mystery. He appears on the stage as Priest of the most High God, and then disappears, leaving us in complete darkness concerning his birth, parentage, and death. "In all these respects," says Mr. Scott, "the silence of the Scripture is *intentional* and refers to the great Antitype." Melchisedek, therefore, we may remark, seems not only to have been designed as a type, but *special care* has been taken, that the record of him should be in all things suited to that design. That the apostle lighted on a happy coincidence, deserving of a passing thought, is not probable, whether this remark be meant to apply to the name, or to other particulars in this remarkable story. Indeed, divest it of its designed typical character, and the grandeur of the passage vanishes. A simple resemblance has been discovered between Christ and a certain character in the Old Testament. This is all the apostle means to affirm ! And for this too, he introduces Melchisedek, with such wondrous caution in ch. v. 11: "Of whom we have many things to say, and hard to be uttered, but ye are dull of hearing." What was hard to be uttered, or difficult to be comprehended about a mere "illustration," or "resemblance ?"

The following remarks of Owen are pertinent and beautiful. "The true cause of all these omissions was the same with that of the institution of his (Melchisedek's) priesthood, and the introduction of his person into the story. And this was, that he might be the more express and signal representative of the Lord Christ in his priesthood. And we may herein consider the sovereign wisdom of the Holy Ghost in bringing forth truth unto light, according as the state and condition of the church doth require. And first he prophesieth only a naked story of a person that was a type of Christ. Something the men of the age wherein he lived, might learn by his ministrations, but not much. For that which was principally instructive in him, for the use of the church, was not of force till

all his circumstances were forgotten. Yea, the contrivance of any tradition concerning his parents, birth, and death, had been contrary to the mind of God, and what instruction he intended the church by him. Afterwards, when, it may be, all thoughts of any use or design in this story were lost, and the church was fully satisfied in a priesthood quite of another nature, the Holy Ghost in one word of prophecy instructs her, not only that the things spoken concerning Melchisedek were not so recorded for his own sake, or on his own account, but with respect to another priest, which was afterwards to arise, by him represented. This gave a new consideration to the whole story; but moreover gave the church to know, that the priesthood, which it then had, was not always to continue, but that one of another nature was to be introduced, as was signified long before the institution of that priesthood which they enjoyed, Ps. cx. 4. Yet the church was left greatly in the dark, and, at the coming of our Saviour, had utterly lost all knowledge of the mystery of the type, and the promise renewed in the Psalm. Wherefore, our apostle entering on the unfolding of this mystery, doth not only preface it with an assertion of its difficulty, but also by a long previous discourse, variously prepareth their minds to a most diligent attention." The excellence of this quotation will, in the reader's estimation, excuse the length of it. On the whole, he who reflects how all things in the ancient economy were ordered of God, and how great a part of that economy was meant to adumbrate the realities of the gospel, while he will be cautious in admitting typical analogies of a doubtful kind, will be slow to believe that the resemblance between Christ's priesthood, and that of the *most* exalted order previously instituted, is casual, or undesigned— slow to believe, that the apostle would make so large a use of *such* accidental analogy, and found on it an argument so great.]

¶ *King of Salem.* Such is the record in Gen. xiv. 18. The word *Salem* —שלם—means *peace;* and from this fact the apostle derives his illustration in ver. 2. He regards it as a fact worth remarking on, that the *name* of the place over which he ruled expressed so strikingly the nature of the kingdom over which the Messiah was placed. In regard to the *place* here denoted by the name *Salem*, the almost uniform opinion has been that it was that afterwards known as Jerusalem. The reasons for this opinion are, (1.) that it is a part of the name Jerusalem itself—the name *Jerus*, altered from *Jebus*, having been after-

ward added, because it was the residence of the *Jebusites.* (2.) The
name *Salem* is itself given to Jerusalem; Ps. lxxvi. 2, " In *Salem* also is
his tabernacle, and his dwelling-place
in Zion." (3.) Jerusalem would be
in the direction through which Abraham would naturally pass on his return
from the slaughter of the kings. He
had pursued them unto Dan (Gen. xiv.
14), and he was returning to Mamre,
that is, Hebron; Gen. xiv. 13. On
his return, therefore, he would pass
in the vicinity of Jerusalem. Rosenmüller, however, supposes that by the
name here, Jerusalem is not intended,
but the whole region occupied by the
Jebusites and Hittites, or the royal
seat of this region, situated not far
from the cities of the plain—the vale
of Siddim where Sodom and Gomorrah
were situated. But I see no reason
for doubting that the common opinion
that Jerusalem is intended, is correct.
That place was favourably situated
for a capital of a nation or tribe; was
easily fortified; and would be likely
to be early selected as a royal residence. ¶ *Priest of the most high God.*
This is the account which is given of
him in Gen. xiv. 18. The leading
office of *priest* was to offer sacrifice.
This duty was probably first performed by the father of the family (comp.
Notes on Job i. 5; see also Gen. viii.
20; xxii. 2), and when he was dead it
devolved on the eldest son. It would
seem also that in the early ages,
among all nations whose records have
reached us, the office of priest and
king were united in the same person.
It was long before it was found that
the interests of religion would be promoted by having the office of priest
pertain to an order of men set apart
for this special work. That Melchisedek, who was a king, should also be a
priest, was not, therefore, remarkable.
The only thing remarkable is, that he
should have been a priest *of the true
God.* In what way he became acquainted with Him, is wholly unknown.
It may have been by tradition preserved from the times of Noah, as it is
possible that the arrival of Abraham
in that land may have been in some
way the means of acquainting him with

the existence and character of Jeno-
vah. The *fact* shows at least that the
knowledge of the true God was not
extinct in the world. ¶ *Who met
Abraham.* He came out to meet
him, and brought with him bread and
wine. *Why* he did this, is not mentioned. It was probably as an expression of gratitude to Abraham for
having freed the country from oppressive and troublesome invaders, and in
order to furnish refreshments to the
party which Abraham headed who had
become weary and exhausted with the
pursuit. There is not the slightest
evidence that the bread and wine which
he brought forth was designed to
typify the Sacrament of the Lord's
Supper, as has been sometimes supposed; comp. Bush on Gen. xiv. 18.
What did he know of this ordinance?
And why should we resort to such a
supposition, when the whole case may
be met by a simple reference to the
ancient rites of hospitality, and by the
fact that the deliverance of the country by Abraham from a grievous inva-
sion made some expression of gratitude on the part of this pious king in
the highest degree proper? ¶ *Returning from the slaughter of the kings*
Amraphel, king of Shinar, Arioch,
king of Ellasar, Chedorlaomer, king
of Elam, and " Tidal, king of nations,"
who had invaded the valley where
Sodom and Gomorrah were, and had
departed with a great amount of booty.
Those kings Abraham had pursued
beyond Dan, and to the neighbourhood
of Damascus, and had smitten them,
and recovered the spoil. ¶ *And blessed him.* For the important service
which he had rendered in taking vengeance on these invaders; in freeing
the land from the apprehension of
being invaded again; and in recovering
the valuable booty which they had
taken away. From vers. 6, 7, it appears that this act of *blessing* was regarded as that of one who was superior
to Abraham. That is, he blessed him
as a priest and a king. As such he
was superior in rank to Abraham, who
never claimed the title of *king*, and
who is not spoken of as a *priest.*
2. *To whom also Abraham gave a
tenth part of all.* That is, a tenth

2 To whom also Abraham gave a tenth part of all; first being by interpretation King of right-

eousness, and after that also King of Salem, which is, King of peace;

part of all the spoils which he had taken (Gen. xiv. 20), thus acknowledging that in dignity of office Melchisedek was greatly his superior; vers. 4, 6, 8. This does not appear to have been on the part of Abraham so much designed as a present to Melchisedek personally, as an act of pious thankfulness to God. He doubtless recognised in Melchisedek one who was a minister of God, and to him as such he devoted the tenth of all which he had taken, as a proper acknowledgment of the goodness of God and of his claims. From this it is evident that the propriety of devoting a tenth part of what was possessed to God, was regarded as a duty before the appointment of the Levitical law. *Some* expression of this kind is obviously demanded, and piety seems early to have fixed on the *tenth* part as being no more than a proper proportion to consecrate to the service of religion. For the propriety of the use which the apostle makes of this fact, see Notes on vers. 4, 6, 8. ¶ *First being.* The *first* idea in the interpretation of his name and office, &c. First being mentioned as king of righteousness, and then as king of peace. ¶ *King of righteousness.* The literal translation of the name Melchisedek; Notes ver. 1. The *argument* implied in this by the remarks of the apostle is, that he bore a name which made him a proper emblem of the Messiah. There was a propriety that one in whose "order" the Messiah was to be found, should have such a name. It would be exactly descriptive of him, and it was *worthy of observation* that he of whose "order" it was said the Messiah would be, should have had such a name. Paul does not say that this name was given to him with any such reference; or that it was *designed* to be symbolical of what the Messiah would be, but that there was a *remarkable coincidence*; that it was a fact which was worth at least *a passing thought.* This is a kind of remark that might occur to any one to make, and where

the slight use which Paul makes of it would not be improper anywhere; but it cannot be denied that to one accustomed to the Jewish mode of reasoning—accustomed to dwell much on hidden meanings, and to trace out concealed analogies, it would be much more obvious and striking than it is with us. We are to place ourselves in the situation of those to whom Paul wrote—trained up with Jewish feelings, and Jewish modes of thought, and to ask how this would strike *their* minds. And this is no more unreasonable than it would be in interpreting a Greek classic, or a work of a Hindoo philosopher, that we should endeavour to place ourselves in the situation of the writer and of those for whom he wrote, and ascertain what ideas would be conveyed to them by certain expressions. It is not meant by these observations that there was really no intrinsic force in what Paul here said respecting the import of the *name.* There was force; and all the use which he makes of it is proper. His meaning appears to be merely that it was a fact worthy of remark, that the *name* had a meaning which corresponded so entirely with the character of him who was to be a high priest of the same "order." ¶ *And after that.* He is mentioned after that with another appellation equally significant. ¶ *King of peace.* A literal translation of the appellation "king of Salem;" ver. 1. The idea of Paul is, that it was *worthy of remark* that the appellation which he bore was appropriate to one whose ministry it was said the priesthood of the Messiah would resemble.

[Admit the typical character of Melchisedek, and the difficulty disappears, and apology of course becomes needless. The apostle does not found an argument on any fanciful analogy, but *seems* to intimate, that the very name, as well as the other circumstances stated concerning Melchisedek, was typical. And why should this surprise us? In the Old Testament we find, that names were frequently given to children by the spirit of prophecy while on other occasions a change

3 Without father, without mother, without 1 descent, having neither beginning of days nor end

1 *pedigree.*

of name was made by command of God. In both these cases, there was always something significant. Melchisedek, doubtless, had his name under the divine direction. In what way, whether at his birth, or by change of name afterwards, it is needless to inquire, and impossible to determine; see for further remarks, Owen, M'Lean, and the Supplementary Note on ch. i. 5, also ii. 6.]

3. *Without father.* The phrase *without father—ἀπάτωρ*—means literally one who has no father; one who has lost his father; one who is an orphan. Then it denotes one who is born after the death of his father; then one whose father is unknown— *spurious. Passow.* The word occurs often in these senses in the classic writers, for numerous examples of which the reader may consult Wetstein *in loc.* It is morally certain, however, that the apostle did not use the word here in either of the senses, for there is no evidence that Melchisedek was *fatherless* in any of these respects. It was very important in the estimation of the Jews that the line of their priesthood should be carefully kept; that their genealogies should be accurately marked and preserved; and that their direct descent from Aaron should be susceptible of easy and certain proof. But the apostle says that there was no such genealogical table in regard to Melchisedek. There was no *record* made of the name either of his father, his mother, or any of his posterity. *He stood alone.* It is simply said that such a man came out to meet Abraham—and that is the first and the last which we hear of him and of his family. Now, says the apostle, it is distinctly said (Ps. cx. 4), that the Messiah was to be a priest *according to his order*—and in this respect there is a remarkable resemblance, *so far as the point of his being a priest* —which was the point under discussion—*was concerned.* The Messiah thus, *as a priest*, STOOD ALONE. His name does not appear in the line of priests. He pertained to another tribe; ver. 14. No one of his ances-

of life; but made like unto the Son of God, abideth a priest continually.

tors is mentioned as a priest; and as a priest he has no descendants, and no followers. He has a lonely conspicuity similar to that of Melchisedek; a standing unlike that of any other priest. This should not, therefore, be construed as meaning that the genealogy of Christ could not be traced out—which is not true, for Matthew (ch. i.), and Luke (ch. iii.), have carefully preserved it; but that he had no genealogical record *as a priest.* As the reasoning of the apostle pertains to this point only, it would be unfair to construe it as implying that the Messiah was to stand unconnected with any ancestor, or that his genealogy would be unknown. The meaning of the word rendered "without father" here is therefore, *one the name of whose father is not recorded in the Hebrew genealogies.* ¶ *Without mother.* The name of whose mother is unknown, or is not recorded in the Hebrew genealogical tables. Philo calls Sarah—ἀμήτορα—*without mother*, probably because her mother is not mentioned in the sacred records. The Syriac has given the correct view of the meaning of the apostle. In that version it is, "Of whom neither the father nor mother are recorded in the genealogies." The meaning here is not that Melchisedek was of low and obscure origin—as the terms "without father and without mother" often signify in the classic writers, and in Arabic, (comp. Wetstein)—for there is no reason to doubt that Melchisedek had an ancestry as honourable as other kings and priests of his time. The simple thought is, that the name of his ancestry does not appear in any record of those in the priestly office. ¶ *Without descent.* Marg. *pedigree.* The Greek word— ἀγενεαλόγητος — means *without genealogy; whose descent is unknown.* He is merely mentioned himself, and nothing is said of his family or of his posterity. ¶ *Having neither beginning of days, nor end of life.* This is a much more difficult expression than any of the others respecting Melchisedek. The obvious meaning of the phrase is, that *in the records of Moses,* neither the beginning nor the close of his life is mentioned. It is not said when he was born, or when he died; nor is it said that he *was* born or that he died. The apostle adverts to this particularly, because it was so unusual in the records of Moses, who is in general so careful to mention the birth and death of the individuals whose lives he mentions. Under the Mosaic dispensation everything respecting the duration of the sacerdotal office was determined accurately by the law. In the time of Moses, and by his arrangement, the Levites were required to serve from the age of thirty to fifty; Num. iv. 3, 23, 35, 43, 47; viii. 24, 25. After the age of fifty, they were released from the more arduous and severe duties of their office. In later periods of the Jewish history they commenced their duties at the age of twenty; 1 Chron. xxiii. 24, 27. The priests, also, and the high priest entered on their office at thirty years of age, though it is not supposed that they retired from it at any particular period of life. The idea of the apostle here is, that nothing of this kind occurs in regard to Melchisedek. No period is mentioned when he entered on his office; none when he retired from it. From anything that *appears* in the sacred record it might be perpetual—though Paul evidently did not mean to be understood as saying that it *was* so. It *cannot* be that he meant to say that Melchisedek had *no beginning of days* literally, that is, that he was from eternity; or that he had *no end of life* literally, that is, that he would exist for ever—for this would be to make him equal with God. The expression used must be interpreted *according to the matter under discussion,* and that was the office of Melchizedek *as a priest.* Of that no beginning is mentioned, and no end. That this is the meaning of Paul there can be no doubt; but there is a much more difficult question about the force and pertinency of this reasoning; about the *use* which he means to make of

this fact, and the strength of the argument which he here designs to employ. This inquiry cannot be easily settled. It may be admitted undoubtedly, that it would strike a Jew with much more force than it would any other person, and to see its pertinency we ought to be able to place ourselves in their condition, and to transfer to ourselves as far as possible their state of feeling. It was mentioned in Ps. cx. 4, that the Messiah was to be a "priest after the order of Melchizedek." It was natural then to turn to the only record which existed of him —the very brief narrative in Gen. xiv. There the account is simple and plain —that he was a pious Canaanitish king, who officiated as a priest. In what point, then, it would be asked, was the Messiah to resemble him? In his personal character; his office; his rank; or in what he did? It would be natural, then, to run out the parallel and seize upon the points in which Melchizedek *differed from the Jewish priests* which would be suggested on reading that account, for it was undoubtedly in those points that the resemblance between Christ and Melchisedek was to consist. Here the *record* was to be the only guide, and the points in which he differed from the Jewish priesthood *according to the record,* were such as these. (1.) That there is no account of his ancestry as a priest—neither father nor mother being mentioned, as was indispensable in the records of the Levitical priesthood. (2.) There was no account of any descendants in his office, and no reason to believe that he had any, and he thus stood alone. (3.) There was no account of the commencement or close of his office as a priest, but *so far as the record goes,* it is just as *it would have been* if his priesthood had neither beginning nor end. It was inevitable, therefore, that those who read the Psalm, and compared it with the account in Gen. xiv., should come to the conclusion that the Messiah was to resemble Melchisedek *in some such points as these*—for these are the points in which he differed from the Levitical priesthood—and to run out these points of

4 Now consider how great this man *was* unto whom even the pa-triarch Abraham gave the tenth of the spoils.

comparison is all that the apostle has done here. It is just what would be done by any Jew, or indeed by any other man, and the reasoning grew directly out of the two accounts in the Old Testament. It is not, then, quibble or quirk—it is sound reasoning, based on these two points, (1.) that it was said in the Old Testament that the Messiah would be a priest after the order of Melchisedek, and (2.) that the only points, *according to the record*, in which there was anything *peculiar* about the priesthood of Melchisedek, or in which he differed from the Levitical priesthood, were such as those which Paul specifies. He reasons *from the record;* and though there is, as was natural, something of a Jewish cast about it, yet it was the *only kind of reasoning that was possible in the case.* ¶ *But made like.* The word here used means to be made like, to be made to resemble ; and then *to be* like, to be compared with. Our translation seems to imply that there was a divine agency or intention by which Melchisedek was *made to resemble* the Son of God, but this does not seem to be the idea of the apostle. In the Psalm it is said that the Messiah would resemble Melchisedek in his priestly office, and this is doubtless the idea here. Paul is seeking to illustrate the nature and perpetuity of the office of the Messiah by comparing it with that of Melchisedek. Hence he pursues the idea of this resemblance, and the true sense of the word used here is, "he was like, or he resembled the Son of God." So Tindal and Coverdale render it, "is likened unto the Son of God." The points of resemblance are those which have been already suggested—(1.) in the *name*—*king of righteousness,* and *king of peace;* (2.) in the fact that he had no ancestors or successors in the priestly office ; (3.) that he was, according to the record, a perpetual priest—there being no account of his death ; and perhaps (4.) that he united in himself the office of king and priest. It may be added, that the expression

here, "was made *like unto* the Son of God," proves that he was not *himself* the Son of God, as many have supposed. How could he be "made like" himself? How could a comparison be formally made *between Christ and himself?* ¶ *Abideth a priest continually.* That is, *as far as the record in Genesis goes*—for it was according to this record that Paul was reasoning. This clause is connected with ver. 1 ; and the intermediate statements are of the nature of a parenthesis, containing important suggestions respecting the character of Melchisedek, which would be useful in preparing the readers for the argument which the apostle proposed to draw from his rank and character. The meaning is, that there is no account of his death, or of his ceasing to exercise the priestly office, and in this respect he may be compared with the Lord Jesus. All other priests cease to exercise their office by death (ver. 23) ; but of the death of Melchisedek there is no mention. It must have been true that the priesthood of Melchisedek terminated at his death ; and it will be also true that that of Christ will cease when his church shall have been redeemed, and when he shall have given up the mediatorial kingdom to the Father; 1 Cor. xv. 25 — 28. The expression, "abideth a priest *continually,*"therefore, is equivalent to saying that he had a *perpetual priesthood* in contradistinction from those whose office terminated at a definite period, or whose office passed over into the hands of others ; see Notes on ver. 24.

4. *Now consider how great this man was.* The object of the apostle was to exalt the rank and dignity of Melchisedek. The Jews had a profound veneration for Abraham, and if it could be shown that Melchisedek was superior to Abraham, then it would be easy to demonstrate the superiority of Christ as a priest to all who descended from Abraham. Accordingly he argues, that he to whom even the patriarch Abraham showed so much respect, must have had an exalted rank. Abraham, according to the

5 And verily they that are of the sons of Levi, who receive the office of the priesthood, have a commandment *a* to take tithes of the people according to the law, that is, of their brethren, though

a Nu.18.21-26.   1 *pedigree.*

they come out of the loins of Abraham :
6 But he, whose 1 descent is not counted from them, received *b* tithes of Abraham, and blessed him that had *c* the promises.

b Ge.14.20.   c Ro 9.4.

views of the East, the illustrious ancestor of the Jewish nation, was regarded as superior to any of his posterity, and of course was to be considered as of higher rank and dignity than the Levitical priests who were descended from him. ¶ *Even the patriarch Abraham.* One so great as he is acknowledged to have been. On the word *patriarch,* see Notes on Acts ii. 29. It occurs only in Acts ii. 29; vii. 8, 9, and in this place. ¶ *Gave the tenth of the spoils.;* Notes ver. 2. The *argument* here is, that Abraham acknowledged the superiority of Melchisedek by thus devoting the usual part of the spoils of war, or of what was possessed, to God by his hands, as the priest of the Most High. Instead of making a direct consecration by himself, he brought them to him as a minister of religion, and recognised in him one who had a higher official standing in the matter of religion than himself. The Greek word here rendered *spoils — ἀκροθίνιων —* means literally, the *top of the heap,* from ἄκρον, top, and Θίν, *heap.* The Greeks were accustomed, after a battle, to collect the spoils together, and throw them into a pile, and then, before they were distributed, to take off a portion from the top, and devote it to the gods ; Xen. Cyro. 7. 5, 35 ; Herod. i. 86. 90; viii. 121, 122; Dion. Hal. ii. In like manner it was customary to place the harvest in a heap, and, as the first thing to take off a portion from the top to consecrate as a thank-offering to God. The word then came to denote the *first-fruits* which were offered to God, and then the best of the spoils of battle. It has that sense here, and denotes the spoils or plunder which Abraham had taken of the discomfited kings.
5. *And verily they that are of the sons of Levi.* The meaning of this verse is, that the Levitical priests had

a right to receive tithes of their brethren, but still that they were inferior to Melchisedek. The apostle admits that their superiority to the rest of the people was shown by the fact that they had a right to require of them the tenth part of the productions of the land for their maintenance, and for the support of religion. But still he says, that their inferiority to Melchisedek, and consequently to Christ as a priest, was shown by the fact that the illustrious ancestor of all the Jewish people, including the priests as well as others, had confessed *his* inferiority to Melchisedek by paying him tithes. ¶ *Who receive the office of the priesthood.* Not all the descendants of Levi were priests. The apostle, therefore, specifies particularly those who "received this office," as being those whom he specially designed, and as those whose inferiority to Christ as a priest it was his object to show. ¶ *Have a commandment to take tithes.* Have by the law a commission, or a right to exact tithes of the people. Deut. xiv. 22, 27—29.
6. *But he whose descent is not counted from them.* Melchisedek. The word *descent* is in the margin *pedigree.* The meaning is, that he was not *in the same genealogy—μὴ γενεαλογούμενος —* he was not of the order of Levitical priests. That Melchisedek is meant there can be no doubt ; at the same time, also, the thought is presented with prominence on which Paul so much insists, that he was of a different order from the Levitical priesthood. ¶ *And blessed him.* Blessed him as a priest of God ; blessed him in such a manner as to imply acknowledged superiority ; see ver. 1. ¶ *That had the promises.* The promise that he should have a numerous posterity ; that in him all the nations of the earth should be blessed ; see ch. vi. 12—16.

7 And without all contradiction the less is blessed of the better.

8 And here men that die receive tithes ; but there he *receiveth them*, of whom *a* it is witnessed that he liveth.

a ch.5.6.

7. *And without all contradiction.* It is an admitted principle ; a point about which there can be no dispute. ¶ *The less is blessed of the better.* The act of pronouncing a blessing is understood to imply superiority of rank, age, or station. So when a father lays his hand on his children and blesses them, it is understood to be the act of one superior in age, venerableness, and authority ; when a prophet pronounced a blessing on the people, the same thing was understood, and the same is true also when a minister of religion pronounces a blessing on a congregation. It is the act of one who is understood to sustain an office above the people on whom the blessing is pronounced. This was understood of the Saviour when parents brought their children to him to lay his hands on them and bless them (Matt. xix. 13) ; and the same was true of Jacob when dying he blessed the sons of Joseph ; Heb. xi. 21 ; Gen. xlviii. 5—20. The word *less* here means the one of inferior rank ; who is *less* in office, honour, or age. It does not imply inferiority of moral or religious character, for this is not the point under consideration. The word *better* means one who is of superior office or rank, not one who has necessarily a purer or holier character. That Melchisedek was thus superior to Abraham, Paul says, is implied by the very declaration that he "blessed him." It is also seen to be true by the whole comparison. Abraham was a petty prince ; an *Emir*—the head of a company of Nomades, or migratory shepherds, having, it is true, a large number of dependants, but still not having the rank here given to Melchisedek. Though called *a prophet* (Gen. xx. 7), yet he is nowhere called either *a priest* or *a king*. In these respects, it was undoubted that he was inferior to Melchisedek.

8. *And here men that die receive tithes.* Another point showing the inferiority of the Levitical priesthood. They who thus received tithes, though by the right to do this they asserted a superiority over their brethren, were mortal. Like others, they would soon die ; and in regard to the most essential things they were on a level with their brethren. They had no exemption from sickness, affliction, or bereavement, and death came to them with just as much certainty as he approached other men. The meaning of this is, that they are mortal like their brethren, and the design is to show the inferiority of their office by this fact. Its obvious and natural signification, in the apprehension of the great mass of readers, would not be, as the meaning has been supposed to be, that it refers " to the *brief* and *mutable* condition of the Levitical priesthood ;" see Stuart *in loco.* Such an interpretation would not occur to any one if it were not to avoid the difficulty existing in the correlative member of the verse where it is said of Melchisedek that "he liveth." But is the difficulty avoided then ? Is it not as difficult to understand what is meant by his having an *immutable* and *perpetual* priesthood, as it is to know what is meant by his not dying literally ? Is the one any more true than the other ? Whatever difficulties, therefore, there may be, we are bound to adhere to the obvious sense of the expression here ; a sense which furnishes also a just and forcible ground of comparison. It seems to me, therefore, that the simple meaning of this passage is, that, under the Levitical economy, those who received tithes were *mortal*, and were thus placed in strong contrast with him of whom it was said "he liveth." Thus they were inferior to him—as a mortal is inferior to one who does not die ; and thus also they must be inferior to him who was made a priest after the " order " of him who thus " lived." ¶ *But there.* In contrast with "here" in the same verse. The

reference here is to the account of Melchisedek, " *Here*," in the Levitical economy, men received tithes who are mortal ;" " there," in the account of Melchisedek, the case is different. ¶ *He* receiveth them Melchisedek— for so the connection evidently demands. ¶ *Of whom it is witnessed.* Of whom the record is. There is not in Genesis, indeed, any direct record that he *lives*, but there is the absence of a record that he *died*, and this seems to have been regarded as in fact a record of permanency in the office ; or as having an office which did not pass over to successors by the death of the then incumbent. ¶ *That he liveth.* This is an exceedingly difficult expression, and one which has always greatly perplexed commentators. The fair and obvious meaning is, that all the record we have of Melchisedek is, that *he was " alive ;"* or as Grotius says, the record is *merely* that he lived. We have no mention of his death. From anything that the *record* shows, it might appear that he continued to live on, and did not die. *Arguing from the record,* therefore, there is a strong contrast between him and the Levitical priests, all of whom we know are mortal ; ver. 23. The apostle is desirous of making out a contrast between them and the priesthood of Christ *on this point* among others, and in doing this, he appeals to the *record* in the Old Testament, and says that there was a case which furnished an intimation that the priestly office of the Messiah was not to pass over from him to others by death. That case was, that he was expressly compared (Ps. cx. 4) with Melchisedek, and that in the account of Melchisedek there was no record of his death. As to the *force* of this argument, it must be admitted that it would strike a Jew more impressively than it does most readers now ; and it may not be improbable that the apostle was reasoning from some interpretation of the passages in Gen. xiv. and Ps. cx., which was then prevalent, and which would then be conceded on all hands to be correct. If this was the admitted interpretation, and if there is no equivocation, or

mere *trick* in the reasoning—as there cannot be shown to be —why should we not allow to the Jew a peculiarity of reasoning as we do to all other people? There are modes of reasoning and illustration in all nations, in all societies, and in all professions, which do not strike others as very forcible. The ancient philosophers had methods of reasoning which now seem weak to us ; the lawyer often argues in a way which appears to be a mere quirk or quibble, and so the lecturer in science sometimes reasons. The cause of all this may not be always that there is *real* quibble or *quirk,* in the mode of argumentation, but that he who reasons in this manner has in his view certain points which he regards as undisputed which do not appear so to us ; or that he argues from what is admitted in the profession, or in the school where he is taught, which are not understood by those whom he addresses. To this should be added also the consideration, that Paul had a constant reference to the Messiah, and that it is possible that in his mind there was here a transition from the type to the antitype, and that the language which he uses may be stronger than if he had been speaking of the *mere* record of Melchisedek if he had found it standing by itself. Still his reasoning turns mainly on the fact that in the case of Melchisedek there was no one who had preceded him in that office, and that he had no successor, and, *in regard to the matter in hand,* it was all one as if he had been a perpetual priest, or *had continued still alive.*

[The reasoning in the whole passage is founded on the Scripture account of Melchisedek. He is not to be regarded *absolutely,* but *typically.* View him just as he appears in the record in Genesis, and the difficulty will be greatly lessened, if it do not altogether disappear. *There,* he is presented to us, in his typical character, as *living.* All notice of his death is studiously omitted with the express design, that, appearing *only* as a living priest, he might the better typify our immortal Redeemer. In this view, which indeed is so well brought out in the commentary above, "the apostle's argument unto the dignity, and pre-eminence of Melchisedek above the Levitical priests, in this instance,

9 And as 1 may so say, Levi also, who receiveth tithes, payed tithes in Abraham.

10 For he was yet in the loins of his father, when Melchisedek met him.

is of an *unquestionable evidence.* For, consider Melchisedek, not in his natural being and existence, which belongs not unto this mystery, but in his Scripture being and existence, and he is immortal, always living, wherein he is more excellent than those who were always obnoxious to death in the exercise of their office."—*Owen.* M'Knight, observing that the Greek verb ζη here is not in the present, but the imperfect of the indicative, translates—*lived,* a PRIEST ALL HIS LIFE, in contradistinction from those who ceased to be priests at a certain age. But whatever view may be taken of the passage, whatever solution of the difficulty may be adopted, apology for the mode of reasoning may well be spared. An inspired writer needs it not. All his reasoning has, doubtless, a solid basis in truth. It is impossible he should proceed on any peculiarities or modes of reasoning, but such as are strictly true, the accuracy of which might, any where, and at any time, be admitted, by those who had the means and patience for a right understanding of them.]

9. *And as I may so say.* So to speak—ὡς ἔπος εἰπεῖν. For numerous examples in the classic writers of this expression, see Wetstein *in loc.* It is used precisely as it is with us when we say "so to speak," or "if I may be allowed the expression." It is employed when what is said is not strictly and literally true, but when it amounts to the same thing, or when about the same idea is conveyed. " It is a *softening down* of an expression which a writer supposes his readers may deem too strong, or which may have the appearance of excess or severity. It amounts to an indirect apology for employing an unusual or unexpected assertion or phrase." *Prof. Stuart.* Here Paul could not mean that Levi had actually paid tithes in Abraham—for he had not then an existence ; or that Abraham was his representative—for there had been no appointment of Abraham to act in that capacity by Levi ; or that the act of Abraham was imputed or reckoned to Levi, for that was not true, and would not have been pertinent to the case if it were so. But it means, that in the circumstances of

the case, the same thing occurred in regard to the superiority of Melchisedek, and the inferiority of the Levitical priesthood, *as if* Levi had been present with Abraham, and had himself actually paid tithes on that occasion. This was so because Abraham was the distinguished ancestor of Levi, and when an ancestor has done an act implying inferiority of rank to another, we feel as if the whole family or all the descendants, by that act recognised the inferiority, unless something occurs to change the relative rank of the persons. Here nothing indicating any such change had occurred. Melchisedek had no descendants of which mention is made, and the act of Abraham, as the head of the Hebrew race, stood therefore as if it were the act of all who descended from him. ¶ *Levi.* The ancestor of the whole Levitical priesthood, and from whom they received their name. He was the third son of Jacob and Leah, and was born in Mesopotamia. On account of the conduct of Simeon and Levi towards Shechem, for the manner in which he had treated their sister Dinah (Gen. xxxiv. 25), and which Jacob characterized as "cruelty" (Gen. xlix. 5, 6), Jacob said that they should be " scattered in Israel." Gen. xlix. 7. Afterwards the whole tribe of Levi was chosen by God to execute the various functions of the priesthood, and were "scattered" over the land, having no inheritance of their own, but deriving their subsistence from the offerings of the people ; Num. iii. 6. seq. Levi is here spoken of as the ancestor of the tribe, or collectively to denote the entire Jewish priesthood. ¶ *Who receiveth tithes.* That is, his descendants, the priests and Levites, receive tithes. ¶ *Payed tithes in Abraham.* It is the same as if he had payed tithes in or by Abraham.

10. *For he was yet in the loins of his father.* Abraham is here called the *father* of Levi, by a common use of the word, referring to a more re-

mote ancestor than the literal father. The meaning of the apostle is, that he was *even then*, in a certain sense, in the loins of Abraham, when Melchisedek met him ; or it was all the same as if he were there, and had then an existence. The relation which subsisted between him and Abraham, in the circumstances of the case, implied the same thing *as if* he had then been born, and had acted for himself by paying tithes. Instances of this occur constantly. A father sells a farm, to which his son would be heir, and it is the same as if the son had sold it. He has no more control over it 'than if he had been present and disposed of it himself. A father acknowledges fealty to a government for a certain title or property which is to descend to his heirs, and it is all one as if the heir had himself done it ; and it is not improper to say that it is the same as if he had been there and acted for himself. For some valuable remarks on the nature of the reasoning here employed, see Stuart on the Hebrews ; Excursus xiv. The reasoning here is, indeed, especially such as would be fitted to impress a Jewish mind, and perhaps more forcibly than it does ours. The Jews valued themselves on the dignity and honour of the Levitical priesthood, and it was important to show them on their own principles, and according to their own sacred writings, that the great ancestor of all the Levitical community had himself acknowledged his inferiority to one who was declared also in their own writings (Ps. cx.) to be like the Messiah, or who was of the same "order." At the same time, the reasoning concedes nothing false ; and conveys no wrong impression. It is not mere fancy or accommodation, nor is it framed on allegory or cabalistic principles. It is founded in truth, and such as might be used anywhere, where regard was shown to pedigree, or respect was claimed on account of the illustrious deeds of an ancestor. It would be regarded as sound reasoning in a country like England, where titles and ranks are recognised, and where various orders of nobility exist. The fact that a re-

mote ancestor had done homage or fealty to the ancestor of another class of titled birth, would be regarded as proof of acknowledged inferiority in the family, and might be used with force and propriety in an argument. Paul has done no more than this.

[Several excellent and evangelical commentators explain the passage on the principle of *representation*, the admission of which relieves it from many difficulties. If we allow that Abraham was the representative of his seed, and of the sons of Levi among the number, then they unquestionably may be said to have paid tithes in him, in a most obvious and intelligible sense. That Abraham is to be here regarded, as not only the natural but covenant head of Israel, is argued from what is said in verse 6, of his having "had the promises," which promises manifestly did not belong to him alone, but to him and to his seed, Gen. xvii. 4—9. The land of Canaan never *was* actually given to Abraham. He obtained the promise or grant of it, as the representative of his posterity, who came to its enjoyment when four hundred years had expired. By those who adopt this view, the passage is supposed to contain an illustration of the manner in which Adam and Christ represent those who respectively belong to them. And here let it be noticed, that the objection against Abraham's representative character, grounded by our author on the fact, "that there had been no appointment of Abraham to act in that capacity by Levi," might with equal force be urged against the representation of Adam and Christ, which the reader will find established in the supplementary Notes on Rom. v. As to the force of the argument, on this principle, there can be no doubt. If the representative, the covenant, as well as the natural head, of the sons of Levi, paid tithes and acknowledged inferiority to Melchisedek, their inferiority follows as a matter of course. They are supposed to be comprehended in their head. "This," says Mr. Scott, "*incontestibly proved* the inferiority of the Levitical priesthood to that of the Messiah, nay, its absolute dependence on him, and subserviency to him;"—and, we may add, is sound reasoning alike in every country, in Palestine and in ours, in England or America. On the whole we cannot but think that whatever difficulties some may have in admitting the principle of representation here, far greater difficulties lie on the other side. Even Prof. Stuart, in his celebrated 14th Excursus, (which for ingenuity deserves, perhaps, all the praise awarded by Bloomfield, Barnes, and others,) resolves the apostle's reasoning into a mere *argumentum ad hominem*, although, in the passage, there is no

11 If ^a therefore perfection were by the Levitical priesthood, (for under it the people received the law,) what further need *was there*

a Ga.2.21; ver.18,19; ch.8.7.

that another priest should rise after the order of Melchisedek, and not be called after the order of Aaron ?

evidence of any such thing. He has indeed instanced two cases of *argumentum ad hominem*, or rather two passages, in both of which the same example occurs Matt. xii. 27; Luke xi. 19. But if the reader consult these passages, he will find that mistake is impossible. The plainest indication is given, that the argument proceeds on the principle of an adversary. It would require no small ingenuity, however, to press this passage into the same rank with those now quoted. It clearly belongs to a different class, and the apostle proceeds with his argument, without the slightest indication that it was grounded rather on what was admitted, than on what was strictly true.]

11. *If therefore perfection were by the Levitical priesthood.* As the Jews supposed. They were accustomed to regard the system as perfect. It was an appointment of God, and they were tenacious of the opinion that it was to be permanent, and that it needed no change. But Paul says that this could not be. Even from their own Scriptures it was apparent that a priest was to arise of another order, and of a more permanent character, and this he says was full proof that there was *defect* of some kind in the previous order. What this defect was, he does not here specify, but the subsequent reasoning shows that it was in such points as these—that it was not permanent; that it could not make the worshippers perfect; that the blood which they offered in sacrifice could not take away sin, and could not render those who offered it holy; comp. vers. 19, 23, 24; ch. x. 1—4. ¶ *For under it the people received the law.* This assertion seems necessary in order to establish the point maintained in ver. 12, that if the priesthood is changed there must be also a change of the law. In order to this, it was necessary to admit that the law was *received* under that economy, and that *it was a part of it*, so that the change of one involved also the change of the other. It was not strictly true that the whole law

was given *after* the various orders of Levitical priests were established—for the law on Sinai, and several other laws, were given before that distinct arrangement was made; but it was true (1.) that a considerable part of the laws of Moses were given under that arrangement; and (2.), that the *whole* of the ceremonial observances was connected with that. They were parts of one system, and mutually dependent on each other. This is all that the argument demands. ¶ *What further need* was there, &c. "If that system would lead to perfection; if it was sufficient to make the conscience pure, and to remove sin, then there was no necessity of any other. Yet the Scriptures have declared that there *would be* another of a different order, implying that there was some defect in the former." This reasoning is founded on the fact that there was an express prediction of the coming of a priest of a different "order" (Ps.cx.4), and that this fact implied that there was some deficiency in the former arrangement. To this reasoning it is impossible to conceive that there can be any objection.

12. *For the priesthood being changed.* According to the prediction in Ps. cx., that it would be. When that occurs, the consequence specified will also follow. ¶ *There is made of necessity a change also of the law.* The law so far as it grew out of that, or was dependent on it. The connection requires us to understand it *only* of the law *so far as it was connected with the Levitical priesthood.* This could not apply to the ten commandments —for they were given *before* the institution of the priesthood; nor could it apply to any other part of the moral law, for that was not dependent on the appointment of the Levitical priests. But the meaning is, that since a large number of laws—constituting a code of considerable extent and importance—was given for the

12 For the priesthood being changed, there is made of necessity a change also of the law.

13 For he of whom these things are spoken pertaineth to another tribe, of which no man gave attendance at the altar.

14 For *it is* evident *a* that our Lord sprang out of Judah ; of which

a Is.11.1; Mat.1.3; Re.5.5.

tribe Moses spake nothing concerning priesthood.

15 And it is yet far more evident : for that after the similitude of Melchisedek there ariseth another priest,

16 Who is made, not after the law of a carnal commandment, but after the power of an endless life.

regulation of the priesthood, and in reference to the rites of religion, which they were to observe or superintend, it followed that when their office was superseded *by one of a wholly different order,* the law which had regulated *them* vanished also, or ceased to be binding. This was a very important point in the introduction of Christianity, and hence it is that it is so often insisted on in the writings of Paul. The *argument* to show that there had been a change or transfer of the priestly office, he proceeds to establish in the sequel.

13. *For he of whom these things are spoken.* The Lord Jesus, the Messiah, to whom they had reference. The *things* here spoken of pertain to his office as priest; his being of the order of Melchisedek. The apostle here *assumes* it as a point concerning which there could be no dispute, that these things referred to the Lord Jesus. Those whom he addressed would not be disposed to call this in question, and his argument had conducted him to this conclusion. ¶ *Pertaineth to another tribe.* To the tribe of Judah ; ver. 14. ¶ *Of which no man gave attendance at the altar.* The priestly office pertained only to the tribe of Levi. No one of the tribe of Judah had any part in the performance of the duties of that office. This was settled by the Jewish law.

14. *For it is evident that our Lord sprang out of Judah.* It is well known: it cannot be a matter of dispute. About the fact that the Lord Jesus was of the tribe of Judah, there could be no doubt; comp. Matt. i. 3. But probably the apostle means here to refer to more than that simple fact. It was a doctrine of the Old Testament, and was admitted by the Jews,

that the Messiah was to be of that tribe; see Gen. xlix. 10 ; Isa. xi. 1 ; Micah v. 2 ; Matt. ii. 6. This was an additional consideration to show that there was to be a change of some kind in the office of the priesthood, since it was declared (Ps. cx.) that the Messiah was to be a *priest.* The fact that the Messiah is to be of the tribe of Judah is still admitted by the Jews. As their distinction of tribes now, however, is broken up, and as it is impossible for them to tell who belongs to the tribe of Judah, it is held by them that when he comes this will be made known *by miracle.* ¶ *Of which tribe Moses spake nothing concerning priesthood.* That is, in the Mosaic laws respecting the office of priest, this tribe is not mentioned. All the arrangements pertain to the tribe of Levi.

15. *And it is yet far more evident.* Not that our Lord would spring out of Judah, but the point which he was endeavouring to establish that there must be a change of the priesthood, was rendered still more evident from another consideration. A strong proof of the necessity of such a change of the priesthood was furnished from the fact that the Messiah was to be of the tribe of Judah ; but a much stronger, because *as a priest* he was to be of the order of Melchisedek—that is, he was of the same rank with one who did not even belong to that tribe. ¶ *After the similitude.* Resembling: that is, he was to be of the order of Melchisedek.

16. *Who is made.* That is, the other priest is made, to wit, the Messiah. He was made a priest by a peculiar law. ¶ *Not after the law of a carnal commandment.* Not according to the law of a commandment per-

17 For he testifieth, [a] Thou *art* a priest for ever after the order of Melchisedek.

18 For there is verily a disannulling of the commandment going

before, for the weakness [b] and unprofitableness thereof.

19 For the law [c] made nothing perfect, but [1] the bringing in of a better hope *did;* by the [d] which we draw nigh unto God.

a Ps.110.4.   *b* Ac.13.39.
c Ro.3.20.   1 or, *but it was.*   *d* Ro.5.2.

taining to the flesh. The word *carnal* means *fleshly;* and the idea is, that the law under which the priests of the old dispensation were made was external, rather than spiritual; it related more to outward observances than to the keeping of the heart. That this was the nature of the Mosaic ritual in the main, it was impossible to doubt, and the apostle proceeds to argue from this undeniable truth. ¶ *But after the power of an endless life.* By an authority of endless duration. That is, it was not concerned mainly with outward observances, and did not pass over from one to another by death, but was unchanging in its character, and spiritual in its nature. It was enduring and perpetual as a priesthood, and was thus far exalted above the service performed by the priests under the former dispensation.

17. *For he testifieth.* "That this is the true account of it is proved by the testimony of God himself, that he was to be a priest *for ever;*" see Note on ch. v. 6.

18. *For there is verily a disannulling.* A setting aside. The law which existed before in regard to the priesthood becomes now abrogated in consequence of the change which has been made in the priesthood; Note ver. 12. ¶ *Of the commandment.* Relating to the office of priest, or to the ceremonial rites in general. This does not refer to the *moral* law, as if that was abrogated, for (1.) the reasoning of the apostle does not pertain to that, and (2.) that law cannot be abrogated. It grows out of the nature of things, and must be perpetual and universal. ¶ *Going before.* Going before the Christian dispensation and introducing it. ¶ *For the weakness and unprofitableness thereof.* That is, it was not adapted to save man; it had not power to accomplish what was necessary to be done in human salvation.

It answered the end for which it was designed—that of introducing a more perfect plan, and then vanished as a matter of course. It did not expiate guilt; it did not give peace to the conscience; it did not produce perfection (ver. 11), and therefore it gave place to a better system.

19. *For the law made nothing perfect.* The Levitical, ceremonial law. It did not produce a perfect state; it did not do what was desirable to be done for a sinner; see Note on ver. 11. That law, as such, did not reconcile man to God; it did not make an atonement; it did not put away guilt; in one word, *it did not restore things to the condition in which they were before the law was broken and man became a sinner.* If man were saved under that system—as many undoubtedly were—it was not in virtue of any intrinsic efficacy which it possessed, but in virtue of that great sacrifice which it typified. ¶ *But the bringing in of a better hope did.* Marg. "But *it was.*" The correct rendering is, probably, " but there is the bringing in of a better hope, by which we have access to God." The law could not effect this. It left the conscience guilty, and sin unexpiated. But there is now the introduction of a better system by which we can approach a reconciled God. The "better hope" here refers to the more sure and certain expectation of heaven introduced by the gospel. There is a better foundation for hope; a more certain way of obtaining the divine favour than the law could furnish. ¶ *By the which.* By which better hope; that is, by means of the ground of hope furnished by the gospel, to wit, that God is now reconciled, and that we can approach him with the assurance that he is ready to save us. ¶ *We draw nigh unto God.* We have access to him ; Notes, Rom. v. 1, 2.

20 And inasmuch as not without an oath *he was made priest*,

21 (For those priests were made without an oath; but this with *in* oath by him that said unto him, 1 or, *swearing of an oath.*

The Lord sware and will not repent, Thou *art* a priest for ever after the order of Melchisedek :) *a*

22 By so much was Jesus made a surety of a better *b* testament.

a Ps. 110.4.   *b* ch.8.6.

20. *And inasmuch as not without an oath.* In addition to every other consideration showing the superiority of Christ as a priest, there was the solemnity of the oath by which he was set apart to the office. The appointment of one to the office of priest by an oath, such as occurred in the case of Jesus, was much more solemn and 'important than where the office was received merely by descent.

21. *For those priests were made without an oath.* The Levitical priests were set apart and consecrated without their office being confirmed to them by an oath on the part of God. They received it by regular descent, and when they arrived at a suitable age they entered on it of course. Jesus received *his* office by special appointment, and it was secured to him by an oath. The word rendered "*oath*" is in the margin *swearing of an oath.* This is the proper meaning of the Greek word, but the sense is not materially varied. ¶ *But this with an oath.* This priest, the Lord Jesus, became a priest in virtue of an oath. ¶ *The Lord sware;* Note ch. vi. 13. The reference here is to Psalm cx. 4. "The Lord hath sworn." ¶ *And will not repent.* That is, *will not regret,* or *will not alter his mind through regret*—for this is the meaning of the Greek word.

22. *By so much.* Inasmuch as an oath is more solemn than a mere appointment. The meaning is, that there is all the additional security in the suretyship of Jesus which arises from the solemnity of an oath. It is not implied that God would not be true to his mere promise, but the argument here is derived from the custom of speaking among men. An oath is regarded as much more sacred and binding than a mere promise, and the fact that God has sworn in a given case furnishes the highest security that what he has promised will be

performed. ¶ *Was Jesus made a surety.* The word *surety* — ἔγγυος — occurs nowhere else in the New Testament nor is it found in the Septuagint. It properly means, a bondsman; one who pledges his name, property, or influence, that a certain thing shall be done. When a contract is made, a debt contracted, or a note given, a friend often becomes the *security* in the case, and is himself responsible if the terms of the contract are not complied with. In the case of the new covenant between God and man, Jesus is the "security" or the bondsman. But of what, and to whom, is he the surety? It cannot be that he is a bondsman *for God* that he will maintain the covenant, and be true to the promise which he makes, as Crellius supposes, for we need no such "security" of the divine faithfulness and veracity. It cannot be that he becomes responsible for the divine conduct in any way—for no such responsibility is needed or possible. But it must mean that he is the security or bondsman on the part of man. He is the pledge that we shall be saved. He becomes responsible, so to speak, to law and justice, that no injury shall be done by our salvation, though we are sinners. He is not a security that we shall be saved *at any rate,* without holiness, repentance, faith, or true religion—for he never could enter into a suretyship of that kind: but his suretyship extends to this point, that the law shall be honoured; that all its demands shall be met; that we may be saved though we have violated it, and that its terrific penalty shall not fall upon us. The case is this. A sinner becomes a true penitent and enters heaven. It might be said that he does this over a broken law; that God treats the good and bad alike, and that no respect has been paid to the law or the penalty in his salvation. Here the Great Surety comes in, and says that it is not so. *He* has become responsible for this; he the surety, the pledge, that all proper honour shall be paid to justice, and that the same good effects shall ensue as if the penalty of the law had been fully borne. He himself has died to honour the law, and to open a way by which its penalty may be fully remitted consistently with justice, and he becomes *the everlasting pledge* or *security* to law, to justice, to the universe, that no injury shall result from the pardon and salvation of the sinner. According to this view, no man can rely on the suretyship of Jesus but he who expects salvation on the terms of the gospel. The suretyship is not at all that he shall be saved in his sins, or that he shall enter heaven no matter what life he leads; it is only that *if* he believes, repents, and is saved, no injury shall be done to the universe; no dishonour to the law. For this the Lord Jesus is responsible. ¶ *Of a better testament.* Rather, "of a better covenant." The former covenant was that which God made with his people under the Mosaic dispensation; the new covenant is that made by means of Christ. This is *better* because (1.) the terms are more simple and easy; (2.) the observances and rites are much less onerous and hard; (3.) it relates to all men, not being confined to the Jewish people; (4.) it is now sure. The former was administered through the instrumentality of the Levitical priesthood, this by the Son of God; that was transitory and changing, this is permanent and eternal.

[The word rendered " Surety," is *εγγυος*. It occurs indeed here only in the New Testament, nor is it found in the Septuagint, *i.e.* the *very word* is not. Yet its derivatives occur there, and bear the sense that is ordinarily, and everywhere expressed by suretyship, Prov. xvii. 18; xxii. 26, and other places. The word itself, too, is found in the Apocrypha, Ecclesiasticus xxix. 15; 2 Mac. x. 28, on which last passage a recent and distinguished writer observes, "we find the word (here) conveying the idea of a covenant engagement, and that too on the part of the Most High. When the Jews joined battle with Timotheus, they are said to have had the Great God for their *εγγυος*, assuring them of victory. They had prostrated themselves before the altar; they had spread ashes

upon their heads, and covered themselves with sackcloth; they had poured out their hearts in prayer, pleading with the Most High, and putting him in mind of his promise—the promise in which he had said that he would be an enemy to their enemies—then seizing their arms and advancing to meet Timotheus, they rushed into the fight, we are told, *εχοντες ευημεριας και νικης*." Indeed, about the meaning of the word, and the accuracy of our English translation, there can be no doubt. Critics who are very far from admitting the doctrine of Christ's suretyship in the covenant of redemption, have freely admitted this. *See Peirce on the place.*

What then is the sense of the word here? Applied to Christ will it bear its ordinary sense or not? Is he a surety in a sense analogous to that in which men are sureties?[f] Hesitating to answer these questions in the affirmative, a host of commentators, following the Greeks, have observed, that *εγγυος* is substituted for, and equivalent to, *μεσιτης*, occurring at ch. viii. 6; ix. 15; xii. 24. But because Christ is called, in these places, the *μεσιτης* or mediator of the covenant, it does not follow that *εγγυος* here has *precisely* the same sense. Or, if so, how shall we account for the introduction of this singular word at all? Why was not *μεσιτης* employed here, as, in other places, in the epistle? This has, indeed been accounted for by observing, that as the apostle, in the 19th verse, had used the word *εγγιζομεν*, we draw near, he employed *εγγυος* in the 22nd, for the sake of the *paronomasia*, to which figure he is alleged to have been much attached. But in whatever way the apostle may have been led to the use of the word (and the above account is probable enough), he never would have used it, in a sense altogether different from that which ordinarily is attached to it, out of fondness for any figure whatever. " A surety has to pay that which they owe, for whom he is engaged; to do, what is to be done by them, which they cannot perform. *And if this be not the notion of a surety in this place, the apostle makes use of a word, nowhere else used in the whole scripture, to teach us that which it doth never signify among men, which is improbable and absurd.* For the sole reason why he did make use of it was, that from the nature and notion of it among men, in other cases, we may understand the signification of it, and what, under that name, he ascribes unto the Lord Jesus."— *Owen.*

Having thus proved that *εγγυος* is properly translated " surety," and that Christ is so styled, in a sense not widely different from that which is usually attached to the word—let us next inquire, how Christ discharges this suretyship, or what he does in his capacity of surety? *Is he surety to us for God?* This last question, by orthodox writers, is

23 And they truly were many priests, because they were not suffered to continue by reason of death :

1 or, *which passeth not from one to another.*

24 But this *man,* because he continueth ever, hath an [1] unchangeable *a* priesthood.

a 1 Sa.2.35.

for the most part, answered in the negative on the ground that there can be no need of security for God, his *promise* and his *oath* being sufficient guarantee that he will fulfil his engagement; on the ground also, that a surety must be some one greater than the party for whom he engages, which, in the case of God, renders the thing impossible, since there is none greater than He. Thus Dr. Owen has argued at great length, and is followed by Guyse, Boston, and many others. Yet there are not wanting writers of great reputation for learning and orthodoxy, who scruple not to say that Christ is surety *for God ;* (see Mr. Scott on this place). He undertook, on the part of the Father, that all the promises should be made good to the seed. He acts in the behalf of God towards us, and assures us of the divine favour. "If it be asked, what need was there of a Mediator to assure us of the fulfilment of the promises made by the God of truth, who cannot lie or deceive us, I answer, the same objection might be made against God's adding his oath to his promise, whereby he intended to give us the greater security of accomplishment."— *Peirce.* The exclusion of this idea from the suretyship of Christ, on the part of so many divines, doubtless arose from the improper use made of it by Socinians, who unwilling to admit that Christ had become bound for our debt of suffering and obedience, and, in this sense, was surety *for us,* resolved the suretyship into a mere engagement *in behalf of God.* They could not allow more, without allowing the atonement. While, however, we see no necessity for discarding this idea, because it has been used for bad purposes, we maintain, that this is neither all, nor even the principal part, of the suretyship of Christ. Revert to the original notion of a surety. He is one who engages, in behalf of another, to pay a debt or discharge a duty, which that other may fail to pay or discharge. Christ engaged to stand in that relation toward us, and therefore he is the *surety for us to God,* that our debt shall be discharged. God the Father, on his part, engages, that Christ shall see his seed, that they shall be saved ; and the Son of God, on his part, becomes bound for the debt of penalty and obedience. This is the covenant of redemption, "the counsel of peace" between the Father and the Son, before all worlds; Zech. vi. 13 ; Isa. liii. 10, 12. It is unnecessary farther to observe, that Christ, in his capacity of surety, has nobly redeemed his pledge, endured the penalty, and honoured

the precept of the broken law, and thereby secured for his people the blessings of the covenant.

Before concluding this Note, we may remark that some difference of opinion exists among those who hold the suretyship of Christ, in reference to another question, viz. Whether he became surety for the faith, repentance, and evangelical obedience of his people ? " I answer," says Thomas Boston, " though the elect's believing, repenting, and sincere obedience are infallibly secured in the covenant, yet I judge, that Christ did not become surety in the covenant, in way of caution to his Father, that the elect should perform these deeds, or any other. These belong rather to the promissory part of the covenant. *They are benefits promised in the covenant* BY GOD UNTO CHRIST, the surety, as a reward of his fulfilling the condition of the covenant. And so they are, by the unchangeable truth of God, and his exact justice, ensured beyond all possibility of failure; Ps. xxii. 27, 30, 31 ; Ps. cx. 3 ; Isa. liii. 10. with ver. 1 ; Ezek. xxxiv. 26, 27, 31 ; Heb. viii. 10, 11."—*Boston on the Covenant of Grace ;* see also Dr. Dick's admirable lectures on the same subject.

It will be seen from this review of the suretyship of Christ, that the sentiments of our author on the subject are not materially different from those of evangelical divines in Scotland. He may not use the same phraseology, but " security to the law, to justice, to the universe, that no injury shall result from the pardon of the sinner," is much the same with " surety to God for us," that our debt shall be discharged, *i. e.* that none of these interests shall suffer.]

23. *And they truly.* Under the Jewish dispensation. The object of this verse and the following is, to state one more reason of the excellence of the priesthood of Christ. It is, that owing to the frailty of human nature, and the shortness of life, the office of priest there was continually changing. But here there was no such change. Christ, being exalted to the heavens to live for ever there, has now an unchangeable priesthood, and everything in regard to his office is permanent.

24. *But this* man. Gr. " But he "— referring to Christ. ¶ *Because he continueth ever.* Gr. " Because he re-

25 Wherefore he is able *a* also to save them ¹ to the uttermost that come unto God by him, seeing he ever liveth to make intercession for *b* them.

a Jude 24.   1 or, *evermore.*

mains for ever." The idea is because he does not die, but ever lives, he has an unchanging priesthood. There is no necessity that he should yield it to others, as was the case with the Jewish priests because they were mortal. The reason in their case, why it passed to others, was not that they did not perform the office well, but that they were *mortal,* and could not continue to hold it. But this reason could not operate in the case of the Lord Jesus, and therefore his priesthood would be permanent. ¶ *Hath an unchangeable priesthood.* Marg. "or, *which passeth not from one to another.*" The margin expresses the sense of the passage. The idea is not strictly that it was *unchangeable,* but that *it did not pass over into other hands.* The Levitical priesthood passed from one to another as successive generations came on the stage of action. This reasoning is not designed to prove that the priesthood of Christ will be literally *eternal*—for its necessity may cease when all the redeemed are in heaven—but that it is permanent, and does not pass from hand to hand.

25. *Wherefore he is able also.* As he ever lives, and ever intercedes, he has power to save. He does not begin the work of salvation, and then relinquish it by reason of death, but he lives on as long as it is necessary that anything should be done for the salvation of his people. We need a Saviour who has *power,* and Christ has shown that he has all the power which is needful to rescue man from eternal death. ¶ *To the uttermost.* This does not mean simply *for ever*— but that he has power to save them so that their salvation shall be *complete*— ἰς τὸ παντελὶς. He does not abandon the work midway; he does not begin a work which he is unable to finish. He can aid us *as long* as we need anything done for our salvation; he

26 For such an high priest became us, *who is* holy, *c* harmless, undefiled, separate from sinners, and made higher than the heavens;

b Ro.8.34; 1John 2.1.   *c* ch.4.15; 1Pe.2.22.

can save *all* who will entrust their salvation to his hands. ¶ *That come unto God by him.* In his name ; or depending on him. To come to God, is to approach him for pardon and salvation. ¶ *Seeing he ever liveth.* He does not die as the Jewish priests did. ¶ *To make intercession for them;* see Note Rom. viii. 34. He constantly presents the merits of his death as a reason why *we* should be saved. The precise mode, however, in which he makes intercession in heaven for his people is not revealed. The *general* meaning is, that he undertakes their cause, and assists them in overcoming their foes and in their endeavours to live a holy life ; comp. 1 John ii. 1. He does in heaven whatever is necessary to obtain for us grace and strength ; secures the aid which we need against our foes ; and is the *pledge* or *security* for us that the law shall be honoured, and the justice and truth of God maintained, though we are saved. It is reasonable to presume that this is somehow by the presentation of the merits of his great sacrifice, and that *that* is the ground on which all this grace is obtained. As that is infinite, we need not fear that it will ever be exhausted.

26. *For such an High Priest became us.* Was fitted to our condition. That is, there was that in our character and circumstances which demanded that a high priest for us should be personally holy. It was not requisite merely that he should have great power ; or that he should be of a rank superior or to that of the Jewish priesthood ; but there was a special propriety that he should surpass all others in *moral* purity. Other priests were mere mortal men, and it was necessary that their office should pass to other hands ; they were *sinful* men also, and it was necessary that sacrifices should be made for themselves as well as others. We need, however, a different priest.

27 Who needeth not daily, as those high priests, to offer up sacrifice, first *a* for his own sins, and then for

a Le.9.7.

the people's : for this he did once, when he offered up himself.

28 For the law maketh men high

We need not only one who ever lives, but one who is perfectly holy, and who has no need to bring an offering for himself, and all the merit of whose sacrifice, therefore, may be ours. Such an high priest we have in the person of the Lord Jesus; and there is no truth more interesting, and no proposition more susceptible of proof, than that HE IS EXACTLY FITTED TO MAN. In his moral character, and in the great work which he has accomplished, he is just such a Saviour as is adapted to the wants of ignorant, fallen, wretched, sinful man. He is benevolent, and pities our woes; wise, and is able to enlighten our ignorance; compassionate, and ready to forgive our faults. He has made such a sacrifice as was necessary to put away our guilt, and offers such intercession as we need to have offered for us in order that we may be preserved from falling. ¶ Who is *holy*. Not merely *outwardly* righteous, but pure in heart. ¶ *Harmless*. Not injuring any one. To no one did he do wrong. Neither to their name, person, or property, did he ever do injury; nor will he ever. He is the only one who has lived on earth of whom it could be said that he never, in any way, did wrong to another. ¶ *Undefiled.* By sin ; by any improper desire or passion. He was unstained by crime ; " unspotted from the world." Sin always defiles the soul ; but from every such pollution the Lord Jesus was free. ¶ *Separate from sinners.* That is, he did not associate with them *as such.* He did not partake of their feelings, plans, pleasures. Though he mingled with them, yet it was merely to do them good, and in all his life there was an entire separation from the feelings, principles, and views of a sinful world. ¶ *And made higher than the heavens.* Exalted above the visible heavens ; that is, at the right hand of God; see Notes on Eph. i. 21 ; Phil. ii. 9. We needed a high priest who is thus ex-

alted that he may manage our cause before the throne of God.

27. *Who needeth not daily, as those high priests.* As the Jewish priests. This is an additional circumstance introduced to show the superior excellency of the High Priest of the Christian profession, and to show also how he was fitted to our wants. The Jewish high priest was a sinful man. He had the same fallen and corrupt nature as others. He needed an expiatory sacrifice for his own sins as really as they did for theirs. When he approached God to offer sacrifice, it was needful to make an atonement for himself, and when all was done it was still a sacrifice offered by a sinful man. But it was not so in the case of Jesus. He was so holy that he needed no sacrifice for himself, and *all* that he did was in behalf of others. Besides, it was necessary that the sacrifices in the Jewish service should be constantly repeated. They were imperfect. They were mere types and shadows. They who offered them were frail, sinful men. It became necessary, therefore, to repeat them every day to keep up the proper sense of their transgressions, and to furnish a suitable acknowledgment of the tendency to sin alike among the people and the priests. Neither in the nature of the offering, nor in the character of those who made it, was there any sufficient reason why it should *cease* to be offered, and it was therefore repeated day by day. But it was not so with the Lord Jesus. The offering which he made, though presented but *once*, was so ample and perfect that it had sufficient merit for all the sins of the world, and needed never to be repeated.—It is not probable that the Jewish high priest himself *personally* officiated at the offering of sacrifice every day ; but the meaning here is, that it was *done* daily, and that there was *need* of a daily sacrifice in his behalf. As one

priests which have infirmity ; but the word of the oath, which was

---

of the Jewish people, the sacrifice was offered on his account as well as on the account of others—for he partook of the common infirmities and sinfulness of the nation. ¶ *For this he did once.* That is, once for all— ἐφάπαξ. He made such an atonement that it was not needful that it should be repeated. Thus he put an end to sacrifice, for when he made the great atonement it was complete, and there was no need that any more blood should be shed for human guilt.

28. *For the law.* The ceremonial law. ¶ *Which have infirmity.* Who are weak, frail, sinful, dying. Such were all who were appointed to the office of priest under the Jewish law. ¶ *But the word of the oath.* By which one was appointed after the order of Melchisedek; Note, ver. 21. ¶ *Maketh the Son.* The Son of God. That appointment has resulted in his being set apart to this work. ¶ *Who is consecrated for evermore.* Marg. *Perfected;* see Note ch. ii. 10. The idea is, that the appointment is *complete* and *permanent.* It does not pass from one to the other. It is perfect in all the arrangements, and will remain so for ever.

REMARKS.

The subject of this chapter is the exalted high-priesthood of the Redeemer. This is a subject which pertains to all Christians, and to all men. All religions imply the priestly office; all suppose sacrifice of some kind. In regard to the priestly office of Christ as illustrated in this chapter, we may observe,

(1.) He stands alone. In that office he had no predecessor, and has no one to succeed him. In this respect he was without father, mother, or descent—and he stands in lonely majesty as the only one who sustains the office ; ver. 3.

(2.) He is superior to Abraham. Abraham never laid claim to the office of priest, but he recognised his inferiority to one whom the Messiah was to resemble ; vers. 2, 4.

---

since the law, *maketh* the Son, who is [1] consecrated for evermore.

[1] or, *perfected.*

(3.) He is superior to all the Jewish priesthood — sustaining a rank and performing an office above them all. The great ancestor of all the Levitical priests recognised his inferiority to one of the rank or "order" of which the Messiah was to be, and received from him a blessing. In our contemplation of Christ, therefore, as priest, we have the privilege of regarding him as superior to the Jewish high priest—exalted as was his office, and important as were the functions of his office ; as more grand, more pure, more worthy of confidence and love.

(4.) The great High Priest of the Christian profession is the only perfect priest ; vers. 11, 19. The Jewish priests were all imperfect and sinful men. The sacrifices which they offered were imperfect, and could not give peace to the conscience. There was need of some better system, and they all looked forward to it. But in the Lord Jesus, and in his work, there is absolute perfection. What he did was complete, and his office needs no change.

(5.) The office now is permanent. It does not change from hand to hand; vers. 23, 24. He who sustains this office does not die, and we may ever apply to him, and cast our cares on him. Men die ; one generation succeeds another ; but our High Priest is the same. We may trust in him in whom our fathers found peace and salvation, and then we may teach our children to confide in the same High Priest—and so send the invaluable lesson down to latest generations.

(6.) His work is firm and sure ; vers. 20—22. His office is founded on an oath, and he has become the *security* for all who will commit their cause to him. Can great interests like those of the soul be entrusted to better hands ? Are they not safer in *his* keeping than in our own ?

(7.) He is able to save to the uttermost ; ver. 25. That power he showed when he was on earth; that power he is constantly evincing. No one has asked aid of him and found him unable to render it ; no one has been suffered to sink down to hell because his arm was weak. What he has done for a few he can do for " all ;" and they who will entrust themselves to him will find him a sure Saviour. Why will not men then be persuaded to commit themselves to him? Can they save themselves? Where is there one who has shown that he was able to do it? Do they not need a Saviour? Let the history of the world answer. Can man conduct his own cause before God? How weak, ignorant, and blind is he ; how little qualified for such an office! Has any one suffered wrong by committing himself to the Redeemer? If there *is* such an one, where is he? Who has ever made this complaint that has tried it? Who ever will make it? In countless millions of instances, the trial has been made whether Christ was " able to save." Men have gone with a troubled spirit; with a guilty conscience; and with awful apprehensions of the wrath to come, and have asked him to save them. Not one of those who have done this has found reason to doubt his ability; not one has regretted that he has committed the deathless interest of the soul into his hands.

(8.) Christ saves to the *uttermost;* ver. 25. He makes the salvation *complete.* So the Bible assures us ; and so we see it *in fact* as far as we can trace the soul. When a Christian friend dies, we stand at his bed-side and accompany him as far as we can into the valley of the shadow of death. We ask him whether he feels that Christ is able to save? He replies, "*yes.*" When he has lost the power of speaking above a whisper, we ask him the same question, and receive the same reply. When he gives us the parting hand, and we, still anxious to know whether all is well, ask the same question, a sign, a smile, a lighting up of the dying eye, declares that all is well. As far as we can trace the departing soul when it goes into the dark valley, we receive the same assurance ; and why should we doubt

that the same grace is bestowed further onward, and that he saves "to the uttermost?" But what else thus saves? Friends give the parting hand at the gloomy entrance to that valley, and the gay and the worldly coolly turn away. The delusions of infidelity there forsake the soul, and minister no comfort then. Flatterers turn away from the dying scene—for who flatters the dying with the praise of beauty or accomplishments? Taste, skill, learning, talent, do not help then, for how can *they* save a dying soul? None but Jesus saves to the "uttermost;" no other friend but he goes with us *entirely through* the valley of death. Is it not better to have such a friend than to go alone through that dark, gloomy path ? Any other gloomy and dangerous way may be more safely trod without a friend, than the vale of death.

(9.) The Christian religion is fitted to our condition ; vers. 26, 27. It has just such a High Priest as we need— holy, harmless, undefiled. Just such an atonement has been made as is necessary—ample, rich, full, and not needing to be made again. It reveals just such truth as we want—that respecting the immortality of the soul, and the glorious state of the redeemed beyond the grave. It imparts just such consolation as is fitted to our condition—pure, rich, unfailing, elevating. It reconciles us to God just as it should be done—in such a way that God can be honoured, and the purity and dignity of his law maintained. It is the religion adapted to dying, ignorant, sinful, wretched man. No other system so much consults the true dignity of our nature, and the honour of God ; no one diffuses such consolations through the life that is, or fills with such hopes in regard to the life to come.

(10.) Since, then, we have now such a Great High Priest ; since the promises of the gospel are settled on so firm a foundation; and since the gospel in its provisions of mercy is all that we can desire it to be, let us yield our hearts entirely to the Saviour, and make this salvation wholly ours. We have the privilege, if we will, of draw-

CHAPTER VIII.

NOW of the things which we have spoken *this is* the sum :

We have such an high priest, [a] who is set on the right hand of the throne of the Majesty in the heavens ;

a Ep.1.20.

ing near to God with boldness. We may come near his throne. Though we are poor, and sinful, and deserve neither notice nor mercy, yet we may come and ask for all that we need. We may go to God, and supplicate his favour, with the assurance that he is ready to hear. We may go feeling that the great atonement has been made for our sins, and that no other offering is now needed ; that the last bloody offering which God required has been presented, and that all that he now asks is the sacrifice of a contrite and a grateful heart. All that was needful to be done on the part of God to provide a way of salvation has been done ; all that remains is for man to forsake his sins and to come back to a God who waits to be gracious.

CHAPTER VIII.

ANALYSIS OF THE CHAPTER.

This chapter is a continuation of the argument which has been prosecuted in the previous chapters respecting the priesthood of Christ. The apostle had demonstrated that he was to be a priest, and that he was to be, not of the Levitical order, but of the order of Melchisedek. As a consequence he had proved that this involved a change of the law appointing the priesthood, and that in respect to permanency, and happy moral influence, the priesthood of Christ far surpassed the Jewish. This thought he pursues in this chapter, and shows particularly that it involved a change in the nature of the covenant between God and his people. In the prosecution of this, he (1.) states the sum or principal point of the whole matter under discussion—that the priesthood of Christ was real and permanent, while that of the Hebrew economy was typical, and was destined in its own nature to be temporary; vers. 1—3. (2.) There was a fitness and propriety in his being removed to heaven to perform the functions of his office there—since if he had remained on

earth he could not have officiated as priest, that duty being by the law of Moses entrusted to others pertaining to another tribe ; vers. 4,5. (3.) Christ had obtained a more exalted ministry than the Jewish priests held, because he was the Mediator in a better covenant—a covenant that related rather to the heart than to external observances ; vers. 6—13. That new covenant excelled the old in the following respects :—(a) It was established on better promises ; ver. 6. (b) It was not a covenant requiring mainly external observances, but pertained to the soul, and the law of that covenant was written there ; vers. 7—10. (c) It was connected with the diffusion of the knowledge of the Lord among all classes from the highest to the lowest; ver. 11. (d) The evidence of forgiveness might be made more clear than it was under the old dispensation, and the way in which sins are pardoned be much better understood ; ver. 12. These considerations involved the consequence, also, which is stated in ver. 13, that the old covenant was of necessity about to vanish away.

1. *Now of the things which we have spoken.* Or, " of the things of which we are speaking" (*Stuart*); or as we should say, *of what is said.* The Greek does not necessarily mean things that *had been* spoken, but may refer to all that he was saying, taking the whole subject into consideration. ¶ This is *the sum.* Or this is the principal thing ; referring to what he was *about* to say, not what he *had* said. Our translators seem to have understood this as referring to a *summing up,* or recapitulation of what he had said, and there can be no doubt that the Greek would bear this interpretation. But another exposition has been proposed, adopted by Bloomfield, Stuart, Michaelis, Storr, among the moderns, and found also in Suidas, Theodoret, Theophylact, and others, among the ancients. It is that which regards the word

2 A minister of ¹ the sanctuary ᵃ and of the true tabernacle,

1 or, *holy things.*

which the Lord pitched, and not man.

a ch.9.8,12,24.

rendered *sum—κεφάλαιον*—as meaning the *principal thing;* the chief matter; the most important point. The reason for this interpretation is, that the apostle in fact goes into no *recapitulation* of what he had said, but enters on a new topic relating to the priesthood of Christ. Instead of *going over* what he *had* demonstrated, he enters on a more important point, that the priesthood of Christ is performed in heaven, and that he has entered into the true tabernacle there. All which preceded was type and shadow ; this was that which the former economy had adumbrated. In the previous chapters the apostle had shown that he who sustained this office was superior in rank to the Jewish priests ; that they were frail and dying, and that the office in their hands was changing from one to another, but that that of Christ was permanent and abiding. He now comes to consider the *real nature* of the office itself; the sacrifice which was offered ; the substance of which all in the former dispensation was the type. This was the *principal thing—κεφάλαιον — the head,* the most important matter ; and the consideration of this is pursued through the viiith, ixth, and xth chapters. ¶ *We have such an high priest.* That is settled ; proved ; indisputable. The Christian system is not destitute of that which was regarded as so essential to the old dispensation—the office of a high priest. ¶ *Who is set on the right hand of a throne,* &c. He is exalted to honour and glory before God. The right hand was regarded as the place of principal honour, and when it is said that Christ is at the right hand of God, the meaning is, that he is exalted to the highest honour in the universe ; see Note Mark xvi. 19. Of course the language is figurative—as God has no hands literally—but the language conveys an important meaning, that he is near to God ; is high in his affection and love, and is raised to the most elevated

situation in heaven ; see Phil. ii. 9 ; Notes Eph. i. 21, 22. 2. *A minister of the sanctuary.* Marg. " or holy things." Gr. τῶν ἁγίων. The Greek may either mean *the sanctuary* —denoting the Holy of Holies ; or *holy things.* The word *sanctuary—* קדש—*kodesh*—was given to the tabernacle or temple as *a holy place,* and the plural form which is here used—τὰ ἅγια—was given to the most holy place by way of eminence — the full form of the name being— קדש קדשים — *kodesh kodáshim,* or, ἅγια ἁγίων—*hagia hagiòn,* (Jahn's Arche. § 328), or as it is here used simply as τὰ ἅγια. The connection seems to require us to understand it of the *most holy place,* and not of holy things. The idea is, that the Lord Jesus the Great High Priest, has entered into the Holy of Holies in heaven, of which that in the tabernacle was an emblem. For a description of the Most Holy place in the temple, see Notes on Matt. xxi. 12. ¶ *And of the true tabernacle.* The *real* tabernacle in heaven, of which that among the Hebrews was but the type. The word *tabernacle—σκηνὴ*—means properly a *booth,* hut, or tent, and was applied to the *tent* which Moses was directed to build as the place for the worship of God. That tabernacle, as the temple was afterwards, was regarded as the peculiar abode of God on earth. Here the reference is to heaven, as the dwelling place of God, of which that tabernacle was the emblem or symbol. It is called the " *true* tabernacle," as it is the *real* dwelling of God, of which the one made by Moses was but the *emblem.* It is not moveable and perishable like that made by man, but is unchanging and eternal. ¶ *Which the Lord pitched, and not man.* The word *pitched* is adapted to express the setting up of a *tent.* When it is said that "the Lord pitched the true tabernacle," that is, the permanent dwelling in heaven ; the meaning is, that heaven has been

3 For every high priest is ordained to offer gifts and sacrifices :
wherefore *it is* of necessity that
this man have somewhat also to
offer. *a*

a Ep.5,2; ch.9.12.

fitted up by God himself, and that
whatever is necessary to constitute
that an appropriate abode for the divine majesty has been done by him.
To that glorious dwelling the Redeemer has been received, and there
he performs the office of high priest
in behalf of man. In what way he
does this, the apostle specifies in the
remainder of this chapter, and in ch.
ix. x.

3. *For every high priest is ordained
to offer gifts and sacrifices.* This is a
general statement about the functions
of the high priest. It was the peculiarity of the office ; it constituted its
essence, that some gift or sacrifice
was to be presented. This was indisputable in regard to the Jewish high
priest, and this is involved in the nature of the priestly office everywhere.
A *priest* is one who offers sacrifice,
mainly in behalf of others. The
principles involved in the office are,
(1.) that there is need that some offering or atonement should be made for
sin; and (2.) that there is a fitness or
propriety that some one should be
designated to do it. If this idea that
a priest must offer sacrifice be correct,
then it follows that the name *priest*
should not be given to any one who
is not appointed to offer sacrifice. It
should not therefore be given to the
ministers of the gospel, for it is no
part of their work to offer sacrifice —
the great sacrifice for sin having been
once offered by the Lord Jesus, and
not being again to be repeated. Accordingly the writers in the New
Testament are perfectly uniform and
consistent on this point. The name
priest is never once given to the ministers of the gospel there. They are
called ministers, ambassadors, pastors, bishops, overseers, &c., but never
priests. Nor should they be so called
in the Christian church. The name
priest as applied to Christian ministers, has been derived from the *pa-*

4 For if he were on earth, he
should not be a priest, seeing that
[1] there are priests that offer gifts
according to the law :
5 Who serve unto the exam-

[1] or, *they.*

pists. They hold that the priest *does*
offer as a sacrifice the real body and
blood of Christ in the mass, and holding this, the name *priest* is given to
the minister who does it consistently.
It is not indeed *right* or *Scriptural*—
for the whole doctrine on which it is
based is absurd and false, but while
that doctrine is held the *name* is consistent. But with what show of consistency or propriety can the name
be given to a Protestant minister of
the gospel? ¶ *Wherefore it is of necessity that this man have somewhat
also to offer.* That the Lord Jesus
should make an offering. That is,
since he is declared to be a *priest,*
and since it is essential to the office
that a priest should make an offering,
it is indispensable that he should
bring a sacrifice to God. He could
not be a priest on the acknowledged
principles on which that office is held,
unless he did it. What the offering
was which the Lord Jesus made, the
apostle specifies more fully in ch. ix.
11—14, 25, 26.

4. *For if he were on earth, he should
not be a priest.* He could not perform
that office. The design of this is, to
show a reason why he was removed
to heaven. The reason was, that on
earth there were those who were set
apart to that office, and that he, not
being of the same tribe with them,
could not officiate as priest. There
was an order of men here on earth
consecrated already to that office, and
hence it was necessary that the Lord
Jesus, in performing the functions of
the office, should be removed to another sphere.

5. *Who serve unto the example.*
Who perform their service by the
mere example and shadow of the
heavenly things ; or in a tabernacle,
and in a mode, that is the mere emblem of the reality which exists in
heaven. The reference is to the tabernacle, which was a mere *example*

ple and shadow [a] of heavenly things, as Moses was admonished of God when he was about to make the ta-

a Col.2.17;ch.10.1.

bernacle: for, See, saith he, [b] *that* thou make all things according to the pattern showed to thee in the mount.

b Ex.25.40;26.30.

or *copy* of heaven. The word here rendered *example*—ὑποδείγμα—means a *copy, likeness,* or *imitation.* The tabernacle was made after a *pattern* which was shown to Moses; it was made so as to have some faint *resemblance* to the reality in heaven, and *in* that "copy," or "example," they were appointed to officiate. Their service, therefore, had some *resemblance* to that in heaven. ¶ *And shadow.* That is, in the tabernacle where they served there was a mere shadow of that which was real and substantial. Compared with what is in heaven, it was what the shadow is compared with the substance. A shadow—as of a man, a house, a tree, will indicate the form, the outline, the size of the object; but it has no substance, or reality. So it was with the rites of the Jewish religion. They were designed merely as a shadow of the substantial realities of the true religion, or to present the dim outlines of what is true and real in heaven ; comp. Notes on Col. ii. 17; Heb. x. 1. The word *shadow* here—σκιά—is used in distinction from the body or reality—σῶμα—(comp. Col. ii. 17), and also from εἰκών—a perfect image or resemblance ; see Heb. x. 1. ¶ *Of heavenly things.* Of the heavenly sanctuary ; of what is real and substantial in heaven. That is, there exists in heaven a reality of which the service in the Jewish sanctuary was but the outline. The reference is, undoubtedly, to the service which the Lord Jesus performs there as the great high priest of his people. ¶ *As Moses was admonished of God.* As he was divinely instructed. The word here used —χρηματίζω—means properly to give oracular responses ; to make communications to men in a supernatural way— by dreams, by direct revelations, &c. ; see Matt. ii. 12, 22 ; Luke ii. 26 ; Acts x. 22 ; Heb. xi. 7. ¶ *For, see, saith he* ; Ex. xxv. 9, 40 ; xxvi. 30. In Ex. xl. it is also repeatedly said that Moses executed all the work of the taberna-

cle as he had been commanded. Great care was taken that an exact copy should be exhibited to him of all which he was to make, and that the work should be exactly like the pattern. The reason doubtless was, that as the Jewish service was to be typical, none but God could judge of the form in which the tabernacle should be made It was not to be an edifice of architectural beauty, skill, or taste, but was designed to adumbrate important realities which were known only to God. Hence it was needful that the exact model of them should be given to Moses, and that it should be scrupulously followed. ¶ That *thou make all things.* Not only the tabernacle itself, but the altars, the ark, the candlestick, &c. The form and materials for each were specified, and the exact pattern shown to Moses in the mount. ¶ *According to the pattern.* Gr. τύπον—*type;* that is, figure, form. The word τύπος, *type,* means properly anything produced by the agency or means of *blows* (from τύπτω, *to strike*); hence a mark, stamp, print, impression—as that made by driving nails in the hands (John xx. 25); then a figure or form, as of an image or statue (Acts vii. 43); the form of a doctrine or opinion (Rom. vi. 17); then an example to be imitated or followed(1 Cor. x. 6, 7; Phil. iii. 17; 1 Thess. i. 7; 2 Thess. iii. 9); and hence a *pattern,* or model after which anything is to be made; Acts vii. 44. This is the meaning here. The allusion is to a pattern such as an architect or sculptor uses; a drawing, or figure made in wood or clay, after which the work is to be modelled. The idea is, that some such drawing or model was exhibited to Moses by God on mount Sinai, so that he might have an exact idea of the tabernacle which was to be made. A similar drawing or model of the temple was given by David to Solomon ; 1 Chron. xxviii. 11, 12. We are not indeed to suppose that there was in the case of the pattern shown to Moses, any min-

6 But now hath he obtained a more excellent *a* ministry, by how much also he is the mediator of a better 1 covenant, which was established upon better promises.

7 For if *b* that first *covenant* had been faultless, then should no place have been sought for the second.

a 2C or.3.6-9; ch.7.22.   1 or, *testament.*
b ch.7.11.

iature model of wood or stone actually created and exhibited, but that the form of the tabernacle was exhibited to Moses in vision (Note Isa. i. 1), or was so vividly impressed on his mind that he would have a distinct view of the edifice which was to be reared. ¶ *In the mount.* In mount Sinai; for it was while Moses was there in the presence of God, that these communications were made. 6. *But now hath he obtained.* That is, Christ. ¶ *A more excellent ministry.* A service of a higher order, or of a more exalted nature. It was the real and substantial service of which the other was but the emblem; it pertained to things in heaven, while that was concerned with the earthly tabernacle; it was enduring, while that was to vanish away; see Notes on 2 Cor. iii. 6—9. ¶ *By how much.* By as much as the new covenant is more important than the old, by so much does his ministry exceed in dignity that under the ancient dispensation. ¶ *He is the mediator;* see Notes on Gal. iii. 19, 20, where the word *mediator* is explained. It means here that Christ officiates between God and man according to the arrangements of the new covenant. ¶ *Of a better covenant.* Marg. " Or *testament.*" This word properly denotes a *disposition, arrangement,* or *ordering* of things; and in the Scriptures is employed to describe the arrangement which God has made to secure the maintenance of his worship on earth, and the salvation of men. It is *uniformly* used in the Septuagint and in the New Testament to denote the *covenant* which God makes with men   The word which *properly* denotes a *covenant* or *compact*—συνθήκη —*suntheke* is never used. The writers of the New Testament evidently derived its use from the Septuagint, but why the authors of that version employed it as denoting a *will* rather than the proper one denoting a *com-*

pact, is unknown. It has been supposed by some, and the conjecture is not wholly improbable, that it was because they were unwilling to represent God as making a *compact* or *agreement* with men, but chose rather to represent him as making a mere *arrangement* or *ordering* of things; * comp. Notes on ver. 8, and ch. ix. 16, 17. This is a *better* covenant than the old, inasmuch as it relates mainly to the pardon of sin; to a spiritual and holy religion; see ver. 10. The former related more to external rites and observances, and was destined to vanish away; see ver. 13. ¶ *Which was established upon better promises.* The promises in the first covenant pertained mainly to the present life. They were promises of length of days; of increase of numbers; of seed time and harvest; of national privileges, and of extraordinary peace, abundance, and prosperity. That there was also the promise of eternal life, it would be wrong to doubt; but this was not the main thing. In the new covenant, however, the promise of spiritual blessings becomes the principal thing. The mind is directed to heaven; the heart is cheered with the hopes of immortal life; the favour of God and the anticipation of heaven are secured in the most ample and solemn manner.

7. *For if that first* covenant *had been faultless;* see Note on ch. vii. 11. It is implied here that God had *said* that that covenant was not perfect or faultless. The meaning is not that that first covenant made under Moses had any real *faults* — or inculcated that which was wrong, but that it did not contain the ample provision for the pardon of sin and the salvation of the soul which was desirable. It was merely *preparatory* to the gospel. ¶ *Then should no place have been*

* See supplementary Note, ch. ix. 16, for the *evidence* of the covenant of grace.

8 For finding fault with them, he ^a saith, Behold, the days come,

a Je.31.31-34.

sought for the second. There could not have been—inasmuch as in that case it would have been impossible to have bettered it, and any change would have been only for the worse. 8. *For finding fault with them.* Or rather, "finding fault, he says to them." The difference is only in the punctuation, and this change is required by the passage itself. This is commonly interpreted as meaning that the fault was not found *with* "*them*"—that is, with the Jewish people, for they had had nothing to do in giving the covenant, but *with the covenant itself.* "Stating its defects, he had said to them that he would give them one more perfect, and of which that was only preparatory." So Grotius, Stuart, Rosenmüller, and Erasmus understand it. Doddridge, Koppe, and many others understand it as it is in our translation, as implying that the fault was found with the people, and they refer to the passage quoted from Jeremiah for proof, where the complaint is of the people. The Greek may bear either construction; but may we not adopt a somewhat different interpretation still? May not this be the meaning? "For using the language of complaint, or language that implied that there was defect or error, he speaks of another covenant. According to this, the idea would be, not that he found fault specifically either with the covenant or the people, but generally that he used language which implied that there was defect somewhere when he promised another and a better covenant. The word rendered "finding fault" properly means to censure, or to blame. It is rendered in Mark vii. 2, "they found fault," to wit, with those who ate with unwashed hands; in Rom. ix. 19, "why doth he yet find fault?" It occurs nowhere else in the New Testament. It is language used where wrong has been done; where there is ground of complaint; where it is desirable that there should be a change. In the passage here quoted from Jeremiah, it is not

saith the Lord, when I will make a new covenant with the house of Israel and with the house of Judah.

expressly stated that God found fault either with the covenant or with the people, but that he promised that he would give another covenant, and that it should be *different* from that which he gave them when they came out of Egypt—implying that there was defect in that, or that it was not *faultless.* The whole meaning is, that there was a deficiency which the giving of a new covenant would remove. ¶ *He saith.* In Jeremiah xxxi. 31—34. The apostle has not quoted the passage literally as it is in the Hebrew, but he has retained the substance, and the sense is not essentially varied. The quotation appears to have been made partly from the Septuagint, and partly from memory. This often occurs in the New Testament. ¶ *Behold.* This particle is designed to call attention to what was about to be said as important, or as having some special claim to notice. It is of very frequent occurrence in the Scriptures, being much more freely used by the sacred writers than it is in the classic authors. ¶ *The days come.* The time is coming. This refers doubtless to the times of the Messiah. Phrases such as these, "in the last days," "in after times," and "the time is coming," are often used in the Old Testament to denote the last dispensation of the world — the dispensation when the affairs of the world would be wound up; see the phrase explained in the Notes ch. i. 2, and Isa. ii. 2. There can be no doubt that as it is used by Jeremiah it refers to the times of the gospel. ¶ *When I will make a new covenant.* A covenant that shall contemplate somewhat different ends; that shall have different conditions, and that shall be more effective in restraining from sin. The word *covenant* here refers to the arrangement, plan, or dispensation into which he would enter in his dealings with men. On the meaning of the word, see Notes on Acts vii. 8, and on ch. ix. 16, 17. The word *covenant* with us commonly denotes a compact or agreement between two parties that are equal, and who are free to enter into the agreement or not. In this sense, of course, it cannot be used in relation to the arrangement which God makes with man. There is (1.) no equality between them, and (2.) man is not at liberty to reject any proposal which God shall make. The word, therefore, is used in a more general sense, and more in accordance with the original meaning of the Greek word. It has been above remarked (Notes on ver. 6), that the *proper* word to denote *covenant*, or *compact* —συνθηκη—*syntheke*—is never used either in the Septuagint or in the New Testament—another word—διαθηκη—*diatheke*—being carefully employed. Whether the reason there suggested for the adoption of this word in the Septuagint be the real one or not, the fact is indisputable. I may be allowed to suggest *as possible* here an additional reason why this so uniformly occurs in the New Testament. It is, that the writers of the New Testament *never meant* to represent the transactions between God and man as a *compact* or *covenant* properly so called. They have studiously avoided it, and their uniform practice, in making this nice distinction between the two words, may show the real sense in which the Hebrew word rendered *covenant*—ברית—*berith*—is used in the Old Testament. The word which they employ —διαθηκη—never means a compact or agreement as between equals. It remotely and secondarily means a *will*, or *testament*—and hence our word "New *Testament*." But *this* is not the sense in which it is used in the Bible —for God has never made a *will* in the sense of a testamentary disposition of what belongs to him. We are referred, therefore, in order to arrive at the true Scripture view of this whole matter, to the original meaning of the word— *diatheke*— διαθηκη —as denoting a *disposition, arrangement, plan;* then that which *is ordered*, a law, precept, promise, &c. Unhappily we have no single word which expresses the idea, and hence a constant error has existed in the church—either keeping up the notion of a *compact*—as if

God could make one with men; or the idea of a *will*—equally repugnant to truth. The word διαθηκη is derived from a verb—διατιθημι—meaning to place apart, to set in order; and then to appoint, to make over, to make an arrangement with. Hence the word διαθηκη —*diatheke* — means properly the *arrangement* or *disposition* which God made with men in regard to salvation; the system of statutes, directions, laws, and promises by which men are to become subject to him, and to be saved. The meaning here is, that he would make a *new* arrangement, contemplating as a primary thing that the law should be written in the *heart;* an arrangement which would be peculiarly spiritual in its character, and which would be attended with the diffusion of just views of the Lord.* ¶ *With the house of Israel.* The *family*, or race of Israel, for so the word *house* is often used in the Scriptures and elsewhere. The word *"Israel"* is used in the Scriptures in the following senses. (1.) As a name given to Jacob because he wrestled with the angel of God and prevailed as a prince; Gen. xxxii. 28. (2.) As denoting all who were descended from him—called "the children of Israel"—or the Jewish nation. (3.) As denoting the kingdom of the ten tribes—or the kingdom of Samaria, or Ephraim—that kingdom having taken the name *Israel* in contradistinction from the other kingdom, which was called *Judah.* (4.) As denoting the people of God in general— his true and sincere friends — his church ; see Notes on Rom. ii. 28, 29; ix. 6. In this place quoted from Jeremiah, it seems to be used to denote the kingdom of Israel in contradistinction from that of Judah, and *together* they denote *the whole people of God*, or *the whole Hebrew nation.* This arrangement was ratified and confirmed by the gift of the Messiah, and by implanting his laws in the heart. It is not necessary to understand this as referring to the whole of the Jews, or to the restoration of the ten tribes; but the words *Israel* and *Judah* are

* See supplementary Note on the existence of the covenant of grace, ch. ix. 16.

9 Not according to the covenant that I made with their fathers in the day when I took them
by the hand to lead them out of

the land of Egypt ; because they
continued not in my covenant,
and I regarded them not, saith the
Lord.

used to denote the people of God in
general, and the idea is, that with the
true Israel under the Messiah the laws
of God would be written in the heart
rather than be mere external observances. ¶ *And with the house of Judah.* The kingdom of Judah. This
kingdom consisted of two tribes—
Judah and Benjamin. The tribe
of Benjamin was, however, small,
and the name was lost in that of Judah.

9. *Not according to the covenant,* &c.
An arrangement or dispensation relating mainly to outward observances,
and to temporal blessings. The meaning is, that the new dispensation
would be different from that which
was made with them when they came
out of Egypt. In what respects it
would differ is specified in vers. 10—
12. ¶ *Because they continued not in
my covenant.* In Jeremiah, in the
Hebrew, this is, " while my covenant
they brake." That is, they failed to
comply with the conditions on which
I promised to bestow blessings upon
them. In Jeremiah this is stated as
a simple fact ; in the manner in which
the apostle quotes it, it is given as a
reason why he would give a new arrangement. The apostle has quoted
it literally from the Septuagint, and
the sense is not materially varied.
The word rendered "because"—ὅτι—
may mean " since "—" since they did
not obey that covenant, and it was
ineffectual in keeping them from sin,
showing that it was not *perfect* or
complete in regard to what was needful to be done for man, a new arrangement shall be made that will be without defect." This accords with the
reasoning of the apostle ; and the idea
is, simply, that an arrangement may
be made for man adapted to produce
important ends in one state of society
or one age of the world, which would
not be well adapted to him in another,
and which would not accomplish *all*
which it would be desirable to accomplish for the race. So an arrange-

ment may be made for teaching children which would not answer the purpose of instructing those of mature
years, and which at that time of life
may be superseded by another. A
system of measures may be adapted
to the infancy of society, or to a comparatively rude period of the world,
which would be ill adapted to a more
advanced state of society. Such was
the Hebrew system. It was well
adapted to the Jewish community in
their circumstances, and answered
the end then in view. It served to
keep them separate from other people ;
to preserve the knowledge and the
worship of the true God, and to introduce the gospel dispensation. ¶ *And
I regarded them not.* In Jeremiah
this is, " Although I was an husband
unto them." The Septuagint is as it
is quoted here by Paul. The Hebrew
is, ראנכי בעלתי בם—which may be rendered, " although I was their Lord;"
or as it is translated by Gesenius,
" and I rejected them." The word
בעל—*Bâăl—* means, (1.) to be lord or
master over anything (Isa. xxvi. 13) ;
(2.) to become the husband of any one
(Deut. xxi. 13 ; xxiv. 1) ; (3.) with ב
to disdain, to reject ; so Jer. iii. 14.
It is very probable that this is the
meaning here, for it is not only adopted by the Septuagint, but by the Syriac. So Abulwalid, Kimchi, and
Rabbi Tanchum understood it. The
Arabic word means *to reject, to loath,
to disdain.* All that is necessary to
observe here is, that it cannot be demonstrated that the apostle has not
given the true sense of the prophet.
The probability is, that the Septuagint translators would give the meaning which was commonly understood
to be correct, and there is still more
probability that the Syriac translator
would adopt the true sense, for (1.)
the Syriac and Hebrew languages
strongly resemble each other ; and (2.)
the old Syriac version—the Peshito—
is incomparably a better translation
than the Septuagint. If this, there-

10 For this *is* the covenant that I will make with the house of Israel after those days, saith the Lord ; I will ¹ put my laws

¹ *give.*   2 or, *upon.*

into their mind, and write them ² in their hearts : and *ª* I will be to them a God, and they shall be to me a people :

a Ho.2.23; Zec.8.8.

fore, be the correct translation, the meaning is, that since they did not regard and obey the laws which he gave them, God would reject them as his people, and give new laws better adapted to save men. Instead of regarding and treating them as his friends, he would punish them for their offences, and visit them with calamities.

10. *For this is the covenant.* This is the arrangement, or the dispensation which shall succeed the old one. ¶ *With the house of Israel.* With the true Israel ; that is, with all those whom he will regard and treat as his friends. ¶ *After those days.* This may either mean, " after those days I will put my laws in their hearts," or, " I will make this covenant with them after those days." This difference is merely in the punctuation, and the sense is not materially affected. It seems, to me, however, that the meaning of the Hebrew in Jeremiah is, "in those *after days*" (comp. Notes on Isa. ii. 1), " I will put my laws into their mind ;" that is, in that subsequent period, called in Scripture "the after times," " the last days," "the ages to come," meaning the last dispensation of the world. Thus interpreted, the sense is, that this would be done in the times of the Messiah. ¶ *I will put my laws into their mind.* Marg. *Give.* The word *give* in Hebrew is often used in the sense of *put.* The meaning here is, that they would not be mere external observances, but would affect the conscience and the heart. The laws of the Hebrews pertained mainly to external rites and ceremonies ; the laws of the new dispensation would relate particularly to the inner man, and be designed to control the heart. The grand peculiarity of the Christian system is, that it regulates the conscience and the principles of the soul rather than external matters. It prescribes few external rites, and those are exceedingly

simple, and are merely the proper *expressions* of the pious feelings supposed to be in the heart ; and all attempts either to increase the *number* of these rites, or to make them imposing by their gorgeousness, have done just so much to mar the simplicity of the gospel, and to corrupt religion. ¶ *And write them in their hearts.* Marg. *Upon.* Not on tables of stone or brass, but on the soul itself. That is, the obedience rendered will not be external. The law of the new system will have living power, and bind the faculties of the soul to obedience. The commandment there will be written in more lasting characters than if engraved on tables of stone. ¶ *And I will be to them a God.* This is quoted literally from the Hebrew. The meaning is, that he would sustain to them the appropriate relation of a God ; or, if the expression may be allowed, he would be to them what a God should be, or what it is desirable that men should find in a God. We speak of a father's acting in a manner appropriate to the character of a father ; and the meaning here is, that *he* would be to his people all that is properly implied in the name of *God.* He would be their lawgiver, their counsellor, their protector, their Redeemer, their guide. He would provide for their wants, defend them in danger, pardon their sins, comfort them in trials, and save their souls. He would be a faithful friend, and would never leave them nor forsake them. It is one of the inestimable privileges of his people that JEHOVAH is their God. The living and ever-blessed Being who made the heavens sustains to them the relation of a Protector and a Friend, and they may look up to heaven feeling that he is all which they could desire in the character of a God. ¶ *And they shall be to me a people.* This is not merely stated as *a fact,* but as *a privilege.* It is an inestimable blessing

11 And they shall not teach every man his neighbour, and every man his brother, saying,

Know the Lord : for all [a] shall know me, from the least to the greatest.

a Is.54.13.

to be regarded as one of the people of God, and to feel that we belong to him — that we are associated with those whom he loves, and whom he treats as his friends.

11. *And they shall not teach every man his neighbour*, &c. That is, no one shall be under a necessity of imparting instruction to another, or of exhorting him to become acquainted with the Lord. This is designed to set forth another of the advantages which would attend the new dispensation. In the previous verse it had been said that one advantage of that economy would be, that the law would be written on the heart, and that they who were thus blessed would be regarded as the people of God. Another advantage over the *old* arrangement or covenant is here stated. It is, that the knowledge of the Lord and of the true religion would be deeply engraved on the minds of all, and that there would be no necessity for mutual exhortation and counsel. "They shall have a much more certain and effectual teaching than they can derive from another." *Doddridge.* This passage does not refer to the fact that the true religion will be universally diffused, but that among those who are interested in the blessings of the new covenant there would be an accurate and just knowledge of the Lord. In some way they would be so taught respecting his character that they would not need the aid to be derived from others. All under that dispensation, or sustaining to him the relation of "*a people,*" would *in fact* have a correct knowledge of the Lord. This could not be said of the old dispensation, for (1.) their religion consisted much in outward observances. (2.) It was not to such an extent as the new system a dispensation of the Holy Spirit. (3.) There were not as many means as now for learning the true character of God. (4.) The fullest revelations had not been made to them of that character.

That was reserved for the coming of the Saviour, and under him it was intended that there should be communicated the full knowledge of the character of God. Many MSS., and those among the best, here have πολίτην — *citizen ; fellow-citizen*, instead of πλησίον, *neighbour*, and this is adopted by Griesbach, Tittman, Rosenmüller, Knapp, Stuart, and by many of the fathers. It is also in the version of the LXX. in the place quoted from Jeremiah. It is not easy to determine the true reading, but the word *neighbour* better accords with the meaning of the Hebrew — ץׁר — and there is strong authority from the MSS. and the versions for this reading. ¶ *And every man his brother.* Another form of expression, meaning that there would be no necessity that one should teach another. ¶ *Saying, Know the Lord.* That is, become acquainted with God; learn his character and his will. The idea is, that the true knowledge of Jehovah would prevail as a characteristic of those times. ¶ *For all shall know me.* That is, all those referred to; all who are interested in the new covenant, and who are partakers of its blessings. It does not mean that all *persons, in all lands,* would then know the Lord—though the time will come when that will be true ; but the expression is to be limited by the point under discussion. That point is not that the knowledge of the Lord will fill the whole world, but that all who are interested in the new dispensation will have a much more full and clear knowledge of God than was possessed under the old. Of the truth of this no one can doubt. Christians have a much more perfect knowledge of God and of his government than could have been learned merely from the revelations of the Old Testament.

12. *For I will be merciful to their unrighteousness*, &c. That is, the blessing of *pardon* will be much more richly enjoyed under the new dispen

12 For I will be merciful to their unrighteousness, and their sins and their iniquities will I remember no more

13 In that he saith, A new *a co-venant*, he hath made the first old. Now that which decayeth and waxeth old *is* ready to vanish away.

a Jer.31.12.

sation than it was under the old. This is the *fourth* circumstance adduced in which the new covenant will surpass the old. That was comparatively severe in its inflictions (see ch. x. 28); marked every offence with strictness, and employed the language of mercy much less frequently than that of justice. It was a system where *law* and *justice* reigned; not where *mercy* was the crowning and prevalent attribute. It was true that it contemplated pardon, and made arrangements for it; but it is still true that this is much more prominent in the new dispensation than in the old. It is there the leading idea. It is that which separates it from all other systems. The entire arrangement is one for the pardon of sin in a manner consistent with the claims of law and justice, and it bestows the benefit of forgiveness in the most ample and perfect manner on all who are interested in the plan. In fact, the peculiarity by which the gospel is distinguished from *all other* systems, ancient and modern, philosophic and moral, pagan and deistical, is that it is a system making provision for the forgiveness of sin, and actually bestowing pardon on the guilty. This is the centre, the crown, the glory of the new dispensation. God is merciful to the unrighteousness of men; and their sins are remembered no more. ¶ *Will I remember no more.* This is evidently spoken of the manner of men, and in accordance with human apprehension. It cannot mean literally that God *forgets* that men are sinners, but it means that he treats them *as if* this were forgotten. Their sins are not charged upon them, and they are no more punished than *if* they had passed entirely out of the recollection. God treats them with just as much kindness, and regards them with as sincere affection, *as if* their sins ceased wholly to be remem-

bered, or which is the same thing, *as if* they had never sinned.

13. *In that he saith, A new* covenant, *he hath made the first old.* That is, the use of the word "*new*" implies that the one which it was to supersede was "*old.*" New and old stand in contradistinction from each other. Thus we speak of a new and old house, a new and old garment, &c. The object of the apostle is to show that by the very fact of the arrangement for a *new* dispensation differing so much from the old, it was implied of necessity that *that* was to be superseded, and would vanish away. This was one of the leading points at which he arrived. ¶ *Now that which decayeth and waxeth old is ready to vanish away.* This is a *general* truth which would be undisputed, and which Paul applies to the case under consideration. An old house, or garment; an ancient tree; an aged man, all have indications that they are soon to disappear. They cannot be expected to remain long. The very fact of their growing *old* is an indication that they will soon be gone. So Paul says it was with the dispensation that was represented as *old.* It had symptoms of decay. It had lost the vigour which it had when it was fresh and new; it had every mark of an antiquated and a declining system; and it had been expressly declared that a new and more perfect dispensation was to be given to the world. Paul concluded, therefore, that the *Jewish* system must soon disappear.

REMARKS.

1. The fact that we have a high priest, is fitted to impart consolation to the pious mind; vers. 1—5. He ever lives, and is ever the same. He is a minister of the true sanctuary, and is ever before the mercy-seat. He enters there not once a year only, but has entered there to abide there for

ever. We can *never* approach the throne of mercy without having a high priest there—for he at all times, day and night, appears before God. The merits of his sacrifice are never exhausted, and God is never wearied with hearing his pleadings in behalf of his people. He is the same that he was when he gave himself on the cross. He has the same love and the same compassion which he had then, and that love which led him to make the atonement, will lead him always to regard with tenderness those for whom he died.

2. It is a privilege to live under the blessings of the Christian system; ver. 6. We have a better covenant than the old one was—one less expensive and less burdensome, and one that is established upon better promises. Now the sacrifice is made, and we do not have to renew it every day. It was made once for all, and need never be repeated. Having now a high priest in heaven who has made the sacrifice, we may approach him in any part of the earth, and at all times, and feel that our offering will be acceptable to him. If there is any blessing for which we ought to be thankful, it is for the Christian religion; for we have only to look at any portion of the heathen world, or even to the condition of the people of God under the comparatively dark and obscure Jewish dispensation, to see abundant reasons for thanksgiving for what we enjoy.

3. Let us often contemplate the mercies of the new dispensation with which we are favoured—the favours of that religion whose smiles and sunshine we are permitted to enjoy; vers. 10—12. It contains all that we want, and is exactly adapted to our condition. It has that for which every man should be thankful; and has not one thing which should lead a man to reject it. It furnishes all the security which we could desire for our salvation; lays upon us no oppressive burdens or charges; and accomplishes all which we ought to desire in our souls. Let us contemplate a moment the arrangements of that "covenant," and see how fitted it is to make man blessed and happy.

First, It writes the laws of God on the mind and the heart; ver. 10. It not only *reveals* them, but it secures their observance. It has made arrangements for *disposing* men to keep the laws—a thing which has not been introduced into any other system. Legislators may enact good laws, but they cannot induce others to obey them; parents may utter good precepts, but they cannot engrave them on the hearts of their children; and sages may express sound maxims and just precepts in morals, but there is no security that they will be regarded. So in all the heathen world—there is no power to inscribe good maxims and rules of living on the *heart*. They may be written; recorded on tablets; hung up in temples; but still men will not regard them. They will still give indulgence to evil passions, and lead wicked lives. But it is not so with the arrangement which God has made in the plan of salvation. One of the very first provisions of that plan is, that the laws shall be inscribed *on the heart*, and that there shall be a DISPOSITION to obey. Such a system is what man wants, and such a system he can nowhere else find.

Secondly, This new arrangement *reveals to us a God* such as we need; ver. 10. It contains the promise that he will be "*our* God." He will be to his people all that can be *desired in God;* all that man could wish. He is just such a God as the human mind, when it is pure, most loves; has all the attributes which it could be desired there should be in his character; has done all that we could desire a God to do; and is ready to do all that we could wish a God to perform. *Man wants a God;* a God in whom he can put confidence, and on whom he can rely. The ancient Greek philosopher *wanted a God*—and he would then have made a beautiful and efficient system of morals; the heathen *want a God*—to dwell in their empty temples, and in their corrupt hearts; the Atheist *wants a God* to make him calm, contented, and happy in this life—for he has no God now, and man everywhere, wretched, sinful, suffering, dying, WANTS A GOD. Such a God is revealed in the Bible —one whose character we may contemplate with ever-increasing admiration; one who has all the attributes which we can desire; one who will minister to us all the consolation which we need in this world; and one who will be to us *the same God for ever and ever.*

Thirdly, The new covenant contemplates the diffusion of *knowledge;* ver. 11. This too was what man needed, for everywhere else he has been ignorant of God and of the way of salvation. The whole heathen world is sunk in ignorance, and indeed all men, except as they are enlightened by the gospel, are in profound darkness on the great questions which most nearly pertain to their welfare. But it is not so with the new arrangement which God has made with his people. It is a fact that they know the Lord, and a dispensation which would produce that is just what man needed. There are two things hinted at in ver. 11 of this chapter, which are worthy of more than a passing notice, illustrating the excellency of the Christian religion. The *first* is, that in the new dispensation *all would know the Lord.* The matter of fact is, that the obscurest and most unlettered Christian often has a knowledge of God which sages never had, and which is never obtained except by the teachings of the Spirit of God. However this may be accounted for, the fact cannot be denied. There is a clear and elevating view of God; a knowledge of him which exerts a practical influence on the heart, and which transforms the soul; and a correctness of apprehension in regard to what truth is, possessed by the humble Christian, though a peasant, which philosophy never imparted to its votaries. Many a sage would be instructed in the truths of religion if he would sit down and converse with the comparatively unlearned Christian, who has no book but his Bible. The other thing hinted at here is, that all would know the Lord *from the least to the greatest.* Children and youth, as well as age

and experience, would have an acquaintance with God. This promise is remarkably verified under the new dispensation. One of the most striking things of the system is, the attention which it pays to the young; one of its most wonderful effects is the knowledge which it is the means of imparting to those in early life. Many a child in the Sabbath-school has a knowledge of God which Grecian sages never had; many a youth in the Church has a more consistent acquaintance with God's real plan of governing and saving men, than all the teachings which philosophy could ever furnish.

Fourthly, The new dispensation contemplates the pardon of sin, and is, therefore, fitted to the condition of man; ver. 12. It is what man needs. The knowledge of some way of pardon is that which human nature has been sighing for for ages; which has been sought in every system of religion, and by every bloody offering; but which has never elsewhere been found. The philosopher had no assurance that God would pardon, and indeed one of the chief aims of the philosopher has been to convince himself that he had no *need* of pardon. The heathen have had no assurance that their offerings have availed to put away the divine anger, and to obtain forgiveness. *The only assurance anywhere furnished that sin may be forgiven, is in the Bible.* This is the great peculiarity of the system recorded there, and this it is which renders it so valuable above all the other systems. It furnishes the *assurance* that sins may be pardoned, and shows *how* it may be done. This is what we *must* have, or perish. And why, since Christianity reveals a way of forgiveness—a way honourable to God and not degrading to man—why should any man reject it? Why should not the guilty embrace a system which proclaims pardon to the guilty, and which assures all that, if they will embrace him who is the " Mediator of the new covenant," " God will be merciful to their unrighteousness, and will remember their iniquities no more."

CHAPTER IX.

THEN verily the first covenant had also [1] ordinances
of divine service, and a worldly
sanctuary. [a]

1 or, *ceremonies.*	a Ex.25.8.

CHAPTER IX.

ANALYSIS OF THE CHAPTER.

The general design of this chapter is the same as the two preceding, to show that Christ as high priest is superior to the Jewish high priest. This the apostle had already shown to be true in regard to his rank, and to the dispensation of which he was the " mediator." He proceeds now to show that this was also true in reference to the efficacy of the sacrifice which he made; and in order to this, he gives an account of the ancient Jewish sacrifices, and compares them with that made by the Redeemer. The essential point is, that the former dispensation was mere shadow, type, or figure, and that the latter was real and efficacious. The chapter comprises, in illustration of this general idea, the following points:

(1.) A description of the ancient tabernacle, and of the utensils that were in it; vers. 1—5.

(2.) A description of the services in it, particularly of that performed by the high priest once a year ; vers. 6, 7

(3.) All this was typical and symbolical, and was a standing demonstration that the way into the most holy place in heaven was not yet fully revealed ; vers. 8—10.

(4.) Christ was now come — the substance of which that was the shadow ; the real sacrifice of which that was the emblem ; vers. 11—14. He pertained as a priest to a more perfect tabernacle (ver. 11); he offered not the blood of bulls and goats, but his own blood (ver. 12) ; with that blood he entered into the most holy place in heaven (ver. 12) ; and if the blood of bulls and goats was admitted to be efficacious in putting away external uncleanness, it must be admitted that the blood of Christ had an efficacy in cleansing the conscience ; vers. 13, 14.

(5.) His blood is efficacious not only in remitting present sins, but it extends in its efficacy even to past ages, and removes the sins of those who had worshipped God under the former covenant ; ver. 15.

(6.) The apostle then proceeds to show that it was necessary that the mediator of the new covenant should shed his own blood, and that the blood thus shed should be applied to purify those for whom the sacrifice was made ; vers. 16—23. This he shows by the following considerations, viz :

(*a*) He argues it from the nature of a covenant or compact, showing that it was ratified only over dead sacrifices, and that of necessity the victim that was set apart to confirm or ratify it must be slain ; see Notes on vers. 16, 17.

(*b*) The first covenant was confirmed or ratified by blood, and hence it was necessary that, since the "patterns" of the heavenly things were sprinkled with blood, the heavenly things themselves should be purified with better sacrifices ; vers. 18—23.

(7.) The offering made by the Redeemer was to be made but once. This arose from the necessity of the case, since it could not be supposed that the mediator would suffer *often*, as the high priest went once every year into the most holy place. He had come and died once in the last dispensation of things on earth, and then had entered into heaven and could suffer no more ; vers. 24—26.

(8.) In the close of the chapter the apostle adverts to the fact that there was a remarkable resemblance, in one respect, between the death of Christ and the death of all men. It was appointed to them to die once, and but once, and so Christ died but once. As a man, it was in accordance with the universal condition of things that he should die once ; and in accordance with the same condition of things it was proper that he should die *but* once. In like manner there was a resemblance or fitness in regard to what would occur after death. Man was to appear at the judgment. He

2 For there was a tabernacle *a* made, the first, wherein *was* the candlestick, and the table, *b* and

was not to cease to be, but would stand hereafter at the bar of God. In like manner, Christ would again appear. He did not cease to exist when he expired, but would appear again that he might save his people ; vers. 27, 28.

1. *Then verily.* Or, moreover. The object is to describe the tabernacle in which the service of God was celebrated under the former dispensation, and to show that it had a reference to what was future, and was only an imperfect representation of the reality. It was important to show this, as the Jews regarded the ordinances of the tabernacle and of the whole Levitical service as of divine appointment, and of perpetual obligation. The object of Paul is to prove that they were to give place to a more perfect system, and hence it was necessary to discuss their real nature. ¶ *The first* covenant. The word "covenant" is not in the Greek, but is not improperly supplied. The meaning is, that the former arrangement or dispensation had religious rites and services connected with it. ¶ *Had also ordinances.* Marg. *Ceremonies.* The Greek word means *laws, precepts, ordinances ;* and the idea is, that there were laws regulating the worship of God. The Jewish institutions abounded with such laws. ¶ *And a worldly sanctuary.* The word *sanctuary* means a holy place, and is applied to a house of worship, or a temple. Here it may refer either to the temple or to the tabernacle. As the temple was constructed after the same form as the tabernacle, and had the same furniture, the description of the apostle may be regarded as applicable to either of them, and it is difficult to determine which he had in his eye. The term "worldly," applied to "sanctuary," here means that it pertained to this world; it was contradistinguished from the heavenly sanctuary not made with hands where Christ was now gone; comp. vers. 11 24. It does not mean that it was *worldly* in the sense in which that

the show-bread ; *c* which is called the Sanctuary. [1]

a Ex.26.1,37. b Ex.40.4. c Ex.25.30. 1 or,*holy*.

word is now used as denoting the opposite of spiritual, serious, religious, but worldly in the sense that it belonged to the earth rather than to heaven; it was made by human hands, not directly by the hands of God.

2. *For there was a tabernacle made.* The word "tabernacle" properly means a tent, a booth, or a hut, and was then given by way of eminence to the tent for public worship made by Moses in the wilderness. For a description of this, see Ex. xxvi. In this place the word means the *outer sanctuary* or room in the tabernacle; that is, the *first* room which was entered—called here "the first." The same word— σκηνή—is used in ver. 3 to denote the *inner* sanctuary, or holy of holies. The tabernacle, like the temple afterwards, was divided into two parts by the veil (Ex. xxvi. 31, 33), one of which was called "the holy place," and the other "the holy of holies." The exact size of the two rooms in the tabernacle is not specified in the Scriptures, but it is commonly supposed that the tabernacle was divided in the same manner as the temple was afterwards; that is, two-thirds of the interior constituted the holy place, and one-third the holy of holies. According to this, the holy place, or "*first* tabernacle" was twenty cubits long by ten broad, and the most holy place was ten cubits square. The whole length of the tabernacle was about fifty-five feet, the breadth eighteen, and the height eighteen. In the temple, the two rooms, though of the same relative proportions, were of course much larger. See a description of the temple in the Notes on Matt. xxi. 12. In both cases, the holy place was at the east, and the Holy of Holies at the west end of the sacred edifice. ¶ *The first.* The first room on entering the sacred edifice, here called the "first tabernacle." The apostle proceeds now to enumerate the various articles of furniture which were in the two rooms of the tabernacle and temple. His object seems to be, not for

information, for it could not be supposed that they to whom he was writing were ignorant on this point, but partly to show that it could not be said that he spoke of that of which he had no information, or that he undervalued it; and partly to show the real nature of the institution, and to prove that it was of an imperfect and typical character, and had a designed reference to something that was to come. It is remarkable that though he maintains that the whole institution was a "figure" of what was to come, and though he specifies by name all the furniture of the tabernacle, he does not attempt to explain their particular typical character, nor does he affirm that they *had* such a character. He does not say that the candlestick, and the table of show-bread, and the ark, and the cherubim were designed to adumbrate some particular truth or fact of the future dispensation, or had a designed spiritual meaning. It would have been happy if all expositors had followed the example of Paul, and had been content, as he was, to state *the facts* about the tabernacle, and the general truth that the dispensation was intended to introduce a more perfect economy, without endeavouring to explain the typical import of every pin and pillar of the ancient place of worship. If those things *had* such a designed typical reference, it is remarkable that Paul did not go into an explanation of that fact in the epistle before us. Never could a better opportunity for doing it occur than was furnished here. Yet it was not done. Paul is silent where many expositors have found occasion for admiration. Where they have seen the profoundest wisdom, he saw none; where they have found spiritual instruction in the various implements of divine service in the sanctuary, he found none. Why should we be more wise than he was? Why attempt to hunt for types and shadows where he found none? And why should we not be limited to the views which he *actually expressed* in regard to the design and import of the ancient dispensation? Following an inspired example we are on solid ground, and

are not in danger. But the moment we leave that, and attempt to spiritualize everything in the ancient economy, we are in an open sea without compass or chart, and no one knows to what fairy lands he may be drifted. As there are frequent allusions in the New Testament to the different parts of the tabernacle furniture here specified, it may be a matter of interest and profit to furnish an illustration of the most material of them.

[Without attempting to explain the typical import of every pin and pillar of the tabernacle, one may be excused for thinking, that such *prominent* parts of its furniture, as the ark, the candlestick, and the cherubim, were designed as types. Nor can it be wrong to inquire into the spiritual significancy of them, under such guidance as the light of Scripture, here or elsewhere affords. This has been done by a host of most sober and learned commentators. It is of no use to allege, that the apostle himself has given no particular explanation of these matters, since this would have kept him back too long from his main object; and is, therefore, expressly declined by him. "Yet," says M'Lean, "his manner of declining it implies, that each of these sacred utensils had a mystical signification. They were all constructed according to particular divine directions, Ex. xxv. The apostle terms them, "the example and shadow of heavenly things," Heb. viii. 5; "the patterns of things in the heavens, ix. 23; and these typical patterns included not only the tabernacle and its services, but every article of its furniture, as is plain from the words of Moses, Ex. xxv. 8, 9. There are also other passages which seem to allude to, and even to explain, some of these articles, such as the golden candlestick, with its seven lamps, Rev. i. 12, 13, 20; the golden censer, viii. 3, 4; the vail, Heb. x. 20; the mercy-seat, Rom. iii. 25; Heb. iv. 16; and, perhaps, the angelic cherubim, 1 Pet. i. 12." It must, however, be acknowledged that too great care and caution cannot be used in investigating such subjects.]

¶ *The candlestick.* For an account of the candlestick, see Ex. xxv. 31—37. It was made of pure gold, and had seven branches, that is, three on each side and one in the centre. These branches had on the extremities seven golden lamps, which were fed with pure olive oil, and which were lighted "to give light over against it;" that is, they shed light on the altar of incense, the table of show-bread, and generally on the furniture of the holy place. These branches were made with three "bowls," "knops," and "flowers" occurring alternately on each one of the six branches ; while on the centre or upright shaft there were *four* "bowls," "knops" and "flowers" of this kind. These ornaments were probably taken from the almond, and represented the flower of that tree in various stages. The "bowls" on the branches of the candlestick probably meant the *calyx* or *cup* of that plant from which the flower springs. The "knops" probably referred to some ornament on the candlestick mingled with the "bowls" and the "flowers," perhaps designed as an imitation of the nut or fruit of the almond. The "flowers" were evidently ornaments resembling the flowers on the almond-tree, wrought, as all the rest were, in pure gold. See Bush's Notes on Exodus xxv. The candlestick was undoubtedly designed to furnish *light* in the dark room of the tabernacle and temple ; and in accordance with the general plan of those edifices, was ornamented after the most chaste and pure views of ornamental architecture of those times—but there is no evidence that its branches, and bowls, and knops, and flowers had each a peculiar typical significance. The sacred writers are wholly silent as to any such reference, and it is not well to attempt to be "wise above that which is written." An expositor of the Scripture cannot have a safer guide than the sacred writers themselves. How should any uninspired man know that these things had such a peculiar typical signification?[*] The candlestick was placed on the south, or left-hand side of the holy place as one entered, the row of lamps being probably parallel with the wall. It was at first placed in the tabernacle, and afterwards removed into the temple built by Solomon. Its subsequent history is unknown. Probably it was destroyed when the temple was taken by the Chaldeans. The form of the candlestick in the second temple, whose figure is preserved on the "Arch of Titus" in Rome, was of somewhat

[*] See supplementary Note p. 183.

different construction. But it is to be remembered that the articles taken away from the temple by Vespasian were not the same as those made by Moses, and Josephus says expressly that the candlestick was altered from its original form. ¶ *And the table.* That is, the table on which the show-bread was placed. This table was made of shittim-wood, overlaid with gold. It was two cubits long, and one cubit broad, and a cubit and a half high ; that is, about three feet and a half in length, one foot and nine inches wide, and two feet and a half in height. It was furnished with rings or staples, through which were passed staves, by which it was carried. These staves, we are informed by Josephus, were removed when the table was at rest, so that they might not be in the way of the priest as they officiated in the tabernacle. It stood lengthwise east and west, on the north side of the holy place. ¶ *And the show-bread.* On the table just described. This bread consisted of twelve loaves, placed on the table, every Sabbath. The Hebrews affirm that they were square loaves, having the four sides covered with leaves of gold. They were arranged in two piles, of course with six in a pile ; Lev. xxiv. 5—9. The number twelve was selected with reference to the twelve tribes of Israel. They were made without leaven ; were renewed each Sabbath, when the old loaves were then taken away to be eaten by the priests only. The Hebrew phrase rendered "show-bread" means properly "bread of faces," or "bread of presence." The LXX. render it ἄρτους ἐνώπιους—*for replaced loaves.* In the New Testament it is, ἡ πρόθεσις τῶν ἄρτων—*the placing of bread;* and in Symmachus, "bread of proposition," or placing. Why it was called "bread of presence" has been a subject on which expositors have been much divided. Some have held that it was because it was *before,* or in the presence of the symbol of the divine presence in the tabernacle, though in another department ; some that it was because it was set there to be seen by *men,* rather than to be seen by God. Others that it had an emblematic de-

3 And after the second veil, *a* the tabernacle, which is called the Holiest of all;

a Ex.26.31,33.

4 Which had the golden *b* censer, and the ark *c* of the covenant overlaid round about with gold, where-

b Le.16.12.   *c* Ex.25.10,&c.

sign, looking forward to the Messiah as the food or nourishment of the soul, and was substantially the same as the table spread with the symbols of the Saviour's body and blood. See Bush, *in loc.* But of this last mentioned opinion, it may be asked where is the proof? It is not found in the account of it in the Old Testament, and there is not the slightest intimation in the New Testament that it had any such design. The *object* for which it was placed there can be only a matter of conjecture, as it is not explained in the Bible, and it is more difficult to ascertain the use and design of the show-bread than of almost any other emblem of the Jewish economy. *Calmet.* Perhaps the true idea, after all that has been written and conjectured is, that the *table* and the *bread* were for the sake of carrying out the idea that the tabernacle was the *dwelling-place* of God, and that there was a propriety that it should be fitted up with the usual appurtenances of a dwelling. Hence there was a candlestick and a table, because these were the common and ordinary furniture of a room; and the idea was to be kept up constantly that that was the dwelling-place of the Most High by lighting and trimming the lamps every day, and by renewing the bread on the table periodically. The most simple explanation of the phrase "bread of faces," or "bread of presence" is, that it was so called because it was set before the *face* or in the *presence* of God in the tabernacle. The various forms which it has been supposed would represent the table of show-bread may be seen in Calmet's Large Dictionary. The Jews say that they were separated by plates of gold. ¶ *Which is called the sanctuary.* Marg. "*Or, holy.*" That is, *the holy place.* The name *sanctuary* was commonly given to the whole edifice, but with strict propriety appertained only to this first room.

3. *And after the second veil.* There

were two *veils* to the tabernacle. The one which is described in Ex. xxvi. 36, 37, was called "the hanging for the door of the tent," and was made of "blue, and purple, and scarlet, and fine twined linen," and was suspended on five pillars of shittim-wood, overlaid with gold. This answered for a *door* to the whole tabernacle. The second or inner veil, here referred to, divided the holy from the most holy place. This is described in Ex. xxvi. 31—33. It was made of the same materials as the other, though it would seem in a more costly manner, and with more embroidered work. On this veil the figures of the cherubim were curiously wrought. The design of this veil was to separate the holy from the most holy place; and in regard to its symbolical meaning we can be at no loss, for the apostle Paul has himself explained it in this chapter; see Notes on vers. 8—14. *The tabernacle.* That is, the *inner* tabernacle; or that which more properly was called the tabernacle. The name was given to either of the two rooms into which it was divided, or to the whole structure. ¶ *Which is called the Holiest of all.* It was called "the Most Holy place;" "the Holy of Holies;" or "the Holiest of all." It was so called because it was the symbol of the divine presence—the *Shekinah*—dwelt there between the Cherubim.

4. *Which had the golden censer.* The censer was a *fire-pan,* made for the purpose of carrying fire, in order to burn incense on it in the place of worship. The forms of the censer were various. Some difficulty has been felt respecting the statement of Paul here that the "golden censer" was in the most holy place, from the fact that no such utensil is mentioned by Moses as pertaining to the tabernacle, nor in the description of Solomon's temple, which was modelled after the tabernacle, is there any account of it given. But the following considerations will probably remove the diffi-

in *was* the golden ^a pot that had
manna, and Aaron's rod ^b that

a Ex.16.33.   b Nu.17.10.

culty. (1.) Paul was a Jew, and was
familiar with what pertained to the
temple, and gave such a description
of it as would be in accordance with
what actually existed in his time.
The fact that Moses does not expressly mention it, does not prove that *in
fact* no such censer was laid up in
the most holy place. (2.) Aaron and
his successors were expressly commanded to burn incense in a "censer"
in the most holy place before the
mercy-seat. This was to be done on
the great day of atonement, and but
once in a year; Lev. xvi. 12, 13. (3.)
There is every probability that the
censer that was used on such an occasion was made of gold. All the
implements that were employed in
the most holy place were made of
gold, or overlaid with gold, and it is
in the highest degree improbable that
the high priest would use any other
on so solemn an occasion; comp. 1
Kings vii. 50. (4.) As the golden
censer was to be used only once in a
year, it would naturally be laid away
in some secure situation, and none
would so obviously occur as the most
holy place. There it would be perfectly safe. No one was permitted
to enter there but the high priest, and
being preserved there it would be always ready for his use. The statement of Paul, therefore, has the highest probability, and undoubtedly accords with what actually occurred in
the tabernacle and the temple. The
object of the incense burned in worship was to produce an agreeable fragrance or smell ; see Notes on Luke
i. 9. ¶ *And the ark of the covenant.*
This ark or *chest* was made of shittim-
wood, was two cubits and a half long,
a cubit and a half broad, and the same
in height ; Ex. xxv. 10. It was completely covered with gold, and had a
lid, which was called the "mercy-
seat," on which rested the Shekinah,
the symbol of the divine presence,
between the outstretched wings of the
cherubim. It was called "the ark of
the covenant," because within it were

budded, and the tables ^c of the
covenant ;

c Ex.34.29; 40.20; De.10.2,5.

the two tables of the covenant, or the
law of God written on tables of stone.
It was a simple *chest, coffer,* or *box,*
with little ornament, though rich in
its materials. A golden crown or
moulding ran around the top, and it
had rings and staves in its sides by
which it might be borne ; Ex. xxv.
12—16. This ark was regarded as
the most sacred of all the appendages
of the tabernacle. Containing the
law, and being the place where the
symbol of the divine presence was
manifested, it was regarded as peculiarly holy, and in the various wars
and revolutions in the Hebrew commonwealth, it was guarded with peculiar care. After the passage over
the Jordan it remained for some time
at Gilgal (Josh. iv. 19), whence it was
removed to Shiloh ; 1 Sam. i. 3. From
hence the Israelites took it to their
camp, apparently to animate them in
battle, but it was taken by the Philistines ; 1 Sam. iv. The Philistines,
however, oppressed by the hand of
God, resolved to return it, and sent it
to Kirjath-Jearim; 1 Sam. vii. 1. In
the reign of Saul it was at Nob. David conveyed it to the house of Obed-
edom, and thence to his palace on
Mount Zion ; 2 Sam. vi. At the
dedication of the temple it was placed
in the Holy of Holies by Solomon,
where it remained for many years.
Subsequently, it is said, the wicked
kings of Judah, abandoning themselves to idolatry, established idols in
the most holy place itself, and the
priests removed the ark, and bore it
from place to place to secure it from
profanation. *Calmet.* When Josiah
ascended the throne he commanded
the priests to restore the ark to its
place in the sanctuary, and forbade
them to carry it about from one place
to another as they had before done ;
2 Chron. xxxv. 3. The subsequent
history of the ark is unknown. It is
probable that it was either destroyed
when the city of Jerusalem was taken
by Nebuchadnezzar, or that it was
carried with other spoils to Babylon.

There is no good reason to suppose that it was ever in the second temple, and it is generally admitted by the Jews that the ark of the covenant was one of the things that were wanting there. Abarbanel says, that the Jews flatter themselves that it will be restored by the Messiah. ¶ *Wherein.* That is, *in the ark*—for so the construction naturally requires. In 1 Kings viii. 9, however, it is said that there was nothing *in* the ark, "save the two tables of stone which Moses put there at Horeb," and it has been supposed by some that the pot of manna and the rod of Aaron were not *in* the ark, but that they were in capsules, or ledges made on its sides for their safe keeping, and that this should be rendered "*by* the ark." But the apostle uses the same language respecting the pot of manna and the rod of Aaron which he does about the two tables of stone, and as they were certainly *in* the ark, the fair construction here is that the pot of manna and the rod of Aaron were in it also. The account in Ex. xvi. 32 — 34 ; Num. xvii. 10, is, that they were laid up in the most holy place, "before the testimony," and there is no improbability whatever in the supposition that they were *in* the ark. Indeed, that would be the most safe place to keep them, as the tabernacle was often taken down and removed from place to place. It is clear from the passage in 1 Kings viii. 9, that they were not *in* the ark in the temple, but there is no improbability in the supposition that before the temple was built they might have been removed from the ark and lost. When the ark was carried from place to place, or during its captivity by the Philistines, it is probable that they were lost, as we never hear of them afterwards. ¶ *The golden pot.* In Ex. xvi. 33, it is simply "a pot," without specifying the material. In the Septuagint it is rendered "golden pot," and as the other utensils of the sanctuary were of gold, it may be fairly presumed that this was also. ¶ *That had manna.* A small quantity of manna which was to be preserved as a perpetual remembrancer of the food which they had eaten in their long journey in the wilderness, and of the goodness of God in miraculously supplying their wants. As the manna, also, would not of itself keep, (Ex. xvi. 20), the fact that this was to be laid up to be preserved from age to age, was a perpetual miracle in proof of the presence and faithfulness of God. On the subject of the manna, see Bush's Notes on Exodus xvi. 15. ¶ *And Aaron's rod that budded.* That budded and blossomed as a proof that God had chosen him to minister to him. The princes of the tribes were disposed to rebel, and to call in question the authority of Aaron. To settle the matter, each one was required to take a rod or staff of office, and to bring it to Moses with the name of the tribe to which it appertained written on it. These were laid up by Moses in the tabernacle, and it was found on the next day that the rod marked with the name of Levi had budded and blossomed, and produced almonds. In perpetual remembrance of this miracle, the rod was preserved in the ark ; Num. xvii. Its subsequent history is unknown. It was not *in* the ark when the temple was built, nor is there any reason to suppose that it was preserved to that time. ¶ *And the tables of the covenant.* The two tables of stone on which the ten commandments were written. They were expressly called "the words of the covenant" in Ex. xxxiv. 28. On the word *covenant*, see Notes on vers. 16 and 17 of this chapter. These two tables were in the ark at the time the temple was dedicated. 1 Kings viii. 9. Their subsequent history is unknown. It is probable that they shared the fate of the ark, and were either carried to Babylon, or were destroyed when the city was taken by Nebuchadnezzar.

5. *And over it.* That is, over the ark. ¶ *The cherubim of glory.* A Hebrew mode of expression, meaning *the glorious cherubim.* The word *cherubim* is the Hebrew form of the plural, of which *cherub* is the singular. The word *glory* used here in connection with "*cherubim*," refers to the splendour, or magnificence of the

5 And over it the cherubim *a* of glory shadowing the mercy-seat ; of which we cannot now speak particularly.

a Ex.25.18,22.

image, as being carved with great skill, and covered with gold. There were two cherubim on the ark, placed on the lid in such a manner that their faces looked inward towards each other, and downward toward the mercy-seat. They stretched out their wings "on high," and covered the mercy-seat, or the lid of the ark; Ex. xxv. 18—20 ; comp. 1 Kings viii. 6, 7; 1 Chron. xxviii. 18. In the temple, the cherubim were made of the olive tree, and were ten cubits high. They were overlaid with gold, and were so placed that the wing of one touched the wall on one side of the Holy of Holies, and that of the other the other side, and their wings met together over the ark; 1 Kings vi. 23—28. It is not probable, however, that this was the form used in the tabernacle, as wings thus expanded would have rendered it inconvenient to carry them from place to place. Of the form and design of the cherubim much has been written, and much that is the mere creation of fancy, and the fruit of wild conjecture. Their design is not explained in the Bible, and silence in regard to it would have been wisdom. If they were intended to be symbolical, as is certainly possible, (comp. Ezek. x. 20 —22), it is impossible now to determine the object of the symbol. Who is authorized to explain it ? Who can give to his speculations anything more than the authority of *pious conjecture ?* And of what advantage, therefore, can speculation be, where the volume of inspiration says nothing?* They who wish to examine this subject more fully, with the various opinions that have been formed on it, may consult the following works, viz. : Calmet's Dictionary, Fragment No. 152, with the numerous illustrations; Bush's Notes on Exodus xxv. 18 ; and the Quarterly Christian Spectator, vol. viii. pp. 368

* See the supplementary Note, ver. 2.

6 Now when these things were thus ordained, the priests *b* went always into the first tabernacle, accomplishing the service *of God.*

b Nu.28.3.

—388. Drawings resembling the cherubim were not uncommon on ancient sculptures. ¶ *Shadowing.* Stretching out its wings so as to cover the mercy-seat. ¶ *The mercy-seat.* The cover of the ark on which rested the cloud or visible symbol of the divine presence. It was called "mercy-seat," or *propitiatory — ἱλαστήριον —* because it was this which was sprinkled over with the blood of atonement or propitiation, and because it was from this place, on which the symbol of the deity rested, that God manifested himself as propitious to sinners. The blood of the atonement was that through or by means of which he declared his mercy to the guilty. Here God was supposed to be seated, and from this place he was supposed to dispense mercy to man when the blood of the atonement was sprinkled there. This was undoubtedly designed to be a symbol of his dispensing mercy to men in virtue of the blood which the Saviour shed as the great sacrifice for guilt; see vers. 13, 14. ¶ *Of which we cannot now speak particularly.* That is, it is not my present design to speak particularly of these things. These matters were well understood by those to whom he wrote, and his object did not require him to go into a fuller explanation.

6. *When these things were thus ordained.* Thus arranged or appointed. Having shown what the tabernacle *was,* the apostle proceeds to show what was *done in it.* ¶ *The priests went always into the first tabernacle.* The outer tabernacle called the holy place. They were not permitted to enter the Holy of Holies, that being entered only once in a year by the High Priest. The holy place was entered every day to make the morning and evening oblation. ¶ *Accomplishing the service* of God. Performing the acts of worship which God had appointed—burning incense, &c. ; Luke i. 9.

7 But into the second *went* the high priest alone *a* once every year, not without blood, which he offered for *b* himself, and *for* the errors of the people :

a Ex.30.10; Le.16.2,&c.   *b* ch.5.3.

---

7. *But into the second.* The second apartment or room, called the most holy place ; ver. 3. ¶ Went *the high priest alone once every year.* On the great day of atonement ; Ex. xxx. 10. On that day he probably entered the Holy of Holies three or four times, first to burn incense, Lev. xvi. 12 ; then to sprinkle the blood of the bullock on the mercy-seat, Lev. xvi. 14 ; then he was to kill the goat of the sin-offering, and bring that blood within the veil and sprinkle it also on the mercy-seat, and then, perhaps, he entered again to bring out the golden censer. The Jewish tradition is, that he entered the Holy of Holies four times on that day. After all, however, the number of times is not certain, nor is it material, the only important point being that he entered it only on one day of the year, while the holy place was entered every day. ¶ *Not without blood.* That is, he bare with him blood to sprinkle on the mercy-seat. This was the blood of the bullock and of the goat—borne in at two different times. ¶ *Which he offered for himself.* The blood of the bullock was offered for himself and for his house or family—thus keeping impressively before his own mind and the mind of the people the fact that the priests even of the highest order were sinners, and needed expiation like others; Lev. ix. 7. ¶ *And for the errors of the people.* The blood of the goat was offered for them ; Lev. xvi. 15. The word rendered *errors—ἀγνόημα*—denotes properly *ignorance, involuntary error ;* and then error or fault in general—the same as the Hebrew משגה —from שגה —to err. The object was to make expiation for *all* the errors and sins of the people, and this occurred *once* in the year. The repetition of these sacrifices was a constant remembrancer of sin, and the design was that neither the priests nor the people should lose sight of the

8 The Holy Ghost this signifying, That the way *c* into the holiest of all was not yet made manifest, while as the first tabernacle was yet standing :

c John 14.6; ch.10.19,20.

---

fact that they were violators of the law of God.

8. *The Holy Ghost.* Who appointed all this. The whole arrangement in the service of the tabernacle is represented as having been under the direction of the Holy Ghost, or this was one of his methods of teaching the great truths of religion, and of keeping them before the minds of men. Sometimes that Spirit taught by direct revelation ; sometimes by the written word, and sometimes by symbols. The tabernacle, with its different apartments, utensils, and services, was a *permanent* means of keeping important truths before the minds of the ancient people of God. ¶ *This signifying.* That is, showing this truth, or making use of this arrangement to impress this truth on the minds of men that the way into the holiest of all was not yet made manifest. ¶ *That the way into the holiest of all.* Into heaven—of which the Most Holy place in the tabernacle was undoubtedly designed to be an emblem. It was the place where the visible symbol of God—the Shekinah —dwelt; where the blood of propitiation was sprinkled, and was, therefore, an appropriate emblem of that holy heaven where God dwells, and whence pardon is obtained by the blood of the atonement. ¶ *Was not yet made manifest.* The way to heaven was not opened or fully understood. It was not known how men could appear before God, or how they could come with the hope of pardon. That way has now been opened by the ascension of the Redeemer to heaven, and by the assurance that all who will may come in his name. ¶ *While as the first tabernacle was yet standing.* As long as it stood, and the appointed services were held in it. The idea is, that until it was superseded by a more perfect system, it was *a proof* that the way to heaven

9 Which *was* a figure for the time then present, in which were offered both gifts and sacrifices, that

a Ps.40.6,7; Ga.3.21; ch.10.1,11.

was not yet fully and freely opened, and that the Holy Ghost *designed* that it should be such a proof. The apostle does not specify in what the proof consisted, but it may have been in something like the following. (1.) It was a mere *symbol*, and not the *reality*—showing that the true way was not yet fully understood. (2.) It was entered but once a year — showing that there was not access at all times. (3.) It was entered only by the High Priest—showing that there was not free and full access to all the people. (4.) It was accessible only by Jews— showing that the way in which all men might be saved was not then fully revealed. The sense is, that it was a system of types and shadows, in which there were many burdensome rites and many things to prevent men from coming before the symbol of the divinity, and was, therefore, an *imperfect* system. All these obstructions are now removed ; the Saviour —the great High Priest of his people —has entered heaven and " opened it to all true believers," and all of every nation may now have free access to God; see ver. 12 ; comp. ch. x. 19—22.

9. *Which was a figure for the time then present.* That is, as long as the tabernacle stood. The word rendered *figure—παραβολὴ*—is not the same as *type —τύπος* — (Rom. v. 14 ; Acts vii. 43, 44 ; John xx. 25 ; 1 Cor. x. 6, 11 ; Phil. iii. 17, *et al.*)—but is the word commonly rendered *parable;* Matt. xiii. 3, 10, 13, 18, 24, 31, 33—36, 53 ; xv. 15, *et sæpe*, and means properly *a placing side by side ;* then *a comparison*, or *similitude.* Here it is used in the sense of *image*, or *symbol —* something to *represent* other things. The idea is, that the arrangements and services of the tabernacle were a *representation* of important realities, and of things which were more fully to be revealed at a future period. There can be no doubt that Paul meant to say that this service in general was symbolical or typical, though this

could not [a] make him that did the service perfect, as pertaining to the [b] conscience ;

b 1 Pet. 3. 21.

will not authorize us to attempt to spiritualize every minute arrangement of it. Some of the things in which it was typical are specified by the apostle himself, and wisdom and safety in explaining the arrangements of the tabernacle and its services con sist in adhering *very closely* to the explanations furnished by the inspired writers. An interpreter is on an open sea, to be driven he knows not whither, when he takes leave of these safe pilots.* ¶ *Both gifts.* Thank-offerings. ¶ *And sacrifices.* Bloody offerings. The idea is, that all kinds of offerings to God were made there. ¶ *That could not make him that did the service perfect.* That could not take away sin, and remove the stains of guilt on the soul ; note ch. vii. 11 ; comp. ch. viii. 7 ; vii. 27 ; x. 1, 11. ¶ *As pertaining to the conscience.* They related mainly to outward and ceremonial rites, and even when offerings were made for *sin* the conscience was not relieved. They could not expiate guilt ; they could not make the soul pure ; they could not of themselves impart peace to the soul by reconciling it to God. They could not fully accomplish what the conscience needed to have done in order to give it peace. Nothing will do this but the blood of the Redeemer.

10. Which stood *only in meats and drinks.* The idea is, that the ordinances of the Jews, in connection with the services of religion, consisted much of laws pertaining to what was lawful to eat and drink, &c. A considerable part of those laws related to the distinction between clean and unclean beasts, and to such arrangements as were designed to keep them externally distinct from other nations. It is possible also that there may be a reference here to meat and drink offerings. On the grammatical difficulties of this verse, see Stuart on the Hebrews, *in loc.* ¶ *And divers washings.* The various ablutions which were required

* See supplementary Note, ver. 2.

10 *Which stood* only in meats *a* and drinks, and divers washings, *b* and carnal [1] ordinances, *c* imposed *on them* until the time of reformation.

a Le.11.2, &c. *b* Nu.19.7,&c.

1 or, *rites* or *ceremonies*. *c* Ep.2.15.

11 But Christ being come an high *d* priest of good *e* things to come, by a greater *f* and more perfect tabernacle, not made with hands, that is to say, not of this building,

d ch.3.1. *e* ch.10.1. *f* ch.8.2.

in the service of the tabernacle and the temple—washing of the hands, of the victim that was to be offered, &c. It was for this purpose that the laver was erected in front of the tabernacle (Ex. xxx. 18; xxxi. 9; xxxv. 16), and that the brazen sea and the lavers were constructed in connection with the temple of Solomon; 2 Chron. iv. 2—5; 1 Kings vii. 26. The Greek word here is *baptisms*. On its meaning, see Notes on Matt. iii. 6; Mark vii. 4. ¶ *And carnal ordinances*. Marg. "Or, *rites*, or *ceremonies*." Gr. "Ordinances of the flesh;" that is, which pertained to the flesh or to external ceremonies. The object was rather to keep them *externally* pure than to cleanse the conscience and make them holy in heart. ¶ *Imposed* on them. *Laid on them*—ἐπικείμενα. It does not mean that there was any *oppression* or *injustice* in regard to these ordinances, but that they were appointed for a temporary purpose. ¶ *Until the time of reformation*. The word here rendered *reformation* — διόρθωσις — means properly *emendation, improvement, reform*. It refers to putting a thing in a right condition; making it better; or raising up and restoring that which is fallen down. *Passow*. Here the reference is undoubtedly to the gospel as being a better system— *a putting things where they ought to be*; comp. Notes on Acts iii. 21. The idea here is, that those ordinances were only temporary in their nature, and were designed to endure till a more perfect system should be introduced. They were of value *to introduce* that better system; they were not adapted to purify the conscience and remove the stains of guilt from the soul.

11. *But Christ being come*. Now that the Messiah has come, a more perfect system is introduced by which the conscience may be made free from guilt. ¶ *An high priest of good things*

to come; see ch. x. 1. The apostle having described the tabernacle, and shown wherein it was defective in regard to the real wants of sinners, proceeds now to describe the Christian system, and to show how that met the real condition of man, and especially how it was adapted to remove sin from the soul. The phrase "high priest of good things to come," seems to refer to those "good things" which belonged to the dispensation that was to come; that is, the dispensation under the Messiah. The Jews anticipated great blessings in that time. They looked forward to better things than they enjoyed under the old dispensation. They expected more signal proofs of the divine favour; a clearer knowledge of the way of pardon; and more eminent spiritual enjoyments. Of these, the apostle says that Christ, who had come, was now the high priest. It was he by whom they were procured; and the time had actually arrived when they might enjoy the long-anticipated good things under the Messiah. ¶ *By a greater and more perfect tabernacle*. The meaning is, that Christ officiated as high priest in a much more magnificent and perfect temple than either the tabernacle or the temple under the old dispensation. He performed the great functions of his priestly office—the sprinkling of the blood of the atonement—in heaven itself, of which the most holy place in the tabernacle was but the emblem. The Jewish high priest entered the sanctuary made with hands to minister before God; Christ entered into heaven itself. The word "*by*" here—διὰ —means probably *through*, and the idea is, that Christ passed *through* a more perfect tabernacle on his way to the mercy-seat in heaven than the Jewish high priest did when he passed *through* the outer tabernacle (ver. 2)

12 Neither by the blood of
goats *a* and calves, but by his *b* own
a ch.10.4.   *b* Ac.20.28; 1 Pe.1.18,19; Re.1.5.

blood, he entered in once into the
holy place, *c* having obtained
eternal redemption *for us.*
c ch.10.19.

and through the veil into the most
holy place. Probably the idea in the
mind of the writer was that of the
Saviour passing through the *visible
heavens* above us, to which the veil,
dividing the holy from the most holy
place in the temple, bore some resemblance. Many, however, have understood the word "tabernacle" here as
denoting the *body* of *Christ* (see Grotius and Bloomfield *in loc.*); and according to this the idea is, that Christ,
by means of his own body and blood
offered as a sacrifice, entered into the
most holy place in heaven. But it
seems to me that the whole scope of
the passage requires us to understand
it of the more perfect temple in heaven where Christ performs his ministry, and of which the tabernacle of
the Hebrews was but the emblem.
Christ did not belong to the tribe of
Levi; he was not an high priest of
the order of Aaron; he did not enter
the holy place on earth, but he entered
the heavens, and perfects the work of
his ministry there. ¶ *Not made with
hands.* A phrase that properly describes heaven as being fitted up by
God himself; see Notes on 2 Cor. v.
1. ¶ *Not of this building,* Gr. "of
this *creation—κτίσεως.* The meaning
is, that the place where he officiates
is not fitted up by human power and
art, but is the work of God. The object is to show that his ministry is
altogether more perfect than that
which could be rendered by a Jewish
priest, and performed in a temple
which could not have been reared by
human skill and power.
12. *Neither by the blood of goats
and calves.* The Jewish sacrifice
consisted of the shedding of the blood
of animals. On the great day of the
atonement the high priest took with
him into the most holy place (1.) the
blood of a young bullock (Lev. xvi. 3,
11), which is here called the blood of
a "calf," which he offered for his own
sin; and (2.) the blood of a goat, as
a sin-offering for others; Lev. xvi. 9.

15. It was *by,* or *by means of—διὰ—*
blood thus sprinkled on the mercy-
seat, that the high priest sought the
forgiveness of his own sins and the
sins of the people. ¶ *But by his own
blood.* That is, by his own blood shed
for the remission of sins. The meaning is, that it was in virtue of his own
blood, or *by means* of that, that he
sought the pardon of his people. That
blood was not shed for himself—for he
had no sin—and consequently there
was a material difference between his
offering and that of the Jewish high
priest. The difference related to such
points as these. (1.) The offering
which Christ made was wholly for
others; that of the Jewish priest for
himself as well as for them. (2.) The
blood offered by the Jewish priest was
that of animals; that offered by the
Saviour was his own. (3.) That offered by the Jewish priest was only an
emblem or type—for it could not take
away sin; that offered by Christ had
a real efficacy, and removes transgression from the soul. ¶ *He entered into
the holy place.* Heaven. The meaning
is, that as the Jewish high priest bore
the blood of the animal into the Holy
of Holies, and sprinkled it there as
the means of expiation, so the offering which Christ has to make in heaven, or the *consideration* on which he
pleads for the pardon of his people, is
the *blood* which he shed on Calvary.
Having made the atonement, he now
pleads the merit of it as a *reason* why
sinners should be saved. It is not of
course meant that he literally *bore*
his own blood into heaven—as the
high priest did the blood of the bullock and the goat into the sanctuary;
or that he literally *sprinkled* it on the
mercy-seat there, but that that blood,
having been shed for sin, is now the
ground of his pleading and intercession for the pardon of sin—as the
sprinkled blood of the Jewish sacrifice
was the ground of the pleading of the
Jewish high priest for the pardon of
himself and the people. ¶ *Having*

13 For if the blood of bulls and
of goats, and the ashes *a* of an

heifer sprinkling the unclean, sanc
tifieth to the purifying of the flesh.

a Nu.19.2—17.

obtained eternal redemption for us.
That is, by the shedding of his blood.
On the meaning of the word *redemption*, see Notes on Gal. iii. 13. The
redemption which the Lord Jesus
effected for his people is *eternal*. It
will continue for ever. It is not a
temporary deliverance leaving the redeemed in danger of falling into sin
and ruin, but it makes salvation
secure, and in its effects extends
through eternity. Who can estimate
the extent of that love which purchased for us *such* a redemption?
Who can be sufficiently grateful that
he is thus redeemed? The *doctrine*
in this verse is, that the blood of
Christ is the means of redemption, or
atones for sin. In the following verses
the apostle shows that it not only
makes atonement for sin, but that it
is the means of sanctifying or purifying the soul.
    13. *For if the blood of bulls and of
goats.* Referring still to the great
day of atonement, when the offering
made was the sacrifice of a bullock
and a goat. ¶ *And the ashes of an
heifer.* For an account of this, see
Numbers xix. 2—10. In ver. 9, it is
said that the ashes of the heifer, after
it was burnt, should be kept "for a
water of separation ; it is a purification for sin." That is, the ashes were
to be carefully preserved, and being
mixed with water were sprinkled on
those who were from any cause ceremonially impure. The *reason* for
this appears to have been that the
heifer was considered as a sacrifice
whose blood has been offered, and the
application of the ashes to which she
had been burnt was regarded as an
evidence of participation *in* that sacrifice. It was needful, where the
laws were so numerous respecting
external pollutions, or where the
members of the Jewish community
were regarded as so frequently "*unclean*" by contact with dead bodies,
and in various other ways, that there
should be some method in which they
could be declared to be cleansed from

their "uncleanness." The nature of
these institutions also required that
this should be in connection with
sacrifice, and in order to this, it was
arranged that there should be this
permanent sacrifice—the ashes of the
heifer that had been sacrificed—of
which they could avail themselves at
any time, without the expense and
delay of making a bloody offering
specifically for the occasion. It was,
therefore, a provision of convenience,
and at the same time was designed to
keep up the idea, that all purification
was somehow connected with the
shedding of blood. ¶ *Sprinkling the
unclean.* Mingled with water, and
sprinkled on the unclean. The word
unclean here refers to such as had
been defiled by contact with dead
bodies, or when one had died in the
family, &c.; see Num. xix. 11—22.
¶ *Sanctifieth to the purifying of the
flesh.* Makes holy so far as the flesh
or body is concerned. The uncleanness here referred to related to the
body only, and of course the means of
cleansing extended only to that. It
was not designed to give peace to the
conscience, or to expiate moral offences. The offering thus made removed the obstructions to the worship
of God so far as to allow him who had
been defiled to approach him in a regular manner. Thus much the apostle allows was accomplished by the
Jewish rites. They *had* an efficacy
in removing ceremonial uncleanness,
and in rendering it proper that he
who had been polluted should be permitted again to approach and worship
God. The apostle goes on to argue
that *if they* had such an efficacy, it
was fair to presume that the blood of
Christ would have far greater efficacy, and would reach to the conscience itself, and make that pure.
    14. *How much more shall the blood
of Christ.* As being infinitely more
precious than the blood of an animal
could possibly be If the blood of an
animal had any efficacy at all, even
in removing ceremonial pollutions,

14 How much more shall the blood of Christ, who *a* through the eternal Spirit offered himself

a 1Pe.3.18.   1 or, *fault.*

without [1] spot to God: purge [b] your conscience from dead works to serve [c] the living God?

b ch.10.22.   *c* 1Pe.4.2.

how much more is it reasonable to suppose may be effected by the blood of the Son of God! ¶ *Who through the eternal Spirit.* This expression is very difficult, and has given rise to a great variety of interpretation.—Some MSS. instead of *eternal* here, read *holy,* making it refer directly to the Holy Spirit; see *Wetstein.* These various readings, however, are not regarded as of sufficient authority to lead to a change in the text, and are of importance only as showing that it was an early opinion that the Holy Spirit is here referred to. The principal opinions which have been entertained of the meaning of this phrase, are the following. (1.) That which regards it as referring to the Holy Spirit, the third person of the Trinity. This was the opinion of Owen, Doddridge, and archbishop Tillotson. (2.) That which refers it to the *divine nature* of Christ. Among those who have maintained this opinion, are Beza, Ernesti, Wolf, Vitringa, Storr, and the late Dr. J. P. Wilson. *MSS. Notes.* (3.) Others, as Grotius, Rosenmüller, Koppe, understand it as meaning *endless* or *immortal life,* in contradistinction from the Jewish sacrifices which were of a perishable nature, and which needed so often to be repeated. (4.) Others regard it as referring to the glorified person of the Saviour, meaning that in his exalted, or spiritual station in heaven, he presents the efficacy of his blood. (5.) Others suppose that it means *divine influence,* and that the idea is, that Christ was actuated and filled with a divine influence when he offered up himself as a sacrifice; an influence which was not of a temporal and fleeting nature, but which was eternal in its efficacy. This is the interpretation preferred by Prof. Stuart. For an examination of these various opinions, see his " Excursus, xviii." on this epistle. It is difficult, if not impossible, to decide what is the true meaning of the passage amidst this

diversity of opinion; but there are some reasons which seem to me to make it probable that the Holy Spirit is intended, and that the idea is, that Christ made his great sacrifice under *the extraordinary influences of that Eternal Spirit.* The reasons which lead me to this opinion, are the following. (1.) It is that which would occur to the great mass of the readers of the New Testament. It is presumed that the great body of sober, plain, and intelligent readers of the Bible, on perusing the passage, suppose that it refers to the Holy Ghost, the third person of the Trinity. There are few better and safer rules for the interpretation of a volume designed like the Bible for the mass of mankind, than to abide by the sense in which they understand it. (2.) This interpretation is one which is most naturally conveyed by the language of the original. The phrase *the spirit—* τὸ πνεῦμα—has so far a technical and established meaning in the New Testament as to denote the Holy Ghost, unless there is something in the connection which renders such an application improper. In this case there is nothing certainly which *necessarily* forbids such an application. The high names and classical authority of those who have held this opinion, are a sufficient guarantee of this. (3.) This interpretation accords with the fact that the Lord Jesus is represented as having been eminently endowed with the influences of the Holy Spirit; comp. Notes on John iii. 34. Though he was divine, yet he was also a man, and as such was under influences similar to those of other pious men. The Holy Spirit is the source and sustainer of all piety in the soul, and it is not improper to suppose that the man Christ Jesus was in a remarkable manner influenced by the Holy Ghost in his readiness to obey God and to suffer according to his will. (4.) If there was *ever* any occasion on which we may suppose he was influenced by the Holy Ghost, that of his sufferings and death here referred to may be supposed eminently to have been such an one. It was expressive of the highest state of piety—of the purest love to God and man—which has ever existed in the human bosom; it was the most trying time of his own life; it was the period when there would be the most strong temptation to abandon his work; and as the redemption of the whole world was dependent on that act, it is reasonable to suppose that the richest heavenly grace would be there imparted to him, and that he would then be eminently under the influence of that Spirit which was granted not *"by measure* unto him." Notes John iii. 34. (5.) This representation is not inconsistent with the belief that the sufferings and death of the Redeemer were *voluntary*, and had all the merit which belongs to a voluntary transaction. Piety in the heart of a Christian now is not less voluntary because it is produced and cherished by the Holy Ghost, nor is there less excellence in it because the Holy Ghost imparts strong faith in the time of temptation and trial. It reems to me, therefore, that the meaning of this expression is, that the Lord Jesus was led by the strong influences of the Spirit of God to devote himself as a sacrifice for sin. It was not by any temporary influence; not by mere excitement; it was by the influence of the *Eternal* Spirit of God, and the sacrifice thus offered could, therefore, accomplish effects which would be *eternal* in their character. It was not like the offering made by the Jewish high priest which was necessarily renewed every year, but it was under the influence of one who was *eternal*, and the effects of whose influence might be everlasting. It may be added, that if this is a correct exposition, it follows that the Holy Ghost is *eternal*, and must, therefore, be divine. ¶ *Offered himself.* That is, as a sacrifice. He did not offer a bullock or a goat, but he offered *himself.* The sacrifice of one's self is the highest offering which he can. make; in this case it was the highest which the universe had to make. ¶ *With-*

out spot. Marg. "Or *fault.*" The animal that was offered in the Jewish sacrifices was to be without blemish; see Lev. i. 10; xxii. 17—22. It was not to be lame, or blind, or diseased. The word which is here used and rendered "without spot"—ἄμωμος—refers to this fact—that there was no defect or blemish. The idea is, that the Lord Jesus, the great sacrifice, was *perfect;* see ch. vii. 26. ¶ *Purge your conscience.* That is, cleanse, purify, or sanctify your conscience. The idea is, that this offering would take away whatever rendered the conscience defiled or sinful. The offerings of the Jews related in the main to external purification, and were not adapted to give peace to a troubled conscience. They could render the worshipper externally pure so that he might draw near to God and not be excluded by any ceremonial pollution or defilement; but the mind, the heart, the conscience, they could not make pure. They could not remove that which troubles a man when he recollects that he has violated a holy law and has offended God, and when he looks forward to an awful judgment-bar. The word *conscience* here is not to be understood as a distinct and independent faculty of the soul, but as *the soul* or *mind itself* reflecting and pronouncing on its own acts. The whole expression refers to a mind alarmed by the recollection of *guilt*— for it is guilt only that disturbs a man's conscience. Guilt originates in the soul remorse and despair; guilt makes a man troubled when he thinks of death and the judgment; it is guilt *only* which alarms a man when he thinks of a holy God; and it is nothing but guilt that makes the entrance into another world terrible and awful. If a man had no guilt he would never dread his Maker, nor would the presence of his God be ever painful to him (comp. Gen. iii. 6—10); if a man had no guilt he would not fear to die—for what have the innocent to fear anywhere? The universe is under the government of a God of goodness and truth, and, under such a government, how *can* those who have done no wrong have anything to dread? The

1b And for this cause he is the Mediator of the New Testament, that by means of death, for the redemption of the transgressions

fear of death, the apprehension of the judgment to come, and *the dread of God*, are strong and irrefragable proofs that every man is a sinner. The only thing, therefore, which ever disturbs the conscience, and makes death dreadful, and God an object of aversion, and eternity awful, is GUILT. If that is removed, man is calm and peaceful; if not, he is the victim of wretchedness and despair. ¶ *From dead works.* From works that are deadly in their nature, or that lead to death. Or it may mean from works that have no spirituality and no life. By *"works"* here the apostle does not refer to their outward religious acts particularly, but to the conduct of the life, to what men *do;* and the idea is, that their acts are not spiritual and saving but such as lead to death ; see Note ch. vi 1. ¶ *To serve the living God.* Not in outward form, but in sincerity and in truth ; to be his true friends and worshippers. The phrase " the *living* God" is commonly used in the Scriptures to describe the true God as distinguished from idols, which are represented as *dead*, or without life; Ps. cxv. 4—7. The idea in this verse is, that it is only the sacrifice made by Christ which can remove the stain of guilt from the soul. It could not be done by the blood of bulls and of goats —for that did not furnish relief to a guilty conscience, but it could be done by the blood of Christ. The sacrifice which he made for sin was so pure and of such value, that God can consistently pardon the offender and restore him to his favour. That blood too can give peace—for Christ poured it out in behalf of the guilty. It is not that he took part with the sinner against God; it is not that he endeavours to convince him who has a troubled conscience that he is needlessly alarmed, or that sin is not as bad as it is represented to be, or that it does not expose the soul to danger. Christ never took the part of the sinner against God ; he never taught that sin

that were under the first testament, they which are called might receive the promise of eternal inheritance :

was a small matter, or that it did not expose to danger. He admitted all that is said of its evil. But he provides for giving peace to the guilty conscience by shedding his blood that it may be forgiven, and by revealing a God of mercy who is willing to receive the offender into favour, and to treat him as though he had never sinned. Thus the troubled conscience may find peace; and thus, though guilty, man may be delivered from the dread of the wrath to come.
   15. *And for this cause.* With this view; that is, to make an effectual atonement for sin, and to provide a way by which the troubled conscience may have peace. ¶ *He is the Mediator;* see Notes on Gal. iii. 19, 20. He is the Mediator between God and man in respect to that new covenant which he has made, or that new dispensation by which men are to be saved. He stands *between* God and man—the parties at variance—and undertakes the work of mediation and reconciliation. ¶ *Of the New Testament.* Not *testament*—for a *testament*, or *will*, needs no mediator; but of the *new covenant*, or the new *arrangement* or *disposition* of things under which he proposes to pardon and save the guilty ; see Notes on vers. 16, 17. ¶ *That by means of death.* His own death as a sacrifice for sin. The *old* covenant or arrangement also contemplated *death*—but it was the death of an *animal.* The purposes of this were to be effected by the death of the Mediator himself; or this covenant was to be ratified in his blood. ¶ *For the redemption of the transgressions* that were *under the first testament.* The covenant or arrangement under Moses. The general idea here is, that these were offences for which no expiation could be made by the sacrifices under that dispensation, or from which the blood then shed could not redeem. This general idea may include two particulars. (1.) That they who had committed transgressions under that

16 For where a testament *is,*
¹ or, *be brought in.*

there must also of necessity ¹ be the death of the testator.

covenant, and who could not be fully pardoned by the imperfect sacrifices then made, would receive a full forgiveness of all their sins in the great day of account through the blood of Christ. Though the blood of bulls and goats could not expiate, yet they offered that blood in faith; they relied on the promised mercy of God; they looked forward to a perfect sacrifice—and now the blood of the great atonement offered as a *full* expiation for all their sins, would be the ground of their acquittal in the last day. (2.) That the blood of Christ would *now* avail for the remission of all those sins which could not be expiated by the sacrifices offered under the law. It not only contemplated the remission of all the offences committed by the truly pious under that law, but would *now* avail to put away sin entirely. No sacrifice which men could offer would avail, but the blood of Christ would remove all that guilt. ¶ *That they which are called.* Alike under the old covenant and the new. ¶ *Might receive the promise of eternal inheritance.* That is, the fulfilment of the promise; or that they might be made partakers of eternal blessings. That blood is effectual alike to save those under the ancient covenant and the new—so that they will be saved in the same manner, and unite in the same song of redeeming love.

16. *For where a testament* is. This is the same word—διαθήκη—which in ch. viii. 6, is rendered *covenant.* For the general signification of the word, see Note on that verse. There is so much depending, however, on the meaning of the word, not only in the interpretation of this passage, but also of other parts of the Bible, that it may be proper to explain it here more at length. The word—διαθήκη—occurs in the New Testament thirty-three times. It is translated *covenant* in the common version, in Luke i. 72; Acts iii. 25; vii. 8; Rom. ix. 4; xi. 27; Gal. iii. 15, 17; iv. 24; Eph. ii. 12; Heb. viii. 6, 9, *twice,* 10; ix. 4, *twice,* x. 16; xii. 24; xiii. 20. In the remain-

ing places it is rendered *testament;* Matt. xxvi. 28; Mark xiv. 24; Luke xxii. 20; 1 Cor. xi 25; 2 Cor. iii. 6. 14; Heb. vii. 22; ix. 15—17, 20; Rev. xi. 19. In four of those instances (Matt. xxvi. 28; Mark xiv. 24; Luke xxii. 20, and 1 Cor. xi. 25), it is used with reference to the institution or celebration of the Lord's Supper. In the Septuagint it occurs not far from three hundred times, in considerably more than two hundred of which it is the translation of the Hebrew word בְּרִית—*Berith.* In one instance (Zech. xi. 14) it is the translation of the word *brotherhood;* once (Deut. ix. 5), of דָּבָר—*word;* once (Jer. xi. 2), of "words of the covenant;" once Lev. xxvi. 11), of *tabernacle;* once (Exod. xxxi. 7), of *testimony ;* it occurs once (Ezek. xx. 37), where the reading of the Greek and Hebrew text is doubtful; and it occurs three times (1 Sam. xi. 2; xx. 8; 1 Kings viii. 9), where there is no corresponding word in the Hebrew text. From this use of the word by the authors of the Septuagint, it is evident that they regarded it as the proper translation of the Hebrew —בְּרִית—*Berith,* and as conveying the same sense which that word does. It cannot be reasonably doubted that the writers of the New Testament were led to the use of the word, in part, at least, by the fact that they found it occurring so frequently in the version in common use, but it cannot be doubted also that they regarded it as *fairly* conveying the sense of the word בְּרִית —*Berith.* On no principle can it be supposed that inspired and honest men would use a word in referring to transactions in the Old Testament which did not *fairly* convey the idea which the writers of the Old Testament meant to express. The use being thus regarded as settled, there are some *facts* in reference to it which are of great importance in interpreting the New Testament, and in understanding the nature of the "covenant" which God makes with man. These facts are the following. (1.) The word διαθήκη —*diatheke*—is not that which properly denotes *compact, agreement,* or *covenant.* That word is συνθήκη—*syntheke* --or in other forms σύνθεσις and συνθεσίας; or if the word *diatheke* is used in that signification it is only remotely, and as a secondary meaning; see *Passow ;* comp. the Septuagint in Isa. xxviii. 15; xxx. 1; Dan. xi. 6, and Wisdom i. 16; 1 Mac. x. 26; 2 Mac. xiii. 25; xiv. 26. It is not the word which a *Greek* would have employed to denote a *compact* or *covenant.* He would have employed it to denote a *disposition, ordering,* or *arrangement* of things, whether of religious rites, civil customs, or property; or if used with reference to a *compact,* it would have been with the idea of an *arrangement,* or *ordering* of matters, not with the primary notion of an agreement with another. (2.) The word properly expressive of a covenant or compact—συνθήκη—is *never* used in the New Testament. In all the allusions to the transactions between God and man, this word never occurs. From some cause, the writers and speakers in the New Testament seem to have supposed that the word would leave an impression which they did not wish to leave. Though it might have been supposed that in speaking of the various transactions between God and man they would have selected this word, yet with entire uniformity they have avoided it. No one of them—though the word διαθήκη—*diatheke*—has been used by no less than six of them—has been betrayed in a single instance into the use of the word συνθήκη—*syntheke,* or has differed from the other writers in the language employed. This cannot be supposed to be the result of concert or collusion, but it must have been founded on some reason which operated equally on all their minds. (3.) In like manner, and with like remarkable uniformity, the word συνθήκη—*syntheke*—is *never* used in the Septuagint with reference to any arrangement or "covenant" between God and man. Once indeed in the Apocrypha, and but once, it is used in that sense. In the three only other instances in which it occurs in the Septuagint, it is with reference to compacts between man and man; Isa.

xxviii. 15; xxx. 1; Dan. xi. 6. This remarkable fact that the authors of that version *never* use the word to denote any transaction between God and man, shows that there must have been some reason for it which acted on *their* minds with entire uniformity. (4.) It is no less remarkable that neither in the Septuagint nor the New Testament is the word διαθήκη—*diatheke*—*ever* used in the sense of *will* or *testament,* unless it be in the case before us. This is conceded on all hands, and is expressly admitted by Prof. Stuart (Com. on Heb. p. 439), though he defends this use of the word in this passage. — A very important inquiry presents itself here, which has never received a solution generally regarded as satisfactory. It is, why the word διαθήκη—*diatheke* —was selected by the writers of the New Testament to express the nature of the transaction between God and man in the plan of salvation. It might be said indeed that they found this word uniformly used in the Septuagint, and that they employed it as expressing the idea which they wished to convey, with sufficient accuracy. But this is only removing the difficulty one step farther back. Why did the LXX. adopt this word? Why did they not rather use the common and appropriate Greek word to express the notion of a covenant? A suggestion on this subject has already been made in the Notes on ch. viii. 6; comp. Bib. Repository, vol. xx. p. 55. Another reason may, however, be suggested for this remarkable fact which is liable to no objection. It is, that in the apprehension of the authors of the Septuagint, and of the writers of the New Testament, the word διαθήκη — *diatheke* — in its original and proper signification *fairly* conveyed the sense of the Hebrew word בְּרִית —*Berith,* and that the word συνθήκη—*syntheke*—or *compact, agreement,* would *not* express that; and *that they never meant to be understood as conveying the idea either that God entered into a* COMPACT *or* COVENANT *with man, or that he made a* WILL. They meant to represent him as making *an arrangement, a disposition, an ordering* of things, by which his service might be kept up among his people, and by which men might be saved ; but they were equally remote from representing him as making a *compact*, or a *will*. In support of this there may be alleged (1.) the remarkable uniformity in which the word διαθηκη—*diatheke*—is used, showing that there was some *settled principle* from which they never departed ; and (2.) it is used mainly as the meaning of the word itself. Prof. Stuart has, undoubtedly, given the accurate original sense of the word. "The real, genuine, and original meaning of διαθηκη [*diatheke*] is, *arrangement, disposition,* or *disposal* of a thing." P. 440. The word from which it is derived—διατί-θημι—means to place apart or asunder ; and then to set, arrange, dispose in a certain order. *Passow.* From this original signification is derived the use which the word has with singular uniformity in the Scriptures. It denotes the *arrangement, disposition,* or *ordering* of things which God made in relation to mankind, by which he designed to keep up his worship on earth, and to save the soul. It means neither covenant nor will ; neither compact nor legacy ; neither agreement nor testament. It is an *arrangement* of an entirely different order from either of them, and the sacred writers with an uniformity which could have been secured only by the presiding influence of the One Eternal Spirit, have avoided the suggestion that God made with man either a *compact* or a *will.* We have no word which precisely expresses this idea, and hence our conceptions are constantly floating between a *compact* and a *will,* and the views which we have are as unsettled as they are unscriptural. The simple idea is, that God has made an *arrangement* by which his worship may be celebrated and souls saved. Under the Jewish economy this arrangement assumed one form ; under the Christian another. In neither was it a compact or covenant between two parties in such a sense that one party would be at liberty to reject the terms proposed ; in neither was it a testa-

ment or will, as if God had left a legacy to man, but in both there were some things in regard to the arrangement such as are found *in* a covenant or compact. One of those things—equally appropriate to a compact between man and man and to this arrangement, the apostle refers to here—that it implied in all cases the death of the victim. If these remarks are well-founded, they should be allowed materially to shape our views in the interpretation of the Bible. Whole treatises of divinity have been written on a mistaken view of the meaning of this word—understood as meaning *covenant.* Volumes of angry controversy have been published on the nature of the "covenant" with Adam, and on its influence on his posterity. The only *literal* "covenant" which can be supposed in the plan of redemption is that between the Father and the Son—though even the existence of such a covenant is rather the result of devout and learned imagining than of any distinct statement in the volume of inspiration. The simple statement there is, that God has made an arrangement for salvation, the execution of which he has entrusted to his Son, and has proposed it to man to be accepted as the only arrangement by which man can be saved, and which he is not at liberty to disregard.

[Whatever merit may attach to these observations on the meaning of διαθηκη, and its corresponding term ברית—and the author displays no small measure of critical research —the doctrine of covenants is not, in any way, affected by them. The advocates of that doctrine deny that it rests on a mistaken view, or on any view of the original term ordinarily rendered covenant. These terms, they most freely allow, occur in various senses, in the sense of simple appointment, promise, command, dispensation, and testament, as well as of stipulation or covenant, Jer. xxxiii. 25; Gen. ix. 11; Heb. viii. 7, &c. "It is not," says an able and accurate modern writer, "from the simple occurrence of the Hebrew or the Greek words, that we are to infer a federal transaction between God and man, or between any other parties, but *from the circumstances of the case,* which alone can determine in what sense the terms are employed. We may meet with them, when no covenant is implied, and we may find a covenant to have been made, where neither of them is used to express it. We should beware," he adds, "of falling into the mistake of some superficial readers of the Scripture, who have occasionally misinterpreted passages in which the word occurs by explaining it of the covenant of works, or the covenant of grace, when something different is intended." Heb. viii. 7, is alleged as an example of passages, in regard to which the mistake is made, whereas the apostle, in that place, is not treating of the covenant of grace absolutely, as opposed to the covenant of works, but of the two great dispensations of religion, the one introduced by Moses, and the other by Christ. It may serve to explain many passages in the epistle to the Hebrews, to observe, that the covenant of grace, strictly so called, is supposed to pervade both the παλαια and καινη διαθηκη of that epistle, its old and new covenant or dispensation alike, that, in fact, these are but different forms, in which the same covenant of grace is administered in different ages. More of this shortly. Meanwhile, it appears that no such fabric, no such treatise of divinity as is alleged, has been built on the slender foundation of erroneous verbal criticism. It is of importance that this should be attended to, for the same statement has recently been put forth with confidence by certain writers in our own country, who, in their antipathy to the doctrine of covenants, have, after the example of the American brethren, greatly lamented, "that so many entire systems of theology and bodies of divinity should have been cast into the mould of a single word, which after all is found out to be but a mistranslation." The reader will admire the temerity that can venture such groundless assertions, and think that lamentations, which have no better foundation, may in future be spared, or kept in reserve, till real cause require them.

What then is the evidence of the doctrine of covenants? Our author, under the conviction that his criticisms had undermined that doctrine, first assails the covenant of works, and, in a single sentence, clears the ground of it, lamenting that volumes of angry controversy should have been written about a thing so visionary. That such a transaction, as divines have usually designated by this name, has a real existence, the reader will find asserted and proved in a supplementary Note on Rom. v. 12. The author is not disposed to deal so summarily with the covenant of redemption or of grace. He seems to allow that something of the kind may possibly exist, though he inclines to believe it has its place only in the "imagination of the devout and learned." But his own countryman, Dr. Dwight, though far from being subject to such pious hallucinations, and

little inclined to receive any doctrine because it had long passed current, finds the covenant of grace distinctly set forth in Isa. liii. 10, 12, and again abundantly evinced in the eighty-ninth Psalm! Having explained the first of these passages, and commented on the engagements of the Son, and the promises of the Father, he thus sums up:—"All these things are exhibited to us *in the form of a covenant*. To this covenant, as to every other, there are two *parties*, GOD who promises; and his servant who was to justify many. A *condition* is specified, to which is annexed a *promise* of reward. The condition is, that Christ should make his soul an offering for sin, and make intercession for the transgressors, or, in other words, execute the whole office of a priest for mankind. The reward is, that he should receive the many for his portion, and that they should prolong their days, or endure for ever."—Sermon xliii. Indeed no one can read the fifty-third of Isaiah without finding in it the *essentials* of a covenant transaction, unless he be predetermined not to find such transaction there, or anywhere else. According to Lowth's translation, the tenth verse runs thus, "IF his soul shall make a propitiatory sacrifice, he SHALL see a seed, which shall prolong their days, and the gracious purpose of Jehovah shall prosper in his hands." That the same transaction is introduced in the eighty-ninth Psalm, is obvious enough. None will doubt the application of this Psalm to Christ, concerning whom Jehovah says, " I have made a covenant with my chosen, I have sworn unto David my servant, thy seed will I establish for ever, and build up thy throne to all generations." The *promise* is the very same as in Isaiah. The only difference between the passages is, that the condition is *expressed* in Isaiah, and *understood* in the Psalm, in consequence of which the covenant there appears rather in the form of a promissory oath. The covenant itself, however, is *expressly named*. " I have made (stricken) a covenant." It is not possible, in the compass of a brief note, to produce all the evidence which the Scripture contains on this subject. For the present we must content ourselves with a simple statement of the chief heads of evidence. Those theologians then who receive the doctrine, suppose that it is necessarily implied, in the surety and representative character of Christ, in the title of the "second Adam" which an apostle gives him, and which is believed to be destitute of meaning, unless, though dissimilar in other respects, he be like the first Adam in this, that he is a covenant head. Many men intervened between Adam and Christ, yet to Christ only is the title applied, and unless the fact now stated be the reason of that application, it must be difficult, if not impossible, to assign any; see supplementary Note on Rom. v. 12, 21. Further, Christ's repeated declarations that he came to do the will of the Father, imply that certain services had been prescribed to him. " Indeed," says an author already quoted, "*the whole scheme of redemption* involves the idea of a covenant; while one divine person prescribes certain services to the other, the other performs them; and the result is not only his own personal exaltation, but the eternal happiness of millions, whose cause he had espoused."—*Dick.*

The reader must have observed that the parties in this covenant are the Father and the Son, and will naturally be anxious to have that *class* of passages explained, in which the parties are God and the saints or the people of Christ, or in which the covenant is supposed to be made WITH THEM; Is. lv. 3; Heb. viii. 10; 2 Sam. xxiii. 5. From the existence of such passages, a double covenant, connected with the salvation of sinners, has been supposed and advocated by certain divines; the one made with Christ in eternity, and the other with his people in time. These have been respectively distinguished as the covenant of redemption, and the covenant of grace. By the generality of accurate writers, however, this distinction has been abandoned as untenable, and these two covenants declared to be but *one*, presented *in different aspects.* The covenant made with the saints is but the administration of that made with Christ, the fulfilment, the performance of it. Hence we read of the "blood of the *covenant,*" not "of the *covenants.*" For a full discussion of this part of the subject, see the admirable treatise of Mr. Bell, late minister in Glasgow, frequently quoted with admiration by Mr. Haldane, in his commentary on the Romans. "What some call the covenant of grace," says he, "in distinction from that of redemption, is nothing but the *promulgation* and *performance* of what was transacted with Christ, in behalf of the elect. Then the Father promised, that on condition he made his soul an offering for sin, he would quicken, justify, sanctify, and save, all those sinners whose substitute he was. Now what is the covenant of grace, but the promulgation and performance of these promises? What was originally made to the surety only, is now directed to sinners themselves. This, however, can in no propriety of speech be called a different covenant from that made with Christ. It is only the revelation of what before lay hid in the cabinet council of heaven; a making good to the children what was promised to their Father before they had a being."

It would appear, therefore, that from the beginning there have been but two covenants, that of works, and that of grace or

redemption, the first made with Adam and the last with Christ, both being regarded as the covenant heads of the parties that respectively belonged to them. But in consistency with this view, how shall we account for the mention of that *other covenant* different from the covenant of works, and with which the new covenant, in this epistle, is contrasted; ch. viii. ix. x. The proper solution of this question lies in the fact already hinted, that but *one* covenant, strictly so called, obtained, *alike under Moses and Christ,* and that the old and the new of the epistle to the Hebrews, point only to *different modes* of its administration. It is certain, that the Sinaitic covenant did not supersede the Abrahamic, which was nothing but the covenant of grace, " the covenant that was confirmed before of God in Christ;" Gal. iii. 15—17. Nay, the ceremonies and sacrifices of the Mosaic dispensation exhibited, in shadow, the blessings of that very covenant that was ultimately to be administered in a more clear and spiritual form.

Let it be noted, in conclusion, that most of the objections, alleged against the doctrine of covenants, arise from misconception or misrepresentation. When a covenant is said to be made between God and man, it is allowed, on all hands, that it differs, in many important particulars, from a human covenant, or covenant between man and man. The parties, in the first case, are not equal, and there is not liberty, on the part of the inferior, to receive or reject the terms at pleasure. Every thing must be set aside, in our conceptions of the subject, that is inconsistent with the majesty and authority of God; see Supplementary Note on Rom. v. 12. And this difference, originating in the unequal character of the parties, may, perhaps, furnish an answer to the question, which the author so frequently puts, concerning the use of διαθηκη, in preference to συνθηκη, and as frequently answers, by resolving into an indisposition on the part of the inspired writers, as well as on the part of the authors of the LXX., to countenance the idea of a covenant or contract between God and man. So thought Owen. " The word בְּרִית" says he, " could not be more properly rendered than by διαθηκη, for it being mostly used to express the covenant between God and man, it is of that nature as cannot properly be termed συνθηκη, which is a covenant or compact upon equal terms of distributive justice between distinct parties." The length of this Note will be excused, on the ground of the very frequent recurrence of the subject of it in the present volume, and the expediency of treating it fully, in some place, to which simple reference might in other places be made, for the economizing of labour.]

There has been much difference of opinion in reference to the meaning of the passage here, and to the design of the illustration introduced. If the word used — διαθήκη — means *testament*, in the sense of *a will*, then the sense of that passage is that " a will is of force only when he who made it dies, for it relates to a disposition of his property after his death." The force of the remark of the apostle then would be, that the fact that the Lord Jesus made or expressed his *will* to mankind, implied that he would die to confirm it ; or that since in the ordinary mode of making a will, it was of force only when he who made it was dead, therefore it was necessary that the Redeemer should die, in order to confirm and ratify that which he made. But the objections to this, which appears to have been the view of our translators, seem to me to be insuperable. They are these. (1.) The word διαθήκη — *diatheke*—is not used in this sense in the New Testament elsewhere ; see the remarks above. (2.) The Lord Jesus made no such *will*. He *had* no property, and the commandments and instructions which he gave to his disciples were not of the nature of a *will* or testament. (3.) Such an illustration would not be pertinent to the design of the apostle, or in keeping with his argument. He is comparing the Jewish and Christian dispensations, and the point of comparison in this chapter relates to the question about the efficacy of sacrifice in the two arrangements. He showed that the arrangement for blood-shedding by sacrifice entered into both ; that the high priest of both offered blood as an expiation ; that the holy place was entered with blood, and that consequently there was *death* in both the arrangements, or dispensations. The former arrangement or dispensation was ratified with blood, and it was equally proper that the new arrangement should be also. The point of comparison is not that Moses made a *will* or *testament* which could be of force only when he died, and that the same thing was required in the *new* dispensation, but it is that the former

covenant was *ratified by blood*, or *by the death of a victim*, and that it might be expected that the new dispensation would be confirmed, and that it was in fact confirmed in the same manner. In this view of the argument, what pertinency would there be in introducing an illustration respecting *a will*, and the manner in which it became efficient ; comp. Notes on ver. 18. It seems clear, therefore, to me, that the word rendered *testament* here is to be taken in the sense in which it is ordinarily used in the New Testament. The opinion that the word here means such a divine arrangement as is commonly denoted a " *covenant*," and not testament, is sanctioned by not a few names of eminence in criticism, such as Pierce, Doddridge, Michaelis, Steudel, and the late Dr. J. P. Wilson. Bloomfield says that the connection here demands this. The principal objections to this view are, (1.) that it is not proved that no covenants or compacts were valid except such as were made by the intervention of sacrifices. (2.) That the word rendered *testator*—διαθέμενος—cannot refer to the death of an animal slain for the purpose of ratifying a covenant, but must mean either a *testator*, or a *contractor*, i. e., one of two contracting parties. (3.) That the word rendered *dead* (ver. 17) — νεκροῖς — means only *dead men*, and never is applied to the dead bodies of animals ; see Stuart on the Heb. p. 442. These objections to the supposition that the passage refers to a covenant or compact, Prof. Stuart says are in his view insuperable, and they are certainly entitled to grave consideration. Whether the view above presented is one which can be sustained, we may be better able to determine after an examination of the words and phrases which the apostle uses. Those objections which depend wholly on the *philological* argument derived from the words used, will be considered of course in such an examination. It is to be remembered at the outset, (1.) that the word διαθήκη—*diatheke*—is *never* used in the New Testament in the sense of *testament*, or *will*, unless in this place; (2.) that it is *never* used in this sense in the Septuagint; and (3.) that the Hebrew word בּרית—*berith—never* has this signification. This is admitted ; see Stuart on the Heb. pp. 439, 440. It must require very strong reasons to prove that it has this meaning here, and that Paul has employed the word in a sense differing from its uniform signification elsewhere in the Bible ; comp., however, the remarks of Prof. Stuart in Bib. Repos. vol. xx. p. 364. ¶ *There must also of necessity be.*—ἀνάγκη— That is, it is necessary in order to confirm the covenant, or it would not be binding in cases where this did not occur. The *necessity* in the case is simply to make it valid or obligatory. So we say now there must "necessarily" be a *seal*, or a deed would not be valid. The fair interpretation of this is, that this was the common and established custom in making a "covenant" with God, or confirming the arrangement with him in regard to salvation. To this it is objected (see the first objection above), that " it is yet to be made out that *no* covenants were valid except those by the intervention of sacrifices." In reply to this, we may observe, (1.) that the point to be made out is *not* that this was a custom in compacts between *man and man*, but between *man and his Maker.* There is no evidence, as it seems to me, that the apostle alludes to a compact between man and man. The mistake on this subject has arisen partly from the use of the word " *testament*" by our translators, in the sense of *will* — supposing that it *must* refer to some transaction relating to man only ; and partly from the insertion of the word " *men*" in ver. 17, in the translation of the phrase—ἐπὶ νεκροῖς—"upon the dead," or "over the dead." But it is not necessary to suppose that there is a reference here to any transaction between man and man at all, as the whole force of the illustration introduced by the apostle will be retained if we suppose him speaking *only* of a covenant between man and God. Then his assertion will be simply that in the arrangement between God and man there

was a *necessity* of the death of something, or of the shedding of blood in order to ratify it. This view will save the necessity of proof that the custom of ratifying compacts between man and man by sacrifice prevailed. Whether that can be made out or not, the assertion of the apostle may be true, that in the arrangement which God makes with man, sacrifice was necessary in order to confirm or ratify it. (2.) The point to be made out is, not that such a custom is or was universal among all nations, but that it was the known and regular opinion among the Hebrews that a sacrifice was necessary in a " covenant" with God, in the same way as if we should say that a deed was not valid without a seal, it would not be necessary to show this in regard to *all* nations, but only that it is the law or the custom in the nation where the writer lived, and at the time when he lived. Other nations may have very different modes of confirming or ratifying a deed, and the same nation may have different methods at various times. The *fact* or *custom* to which I suppose there is allusion here, is that of sacrificing an animal to ratify the arrangement between man and his Maker, commonly called a " covenant." In regard to the existence of such a custom, particularly among the Hebrews, we may make the following observations. It was the common mode of ratifying the " covenant" between God and man. That was done over a sacrifice, or by the shedding of blood. So the covenant with Abraham was ratified by slaying a heifer, a she-goat, a ram, a turtle-dove, and a young pigeon. The animals were divided and a burning lamp passed between them ; Gen. xv. 9, 18. So the covenant made with the Hebrews in the wilderness was ratified in the same manner ; Ex. xxiv. 6, seq. Thus in Jer. xxxiv. 18, God speaks of the " men that had transgressed his covenant which they had made before him when *they cut the calf in twain, and passed between the parts thereof;*" see also Zech. ix. 11. Indeed all the Jewish sacrifices were regarded as a ratification of the covenant. It was never supposed that it was ratified or confirmed in a proper manner without such a sacrifice. Instances occur, indeed, in which there was *no* sacrifice offered when a covenant was made between man and man (see Gen. xxiii. 16; xxiv. 9; Deut. xxv. 7, 9; Ruth iv. 7), but these cases do not establish the point that the custom did not prevail of ratifying a covenant with God by the blood of sacrifice. Further; the *terms* used in the Hebrew in regard to making a covenant with God, prove that it was understood to be ratified by sacrifice, or that the death of a victim was necessary.(—פרת ברית—*Kârăth Berith*) "to cut a covenant"—the word פרת *kârăth* meaning to cut; to cut off; to cut down, and the allusion being to the victims offered in sacrifice, and *cut in pieces* on occasion of entering into a covenant; see Gen. xv. 10; Jer. xxxiv. 18, 19. The same idea is expressed in the Greek phrases ὅρκια τέμνειν, τέμνειν σπονδάς, and in the Latin *icere fœdus*; comp. Virgil Æn. viii. 941.

> Et cæsa jungebant fœdera porca.

These considerations show that it was the common sentiment, alike among the Hebrews and the heathen, that a covenant with God was to be ratified or sanctioned by sacrifice; and the statement of Paul here is, that the death of a sacrificial victim was needful to confirm or ratify such a covenant with God. It was not secure, or confirmed, until blood was thus shed. This was well understood among the Hebrews, that all their covenant transactions with God were to be ratified by a sacrifice; and Paul says that the same principle must apply to any arrangement between God and men. Hence he goes on to show that it was *necessary* that a sacrificial victim should die in the new covenant which God established by man through the Mediator; see ver. 23. This I understand to be the sum of the argument here. It is not that every contract made between man and man was to be ratified or confirmed by a sacrifice—for the apostle is not discussing that point; but it is that every similar transaction with God must be based on such a sacrifice, and that no covenant with him could be complete without such a sacrifice. This was provided for in the ancient dispensation by the sacrifices which were constantly offered in their worship; in the new, by the one great sacrifice offered on the cross. Hence all our approaches to God are based on the supposition of such a sacrifice, and are, as it were, ratified over it. *We* ratify or confirm such a covenant arrangement, not by offering the sacrifice anew, but by recalling it in a proper manner when we celebrate the death of Christ, and when in view of his cross we solemnly pledge ourselves to be the Lord's.

¶ *The death of the testator.* According to our common version, *the death of him who makes a will.* But if the views above expressed are correct, this should be rendered the *covenanter,* or "the victim set apart to be slain." The Greek will admit of the translation of the word διαθέμενος, *diathemenos,* by the word *covenanter,* if the word διαθήκη—*diatheke*—is rendered *covenant.* To such a translation here as would make the word refer *to a victim slain in order to ratify a covenant,* it is objected that the "word has no such meaning anywhere else. It must either mean a *testator,* or a *contractor,* i. e. one of two covenanting parties. But where is the death of a person covenanting made necessary in order to confirm the covenant?" *Prof. Stuart, in loc.* To this objection I remark respectfully, (1.) that the word is *never* used in the sense of *testator* either in the New Testament or the Old, unless it be here. It is admitted of the word διαθήκη — *diatheke* — by Prof. Stuart himself, that it never means *will,* or *testament,* unless it be here, and it is equally true of the word used here that it never means one *who makes a will.* If, therefore, it should be that a meaning quite uncommon, or wholly unknown in the usage of the Scriptures, is to be assigned to the use of the word here, why should it be *assumed* that that unusual meaning should be that of *making a will,* and *not* that of confirming a covenant? (2.) If the apos-

17 For a testament *is* of force after men are dead; otherwise it is tle used the word διαθήκη—*diatheke*—in the sense of *a covenant* in this passage, nothing is more natural than that he should use the corresponding word διαθέμενος—*diathemenos*—in the sense of that by which a covenant was ratified. He wished to express the idea that the covenant was always ratified by the death of a victim—a sacrifice of an animal under the law, and the sacrifice of the Redeemer under the gospel—and no word would so naturally convey that idea as the one from which the word *covenant* was derived. It is to be remembered also that there *was* no word to express that thought. Neither the Hebrew nor the Greek furnished such a word; nor have *we* now any word to express that thought, but are obliged to use circumlocution to convey the idea. The word *covenanter* would not do it; nor the words victim, or sacrifice. *We* can express the idea only by some phrase like this—"the victim set apart to be slain to ratify the covenant." But it was not an unusual thing for the apostle Paul to make use of a word in a sense quite peculiar to himself; comp. 2 Cor. iv. 17. (3.) The word διατίθημι—*diatithemi*—properly means, *to place apart, to set in order, to arrange*. It is rendered *appoint* in Luke xxii. 29; *made*, and *make*, with reference to a covenant, Acts iii. 25; Heb. viii. 10; x. 16. It occurs nowhere else in the New Testament, except in the passage before us. The idea of *placing, laying, disposing, arranging*, &c., enters into the word—as to place wares or merchandise for sale, to arrange a contract, &c; see *Passow*. The fair meaning of the word here may be, whatever goes to arrange, dispose, or settle the covenant, or to make the covenant secure and firm. If the reference be to a compact, it cannot relate to one of the contracting parties, because the death of neither is necessary to confirm it. But it may refer to that which was well-known as an established opinion, that a covenant with God was ratified only by a sacrifice.

of no strength at all while the testator liveth.

Still, it must be admitted that this use of the word is not elsewhere found, and the only material question is, whether it is to be presumed that the apostle would employ a word in a single instance in a peculiar signification, where the connection would not render it difficult to be understood. This *must* be admitted, that he might, whichever view is taken of the meaning of this passage, for on the supposition that he refers here to a *will*, it is conceded that he uses the word in a sense which does not once occur elsewhere either in the Old Testament or the New. It seems to me, therefore, that the word here may, without impropriety, be regarded as referring to *the victim that was slain in order to ratify a covenant with God*, and that the meaning is, that such a covenant was not regarded as confirmed until the victim was slain. It may be added that the authority of Michaelis, Macknight, Doddridge, Bloomfield, and Dr. J. P. Wilson, is a proof that such an interpretation cannot be a very serious departure from the proper use of a Greek word.

17. *For a testament.* Such an arrangement as God enters into with man; see the remarks on ver. 16. ¶ Is *of force.* Is ratified, or confirmed—in the same way as a deed or compact is confirmed by affixing a seal. ¶ *After men are dead.* ἐπὶ νεκροῖς. "Over the dead." That is, in accordance with the view given above, after the animal is dead; or over the body of the animal slain for sacrifice, and to confirm the covenant. "For a covenant is completed or confirmed over dead sacrifices, seeing it is never of force as long as the victim set apart for its ratification is still living." MS. Notes of Dr. J. P. Wilson. To this interpretation it is objected, that "νεκροῖς—*nekrois*—means only *dead men;* but *men* surely were not sacrificed by the Jews, as a mediating sacrifice in order to confirm a covenant." Prof. Stuart *in loc.* In regard to this objection, and to the proper meaning of the passage, we may re-

mark, (1.) that the word "*men*" is not in the Greek, nor is it necessarily implied, unless it be in the use of the Greek word rendered *dead*. The proper translation is, "*upon*, or *over the dead*." The use of the word "men" here by our translators would seem to limit it to the making of a will. (2.) It is to be presumed, unless there is positive proof to the contrary, that the Greeks and Hebrews used the word *dead* as it is used by other people, and that it *might* refer to deceased animals, or vegetables, as well as to *men*. A sacrifice that had been offered was dead ; a tree that had fallen was dead ; an animal that had been torn by other wild animals was dead. It is *possible* that a people might have one word to refer to *dead men*, and another to *dead animals*, and another to *dead vegetables :* but what is the evidence that the Hebrews or the Greeks had such words? (3.) What is the meaning of this very word— *νεκρός—nekros*—in ch. vi. 1 ; ix. 14. of this very epistle when it is applied to *works* —"dead works"—if it never refer to anything but *men?* comp. James ii. 17, 20, 26; Eph. ii. 1. 5; Rev. iii. 1. In Eccl. ix. 4, it is applied to a dead lion. I suppose, therefore, that the Greek phrase here will admit of the interpretation which the "exigency of the place" seems to demand, and that the idea is, that a covenant with God was ratified over the animals slain in sacrifice, and was not considered as confirmed until the sacrifice was killed. ¶ *Otherwise*. Since —ἐπεί. That is, unless this takes place it will be of no force. ¶ *It is of no strength*. It is not *strong—ἰσχύει—*it is not confirmed or ratified. ¶ *While the testator liveth*. Or while the animal selected to confirm the covenant is alive. It can be confirmed only by its being slain. A full examination of the meaning of this passage (Heb. ix. 16, 17) may be found in an article in the Biblical Repository, vol. xx. pp. 51 —71, and in Prof. Stuart's reply to that article. Bib. Repos. xx. pp. 356 —381.

[The reader must admire the critical skill which the author has brought to bear on this intricate and long-contested question.

The design of the following Note is by no means to enter into the controversy, and adjudicate between contending parties, a task as difficult as presumptuous, where, on both sides, are found many of the most eminent names in the history of sacred criticism, where such men as Pierce, Doddridge, M'-Knight, and Barnes, stand opposed to Calvin, Newcombe, Kinnoel, and Stuart. A very brief digest of the argument by which the common translation is defended, is alone intended in this place.

1. As to the word διαθηκη, it is allowed, that neither in the New Testament, nor in the LXX. has it, anywhere, the sense of "*will*" or testamentary deed, unless this place be held an exception, to which many, with Bloomfield, are disposed to add Gal. iii. 15. Yet the classical use of δ. as is alleged on the one hand, and admitted on the other, is altogether in favour of "testament." It need not therefore excite surprise, that the apostle, in a few instances, should employ it in that sense.

2. As to the sense of διαθεμενος, it is contended, in opposition to M'Knight, who renders it "appointed sacrifice," that διατιθημι is never used in the sense of "ordain," "appoint." That author quotes but one passage, Luke xxii. 29, in which, however, the word obviously has the sense of "grant." Διαθεμενος, besides, being the participle of the 2 Aor. middle voice, demands, for the most part, an active signification, and if the word "appoint" be used at all, should be here translated "appointer." Accordingly, Pierce gives the active sense, and adopts the term "pacifier." Others render "mediating sacrifice," but the word cannot have such meaning, and must signify either testator or contractor. And Scholefield himself, the author of this conjecture, admits that it is quite unsupported by the *usus loquendi*. Indeed, the same may be affirmed of all, or most of the emendations, that have yet been proposed. The philological argument is against them, and their authors justify them, for the most part, on the ground that they are necessary to the just course of the apostle's reasoning. Those who, with M'Knight, render "victim set apart," or "appointed sacrifice," may be reminded of the difficulty which that author has experienced, in reconciling the masculine gender of ὁ διαθεμενος with the various substantives he has found it necessary to supply in his paraphrase. Had the word referred to a sacrifice or victim, we should have expected the neuter gender το διαθεμενον. "The Greek scholar," says Donald Fraser, in an elaborate Note on this question, appended to his translation of Witsius on the creed, and which contains the ablest digest of argument, in favour of the old rendering

18 Whereupon neither the first | *testament* was 1 dedicated without
1 or, *purified*. | blood.

of " testament" or " will," that the writer of this Note has anywhere found within the same limited compass—" The Greek scholar is requested to observe, that according to M'Knight θυματος, a sacrifice, or ζωον, an animal, should be supplied to agree with τον διαθεμενου, verse 16th, while he supplies a different word, μοσχος, τραγος or ταυρος, a calf, goat, or bull, to agree with ὁ διαθεμενος, verse 17th. The truth is that ὁ διαθεμενος is necessarily masculine, and του διαθεμενου may be either masculine or neuter, as the structure of the sentence requires. In this passage, both these expressions unquestionably refer to the *very same person, or else the very same thing*. Why then, does the doctor entertain the unnatural supposition of a diversity of genders? The reason is manifest. The Lexicons could not readily furnish him with a Greek word, in the masculine gender, that signifies an animal, victim, or sacrifice, and it might have thrown discredit on his version, had he alleged that του διαθεμενου, verse 16th, must denote distinctly a calf, goat, or bull. It was equally impossible, on the other side, to compel ὁ διαθ. verse 17th, to agree with θυμα or ζωον, and thus to signify in general a sacrifice, or animal ; and in consequence, he sagaciously alleges, that a calf, goat, or bull, must be supplied, while, in order to make his version the more plausible, he takes the liberty to repeat the general term " *sacrifice*." The result of the whole is, that the *neuter gender* is requisite to the new rendering, but *no manuscript sanctions* το διαθεμενον."

3. It is important, in connection with this controversy, to ascertain the just sense of ιικροις. Our author has reasoned with ingenuity on this word. The reader, however, must bear in mind, that the question is not, whether ιικ. be not sometimes applied to designate dead works, animals, or vegetables—not whether it be a word of equally universal application with its corresponding English adjective, but whether, *when occurring without a substantive*, it have, in the New Testament, any such extensive application. In such cases, it is affirmed that there is not a *single example of the application to dead animals, or sacrifices*. The author has not produced an example of this kind.

4. As to the alleged fact, on the reality of which the new translation is founded, what the author asserts carries great weight with it ; and, in the estimation of many, will be regarded as conclusive, in regard to one part of the question. The allegation is, that covenants are ratified only by the death of a victim, which Mr. Barnes has above explained of covenants of a special kind, *i. e.* such as

are made between God and men. On the other side, it is affirmed, that " the proposition is too general here (ὁπου διαθηκη) to admit of limitation merely to covenants of a special nature."

Finally. According to the old translation of διαθηκη by " *testament*" the connection of the passage is not, in the view of those who adopt it, in the least injured. They suppose that the apostle having, in the 15th verse, introduced the " promise of the eternal *inheritance*" most naturally falls into the idea of testament or will, by which inheritances are usually conveyed. They contend that this idea in connection with the death of Christ is exceedingly beautiful. Nor should the circumstance of its frequent abuse, on the part of interpreters more ingenious than solid, lead to its rejection.]

18. *Whereupon.* "Οθεν — *Whence.* Or since this is a settled principle, or an indisputable fact, it occurred in accordance with this, that the first covenant was confirmed by the shedding of blood. The admitted principle which the apostle had stated, that the death of the victim was necessary to confirm the covenant, was the *reason* why the first covenant was ratified with blood. If there were any doubt about the correctness of the interpretation given above, that vers. 16, 17, refer to a *covenant,* and not a *will,* this verse would seem to be enough to remove it. For how could the fact that *a will* is not binding until he who makes it is dead, be a reason why *a covenant* should be confirmed by blood? What bearing would such a fact have on the question whether it ought or ought not to be confirmed in this manner? Or how could that fact, though it is universal, be given as *a reason* to account for the fact that the covenant made by the instrumentality of Moses was ratified with blood? No possible connection can be seen in such reasoning. But admit that Paul had stated in vers. 16, 17, a general principle that in all covenant transactions with God, the death of a victim was necessary, and everything is plain. We then see why he offered the sacrifice and sprinkled the blood. It was not on the basis of such reasoning as this : " The death of a man who makes a will is

19 For when *a* Moses had spoken every precept to all the people according to the law, he took the blood of calves and of

a Ex.24.6,&c.; Le.14. & 16.

indispensable before the will is of binding force, THEREFORE it was that Moses confirmed the covenant made with our fathers by the blood of a sacrifice;" but by such reasoning as this: "It is a great principle that in order to ratify a covenant between God and his people a victim should be slain, *therefore* it was that Moses ratified the old covenant in this manner, and *therefore* it was also that the death of a victim was necessary under the new dispensation." Here the reasoning of Paul is clear and explicit; but who could see the force of the former? Prof. Stuart indeed connects this verse with ver. 15, and says that the course of thought is, "The new covenant or redemption from sin was sanctioned by the death of Jesus; consequently, or wherefore (*ὅθεν*) the old covenant, which is a type of the new, was sanctioned by the blood of victims." But is this the reasoning of Paul? Does he say that *because* the blood of a Mediator was to be shed under the new dispensation, and *because* the old was a type of this, that THEREFORE the old was confirmed by blood? Is he not rather accounting for the shedding of blood at all, and showing that it was *necessary* that the blood of the Mediator should be shed, rather than *assuming* that, and from that arguing that a typical shedding of blood was needful? Besides, on this supposition, why is the statement in vers. 16, 17, introduced? What bearing have these verses in the train of thought? What are they but an inexplicable obstruction? ¶ *The first testament.* Or rather covenant—the word testament being supplied by the translators. ¶ *Was dedicated.* Marg. *Purified.* The word used to *ratify*, to *confirm*, to *consecrate*, to *sanction.* Literally, *to renew.* ¶ *Without blood.* It was ratified by the blood of the animals that were slain in sacrifice. The blood was then sprinkled on the principal objects that were regarded as holy under that dispensation.

goats, with water, and [1] scarlet wool, and hyssop, and sprinkled both the book and all the people,

[1] or, *purple.*

19. *For when Moses had spoken every precept to all the people.* When he had recited all the law, and had given all the commandments entrusted him to deliver; Ex. xxiv. 3. ¶ *He took the blood of calves and of goats.* This passage has given great perplexity to commentators from the fact that Moses in his account of the transactions connected with the ratification of the covenant with the people, (Ex. xxiv.), mentions only a part of the circumstances here referred to. He says nothing of the blood of calves and of goats; nothing of water, and scarlet-wool, and hyssop; nothing of sprinkling the book, the tabernacle, or the vessels of the ministry. It has been made a question, therefore, whence Paul obtained a knowledge of these circumstances? Since the account is not contained in the Old Testament, it must have been either by tradition, or by direct inspiration. The latter supposition is hardly probable, for (1.) the information here can hardly be regarded as of sufficient importance to have required an original revelation; for the illustration would have had sufficient force to sustain his conclusion if the literal account in Exodus only had been given, that Moses sprinkled the people; but (2.) such an original act of inspiration here would not have been consistent with the object of the apostle. In that argument it was essential that he should state only the facts about the ancient dispensation which were admitted by the Hebrews themselves. Any statement of his own about things which they did not concede to be true, or which was not well understood as a custom, might have been called in question, and would have done much to invalidate the entire force of the argument. It is to be presumed, therefore, that the facts here referred to had been preserved by tradition; and in regard to this, and the authority due to such a tradition, we may remark, (1.) that it

is well known that the Jews had a great number of traditions which they carefully preserved; (2.) that there is no improbability in the supposition that many events in their history would be preserved in this manner, since in the small compass of a volume like the Old Testament it cannot be presumed that *all* the events of their nation had been recorded; (3.) though they had many traditions of a trifling nature, and many which were false (comp. Notes on Matt. xv. 2), yet they doubtless had many that were true; (4.) in referring to those traditions, there is no impropriety in supposing that Paul may have been guided by the Spirit of inspiration in selecting only those which were true; and (5.) nothing is more *probable* than what is here stated. If Moses sprinkled "the people ;" if he read "the book of the law" then (Ex. xxiv. 7), and if this was regarded as a solemn act of ratifying a covenant with God, nothing would be more natural than that he should sprinkle the book of the covenant, and even the tabernacle and its various sacred utensils. We are to remember also, that it was common among the Hebrews to sprinkle blood for the purpose of consecrating, or as an emblem of purifying. Thus Aaron and his sons and their garments were sprinkled with blood when they were consecrated to the office of priests, Ex. xxix. 19—21; the blood of sacrifices was sprinkled on the altar, Lev. i. 5, 11 ; iii. 2, 13 ; and blood was sprinkled before the veil of the sanctuary, Lev. iv. 16, 17; comp. Lev. vi. 27; vii. 14. So Josephus speaks of the garments of Aaron and of his sons being sprinkled with "the blood of the slain beasts, and with spring water." "Having consecrated them and their garments," he says, "for seven days together, he did the same to the tabernacle, and the vessels thereto belonging, both with oil and with the blood of bulls and of rams." Ant. B. iii. ch. viii. § 6. These circumstances show the strong *probability* of the truth of what is here affirmed by Paul, while it is impossible to prove that Moses did *not* sprinkle the book and the tabernacle in the manner stated. The

mere omission by Moses cannot demonstrate that it was not done. On the phrase "the blood of calves and of goats," see Note on ver. 12. ¶ *With water.* Agreeably to the declaration of Josephus that "spring water was used." In Lev. xiv. 49—51, it is expressly mentioned that the blood of the bird that was killed to cleanse a house from the plague of leprosy should be shed over running water, and that the blood and the water should be sprinkled on the walls. It has been suggested also (see Bloomfield), that the use of water was necessary in order to prevent the blood from coagulating, or so as to make it *possible* to sprinkle it. ¶ *And scarlet wool.* Marg. *Purple.* The word here used denotes crimson, or deep-scarlet. The colour was obtained from a small insect which was found adhering to the shoots of a species of oak in Spain and in Western Asia, of about the size of a pea. It was regarded as the most valuable of the colours for dyeing, and was very expensive. Why the wool used by Moses was of this colour is not known, unless it be because it was the most expensive of colours, and thus accorded with everything employed in the construction of the tabernacle and its utensils. *Wool* appears to have been used in order to *absorb* and *retain* the blood. ¶ *And hyssop.* That is, a bunch of hyssop intermingled with the wool, or so connected with it as to constitute a convenient instrument for sprinkling; comp. Lev. xiv. 51. Hyssop is a low shrub, regarded as one of the smallest of the plants, and hence put in contrast with the cedar of Lebanon. It sprung out of the rocks or walls, 1 Kings iv. 33, and was used for purposes of purification. The term seems to have comprised not only the common hyssop, but also lavender and other aromatic plants. Its *fragrance*, as well as its size, may have suggested the idea of using it in the sacred services of the tabernacle. ¶ *And sprinkled both the book.* This circumstance is not mentioned by Moses, but it has been shown above not to be improbable. Some expositors, however, in order to avoid the difficulty in the passage, have taken

20 Saying, This *is* the blood *a* of the testament which God hath enjoined unto you.

21 Moreover *b* he sprinkled likewise with blood both the taberna-

1 Matt.26.28.   *b* Ex.29.12,36.   *c* Lev.17.11.

cle, and all the vessels of the ministry.

22 And almost all things are by the law purged with blood ; and without shedding of blood *c* is no remission.

this in connection with the word λαβὼν —rendered *"he took"*—meaning "taking the blood, and the book itself;" but the more natural and proper construction is, that the book was sprinkled with the blood. ¶ *And all the people.* Moses says, "and sprinkled it on the people;" Ex. xxiv. 8. We are not to suppose that either Moses or Paul designs to say that the blood was actually sprinkled on each one of the three millions of people in the wilderness, but the meaning doubtless is that the blood was sprinkled over the people, though in fact it might have fallen on a few. So a man now standing on an elevated place, and surrounded by a large assembly, if he should sprinkle water over them from the place where he stood, might be said to sprinkle it *on the people,* though in fact but few might have been touched by it. The act would be equally significant whether the emblem fell on few or many.

20. *Saying, This is the blood of the testament.* Of the covenant ; see Notes on vers. 16, 17. That is, this is the blood by which the covenant is ratified. It was the means used to confirm it ; the sacred and solemn form by which it was made sure. When this was done, the covenant between God and the people was confirmed—as a covenant between man and man is when it is sealed. ¶ *Which God hath enjoined unto you.* In Ex. xxiv. 8, "which God hath made with you." The language used by Paul, "which God hath *enjoined* —ἐνετείλατο—*commanded*—shows that he did not regard this as strictly of the nature of a *covenant,* or *compact.* When a compact is made between parties, one does not *enjoin* or *command* the other, but it is a mutual *agreement.* In the transactions between God and man, though called בְּרִית, *Berith,* or διαθήκη, *diatheke,* the

idea of a *covenant* or *compact* is so far excluded that God never loses his right to *command* or *enjoin.* It is not a transaction between equals, or an *agreement;* it is a solemn *arrangement* on the part of God which he proposes to men, and which he enjoins them to embrace ; which they are not indeed at liberty to disregard, but which when embraced is appropriately ratified by some solemn act on their part ; comp. Notes on ch. viii. 6.*

21. *He sprinkled—both the taberna-cle.* This circumstance is not stated by Moses. On the probability that this was done, see Notes on ver. 19. The account of setting up the tabernacle occurs in Ex. xl. In that account it is said that Moses *anointed* the tabernacle with the holy anointing oil ; vers. 9—11. Josephus (Ant. B. III. ch. viii. § 6), says that he consecrated it and the vessels thereto belonging with the blood of bulls and of rams. This was undoubtedly the tradition in the time of Paul, and no one can *prove* that it is not correct. ¶ *And all the vessels of the ministry.* Employed in the service of God. The altar, the laver, (Ex. xl. 10, 11), the censers, dishes, bowls, &c., which were used in the tabernacle.

22. *And almost all things.* It is a general custom to purify everything by blood. This rule was not universal, for some things were purified by fire and water, (Num. xxxi. 22, 23), and some by water only ; Num. xxxi. 24 ; Lev. xvi. 26, 28. But the exceptions to the general rule were few. Almost everything in the tabernacle and temple service, was consecrated or purified by blood. ¶ *And without shedding of blood is no remission.* Remission or forgiveness of sins. That is, though some things were purified

* See also supplementary Note on ch. ix. 16. and on Rom. v. 12, page 119.

23 *It was* therefore necessary that the patterns of things in the heavens should be purified with these ; but the heavenly things themselves with better sacrifices than these.

24 For Christ is not entered into the holy places made with hands, *which are* the figures of the true ; but into heaven itself, now to appear *a* in the presence of God for us :

a Rom.8.34.

by fire and water, yet when the matter pertained to the forgiveness of sins, it was *universally* true that no sins were pardoned except by the shedding of blood. *Some* impurities might be removed by water and fire, but the stain of *sin* could be removed only by blood. This declaration referred in its primary meaning, to the Jewish rites, and the sense is, that under that dispensation it was universally true that in order to the forgiveness of sin blood must be shed. But it contains a truth of higher order and importance still. *It is universally true that sin never has been, and never will be forgiven, except in connection with, and in virtue of the shedding of blood.* It is on this principle that the plan of salvation by the atonement is based, and on this that God in fact bestows pardon on men. There is not the slightest evidence that any man has ever been pardoned except through the blood shed for the remission of sins. The infidel who rejects the atonement has no evidence that his sins are pardoned ; the man who lives in the neglect of the gospel, though he has abundant evidence that he is a sinner, furnishes none that his sins are forgiven ; and the Mussulman and the heathen can point to no proof that their sins are blotted out. It remains to be demonstrated that one single member of the human family has ever had the slightest evidence of pardoned sin, except through the blood of expiation. In the divine arrangement there is no principle better established than this, that all sin which is forgiven is remitted through the blood of the atonement ; a principle which has never been departed from hitherto, and which never will be. It follows, therefore, (1.) that no sinner can hope for forgiveness except through the blood of Christ ;

(2.) that if men are ever saved they must be willing to rely on the merits of that blood ; (3.) that all men are on a level in regard to salvation, since all are to be saved in the same way ; and (4.) that there will be one and the same song in heaven – the song of redeeming love. 23. *The patterns of things in the heavens.* The tabernacle and its various utensils ; see Notes on ch. viii. 5. ¶*Be purified with these.* With water and blood, and by these ceremonies. ¶*But the heavenly things themselves.* The heavenly tabernacle or sanctuary into which Christ has entered, and where he performs the functions of his ministry. The use of the word *purified* here applied to heaven, does not imply that heaven was before *unholy*, but it denotes that it is now made accessible to sinners ; or that they may come and worship there in an acceptable manner. The ancient tabernacle was purified or consecrated by the blood of the victims slain, so that men might approach with acceptance and worship ; the heavens by purer blood are rendered accessible to the guilty. The necessity for "better sacrifices" in regard to the latter was, that it was designed to make the conscience pure, and because the service in heaven is more holy than any rendered on earth. ¶ *With better sacrifices than these.* To wit, the sacrifice made by the offering of the Lord Jesus on the cross. This infinitely surpassed in value all that had been offered under the Jewish dispensation. 24. *For Christ is not entered into the holy places made with hands.* Into the temple or tabernacle. The Jewish high priest alone entered into the most holy place ; and the other priests into the holy place. Jesus, being of the tribe of Judah, and not of Levi, never entered the temple proper. He had

25 Nor yet that he should offer himself often, as the high priest entereth into the holy place every year with blood of others;

26 For then must he often have suffered since the foundation of the world: but now once in the end of the world hath he appeared, to put away sin by the sacrifice of himself.

27 And as it is appointed *a* unto men once to die, but after this *b* the judgment;

a Gen.3.19.

b Ec.12.14.

access only to the courts of the temple, in the same way as any other Jew had; see Notes on Matt. xxi. 12. He has entered into the true temple—heaven —of which the earthly tabernacle was the type. ¶ *Which are the figures of the true.* Literally, *the antitypes—* ἀντίτυπα. The word properly means that which is formed after a model, pattern, or type; and then that which corresponds to something or answers to it. The idea here is, that the *type* or *fashion*—the *true* figure or form— was shown to Moses in the Mount, and then the tabernacle was made after that model, or corresponded to it. The *true original* figure is heaven itself; the tabernacle was an *antitype* of that—or was so formed as in some sense to correspond to it. That is, it corresponded in regard to the matters under consideration—the most holy place denoted heaven; the mercy-seat and the shekinah were symbols of the presence of God, and of the fact that he shows mercy in heaven; the entrance of the high priest was emblematical of the entrance of the Redeemer into heaven; the sprinkling of the blood there was a type of what the Redeemer would do in heaven. ¶ *Now to appear in the presence of God for us.* As the Jewish high priest appeared before the shekinah, the symbol of the divine presence in the tabernacle, so Christ appears before God himself in our behalf in heaven. He has gone to plead for our salvation; to present the merits of his blood as a permanent reason why we should be saved; Notes Rom. viii. 34; Heb. vii. 25

25. *Nor yet that he should offer himself often.* The Jewish high priest entered the most holy place with blood once every year. In this respect the offering made by Christ, and the work which he performed, differed from that of the Jewish high priest.

It was not needful that he should enter the holy place but once. Having entered there, he permanently remains there. ¶ *With the blood of others.* That is, with the blood of calves, and goats. This is a second point in which the work of Christ differs from that of the Jewish high priest. Christ entered there with his own blood; Notes on ver. 12.

26. *For then must he often have suffered.* That is, if his blood had no more efficacy than that which the Jewish high priest offered, and which was so often repeated, it would have been necessary that Christ should have often died. ¶ *But now once.* Once for all; once in the sense that it is not to be repeated again—ἅπαξ. ¶ *In the end of the world.* In the last dispensation or economy; that under which the affairs of the world will be wound up; see the phrase fully explained in Notes ch. i. 2, and Acts ii. 17; 1 Cor. x. 11, and Isa. ii. 2. ¶ *Hath he appeared.* He has been manifested in human form. ¶ *To put away sin.* (1.) To remove the punishment due to sin, or to provide a way of pardon; and (2.) to remove the stain of sin from the soul; see Notes on ver. 14. ¶ *By the sacrifice of himself;* see Notes on ch. i. 3; ii. 14; vii. 27.

27. *And as it is appointed unto men once to die.* Or, "since it is appointed unto men to die once *only.*" The object of this is to illustrate the fact that Christ died but *once* for sin, and that is done by showing that the most important events pertaining to man occur but once. Thus it is with *death.* That does not, and cannot occur many times. It is the great law of our being that men die *but once,* and hence the same thing was to be expected to occur in regard to him who made the atonement. It could not be supposed that this great law pertaining to man

would be departed from in the case of him who died to make the atonement, and that he would repeatedly undergo the pains of death. The same thing was true in regard to the *judgment*. Man is to be judged once, and but once. The decision is to be final, and is not to be repeated. In like manner there was a fitness that the great Redeemer should die *but once*, and that his death should, without being repeated, determine the destiny of man. There was a remarkable *oneness* in the great events which most affected men; and neither death, the judgment, nor the atonement could be repeated. In regard to the declaration here that "it is appointed unto men once to die," we may observe, (1.) that death is the result of *appointment;* Gen. iii. 19. It is not the effect of chance, or hap-hazard. It is not a "debt of nature." It is not the condition to which man was subject by the laws of his creation. It is not to be accounted for by the mere principles of physiology. God could as well have made the heart to play for ever as for fifty years. Death is no more the regular result of physical laws than the guillotine and the gallows are. It is in all cases the result of *intelligent appointment*, and for *an adequate cause*. (2.) That cause, or the reason of that appointment, is sin; Notes Rom. vi. 23. This is the adequate cause; this explains the whole of it. Holy beings do not die. There is not the slightest proof that an angel in heaven has died, or that any perfectly holy being has ever died except the Lord Jesus. In every death, then, we have a demonstration that the race is guilty; in each case of mortality we have an affecting memento that we are individually transgressors. (3.) Death occurs but *once* in this world. It cannot be repeated if we should desire to have it repeated. Whatever truths or facts then pertain to death; whatever lessons it is calculated to convey, pertain to it as an event which is not to occur again. That which is to occur but *once* in an eternity of existence acquires, from that very fact, if there were no other circumstances, an immense import-

ance. What is to be done but once, we should wish to be done well. We should make all proper preparation for it; we should regard it with singular interest. If preparation is to be made for it, we should make *all* which we expect *ever* to make. A man who is to cross the ocean *but once;* to go away from his home never to return, should make the right kind of preparation. He cannot come back to take that which he has forgotten; to arrange that which he has neglected; to give counsel which he has failed to do; to ask forgiveness for offences for which he has neglected to seek pardon. And so of death. A man who dies, dies but once. He cannot come back again to make preparation if he has neglected it; to repair the evils which he has caused by a wicked life; or to implore pardon for sins for which he had failed to ask forgiveness. Whatever is *to be done* with reference to death, is to be done *once for all* before he dies. (4.) Death occurs to all. "It is appointed unto men" — to the race. It is not an appointment for one, but for all. No one is appointed by name to die; and not an individual is designated as one who shall escape. No exception is made in favour of youth, beauty, or blood; no rank or station is exempt; no merit, no virtue, no patriotism, no talent, can purchase freedom from it. In every other sentence which goes out against men there may be *some* hope of reprieve. Here there is none. We cannot meet an individual who is not *under sentence of death*. It is not only the poor wretch in the dungeon doomed to the gallows who is to die, it is the rich man in his palace; the gay trifler in the assembly room; the friend that we embrace and love; and she whom we meet in the crowded saloon of fashion with all the graces of accomplishment and adorning. Each one of these is just as much under sentence of death as the poor wretch in the cell, and the execution on any one of them may occur before his. It is too for substantially the same cause, and is as really deserved. It is for *sin* that all are doomed to death, and the *fact* that we must

28 So Christ *a* was once of-
a 1 Pet. 2. 24; 3. 18; 1 John 3. 5.

die should be a constant remembrancer of our guilt. (5.) As death
is to occur to us but once, there is a
cheering interest in the reflection that
when it is passed it is passed *for ever.*
The dying pang, the chill, the cold
sweat, are not to be repeated. Death
is not to approach us often—he is to
be allowed to come to us but once.
When we have once passed through
the dark valley, we shall have the assurance that we shall never tread its
gloomy way again. Once, then, let
us be willing to die— since we can
die *but* once ; and let us rejoice in
the assurance which the gospel furnishes, that they who die in the Lord
leave the world to go where death in
any form is unknown. ¶ *But after
this the judgment.* The apostle does
not say *how long* after death this will
be, nor is it possible for us to know ;
Acts i. 7; comp. Matt. xxiv. 36. We
may suppose, however, that there
will be two periods in which there
will be an act of judgment passed
on those who die. (1.) Immediately
after death when they pass into the
eternal world, when their destiny will
be made known to them. This seems
to be necessarily implied in the supposition that they will continue to
live, and to be happy or miserable
after death. This act of judgment
may not be formal or public, but it
will be such as to show them what
must be the issues of the final day,
and as the result of that interview
with God, they will be made happy or
miserable until the final doom shall
be pronounced. (2.) The more public
and formal act of judgment, when
the whole world will be assembled at
the bar of Christ; Matt. xxv. The decision of that day will not change or
reverse the former; but the trial will
be of such a nature as to bring out all
the deeds done on earth, and the sentence which will be pronounced will
be in view of the universe, and will
fix the everlasting doom. Then the
body will have been raised; the affairs of the world will be wound up ;
the elect will all be gathered in, and

fered to bear the sins of *b* many;
b Is.53.12; Matt.26.28.

the state of retribution will commence,
to continue for ever. The main
thought of the apostle here may be,
that after death will commence a state
of *retribution* which can never change.
Hence there was a propriety that
Christ should die but once. In that
future world he would not die to make
atonement, for there all will be fixed
and final. If men, therefore, neglect
to avail themselves of the benefits of
the atonement here, the opportunity
will be lost for ever. In that changeless state which constitutes the eternal judgment no sacrifice will be again
offered for sin ; there will be no opportunity to embrace that Saviour who
was rejected here on earth.
28. *So Christ was once offered.* As
men are to die but once ; and as all
beyond the grave is fixed by the
judgment, so that his death there
would make no change in the destiny,
there was a propriety that he should
die but once for sin. The argument
is, there is *one* probation only, and
therefore there was need of but one
sacrifice, or of his dying but once.
If death were to occur frequently in
the existence of each individual, and
if each intermediate period were a
state of probation, then there might
be a propriety that an atonement
should be made with reference to each
state. Or if beyond the grave●there
were a state of probation still, then
also there might be a propriety that
an atoning sacrifice should be offered
there. But since neither of these
things is true, there was a fitness that
the great victim should die but once.

[Rather, perhaps, as in the original sentence,
"once dying" was the penalty denounced on
the sinner, so the substitute in enduring it, is
in like manner, under necessity of dying but
once. By this he fully answers the requirement of the law. Or, there may be in the
passage a simple intimation that, in this respect, as in others, Christ is like us, viz. in
being but once subject to death. It would be
inconsistent with the nature which he sustains, to suppose him a second time subject
to death.]

¶ *To bear the sins of many.* To suffer

and unto them that look *a* for him shall he appear *b* the se-

a Tit.2.13; 2 Pet.3.12.

cond time, without sin, *c* unto salvation.

b Ac.1.11; Rev.1.7.　　　*c* Is.25.9.

and die on account of their sins; see Notes on Isa. liii. 6, 11 ; Gal. iii. 13. The phrase does not mean (1.) that Christ was a *sinner*—for that was in no sense true. See ch. vii. 26. Nor (2.) that he literally bore the *penalty* due to transgression—for that is equally untrue. The penalty of the law for sin is *all* which the law when executed inflicts on the offender for his transgression, and includes, *in fact*, remorse of conscience, overwhelming despair, and eternal punishment. But Christ did not suffer for ever, nor did he experience remorse of conscience, nor did he endure utter despair. Nor (3.) does it mean that he was literally *punished* for our sins. Punishment pertains only to the guilty. An innocent being may *suffer* for what another does, but there is no propriety in saying that he is *punished* for it. A father suffers much from the misconduct of a son, but we do not say that he is *punished* for it ; a child suffers much from the intemperance of a parent—but no one would say that it was a *punishment* on the child. Men always connect the idea of criminality with punishment, and when we say that a man is *punished*, we suppose at once that there is *guilt*. The phrase here means simply, that Christ endured sufferings in his own person, which, if they had been inflicted on us, would have been the proper punishment of sin. He who was innocent interposed, and received on himself what was descending to meet us, and consented to be treated *as he would have deserved if he had been a sinner*. Thus he bore what was due to us; and this, in Scripture phrase, is what is meant by *bearing our iniquities;* see Notes Isa. liii. 4.

[It is indeed true, that Christ did not endure the *very* penalty which we had incurred, and, but for his interference, should have endured. His sufferings must be regarded in the light of an *equivalent* to the law's original claim, of a *satisfaction* to its injured honour, which the Lawgiver has been pleased to accept. It is, however, equally true, that the sufferings of Christ were strictly *penal*. They were the punishment of sin. The true meaning of the important phrase in this verse, "to bear sin," establishes this point. It can have no other meaning than bearing the punishment of sin. See Stuart's xix. Excursus. That punishment supposes guilt is not denied. What then ? Not certainly that Christ was personally guilty, but that our guilt has been *imputed* to him—that he has taken the place of the guilty, and become answerable for their transgressions. See Supp. Note, 2 Cor. v. 21.]

¶ *And unto them that look for him.* To his people. It is one of the characteristics of Christians that they *look for* the return of their Lord ; Titus ii. 13 ; 2 Pet. iii. 12 ; comp. Notes 1 Thess. i. 10. They fully *believe* that he will come. They earnestly *desire* that he will come ; 2 Tim. iv. 8 ; Rev. xxii. 20. They are *waiting* for his appearing ; 1 Thess. i. 10. He left the world and ascended to heaven, but he will again return to earth, and his people are looking for that time as the period when they shall be raised up from their graves; when they shall be publicly acknowledged to be his, and when they shall be admitted to heaven ; see Notes on John xiv. 3. ¶ *Shall he appear the second time.* He first appeared as the man of sorrows to make atonement for sin. His second appearance will be as the Lord of his people, and the Judge of the quick and the dead ; Matt. xxv. 31 ; see Notes Acts i. 11. The apostle does not say *when* this would be, nor is any intimation given in the Scriptures when it will occur. It is on the contrary everywhere declared that this is concealed from men (Acts i. 7 ; Matt. xxiv. 36), and all that is known respecting the time is, that it will be suddenly and at an unexpected moment; Matt. xxiv. 42, 44, 50. ¶ *Without sin.* That is, when he comes again he will not make himself a sin-offering ; or will not come in order to make atonement for sin. It is not implied that when he came the first time he was in any sense a *sinner*, but that he came then with reference to sin, or that the main object of his incarnation was to " put away sin by the sacrifice of himself." When he comes the second time, it will be with reference to another object. ¶ *Unto salvation.* That is, to receive his friends and followers to eternal salvation. He will come to save them from all their sins and temptations; to raise them from their graves ; to place them at his right hand in glory, and to confirm them in the everlasting inheritance which he has promised to all who truly love him, and who wait for his appearing.

In view of this anticipated return of the Redeemer, we may remark—

(1.) There is a propriety that the Lord Jesus should thus return. He came once to be humbled, despised, and put to death ; and there is a fitness that he should come to be honoured in his own world.

(2.) Every person on earth is interested in the fact that he will return, for "every eye shall see him;" Rev. i. 7. All who are now in their graves, and all who now live, and all who will hereafter live, will behold the Redeemer in his glory.

(3.) It will not be merely to gaze upon him, and to admire his magnificence that they will see him. It will be for greater and more momentous purposes—with reference to an eternal doom.

(4.) The great mass of men are not prepared to meet him. They do not believe that he will return; they do not desire that he should appear; they are not ready for the solemn interview which they will have with him. His appearing now would overwhelm them with surprise and horror. There is nothing in the future which they less expect and desire than the second coming of the Son of God, and in the present state of the world his appearance would produce almost universal consternation and despair. It would be like the coming of the flood of waters on the old world; like the sheets of flame on the cities of the plain ; or as *death* now comes to the great mass of those who die.

(5.) Christians *are* prepared for his coming. They believe in it; they desire it ; they are expecting it. In

this they are distinguished from all the world besides, and they would be ready to hail his coming as that of a friend, and to rejoice in his appearance as that of *their* Saviour.

(6.) Let us then live in habitual preparation for his advent. To each one of us he will come soon ; to all he will come suddenly. Whether he come to remove us by death, or whether in the clouds of heaven to judge the world, the period is not far distant when *we* shall see him. Yes, our eyes shall behold the Son of God in his glory! That which we have long desired—a sight of *our* Saviour who died for us, shall soon, very soon be granted unto us. No Christian begins a week or a day in which there is not a possibility that, before its close, he may have seen the Son of God in his glory ; none lies down upon his bed at night who may not, when the morning dawns upon this world, be gazing with infinite delight on the glories of the Great Redeemer in the heavens.

CHAPTER X.

ANALYSIS OF THE CHAPTER.

The general subject of this chapter is the sacrifice which Christ has made for sin, and the consequences which flow from the fact, that he has made a sufficient atonement. In chapter IX. the apostle had shown that the Jewish rites were designed to be temporary and typical, and that the offerings which were made under that dispensation could never remove sin. In this chapter he shows that the true sacrifice had been made, by which sin could be pardoned, and that certain very important consequences followed from that fact. The subject of *sacrifice* was the most important part of the Jewish economy, and was also the essential thing in the Christian dispensation, and hence it is that the apostle dwells upon it at so great length. The chapter embraces the following topics.

I. The apostle repeats what he had said before about the inefficacy of the sacrifices made under the law; ver. 1—4. The law was a mere shadow of good things to come, and the sacrifices which were made under it could

CHAPTER X.

FOR the law, having a shadow ^a of good things to come, and

^a Col. 2. 17.

never render those who offered them perfect. This was conclusively proved by the fact, that they continued constantly to be offered.

II. Since this was the fact in regard to those sacrifices, a better offering had been provided in the gospel by the Redeemer; ver. 5—10. A body had been prepared him for this work; and when God had said that he had no pleasure in the offerings under the law, Christ had come and offered *his* body once for all, in order that an effectual atonement might be made for sin.

III. This sentiment the apostle further illustrates, by showing how this one great offering was connected with the forgiveness of sins; ver. 11—18. Under the Jewish dispensation, sacrifices were repeated every day; but under the Christian economy, when the sacrifice was once made, he who had offered it sat down for ever on the right hand of God, for his great work was done. Having done this, he looked forward to the time when his work would have full effect, and when his enemies would be made his footstool. That this was to be the effect of the offering made by the Messiah, the apostle then shows from the Scriptures themselves, where it is said (Jer. xxxi. 33, 34), that under the gospel the laws of God would be written on the heart, and sin would be remembered no more. There must then be, the apostle inferred, some way by which this was to be secured, and this was by the great sacrifice on the cross, which had the effect of perfecting for ever those who were sanctified.

IV. Since it was a fact that such an atonement had been made; that one great offering for sin had been presented to God which was never to be repeated, there were certain consequences which followed from that, which the apostle proceeds to state; ver. 19—25. They were these (a), the privilege of drawing near to God

not the very image of the things, can never with those sacrifices which they offered year by year

with full assurance of faith (ver. 22); (b) the duty of holding fast the profession of faith without wavering (ver. 23); (c) the duty of exhorting one another to fidelity and to good works (ver. 24); (d) the duty of assembling for public worship, since they had a High Priest in heaven, and might now draw near to God; ver. 25.

V. As a *reason* for fidelity in the divine life, and for embracing the offer of mercy now made through the one sacrifice on the cross, the apostle urges the consequence which *must* follow from the rejection of that atonement, and especially after having been made acquainted with the truth; ver. 26—31. The result, says he, *must* be certain destruction. If that was rejected, there could remain nothing but a fearful looking for of judgment, for there was no other way of salvation. In support of this, the apostle refers to what was the effect, under the law of Moses, of disobedience, and says that, under the greater light of the gospel, much more fearful results must follow.

VI. The chapter closes (ver. 32—39) with an exhortation to fidelity and perseverance. The apostle reminds those to whom he wrote of what they had already endured; encourages them by the commendation of what they had already done, and especially by the kindness which they had shown to him; says that they had need only of patience, and that the time of their deliverance from all trial was not far off, for that he who was to come would come; says that it was their duty to live by faith, but that if any one drew back, God could have no pleasure in him. Having thus in the close of the chapter alluded to the subject of faith, he proceeds in the following chapter to illustrate its value at length. The object of the whole is to encourage Christians to make strenuous efforts for salvation; to guard them against the danger of apostasy; and to exhort them to bear their trials with pa-

continually make the comers thereunto perfect.

2 For then [1] would they not
have ceased to be offered? because

that the worshippers once purged
should have had no more conscience of sins.

1 or, *they would have.*

tience, and with submission to the will
of God.

1. *For the law having a shadow.*
That is, the whole of the Mosaic economy was a shadow ; for so the word
law is often used. The word *shadow*
here refers to a rough outline of anything, a mere sketch, such as a carpenter draws with a piece of chalk,
or such as an artist delineates when
he is about to make a picture. He
sketches an outline of the object which
he designs to draw, which has *some*
resemblance to it, but is not the
" very image ; " for it is not yet complete. The words rendered " the very
image" refer to a painting or statue
which is finished, where every part is
an exact copy of the original. The
" good things to come" here refer to
the future blessings which would be
conferred on man by the gospel. The
idea is, that under the ancient sacrifices there was an imperfect representation ; a dim outline of the blessings
which the gospel would impart to
men. They were a typical representation ; they were not such that it
could be pretended that they would
answer the purpose of the things
themselves which they were to represent, and would make those who offered them perfect. Such a rude outline ; such a mere sketch, or imperfect
delineation, could no more answer the
purpose of saving the soul than the
rough sketch which an architect
makes would answer the purpose of a
house, or than the first outline which
a painter draws would answer the
purpose of a perfect and finished por-
trait. All that could be done by either
would be to convey some distant and
obscure idea of what the house or the
picture might be, and this was all that
was done by the law of Moses. ¶ *Can
never with those sacrifices which they
offered year by year continually.* The
sacrifices here particularly referred to
were those which were offered on the
great day of atonement. These were
regarded as the most sacred and ef-

ficacious of all, and yet the apostle
says that the very fact that they were
offered every year showed that there
must be some deficiency about them,
or they would have ceased to be offered. ¶ *Make the comers thereunto perfect.* They could not free them from
the stains of guilt ; they could not give
ease to a troubled conscience; there
was in them no efficacy by which sin
could be put away; comp. Notes on
ch. vii. 11; ix. 9.

2. *For then would they not have
ceased to be offered?* Marg. " Or *they
would have.*" The sense is the same.
The idea is, that the very fact that
they were repeated showed that there
was some deficiency in them as to
the matter of cleansing the soul from
sin. If they had answered all the
purposes of a sacrifice in putting away
guilt, there would have been no need
of repeating them in this manner.
They were in this respect like medicine. If that which is given to a patient heals him, there is no need of
repeating it ; but if it is repeated often
it shows that there was some deficiency
in it, and if taken periodically through
a man's life, and the disease should
still remain, it would show that it was
not sufficient to effect his cure. So it
was with the offerings made by the
Jews. They were offered every year,
and indeed every day, and still the
disease of sin remained. The conscience was not satisfied; and the
guilty felt that it was necessary that the
sacrifice should be repeated again and
again. ¶ *Because that the worshippers
once purged should have had no more
conscience of sin.* That is, if their
sacrifices had so availed as to remove
their past sins, and to procure forgiveness, they would have had no
more trouble of conscience on account
of them. They would not have felt
that it was necessary to make these
sacrifices over and over again in order
to find peace. When a man has full
evidence that an atonement has been
made which will meet all the demands

3 But in those *sacrifices there is* a remembrance again *made* of sins every year. *a*

a Le.16.34.

4 For *it is* not possible that the blood of bulls and of goats should take away sins.*b*

b Ps. 51. 16.

of the law, and which secures the remission of sin, he feels that it is enough. It is all that the case demands, and his conscience may have peace. But when he does *not* feel this, or has not evidence that his sins are all forgiven, those sins will rise to remembrance, and he will be alarmed. He may be punished for them after all. Thence it follows that if a man wants peace he should have good evidence that his sins are forgiven through the blood of the atonement. No temporary expedient; no attempt to cover them up; no effort to forget them will answer the purpose. They *must be blotted out* if he will have peace — and that can be only through a perfect sacrifice. By the use of the word rendered "*conscience*" here, it is not meant that he who was pardoned would have no *consciousness* that he was a sinner, or that he would forget it, but that he would have no trouble of conscience ; he would have no apprehension of future wrath. The pardon of sin does not cause it to cease to be remembered. He who is forgiven may have a deeper conviction of its evil than he had ever had before. But he will not be troubled or distressed by it as if it were to expose him to the wrath of God. The remembrance of it will humble him; it will serve to exalt his conceptions of the mercy of God and the glory of the atonement, but it will no longer overwhelm the mind with the dread of hell. This effect, the apostle says, was not produced on the minds of those who offered sacrifices every year. The very fact that they did it, showed that the conscience was not at peace.

3. *But in those* sacrifices there is *a remembrance again* made *of sins every year.* The reference here is to the sacrifices made on the great day of atonement. This occurred once in a year. Of course as often as a sacrifice was offered, it was an acknowledgment of guilt on the part of those for whom it was made. As these sacrifices con-

tinued to be offered every year, they who made the offering were reminded of their guilt and their desert of punishment. All the efficacy which could be pretended to belong those sacrifices, was that they made expiation for the past year. Their efficacy did not extend into the future, nor did it embrace any but those who were engaged in offering them. These sacrifices, therefore, could not make the atonement which man needed. They could not make the conscience easy ; they could not be regarded as a sufficient expiation for the time to come, so that the sinner at any time could plead an offering which was already made as a ground of pardon, and they could not meet the wants of all men in all lands and at all times. These things are to be found only in that great sacrifice made by the Redeemer on the cross.

4. *For it is not possible that the blood of bulls and of goats should take away sins.* The reference here is to the sacrifices which were made on the great day of the atonement, for on that day the blood of bulls and of goats alone was offered ; see Notes on ch. ix. 7. Paul here means to say, doubtless, that it was not possible that the blood of these animals should make a complete expiation so as to purify the conscience, and so as to save the sinner from deserved wrath. According to the divine arrangement, expiation was made by those sacrifices for offences of various kinds against the ritual law of Moses, and pardon for such offences was thus obtained. But the meaning here is, that there was no efficacy in the blood of a mere animal to wash away a *moral* offence. It could not repair the law; it could not do anything to maintain the justice of God ; it had no efficacy to make the heart pure. The mere shedding of the blood of an animal never *could* make the soul pure. This the apostle states as a truth which must be admitted at once as indisputable, and yet it is probable that many of the Jews had

5 Wherefore, when he cometh into the world, he saith, *a* Sacri-

a Ps.40.6—8.

fice and offering thou wouldest not, but a body hast thou prepared[1] me.

1 or, *thou hast fitted.*

imbibed the opinion that there was such efficacy in blood shed according to the divine direction, as to remove all stains of guilt from the soul; see Notes ch. ix. 9, 10.

5. *Wherefore.* This word shows that the apostle means to sustain what he had said by a reference to the Old Testament itself. Nothing could be more opposite to the prevailing Jewish opinions about the efficacy of sacrifice, than what he had just said. It was, therefore, of the highest importance to defend the position which he had laid down by authority which they would not presume to call in question, and he therefore makes his appeal to their own Scriptures. ¶ *When he cometh into the world.* When the Messiah came, for the passage evidently referred to him. The Greek is, "Wherefore coming into the world, he saith." It has been made a question *when* this is to be understood as spoken—whether when he was born, or when he entered on the work of his ministry. Grotius understands it of the latter. But it is not material to a proper understanding of the passage to determine this. The simple idea is, that since it was impossible that the blood of bulls and goats should take away sin, Christ coming into the world made arrangements for a better sacrifice. ¶ *He saith.* That is, this is the language denoted by his great undertaking; this is what his coming to make an atonement implies. We are not to suppose that Christ formally used these words on any occasion—for we have no record that he did—but this language is that which appropriately expresses the nature of his work. Perhaps also the apostle means to say that it was originally employed in the Psalm from which it is quoted in reference to him, or was indited by him with reference to his future advent. ¶ *Sacrifice and offering thou wouldest not.* This is quoted from Ps. xl. 6. 8. There has been much perplexity felt by expositors in reference to this quotation, and

after all which has been written, it is not entirely removed. The difficulty relates to these points. (1.) To the question whether the Psalm originally had any reference to the Messiah. The Psalm *appears* to have pertained merely to David, and it would probably occur to no one on reading it to suppose that it referred to the Messiah, unless it had been so applied by the apostle in this place. (2.) There are many parts of the Psalm, it has been said, which cannot, without a very forced interpretation, be applied to Christ; see vers. 2. 12. 14—16. (3.) The argument of the apostle in the expression "a body hast thou prepared me," seems to be based on a false translation of the Septuagint, which he has adopted, and it is difficult to see on what principles he has done it.—It is not the design of these Notes to go into an extended examination of questions of this nature. Such examination must be sought in more extended commentaries, and in treatises expressly relating to points of this kind. On the design of Ps. xl., and its applicability to the Messiah, the reader may consult Prof. Stuart on the Hebrews, Excursus xx. and Kuinoel *in loc.* After the most attentive examination which I can give of the Psalm, it seems to me probable that it is one of the Psalms which had an original and exclusive reference to the Messiah, and that the apostle has quoted it just as it was meant to be understood by the Holy Spirit, as applicable to him. The reasons for this opinion are briefly these. (1.) There *are* such Psalms, as is admitted by all. The Messiah was the hope of the Jewish people; he was made the subject of their most sublime prophecies, and nothing was more natural than that he should be the subject of the songs of their sacred bards. By the spirit of inspiration they saw him in the distant future in the various circumstances in which he would be placed, and they dwelt with delight upon the vision; comp. Intro. to Isaiah, § 7.

iii. (2.) The fact that it is here applied to the Messiah, is a strong circumstance to demonstrate that it had an original applicability to him. This proof is of two kinds. *First*, that it is so applied by an inspired apostle, which with all who admit his inspiration seems decisive of the question. *Second*, the fact that he so applied it shows that this was an ancient and admitted interpretation. The apostle was writing to those who had been Jews, and whom he was desirous to convince of the truth of what he was alleging in regard to the nature of the Hebrew sacrifices. For this purpose it was necessary to appeal to the Scriptures of the Old Testament, but it cannot be supposed that he would adduce a passage for proof whose relevancy would not be admitted. The presumption is, that the passage was in fact commonly applied as here. (3.) The whole of the Psalm may be referred to the Messiah without anything forced or unnatural. The Psalm throughout seems to be made up of expressions used by a suffering person, who had indeed been delivered from some evils, but who was expecting many more. The principal difficulties in the way of such an interpretation, relate to the following points. (*a*) In ver. 2, the speaker in the Psalm says, " He brought me up out of an horrible pit, out of the miry clay, and set my feet upon a rock," and on the ground of this he gives thanks to God. But there is no real difficulty in supposing that this may refer to the Messiah. His enemies often plotted against his life; laid snares for him and endeavoured to destroy him, and it may be that he refers to some deliverance from such machinations. If it is objected to this that it is spoken of as having been uttered " when he came into the world," it may be replied that that phrase does not necessarily refer to the time of his birth, but that he uttered this sentiment sometime *during* the period of his incarnation. " He coming into the world for the purpose of redemption made use of this language." In a similar manner we would say of Lafayette, that " he coming to the United States to aid in the cause of

liberty, suffered a wound in battle." That is, during the period in which he was engaged in this cause, he suffered in this manner. (*b*.) The next objection or difficulty relates to the application of ver. 12 to the Messiah. " Mine iniquities have taken hold upon me, so that I am not able to look up; they are more than the hairs of my head; therefore my heart faileth me." To meet this some have suggested that he refers to the sins of men which he took upon himself, and which he here speaks of as *his own*. But it is not true that the Lord Jesus so took upon himself the sins of others that they could be *his*. They were *not* his, for he was in every sense "holy, harmless, and undefiled."* The true solution of this difficulty, probably is, that the word rendered *iniquity*—עון—means *calamity, misfortune, trouble*; see Ps. xxxi. 10; 1 Sam. xxviii. 10; 2 Kings vii. 9; Ps. xxviii. 6; comp. Ps. xlix. 5. The proper idea in the word is that of *turning away, curving, making crooked*; and it is thus applied to anything which is *perverted* or turned from the right way; as when one is turned from the path of rectitude, or commits sin; when one is turned from the way of prosperity or happiness, or is exposed to calamity. This seems to be the idea demanded by the scope of the Psalm, for it is not a penitential Psalm, in which the speaker is recounting his *sins*, but one in which he is enumerating his *sorrows ;* praising God in the first part of the Psalm for some deliverance already experienced, and supplicating his interposition in view of calamities that he saw to be coming upon him. This interpretation also seems to be demanded in ver. 12 of the Psalm by the *parallelism*. In the former part of the verse, the word to which " iniquity" corresponds, is not *sin*, but *evil*, i. e. calamity.

"For innumerable *evils* have compassed me about ;
Mine *iniquities* [calamities] have taken hold upon me."

If the word, therefore, be used here as it often is, and as the scope of the Psalm and the connection seem to demand, there is no solid objection

*See supplementary Note ix. 28.

against applying this verse to the Messiah. (c.) A third objection to this application of the Psalm to the Messiah is, that it cannot be supposed that he would utter such imprecations on his enemies as are found in vers. 14, 15. "Let them be ashamed and confounded; let them be driven backward; let them be desolate." To this it may be replied, that such imprecations are as proper in the mouth of the Messiah as of David; but particularly, it may be said also, that they are improper in the mouth of neither. Both David and the Messiah *did* in fact utter denunciations against the enemies of piety and of God. God does the same thing in his word and by his Providence. There is no evidence of any *malignant* feeling in this; nor is it inconsistent with the highest benevolence. The lawgiver who says that the murderer shall die, may have a heart full of benevolence; the judge who sentences him to death, may do it with eyes filled with tears. The objections, then, are not of such a nature that it is improper to regard this Psalm as wholly applicable to the Messiah. (4.) The Psalm cannot be applied with propriety to David, nor do we know of any one to whom it can be but to the Messiah. When was it true of David that he said that he "had come to do the will of God in view of the fact that God did not require sacrifice and offerings?" In what "volume of a book" was it written of him before his birth that he "delighted to do the will of God?" When was it true that he had "preached righteousness in the great congregation?" These expressions are such as can be applied properly only to the Messiah, as Paul does here; and taking all these circumstances together it will probably be regarded as the most proper interpretation to refer the whole Psalm at once to the Redeemer, and to suppose that Paul has used it in strict accordance with its original design. The other difficulties referred to will be considered in the exposition of the passage.—The difference between *sacrifice* and *offering* is, that the former refers to *bloody* sacrifices; the latter to *any* oblation made to God

—as a thank-offering; an offering of flour, oil, &c; see Notes on Isa. i. 11. When it is said "sacrifice and offering *thou wouldest not,*" the meaning is not that such oblations were *in no sense* acceptable to God—for as his appointment, and when offered with a sincere heart, they doubtless were; but that they were not *as* acceptable to him as obedience, and especially as the expression is used here that they could not avail to secure the forgiveness of sins. They were not in their own nature such as was demanded to make an expiation for sin, and hence a body was prepared for the Messiah by which a more perfect sacrifice could be made. The sentiment here expressed occurs more than once in the Old Testament. Thus, 1 Sam. xv. 22. "Behold, to obey is better than sacrifice, and to hearken than the fat of rams," Hos. vi. 6, "For I desired mercy and not sacrifice; and the knowledge of God more than burnt-offerings;" comp. Ps. li. 16, 17, "For thou desirest not sacrifice, else would I give it; thou delightest not in burnt-offering. The sacrifices of God are a broken spirit." This was an indisputable principle of the Old Testament, though it was much obscured and forgotten in the common estimation among the Jews. In accordance with this principle the Messiah came to render obedience of the highest order, even to such an extent that he was willing to lay down his own life. ¶ *But a body hast thou prepared me.* This is one of the passages which has caused a difficulty in understanding this quotation from the Psalm. The difficulty is, that it differs from the Hebrew, and *that the apostle builds an argument upon it.* It is not unusual indeed in the New Testament to make use of the language of the Septuagint even where it varies somewhat from the Hebrew; and where no *argument* is based on such a passage, there can be no difficulty in such a usage, since it is not uncommon to make use of the language of others to express our own thoughts. But the apostle does not appear to have made such a use of the passage here, but to have applied it in the way of *argument*. The argument, indeed, does not rest *wholly*, perhaps not *principally*, on the fact that a " body had been prepared" for the Messiah ; but still this was evidently in the view of the apostle an important consideration, and this is the passage on which the proof of this is based. The Hebrew (Ps. xl. 6) "Mine ears hast thou opened," or as it is in the margin, *digged*. The idea there is, that the ear had been, as it were, excavated, or dug out, so as to be made to hear distinctly ; that is, certain truths had been clearly revealed to the speaker ; or perhaps it may mean that he had been made " readily and attentively obedient." *Stuart ;* comp. Isa. l. 5. " The Lord God hath opened mine ear, and I was not rebellious." In the Psalm, the proper connection would seem to be, that the speaker had been made obedient, or had been so led that he was disposed to do the will of God. This may be expressed by the fact that the ear had been opened so as to be quick to hear, since an indisposition to obey is often expressed by the fact that the ears are *stopped*. There is manifestly no allusion here, as has been sometimes supposed, to the custom of boring through the ear of a servant with an awl as a sign that he was willing to remain and serve his master ; Ex. xxi. 6 ; Deut. xv. 17. In that case, the outer circle, or rim of the ear was bored through with an awl ; here the idea is that of hollowing out, digging, or excavating—a process to make the passage clear, not to pierce the outward ear. The Hebrew in the Psalm the Septuagint translates, " a body hast thou prepared me," and this rendering has been adopted by the apostle. Various ways have been resorted to of explaining the fact that the translators of the Septuagint rendered it in this manner, none of which are entirely free from difficulty. Some critics, as Cappell, Ernesti, and others have endeavoured to show that it is probable that the Septuagint reading in Ps. xl. 6, was— ὠτίον κατηρτίσω μοι— "my ear thou hast prepared ;" that is, for obedience. But of this there is no proof, and indeed it is evident that

the apostle quoted it as if it were σῶμα, *body ;* see ver. 10. It is probably altogether impossible now to explain the reason why the translators of the Septuagint rendered the phrase as they did ; and this remark may be extended to many other places of their version. It is to be admitted here, beyond all doubt, whatever consequences may follow, (1.) that their version does not accord with the Hebrew ; (2.) that the apostle has quoted their version as it stood, without attempting to correct it ; (3.) that his use of the passage is designed, to some extent at least, as *proof* of what he was demonstrating. The leading idea ; the important and essential point in the argument, is, indeed, not that *a body was prepared*, but that *he came to do the will of God ;* but still it is clear that the apostle meant to lay some stress on the fact that a body had been prepared for the Redeemer. Sacrifice and offering by the bodies of lambs and goats were not what was required, but instead of that the Messiah came to do the will of God by offering a more perfect sacrifice, and in accomplishing that it was necessary that he should be endowed with a body. But on what principle the apostle has quoted a passage to prove this which differs from the Hebrew, I confess I cannot see, nor do any of the explanations offered commend themselves as satisfactory. The only circumstances which seem to furnish any relief to the difficulty are these two— (1.) that the *main point* in the argument of the apostle was not that " a body had been prepared," but that the Messiah came to do the "will of God," and that the preparation of a body for that was rather an incidental circumstance ; and (2.) that the translation by the Septuagint was not a material departure from the *scope* of the whole Hebrew passage. The *main* thought —that of doing the will of God in the place of offering sacrifice—was still retained ; the opening of the ears, i. e. rendering the person attentive and disposed to obey, and the preparing of a body in order to obedience, were not circumstances *so* unlike as to make it necessary for the apostle to

6 In burnt-offerings and *sacrifices* for sins thou hast had no pleasure :

re-translate the whole passage in order to the main end which he had in view. Still, I admit, that these considerations do not seem to me to be wholly satisfactory. Those who are disposed to examine the various opinions which have been entertained of this passage may find them in Kuinoel, *in loc.*, Rosenmüller, Stuart on the Hebrews, Excursus xx., and Kennicott on Ps. xl. 6. Kennicott supposes that there has been a change in the Hebrew text, and that instead of the present reading—אזנים—*oznaim, ears,* the reading was אז גיף—*oz, guph—then a body;* and that these words became united by the error of transcribers, and by a slight change then became as the present copies of the Hebrew text stands. This conjecture is ingenious, and if it were ever allowable to follow a *mere* conjecture, I should be disposed to do it here. But there is no authority from MSS. for any change, nor do any of the old versions justify it, or agree with this except the Arabic.

6. *In burnt-offerings and* sacrifices *for sin thou hast had no pleasure.* This is not quoted literally from the Psalm, but the sense is retained. The reading there is, " burnt-offering and sin-offering hast thou not required." The quotation by the apostle is taken from the Septuagint, with the change of a single word, which does not materially affect the sense—the word ὀυκ ἰυδόκησας—*ouk eudokesas—*"thou hast no pleasure," instead of ὀυκ ἠθέλησας —*ouk ethelesas—*"thou dost not will." The idea is, that God had no pleasure in them as compared with obedience. He preferred the latter, and they could not be made to come in the place of it, or to answer the same purpose. When they were performed with a pure heart, he was doubtless pleased with the offering. As used here in reference to the Messiah, the meaning is, that they would not be what was required of *him.* Such offerings would not answer the end for which he was sent into the world, for that end was

7 Then said I, Lo, I come (in the volume of the book it is written of me) to do thy will, O God.

to be accomplished only by his being " obedient unto death."

7. *Then said I.* I the Messiah. Paul applies this directly to Christ, showing that he regarded the passage in the Psalms as referring to him as the speaker. ¶ *Lo, I come.* Come into the world ; ver. 5. It is not easy to see how this *could* be applied to David in any circumstance of his life. There was no situation in which he could say that, since sacrifices and offerings were not what was demanded, he *came* to do the will of God in the place or stead of them. The *time* here referred to by the word "then" is when it was manifest that sacrifices and offerings for sin would not answer all the purposes desirable, or when in view of that fact the purpose of the Redeemer is conceived as formed to enter upon a work which *would* effect what they could not. ¶ *In the volume of the book it is written of me.* The word here rendered "volume"—*κεφα-λίς—*means properly *a little head ;* and then *a knob,* and here refers doubtless to the *head* or *knob* of the rod on which the Hebrew manuscripts were rolled. Books were usually so written as to be rolled up, and when they were read they were unrolled at one end of the manuscript, and rolled up at the other as fast as they were read ; see Notes on Luke iv. 17. The rods on which they were rolled had small heads, either for the purpose of holding them, or for ornament, and hence the name *head* came metaphorically to be given to the roll or volume. But what volume is here intended? And where is that written which is here referred to? If David was the author of the Psalm from which this is quoted (Ps. xl.), then the book or volume which was then in existence must have been principally, if not entirely, the five books of Moses, and perhaps the books of Job, Joshua, and Judges, with probably a few of the Psalms. It is most natural to understand this of the Pentateuch, or the five books of Moses, as the word "volume" at that time

8 Above when he said, Sacrifice and offering and burnt-offerings and *offering* for sin thou

would undoubtedly have most naturally suggested that. But plainly, this could not refer to *David himself*, for in what part of the law of Moses, or in any of the volumes then extant, can a reference of this kind be found to David? There is no promise, no intimation that *he* would come to "do the will of God" with a view to effect that which could not be done by the sacrifices prescribed by the Jewish law. The reference of the language, therefore, must be to the Messiah—to some place where it is represented that he would come to effect by his obedience what could not be done by the sacrifices and offerings under the law. But still, in the books of Moses, this language is not *literally* found, and the meaning must be, that this was the language which was there *implied* respecting the Messiah; or this was the substance of the description given of him, that he would come to take the place of those sacrifices, and by his obedience unto death would accomplish what they could not do. They had a reference to him; and it was contemplated in their appointment that their inefficiency would be such that there should be felt a necessity for a higher sacrifice, and when he should come they would all be done away. The whole language of the institution of sacrifices, and of the Mosaic economy, was, that a Saviour would hereafter come to do the will of God in making an atonement for the sin of the world. That there are places in the books of Moses which refer to the Saviour, is expressly affirmed by Christ himself (John v. 46), and by the apostles (comp. Acts xxvi.22,3), and that the general spirit of the institutions of Moses had reference to him is abundantly demonstrated in this epistle. The meaning here is, "I come to do thy will in making an atonement, for no other offering would expiate sin. That I would do this is the language of the Scriptures which predict my coming, and of the whole spirit and design of the ancient dispensation."

wouldest not, neither hadst pleasure *therein;* which are offered by the law ;

¶ *To do thy will, O God.* This expresses the amount of all that the Redeemer came to do. He came to do the will of God (1.) by perfect obedience to his law, and (2.) by making an atonement for sin—becoming "obedient unto death;" Phil. ii. 8. The latter is the principal thought here, for the apostle is showing that sacrifice and offering such as were made under the law would not put away sin, and that Christ came in contradistinction from them to make a sacrifice that would be efficacious. Everywhere in the Scriptures it is held out as being the "will of God" that such an atonement should be made. There was salvation in no other way, nor was it possible that the race should be saved unless the Redeemer drank that cup of bitter sorrows; see Matt. xxvi. 39. We are not to suppose, however, that it was by mere arbitrary *will* that those sufferings were demanded. There were good *reasons* for all that the Saviour was to endure, though those reasons are not all made known to us.

8. *Above when he said.* That is, the Messiah. The word "above" refers here to the former part of the quotation. That is, "having in the former part of what was quoted said that God did not require sacrifices, in the latter part he says that he came to do the will of God in the place of them." ¶ *Sacrifice and offering, and burnt-offerings,* &c. These words are not all used in the Psalm from which the apostle quotes, but the idea is, that the specification there included all kinds of offerings. The apostle dwells upon it because it was important to show that the same remark applied to all the sacrifices which could be offered by man. When the Redeemer made the observation about the inefficacy of sacrifices, he meant that there was none of them which would be sufficient to take away sin.

9. *Then said he.* In another part of the passage quoted. When he had said that no offering which man could make would avail, *then* he said that he

9 Then said he, Lo, I come to do thy will, O God. He taketh away the first, that he may establish the second,

10 By the which will we are sanctified, *a* through the offering *b*

a John 17.19.　　　*b* ch.9.14.

---

of the blood of Jesus Christ once *for all.*

11 And every priest standeth daily *c* ministering, and offering oftentimes the same sacrifices, which can never *d* take away sins:

c Nu.28.3.　　　*d* Ps.50.8–13.Is.1.11.

---

would come himself. ¶ *He taketh away the first.* The word *"first"* here refers to sacrifices and offerings. He takes *them* away; that is, he shows that they are of no value in removing sin. He states their inefficacy, and declares his purpose to abolish them. ¶ *That he may establish the second.* To wit, the doing of the will of God. The two stand in contrast with each other, and he shows the inefficacy of the former, in order that the necessity for his coming to do the will of God may be fully seen. If *they* had been efficacious, there would have been no need of his coming to make an atonement.

10. *By the which will.* That is, by his obeying God in the manner specified. It is in virtue of his obedience that we are sanctified. The apostle immediately specifies what he means, and furnishes the key to his whole argument, when he says that it was *through the offering of the body of Jesus Christ.* It was not merely his doing the will of God *in general*, but it was the specific thing of offering his body in the place of the Jewish sacrifices; comp. Phil. ii. 8. Whatever part his personal *obedience* had in our salvation, yet the particular thing here specified is, that it was his doing the will of God by offering himself as a sacrifice for sin that was the means of our sanctification. ¶ *We are sanctified.* We are made holy. The word here is not confined to the specific work which is commonly called *sanctification*—or the process of making the soul holy *after* it is renewed, but it includes *everything* by which we are made holy in the sight of God. It embraces, therefore, justification and regeneration as well as what is commonly known as sanctification. The idea is, that whatever there is in our hearts which is holy, or whatever influences are brought to bear upon us

to make us holy, is all to be traced to the fact that the Redeemer became obedient unto death, and was willing to offer his body as a sacrifice for sin. ¶ *Through the offering of the body.* As a sacrifice. A body just adapted to such a purpose had been prepared for him; ver. 5. It was perfectly holy; it was so organized as to be keenly sensitive to suffering; it was the dwelling-place of the incarnate Deity. ¶ *Once* for all. In the sense that it is not to be offered again ; see Notes on ch. ix. 28. This idea is repeated here because it was very important to be clearly understood in order to show the contrast between the offering made by Christ, and those made under the law. The object of the apostle is to exalt the sacrifice made by him above those made by the Jewish high priests. This he does by showing that such was the efficacy of the atonement made by him that it did not need to be repeated ; the sacrifices made by them, however, were to be renewed every year.

11. *And every priest standeth daily ministering.* That is, this is done every day. It does not mean literally that *every* priest was daily concerned in offering sacrifices, for they took turns according to their courses, (Notes on Luke i. 5), but that this was done each day, and that every priest was to take his regular place in doing it ; Num. xxviii. 3. The object of the apostle is to prove that under the Jewish economy sacrifices were *repeated* constantly, showing their imperfection, but that under the Christian economy the great sacrifice had been offered once, which was sufficient for all. ¶ *And offering oftentimes the same sacrifices.* The same sacrifices were offered morning and evening every day. ¶ *Which can never take away sins*; Notes ch. ix. 9 ; x. 1.

12. *But this man.* The Lord Jesus.

12 But this man, after he had offered one sacrifice for sins, for ever sat*a* down on the right hand of God;

13 From henceforth expecting

a Col. 3.1.

The word *man* is not in the original here. The Greek is literally "but this ;" to wit, this priest. The apostle does not state here whether he was a *man*, or a being of a higher order. He merely mentions him as *a priest* in contradistinction from the Jewish priests. ¶ *After he had offered one sacrifice for sins.* By dying on the cross. This he did but once ; this *could* not be repeated ; and *need* not be repeated, for it was sufficient for the sins of the world. ¶ *For ever sat down.* That is, he sat down then to return no more for the purpose of offering sacrifice for sin. He will no more submit himself to scenes of suffering and death to expiate human guilt. ¶ *On the right hand of God ;* see Notes on Mark xvi. 19; comp. Notes on Eph. i. 20—22.

13 *From henceforth expecting.* Or *waiting.* He *waits* there until this shall be accomplished according to the promise made to him that all things shall be subdued under him; see notes on 1 Cor. xv. 25—27. ¶ *Till his enemies.* There is an allusion here to Ps. cx. 1, where it is said, "The Lord said unto my Lord, Sit thou at my right hand until I make thine enemies thy footstool." The enemies of the Redeemer are Satan, the wicked of the earth, and all the evil passions of the heart. The idea is, that all things are yet to be made subject to his will—either by a cheerful and cordial submission to his authority, or by being crushed beneath his power. The Redeemer, having performed his great work of redemption by giving himself as a sacrifice on the cross, is represented now as calmly waiting until this glorious triumph is achieved, and this promise is fulfilled. We are not to suppose that he is *inactive*, or that he takes no share in the agency by which this is to be done, but the meaning is, that he looks to the certain fulfilment of the promise. ¶ *His foot-*

till his enemies *b* be made his footstool.

14 For by one offering he*c* hath perfected for ever them that are sanctified.

b Ps. 110.1.   c ver. 10.

stool. That is, they shall be thoroughly and completely subdued. The same idea is expressed in 1 Cor. xv. 25, by saying that all his enemies shall be put under his feet. The language arose from the custom of conquerors in putting their feet on the necks of their enemies, as a symbol of subjection; see Josh. x. 24 ; Notes Isa. xxvi. 5, 6.

14. *For by one offering.* By offering himself once on the cross. The Jewish priest offered his sacrifices often, and still they did not avail to put away sin ; the Saviour made one sacrifice, and it was sufficient for the sins of the world. ¶ *He hath perfected for ever.* He hath laid the foundation of the eternal perfection. The offering is of such a character that it secures their final freedom from sin, and will make them for ever holy. It cannot mean that those for whom he died are made at once perfectly holy, for that is not true ; but the idea is, that the offering was complete, and did not need to be repeated ; and that it was of such a nature as entirely to remove the penalty due to sin, and to lay the foundation for their final and eternal holiness. The offerings made under the Jewish law were so defective that there was a necessity for repeating them every day ; the offering made by the Saviour was so perfect that it needed not to be repeated, and that it secured the complete and final salvation of those who availed themselves of it. ¶ *Them that are sanctified.* Those who are made holy by that offering. It does not mean that they are as yet *wholly* sanctified, but that they have been brought under the influence of that gospel which sanctifies and saves ; see ch. ii. 11; ix. 14. The doctrine taught in this verse is, that all those who are in any measure sanctified *will* be perfected for ever. It is not a temporary work which has been begun in their souls, but one which is designed to be car-

15 *Whereof* the Holy Ghost also is a witness to us ; for after that he had said before,

16 This *ᵃ is* the covenant that I will make with them after those

a Je.31.33.34.

ried forward to perfection. In the atonement made by the Redeemer there is the foundation laid for their eternal perfection, and it was with reference to that, that it was offered. Respecting this work and the consequences of it, we may remark, that there is (1.) perfection in its nature, it being of such a character that it needs not to be repeated ; (2.) there is perfection in regard to the pardon of sin —*all* past sins being forgiven to those who embrace it, and being *for ever* forgiven ; and (3.) there *is to be* absolute perfection for them for ever. They *will be* made perfect at some future period, and when that shall take place it will be to continue for ever and ever.

[The perfection, in this place, is not to be understood of the perfection of grace or of glory. It is perfection, in regard to the matter in hand, in regard to that which was the chief design of sacrifices, namely, expiation and consequent pardon and acceptance of God. And this indeed is the Τελειωσις of the epistle to the Hebrews generally, vii. 11; ix. 9; x. 1. Perfect moral purity and consummate happiness will doubtless follow as consequences of the sacrifice of Christ, but the completeness of his expiation, and its power to bring pardon and peace to the guilty and trembling sinner, to *justify* him unto eternal life, is here, at all events, *principally* intended. The parties thus perfected or completely justified, are τους αγιαζομενους, the "sanctified." 'Αγιαζω, however, besides the general sense of "sanctify" has in this epistle, like τελειοω, its *sacrificial* sense of cleansing from *guilt.* " Whether ceremonially, as under the Levitical dispensation ; Heb. ix. 13 ; comp, Lev. xvi. 19 ; or really and truly, by the offering of the body of Christ ; Heb. x. 10, 14, 29 ; comp. ver. 2, and ch. ii. 11 ; ix. 14."—Parkhurst's Greek Lexicon. The meaning, then, may be, that they who are purged or cleansed by *this* sacrifice, in other words, those to whom *its* virtue is applied, are perfectly justified. Wherever this divine remedy is used, it will effectually save. By one offering Christ hath for ever *justified* such as are purged or cleansed by *it.* This could not be said of those sanctified or purged by the legal sacrifices. Mr. Scott gives the

days, saith the Lord ; I will put my laws into their hearts, and in their minds will I write them.

17 And ¹ their sins and iniquities will I remember no more.

1 Some copies have, *Then he said, And their.*

sacrificial sense of the word, but combines with it the sense of sanctifying morally, in the following excellent paraphrase. " By his one oblation he hath provided effectually for the perfect justification unto eternal life, of all those who should ever receive his atonement, by faith springing from regeneration, and evidenced ' by the sanctification of the Spirit unto obedience,' and who were thus set apart and consecrated to the service of God."]

15—17. Whereof *the Holy Ghost is a witness to us.* That is, the Holy Ghost is a proof of the truth of the position here laid down—that the one atonement made by the Redeemer lays the foundation for the eternal perfection of all who are sanctified. The witness of the Holy Ghost here referred to is that which is furnished in the Scriptures, and not any witness in ourselves. Paul immediately makes his appeal to a passage of the Old Testament, and he thus shows his firm conviction that the Scriptures were inspired by the Holy Ghost. ¶ *For after that he had said before.* The apostle here appeals to a passage which he had before quoted from Jer. xxxi. 33, 34; see it explained in the Notes on ch. viii. 8—12. The object of the quotation in both cases is, to show that the new covenant contemplated the formation of a *holy* character or a holy people. It was not to set apart a people who should be externally holy only, or be distinguished for conformity to external rites and ceremonies, but who should be holy in heart and in life. There has been some difficulty felt by expositors in ascertaining what corresponds to the expression "after that he had said before," and some have supposed that the phrase " then he saith" should be understood before ver. 17. But probably the apostle means to refer to two distinct parts of the quotation from Jeremiah, the former of which expresses the fact that God meant to make a new covenant with his people,

18 Now where remission of these *is, there is* no more offering for sin.

1 or, *liberty.*

and the latter expresses the nature of that covenant, and it is particularly to the latter that he refers. This is seen more distinctly in the passage in Jeremiah than it is in our translation of the quotation in this epistle. The meaning is this, "The Holy Ghost first said, this is the covenant that I will make with them:" and having said this, he then added, "After those days, I will put my laws into their hearts, and in their minds will I write them, and their sins and their iniquities will I remember no more." The first part of it expresses the purpose to form such a covenant; the latter states what that covenant would be. The quotation is not, indeed, literally made, but the sense is retained; comp. Notes on ch. viii. 8—12. Still, it may be asked, how this quotation *proves* the point for which it is adduced— that the design of the atonement of Christ was "to perfect for ever them that are sanctified?" In regard to this, we may observe, (1.) that it was declared that those who were interested in it would be *holy*, for the law would be in their *hearts* and written on their *minds;* and (2.) that this would be *entire* and *perpetual.* Their sins would be *wholly* forgiven; they would *never* be remembered again— and thus they would be "perfected for ever."

18. *Now where remission of these* is. Remission or forgiveness of sins; that is, of the sins mentioned in the previous verse. ¶ There is *no more offering for sin.* If those sins are wholly blotted out, there is no more need of sacrifice to atone for them, any more than there is need to pay a debt again which has been once paid. The idea of Paul is, that in the Jewish dispensation there was a constant repeating of the remembrance of sins by the sacrifices which were offered, but that in reference to the dispensation under the Messiah, sin would be entirely cancelled. There would be one great and all-sufficient sacrifice,

19 Having therefore, brethren, [1] boldness to enter into the holiest *a* by the blood of Jesus.

a ch.9.8,12.

and when there was faith in that offering, sin would be absolutely forgiven. If that was the case, there would be no occasion for any further sacrifice for it, and the offering need not be repeated. This circumstance, on which the apostle insists so much, made a very important difference between the new covenant and the old. In the one, sacrifices were offered every day; in the other, the sacrifice once made was final and complete; in the one case, there was no *such* forgiveness but that the offender was constantly reminded of his sins by the necessity of the repetition of sacrifice; in the other, the pardon was so complete that all dread of wrath was taken away, and the sinner might look up to God as calmly and joyfully as if he had never been guilty of transgression.

19. *Having therefore, brethren.* The apostle, in this verse, enters on the hortatory part of his epistle, which continues to the end of it. He had gone into an extensive examination of the Jewish and Christian systems; he had compared the Founders of the two—Moses and the Son of God, and shown how far superior the latter was to the former; he had compared the Christian Great High Priest with the Jewish high priest, and shown his superiority; he had compared the sacrifices under the two dispensations, and showed that in all respects the Christian sacrifice was superior to the Jewish—that it was an offering that cleansed from sin; that it was sufficient when once offered without being repeated, while the Jewish offerings were only typical, and were unable to put away sin; and he had shown that the great High Priest of the Christian profession had opened a way to the mercy-seat in heaven, and was himself now seated there; and having shown this, he now exhorts Christians to avail themselves fully of all their advantages, and to enjoy to the widest extent all the privileges now conferred on them. One of the first of these

20 By a new and living way ^a which he hath ¹ consecrated for

a John14.6.

us through the veil, that is to say, his flesh;

1 or, *new-made.*

benefits was, that they had now free access to the mercy-seat. ¶ *Boldness to enter into the holiest.* Marg. *liberty.* The word rendered *boldness—παρρησίαν* —properly means *boldness of speech,* or freedom where one speaks all that he thinks (Notes, Acts iv. 13); and then it means boldness in general, license, authority, pardon. Here the idea is, that before Christ died and entered into heaven, there was no such access to the throne of grace as man needed. Man had no offering which he could bring that would make him acceptable to God. But now the way was open. Access was free for all, and all might come with the utmost freedom. The word *holiest* here is taken from the holy of holies in the temple (Notes on ch. ix. 3), and is there applied to heaven, of which that was the emblem. The entrance into the most holy place was forbidden to all but the high priest; but now access to the *real* "holy of holies" was granted to all in the name of the great High Priest of the Christian profession. ¶ *By the blood of Jesus.* The blood of Jesus is the *means* by which this access to heaven is procured. The Jewish high priest entered the holy of holies with the blood of bullocks and of rams (Notes ch. ix. 7.); but the Saviour offered his own blood, and that became the means by which we may have access to God.

20. *By a new and living way.* By a new *method* or *manner.* It was a mode of access that was till then unknown. No doubt many were saved before the Redeemer came, but the method by which they approached God was imperfect and difficult. The word which is here rendered *new—* *πρόσφατον*—occurs nowhere else in the New Testament. It properly means *slain,* or *killed thereto;* i. e. *newly killed, just dead ;* and then *fresh, recent.* *Passow.* It does not so much convey the idea that it is *new* in the sense that it had never existed before, as new in the sense that it is *recent,* or *fresh.* It was a way which was

recently disclosed, and which had all the freshness of novelty. It is called a "*living* way," because it is a method that *imparts* life, or because it leads to life and happiness. Doddridge renders it "*ever-living way,*" and supposes, in accordance with the opinion of Dr. Owen, that the allusion is to the fact that under the old dispensation the blood was to be offered as soon as it was shed, and that it could not be offered when it was cold and coagulated. The way by Christ was, however, *always* open. His blood was, as it were, always *warm,* and as if it had been recently shed. This interpretation seems to derive some support from the word which is rendered "*new.*" See above. The word *living,* also, has often the sense of perennial, or perpetual, as when applied to a fountain always running, in opposition to a pool that dries up (see Notes on John iv. 10), and the new way to heaven may be called *living* —in all these respects. It is a way that conducts *to* life. It is *ever-living* as if the blood which was shed always retained the freshness of that which is flowing from the vein. And it is *perpetual* and *constant*—like a fountain that always flows—for it is by a sacrifice whose power is perpetual and unchanging. ¶ *Which he hath consecrated for us.* Marg. "or *new made.*" The word here used means properly *to renew,* and then to initiate, to consecrate, to sanction. The idea is, that he has dedicated this way for our use; as if a temple or house were set apart for our service. It is a part consecrated by him for the service and salvation of man; a way of access to the eternal sanctuary for the sinner which has been set apart by the Redeemer for this service alone. ¶ *Through the veil, that is to say, his flesh.* The Jewish high priest entered into the most holy place through the veil that divided the holy from the most holy place. That entrance was made by his drawing the veil aside, and thus the interior sanctuary was

21 And *having* an high priest *a* over the house of God ;

22 Let us draw near with a true heart, in *b* full assurance

a ch.4,14-16.　　　*b* Ep.3.12.

of faith, having our hearts sprinkled *c* from an evil conscience, and our bodies washed with pure water;

c Eze.36.25.

laid open. But there has been much difficulty felt in regard to the sense of the expression here used. The plain meaning of the expression is, that the way to heaven was opened by means, or through the medium of the flesh of Jesus; that is, of his body sacrificed for sin, as the most holy place in the temple was entered by means or through the medium of the veil. We are not to suppose, however, that the apostle meant to say that there was *in all respects* a resemblance between the veil and the flesh of Jesus, nor that the veil was in any manner typical of his body, but there was a resemblance *in the respect under consideration*—to wit, in the fact that the holy place was rendered accessible by withdrawing the veil, and that heaven was rendered accessible through the slain body of Jesus. The idea is, that there is by means both of the veil of the temple, and of the body of Jesus, *a medium of access to God.* God dwelt in the most holy place in the temple behind the veil by visible symbols, and was to be approached by removing the veil; and God dwells in heaven, in the most holy place there, and is to be approached only through the offering of the body of Christ. Prof. Stuart supposes that the point of the comparison may be, that the veil of the temple operated as a screen to hide the visible symbol of the presence of God from human view, and that in like manner the body of Jesus might be regarded as a "kind of temporary tabernacle, or *veil* of the divine nature which dwelt within him." and that "as the veil of the tabernacle concealed the glory of Jehovah in the holy of holies, from the view of men, so Christ's flesh or body screened or concealed the higher nature from our view, which dwelt within this veil, as God did of old within the veil of the temple." See this and other views explained at length in the larger commentaries. It does not seem to me

to be necessary to attempt to carry out the point of the comparison in all respects. The simple idea which seems to have been in the mind of the apostle was, that the veil of the temple and the body of Jesus were alike *in this respect*, that they were *the medium of access to God.* It is by the offering of the body of Jesus ; by the fact that he was clothed with flesh, and that in his body he made an atonement for sin, and that with his body raised up from the dead he has ascended to heaven, that we have access now to the throne of mercy.

21. *And* having *an High Priest over the house of God.* Over the spiritual house of God; that is, the church; comp. Notes on ch. iii. 1 – 6. Under the Jewish dispensation there was a great high priest, and the same is true under the Christian dispensation. This the apostle had shown at length in the previous part of the epistle. The idea here is, that as under the former dispensation it was regarded as a privilege that the people of God might have access to the mercy-seat by means of the high priest ; so it is true in a much higher sense that we may now have access to God through our greater and more glorious High Priest.

22. *Let us draw near with a true heart.* In prayer and praise ; in every act of confidence and of worship. A sincere heart was required under the ancient dispensation ; it is always demanded of men when they draw near to God to worship him ; see John iv. 23, 24. Every form of religion which God has revealed requires the worshippers to come with pure and holy hearts. ¶ *In full assurance of faith;* see the word here used explained in the Notes on ch. vi. 11. The "full assurance of faith" means *unwavering confidence ;* a fulness of faith in God which leaves no room for doubt. Christians are permitted to come thus because God has reveal-

ed himself through the Redeemer as in every way deserving their fullest confidence. No one approaches God in an acceptable manner who does not come to him in this manner. What parent would feel that a child came with any right feelings to ask a favour of him who had not *the fullest confidence* in him?

["This πληροφορια, or full assurance of faith, is not, as many imagine, absolute certainty of a man's own particular salvation, for that is termed *the full assurance of hope*, ch. vi. 11, and arises from faith and its fruits. But the full assurance of faith is the assurance of that truth, which is testified and proposed in the gospel, to all the hearers of it in common, to be believed by them, unto their salvation, and is also termed *the full assurance of understanding ;* Col. ii. 2. Though all that the gospel reveals, claims the full assurance of faith, yet here it seems more particularly to respect the efficacy and all-sufficiency of Christ's offering for procuring pardon and acceptance."—*M'Lean*.

¶ *Having our hearts sprinkled from an evil conscience.* By the blood of Jesus. This was fitted to make the conscience pure. The Jewish cleansing or sprinkling with blood related only to that which was external, and could not make the conscience perfect (ch. ix. 9), but the sacrifice offered by the Saviour was designed to give peace to the troubled mind, and to make it pure and holy. An "evil conscience" is a consciousness of evil, or a conscience oppressed with sin ; that is, a conscience that accuses of guilt. We are made free from such a conscience through the atonement of Jesus, not because we become convinced that we have not committed sin, and not because we are led to suppose that our sins are less than we had otherwise supposed—for the reverse of both these is true—but because our sins are forgiven, and since they are freely pardoned they no longer produce remorse and the fear of future wrath. A child that has been forgiven may feel that he has done very wrong, but still he will not be then overpowered with distress in view of his guilt, or with the apprehension of punishment. ¶ *And our bodies washed with pure water.* It was common for the Jews to wash themselves, or to perform va-

rious ablutions in their services ; see Ex. xxix. 4 ; xxx. 19—21 ; xl. 12 ; Lev. vi. 27 ; xiii. 54, 58 ; xiv. 8, 9 ; xv. 16 ; xvi. 4, 24 ; xxii. 6 ; comp. Notes on Mark vii. 3. The same thing was also true among the heathen. There was usually, at the entrance of their temples, a vessel placed with consecrated water, in which, as Pliny says (Hist. Nat. lib. xv. c. 30), there was a branch of laurel placed with which the priests sprinkled all who approached for worship. It was necessary that this water should be pure, and it was drawn fresh from wells or fountains for the purpose. Water from pools and ponds was regarded as unsuitable, as was also even the purest water of the fountain, if it had stood long. Æneas sprinkled himself in this manner, as he was about to enter the invisible world (Æn. vi. 635), with fresh water. Porphyry says that the Essenes were accustomed to cleanse themselves with the purest water. Thus Ezekiel also says, " Then will I sprinkle clean water upon you, and you shall be clean." Sea-water was usually regarded as best adapted to this purpose, as the salt was supposed to have a cleansing property. The Jews who dwelt near the sea, were thence accustomed, as Aristides says, to wash their hands every morning on this account in the sea-water. Potter's Gr. Archæ. i. 222. Rosenmüller, Alte und Neue Morgenland, *in loc*. It was from the heathen custom of placing a vessel with consecrated water at the entrance of their temples, that the Roman Catholic custom is derived in their churches of placing " holy water" near the door, that those who worship there may " cross themselves." In accordance with the Jewish custom, the apostle says, that it was proper that under the Christian dispensation we should approach God, having performed an act emblematic of purity by the application of water to the body. That there is an allusion to baptism is clear. The apostle is comparing the two dispensations, and his aim is to show that in the Christian dispensation there was everything which was regarded as valuable and

23 Let us hold fast the profession of *our* faith without wavering ; (for he *a is* faithful that promised ;)

a 1 Th. 5. 24.

important in the old. So he had shown it to have been in regard to the fact that there was a Lawgiver ; that there was a great High Priest ; and that there were sacrifices and ordinances of religion in the Christian dispensation as well as the Jewish. In regard to each of these, he had shown that they existed in the Christian religion in a much more valuable and important sense than under the ancient dispensation. In like manner it was true, that as *they* were required to come to the service of God, having performed various ablutions to keep the body pure, so it was with Christians. Water was applied to the Jews as emblematic of purity, and Christians came, having had it applied to them also in baptism, as a symbol of holiness. It is not necessary, in order to see the force of this, to suppose that water had been applied to the *whole* of the body, or that they had been completely *immersed,* for all the force of the reasoning is retained by the supposition that it was a mere *symbol* or *emblem* of purification. The whole stress of the argument here turns, not on the fact that *the body had been washed all over,* but that the worshipper had been qualified for the *spiritual* service of the Most High in connection with an appropriate emblematic ceremony. The *quantity* of water used for this is not a material point, any more than the *quantity* of oil was in the ceremony of inaugurating kings and priests. This was not done in the Christian dispensation by washing the body *frequently,* as in the ancient system, nor even necessarily by washing the *whole* body —which would no more contribute to the purity of *the heart* than by application of water to any part of the body, but by the fact that water had been used as emblematic of the purifying of the soul. The passage before us proves, undoubtedly, (1.) that *water* should be applied under the new dispensation as an ordinance of religion ; and (2.) that *pure* water

should be used—for that only is a proper emblem of the purity of the heart.

23. *Let us hold fast the profession of our faith without wavering.* To secure this was one of the leading designs of this epistle, and hence the apostle adverts to it so frequently. It is evident that those to whom he wrote were suffering persecution (ch. xii.), and that there was great danger that they would apostatize. As these persecutions came probably from the Jews, and as the aim was to induce them to return to their former opinions, the object of the apostle is to show that there was in the Christian scheme every advantage of which the Jews could boast ; everything pertaining to the dignity of the great Founder of the system, the character of the High Priest, and the nature and value of the sacrifices offered, and that all this was possessed far more abundantly in the permanent Christian system than in that which was typical in its character, and which were designed soon to vanish away. In view of all this, therefore, the apostle adds that they should hold fast the profession of their faith without being shaken by their trials, or by the arguments of their enemies. *We* have the same inducement to hold fast the profession of our faith—for it is the same religion still ; we have the same Saviour, and there is held out to us still the same prospect of heaven. ¶ *For he is faithful that promised.* To induce them to hold fast their profession, the apostle adds this additional consideration. God, who had promised eternal life to them, was faithful to all that he had said. The argument here is, (1.) That since *God* is so faithful to us, we ought to be faithful to him. (2.) The fact that *he is faithful is an encouragement* to us. We are dependent on him for grace to hold fast our profession. If he were to prove unfaithful, we should have no strength to do it. But this he never does ; and we may be assured, that *all* that he has promised he will

24 And let us consider one another, to provoke unto love and to
good works :

25 Not forsaking the assembling
of ourselves together, as the manner of some *is ;* but exhorting

perform. To the service of *such* a
God, therefore, we should adhere
without wavering ; compare Notes on
1 Cor. x. 13.

24. *And let us consider one another.*
Let us so regard the welfare of others
as to endeavour to excite them to persevere in the Christian life. The idea
is, that much might be done, in securing perseverance and fidelity, by mutual kind exhortation. They were
not to be selfish ; they were not to regard their own interests only (Notes
Phil. ii. 4) ; they were to have a kind
sympathy in the concerns of each
other. They had, as Christians have
now, the same duties to perform, and
the same trials to meet, and they
should strengthen each other in their
trials and encourage them in their
work. ¶ *To provoke unto love.* We
use the word *provoke* now in a somewhat different sense, as meaning to
offend, to irritate, to incense ; but its
original meaning is *to arouse, to excite, to call into action,* and it is used
in this sense here. The Greek is,
literally, " unto a *paroxysm* of love "
—εἰς παροξυσμὸν—the word *paroxysm*
meaning *excitement* or *impulse,* and
the idea is, that they were to endeavour to *arouse* or *excite* each other to
the manifestation of love. The word
is that which properly expresses *excitement,* and means that Christians
should endeavour to *excite* each other.
Men are sometimes afraid of excitement in religion. But there is no danger that Christians will ever be *excited*
to love each other too much, or to perform too many *good works.*
25. *Not forsaking the assembling
of ourselves together.* That is, for purposes of public worship. Some expositors have understood the word here
rendered *assembling*—ἐπισυναγωγὴν—
as meaning *the society of Christians,*
or the church ; and they have supposed that the object of the apostle
here is, to exhort them not to *apostatize* from the church. The arguments
for this opinion may be seen at length
in Kuinoel, *in loc.* But the more

obvious interpretation is that which
is commonly adopted, that it refers
to public worship. The Greek word
(the noun) is used nowhere else in
the New Testament, except in 2
Thess. ii. 1, where it is rendered *gathering together.* The *verb* is used
in Matt. xxiii. 37 ; xxiv. 31 ; Mark i.
33 ; xiii. 27 ; Luke xii. 1 ; xiii. 34, in
all which places it is rendered *gathered together.* It properly means *an
act of assembling,* or a *gathering together,* and is nowhere used in the
New Testament in the sense of *an
assembly,* or *the church.* The command, then, here is, to *meet together*
for the worship of God, and it is enjoined on Christians as an important
duty to do it. It is *implied,* also,
that there is blame or fault where this
is " neglected." ¶ *As the manner of
some is.* *Why* those here referred to
neglected public worship, is not specified. It may have been from such
causes as the following. (1.) Some
may have been deterred by the fear
of persecution, as those who were
thus assembled would be more exposed to danger than others. (2.) Some
may have neglected the duty because
they felt no interest in it—as professing Christians now sometimes do. (3.)
It is possible that some may have had
doubts about the necessity and propriety of this duty, and on that account may have neglected it. (4.) Or
it may perhaps have been, though we
can hardly suppose that this reason
existed, that some may have neglected it from a cause which now sometimes operates—from dissatisfaction
with a preacher, or with some member or members of the church, or
with some measure in the church.
Whatever were the reasons, the apostle says that they should not be allowed to operate, but that Christians
should regard it as a sacred duty to
meet together for the worship of God.
None of the causes above suggested
should deter men from this duty.
With all who bear the Christian name,
with all who expect to make advances

one another: and so much the
a Rom. 13.11.

in piety and religious knowledge, it should be regarded as a sacred duty to assemble together for public worship. Religion is social; and our graces are to be strengthened and invigorated by waiting together on the Lord. There is an obvious propriety that men should assemble together for the worship of the Most High, and no Christian can hope that his graces will grow, or that he can perform his duty to his Maker, without uniting thus with those who love the service of God. ¶ *But exhorting* one another. That is, in your assembling together—a direction which proves that it is proper for Christians to exhort one another when they are gathered together for public worship. Indeed there is reason to believe that the preaching in the early Christian assemblies partook much of the character of mutual exhortation. ¶ *And so much the more as ye see the day approaching.* The term "day" here refers to some event which was certainly anticipated, and which was so well understood by them that no particular explanation was necessary. It was also some event that was expected soon to occur, and in relation to which there were indications then of its speedily arriving. If it had not been something which was expected soon to happen, the apostle would have gone into a more full explanation of it, and would have stated at length what these indications were. There has been some diversity of opinion about what is here referred to, many commentators supposing that the reference is to the anticipated second coming of the Lord Jesus to set up a visible kingdom on the earth; and others to the fact that the period was approaching when Jerusalem was to be destroyed, and when the services of the temple were to cease. So far as the *language* is concerned, the reference might be to either event, for the word a "day" is applied to both in the New Testament. The word would properly be understood as referring to an expected period when

more as *a*ye see the day approaching.

something *remarkable* was to happen which ought to have an important influence on their character and conduct. In support of the opinion that it refers to the approaching destruction of Jerusalem, and not to the coming of the Lord Jesus to set up a visible kingdom, we may adduce the following considerations. (1.) The term used—"day"—will as properly refer to that event as to any other. It is a word which would be *likely* to suggest the idea of distress, calamity, or judgment of some kind, for so it is often used in the Scriptures; comp. Ps. xxvii. 13; 1 Sam. xxvi. 10; Jer. xxx. 7; Ezek. xxi. 5; Notes Isa. ii. 12. (2.) Such a period was distinctly predicted by the Saviour, and the indications which would precede it were clearly pointed out; see Matt. xxiv. That event was then so near that the Saviour said that "that generation would not pass" until the prediction had been fulfilled; Matt. xxiv. 34. (3.) The destruction of Jerusalem was an event of great importance to the Hebrews, and to the Hebrew Christians to whom this epistle was directed, and it might be reasonable to suppose that the apostle Paul would refer to it. (4.) It is not improbable that at the time of writing this epistle there *were* indications that that day was approaching. Those indications were of so marked a character that when the time approached they could not well be mistaken (see Matt. xxiv. 6—12, 24, 26), and it is probable that they had already begun to appear. (5.) There *were* no such indications that the Lord Jesus was about to appear to set up a visible kingdom. It was not *a fact* that that was about to occur, as the result has shown; nor is there any positive proof that the mass of Christians were expecting it, and *no* reason to believe that the apostle Paul had any such expectation; see 2 Thess. ii. 1—5. (6.) The expectation that the destruction of Jerusalem was referred to, and was about to occur, was just that which might be expected to

26 For if *a* we sin wilfully after that we have received the know-

a Num.15.30. ch.6.4, &c.

ledge of the truth, there remaineth no more sacrifice for sins,

produce the effect on the minds of the Hebrew Christians which the apostle here refers to. It was to be a solemn and fearful event. It would be a remarkable manifestation of God. It would break up the civil and ecclesiastical polity of the nation, and would scatter them abroad. It would require all the exercise of their patience and faith in passing through these scenes. It might be expected to be a time when many would be tempted to apostatize, and it was proper, therefore, to exhort them to meet together, and to strengthen and encourage each other as they saw that that event was drawing near. The argument then would be this. The danger against which the apostle desired to guard those to whom he was writing was, that of apostasy from Christianity to Judaism. To preserve them from this, he urges the fact that the downfall of Judaism was near, and that every indication which they saw of its approach ought to be allowed to influence them, and to guard them from that danger. It is for reasons such as these that I suppose the reference here is not to the " second advent" of the Redeemer, but to the approaching destruction of' Jerusalem. At the same time, it is not improper to use this passage as an exhortation to Christians to fidelity when they shall see that the end of the world draws nigh, and when they shall perceive indications that the Lord Jesus is about to come. And so of death. We should be the more diligent when we see the indications that the great Messenger is about to come to summon us into the presence of our final Judge. And who does not know that he is approaching him with silent and steady footsteps, and that even now he may be very near ? Who can fail to see in himself indications that the time approaches when he must lie down and die? Every pang that we suffer should remind us of this ; and when the hair changes its hue, and time makes furrows in the cheek, and

the limbs become feeble, we should regard them as premonitions that he is coming, and should be more diligent as we see that he is drawing near.

26. *For if we sin wilfully after that we have received the knowledge of the truth.* If after we are converted and become true Christians we should apostatize, it would be impossible to be recovered again, for there would be no other sacrifice for sin ; no way by which we could be saved. This passage, however, like ch. vi. 4—6, has given rise to much difference of opinion. But that the above is the correct interpretation, seems evident to me from the following considerations. (1.) It is the natural and obvious interpretation, such as would occur probably to ninety-nine readers in a hundred, if there were no theory to support, and no fear that it would conflict with some other doctrine. (2.) It accords with the scope of the epistle, which is, to keep those whom the apostle addressed from returning again to the Jewish religion, under the trials to which they were subjected. (3.) It is in accordance with the fair meaning of the language —the words " after that we have received the knowledge of the truth," referring more naturally to true conversion than to any other state of mind. (4.) The sentiment would not be correct if it referred to any but real Christians. It would not be true that one who had been somewhat enlightened, and who then sinned " wilfully," must look on fearfully to the judgment without a possibility of being saved. There are multitudes of cases where such persons *are* saved. They *wilfully* resist the Holy Spirit ; they strive against him ; they for a long time refuse to yield, but they are brought again to reflection, and are led to give their hearts to God. (5.) It is true, and always will be true, that *if* a sincere Christian should apostatize he could *never* be converted again ; see Notes on ch. vi. 4—6.

27 But a certain fearful looking
for of judgment, and fiery *a* indig-

a Zeph.1.18; 3.8.

nation which shall devour the adversaries.

The reasons are obvious. He would
have tried the *only* plan of salvation,
and it would have failed. He would
have embraced the Saviour, and there
would not have been efficacy enough
in *his* blood to keep him, and there
would be no more powerful Saviour
and no more efficacious blood of atonement   He would have renounced the
Holy   Spirit, and would have shown
that *his* influences were not effectual
to keep him, and there would be no
other agent of greater power to renew
and save him after he had apostatized.
For these reasons it seems clear to
me that this passage refers to true
Christians, and that the doctrine here
taught is, that if such an one should
apostatize, he must look forward only
to the terrors of the judgment, and to
final condemnation. Whether this *in
fact* ever occurs, is quite another
question. In regard to that inquiry,
see Notes on ch. vi. 4—6. If this
view be correct, we may add, that the
passage should not be regarded as
applying to what is commonly known
as the " sin against the Holy Ghost,"
or "the unpardonable sin." The word
rendered "wilfully"—ἑκουσίως—occurs
nowhere else in the New Testament,
except in 1 Pet. v. 2, where it is rendered *willingly* — " taking the oversight thereof [of the church] not by
constraint, but *willingly.*" It properly means, *willingly, voluntarily, of
our own accord,* and applies to cases
where no constraint is used. It is
not to be construed here *strictly,* or
metaphysically, for *all* sin is voluntary,
or is committed *willingly,* but must
refer to *a deliberate act,* where a man
MEANS to abandon his religion, and to
turn away from God. If it were to
be taken with metaphysical exactness,
it would demonstrate that every Christian who ever does *anything* wrong,
no matter how small, would be lost.
But this cannot, from the nature of
the case, be the meaning. The apostle well knew that Christians *do* commit such sins (see Notes on Rom. vii.),
and his object here is not to set forth

the danger of *such* sins, but to guard
Christians against apostasy from their
religion. In the Jewish law, as is indeed the case everywhere, a distinction is made between sins of *oversight,
inadvertence,* or *ignorance,* (Lev. iv. 2,
13, 22, 27; v. 15 ; Num. xv. 24, 27,
28, 29 ; comp. Acts iii. 17 ; xvii. 30),
and sins of *presumption;* sins that are
deliberately and *intentionally* committed ; see Ex. xxi. 14 ; Num. xv. 30 ;
Deut. xvii. 12 ; Ps. xix. 13.   The
apostle here has reference, evidently,
to such a distinction, and means to
speak of a decided and deliberate
purpose to break away from the restraints and obligations of the Christian religion.   ¶ *There remaineth no
more sacrifice for sins.* Should a man
do this, there is no sacrifice for sins
which could save him.   He would
have rejected deliberately the only
atonement made for sin, and there
will be no other made.   It is as if a
man should reject the only medicine
that could heal him, or push away
the only boat that could save him
when shipwrecked ; see Notes ch. vi.
6.   The sacrifice made for sin by the
Redeemer is never to be repeated,
and if that is deliberately rejected,
the soul must be lost.
  27. *But a certain fearful looking for
of judgment.* The word "*certain*" here
does not mean *fixed, sure, inevitable,*
as our translation would seem to imply.   The Greek is the same as " *a*
(τις) fearful expectation," &c.   So it
is rendered by Tindall.   The idea is,
that if there was voluntary apostasy
after having embraced the Christian
religion, there *could be* nothing but an
expectation of the judgment to come.
There could be no other hope but
that through the gospel, and as this
would have been renounced, it would
follow that the soul must perish. The
"fearful apprehension" or expectation
here does not refer so much to what
would be *in the mind itself,* or what
would be experienced, as to what
must follow.   It might be that the
person referred to would have no re-

28 He *a* that despised Moses' law died without mercy under two or three witnesses :

a De.17.2-7,13.

29 Of *b* how much sorer punishment, suppose ye, shall he be thought worthy, who hath trod-

b ch.2.3.

alizing sense of all this, and still his situation be that of one who had nothing to expect but the terrors of the judgment to come. ¶ *And fiery indignation.* Fire is often used in the Scriptures as an emblem of fierce punishment. The idea is, that the person referred to could expect nothing but the wrath of God. ¶ *Which shall devour the adversaries.* All who become the adversaries or enemies of the Lord. Fire is often said to *devour*, or *consume*, and the meaning here is, that those who should thus become the enemies of the Lord must perish.
28. *He that despised Moses' law.* That is, the apostate from the religion of Moses. It does not mean that *in all cases* the offender against the law of Moses died without mercy, but only where offences were punishable with death, and probably the apostle had in his eye particularly the case of apostasy from the Jewish religion. The subject of apostasy from the Christian religion is particularly under discussion here, and it was natural to illustrate this by a reference to a similar case under the law of Moses. The law in regard to apostates from the Jewish religion was positive. There was no reprieve ; Deut. xiii. 6—10. ¶ *Died without mercy.* That is, there was no provision for pardon. ¶ *Under two or three witnesses.* It was the settled law among the Hebrews that in all cases involving capital punishment, two or three witnesses should be necessary. That is, no one was to be executed unless two persons certainly bore testimony, and it was regarded as important, if possible, that *three* witnesses should concur in the statement. The object was the security of the accused person if innocent. The *principle* in the law was, that it was to be presumed that two or three persons would be much less likely to conspire to render a false testimony than one would be, and that two or three would not be likely to be de-

ceived in regard to a fact which the had observed.
29. *Of how much sorer punishment, suppose ye, shall he be thought worthy.* That is, he who renounces Christianity *ought* to be regarded as deserving a much severer punishment than the man who apostatized from the Jewish religion, and if he *ought* to be so regarded he will be—for God will treat every man as he *ought* to be treated. This must refer to future punishment, for the severest punishment was inflicted on the apostate from the Jewish religion which *can be* in this world—*death;* and yet the apostle here says that a severer punishment than that would be deserved by him who should apostatize from the Christian faith. The *reasons* why so much severer punishment would be deserved, are such as these :—the Author of the Christian system was far more exalted than Moses, the founder of the Jewish system ; he had revealed more important truths ; he had increased and confirmed the motives to holiness ; he had furnished more means for leading a holy life ; he had given himself as a sacrifice to redeem the soul from death, and he had revealed with far greater clearness the truth that there is a heaven of glory and of holiness. He who should apostatize from the Christian faith, the apostle goes on to say, would also be guilty of the most aggravated crime of which man could be guilty — the crime of trampling under foot the Son of God, of showing contempt for his holy blood. and despising the Spirit of grace. ¶ *Who hath trodden under foot the Son of God.* This language is taken either from the custom of ancient conquerors who were accustomed to tread on the necks of their enemies in token of their being subdued, or from the fact that men tread on that which they despise and contemn. The idea is, that he who should apostatize from the Christian faith would act *as if* he should indig-

den under foot the Son of God, and hath counted the blood of the covenant, wherewith he was sanc-

tified, an unholy thing, and hath done despite unto the Spirit *a* of grace?

a Mat.12.31,32.

nantly and contemptuously trample on God's only Son. What crime could be more aggravated than this? ¶ *And hath counted the blood of the covenant.* The blood of Jesus by which the new covenant between God and man was ratified; see Notes on ch. ix. 16—20; comp. Notes on Matt. xxvi. 28. ¶ *Wherewith he was sanctified.* Made holy, or set apart to the service of God. The word *sanctify* is used in both these senses. Prof. Stuart renders it, "by which expiation is made;" and many others, in accordance with this view, have supposed that it refers to the Lord Jesus. But it seems to me that it refers to the person who is here supposed to renounce the Christian religion, or to apostatize from it. The reasons for this are such as these. (1.) It is the natural and proper meaning of the word here rendered *sanctified.* This word is commonly applied to Christians in the sense that they are made holy; see Acts xx. 32; xxvi. 18; 1 Cor. i. 2; Jude 1; comp. John x. 36; xvii. 17. (2.) It is unusual to apply this word to the Saviour. It is true, indeed, that he says (John xvii. 19), "for their sakes I sanctify myself," but there is no instance in which he says that he was *sanctified by his own blood.* And where is there an instance in which the word is used as meaning "to make expiation?" (3.) The supposition that it refers to one who is here spoken of as in danger of apostasy, and not of the Lord Jesus, agrees with the scope of the argument. The apostle is showing the great guilt, and the certain destruction, of one who should apostatize from the Christian religion. In doing this it was natural to speak of the dishonour which would thus be done to the means which had been used for his sanctification—the blood of the Redeemer. It would be treating it as if it were a common thing, or as if it might be disregarded like anything else which was of no value. ¶ *An unholy thing.*

Gr. *common;* often used in the sense of unholy. The word is so used because that which was holy was separated from a common to a sacred use. What was *not* thus consecrated was free to all, or was for common use, and hence also the word is used to denote that which is unholy. ¶ *And hath done despite unto the Spirit of grace.* The Holy Spirit, called "the Spirit of grace," because he confers favour or grace on men. The meaning of the phrase "done despite unto" —ἐνυβρίσας—is, "having reproached, or treated with malignity, or contempt." The idea is, that if they were thus to apostatize, they would by such an act treat the Spirit of God with disdain and contempt. It was by him that they had been renewed; by him that they had been brought to embrace the Saviour and to love God; by him that they had any holy feelings or pure desires; and if they now apostatized from religion, such an act would be in fact treating the Holy Spirit with the highest indignity. It would be saying that all his influences were valueless, and that they needed no help from him. From such considerations, the apostle shows that *if* a true Christian were to apostatize, nothing would remain for him but the terrific prospect of eternal condemnation. He would have rejected the only Saviour; he would have in fact treated him with the highest indignity; he would have considered his sacred blood, shed to sanctify men, as a common thing, and would have shown the highest disregard for the only agent who can save the soul—the Spirit of God. How could such an one afterwards be saved? The apostle does not indeed say that any one ever *would* thus apostatize from the true religion, nor is there any reason to believe that such a case ever *has* occurred, but if it *should* occur the doom would be inevitable. How dangerous then is every step which would lead to such a precipice!

30 For we know him that hath said, Vengeance ^a *belongeth* unto me,

a De.32.35,36.   b Ps.135.14.

And how strange and unscriptural the opinion held by so many that sincere Christians *may* "*fall away*" and be renewed, again and again !

[See the supplementary Note on ch. vi. 6. where certain principles are laid down, for the interpretation of this and similar passages, in consistency with the doctrine of the saints' perseverance. If that doctrine be maintained, and our author's view of the passage at the same be correct, then plainly it contains an *impossible* case. It is descriptive of real Christians, yet *they* never can fall away. The utility of the warning, in this case, may indeed successfully be vindicated, on the ground that it is the *means* of preventing apostasy in the saints, the means by which the decree of God in reference to their stability is effected. Most, however, will incline to the view which regards this case, as something more than imaginary, as *possible*, as ˉ*real*. The warning is addressed to *professors* generally, without· any attempt of distinguishing or separating into *true* or *false*. Doubtless there might be *some* even of the latter class in the churches whose members the apostles, presuming on their professed character, addressed as "saints," " elect," and "faithful," without distinction. Of course, in consistency with the doctrine of perseverance only the "*false*," in whom the "root of the matter" had never existed, could apostatize ; yet at the same time, when no distinction was made, when the apostle made none, but addressed all in the language of charity, when Christians themselves might find it difficult at all times to affirm decidedly on their own case, *universal vigilance* was secured, or at all events designed. But is not the party whose apostasy is here supposed, described by two attributes which belong to none but genuine Christians, viz. the " reception of the knowledge of the truth," and " sanctification through the blood of the covenant ?" The answer which has been given to this question is generally, that neither of these things necessarily involves more than *external* dedication to God. The first is parallel to the " once enlightened" of Heb. vi. 4. and of course admits of the same explanation ; see supplementary Note there. The second thing, viz. the sanctification of the party " is not real or internal sanctification, and all the disputes concerning the total and final apostasy from the faith of them who have been really and internally sanctified from this place, are altogether vain. As at the giving of the law, the people being

I will recompense, saith the Lord. And again, ^b The Lord shall judge his people.

sprinkled with blood, were *sanctified* or dedicated to God in a peculiar manner, so those who, by baptism and confession of faith in the church of Christ, were separated from all others were peculiarly dedicated to God thereby."—*Owen*. Yet, this eminent writer is rather disposed to adopt the opinion of those who construe, εν ᾧ ἡγιασθη with the immediate antecedent, τον Ὑιον του Θεου, thus referring the sanctification to Christ, and not to the apostate ; see John xvii. 19. Whichever of these views we receive, the great doctrine of perseverance is, of course, unaffected. In reference to an objection which the author has urged, that " the sentiment (in the 26th and 27th verses) would not be correct, if it referred to any but true Christians," let it be noticed that while many may be saved, who have long resisted the Spirit, yet the assertion must appear hazardous in the extreme, that *any* can be saved, who do ALL that the apostate in this passage is alleged to do. The sin described seems to be that of a determined, insulting, final rejection of the *only* remedy for sin.]

30. *For we know him that hath said.* We know who has said this — God. They knew this because it was recorded in their own sacred books. ¶ *Vengeance* belongeth *unto me*, &c. This is found in Deut. xxxii. 35 ; see it explained in the Notes on Romans xii. 19. It is there quoted to show that *we* should not avenge ourselves ; it is here quoted to show that God will *certainly* inflict punishment on those who deserve it. If any should apostatize in the manner here referred to by the apostle, they would, says he, be guilty of great and unparalleled wickedness, and would have the certainty that they *must* meet the wrath of God. ¶ *And again, The Lord shall judge his people.* This is quoted from Deut. xxxii. 36. That is, he will judge them when they deserve it, and punish them if they ought to be punished. The mere fact that they *are* his people will not save them from punishment if they deserve it, any more than the fact that one is a beloved child will save him from correction when he does wrong. This truth was abundantly illustrated in the history of the Israelites ; and the same great prin-

31 *It is* a fearful thing to fall into the hands of the living God.

32 But call to remembrance the

former days, in which, after ye were illuminated, ye endured a great fight of afflictions ;

---

ciple would be applied should any sincere Christian apostatize from his religion. He would have before him the certainty of the most fearful and severe of all punishments.

31. It is *a fearful thing to fall into the hands of the living God.* There may be an allusion here to the request of David to "fall into the hands of the Lord and not into the hands of men," when it was submitted to him for the sin of numbering the people, whether he would choose seven years of famine, or flee three months before his enemies, or have three days of pestilence ; 2 Sam. xxiv. He preferred "to fall into the hands of the Lord," and God smote seventy thousand men by the pestilence. The idea here is, that to fall into the hands of the Lord, after having despised his mercy and rejected his salvation, would be terrific ; and the fear of this should deter from the commission of the dreadful crime. The phrase "living God" is used in the Scripture in opposition to *idols.* God always lives ; his power is capable of being always exerted. He is not like the idols of wood or stone which have no life, and which are not to be dreaded, but he always lives. It is the more fearful to fall into his hands because he will live *for ever.* A man who inflicts punishment will die, and the punishment will come to an end ; but God will never cease to exist, and the punishment which he is capable of inflicting to-day he will be capable of inflicting for ever and ever. To fall into his hands, therefore, *for the purpose of punishment* — which is the idea here—is fearful (1.) because he has all power, and can inflict just what punishment he pleases ; (2.) because he is strictly just, and will inflict the punishment which ought to be inflicted ; (3.) because he lives for ever, and can carry on his purpose of punishment to eternal ages, and (4.) because the actual inflictions of punishment which have occurred show what is to be dreaded. So it was on

the old world ; on the cities of the plain ; on Babylon, Idumea, Capernaum, and Jerusalem ; and so it is in the world of wo—the eternal abodes of despair, where the worm never dies. All men *must,* in one sense, fall into his hands. They *must* appear before him. They *must* be brought to his bar when they die. How unspeakably important it is then now to embrace his offers of salvation, that we may not fall into his hands as a righteous, avenging judge, and sink beneath his uplifted arm for ever !

32. *But call to remembrance the former days.* It would seem from this, that at the time when the apostle wrote this epistle they were suffering some severe trials, in which they were in great danger of apostatizing from their religion. It is also manifest that they had on some former occasion endured a similar trial, and had been enabled to bear it with a Christian spirit, and with resignation. The object of the apostle now is to remind them that they were sustained under those trials, and he would encourage them now to similar patience by the recollection of the grace then conferred on them. What was the nature of their former trials, or of that which they were then experiencing, is not certainly known. It would seem probable, however, that the reference in both instances is to some form of persecution by their own countrymen. The meaning is, that *when we have been enabled to pass through trials once, we are to make the remembrance of the grace then bestowed on us a means of supporting and encouraging us in future trials.* ¶ *After ye were illuminated.* After you became Christians, or were enlightened to see the truth. This phrase, referring here undoubtedly to the fact that they were Christians, may serve to explain the disputed phrase in ch. vi. 4 ; see Notes on that passage. ¶ *A great fight of afflictions.* The *language* here seems to be taken from the Grecian games. The word "fight"

33 Partly, whilst ye were made a gazing-stock, both by reproaches and afflictions; and partly, whilst ye became *a* companions of them that were so used.

34 For ye had compassion of me in my bonds, and took joyfully the spoiling of your goods, knowing [1] in yourselves that ye have in *b* heaven a better and an enduring substance.

1 or, *that ye have in yourselves;* or, *for yourselves.* *b* Luke 12.33.

means properly *contention, combat,* such as occurred in the public games. Here the idea is, that in the trials referred to, they had a great *struggle;* that is, a struggle to maintain their faith without wavering, or against those who would have led them to apostatize from their religion. Some of the circumstances attending this conflict are alluded to in the following verses.

33. *Partly.* That is, your affliction consisted partly in this. The Greek is, "this"—specifying one kind of affliction that they were called to endure. ¶ *Whilst ye were made a gazing-stock.* Gr. Θεατριζόμενοι—you were made a public spectacle, as if in a theatre; you were held up to public view, or exposed to public scorn. When this was done, or in precisely what manner, we are not told. It was not an uncommon thing, however, for the early Christians to be held up to reproach and scorn, and probably this refers to some time when it was done by rulers or magistrates. It was a common custom among the Greeks and Romans to lead criminals, before they were put to death, through the theatre, and thus to expose them to the insults and reproaches of the multitude. See the proofs of this adduced by Kuinoel on this passage. The *language* here seems to have been taken from this custom, though there is no evidence that the Christians to whom Paul refers had been treated in this manner. ¶ *By reproaches.* Reproached as being the followers of Jesus of Nazareth; probably as weak and fanatical. ¶ *And afflictions.* Various *sufferings* inflicted on them. They were not merely reviled *in words,* but they were made to endure positive sufferings of various kinds. ¶ *And partly, while ye became companions of them that were so used.* That is, even when they had not themselves

been subjected to these trials, they had sympathized with those who were. They doubtless imparted to them of their property; sent to them relief, and identified themselves with them. It is not known to what particular occasion the apostle here refers. In the next verse he mentions *one* instance in which they had done this, in aiding *him* when he was a prisoner.

34. *For ye had compassion of me in my bonds.* You sympathized with me when a prisoner, and sent to my relief. It is not known to what particular instance of imprisonment the apostle here refers. It is probable, however, that it was on some occasion when he was a prisoner in Judea, for the persons to whom this epistle was sent most probably resided there. Paul was at one time a prisoner more than two years at Cesarea (Acts xxiv. 27), and during this time he was kept in the charge of a centurion, and his friends had free access to him ; Acts xxiv. 23. It would seem not improbable that this was the occasion to which he here refers. ¶ *And took joyfully the spoiling of your goods.* The *plunder* of your property. It was not an uncommon thing for the early Christians to be plundered. This was doubtless a part of the "afflictions" to which the apostle refers in this case. The meaning is, that they yielded their property not only without resistance, but with joy. They, in common with all the early Christians, counted it a privilege and honour to suffer in the cause of their Master ; see Notes on Phil. iii. 10 ; comp. Rom. v. 3. Men *may* be brought to such a state of mind as to part with their property *with joy.* It is not usually the case ; but religion will enable a man to do it. ¶ *Knowing in yourselves.* Marg "or, *that ye have in yourselves;* or, *for yourselves.*" The true rendering is, "knowing that ye have for yourselves."

35 Cast not away therefore your confidence, which hath great *a* recompense of reward.

a Matt.5.12.

It does not refer to any *internal* knowledge which they had of this, but to the fact that they were assured that they had laid up for themselves a better inheritance in heaven. ¶ *That ye have in heaven a better and an enduring substance.* Better than any earthly possession, and more permanent. It is (1.) *better ;* it is worth more ; it gives more comfort ; it makes a man really *richer.* The treasure laid up in heaven is *worth more* to a man than all the wealth of Crœsus. It will give him more solid peace and comfort ; will better serve his turn in the various situations in which he may be placed in life, and will do more on the whole to make him happy. It is not said here that property is worth *nothing* to a man — which is not true, if he uses it well — but that the treasures of heaven are worth *more.* (2.) It is more *enduring.* Property here soon vanishes. Riches take to themselves wings and fly away, or at any rate all that we possess must soon be left. But in heaven all is permanent and secure. No calamity of war, pestilence, or famine ; no change of times ; no commercial embarrassments ; no failure of a crop, or a bank ; no fraud of sharpers and swindlers, and no act of a pick-pocket or highwayman can take it away ; nor does death ever come there to remove the inhabitants of heaven from their "mansions." With this hope, therefore, Christians may cheerfully see their earthly wealth vanish, for they can look forward to their enduring and their better inheritance.

35. *Cast not away therefore your confidence.* Gr. "your boldness;" referring to their confident hope in God. They were not to cast this away, and to become timid, disheartened, and discouraged. They were to bear up manfully under all their trials, and to maintain a steadfast adherence to God and to his cause. The command is not to " cast this away." Nothing

36 For ye have need of *b* patience; that, after ye have done the will of God, ye might receive the promise.

b Luke 21.19.

could take it from them if they trusted in God, and it could be lost only by their own neglect or imprudence. Rosenmüller supposes (Alte und Neue Morgenland, *in loc.*) that there may be an allusion here to the disgrace which was attached to the act of a warrior if he cast away his shield. Among the Greeks this was a crime which was punishable with death. Alexander ab Alexand. Gen. Dier. L. ii. c. 13. Among the ancient Germans, Tacitus says, that to lose the shield in battle was regarded as the deepest dishonour, and that those who were guilty of it were not allowed to be present at the sacrifices or in the assembly of the people. Many, says he, who had suffered this calamity, closed their own lives with the halter under the loss of honour. Tac. Germ. c. 6. A similar disgrace would attend the Christian soldier if he should cast away his shield of faith ; comp. Notes Eph. vi. 16. ¶ *Which hath great recompense of reward.* It will furnish a reward by the peace of mind which it gives here, and will be connected with the rewards of heaven.

36. *For ye have need of patience.* They were then suffering, and in all trials we have need of patience. We have need of it because there is in us so much disposition to murmur and repine ; because our nature is liable to sink under sufferings ; and because our trials are often protracted. All that Christians can do in such cases is to be *patient*—to lie calmly in the hands of God, and submit to his will day by day, and year by year ; see James i. 3, 4 ; Notes Rom. v. 4. ¶ *That after ye have done the will of God.* That is, in bearing trials, for the reference here is particularly to afflictions. ¶ *Ye might receive the promise.* The promised inheritance or reward—in heaven. It is implied here that this promise will not be received unless we are patient in our trials, and the prospect of this reward should encourage us to endure them.

37 For yet a little while, and he that shall come will come, and will not tarry.*a*

a Hab.2.3.

38 Now the just shall live by faith:*b* but if *any man* draw back, my soul shall have no pleasure in him.   *b* Hab.2.4.

37. *For yet a little while.* There seems to be an allusion here to what the Saviour himself said, " A little while, and ye shall not see me ; and again, a little while and ye shall see me ;" John xvi. 16. Or more probably it may be to Hab. ii. 3. " For the vision is yet for an appointed time, but at the end it shall speak, and not lie : though it tarry, wait for it ; because it will surely come, it will not tarry." The idea which the apostle means to convey evidently is, that the time of their deliverance from their trials was not far remote. ¶ *And he that shall come will come.* The reference here is, doubtless, to the Messiah. But what *"coming"* of his is referred to here, is more uncertain. Most probably the idea is, that the Messiah who was coming to destroy Jerusalem, and to overthrow the Jewish power (Matt. xxiv.), would soon do this. In this way he would put a period to their persecutions and trials, as the power of the Jewish people to afflict them would be at an end. A similar idea occurs in Luke xxi. 28. " And when these things begin to come to pass, then look up, and lift up your heads ; *for your redemption draweth nigh ;*" see Notes on that passage. The Christians in Palestine were oppressed, reviled, and persecuted by the Jews. The destruction of the city and the temple would put an end to that power, and would be in fact the time of deliverance for those who had been persecuted. In the passage before us, Paul intimates that that period was not far distant. Perhaps there were already " signs" of his coming, or indications that he was about to appear, and he therefore urges them patiently to persevere in their fidelity to him during the little time of trial that remained. The same encouragement and consolation may be employed still. To all the afflicted it may be said that "he that shall come will come" soon. The time of affliction is not long. Soon

the Redeemer will appear to deliver his afflicted people from all their sorrows ; to remove them from a world of pain and tears ; and to raise their bodies from the dust, and to receive them to mansions where trials are for ever unknown ; Notes John xiv. 3 ; 1 Thess. iv. 13—18.

38. *Now the just shall live by faith.* This is a part of the quotation from Habakkuk (ii. 3, 4), which was probably commenced in the previous verse ; see the passage fully explained in the Notes on Rom. i. 17. The meaning in the connection in which it stands here, in accordance with the sense in which it was used by Habakkuk, is, that the righteous should live by *continued confidence* in God. They should pass their lives, not in doubt, and fear, and trembling apprehension, but in the exercise of a calm trust in God. In this sense it accords with the scope of what the apostle is here saying. He is exhorting the Christians whom he addressed, to perseverance in their religion even in the midst of many persecutions. To encourage this he says, that it was a great principle that the just, that is, all the pious, ought to live in the constant exercise of *faith in God.* They should not confide in their own merits, works, or strength. They should exercise constant reliance on their Maker, and he would keep them even unto eternal life. The sense is, that a persevering confidence or belief in the Lord will preserve us amidst all the trials and calamities to which we are exposed. ¶ *But if* any man *draw back, my soul shall have no pleasure in him.* This also is a quotation from Hab. ii. 4, but from the Septuagint, not from the Hebrew. *Why* the authors of the Septuagint thus translated the passage, it is impossible now to say. The Hebrew is rendered in the common version, " Behold, his soul which is lifted up is not upright in him ;" or more literally, " Behold the scorn-

39 But we are not of them who draw back *a* unto perdition, but of

them that believe to the saving of the soul.

ful ; his mind shall not be happy" (*Stuart*) ; or as Gesenius renders it, " See, he whose soul is unbelieving shall, on this account, be unhappy." The sentiment there is, that the scorner or unbeliever in that day would be unhappy, or would not prosper— לֹא יִשְׁרָה. The apostle has retained the general sense of the passage, and the idea which *he* expresses is, that the unbeliever, or he who renounces his religion, will incur the divine displeasure. He will be a man exposed to the divine wrath ; a man on whom God cannot look but with disapprobation. By this solemn consideration, therefore, the apostle urges on them the importance of perseverance, and the guilt and danger of apostasy from the Christian faith. *If* such a case should occur, no matter what might have been the former condition, and no matter what love or zeal might have been evinced, yet such an apostasy would expose the individual to the certain wrath of God. His former love could not save him, any more than the former obedience of the angels saved them from the horrors of eternal chains and darkness, or than the holiness in which Adam was created saved him and his posterity from the calamities which his apostasy incurred.

39. *But we are not of them,* &c. We who are true Christians do not belong to such a class. In this the apostle expresses the fullest conviction that none of those to whom he wrote would apostatize. The case which he had been describing was only a supposable case, not one which he believed would occur. He had only been stating what *must* happen if a sincere Christian should apostatize. But he did not mean to say that this *would* occur in regard to them, or in any case. He made a statement of a general principle under the divine administration, and he designed that this should be a means of keeping them in the path to life. What could be a more effectual means

than the assurance that *if* a Christian should apostatize *he must inevitably perish for ever ?* See the sentiment in this verse illustrated at length in the Notes on ch. vi. 4—10

REMARKS.

(1.) It is a subject of rejoicing that we are brought under a more perfect system than the ancient people of God were. We have not merely a rude outline — a dim and shadowy sketch of religion, as they had. We are not now required to go before a bloody altar every day, and lead up a victim to be slain. We may come to the altar of God feeling that the great sacrifice has been made, and that the last drop of blood to make atonement has been shed. A pure, glorious, holy body was prepared for the Great Victim, and in that body he did the will of God and died for our sins ; vers. 1—10.

(2.) Like that Great Redeemer, let *us* do the will of God. It may lead us through sufferings, and we may be called to meet trials strongly resembling his. But the will of God is to be done alike in bearing trials, and in prayer and praise. *Obedience* is the great thing which he demands ; which he has always sought. When his ancient people led up, in faith, a lamb to the altar, still he preferred obedience to sacrifice ; and when his Son came into the world to teach us how to live, and how to die, still the great thing was obedience. He came to illustrate the nature of perfect conformity to the will of God, and he did that by a most holy life, and by the most patient submission to all the trials appointed him in his purpose to make atonement for the sins of the world. Our model, alike in holy living and holy dying, is to be the Saviour ; and like him we are required to exercise simple submission to the will of God ; vers. 1—10.

(3.) The Redeemer looks calmly forward to the time when all his foes will be brought in submission to his feet ;

vers. 12, 13. He is at the right hand of God. His great work on earth is done. He is to suffer no more. He is exalted beyond the possibility of pain and sorrow, and he is seated now on high looking to the period when all his foes shall be subdued and he will be acknowledged as universal Lord.

(4.) The Christian has exalted advantages. He has access to the mercy-seat of God. He may enter by faith into the "Holiest" — the very heavens where God dwells. Christ, his great High Priest, has entered there; has sprinkled over the mercy-seat with his blood, and ever lives there to plead his cause. There is no privilege granted to men like that of a near and constant access to the mercy-seat. This is the privilege not of a few; and not to be enjoyed but once in a year, or at distant intervals, but which the most humble Christian possesses, and which may be enjoyed at all times, and in all places. There is not a Christian so obscure, so poor, so ignorant that he may not come and speak to God; and there is not a situation of poverty, want, or wo, where he may not make his wants known with the assurance that his prayers will be heard through faith in the great Redeemer; vers. 19, 20.

(5.) When we come before God, let our hearts be pure; ver. 22. The body has been washed with pure water in baptism, emblematic of the purifying influences of the Holy Spirit. Let the conscience be also pure. Let us lay aside every unholy thought. Our worship will not be acceptable; our prayers will not be heard, if it is not so. "If we regard iniquity in our hearts the Lord will not hear us." No matter though there be a great High Priest; no matter though he have offered a perfect sacrifice for sin, and no matter though the throne of God be accessible to men, yet if there is in the heart the love of sin; if the conscience is not pure, our prayers will not be heard. Is this not one great reason why our worship is so barren and unprofitable?

(6.) It is the duty of Christians to exhort one another to mutual fidelity;

ver. 24. We should so far regard the interests of each other, as to strive to promote our mutual advance in piety. The church is one. All true Christians are brethren. Each one has an interest in the spiritual welfare of every one who loves the Lord Jesus, and should strive to increase his spiritual joy and usefulness. A Christian brother often goes astray and needs kind admonition to reclaim him; or he becomes disheartened and needs encouragement to cheer him or his Christian way.

(7.) Christians should not neglect to assemble together for the worship of God; ver. 25. It is a duty which they owe to God to acknowledge him publicly, and their own growth in piety is essentially connected with public worship. It is impossible for a man to secure the advancement of religion in his soul who habitually neglects public worship, and religion will not flourish in any community where this duty is not performed. There are great benefits growing out of the worship of God, which can be secured in no other way. God has made us social beings, and he intends that the social principle shall be called into exercise in religion, as well as in other things. We have common wants, and it is proper to present them together before the mercy-seat. We have received common blessings in our creation, in the providence of God, and in redemption, and it is proper that we should assemble together and render united praise to our Maker for his goodness. Besides, in any community, the public worship of God does more to promote intelligence, order, peace, harmony, friendship, neatness of apparel, and purity and propriety of intercourse between neighbours, than anything else can, and for which nothing else can be a compensation. Every Christian, and every other man, therefore, is bound to lend his influence in thus keeping up the worship of God, and should always be in his place in the sanctuary. The particular thing in the exhortation of the apostle is, that this should be done *even in the face of persecution.* The early Christians felt so much the importance of this, that we are told they were accustomed to assemble at night. Forbidden to meet in public houses of worship, they met in caves, and even when threatened with death they continued to maintain the worship of God. It may be added, that so important is this, that it should be preserved even when the preaching of the gospel is not enjoyed. Let Christians assemble together. Let them pray and offer praise. Let them read the word of God, and an appropriate sermon. Even *this* will exert an influence on them and on the community of incalculable importance, and will serve to keep the flame of piety burning on the altar of their own hearts, and in the community around them.

(8.) We may see the danger of indulging in any sin; vers. 26, 27. None can tell to what it may lead. No matter how small and unimportant it may appear at the time, yet if indulged in it will prove that there is no true religion, and will lead on to those greater offences which make shipwreck of the Christian name, and ruin the soul. He that "wilfully" and deliberately sins "after he professes to have received the knowledge of the truth," shows that his religion is but a name, and that he has never known any thing of its power.

(9.) We should guard with sacred vigilance against everything which might lead to apostasy; vers. 26—29. If a sincere Christian *should* apostatize from God, he could never be renewed and saved. There would remain no more sacrifice for sins; there is no other Saviour to be provided; there is no other Holy Spirit to be sent down to recover the apostate. Since, therefore, so fearful a punishment *would* follow apostasy from the true religion, we may see the guilt of everything which has a *tendency* to it. That guilt is to be measured by the fearful consequences which would ensue if it were followed out; and the Christian should, therefore, tremble when he is on the verge of committing any sin whose legitimate tendency would be such a result.

(10.) We may learn from the views presented in this chapter (vers. 26—29), the error of those who suppose that a true Christian may fall away and be renewed again and saved. If there is any principle clearly settled in the New Testament, it is, that *if* a sincere Christian should apostatize, *he must perish*. There would be no possibility of renewing him. He would have tried the only religion which saves men, and it would in his case have failed; he would have applied to the only blood which purifies the soul, and it would have been found inefficacious; he would have been brought under the only influence which renews the soul, and that would not have been sufficient to save him. What hope *could* there be? What would then save him if these would not? To what would he apply — to what Saviour, to what blood of atonement, to what renewing and sanctifying agent, if the gospel, and the Redeemer, and the Holy Spirit had all been tried in vain? There are few errors in the community more directly at variance with the express teachings of the Bible than the belief that a Christian may fall away and be again renewed.

(11.) Christians, in their conflicts, their trials, and their temptations, should be strengthened by what is past; vers. 32—35. They should remember the days when they were afflicted and God sustained them, when they were persecuted and he brought them relief. It is proper also to remember for their own encouragement now, the spirit of patience and submission which they were enabled to manifest in those times of trial, and the sacrifices which they were enabled to make. They may find in such things evidence that they are the children of God; and they should find in their past experience proof that he who has borne them through past trials, is able to keep them unto his everlasting kingdom.

(12.) We need patience—but it is only for a little time; vers. 36—39. Soon all our conflicts will be over. "He that shall come will come and will not tarry." He will come to de-

CHAPTER XI.

NOW faith is the [1] substance of things hoped for, the

evidence of things [a] not seen.

1 or, *ground*, or, *confidence*.
a Rom.8.24,25.

liver his suffering people from all their trials. He will come to rescue the persecuted from the persecutor ; the oppressed from the oppressor; the down-trodden from the tyrant; and the sorrowful and sad from their woes. The coming of the Saviour to each one of the afflicted is the signal of release from sorrow, and his advent at the end of the world will be proof that all the trials of the bleeding and persecuted church are at an end. The time too is short before he will appear. In each individual case it is to be but a brief period before he will come to relieve the sufferer from his woes, and in the case of the church at large the time is not far remote when the Great Deliverer shall appear to receive "the bride," the church redeemed, to the "mansions" which he has gone to prepare.

CHAPTER XI.

ANALYSIS OF THE CHAPTER.

In the close of the previous chapter, the apostle had incidentally made mention of faith (vers. 38, 39), and said that the just should live by faith. The object of the whole argument in this epistle was to keep those to whom it was addressed from apostatizing from the Christian religion, and especially from relapsing again into Judaism. They were in the midst of trials, and were evidently suffering some form of persecution, the tendency of which was to expose them to the danger of relapsing. The indispensable means of securing them from apostasy was *faith*, and with a view to show its efficacy in this respect, the apostle goes into an extended account of its nature and effects, occupying this entire chapter. As the persons whom he addressed had been Hebrews, and as the Old Testament contained an account of numerous instances of persons in substantially the same circumstances in which they were, the reference is made to the illustrious examples of the efficacy of faith in the Jewish history. The object is, to show that *faith*, or confi-

dence in the divine promises, has been in all ages the means of perseverance in the true religion, and consequently of salvation. In this chapter, therefore, the apostle first describes or defines the nature of faith (ver. 1), and then illustrates its efficacy and power by reference to numerous instances ; vers. 2—40. In these illustrations he refers to the steady belief which we have that God made the worlds, and then to the examples of Abel, Enoch, Noah, Abraham, Sarah, Isaac, Jacob, Joseph, Moses, and Rahab in particular, and then to numerous other examples without mentioning their names. The object is to show that there is power in faith to keep the mind and heart in the midst of trials, and that having these examples before them, those whom he addressed should continue to adhere steadfastly to the profession of the true religion.

1. *Now faith is the substance of things hoped for.* On the general nature of faith, see Notes on Mark xvi. 16. The margin here is, "*ground* or *confidence*." There is scarcely any verse of the New Testament more important than this, for it states what is the nature of all true faith, and is the only definition of it which is attempted in the Scriptures. Eternal life depends on the existence and exercise of faith (Mark xvi. 16), and hence the importance of an accurate understanding of its nature. The word rendered *substance*—ὑπόστασις—occurs in the New Testament only in the following places. In 2 Cor. ix. 4 ; xi. 17; Heb. iii. 14, where it is rendered *confident* and *confidence ;* and in Heb. i. 3, where it is rendered *person*, and in the passage before us ; comp. Notes on ch. i. 3. Prof. Stuart renders it here *confidence ;* Chrysostom, "Faith gives reality or substance to things hoped for." The word properly means *that which is placed under* (Germ. *Unterstellen*); then *ground, basis, foundation, support.* Then it means also *reality, substance, existence,* in contradistinction from that

which is unreal, imaginary, or deceptive (*täuschung*). *Passow.* It seems to me, therefore, that the word here has reference to something which imparts reality in the view of the mind to those things which·are not seen, and which serves to distinguish them from those things which are unreal and illusive. It is that which enables us to feel and act *as if* they were real, or which causes them to exert an influence over us *as if* we saw them. Faith does this on all other subjects as well as religion. A belief that there is such a place as London or Calcutta, leads us to act *as if* this were so, if we have occasion to go to either ; a belief that money may be made in a certain undertaking, leads men to act *as if* this were so ; a belief in the veracity of another leads us to act *as if* this were so. As long as the faith continues, whether it be well-founded or not, it gives all the force of reality to that which is believed. We feel and act *just as if* it were so, or *as if* we saw the object before our eyes. This, I think, is the clear meaning here. We do not *see* the things of eternity. We do not see God, or heaven, or the angels, or the redeemed in glory, or the crowns of victory, or the harps of praise; but we have faith in them, and this leads us to act *as if* we saw them. And this is, undoubtedly, the fact in regard to all who live by faith and who are fairly under its influence. ¶ *Of things hoped for.* In heaven. Faith gives them reality in the view of the mind. The Christian hopes to be admitted into heaven ; to be raised up in the last day from the slumbers of the tomb, to be made perfectly free from sin ; to be everlastingly happy. Under the influence of faith he allows these things to control his mind *as if* they were a most affecting reality. ¶ *The evidence of things not seen.* Of the existence of God ; of heaven ; of angels ; of the glories of the world prepared for the redeemed. The word rendered *evidence*—ἔλεγχος—occurs in the New Testament only in this place and in 2 Tim. iii. 16, where it is rendered *reproof.* It means properly proof, or means of proving, to wit,

evidence ; then proof which convinces another of error or guilt ; then vindication, or defence ; then summary or contents ; see *Passow.* The idea of *evidence* which goes to demonstrate the thing under consideration, or which is adapted to produce *conviction* in the mind, seems to be the elementary idea in the word. So when a proposition is demonstrated ; when a man is arraigned and evidence is furnished of his guilt, or when he establishes his innocence ; or when one by argument refutes his adversaries, the idea of *convincing argument* enters into the use of the word in each case. This, I think, is clearly the meaning of the word here. " Faith in the divine declarations answers all the purposes of a convincing argument, or is itself a convincing argument to the mind, of the real existence of those things which are not seen." But is it a good argument ? Is it rational to rely on such a means of being convinced ? Is mere *faith* a consideration which should ever convince a rational mind ? The infidel says *no ;* and we know there may be a faith which is no argument of the truth of what is believed. But when a man who has never seen it believes that there is such a place as London, his belief in the numerous testimonies respecting it which he has heard and read is to his mind a good and rational proof of its existence, and he would act on that belief without hesitation. When a son credits the declaration or the promise of a father who has never deceived him, and acts *as though* that declaration and promise were true, his faith is to him a ground of conviction and of action, and he will act as if these things were so. In like manner the Christian believes what God says. He has never seen heaven ; he has never seen an angel ; he has never seen the Redeemer ; he has never seen a body raised from the grave. *But he has evidence which is satisfactory to his mind that God has spoken on these subjects,* and his very nature prompts him to confide in the declarations of his Creator. Those declarations are to his mind more **convincing proof**

2 For by it the elders obtained a good report.

3 Through faith we understand *a* that the worlds were

a Gen.1.1; Ps.33.6.

than anything else would be. They are more conclusive evidence than would be the deductions of his own reason ; far better and more rational than all the reasonings and declarations of the infidel to the contrary. He feels and acts, therefore, *as if* these things were so—for his faith in the declarations of God has convinced him that they *are* so —The object of the apostle, in this chapter, is not to illustrate the nature of what is called *saving faith*, but to show the power of *unwavering confidence in God* in sustaining the soul, especially in times of trial ; and particularly in leading us to act in view of promises and of things not seen *as if* they were so. " Saving faith" is the same kind of confidence directed to the Messiah— the Lord Jesus—as the Saviour of the soul.

2. *For by it.* That is, by that faith which gives reality to things hoped for, and a certain persuasion to the mind of the existence of those things which are not seen. ¶ *The elders.* The ancients ; the Hebrew patriarchs and fathers. ¶ *Obtained a good report.* Literally, "were witnessed of ;" that is, an honourable testimony was borne to them in consequence of their faith. The idea is, that their acting under the influence of faith, in the circumstances in which they were, was the ground of the honourable testimony which was borne to them in the Old Testament ; see this use of the word in ch. vii. 8, and in ver. 4 of this chapter. Also Luke iv. 22 ; Acts xv. 8. In the cases which the apostle proceeds to enumerate in the subsequent part of the chapter, he mentions those whose piety is particularly commended in the Old Testament, and who showed in trying circumstances that they had unwavering confidence in God.

3. *Through faith we understand that the worlds were framed.* The first instance of the strength of faith which the apostle refers to is that by which we give credence to the decla-

rations in the Scriptures about the work of creation ; Gen. i. 1. This is selected first, evidently because it is the first thing that occurs in the Bible, or is the first thing there narrated in relation to which there is the exercise of faith. He points to no particular instance in which this faith was exercised—for none is especially mentioned—but refers to it as an illustration of the nature of faith which every one might observe in himself. The *faith* here exercised is confidence in the truth of the divine declarations in regard to the creation. The meaning is, that our knowledge on this subject is a mere matter of faith in the divine testimony. It is not that we could *reason* this out, and demonstrate that the worlds were thus made ; it is not that profane history goes back to that period and informs us of it ; it is simply that God has told us so in his word. The *strength* of the faith in this case is measured (1.) by the fact that it is *mere faith*— that there is nothing else on which to rely in the case, and (2.) by the greatness of the truth believed. After all the acts of faith which have ever been exercised in this world, perhaps there is none which is really more strong, or which requires higher confidence in God, than the declaration that this vast universe has been brought into existence by a word ! ¶ *We understand.* We attain to the apprehension of ; we receive and comprehend the idea. Our knowledge of this fact is derived only from faith, and not from our own reasoning. ¶ *That the worlds.* In Gen. i. 1, it is " the heaven and the earth." The phrase which the apostle uses denotes a plurality of worlds, and is proof that he supposed there were other worlds besides our earth. How far his knowledge extended on this point, we have no means of ascertaining, but there is no reason to doubt that he regarded the stars as " worlds" in some respects like our own. On the meaning of the Greek word used here, see Notes

framed by the word of God, so that things which are seen were not made of things which do appear.

4 By faith Abel [a] offered unto God a more excellent sacrifice than Cain, by which he obtain-

a Gen. 4.4,5.

on ch. i. 2. The plural form is used there also, and in both cases, it seems to me, not without design. ¶ *Were framed.* It is observable that the apostle does not here use the word *make* or *create.* That which he does use—*καταρτίζω*—means to put in order, to arrange, to complete, and may be applied to that which before had an existence, and which is to be put in order, or re-fitted ; Matt. iv. 24; Mark i. 19 ; Matt. xxi. 6 ; Heb. x. 5. The meaning here is, that they *were set in order* by the word of God. This implies the act of creation, but the specific idea is that of *arranging* them in the beautiful order in which they are now. Doddridge · renders it "*adjusted.*" Kuinoel, however, supposes that the word is used here in the sense of *form*, or *make.* It has probably about the meaning which we attach to the phrase "*fitting up anything*," as, for example, a dwelling, and includes all the previous arrangements, though the thing which is particularly denoted is not the *making*, but the *arrangement.* So in the work here referred to. "We arrive at the conviction that the universe was *fitted up* or *arranged* in the present manner by the word of God." ¶ *By the word of God.* This does not mean here, by the *Logos*, or the second person of the Trinity, for Paul does not use that term here or elsewhere. The word which he employs is *ῥῆμα*—*rema* —meaning properly a word spoken, and in this place *command;* comp. Gen. i. 3, 6, 9, 11, 14, 20 ; Ps. xxxiii. 6. "By the word of the Lord were the heavens made ; and all the host of them by the breath of his mouth." In regard to the agency of the Son of God in the work of the creation, see Notes on ch. i. 2 ; comp. Notes on John i. 3. ¶ *So that things which are seen.* The point of the remark here is, that the visible creation was not moulded out of pre-existing materials, but was made out of nothing. In reference to the grammatical con-

struction of the passage, see Stuart, Comm. *in loc.* The doctrine taught is, that matter was not eternal ; that the materials of the universe, as well as the arrangement, were formed by God, and that all this was done by a simple command. The *argument* here, so far as it is adapted to the purpose of the apostle, seems to be, that there was nothing which *appeared*, or which was to be *seen*, that could lay the foundation of a belief that God made the worlds ; and in like manner our faith now is not to be based on what "*appears*," by which we could infer or *reason out* what would be, but that we must exercise strong confidence in Him who had power to create the universe out of nothing. If this vast universe has been called into existence by the mere *word* of God, there is nothing which we may not believe he has ample power to perform.

4. *By faith Abel offered ;* see Gen. iv. 4, 5. In the account in Genesis of the offering made by Abel, there is no mention of *faith*—as is true also indeed of most of the instances referred to by the apostle. The account in Genesis is, simply, that Abel "brought of the firstlings of his flock, and the fat thereof, and that the Lord had respect to Abel and his offering." Men have speculated much as to the reason why the offering of Abel was accepted, and that of Cain rejected ; but such speculation rests on no certain basis, and the solution of the apostle should be regarded as decisive and satisfactory, that in the one case there was faith, in the other not. It could not have been because an offering of the fruits of the ground was not pleasing to God, for such an offering was commanded under the Jewish law, and was not in itself improper. Both the brothers selected that which was to them most obvious ; which they had reared with their own hands ; which they regarded as most valuable. Cain had cultivated the earth, and he naturally brought what had

ed witness that he was righteous, God testifying of his gifts: and by it he, be ng dead, [1]yet speaketh.

or, is yet spoken of.

grown under his care ; Abel kept a flock, and *he* as naturally brought what he had raised : and had the temper of mind in both been the same, there is no reason to doubt that the offering of each would have been accepted. To this conclusion we are led by the nature of the case, and the apostle advances substantially the same sentiment, for he says that the particular state of mind on which the whole turned was, that the one had faith, and the other not. *How* the apostle himself was informed of the fact that it was *faith* which made the difference, he has not informed us. The belief that he was inspired will, however, relieve the subject of this difficulty, for according to such a belief, all his statements here, whether recorded in the Old Testament or not, are founded in truth. It is equally impossible to tell with certainty *what* was the nature of the faith of Abel. It has been commonly asserted, that it was faith in Christ—looking forward to his coming, and depending on his sacrifice when offering that which was to be a type of him. But of this there is no positive evidence, though from Heb. xii. 24, it seems to be not improbable. Sacrifice, as a type of the Redeemer's great offering, was instituted early in the history of the world. There can be no reason assigned for the offering of *blood* as an atonement for sin, except that it had originally a reference to the great atonement which was to be made by blood ; and as the salvation of man depended on this entirely, it is probable that that would be one of the truths which would be first communicated to man after the fall. The bloody offering of Abel is the first of the kind which is definitely mentioned in the Scriptures (though it is not improbable that such sacrifices were offered by Adam, comp. Gen. iii. 21), and consequently Abel may be regarded as *the recorded head of the whole typical system, of which Christ was the antitype and the ful-*

fillment. Comp. Notes ch. xii. 24. ¶ *A more excellent sacrifice.* Πλείονα θυσίαν —as rendered by Tindal, "a more plenteous sacrifice" ; or, as Wickliff renders it more literally, " a much more sacrifice ;" that is, a more full or complete sacrifice ; a better sacrifice. The meaning is, that it had in it much more to render it acceptable to God. In the estimate of its value, the views of him who offered it would be more to be regarded than the nature of the offering itself.

[" By offering victims of the choice of his flock, Abel not only showed a more decided attachment to God, but there is great reason to suppose (as Abp. Magee on Atonement, p. 52, shows) that his faith was especially superior, as being not only directed to God alone (recognising his existence, authority, and providence) but also to the Great Redeemer, promised immediately after the fall, (Gen. iii. 15) whose expiatory death was typified by animal sacrifice, by offering which Abel had evinced his faith in the great sacrifice of the Redeemer, prefigured by it : and then he obtained that acceptance from God, and witnessing of his offering, which was refused to Cain ; see more in Macknight and Scott."—*Bloomfield.*

¶ *By which.* By which sacrifice so offered. The way in which he obtained the testimony of divine approbation was by the sacrifice offered in this manner. It was not *merely* by faith, it was by the offering of a sacrifice in connection with, and under the influence of faith. ¶ *He obtained witness that he was righteous.* That is, from God. His offering made in faith was the means of his obtaining the divine testimonial that he was a righteous man. Comp. Notes on ver. 2. This is implied in what is said in Gen. iv. 4. " And the Lord had respect unto Abel and his offering ;" that is, he regarded it as the offering of a righteous man. ¶ *God testifying of his gifts.* In what way this was done is not mentioned either here or in Genesis. Commentators have usually supposed that it was by fire descending from heaven to consume the sacrifice. But there is no evidence of this, for there is no intimation of it in the Bible. It is true that this frequently occurred when an offering was made to God, (see Gen. xv. 17; Lev. ix. 24; Judges vi. 21; 1 Kings xviii. 38), but the sacred writers give us no hint that this happened in the case of the sacrifice made by Abel, and since it is expressly mentioned in other cases and not here, the presumption rather is that no such miracle occurred on the occasion. So remarkable a fact—the first one in all history if it were so—could hardly have failed to be noticed by the sacred writer. It seems to me, therefore, that there was some method by which God "testified" his approbation of the offering of Abel which is unknown to us, but in regard to what it was conjecture is vain. ¶ *And by it he, being dead, yet speaketh.* Marg. *Is yet spoken of.* This difference of translation arises from a difference of reading in the MSS. That from which the translation in the text is derived, is λαλεῖ— *he speaketh.* That from which the rendering in the margin is derived, is λαλεῖται—*is spoken of;* that is, *is praised* or *commended.* The latter is the common reading in the Greek text, and is found in Walton, Wetstein, Matthæi, Titman, and Mill; the former is adopted by Griesbach, Koppe, Knapp, Grotius, Hammond, Storr, Rosenmüller, Prof. Stuart, Bloomfield, and Hahn, and is found in the Syriac and Coptic, and is that which is favoured by most of the Fathers. See *Wetstein.* The authority of MSS. is in favour of the reading λαλεῖται—*is spoken of.* It is impossible, in this variety of opinion, to determine which is the true reading, and this is one of the cases where the original text must probably be for ever undecided. Happily no important doctrine or duty is depending on it. Either of the modes of reading will give a good sense. The apostle is saying that it is by faith that the "elders have obtained a good report" (ver. 2); he had said (ver. 4), that it was by faith that Abel obtained the testimony of God in his favour, and if the reading "is spoken of" be adopted, the apostle means that in

consequence of that offering thus made, Abel continued even to his time to receive an honourable mention. This act was commended still; and the "good report" of which it had been the occasion, had been transmitted from age to age. A sentiment thus of great beauty and value *may* be derived from the passage — that true piety is the occasion of transmitting a good report—or an honourable reputation, even down to the latest generation. It is that which will embalm the memory in the grateful recollection of mankind; that on which they will reflect with pleasure, and which they will love to transmit to future ages. But after all, it seems to me to be probable that the true sentiment in this passage is that which is expressed in the common version, "he yet speaketh." The reasons are briefly these. (1.) The authority of MSS., versions, editions, and critics, is so nearly equal, that it is impossible from this source to determine the true reading, and we must, therefore, form our judgment from the connection. (2.) The apostle had twice in this verse expressed substantially the idea that he was honourably testified of by his faith, and it is hardly probable that he would again repeat it so soon. (3.) There seems to be an allusion here to the *language* used respecting Abel (Gen. iv. 10), "The voice of thy brother's blood *crieth* unto me from the ground;"— or utters a distinct voice—and the apostle seems to design to represent Abel as still speaking. (4.) In Heb. xii. 24, he represents both Abel and Christ as still *speaking*—as if Abel continued to utter a voice of admonition. The reference there is to the fact that he continued to proclaim from age to age, even to the time of the apostle, the great truth that salvation was only *by blood.* He had proclaimed it at first by his faith when he offered the sacrifice of the lamb; he continued to speak from generation to generation, and to show that it was one of the earliest principles of religion that there could be redemption from sin in no other way. (5.) The expression "yet *speaketh*" accords better with the connection. The other interpretation is cold compared with this, and less fits the case before us. On the faith of Noah, Abraham, and Moses, it might be said with equal propriety that it is still commended or celebrated as well as that of Abel, but the apostle evidently means to say that there was a voice in that of Abel which was peculiar ; there was something in *his* life and character which continued to speak from age to age. His sacrifice, his faith, his death, his blood, *all* continued to lift up the voice, and to proclaim the excellence and value of confidence in God, and to admonish the world how to live. (6.) This accords with usage in classic writers, where it is common to say of the dead that they continue to speak. Comp. Virg. Æn. vi. 618.

Et magna testatur voce per umbras:
Discite justitiam moniti, et non temnere Divos.

If this be the true meaning, then the sense is that there is an influence from the piety of Abel which continues to admonish all coming ages of the value of religion, and especially of the great doctrine of the necessity of an atonement by blood. His faith and his sacrifice proclaimed from age to age that this was one of the first great truths made known to fallen man ; and on this he continues to address the world *as if* he were still living. Thus all who are pious continue to exert an influence in favour of religion long after the soul is removed to heaven, and the body consigned to the grave. This is true in the following respects. (1.) They speak by their *example.* The example of a pious father, mother, neighbour, will be remembered. It will often have an effect after their death in influencing those over whom it had little control while living. (2.) They continue to speak by their *precepts.* The precepts of a father may be remembered, with profit, when he is in his grave, though they were heard with indifference when he lived ; the counsels of a minister may be recollected with benefit though they were heard with scorn. (3.) They conti-

nue to speak from the fact that the good are remembered with increasing respect and honour as long as they are remembered at all. The character of Abel, Noah, and Abraham, is brighter now than it was when they lived, and will continue to grow brighter to the end of time. " The name of the wicked will rot," and the influence which they had when living will grow feebler and feebler till it wholly dies away. Howard will be remembered, and will proclaim from age to age the excellence of a life of benevolence ; the character of Nero, Caligula, and Richard III., has long since ceased to exercise *any* influence whatever in favour of evil, but rather shows the world, by contrast, the excellence of virtue :—and the same will yet be true of Paine, and Voltaire, and Byron, and Gibbon, and Hume. The time will come when they shall cease to exert any influence in favour of infidelity and sin, and when the world shall be so satisfied of the error of their sentiments, and the abuse of their talents, and the corruption of their hearts, that their names, by contrast, will be made to promote the cause of piety and virtue. If a man wishes to exert any permanent influence after he is dead, he should be a good man.—The *strength* of the faith of Abel here commended, will be seen by a reference to a few circumstances. (1.) It was manifested shortly after the apostasy, and not long after the fearful sentence had been pronounced in view of the sin of man. The serpent had been cursed ; the earth had been cursed ; woe had been denounced on the mother of mankind ; and the father of the apostate race, and all his posterity, doomed to toil and death. The thunder of this curse had scarcely died away ; man had been ejected from Paradise and sent out to enter on his career of woes; and the earth was trembling under the malediction, and yet Abel maintained his confidence in God. (2.) There was then little truth revealed, and only the slightest intimation of mercy. The promise in Gen. iii. 15, that the seed of the woman should bruise the head of the serpent, is so enigmatical

5 By faith Enoch *a* was trans-

a Gen. 5. 22,24.

and obscure that it is not easy even now to see its exact meaning, and it cannot be supposed that Abel could have had a full understanding of what was denoted by it. Yet this appears to have been *all* the truth respecting the salvation of man then revealed, and on this Abel maintained his faith steadfast in God. (3) Abel had an elder brother, undoubtedly an infidel, a scoffer, a mocker of religion. He was evidently endowed with a talent for sarcasm (Gen. iv. 9), and there is no reason to doubt, that, like other infidels and scoffers, he would be disposed to use that talent when occasion offered, to hold up religion to contempt. The power with which he used this, and the talent with which he did this, may be seen illustrated probably with melancholy fidelity in Lord Byron's "Cain." No man ever lived who could more forcibly express the feelings that passed through the mind of Cain—for there is too much reason to think that his extraordinary talents were employed on this occasion to give vent to the feelings of his own heart in the sentiments put into the mouth of Cain. Yet, notwithstanding the infidelity of his elder brother, Abel adhered to God, and his cause. Whatever influence that infidel brother might have sought to use over him—and there can be no reason to doubt that such an influence *would be* attempted—yet he never swerved, but maintained with steadfastness his belief in religion, and his faith in God.

5. *By faith Enoch was translated.* The account of Enoch is found in Gen. v. 21—24. It is very brief, and is this, that "Enoch walked with God, and was not, for God took him." There is no particular mention of his *faith*, and the apostle attributes this to him, as in the case of Abel, either because it was involved in the very nature of piety, or because the fact was communicated to him by direct revelation. In the account in Genesis, there is nothing inconsistent with the belief that Enoch was characterized

lated that he should not see death ; and was not found, be-

by eminent faith, but it is rather implied in the expression, "he walked with God." Comp. 2 Cor. v. 7. It may also be implied in what is said by the apostle Jude (vers. 14, 15), that "he prophesied, saying, Behold the Lord cometh with ten thousand of his saints," &c. From this it would appear that he was a preacher : that he predicted the coming of the Lord to judgment, and that he lived in the firm *belief* of what was to occur in future times. Moses does not say expressly that Enoch was translated. He says "he was not, for God took him." The expression "he was not," means he was no more among men ; or he was removed from the earth. *This* language would be applicable to any method by which he was removed, whether by dying, or by being translated. A similar expression respecting Romulus occurs in Livy (i. 16), Nec deinde in terris Romulus fuit. The translation of the Septuagint on this part of the verse in Genesis is, οὐχ εὑρίσκετο—"was not found ;" that is, he disappeared. The authority for what the apostle says here, that he "was translated," is found in the other phrase in Genesis, " God took him." The reasons which led to the statement that he was translated without seeing death, or that show that this is a fair conclusion from the words in Genesis, are such as these. (1.) There is no mention made of his death, and in this respect the account of Enoch stands by itself. It is, except in this case, the uniform custom of Moses to mention the age and the death of the individuals whose biography he records, and in many cases this is about all that is said of them. But in regard to Enoch there is this remarkable exception that no record is made of his death—showing that there was something unusual in the manner of his removal from the world. (2.) The Hebrew word used by Moses, found in such a connection, is one which would rather suggest the idea that he had been taken in some extraordinary manner from the

cause God had translated him: for before his translation he had world. That word—לקח—means to take—with the idea of taking to one's self. Thus Gen. viii. 20, "Noah took of all beasts and offered a burnt-offering." Thus it is often used in the sense of taking a wife—that is, to one's self (Gen. iv. 19; vi. 2 ; xii. 19 ; xix. 14) ; and then it is used in the sense of taking away; Gen. xiv. 12 ; xxvii. 35 ; Job i. 21; xii. 20 ; Ps. xxxi. 13; Jer. xv. 15. The word, therefore, would naturally suggest the idea that he had been taken by God to himself, or had been removed in an extraordinary manner from the earth. This is confirmed by the fact that the word is not used anywhere in the Scriptures to denote a removal by death, and that in the only other instance in which it (לקח) is used in relation to a removal from this world, it occurs in the statement respecting the translation of Elijah. "And the sons of the prophets that were at Bethel, came forth to Elisha, and said to him, Knowest thou that the Lord will take away (לקח) thy master from thy head to-day?" 2 Kings ii. 3, 5; comp. ver. 11. This transaction, where there could be no doubt about the manner of the removal, shows in what sense the word is used in Genesis. (3.) It was so understood by the translators of the Septuagint. The apostle has used the same word in this place which is employed by the Seventy in Gen. v. 24 — μετατίθημι. This word means to transpose, to put in another place ; and then to transport, transfer, translate; Acts vii. 16 ; Heb. vii. 12. It properly expresses the removal to another place, and is the very word which would be used on the supposition that one was taken to heaven without dying. (4.) This interpretation of the passage in Genesis by Paul is in accordance with the uniform interpretation of the Jews. In the Targum of Onkelos it is evidently supposed that Enoch was translated without dying. In that Targum the passage in Gen. v. 24 is rendered, "And Enoch walked in the fear of the Lord, and was not, for the Lord did not put him to death"

this testimony, that he pleased God.

—לא.—אמרת ותיה יי. So also in Ecclesiasticus or the Son of Sirach (xlix. 14), " But upon the earth was no man created like Enoch ; for he was taken from the earth." These opinions of the Jews and of the early translators, are of value only as showing that the interpretation which Paul has put upon Gen. v. 2 is the natural interpretation. It is such as occurs to separate writers, without collusion, and thus shows that this is the meaning most naturally suggested by the passage. ¶ That he should not see death. That is, that he should not experience death, or be made personally acquainted with it. The word taste often occurs in the same sense. Heb. ii. 9, "That he should taste death for every man ;" comp. Matt. xvi. 28 ; Mark ix. 1 ; Luke ix 27. ¶ And was not found; Gen. v. 24, "And he was not." That is, he was not in the land of the living. Paul retains the word used in the Septuagint. ¶ He had this testimony, that he pleased God. Implied in the declaration in Gen. v. 22, that he "walked with God." This denotes a state of friendship between God and him, and of course implies that his conduct was pleasing to God. The apostle appeals here to the sense of the account in Genesis, but does not retain the very words. The meaning here is not that the testimony respecting Enoch was actually given before his translation, but that the testimony relates to his having pleased God before he was removed. Stuart. In regard to this instructive fragment of history, and to the reasons why Enoch was thus removed, we may make the following remarks. (1.) The age in which he lived was undoubtedly one of great wickedness. Enoch is selected as the only one of that generation signalized by eminent piety, and he appears to have spent his life in publicly reproving a sinful generation, and in warning them of the approaching judgment; Jude 14, 15. The wickedness which ultimately led to the universal deluge seems already to have commenced in the earth, and

Enoch, like Noah, his great-grand-son, was raised up as a preacher of righteousness to reprove a sinful generation. (2.) It is not improbable that the great truths of religion in that age were extensively denied, and probably among other things the future state, the resurrection, the belief that man would exist in another world, and that it was maintained that death was the end of being—was an eternal sleep. If so, nothing could be better adapted to correct the prevailing evils than the removal of an eminent man, without dying, from the world. His departure would thus confirm the instructions of his life, and his removal, like the death of saints often now, would serve to make an impression which his living instructions would not. (3.) His removal is, in itself, a very important and instructive fact in history. It has occurred in no other instance except that of Elijah ; nor has any other living man been translated to heaven except the Lord Jesus. That fact was instructive in a great many respects. (a) It showed that there was a future state—another world. (b) It showed that the *body* might exist in that future state—though doubtless so changed as to adapt it to the condition of things there. (c) It prepared the world to credit the account of the ascension of the Redeemer. If Enoch and Elijah were removed thus without dying, there was no intrinsic improbability that the Lord Jesus would be removed after having died and risen again. (d) It furnishes a demonstration of the doctrine that the saints will exist hereafter, which meets all the arguments of the sceptic and the infidel. One single *fact* overturns all the mere *speculations* of philosophy, and renders nugatory all the objections of the sceptic. The infidel argues against the truth of the resurrection and of the future state from the *difficulties* attending the doctrine. A single *case* of one who has been raised up from the dead, or who has been removed to heaven, annihilates all such arguments—for how can supposed difficulties destroy a well-authenticated *fact?* (e) It is an encouragement to piety.

It shows that God regards his friends ; that their fidelity and holy living please him ; and that *in the midst of eminent wickedness and a scoffing world it is possible so to live as to please God.* The conduct of this holy man, therefore, is an encouragement to us to do our duty though we stand alone ; and to defend the truth though all who live with us upon the earth deny and deride it. (4.) The removal of Enoch shows that the same thing would be *possible* in the case of every saint. God could do it in other cases, as well as in his, with equal ease. That his friends, therefore, are suffered ·to remain on the earth ; that they linger on in enfeebled health, or are crushed by calamity, or are stricken down by the pestilence as others are, is not because God *could* not remove them as Enoch was without dying, but because there is some important *reason* why they should remain and linger, and suffer, and die. Among those reasons may be such as the following. (a) The regular operation of the laws of nature as now constituted, require it. Vegetables die ; the inhabitants of the deep die ; the fowls that fly in the air, and the beasts that roam over hills and plains die ; and man, by his sins, is brought under the operation of this great universal law. It would be *possible* indeed for God to save his people from this law, but it would require the interposition of continued *miracles,* and it is better to have the laws of nature regularly operating, than to have them constantly set aside by divine interposition. (b) The power of religion is now better illustrated in the way in which the saints are actually removed from the earth, than it would be if they were all translated. Its power is now seen in its enabling us to overcome the dread of death, and in its supporting us in the pains and sorrows of the departing hour. It is a good thing to discipline the soul so that it will not fear to die ; it shows how superior religion is to all the forms of philosophy, that it enables the believer to look calmly forward to his own certain approaching death. It is an important matter to keep this

6 But without faith *it is* impossible to please *a him:* for he that cometh to God must believe that

up from age to age, and to show to each generation that religion can overcome the natural apprehension of the most fearful calamity which befalls a creature — death ; and can make man calm in the prospect of lying beneath the clods of the valley, cold, dark, alone, to moulder back to his native dust. (*c*) The death of the Christian does good. It preaches to the living. The calm resignation ; the peace ; the triumph of the dying believer, is a constant admonition to a thoughtless and wicked world. The deathbed of the Christian proclaims the mercy of God from generation to generation, and there is not a dying saint who may not, and who probably *does* not do great good in the closing hours of his earthly being. (*d*) It may be added that the present arrangement falls in with the general laws of religion that we are to be influenced by *faith*, not by *sight*. If all Christians were removed like Enoch, it would be an argument for the truth of religion addressed constantly to the senses. But this is not the way in which the evidence of the truth of religion is proposed to man. It is submitted to his understanding, his conscience, his heart ; and in this there is of design a broad distinction between religion and other things. Men act in other matters under the influence of the senses ; it is designed that in religion they shall act under the influence of higher and nobler considerations, and that they shall be influenced not solely by a reference to what is passing before their eyes, but to the things which are not seen.

6. *But without faith* it is *impossible* to please him. Without *confidence* in God — in his fidelity, his truth, his wisdom, his promises. And this is as true in other things as in religion. It is impossible for a child to please his father unless he has confidence in him. It is impossible for a wife to please her husband, or a husband a wife, unless they have confidence in each other. If there is distrust and

he is, and *that* he is a rewarder of them that diligently seek him.
a Ps.106.24-26.

jealousy on either part, there is discord and misery. We cannot be pleased with a professed friend unless he has such confidence in us as to believe our declarations and promises. The same thing is true of God. He cannot be pleased with the man who has no confidence in him ; who doubts the truth of his declarations and promises ; who does not believe that his ways are right, or that he is qualified for universal empire. The requirement of faith or confidence in God is not arbitrary ; it is just what we require of our children, and partners in life, and friends, as the indispensable condition of *our* being pleased with them. ¶ *For he that cometh to God.* In any way—as a worshipper. This is alike required in public worship, in the family, and in secret devotion. ¶ *Must believe that he is.* That God exists. This is the first thing required in worship. Evidently we cannot come to him in an acceptable manner if we doubt his existence. We do not see him, but we must believe that he is ; we cannot form in our mind a correct image of God, but this should not prevent a conviction that there *is* such a Being. But the declaration here implies more than that there should be a general persuasion of the truth that there is a God. It is necessary that we have this belief in lively exercise in the act of drawing near to him, and that we should realize that we are actually in the presence of the all-seeing JEHOVAH. ¶*And* that he *is a rewarder of them that diligently seek him.* This is equally necessary as the belief that he exists. If we could not believe that God would hear and answer our prayers, there could be no encouragement to call upon him. It is not meant here that the desire of the reward is to be the *motive* for seeking God—for the apostle makes no affirmation on that point ; but that it is impossible to make an acceptable approach to him unless we have this belief.

7. *By faith Noah.* It is less diffi-

7 By faith Noah, ^a being warned of God of things not seen as yet, ¹ moved with fear, prepared an ark to the saving of his house; by the which he condemned the world, and became heir of the righteousness which is by faith.

a Gen.6.14-22.　　　1 or, *being wary.*

cult to see that Noah must have been influenced *by faith* than that Abel and Enoch were. Everything which Noah did in reference to the threatened deluge, was done in virtue of simple faith or belief of what God said. It was not because he could show from the course of events that things were tending to such a catastrophe; or because such an event had occurred before, rendering it probable that it would be likely to occur again; or because this was the common belief of men, and it was easy to fall into this himself. It was simply because God had informed him of it, and he put unwavering reliance on the truth of the divine declaration. ¶ *Being warned of God;* Gen. vi. 13. The Greek word here used means *divinely admonished;* comp. ch. viii. 5. ¶ *Of things not seen as yet.* Of the flood which was yet future. The meaning is, that there were no visible signs of it; there was nothing which could be a basis of calculation that it would occur. This admonition was given an hundred and twenty years before the deluge, and of course long before there could have been any natural indications that it would occur. ¶ *Moved with fear.* Marg. *Being wary.* The Greek word—ευλαβη-θεις—occurs only here and in Acts xxiii. 10, "The chief captain *fearing* lest Paul," &c. The *noun* occurs in Heb. v. 7, "And was heard in that he *feared,*" (see Note on that place), and in Heb. xii. 28, "With reverence and *godly fear.*" The verb properly means, *to act with caution, to be circumspect,* and then *to fear, to be afraid.* So far as the *word* is concerned, it might mean here that Noah was influenced by the dread of what was coming, or it may mean that he was influenced by proper caution and reverence for God. The latter meaning agrees better with the scope of the remarks of Paul, and is probably the true sense. His reverence and respect for God induced him to act

under the belief that what he had said was true, and that the calamity which he had predicted would certainly come upon the world. ¶ *Prepared an ark to the saving of his house.* In order that his family might be saved. Gen. vi. 14—22. The *salvation* here referred to was preservation from the flood. ¶ *By the which.* By which faith. ¶ *He condemned the world.* That is, the wicked world around him. The meaning is, that by his confidence in God, and his preparation for the flood, he showed the wisdom of his own course and the folly of theirs. We have the same phrase now in common use where one who sets a good example is said to "condemn others." He shows the guilt and folly of their lives by the contrast between his conduct and theirs. The wickedness of the sinner is condemned not only by preaching, and by the admonitions and threatenings of the law of God, but by the conduct of every good man. The language of such a life is as plain a rebuke of the sinner as the most fearful denunciations of divine wrath. ¶ *And became heir of the righteousness which is by faith.* The phrase "heir of righteousness" here means properly that he acquired, gained, or became possessed of that righteousness. It does not refer so much to the *mode* by which it was done as if it were by inheritance, as to the *fact* that he obtained it. The word *heir* is used in this general sense in Rom. iv. 13, 14; Titus iii. 7; Heb. i. 2; vi. 17. Noah was not the *heir* to that righteousness by *inheriting* it from his ancestors, but in virtue of it he was regarded as among the heirs or sons of God, and as being a possessor of that righteousness which is connected with faith. The phrase "righteousness which is by faith" refers to the fact that he was regarded and treated as a righteous man. Notes on Rom. i. 17. It is observable here that it is not said that Noah had specific faith in Christ, or that his being made heir of the righteousness of faith depended on that, but it was in connection with his believing what God said respecting the deluge. It was *faith* or *confidence* in God which was the ground of his justification, in accordance with the general doctrine of the Scriptures that it is only by faith that man can be saved, though the specific mode of faith was not that which is required now under the gospel In the early ages of the world, when few truths were revealed, a cordial belief of *any* of those truths showed that there was real confidence in God, or that the *principle* of faith was in the heart ; in the fuller revelation which *we* enjoy, we are not only to believe those truths, but specifically to believe in him who has made the great atonement for sin, and by whose merits all have been saved who have entered heaven. The same faith or confidence in God which led Noah to believe what God said about the deluge would have led him to believe what he has said about the Redeemer ; and the same confidence in God which led him to commit himself to his safe keeping in an ark on the world of waters, would have led him to commit his soul to the safe keeping of the Redeemer, the true ark of safety. As the *principle* of faith, therefore, existed in the heart of Noah, it was proper that he should become, with others, an "heir of the righteousness which is by faith."

[If this righteousness which is by faith be the same with that in Rom. i. 17 ; iii. 21 ; and of this there can be no doubt—if it be the same with that which forms the ground of the sinner's justification in every age, namely, the glorious righteousness which Christ has wrought out in his active and passive obedience—then clearly there is no way of getting possession of this, but by faith in Jesus, And, without doubt, by *this* faith, Noah was saved. It is absurd to suppose that the doctrine of salvation by the Redeemer was unknown to him. Was not the ark itself a type and pledge of this salvation? 1 Peter iii. 21. Was Noah ignorant of the promise concerning the Messiah? Dr. Owen can scarce speak with patience of the view that excludes Christ as the specific object of Noah's faith, "That in this faith of the patriarchs no respect was had unto Christ and

his righteousness, is such a putid figment, is so destructive of the first promises, and of all true faith in the church of old, is so inconsistent with, and contrary to the design of the apostle, and is so utterly destructive of the whole force of his argument, that it deserves no consideration." The idea indeed *seems* to derogate from the glory of Christ as the *alone* object of faith and salvation in every age ; see also Scott, Bloomfield, M'Lean.]

In regard to the circumstances which show the strength of his faith, we may make the following remarks. (1.) It pertained to a very distant future event. It looked forward to that which was to happen after a lapse of an hundred and twenty years. This was known to Noah (Gen. vi. 3), and at this long period before it occurred, he was to begin to build an ark to save himself and family ; to act as though this would be undoubtedly true. This is a much longer period than man *now* is required to exercise faith before that is realized which is the object of belief. Rare is it that three score years intervene between the time when a man first believes in God and when he enters into heaven ; much more frequently it is but a few months or days ; not an instance now occurs in which the period is lengthened out to an hundred and twenty years. (2.) There was no outward *evidence* that what Noah believed would occur. There were no appearances in nature which indicated that there would be such a flood of waters after more than a century had passed away. There were no breakings up of the fountains of the deep ; no marks of the far distant storm gathering on the sky which could be the basis of the calculation. The *word of God* was the only ground of evidence ; the only thing to which he could refer gainsayers and revilers. It is so now. There are no visible signs of the coming of the Saviour to judge the world. Yet the true believer feels and acts *as if* it were so —resting on the sure word of God. (3.) The course of things was much against the truth of what Noah believed. No such event had ever occurred. There is no evidence that there had ever been a storm of rain half sufficient to drown the world ; or that there had ever been the breaking up of the deep, or that there had been ever a partial deluge. For sixteen hundred years the course of nature had been uniform, and all the force of this uniformity would be felt and urged when it should be alleged that this was to be disturbed and to give place to an entire new order of events. Comp. 2 Pet. iii. 4. The same thing is now felt in regard to the objects of the Christian faith. The course of events is uniform. The laws of nature are regular and steady. The dead do not leave their graves. Seasons succeed each other in regular succession; men are born, live, and die, as in former times; fire does not wrap the earth in flames; the elements do not melt with fervent heat; seed-time and harvest, cold and heat, summer and winter follow each other, and "all things continue as they were from the beginning of the creation." How many probabilities are there now, therefore, as there were in the time of Noah, against that which is the object of faith! (4.) It is not improbable that when Noah proclaimed the approaching destruction of the world by a deluge, the *possibility* of such an event was strongly denied by the philosophers of that age. The fact that such an event could have occurred has been denied by infidel philosophers in our own times, and attempts have been gravely made to show that the earth did not contain water enough to cover its surface to the height mentioned in the Scriptures, and that no condensation of the vapour in the atmosphere could produce such an effect. It is not improbable that some such arguments may have been used in the time of Noah, and *it is morally certain that he could not meet those arguments by any philosophy of his own.* There is no reason to think that he was endowed with such a knowledge of chemistry as to be able to show that such a thing was possible, or that he had such an acquaintance with the structure of the earth as to demonstrate that it contained within itself the elements of its own destruction. All that he could oppose to such speculations was the simple declaration of God; and the same thing is also true now in regard to the cavils and philosophical arguments of infidelity. Objections drawn from philosophy are often made against the doctrine of the resurrection of the body; the destruction of the earth by the agency of fire; and even the existence of the soul after death. These difficulties may be obviated partly by science; but the proof that these events will occur, does not depend on science. It is a matter of simple faith; and all that we can in fact oppose to these objections is the declaration of God. The result showed that Noah was not a fool or a fanatic in trusting to the word of God against the philosophy of his age; and the result will show the same of the Christian in his confiding in the truth of the divine declarations against the philosophy of *his* age. (5.) It is beyond all question that Noah would be subjected to much ridicule and scorn. He would be regarded as a dreamer; a fanatic; an alarmist; a wild projector. The purpose of making preparation for such an event as the flood, to occur after the lapse of an hundred and twenty years, and when there were no indications of it, and all appearances were against it, would be regarded as in the highest degree wild and visionary. The design of building a vessel which would outride the storm, and which would live in such an open sea, and which would contain all sorts of animals, with the food for them for 'an indefinite period, could not but have been regarded as eminently ridiculous. When the ark was preparing, nothing could have been a more happy subject for scoffing and jibes. In such an age, therefore, and in such circumstances, we may suppose that all the means possible would have been resorted to, to pour contempt on such an undertaking. They who had wit, would find here an ample subject for its exercise; if ballads were made then, no more fertile theme for a profane song could be desired than this; and in the haunts of revelry, intemperance, and pollution, nothing would furnish a finer topic to give point to a jest, than the credulity and folly of

8 By faith Abraham *a* when
he was called to go out into a
place which he should after re-

a Gen.12.1,4,&c.

the old man who was building the
ark. It would require strong faith
to contend thus with the wit, the sarcasm, the contempt, the raillery, and
the low jesting, as well as with the
wisdom and philosophy of a whole
world. Yet it is a fair illustration of
what occurs often now, and of the
strength of that faith in the Christian
heart which meets meekly and calmly
the scoffs and jeers of a wicked generation. (6.) All this would be height-
ened by delay. The time was distant.
What now completes four generations
would have passed away before the
event predicted would occur. Youth
grew up to manhood, and manhood
passed on to old age, and still there
were no signs of the coming storm.
That was no feeble faith which could
hold on in this manner, for an hundred and twenty years, believing un-
waveringly that all which God had
said would be accomplished. But it
is an illustration of faith in the Christian church now. The church maintains the same confidence in God from
age to age—and regardless of all the
reproaches of scoffers, and all the arguments of philosophy, still adheres to
the truths which God has revealed.
So with individual Christians. They
look for the promise. They are expecting heaven. They doubt not that
the time will come when they will be
received to glory; when their bodies
will be raised up glorified and immortal, and when sin and sorrow
will be no more. In the conflicts
and trials of life the time of their deliverance may seem to be long delayed. The world may reproach
them, and Satan may tempt them to
doubt whether all their hope of heaven is not delusion. But their faith
fails not, and though hope seems delayed, and the heart is sick, yet they
keep the eye on heaven. So it is in
regard to the final triumphs of the
gospel. The Christian looks forward
to the time when the earth shall be
full of the knowledge of God as the

ceive for an inheritance, obeyed;
and he went out, not knowing whither he went.

waters cover the sea. Yet that time
may seem to be long delayed. Wickedness triumphs. A large part of the
earth is still filled with the habitations of cruelty. The progress of the
gospel is slow. The church comes
up reluctantly to the work. The enemies of the cause exult and rejoice,
and ask with scoffing triumph where
is the evidence that the nations will
be converted to God? They suggest
difficulties; they refer to the numbers, and to the opposition of the enemies of the true religion; to the
might of kingdoms, and to the power
of fixed opinion, and to the hold which
idolatry has on mankind, and they
sneeringly inquire at what period will
the world be converted to Christ?
Yet in the face of all difficulties, and
arguments, and sneers, *faith* confides
in the promise of the Father to the
Son, that the "heathen shall be given
to him for an inheritance, and the
uttermost parts of the earth for a
possession," Ps. ii. 8. The faith of
the true Christian is as strong in the
fulfilment of this promise, as that of
Noah was in the assurance that the
guilty world would be destroyed by a
flood of waters.

8. *By faith Abraham.* There is
no difficulty in determining that Abraham was influenced by faith in God.
The case is even stronger than that
of Noah, for it is expressly declared,
Gen. xv. 6, "And he believed in the
Lord; and he counted it to him for
righteousness." Comp. Notes Rom.
iv. 1—5. In the illustrations of the
power of faith in this chapter, the
apostle appeals to two instances in
which it was exhibited by Abraham,
"the father of the faithful." Each of
these required confidence in God of
extraordinary strength, and each of
them demanded a special and honourable mention. The first was that
when he left his own country to go
to a distant land of strangers (vs. 8—
10); the other when he showed his
readiness to sacrifice his own son in

9 By faith he sojourned in the land of promise, as in a strange country, ^{a} dwelling in tabernacles

obedience to the will of God, vers. 17 —19. ¶ *When he was called.* Gen. xii. 1, " Now the Lord had said unto Abraham, Get thee out of thy country, and from thy kindred, and from thy father's house, ur to a land that I will show thee." ¶ *Into a place which he should after receive for an inheritance, obeyed.* To Palestine, or the land of Canaan, though that was not indicated at the time. ¶ *And he went out, not knowing whither he went.* Gen. xii. 4. Abraham at that time took with him Sarai, and Lot the son of his brother, and "the souls that they had gotten in Haran." Terah, the father of Abraham, started on the journey with them, but died in Haran; Gen. xi. 31, 32. The original call was made to Abraham, (Gen. xii. 1; Acts vii. 2, 3), but he appears to have induced his father and his nephew to accompany him. At this time he had no children (Gen. xi. 30), though it seems probable that Lot had ; Gen. xii. 5. Some, however, understand the expression in Gen. xii. 5, "and the souls they had gotten in Haran," as referring to the servants or domestics that they had in various ways procured, and to the fact that Abraham and Lot gradually drew around them a train of dependents and followers who were disposed to unite with them, and accompany them wherever they went. The Chaldee Paraphrast understands it of the *proselytes* which Abraham had made there—" All the souls which he had subdued unto the law." When it is said that Abraham " went out, not knowing whither he went," it must be understood as meaning that he was ignorant to what country he would in fact be led. If it be supposed that he had some general intimation of the nature of that country, and of the direction in which it was situated, yet it must be remembered that the knowledge of geography was then exceedingly imperfect ; that this was a distant country ; that it lay beyond a pathless desert, and that probably no traveller had ever come from that

with Isaac and Jacob, the heirs with him of the same promise.
a Gen.13.3,18; '8.1,9.

land to apprize him what it was. All this serves to show what was the strength of the faith of Abraham. 9. *By faith he sojourned in the land of promise, as in a strange country.* The land of Canaan that had been promised to him and his posterity. He resided there *as if* he were a stranger and sojourner. He had no possessions there which he did not procure by honest purchase ; he owned no land in fee-simple except the small piece which he bought for a burial-place ; see Gen. xxiii. 7—20. In all respects he lived there as if he had no peculiar right in the soil ; as if he never expected to own it ; as if he were in a country wholly owned by others. He exercised no privileges which might not have been exercised by any foreigner, and which was not regarded as a right of common—that of feeding his cattle in any unoccupied part of the land ; and he would have had no power of ejecting any other persons excepting that which any one might have enjoyed by the pre-occupancy of the pasture-grounds. To all intents and purposes he was a stranger. Yet he seems to have lived in the confident and quiet expectation that that land would at some period come into the possession of his posterity. It was a strong instance of *faith* that he should cherish this belief for so long a time, when he was a stranger there ; when he gained no right in the soil except in the small piece that was purchased as a burial-place for his wife, and when he saw old age coming on and still the whole land in the possession of others. ¶ *Dwelling in tabernacles.* In tents — the common mode of living in countries where the principal occupation is that of keeping flocks and herds. His dwelling thus in moveable tents looked little like its being his permanent possession. ¶ *With Isaac and Jacob, the heirs with him of the same promise.* That is, the same thing oc curred in regard to them, which had to Abraham. *They* also lived in tents.

10 For he looked for a city ^awhich
a ch.12.22; 13.14.   b Re.21.2,10.

They acquired no fixed property, and no title to the land except to the small portion purchased as a burial-place. Yet they were heirs of the same promise as Abraham, that the land would be theirs. Though it was still owned by others, and filled with its native inhabitants, yet they adhered to the belief that it would come into the possession of their families. In their moveable habitations; in their migrations from place to place, they seem never to have doubted that the fixed habitation of their posterity was to be there, and that all that had been promised would be certainly fulfilled.
10. *For he looked for a city which hath foundations.* It has been doubted to what the apostle here refers. Grotius and some others suppose, that he refers to Jerusalem, as a permanent dwelling for his posterity, in contradistinction from the unsettled mode of life which Abraham, Isaac, and Jacob led. But there is no evidence that Abraham looked forward to the building of such a city, for no promise was made to him of this kind; and this interpretation falls evidently below the whole drift of the passage; comp. vers. 14—16; ch. xii. 22; xiii.
14. Phrases like that of "the city of God," "a city with foundations," "the new Jerusalem," and "the heavenly Jerusalem" in the time of the apostle, appear to have acquired a kind of technical signification. They referred to *heaven*—of which Jerusalem, the seat of the worship of God, seems to have been regarded as the emblem. Thus in ch. xii. 22, the apostle speaks of the "heavenly Jerusalem," and in ch. xiii. 14, he says, "here have we no continuing city, but we seek one to come." In Rev. xxi. 2, John says that he "saw the holy city, new Jerusalem, coming down from God, out of heaven," and proceeds in that chapter and the following to give a most beautiful description of it. Even so early as the time of Abraham, it would seem that the future blessedness of the righteous was foretold under the image of a splendid city reared on per-

hath foundations, whose builder and
b maker *is* God.

manent foundations. It is remarkable that Moses does not mention this as an object of the faith of Abraham, and it is impossible to ascertain the degree of distinctness which this had in his view. It is probable that the apostle in speaking of his faith in this particular did not rely on any distinct record, or even any tradition, but spoke of his piety in the language which he would use to characterize religion of any age, or in any individual. He was accustomed, in common with others of his time, to contemplate the future blessedness of the righteous under the image of a beautiful city; a place where the worship of God would be celebrated for ever—a city of which Jerusalem was the most striking representation to the mind of a Jew. It was natural for him to speak of strong piety in this manner wherever it existed, and especially in such a case as that of Abraham, who left his own habitation to wander in a distant land. This fact showed that he regarded himself as a stranger and sojourner, and yet he had a strong expectation of a fixed habitation, and a permanent inheritance. He must, therefore, have looked on to the permanent abodes of the righteous; the heavenly city;— and though he had an undoubted confidence that the promised land would be given to his posterity, yet as he did not possess it himself, he must have looked for his own permanent abode to the fixed residence of the just in heaven This passage seems to me to prove that Abraham had an expectation of future happiness after death. There is not the slightest evidence that he supposed there would be a magnificent and glorious capital where the Messiah would personally reign, and where the righteous dead, raised from their graves, would dwell in the second advent of the Redeemer. All that the passage fairly implies is, that while Abraham expected the possession of the promised land for his posterity, yet his faith looked beyond this for a permanent home in a future

11 Through faith also ^a Sarah | herself received strength to con-
a Gen.21.1,2.

world. ¶ *Whose builder and maker is God.* Which would not be reared by the agency of man, but of which God was the immediate and direct architect. This shows conclusively, I think, that the reference in this allusion to the "city" is not to Jerusalem, as Grotius supposes; but the language is just such as will appropriately describe heaven, represented as a city reared without human hands or art, and founded and fashioned by the skill and power of the Deity; comp. Notes on 2 Cor. v. 1. The language here applied to God as the "architect" or framer of the universe, is often used in the classic writers. See Kuinoel and Wetstein. The apostle here commends the faith of Abraham as eminently strong. The following *hints* will furnish topics of reflection to those who are disposed to inquire more fully into its strength. (1.) The journey which he undertook was then a long and dangerous one. The distance from Haran to Palestine by a direct route was not less than four hundred miles, and this journey lay across a vast desert—a part of Arabia Deserta. That journey has always been tedious and perilous; but to see its real difficulty, we must put ourselves into the position in which the world was four thousand years ago. There was no knowledge of the way; no frequented path; no facility for travelling; no turnpike or rail-way; and such a journey then must have appeared incomparably more perilous than almost any which could now be undertaken. (2.) He was going among strangers. Who they were he knew not; but the impression could not but have been made on his mind that they were strangers to religion, and that a residence among them would be anything but desirable. (3.) He was leaving country, and home, and friends; the place of his birth and the graves of his fathers, with the moral certainty that he would see them no more. (4.) He had no right to the country which he went to receive. He could urge no claim

on the ground of discovery, or inheritance, or conquest at any former period; but though he went in a peaceful manner, and with no power to take it, and could urge no claim to it whatever, yet he went with the utmost confidence that it would be his. He did not even expect to buy it—for he had no means to do this, and it seems never to have entered his mind to bargain for it in any way, except for the small portion that he needed for a burying-ground. (5.) He had no means of obtaining possession. He had no wealth to purchase it; no armies to conquer it; no title to it which could be enforced before the tribunals of the land. The prospect of obtaining it must have been distant, and probably he saw no means by which it was to be done. In such a case, his only hope could be in God. (6.) It is not impossible that the enterprise in that age might have been treated by the friends of the patriarch as perfectly wild and visionary. The prevailing religion evidently was idolatry, and the claim which Abraham set up to a special call from the Most High, might have been deemed entirely fanatical. To start off on a journey through a pathless desert; to leave his country and home, and all that he held dear, when he himself knew not whither he went; to go with no means of conquest, but with the expectation that the distant and unknown land would be given him, could not but have been regarded as a singular instance of visionary hope. The whole transaction, therefore, was in the highest degree an act of simple confidence in God, where there was no human basis of calculation, and where all the principles on which men commonly act would have led him to pursue just the contrary course. It is, therefore, not without reason that the faith of Abraham is so commended.

11. *Through faith also Sarah herself received strength to conceive seed.* The word "herself" here—αὐτὴ—implies that there was something remarkable in the fact that *she* should

ceive seed and was delivered of a
child when she was past age, be
cause she judged him faithful *a* who
had promised.

12 Therefore sprang there even
of one, and him as good as dead,
so many b as the stars of the sky

a ch.10.23.   b Gen.22.17; Rom.4.17.
1 *according to.*   c 1Ch.29.15; 1Pet.2.11.

manifest this faith.   Perhaps there
may be reference here to the incredulity with which she at first received
the announcement that she should
have a child; Gen. xviii. 11, 13. Even
her strong incredulity was overcome,
and though everything seemed to
render what was announced impossible, and though she was so much
disposed to laugh at the very suggestion at first, yet her unbelief was overcome, and she ultimately credited the
divine promise.   The apostle does not
state the authority for his assertion
that the strength of Sarah was derived from her faith, nor *when* particularly it was exercised.   The argument seems to be, that here was a
case where all human probabilities
were against what was predicted, and
where, therefore, there must have
been simple trust in God.   Nothing
else *but* faith could have led her to
believe that in her old age she would
have borne a son.   ¶ *When she was
past age.*   She was at this time more
than ninety years of age ; Gen. xvii.
17 ; comp. Gen. xviii. 11.   ¶ *Because
she judged him faithful who had promised.*   She had no other ground of
confidence or expectation.   All human probability was against the supposition that at her time of life she
would be a mother.

12. *Therefore sprang there even of
one.*   From a single individual.   What
is observed here by the apostle as worthy of remark, is, that the whole Jewish people sprang from one man, and
that as the reward of his strong faith
he was made the father and founder
of a nation.   ¶ *And him as good as
dead.*   So far as the subject under
discussion is concerned.   To human
appearance there was no more probability, that he would have a son at
that period of life, than that the dead

in multitude, and as the sand
which is by the sea shore innumerable.

13 These all died 1 in faith, not
having received the promises, but
having seen them afar off, and were
persuaded of *them*, and embraced
them, and confessed *c* that they

would have.   ¶ So many *as the stars
in the sky,* &c.   An innumerable multitude.   This was agreeable to the
promise ; Gen. xv. 5 ; xxii. 17.   The
phrases here used are often employed
to denote a vast multitude, as nothing
appears more numerous than the stars
of heaven, or than the sands that lie
on the shores of the ocean.   The
strength of faith in this case was, that
there was simple confidence in God
in the fulfilment of a promise where
all human probabilities were against
it.   This is, therefore, an illustration
of the nature of faith.   It does not
depend on human reasoning ; on analogy ; on philosophical probabilities ; on
the foreseen operation of natural laws;
but on the mere assurance of God—
no matter what may be the difficulties to human view, or the improbabilities against it.

13. *These all died in faith.*   That
is, those who had been just mentioned
—Abraham, Isaac, Jacob, and Sarah.
It was true of Abel and Noah also
that they died in faith, but they are
not included in *this* declaration, for
the " promises" were not particularly
entrusted to them, and if the word
" these" be made to include them it
must include Enoch also, who did not
die at all.   The phrase here used,
"these all died *in faith*," does not mean
that they died in the exercise or possession of religion, but more strictly
that they died not having possessed
what was the object of their faith.
They had been looking for something
future, which they did not obtain
during their lifetime, and died believing that it would yet be theirs.   ¶ *Not
having received the promises.*   That is,
not having received the *fulfilment* of
the promises ; or *the promised blessings.*   The promises themselves they
had received ; comp. Luke xxiv. 49 ;

were strangers and pilgrims on the earth.

14 For they that say such things

Acts i. 4; ii. 39; Gal. iii. 14, and vers. 33, 39 of this chapter. In all these places the word *promise* is used by metonymy *for the thing promised.* ¶ *But having seen them afar off.* Having seen that they would be fulfilled in future times; comp. John viii. 56. It is probable that the apostle here means that they saw *the entire fulfilment* of all that the promises embraced in the future—that is, the bestowment of the land of Canaan, the certainty of a numerous posterity, and of the entrance into the heavenly Canaan —the world of fixed and permanent rest. According to the reasoning of the apostle here the "promises" to which they trusted included all these things. ¶ *And were persuaded of them.* Had no doubt of their reality. ¶ *And embraced* them. This word implies more than our word *embrace* frequently does; that is, *to receive as true.* It means properly *to draw to one's self;* and then to embrace as one does a friend from whom he has been separated. It then means to greet, salute, welcome, and here means a joyful greeting of those promises; or a pressing them to the heart as we do a friend. It was not a cold and formal reception of them, but a warm and hearty welcome. Such is the nature of true faith when it embraces the promises of salvation. No act of pressing a friend to the bosom is ever more warm and cordial. ¶ *And confessed that they were strangers.* Thus Abraham said (Gen. xxiii. 4), "I am a stranger and a sojourner with you." That is, he regarded himself as a foreigner; as having no home and no possessions there. It was on this ground that he proposed to *buy* a burial-place of the sons of Heth. ¶ *And pilgrims.* This is the word —παρεπιδη-μος—which is used by Abraham, as rendered by the LXX. in Gen. xxiii. 4, and which is there translated "sojourner" in the common English version. The word *pilgrim* means properly *a wanderer, a traveller,* and particularly one who leaves his own

declare plainly that they seek a country.

country to visit a holy place. This sense does not *quite* suit the meaning here, or in Gen. xxiii. 4. The Hebrew word—תושב—means properly one who *dwells in a place,* and particularly one who is a *mere* resident without the rights of a citizen. The Greek word means a *by-resident;* one who lives *by* another; or among a people not his own. This is the idea here. It is not that they confessed themselves to be wanderers; or that they had left their home to visit a holy place, but that they *resided* as mere sojourners in a country that was not theirs. What might be their ultimate destination, or their purpose, is not implied in the meaning of the word. They were such as reside awhile among another people, but have no permanent home there. ¶ *On the earth.* The phrase here used—ἐπὶ τῆς γῆς— might mean merely on the land of Canaan, but the apostle evidently uses it in a larger sense as denoting the earth in general. There can be no doubt that this accords with the views which the patriarchs had—regarding themselves not only as strangers in the land of Canaan, but feeling that the same thing was true in reference to their whole residence upon the earth —that it was not their permanent *home.*

14. *For they that say such things,* &c. That speak of themselves as having come into a land of strangers; and that negotiate for a small piece of land, not to cultivate, but to bury their dead. So we should think of any strange people coming among us now —who lived in tents; who frequently changed their residence; who became the purchasers of no land except to bury their dead, and who never spake of becoming permanent residents. We should think that they were in search of some place as their home, and that they had not yet found it. Such people were the Hebrew patriarchs. They lived and acted just *as if* they had not yet found a permanent habitation, but were travelling in search of one.

15 And truly if they had been mindful of that *country* from whence they came out, they might have had opportunity to have returned :

16 But now they desire a

15. *And truly if they had been mindful of that* country, &c. If they had remembered it with sufficient interest and affection to have made them desirous to return. ¶ *They might have had opportunity to have returned.* The journey was not so long or perilous that they could not have retraced their steps. It would have been no more difficult or dangerous for them to do that than it was to make the journey at first. This shows that their remaining as strangers and sojourners in the land of Canaan was voluntary. They preferred it, with all its inconveniences and hardships, to a return to their native land. The same thing is true of all the people of God now. If they choose to return to the world, and to engage again in all its vain pursuits, there is nothing to hinder them. There are " opportunities" enough. There are abundant inducements held out. There are numerous gay and worldly friends who would regard it as a matter of joy and triumph to have them return to vanity and folly again. They would welcome them to their society ; rejoice to have them participate in their pleasures ; and be willing that they should share in the honours and the wealth of the world. And they might do it. There are multitudes of Christians who could grace, as they once did, the ball-room : who could charm the social party by song and wit ; who could rise to the highest posts of office, or compete successfully with others in the race for the acquisition of fame. They have seen and tasted enough of the vain pursuits of the world to satisfy them with their vanity ; they are convinced of the sinfulness of making these things the great objects of living ; their affections are now fixed on higher and nobler objects, and they *choose* not to return to those pursuits again, but to live as strangers and sojourners on

better *country*, that is, an heavenly : wherefore God is not ashamed to be called their God : *a* for he hath prepared for them a city.*b*

a Ex. 3.6,15.   b ver. 10.

the earth—for there is nothing more *voluntary* than religion.

16. *But now they desire a better* country, *that is, an heavenly.* That is, at the time referred to when they confessed that they were strangers and sojourners, they showed that they sought a better country than the one which they had left. They lived as if they had no expectation of a permanent residence on earth, and were looking to another world. The argument of the apostle here appears to be based upon what is apparent from the whole history, that they had a confident belief that the land of Canaan would be given to *their posterity,* but as for *themselves* they had no expectation of permanently dwelling there, but looked to a home in the heavenly country. Hence they formed no plans for conquest ; they laid claim to no title in the soil ; they made no purchases of farms for cultivation ; they lived and died without owning any land except enough to bury their dead All this appears as if *they* looked for a final home in a "better country, even a heavenly." ¶ *Wherefore God is not ashamed to be called their God.* Since they had such an elevated aim, he was willing to speak of himself as their God and Friend. They acted as became his friends, and he was not ashamed of the relation which he sustained to them. The language to which the apostle evidently refers here is that which is found in Ex. iii. 6, " I am the God*l*of Abraham, the God of Isaac, and the God of Jacob." We are not to suppose that God is ever *ashamed* of anything that he does. The meaning here is, that they had acted in such a manner that it was fit that he should show towards them the character of a Benefactor, Protector, and Friend. ¶ *For he hath prepared for them a city.* Such as they had expected—a heavenly residence ; ver. 10. There is

17 By faith Abraham, when [a]
he was tried, offered up Isaac;
and he that had received the pro-
a Gen. 22. 1, &c.; Ja. 2.21.

mises offered up his only begotten
son,
18 [1] Of whom it was said, [b]
1 or, *To.*   *b* Gen. 21.12.

evidently here a reference to heaven,
represented as a city—the new Jerusalem—prepared for his people by God
himself; comp. Notes on Matt. xxv.
34. Thus they obtained what they
had looked for by faith. The wandering and unsettled patriarchs to
whom the promise was made, and
who showed all their lives that they
regarded themselves as strangers and
pilgrims, were admitted to the home
of permanent rest, and their posterity was ultimately admitted to the
possession of the promised land. Nothing could more certainly demonstrate that the patriarchs believed in
a future state than this passage.
They did not expect a permanent
home on earth. They made no efforts
to enter into the possession of the promised land themselves. They quietly
and calmly waited for the time when
God would give it to their posterity,
and in the meantime for themselves
they looked forward to their permanent home in the heavens. Even in
this early period of the world, therefore, there was the confident expectation of the future state; comp. Notes
on Matt. xxii. 31, 32. We may remark, that the life of the patriarchs
was, in all essential respects, such as
we should lead. They looked forward
to heaven; they sought no permanent
possessions here; they regarded themselves as strangers and pilgrims on
the earth. So should we be. In our
more fixed and settled habits of life;
in our quiet homes; in our residence
in the land in which we were born,
and in the society of old and tried
friends, we should yet regard ourselves as "strangers and sojourners."
We have here no fixed abode. The
houses in which we dwell will soon
be occupied by others; the paths in
which we go will soon be trod by the
feet of others; the fields which we
cultivate will soon be ploughed and
sown and reaped by others. Others
will read the books which we read;
sit down at the tables where we sit;

lie on the beds where we repose;
occupy the chambers where we shall
die, and from whence we shall be
removed to our graves. If we *have*
any permanent home, it is in heaven;
and that we have, the faithful lives
of the patriarchs teach us, and the
unerring word of God everywhere
assures us.
17. *By faith Abraham.* The apostle had stated one strong instance of
the faith of Abraham, and he now refers to one still more remarkable—
the strongest illustration of faith, undoubtedly, which has ever been evinced
in our world. ¶ *When he was tried.*
The word here used is rendered *tempted*, in Matt. iv. 1, 3; xvi. 1; xix. 3;
xxii. 18, 35, and in twenty-two other
places in the New Testament; *prove*,
in John vi. 6; *hath gone about*, in Acts
xxiv. 6; *examine*, 2 Cor. xiii. 5; and
tried, in Rev. ii. 2, 10; iii. 10. It
does not mean here, as it often does,
to place inducements before one to
lead him to do wrong, but to subject
his faith to a *trial* in order to test its
genuineness and strength. The meaning here is, that Abraham was placed
in circumstances which showed what
was the real strength of his confidence in God. ¶ *Offered up Isaac.*
That is, he showed that he was ready
and willing to make the sacrifice, and
would have done it if he had not
been restrained by the voice of the
angel; Gen. xxii. 11, 12. So far as
the intention of Abraham was concerned, the deed was done, for he had
made every preparation for the offering, and was actually about to take
the life of his son. ¶ *And he that
had received the promises offered up
his only begotten son.* The promises
particularly of a numerous posterity.
The fulfilment of those promises depended on him whom he was now
about to offer as a sacrifice. If Abraham had been surrounded with children, or if no special promise of a numerous posterity had been made to
him, this act would not have been so

That in Isaac shall thy seed be called :

19 Accounting that God *was* able

remarkable. It would in any case have been a strong act of faith; it was *peculiarly* strong in his case from the circumstances that he had an only son, and that the fulfilment of the promise depended on his life.

18. *Of whom it was said, That in Isaac shall thy seed be called ;* Gen. xxi. 12. A numerous posterity had been promised to him. It was there said expressly that this promise was not to be fulfilled through the son of Abraham, by the bondwoman Hagar, but through Isaac. Of course, it was implied that Isaac was to reach manhood, and yet notwithstanding this, and notwithstanding Abraham fully believed it, he prepared deliberately, in obedience to the divine command, to put him to death. The phrase "thy seed be called" means, that his posterity was to be named after Isaac, or was to descend only from him. The word "*called*" in the Scriptures is often equivalent to the verb *to be ;* see Isa. lvi. 7. To *name* or *call* a thing was the same as to say that it was, or that it existed. It does not mean here that his *spiritual* children were to be called or selected from among the posterity of Isaac, but that the posterity promised to Abraham would descend neither from Ishmael nor the sons of Keturah, but in the line of Isaac. This is a strong circumstance insisted on by the apostle to show the strength of Abraham's faith. It was shown not only by his willingness to offer up the child of his old age—his only son by his beloved wife, but by his readiness, at the command of God, to sacrifice even him on whom the fulfilment of the promises depended.

19. *Accounting that God* was *able to raise* him *up even from the dead.* And that he *would* do it; for so Abraham evidently believed, and this idea is plainly implied in the whole narrative. There was no other way in which the promise could be fulfilled ; and Abraham reasoned justly in the case. He had received the promise

to raise *him* up, even from the dead ; from whence also he received him in a figure.

of a numerous posterity. He had been told expressly that it was to be through this favourite child. He was now commanded to put him to death as a sacrifice, and he prepared to do it. To fulfil these promises, therefore, there was no other way possible but for him to be raised up from the dead, and Abraham fully believed that it would be done. The child had been given to him at first in a supernatural manner, and he was prepared, therefore, to believe that he would be restored to him again by miracle. He did not doubt that he who had given him to him in a manner at first so contrary to all human probability, could restore him again in a method as extraordinary. He, therefore, anticipated that he would raise him up immediately from the dead. That this was the expectation of Abraham is apparent from the narrative in Gen. xxii. 5, "And Abraham said unto his young men, Abide ye here with the ass ; and I and the lad will go yonder and worship, *and come again to you ;*" in the plural—וְנָשׁוּבָה אֲלֵיכֶם— "and we will return ;" that is, I and Isaac will return, for no other persons went with them, ver. 6. As Abraham went with the full expectation of sacrificing Isaac, and as he expected Isaac to return with him, it follows that he believed that God would raise him up immediately from the dead. ¶ *From whence also he received him in a figure.* There has been great difference of opinion as to the sense of this passage, but it seems to me to be plain. The obvious interpretation is that he then received him by his being raised up from the altar *as if* from the dead. He was to Abraham dead. He had given him up. He had prepared to offer him as a sacrifice. He lay there before him as one who was dead From that altar he was raised up by direct divine interposition, *as if* he was raised from the grave, and this was to Abraham a *figure* or a representation of the resurrection. Other interpretations may be seen in Stuart *in loc.* — The following circumstances will illustrate the strength of Abraham's faith in this remarkable transaction. (1.) The strong persuasion on his mind that God had commanded this. In a case of this nature— where such a sacrifice was required —how natural would it have been for a more feeble faith to have doubted whether the command came from God! It might have been suggested to such a mind that this *must* be a delusion, or a temptation of Satan ; that God *could not* require such a thing ; and that whatever might be the *appearance* of a divine command in the case, there *must be* some deception about it. Yet Abraham does not appear to have reasoned about it at all, or to have allowed the strong feelings of a father to come in to modify his conviction that God had commanded him to give up his son. What an example is this to us! And how ready should *we* be to yield up a son— an only son—when God comes himself and removes him from us. (2.) The strength of his faith was seen in the fact that in obedience to the simple command of God, all the strong feelings of a father were overcome. On the one hand there were his warm affections for an only son ; and on the other there was the simple command of God. They came in collision— but Abraham did not hesitate a moment. The strong paternal feeling was sacrificed at once. What an example this too for us! When the command of God and our own attachments come into collision, we should not hesitate a moment. God is to be obeyed. His command and arrangements are to be yielded to, though most tender ties are rent asunder, and though the heart bleeds. (3.) The strength of his faith was seen in the fact, that, in obedience to the command of God, he resolved to do what in the eyes of the world would be regarded as a most awful crime. There is no crime of a higher grade than the murder of a son by the hand of a father. So it is now estimated by the world, and so it would have been in the time of Abraham. All the laws of God and

of society appeared to be against the act which Abraham was about to commit, and he went forth not ignorant of the estimate which the world would put on this deed if it were known. How natural in such circumstances would it have been to argue that God *could not* possibly give such a command ; that it was against all the laws of heaven and earth ; that there was required in this what God and man alike must and would pronounce to be wrong and abominable! Yet Abraham did not hesitate. The command of God in the case was to his mind a sufficient proof that this was right— and it should teach *us* that whatever our Maker commands us should be done—no matter what may be the estimate affixed to it by human laws, and no matter how it may be regarded by the world. (4.) The strength of his faith was seen in the fact that there was a positive promise of God to himself which would *seem* to be frustrated by what he was about to do. God had expressly promised to him a numerous posterity, and had said that it was to be through this son. How could this be if he was put to death as a sacrifice? And how *could* God command such a thing when his promise was thus positive ? Yet Abraham did not hesitate. It was not for him to *reconcile* these things ; it was his to *obey*. He did not doubt that *somehow* all that God had said would prove to be true ; and as he saw but *one way* in which it could be done—by his being immediately restored to life—he concluded that *that* was to be the way. So when God utters his will to us, it is ours simply to obey. It is not to inquire in what way his commands or revealed truth can be reconciled with other things. He will himself take care of that. It is ours at once to yield to what he commands, and to believe that *somehow* all that he has required and said will be consistent with everything else which he has uttered. (5.) The strength of the faith of Abraham was seen in his belief that God would raise his son from the dead. Of that he had no doubt. But what evidence had he of that ? It had not

20 By faith Isaac *a* blessed Jacob and Esau concerning things to come.
21 By faith Jacob, when he

a Gen.27.27-40.

been promised. No case of the kind had ever occurred ; and the subject was attended with all the difficulties which attend it now. But Abraham believed it ; for, *first,* there was no other way in which the promise of God could be fulfilled ; and *second,* such a thing would be no more remarkable than what had already occurred. It was as easy for God to raise him from the dead as it was to give him at first contrary to all the probabilities of the case, and he did not, therefore, doubt that it would be so. Is it less easy for *us* to believe the doctrine of the resurrection than it was for Abraham ? Is the subject attended with more difficulties now than it was then ? The faith of Abraham in this remarkable instance shows us that the doctrine of the resurrection of the dead, notwithstanding the limited revelations then enjoyed, and all the obvious difficulties of the case, was early believed in the world ; and as those difficulties are no greater now, and as no new light has been shed upon it by subsequent revelations, and especially as in more than one instance the dead have been actually raised, those difficulties should not be allowed to make us doubt it now.

20. *By faith Isaac blessed Jacob and Esau concerning things to come ;* see Gen. xxvii. 26 — 40. The meaning is, that he pronounced a blessing on them in respect to their future condition. This was by faith in God who had communicated it to him, and in full confidence that he would accomplish all that was here predicted. The act of faith here was simply that which believes that all that God says is true. There were no human probabilities at the time when these prophetic announcements were made, which could have been the basis of his calculation, but all that he said must have rested merely on the belief that God had revealed it to him. A blessing was pronounced on each, of

was a dying, blessed *b* both the sons of Joseph ; and worshipped, leaning *c* upon the top of his staff.

b Gen.48.5-20.　　　*c* Gen.47.31.

a very different nature, but Isaac had no doubt that both would be fulfilled.

21. *By faith Jacob, when he was a dying ;* Gen. xlvii. 31 ; xlviii. 1—20. That is, when he was about to die. He saw his death near when he pronounced this blessing on Ephraim and Manasseh, the sons of Joseph. ¶ *And worshipped,* leaning *upon the top of his staff.* This is an exact quotation from the Septuagint in Gen. xlvii. 31. The English version of that place is, "and Israel bowed himself upon the bed's head," which is a proper translation, in the main, of the word מטה—*mittĕh.* That word, however, with different points — מטה *mǎttĕh,* means a branch, a bough, a rod, a staff, and the translators of the Septuagint have so rendered it. The Masoretic points are of no authority, and either translation, therefore, would be proper. The word rendered "head" in Gen. xlvii. 31.—"bed's *head"—* ראש—*rōsh,* means properly *head,* but may there mean the *top* of anything, and there is no impropriety in applying it to the *head* or *top* of a staff. The word rendered in Gen. xlvii. 31. *bowed—*וישתחו—implies properly the idea of *worshipping.* It is *bowing,* or *prostration* for the purpose of worship or homage. Though the Septuagint and the apostle here have, therefore, given a somewhat different version from that commonly given of the Hebrew, and sustained by the Masoretic pointing, yet it cannot be demonstrated that the version is unauthorized, or that it is not a fair translation of the Hebrew. It has also the probabilities of the case in its favour. Jacob was tenderly affected in view of the goodness of God, and of the assurance that he would be conveyed from Egypt when he died, and buried in the land of his fathers. Deeply impressed with this, nothing was more natural than that the old man should lean reverently forward and incline his head upon the top of his staff, and

22 By faith Joseph, *a* when he died, made [1] mention of the departing of the children of Israel ; and gave commandment concerning his bones.

a Gen.50.24,25.   1 or, *remembered.*

adore the covenant faithfulness of his God. Such an image is much more natural and probable than that he should "bow upon his bed's head"—a phrase which at best is not very intelligible. If this be the true account, then the apostle does not refer here to what was done when he "blessed the sons of Joseph," but to an act expressive of strong faith in God which had occurred just before. The meaning then is, "By faith when about to die he blessed the sons of Joseph ; and by faith also he reverently bowed before God in the belief that when he died his remains would be conveyed to the promised land, and expressed his gratitude in an act of worship, leaning reverently on the top of his staff." The order in which these things are mentioned is of no consequence, and thus the whole difficulty in the case vanishes. *Both* the acts here referred to were expressive of strong confidence in God.

22. *By faith Joseph, when he died.* When about to die ; see Gen. l. 24, 25. ¶ *Made mention of the departing of the children of Israel.* Marg. "*remembered.*" The meaning is, that he called this to their mind ; he spake of it. "And Joseph said unto his brethren, I die ; and God will surely visit you, and bring you out of this land unto the land which he sware to Abraham, to Isaac, and to Jacob." This prediction of Joseph *could* have rested only on faith in the promise of God. There were no events then occurring which would be likely to lead to this, and nothing which could be a basis of calculation that it would be so, except what God had spoken. The faith of Joseph, then, was simple confidence in God ; and its *strength* was seen in his firm conviction that what had been promised would be fulfilled, even when there were no appearances that to human view justified it. ¶ *And gave commandment*

23 By faith Moses, when he was born, was hid *b* three months of his parents, because they saw *he was* a proper child ; and they were not afraid of the king's *c* commandment.

b Ex.2.2.   *c* Ex.1.16,22.

concerning his bones ; Gen. 1. 25. "And Joseph took an oath of the children of Israel, saying, God will surely visit you, and ye shall carry up my bones from hence." He had such a firm belief that they would possess the land of promise, that he exacted an oath of them that they would remove his remains with them, that he might be buried in the land of his fathers. He could not have exacted this oath, nor could they have taken it, unless both he and they had a sure confidence that what God had spoken would be performed.

23. *By faith Moses, when he was born.* That is, by the faith of his parents. The faith of Moses himself is commended in the following verses. The statement of the apostle here is, that his parents were led to preserve his life by *their* confidence in God. They *believed* that he was destined to some great purpose, and that he would be spared, notwithstanding all the probabilities against it, and all the difficulties in the case. ¶ *Was hid three months of his parents.* By his parents. In Ex. ii. 2, it is said that it was done *by his mother.* The truth doubtless was, that the mother was the agent in doing it—since the concealment, probably, could be better effected by one than where two were employed—but that the father also concurred in it is morally certain. The concealment was, at first, probably in their own house. The command seems to have been (Ex. i. 22), that the child should be cast into the river as soon as born. This child was concealed in the hope that some way might be found out by which his life might be spared. ¶ *Because they saw* he was *a proper child.* A fair, or beautiful child — ἀστεῖον. The word properly means *pertaining to a city* — (from ἄστυ, *a city*); then urbane, polished, elegant ; then fair, beautiful. In Acts vii. 20, it is said that he was "*fair to*

24 By faith Moses, *a* when he was come to years, refused to be

a Ex.2 10.11.

God," (Marg.) ; that is, exceedingly fair, or very handsome. His extraordinary beauty seems to have been the reason which particularly influenced his parents to attempt to preserve him. It is not impossible that they supposed that his uncommon beauty indicated that he was destined to some important service in life, and that they were on that account the more anxious to save him. ¶ *And they were not afraid of the king's commandment.* Requiring that *all* male children should be given up to be thrown into the Nile. That is, they were not *so* alarmed, or did not *so* dread the king, as to be induced to comply with the command. The strength of the faith of the parents of Moses, appears (1.) because the command of Pharaoh to destroy all the male children was positive, but they had so much confidence in God as to disregard it. (2.) Because there was a strong improbability that their child could be saved. They themselves found it impossible to conceal him longer than three months, and when it was discovered, there was every probability that the law would be enforced and that the child would be put to death. Perhaps there was reason also to apprehend that the parents would be punished for disregarding the authority of the king. (3.) Because they probably believed that their child was destined to some important work. They thus committed him to God instead of complying with the command of an earthly monarch, and against strong probabilities in the case, they *believed* that it was possible that in some way he might be preserved alive. The remarkable result showed that their faith was not unfounded.

24. *By faith Moses.* He had confidence in God when he called him to be the leader of his people. He believed that he was able to deliver them, and he so trusted in him that he was willing at his command to forego the splendid prospects which called the son of Pharaoh's daughter ;

opened before him in Egypt. ¶ *When he was come to years.* Gr. " being great ;" that is, when he was grown up to manhood. He was at that time forty years of age ; see Notes on Acts vii. 23. He took this step, therefore, in the full maturity of his judgment, and when there was no danger of being influenced by the ardent passions of youth. ¶ *Refused to be called the son of Pharaoh's daughter.* When saved from the ark in which he was placed on the Nile, he was brought up for the daughter of Pharaoh ; Ex. ii. 9. He seems to have been *adopted* by her, and trained up as her own son. What prospects this opened before him is not certainly known. There is no probability that he would be the heir to the crown of Egypt, as is often affirmed, for there is no proof that the crown descended in the line of daughters ; nor if it did, is there any probability that it would descend on an *adopted* son of a daughter. But his situation could not but be regarded as highly honourable, and as attended with great advantages. It gave him the opportunity of receiving the best education which the times and country afforded—an opportunity of which he seems to have availed himself to the utmost ; Notes, Acts vii. 22. It would doubtless be connected with important offices in the state. It furnished the opportunity of a life of ease and pleasure — such as they commonly delight in who reside at courts. And it doubtless opened before him the prospect of wealth—for there is no improbability in supposing that he would be the *heir* of the daughter of a rich monarch. Yet all this, it is said, he "*refused.*" There is indeed no express mention made of his *formally* and *openly* refusing it, but his leaving the court, and identifying himself with his oppressed countrymen, was *in fact* a refusal of these high honours, and of these brilliant prospects. It is not impossible that when he became acquainted with his real history,

25 Choosing ^a rather to suffer
affliction with the people of God,

than to enjoy the pleasures of sin
for a season ;

there was some open and decided refusal on his part, to be regarded as
the son of the daughter of this heathen monarch.
25. *Choosing rather to suffer affliction with the people of God.* With
those whom God had chosen to be his
people—the Israelites. They were
then oppressed and down-trodden ;
but they were the descendants of
Abraham, and were those whom God
had designed to be his peculiar people. Moses saw that if he cast in
his lot with them, he must expect
trials. They were poor, and crushed,
and despised—a nation of slaves. If
he identified himself with them, his
condition would be like theirs—one
of great trial ; if he sought to elevate
and deliver them, such an undertaking could not but be one of great
peril and hardship. Trial and danger, want and care would follow from
any course which he could adopt, and
he knew that an effort to rescue them
from bondage must be attended with
the sacrifice of all the comforts and
honour which he enjoyed at court.
Yet he "*chose*" this. He on the whole
preferred it. He left the court, not
because he was driven away ; not because there was nothing there to gratify ambition or to be a stimulus to
avarice ; and not on account of harsh
treatment—for there is no intimation
that he was not treated with all the
respect and honour due to his station,
his talents, and his learning, but because he deliberately *preferred* to
share the trials and sorrows of the
friends of God. So every one who
becomes a friend of God and casts
in his lot with his people, though he
may anticipate that it will be attended with persecution, with poverty, and
with scorn, *prefers* this to all the pleasures of a life of gaiety and sin, and
to the most brilliant prospects of
wealth and fame which this world
can offer. ¶ *Than to enjoy the pleasures of sin for a season.* We are
not to suppose that Moses, even at the
court of Pharaoh, was leading a life

of vicious indulgence. The idea is,
that sins were practised there such
as those in which pleasure is sought,
and that if he had remained there it
must have been because he loved the
pleasures of a sinful court and a sinful life rather than the favour of God.
We may learn from this (1.) that there
is a degree of *pleasure* in sin. It does
not deserve to be called *happiness*, and
the apostle does not call it so. It is
"*pleasure*," excitement, hilarity, mer-
riment, amusement. *Happiness* is
more solid and enduring than "*pleasure ;*" and solid happiness is not
found in the ways of sin. But it cannot be denied that there is a degree
of *pleasure* which may be found in
amusement ; in the excitement of the
ball-room ; in feasting and revelry ;
in sensual enjoyments. All which
wealth and splendour ; music and
dancing ; sensual gratifications, and
the more refined pursuits in the circles of fashion, can furnish, may be
found in a life of irreligion ; and if
disappointment, and envy, and sickness, and mortified pride, and bereavements do not occur, the children of vanity and sin can find no
inconsiderable enjoyment in these
things. They *say* they do ; and there
is no reason to doubt the truth of their
own testimony in the case. They
call it a "life of pleasure ;" and it is
not proper to withhold from it the
appellation which they choose to give
it. It is not the most pure or elevated kind of enjoyment, but it would
be unjust to deny that there is *any*
enjoyment in such a course. (2.) It
is only "for a season." It will all soon
pass away. Had Moses lived at the
court of Pharaoh all his days, it would
have been only for a little " season."
These pleasures soon vanish, for (*a*)
life itself is short at best, and if a
career of " pleasure " is pursued
through the whole of the ordinary
period allotted to man, it is *very* brief.
(*b*) Those who live for pleasure often
abridge their own lives. Indulgence
brings disease in its train, and the

26 Esteeming the reproach [1] of Christ [a] greater riches than the

1 or, *for.*   *a* ch.13.13.   *b* ch.10.35.

votaries of sensuality usually die young. The art has never been yet discovered of combining intemperance and sensuality with length of days. If a man wishes a reasonable prospect of long life, he must be temperate and virtuous. Indulgence in vice wears out the nervous and muscular system, and destroys the powers of life—just as a machine without balance-wheel or governor would soon tear itself to pieces. (*c*) Calamity, disappointment, envy, and rivalship mar such a life of pleasure—and he who enters on it, from causes which he cannot control, finds it *very short.* And, (*d*) compared with eternity, O how brief is the longest life spent in the ways of sin! Soon it *must* be over—and then the unpardoned sinner enters on an immortal career where *pleasure* is for ever unknown! (3.) In view of all the "pleasures" which sin *can* furnish, and in view of the most brilliant prospects which this world *can* hold out, religion enables man to pursue a different path. They who become the friends of God are willing to give up all those fair and glittering anticipations, and to submit to whatever trials may be incident to a life of self-denying piety. Religion, with all its privations and sacrifices, is *preferred,* nor is there ever occasion to regret the choice. Moses deliberately made that choice; —nor in all the trials which succeeded it—in all the cares incident to his great office in conducting the children of Israel to the promised land— in all their ingratitude and rebellion —is there the least evidence that he ever once wished himself back again that he might enjoy "the pleasures of sin" in Egypt.

26. *Esteeming the reproach of Christ.* Marg. "*For;*" that is, on account of Christ. This means either that he was willing to bear the reproaches incident to his belief that the Messiah would come, and that he gave up his fair prospects in Egypt with that expectation; or that he endured

treasures in Egypt : for he had respect unto the recompense [b] of the reward.

such reproaches as Christ suffered; or the apostle uses the expression as a sort of *technical* phrase, well understood in his time, to denote sufferings endured in the cause of religion. Christians at that time would naturally describe all sufferings on account of religion as endured *in the cause of Christ;* and Paul, therefore, may have used this phrase to denote sufferings in the cause of religion—meaning that Moses suffered what, when the apostle wrote, would be called "the reproaches of Christ." It is not easy, or perhaps possible, to determine which of these interpretations is the correct one. The most respectable *names* may be adduced in favour of each, and every reader must be left to adopt his own view of that which is correct. The original will admit of either of them. The general idea is, that he would be reproached for the course which he pursued. He could not expect to leave the splendours of a court and undertake what he did, without subjecting himself to trials. He would be *blamed* by the Egyptians for his interference in freeing their "slaves," and in bringing so many calamities upon their country; and he would be exposed to ridicule for his folly in leaving his brilliant prospects at court to become identified with an oppressed and despised people. It is rare that men are zealous in doing good without exposing themselves both to blame and to ridicule. ¶ *Greater riches.* Worth more; of greater value. Reproach *itself* is not desirable ; but reproach, when a man receives it in an effort to do good to others, is worth more to him than gold , 1 Pet. iv. 13, 14. The scars which an old soldier has received in the defence of his country are more valued by him than his pension ; and the reproach which a good man receives in endeavouring to save others is a subject of greater joy to him than would be all the wealth which could be gained in a life of sin. ¶ *Than the treasures in Egypt.* It

27 By faith he forsook Egypt, not fearing *a* the wrath of the king: for he endured, as seeing him who is invisible.*b*

a Ex.10.28,29; 12.31.　　　*b* 1Ti.1.17.

is implied here, that Moses had a prospect of inheriting large treasures in Egypt, and that he voluntarily gave them up to be the means of delivering his nation from bondage. Egypt abounded in wealth ; and the adopted son of the daughter of the king would naturally be heir to a great estate. ¶ *For he had respect unto the recompense of the reward.* The "recompense of the reward" here referred to must mean the blessedness of heaven—for he had no earthly reward to look to. He had no prospect of pleasure, or wealth, or honour, in his undertaking. If he had sought these, so far as human sagacity could foresee, he would have remained at the court of Pharaoh. The declaration here proves that it is right to have respect to the rewards of heaven in serving God. It does not prove that this was the *only* or the *main* motive which induced Moses to abandon his prospects at court ; nor does it prove that this should be *our* main or only motive in leading a life of piety. If it were, our religion would be mere selfishness. But it is right that we should desire the rewards and joys of heaven, and that we should allow the prospect of those rewards and joys to influence us as *a* motive to do our duty to God, and to sustain us in our trials; comp. Phil. iii. 8—11, 13, 14.

27. *By faith he forsook Egypt.* Some have understood this of the first time in which Moses forsook Egypt, when he fled into Midian, as recorded in Ex. ii. ; the majority of expositors have supposed that it refers to the time when he left Egypt to conduct the Israelites to the promised land. That the latter is the time referred to is evident from the fact that it is said that he did "not fear the wrath of the king." When Moses first fled to the land of Midian it is expressly said that he went because he *did* fear the anger of Pharaoh for his having killed an Egyptian ; Ex.

28 Through faith he kept the passover *c* and the sprinkling of blood, lest he that destroyed the first-born should touch them.

c Ex.12.21,&c.

ii. 14, 15. He was at that time in fear of his life ; but when he left Egypt at the head of the Hebrew people, he had no such apprehensions. God conducted him out with "an high hand," and throughout all the events connected with that remarkable deliverance, he manifested no dread of Pharaoh, and had no apprehension from what he could do. He went forth, indeed, at the head of his people when all the power of the king was excited to destroy them, but he went confiding in God : and this is the faith referred to here. ¶ *For he endured.* He persevered, amidst all the trials and difficulties connected with his leading forth the people from bondage. ¶ *As seeing him who is invisible. As if* he saw God. He had no more doubt that God had called him to this work, and that he would sustain him, than if he saw him with his bodily eyes. This is a most accurate account of the nature of faith; comp. Notes on ver. 1.

28. *Through faith he kept the passover.* Greek, "he *made*—πεποίηκε—the passover," which means more, it seems to me, than that he merely *kept* or *celebrated* it. It implies that he *instituted* this rite, and *made* the arrangements for its observance. There is reference to the special agency, and the special faith which he had in its institution. The faith in the case was *confidence* that this would be the means of preserving the first-born of the Israelites, when the angel should destroy the first-born of the Egyptians, and also that it would be celebrated as a perpetual memorial of this great deliverance. On the passover, see Notes on Matt. xxvi. 2. ¶ *And the sprinkling of blood.* The blood of the paschal lamb on the lintels and door-posts of the houses; Ex. xii. 22. ¶ *Lest he that destroyed the first-born should touch them.* The first-born of the Egyptians; Ex.xii.23. The apostle has thus enumerated

some of the things which illustrated the faith of Moses. The *strength* of his faith may be seen by a reference to some of the circumstances which characterized it. (1.) It was such confidence in God as to lead him to forsake the most flattering prospects of worldly enjoyment. I see no evidence, indeed, that he was the heir to the throne ; but he was evidently heir to great wealth ; he was encompassed with all the means of worldly pleasure ; he had every opportunity for a life of literary and scientific pursuits ; he was eligible to high and important trusts ; he had a rank and station which would be regarded as one of the most honoured and enviable on earth. None of those who are mentioned before in this chapter were required to make just such sacrifices as this. Neither Abel, nor Noah, nor Enoch, was called to forsake so brilliant worldly prospects ; and though Abraham was called to a higher act of faith when commanded to give up his beloved son, yet there were some circumstances of trial in the case of Moses illustrating the nature of faith which did not exist in the case of Abraham. Moses, in the maturity of life, and with everything around him that is usually regarded by men as objects of ambition, was ready to forego it all. So *wherever* true faith exists, there is a readiness to abandon the hope of gain, and brilliant prospects of distinction, and fascinating pleasures, in obedience to the command of God. (2.) Moses entered on an undertaking wholly beyond the power of man to accomplish, and against every human probability of success. It was no less than that of restoring to freedom two millions of down-trodden, oppressed, and dispirited *slaves*, and conducting aged and feeble men, tender females, helpless children, with numerous flocks and herds, across barren wastes to a distant land. He undertook this against the power of probably the most mighty monarch of his time ; from the midst of a warlike nation ; and when the whole nation would be kindled into rage at *the loss of so many slaves*, and when he might ex-

pect that all the power of their wrath would descend on him and his undisciplined and feeble hosts. He did this when he had no wealth that he could employ to furnish provisions or the means of defence ; no armies at his command to encircle his people on their march ; and even no influence among the people himself, and with every probability that they would disregard him ; comp. Ex. iii. 11 ; iv. 1. He did this when the whole Hebrew people were to be aroused to *willingness* to enter on the great undertaking ; when there was every probability that they would meet with formidable enemies in the way, and when there was nothing human whatever on which the mind could fix as a basis of calculation of success. If there ever was any undertaking commenced opposed to every human probability of success, it was that of delivering the Hebrew people and conducting them to the promised land. To human view it was quite as hopeless and impracticable as it would be now for a stranger from Africa, claiming to be a native prince there, and to have a commission from God to liberate the two and a half millions of slaves in the U. States and conduct them to the land of their fathers. In all the difficulties and discouragements of the undertaking of Moses, therefore, his only hope of success must have arisen from his confidence in God. (3.) It was an undertaking where there were many certain trials before him. The people whom he sought to deliver were poor and oppressed. An attempt to rescue them would bring down the wrath of the mighty monarch under whom they were. They were a people unaccustomed to self-government, and as the result proved, prone to ingratitude and rebellion. The journey before him lay through a dreary waste, where there was every prospect that there would be a want of food and water, and where he might expect to meet with formidable enemies. In all these things his only hope must have been in God. It was he only who could deliver them from the grasp of the tyrant ; who could conduct them through the wilderness ,

29 By faith they passed ^a through the Red sea as by dry *land :* which the Egyptians assaying to do, were drowned.

a Ex.14.22,29.

who could provide for their wants in the desert; and who could defend a vast multitude of women and children from the enemies which they would be likely to encounter. (4.) There was nothing in this to gratify ambition, or to promise an earthly reward. All these prospects he gave up when he left the court of Pharaoh. To be the leader of a company of emancipated slaves through a pathless desert to a distant land, had nothing in itself that could gratify the ambition of one who had been bred at the most magnificent court on earth, and who had enjoyed every advantage which the age afforded to qualify him to fill any exalted office. The result showed that Moses never designed to be himself the king of the people whom he led forth, and that he had no intention of aggrandizing his own family in the case.

29. *By faith they passed through the Red sea as by dry* land; Ex. xiv. 22, 29. That is, it was only by confidence in God that they were able to do this. It was not by power which they had to remove the waters and to make a passage for themselves ; and it was not by the operation of any natural causes. It is not to be supposed that *all* who passed through the Red sea had saving faith. The assertion of the apostle is, that the passage was made in virtue of strong confidence in God, and that if it had not been for this confidence the passage could not have been made at all. Of this no one can entertain a doubt who reads the history of that remarkable transaction. ¶ *Which the Egyptians assaying to do, were drowned;* Ex. xiv. 27, 28. Evidently referred to here as showing the effects of *not* having faith in God, and of what must inevitably have befallen the Israelites if they had had no faith. The destruction of the Egyptians by the return of the waters in accordance with natural laws, showed that the

30 By faith the walls of Jericho ^b fell down, after they were encompassed about seven days.

b Jos.6.12—20.

Israelites would have been destroyed in the passage if a divine energy had not been employed to prevent it. On the passage through the Red sea, see Robinson's Biblical Researches, vol. i. pp. 81—86.

30. *By faith the walls of Jericho fell down,* &c. Jos. vi. 12—20. That is, it was not by any natural causes, or by any means that were in themselves adapted to secure such a result. It was not because they fell of themselves; nor because they were assailed by the hosts of the Israelites ; nor was it because there was any natural tendency in the blowing of horns to cause them to fall. None of these things were true ; and it was only by confidence in God that means so little adapted to such a purpose could have been employed at all; and it was only by continued faith in him that they could have been persevered in day by day, when no impression whatever was made. The *strength* of the faith evinced on this occasion appears from such circumstances as these :—that there was no natural tendency in the means used to produce the effect; that there was great apparent improbability that the effect would follow ; that they might be exposed to much ridicule from those within the city for attempting to demolish their strong walls in this manner, and from the fact that the city was encircled day after day without producing any result. This may teach us the propriety and necessity of faith in similar circumstances. Ministers of the gospel often preach where there seems to be as little prospect of beating down the opposition in the human heart by the message which they deliver, as there was of demolishing the walls of Jericho by the blowing of rams' horns. They blow the gospel trumpet from week to week and month to month, and there seems to be no tendency in the strong citadel of the heart to yield. Perhaps the

31 By faith the harlot Rahab [a] perished not with them that [1] be-

a Jos.6.23; Ja.2.25.

only apparent result is to excite ridicule and scorn. Yet let them not despair. Let them blow on. Let them still lift up their voice with faith in God, and in due time the walls of the citadel will totter and fall. God has power over the human heart as he had over Jericho ; and in our darkest day of discouragement let us remember that we are never in circumstances indicating *less* probability of success from any apparent tendency in the means used to accomplish the result, than those were who encompassed this heathen city. With similar confidence in God we may hope for similar success.

31. *By faith the harlot Rahab.* She resided in Jericho ; Josh. ii. 1. When Joshua crossed the Jordan, he sent two men as spies to her house, and she saved them by concealment from the enemies that would have destroyed their lives. For this act of hospitality and kindness, they assured her of safety when the city should be destroyed, and directed her to give an indication of her place of abode to the invading Israelites, that her house might be spared ; Josh. ii. 18, 19. In the destruction of the city, she was accordingly preserved ; Josh. vi. The apostle seems to have selected this case as illustrating the nature of faith, partly because it occurred at Jericho, of which he had just made mention, and partly to show that strong faith had been exercised not only by the patriarchs, and by those who were confessed to be great and good, but by those in humble life, and whose earlier conduct had been far from the ways of virtue. *Calvin.* Much perplexity has been felt in reference to this case, and many attempts have been made to remove the difficulty. The main difficulty has been that a woman of this character should be enumerated among those who were eminent for piety, and many expositors have endeavoured to show that the word rendered *harlot* does not necessarily denote a woman of aban-

lieved not, when she had received the spies [b] with peace.

1 or, *were disobedient.* b Jos.2.4,&c.

doned character, but may be used to denote a *hostess.* This definition is given by Schleusner, who says that the word may mean one who prepares and sells food and who receives strangers to entertain them. Others have supposed that the word means an *idolatress,* because those devoted to idolatry were frequently of abandoned character. But there are no clear instances in which the Greek word, and the corresponding Hebrew word—זונה—is used in this sense. The usual and the fair meaning of the word is that which is given in our translation, and there is no good reason why that signification should not be retained here. It is not implied by the use of the word here, however, that Rahab was an harlot at the time to which the apostle refers ; but the meaning is, that this *had been* her character, so that it was proper to designate her by this appellation. In regard to this case, therefore, and in explanation of the difficulties which have been felt in reference to it, we may remark, (1.) that the obvious meaning of this word here and of the corresponding place in Josh. ii. is, that she had been a woman of abandoned character, and that she was known as such. That she might have been *also* a hostess, or one who kept a house of entertainment for strangers, is at the same time by no means improbable, since it not unfrequently happened in ancient as well as modern times, that females of this character kept such houses. It might have been the fact that her house was *known* merely as a house of entertainment that led the spies who went to Jericho to seek a lodging there. It would be natural that strangers coming into a place should act in this respect as all other travellers did, and should apply for entertainment at what was known as a public house. (2.) There is no improbability in supposing that her course of life had been changed either before their arrival, or in consequence

32 And what shall I more
say? for the time would fail
me to tell of ᵃ Gedeon, and of
Barak, ᵇ and of Samson, ᶜ and

a Ju.vi.vii.   *b* Ju.4.6,&c.

of Jephthae; ᵈ of David ᵉ also,
and Samuel, ᶠ and of the prophets.

c Ju.xv.xvi.   *d* Ju.11.32,&c.
e 1Sa.17.45,&c.   *f* 1Sa.7.9.8c.

of it. They were doubtless wise and holy men. Men would not be selected for an enterprise like this, in whom the leader of the Hebrew army could not put entire confidence. It is not unfair then to suppose that they were men of eminent piety, as well as sagacity. Nor is there any improbability in supposing that they would acquaint this female with the history of their people, with their remarkable deliverance from Egypt, and with the design for which they were about to invade the land of Canaan. There is evidence that some such representations made a deep impression on her mind, and led to a change in her views and feelings, for she not only received them with the usual proofs of hospitality, but jeoparded her own life in their defence, when she might easily have betrayed them. This fact showed that she had a firm belief that they were what they professed to be—the people of God, and that she was willing to identify her interests with theirs. (3.) This case—supposing that she had been a woman of bad character, but now was truly converted—does not stand alone. Other females of a similar character have been converted, and have subsequently led lives of piety; and though the number is not comparatively great, yet the truth of God has shown its power in renewing and sanctifying some at least of this, the most abandoned and degraded class of human beings. "Publicans and *harlots,*" said the Saviour, "go into the kingdom of God;" Matt. xxi. 31. Rahab seems to have been one of them; and her case shows that such instances of depravity are not hopeless. This record, therefore, is one of encouragement for the most abandoned sinners; and one too which shows that strangers, even in a public house, may do good to those who have wandered far from God and virtue, and that we should never despair of saving the

most abandoned of our race. (4.) There is no need of supposing that the apostle in commending this woman approved of all that she did. That she was not perfect is true. That she did some things which cannot be vindicated is true also—and who does not? But admitting all that may be said about any imperfection in her character, (comp. Josh. ii. 4), it was still true that she had *strong faith*—and that is *all* that the apostle commends. We are under no more necessity of vindicating *all* that she did, than we are all that David or Peter did—or all that is now done by those who have the highest claims to virtue. (5.) She had strong faith. It was only a strong belief that Jehovah was the true God, and that the children of Israel were his people, which would have led her to screen the strangers at the peril of her own life; and when the city was encompassed, and the walls fell, and the tumult of battle raged she showed her steady confidence in their fidelity, and in God, by using the simple means on which she was told the safety of herself and her family depended; Josh. vi. 22, 23. ¶ *With them that believed not.* The inhabitants of the idolatrous city of Jericho. The margin is, "*were disobedient.*" The more correct rendering, however, is, as in the text, *believed not.* They evinced no such faith as Rahab had, and they were therefore destroyed. ¶ *Received the spies with peace.* With friendliness and kindness; Josh. ii. 1, *seq.*

32. *And what shall I more say?* "There are numerous other instances showing the strength of faith which there is not time to mention. ¶ *For the time would fail me to tell.* To recount all that they did; all the illustrations of the strength and power of faith evinced in their lives. ¶ *Of Gedeon.* The history of Gideon is detailed at length in Judges vi. vii., and there can be no doubt that in his

wars he was sustained and animated by strong confidence in God. ¶ *And of Barak;* Judges iv. Barak, at the command of Deborah the prophetess, who summoned him to war in the name of the Lord, encountered and overthrew the hosts of Sisera. His yielding to her summons, and his valour in battle against the enemies of the Lord, showed that he was animated by faith. ¶ *And of Samson;* see the history of Samson in Judges xiv—xvi. It is not by any means necessary to suppose that in making mention of Samson, the apostle approved of *all* that he did. All that he commends is his *faith,* and though he was a very imperfect man, and there were many things in his life which neither sound morality nor religion can approve, yet it was still true that he evinced, on some occasions, remarkable confidence in God, by relying on the strength which he gave him. This was particularly true in the instance where he made a great slaughter of the enemies of the Lord, and of his country; see Judges xv. 16 ; xvi. 30. ¶ *And* of *Jephthae.* The story of Jephtha is recorded in Judges xi. The mention of his name among those who were distinguished for *faith,* has given occasion to much perplexity among expositors. That a man of so harsh and severe a character, a man who sacrificed his own daughter, in consequence of a rash vow, should be numbered among those who were eminent for piety, as if he were one distinguished for piety also, has seemed to be wholly inconsistent and improper. The same remark, however, may be made respecting Jephtha which has been made of Samson and others. The apostle does not commend *all* which they did. He does not deny that they were very imperfect men, nor that they did many things which cannot be approved or vindicated. He commends only *one thing—their faith ;* and in these instances he particularly alludes, doubtless, to their remarkable valour and success in delivering their country from their foes and from the foes of God. In this it is implied that they

regarded themselves as called to this work by the Lord, and as engaged in his service ; and that they went forth to battle, depending on *his* protection and nerved by confidence in *him* as the God of their country. Their views of God himself might be very erroneous ; their notions of religion —as was the case with Jephtha—very imperfect and obscure ; many things in their lives might be wholly inconsistent with what *we* should now regard as demanded by religion, and still it might be true that in their efforts to deliver their country, they relied on the aid of God, and were animated to put forth extraordinary efforts, and were favoured with extraordinary success from their confidence in him. In the case of Jephtha, all that it is necessary to suppose, in order to see the force of the illustration of the apostle is, that he had strong confidence in God—the God of his nation, and that, under the influence of this, he made extraordinary efforts in repelling his foes. And this is not unnatural or improbable, even on the supposition that he was not a pious man. How many a Greek, and Roman, and Goth, and Mohammedan, has been animated to extraordinary courage in battle, by confidence in the gods which they worshipped ! That Jephtha had this, no one can doubt ; see Judges xi. 29—32.

[It is not likely that Jephtha's faith would have found a record *here*, had it been of no higher kind than this. Peirce admits his unnatural crime, but supposes him to have repented. " It must be owned," says he, "that if Jephtha had not repented of this very heinous wickedness, he could not have been entitled to salvation. The apostle, therefore, who has assured us of his salvation, must undoubtedly have gone upon the supposition that Jephtha actually repented of it before he died. That he had *time* to repent is beyond dispute, because he lived near *six* years after this. For it is expressly said *he judged Israel six years,* Judges xii. 7, and it is as certain he made this vow in the beginning of his government. What evidence the apostle had of Jephtha's repentance, I cannot say. He might know it by the help of old Jewish histories, or by inspiration."]

Even in the great and improper sacrifice of his only daughter which the obvious interpretation of the record

33 Who through faith subdued kingdoms, wrought righteousness, obtained promises, *a* stopped the mouths of lions,*b*
34 Quenched the violence of

a Gen. 15. 5.   *b* Da.6.22.

respecting him in Judges xi. 30, leads us to suppose he made, he did it as an offering to the Lord, and under these mistaken views of duty, he showed by the greatest sacrifice which a man *could* make—that of an only child—that he was disposed to do what he believed was required by religion A full examination of the case of Jephtha, and of the question whether he really sacrificed his daughter, may be found in Warburton's Divine Legation of Moses, book ix. Notes; in Bush's Notes on Judges xi.; and in the Biblical Repository for January 1843. It is not necessary to go into the much litigated inquiry here whether he really put his daughter to death, for whether he did or not, it is equally true that he evinced strong confidence in God. If he *did* do it, in obedience as he supposed to duty and to the divine command, no higher instance of faith in God as having a right to dispose of all that he had, could be furnished; if he did *not*, his eminent valour and success in battle show that he relied for strength and victory on the arm of Jehovah. The single reason why the piety of Jephtha has ever been called in question has been the fact that he sacrificed his own daughter. If he did *not* do that, no one will doubt his claims to an honoured rank among those who have evinced faith in God. ¶ Of *David also.* Commended justly as an eminent example of a man who had faith in God, though it cannot be supposed that *all* that he did was approved. ¶ *And Samuel.* In early youth distinguished for his piety, and manifesting it through his life; see 1 Sam. ¶ *And of the prophets.* They were men who had strong confidence in the truth of what God directed them to foretell, and who were ever ready, depending on him, to make known the most unwelcome truths to their fellow men, even at the peril of their lives.

fire, *c* escaped *d* the edge of the sword, out of weakness were made strong, waxed valiant in fight, turned to flight the armies of the aliens.

c Da.3.25.   *d* 1Ki.19.3; 2Ki.6.16.

33. *Who through faith subdued kingdoms.* That is, those specified in the previous verses, and others like them. The meaning is, that some of them subdued kingdoms, others obtained promises, &c. Thus, Joshua subdued the nations of Canaan; Gideon the Midianites; Jephtha the Ammonites; David the Philistines, Amalekites, Jebusites, Edomites, &c. ¶ *Wrought righteousness.* Carried the laws of justice into execution, particularly on guilty nations. They executed the great purposes of God in punishing the wicked, and in cutting off his foes. ¶ *Obtained promises.* Or obtained *promised blessings (Bloomfield, Stuart);* that is, they obtained as a result of their faith, promises of blessings on their posterity in future times. ¶ *Stopped the mouths of lions.* As Samson, Judges xiv. 6; David, 1 Sam. xvii. 34, seq.; and particularly Daniel; Dan. vi. 7, seq. To be able to subdue and render harmless the king of the forest—the animal most dreaded in early times—was regarded as an eminent achievement.

34. *Quenched the violence of fire.* As Shadrach, Meshach, and Abednego did; Dan. iii. 15—26. ¶ *Escaped the edge of the sword.* As Elijah did when he fled from Ahab, 1 Kings xix. 3; as Elijah did when he was delivered from the king of Syria, 2 Kings vi. 16; and as David did when he fled from Saul. ¶ *Out of weakness were made strong.* Enabled to perform exploits beyond their natural strength, or raised up from a state of bodily infirmity, and invigorated for conflict. Such a case as that of Samson may be referred to, Judges xv. 15; xvi. 26—30; or as that of Hezekiah, 2 Kings xx., who was restored from dangerous sickness by the immediate interposition of God; see Notes on Isa. xxxviii. ¶ *Waxed valiant in fight.* Became valiant. Like Joshua. Barak, David, &c. The books

35 Women [a] received their dead raised to life again : and others were tortured, not accepting [b] deliverance ; that they might obtain a better resurrection :

36 And others had trial of *cruel*

a 1Ki.17.22; 2Ki.4.35,36.
b Ac.4.19,20.

of Joshua, Judges, Samuel, and Kings supply instances of this in abundance. ¶ *Turned to flight the armies of the aliens.* The foreigners—as the invading Philistines, Ammonites, Moabites, Assyrians, &c.

35. *Women received their dead raised to life again.* As in the case of the woman of Zarephath, whose child was restored to life by Elijah, 1 Kings xvii. 19—24; and of the son of the Shunamite woman whose child was restored to life by Elisha ; 2 Kings iv. 18—37. ¶ *And others were tortured.* The word which is here used —τυμπανίζω—to *tympanize*, refers to a form of severe *torture* which was sometimes practised. It is derived from τύμπανον—*tympanum*—a drum, tabret, timbrel ; and the instrument was probably so called from resembling the drum or the timbrel. This instrument consisted in the East of a thin wooden rim covered over with skin, as a tambourine is with us ; see it described in the Notes on Isa. v. 12. The engine of torture here referred to, probably resembled the drum in form, on which the body of a criminal was *bent* so as to give greater severity to the wounds which were inflicted by scourging. The lash would cut deeper when the body was so extended, and the open gashes exposed to the air would increase the torture ; see 2 Mac. vi. 19—29. The punishment here referred to seems to have consisted of two things—the stretching upon the instrument, and the scourging ; see Robinson's Lex. and Stuart *in loc.* Bloomfield, however, supposes that the mode of the torture can be best learned from the original meaning of the word τύμπανον—*tympanum*—as meaning (1) a beating-stick, and (2) a beating-post which was in the form of a T, thus suggesting the posture of the sufferer. This beating, says he, was sometimes administered with sticks or rods ; and sometimes with leather thongs inclosing pieces of lead. The former ac-

count, however, better agrees with the usual meaning of the word. ¶ *Not accepting deliverance.* When it was offered them ; that is, on condition that they would renounce their opinions, or do what was required of them. This is the very nature of the spirit of martyrdom. ¶ *That they might obtain a better resurrection.* That is, when they were subjected to this kind of torture they were looked upon as certainly *dead.* To have accepted deliverance *then,* would have been a kind of restoration to life, or a species of *resurrection.* But they refused this, and looked forward to a more honourable and glorious restoration to life ; a resurrection, therefore, which would be better than this. It would be in itself more noble and honourable, and would be permanent, and therefore better. No particular instance of this kind is mentioned in the Old Testament ; but amidst the multitude of cases of persecution to which good men were subjected, there is no improbability in supposing that this may have occurred. The case of Eleazer, recorded in 2 Mac. 6, so strongly resembles what the apostle says here, that it is very possible he may have had it in his eye. The passage before us *proves* that the doctrine of the resurrection was understood and believed before the coming of the Saviour, and that it was one of the doctrines which sustained and animated those who were called to suffer on account of their religion. In the prospect of death under the infliction of torture on account of religion, or under the pain produced by disease, nothing will better enable us to bear up under the suffering than the expectation that the body will be restored to immortal vigour, and raised to a mode of life where it will be no longer susceptible of pain. To be raised up to *that* life is a " better resurrection" than to be saved from death when persecuted, or to be raised up from a bed of pain.

36. *And others had trial of* cruel

mockings and scourgings, yea, moreover, of bonds [a] and imprisonment. [b]
37 They were stoned, [c] they
were sawn asunder, were tempt-

a Gen.39.20.　　　*b* Je.20.2.

mockings. Referring to the scorn and
derision which the ancient victims of
persecution experienced. This has
been often experienced by martyrs,
and doubtless it was the case with
those who suffered on account of their
religion, before the advent of the
Saviour as well as afterwards. Some
instances of this kind are mentioned
in the Old Testament (2 Kings ii.
23; 1 Kings xxii. 24); and it was
frequent in the time of the Maccabees.
¶ *And scourging.* Whipping. This
was a common mode of punishment,
and was usually inflicted before a
martyr was put to death; see Notes
on Matt. x. 17; xxvii. 26. For instances of this, see Jer. xx. 2; 2 Mac.
vii. 1; v. 17. ¶ *Of bonds.* Chains.
Gen. xxxix. 20. ¶ *And imprisonment;*
see 1 Kings xxii. 27; Jer. xx. 2.
37. *They were stoned.* A common
method of punishment among the
Jews; see Notes on Matt. xxi.35,44.
Thus Zechariah, the son of Jehoiada
the priest, was stoned; see 2 Chron.
xxiv. 21; comp. 1 Kings xxi. 1—14.
It is not improbable that this was
often resorted to in times of popular
tumult, as in the case of Stephen;
Acts vii. 59; comp. John x. 31; Acts
xiv. 5. In the time of the terrible
persecutions under Antiochus Epi-
phanes, and under Manasseh, such instances also probably occurred. ¶ *They
were sawn asunder.* It is commonly
supposed that Isaiah was put to death
in this manner. For the evidence of
this, see introduction to Isaiah, § 2.
It is known that this mode of punishment, though not common, did exist
in ancient times. Among the Romans, the laws of the twelve tables
affixed this as the punishment of certain crimes, but this mode of execution was very rare, since Aulius Gel-
lius says that in his time no one remembered to have seen it practised.
It appears, however, from Suetonius
that the emperor Caligula often condemned persons of rank to be sawn

ed, were slain with the sword:
they wandered about in sheepskins and goatskins; being destitute, afflicted, tormented;

c Ac.7.59.

through the middle. Calmet, writing
above a hundred years ago, says, " I
am assured that the punishment of
the saw is still in use among the Swit-
zers, and that they put it in practice
not many years ago upon one of their
countrymen, guilty of a great crime,
in the plain of Grenelles, near Paris.
They put him into a kind of coffin,
and sawed him lengthwise, beginning
at the head, as a piece of wood is
sawn; *Pict. Bib.* It was not an unusual mode of punishment to *cut* a
person asunder, and to suspend the
different parts of the body to walls
and towers, as a warning to the living; see 1 Sam. xxxi. 10, and Mo-
rier's Second Journey to Persia, p. 96.
¶ *Were tempted.* On this expression,
which has given much perplexity to
critics, see the Notes of Prof. Stuart,
Bloomfield, and Kuinoel. There is a
great variety of reading in the MSS.
and editions of the New Testament,
and many have regarded it as an in-
terpolation. The difficulty which has
been felt in reference to it has been,
that it is a much *milder* word than
those just used, and that it is hardly
probable that the apostle would enumerate this among those which he
had just specified, as if *to be tempted*
deserved to be mentioned among sufferings of so severe a nature. But it
seems to me there need be no real
difficulty in the case. The apostle
here, among other sufferings which
they were called to endure, may have
referred to the *temptations* which were
presented to the martyrs when about
to die to abandon their religion and
live. It is very possible to conceive
that this might have been among the
highest aggravations of their sufferings. We know that in later times
it was a common practice to offer life
to those who were doomed to a horrid
death on condition that they would
throw incense on the altars of a heathen god, and we may easily suppose
that a temptation of that kind, art-

38 (Of whom the world was not worthy:) they wandered in deserts, and *in* mountains, and *in* dens and caves of the earth.

39 And these all, having obtained a good report through

1 or, *foreseen.*

fully presented in the midst of keen tortures, would greatly aggravate their sufferings. Or suppose when a father was about to be put to death for his religion, his wife and children were placed before him and should plead with him to save his life by abandoning his religion, we can easily imagine that no pain of the rack would cause so keen torture to the soul as their cries and tears would. Amidst the sorrows of martyrs, therefore, it was not improper to say that they were *tempted,* and to place this among their most aggravated woes. For instances of this nature, see 2 Mac. vi. 21, 22 ; vii. 17, 24. ¶ *Were slain with the sword.* As in the case of the eighty-five priests slain by Doeg (1 Sam. xxii. 18) ; and the prophets, of whose slaughter by the sword Elijah complains ; 1 Kings xix. 10. ¶ *They wandered about in sheepskins and goatskins.* Driven away from their homes, and compelled to clothe themselves in this rude and uncomfortable manner. A dress of this kind, or a dress made of hair, was not uncommon with the prophets, and seems indeed to have been regarded as an appropriate badge of their office ; see 2 Kings i. 8 ; Zech. xiii. 4. ¶ *Being destitute, afflicted, tormented.* The word *tormented* here means *tortured.* The apostle expresses here in general what in the previous verses he had specified in detail. 38. *Of whom the world was not worthy.* The world was so wicked that it had no claim that such holy men should live in it. These poor, despised, and persecuted men, living as outcasts and wanderers, were of a character far elevated above the world. This is a most beautiful expression. It is at once a statement of *their* eminent holiness, and of the wickedness of the rest of mankind. ¶ *They wandered in deserts,* &c. On the Scrip-

faith, received not the promise :

40 God having [1] provided some better thing for us, that they without *a* us should not be made perfect.

a Matt.13.16.17.

ture meaning of the word *desert* or *wilderness,* see Notes on Matt. iii. 1. This is a description of persons driven away from their homes, and wandering about from place to place to procure a scanty subsistence ; comp. 1 Mac. i. 53 ; 2 Mac. v. 27 ; vi. 7. The instances mentioned in the Books of Maccabees are so much in point, that there is no impropriety in supposing that Paul referred to some such cases, if not these very cases. As there is no doubt about their historic truth, there was no impropriety in referring to them, though they are not mentioned in the canonical books of Scripture. One of those cases may be referred to as strikingly illustrating what is here said. " But Judas Maccabeus with nine others or thereabout, withdrew himself into the wilderness, and lived in the mountains after the manner of beasts, with his company, who fed on herbs continually lest they should be partakers of the pollution ;" 2 Mac. v. 27.

39. *And these all, having obtained a good report through faith.* They were all commended and approved on account of their confidence in God ; see Notes on ver. 2. ¶ *Received not the promise.* That is, did not receive the fulfilment of the promise ; or did not receive *all* that was promised. They all still looked forward to some future blessings ; Notes, ver. 13.

40. *God having provided some better thing for us;* Marg. *foreseen.* That is, "God having provided, or determined on giving some better thing than any of them realized, and which we are now permitted to enjoy." That is, God gave them promises ; but they were not allowed to see their fulfilment. *We* are permitted now to see what they referred to, and in part, at least, to witness their completion ; and though the *promise* was made to them, the *fulfilment* more particularly

pertains to us. ¶ *That they without us should not be made perfect.* That is, *complete.* The whole system of revelation was not complete at once, or in one generation. It required successive ages to make the system complete, so that it might be said that it was *finished*, or *perfect.* Our exist ence, therefore, and the developments in our times, were as necessary to the perfection of the system, as the promise made to the patriarchs. And as the system would not have been complete if the blessings had been simply conferred on us without the previous arrangements, and the long scheme of introductory measures, so it would not have been complete if the promises had been merely given to them without the corresponding fulfilment in our times. They are like the two parts of a *tally.* The fathers had one part *in the promises*, and we the other *in the fulfilment*, and neither would have been complete without the other. The "better things" then referred to here as possessed by Christians, are the privilege of seeing those promises fulfilled in the Messiah; the blessings resulting from the atonement; the more expanded views which they have under the gospel; the brighter hopes of heaven itself, and the clearer apprehension of what heaven will be, which they are permitted to enjoy. This, therefore, accords entirely with the argument which the apostle is pursuing—which is, to show that the Christians whom he addressed should not apostatize from their religion. The argument is, that in numerous instances, as specified, the saints of ancient times, even under fiery trials, were sustained by faith in God, and that too when they had not seen the fulfilment of the promises, and when they had much more obscure views than we are permitted to enjoy. If they, under the influence of the mere *promise* of future blessings, were enabled thus to persevere, how much more reason is there for us to persevere who have been permitted, by the coming of the Messiah, to witness the perfection of the system !

There is no part of the New Tes-tament of more value than this chapter ; none which deserves to be more patiently studied, or which may be more frequently applied to the circumstances of Christians. These invaluable records are adapted to sustain us in times of trial, temptation, and persecution ; to show us what faith has done in days that are past, and what it may do still in similar circumstances. Nothing can better show the value and the power of faith, or of true religion, than the records in this chapter. It has done what nothing else could do. It has enabled men to endure what nothing else would enable them to bear, and it has shown its power in inducing them to give up, at the command of God, what the human heart holds most dear. And among the lessons which we may derive from the study of this portion of divine truth, let us learn from the example of Abel to continue to offer to God the sacrifice of true piety which he requires, though we may be taunted or opposed by our nearest kindred ; from that of Enoch to walk with God, though surrounded by a wicked world, and to look to the blessed translation to heaven which awaits all the righteous ; from that of Noah to comply with all the directions of God, and to make all needful preparations for the future events which he has predicted, in which we are to be interested – as death, judgment, and eternity—though the events may seem to be remote, and though there may be no visible indications of their coming, and though the world may deride our faith and our fears ; from that of Abraham to leave country, and home, and kindred, if God calls us to, and to go just where he commands, through deserts and wilds, and among strange men, and like him also to be ready to give up the dearest objects of our earthly affection, even when attended with all that can try or torture our feelings of affection—feeling that God who gave has a right to require their removal in his own way, and that however much we may fix our hopes on a dear child, he can fulfil all his purposes and promises to us though such a

CHAPTER XII.

WHEREFORE seeing we also are compassed about with

child should be removed by death: from that of Abraham, Isaac, and Jacob, to regard ourselves as strangers and pilgrims on earth, having here no permanent home, and seeking a better country; from that of Moses to be willing to leave all the pomp and splendour of the world, all our brilliant prospects and hopes, and to welcome poverty, reproach, and suffering, that we may identify ourselves with the people of God; by the remembrance of the host of worthies who met danger, and encountered mighty foes, and vanquished them, let us learn to go forth in our spiritual conflicts against the enemies of our souls and of the church, assured of victory; and from the example of those who were driven from the abodes of men, and exposed to the storms of persecution, let us learn to bear every trial, and to be ready at any moment to lay down *our* lives in the cause of truth and of God. Of all those holy men who made these sacrifices, which of them ever regretted it, when he came calmly to look over his life, and to review it on the borders of the eternal world? None. Not one of them ever expressed regret that he had given up the world; or that he had obeyed the Lord too early, too faithfully, or too long. Not Abraham who left his country and kindred; not Moses who abandoned his brilliant prospects in Egypt; not Noah who subjected himself to ridicule and scorn for an hundred and twenty years; and not one of those who were exposed to lions, to fire, to the edge of the sword, or who were driven away from society as outcasts to wander in pathless deserts or to take up their abodes in caverns, ever regretted the course which they had chosen. And who of them all *now* regrets it? Who, of these worthies, now looks from heaven and feels that he suffered one privation too much, or that he has not had an ample recompense for all the ills he experienced in the cause of religion? So

so great a cloud of witnesses, let us lay aside *a* every weight,

a 2Cor.7.1.

we shall feel when from the bed of death we look over the present life, and look out on eternity Whatever our religion may have cost us, we shall not feel that we began to serve God too early, or served him too faithfully. Whatever pleasure, gain, or splendid prospects we gave up in order to become Christians, we shall feel that it was the way of wisdom, and shall rejoice that we were able to do it. Whatever sacrifices, trials, persecution, and pain, we may meet with, we shall feel that there has been more than a compensation in the consolations of religion, and in the hope of heaven, and that by every sacrifice we have been the gainers. When we reach heaven, we shall see that we have not endured one pain too much, and that through whatever trials we may have passed, the result is worth all which it has cost. Strengthened then in our trials by the remembrance of what faith has done in times that are past; recalling the example of those who through faith and patience have inherited the promises, let us go cheerfully on our way. Soon the journey of trials will be ended, and soon what are now objects of faith will become objects of fruition, and in their enjoyment how trifling and brief will seem all the sorrows of our pilgrimage below!

CHAPTER XII.

ANALYSIS OF THE CHAPTER.

The apostle having illustrated the nature and power of faith in the previous chapter, proceeds in this to exhort those to whom he wrote to apply the same principles to their own case, and to urge them to manifest the same steady confidence in God and perseverance in their holy walk. For this purpose, he adverts to the following arguments or considerations:

I. He represents the ancient worthies who had so faithfully persevered and so gloriously triumphed, as witnesses of their strife in the Christian race, and as cheering them on to victory; ver. 1.

II. He appeals to the example of the Saviour; vers. 2—4. This was a more illustrious instance than any of those which had been adverted to, and is not referred to *with* theirs, but is adduced as deserving a separate and a special specification. The circumstances in his case which are an encouragement to perseverance in the Christian conflict, are these. (1.) He endured the cross, and is now exalted to the right hand of God. (2.) He bore the contradiction of sinners against himself, as those were called to do to whom Paul wrote. (3.) He went *beyond* them in his trials and temptations—beyond anything which they could have reason to apprehend — for he had "resisted unto blood, striving against sin."

III. He encourages them by showing that their trials would result in their own good, and particularly that the hand of a *Father* was in them; vers. 5—13. Particularly he urges (1.) that God addressed those who suffered as his *sons*, and called on them not to receive with improper feeling the chastening of the Lord, ver. 5; (2.) that it was a general principle that the Lord chastened those whom he loved, and the fact that we received chastening was to be regarded as evidence that we are under his paternal care, and that he has not forsaken us, vers. 6—8; (3.) that they had been subject to the correction of earthly fathers and had learned to be submissive, and that there was much higher reason for submitting to God, vers. 9, 10; (4.) and that however painful chastisement might be at present, yet it would ultimately produce important benefits; ver. 11. By these considerations he encourages them to bear their trials with patience, and to assume new courage in their efforts to live a Christian life; vers. 12, 13.

IV. He exhorts them to perseverance and fidelity by the fact that if they should become remiss, and renounce their confidence in God, it would be impossible to retrieve what was lost; vers. 14—17. In illustrating this, he appeals to the case of Esau. For a trifling consideration, when in distress, he parted with an invaluable blessing. When it was gone, it was impossible to recover it. No consideration could induce a change, though he sought it earnestly with tears. So it would be with Christians, if, under the power of temptation, they should renounce their religion, and go back to their former state.

V. He urges them to perseverance by the nature of the dispensation under which they were, as compared with the one under which they had formerly been—the Jewish; vers. 18 —29. Under the former, everything was fitted to alarm and terrify the soul; vers. 18—21. The new dispensation was of a different character. It was adapted to encourage and to win the heart. The real Mount Zion —the city of the living God—the New Jerusalem—the company of the angels—the church of the first-born— the Judge of all—the great Mediator —to which they had come under the new dispensation, all these were fitted to encourage the fainting heart, and to win the affections of the soul; vers. 22—24. Yet, in proportion to the sacredness and tenderness of these considerations, and to the light and privileges which they now enjoyed, would be their guilt if they should renounce their religion—for under this dispensation, as under the old, God was a consuming fire; vers. 25—29.

1. *Wherefore.* In view of what has been said in the previous chapter. ¶ *Seeing we also are encompassed about with so great a cloud of witnesses.* The apostle represents those to whom he had referred in the previous chapter, as *looking on* to witness the efforts which Christians make, and the manner in which they live There is allusion here, doubtless, to the ancient games. A great multitude of spectators usually occupied the circular seats in the amphitheatre, from which they could easily behold the combatants; see Notes on 1 Cor. ix. 24—27. In like manner, the apostle represents Christians as encompassed with the multitude of worthies to whom he had referred in the previous chapter. It cannot be fairly

and the sin which doth so easily beset *us*, and let us run with patience the race that is set before us.

inferred from this that he means to say that all those ancient worthies were *actually* looking at the conduct of Christians, and saw their conflicts. It is a figurative representation, such as is common, and means that we ought to act *as if* they were in sight, and cheered us on. How far the spirits of the just who are departed from this world are permitted to behold what is done on earth—if at all —is not revealed in the Scriptures. The phrase, " a *cloud* of witnesses," means *many* witnesses, or a number so great that they seem to be *a cloud*. The comparison of a *multitude* of persons to a cloud is common in the classic writers ; see Homer Il. iv. 274, xxiii. 133 ; Statius i. 340, and other instances adduced in Wetstein, *in loc. ;* comp. Notes on 1 Thess. iv. 17. ¶ *Let us lay aside every weight.* The word rendered *weight*—ὄγκον— means that which is *crooked* or *hooked*, and thence any thing that is attached or suspended by a hook—that is, by its whole weight, and hence means *weight ;* see *Passow.* It does not occur elsewhere in the New Testament. The word is often used in the classic writers in the sense of swelling, tumour, pride. Its usual meaning is that of *weight* or *burden*, and there is allusion here, doubtless, to the runners in the games who were careful not to encumber themselves with anything that was heavy. Hence their clothes were so made as not to impede their running, and hence they were careful in their training not to overburden themselves with food, and in every way to remove what would be an impediment or hindrance. As applied to the racers it does not mean that they began to run with anything like a burden, and then threw it away —as persons sometimes aid their jumping by taking a stone in their hands to acquire increased *momentum*—but that they were careful *not to allow* anything that would be a weight or an encumbrance. As applied to Christians it means that they should remove *all* which would obstruct their progress in the Christian course. Thus it is fair to apply it to whatever would be an impediment in our efforts to win the crown of life. It is not the same thing in all persons. In one it may be pride ; in another vanity ; in another worldliness ; in another a violent and almost ungovernable temper; in another a corrupt imagination ; in another a heavy, leaden, insensible heart ; in another some improper and unholy attachment. Whatever it may be, we are exhorted to lay it aside, and this general direction may be applied to anything which prevents our making the highest possible attainment in the divine life. Some persons would make much more progress if they would throw away many of their personal ornaments ; some, if they would disencumber themselves of the heavy *weight* of gold which they are endeavouring to carry with them. So some very light objects, in themselves considered, become material encumbrances. Even a feather or a ring—such may be the fondness for these toys — may become such a weight that they will never make much progress towards the prize. ¶ *And the sin which doth so easily beset* us. The word which is here rendered " *easily beset*"—εὐπερίστατον—*euperistaton*—does not elsewhere occur in the New Testament. It properly means, " *standing well around;*" and hence denotes that which is near, or at hand, or readily occurring. So Chrysostom explains it. Passow defines it as meaning "easy to encircle." Tindal renders it " the sin that hangeth on us." Theodoret and others explain the word as if derived from περίστασις —*peristasis*—a word which sometimes means affliction, peril—and hence regard it as denoting that *which is full of peril*, or the sin which so easily subjects one to calamity. Bloomfield supposes, in accordance with the opinion of Grotius, Crellius, Kype, Kuinoel, and others, that it means "the sin which especially winds around us, and hinders our

2 Looking unto Jesus the [1] au-
1 or, *beginner*.　　　*a* Lu.24.26.

thor and finisher of *our* faith ;
who, for the *a* joy that was set

course," with allusion to the long
Oriental garments. According to
this, the meaning would be, that as a
runner would be careful not to encumber himself with a garment which
would be apt to wind around his legs
in running, and hinder him, so it
should be with the Christian, who
especially ought to lay aside everything
which resembles this ; that is, all sin,
which *must* impede his course. The
former of these interpretations, however, is most commonly adopted, and
best agrees with the established sense
of the word. It will then mean
that we are to lay aside every encumbrance, *particularly* or *especially* —
for so the word καὶ "and," should be
rendered here—the sins to which we
are most exposed. Such sins are
appropriately called " easily besetting
sins." They are those to which *we*
are particularly liable. They are
such sins as the following. (1.) Those
to which we are particularly exposed
by our natural temperament, or disposition. In some this is pride, in
others indolence, or gaiety, or levity,
or avarice, or ambition, or sensuality.
(2.) Those in which we freely indulged
before we became Christians. They
will be likely to return with power,
and we are far more likely from the
laws of association, to fall into them
than into any other. Thus a man
who has been intemperate is in special danger from that quarter ; a man
who has been an infidel, is in special
danger of scepticism : one who has
been avaricious, proud, gay, or ambitious, is in special danger, even after
conversion, of again committing these
sins. (3.) Sins to which we are exposed by our profession, by our relations to others, or by our situation
in life. They whose condition will
entitle them to associate with what
are regarded as the more elevated
classes of society, are in special danger of indulging in the methods of
living, and of amusement that are
common among them ; they who are
prospered in the world are in danger
of losing the simplicity and spirit-

uality of their religion ; they who
hold a civil office are in danger of becoming mere politicians, and of losing
the very form and substance of piety.
(4.) Sins to which we are exposed
from some peculiar *weakness* in our
character. On some points we may
be in no danger. We may be constitutionally so firm as not to be especially liable to certain forms of sin.
But every man has one or more *weak
points* in his character ; and it is
there that he is particularly exposed.
A bow may be in the main very
strong. All along its length there
may be no danger of its giving way
— save at one place where it has been
made too thin, or where the material
was defective—and if it ever breaks,
it will of course be at that point. *That*
is the point, therefore, which needs
to be guarded and strengthened. So
in reference to *character*. There is
always some weak point which needs
specially to be guarded, and our principal danger is there. Self-knowledge,
so necessary in leading a holy life,
consists much in searching out those
weak points of character where we
are most exposed ; and our progress
in the Christian course will be determined much by the fidelity with which
we guard and strengthen them. ¶ *And
let us run with patience the race
that is set before us.* The word
rendered "patience" rather means in
this place, *perseverance*. We are to
run the race without allowing ourselves to be hindered by any obstructions, and without giving out or fainting in the way. Encouraged by the
example of the multitudes who have
run the same race before us, and who
are now looking out upon us from
heaven, where they dwell, we are to
persevere as they did to the end.
2. *Looking unto Jesus.* As a farther
inducement to do this, the apostle
exhorts us to look to the Saviour. We
are to look to his holy life ; to his
patience and perseverance in trials ;
to what he endured in order to obtain
the crown, and to his final success
and triumph. ¶ *The author and fin-*

before him, endured the cross, despising the shame, and is set down

isher of our *faith.* The word *"our"*
is not in the original here, and obscures the sense.   The meaning is,
he is the *first* and the *last* as an
example of faith or of confidence in
God—occupying in this, as in all other
things, the pre-eminence, and being
the most complete model that can be
placed before us. The apostle had
not enumerated him among those
who had been distinguished for their
faith, but he now refers to him as
above them all ; as a case that deserved to stand by itself. It is probable that there is a continuance here
of the allusion to the Grecian games
which the apostle had commenced in
the previous verse. The word *author*
—ἀρχηγὸν—(marg. *beginner*)—means
properly *the source,* or *cause* of any
thing ; or one who makes a beginning. It is rendered in Acts iii. 15,
v. 31, *Prince;* in Heb. ii. 10, *Captain;*
and in the place before us, *Author.* It
does not elsewhere occur in the New
Testament. The phrase " the beginner of faith," or the *leader on* of faith,
would express the idea. He is at the
head of all those who have furnished
an example of confidence in God, for
he was himself the most illustrious
instance of it. The expression, then,
does not mean properly that he produces faith *in us,* or that we believe
because he causes us to believe—whatever may be the truth about that—but
that he stands at the head as the most
eminent example that can be referred
to on the subject of faith. We are
exhorted to look to him, as if at the
Grecian games there was *one* who
stood before the racer who had previously carried away every palm of victory; who had always been triumphant,
and with whom there was no one who
could be compared. The word *finisher*—τελειωτὴν—corresponds in meaning with the word *author.* It means
that he is the *completer* as well as the
beginner ; the *last* as well as the *first.*
As there has been no one hitherto
who could be compared with him, so
there will be no one hereafter ; comp.
Rev. i. 8, 11. " I am Alpha and Ome-

at the right hand of the throne
of God.

ga, the beginning and the ending, the
first and the last."   The word does
not mean that he was the " finisher"
of faith in the sense that he makes
our faith complete or perfects it—
whatever may be true about that—
but that he occupies this elevated position of being beyond comparison
above all others. Alike in the commencement and the close, in the beginning of faith, and in its ending, *he*
stands pre-eminent. To this illustrious model we should look—as a racer
would on one who had been always
so successful that he surpassed all
competitors and rivals. If this be the
meaning, then it is not properly explained, as it is commonly (see Bloomfield and Stuart *in loc.*), by saying that
the word here is synonymous with
rewarder, and refers to the βραβευτὴς
—*brabeutes*—or *the distributor of the
prize ;* comp. Notes on Col. iii. 15.
There is no instance where the word
is used in this sense in the New Testament (comp. *Passow*), nor would such
an interpretation present so beautiful
and appropriate a thought as the one
suggested above. ¶ *Who for the joy
that was set before him.* That is, who
in view of all the honour which he
would have at the right hand of God,
and the happiness which he would experience from the consciousness that
he had redeemed a world, was willing
to bear the sorrows connected with
the atonement. ¶ *Endured the cross.*
Endured patiently the ignominy and
pain connected with the suffering of
death on the cross. ¶ *Despising the
shame.* Disregarding the ignominy
of such a mode of death.   It is difficult for us now to realize the force of
the expression, " enduring the shame
of the cross," as it was understood in
the time of the Saviour and the apostles.   The views of the world have
changed, and it is now difficult to divest the " cross" of the associations of
honour and glory which the word
suggests, so as to appreciate the ideas
which encompassed it then. There
is a degree of dishonour which we
attach to the guillotine, but the igno-

3 For consider him that endured such contradiction of sinners against himself, lest ye be wearied and faint in your minds.

miny of a death on the cross was greater than that; there is disgrace attached to the block, but the ignominy of the cross was greater than that; there is a much deeper infamy attached to the gallows, but the ignominy of the cross was greater than that. And that word—*the cross*— which when now proclaimed in the ears of the refined, the intelligent, and even the gay, excites an idea of honour, in the ears of the people of Athens, of Corinth, and of Rome, excited deeper disgust than the word *gallows* does with us—for it was regarded as the appropriate punishment of the most infamous of mankind. We can now scarcely appreciate these feelings, and of course the declaration that Jesus " endured the cross, despising the shame," does not make the impression on our minds in regard to the nature of his sufferings, and the value of his example, which it should do. When we now think of the "cross," it is not of the multitude of slaves, and robbers, and thieves, and rebels, who have died on it, but of the one great Victim, whose death has ennobled even this instrument of torture, and encircled it with a halo of glory. We have been accustomed to read of it as an imperial standard in war in the days of Constantine, and as the banner under which armies have marched to conquest; it is intermingled with the sweetest poetry; it is a sacred thing in the most magnificent cathedrals; it adorns the altar, and is even an object of adoration; it is in the most elegant engravings; it is worn by beauty and piety as an ornament near the heart; it is associated with all that is pure in love, great in self-sacrifice, and holy in religion. To see the true force of the expression here, therefore, it is necessary to divest ourselves of these ideas of glory which encircle the " cross," and to place ourselves in the times and lands in which, when the most infamous of mankind were stretched upon it, it was regarded for such men as an appropriate mode of punishment. That

infamy Jesus was willing to bear, and the strength of his confidence in God, his love for man, and the depth of his humiliation, was shown in the readiness and firmness with which he went forward to such a death. ¶ *And is set down at the right hand of the throne of God.* Exalted to the highest place of dignity and honour in the universe; Notes, Mark xvi. 19; Eph. i. 20—22. The sentiment here is, "Imitate the example of the great Author of our religion. He, in view of the honour and joy before him, endured the most severe sufferings to which the human frame can be subjected, and the form of death which is regarded as the most shameful. So amidst all the severe trials to which you are exposed on account of religion, patiently endure all—for the glorious rewards, the happiness and the triumph of heaven, are before you."

3. *For consider him.* Attentively reflect on his example that you may be able to bear your trials in a proper manner. ¶ *That endured such contradiction of sinners.* Such opposition. The reference is to the Jews of the time of the Saviour, who opposed his plans, perverted his sayings, and ridiculed his claims. Yet, regardless of their opposition, he persevered in the course which he had marked out, and went patiently forward in the execution of his plans. The idea is, that we are to pursue the path of duty and follow the dictates of conscience, let the world say what they will about it. In doing this we cannot find a better example than the Saviour. No opposition of sinners ever turned him from the way which he regarded as right; no ridicule ever caused him to abandon any of his plans; no argument, or expression of scorn, ever caused him for a moment to deviate from his course. ¶ *Lest ye be wearied and faint in your minds.* The meaning is, that there is great danger of being disheartened and wearied out by the opposition which you meet with. But with the bright example

4 Ye have not yet resisted

of one who was *never* disheartened, and who never became weary in doing the will of God, you may persevere. The best means of leading a faithful Christian life amidst the opposition which we may encounter, is to keep the eye steadily fixed on the Saviour.

4. *Ye have not yet resisted unto blood, striving against sin.* The general sense of this passage is, "you have not yet been called in your Christian struggles to the highest kind of sufferings and sacrifices. Great as your trials may seem to have been, yet your faith has not yet been put to the severest test. And since this is so, you ought not to yield in the conflict with evil, but manfully resist it." In the *language* here used there is undoubtedly a continuance of the allusion to the *agonistic* games—the strugglings and wrestlings for mastery there. In those games, the boxers were accustomed to arm themselves for the fight with the cæstus. This at first consisted of strong leathern thongs wound around the hands, and extending only to the wrist, to give greater solidity to the *fist*. Afterwards these were made to extend to the elbow, and then to the shoulder, and finally, they sewed pieces of lead or iron in them that they might strike a heavier and more destructive blow. The consequence was, that those who were engaged in the fight were often covered with blood, and that resistance "unto blood" showed a determined courage, and a purpose not to yield. But though the *language* here may be taken from this custom, the *fact* to which the apostle alludes, it seems to me, is the struggling of the Saviour in the garden of Gethsemane, when his conflict was so severe that great drops of blood fell down to the ground; see Notes on Matt. xxvi. 36—44. It is, indeed, commonly understood to mean that they had not yet been called to shed their blood as martyrs in the cause of religion; see Stuart, Bloomfield, Doddridge, Clarke, Whitby, Kuinoel, &c. Indeed, I find in none of the commentators what seems to me to be the true sense of this pas-

unto blood, striving against sin.

sage, and what gives an exquisite beauty to it, the allusion to the sufferings of the Saviour in the garden. The reasons which lead me to believe that there *is* such an allusion, are briefly these. (1.) The connection. The apostle is appealing to the example of the Saviour, and urging Christians to persevere amidst their trials by looking to him. Nothing would be more natural in this connection, than to refer to that dark night, when in the severest conflict with temptation which he ever encountered, he so signally showed his own firmness of purpose, and the effects of resistance on his own bleeding body, and his signal victory—in the garden of Gethsemane. (2.) The expression "striving against sin" seems to demand the same interpretation. On the common interpretation, the allusion would be merely to their resisting *persecution;* but here the allusion is to some struggle in their minds against *committing sin.* The apostle exhorts them to strive manfully and perseveringly against *sin* in every form, and especially against the sin of apostasy. To encourage them he refers them to the highest instance on record where there was a "striving against sin"—the struggle of the Redeemer in the garden with the great enemy who there made his most violent assault, and where the resistance of the Redeemer was so great as to force the blood through his pores. What was the exact *form* of the temptation there, we are not informed. It *may* have been to induce him to abandon his work even then and to yield, in view of the severe sufferings of his approaching death on the cross. If there ever was a point where temptation would be powerful, it would be there. When a man is about to be put to death, how strong is the inducement to abandon his purpose, his plans, or his principles, if he may save his life! How many, of feeble virtue, have yielded just there! If to this consideration we add the thought that the Redeemer was engaged in a

5 And ye have forgotten the exhortation ^a which speaketh unto you as unto children, My son, de-

a Pr.3.11,12.

spise not thou the chastening of the Lord, nor faint when thou art rebuked of him:

---

work never before undertaken ; that he designed to make an atonement never before made; that he was about to endure sorrows never before endured ; and that on the decision of that moment depended the ascendency of sin or holiness on the earth, the triumph or the fall of Satan's kingdom, the success or the defeat of all the plans of the great adversary of God and man, and that, on such an occasion as this, the tempter would use all his power to crush the lonely and unprotected man of sorrows in the garden of Gethsemane, it is easy to imagine what may have been the terror of that fearful conflict, and what virtue it would require in him to resist the concentrated energy of Satan's might to induce him even then to abandon his work. The apostle says of those to whom he wrote, that they had not *yet* reached that point ; comp. Notes on ch. v. 7 (3.) This view furnishes a proper *climax* to the argument of the apostle for perseverance. It presents the Redeemer before the mind as *the* great example; directs the mind to him in various scenes of his life—as looking to the joy before him — disregarding the ignominy of his sufferings—enduring the opposition of sinners—and *then* in the garden as engaged in a conflict with his great foe, and so resisting *sin* that rather than yield he endured that fearful mental struggle which was attended with such remarkable consequences. This is the highest consideration which *could* be presented to the mind of a believer to keep him from yielding in the conflict with evil; and if we could keep him in the eye resisting even unto blood rather than yield in the least degree, it would do more than all other things to restrain us from sin. How different his case from ours! How readily we yield to sin! We offer a faint and feeble resistance, and then surrender. We think it will be unknown; or that others do it; or

that we may repent of it ; or that we have no power to resist it ; or that it is of little consequence, and our resolution gives way. Not so the Redeemer. Rather than yield in any form to sin, he measured strength with the great adversary when alone with him in the darkness of the night, and gloriously triumphed ! And so would *we* always triumph if we had the same settled purpose to resist sin in every form *even unto blood*.

5. *And ye have forgotten the exhortation.* This exhortation is found in Prov. iii. 11, 12. The object of the apostle in introducing it here is, to show that afflictions were designed on the part of God to produce some happy effects in the lives of his people, and that they ought, therefore, to bear them patiently. In the previous verses, he directs them to the example of the Saviour. In this verse and the following, for the same object he directs their attention to the design of trials, showing that they are necessary to our welfare, and that they are in fact proof of the paternal care of God. This verse might be rendered as a question. "And have ye forgotten?" &c. This mode of rendering it will agree somewhat better with the design of the apostle. ¶ *Which speaketh unto you.* Which may be regarded as addressed to you ; or which involves a principle as applicable to you as to others. He does not mean that when Solomon used the words, he had reference to *them* particularly, but that he used them with reference to the children of God, and they might therefore be applied to them. In this way we may regard the language of the Scriptures as addressed to *us*. ¶ *As unto children.* As if he were addressing children. The language is such as a father uses. ¶ *My son.* It is *possible* that in these words Solomon may have intended to address a son literally, giving him paternal counsel ; or he may have spoken as the Head of the Jewish peo-

6 For *a* whom the Lord loveth
a Re.3.19.

he chasteneth, and scourgeth every son whom he receiveth.

ple, designing to address all the pious, to whom he sustained, as it were, the relation of a father. Or, it is possible also, that it may be regarded as the language of God himself addressing his children. Whichever supposition is adopted, the sense is substantially the same. ¶ *Despise not thou the chastening of the Lord.* Literally, "Do not regard it as a small matter, or as a trivial thing,—ὀλιγώρει. The Greek word here used does not occur elsewhere in the New Testament. The word here rendered *chastening—παιδεία*—and also in vers. 6, 7, 8, and in ver. 9, "corrected"—*παιδευτὰς*—does not refer to affliction in general, but that kind of affliction which is designed to *correct* us for our faults, or which is of the nature of *discipline.* The verb properly relates to the training up of a child—including instruction, counsel, discipline, and correction (see this use of the verb in Acts vii. 22 ; 2 Tim. ii. 25 ; Titus ii. 12), and then especially discipline or correction for faults—to *correct, chastise, chasten ;* 1 Cor. xi. 32; 2 Cor. vi. 9 ; Rev. iii. 19. This is the meaning here ; and the idea is, not that God will *afflict* his people in general, but that if they wander away he will *correct* them for their faults. He will bring calamity upon them as a *punishment* for their offences, and in order to bring them back to himself. He will not suffer them to wander away unrebuked and unchecked, but will mercifully reclaim them though by great sufferings. Afflictions have many objects, or produce many happy effects. That referred to here is, that they are means of reclaiming the wandering and erring children of God, and are proofs of his paternal care and love; comp. 2 Sam. vii. 14 ; xii. 13, 14 ; Ps. lxxxix. 31—34 ; Prov. iii. 11, 12. Afflictions, which are always sent by God, should not be regarded as small matters, for these reasons. (1.) The fact that they *are* sent by God. Whatever he does is of importance, and is worthy the profound attention of men. (2.) They

are sent for some important purpose, and they should be regarded, therefore, with attentive concern. Men *despise* them when (1) they treat them with affected or real unconcern ; (2) when they fail to receive them as divine admonitions, and regard them as without any intelligent design ; and (3) when they receive them with *expressions* of contempt, and speak of them and of the government of God with scorn. It should be a matter of deep concern when we are afflicted in any manner, not to treat the matter *lightly,* but to derive from our trials all the lessons which they are adapted to produce on the mind. ¶ *Nor faint,* &c. Bear up patiently under them. This is the second duty. We are first to study their character and design ; and secondly, to bear up under them, however severe they may be, and however long they may be continued. " Avoid the extremes of proud insensibility and entire dejection."—*Doddridge.*

6. *For whom the Lord loveth he chasteneth.* This is also a quotation from Proverbs iii. It means that it is a universal rule that God sends trials on those whom he truly loves. It does not, of course, mean that he sends chastisement which is not deserved ; or that he sends it *for the mere purpose* of inflicting pain. That cannot be. But it means that by his chastisements he shows that he has a paternal care for us. He does not treat us with neglect and unconcern, as a father often does his illegitimate child. The very fact that he corrects us shows that he has towards us a father's feelings, and exercises towards us a paternal care. If he did not, he would let us go on without any attention, and leave us to pursue a course of sin that would involve us in ruin. To restrain and govern a child; to correct him when he errs, shows that there is a parental solicitude for him, and that he is not an outcast. And as there is in the life of every child of God *something* that deserves correction, it happens that it

7 If ye endure chastening, God dealeth with you as with sons; for *a* what son is he whom the father chasteneth not?

8 But if ye be without chas-

a Pr.13.24.

is universally true that "whom the Lord loveth he chasteneth." ¶ *And scourgeth every son whom he receiveth.* Whom he receives or acknowledges as his child. This is not quoted literally from the Hebrew, but from the Septuagint. The Hebrew is, " even as a father the son in whom he delighteth." The general sense of the passage is retained, as is often the case in the quotations from the Old Testament. The meaning is the same as in the former part of the verse, that every one who becomes a child of God is treated by him with that watchful care which shows that he sustains towards him the paternal relation.

7. *If ye endure chastening.* That is, if you undergo, or are called to experience correction. It does not mean here, "if you endure it patiently; or if you bear up under it;" but "if you *are* chastised or corrected by God." The affirmation does not relate to the manner of *bearing* it, but to the *fact* that we are disciplined. ¶ *God dealeth with you as with sons.* He does not cast you off and regard you as if you were in no way related to him. ¶ *For what son is he whom the father chasteneth not.* That is, he evinces towards his son the care which shows that he sustains the relation of a father. If he deserves correction, he corrects him; and he aims by all proper means to exhibit the appropriate care and character of a father. And as we receive such attention from an earthly parent, we ought to expect to receive similar notice from our Father in heaven.

8. *But if ye be without chastisement.* If you never meet with anything that is adapted to correct your faults; to subdue your temper; to chide your wanderings, it would prove that you were in the condition of illegitimate children—cast off and disregarded by their father. ¶ *Whereof all are partakers.* All who are the true children

tisement, whereof all are partakers, then are ye bastards, and not sons.

9 Furthermore we have had fathers of our flesh which cor-

of God. ¶ *Then are ye bastards, and not sons.* The reference here is to the neglect with which such children are treated, and to the general want of care and discipline over them :

" Lost in the world's wide range; enjoin'd
        no aim,
Prescrib'd no duty, and assign'd no
        name." *Savage.*

In the English law, a bastard is termed *nullius filius.* Illegitimate children are usually abandoned by their father. The care of them is left to the mother, and the father endeavours to avoid all responsibility, and usually to be concealed and unknown. His own child he does not wish to recognise; he neither provides for him ; nor instructs him ; nor governs him; nor disciplines him. A *father*, who is worthy of the name, will do all these things. So Paul says it is with Christians. God has not cast them off. In every way he evinces towards them the character of a father. And if it should be that they passed along through life without any occurrence that would indicate the paternal care and attention designed to correct their faults, it would show that they never had been his children, but were cast off and wholly disregarded. This is a beautiful argument; and we should receive every affliction as full proof that we are not forgotten by the High and Holy One who condescends to sustain to us the character, and to evince towards us, in our wanderings, the watchful care of a Father.

9. *Furthermore.* As an additional consideration to induce us to receive chastisement with submission. The argument in this verse is derived from the difference in the spirit and design with which we are corrected by God and by an earthly parent. In God everything is without any intermingling of passion or any improper feeling. In an earthly parent there is often much that is the result of hasty

rected *us*, and we gave *them* reverence : shall we not much rather

emotion, of an irascible temper, perhaps of the mere love of power. There is much that is inflicted without due reflection, and that produces only pain in the bosom of the parent himself in the recollection. Yet with all this imperfection of parental government, we were patient and unmurmuring. How much more should we submit to one whose paternal discipline is caused by no excited feeling ; by no love of power ; by no want of reflection, and which never furnishes occasion for regret ! ¶ *Fathers of our flesh.* Earthly fathers ; those from whom we have derived our being here. They are contrasted here with God, who is called "the Father of spirits," not because the father does not sustain the paternal relation to the soul as well as the body, but to designate the nature of the dominion over us. The dominion of God is that which pertains to a spiritual kingdom, having more direct reference to the discipline of the soul, and being designed to prepare us for the spiritual world ; that of the earthly father pertains primarily to our condition here, and the discipline is designed to subdue our unruly passions, to teach us to restrain our appetites, to inculcate maxims of health and prosperity, and to prevent those things which would impede our happiness in the present world. See, however, many curious instances of the manner in which these phrases were used by the Jewish writers, collected by Wetstein. ¶ *We gave* them *reverence.* We submitted to them ; honoured them ; loved them Painful at the time as correction may have been, yet when we have fully understood the design of it, we have loved them the more. The effect of such discipline, properly administered, is to produce real veneration for a parent—for he who in a timely and appropriate manner restrains his child is the only one who will secure ultimate reverence and respect. ¶ *Shall we not much rather be in subjection.* Since God's govern-

be in subjection unto the *a* Father of spirits, and live ?

10 For they verily for a few ment is so much more perfect ; since he has so much better right to control us ; and since his administration is free from all the defects which attend parental discipline on earth, there is a much higher reason for bowing with submission and reverence to him. ¶ *The Father of spirits.* Thus in Numbers xvi. 22, God is called " the God of the spirits of all flesh ;" so also Num. xxvii. 16; comp. Job xxxiii. 4. The idea seems to be that, as the soul is the most important part of man, this name is given to God by way of eminence, or he is eminently and supremely our Father. It was his to create the immortal part, and to that spirit which is never to die he sustains the relation of Father. The earthly father is parent to the man as mortal; God is the Father of man as immortal. God is himself a spirit. Angels and human souls, therefore, may be represented as peculiarly his offspring. It is the highest designation which could be given to God to say that he is at the head of the universe of mind ; not implying that he is not also at the head of the material universe, but designing to bring into view this high characteristic of the Almighty, that all created minds throughout the universe sustain to him the relation of children. To this Great Being we should, therefore, more cheerfully subject ourselves than to an earthly parent. ¶ *And live.* Meaning that his fatherly chastisements are adapted to secure our spiritual life. He corrects us that he may promote our final happiness, and his inflictions are the means of saving us from eternal death. 10. *For they verily for a few days.* That is, with reference to a few days (πρὸς) ; or it was a chastisement that had reference mainly to this short life. The apostle seems to bring in this circumstance to contrast the dealings of earthly parents with those of God. One of the circumstances is, that the corrections of earthly parents had a much less important object

days chastened *us* [1] after their own pleasure : but he for *our* profit,

1 or, *as seemed good*, or, *meet*, to them.

than those of God. They related to this life—a life so brief that it may be said to continue but a " few days." Yet, in order to secure the benefit to be derived for so short a period from fatherly correction, we submitted without murmuring. Much more cheerfully ought we to submit to that discipline from the hand of our heavenly Father which is designed to extend its benefits through eternity. This seems to me to afford a better sense than that adopted by Prof. Stuart and others, that it means " during our childhood or minority ;" or than that proposed by Doddridge, that it refers *both* to our earthly parents and to our heavenly Father. ¶ *After their own pleasure.* Marg. "as *seemed good*, or *meet* to them." Meaning that it was sometimes done arbitrarily, or from caprice, or under the influence of passion. This is an additional reason why we should submit to God. We submitted to our earthly parents, though their correction was sometimes passionate, and was designed to gratify their own pleasure rather than to promote our good. There is much of this kind of punishment in families ; but there is none of it under the administration of God. ¶ *But he for* our *profit.* Never from passion, from caprice, from the love of power or superiority, but always for our good. The exact benefit which he designs to produce we may not be able always to understand, but we may be assured that no other cause influences him than a desire to promote our real welfare, and as he can never be mistaken in regard to the proper means to secure that, we may be assured that our trials are always *adapted* to that end. ¶ *That* we *might be partakers of his holiness.* Become so holy that it may be said that we are partakers of the very holiness of God ; comp. 2 Pet. i. 4. This is the elevated object at which God aims by our trials. It is not that he delights to produce pain ; not that he envies us and would rob us of our little com-

that *we* might be partakers of his holiness.

11 Now no chastening for the

forts ; not that he needs what we prize to increase his own enjoyment, and therefore rudely takes it away ; and not that he acts from caprice—now conferring a blessing and then withdrawing it without any reason : it is, that he may make us more pure and holy, and thus promote our own best interest. To be holy as God is holy ; to be so holy that it may be said that we "are partakers of *his* holiness," is a richer blessing than health, and property, and friends, without it ; and when by the exchange of the one we acquire the other, we have secured infinitely more than we have lost. To obtain the greater good we should be willing to part with the less ; to secure the everlasting friendship and favour of God we should be willing, if necessary, to surrender the last farthing of our property ; the last friend that is left us ; the last feeble and fluttering pulsation of life in our veins.

11. *Now no chastening for the present seemeth to be joyous, but grievous.* It does not impart pleasure, nor is this its design. All chastisement is *intended* to produce pain, and the Christian is as sensitive to pain as others. His religion does not blunt his sensibilities and make him a stoic, but it rather *increases* his susceptibility to suffering. The Lord Jesus, probably, felt pain, reproach, and contempt more keenly than any other human being ever did ; and the Christian feels the loss of a child, or bodily suffering, as keenly as any one. But while religion does not render him insensible to suffering, it does two things—(1) it enables him to bear the pain without murmuring ; and (2) it turns the affliction into a blessing on his soul. ¶ *Nevertheless afterward.* In future life. The effect is seen in a pure life, and in a more entire devotedness to God. We are not to look for the proper fruits of affliction *while* we are suffering, but *afterwards.* ¶ *It yieldeth the peaceable fruit of righteousness.* It is a tree that bears

present seemeth to be joyous, but grievous : nevertheless, afterward it yieldeth the peaceable fruit *a* of righteousness unto them which are exercised thereby.

good fruit, and we do not expect the fruit to form and ripen at once. It may be long maturing, but it will be rich and mellow when it is ripe. It frequently requires a long time before all the results of affliction appear—as it requires months to form and ripen fruit. Like fruit it may appear at first sour, crabbed, and unpalatable ; but it will be at last like the ruddy peach or the golden orange. When those fruits *are* ripened, they are (1) fruits of *righteousness.*" They make us more holy, more dead to sin and the world, and more alive to God. And they are (2) "*peaceable.*" They produce peace, calmness, submission in the soul. They make the heart more tranquil in its confidence in God, and more disposed to promote the religion of peace. The apostle speaks of this as if it were a *universal* truth in regard to Christians who are afflicted. And it is so. There is no Christian who is not ultimately benefited by trials, and who is not able at some period subsequently to say, " It was good for me that I was afflicted. Before I was afflicted I went astray; but now have I kept thy word." When a Christian comes to die, he does not feel that he has had one trial too many, or one which he did not deserve. He can then look back and see the effect of some early trial so severe that he once thought he could hardly endure it, spreading a hallowed influence over his future years, and scattering its golden fruit all along the pathway of life. I have never known a Christian who was not benefited by afflictions ; I have seen none who was not able to say that his trials produced some happy effect on his religious character, and on his real happiness in life. If this be so, then no matter how severe our trials, we should submit to them without a murmur. The more severe they are, the more we shall yet be blessed—on earth or in heaven.

12 Wherefore lift *b* up the hands which hang down, and the feeble knees :

13 And make 1 straight *o* paths

a Is.32.17; Ja 3.18.   b Is.35.3.
1 or, *even.*   o Pr.4.26,27.

12. *Wherefore.* In view of the facts which have been now stated--that afflictions are sent from God, and are evidences of his paternal watchfulness. ¶ *Lift up the hands which hang down.* As if from weariness and exhaustion. Renew your courage ; make a new effort to bear them. The hands fall by the side when we are exhausted with toil, or worn down by disease ; see Notes on Isa. xxxv. 3, from which place this exhortation is taken. ¶ *And the feeble knees.* The knees also become enfeebled by long effort, and tremble as if their strength were gone. Courage and resolution may do much, however, to make them firm, and it is to this that the apostle exhorts those to whom he wrote. They were to make every effort to bear up under their trials. The hope of victory will do much to strengthen one almost exhausted in battle ; the desire to reach home invigorates the frame of the weary traveller. So it is with the Christian. In persecution, and sickness, and bereavement, he may be ready to sink under his burdens. The hands fall, and the knees tremble, and the heart sinks within us. But confidence in God, and the hope of heaven, and the assurance that all this is for our good, will reinvigorate the enfeebled frame, and enable us to bear what we once supposed would crush us to the dust. A courageous mind braces a feeble body, and hope makes it fresh for new conflicts.

13. *And make straight paths for your feet ;* Marg. *even.* The word here used means properly *straight,* in the sense of *upright, erect ;* Acts xiv. 10; but it is here used in the sense of straight *horizontally,* that is, *level, plain, smooth.* The meaning is, that they were to remove all obstacles out of the way, so that they need not stumble and fall. There is probably an allusion here to Prov. iv. 25—27. " Let thine eyes look right on, and

for your feet, lest that which is lame be turned out of the way ; but *a* let it rather be healed.

a Ga. 6.1.　　　b Ps.34.14.

let thine eyelids look straight before thee. Ponder the path of thy feet, and let all thy ways be established. Turn not to the right hand nor to the left ; remove thy foot from evil." The idea is, that by every proper means they were to make the way to heaven as plain and easy as possible. They were to allow no obstructions in the path over which the lame and feeble might fall. ¶ *Lest that which is lame be turned out of the way.* A lame man needs a smooth path to walk in. The idea is here, that everything which would prevent those in the church who were in any danger of falling—the feeble, the unestablished, the weak—from walking in the path to heaven, or which might be an occasion to them of falling, should be removed. Or it may mean, that in a road that was not level, those who were lame would be in danger of spraining, distorting, or wrenching a lame limb ; and the counsel is, that whatever would have a tendency to this should be removed. Divested of the figure, the passage means, that everything should be removed which would hinder any one from walking in the path to life. ¶ *But let it rather be healed.* As in the case of lameness, pains should be taken to heal it rather than to suffer it to be increased by careless exposure to a new sprain or fracture, so it should be in our religious and moral character. Whatever is defective we should endeavour to restore to soundness, rather than to suffer the defect to be increased. Whatever is feeble in our faith or hope ; whatever evil tendency there is in our hearts, we should endeavour to strengthen and amend, lest it should become worse, and we should entirely fall.

14. *Follow peace with all men.* Do not give indulgence to those passions which lead to litigations, strifes, wars; see Notes on Rom. xiv. 19 The connection here requires us to understand this mainly of persecutors. The

14 Follow peace *b* with all *men,* and holiness, without *c* which no man shall see the Lord :

c Matt.5.8; Ep.5.5.

apostle is referring to the trials which those whom he addressed were experiencing. Those trials seem to have arisen mainly from persecution, and he exhorts them to manifest a spirit of kindness towards *all*—even though they were engaged in persecuting them. This is the temper of the gospel. We are to make war with *sin*, but not with *men ;* with bad passions and corrupt desires, but not with our fellow-worms. ¶ *And holiness.* Instead of yielding to contending passions and to a spirit of war ; instead of seeking revenge on your persecutors and foes, make it rather your aim to be holy. Let *that* be the object of your pursuit; the great purpose of your life. Men might in such cases counsel them to seek revenge ; the spirit of religion would counsel them to strive to be holy. In such times they were in great danger of giving indulgence to evil passions, and hence the special propriety of the exhortation to endeavour to be holy. ¶ *Without which no man shall see the Lord.* That is, shall see him in peace ; or shall so see him as to dwell with him. *All* will see him in the day of judgment, but to " *see*" one is often used in the sense of being with one ; dwelling with one ; enjoying one ; see Notes on Matt. v. 8. The principle here stated is one which is never departed from ; Rev. xxi. 27 ; Isa. xxxv. 8 ; lii. 1 ; lx. 21 ; Joel iii. 17 ; Matt. xiii. 41 ; 1 Cor. vi. 9, 10. No one *has* ever been admitted to heaven in his sins ; nor is it desirable that any one ever should be. Desirable as it is that lost men should be happy, yet it is *benevolence* which excludes the profane, the impious, and the unbelieving from heaven—just as it is benevolence to a family to exclude profligates and seducers, and as it is benevolence to a community to confine thieves and robbers in prison. This great principle in the divine administration will *always* be adhered to ; and hence they who are expect-

15 Looking diligently *a* lest any man fail [1] of the grace of God ; lest

a 2Pet.1.   ¹ or, *fall from.*   *b* De.29.18.

ing to be saved without holiness or religion, are destined to certain disappointment. Heaven and earth will pass away, but God will not admit one unrepenting and unpardoned sinner to heaven. It was the importance and the certainty of this principle which made the apostle insist on it here with so much earnestness. Amidst all their trials ; when exposed to persecution ; and when everything might tempt them to the indulgence of feelings which were the opposite of holiness, they were to make it their great object to be like God. For this they were to seek, to strive. to labour, to pray. This with *us* in all our trials should also be the great aim of life. How deeply affecting then is the inquiry whether *we* have that holiness which is indispensable to salvation! Let us not deceive ourselves. We may have many things else—many things which are in themselves desirable, but without this *one* thing we shall never see the Lord in peace. We may have wealth, genius, learning, beauty, accomplishments, houses, lands, books, friends — but without religion they will be all in vain. Never *can* we see God in peace without a holy heart ; never can we be admitted into heaven without that religion which will identify us with the angels around the throne ! 15. *Looking diligently.* This phrase implies close attention. It is implied that there are *reasons* why we should take special care. Those reasons are found in the propensities of our hearts to evil ; in the temptations of the world ; in the allurements to apostasy presented by the great adversary of our souls. ¶ *Lest any man fail.* As every man is in danger, it is his personal duty to see to it that his salvation be secure. ¶ *Fail of the grace of God.* Marg. *fail from.* The Greek is, " lest any one *be wanting* or *lacking*"—ὑστερῶν. There is no intimation in the words used here that they already *had* grace and might fall away —whatever might be true about that

any *b* root of bitterness springing up trouble *you,* and thereby many be defiled ;

—but that there was danger that they might be found at last to be *deficient* in that religion which was necessary to save them. Whether this was to be by *losing* the religion which they now had, or by the fact that they never *had* any—however near they may have come to it — the apostle does not here intimate, and *this* passage should not be used in the discussion of the question about falling from grace. It is a proper exhortation to be addressed to any man in the church or out of it, to inquire diligently whether there is not reason to apprehend that when he comes to appear before God he will be found to be wholly destitute of religion. ¶ *Lest any root of bitterness springing up.* Any bitter root. There is doubtless an allusion here to Deut. xxix. 18. " Lest there should be among you man, or woman, or family, or tribe, whose heart turneth away this day from the Lord our God, to go and serve the gods of these nations ; lest there should be among you a root that beareth gall and wormwood." The allusion there is to those who were idolaters, and who instead of bearing the fruits of righteousness, and promoting the piety and happiness of the nation, would bear the fruits of idolatry, and spread abroad irreligion and sin. The allusion, in both cases, is to a bitter plant springing up among those that were cultivated for ornament or use, or to a tree bearing bitter and poisonous fruit, among those that produced good fruit. The reference of the apostle is to some person who should produce a similar effect in the church —to one who should inculcate false doctrines ; or who should apostatize ; or who should lead an unholy life, and thus be the means of corrupting and destroying others. They were to be at especial pains that no such person should start up from among themselves, or be tolerated by them. ¶ *Trouble you.* By his doctrines and example. ¶ *And thereby many be de-*

16 Lest there *be* any fornicator, *a* or profane person, as Esau,

a 1Cor.5.11;6.18.

who *b* for one morsel of meat sold
his birth-right.

b Gen.25.33.

filed. Led away from the faith and
corrupted. One wicked man, and especially one hypocrite in the church,
may be the means of destroying many
others.

16. *Lest there be any fornicator.*
The sin here referred to is one of
those which would spread corruption
in the church, and against which
they ought to be especially on their
guard. Allusion is made to Esau as
an example, who, himself a corrupt
and profane man, for a trifle threw
away the highest honour which as a
son he could have. Many have regarded the word here used as referring to *idolatry,* or defection from the
true religion to a false one—as the
word is often used in the Old Testament—but it is more natural to understand it literally. The crime here
mentioned was one which abounded
everywhere in ancient times, as it
does now, and it was important to
guard the church against it ; see
Notes on Acts xv. 20 ; 1 Cor. vi. 18.
¶ *Or profane person.* The word *profane* here refers to one who by word
or conduct treats religion with contempt, or has no reverence for that
which is sacred. This may be shown
by words ; by the manner ; by a
sneer ; by neglect of religion ; or
by openly renouncing the privileges
which might be connected with our
salvation. The allusion here is to
one who should openly cast off all the
hopes of religion for indulgence in
temporary pleasure, as Esau gave up
his birthright for a trifling gratification. In a similar manner, the young,
for temporary gratification, neglect
or despise all the privileges and hopes
resulting from their being born in the
bosom of the church ; from being
baptized and consecrated to God ; and
from being trained up in the lap of
piety. ¶ *As Esau.* It is clearly implied here that Esau sustained the
character of a fornicator and a profane person. The former appellation
is probably given to him to denote
his licentiousness shown by his mar-

rying many wives, and particularly
foreigners, or the daughters of Canaan : see Gen. xxxvi. 2 ; comp.
Gen. xxvi. 34, 35. The Jewish writers abundantly declare that that was
his character ; see *Wetstein, in loc.*
In proof that the latter appellation—
that of a profane person—belonged to
him, see Gen. xxv. 29—34. It is
true that it is rather by inference,
than by direct assertion, that it is
known that he sustained this character. The birth-right, in his circumstances, was a high honour. The
promise respecting the inheritance of
the land of Canaan, the coming of the
Messiah, and the preservation of the
true religion, had been given to Abraham and Isaac, and was to be transmitted by them. As the eldest son,
all the honour connected with this,
and which is now associated with the
name *Jacob,* would have properly appertained to Esau. But he undervalued it. He lived a licentious life.
He followed his corrupt propensities,
and gave the reins to indulgence. In
a time of temporary distress, also, he
showed how little he really valued all
th.s, by bartering it away for a single
meal of victuals. Rather than bear
the evils of hunger for a short period,
and evidently in a manner implying
a great undervaluing of the honour
which he held as the first-born son
in a pious line, he agreed to surrender all the privileges connected with
his birth. It was this which made
the appellation appropriate to him ;
and this will make the appellation
appropriate in any similar instance.
¶ *Who for one morsel of meat.* The
word *meat* here is used, as it is commonly in the Scriptures, in its primitive sense in English, to denote *food;*
Gen. xxv. 34. The phrase here, "morsel of meat," would be better rendered
by "a single meal." ¶ *Sold his birth-
right.* The birth-right seems to have
implied the first place or rank in the
family ; the privilege of offering sacrifice and conducting worship in the
absence or death of the father ; a

17 For ye know how that after-ward, when *a* he would have inherited the blessing, he was rejected ;

a Gen.27.34–38.

double share of the inheritance, and in this instance the honour of being in the line of the patriarchs, and transmitting the promises made to Abraham and Isaac. What Esau parted with, we can easily understand by reflecting on the honours which have clustered around the name of Jacob.

17. *For ye know how that afterward, &c.* When he came to his father, and earnestly besought him to reverse the sentence which he had pronounced ; see Gen. xxvii. 34—40. The " blessing" here referred to was not that of the birth-right, which he knew he could not regain, but that pronounced by the father Isaac on him whom he regarded as his first-born son. This Jacob obtained by fraud, when Isaac really *meant* to bestow it on Esau. Isaac appears to have been ignorant wholly of the bargain which Jacob and Esau had made in regard to the birth-right, and Jacob and his mother contrived in this way to have that confirmed which Jacob had obtained of Esau by contract. The sanction of the father, it seems, was necessary, before it could be made sure, and Rebecca and Jacob understood that the dying blessing of the aged patriarch would establish it all. It was obtained by dishonesty on the part of Jacob ; but so far as Esau was concerned, it was an act of righteous retribution for the little regard he had shown for the honour of his birth. ¶ *For he found no place of repentance.* Marg. *"Way to change his mind,"* That is, no place for repentance *in the mind of Isaac,* or no way to change *his* mind. It does not mean that Esau earnestly sought to repent and could not, but that when once the blessing had passed the lips of his father, he found it impossible to change it. Isaac firmly declared that he *had pronounced* the blessing, and though it had been obtained by fraud, yet as it was of the nature of a divine prediction, it *could* not now be changed.

for he found no place [1] of repentance, though he sought it carefully with tears.

1 or, *way to change his mind.*

He had not indeed intended that it should be thus. He had pronounced a blessing on another which had been designed for him. But still the benediction had been given. The prophetic words had been pronounced. By divine direction the *truth* had been spoken, and how *could* it be changed? It was impossible now to reverse the divine purposes in the case, and hence the "blessing" must stand as it had been spoken. Isaac did, however, all that *could* be done. He *gave* a benediction to his son Esau, though of far inferior value to that which he had pronounced on the fraudulent Jacob ; Gen. xxvii. 39, 40. ¶ *Though he sought it carefully with tears;* Gen. xxvii. 34. He sought to change the purpose of his father, but could not do it. The meaning and bearing of this passage, as used by the apostle, may be easily understood. (1.) The decision of God on the human character and destiny will soon be pronounced. That decision will be according to truth, and cannot be changed. (2.) If we should despise our privileges as Esau did his birth-right, and renounce our religion, it would be impossible to recover what we had lost. There would be no possibility of changing the divine decision in the case, for it would be determined for ever. This passage, therefore, should not be alleged to show that a sinner *cannot* repent, or that he cannot find " place for repentance," or assistance to enable him to repent, or that tears and sorrow for sin would be of no avail, for it teaches none of these things ; but it *should* be used to keep us from disregarding our privileges, from turning away from the true religion, from slighting the favours of the gospel, and from neglecting religion till death comes ; because when God has once pronounced a sentence excluding us from his favour, no tears, or pleading, or effort of our own can change *him.* The sentence which *he* pronounces on the scoffer, the impen-

18 For ye are not come unto the *a* mount that might be touched, and that burned with fire, nor unto blackness, and darkness, and tempest,

a Ex.19,12—19.

19 And the sound of a trumpet, and the voice of words ; *a* which *voice* they that heard, entreated that the word should not be spoken to them any more :

a Ex.20.18,19.

itent, the hypocrite, and the apostate, is one that will abide for ever without change. This passage, therefore, is in accordance with the doctrine more than once stated before in this epistle, that if a Christian should really apostatize it would be impossible that he should be saved ; see Notes on ch. vi. 1—6.

18. *For ye are not come.* To enforce the considerations already urged, the apostle introduces this sublime comparison between the old and new dispensations ; vers. 18—24. The object, in accordance with the principal scope of the epistle, is, to guard them against apostasy. To do this, he shows that under the new dispensation there was much more to bind them to fidelity, and to make apostasy dangerous, than there was under the old. The main point of the comparison is, that under the Jewish dispensation, everything was adapted to awe the mind, and to restrain by the exhibition of grandeur and of power ; but that under the Christian dispensation, while there was as much that was sublime, there was much more that was adapted to win and hold the affections. There were revelations of higher truths. There were more affecting motives to lead to obedience. There was that of which the former was but the type and emblem. There was the clear revelation of the glories of heaven, and of the blessed society there, all adapted to prompt to the earnest desire that they might be our own. The considerations presented in this passage constitute the climax of the argument so beautifully pursued through this epistle, showing that the Christian system was far superior in every respect to the Jewish. In presenting this closing argument, the apostle first refers to some of the circumstances attending the former dispensation which were designed to keep the people of God from aposta-

sy, and then the considerations of su perior weight existing under the Christian economy. ¶ *The mount that might be touched.* Mount Sinai. The meaning here is, that *that* mountain was *palpable, material, touchable*—in contradistinction from the Mount Zion to which the church had now come, which is above the reach of the external senses ; ver. 22. The apostle does not mean that it was *permitted* to the Israelites to touch Mount Sinai—for this was strictly forbidden, Ex. xix. 12 ; but he evidently alludes to that prohibition, and means to say that a command forbidding them to "*touch*" the mountain, implied that it was a material or palpable object. The sense of the passage is, that every circumstance that occurred there was fitted to fill the soul with terror. Everything accompanying the giving of the law, the setting of bounds around the mountain which they might not pass, and the darkness and tempest on the mountain itself, was adopted to overawe the soul. The phrase " the *touchable* mountain"—if such a phrase is proper—would express the meaning of the apostle here. The "Mount Zion" to which the church now has come, is of a different character. It is not thus visible and palpable. It is not enveloped in smoke and flame, and the thunders of the Almighty do not roll and re-echo among its lofty peaks as at Horeb ; yet it presents *stronger* motives to perseverance in the service of God. ¶ *And that burned with fire ;* Ex. xix. 18 ; comp. Deut. iv. 11 ; xxxiii. 2. ¶ *Nor unto blackness, and darkness, and tempest ;* see Ex. xix. 16.

19. *And the voice of a trumpet ;* Ex. xix. 19. The sound of the trumpet amidst the tempest was fitted to increase the terror of the scene. ¶ *And the voice of words.* Spoken by God ; Ex. xix. 19. It is easy to conceive what must have been the awe

20 (For they could not endure that which was commanded, ^a And if so much as a beast touch the

a Ex.19.12,13.

produced by a voice uttered from the midst of the tempest so distinct as to be heard by the hundreds of thousands of Israel, when the speaker was invisible. ¶ *Which* voice *they that heard*, &c.; Ex. xx. 18, 19. It was so fearful and overpowering that the people earnestly prayed that if they must be addressed, it might be by the familiar voice of Moses and not by the awful voice of the Deity.

20. *For they could not endure that which was commanded.* They could not sustain the awe produced by the fact that God uttered his commands himself. The meaning is not that the commands themselves were intolerable, but that the *manner* in which they were communicated inspired a terror which they could not bear. They feared that they should die ; Ex. xx. 19. ¶ *And if so much as a beast touch the mountain, it shall be stoned ;* Ex. xix. 13. The prohibition was, that neither beast nor man should touch it on pain of death. The punishment was to be either by stoning, or being "shot through." ¶ *Or thrust through with a dart;* Ex. xix. 13. " Or shot through." This phrase, however, though it is found in the common editions of the New Testament, is wanting in all the more valuable manuscripts ; in all the ancient versions ; and it occurs in none of the Greek ecclesiastical writers, with one exception. It is omitted now by almost all editors of the New Testament. It is beyond all doubt an addition of later times, taken from the Septuagint of Ex. xix. 13. Its omission does not injure the sense.

21. *And so terrible was the sight,* that *Moses said,* &c. This is not recorded in the account of the giving of the law in Exodus, and it has been made a question on what authority the apostle made this declaration respecting Moses. In Deut. ix. 19, Moses indeed says, of himself, after he had come down from the mountain, and had broken the two tables of

mountain, it shall be stoned, or thrust through with a dart.

21 And so terrible was the sight,

stone that were in his hand, that he was greatly afraid of the anger of the Lord on account of the sin of the people. " I was afraid of the anger and hot displeasure wherewith the Lord was wroth against you to destroy you ;" and it has been supposed by many that this is the passage to which the apostle here alludes. But it is very evident that was spoken on a different occasion from the one which is referred to in the passage before us. That was *after* the law was promulgated, and Moses had descended from the mount ; and it was not said in view of the terrors of the scene *when* the law was given, but of the apprehension of the wrath of God against the people for their sin in making the golden calf. I know not how to explain this, except by the supposition that the apostle here refers to some tradition that the scene produced this effect on his mind. In itself it is not improbable that Moses thus trembled with alarm (comp. Ex. xix. 16), nor that the remembrance of it should have been handed down among the numerous traditions which the Jews transmitted from age to age. There must have been many things that occurred in their journey through the wilderness which are not recorded in the Books of Moses. Many of them would be preserved naturally in the memory of the people, and transmitted to their posterity ; and though those truths might become intermingled with much that was fabulous, yet it is not irrational to suppose that an inspired writer may have adduced pertinent and true examples from these traditions of what actually occurred. It was one method of preserving *the truth*, thus to select such instances of what actually took place from the mass of traditions which were destined to perish, as would be useful in future times. The circumstance here mentioned was greatly fitted to increase the impression of

that Moses said, I exceedingly fear and quake :)

22 But ye are come unto Mount Sion, and unto the city *a* of the

living God, the heavenly Jerusalem, and to an innumerabl company of angels, *b*

a Re.3.12.　　　　*b* Ps. 68.17.

the sublimity and fearfulness of the scene. Moses was accustomed to commune with God. He had met him at the "bush," and had been addressed by him face to face, and yet so awful were the scenes at Horeb that even *he* could not bear it with composure. What may we then suppose to have been the alarm of the body of the people, when the mind of the great leader himself was thus overpowered! 22. *But ye are come unto Mount Sion.* You who are Christians ; all who are under the new dispensation. The design is to *contrast* the Christian dispensation with the Jewish, and to show that its excellencies and advantages were far superior to the religion of their fathers. It had more to win the affections ; more to elevate the soul ; more to inspire with hope. It had less that was terrific and alarming ; it appealed less to the fears and more to the hopes of mankind ; but still apostasy from this religion could not be less terrible in its consequences than apostasy from the religion of Moses. In the passage before us, the apostle evidently contrasts Sinai with Mount Zion, and means to say that there was more about the latter that was adapted to win the heart and to preserve allegiance than there was about the former. Mount Zion literally denoted the Southern hill in Jerusalem, on which a part of the city was built. That part of the city made by David and his successors the residence of the court, and soon the name *Zion* was given familiarly to the whole city. Jerusalem was the centre of religion in the land ; the place where the temple stood, and where the worship of God was celebrated, and where God dwelt by a visible symbol, and it became the type and emblem of the holy abode where He dwells in heaven. It cannot be literally meant here that they had come to the Mount Zion in Jerusalem, for that was as true of the whole Jewish people as of those whom the apos-

tle addressed, but it must mean that they had come to the Mount Zion of which the holy city was an emblem ; to the glorious mount which is revealed as the dwelling-place of God, of angels, of saints. That is, they had " come" to this by the revelations and hopes of the gospel. They were not indeed literally in heaven, nor was that glorious city literally on earth, but the dispensation to which they had been brought was that which conducted them directly up to the city of the living God, and to the holy mount where he dwelt above. The view was not confined to an earthly mountain enveloped in smoke and flame, but opened at once on the holy place where God abides. By the phrase, "ye *are* come," the apostle means that this was the characteristic of the new dispensation that it conducted them there, and that they were already in fact inhabitants of that glorious city. They were citizens of the heavenly Jerusalem (comp. Note Phil. iii. 20), and were entitled to its privileges. ¶ *And unto the city of the living God.* The city where the living God dwells—the heavenly Jerusalem : comp. Notes on ch. xi. 10. God dwelt by a visible symbol in the temple at Jerusalem—and to *that* his people came under the old dispensation. In a more literal and glorious sense his abode is in heaven, and to *that* his people have now come. ¶ *The heavenly Jerusalem.* Heaven is not unfrequently represented as a magnificent city where God and angels dwell ; and the Christian revelation discloses this to Christians as certainly their final home. They should regard themselves already as dwellers in that city, and live and act *as if* they saw its splendour and partook of its joy. In regard to this representation of heaven as *a city* where God dwells, the following places may be consulted : Heb. xi. 10, 14—16 ; xii. 28 ; xiii. 14 ; Gal. iv. 26 ; Rev. iii. 12 ; xxi. 2, 10—27. It is true that

23 To the general assembly
and church of the first-born, *a*
which are ¹ written *b* in heaven,
a Re.14.4.   1 or, *enrolled*.   b Lu.10.20.

and to God, the Judge *c* of all,
and to the spirits of just *d* men
made perfect,
c Gen.18.25.   d 1 Cor.15.49,54.

Christians have not yet *seen* that city
by the bodily eye, but they look to it
with the eye of faith. It is revealed
to them ; they are permitted by anticipation to contemplate its glories,
and to feel that it is to be their eternal home. They are permitted to
live and act *as if* they saw the glorious God whose dwelling is there, and
were already surrounded by the angels and the redeemed. The apostle
does not represent them as if they
were expecting that it would be visi-
bly set up on the earth, but as being
now actually dwellers in that city,
and bound to live and act *as if* they
were amidst its splendours. ¶ *And
to an innumerable company of angels.*
The Greek here is, "to myriads [or
ten thousands] of angels in an assembly or joyful convocation." The
phrase "tens of thousands" is often
used to denote a great and indefinite
number. The word rendered "general assemb'y," (ver. 22)—πανήγυρις—
refers properly to an "assembly, or
convocation of the whole people in
order to celebrate any public festival
or solemnity, as the public games or
sacrifices ; *Rob. Lex.* It occurs nowhere else in the New Testament,
and refers here to the angels viewed
as assembled around the throne of
God and celebrating his praises. It
should be regarded as connected with
the word *angels*, referring to *their*
convocation in heaven, and not to the
church of the first-born. This construction is demanded by the Greek.
Our common translation renders it as
if it were to be united with the church
—"to the general assembly *and* church
of the first-born ;" but the Greek will
not admit of this construction. The
interpretation which unites it with
the *angels* is adopted now by almost
all critics, and in almost all the editions of the New Testament. On the
convocation of angels, see Notes on
Job i. 6. The writer intends, doubtless, to contrast that joyful assem-
blage of the angels in heaven with

those who appeared in the giving of
the law on Mount Sinai. God is always represented as surrounded by
hosts of angels in heaven ; see Deut.
xxxiii. 2 ; 1 Kings xxii. 19 ; Dan. vii.
10 ; Ps. lxviii. 17; comp. Notes Heb.
xii. 1 ; see also Rev. v. 11.; Matt. xxvi.
53 ; Luke ii. 13. The meaning is,
that under the Christian dispensation
Christians in their feelings and worship become united to this vast host
of holy angelic beings. It is, of
course, not meant that they are *visible*, but they are seen by the eye of
faith. The *argument* here is, that as,
in virtue of the Christian revelation,
we become associated with those pure
and happy spirits, we should not apostatize from such a religion, for we
should regard it as honourable and
glorious to be identified with them.
    23. *To the general assembly ;* see
Notes on ver. 22. ¶ *And church of
the first-born.* That is, you are united
with the church of the first-born.
They who were first-born among the
Hebrews enjoyed peculiar privileges,
and especially pre-eminence of rank ;
see Notes on Col. i. 15. The reference here is, evidently, to those saints
who had been distinguished for their
piety, and who may be supposed to
be exalted to peculiar honours in heaven—such as the patriarchs, prophets,
martyrs. The meaning is, that by
becoming Christians, we have become
in fact identified with that happy and
honoured church, and that this is a
powerful motive to induce us to persevere. It is a consideration which
should make us adhere to our religion
amidst all temptations and persecutions, that we are identified with the
most eminently holy men who have
lived, and that we are to share their
honours and their joys. The Christian is united in feeling,, in honour,
and in destiny, with the excellent of
all the earth, and of all times. He
should feel it, therefore, an honour t:
be a Christian ; he should yield to no
temptation which would induce him

24 And to Jesus the *a* Mediator of the new covenant, [1] and to the

a ch.8.6.   [1] or, *testament.*

blood *b* of sprinkling, that speaketh better things than *that of* Abel.*c*

b Ex.24.8.   *c* Gen 4.10.

to part from so goodly a fellowship. ¶ *Which are written in heaven.* Marg. *enrolled.* The word here was employed by the Greeks to denote that one was enrolled as a citizen, or entitled to the privileges of citizenship. Here it means that the names of the persons referred to were registered or enrolled among the inhabitants of the heavenly world; see Notes, Luke x. 20. ¶ *And to God the Judge of all.* God, who will pronounce the final sentence on all mankind. The object of the reference here to God as *judge* does not appear to be to contrast the condition of Christians with that of the Jews, as is the case in some of the circumstances alluded to, but to bring impressively before their minds the fact that they sustained a peculiarly near relation to him from whom all were to receive their final allotment. As the destiny of all depended on him, they should be careful not to provoke his wrath. The design of the apostle seems to be to give a rapid glance of what there was in heaven, as disclosed by the eye of faith to the Christian, which should operate as a motive to induce him to persevere in his Christian course. The thought that seems to have struck his mind in regard to God was, that he would do right to all. They had, therefore, everything to fear if they revolted from him; they had everything to hope if they bore their trials with patience, and persevered to the end. ¶ *And to the spirits of just men made perfect.* Not only to the more eminent saints—the "church of the first-born"—but to *all* who were made perfect in heaven. They were not only united with the imperfect Christians on earth, but with those who have become completely delivered from sin, and admitted to the world of glory. This is a consideration which ought to influence the minds of all believers. They are even now united with *all* the redeemed in heaven. They should so live as not to be separated from them in the final day. Most Chris-

tians have among the redeemed already not a few of their most tenderly beloved friends. A father may be there; a mother, a sister, a smiling babe. It should be a powerful motive with us so to live as to be prepared to be reunited with them in heaven. 24. *And to Jesus the Mediator of the new covenant.* This was the crowning excellence of the new dispensation in contradistinction from the old. They had been made acquainted with the true Messiah; they were united to him by faith; they had been sprinkled with his blood; see Notes on ch. vii. 22, and ch. viii. 6. The highest consideration which can be urged to induce any one to persevere in a life of piety is the fact that the Son of God has come into the world and died to save sinners; comp. Notes on vers. 2—4 of this chapter. ¶ *And to the blood of sprinkling.* The blood which Jesus shed, and which is sprinkled upon us to ratify the covenant; see Notes on ch. ix. 18—23. ¶ *That speaketh better things than* that of *Abel.* Gr. "Than Abel;" the words "*that of*" being supplied by the translators. In the original there is no reference to the blood of Abel shed by Cain, as our translators seem to have supposed, but the allusion is to the faith of Abel, or to the testimony which he bore to a great and vital truth of religion. The meaning here is, that the blood of Jesus speaks better things than Abel did; that is, that the blood of Jesus is the *reality* of which the offering of Abel was a *type.* Abel proclaimed by the sacrifice which he made the great truth that salvation could be only by a bloody offering—but he did this only in a typical and obscure manner; Jesus proclaimed it in a more distinct and better manner by the reality. The object here is to compare the Redeemer with Abel, not in the sense that the blood shed in either case calls for vengeance, but that salvation by blood is more clearly revealed in the Christian plan than in the ancient history; and

25 See that ye refuse not him
that speaketh. For if they escaped not who refused him that spake
on earth, much more *shall not* we

hence illustrating, in accordance with
the design of this epistle, the superior
excellency of the Christian scheme
over all which had preceded it. There
were *other* points of resemblance between Abel and the Redeemer, but on
them the apostle does not insist. Abel
was a martyr, and so was Christ ;
Abel was cruelly murdered, and so
was Christ ; there was aggravated
guilt in the murder of Abel by his
brother, and so there was in that
of Jesus by his brethren — his own
countrymen ; the blood of Abel called
for vengeance, and was followed by
a fearful penalty on Cain, and so was
the death of the Redeemer on his murderers—for they said, " his blood be on
us and on our children," and are
yet suffering under the fearful malediction then invoked ;—but the point of
contrast here is, that the blood of Jesus makes a more full, distinct, and
clear proclamation of the truth that
salvation is by blood than the offering
made by Abel did. The apostle alludes here to what he had said in ch.
xi. 4; see Notes on that verse. Such
is the contrast between the former
and the latter dispensations; and such
the motives to perseverance presented
by both. In the former, the Jewish,
all was imperfect, terrible, and alarming. In the latter, everything was
comparatively mild, winning, alluring, animating. Terror was not the
principal element, but heaven was
opened to the eye of faith, and the
Christian was permitted to survey the
Mount Zion ; the New Jerusalem ;
the angels ; the redeemed ; the blessed
God ; the glorious Mediator, and to
feel that that blessed abode was to be
his home. To that happy world he
was tending ; and with all these pure
and glorious beings he was identified.
Having stated and urged this argument, the apostle in the remainder
of the chapter warns those whom he
addressed in a most solemn manner
against a renunciation of their Christian faith

escape if we turn away from him
that *speaketh* from heaven :
26 Whose voice then shook the
earth : but now he hath promised,

25. *See that ye refuse not.* That
you do not reject or disregard. ¶ *Him
that speaketh.* That is, in the gospel.
Do not turn away from him who has
addressed you in the new dispensation, and called you to obey and serve
him. The meaning is, that God had
addressed *them* in the gospel as really
as he had done the Hebrews on Mount
Sinai, and that there was as much to
be dreaded in disregarding his voice
now as there was then. He does not
speak, indeed, amidst lightnings, and
thunders, and clouds, but he speaks
by every message of mercy ; by every
invitation ; by every tender appeal.
He spake by his Son (ch. i. 1) ; he
speaks by the Holy Spirit, and by all
his calls and warnings in the gospel.
¶ *For if they escaped not.* If they
who heard God under the old dispensation, who refused to obey him, were
cut off ; Notes ch. x. 28. ¶ *Who refused him that spake on earth.* That
is, Moses. The contrast here is between Moses and the Son of God—
the head of the Jewish and the head
of the Christian dispensation. Moses
was a mere man, and spake as such,
though in the name of God. The Son
of God was from above, and spake as
an inhabitant of heaven. ¶ *Much
more*, &c. ; see Notes on ch. ii. 2, 3 ;
x. 29.
26. *Whose voice then shook the earth.*
When he spake at Mount Sinai. The
meaning is, that the mountain and
the region around quaked ; Ex. xix.
18. The "voice" here referred to is
that of God speaking from the holy
mount. ¶ *But now hath he promised,
saying.* The words here quoted are
taken from Haggai ii. 6, where they
refer to the changes which would take
place under the Messiah. The meaning is, that there would be great revolutions in his coming, as *if* the
universe were shaken to its centre.
The apostle evidently applies this
passage as it is done in Haggai, to
the first advent of the Redeemer.
¶ *I shake not the earth only.* This is

saying, ^a Yet once more I shake | 27 And this *word,* Yet once
not the earth only, but also heaven. | ^a Hag. 2.6.

not quoted literally from the Hebrew, but the sense is retained. In Haggai it is, "Yet once it is a little while, and I will shake the heavens and the earth, and the sea, and the dry land; and I will shake all nations, and the desire of all nations shall come." The apostle lays emphasis on the fact that not only the *earth* was to be shaken but also *heaven.* The shaking of the earth here evidently refers to the commotions among the nations that would prepare the way for the coming of the Messiah. ¶ *But also heaven.* This may refer either (1) to the extraordinary phenomena in the heavens at the birth, the death, and the ascension of Christ; or (2) to the revolutions in morals and religion which would be caused by the introduction of the gospel, as if everything were to be changed—expressed by "a shaking of the heavens and the earth;" or (3) it may be more literally taken as denoting that there was a remarkable agitation in the heavens—in the bosoms of its inhabitants—arising from a fact so wonderful as that the Son of God should descend to earth, suffer, and die. I see no reason to doubt that the latter idea may have been included here; and the meaning of the whole then is, that while the giving of the law at Mount Sinai, fearful and solemn as it was, was an event that merely shook the earth in the vicinity of the holy Mount, the introduction of the gospel agitated the universe. Great changes upon the earth were to precede it; one revolution was to succeed another preparatory to it, and the whole universe would be moved at an event so extraordinary. The meaning is, that the introduction of the gospel was a much more solemn and momentous thing than the giving of the law—and that, therefore, it was much more fearful and dangerous to apostatize from it.

27. *And this* word, Yet once *more.* That is, this reference to a great agitation or commotion in some future time. This is designed as an explanation of the prophecy in Haggai,

and the idea is, that there would be such agitations that everything which was not fixed on a permanent and immovable basis would be thrown down as in an earthquake. Everything which was temporary in human institutions; everything which was wrong in customs and morals; and everything in the ancient system of religion, which was merely of a preparatory and typical character, would be removed. What was of permanent value would be retained, and a kingdom would be established which nothing could move. The effect of the gospel would be to overturn everything which was of a temporary character in the previous system, and everything in morals which was not founded on a solid basis, and to set up in the place of it principles which no revolution and no time could change. The coming of the Saviour, and the influence of his religion on mankind, had this effect in such respects as the following. (1.) All that was of a sound and permanent nature in the Jewish economy was retained; all that was typical and temporary was removed. The whole mass of sacrifices and ceremonies that were designed to prefigure the Messiah of course then ceased; all that was of permanent value in the law of God, and in the principles of religion, was incorporated in the new system, and perpetuated. (2.) The same is true in regard to morals. There was much truth on the earth before the time of the Saviour; but it was intermingled with much that was false. The effect of his coming has been to distinguish what is true and what is false; to give permanency to the one, and to cause the other to vanish. (3.) The same is true of religion. There are some views of religion which men have by nature which are correct; there are many which are false. The Christian religion gives permanence and stability to the one, and causes the other to disappear. And in general, it may be remarked, that the effect of Christianity is to give sta-

more, signifieth the removing of those things that are [1] shaken, as of things that are made, that those

1 or, *may be.*

bility to all that is founded on truth, and to drive error from the world. Christ came that he might destroy all the systems of error—that is, all that *could* be shaken on earth, and to confirm all that is true. The result of all will be that he will preside over a *permanent* kingdom, and that his people will inherit " a kingdom which cannot be moved"; ver. 28. ¶ *The removing of those things that are shaken.* Marg. more correctly *"may be."* The meaning is, that those principles of religion and morals which were not founded on truth would be removed by his coming. ¶ *As of things that are made.* Much perplexity has been felt by expositors in regard to this phrase, but the meaning seems to be plain. The apostle is contrasting the things which are fixed and stable with those which are temporary in their nature, or which are settled on no firm foundation. The former he speaks of as if they were uncreated and eternal principles of truth and righteousness. The latter he speaks of as if they were *created*, and therefore liable," like all things which are "made," to decay, to change, to dissolution. ¶ *That those things which cannot be shaken may remain.* The eternal principles of truth, and law, and righteousness. These would enter into the new kingdom which was to be set up, and of course *that* kingdom would be permanent. These are not changed or modified by time, circumstances, human opinions, or laws. They remain the same from age to age, in every land, and in all worlds. They have been permanent in all the fluctuations of opinion; in all the varied forms of government on earth; in all the revolutions of states and empires. To bring out these is the result of the events of divine Providence, and the object of the coming of the Redeemer; and on these principles that great kingdom is to be reared which is to endure for ever and ever.

things which cannot be shaken may remain.

28 Wherefore we receiving a

. 28. *Wherefore we receiving a kingdom which cannot be moved.* We who are Christians. We pertain to a kingdom that is permanent and unchanging. The meaning is, that the kingdom of the Redeemer is never to pass away. It is not like the Jewish dispensation, to give place to another, nor is there any power that can destroy it; see Notes on Matt. xvi. 18. It has *now* endured for eighteen hundred years, amidst all the revolutions on earth, and in spite of all the attempts which have been made to destroy it; and it is now as vigorous and stable as it ever was. The past has shown that there is no power of earth or hell that can destroy it, and that in the midst of all revolutions this kingdom still survives. Its great principles and laws will endure on earth to the end of time, and will be made permanent in heaven. This is the *only* kingdom in which we can be certain that there will be no revolution; the only empire which is destined never to fall. ¶ *Let us have grace, whereby we may serve God.* Marg. " *let us hold fast.*" The Greek is, literally, *let us have grace;* the meaning is, " let us hold fast the grace or favour which we have received in being admitted to the privileges of that kingdom." The object of the apostle is, to keep them in the reverent fear and service of God. The *argument* which he presents is, that this kingdom is permanent. There is no danger of its being overthrown. It is to continue on earth to the end of time; it is to be established in heaven for ever. If it were temporary, changeable, liable to be overthrown at any moment, there would be much less encouragement to perseverance. But in a kingdom like this there is every encouragement, for there is the assurance (1) that all our interests there are safe; (2) that all our exertions will be crowned with ultimate success, (3) that the efforts which we make to do

kingdom which cannot be moved, let us [1] have grace, whereby we way serve God acceptably with reverence and godly fear :

29 For [a] our God *is* a consuming fire.

1 or, *hold fast.*   a De.4.24.

good will have a permanent influence on mankind, and will bless future ages; and (4) that the reward is certain. A man subject to a government about whose continuance there would be the utmost uncertainty, would have little encouragement to labour with a view to any permanent interest. In a government where nothing is settled; where all policy is changing, and where there are constantly vacillating plans, there is no inducement to enter on any enterprise demanding time and risk. But where the policy is settled; where the principles and the laws are firm; where there is evidence of permanency, there is the highest encouragement. The highest possible encouragement of this kind is in the permanent and established kingdom of God. All other governments may be revolutionized; this never will be : — all others may have a changeful policy; this has none : — all others will be overthrown; this never will. ¶ *With reverence and godly fear.* With true veneration for God, and with pious devotedness.

29. *For our God is a consuming fire.* This is a further reason why we should serve God with profound reverence and unwavering fidelity. The quotation is made from Deut. iv. 24. "For the LORD thy God is a consuming fire, even a jealous God." The object of the apostle here seems to be, to show that there was the same reason for fearing the displeasure of God under the new dispensation which there was under the old. It was the same God who was served. There had been no change in his attributes, or in the principles of his government. He was no more the friend of sin now than he was then; and the same perfections of his nature which would then lead him to punish transgression would also lead him to do it now.

CHAPTER XIII.

LET brotherly [b] love continue.
2 Be not forgetful to entertain strangers : for thereby some [c] have entertained angels unawares.

b 1Pet.1.22; 1John4.7,20.   c Gen.18.3; 19.2.

His anger was really as terrible, and as much to be dreaded as it was at Mount Sinai; and the destruction which he would inflict on his foes would be as terrible now as it was then. The fearfulness with which he would come forth to destroy the wicked might be compared to a *fire* that consumed all before it; see Notes, Mark ix. 44—46. The image here is a most fearful one, and is in accordance with all the representations of God in the Bible and with all that we see in the divine dealings with wicked men, that punishment as inflicted by him is awful and overwhelming. So it was on the old world; on the cities of the plain; on the hosts of Sennacherib; and on Jerusalem—and so it has been in the calamities of pestilence, war, flood, and famine with which God has visited guilty men. By all these tender and solemn considerations, therefore, the apostle urges the friends of God to perseverance and fidelity in his service. His goodness and mercy; the gift of a Saviour to redeem us; the revelation of a glorious world; the assurance that all may soon be united in fellowship with the angels and the redeemed; the certainty that the kingdom of the Saviour is established on a permanent basis, and the apprehension of the dreadful wrath of God against the guilty, all should lead us to persevere in the duties of our Christian calling, and to avoid those things which would jeopard the eternal interests of our souls.

CHAPTER XIII.
ANALYSIS OF THE CHAPTER.

The closing chapter of this epistle is made up almost entirely of exhortations to the performance of various practical duties. The exhortations relate to the following points : brotherly love, ver. 1; hospitality, ver. 2; sympathy with those in bonds, ver.

3 Remember them that are in bonds, *a* as bound with them ; *and*

a Matt. 25. 36.

3 ; fidelity in the marriage relation, ver. 4; contentment, vers. 5, 6 ; submission to those in authority, vers. 7, 8 ; stability in the doctrines of religion, vers. 9—15 ; benevolence, ver. 16; obedience to those entrusted with office, ver. 17 ; and special prayer for him who wrote this epistle, vers. 18, 19. The epistle then closes with a beautiful and impressive benediction, vers. 20, 21 ; with an entreaty that they would receive with favour what had been written, ver. 22 ; with the grateful announcement that Timothy, in whom they doubtless felt a great interest, was set at liberty, ver. 23 ; and with a salutation to all the saints, ver. 24, 25.

1. *Let brotherly love continue.* Implying that it now existed among them. The apostle had no occasion to reprove them for the want of it, as he had in regard to some to whom he wrote, but he aims merely to impress on them the importance of this virtue, and to caution them against the danger of allowing it ever to be interrupted ; see Notes on John xiii. 34.

2. *Be not forgetful to entertain strangers.* On the duty of hospitality, see a full explanation in the Notes on Rom. xii. 13. ¶ *For thereby some have entertained angels unawares.* Without knowing that they were angels. As Abraham (Gen. xviii. 2, seq.), and Lot did ; Gen. xix. The *motive* here urged for doing it is, that by entertaining the stranger we may perhaps be honoured with the presence of those whose society will be to us an honour and a blessing. It is not well for us to miss the opportunity of the presence, the conversation, and the prayers of the good. The influence of such guests in a family is worth more than it costs to entertain them. If there is danger that we may sometimes receive those of an opposite character, yet it is not wise on account of such possible danger, to lose the opportunity of entertaining those whose presence would be a blessing. Many a parent owes the conversion of a child to the influ-

ence of a pious stranger in his family; and the hope that this *may* occur, or that our own souls may be blessed, should make us ready, at all proper times, to welcome the feet of the stranger to our doors. Many a man, if he had been accosted as Abraham was at the door of his tent by strangers, would have turned them rudely away ; many a one in the situation of Lot would have sent the unknown guests rudely from his door ; but who can estimate what would have been the results of such a course on the destiny of those good men and their families ? For a great number of instances in which the heathen were supposed to have entertained the *gods*, though unknown to them, see Wetstein *in loc.*

3. *Remember them that are in bonds.* All who are *bound ;* whether prisoners of war ; captives in dungeons ; those detained in custody for trial ; those who are imprisoned for righteousness' sake, or those held in slavery. The word used here will include *all* instances where *bonds, shackles, chains* were ever used. Perhaps there is an immediate allusion to their fellow-Christians who were suffering imprisonment on account of their religion, of whom there were doubtless many at that time, but the *principle* will apply to every case of those who are imprisoned or oppressed. The word *remember* implies more than that we are merely to *think* of them ; comp. Ex. xx. 8 ; Eccl. xii. 1. It means that we are to remember them *with appropriate sympathy;* or as we should wish others to remember us if we were in their circumstances. That is, we are (1) to feel deep compassion for them ; (2) we are to remember them in our prayers ; (3) we are to remember them, as far as practicable, with aid for their relief. Christianity teaches us to sympathize with all the oppressed, the suffering, and the sad ; and there are more of this class than we commonly suppose, and they have stronger claims on our sympathy than we commonly realize. In America

them which suffer adversity, as being yourselves also in the body.

there are not far from *ten thousand* confined in prison—the father separated from his children ; the husband from his wife ; the brother from his sister ; and all cut off from the living world. Their fare is coarse, and their couches hard, and the ties which bound them to the living world are rudely snapped asunder. Many of them are in solitary dungeons ; all of them are sad and melancholy men. True, they are there for crime ; but they are men —they are our brothers. They have still the feelings of our common humanity, and many of them *feel* their separation from wife, and children, and home, as keenly as we would. That God who has mercifully made our lot different from theirs, has commanded us to sympathize with them—and we should sympathize all the more when we remember that but for *his* restraining grace we should have been in the same condition. There are in this land of "liberty" also nearly three millions who are held in the hard bondage of slavery. There is the father, the mother, the child, the brother, the sister. They are held as property ; liable to be sold ; having no right to the avails of their own labour ; exposed to the danger of having the tenderest ties sundered at the will of their master; shut out from the privilege of reading the word of God ; fed on coarse fare ; living in wretched hovels ; and often subjected to the painful inflictions of the lash at the caprice of a passionate driver. Wives and daughters are made the victims of degrading sensuality without the power of resistance or redress; the security of home is unknown ; and they are dependent on the will of another man whether they shall or shall not worship their Creator. We should remember them, and sympathize with them as if they were *our* fathers, mothers, sisters, brothers, or sons and daughters. Though of different colour, yet the same blood flows in their veins as in ours (Acts xvii. 26) ; they are bone of our bone, and flesh of our flesh. By nature they

4 Marriage *a is* honourable in

a Pr.5.15—23.

have the same right to "life, liberty, and the pursuit of happiness" which we and our children have, and to deprive *them* of that right is as unjust as it would be to deprive *us* and *ours* of it. They have a *claim* on our sympathy, for they are our brethren. They *need* it, for they are poor and helpless. They should have it, for the same God who has kept *us* from that hard lot has commanded us to remember *them*. That kind remembrance of them should be shown in every practicable way. By prayer ; by plans contemplating their freedom ; by efforts to send them the gospel ; by diffusing abroad the principles of liberty and of the rights of man, by using our influence to arouse the public mind in their behalf, we should endeavour to relieve those who are in bonds, and to hasten the time when "the oppressed shall go free." On this subject, see Notes on Isa. ch. lviii. 6. ¶ *As bound with them.* There is great force and beauty in this expression. Religion teaches us to identify ourselves with all who are oppressed, and to feel what they suffer as if we endured it ourselves. Infidelity and atheism are cold and distant. They stand aloof from the oppressed and the sad. But Christianity unites all hearts in one ; binds us to all the race, and reveals to us in the case of each one oppressed and injured, a brother. ¶ *And them which suffer adversity.* The word here used refers properly to those who are maltreated, or who are injured by others. It does not properly refer to those who merely experience calamity. ¶ *As being ourselves also in the body.* As being yourselves exposed to persecution and suffering, and liable to be injured. That is, do to them as you would wish them to do to you if you were the sufferer. When we see an oppressed and injured man, we should remember that it is possible that we may be in the same circumstances, and that then we shall need and desire the sympathy of others.

4. *Marriage is honourable in all.*

all, and the bed undefiled : *a* but whoremongers and adulterers God will judge.

5 *Let your* conversation *be* without covetousness ; *and be* *b* content with such things as ye have : for

a 1 Cor.6.9; Re.22.15.
b Matt.6.25.34.

The object here is to state that *honour* is to be shown to the marriage relation. It is not to be undervalued by the pretence of the superior purity of a state of celibacy, as if marriage were improper for any class of men or any condition of life ; and it should not be dishonoured by any violation of the marriage contract. The course of things has shown that there was abundant reason for the apostle to assert with emphasis, that "marriage was an honourable condition of life." There has been a constant effort made to show that celibacy was a more holy state ; that there was something in marriage that rendered it *dishonourable* for those who are in the ministry, and for those of either sex who would be eminently pure. This sentiment has been the cause of more abomination in the world than any other single opinion claiming to have a religious sanction. It is one of the supports on which the Papal system rests, and has been one of the principal upholders of all the corruptions in monasteries and nunneries. The apostle asserts, without any restriction or qualification, that marriage is honourable in all ; and this *proves* that it is lawful for the ministers of religion to marry, and that the whole doctrine of the superior purity of a state of celibacy is false ; see this subject examined in the Notes on 1 Cor. vii. ¶ *And the bed undefiled.* Fidelity to the marriage vow. ¶ *But whoremongers and adulterers God will judge.* All licentiousness of life, and all violations of the marriage covenant, will be severely punished by God; see Notes on 1 Cor. vi. 9. The sins here referred to prevailed everywhere, and hence there was the more propriety for the frequent and solemn injunctions to avoid them which we find in the Scriptures.

he hath said, *c* I will never leave thee, nor forsake thee.

6 So that we may boldly say, *d* The Lord *is* my helper, and I will not fear what man shall do unto me.

c Gen.28.15; De.31.6,8; 1Ch.28.20.
d Ps.118.6.

5. Let your *conversation.* Your *conduct*—for so the word conversation is used in the Scriptures ; Notes, Phil. i. 27. ¶ Be *without covetousness ;* Notes on Eph. v. 3; Col. iii. 5. ¶ And be *content with such things as ye have;* see Notes on Phil. iv. 11, 12 ; Matt. vi. 25—34. The particular *reason* here given for contentment is, that God has promised never to leave his people. Compare with this the beautiful argument of the Saviour in Matt. vi. 25, seq. ¶ *For he hath said.* That is, God has said. ¶ *I will never leave thee nor forsake thee;* see Deut. xxxi. 6 ; Josh. i. 5 ; 1 Chron. xxviii. 20. Substantially the same expression is found in each of those places, and all of them contain the *principle* on which the apostle here relies, that God will not forsake his people.

6. So that we may boldly say. Without any hesitation or doubt. In all times of perplexity and threatening want ; in all times when we scarcely know whence the supplies for our necessities are to come, we may put our trust in God, and be assured that he will not leave us to suffer. In the facts which occur under the providential dealings, there is a ground for confidence on this subject which is not always exercised even by good men. It remains yet to be shown that they who exercise simple trust in God for the supply of their wants are ever forsaken ; comp. Ps. xxxvii. 25. ¶ *The Lord* is *my helper.* Substantially this sentiment is found in Ps. xxvii. 1, and Ps. cxviii. 6. The apostle does not adduce it as a *quotation,* but as language which a true Christian may employ. The sentiment is beautiful and full of consolation. What can we fear if we have the assurance that the Lord is on our side, and that he will help us ? Man can do no more to us than he permits,

7 Remember them which [1] have the rule over you, who have spoken unto you the word of God : whose

1 or, *are the guides.*   *a* ch 6.12.   *b* Re.1.4.

faith *a* follow, considering the end of *their* conversation :

8 Jesus Christ the same[b] yesterday, and to-day, and for ever.

and of course no more than will be for our own good ; and under whatever trials we may be placed, we need be under no painful apprehensions, for God will be our protector and our friend.

7. *Remember them which have the rule over you.* Marg. "*are the guides.*" The word here used means properly *leaders, guides, directors.* It is often applied to military commanders. Here it means *teachers*—appointed to lead or guide them to eternal life. It does not refer to them so much as *rulers* or *governors,* as *teachers,* or *guides.* In ver. 17, however, it is used in the former sense. The duty here enjoined is that of *remembering* them ; that is, remembering their counsel ; their instructions; their example. ¶ *Who have spoken to you the word of God.* Preachers; either apostles or others. Respect is to be shown to the ministerial office, by whomsoever it is borne. ¶ *Whose faith follow.* That is, imitate ; see Notes on ch. vi. 12. ¶ *Considering the end of their conversation.* Of their conduct ; of their manner of life. The word here rendered "*the end*"—ἔκβασις—occurs only here and in 1 Cor. x. 13, where it is rendered "*a way* of escape." It properly means, *a going out, an egress,* and is hence spoken of as a going out from life, or of an exit from the world—*death.* This is probably the meaning here. It does not mean, as our translation would seem to imply, that Jesus Christ, the same yesterday, to-day, and for ever, was the *aim* or *end* for which they lived—for the Greek will not bear that construction ; but it means that they were attentively to contemplate the *end* or the *issue* of the conduct of those holy teachers— the close or *going out* of all that they did; to wit, in a peaceful death. Their faith sustained them. They were enabled to persevere in a Christian course, and did not faint or fail. There is allusion, doubtless, to those who had been their religious instructors,

and who had died in the faith of the gospel, either by persecution or by an ordinary death, and the apostle points to them as examples of that to which he would exhort those whom he addressed—of perseverance in the faith until death. Thus explained, this verse does not refer to the duty of Christians towards *living* teachers, but towards those who are *dead.* Their duty towards living teachers is enforced in ver. 17. The sentiment here is, that the proper remembrance of those now deceased who were once our spiritual instructors and guides, should be allowed to have an important influence in inducing us to lead a holy life. We should remember them with affection and gratitude ; we should recal the truths which they taught, and the exhortations which they addressed to us ; we should cherish with kind affection the memory of all that they did for our welfare, and we should not forget the effect of the truths which they taught in sustaining their own souls when they died.

8. *Jesus Christ the same yesterday,* &c. As this stands in our common translation, it conveys an idea which is not in the original. It would seem to mean that Jesus Christ, the unchangeable Saviour, was the *end* or *aim* of the conduct of those referred to, or that they lived to imitate and glorify him. But this is by no means the meaning in the original. There it stands as an absolute proposition, that " Jesus Christ *is* the same yesterday, to-day, and for ever ;" that is, that he is unchangeable. The evident design of this independent proposition here is, to encourage them to persevere by showing that their Saviour was always the same ; that he who had sustained his people in former times, was the same still, and would be the same for ever. The *argument* here, therefore, for perseverance is founded on the *immutability* of the Redeemer. If he were fickle, vacillating, changing in his character and

9 Be [a] not carried about with
divers and strange doctrines. For
it is a good thing that the heart

a 1 John 4.1.

plans; if to-day he aids his people,
and to-morrow will forsake them; if
at one time he loves the virtuous, and
at another equally loves the vicious;
if he formed a plan yesterday which
he has abandoned to-day; or if he is
ever to be a different being from what
he is now, there would be no encouragement to effort. Who would know
what to depend on? Who would know
what to expect to-morrow? For who
could have any certainty that he
could ever please a capricious or a
vacillating being? Who could know
how to shape his conduct if the principles of the divine administration
were not always the same? At the
same time, also, that this passage furnishes the strongest argument for
fidelity and perseverance, it is an irrefragable proof of the divinity of the
Saviour. It asserts immutability—
sameness in the past, the present, and
to all eternity—but of whom can this
be affirmed but God? It would not
be possible to conceive of a declaration which would more strongly
assert immutability than this.

9. *Be not carried about with divers
and strange doctrines.* That is, they
should have settled and fixed points
of belief, and not yield to every new
opinion which was started. The apostle does not exhort them to adhere to
an opinion merely because they *had*
before held it, or because it was an
old opinion, nor does he forbid their
following the leadings of truth though
they might be required to abandon
what they had before held; but he
cautions them against that vacillating
spirit, and that easy credulity, which
would lead them to yield to any novelty, and to embrace an opinion because it was new or strange. Probably
the principal reference here is to the
Judaizing teachers, and to their various doctrines about their ceremonial
observances and traditions. But the
exhortation is applicable to Christians
at all times. A religious opinion,
once embraced on what was regarded

be established with grace; not with
meats, which have not profited them
that have been occupied therein.

a good evidence, or in which we have
been trained, should not be abandoned
for slight causes. Truth indeed should
always be followed, but it should be
only after careful inquiry. ¶ *For it
is a good thing that the heart be established with grace.* This is the proper
foundation of adherence to the truth.
The *heart* should be established with
the love of God, with pure religion,
and then we shall love the truth, and
love it in the right manner. If it is the
head merely which is convinced, the
consequence is bigotry, pride, narrow-
mindedness. If the belief of the truth
has its seat in the *heart*, it will be accompanied with charity, kindness,
good-will to all men. In *such* a belief of the truth it is a good thing to
have the heart established. It will
produce (1) firmness and stability of
character; (2) charity and kindnes‹
to others; (3) consolation and suppor‹
in trials and temptations. When a
man is thrown into trials and temptations, he *ought* to have some settled
principles on which he can rely; some
fixed points of belief that will sustain
his soul. ¶ *Not with meats.* The
meaning is, that it is better to have
the heart established with grace, or
with the principles of pure religion,
than with the most accurate knowledge of the rules of distinguishing
the clean from the unclean among the
various articles of food. Many such
rules were found in the law of Moses,
and many more had been added by
the refinements of Jewish rulers and
by tradition. To distinguish and remember all these, required no small
amount of knowledge, and the Jewish
teachers, doubtless, prided themselves
much on it. Paul says that it would
be much better to have the principles
of grace in the heart than all this
knowledge; to have the mind settled
on the great truths of religion than
to be able to make the most accurate
and learned distinctions in this matter.
The same remark may be made about
a great many other points besides the

10 We have an altar, whereof they have no right to eat which serve the tabernacle.

11 For the bodies of those beasts, whose blood is brought into the sanctuary by the high priest for sin, are burned without ^a the camp.

12 Wherefore Jesus also, that he might sanctify the people with his own blood, suffered ^b without the gate.

a Le.16.27.   b John19.17,18.

Jewish distinctions respecting meats. The principle is, that it is better to have the *heart* established in the grace of God than to have the most accurate knowledge of the distinctions which are made on useless or unimportant subjects of religion. This observation would extend to many of the shibboleths of party ; to many of the metaphysical distinctions in a hair-splitting theology ; to many of the points of controversy which divide the Christian world. ¶ *Which have not profited,* &c. Which have been of no real benefit to their souls ; see Notes on 1 Cor. viii. 8.

10. *We have an altar.* We who are Christians. The Jews had an altar on which their sacrifices were offered which was regarded as sacred, and of the benefit of which no others might partake. The design of the apostle is to show that the same thing substantially, so far as *privilege* and *sanctifying influence* were concerned, was enjoyed by Christians. The "altar" to which he here refers is evidently the cross on which the great sacrifice was made. ¶ *Whereof they have no right to eat which serve the tabernacle.* A part of the meat offered in sacrifice among the Jews became the property of the priests and Levites, and they had, by the law, a *right* to this as a part of their support ; see Lev. vi. 25, 26 ; Num. xviii. 9, 10. But the apostle says that there is a higher and more valuable sacrifice of which they have no right to partake while they remain in the service of the "tabernacle" or temple ; that is, while they remain Jews. The participation in the great Christian sacrifice appertained only to those who were the friends of the Redeemer, and however much they might value themselves on the privilege of partaking of the sacrifices offered under the Jewish law, that of partaking of the great sacrifice made by the Son of God was much greater. ¶ *Which serve the tabernacle;* Notes ch. ix. 2, 3. The Jewish priests and Levites.

11. *For the bodies of those beasts,* &c. The word here rendered "*for*" — γὰρ — would be here more properly rendered "*moreover.*" *Stuart.* The apostle is not urging a reason for what he had said in the previous verse, but is suggesting a *new* consideration to excite those whom he addressed to fidelity and perseverance. In the previous verse the consideration was, that Christians are permitted to partake of the benefits of a higher and more perfect sacrifice than the Jews were, and *therefore* should not relapse into that religion. In this verse the consideration is, that the bodies of the beasts that were burnt were taken without the camp, and that in like manner the Lord Jesus suffered *without* the gate of Jerusalem, and that we should be willing to go out with him to that sacrifice, whatever reproach or shame it might be attended with. ¶ *Whose blood is brought into the sanctuary,* &c.; see Notes on ch. ix. 7, 12. ¶ *Are burned without the camp ;* Lev. iv. 12, 21; xvi. 27. The "camp" here refers to the time when the Israelites were in the wilderness, and lived in encampments. The same custom was observed after the temple was built by conveying the body of the animal slain for a sin-offering on the great day of atonement beyond the walls of Jerusalem to be consumed there. "Whatever," says Grotius, "was not lawful to be done in the camp, afterwards was not lawful to be done in the city."

12. *Wherefore, Jesus also, that he might sanctify the people with his own blood.* That there might be a conformity between his death for sin and the sacrifices which typified it. It is implied here that it was *voluntary* on

13 Let us go forth therefore unto him without the camp, bearing [z] his reproach.

a Ac.5.41.

the part of Jesus that he suffered out of the city; that is, it was so ordered by Providence that it should be so. This was secured by his being put to death as the result of a judicial trial, and not by popular tumult; see Notes on Isa. liii. 8. If he had been killed in a tumult, it is possible that it might have been done as in other cases (comp. the case of Zacharias son of Barachias, Matt. xxiii. 35), even at the altar. As he was subjected, however, to a judicial process, his death was effected with more deliberation, and in the usual form. Hence he was conducted *out* of the city, because no criminal was executed within the walls of Jerusalem. ¶ *Without the gate.* Without the gate of Jerusalem; John xix. 17, 18. The place where he was put to death was called Golgotha, the place of a skull, and hence the Latin word which we commonly use in speaking of it, *Calvary*, Luke xxiii. 33; comp. Notes on Matt. xxvii. 33. Calvary, as it is now shown, is within the walls of Jerusalem, but there is no reason to believe that this is the place where the Lord Jesus was crucified, for that was outside of the walls of the city. The precise direction from the city is not designated by the sacred writers, nor are there any historical records, or traditional marks by which it can now be known where the exact place was. All that we know on the subject from the New Testament is, that the *name* was Golgotha; that the place of the crucifixion and sepulchre were near each other; that they were without the gate and nigh to the city, and that they were in a frequented spot; John xix. 20. " This would favour the conclusion that the place was probably upon a great road leading from one of the gates : and such a spot would only be found upon the western or northern sides of the city, on the roads leading towards Joppa or Damascus." See the question about the place of the crucifixion examined at length in

14 For here [b] have we no continuing city, but we seek one to come.

b Mi.2.10.

Robinson's Bibli. Research., vol. ii. pp. 69—80, and Bibliotheca Sacra, No. 1.

13. *Let us go forth therefore unto him without the camp.* As if we were going forth with him when he was led away to be crucified. He was put to death as a malefactor. He was the object of contempt and scorn. He was held up to derision, and was taunted and reviled on his way to the place of death, and even on the cross. To be identified with him there ; to follow him ; to sympathize with him ; to be regarded as his friend, would have subjected one to similar shame and reproach. The meaning here is, that we should be willing to regard ourselves as identified with the Lord Jesus, and to bear the same shame and reproaches which he did. When he was led away amidst scoffing and reviling to be put to death, would *we*, if we had been there, been willing to be regarded as his followers, and to have gone out with him as his avowed disciples and friends ? Alas, how many are there who profess to love him when religion subjects them to no reproach, who would have shrunk from following him to Calvary ! ¶ *Bearing his reproach.* Sympathizing with him ; or bearing such reproach as he did ; see 1 Pet. iv. 13 ; comp. Notes on ch. xii. 2 ; Phil. iii. 10 ; Col. i. 24.

14. *For here we have no continuing city, &c.* We do not regard this as our final home, or our fixed abode, and we should be willing to bear reproaches during the little time that we are to remain here ; comp. Notes, ch. xi. 10, 13, 14. If, therefore, in consequence of our professed attachment to the Saviour, we should be driven away from our habitations, and compelled to wander, we should be willing to submit to it, for our permanent home is not here, but in heaven. The *object* of the writer seems to be to comfort the Hebrew Chris-

15 By him *a* therefore let us offer the sacrifice of praise to God continually, that is, the fruit *b* of *our* lips 1 giving thanks to *his* name.

a Ep.5.20.   b Ho.14.2.   1 *confessing.*

16 But to do good, and to communicate, *c* forget not: for with such *d* sacrifices God is well pleased.

17 Obey *e* them that 1 have the

c Rom.12.13.   d Phi.4 18.
11 h.5.12.13.   1 or, *guide.*

tians on the supposition that they would be driven by persecution from the city of Jerusalem, and doomed to wander as exiles. He tells them that their Lord was led from that city to be put to death, and they should be willing to go forth also ; that their permanent home was not Jerusalem, but heaven, and they should be willing in view of that blessed abode to be exiled from the city where they dwelt, and made wanderers in the earth.

15. *By him, therefore.* The Jews approached God by the blood of the sacrifice and by the ministry of their high priest. The exhortation of the apostle here is founded on the general course of argument in the epistle " In view of all the considerations presented respecting the Christian High Priest—his dignity, purity, and love ; his sacrifice and his intercession, let us persevere in offering through him praise to God." That is, let us persevere in adherence to our religion. ¶ *The sacrifice of praise.* For all the mercies of redemption. The Jews, says Rosenmüller (Alte u. neue Morgenland, *in loc.*), had a species of offerings which they called *peace-offerings,*or*friendship-offerings.* They were designed not to *produce* peace or friendship with God, but to *preserve* it. Burnt-offerings, sin-offerings, and trespass-offerings, were all on account of transgression, and were designed to remove transgression. But in their peace-offerings, the offerer was regarded as one who stood in the relation of a friend with God, and the oblation was a sign of thankful acknowledgment for favours received, or they were connected with vows in order that further blessings might be obtained, or they were brought voluntarily as a means to continue themselves in the friendship and favour of God ; Lev. vii. 11, 12 ;

comp. Jenning's Jew. Ant. i. 335. ¶ *That is, the fruit of* our *lips.* The phrase " fruit of the lips," is a Hebraism, meaning what the lips *produce ;* that is, *words ;* comp. Prov. xviii. 20 ; Hos. xiv. 2. ¶ *Giving thanks to his name.* To God ; the *name* of one being often put for the person himself. *Praise* now is one of the great duties of the redeemed. It will be their employment for ever.

16. *But to do good, and to communicate, forget not.* To communicate or *impart* to others ; that is, to share with them what we have. The Greek word means *having in common* with others. The meaning is, that they were to show *liberality* to those who were in want, and were to take special pains not to *forget* this duty. We are prone to think constantly of our own interests, and there is great danger of *forgetting* the duty which we owe to the poor and the needy. On the duty here enjoined, see Notes on Gal. vi. 10. ¶ *For with such sacrifices God is well pleased* He is pleased with the sacrifices of prayer and of praise ; with the offerings of a broken and a contrite heart : but he is especially pleased with the religion which leads us to do good to others. This was eminently the religion of his Son, the Lord Jesus ; and to this all true religion prompts. The word " sacrifices" here is not taken in a strict sense, as denoting that which is offered as an expiation for sin, or in the sense that we are by doing good to attempt to make atonement for our transgressions, but in the general sense of an *offering* made to God. God is pleased with this, (1) because it shows in us a right state of heart ; (2) because it accords with his own nature. *He* does good continually, and he is pleased with all who evince the same spirit.

17. *Obey them that have the rule*

rule over you, and submit yourselves : for they watch *a* for your souls, as they that must give account, that they may do it with

a Eze.3.17.   *b* Ac.24.16.

over you. Marg. *guide ;* see Notes on ver. 7. The reference here is to their religious teachers, and not to civil rulers. They were to show them proper respect, and to submit to their authority in the church, so far as it was administered in accordance with the precepts of the Saviour. The obligation to obedience does not, of course, extend to anything which is wrong in itself, or which would be a violation of conscience. The doctrine is, that subordination is necessary to the welfare of the church, and that there ought to be a disposition to yield all proper obedience to those who are set over us in the Lord; comp. Notes on 1 Thess. v. 12, 13. ¶ *And submit yourselves.* That is, to all which they enjoin that is lawful and right. There are in relation to a society (1.) those things which God has positively commanded — which are always to be obeyed. (2.) Many things which have been *agreed on* by the society as needful for its welfare—and these are to be submitted to unless they violate the rights of conscience ; and (3.) many things which are in themselves a matter of no express divine command, and of no formal enactment by the community. They are matters of convenience ; things that tend to the order and harmony of the community, and of the propriety of these, " rulers" in the church and elsewhere should be allowed to judge, and we should submit to them patiently. Hence in the church we are to submit to all the proper regulations for conducting public worship; for the promotion of religion ; and for the administration of discipline. ¶ *For they watch for your souls.* They have no selfish aim in this. They do not seek " to lord it over God's heritage." It is for your own good that they do this, and you should therefore submit to these arrangements. And this shows also the true principle on which authority should be exercised

joy, and not with grief : for that *is* unprofitable for you.

18 Pray for us : for we trust we have a good conscience, *b* in all things willing to live honestly.

in a church. It should be in such a way as to promote the salvation of the people ; and all the arrangements should be with that end. The measures adopted, therefore, and the obedience enjoined, should not be arbitrary, oppressive, or severe, but should be such as will really promote salvation. ¶ *As they that must give account.* To God. The ministers of religion must give account to God for their fidelity. For all that they teach, and for every measure which they adopt, they must soon be called into judgment. There is, therefore, the best security that under the influence of this solemn truth they will pursue only that course which will be for your good. ¶ *That they may do it with joy, and not with grief.* Gr. μὴ στενάζοντες—not sighing, or *groaning;* as they would who had been unsuccessful. The meaning is, that they should *so* obey, that when their teachers came to give up their account they need not do it with sorrow over their perverseness and disobedience ¶ *For this* is *unprofitable for you.* That is, their giving up their account in that manner—as unsuccessful in their efforts to save you—would not be of advantage to you, but would be highly injurious. This is a strong mode of expressing the idea that it *must* be attended with eminent peril to their souls to have their religious teachers go and give an account against them. As they would wish, therefore, to avoid that, they should render to them all proper honour and obedience.

18. *Pray for us.* This is a request which the apostle often makes in hi own behalf, and in behalf of his fellow labourers in the gospel ; see 1 Thess v. 25. Notes, Eph. vi. 18, 19. ¶ *Fo we trust we have a good conscience.* &c. ; see Notes on Acts xxiv. 16. The apostle here appeals to the uprightness of his Christian life as a reason why he might claim their sym

19 But I beseech *you* the rather to do this, that I may be restored to you the sooner. 20 Now the God *a* of peace, that brought again from the dead *b* our

Lord Jesus, that great *c* Shepherd of the sheep, *d* through the blood of the everlasting ¹ covenant, 21 Make you perfect *e* in every good work to do his will, ² work-

a 1 Th.5.23.　*b* 1 Pe.1.21.
c Eze.34.23.　*d* Zec.9.11.

1 testament.　*e* 1 Pe.5.10.
2 or, doing.

,athy. He was conscious of an aim to do good; he sought the welfare of the church; and having this aim he felt that he might appeal to the sympathy of all Christians in his behalf. It is only when we aim to do right, and to maintain a good conscience, that we can with propriety ask the prayers of others, or claim their sympathy. And if we are "*willing* in all things to live honestly," we may expect the sympathy, the prayers, and the affections of all good men. 19. *That I may be restored to you the sooner.* It is here clearly implied that the writer was deterred from visiting them by some adverse circumstances over which he had no control. This might be either by imprisonment, or sickness, or the want of a convenient opportunity of reaching them. The probability is, judging particularly from the statement in ver. 23, that he was then a prisoner, and that his detention was on that account; see Intro. § 4. (6) The language here is such as Paul would use on the supposition that he was then a prisoner at Rome, and this is a slight circumstance going to show the probability that the epistle was composed by him. 20. *Now the God of peace.* God who is the Author, or the source of peace ; Notes, 1 Thess. v. 23. The word *peace* in the New Testament is used to denote every kind of blessing or happiness. It is opposed to all that would disturb or trouble the mind, and may refer, therefore, to reconciliation with God ; to a quiet conscience ; to the evidence of pardoned sin ; to health and prosperity, and to the hope of heaven ; see Notes on John xiv. 27. ¶ *That brought again from the dead our Lord Jesus;* Notes, Acts ii. 32 ; 1 Cor. xv. 15. It is only by the fact of the resurrection of the Lord Jesus that we have peace, for it

is only by him that we have the prospect of an admission into heaven. ¶ *That great Shepherd of the sheep;* Notes, John x. 1, 14. The idea here is, that it is through the tender care of that great Shepherd that true happiness is bestowed on the people of God. ¶ *Through the blood of the everlasting covenant.* The blood shed to ratify the everlasting covenant that God makes with his people; Notes, ch. ix. 14—23. This phrase, in the original, is not connected, as it is in our translation, with his being raised from the dead, nor should it be so rendered, for what can be the sense of "raising Christ from the dead *by the blood of the covenant ?*" In the Greek it is, "the God of peace, who brought again from the dead the shepherd of the sheep, great by the blood of the everlasting covenant, our Lord Jesus," &c. The meaning is, that he was made or constituted the great Shepherd of the sheep—the great Lord and ruler of his people, by that blood. That which makes him so eminently distinguished ; that by which he was made superior to all others who ever ruled over the people of God, was the fact that he offered the blood by which the eternal covenant was ratified. It is called everlasting or eternal, because (1) it was formed in the councils of eternity, or has been an eternal plan in the divine mind ; and (2) because it is to continue for ever. Through such a covenant God can bestow permanent and solid "peace" on his people, for it lays the foundation of the assurance of eternal happiness. 21. *Make you perfect.* The apostle here does not affirm that they were then perfect, or that they would be in this life. The word here used— χαταϱτιζω—means *to make fully ready; to put in full order ; to make complete.* The meaning here is, that Paul

ing ͣ in you that which is well-pleasing in his sight, through Jesus Christ ; to whom be glory for ever and ever. Amen.

22 And I beseech you, brethren, suffer the word of exhortation :

a Phi. 2. 13.

prayed that God would fully endow them with whatever grace was necessary to do his will and to keep his commandments ; see the word explained in the Notes on ch. xi. 3. It is an appropriate prayer to be offered at all times, and by all who love the church, that God would make all his people perfectly qualified to do all his will. ¶ *Working in you*. Marg. *Doing*. The idea here is, that the only hope that they would do the will of God was, that *he* would, by his own agency, cause them to do what was well-pleasing in his sight ; comp. Notes on Phil. ii. 12. It is not from any expectation that man would do it himself. ¶ *Through Jesus Christ*. The idea is, that God does not directly, and by his own immediate agency, convert and sanctify the heart, but it is through the gospel of Christ, and all good influences on the soul must be expected through the Saviour. ¶ *To whom* be *glory for ever and ever*. That is, to Christ; for so the connection evidently demands. It is not uncommon for the apostle Paul to introduce doxologies in this way in the midst of a letter ; see Notes, Rom. ix. 5. It was common among the Jews, as it is now in the writings and conversation of the Mohammedans, when the name of God was mentioned to accompany it with an expression of praise.

22. *Suffer the word of exhortation*. Referring to the arguments and counsels in this whole epistle, which is in fact a practical exhortation to perseverance in adhering to the Christian religion amidst all the temptations which existed to apostasy. ¶ *For I have written a letter unto you in few words*. This does not mean that this epistle is short compared with the others that the author had written, for most of the epistles of Paul are shorter than this. But it means, that

for I have written a letter unto you in few words.

23 Know ye that our brothei Timothy is set at liberty ; with whom, if he come shortly, I will see you.

it was brief compared with the importance and difficulty of the subjects of which he had treated. The topics introduced would have allowed a much more extended discussion ; but in handling them he had made use of as few words as possible. No one can deny this who considers the sen tentious manner of this epistle. As an illustration of this, perhaps we may remark that it is easy to *expand* the thoughts of this epistle into ample volumes of exposition, and that in fact it is difficult to give an explanation of it without a commentary that shall greatly surpass in extent the text. None can doubt, also, that the author of this epistle could have himself greatly expanded the thoughts and the illustrations if he had chosen,. It is with reference to such considerations, probably, that he says that the epistle was *brief*.

23. *Know ye that* our *brother Timothy is set at liberty*. Or, *is sent away*. So it is rendered by Prof. Stuart and others. On the meaning of this, and its importance in determining who was the author of the epistle, see the Intro. § 3, (5) 4, and Prof. Stuart's Intro. § 19. This is a strong circumstance showing that Paul was the author of the epistle, for from the first acquaintance of Timothy with Paul he is represented as his constant companion, and spoken of as a brother ; Notes, 2 Cor. i. 1 ; Phil. i. 1 ; Col. i 1 ; Phil. i. There is no other one of the apostles who would so naturally have used this term respecting Timothy, and this kind mention is made of him here because he was so dear to the heart of the writer, and because he felt that they to whom he wrote would also feel an interest in his circumstances. As to the meaning of the word rendered " set at liberty"—ἀπολελυμένον—there has been much difference of opinion whether

24 Salute all them that have the rule over you, and all the saints. They of Italy salute you.

25 Grace *be* with you all. Amen. Written to the Hebrews from Italy by Timothy.

it means "set at liberty from confinement," or, "sent away on some message to some other place." That the latter is the meaning of the expression appears probable from these considerations. (1.) The connection seems to demand it. The writer speaks of him as if he were now away, and as if he hoped that he might soon return. "With whom, if he come shortly, I will see you." This is language which would be used rather of one who had been sent on some embassy than of one who was just released from prison. At all events, he was at this time away, and there was some expectation that he might soon return. But on the supposition that the expression relates to release from imprisonment, there would be an entire incongruity in the language. It is not, as we should then suppose, " our brother Timothy is now released from prison, and *therefore* I will come soon with him and see you;" but, " our brother Timothy is now sent away, and if he return soon I will come with him to you." (2.) In Phil. ii. 19, 23, Paul, then a prisoner at Rome, speaks of the hope which he entertained that he would be able to send Timothy to them as soon as he should know how it would go with him. He designed to retain him until that point was settled, as his presence with him would be important until then, and then to send him to give consolation to the Philippians, and to look into the condition of the church. Now the passage before us agrees well with the supposition that that event had occurred—that Paul had ascertained with sufficient clearness that he would be released, so that he might be permitted yet to visit the Hebrew Christians, that he had sent Timothy to Philippi and was waiting for his return ; that as soon as he should return he would be prepared to visit them ; and that in the mean time while Timothy was absent, he wrote to them this epistle. (3.) The supposition agrees well with

the meaning of the word here used— ἀπολύω. It denotes properly, to let loose from : to loosen ; to unbind ; to release; to let go free ; to put away or divorce ; to *dismiss* simply, or let go, or send away ; see Matt. xiv. 15, 22, 23 ; xv. 32, 39 ; Luke ix. 12, *et al.;* comp. Rob. Lex. and Stuart's Intro. § 19. The meaning, then, I take to be this, that Timothy was then sent away on some important embassage ; that the apostle expected his speedy return; and that then he trusted that he would be able with him to visit those to whom this epistle was written.

24. *Salute all them ;* see Notes on Rom. xvi. 3, seq. It was customary for the apostle Paul to close his epistles with an affectionate salutation. ¶ *That have the rule over you;* Notes ver. 7, 17. None are mentioned by name, as is usual in the epistles of Paul. The cause of this omission is unknown. ¶ *And all the saints.* The common name given to Christians in the Scriptures ; see Notes on Rom. i. 7. ¶ *They of Italy salute you.* The saints or Christians in Italy. Showing that the writer of the epistle was then in Italy. He was probably in Rome ; see the Intro. § 4.

25. *Grace be with you all ;* Notes Rom. xvi. 20, 24.

The subscription at the close of the epistle " written to the Hebrews from Italy by Timothy," like the other subscriptions, is of no authority ; see Notes at the end of 1 Cor. It is demonstrably erroneous here, for it is expressly said by the author of the epistle that at the time he wrote it, Timothy was absent ; ch. xiii. 23. In regard to the time and place of writing it, see the Intro. § 4.

At the close of this exposition, it is not improper to refer the reader to the remarks on its design at the end of the introduction, § 6. Having passed through the exposition, we may see more clearly the importance of the views there presented. There is no book of the New Testament more important than this, and of course none whose want would be more perceptible in the canon of the Scriptures. Every reader of the Old Testament *needs* such a guide as this epistle, written by some one who had an intimate acquaintance from childhood with the Jewish system; who had all the advantages of the most able and faithful instruction, and who was under the influence of inspiration, to make us acquainted with the true nature of those institutions Nothing was more important than to settle the principles in regard to the nature of the Jewish economy; to show what was typical, and how those institutions were the means of introducing a far more perfect system—the system of the Christian religion. If we have right feelings, we shall have sincere gratitude to God that he caused the Christian religion to be prefigured by a system in itself so magnificent and grand as that of the Jewish, and higher gratitude for that sublime system of religion of which the Jewish, with all its splendour, was only the shadow. There was much that was beautiful, cheering, and sublime in the Jewish system. There was much that was grand and awful in the giving of the law, and much that was imposing in its ceremonies. In its palmy and pure days, it was incomparably the purest and noblest system of religion then on earth. It taught the knowledge of the one true God; inculcated a pure system of morals; preserved the record of the truth on

the earth, and held up constantly before man the hope of a better system still in days to come. But it was expensive, burdensome, precise in its prescriptions, and wearisome in its ceremonies; Acts xv. 10. It was adapted to one people—a people who occupied a small territory, and who could conveniently assemble at the central place of their worship three times in a year. It was not a system adapted to the whole world, nor was it designed for the whole world. When the Saviour came, therefore, to introduce whom was the design of the Jewish economy, it ceased as a matter of course. The Jewish altars were soon thrown down; the temple was razed to the ground, and the city of their solemnities was destroyed. The religion of the Hebrews passed away to be revived no more in its splendour and power, and it has never lived since, except as an empty form.

This epistle teaches us why it passed away, and why it can never be restored. It is the true key with which to unlock the Old Testament; and with these views, we may remark in conclusion, that he who would understand the Bible thoroughly should make himself familiar with this epistle; that the canon of Scripture would be incomplete without it; and that, to one who wishes to understand the Revelation which God has given, there is no portion of the volume whose loss would be a more irreparable calamity than that of the Epistle to the Hebrews.

Notes
on the
New Testament

Albert Barnes

Edited by
Robert Frew

JAMES TO JUDE

BAKER BOOK HOUSE
Grand Rapids, Michigan 49506

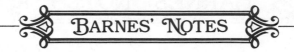

Heritage Edition

Fourteen Volumes 0834-4

When ordering by ISBN (International Standard Book Number), numbers listed above should be preceded by 0-8010-.

Reprinted from the 1884-85 edition published by Blackie & Son, London, edited by Robert Frew

ISBN: 0-8010-0848-4

Printed and bound in the United States of America

GENERAL INTRODUCTION

TO THE

SEVEN CATHOLIC EPISTLES.

§ 1. *The Antiquity and Reason of the term* GENERAL *or* CATHOLIC, *applied to these Epistles.*

THE seven Epistles embraced in the New Testament between the Epistle to the Hebrews and the book of Revelation, are denoted by the term *General* or *Catholic* (καθολικαί). This word does not occur in the New Testament, except in the inscriptions to these epistles ; and these inscriptions are no part of the inspired writings, and are of no authority, as it is evident that the writers themselves would not affix the title to them. Indeed, the term is not applied with strict propriety to the second and third Epistles of John ; but those Epistles are ranked under the general appellation, because they were usually annexed to his first Epistle in transcribing, partly because they were the work of the same author, and partly because they were so small, that there might otherwise be danger of their being lost.—*Michaelis.* Tho Greek word *catholic* (καθολικαί) applied to these Epistles, means *general, universal;* and it was given to them because they were not addressed to particular churches or individuals, but to Christians at large. Even the Epistles of Peter, however, as well as the second and third of John, had originally a definite direction, and were designed for certain specified churches and Christians, as really as the Epistle to the Romans or Corinthians ; see 1 Pet. i. 1. There is, therefore, no good reason for retaining the title now, and it is omitted in the editions of Tittman and Hahn. It was, however, early applied to the Epistles, and is found in most of the editions and versions of the New Testament. Thus Eusebius, having given an account of James, called the Just, and our Lord's brother, says, " Thus far concerning this James, who is said to be the author of the first of the Epistles called *catholic.*" In another place he says, " That, in his Institutions, Clement of Alexandria had given short explications of all the canonical Scriptures, not omitting those which are contradicted—I mean the Epistle of Jude, and the other *catholic* Epistles." John's first Epistle is several times called catholic by Origen. So Athanasius, Epiphanius, and other Greek writers, mention the seven Epistles under the term *catholic.*—Lardner, Works, vi. 158. Ed. Lond., 1829. Comp. Hug's Intro., ch. iii., § 151. " The didactic writings of the apostles were separated into two collections ; the one comprising the Epistles of Paul, and bearing generally the title ἀπόστολος (*apostle*); the other containing the Epistles of the rest of the apostles, with the title καθολικαὶ ἐπιστολαί (*catholic epistles*), or καθολικαὶ ἐπιστολαὶ τῶν ἀποστόλων (*catholic epistles of the apostles*)."—*Hug*. Hug supposes that the appellation was given to them to designate them as a class of biblical writings, comprising the writings of *all* the apostles, except those of Paul. The Gospels and the Acts, he supposes, comprised one class by themselves; the Epistles of Paul a second; and these seven Epistles, under the title of *general* or *catholic*, a third, embracing the writings of all the apostles, Paul excepted. In the course of time, however, the signification of the term became changed, and they were called catholic, because they were not addressed to any church in particular.—Intro., pp. 605, 606. Ed. And., 1836. At all events, this last is the sense in which the word is used by Theodoret, and by subsequent commentators. On this point, see also Koppe, New Tes., vol. ix. 1, seq., and Noesselt, In conjecturis ad historiam catholicæ Jacobi epistolæ. Opusc. Fasc., ii., p. 303, seq., and Bertholdt, Historisch-kritische Einleitung in sammtliche kanonische und apokryphische Scriften des A. und N. T., i. p. 216, seq.

It may be added, that the term 'canonical' was given to these Epistles, about the middle of the sixth century, by Cassiodorius, and by the writer of the prologue to these Epistles, ascribed to Jerome, though not his. The reason why this appellation was given is not known.—Lardner, Works, vi. 160.

§ 2. *The canonical Authority of these Epistles.*

"Before the fourth century," says Hug, Intro., p. 606, "in which, for the first time, undeviating unanimity in all the churches, in respect to the canon, was effected, Christian writers with perfect freedom advocated or denied the authenticity of certain writings of the New Testament. Individual Fathers admitted or rejected certain books, according as their judgment dictated. Besides the Epistle to the Hebrews and the Apocalypse, this was the case, as is well known, in regard to several of the catholic Epistles, viz., that of James, the second and third of John, the second of Peter, and that of Jude." It is of some importance here to inquire what bearing this fact should have on the question of the canonical authority of these Epistles, or the question whether they are to be regarded as constituting a part of the inspired writings. Some general remarks only will be made here; a more particular examination will be proper in considering the evidences of the genuineness of the several Epistles. See the Introduction to James, to second Peter, to second and third John, and to Jude.

The *facts* in the case, in regard to these disputed Epistles, were these:—

(1.) They were always circulated under the names of the respective authors whose names they bear, and, by established custom, were subjoined to the other biblical books, though they had not universally the estimation which was given to the others.

(2.) In most of the churches, these Epistles were made use of, as Eusebius testifies, equally with the other Scriptures.

(3.) There was supposed by many to be a want of *positive* historical testimony in their favour; at least of the evidence which existed in favour of the other books of the New Testament.

(4.) It was not supposed that there was any positive testimony *against* the genuineness of these writings. The sole ground of doubt with *any* of the Fathers was, that there were not the same historical vouchers for their genuineness which there were for the other books.

(5.) They were never regarded as books that were certainly to be rejected. Those who entertained doubts in regard to them did not argue *against* their genuineness, but only expressed *doubts* in respect to their canonical authority.

(6.) Even these doubts were in time removed, and after the fourth century these Epistles were everywhere received as a part of the genuine inspired writings. The progress of investigation removed *all* doubt from the mind, and they were allowed a place among the undisputed writings of the apostles, as a part of the word of God.

In regard, therefore, to the influence which this fact should have on the estimate which we form of their genuineness and canonical authority, we may observe,

(1.) That the settled and established voice of antiquity is in their favour. That opinion became at length harmonious, and was all the more valuable, from the fact that there ever had been any doubts. The general judgment of the church now in their favour is the result of long and careful inquiry; and an opinion is always more valuable when it is known to have been the result of long and careful investigation.

(2.) The facts in regard to these epistles showed that there was great *caution* in the early Christian church about admitting books into the canon. None were received without examination; none where the evidence was not supposed to be clear. The honest doubts of the early Christian Fathers were stated and canvassed, and passed for what they were worth; and the highest care was taken to remove the doubts, when any existed. No books were admitted into the canon by a mere *vote* of a synod or council, or by any ecclesiastical body. The books which were admitted were received because there was *evidence* that they were genuine, which satisfied the church at large, and they were recognised as canonical by common consent.

(3.) It has been observed above, that there never was any *positive* evidence against the authority and genuineness of the disputed books. But, as Hug has remarked (p. 607), even the *negative* argument loses much of its force when its character is considered. Such is their brevity, that it was less easy to establish their authority, or to demonstrate their authorship by any *internal* evidence, than in regard to the longer Epistles. It happened, also, from the brevity of the Epistles, that they were less frequently quoted by the early Fathers than the longer ones were, and hence it was more difficult to demonstrate that they were early received. But it is clear that this arose, not from any thing *in* the Epistles which was calculated to excite suspicion as to their origin, but from the nature of the case. On the supposition that they are genuine, and were early regarded as genuine, this difficulty would be as great as on the supposition that they are not. But if so, the difficulty is manifestly of no force. On this whole subject, the reader may find all that is necessary to be said in the Prolegomena of Koppe in Epistolas Catholicas. See also Hug's Intro., § 151, 152.

THE GENERAL

EPISTLE OF JAMES.

INTRODUCTION

§ 1. *The Question who was the Author of this Epistle.*

THERE have been more difficult questions raised in regard to the Epistle of James than perhaps any other portion of the New Testament. Those questions it is of importance to examine as fully as is consistent with the design of these Notes; that is, so far as to enable a candid inquirer to see what is the *real* difficulty in the case, and what is, so far as can be ascertained, the truth.

The first question is, Who was the author? It has been attributed to one of three persons :—to James ' the elder,' the son of Zebedee, and brother of John; to James ' the less,' son of Alpheus or Cleophas ; and to a James of whom nothing more is known. Some have supposed, also, that the James who is mentioned as the ' Lord's brother,' (Gal. i. 19,) was a different person from James the son of Alpheus.

There are no methods of determining this point from the Epistle itself. All that can be established from the Epistle is, (1.) That the name of the author was *James*, ch. i. 1; (2.) That he professed to be a "servant of God," ch. i. 1; (3.) That he had been probably a Jew, and sustained such a relation to those to whom he wrote, as to make it proper for him to address them with authority; and, (4.) That he was a follower of the Lord Jesus Christ, ch. ii. 1; v. 8.

There are two persons, if not three, of the name of *James*, mentioned in the New Testament. The one is James, the son of Zebedee, Matt. iv. 21; Mark iii. 17; Luke vi. 14; Acts i. 13, *et al.* He was the brother of John, and is usually mentioned in connection with him ; Matt. iv. 21; xvii. 1; Mark v. 37; xiii. 3, *et al.* The name of their mother was Salome. Comp. Matt. xxvii. 56, with Mark xv. 40. He was put to death by Herod Agrippa, about A.D. 41. Acts xii. 2. He was called the major, or the elder—to distinguish him from the other James, the younger, or the *less*, Mark xv. 40; called also, in ancient history, James the Just.

The other James was a son of Alpheus or Cleophas ; Matt. x. 3; Mark iii. 18; Acts i. 13; Luke xxiv. 18. That Alpheus and Cleophas was the same person is evident from the fact that both the words are derived from the Hebrew הלפי— *hhalphi*. The name of the mother of this James was Mary, (Mark xv. 40;) and James, and Joses, and Simon, and Judas, are mentioned as brethren ; Matt. xiii. 55. There is also a James mentioned in Matt. xiii. 55; Mark vi. 3; and Gal. i. 19, as a "brother of our Lord." On the meaning of this expression, see Notes on Gal. i. 19.

It has been a question which has been agitated from the earliest times, whether the James who is mentioned as the son of Alpheus, and the James who is men-tioned as the "Lord's brother," were the same or different persons. It is not necessary for the purposes of these Notes to go into an examination of this ques-tion. Those who are disposed to see it pursued, may consult Hug's Intro., § 158, and the works there referred to; Neander's History of the Planting and Training of the Christian Church, vol. ii. p. 2, seq., Edin. Ed.; and Michaelis' Intro., vol. iv. 271, seq. The question, says Neander, is one of the most difficult in the apostolic history. Hug supposes that James the son of Alpheus, and James the brother of the Lord, were the same. Neander supposes that the James mentioned by the title of the "Lord's brother" was a son of Joseph, either by a former marriage, or by Mary, and consequently a "brother" in the stricter sense.

It is remarked by Michaelis, that James may have been called "the Lord's brother," or mentioned as one of his brethren, in one of the following senses :— (1.) That the persons accounted as the "brethren of the Lord" (Matt. xiii. 55, *et al.*) were the sons of Joseph, not by Mary the mother of Jesus, but by a former wife. This, says he, was the most ancient opinion, and there is in it nothing improbable. If so, they were older than Jesus. (2.) It may mean that they were the sons of Joseph by Mary, the mother of Jesus. Comp. Notes on Matt. xiii. 55. If so, James was an own brother of Jesus, but younger than he. There is nothing in this opinion inconsistent with any statement in the Bible ; for the notion of the perpetual virginity of Mary is not founded on the authority of the Scriptures. If either of these suppositions were true, however, and James and Judas, the authors of the Epistles which bear their names, were literally the brothers of Christ, it would follow that they were not apostles ; for the elder apostle James was the son of Zebedee, and James the younger was the son of Alpheus. (3.) A third opinion in relation to James, and Joses, and Simon, and Judas, is, that they were the sons of Joseph by the widow of a brother who had died without children, and to whom, therefore, Joseph, by the Mosaic laws, was obliged to raise up issue. This opinion, however, is entirely unsupported, and is wholly improbable ; for (*a*) the law which obliged the Jews to take their brothers' widows applied only to those who were single (*Michaelis*) ; and (*b*) if this had been an instance of that kind, all the requirement of the law in the case would have been satisfied when one heir was born. (4.) It might be maintained that, according to the preceding opinion, the brother of Joseph was *Alpheus*, and then they would be reckoned as his sons ; and in this case, the James and Judas who are called the brothers of Jesus, would have been the same as the apostles of that name. But, in that case, Alpheus would not have been the same as Cleopas, for Cleopas had a wife—the sister of Joseph's wife. (5.) A fifth opinion, and one which was advanced by Jerome, and which has been extensively maintained, is, that the persons referred to were called 'brethren' of the Lord Jesus only in a somewhat lax sense, as denoting his near kinsmen. See Notes on Gal. i. 19. According to this, they would have been *cousins* of the Lord Jesus, and the relationship was of this kind :—James and Judas, sons of Alpheus, were the apostles, and consequently Alpheus was the father of Simon and Joses. Farther, Alpheus is the same as Cleopas, who married Mary, the sister of the mother of Jesus (John xix. 25), and consequently the sons of Cleopas were cousins of the Saviour.

Which of these opinions is the correct one, it is impossible now to determine. The latter is the common opinion, and perhaps, on the whole, best sustained ; and if so, then there were but two Jameses referred to, both apostles, and the one who wrote this Epistle was a cousin of the Lord Jesus. Neander, however, supposes that there were two Jameses besides James the brother of John, the son of Zebedee, and that the one who wrote this Epistle was not the apostle, the son of Alpheus, but was, in the stricter sense, the 'brother' of our Lord, and was trained up with him. Hist. of the Planting of Christianity, ii., p. 3, seq.

It is a circumstance of some importance, in showing that there was but one James besides James the brother of John, and that this was the apostle, the son of Alpheus, that after the death of the elder James (Acts xii. 1,) no mention is made of more than one of that name. If there had been, it is hardly possible, says Hug, that there should not have been some allusion to him. This, however, is not conclusive; for there is no mention of Simon, or Bartholomew, or Thomas after that time.

There is but one serious objection, perhaps, to this theory, which is, that it is said (John vii. 5) that "his brethren did not believe on him." It is possible, however, that the word 'brethren' in that place may not have included *all* his kinsmen, but may have had particular reference to the larger portion of them (ver. 3,) who were not believers, though it might have been that some of them *were* believers.

On the whole, it seems probable that the James who was the author of this Epistle was one of the apostles of that name, the son of Alpheus, and that he was a cousin of our Lord. Entire certainty on that point, however, cannot be hoped for.

If the author of this Epistle was a different person from the one who resided at Jerusalem, and who is often mentioned in the Acts of the Apostles, then nothing more is known of him. That James was evidently an apostle (Gal. i. 19,) and perhaps, from his relationship to the Lord Jesus, would have a special influence and authority there.

Of this James, little more is certainly known than what is mentioned in the Acts of the Apostles. Hegesippus, as quoted by Neander, says, that from childhood he led the life of a Nazarene. He is described by Josephus (Archæol. xx. 9,) as well as by Hegesippus and Eusebius, as a man eminent for his integrity of life, and as well meriting the appellation or surname which he bore among the Jews, of צַדִּיק, δίκαιος, *the Just.* He is mentioned as one who set himself against the corruptions of the age, and who was thence termed the bulwark of the people —עַם לְבֵּל—περιοχη τοῦ λαοῦ. His manner of life is represented as strict and holy, and such as to command in an eminent degree the confidence of his country-men, the Jews. Hegesippus says that he frequently prostrated himself on his knees in the Temple, calling on God to forgive the sins of his people, praying that the divine judgments on the unbelievers might be averted, and that they might be led to repentance and faith, and thus to a participation of the kingdom of the glorified Messiah. Neander, as quoted before, p. 10.

In the New Testament, James appears as a prominent and leading man in the church at Jerusalem. In later times he is mentioned by the ecclesiastical writers as 'Bishop of Jerusalem;' but this title is not given to him in the New Testament, nor is there any reason to suppose that he filled the office which is now usually denoted by the word *bishop*. He appears, however, from some cause, to have had his home permanently in Jerusalem, and, for a considerable portion of his life, to have been the only apostle residing there. As such, as well as from his near relationship to the Lord Jesus, and his own personal worth, he was entitled to, and received, marked respect. His prominence, and the respect which was shown to him at Jerusalem, appear in the following circumstances : (1.) In the council that was held respecting the rules that were to be imposed on the converts from the Gentiles, and the manner in which they were to be regarded and treated (Acts xv.), after the other apostles had fully delivered their sentiments, the views of James were expressed, and his counsel was followed. Acts xv. 13–29. (2.) When Peter was released from prison, in answer to the prayers of the assembled church, he directed those whom he first saw to 'go and show these things to *James*, and to the brethren.' Acts xii. 17. (3.) When Paul visited Jerusalem after his conversion, James is twice mentioned by him as occupying a prominent position there. First, Paul says that when he went there on the first occasion, he saw none of the apostles but Peter, and 'James the Lord's brother.' Gal. i. 18, 19. He is here mentioned as one of the apostles, and as sustaining a near relation to the Lord Jesus. On the second occasion, when Paul went up there fourteen years after, he is mentioned, in enumerating those who gave to him the right hand of fellowship, as one of the 'pillars' of the church; and among those who recognised him as an apostle, he is mentioned first. "And when James, Cephas, and John, who seemed to be pillars, perceived the grace that was given unto me, they gave me and Barnabas the right hand of fellow-ship." Gal. ii. 9. (4.) When Paul went up to Jerusalem after his visit to Asia

Minor and to Greece, the whole matter pertaining to his visit was laid before James, and his counsel was followed by Paul. Acts xxi. 18—24.
The leading points in the character of James seem to have been these:—(1.) Incorruptible integrity; integrity such as to secure the confidence of all men, and to deserve the appellation of 'the Just.' (2.) An exalted regard for the rites and ceremonies of the ancient religion, and a desire that they should be respected everywhere and honoured. He was more slow in coming to the conclusion that they were to be superseded by Christianity than Paul or Peter was (comp. Acts xxi. 18; Gal. ii. 12), though he admitted that they were not to be *imposed* on the Gentile converts as absolutely binding. Acts xv. 19-21, 24-29. Repeated intimations of his great respect for the laws of Moses are found in the Epistle before us, thus furnishing an internal proof of its genuineness. If he was educated as a Nazarene, and if he always resided with the Jews, in the very vicinity of the Temple, this is not difficult to be accounted for, and this might be expected to tinge his writings. (3.) The point from which he contemplated religion particularly was, *conformity to the law*. He looked at it as it was intended, to regulate the life, and to produce holiness of deportment, in opposition to all lax views of morals and low conceptions of holiness. He lived in a corrupt age, and among corrupt people; among those who sought to be justified before God by the mere fact that they were Jews, that they had the true religion, and that they were the chosen people of God, and who, in consequence, were lax in their morals, and comparatively regardless of the obligations to personal holiness. He therefore contemplated religion, not so much in respect to the question how man may be justified, as to the question to what kind of *life* it will lead us; and his great object was to show that *personal holiness* is necessary to salvation. Paul, on the other hand, was led to contemplate it mainly with reference to another question—how man may be justified; and it became necessary for him to show that men cannot be justified by their own works, but that it must be by faith in the Redeemer. The error which Paul particularly combats, is an error on the subject of justification; the error which James particularly opposes, is a practical error on the influence of religion on the life. It was because religion was contemplated by these two writers from those different points of view, and not from any real contradiction, that the apparent discrepancy arose between the Epistle of James and the writings of Paul. The peculiarity in the character and circumstances of James will account for the views which he took of religion; and, keeping this in mind, it will be easy to show that there is no real contradiction between these writers. It was of great importance to guard against each of the errors referred to; and the views expressed by both of the apostles are necessary to understand the nature and to see the full developement of religion.

How long James lived, and when and how he died, is not certainly known. It is agreed by all that he spent his last days in Jerusalem, and that he probably died there. On the subject of his death there is a remarkable passage in Josephus, which, though its genuineness has been disputed, is worth transcribing, as, if genuine, it shows the respect in which James was held, and contains an interesting account of his death. It is as follows:—" The emperor [Roman] being informed of the death of Festus, sent Albinus to be prefect of Judea. But the younger Ananus, who, as we said before, was made high priest, was haughty in his behaviour, and was very ambitious. And, moreover, he was of the sect of the Sadducees, who, as we have also observed before, are, above all other Jews, severe in their judicial sentences. This, then, being the temper of Ananus, he, thinking he had a fit opportunity, because Festus was dead, and Albinus was yet on the road, calls a council. And, bringing before them James, the brother of him who is called Christ, and some others, he accused them as transgressors of the laws, and had them stoned to death. But the most moderate men of the city, who were also reckoned most skilful in the laws, were offended at this proceeding. They therefore sent privately to the king [Agrippa the younger], entreating him to send orders to Ananus no more to attempt any such things."—

Ant., B. xx. A long account of the manner of his death, by Hegesippus, is preserved in Eusebius, going much more into detail, and evidently introducing much that is fabulous. The *amount* of all that can now be known in regard to his decease would seem to be, that he was put to death by violence in Jerusalem, a short time before the destruction of the Temple. From the well-known character of the Jews, this account is by no means improbable. On the subject of his life and death, the reader may find all that is known in Lardner's Works, vol. vi. pp. 162–195; Bacon's Lives of the Apostles, pp. 411–433; and Neander, Hist. of the Planting of the Christian Church, ii., pp. 1–23, Edin. Ed.

The belief that it was this James, the son of Alpheus, who resided so long at Jerusalem, who was the author of this Epistle, has been the common, though not the unanimous opinion of the Christian church, and seems to be supported by satisfactory arguments. It must evidently have been written either by him or by James the elder, the son of Zebedee, or by some other James, the supposed literal brother of our Lord.

In regard to these opinions, we may observe,

I. That the supposition that it was written by some third one of that name, 'wholly unknown to fame,' is mere hypothesis. It has no evidence whatever in its support.

II. There are strong reasons for supposing that it was not written by James the elder, the son of Zebedee, and brother of John. It has been indeed ascribed to him. In the old Syriac version, in the earlier editions, it is expressly attributed to him. But against this opinion the following objections may be urged, which seem to be conclusive. (1.) James the elder was beheaded about the year 43, or 44, and if this epistle was written by him, it is the oldest of the writings of the New Testament. It is possible, indeed, that the epistle may have been written at as early a period as that, but the considerations which remain to be stated, will show that this epistle has sufficient internal marks to prove that it was of later origin. (2.) Before the death of James the elder, the preaching of the gospel was chiefly confined within the limits of Palestine; but this epistle was written to Christians 'of the dispersion,' that is, to those who resided out of Palestine. It is hardly credible that in so short a time after the ascension of our Lord, there were so many Christians scattered abroad as to make it probable that a letter would be sent to them. (3.) This epistle is occupied very much with a consideration of a false and perverted view of the doctrine of justification by faith. It is evident that false views on that subject prevailed, and that a considerable corruption of morals was the consequence. But this supposes that the doctrine of justification by faith had been extensively preached; consequently that considerable time had elapsed from the time when the doctrine had been first promulgated. The perversion of a doctrine, so as to produce injurious effects, seldom occurs until some time after the doctrine was first preached, and it can hardly be supposed that this would have occurred before the death of James, the son of Zebedee. See these reasons stated more at length in *Benson.*

III. There are strong probabilities, from the epistle itself, to show that it was written by James the Less. (1.) His position at Jerusalem, and his eminence among the apostles, as well as his established character, made it proper that he should address such an epistle to those who were scattered abroad. There was no one among the apostles who would command greater respect from those abroad who were of Jewish origin than James. If he had his residence at Jerusalem; if he was in any manner regarded as the head of the church there; if he sustained a near relation to the Lord Jesus; and if his character was such as has been commonly represented, there was no one among the apostles whose opinions would be treated with greater respect, or who would be considered as having a clearer right to address those who were scattered abroad. (2.) The character of the epistle accords with the well-known character of James the Less. His strong regard for the law; his zeal for incorruptible integrity ; his opposition to

INTRODUCTION. 9

lax notions of morals; his opposition to all reliance on faith that was not productive of good works, all appear in this epistle. The necessity of conformity to the law of God, and of a holy life, is everywhere apparent, and the views expressed in the epistle agree with all that is stated of the early education and the established character of James. While there is no real contradiction between this epistle and the writings of Paul, yet it is much more easy to show that this is a production of James than it would be to prove that it was written by Paul. Comp. *Hug*, Intro., § 159.

§ 2. *To whom was the Epistle written ?*

The epistle purports to have been written to 'the twelve tribes scattered abroad' —or the 'twelve tribes *of the dispersion*'—ἐν τῇ διασπορᾷ; ch. i. 1. See Notes on 1 Pet. i. 1, and Notes on ch. i. 1 of this epistle. No mention of the *place* where they resided is made; nor can it be determined to what portion of the world it was first sent, or whether more than one copy was sent. All that can be conclusively determined in regard to the persons to whom it was addressed, is, (1.) That they were of Jewish descent—as is implied in the phrase 'to the twelve tribes' (ch. i. 1), and as is manifest in all the reasonings of the epistle; and, (2.) That they were Christian converts, ch. ii. 1. But by whose labours they were converted, is wholly unknown. The Jewish people who were 'scattered abroad' had two central points of union, the dispersion in the East, of which Babylon was the head, and the dispersion in the West, of which Alexandria was the head, Hug. § 156. Peter wrote his epistles to the latter (1 Pet. i. 1), though he was at Babylon when he wrote them (1 Pet. v. 13), and it would seem probable that this epistle was addressed to the former. Beza supposed that this epistle was sent to the believing Jews, dispersed all over the world; Grotius, that it was written to all the Jews living out of Judea; Lardner, that it was written to all Jews, descendants of Jacob, of every denomination, in Judea, and out of it. It seems plain, however, from the epistle itself, that it was not addressed to the Jews *as such*, or without respect to their being already Christians, for (*a*) if it had been, it is hardly conceivable that there should have been no arguments to prove that Jesus was the Messiah, and no extended statements of the nature of the Christian system; and (*b*) it bears on the face of it evidence of having been addressed to those who were regarded as Christians; ch. ii. 1; v. 7, 11, 14. It may be difficult to account for the fact, on any principles, that there are no more definite allusions to the nature of the Christian doctrines in the epistle, but it is morally certain that if it had been written to Jews *as such*, by a Christian apostle, there would have been a more formal defence and statement of the Christian religion. Compare the arguments of the apostles with the Jews in the Acts, *passim.* I regard the epistle, therefore, as having been sent to those who were of Jewish origin, but who had embraced the Christian faith, by one who had been himself a Jew, and who, though now a Christian apostle, retained much of his early habits of thinking and reasoning in addressing his own countrymen.

§ 3. *Where and when was the Epistle written ?*

There are no certain indications by which it can be determined *where* this epistle was written, but if the considerations above suggested are well founded, there can be little doubt that it was at Jerusalem. There are indeed certain internal marks, as Hug has observed (Intro. § 155), pertaining to the *country* with which the writer was familiar, and to certain features of natural scenery incidentally alluded to in the epistle. Thus, his native land was situated not far from the sea (ch. i. 6; iii. 4); it was blessed with valuable productions, as figs, oil, and wine (ch. iii. 12); there were springs of saline and fresh water with which he was familiar (ch. iii. 11); the land was much exposed to drought, and there were frequently reasons to apprehend famine from the want of rain (ch. v. 17, 28)·

there were sad devastations produced, and to be dreaded, from a consuming, burning wind (ch. i. 11); and it was a land in which the phenomena known as ' early and latter rains ' were familiarly understood ; ch. v. 7. All these allusions apply well to Palestine, and were such as would be employed by one who resided in that country, and they may be regarded as an incidental proof that the epistle was written in that land.

There is no way of determining with certainty *when* the epistle was written. Hug supposes that it was after the epistle to the Hebrews, and not before the beginning of the tenth year of Nero, nor after the accession of Albinus ; *i. e.* the close of the same year. Mill and Fabricius suppose it was before the destruction of Jerusalem, and about a year and a half before the death of James. Lardner supposes that James was put to death about the year 62, and that this epistle was written about a year before. He supposes also that his death was hastened by the strong language of reprehension employed in the epistle. It is probable that the year in which it was written was not far from A.D. 58 or 60, some ten or twelve years before the destruction of Jerusalem.

§ 4. *The canonical Authority of the Epistle.*

On the question generally respecting the canonical authority of the disputed epistles, see the Intro. to the Catholic Epistles, § 2. The particular proof of the canonical authority of this epistle is contained in the evidence that it was written by one of the apostles. If it was written, as suggested above (§ 1), by James the Less, or if it be supposed that it was written by James the elder, both of whom were apostles, its canonical authority will be admitted. As there is no evidence that it was written by any other James, the point seems to be clear.

But there are additional considerations, derived from its reception in the church, which may furnish some degree of confirmation of its authority. These are, (*a*) It was included in the old Syriac version, the Peshita, made either in the first century or in the early part of the second, thus showing that it was recognised in the country to which it was probably sent ; (*b*) Ephrem the Syrian, in his Greek works, made use of it in many places, and attributed it to James, the brother of our Lord (*Hug*); (*c*) It is quoted as of authority by several of the Fathers ; by Clement of Rome, who does not indeed mention the *name* of the writer, but quotes the words of the epistle (James iii. 13; iv. 6, 11; ii. 21, 23) ; by Hermas ; and by Jerome. See Lardner, vol. vi. pp. 195–199, and Hug, § 161.

§ 5. *The evidence that the writer was acquainted with the writings of Paul; the alleged contradiction between them; and the question how they can be reconciled.*

It has been frequently supposed, and sometimes affirmed, that this epistle is directly contradictory to Paul on the great doctrine of justification, and that it was written to counteract the tendency of his writings on that subject. Thus Hug strangely says, " In this epistle, Paul is (if I may be allowed to use so harsh an expression for a while) contradicted so flatly, that it would seem to have been written in opposition to some of his doctrines and opinions." § 157. It is of importance, therefore, to inquire into the foundation of this charge, for if it be so, it is clear that either this epistle or those of Paul would not be entitled to a place in the sacred canon. In order to this investigation, it is necessary to inquire to what extent the author was acquainted with the writings of Paul, and then to ask whether the statements of James are susceptible of any explanation which will reconcile them with those of Paul.

(1.) There is undoubted evidence that the author was acquainted with the writings of Paul. This evidence is found in the *similarity* of the expressions occurring in the epistles of Paul and James ; a similarity such as would occur not merely from the fact that two men were writing on the same subject, but such as occurs only where one is acquainted with the writings of the other. Between two persons writing on the same subject, and resting their opinions on the same general reasons, there might be indeed a general resemblance, and possibly there might be expressions used which would be precisely the same. But it might happen that the resemblance would be so minute and particular, and on points where there could be naturally no such similarity, as to demonstrate that one of the writers was familiar with the productions of the other. For example, a man writing on a religious subject, if he had never heard of the Bible, *might* use expressions coincident with some that are found there ; but it is clear also that he might in so many cases use the same expressions which occur there, and on points where the statements in the Bible are so peculiar, as to show conclusively that he was familiar with that book. So also a man might show that he was familiar with the Rambler or the Spectator, with Shakspeare or Milton. Such, it is supposed, are the allusions in the epistle of James, showing that he was acquainted with the writings of Paul. Among these passages are the following :—

JAMES.	PAUL.
i. 3. Knowing this, that the trying of your faith worketh patience.	Rom. v. 3. Knowing that tribulation worketh patience.
i. 2. Count it all joy when ye fall into divers temptations.	Rom. v. 3. We glory in tribulations also.
i. 4. Wanting nothing.	1 Cor. i. 7. Ye come behind in no gift.
i. 6. He that wavereth is like a wave of the sea, driven with the wind and tossed.	Eph. iv. 14. Tossed to and fro, carried about with every wind of doctrine.
i. 12. When he is tried, he shall receive the crown of life.	2 Tim. iv. 8. There is laid up for me a crown of righteousness.
i. 15. When lust hath conceived, it bringeth forth sin ; and sin, when it is finished, bringeth forth death.	Rom. vii. 7, 8. I had not known lust, except the law had said, Thou shalt not covet. But sin, taking occasion by the commandment, wrought in me all manner of concupiscence.
i. 18. That we should be a kind of first-fruits of his creatures.	Rom. viii. 23. Ourselves also which have the first-fruits of the Spirit.
i. 21. Lay apart all filthiness and superfluity of naughtiness, &c.	Col. iv. 8. But now ye also put off all these ; anger, wrath, malice, blasphemy, filthy communications out of your mouth.
i. 22. But be ye doers of the word, and not hearers only, &c.	Rom. ii. 13. For not the hearers of the law are just before God, but the doers of the law.
ii. 5. Hath not God chosen the poor of this world, rich in faith, &c.	1 Cor. i. 27. But God hath chosen the foolish things of the world, to confound the wise, &c.

Compare also, on this subject, the passage in James v. 14–26, with Romans iii. 20, seq.; the examples of Abraham and Rahab, referred to in ch. ii. 21, 25, with the reference to Abraham in Rom. iv.; and James iv. 12, with Rom. ii. 1, and xiv. 4.

These passages will show that James had an acquaintance with the writings of Paul, and that he was familiar with his usual method of expressing his thoughts. These allusions are not such as two men would be likely to make who were total strangers to each other's mode of speaking and of writing.

It may be added here, also, that some critics have supposed that there is another kind of evidence that James was acquainted with the writings of Paul.

than that which arises from mere similarity of expression, and that he *meant* to refer to him, with a view to correct the influence of some of his views. Thus, Hug, in the passage already referred to (§ 157), says, " In this Epistle, the apostle Paul is (if I may be allowed to use so harsh an expression for a while) contradicted so flatly, that it would seem to have been written in opposition to some of his doctrines and opinions. All that Paul has taught respecting faith, its efficacy in justification, and the inutility of works, is here directly contravened." After citing examples from the Epistle to the Romans, and the Epistle of James, in support of this, Hug adds, " The Epistle was therefore written of set purpose against Paul, against the doctrine that faith procures man justification and the divine favour." The contradiction between James and Paul appeared so palpable to Luther, and the difficulty of reconciling them seemed to him to be so great, that for a long time he rejected the Epistle of James altogether. He subsequently, however, became satisfied that it was a part of the inspired canon of Scripture.

(2.) It has been, therefore, an object of much solicitude to know how the views of Paul and James, apparently so contradictory, can be reconciled ; and many attempts have been made to do it. Those who wish to pursue this inquiry to greater length than is consistent with the design of these Notes, may consult Neander's History of the Planting of the Christian Church, vol. ii., pp. 1–23, 228–239, and Dr. Dwight's Theology, serm. lxviii. The particular consideration of this pertains more appropriately to the exposition of the Epistle (see the remarks at the close of ch. iii.) ; but a few general principles may be laid down here, which may aid those who are disposed to make the comparison between the two, and which may show that there is no *designed*, and no *real* contradiction.

(*a*) The view which is taken of any object depends much on the point of vision from which it is beheld—the *stand-point*, as the Germans say ; and in order to estimate the truthfulness or value of a description or a picture, it is necessary for us to place ourselves in the same position with him who has given the description, or who has made the picture. Two men, painting or describing a mountain, a valley, a waterfall, or an edifice, might take such different positions in regard to it, that the descriptions which they give would seem to be quite contradictory and irreconcilable, unless this were taken into the account. A landscape, sketched from the top of a high tower or on a level plain ; a view of Niagara Falls, taken above or below the falls—on the American or Canada side ; a view of St. Paul's, taken from one side or another, from the dome or when on the ground, might be very different ; and two such views might present features which it would be scarcely possible to reconcile with each other. So it is of moral subjects. Much depends on the point from which they are viewed, and from the bearings and tendencies of the doctrine which is the particular subject of contemplation. The subject of *temperance*, for example, may be contemplated with reference, on the one hand, to the dangers arising from too lax a view of the matter, or, on the other, to the danger of pressing the principle too far ; and in order to know a man's views, and not to do injustice to him, it is proper to understand the particular aspect in which he looked at it, and the particular object which he had in view.

(*b*) The *object* of Paul—the ' stand-point ' from which he viewed the subject of justification—on which point alone it has been supposed that he and James differ—was to show that there is no justification before God, except by faith ; that the meritorious cause of justification is the atonement ; that good works do not enter into the question of justification as a matter of merit, or as the ground of acceptance ; that if it were not for faith in Christ, it would not be possible for man to be justified. The point which he *opposes* is, that men can be justified by good works, by conformity to the law, by dependence on rites and ceremonies, by birth or blood. The aim of Paul is not to demonstrate that good works are not necessary or desirable in religion, but that they are not the ground of justification. The point of view in which he contemplates man, is *before* he is converted, and with reference to the question on *what ground* he can be justified :

and he affirms that it is only by faith, and that good works come in for no share in justification, as a ground of merit.

(c) The object of James—the 'stand-point' from which he viewed the subject —was, to show that a man cannot have evidence that he is justified, or that his faith is genuine, unless he is characterized by good works, or by holy living. His aim is to show, not that faith is not essential to justification, and not that the real ground of dependence is not the merit of the Saviour, but that conformity to the law of God is indispensable to true religion. The point of view in which he contemplates the subject, is *after* a man professes to be justified, and with reference to the question whether his faith is *genuine;* and he affirms that no faith is of value in justification but that which is productive of good works. By his own character, by education, by the habits of his whole life, he was accustomed to look on religion as obedience to the will of God; and every thing in his character led him to oppose all that was lax in principle, and loose in tendency, in religion. The point which he *opposed,* thererore, was, that mere *faith* in religion, as a revelation from God; a mere assent to certain doctrines, without a corresponding life, could be a ground of justification before God. This was the prevalent error of his countrymen; and while the Jews held to the belief of divine revelation as a matter of speculative faith, the most lax views of morals prevailed, and they freely indulged in practices entirely inconsistent with true piety, and subversive of all proper views of religion. It was not improper, therefore, as Paul had given prominence to one aspect of the doctrine of justification, showing that a man could not be saved by dependence on the works of the law, but that it must be by the work of Christ, that James should give due prominence to the other form of the doctrine, by showing that the essential and necessary tendency of the true doctrine of justification was to lead to a holy life; and that a man whose life was not conformed to the law of God, *could* not depend on any mere assent to the truth of religion, or any speculative faith whatever. Both these statements are necessary to a full exposition of the doctrine of justification; both are opposed to dangerous errors; and both, therefore, are essential in order to a full understanding of that important subject.

(d) Both these statements are true. (1.) That of Paul is true, that there can be no justification before God on the ground of our own works, but that the real ground of justification is faith in the great sacrifice made for sin. (2.) That of James is no less true, that there can be no genuine faith which is not productive of good works, and that good works furnish the evidence that we have true religion, and are just before God. A mere faith; a naked assent to dogmas, accompanied with lax views of morals, can furnish no evidence of true piety. It is as true, that where there is not a holy life there is no religion, as it is in cases where there is no faith.

It may be added, therefore, that the Epistle of James occupies an important place in the New Testament, and that it could not be withdrawn without materially marring the proportions of the scheme of religion which is there revealed. Instead, therefore, of being regarded as contradictory to any part of the New Testament, it should rather be deemed indispensable to the concinnity and beauty of the whole.

Keeping in view, therefore, the general design of the Epistle, and the point of view from which James contemplated the subject of religion; the general corruptions of the age in which he lived, in regard to morals; the tendency of the Jews to suppose that mere assent to the truths of religion was enough to save them; the liability which there was to abuse the doctrine of Paul on the subject of justification,—it will not be difficult to understand the general drift of this Epistle, or to appreciate its value. A summary of its contents, and a more particular view of its design, will be found in the Analyses prefixed to the several chapters.

EPISTLE OF JAMES.

CHAPTER I.

JAMES, a servant *a* of God and of the Lord Jesus Christ, to the twelve *b* tribes which are scattered *c* abroad, greeting.

a Jude 1.   *b* Ac.26.7.   *c* Ac.8.1.

CHAPTER I.

ANALYSIS OF THE CHAPTER.

This chapter seems to comprise two general classes of subjects; the statement in regard to the first of which is complete, but the second is only commenced in this chapter, and is continued in the second. The first is the general subject of temptation and trial (vs. 1-15); the second is the nature of true religion:— the statement that all true religion has its origin in God, the source of purity and truth, and that it requires us to be docile and meek; to be doers of the word; to bridle the tongue, and to be the friends of the fatherless and the widow, vs. 16-27.

I. The general subject of temptation or trial, vs. 1-15. It is evident that those to whom the epistle was directed were, at that time, suffering in some form, or that they were called to pass through temptations, and that they needed counsel and support. They were in danger of sinking in despondency; of murmuring and complaining, and of charging God as the author of temptation and of sin. This part of the chapter comprises the following topics:

1. The salutation, ver. 1.

2. The subject of temptations or trials. They were to regard it, not as a subject of sorrow, but of gladness and joy, that they were called to pass through trials; for, if borne in a proper manner, they would produce the grace of patience, and this was to be regarded as an object worth being secured, even by much suffering, vs. 2-4.

3. If in their trials they felt that they had lacked the wisdom which they needed to enable them to bear them in a proper manner, they had the privilege of looking to God, and seeking it at his hand. This was a privilege conceded to all, and if it were asked in faith, without any wavering, it would certainly be granted, vs. 5-7.

4. The importance and value of stability, especially in trials; of being firm in principle, and of having one single great aim in life. A man who wavered in his faith would waver in every thing, ver. 8.

5. An encouragement to those who, in the trials which they experienced, passed through rapid changes of circumstances. Whatever those changes were, they were to rejoice in them as ordered by the Lord. They were to remember the essential instability of all earthly things. The rich especially, who were most disposed to murmur and complain when their circumstances were changed, were to remember how the burning heat blasts the beauty of the flower, and that in like manner all worldly splendour must fade away, vs. 9-11.

6. Every man is blessed who endures trials in a proper manner, for such an endurance of trial will be connected with a rich reward—the crown of life, ver. 12.

7. In their trials, however, in the allurements to sin which might be set before them; in the temptations to apostatize, or to do any thing wrong, which might be connected with their suffering condition, they were to be careful never to charge *temptation as such* on God. They were never to allow their minds to feel for a moment that

he allured them to sin, or placed an inducement of any kind before them to do wrong. Every thing of that kind, every disposition to commit sin, originated in their own hearts, and they should never allow themselves to charge it on God, vs. 13–15.

II. The nature of true religion, vs. 16–27.

1. It has its origin in God, the source of every good gift, the Father of lights, who has of his own will begotten us again, that he might raise us to an exalted rank among his creatures. God, therefore, should be regarded not as the author of sin, but as the source of all the good that is in us, vs. 16–18.

2. Religion requires us to be meek and docile; to lay aside all disposition to dictate or prescribe, all irritability against the truth, and all corruption of heart, and to receive meekly the ingrafted word, vs. 19–21.

3. Religion requires us to be doers of the word, and not hearers only, vs. 23, 24, 25.

4. Religion requires us to bridle the tongue, to set a special guard on our words, ver. 26.

5. Religion requires us to be the friends of the fatherless and the widow, and to keep ourselves unspotted from the world, ver. 27.

1. *James, a servant of God.* On the meaning of the word *servant* in this connexion, see Note on Rom. i. 1. Comp. Note on Philem. 16. It is remarkable that James does not call himself *an apostle;* but this does not prove that the writer of the epistle was not an apostle, for the same omission occurs in the epistle of John, and in the epistle of Paul to the Philippians, the Thessalonians, and to Philemon. It is remarkable, also, considering the relation which James is supposed to have borne to the Lord Jesus as his 'brother' (Gal. i. 19; Intro. § 1). that he did not refer to that as constituting a ground of claim to his right to address others; but this is only one instance out of many, in the New Testament, in which it is regarded as a higher honour to be the 'servant of God,' and to belong to his family, than to sustain *any* relations of blood or kindred. Comp. Matth. xii 50. It may be ob-

served also (Comp. the Intro. § 1), that this term is one which was peculiarly appropriate to James, as a man eminent for his integrity. His claim to respect and deference was not primarily founded on any relationship which he sustained; any honour of birth or blood; or even any external office, but on the fact that he was a '*servant of God.*' ¶ *And of the Lord Jesus Christ.* The 'servant of the Lord Jesus,' is an appellation which is often given to Christians, and particularly to the ministers of religion. They are his servants, not in the sense that they are *slaves,* but in the sense that they voluntarily obey his will, and labour for him, and not for themselves. ¶ *To the twelve tribes which are scattered abroad.* Gr. 'The twelve tribes which are *in the dispersion,*' or of the dispersion (ἐν τῇ διασπορᾷ). This word occurs only here and in 1 Pet. i. 1, and John vii. 35. It refers properly to those who lived out of Palestine, or who were scattered among the Gentiles. There were *two* great 'dispersions;' the Eastern and the Western. The first had its origin about the time when the ten tribes were carried away to Assyria, and in the time of the Babylonian captivity. In consequence of these events, and of the fact that large numbers of the Jews went to Babylon, and other Eastern countries, for purposes of travel, commerce, &c., there were many Jews in the East in the times of the apostles. The other was the Western 'dispersion,' which commenced about the time of Alexander the Great, and which was promoted by various causes, until there were large numbers of Jews in Egypt and along Northern Africa, in Asia Minor, in Greece proper, and even in Rome. To which of these classes this epistle was directed is not known; but most probably the writer had particular reference to those in the East. See the Intro. § 2. The phrase 'the twelve tribes,' was the common term by which the Jewish people were designated, and was in use long after the ten tribes were carried away, leaving, in fact, but two of the twelve in Palestine. Comp. Notes on Acts xxvi. 7. Many have supposed that James here addressed them as Jews, and that the epistle was sent

2 My brethren, count it all joy *a* when ye fall into divers temptations;

a Matt.5.12.   1 Pet.4.13-16.

3 Knowing *this*, that the trying of your faith worketh *b* patience.
4 But let patience *c* have *her*

b Ro.5.3.   *c* Lu. 8.15; 21.19.

to them *as* such. But this opinion has no probability; for (1) had this been the case, he would not have been likely to begin his epistle by saying that he was ' a servant of Jesus Christ,' a name so odious to the Jews ; and (2) if he *had* spoken of himself as a Christian, and had addressed his countrymen as himself a believer in Jesus as the Messiah, though regarding them *as Jews*, it is incredible that he did not make a more distinct reference to the principles of the Christian religion ; that he used no arguments to convince them that Jesus was the Messiah ; that he did not attempt to convert them to the Christian faith. It should be added, that at first most converts were made from those who had been trained in the Jewish faith, and it is not improbable that one in Jerusalem, addressing those who were Christians out of Palestine, would naturally think of them as of Jewish origin, and would be likely to address them as appertaining to the ' twelve tribes.' The phrase ' the twelve tribes ' became also a sort of technical expression to denote the people of God—the church. ¶ *Greeting*. A customary form of salutation, meaning, in Greek, *to joy, to rejoice;* and implying that he wished their welfare. Comp. Acts xv. 23.

2. *My brethren*. Not brethren *as Jews*, but *as Christians*. Comp. ch. ii. 1. ¶ *Count it all joy*. Regard it as a thing to rejoice in ; a matter which should afford you happiness. You are not to consider it as a punishment, a curse, or a calamity, but as a fit subject of felicitation. Comp. Notes Matt. v. 12. ¶ *When ye fall into divers temptations*. On the meaning of the word *temptations*, see Notes on Matt. iv. 1. It is now commonly used in the sense of placing allurements before others to induce them to sin, and in this sense the word seems to be used in vs. 13, 14 of this chapter. Here, however, the word is used in the sense of *trials*, to wit, by persecution, poverty, calamity of any kind. These cannot be said to be direct inducements or allurements to sin, but

they try the faith, and they show whether he who is tried is disposed to adhere to his faith in God, or whether he will apostatise. They so far *coincide* with temptations, properly so called, as to *test* the religion of men. They *differ* from temptations, properly so called, in that they are not brought before the mind *for the express purpose* of inducing men to sin. In this sense it is true that God never *tempts* men, vs. 13, 14. On the sentiment in the passage before us, see Notes on 1 Pet. i. 6, 7. The word *divers* here refers to the various kinds of trials which they might experience—sickness, poverty, bereavement, persecution, &c. They were to count it a matter of joy that their religion was subjected to any thing that tried it. It is well for us to have the reality of our religion tested, in whatever way it may be done.

3. *Knowing this, that the trying of your faith worketh patience*. Patience is one of the fruits of such a trial, and the grace of patience is *worth* the trial which it may cost to procure it. This is one of the passages which show that James was acquainted with the writings of Paul. See the Intro. § 5. The sentiment expressed here is found in Rom. v. 3. See Notes on that verse. Paul has carried the sentiment out farther, and shows that tribulation produces other effects than patience. James only asks that patience may have its perfect work, supposing that every Christian grace is implied in this.

4. *But let patience have* her *perfect work*. Let it be fairly developed ; let it produce its appropriate effects without being hindered. Let it not be obstructed in its fair influence on the soul by murmurings, complaining, or rebellion. Patience under trials is fitted to produce important effects on the soul, and we are not to hinder them in any manner by a perverse spirit, or by opposition to the will of God. Every one who is afflicted should desire that the *fair* effects of affliction should be produced on his mind, or that there should be pro-

perfect work, that ye may be perfect and entire, wanting nothing.
5 If any of you lack wisdom, let

him ask of God, that *z* giveth to all
men liberally, and upbraideth not;
and *b* it shall be given him.

a Pr.2.3-6.   *b* Je.29.12.

duced in his soul precisely the results
which his trials are adapted to accomplish. ¶ *That ye may be perfect and
entire.* The meaning of this is explained
in the following phrase—'wanting nothing;' that is, that there may be nothing lacking to complete your character. There may be the elements of a
good character; there may be sound
principles, but those principles may not
be fully carried out so as to show what
they are. Afflictions, perhaps more than
any thing else, will do this, and we
should therefore allow them to do all
that they are adapted to do in developing
what is good in us. The idea here is,
that it is desirable not only to have the
elements or *principles* of piety in the
soul, but to have them fairly carried
out, so as to show what is their real
tendency and value. Comp. Notes on 1
Pet. i. 7. On the word *perfect*, as used
in the Scriptures, see Notes on Job i. 1.
The word rendered *entire* (ὁλόκληροι)
means, *whole in every part.* Comp.
Notes on 1 Thess. v. 23. The word
occurs only in these two places. The
corresponding noun (ὁλοκληρία) occurs in
Acts iii. 16, rendered *perfect soundness.*
¶ *Wanting nothing.* 'Being left in
nothing;' that is, every thing being
complete, or fully carried out.
  5. *If any of you lack wisdom.* Probably this refers particularly to the
kind of wisdom which they would need
in their trials, to enable them to bear
them in a proper manner, for there is
nothing in which Christians more feel
the need of heavenly wisdom than in regard to the manner in which they should
bear trials, and what they should *do* in
the perplexities, and disappointments,
and bereavements that come upon them;
but the language employed is so general,
that what is here said may be applied to
the need of wisdom in all respects. The
particular kind of wisdom which we need
in trials is to enable us to understand
their design and tendency; to perform
our duty under them, or the new duties which may grow out of them; to
learn the lessons which God designs

to teach, for he always designs to teach
us *some* valuable lessons by affliction;
and to cultivate such views and feelings
as are appropriate under the peculiar
forms of trial which are brought upon
us; to find out the sins for which we
have been afflicted, and to learn how
we may avoid them in time to come.
We are in great danger of going wrong
when we are afflicted; of complaining
and murmuring; of evincing a spirit of
insubmission, and of losing the benefits
which we *might* have obtained if we had
submitted to the trial in a proper manner. So in all things we 'lack wisdom.'
We are short-sighted; we have hearts
prone to sin; and there are great and
important matters pertaining to duty
and salvation on which we cannot but
feel that we need heavenly guidance.
¶ *Let him ask of God.* That is, for the
specific wisdom which he needs; the
very wisdom which is necessary for him
in the particular case. It is proper to
bear the very case before God; to make
mention of the specific want; to ask of
God to guide us in the very matter
where we feel so much embarrassment.
It is one of the privileges of Christians,
that they may not only go to God and
ask him for that *general* wisdom which
is needful for them in life, but that
whenever a particular emergency arises,
a case of perplexity and difficulty in
regard to duty, they may bring that
particular thing before his throne, with
the assurance that he will guide them.
Comp. Ps. xxv. 9; Isa. xxxvii. 14; Joel
ii. 17. ¶ *That giveth to all* men *liberally.* The word *men* here is supplied
by the translators, but not improperly,
though the promise should be regarded
as restricted to those who *ask.* The
object of the writer was to encourage
those who felt their need of wisdom, to
go and ask it of God; and it would not
contribute any thing to furnish such a
specific encouragement to say of God
that he gives to all men liberally *whether
they ask or not.* In the Scriptures, the
promise of divine aid is always limited
to the desire. No blessing is promised

6 But *a* let him ask in faith, nothing wavering. For he that

a Mar.11.24.

wavereth, is like a wave of the sea, driven with the wind and tossed.

---

to man that is not sought; no man can feel that he has a right to hope for the favour of God, who does not value it enough to pray for it; no one *ought* to obtain it, who does *not* prize it enough to ask for it. Comp. Matt. vii. 7, 8. The word rendered *liberally* (ἁπλῶς) means, properly, *simply;* that is, in simplicity, sincerity, reality. It occurs nowhere else in the New Testament, though the corresponding *noun* occurs in Rom. xii. 8; 2 Cor. i. 12; xi. 3, rendered *simplicity;* in 2 Cor. viii. 2; ix. 13, rendered *liberality,* and *liberal;* 2 Cor. ix. 11, rendered *bountifulness;* and Eph. vi. 5; Col. iii. 22, rendered *singleness,* scil., of the heart. The idea seems to be that of openness, frankness, generosity; the absence of all that is sordid and contracted; where there is the manifestation of generous feeling, and liberal conduct. In a higher sense than in the case of any man, all that is excellent in these things is to be found in God; and we may therefore come to him feeling that in his heart there is more that is noble and generous in bestowing favours than in any other being. There is nothing that is stinted and close; there is no partiality; there is no withholding of his favour because we are poor, and unlettered, and unknown. ¶ *And upbraideth not.* Does not reproach, rebuke, or treat harshly. He does not coldly repel us, if we come and ask what we need, though we do it often and with importunity. Comp. Luke xviii. 1–7. The proper meaning of the Greek word is to rail at, reproach, revile, chide; and the object here is probably to place the manner in which God bestows his favours in contrast with what sometimes occurs among men. He does not reproach or chide us for our past conduct; for our foolishness; for our importunity in asking. He permits us to come in the most free manner, and meets us with a spirit of entire kindness, and with promptness in granting our requests. We are not always sure, when we ask a favour of a man, that we shall not encounter something that we will be repulsive, or that will

mortify us; we are certain, however, when we ask a favour of God, that we shall never be reproached in an unfeeling manner, or meet with a harsh response. ¶ *And it shall be given him.* Comp. Jer. xxix. 12, 13, "Then shall ye call upon me, and go and pray unto me, and I will hearken unto you. And ye shall seek me, and find me, when ye shall search for me with your whole heart." See also Matt. vii. 7, 8; xxi. 22; Mark xi. 24; 1 John iii. 22; v. 14. This promise in regard to the *wisdom* that may be necessary for us, is absolute ; and we may be sure that if it be asked in a proper manner it will be granted us. There can be no doubt that it is one of the things which God is able to impart; which will be for our own good; and which, therefore, he is ever ready to bestow. About many things there might be doubt whether, if they were granted, they would be for our real welfare, and therefore there may be a doubt whether it would be consistent for God to bestow them; but there can be no such doubt about *wisdom.* That is always for our good ; and we may be sure, therefore, that we shall obtain that, if the request be made with a right spirit. If it be asked in what way we may expect he will bestow it on us, it may be replied, (1.) That it is through his word—by enabling us to see clearly the meaning of the sacred volume, and to understand the directions which he has there given to guide us; (2.) By the secret influences of his Spirit (*a*) *suggesting* to us the way in which we should go, and (*b*) *inclining* us to do that which is prudent and wise ; and (3.) By the events of his Providence making plain to us the path of duty, and removing the obstructions which may be in our path. It is easy for God to guide his people ; and they who 'watch daily at the gates, and wait at the posts of the doors' of wisdom (Prov. viii. 34), will not be in danger of going astray. Ps. xxv. 9.

6. *But let him ask in faith.* See the passages referred to in ver. 5. Comp. Notes on Matt. vii. 7, and on Heb. xi.

7 For let not that man think that he shall receive any thing of the Lord.

8 A double-minded man *is* un-stable in all his ways.

6. We cannot hope to obtain any favour from God if there is not faith; and where, as in regard to the *wisdom* necessary to guide us, we are sure that it is in accordance with his will to grant it to us, we may come to him with the utmost confidence, the most entire as-surance, that it will be granted. In this case, we should come to God without a doubt that, if we ask with a proper spirit, the very thing that we ask will be be-stowed on us. We cannot in all other cases be so sure that what we ask will be for our good, or that it will be in accordance with his will to bestow it; and hence we cannot in such cases come with the same kind of faith. We can then only come with unwavering con-fidence in God, that he will do what is right and best; and that if he sees that what we ask will be for our good, he will bestow it upon us. Here, however, nothing prevents our coming with the assurance that *the very thing* which we ask will be conferred on us. ¶ *Nothing wavering.* (μηδὲν διακρινόμενος.) 'Doubt-ing or hesitating as to nothing, or in no respect.' See Acts xx. 20; xi. 12. In regard to the matter under considera-tion, there is to be no hesitancy, no doubting, no vacillation of the mind. We are to come to God with the utmost confidence and assurance. ¶ *For he that wavereth, is like a wave of the sea,* &c. The propriety and beauty of this comparison will be seen at once. The wave of the sea has no stability. It is at the mercy of every wind, and seems to be driven and tossed every way. So he that comes to God with unsettled convictions and hopes, is liable to be driven about by every new feeling that may spring up in the mind. At one moment, hope and faith impel him to come to God; then the mind is at once filled with uncertainty and doubt, and the soul is agitated and restless as the ocean. Comp. Isa. lvii. 20. Hope on the one hand, and the fear of not ob-taining the favour which is desired on the other, keep the mind restless and discomposed.

7. *For let not that man think that he shall receive any thing of the Lord.* Comp. Heb. xi. 6. A man can hope for favour from God only as he puts confidence in him. He sees the heart; and if he sees that there is no belief in his existence, or his perfections—no real trust in him—no reliance on his pro-mises, his wisdom, his grace—it cannot be proper that he should grant an an-swer to our petitions. That will account sufficiently for the fact that there are so many prayers unanswered; that we so frequently go to the throne of grace, and are sent empty away. A man that goes to God in such a state of mind, should not *expect* to receive any favour. 8. *A double-minded man.* The word here used, δίψυχος occurs only here and in ch. iv. 8. It means, properly, one who has two souls; then one who is wavering or inconstant. It is applica-ble to a man who has no settled princi-ples; who is controlled by passion; who is influenced by popular feeling; who is now inclined to one opinion or course of conduct, and now to another. ¶ *Is unstable in all his ways.* That is, not merely in regard to prayer, the point particularly under discussion, but in respect to every thing. From the in-stability which the wavering must evince in regard to *prayer*, the apostle takes occasion to make the general remark concerning such a man, that stability and firmness could be expected on no subject. The hesitancy which he mani-fested on that one subject would extend to all; and we might expect to find such a man irresolute and undetermined in all things. This is always true. If we find a man who takes hold of the pro-mises of God with firmness; who feels the deepest assurance when he prays that God will hear prayer; who always goes to him without hesitation in his perplexities and trials, never wavering, we shall find one who is firm in his prin-ciples, steady in his integrity, settled in his determinations, and steadfast in his plans of life—a man whose character we shall feel that we understand, and in

9 Let the brother of low degree ¹ rejoice in that he is exalted:

1 Or, *glory.*

whom we can confide. Such a man eminently was Luther; and the spirit which is thus evinced by taking firmly hold of the promises of God is the best kind of religion.

9. *Let the brother of low degree.* This verse seems to introduce a new topic, which has no other connection with what precedes than that the apostle is discussing the general subject of trials. Comp. ver. 2. Turning from the consideration of trials in general, he passes to the consideration of a particular kind of trials, that which results from a change of circumstances in life, from poverty to affluence, and from affluence to poverty. The idea which seems to have been in the mind of the apostle is, that there is a great and important *trial of faith* in *any* reverse of circumstances; a trial in being elevated from poverty to riches, or in being depressed from a state of affluence to want. Wherever *change* occurs in the external circumstances of life, there a man's religion is put to the test, and there he should feel that God is trying the reality of his faith. The phrase ' of low degree' (*ταπεινὸς*) means one in humble circumstances; one of lowly rank or employment; one in a condition of dependence or poverty. It stands here particularly opposed to one who is *rich;* and the apostle doubtless had his eye, in the use of this word, on those who had been poor. ¶ *Rejoice,* marg. *glory.* Not because, being made rich, he has the means of sensual gratification and indulgence ; not because he will now be regarded as a rich man, and will feel that he is above want ; not even because he will have the means of doing good to others. Neither of these was the idea in the mind of the apostle ; but it was, that the poor man that is made rich should rejoice *because his faith and the reality of his religion are now tried;* because a *test* is furnished which will show, in the new circumstances in which he is placed, whether his piety is genuine. In fact, there is almost no trial of religion which is more certain and decisive than that furnished by a sudden transition from poverty to affluence,

from adversity to prosperity, from sickness to health. There is much religion in the world that will bear the ills of poverty, sickness, and persecution, or that will bear the temptations arising from prosperity, and even affluence, which will not bear the transition from one to the other ; as there is many a human frame that could become accustomed to bear either the steady heat of the equator, or the intense cold of the north, that could not bear a rapid transition from the one to the other. See this thought illustrated in the Notes on Phil. iv. 12. ¶ *In that he is exalted.* A good man *might* rejoice in such a transition, because it would furnish him the means of being more extensively useful ; most persons *would* rejoice because such a condition is that for which men commonly aim, and because it would furnish them the means of display, of sensual gratification, or of ease ; but neither of these is the idea of the apostle. The thing in which we are to rejoice in the transitions of life is, that a test is furnished of our piety ; that a trial is applied to it which enables us to determine whether it is genuine. The most important thing conceivable for us is to know whether we are true Christians, and we should rejoice in every thing that will enable us to settle this point.

[Yet it seems not at all likely that an Apostle would exhort a poor man to *rejoice* in his exaltation to wealth. An exhortation to fear and trembling appears more suitable. Wealth brings along with it so many dangerous temptations, that a man must have greater confidence in his faith and stability than he ought to have, who can rejoice in its acquisition, simply as furnishing occasion to *try* him: the same may be said of poverty, or of the transition from riches to poverty. The spirit of Agar is more suitable to the humility of piety, "Give me neither poverty nor riches; feed me with food convenient for me, lest I be full and deny thee, and say, Who is the Lord ? or lest I be poor, and steal, and take the name of my God in vain," Prov. xxx. 8, 9. Besides, there is no necessity for resorting to this interpretation. The words will, without any straining, bear another sense, which is both excellent in itself, and suitable in its connection. The poor man, or man in humble life, may

10 But the rich, in that he is made low: because as the flower of the grass *a* he shall pass away.

11 For the sun is no sooner risen with a burning heat, but it wither-

eth the grass, and the flower thereof falleth, and the grace of the fashion of it perisheth: so also shall the rich man fade away in his ways.

a Is.40.6.

---

well rejoice "in that he is exalted" to the dignity of a child of God, and heir of glory. If he be depressed with his humble rank in this life, let him but think of his spiritual elevation, of his relation to God and Christ, and he shall have an antidote for his dejection. What is the world's dignity in comparison of his! The rich man, or the man of rank, on the other hand, has reason to rejoice "in that he is made low" through the possession of a meek and humble spirit which his affluence illustrates, but neither destroys nor impairs. It would be matter of *grief* were he otherwise minded; since all his adventitious splendour is as evanescent as the flower which, forming for a time the crown of the green stalk on which it hangs, perishes before it. This falls admirably in with the design of the Apostle, which was to fortify Christians against trial. Every condition in life had its own trials. The two great conditions of poverty and wealth had theirs; but Christianity guards against the danger, both of the one state and of the other. It elevates the poor under his depression, and humbles the rich in his elevation, and bids both rejoice in its power to shield and bless them. The passage in this view is conceived in the same spirit with one of Paul, in which he beautifully balances the respective conditions of slaves and freemen, by honouring the former with the appellation of the *Lord's freemen*, and imposing on the latter that of *Christ's servants*, 1 Cor. vii. 22.]

10. *But the rich, in that he is made low*. That is, because his property is taken away, and he is made poor. Such a transition is often the source of the deepest sorrow; but the apostle says that even in that a Christian may find occasion for thanksgiving. The *reasons* for rejoicing in this manner, which the apostle seems to have had in view, were these: (1) because it furnished a *test* of the reality of religion, by showing that it is adapted to sustain the soul in this great trial; that it cannot only bear prosperity, but that it can bear the rapid transition from that state to one of poverty; and (2) because it would furnish to the mind an impressive and salutary illustration of the fact that *all* earthly glory is soon to fade away. I may remark here, that the transition from affluence to poverty

is often borne by Christians with the manifestation of a most lovely spirit, and with an entire freedom from murmuring and complaining. Indeed, there are more Christians who could safely bear a transition from affluence to poverty, from prosperity to adversity, than there are who could bear a sudden transition from poverty to affluence. Some of the loveliest exhibitions of piety which I have ever witnessed have been in such transitions; nor have I seen occasion anywhere to love religion more than in the ease, and grace, and cheerfulness with which it has enabled those accustomed long to more elevated walks, to descend to the comparatively humble lot where God places them. New grace is imparted for this new form of trial, and new traits of Christian character are developed in these rapid transitions, as some of the most beautiful exhibitions of the laws of matter are brought out in the rapid transitions in the laboratory of the chemist. ¶ *Because as the flower of the grass he shall pass away.* That is, since it is *a fact* that he will thus pass away, he should rejoice that he is reminded of it. He should, therefore, esteem it a favour that this lesson is brought impressively before his mind. To learn this effectually, though by the loss of property, is of more value to him than all his wealth would be if he were forgetful of it. The comparison of worldly splendour with the fading flower of the field, is one that is common in Scripture. It is probable that James had his eye on the passage in Isaiah xl. 6–8. See Notes on that passage. Comp. Notes on 1 Pet. i. 24, 25. See also Ps. ciii. 15; Matt. vi. 28–30.

11. *For the sun is no sooner risen with a burning heat.* Isaiah (xl. 7) employs the word *wind*, referring to a burning wind that dries up the flowers. It is probable that the apostle also refers not so much to the sun itself, as to the hot and fiery wind called the *simoom*, which often rises *with* the sun, and

12 Blessed *is* the man that endureth temptation: for when he is tried, he shall receive the crown *a* of life, which *b* the Lord hath promised to them that love him.

a 2 Ti.4.8. Re.2.10.   b Is.64.4.

which consumes the green herbage of the fields. So Rosenmüller and Bloomfield interpret it. ¶ *It withereth the grass.* Isa. xl. 7. It withereth the *stalk*, or that which, when dried, produces hay or fodder—the word here used being commonly employed in the latter sense. The meaning is, that the effect of the hot wind is to wither the stalk or spire which supports the flower, and when that is dried up, the flower itself falls. This idea will give increased beauty and appropriateness to the figure —that *man himself* is blasted and withered, and then that all the external splendour which encircled him falls to the ground, like a flower whose support is gone. ¶ *And the grace of the fashion of it perisheth.* Its beauty disappears. ¶ *So shall the rich man fade away in his ways.* That is, his splendour, and all on which he prideth himself, shall vanish. The phrase 'in his ways,' according to Rosenmüller, refers to his counsels, his plans, his purposes ; and the meaning is, that the rich man, with all by which he is known, shall vanish. A man's 'ways,' that is, his mode of life, or those things by which he appears before the world, may have somewhat the same relation to him which the flower has to the stalk on which it grows, and by which it is sustained. The idea of James seems to be, that as it was indisputable that the rich man *must* soon disappear, with all that he had of pomp and splendour in the view of the world, it was well for him to be reminded of it by every change of condition ; and that he should therefore rejoice in the providential dispensation by which his property would be taken away, and by which the reality of his religion would be tested. We should rejoice in *anything* by which it can be shown whether we are prepared for heaven or not.

12. *Blessed* is *the man that endureth temptation.* The apostle seems here to use the word *temptation* in the most general sense, as denoting *anything* that will try the reality of religion, whether

affliction, or persecution, or a direct inducement to sin placed before the mind. The word *temptation* appears in this chapter to be used in two senses ; and the question may arise, why the apostle so employs it. Comp. vs. 2, 13. But, in fact, the word *temptation* is in itself of so general a character as to cover the whole usage, and to justify the manner in which it is employed. It denotes *anything* that will try or test the reality of our religion ; and it may be applied, therefore, either to afflictions or to direct solicitations to sin—the latter being the sense in which it is now commonly employed. In another respect, also, essentially the same idea enters into both the ways in which the word is employed. Affliction, persecution, sickness, &c., may be regarded as, in a certain sense, temptations to sin ; that is, the question comes before us whether we will adhere to the religion on account of which we are persecuted, or apostatize from it, and escape these sufferings ; whether in sickness and losses we will be patient and submissive to that God who lays his hand upon us, or revolt and murmur. In each and every case, whether by affliction, or by direct allurements to do wrong, the question comes before the mind whether we have religion enough to keep us, or whether we will yield to murmuring, to rebellion, and to sin. In these respects, in a general sense, *all* forms of trial may be regarded as *temptation.* Yet in the following verse (13) the apostle would guard this from abuse. So far as the form of trial involved an allurement or inducement *to sin*, he says that no man should regard it as from God. *That* cannot be his design. The *trial* is what he aims at, not the *sin.* In the verse before us he says, that whatever may be the form of the trial, a Christian should rejoice in it, for it will furnish an evidence that he is a child of God. ¶ *For when he is tried.* In any way—if he bears the trial. ¶ *He shall receive the crown of life.* See Notes on 2 Tim. iv. 8. It is *possible* that James had that passage in his eye

13 Let no man say when he is tempted, I am tempted of God: for

1 Or, *evils*.

God cannot be tempted with [1] evil, neither tempteth he any man.

Comp. the Intro., § 5. ¶ *Which the Lord hath promised.* The sacred writers often speak of such a crown as promised, or as in reserve for the children of God. 2 Tim. iv. 8; 1 Pet. v. 4; Rev. ii. 10; iii. 11; iv. 4. ¶ *Them that love him.* A common expression to denote those who are truly pious, or who are his friends. It is sufficiently distinctive to characterize them, for the great mass of men do not love God. Comp. Rom. i. 30.

13. *Let no man say when he is tempted, I am tempted of God.* See the remarks on the previous verse. The apostle here seems to have had his eye on whatever there was in trial of any kind to induce us to commit *sin*—whether by complaining, by murmuring, by apostacy, or by yielding to sin. So far as *that* was concerned, he said that no one should charge it on God. He did nothing in any way with a view to *induce* men to do evil. That was only an incidental thing in the trial, and was no part of the divine purpose or design. The apostle felt evidently that there was great danger, from the general manner in which the word *temptation* was used, and from the perverse tendency of the heart, that it would be charged on God that he so arranged these trials, and so influenced the mind, as to present *inducements* to sin. Against this, it was proper that an inspired apostle should bear his solemn testimony; so to guard the whole subject as to show that whatever there was in *any* form of trial that could be regarded as an inducement or allurement to sin, is not the thing which he contemplated in the arrangement, and does not proceed from him. It has its origin in other causes; and if there was nothing *in the corrupt human mind itself* leading to sin, there would be nothing in the divine arrangement that would produce it. ¶ *For God cannot be tempted with evil.* Marg. *evils.* The sense is the same. The object seems to be to show that, in regard to the whole matter of temptation, it does not pertain to God. Nothing can be presented to *his* mind as an in-

ducement to do wrong, and as little can be present any thing to the mind of man to induce *him* to sin. Temptation is a subject which does not pertain to him. He stands aloof from it altogether. In regard to the *particular* statement here, that 'God cannot be tempted with evil,' or to do evil, there can be no doubt of its truth, and it furnishes the highest security for the welfare of the universe. There is nothing *in* him that has a tendency to wrong; there can be nothing presented from without to induce him to do wrong. (1.) There is no evil *passion* to be gratified, as there is in men; (2.) There is no want of *power*, so that an allurement could be presented to seek what he has not; (3.) There is no want of *wealth*, for he has infinite resources, and all that there is or can be is his (Ps. l. 10, 11); (4.) There is no want of *happiness*, that he should seek happiness in sources which are not now in his possession. Nothing, therefore, could be presented to the divine mind as an *inducement* to do evil. ¶ *Neither tempteth he any man.* That is, he places nothing before any human being with a view to induce him to do wrong. This is one of the most positive and unambiguous of all the declarations in the Bible, and one of the most important. It may be added, that it is one which stands in opposition to as many feelings of the human heart as perhaps any other one. We are perpetually thinking—the *heart* suggests it constantly— that God *does* place before us inducements to evil, with a view to lead us to sin. This is done in many ways: (*a*) Men take such views of his decrees as if the doctrine implied that he *meant* that we should sin, and that it could not be otherwise than that we should sin. (*b*) It is felt that all things are under his control, and that he has made his arrangements with a *design* that men should do as they actually do. (*c*) It is said that he has created us with just such dispositions as we actually have, and knowing that we would sin. (*d*) It is said that, by the arrange-

14 But every man is tempted, | when he is drawn away of his own
a Hos.13.9. | a lust, and enticed.

ments of his Providence, he actually places inducements before us to sin, knowing that the effect will be that we will fall into sin, when we might easily have prevented it. (e) It is said that he suffers some to tempt others, when he might easily prevent it if he chose, and that this is the same as tempting them himself. Now, in regard to these things, there may be much which we cannot explain, and much which often troubles the heart even of the good; yet the passage before us is explicit on one point, and all these things *must* be held in consistency with that—that God does not place inducements before us *with a view* that we should sin, or *in order* to lead us into sin. None of his decrees, or his arrangements, or his desires, are based on that, but all have some other purpose and end. The real force of temptation is to be traced to some other source—to ourselves, and not to God. See the next verse.

14. *But every man is tempted, when he is drawn away of his own lust.* That is, the fountain or source of *all* temptation is in man himself. It is true that external inducements to sin may be placed before him, but they would have no force if there was not something in himself to which they corresponded, and over which they might have power. There must be some ' lust;' some desire; some inclination; something which is unsatisfied now, which is made the foundation of the temptation, and which gives it all its power. If there were no capacity for receiving food, or desire for it, objects placed before us appealing to the appetite could never be made a source of temptation; if there were nothing in the soul which could be regarded as the love of acquisition or possession, gold would furnish no temptation; if there were no sensual propensities, we should be in that quarter above the power of temptation. In each case, and in every form, the power of the temptation is laid in some propensity of our nature, some desire of that which we do not now possess. The word rendered ' lust' in this place (ἐπιθυμία), is not employed here in the

narrow sense in which it is now commonly used, as denoting libidinousness. It means *desire* in general; an earnest wish for any thing. Notes, Eph. iv. 22 It seems here to be used with reference to the original propensities of our nature —the desires implanted in us, which are a stimulus to employment—as the desire of knowledge, of food, of power, of sensual gratifications; and the idea is, that a man may be *drawn along* by these *beyond* the prescribed limits of indulgence, and in the pursuit of objects that are forbidden. He does not stop at the point at which the law requires him to stop, and is therefore guilty of *transgression*. This is the source of all sin. The original propensity *may* not be wrong, but may be perfectly harmless—as in the case of the desire of food, &c. Nay, it may furnish a most desirable stimulus to action; for how could the human powers be called forth, if it were not for this? The error, the fault, the sin, is, not restraining the indulgence where we are *commanded* to do it, either in regard to the *objects* sought, or in regard to the *degree* of indulgence. ¶ *And enticed.* Entrapped, caught; that is, he is seized by this power, and held fast; or he is led along and beguiled, until he falls into sin, as in a snare that springs suddenly upon him.

[Ἐπιθυμία in the New Testament, is sometimes employed in a good sense, Luke xxii. 15; 1 Phil. i. 23; 1 Thess. ii. 17: often in a bad sense, as in Mark iv. 19; John viii. 44; Rom. i. 24; vi. 12; vii. 7; 1 John ii. 16; but there is no difficulty in making the distinction; the context easily determining the matter. And this passage in James seems at once to fix down on Ἐπιθυμία the sense of *evil* or *corrupt* desire. That it can mean a ' harmless propensity;' or that it is a propensity on whose *character* the apostle does not at all pronounce, is incredible. It is said to ' draw away a man and entice him;' to ' conceive and bring forth sin:' and a principle from which such fruit springs cannot be very *harmless*. Without doubt, the apostle traces the whole evil of temptation, which some falsely ascribed to God, to the *sinful* desires of the human heart; and, as our author remarks, he seems to take the common sense view without entertaining any thought of nice philosophical distinction. We cannot for a moment suppose the apostle to say

15 Then when lust hath *a* conceived, it bringeth forth sin : and sin, when it is finished, bringeth forth death.*b*

a Job 15.35.   *b* Ro.6.21-23.

—'the evil is not to be traced to God, but to a harmless propensity.' The whole passage, with *the words and figures which are used*, show that the idea in the apostle's mind was that of an enticing harlot. The ιπιθ. is personified. She persuades the understanding and will into her impure embrace. The result of this fatal union is the 'conception' and ultimate 'bringing forth' of actual sin, which again brings forth death. This is the true genealogy of sin (M'Knight); and to say that the ιπιθ., or evil desire, of which the apostle says that it is the *origo mali*, is harmless, —is to contradict him, and Paul also, who in a parallel passage says that he had not known the ιπιθ., or inward desire after forbidden objects, to be sinful, unless the law had enlightened him and said 'thou shalt not covet.' Mr. Scott has spoken in strong terms of the folly of some parties who understand ιπιθ. here only of the desire of sensual gross indulgence, to the exclusion of other sinful desires; but the extreme of interpreting it as meaning nothing sinful at all, deserves equal reprehension. The reader, however, will notice that the author does not venture on this assertion. He says " it *may* be so," and otherwise modifies his view.]

15. *Then when lust hath conceived.* Comp. Job xv. 35. The allusion here is obvious. The meaning is, when the desire which we have naturally is quickened, or made to act, the result is that sin is produced. As our desires of good lie in the mind by nature, as our propensities exist as they were created, they cannot be regarded as sin, or treated as such; but when they are indulged, when plans of gratification are formed, when they are developed in actual life, the effect is sin. In the mere desire of good, of happiness, of food, of raiment, there is no sin ; it becomes sin when indulged in an improper manner, and when it leads us to seek that which is forbidden—to invade the rights of others, or in any way to violate the laws of God. The Rabbins have a metaphor which strongly expresses the general sense of this passage :—" Evil concupiscence is at the beginning like the thread of a spider's web; afterwards it is like a cart rope." *Sanhedrin*, fol. 99. ¶ *It bringeth forth sin.* The result is sin— open, actual sin. When that which is conceived in the heart is matured, it is

seen to be sin. The *design* of all this is to show that sin is not to be traced to God, but to man himself ; and in order to this, the apostle says that there is enough in the heart of man to account for all actual sin, without supposing that it is caused by God. The solution which he gives is, that there are certain propensities in man which, when they are suffered to act themselves out, will account for all the sin in the world. In regard to those native propensities themselves, he does not *say* whether he regards them as sinful and blameworthy or not; and the probability is, that he did not design to enter into a formal examination, or to make a formal statement, of the nature of these propensities themselves. He looked at man as he is—as a creature of God—as endowed with certain animal propensities —as seen, in fact, to have strong passions by nature ; and he showed that there was enough in him to account for the existence of sin, without bringing in the agency of God, or charging it on him. In reference to those propensities, it may be observed that there are two kinds, either of which may account for the existence of sin, but which are frequently both combined. There are, first, our natural propensities ; those which we have as men, as endowed with an animal nature, as having constitutional desires to be gratified, and wants to be supplied. Such Adam had in innocence ; such the Saviour had ; and such are to be regarded as in no respect in themselves sinful and wrong. Yet they may, in our case, as they did in Adam, lead us to sin, because, under their strong influence, we may be led to desire that which is forbidden, or which belongs to another. But there are, secondly, the propensities and inclinations which we have as the result of the fall, and which are evil in their nature and tendency; which as a matter of course, and especially when combined with the former, lead to open transgression. It is not always easy to separate these, and in fact they are often com-

16 Do not err, my beloved brethren.

17 Every ᵃgood gift and every

bined in producing the actual guilt of
the world. It often requires a close
analysis of a man's own mind to detect
these different ingredients in his conduct, and the one often gets the credit of
the other. The apostle James seems to
have looked at it as a simple matter of
fact, with a common sense view, by saying that there were *desires* (ἐπιθυμίας)
in a man's own mind which would *account* for all the actual sin in the world,
without charging it on God. Of the truth
of this, no one can entertain a doubt.
—[See Supplementary Note above on
v. 14.] ¶ *And sin, when it is finished,
bringeth forth death.* The result of sin,
when it is fully carried out, is death—
death in all forms. The idea is, that
death, in whatever form it exists, is to
be traced to sin, and that sin will naturally and regularly produce it. There
is a strong similarity between this
declaration and that of the apostle Paul
(Rom. vi. 21–23); and it is probable
that James had that passage in his eye.
See the sentiment illustrated in the
Notes on that passage, and on Romans
v. 12. Any one who indulges in a sinful thought or corrupt desire, should
reflect that it *may* end in death—death
temporal and eternal. Its natural tendency will be to produce such a death.
This reflection should induce us to check
an evil thought or desire at the beginning. Not for one moment should we
indulge in it, for soon it may secure the
mastery and be beyond our control; and
the end may be seen in the grave, and
the awful world of woe.

16. *Do not err, my beloved brethren.*
This is said as if there were great danger of error in the point under consideration. The *point* on which he would
guard them, seems to have been in respect to the opinion that God was the
author of sin, and that the evils in the
world are to be traced to him. There
was great danger that they would embrace that opinion, for experience has
shown that it is a danger into which
men are always prone to fall. Some of
the sources of this danger have been
already alluded to. Notes on ver. 13.

perfect gift is from above, and
cometh down from the Father of

ᵃ Jno.3.27. 1 Co.4.7.

To meet the danger he says that, so far is
it from being true that God is the source
of evil, he is in fact the author of all that
is good : every *good* gift, and every *perfect* gift (ver. 17), is from him, ver. 18
17. *Every good gift and every perfect gift.* The difference between *good*
and *perfect* here, it is not easy to mark
accurately. It may be that the former
means that which is *benevolent* in its
character and tendency ; the latter that
which is *entire*, where there is nothing
even apparently wanting to complete
it ; where it can be regarded as good as
a whole and in all its parts. The general sense is, that God is the author of
all good. Every thing that is good on
the earth we are to trace to him ; evil
has another origin. Comp. Matt. xiii.
28. ¶ *Is from above.* From God, who
is often represented as dwelling above—
in heaven. ¶ *And cometh down from
the Father of lights.* From God, the
source and fountain of all light. Light,
in the Scriptures, is the emblem of
knowledge, purity, happiness; and God
is often represented as *light*. Comp. 1
John i. 5. Notes 1 Tim. vi. 16. There
is, doubtless, an allusion here to the
heavenly bodies, among which the sun
is the most brilliant. It appears to us
to be the great original fountain of light,
diffusing its radiance over all worlds.
No cloud, no darkness seems to come
from the sun, but it pours its rich efful-
gence on the farthest part of the universe. So it is with God. There is no
darkness in him (1 John i. 5); and all
the moral light and purity which there
is in the universe is to be traced to him.
The word *Father* here is used in a sense
which is common in Hebrew (Comp.
Notes Matt. i. 1) as denoting that which
is the source of any thing, or that from
which any thing proceeds. Comp. Notes
on Isa. ix. 6. ¶ *With whom is no variableness, neither shadow of turning.*
The design here is clearly to contrast
God with the sun in a certain respect.
As the source of light, there is a strong
resemblance. But in the sun there are
certain changes. It does not shine on
all parts of the earth at the same time,

lights, with whom *is no variableness, neither shadow of turning.

a 1 Sa.15.29. Mal.3.6.   b Jno.1.13.
c Je.2.3. Ep.1.12. Re.14.4.

nor in the same manner all the year.
It rises and sets; it crosses the line,
and seems to go far to the south, and
sends its rays obliquely on the earth;
then it ascends to the north, recrosses
the line, and sends its rays obliquely
on southern regions. By its revolutions it produces the changes of the
seasons, and makes a constant variety
on the earth in the productions of different climes. In this respect God is
not indeed like the sun. With him there
is *no* variableness, not even the appearance of turning. He is always the same,
at all seasons of the year, and in all
ages; there is no change in his character,
his mode of being, his purposes and plans.
What he was millions of ages before the
worlds were made, he is now; what he
is now, he will be countless millions of
ages hence. We may be sure that whatever changes there may be in human
affairs; whatever reverses we may undergo; whatever oceans we may cross,
or whatever mountains we may climb,
or in whatever worlds we may hereafter
take up our abode, *God* is the same.—
The *word* which is here rendered *variableness* (παραλλαγὴ) occurs nowhere
else in the New Testament. It means
change, alteration, vicissitude, and would
properly be applied to the changes observed in astronomy. See the examples
quoted in Wetstein. The phrase rendered *shadow of turning* would properly
refer to the different *shade* or *shadow*
cast by the sun from an object, in its
various revolutions, in rising and setting, and in its changes at the different
seasons of the year. God, on the other
hand, is as if the sun stood in the meri-
dian at noon-day, and never cast *any*
shadow.

18. *Of his own will.* Gr. *willing.*
βουληθεὶς. The idea is, that the fact
that we are 'begotten' to be his children
is to be traced solely to his *will.* He
purposed it, and it was done. The *antecedent* in the case on which all depended was the sovereign will of God.
See this sentiment explained in the
Notes on John i. 13. Comp. Notes on

18 Of *his own will begat he us
with the word of truth, that we
should be a kind of first-fruits *of
his creatures.

Eph. i. 5. When it is said, however,
that he has done this by his mere *will,*
it is not to be inferred that there was
no *reason* why it should be done, or that
the exercise of his will was arbitrary,
but only that his will determined the
matter, and that is the cause of our
conversion. It is not to be inferred
that there are not in all cases good reasons why God wills as he does, though
those reasons are not often stated to us,
and perhaps we could not comprehend
them if they were. The *object* of the
statement here seems to be to direct the
mind up to God as the source of *good*
and not *evil;* and among the most eminent illustrations of his goodness is this,
that by his mere *will,* without any external power to control him, and where
there *could* be nothing but benevolence,
he has adopted us into his family, and
given us a most exalted condition, as
renovated beings, among his creatures.
¶ *Begat he us.* The Greek word here
is the same which in ver. 15 is rendered
'bringeth forth,'—'sin *bringeth forth*
death.' The word is perhaps designedly
used here in contrast with that, and the
object is to refer to a different kind of
production, or bringing forth, under the
agency of *sin,* and the agency of *God.*
The meaning here is, that we owe the
beginning of our spiritual life to God.
¶ *With the word of truth.* By the
instrumentality of *truth.* It was not a
mere creative act, but it was by truth
as the seed or germ. There is no effect
produced in our minds in regeneration
which the *truth* is not fitted to produce,
and the agency of God in the case is to
secure its fair and full influence on the
soul. ¶ *That we should be a kind of
first-fruits of his creatures.* Comp.
Eph. i. 12. For the meaning of the
word rendered *first-fruits,* see Note on
Rom. viii. 23. Comp. Rom. xi. 6; xvi.
5; 1 Cor. xv. 20, 23; xvi. 15; Rev. xiv.
4. It does not elsewhere occur in the
New Testament. It denotes, properly,
that which is first taken from any thing;
the portion which was usually offered to
God. The phrase here does not primarily

19 Wherefore, my beloved bre-

a E.e.5.2. b Pr.16.32.

thren, let every man be swift to hear, slow *a* to speak, slow *b* to wrath :

denote eminence in honour or degree, but refers rather to *time*—the first in time ; and in a secondary sense it is then used to denote the honour attached to that circumstance. The meaning here is, either (1) that, under the gospel, those who were addressed by the apostles had the honour of being first called into his kingdom as a part of that glorious harvest which it was designed to gather in this world, and that the *goodness* of God was manifested in thus furnishing the first-fruits of a most glorious harvest ; or (2) the reference may be to the rank and dignity which all who are born again would have among the creatures of God in virtue of the new birth.

19. *Wherefore, my beloved brethren.* The connection is this : ' since God is the only source of good ; since he tempts no man ; and since by his mere sovereign goodness, without any claim on our part, we have had the high honour conferred on us of being made the first-fruits of his creatures, we ought to be ready to hear his voice, to subdue all our evil passions, and to bring our souls to entire practical obedience.' The necessity of *obedience*, or the doctrine that the gospel is not only to be *learned* but *practised*, is pursued at length in this and the following chapter. The particular statement here (vs. 19–21) is, that religion requires us to be meek and docile ; to lay aside all irritability against the truth, and all pride of opinion, and all corruption of heart, and to receive meekly the ingrafted word. See the analysis of the chapter. ¶ *Let every man be swift to hear, slow to speak.* That is, primarily, to hear God ; to listen to the instructions of that *truth* by which we have been begotten, and brought into so near relation to him. At the same time, though this is the primary sense of the phrase here, it may be regarded as inculcating the *general* doctrine that we are to be more ready to hear than to speak ; or that we are to be disposed to *learn* always, and from any source. Our appropriate condition is rather that of *learners* than *instructors;* and the attitude of mind which we should cultivate is that of a readiness to receive information from

any quarter. The ancients have some sayings on this subject which are well worthy of our attention. ' Men have two ears, and but one tongue, that they should hear more than they speak.' ' The ears are always open, ever ready to receive instruction ; but the tongue is surrounded with a double row of teeth, to hedge it in, and to keep it within proper bounds.' See *Benson.* So Valerius Maximus, vii. 2. ' How noble was the response of Xenocrates ! When he met the reproaches of others with a profound silence, some one asked him why he alone was silent ? Because, says he, I have sometimes had occasion to regret that I have spoken, *never that I was silent.*' See Wetstein. So the son of Sirach, ' Be swift to hear, and with deep consideration (ἐν μακροθυμίᾳ) give answer,' ch. v. 11. So the Rabbins have some similar sentiments. ' Talk little and work much.' Pirkey Aboth. c. i. 15. ' The righteous speak little and do much ; the wicked speak much and do nothing.' Bava Metsia, fol. 87. A sentiment similar to that before us is found in Ecclesiastes v. 2. ' Be not rash with thy mouth, and let not thine heart be hasty to utter any thing before God.' So Prov. x. 19. ' In the multitude of words there wanteth not sin.' xiii. 3. ' He that keepeth his mouth keepeth his life.' xv. 2. ' The tongue of the wise useth knowledge aright, but the mouth of fools poureth out foolishness.' ¶ *Slow to wrath.* That is, we are to govern and restrain our temper ; we are not to give indulgence to excited and angry passions. Comp. Prov. xvi. 32, ' He that is slow to anger is greater than the mighty ; and he that ruleth his spirit than he that taketh a city.' See also on this subject, Job v. 2; Prov. xxxvii. 8; xi. 17; xiii. 10; xiv. 16; xv. 18; xix. 19; xxii. 24; xxv. 28; Eccl. vii. 9; Rom. xii. 17; 1 Thess. v. 14; 1 Pet. iii. 8. The particular point here is, however, not that we should be slow to wrath as a general habit of mind, which is indeed most true, but in reference particularly *to the reception of the truth.* We should lay aside all anger and wrath, and should

20 For the wrath of man worketh not the righteousness of God.

21 Wherefore lay apart *a* all filthiness and superfluity of naughtiness,

and receive with meekness the engrafted word, which is able to save your souls.

a Col.3.5-8. He.12.1. 1 Pe.2.1,2.

come to the investigation of truth with a calm mind, and an imperturbed spirit. A state of wrath or anger is always unfavourable to the investigation of truth. Such an investigation demands a calm spirit, and he whose mind is excited and enraged is not in a condition to see the value of truth, or to weigh the evidence for it. 20. *For the wrath of man worketh not the righteousness of God.* Does not produce in the life that righteousness which God requires. Its tendency is not to incline us to keep the law, but to break it; not to induce us to embrace the truth, but the opposite. The meaning of this passage is not that our wrath will make God either more or less righteous; but that its tendency is not to produce that upright course of life, and love of truth, which God requires. A man is never sure of doing right under the influence of excited feelings; he *may* do that which is in the highest sense wrong, and which he will regret all his life. The particular meaning of this passage is, that wrath in the mind of man will not have any tendency to make him righteous. It is only that candid state of mind which will lead him to embrace the truth which can be hoped to have such an effect. 21. *Wherefore.* In view of the fact that God has begotten us for his own service; in view of the fact that excited feeling tends only to wrong, let us lay aside *all* that is evil, and submit ourselves wholly to the influence of truth. ¶ *Lay apart all filthiness.* The word here rendered *filthiness*, occurs nowhere else in the New Testament. It means properly *filth;* and then is applied to evil conduct considered as *disgusting* or *offensive.* Sin may be contemplated as a *wrong* thing; as a violation of law; as evil in its nature and tendency, and *therefore* to be avoided; or it may be contemplated as *disgusting, offensive, loathsome.* To a pure mind, this is one of its most odious characteristics; for, to such a mind, sin in any form is more

loathsome than the most offensive object can be to any of the senses. ¶ *And superfluity of naughtiness.* Literally, 'abounding of evil.' It is rendered by Doddridge, 'overflowing of malignity;' by Tindal, 'superfluity of maliciousness;' by Benson, 'superfluity of malice;' by Bloomfield, 'petulance.' The phrase ' *superfluity* of naughtiness,' or of evil, does not exactly express the sense, as if we were only to lay aside that which *abounded*, or which is *superfluous*, though we might retain that which does not come under this description; but the object of the apostle is to express his deep abhorrence of the thing referred to by strong and emphatic language. He had just spoken of sin in one aspect, as *filthy, loathsome, detestable;* here he designs to express his abhorrence of it by a still more emphatic description, and he speaks of it not merely as an *evil*, but as an evil *abounding, overflowing;* an evil in the highest degree. The thing referred to had the essence of *evil* in it (*κακία*); but it was not merely *evil*, it was evil that was aggravated, that was overflowing, that was eminent in degree (*περισσία*). The particular reference in these passages is to the reception of the truth; and the doctrine taught is, that a *corrupt* mind, a mind full of sensuality and wickednesss, is not favourable to the reception of the truth. It is not fitted to see its beauty, to appreciate its value, to understand its just claims, or to welcome it to the soul. Purity of heart is the best preparation always for seeing the force of truth. ¶ *And receive with meekness.* That is, open the mind and heart to instruction, and to the fair influence of truth. Meekness, gentleness, docility, are everywhere required in receiving the instructions of religion, as they are in obtaining knowledge of any kind. See Notes on Matt. xviii. 2, 3. ¶ *The engrafted word.* The gospel is here represented under the image of that which is implanted or engrafted from another source; by a figure

22 But be ye doers *a* of the word, and not hearers only, deceiving your own selves.

23 For if any be a hearer of the word, and not a doer, he is like

a Mat.7.21.

unto a man beholding his natural face in a glass:

24 For he beholdeth himself, and goeth his way, and straightway forgetteth what manner of man he was.

---

that would be readily understood, for the art of *engrafting* is everywhere known. Sometimes the gospel is represented under the image of seed sown (Comp. Mark vi. 14, seq.); but here it is under the figure of *a shoot* implanted or engrafted, that produces fruit of its own, whatever may be the original character of the tree into which it is engrafted. Comp. Notes on Rom. xi. 17. The meaning here is, that we should allow the principles of the gospel to be thus *engrafted* on our nature; that however crabbed or perverse our nature may be, or however bitter and vile the fruits which it might bring forth of its own accord, it might, through the engrafted word, produce the fruits of righteousness. ¶ *Which is able to save your souls.* It is not, therefore, a weak and powerless thing, merely designed to show its own feebleness, and to give occasion for God to work *a miracle;* but it has *power*, and is *adapted* to save. Comp. Notes on Rom. i. 16; 1 Cor. i. 18; 2 Tim. iii. 15.

22. *But be ye doers of the word, and not hearers only.* Obey the gospel, and do not merely listen to it. Comp. Matt. vii. 21. ¶ *Deceiving your own selves.* It is implied here, that by merely *hearing* the word but not *doing* it, they would deceive their own souls. The nature of this deception was this, that they would imagine that that was all which was required, whereas the main thing was that they should be obedient. If a man supposes that by a mere punctual attendance on preaching, or a respectful attention to it, he has done all that is required of him, he is labouring under a most gross self-deception. And yet there are multitudes who seem to imagine that they have done all that is demanded of them when they have heard attentively the word preached. Of its influence on their lives, and its claims to obedience, they are utterly regardless.

23, 24. *For if any be,* &c. The ground of the comparison in these verses is obvious. The apostle refers to what all persons experience, the fact that we do not retain a distinct impression of ourselves after we have looked in a mirror. While actually looking in the mirror, we see all our features, and can trace them distinctly; when we turn away, the image and the impression both vanish. When looking in the mirror, we can see all the defects and blemishes of our person; if there is a scar, a deformity, a feature of ugliness, it is distinctly before the mind; but when we turn away, that is 'out of sight and out of mind.' When unseen it gives no uneasiness, and, even if capable of correction, we take no pains to remove it. So when we hear the word of God. It is like a mirror held up before us. In the perfect precepts of the law, and the perfect requirements of the gospel, we see our own short-comings and defects, and perhaps think that we will correct them. But we turn away immediately, and forget it all. If, however, we were ' *doers* of the word,' we should endeavour to remove all those defects and blemishes in our moral character, and to bring our whole souls into conformity with what the law and the gospel require. The phrase 'natural face,' (Gr. face of birth), means, the face or appearance which we have in virtue of our natural birth. The word *glass* here means *mirror*. Glass was not commonly used for mirrors among the ancients, but they were made of polished plates of metal. See Notes on Isa. iii. 24, and Job xxxvii. 18.

24. *For he beholdeth himself.* While he looks in the mirror he sees his true appearance. ¶ *And goeth his way, and straightway forgetteth.* As soon as he goes away, he forgets it. The apostle does not refer to any *intention* on his part, but to what is known to occur as a matter of fact. ¶ *What manner of*

25 But whoso looketh *a* into the perfect law of liberty, *b* and continueth *therein*, he being not a forgetful hearer, but a doer of the

a 2 Co. 3.18.

work, this man *c* shall be blessed in his 1 deed.

26 If any man among you seem to be religious, and bridleth not his

b Ps. 119.45.   *c* Lu. 6.47, &c.   1 Or, *doing*.

---

man he was. How he looked; and especially if there was any thing in his appearance that required correction. 25. *But whoso looketh* (παρακύψας). This word means, to stoop down near by any thing; to bend forward near, so as to look at any thing more closely. See the word explained in the Notes on 1 Pet. i. 12. The idea here is that of a close and attentive observation. The object is not to contrast the *manner* of looking in the glass, and in the law of liberty, implying that the former was a '*careless* beholding,' and the latter an attentive and careful looking, as Doddridge, Rosenmüller, Bloomfield, and others suppose; for the word used in the former case (κατενόησε) implies intense or accurate observation, as really as the word used here; but the object is to show that if a man would attentively look into, and *continue* in the law of liberty, and not do as one who went away and forgot how he looked, he would be blessed. The emphasis is not in the manner of *looking*, it is on the duty of *continuing* or persevering in the observance of the law. ¶ *The perfect law of liberty.* Referring to the law of God, or his will, however made known, as the correct standard of conduct. It is called the *perfect* law, as being wholly free from all defects; being just such as a law *ought* to be. Comp. Ps. xix. 7. It is called *the law of liberty*, or freedom, because it is a law producing freedom from the servitude of sinful passions and lusts. Comp. Ps. cxix. 45; Notes on Rom. vi. 16–18. ¶ *And continueth therein.* He must not merely *look* at the law, or see what he *is* by comparing himself with its requirements, but he must yield steady obedience to it. See Notes on John xiv. 21. ¶ *This man shall be blessed in his deed.* Marg. *doing.* The meaning is, that he shall be blessed in the very act of keeping the law. It will produce peace of conscience; it will impart happiness of a high order to his mind; it will exert a good influence over

his whole soul. Ps. xix. 11. 'In keeping of them there is great reward.' 26. *If any man among you seem to be religious.* Pious, or devout. That is, if he does not restrain his tongue, his other evidences of religion are worthless. A man may undoubtedly have many things in his character which *seem* to be evidences of the existence of religion in his heart, and yet there may be some one thing that shall show that all those evidences are false. Religion is designed to produce an effect on our whole conduct; and if there is any one thing in reference to which it does not bring us under its control, that one thing may show that *all* other appearances of piety are worthless. ¶ *And bridleth not his tongue.* Restrains or curbs it not, as a horse is restrained with a bridle. There may have been some reason why the apostle referred to this particular sin which is now unknown to us; or he may perhaps have intended to select this as a *specimen* to illustrate this idea, that if there is any one evil propensity which religion does not control, or if there is any one thing in respect to which its influence is not felt, whatever other evidences of piety there may be, this will demonstrate that all those appearances of religion are vain. For religion is designed to bring the whole man under control, and to subdue every faculty of the body and mind to its demands. If the tongue is not restrained, or if there is *any* unsubdued propensity to sin whatever, it proves that there is no true religion. ¶ *But deceiveth his own heart.* Implying that he *does* deceive his heart by supposing that any evidence can prove that he is under the influence of religion if his tongue is unrestrained. Whatever love, or zeal, or orthodoxy, or gift in preaching or in prayer he may have, this one evil propensity will neutralize it all, and show that there is no true religion at heart. ¶ *This man's religion* is *vain.* As all religion must be which does not control all the faculties of the

tongue, *but deceiveth his own heart, this man's religion *is* vain. 27 Pure religion, and undefiled before God and the Father, is this,

To visit *b* the fatherless and widows in their affliction, *and* to keep himself unspotted *c* from the world.

a Ps.34.13.   *b* Is.1.16,17; 58.6,7.   *c* Ro.12.2.

body and the mind. The truths, then, which are taught in this verse are, (1.) That there may be evidences of piety which seem to be very plausible or clear, but which in themselves do not prove that there is any true religion. There may be much zeal, as in the case of the Pharisees; there may be much apparent love of Christians, or much outward benevolence; there may be an uncommon gift in prayer; there may be much self-denial, as among those who withdraw from the world in monasteries or nunneries; or there may have been deep conviction for sin, and much joy at the time of the supposed conversion, and still there be no true religion. Each and all of these things may exist in the heart where there is no true religion. (2.) A single unsubdued sinful propensity neutralizes all these things, and shows that there is no true religion. If the tongue is not subdued; if *any* sin is indulged, it will show that the *seat* of the evil has not been reached, and that the soul, *as such,* has never been brought into subjection to the law of God. For the very *essence* of all the sin that there was in the soul may have been concentrated on that one propensity. Every thing else which may be manifested may be accounted for on the supposition that there is no religion; this cannot be accounted for on the supposition that there is any.

27. *Pure religion.* On the word here rendered *religion* (Θρησκεία), see Notes on Col. ii. 18. It is used here evidently in the sense of *piety,* or as we commonly employ the word *religion.* The object of the apostle is to describe what enters essentially into religion; what it will do when it is properly and fairly developed. The phrase '*pure* religion' means that which is genuine and sincere, or which is free from any improper mixture. ¶ *And undefiled before God and the Father.* That which God sees to be pure and undefiled. Rosenmüller supposes that there is a metaphor here taken from pearls or gems, which should

be pure, or without stain. ¶ *Is this.* That is, this enters into it; or this *is* religion such as God approves. The apostle does not say that this is *the whole* of religion, or that there is nothing else essential to it; but his general design clearly is, to show that religion will lead to a holy life, and he mentions this as a specimen, or an instance of what it will lead us to do. The *things* which he specifies here are in fact two: (1.) That pure religion will lead to a life of practical benevolence; and (2.) That it will keep us unspotted from the world. If these things are found, they show that there is true piety. If they are not, there is none. ¶ *To visit the fatherless and widows in their affliction.* To go to see, to look after, to be ready to aid them. This is an instance or specimen of what true religion will do, showing that it will lead to a life of practical benevolence. It may be remarked in respect to this, (1.) That this has always been regarded as an essential thing in true religion; for (*a*) it is thus an imitation of God, who is 'a father of the fatherless, and a judge of the widows in his holy habitation,' (Ps. lxviii. 5); and who has always revealed himself as their friend, Deut. x. 18; xiv. 29; Ps. x. 14; lxxxii. 3; Isa. i. 17; Jer. vii. 7; xlix. 11; Hos. xiv. 3; (*b*) religion is represented as leading its friends to do this, or this is required everywhere of those who claim to be religious, Isa. i. 17; Deut. xxiv. 17; xiv. 29; Ex. xxii. 22; Job xxix. 11–13. (2.) Where this disposition to be the real friend of the widow and the orphan exists, there will also exist other corresponding things which go to make up the religious character. This will not stand alone. It will show what the heart is, and prove that it will ever be ready to do good. If a man, from proper motives, is the real friend of the widow and the fatherless, he will be the friend of every good word and work, and we may rely on him in any and every way in doing

CHAPTER II.

MY brethren, have not the faith of our Lord Jesus Christ, *the*

Lord of glory, with respect *a* of persons.

2 For if there come unto your

a Pr.28.21; Jude 16.

good. ¶ And *to keep himself unspotted from the world.* Comp. Notes Rom. xii. 2; James iv. 4; 1 John ii. 15–17. That is, religion will keep us from the maxims, vices, and corruptions which prevail in the world, and make us holy. These two things may, in fact, be said to constitute religion. If a man is truly benevolent, he bears the image of that God who is the fountain of benevolence; if he is pure and uncontaminated in his walk and deportment, he also resembles his Maker, for he is holy. If he has *not* these things, he cannot have any well-founded evidence that he is a Christian; for it is always the nature and tendency of religion to produce these things. It is, therefore, an easy matter for a man to determine whether he has any religion; and equally easy to see that religion is eminently desirable. Who can doubt that that is good which leads to compassion for the poor and the helpless, and which makes the heart and the life pure?

CHAPTER II.

ANALYSIS OF THE CHAPTER.

THIS chapter is evidently made up of three parts, or three subjects are discussed :—

I. The duty of impartiality in the treatment of others, vs. 1–9. There was to be no favouritism on account of rank, birth, wealth, or apparel. The *case* to which the apostle refers for an illustration of this, is that where two persons should come into an assembly of Christian worshippers, one elegantly dressed, and the other meanly clad, and they should show special favour to the former, and should assign to the latter a more humble place. The *reasons* which the apostle assigns why they should not do this are, (*a*) that God has chosen the poor for his own people, having selected *his* friends mainly from them ; (*b*) because rich men in fact oppressed them, and showed that they were worthy of no special regard; (*c*) because they were often found among revilers, and in fact despised their reli-

gion ; and (*d*) because the law required that they should love their neighbours as themselves, and if they did this, it was all that was demanded ; that is, that the love of the *man* was not to be set aside by the love of splendid apparel.

II. The duty of yielding obedience to the *whole* law in order to have evidence of true religion, vs. 10–13. This subject seems to have been introduced in accordance with the general principles and aims of James (see the Intro.) that religion consists in obeying the law of God, and that there can be none when this is not done. It is not improbable that, among those to whom he wrote, there were some who denied this, or who had embraced some views of religion which led them to doubt it. He therefore enforces the duty by the following considerations : (1.) That if a man should obey every part of the law, and yet be guilty of offending in one point, he was in fact guilty of all ; for he showed that he had no genuine principle of obedience, and was guilty of violating the law as a whole, ver. 10. (2.) Every part of the law rests on the same authority, and one part, therefore, is as binding as another. The same God that has forbidden murder, has also forbidden adultery; and he who does the one as really violates the law as he who does the other, ver. 11. (3.) The judgment is before us, and we shall be tried on impartial principles, not with reference to obeying one part of the law, but with reference to its whole claim ; and we should so act as becomes those who expect to be judged by the whole law, or on the question whether we have conformed to every part of it, vs. 12, 13.

III. The subject of justification, showing that *works* are necessary in order that a man may be justified, or esteemed righteous before God, vs. 14–26. For a general view of the design of this part of the epistle, see Intro., § 5. The object here is to show that *in fact* no one can be regarded as truly righteous before God who does not lead

¹ assembly a man with a gold ring,
  1 *synagogue.*

in goodly apparel; and there come
in also a poor man in vile raiment;

an upright life; and that if a man professes to have faith, and has not works, he cannot be justified; or that if he have *real* faith, it will be shown by his works. If it is *not* shown by works corresponding to its nature, it will be certain that there is *no* true religion, or that his professed faith is worth nothing. The 'stand-point' from which James views the subject, is not that faith is unnecessary or worthless, or that a man is not justified by faith rather than by his own works, in the sense of its being the ground of acceptance with God; or, in other words, the place where the apostle takes his position, and which is the point from which he views the subject, is not *before* a man is justified, to inquire in what way he *may be* accepted of God, but it is *after* the act of justification by faith, to show that if faith does not lead to good works it is 'dead,' or is of no value; and that, in fact, therefore, the evidence of justification is to be found in good living, and that when this is not manifest, all a man's professed religion is worth nothing. In doing this, he (*a*) makes the general statement, by a pointed interrogatory, that faith cannot *profit*, that is, cannot *save* a man, unless there be also works, ver. 14. He then (*b*) appeals, for an illustration, to the case of one who is hungry or naked, and asks what mere *faith* could do in his case, if it were not accompanied with proper acts of benevolence, vs. 15–17. He then, (*c*) by a strong supposable case, says that real faith will be evinced *by* works, or that works are the proper evidence of its existence, ver. 18. He then (*d*) shows that there is a kind of faith which even the devils have on one of the most important doctrines of religion, and which can be of no value; showing that it cannot be by *mere* faith, irrespective of the question of what sort the faith is, that a man is to be saved, ver. 19. He then (*e*) appeals to the case of Abraham, showing that *in fact* works performed an important part in his acceptance with God; or that if it had not been for his works—that is, if there had been

no spirit of true obedience in his case, he could have had no evidence that he was justified, or that his works were the proper *carrying out* or *fulfilment* of his faith, vs. 20–24. He then (*f*) shows that the same thing was true of another case recorded in the Old Testament— that of Rahab (ver. 25); and then observes (ver. 26) that faith without works would have no more claim to being true religion than a dead body, without a soul, would be regarded as a living man.

1. *My brethren.* Perhaps meaning brethren in two respects—as Jews, and as Christians. In both respects the form of address would be proper. ¶ *Have not the faith of our Lord Jesus Christ.* Faith is the distinguishing thing in the Christian religion, for it is this by which man is justified, and hence it comes to be put for religion itself. Notes on 1 Tim. iii. 9. The meaning here is, 'do not hold such views of the religion of Christ, as to lead you to manifest partiality to others on account of their difference of rank or outward circumstances.' ¶ The Lord *of glory.* The glorious Lord; he who is glorious himself, and who is encompassed with glory. See Notes on 1 Cor. ii. 8. The *design* here seems to be to show that the religion of such a Lord should be in no way dishonoured. ¶ *With respect of persons.* That is, you are not to show respect of persons, or to evince partiality to others on account of their rank, wealth, apparel, &c. Comp. Prov. xxiv. 23; xxviii. 21; Lev. xix. 15; Deut. i. 17; x. 17; 2 Chron. xix. 7; Ps. xl. 4. See the subject explained in the Notes on Acts x. 34; Rom. ii. 11.

2. *For if there come into your assembly.* Marg., as in Gr., *synagogue.* It is remarkable that this is the only place in the New Testament where the word *synagogue* is applied to the Christian church. It is probably employed here because the apostle was writing to those who had been Jews; and it is to be presumed that the word *synagogue* would be naturally used by the early converts from Judaism to designate a Christian place of worship, or a Chris-

3 And ye have respect to him that weareth the gay clothing, and say unto him, Sit thou here ¹ in a

1 or, *well;* or, *seemly.*

good place; and say to the poor, Stand thou there, or sit here under my footstool:

---

tian congregation, and it was probably so employed until it was superseded by a word which the Gentile converts would be more likely to employ, and which would, in fact, be better and more expressive—the word *church.* The word *synagogue* (*συναγωγην*) would properly refer to the whole congregation, considered *as assembled together,* without respect to the question whether all were truly pious or not; the word *church* (*ικκλησία*) would refer to the assembly convened for worship as *called out,* referring to the fact that they were called out from the world, and convened as worshippers of God, and would, therefore, be more applicable to a body of spiritual worshippers. It is probable that the Christian church was modelled, in its general arrangements, after the Jewish synagogue; but there would be obviously some disadvantages in retaining the name, as applicable to Christian worship. It would be difficult to avoid the associations connected with the *name,* and hence it was better to adopt some other name which would be free from this disadvantage, and on which might be engrafted all the ideas which it was necessary to connect with the notion of the Christian organization. Hence the word *church,* liable to no such objection as that of synagogue, was soon adopted, and ultimately prevailed, though the passage before us shows that the word *synagogue* would be in some places, and for a time, employed to designate a Christian congregation. We should express the idea here by saying, 'If a man of this description should come *into the church.'* ¶ *A man with a gold ring.* Indicative of rank or property. Rings were common ornaments of the rich; and probably then, as now, of those who desired to be *esteemed* to be rich. For proof that they were commonly worn, see the quotations in Wetstein, *in loc.* ¶ *In goodly apparel.* Rich and splendid dress. Comp. Luke xvi. 19. ¶ *A poor man in vile raiment.* The Greek here is, *filthy, foul;* the

meaning of the passage is, in sordid, shabby clothes. The reference here seems to be, not to those who commonly attended on public worship, or who were members of the church, but to those who might accidentally drop in to witness the services of Christians. See 1 Cor. xiv. 24.

3. *And ye have respect to him that weareth the gay clothing.* If you show him superior attention on account of his rich and gay apparel, giving him a seat by himself, and treating others with neglect or contempt. Religion does not forbid proper respect to rank, to office, to age, or to distinguished talents and services, though even in such cases it does not require that we should feel that such persons have any peculiar claims to salvation, or that they are not on a level with all others, as sinners before God; it does not forbid that a man who has the means of procuring for himself an eligible pew in a church should be permitted to do so; but it requires that men shall be regarded and treated according to their moral worth, and not according to their external adorning; that all shall be considered as in fact on a level before God, and entitled to the privileges which grow out of the worship of the Creator. A stranger coming into any place of worship, no matter what his rank, dress, or complexion, should be treated with respect, and every thing should be done that can be to win his heart to the service of God. ¶ *And say unto him, Sit thou here in a good place.* Marg., as in Gr., *well* or *seemly;* that is, in an honourable place near the pulpit ; or in some elevated place where he would be conspicuous. The meaning is, you treat him with distinguished marks of respect on the first appearance, merely from the indications that he is a rich man, without knowing any thing about his character. ¶ *And say to the poor, Stand thou there.* Without even the civility of offering him a seat at all. This may be presumed not *often* to occur

4 Are ye not then partial in yourselves, and are become judges of evil thoughts?

5 Hearken, my beloved brethren, *a* Hath not God chosen the poor of this world, rich *b* in faith, and heirs

of [1] the kingdom *c* which he hath promised to them that love him?

6 But ye have despised the poor. Do not rich men oppress you, and

a 1 Co.1.26-28.   *b* Re.2.9.   1 or, *that*.   *c* Mat.5.3.
Lu.12.32; 22.29.

in a Christian church; yet it practically does sometimes, when no disposition is evinced to furnish a stranger with a seat. ¶ *Or sit here under my footstool.* Perhaps some seats in the places of worship were raised, so that even the footstool would be elevated above a lower seat. The meaning is, that he would be treated as if he were not worth the least attention.

4. *Are ye not then partial in yourselves?* Among yourselves. Do you not show that you are partial? ¶ *And are become judges of evil thoughts.* There has been considerable difference of opinion respecting this passage, yet the sense seems not to be difficult. There are two ideas in it: one is, that they showed by this conduct that they took it upon themselves to be *judges*, to pronounce on the character of men who were strangers, and on their claims to respect (Comp. Matt. vii. 1); the other is, that in doing this, they were not guided by just rules, but that they did it under the influence of improper ' thoughts.' They did it not from benevolence ; not from a desire to do justice to all according to their moral character; but from that improper feeling which leads us to show honour to men on account of their external appearance, rather than their real worth. The *wrong* in the case was in their presuming to 'judge' these strangers at all, as they practically did by making this distinction, and then by doing it under the influence of such an unjust rule of judgment. The sense is, that we have no right to form a decisive judgment of men on their first appearance, as we do when we treat one with respect and the other not; and that when we make up our opinion in regard to them, it should be by some other means of judging than the question whether they can wear gold rings, and dress well, or not. Beza and Doddridge render this, ' ye become judges who reason ill.'

5. *Hearken, my beloved brethren.* The apostle now proceeds to show that the rich, as such, had no special claim on their favour, and that the poor in fact might be made more entitled to esteem than they were. For a view of the arguments by which he does this, compare the analysis of the chapter. ¶ *Hath not God chosen the poor of this world?* Those who are poor so far as this world is concerned, or those who have not wealth. This is the first argument which the apostle suggests why the poor should not be treated with neglect. It is, that God has had special reference to them in choosing those who should be his children. The meaning is not that he is not as *willing* to save the rich as the poor, for he has no partiality; but that there are circumstances in the condition of the poor which make it more likely that they will embrace the offers of the gospel than the rich ; and that in fact the great mass of believers is taken from those who are in comparatively humble life. Comp. Notes on 1 Cor. i. 26–28. The fact that God has chosen one to be an 'heir of the kingdom' is as good a reason now why he should not be treated with neglect, as it was in the times of the apostles. ¶ *Rich in faith.* Though poor in this world's goods, they are rich in a higher and more important sense. They have faith in God their Saviour; and in this world of trial and of sin, that is a more valuable possession than piles of hoarded silver or gold. A man who has that is sure that he will have all that is truly needful for him in this world and the next ; a man who has it not, though he may have the wealth of Crœsus, will be utterly without resources in respect to the great wants of his existence.

"Give what thou wilt, without thee we are poor ;
And with thee rich, take what thou wilt away."

Faith in God the Saviour will answer more purposes, and accomplish more valuable ends for man, than the wealth

draw you before the judgment-
seats?
7 Do they not blaspheme that
a worthy name by the which ye are
called?

8 If ye fulfil the royal law, according to the Scripture, *b* Thou
shalt love thy neighbour as thyself,
ye do well :

a Ps.111.9.   b Le.19.18.

of the Indies could: and this the poor
may have as well as the rich. Comp.
Rev. ii. 9. ¶ *And heirs of the kingdom, &c.* Marg. *that.* Comp. Notes
on Matt. v. 3.
6. *But ye have despised the poor.*
Koppe reads this as an interrogation:
'Do ye despise the poor?' Perhaps
it might be understood somewhat ironi-
cally : 'You despise the poor, do you,
and are disposed to honour the rich!
Look then, and see how the rich treat
you, and see whether you have so much
occasion to regard them with any
peculiar respect.' The *object* of the
apostle is to fix the attention on the
impropriety of that partiality which
many were disposed to show to the rich,
by reminding them that the rich had
never evinced towards them any such
treatment as to lay the foundation of a
claim to the honour which they were
disposed to render them. ¶ *Do not
rich men oppress you?* Referring probably to something in their conduct
which existed particularly then. The
meaning is not that they oppressed the
poor as such, but that they oppressed
those whom James addressed. It is
probable that then, as since, a considerable portion of those who were Christians
were in fact poor, and that this would
have all the force of a personal appeal;
but still the particular thought is, that
it was a characteristic of the rich and
the great, whom they were disposed
peculiarly to honour, to oppress and
crush the poor. The Greek here is
very expressive : 'Do they not imperi-
ously lord it over you?' The statement
here will apply with too much force to
the rich in every age. ¶ *And draw
you before the judgment-seats.* That is,
they are your persecutors rather than
your friends. It was undoubtedly the
case that many of the rich were engaged
in persecuting Christians, and that on
various pretences they dragged them
before the judicial tribunals.
7. *Do they not blaspheme that worthy*

name? This is another argument to
show that the rich had no special claim
to the honour which they were disposed
to show them. The 'worthy name'
here referred to is, doubtless, the name
of the Saviour. The thing here affirmed
would, of course, accompany persecution.
They who persecuted Christians, would
revile the name which they bore. This
has always occurred. But besides this,
it is no improbable supposition that
many of those who were *not* disposed to
engage in open persecution, would revile
the name of Christ, by speaking contemptuously of him and his religion.
This has been sufficiently common in
every age of the world, to make the
description here not improper. And
yet nothing has been more remarkable
than the very thing adverted to here by
James, that notwithstanding this, many
who profess to be Christians have been
more disposed to treat even such persons
with respect and attention than they
have their own brethren, if they were
poor ; that they have cultivated the
favour, sought the friendship, desired the
smiles, aped the manners, and coveted
the society of such persons, rather than
the friendship and the favour of their
poorer Christian brethren. Even though
they are known to despise religion in
their hearts, and not to be sparing of
their words of reproach and scorn towards Christianity; though they are
known to be blasphemers, and to have
the most thorough contempt for serious,
spiritual religion, yet there is many a
professing Christian who would prefer
to be at a party given by such persons
than at a prayer-meeting where their
poorer brethren are assembled ; who
would rather be known by the world to
be the associates and friends of such
persons, than of those humble believers
who can make no boast of rank or
wealth, and who are looked down upon
with contempt by the great and the gay.
8. *If ye fulfil the royal law.* That
is, the law which he immediately men-

9 But if ye have respect *a* to persons, ye commit sin, and are convinced of the law as transgressors.

a ver. 1.

10 For whosoever shall keep the whole law, and yet offend in one point, he *b* is guilty of all.

b De.27.26.

---

tions requiring us to love our neighbour as ourselves. It is called a '*royal law*,' or *kingly law*, on account of its excellence or nobleness ; not because it is ordained by God *as a king*, but because it has some such prominence and importance among other laws as a king has among other men ; that is, it is majestic, noble, worthy of veneration. It is a law which ought to govern and direct us in all our intercourse with men —as a king rules his subjects. ¶ *According to the Scripture, Thou shalt love thy neighbour as thyself.* Lev. xix. 18. Comp. Matt. xix. 19. See it explained by the Saviour, in the parable of the good Samaritan, Luke x. 25–37. In regard to its meaning, see Notes on Matt. xix. 19. ¶ *Ye do well.* That is, ' if you fairly comply with the spirit of this law, you do all that is required of you in regulating your intercourse with others. You are to regard all persons as your " neighbours," and are to treat them according to their real worth ; you are not to be influenced in judging of them, or in your treatment of them, by their apparel, or their complexion, or the circumstances of their birth, but by the fact that they are fellow-beings.' This is another reason why they should not show partiality in their treatment of others, for if, in the true sense, they regarded all others as ' neighbours,' they would treat no one with neglect or contempt.

9. *But if ye have respect to persons, ye commit sin.* You transgress the plain law of God, and do wrong. See the references on ver. 1. ¶ *And are convinced of the law as transgressors.* Gr. '*By* the law.' The word *convinced* is now used in a somewhat different sense from what it was formerly. It now commonly refers to the impression made on a man's mind by showing him the truth of a thing which before was doubted, or in respect to which the evidence was not clear. A man who doubted the truth of a report or a proposition may be *convinced* or *satisfied*

of its truth ; a man who has done wrong, though he supposed he was doing what was proper, may be *convinced* of his error. So a man may be *convinced* that he is a sinner, though before he had no belief of it, and no concern about it ; and this may produce in his mind the feeling which is technically known as *conviction*, producing deep distress and anguish. See Notes on John xvi. 8. Here, however, the word does not refer so much to the effect produced on the mind itself, as to the fact that the law would hold such an one to be guilty ; that is, the law pronounces what is done to be wrong. Whether they would be personally *convinced* of it, and troubled about it as convicted sinners, would be a different question, and one to which the apostle does not refer ; for his object is not to show that they would be *troubled* about it, but to show that the law of God condemned this course, and would hold them to be guilty. The *argument* here is not from the *personal distress* which this course would produce in their own minds, but from the fact that the law of God *condemned* it.

10. *For whosoever shall keep the whole law.* All except the single point referred to. The apostle does not say that this in fact ever *did* occur, but he says that if it *should*, and yet a man should have failed in only one particular, he must be judged to be guilty. The case supposed seems to be that of one who *claimed* that he had kept the whole law. The apostle says that even if this should be admitted for the time to be true in all other respects, yet, if he had failed in any *one* particular—in showing respect to persons, or in anything else— he could not but be held to be a transgressor. The design of this is to show the importance of yielding *universal* obedience, and to impress upon the mind a sense of the enormity of sin from the fact that the violation of any one precept is in fact an offence against the whole law of God. The *whole law* here means all the law of God ; all that he has re-

11 For ¹he that said, *a* Do not commit adultery, said also, Do not kill. Now if thou commit no adul-tery, yet if thou kill, thou art become a transgressor of the law.

1 Or, *that* law *which said.*   *a* Ex.20.13,14.

quired; all that he has given to regulate us in our lives. ¶ *And yet offend in one* point. In one respect; or shall violate any one of the commands included in the general word *law*. The word *offend* here means, properly, to stumble, to fall; then to err, or fail in duty. See Notes on Matt. v. 29; xxvi. 31. ¶ *He is guilty of all.* He is guilty of violating the law as a whole, or of violating the law of God as such; he has rendered it impossible that he should be justified and saved *by* the law. This does not affirm that he is *as* guilty as if he had violated *every* law of God; or that all sinners are of equal grade because all have violated some one or more of the laws of God; but the meaning is, that he is guilty of violating the law of God *as such;* he shows that he has not the true spirit of obedience; he has exposed himself to the penalty of the law, and made it impossible now to be saved *by* it. His acts of obedience in other respects, no matter how many, will not screen him from the charge of being a violator of the law, or from its penalty. He must be held and treated as a transgressor for *that* offence, however upright he may be in other respects, and must meet the penalty of the law as certainly as though he had violated every commandment. One portion of the law is as much binding as another, and if a man violates any one plain commandment, he sets at nought the authority of God. This is a simple principle which is everywhere recognised, and the apostle means no more by it than occurs every day. A man who has stolen a horse is held to be a violator of the law, no matter in how many other respects he has kept it, and the law condemns him for it. He cannot plead his obedience to the law in other things as a reason why he should not be punished for this sin; but however upright he may have been in general, even though it may have been through a long life, the law holds him to be a transgressor, and condemns him. He is as *really* condemned, and as much thrown from the protection of law, as though he had violated every command. So of murder, arson, treason, or any other crime. The law judges a man for what he has done *in this specific case*, and he cannot plead in justification of it that he has been obedient in other things. It follows, therefore, that if a man has been guilty of violating the law of God in any one instance, or is not perfectly holy, he cannot be justified and saved by it, though he should have obeyed it in every other respect, any more than a man who has been guilty of murder can be saved from the gallows *because* he has, in other respects, been a good citizen, a kind father, an honest neighbour, or has been compassionate to the poor and the needy. He cannot plead his act of truth in one case as an offset to the sin of falsehood in another; he cannot defend himself from the charge of dishonesty in one instance by the plea that he has been honest in another; he cannot urge the fact that he has done a good thing as a reason why he should not be punished for a bad one. He must answer for the specific charge against him, and none of these other things can be an *offset* against this one act of wrong. Let it be remarked, also, in respect to our being justified by obedience to the law, that no man can plead before God that he has kept all his law *except* in one point. Who is there that has not, in spirit at least, broken each one of the ten commandments? The sentiment here expressed by James was not new with him. It was often expressed by the Jewish writers, and seems to have been an admitted principle among the Jews. See Wetstein, *in loc.*, for examples.

11. *For he that said, Do not commit adultery, said also, Do not kill.* That is, these are parts of the same law of God, and one is as obligatory as the other. If, therefore, you violate either of these precepts, you transgress the law of God *as such*, and must be held to be guilty of violating it as a whole. The penalty of the law will be incurred, whatever precept you violate.

12 So speak ye, and so do, as they that shall be judged by the law *a* of liberty.

13 For he *b* shall have judgment

without mercy, that hath showed no mercy, and mercy [1]rejoiceth *c* against judgment.

a James 1.25.   *b* Pr.21.13. Mat.6.15; 7.1,2.
1 Or, *glorieth.*   *c* Ps.85.10.

---

12. *So speak ye, and so do, as they that shall be judged by the law of liberty.* On the phrase, 'the law of liberty,' see Notes on ch. i. 25. Comp. Notes on ch. iv. 11. The meaning is, that in all our conduct we are to act under the constant impression of the truth that we are soon to be brought into judgment, and that the law by which we are to be judged is that by which it is contemplated that we shall be set free from the dominion of sin. In the rule which God has laid down in his word, called ' the law of liberty,' or the rule by which true *freedom* is to be secured, a system of religion is revealed by which it is designed that man shall be emancipated not only from *one* sin, but from *all.* Now, it is with reference to such a law that we are to be judged; that is, we shall not be able to plead on our trial that we were under a necessity of sinning, but we shall be judged under that law by which the arrangement was made that we might be free from sin. If we might be free from sin ; if an arrangement was made by which we could have led holy lives, then it will be proper that we shall be judged and condemned if we are not righteous. The sense is, ' In all your conduct, whatever you do or say, remember that you *are to be judged,* or that you are to give an impartial account ; and remember also that the *rule* by which you are to be judged is that by which provision is made for being delivered from the dominion of sin, and brought into the freedom of the gospel.' The argument here seems to be, that he who habitually feels that he is soon to be judged by a law under which it was contemplated that he *might* be, and *should* be, free from the bondage of sin, has one of the strongest of all inducements to lead a holy life.

13. *For he shall have judgment without mercy, that hath showed no mercy.* This is obviously an equitable principle, and is one which is everywhere found in the Bible. Prov. xxi. 13. ' Whoso stoppeth his ears at the

cry of the poor, he also shall cry himself, but will not be heard.' 2 Sam. xxii. 26, 27, ' With the merciful thou wilt show thyself merciful, and with the froward thou wilt show thyself unsavoury.' Comp. Ps. xviii. 25, 26 ; Matt. vi. 15; vii. 1, 2. The idea which the apostle seems to design to convey here is, that there will certainly be a judgment, and that we must expect that it will be conducted on equitable principles ; that no mercy is to be shown when the character is not such that it will be proper that it should be; and that we should habitually feel in our conduct that God will be impartial, and should frame our lives accordingly. ¶ *And mercy rejoiceth against judgment.* Marg. *glorieth.* Gr. Boasts, glories, or exults. The idea is that of glorying over, as where one is superior to another, or has gained a victory over another. The reference all along here is to the judgment, the trial of the great day ; and the apostle is stating the principles on which the trial at that day will be conducted—on which one class shall be condemned, and the other acquitted and saved. In reference to one class, the wicked, he says that where there has been no mercy shown to others—referring to this as *one* evidence of piety—that is, where there is no true piety, there will be judgment without mercy; in the other case there will be, as it were, a *triumph* of mercy, or mercy will appear to have gained a victory over judgment. Strict justice would indeed plead for their condemnation, but the attribute of mercy will triumph, and they will be acquitted. The attributes of mercy and justice would seem to come in conflict, but mercy would prevail. This is a true statement of the plan of salvation, and of what actually occurs in the redemption of a sinner. Justice *demands,* as what is her due, that the sinner should be condemned; mercy *pleads* that he may be saved—and mercy prevails. It is not uncommon that there

14 What *ᵃ doth it* profit, my bre- | faith, and have not works? Can
thren, though a man say he hath | faith save him?

a Mat.7.26.

seems to be a conflict between the
two. In the dispensations of justice before human tribunals, this often occurs.
Strict justice *demands* the punishment
of the offender ; and yet there are cases
when mercy pleads, and when every man
feels that it would be desirable that pardon should be extended to the guilty,
and when we always rejoice if mercy
triumphs. In such a case, for example,
as that ot Major André, this is strikingly seen. On the one hand, there was
the undoubted proof that he was guilty;
that he had been taken as a spy ; that
by the laws of war he ought to be put to
death ; that as what he had done had
tended to the ruin of the American
cause, and as such an act, if unpunished,
would always expose an army to surprise
and destruction, he ought, in accordance
with the law of nations, to die. On the
other hand, there were his youth, his
high attainments, his honourable connections, his brilliant hopes, all pleading
that he might live, and that he might
be pardoned. In the bosom of Washington, the promptings of justice and mercy
thus came into collision. Both could
not be gratified, and there seemed to be
but one course to be pursued. His sense
of justice was shown in the act by which
he signed the death-warrant ; his feelings of compassion in the fact that when
he did it his eyes poured forth a flood
of tears. How every generous feeling
of our nature would have been gratified
if mercy could have triumphed, and the
youthful and accomplished officer could
have been spared ! In the plan of salvation, this does occur. Respect is done
to justice, but mercy triumphs. Justice
indeed pleaded for the condemnation of
the sinner, but mercy interposed, and
he is saved. Justice is not disregarded,
for the great Redeemer of mankind has
done all that is needful to uphold it ;
but there is the most free and full exercise of mercy, and, while the justice of
God is maintained, every benevolent
feeling in the breasts of all holy beings
can be gratified in the salvation of countless thousands.

14. *What* doth it *profit, my brethren,
though a man say he hath faith ?* The
apostle here returns to the subject adverted to in ch. i. 22–27, the importance
of a practical attention to the duties of
religion, and the assurance that men
cannot be saved by a mere speculative
opinion, or merely by holding correct
sentiments. He doubtless had in his
eye those who abused the doctrine of
justification by faith, by holding that
good works are unnecessary to salvation,
provided they maintain an orthodox belief. As this abuse probably existed in
the time of the apostles, and as the Holy
Ghost saw that there would be danger
that in later times the great and glorious doctrine of justification by faith
would be thus abused, it was important
that the error should be rebuked, and
that the doctrine should be distinctly
laid down that good works *are* necessary
to salvation. The apostle, therefore, i
the question before us, implicitly asserts
that faith would not ' profit' at all unless accompanied with a holy life, and
this doctrine he proceeds to illustrate
in the following verses. See the analysis
of this chapter ; and Intro. § 5, (2).
In order to a proper interpretation of
this passage, it should be observed that
the *stand-point* from which the apostle
views this subject is not *before* a man
is converted, inquiring in what way he
may be justified before God, or on what
ground his sins may be forgiven; but it
is *after* a man is converted, showing
that that faith can have no value which
is not followed by good works ; that is,
that it is not *real* faith, and that good
works are necessary if a man would
have evidence that he is justified. Thus
understood, all that James says is in
entire accordance with what is taught
elsewhere in the New Testament. ¶ *Can
faith save him ?* It is implied in
this question that faith *cannot* save
him, for very often the most emphatic way of making an affirmation is by
asking a question. The meaning here is,
that that faith which does *not* produce
good works, or which would not produce

15 If a brother or sister be naked, and destitute of daily food,

16 And one of you say unto them, Depart in peace, be *ye* warmed and filled; notwithstanding ye give them

not those things which are needful to the body; what *a doth it* profit?

17 Even so faith, if it hath not works, is dead, being [1] alone.

a 1 Jno.3.18.   1 *by itself.*

holy living if fairly acted out, will save no man, for it is not genuine faith. 15, 16, 17. *If a brother or sister be naked,* &c. The comparison in these verses is very obvious and striking. The sense is, that faith in itself, without the acts that correspond to it, and to which it would prompt, is as cold, and heartless, and unmeaning, and useless, as it would be to say to one who was destitute of the necessaries of life, ' depart in peace.' In itself considered, it might seem to have something that was good ; but it would answer none of the purposes of faith unless it should prompt to action. In the case of one who was hungry or naked, what he wanted was not good wishes or kind words merely, but the *acts* to which good wishes and kind words prompt. And so in religion, what is wanted is not merely the abstract state of mind which would be indicated by faith, but the life of goodness to which it ought to lead. Good wishes and kind words, in order to make them what they should be for the welfare of the world, should be accompanied with corresponding action. So it is with faith. It is not enough for salvation without the benevolent and holy acts to which it would prompt, any more than the good wishes and kind words of the benevolent are enough to satisfy the wants of the hungry, and to clothe the naked, without correspondent action. Faith is not and cannot be shown to be genuine, unless it is accompanied with corresponding acts; as our good wishes for the poor and needy can be shown to be genuine, when we have the means of aiding them, only by actually ministering to their necessities. In the one case, our wishes would be shown to be unmeaning and heartless ; in the other, our faith would be equally so. In regard to this passage, therefore, it may be observed, (1), that in fact faith is of no more value, and has no more evidence of genuineness when it is unaccompanied with good works, than such

empty wishes for the welfare of the poor would be when unaccompanied with the means of relieving their wants. Faith is designed to lead to good works. It is intended to produce a holy life ; a life of activity in the service of the Saviour. This is its very essence ; it is what it always produces when it is genuine. Religion is not designed to be a cold abstraction ; it is to be a living and vivifying principle. (2) There is a great deal of that kindness and charity in the world which is expressed by mere good wishes. If we really have not the means of relieving the poor and the needy, then the expression of a kind wish may be in itself an alleviation to their sorrows, for even sympathy in such a case is of value, and it is much to us to know that others *feel* for us ; but if we *have* the means, and the object is a worthy one, then such expressions are mere mockery, and aggravate rather than soothe the feelings of the sufferer. Such wishes will neither clothe nor feed them ; and they will only make deeper the sorrows which we ought to heal. But how much of this is there in the world, when the sufferer cannot but feel that all these wishes, however kindly expressed, are hollow and false, and when he cannot but feel that relief would be easy ! (3) In like manner there is much of this same kind of worthless *faith* in the world—faith that is dead; faith that produces no good works; faith that exerts no practical influence whatever on the life. The individual professes indeed to believe the truths of the gospel; he may be in the church of Christ; he would esteem it a gross calumny to be spoken of as an infidel; but as to any influence which his faith exerts over him, his life would be the same if he had never heard of the gospel. There is not one of the truths of religion which is bodied forth in his life; not a deed to which he is prompted by religion ; not an act which could not be accounted for on the supposition that

18 Yea, a man may say, Thou hast faith, and I have works: show me thy faith ¹ without thy works, and I ª will show thee my faith by my works.

1 some copies read, *by.* a James 3.18.

he has no true piety. In such a case, faith may with propriety be said to be dead. ¶ *Being alone.* Marg., *by itself.* The sense is, ' being by itself;' that is, destitute of any accompanying fruits or results, it shows that it is dead. That which is alive bodies itself forth, produces effects, makes itself visible; that which is dead produces no effect, and is as if it were not.

18. *Yea, a man may say,* &c. The word which is rendered '*yea*' (ἀλλὰ) would be better rendered by *but.* The apostle designs to introduce an objection, not to make an affirmation. The sense is, ' some one might say,' or, ' to this it might be urged in reply.' That is, it might perhaps be said that religion is not always manifested in the same way, or we should not suppose that, because it is not always exhibited in the same form, it does not exist. One man may manifest it in one way, and another in another, and still both have true piety. One may be distinguished for his faith, and another for his works, and both may have real religion. This objection would certainly have some plausibility, and it was important to meet it. It would *seem* that all religion was not to be manifested in the same way, as all virtue is not; and that it *might* occur that one man might be particularly eminent for one form of religion, and another for another; as one man may be distinguished for zeal, and another for meekness, and another for integrity, and another for truth, and another for his gifts in prayer, and another for his large-hearted benevolence. To this the apostle replies, that the two things referred to, faith and works, were not independent things, which could exist separately, without the one materially influencing another— as, for example, charity and chastity, zeal and meekness; but that the one was the *germ* or *source* of the other, and that the existence of the one was to be known only by its developing itself in the form of the other. A man could not show that he possessed the one un-

less it developed itself in the form of the other. In proof of this, he could boldly appeal to any one to show a case where faith existed without works. He was himself willing to submit to this just trial in regard to this point, and to demonstrate the existence of his own faith *by* his works. ¶ *Thou hast faith, and I have works.* You have one form or manifestation of religion in an eminent or prominent degree, and I have another. You are characterized particularly for one of the virtues of religion, and I am for another; as one man may be particularly eminent for meekness, and another for zeal, and another for benevolence, and each be a virtuous man. The expression here is equivalent to saying, ' One may have faith, and another works.' ¶ *Show me thy faith without thy works.* That is, you who maintain that faith is enough to prove the existence of religion; that a man may be justified and saved by that alone, or where it does not develope itself in holy living; or that all that is necessary in order to be saved is merely *to believe.* Let the reality of any *such* faith as that be shown, if it can be; let *any* real faith be shown to exist *without* a life of good works, and the point will be settled. *I,* says the apostle, will undertake to exhibit the evidence of *my* faith in a different way—in a way about which there can be no doubt, and which is the *appropriate* method. It is clear, if the common reading here is correct, that the apostle meant to *deny* that true faith could be evinced without appropriate works. It should be said, however, that there is a difference of reading here of considerable importance. Many manuscripts and printed editions of the New Testament, instead of *without* [works—χωρίς], read *from* or *by* (ἐκ), as in the other part of the verse, ' show me thy faith by thy works, and I will show thee my faith by my works.' This reading is found in Walton, Wetstein, Mill, and in the received text generally; the other [*without*] is found in many MSS., and in the Vulgate, Syriac,

19 Thou believest that there is
one God; thou doest well: the devils
*also believe, and tremble.

a Mar.1.24; 5 7.

Coptic, English, and Armenian versions; and is adopted by Beza, Castalio, Grotius, Bengel, Hammond, Whitby, Drusius, Griesbach, Tittman, and Hahn, and is now commonly received as the correct reading. It may be added that this reading seems to be demanded by the similar reading in ver. 20, 'But wilt thou know that faith *without works* (χωρὶς τῶν ἔργων) is dead,' evidently implying that something had been said before about ' faith *without* works.' This reading also is so natural, and makes so good sense in the connection, that it would seem to be demanded. Doddridge felt the difficulty in the other reading, and has given a version of the passage which showed his great perplexity, and which is one of the most unhappy that he ever made. ¶ *And I will show thee my faith by my works.* I will furnish in this way the best and most certain proof of the existence of faith. It is implied here that true faith is adapted to lead to a holy life, and that such a life would be the appropriate evidence of the existence of faith. By their fruits the principles held by men are known, See Notes on Matt. vii. 16.

19. *Thou believest that there is one God.* One of the great and cardinal doctrines of religion is here selected as an illustration of all. The design of the apostle seems to have been to select one of the doctrines of religion, the belief of which would—if mere belief in *any* doctrine could—save the soul; and to show that even *this* might be held as an article of faith by those who could be supposed by no one to have any claim to the name of Christian. He selects, therefore, the great fundamental doctrine of all religion,—the doctrine of the existence of one Supreme Being,—and shows that if even this were held in such a way as it might be, and as it was held by devils, it could not save men. The apostle here is not to be supposed to be addressing such an one as *Paul*, who held to the doctrine that we are justified by faith; nor is he to be supposed to be *combating* the doctrine of Paul, as some have maintained, (see the

Intro.); but he is to be regarded as addressing one who held, in the broadest and most unqualified sense, that provided there was *faith*, a man would be saved. To this he replies, that even the devils might have faith of a certain sort, and faith that would produce sensible effects on them of a certain kind, and still it could not be supposed that they had true religion, or that they would be saved. Why might not the same thing occur in regard to man? ¶ *Thou doest well.* So far as this is concerned, or so far as it goes. It is a doctrine which *ought* to be held, for it is one of the great fundamental truths of religion. ¶ *The devils.* The demons,—(τὰ δαιμόνια.) There is, properly, but *one* being spoken of in the New Testament as *the devil*—ὁ διάβολος, and ὁ Σατᾶν—though *demons* are frequently spoken of in the plural number. They are represented as evil spirits, subject to Satan, or under his control, and engaged with him in carrying out his plans of wickedness. These spirits or demons were supposed to wander in desert and desolate places, (Math. xii. 43), or to dwell in the atmosphere, (Notes, Eph. ii. 2); they were thought to have the power of working miracles, but not for good, (Rev. xvi. 14; comp. John x. 21); to be hostile to mankind, (John viii. 44); to utter the heathen oracles, (Acts xvi. 17); to lurk in the idols of the heathen, (1 Cor. x. 20); and to take up their abodes in the bodies of men, afflicting them with various kinds of diseases, Matt. vii. 22; ix. 34; x. 8; xvii. 18; Mark vii. 29, 30; Luke iv. 33; viii. 27, 30, *et sæpe.* It is of *these* evil spirits that the apostle speaks when he says that they believe. ¶ *Also believe.* That is, particularly, they believe in the existence of the one God. How far their knowledge may extend respecting God, we cannot know; but they are never represented in the Scriptures as denying his existence, or as doubting the great truths of religion. They are never described as *atheists.* That is a sin of this world only They are not represented as *sceptics.* That, too, is a peculiar sin of the earth; and

20 But wilt thou know, O vain man, that faith without works is dead?

21 Was not Abraham our father justified by works, when *a* he had offered Isaac his son upon the altar?

a Ge.22.9,12.

---

probably, in all the universe besides, there are no beings but those who dwell on this globe, who doubt or deny the existence of God, or the other great truths of religion. ¶ *And tremble.* The word here used (φρίσσω) occurs nowhere else in the New Testament. It means, properly, to be rough, uneven, jaggy, sc., with bristling hair; to bristle, to stand on end, as the hair does in a fright; and then to shudder or quake with fear, &c. Here the meaning is, that there was much more in the case referred to than mere speculative faith. There was a faith that produced *some* effect, and an effect of a very decided character. It did not, indeed, produce good works, or a holy life, but it made it manifest that there *was faith;* and, consequently, it followed that the existence of mere faith was not all that was necessary to save men, or to make it certain that they would be secure, unless it were held that the devils would be justified and saved by it. If they might hold such faith, and still *remain* in perdition, men might hold it, and *go* to perdition. A man should not infer, therefore, because he has faith, even that faith in God which will fill him with alarm, that therefore he is safe. He must have a faith which will produce another effect altogether—that which will lead to a holy life.

20. *But wilt thou know.* Will you have a full demonstration of it; will you have the clearest proof in the case. The apostle evidently felt that the instances to which he was about to refer, those of Abraham and Rahab, were decisive. ¶ *O vain man.* The reference by this language is to a man who held an opinion that could not be defended. The word *vain* here used (κενός) means properly *empty,* as opposed to *full*—as empty hands, having nothing in them; then fruitless, or without utility or success; then false, fallacious. The meaning here, properly, would be 'empty,' in the sense of being void of understanding; and this would be a mild and gen-

tle way of saying of one that he was *foolish,* or that he maintained an argument that was *without sense.* James means, doubtless, to represent it as a perfectly plain matter, a matter about which no man of sense could have any reasonable doubt. If we *must* call a man *foolish,* as is sometimes necessary, let us use as mild and inoffensive a term as possible—a term which, while it will convey our meaning, will not unnecessarily wound and irritate. ¶ *That faith without works is dead.* That the faith which does not produce good works is useless in the matter of salvation. He does not mean to say that it would produce *no* effect, for in the case of the demons it *did* produce trembling and alarm; but that it would be valueless in the matter of salvation. The faith of Abraham and of Rahab was entirely different from this.

21. *Was not Abraham our father.* Our progenitor, our ancestor; using the word *father,* as frequently occurs in the Bible, to denote a remote ancestor. Comp. Notes on Matt. i. 1. A reference to his case would have great weight with those who were Jews by birth, and probably most of those to whom this epistle was addressed were of this character. See the Intro. ¶ *Justified by works.* That is, in the sense in which James is maintaining that a man professing religion is to be justified by his works. He does not affirm that the ground of acceptance with God is that we keep the law, or are perfect; or that our good works make an atonement for our sins, and that it is on their account that we are pardoned; nor does he deny that it is necessary that a man should *believe* in order to be saved. In this sense he does not deny that men are justified by faith; and thus he does not contradict the doctrine of the apostle Paul. But he *does* teach that where there are no good works, or where there is not a holy life, there is no true religion; that that faith which is not productive of good works is of no value;

22 ¹ Seest thou how faith *a* wrought with his works, and by works was faith made perfect?

that if a man has that faith only, it would be impossible that he could be regarded as justified, or could be saved; and that consequently, in that large sense, a man is justified by his works; that is, they are the evidence that he is a justified man, or is regarded and treated as righteous by his Maker. The point on which the apostle has his eye is the nature of saving faith; and his design is to show that a mere faith which would produce no more effect than that of the demons did, could not save. In this he states no doctrine which contradicts that of Paul. The *evidence* to which he appeals in regard to faith, is good works and a holy life; and where that exists it shows that the faith is genuine. The case of Abraham is one directly in point. He showed that he had that kind of faith which was *not* dead. He gave the most affecting evidence that his faith was of such a kind as to lead him to implicit obedience, and to painful sacrifices. Such an act as that referred to—the act of offering up his son—demonstrated, if any thing could, that his faith was genuine, and that his religion was deep and pure. In the sight of heaven and earth it would *justify* him as a righteous man, or would *prove* that he was a righteous man. In regard to the strength of his faith, and the nature of his obedience in this sacrifice, see Notes on Heb. xi. 19. That the apostle here cannot refer to the act of justification as the term is commonly understood, referring by that to the moment when he was accepted of God as a righteous man, is clear from the fact that in a passage of the Scriptures which he himself quotes, that is declared to be consequent on his *believing:* 'Abraham believed God, and it was imputed unto him for righteousness.' The act here referred to occurred long *subsequent* to that, and was thus a fulfilment or confirmation of the declaration of Scripture, which says that ' he *believed* God.' It showed that his faith was not merely speculative, but was an active principle, leading to holy living. See Notes on ver. 23. This demonstrates that what the apostle refers to here is

the evidence by which it is shown that a man's faith is genuine, and that he does not refer to the question whether the act of justification, where a sinner is converted, is solely in consequence of believing. Thus the case proves what James purposes to prove, that the faith which justifies is only that which leads to good works. ¶ *When he had offered Isaac his son upon the altar.* This was long after he believed, and was an act which, if any could, would show that his faith was genuine and sincere. On the meaning of this passage, see Notes on Heb. xi. 17.

22. *Seest thou.* Marg. *Thou seest.* Either rendering is correct, and the sense is the same. The apostle means to say that this was so plain that they could not but see it. ¶ *How faith wrought with his works.* συνήργει. Co-operated with. The meaning of the word is, *to work together with any one; to co-operate,* (1 Cor. xvi. 16; 2 Cor. vi. 1); then to aid, or help, (Mark xvi. 20); to contribute to the production of any result, where two or more persons or agents are united. Comp. Rom. viii. 28. The idea here is, that the result in the case of Abraham, that is, his salvation, or his religion, was secured, not by *one* of these things alone, but that *both* contributed to it. The result which *was* reached, to wit, his acceptance with God, could *not* have been obtained by either one of them separately, but both, in some sense, entered into it. The apostle does not say that, in regard to the *merit* which justifies, they came in for an equal share, for he makes no affirmation on that point; he does not deny that in the sight of God, who foresees and knows all things, he was regarded as a justified man the moment he believed, but he looks at the result *as it was,* at Abraham as he appeared under the trial of his faith, and says that *in* that result there was to be seen the co-operation of faith *and* good works. Both contributed to the end, as they do now in all cases where there is true religion.

[By the somewhat unhappy term 'merit,' the author clearly means nothing more than 'prin-

23 And the Scripture was fulfilled which saith, *a* Abraham believed God, and it was imputed

a Ge.15.6.

unto him for righteousness: and he was called *b* the friend of God.

24 Ye see then how that by works

b 2 Ch.20.7. Is.41.8.

ciple,' as is obvious from his acute and evangelical comment on the verse; as well as from the admirable reconciliation of Paul and James below.]

¶ *And by works was faith made perfect.* Made *complete, finished,* or *entire.* It was so *carried out* as to show its legitimate and fair results. This does not mean that the faith in itself was defective before this, and that the defect was *remedied* by good works; or that there is any deficiency in what the right kind of faith can do in the matter of justification, which is to be *helped out* by good works; but that there was that kind of completion which a thing has when it is fully developed, or is fairly carried out.

23. *And the Scripture was fulfilled which saith.* That is, the fair and full meaning of the language of Scripture was expressed by this act, showing in the highest sense that his faith was genuine; or the declaration that he truly believed, was *confirmed* or *established* by this act. His faith was shown to be genuine; and the fair meaning of the declaration that he *believed* God was carried out in the subsequent act. The passage here referred to occurs in Gen. xv. 6. That which it is said Abraham believed, or in which he believed God, was this : ' This shall not be thine heir (viz. Eliezer of Damascus), but he that shall come forth out of thine own bowels, shall be thine heir.' And again, ' Look now toward heaven, and tell the stars, if thou be able to number them. And he said unto him, So shall thy seed be,' vs. 3–5. The act of confiding in these promises, was that act of which it is said that ' he believed in the Lord ; and he counted it to him for righteousness.' The act of offering his son on the altar, by which James says this Scripture was fulfilled, occurred some twenty years afterwards. That act confirmed or fulfilled the declaration. It showed that his faith was genuine, and that the declaration that he believed in God was true; for what could do more to confirm that, than a readiness to offer his own son at the command of God? It cannot

be supposed that James meant to say that Abraham was justified by *works* without respect to faith, or to deny that the primary ground of his justification in the sight of God was *faith,* for the very passage which he quotes shows that faith was the primary consideration : ' Abraham *believed* God, and *it* was imputed,' &c. The meaning, therefore, can only be, that this declaration received its fair and full expression when Abraham, by an act of obedience of the most striking character, long after he first exercised that faith by which he was accepted of God, showed that his faith was genuine. If he had not thus obeyed, his faith would have been inoperative and of no value. As it was, his act showed that the declaration of the Scripture that, he ' *believed* ' was well founded. ¶ *Abraham believed God, and it was imputed,* &c. See this passage fully explained in the Notes on Rom. iv. 3. ¶ *And he was called the friend of God.* In virtue of his strong faith and obedience. See 2 Chron. xx. 7: 'Art not thou our God, who didst drive out the inhabitants of this land before thy people Israel, and gavest it to the seed of Abraham *thy friend* for ever ?' Isa. xli. 8. ' But thou, Israel, art my servant, Jacob whom I have chosen, the seed of Abraham *my friend.*' This was a most honourable appellation ; but it is one which, in all cases, will result from true faith and obedience.

24. *Ye see then.* From the course of reasoning pursued, and the example referred to. ¶ *How that by works a man is justified, and not by faith only.* Not by a cold, abstract, inoperative faith. It must be by a faith that shall *produce* good works, and whose existence will be shown to men by good works. As justification takes place in the sight of God, it is by faith, for he sees that the faith is genuine, and that it will produce good works if the individual who exercises faith shall live; and he justifies men in view of *that* faith, and no other. If he sees that the faith is merely speculative; that it is cold and

ᵃ a man is justified, and not by faith only.

25 Likewise also was not Rahab ᵇ the harlot ᶜ justified by works, when she had received the messen-

a Re.20.12.　　b Jos.2.1,&c. He.11.31.

c Mat.21.31.

dead, and would *not* produce good works, the man is *not* justified in his sight. As a matter of fact, therefore, it is only the faith that produces good works that justifies; and good works, therefore, as the proper expression of the nature of faith, *foreseen* by God as the certain result of faith, and actually *performed* as seen by men, are necessary in order to justification. In other words, no man will be justified who has not a faith which will produce good works, and which is of an operative and practical character. The *ground* of justification in the case is faith, and that only; the *evidence* of it, the carrying it out, the proof of the existence of the faith, is good works; and thus men are justified and saved not by mere abstract and cold faith, but by a faith necessarily connected with good works, and where good works perform an important part. James, therefore, does not contradict Paul, but he contradicts a false explanation of Paul's doctrine. He does not deny that a man is justified in the sight of God by faith, for the very passage which he quotes shows that he believes that; but he *does* deny that a man is justified by a faith which would not produce good works, and which is not expressed by good works; and thus he maintains, as Paul always did, that nothing else than a holy life can show that a man is a true Christian, and is accepted of God.

25. *Likewise also was not Rahab the harlot justified by works?* In the same sense in which Abraham was, as explained above—showing by her act that her faith was genuine, and that it was not a mere cold and speculative assent to the truths of religion. Her act showed that she truly believed God. If that act had not been performed, the fact would have shown that her faith was not genuine, and she could not have been justified. God saw her faith as it was; he saw that it *would* produce acts

gers, and had sent *them* out another way?

26 For as the body without the ¹ spirit is dead, so faith without works is dead also.

1 Or, *breath.*

of obedience, and he accepted her as righteous. The act which she performed was the public manifestation of her faith, the evidence that she was justified. See the case of Rahab fully explained in the Notes on Heb. xi. 31. It may be observed here, that we are not to suppose that *everything* in the life and character of this woman is commended. She is commended for her *faith*, and for the fair expression of it; a faith which, as it induced her to receive the messengers of the true God, and to send them forth in peace, and as it led her to identify herself with the people of God, was also influential, we have every reason to suppose, in inducing her to abandon her former course of life. When we commend the faith of a man who has been a profane swearer, or an adulterer, or a robber, or a drunkard, we do not commend his former life, or give a sanction to it. We commend that which has induced him to abandon his evil course, and to turn to the ways of righteousness. The more evil his former course has been, the more wonderful, and the more worthy of commendation, is that faith by which he is reformed and saved.

26. *For as the body without the spirit is dead.* Marg. *breath.* The Greek word πνεῦμα is commonly used to denote *spirit* or *soul*, as referring to the intelligent nature. The meaning here is the obvious one, that the body is animated or kept alive by the presence of the soul, and that when that is withdrawn, hope departs. The body has no life independent of the presence of the soul. ¶ *So faith without works is dead also.* There is as much necessity that faith and works should be united to constitute true religion, as there is that the body and soul should be united to constitute a living man. If good works do not follow, it is clear that there is no true and proper faith; none that justifies and saves. If faith pro-

duces no fruit of good living, that fact proves that it is dead, that it has no power, and that it is of no value. This shows that James was not arguing against real and genuine faith, nor against its importance in justification, but against the supposition that mere faith was all that was necessary to save a man, whether it was accompanied by good works or not. *He* maintains that if there is genuine faith it will always be accompanied by good works, and that it is only *that* faith which can justify and save. If it leads to no practical holiness of life, it is like the body without the soul, and is of no value whatever. James and Paul both agree in the necessity of true faith in order to salvation; they both agree that the tendency of true faith is to produce a holy life; they both agree that where there is not a holy life there is no true religion, and that a man cannot be saved. We may learn, then, from the whole doctrine of the New Testament on the subject, that unless we believe in the Lord Jesus we cannot be justified before God; and that unless our faith is of that kind which will produce holy living, it has no more of the character-istics of true religion than a dead body has of a living man.

Reconciliation of Paul and James.

At the close of the exposition of this chapter, it may be proper to make a few additional remarks on the question in what way the statements of James can be reconciled with those of Paul, on the subject of justification. A difficulty has always been felt to exist on the sub-ject; and there are, perhaps, no readers of the New Testament who are not per-plexed with it. Infidels, and particu-larly Voltaire, have seized the occasion which they supposed they found here to sneer against the Scriptures, and to pronounce them to be contradictory. Luther felt the difficulty to be so great that, in the early part of his career, he regarded it as insuperable, and denied the inspiration of James, though he afterwards changed his opinion, and be-lieved that his epistle was a part of the inspired canon; and one of Luther's fol-lowers was so displeased with the state-ments of James, as to charge him with

wilful falsehood.—Dr. Dwight's Theo-logy, Serm. lxviii. The question is, whether their statements can be so re-conciled, or can be shown to be so con-sistent with each other, that it is proper to regard them both as inspired men? Or, are their statements so opposite and contradictory, that it cannot be believed that both were under the influences of an infallible Spirit? In order to answer these questions, there are two points to be considered: I. What the real diffi-culty is; and, II. How the statements of the two writers can be reconciled, or whether there is any way of explanation which will remove the difficulty.

I. What the difficulty is. This re-lates to two points—that James seems to contradict Paul in express terms, and that both writers make use of the same case to illustrate their opposite sentiments.

(1.) That James seems to contradict Paul in express terms. The doctrine of Paul on the subject of justification is stated in such language as the following: 'By the deeds of the law there shall no flesh be justified in his sight,' Rom. iii. 20. 'We conclude that a man is justi-fied by faith without the deeds of the law,' Rom. iii. 28. 'Being justified by faith,' Rom. v. 1. 'Knowing that a man is not justified by the works of the law, but by the faith of Jesus Christ,' Gal. ii. 16. Comp. Rom. iii. 24-26; Gal. iii. 11; Titus iii. 5, 6. On the other hand, the statement of James seems to be equally explicit that a man is *not* justified by faith only, but that good works come in for an important share in the matter. 'Was not Abra-ham our father justified by works?' ver. 21. 'Seest thou how faith wrought with his works?' ver. 22. 'Ye see then how that by works a man is justified, and not by faith only,' ver. 24.

(2.) Both writers refer to the same case to illustrate their views—the case of Abraham. Thus Paul (Rom. iv. 1-3) refers to it to prove that justification is wholly by faith. 'For if Abraham were justified by works, he hath whereof to glory; but not before God. For what saith the Scripture? Abraham believed God, and it was imputed unto him for righteousness.' And thus James (vs. 21, 22) refers to it to prove that justification is by works : ' Was not Abraham our father justified by works when he had offered Isaac his son upon the altar?' The difficulty of reconciling these statements would be more clearly seen if they occurred in the writings of the same author; by supposing, for example, that the statements of James were appended to the fourth chapter of the epistle to the Romans, and were to be read in connection with that chapter. Who, the infidel would ask, would not be struck with the contradiction? Who would undertake to harmonize statements so contradictory? Yet the statements are equally contradictory, though they occur in different writers, and especially when it is claimed for both that they wrote under the influence of inspiration.

II. The inquiry then is, how these apparently contradictory statements may be reconciled, or whether there is any way of explanation that will remove the difficulty. This inquiry resolves itself into two—whether there is any theory that can be proposed that would relieve the difficulty, and whether that theory can be shown to be well founded.

(1.) Is there any theory which would remove the difficulty—any explanation which can be given on this point which, if true, would show that the two statements may be in accordance with each other and with truth ?

Before suggesting such an explanation, it may be further observed, that, as all history has shown, the statements of Paul on the subject of justification are liable to great abuse. All the forms of Antinomianism have grown out of such abuse, and are only perverted statements of his doctrine. It has been said, that if Christ has freed us from the necessity of obeying the law in order to justification; if he has fulfilled it in our stead, and borne its penalty, then the law is no longer binding on those who are justified, and they are at liberty to live as they please. It has been further said, that if we are saved by faith alone, a man is safe the moment he believes, and good works are therefore not necessary. It is possible that such views as these began to prevail as early as the time of James, and, if so, it was proper that there should be an authoritative

apostolic statement to correct them, and to check these growing abuses. If, therefore, James had, as it has been supposed he had, any reference to the sentiments of Paul, it was not to correct his sentiments, or to controvert them. but it was to correct the *abuses* which began already to flow from his doctrines, and to show that the alleged inferences did not properly follow from the opinions which he held ; or, in other words, to show that the Christian religion required men to lead holy lives, and that the faith by which it was acknowledged that the sinner must be justified, was a faith which was productive of good works.

Now, all that is necessary to reconcile the statements of Paul and James, is to suppose that they contemplate the subject of justification from different points of view, and with reference to different inquiries. Paul looks at it *before* a man is converted, with reference to the question how a sinner may be justified before God ; James *after* a man is converted, with reference to the question how he may show that he has the genuine faith which justifies. Paul affirms that the sinner is justified before God only by faith in the Lord Jesus, and not by his own works ; James affirms that it is not a mere speculative or dead faith which justifies, but only a faith that is productive of good works, and that its genuineness is seen only *by* good works. Paul affirms that whatever else a man has, if he have not faith in the Lord Jesus, he cannot be justified ; James affirms that no matter what pretended faith a man has, if it is not a faith which is adapted to produce good works, it is of no value in the matter of justification. Supposing this to be the true explanation, and that these are the 'stand-points' from which they view the subject, the reconciliation of these two writers is easy: for it was and is still true, that if the question is asked how a sinner is to be justified before God, the answer is to be that of Paul, that it is by faith alone, ' without the works of the law;' if the question be asked, how it can be shown what is the kind of faith that justifies, the answer is that of James, that it is only that which is productive of holy living and practical obedience

(2.) Is this a true theory? Can it be shown to be in accordance with the statements of the two writers? Would it be a proper explanation if the same statements had been made by the same writer? That it is a correct theory, or that it is an explanation founded in truth, will be apparent if (a) the language used by the two writers will warrant it ; (b) if it accords with a fair interpretation of the declarations of both writers ; and (c) if, in fact, each of the two writers held respectively the same doctrine on the subject.

(a) Will the language bear this explanation? That is, will the word *justify*, as used by the two writers, admit of this explanation? That it will, there need be no reasonable doubt ; for both are speaking of the way in which man, who is a sinner, may be regarded and treated by God *as if* he were righteous —the true notion of justification. It is not of justification in the sight *of men* that they speak, but of justification in the sight of God. Both use the word justify in this sense—Paul as affirming that it is only by faith that it can be done ; James as affirming, in *addition*, not in *contradiction*, that it is by a faith that produces holiness, and no other.

(b) Does this view accord with the fair interpretation of the declarations of both writers ?

In regard to Paul, there can be no doubt that this is the point from which he contemplates the subject, to wit, with reference to the question *how a sinner may be justified*. Thus, in the epistle to the Romans, where his principal statements on the subject occur, he shows, first, that the Gentiles cannot be justified by the works of the law, (ch. i.), and then that the same thing is true in regard to the Jews, (chs. ii., iii.), by demonstrating that both had violated the law given them, and were transgressors, and then (ch. iii. 20) draws his conclusion, ' Therefore by the deeds of the law there shall no flesh be justified in his sight '—the whole argument showing conclusively that he is contemplating the subject *before* a man is justified, and with reference to the question how he *may be.*

In regard to James, there can be as little doubt that the point of view from which he contemplates the subject, is *after* a man professes to have been justified by faith, with reference to the question *what kind of faith justifies*, or *how it may be shown that faith is genuine*. This is clear, (a) because the whole question is introduced by him with almost express reference to that inquiry : ' What doth it *profit*, my brethren, though a man *say* he hath faith, and have not works? Can faith save him?' ver. 14. That is, can *such* faith —can *this* faith (η $\pi i \sigma \tau i s$) save him? In other words, He must have a different kind of faith in order to save him. The point of James' denial is not that faith, if genuine, would save ; but it is, that *such* a faith, or a faith without works, would save. (b) That this is the very point which he discusses, is further shown by his illustrations, vs. 15, 16, 19. He shows (vs. 15, 16) that mere faith in religion would be of no more value in regard to salvation, than if one were naked and destitute of food, it would meet his wants to say, 'Depart in peace, be ye warmed and filled ;' and then (ver. 19), that even the demons had a certain kind of faith in one of the cardinal doctrines of religion, but that it was a faith which was valueless—thus showing that his mind was on the question what is true and genuine faith. (c) Then he shows by the case to which he refers (vs. 21–23)—the case of Abraham—that this was the question before his mind. He refers not to the act *when* Abraham first believed—the act by which as a sinner he was justified before God ; but to an act that occurred twenty years after—the offering up of his son Isaac. See Notes on those verses. He affirms that the faith of Abraham was of such a kind that it led him to obey the will of God ; that is, to good works. Though, as is implied in the objection referred to above, he does refer to the same *case* to which Paul referred—the case of Abraham—yet it is not to the same *act* in Abraham. Paul (Rom. iv. 1–3) refers to him when he first believed, affirming that he was then justified by faith ; James refers indeed to an act of the same man, but occurring twenty years after, showing that the faith by which he had been justified was genuine. Abraham was, in fact, according to Paul, justified when he believed, and, had he died then, he would have been saved; but according to James, the faith which justified him was not a dead faith, but was living and operative, as was shown by his readiness to offer his son on the altar.

(c) Did each of these two writers in reality hold the same doctrine on the subject? This will be seen, if it can be shown that James held to the doctrine of justification by faith, as really as Paul did; and that Paul held that good works were necessary to show the genuineness of faith, as really as James did.

(1.) They both agreed in holding the doctrine of justification by faith. Of Paul's belief there can be no doubt. That *James* held the doctrine is apparent from the fact that he quotes the very passage in Genesis, (xv. 6), and the one on which Paul relies, (Rom. iv. 1–3), as expressing his own views— 'Abraham believed God, and it was imputed unto him for righteousness.' The truth of this, James does not deny, but affirms that the Scripture which made this declaration was fulfilled or confirmed by the act to which he refers.

(2.) They both agreed in holding that good works are necessary to show the genuineness of faith. Of *James'* views on that point there can be no doubt. That *Paul* held the same opinion is clear (a) from his own life, no man ever having been more solicitous to keep the whole law of God than he was. (b) From his constant exhortations and declarations, such as these: ' Created in Christ Jesus unto good works,' (Eph. ii. 10); ' Charge them that are rich, that they be rich in good works,' 1 Tim. vi. 17, 18 ; ' In all things showing thyself a pattern of good works,' (Titus ii. 7); ' Who gave himself for us, that he might purify unto himself a peculiar people, zealous of good works,' (Titus ii. 14); ' These things I will that thou affirm constantly, that they which have believed in God might be careful to maintain good works,' Titus iii. 8. (c) It appears from the fact that Paul believed that the rewards of heaven are to be apportioned according to our good works, or according to our character and our attainments in the divine life. The *title* indeed to eternal life is, ac-

cording to him, in consequence of faith; the measure of the reward is to be our holiness, or what we do. Thus he says, (2 Cor. v. 10), ' For we must all appear before the judgment-seat of Christ, that every one may receive the things done in his body.' Thus also he says, (2 Cor. ix. 6), ' He which soweth sparingly, shall reap also sparingly; and he which soweth bountifully, shall reap also bountifully.' And thus also he says, (Rom. ii. 6), that God ' will render to every man according to his deeds.' See also the influence which faith had on Paul personally, as described in the third chapter of his epistle to the Philippians. If these things are so, then these two writers have not contradicted each other, but, viewing the subject from different points, they have together stated important truths which might have been made by any one writer without contradiction ; first, that it is only by faith that a sinner can be justified—and second, that the faith which justifies is that only which leads to a holy life, and that no other is of value in saving the soul. Thus, on the one hand, men would be guarded from depending on their own righteousness for eternal life ; and, on the other, from all the evils of Antinomianism. The great object of religion would be secured—the sinner would be justified, and would become personally holy.

CHAPTER III.

ANALYSIS OF THE CHAPTER.

THE *evil* which the apostle seems to have referred to in this chapter, was a desire, which appears to have prevailed among those to whom he wrote, *to be public teachers* (διδάσκαλοι, ver. 1), and to be such even where there was no proper qualification. It is not easy to see any *connection* between what is said in this chapter, and what is found in other parts of the epistle ; and indeed the plan of the epistle seems to have been to notice such things as the apostle supposed claimed their attention, without particular regard to a logical connection. Some of the errors and improprieties which existed among them had been noticed in the previous chapters, and others are referred to in chs. iv. v. Those which are noticed in this

CHAPTER III.

M Y brethren, be not many *a* masters, knowing that we

shall receive the greater condemnation.[1]

a Mat.23.8,14. 1 Pe.5.3.   1 Or, *judgment.*

chapter grew out of the desire of being public teachers of religion. It seems probable that he had this subject in his eye in the whole of this chapter, and this will give a clue to the course of thought which he pursues. Let it be supposed that there was a *prevailing desire among those to whom he wrote to become public teachers, without much regard for the proper qualifications for that office,* and the interpretation of the chapter will become easy. Its design and drift then may be thus expressed :
I. The general subject of the chapter, a caution against the desire prevailing among many to be ranked among public teachers, ver. 1, first clause.
II. Considerations to check and modify that desire, ver. 1 (last clause), ver. 18. These considerations are the following :
(1.) The fact that public teachers must give a more solemn account than other men, and that they expose themselves to the danger of a deeper condemnation, ver. 1, last clause.
(2.) The evils which grow out of an improper use of the *tongue; evils to* which those are particularly liable whose business is *speaking,* vs. 2–12. This leads the apostle into a general statement of the importance of the tongue as a member of the human body ; of the fact that we are peculiarly liable to offend in that (ver. 2); of the fact that if that is regulated aright, the whole man is—as a horse is managed by the bit, and a ship is steered by the rudder (vs. 2–4); of the fact that the tongue, though a little member, is capable of accomplishing great things, and is peculiarly liable, when not under proper regulations, to do mischief, (vs. 5, 6); of the fact that, while every thing else has been tamed, it has been found impossible to bring the tongue under proper restraints, and that it performs the most discordant and opposite functions, (vs. 7–9); and of the impropriety and absurdity of this, as if the same fountain should bring forth sweet water and bitter, vs. 10–12. By these considera-

tions, the apostle seems to have designed to repress the prevailing desire of leaving other employments, and of becoming public instructors without suitable qualifications.
(3.) The apostle adverts to the importance of *wisdom,* with reference to the same end ; that is, of suitable qualifications to give public instruction, vs. 13–18. He shows (ver. 13) that if there was a truly wise man among them, he should show this by his works, with ' meekness,' and not by obtruding himself upon the attention of others ; that if there was a want of it evinced in a spirit of rivalry and contention, there would be confusion and every evil work, (vs. 14–16) ; and that where there was true wisdom, it was unambitious and unostentatious ; it was modest, retiring, and pure. It would lead to a peaceful life of virtue, and its existence would be seen in the ' fruits of righteousness sown in peace,' vs. 17, 18. It might be inferred that they who had *this* spirit would not be ambitious of becoming public teachers ; they would not place themselves at the head of parties ; they would show the true spirit of religion in an unobtrusive and humble life. We are not to suppose, in the interpretation of this chapter, that the apostle argued against a desire to enter the ministry, in itself considered, and where there are proper qualifications ; but he endeavoured to suppress a spirit which has not been uncommon in the world, to become public teachers as a means of more influence and power, and without any suitable regard to the proper endowments for such an office.
1. *My brethren, be not many masters.* ' Be not many of you teachers.' The evil referred to is that where *many* desired to be teachers, though but *few* could be qualified for the office, and though, in fact, comparatively few were required. A small number, well qualified, would better discharge the duties of the office, and do more good, than many would ; and there would be great evil in having many crowding themselves un-

qualified into the office. The word here rendered *masters* (διδάσκαλοι) should have been rendered *teachers*. It is so rendered in John iii. 2; Acts xiii. 1; Rom. ii. 20; 1 Cor. xii. 28, 29; Eph. iv. 11; 1 Tim. ii. 11; iv. 3; Heb. v. 12; though it is elsewhere frequently rendered *master*. It has, however, in it primarily the notion of *teaching* (διδά-σκω), even when rendered *master;* and the word *master* is often used in the New Testament, as it is with us, to denote an *instructor*—as the ' school-master.' Comp. Matt. x. 24, 25; xxii. 16; Mark x. 17; xii. 19, *et al.* The word is not properly used in the sense of *master*, as distinguished from a *servant*, but as distinguished from a *disciple* or *learner.* Such a position, indeed, implies *authority*, but it is authority based not on power, but on superior qualifications. The connection implies that the word is used in that sense in this place; and the evil reprehended is that of seeking the office of public instructor, especially the sacred office. It would seem that this was a prevailing fault among those to whom the apostle wrote. This desire was common among the Jewish people, who coveted the name and the office of *Rabbi*, equivalent to that here used, (comp. Matt. xxiii. 7), and who were ambitious to be doctors and teachers. See Rom. ii. 19; 1 Tim. i. 7. This fondness for the office of teachers they naturally carried with them into the Christian church when they were converted, and it is this which the apostle here rebukes.* The same spirit the passage before us would rebuke now, and for the same reasons; for although a man should be willing to become a public instructor in religion when called to it by the Spirit and Providence of God, and should esteem it a privilege when so called, yet there would be

* A proof of some importance that this prevailed in the early Christian church, among those who had been Jews, is furnished by a passage in the Apocryphal work called ' The Ascension of Isaiah the Prophet;' a work which Dr. Lawrence, the editor, supposes was written not far from the apostolic age. ' In those days (the days of the Messiah) shall many be attached to office, destitute of wisdom; multitudes of iniquitous elders and pastors, injurious to their flocks, and addicted to rapine, nor shall the holy pastors themselves diligently discharge their duty.' Ch. iii. 23, 24

scarcely any thing more injurious to the cause of true religion, or that would tend more to produce disorder and confusion, than a prevailing desire of the prominence and importance which a man has in virtue of being a public instructor. If there is any thing which ought to be managed with extreme prudence and caution, it is that of introducing men into the Christian ministry. Comp. 1 Tim. v. 22; Acts i. 15-26; xiii. 2, 3. ¶ *Knowing that we shall receive the greater condemnation,* (μεῖζον κρίμα). Or rather, *a severer judgment;* that is, we shall have a severer trial, and give a stricter account. The word here used does not necessarily mean *condemnation*, but *judgment, trial, account;* and the consideration which the apostle suggests is not that those who were public teachers would be *condemned*, but that there would be a much more solemn account to be rendered by them than by other men, and that they ought duly to reflect on this in seeking the office of the ministry. He would carry them in anticipation before the judgment-seat, and have them determine the question of entering the ministry there. No better ' standpoint' can be taken in making up the mind in regard to this work; and if that had been the position assumed in order to estimate the work, and to make up the mind in regard to the choice of this profession, many a one who has sought the office would have been deterred from it; and it may be added, also, that many a pious and educated youth *would* have sought the office, who has devoted his life to other pursuits. A young man, when about to make choice of a calling in life, should place himself by anticipation at the judgment-bar of Christ, and ask himself how human pursuits and plans will appear there. If *that* were the point of view taken, how many would have been deterred from the ministry who have sought it with a view to honour or emolument! How many, too, who have devoted themselves to the profession of the law, to the army or navy, or to the pursuits of elegant literature, would have felt that it was their duty to serve God in the ministry of reconciliation? How many at the close of life, in the

2 For *a* in many things we offend all. If any man offend not in word, *b* the same *is* a perfect man, *and* able also to bridle the whole body.

3 Behold, we put bits *c* in the

horses' mouths, that they may obey us; and we turn about their whole body.

4 Behold also the ships, which though *they be* so great, and *are*

ministry and out of it, feel, when too late to make a change, that they have wholly mistaken the purpose for which they should have lived!

2. *For in many things we offend all.* We all offend. The word here rendered *offend,* means to stumble, to fall; then to err, to fail in duty; and the meaning here is, that all were liable to commit error, and that this consideration should induce men to be cautious in seeking an office where an error would be likely to do so much injury. The particular thing, doubtless, which the apostle had in his eye, was the peculiar liability to commit error, or to do wrong with the tongue. Of course, this liability is very great in an office where the *very business* is public speaking. If anywhere the improper use of the tongue will do mischief, it is in the office of a religious teacher; and to show the danger of this, and the importance of caution in seeking that office, the apostle proceeds to show what mischief the *tongue* is capable of effecting. ¶ *If any man offend not in word.* In his speech; in the use of his tongue. ¶ *The same* is *a perfect man.* Perfect in the sense in which the apostle immediately explains himself; that he is able to keep every other member of his body in subjection. His object is not to represent the man as absolutely spotless in every sense, and as wholly free from sin, for he had himself just said that ' all offend in many things;' but the design is to show that if a man can cóntrol his tongue, he has complete dominion over himself, as much as a man has over a horse by the bit, or as a steersman has over a ship if he has hold of the rudder. He is perfect in that sense, that he has complete control over himself, and will not be liable to error in any thing. The design is to show the important position which the tongue occupies, as governing the whole man. On the meaning of the word *perfect,* see Notes on Job i. 1. ¶ And *able*

also to bridle the whole body. To control his whole body, that is, every other part of himself, as a man does a horse by the bridle. The word rendered ' to bridle,' means to lead or guide with a bit; then to rein in, to check, to moderate, to restrain. A man always has complete government over himself if he has the entire control of his tongue. It is that by which he gives expression to his thoughts and passions; and if that is kept under proper restraint, all the rest of his members are as easily controlled as the horse is by having the control of the bit.

3. *Behold, we put bits in the horses' mouths,* &c. The meaning of this simple illustration is, that as we control a horse by the bit—though the bit is a small thing—so the body is controlled by the tongue. He who has a proper control over his tongue can govern his whole body, as he who holds a bridle governs and turns about the horse.

4. *Behold also the ships.* This illustration is equally striking and obvious. A ship is a large object. It seems to be unmanageable by its vastness, and it is also impelled by driving storms. Yet it is easily managed by a small rudder; and he that has control of that, has control of the ship itself. So with the tongue. It is a small member as compared with the body; in its size not unlike the rudder as compared with the ship. Yet the proper control of the tongue in respect to its influence on the whole man, is not unlike the control of the rudder in its power over the ship. ¶ *Which though* they be *so great.* So great in themselves, and in comparison with the rudder. Even such bulky and unwieldy objects are controlled by a very small thing. ¶ *And* are *driven of fierce winds.* By winds that would seem to leave the ship beyond control. It is probable that by the ' fierce winds' here as impelling the ship, the apostle meant to illustrate the power of the

driven of fierce winds, yet are they turned about with a very small helm, whithersoever the governor listeth.

5 Even so the tongue is *a* a little

a Pr.12.18.

member, and boasteth *b*great things. Behold, how great ¹ a matter a little fire kindleth!

6 And the tongue *is* a fire, *c* a world of iniquity: so is the tongue

b Ps.12.3.   1 Or, *wood.*   *c* Pr.16.27.

passions in impelling man. Even a man under impetuous passion would be restrained, if the tongue is properly controlled, as the ship driven by the winds is by the helm. ¶ *Yet are they turned about with a very small helm.* The ancient rudder or helm was made in the shape of an oar. This was very small when compared with the size of the vessel— about as small as the tongue is as compared with the body. ¶ *Whithersoever the governor listeth.* As the helmsman pleases. It is entirely under his control. 5. *Even so the tongue is a little member.* Little compared with the body, as the bit or the rudder is, compared with the horse or the ship. ¶ *And boasteth great things.* The design of the apostle is to illustrate the *power* and *influence* of the tongue. This may be done in a great many respects: and the apostle does it by referring to its boasting; to the effects which it produces, resembling that of fire, (ver. 6); to its untameableness, (vs. 8, 9); and to its giving utterance to the most inconsistent and incongruous thoughts, vs. 9, 10. The particular idea here is, that the tongue seems to be conscious of its influence and power, and *boasts* largely of what it can do. The apostle means doubtless to convey the idea that it boasts not *unjustly* of its importance. It *has* all the influence in the world, for good or for evil, which it claims. ¶ *Behold, how great a matter a little fire kindleth!* Marg. *wood.* The Greek word (ὕλη), means a wood, forest, grove; and then fire-wood, fuel. This is the meaning here. The sense is, that a very little fire is sufficient to ignite a large quantity of combustible materials, and that the tongue produces effects similar to that. A spark will kindle a lofty pile; and a word spoken by the tongue may set a neighbourhood or a village 'in a flame.' 6. *And the tongue is a fire.* In this sense, that it produces a 'blaze,' or a great conflagration. It produces a dis-

turbance and an agitation that may be compared with the conflagration often produced by a spark. ¶ *A world of iniquity.* A little world of evil in itself. This is a very expressive phrase, and is similar to one which we often employ, as when we speak of a town as being *a world* in miniature. We mean by it that it is an epitome of the world; that all that there is in the world is represented there on a small scale. So when the tongue is spoken of as being 'a world of iniquity,' it is meant that all kinds of evil that are in the world are exhibited there in miniature; it seems to concentrate all sorts of iniquity that exist on the earth. And what evil is there which may not be originated or fomented by the tongue? What else is there that might, with so much propriety, be represented as a little world of iniquity? With all the good which it does, who can estimate the amount of evil which it causes? Who can measure the evils which arise from scandal, and slander, and profaneness, and perjury, and falsehood, and blasphemy, and obscenity, and the inculcation of error, by the tongue? Who can gauge the amount of broils, and contentions, and strifes, and wars, and suspicions, and enmities, and alienations among friends and neighbours, which it produces? Who can number the evils produced by the 'honeyed' words of the seducer; or by the tongue of the eloquent in the maintenance of error, and the defence of wrong? If all men were *dumb*, what a portion of the crimes of the world would soon cease! If all men would speak only that which *ought* to be spoken, what a change would come over the face of human affairs! ¶ *So is the tongue among our members, that it defileth the whole body.* It stains or pollutes the whole body. It occupies a position and relation so important in respect to every part of our moral frame, that there is no portion which is not affected by it. Of the truth of this, no

among our members, that it defileth [a] the whole body, and setteth on fire the [1] course of nature ; and it is set on fire of hell.

7 For every [2] kind of beasts, and of birds, and of serpents, and of things in the sea, is tamed, and hath been tamed of [3] mankind.

one can have any doubt. There is nothing else pertaining to us as moral and intellectual beings, which exerts such an influence over *ourselves* as the tongue. A man of pure conversation is understood and felt to be pure in every respect; but who has any confidence in the virtue of the blasphemer, or the man of obscene lips, or the calumniator and slanderer? We always regard such a man as corrupt to the core. ¶ *And setteth on fire the course of nature.* The margin is ' the *wheel* of nature.' The Greek word also (τροχός) means a *wheel*, or any thing made for revolving and running. Then it means the course run by a wheel; a circular course or circuit. The word rendered *nature* (γίνεσις), means *procreation, birth, nativity;* and therefore the phrase means, literally, *the wheel of birth*—that is, the wheel which is set in motion at birth, and which runs on through life. —*Rob. Lex.* sub voce γίνεσις. It may be a matter of doubt whether this refers to successive generations, or to the course of individual life. The more literal sense would be that which refers to an individual ; but perhaps the apostle meant to speak in a popular sense, and thought of the affairs of the world as they roll on from age to age, as all enkindled by the tongue, keeping the world in a constant blaze of excitement. Whether applied to an individual life, or to the world at large, every one can see the justice of the comparison. One naturally thinks, when this expression is used, of a chariot driven on with so much speed that its wheels by their rapid motion become self-ignited, and the chariot moves on amidst flames. ¶ *And it is set on fire of hell.* Hell, or Gehenna, is represented as a place where the fires continually burn. See Notes on Matt. v. 22. The idea here is, that that which causes the tongue to do so much evil derives its origin from hell. Nothing could better characterize much of that which the tongues does, than to say that it has its origin in

hell, and has the spirit which reigns there. The very spirit of that world of fire and wickedness—a spirit of falsehood, and slander, and blasphemy, and pollution—seems to inspire the tongue. The *image* which seems to have been before the mind of the apostle was that of a torch which enkindles and burns every thing as it goes along—a torch itself lighted at the fires of hell. One of the most striking descriptions of the woes and curses which there may be in hell, would be to pourtray the sorrows caused on the earth by the tongue. 7. *For every kind of beasts.* The apostle proceeds to state another thing showing the power of the tongue, the fact that it is ungovernable, and that there is no power of man to keep it under control. Every thing else but this has been tamed. It is unnecessary to refine on the expressions used here, by attempting to prove that it is *literally* true that every species of beasts, and birds, and fishes has been tamed. The apostle is to be understood as speaking in a general and popular sense, showing the remarkable power of man over those things which are by nature savage and wild. The power of man in taming wild beasts is wonderful. Indeed, it is to be remembered that nearly all those beasts which we now speak of as ' domestic' animals, and which we are accustomed to see only when they are tame, were once fierce and savage races. This is the case with the horse, the ox, the ass, (see Notes on Job xi. 12; xxxix. 5), the swine, the dog, the cat, &c. The editor of the Pictorial Bible well remarks, ' There is perhaps no kind of creature, to which man has access, which might not be tamed by him with proper perseverance. The ancients seem to have made more exertions to this end, and with much better success, than ourselves. The examples given by Pliny, of creatures tamed by men, relate to elephants, lions, and tigers, among beasts ; to the eagle, among birds ; to asps, and other serpents ; and to croco-

8 But the tongue can no man tame ; *it is* an unruly evil, full of deadly *a* poison.

a Ps.140.3. Ro.3.13.

diles, and various fishes, among the inhabitants of the water. Nat. His. viii. 9, 16, 17; x. 5, 44. The lion was very commonly tamed by the ancient Egyptians, and trained to assist both in hunting and in war.' Notes *in loc.* The only animal which it has been supposed has defied the power of man to tame it, is the hyena, and even this, it is said, has been subdued, in modern times. There is a passage in Euripides which has a strong resemblance to this of James:—

Βραχὺ τοι σθένος ἀνέρος
᾿Αλλὰ ποικιλίαις πραπίδων
Δαμᾷ φῦλα πόντου,
Χθονίων τ᾽ ἀερίων τε παιδεύματα.

'Small is the power which nature has given to man; but, by various acts of his superior understanding, he has subdued the tribes of the sea, the earth, and the air.' Comp. on this subject, the passages quoted by Pricæus in the Critici Sacri, *in loc.* ¶ *And of birds.* It is a common thing to tame birds, and even the most wild are susceptible of being tamed. A portion of the feathered race, as the hen, the goose, the duck, is thoroughly domesticated. The pigeon, the martin, the hawk, the eagle, may be; and perhaps there are none of that race which might not be made subject to the will of man. ¶ *And of serpents.* The ancients showed great skill in this art, in reference to asps and other venomous serpents, and it is common now in India. In many instances, indeed, it is known that the fangs of the serpents are extracted; but even when this is not done, they who practise the art learn to handle them with impunity. ¶ *And of things in the sea.* As the crocodile, mentioned by Pliny. It may be affirmed with confidence that there is no animal which might not, by proper skill and perseverance, be rendered tame, or made obedient to the will of man. It is not necessary, however, to understand the apostle as affirming that literally every animal has been tamed, or ever can be. He evidently speaks in a popular sense

9 Therewith bless we God, even the Father ; and therewith curse we men, which are made after the similitude of God.

of the great power which man undeniably has over all kinds of wild animals —over the creation beneath him.

8. *But the tongue can no man tame.* This does not mean that it is *never* brought under control, but that it is impossible effectually and certainly to subdue it. It would be possible to subdue and domesticate any kind of beasts, but this could not be done with the tongue. ¶ It is *an unruly evil.* An evil without restraint, to which no certain and effectual check can be applied. Of the truth of this no one can have any doubt, who looks at the condition of the world. ¶ *Full of deadly poison.* That is, it acts on the happiness of man, and on the peace of society, as poison does on the human frame. The allusion here seems to be to the bite of a venomous reptile. Comp. Ps. cxl. 3, 'They have sharpened their tongues like serpent; adders' poison is under their lips.' Rom. iii. 13, 'With their tongues they have used deceit; the poison of asps is under their lips.' Nothing would better describe the mischief that may be done by the tongue. There is no sting of a serpent that does so much evil in the world; there is no poison more deadly to the frame than the poison of the tongue is to the happiness of man. Who, for example, can stand before the power of the slanderer? What mischief can be done in society that can be compared with that which he may do?

'Tis slander;
Whose edge is sharper than the sword; whose tongue
Outvenoms all the worms of Nile ; whose breath
Rides on the posting winds, and doth belie
All corners of the world : kings, queens, and states,
Maids, matrons, nay, the secrets of the grave
This viperous slander enters.

Shaks. in Cymbeline.

9. *Therewith bless we God.* We men do this; that is, all this is done by the tongue. The apostle does not mean that the *same* man does this, but that all this is done by the same organ—the tongue. ¶ *Even the Father.* Who sustains to us the relation of a father.

10 Out of the same mouth proceedeth blessing and cursing. My brethren, these things ought not so to be.

11 Doth a fountain send forth at the same ¹ place sweet *water* and bitter?

1 Or, *hole.*

12 Can the fig-tree, *ª* my brethren, bear olive-berries? either a vine, figs? so *can* no fountain both yield salt water and fresh.

13 Who *ᵇ is* a wise man and endued with knowledge among you? let him show out of a good conver-

a Mat.7.16.   b Ps.107.43.

The point in the remark of the apostle is, the absurdity of employing the tongue in such contradictory uses as to bless one who has to us the relation of a *father*, and to *curse* any being, especially those who are made in his image. The word *bless* here is used in the sense of *praise, thank, worship.* ¶ *And therewith curse we men.* That is, it is done by the same organ by which God is praised and honoured. ¶ *Which are made after the similitude of God.* After his image, Gen. i. 26, 27. As we bless God, we ought with the same organ to bless those who are like him. There is an absurdity in cursing men who are thus made, like what there would be in both blessing and cursing the Creator himself.

10. *Out of the same mouth proceedeth blessing and cursing.* The meaning here may be, either that out of the mouth of man two such opposite things proceed, not referring to the same individual, but to different persons; or, out of the mouth of the same individual. Both of these are true; and both are equally incongruous and wrong. No organ should be devoted to uses so unlike, and the mouth should be employed in giving utterance only to that which is just, benevolent, and good. It is true, however, that the mouth *is* devoted to these opposite employments; and that while one part of the race employ it for purposes of praise, the other employ it in uttering maledictions. It is also true of many individuals that at pne time they praise their Maker, and then, with the same organ, calumniate, and slander, and revile their fellow-men. After an act of solemn devotion in the house of God, the professed worshipper goes forth with the feelings of malice in his heart, and the language of slander, detraction, or even blasphemy on his lips. ¶ *My brethren, these things ought*

not so to be. They are as incongruous as it would be for the same fountain to send forth both salt water and fresh; or for the same tree to bear different kinds of fruit.

11. *Doth a fountain send forth at the same place.* Marg. *hole.* The Greek word means *opening, fissure,* such as there is in the earth, or in rocks from which a fountain gushes. ¶ *Sweet* water *and bitter.* Fresh water and salt, ver. 12. Such things do not occur in the works of nature, and they should not be found in man.

12. *Can the fig-tree, my brethren, bear olive-berries?* Such a thing is *impossible* in nature, and equally *absurd* in morals. A fig-tree bears only figs; and so the tongue ought to give utterance only to one class of sentiments and emotions. These illustrations are very striking, and show the absurdity of that which the apostle reproves. At the same time, they accomplish the main purpose which he had in view, to repress the desire of becoming public teachers without suitable qualifications. They show the power of the tongue; they show what a dangerous power it is for a man to wield who has not the proper qualifications; they show that no one should put himself in the position where he may wield this power without such a degree of tried prudence, wisdom, discretion, and piety, that there shall be a moral certainty that he will use it aright.

13. *Who is a wise man, and endued with knowledge among you?* This is spoken with reference to the work of public teaching; and the meaning of the apostle is, that if there were such persons among them, *they* should be selected for that office. The characteristics here stated as necessary qualifications, are *wisdom* and *knowledge.* Those, it would seem, on which reliance

sation *a* his works with meekness of wisdom.

14 But if ye have bitter envying and strife in your hearts, glory not; and lie not against the truth.

15 This *b* wisdom descendeth not from above, but *is* earthly, [1] sensual, devilish.

a Ph.1.27.

b 1 Co.3.3.　　　　　1 Or, *natural.*

had been placed, were chiefly those which were connected with a ready elocution, or the mere faculty of speaking. The apostle had stated the dangers which would follow if reliance were placed on that alone, and he now says that something more is necessary, that the main qualifications for the office are wisdom and knowledge. No mere power of speaking, however eloquent it might be, was a sufficient qualification. The primary things to be sought in reference to that office were wisdom and knowledge, and they who were endowed with these things should be selected for public instructors. ¶ *Let him show out of a good conversation.* From a correct and consistent life and deportment. On the meaning of the word *conversation*, see Notes on Phil. i. 27. The meaning here is, that there should be an upright *life*, and that this should be the basis in forming the judgment in appointing persons to fill stations of importance, and especially in the office of teaching in the church. ¶ *His works.* His acts of uprightness and piety. He should be a man of a holy life. ¶ *With meekness of wisdom.* With a wise and prudent gentleness of life ; not in a noisy, arrogant, and boastful manner. True wisdom is always meek, mild, gentle ; and that is the wisdom which is needful, if men would become public teachers. It is remarkable that the truly wise man is always characterized by a calm spirit, a mild and placid demeanour, and by a gentle, though firm, enunciation of his sentiments. A noisy, boisterous, and stormy declaimer we never select as a safe counsellor. He may accomplish much in his way by his bold eloquence of manner, but we do not put him in places where we need far-reaching thought, or where we expect the exercise of profound philosophical views. In an eminent degree, the ministry of the gospel should be characterized by a calm, gentle, and thoughtful wisdom—a wisdom which shines in all the actions of the life.

14. *But if ye have bitter envying and strife in your hearts.* If that is your characteristic. There is reference here to a fierce and unholy zeal against each other ; a spirit of ambition and contention. ¶ *Glory not.* Do not boast, in such a case, of your qualifications to be public teachers. Nothing would render you more unfit for such an office than such a spirit. ¶ *And lie not against the truth.* You would lie against what is true by setting up a claim to the requisite qualifications for such an office, if this is your spirit. Men should seek no office or station which they could not properly seek if the whole truth about them were known. 15. *This wisdom descendeth not from above.* Comp. Notes on 1 Cor. iii. 3. The *wisdom* here referred to is that carnal or worldly wisdom which produces strife and contention ; that kind of knowledge which leads to self-conceit, and which prompts a man to defend his opinions with over-heated zeal. In the contentions which are in the world, in church and state, in neighbourhoods and families, at the bar, in political life, and in theological disputes, even where there is the manifestation of enraged and irascible feeling, there is often much of a certain kind of *wisdom.* There is learning, shrewdness, tact, logical skill, subtle and skilful argumentation—' making the worse appear the better reason ;' but all this is often connected with a spirit so narrow, bigoted, and contentious, as to show clearly that it has not its origin in heaven. The spirit which is originated there is always connected with gentleness, calmness, and a love of truth. ¶ *But is earthly.* Has its origin in this world, and partakes of its spirit. It is such as men exhibit who are governed only by worldly maxims and principles. ¶ *Sensual.* Marg. *natural.* The meaning is, that it has its origin in our sensual rather than in our intellectual and moral nature. It is that which takes counsel of our natural appetites and pro-

16 For where envying and strife
is, there *is* ¹ confusion and every
evil work.

17 But the wisdom *ᵃ* that is from

1 *tumult*, or *unquietness*.   *a* 1 Co.2.6,7.

above is first pure, *ᵇ* then peaceable, *ᶜ* gentle, *ᵈ and* easy to be
entreated, full of mercy and good
fruits, without ² partiality, and
without hypocrisy.

b Ph.4.8. *c* He.12.14. *d* Ga.5.22.   2 Or, *wrangling*.

pensities, and not of high and spiritual
influences. ¶ *Devilish.* Demoniacal
(δαιμονιώδης). Such as the *demons* exhibit. See Notes on ch. ii. 19. There
may be indeed *talent* in it, but there is
the intermingling of malignant passions,
and it leads to contentions, strifes, divisions, and 'every evil work.'
16. *For where envying and strife* is,
there is *confusion.* Marg., *tumult* or
unquietness. Every thing is unsettled
and agitated. There is no mutual confidence ; there is no union of plan and
effort ; there is no co-operation in promoting a common object ; there is no
stability in any plan ; for a purpose,
though for good, formed by one portion,
is defeated by another. ¶ *And every
evil work.* Of the truth of this no one
can have any doubt who has observed
the effects in a family or neighbourhood
where a spirit of strife prevails. All
love and harmony of course are banished;
all happiness disappears ; all prosperity
is at an end. In place of the peaceful
virtues which ought to prevail, there
springs up every evil passion that tends
to mar the peace of a community. Where
this spirit prevails in a church, it is of
course impossible to expect any progress
in divine things ; and in such a church
any effort to do good is vain.

"The Spirit, like a peaceful dove,
Flies from the realms of noise and strife."

17. *But the wisdom that is from above.*
Comp. Notes on 1 Cor. ii. 6, 7. The
wisdom which has a heavenly origin, or
which is from God. The man who is
characterised by that wisdom will be
pure, peaceable, &c. This does not
refer to the *doctrines* of religion, but to
its *spirit.* ¶ *Is first pure.* That is, the
first effect of it on the mind is to make
it *pure.* The influence on the man is
to make him upright, sincere, candid,
holy. The word here used (ἁγνός) is
that which would be applied to one who
is innocent, or free from crime or blame.

Comp. Phil. iv. 8; 1 Tim. v. 22; 1 John
iii. 3, where the word is rendered, as
here, *pure;* 2 Cor. vii. 11, where it is
rendered *clear,* [in this matter]; 2 Cor.
xi. 2 ; Titus ii. 5 ; 1 Pet. iii. 2, where
it is rendered *chaste.* The meaning
here is, that the first and immediate
effect of religion is not on the intellect,
to make it more enlightened ; or on the
imagination, to make it more discursive
and brilliant ; or on the memory and
judgment, to make them clearer and
stronger ; but it is to *purify* the heart,
to make the man upright, inoffensive,
and good. This passage should not be
applied, as it often is, to the *doctrines*
of religion, as if it were the first duty
of a church to keep itself free from
errors in doctrine, and that this ought
to be sought even in preference to the
maintenance of peace—as if it meant
that in doctrine a church should be
'*first* pure, *then* peaceable ;' but it
should be applied *to the individual
consciences of men,* as showing the
effect of religion on the heart and life.
The *first* thing which it produces is to
make the man himself pure and good ;
then follows the train of blessings which
the apostle enumerates as flowing from
that. It is true that a church should
be *pure* in doctrinal belief, but that is
not the truth taught here. It is *not*
true that the scripture teaches, here or
elsewhere, that purity of doctrine is to
be preferred to a peaceful spirit ; or that
it always leads to a peaceful spirit; or
that it is proper for professed Christians
and Christian ministers to sacrifice, as
is often done, a peaceful spirit, in an
attempt to preserve purity of doctrine.
Most of the persecutions in the church
have grown out of this maxim. This
led to the establishment of the Inquisi-
tion; this kindled the fires of Smith-
field; this inspirited Laud and his friends;
this has been the origin of no small part
of the schisms in the church. A pure
spirit is the best promoter of peace, and

will do more than any thing else to secure the prevalence of truth.

[It is but too true that much unseemly strife has had the *aegis* of this text thrown over it. The 'wrath of man' accounts itself zeal for God, and strange fire usurps the place of the true fire of the sanctuary. Yet the author's statement here seems somewhat overcharged; possibly his own personal history may have contributed a little to this result. Although the Greek word *ἀγνὴ* here qualifying the *σοφία*, or wisdom, refers to purity of *heart*, still it remains true that a pure heart will never relinquish its hold on God's truth for the sake of a peace that at such a price would be too dearly purchased. A pure heart cannot but be faithful to the truth; it could not otherwise be pure, provided *conscientiousness* and *love of truth* form any part of moral purity. Surely, then, an individual solicited to yield up what he believed to be truth, or what were cherished convictions, might properly assign this text as a reason why he could not, and ought not; and if an individual might, why not any number associated into a church? It is true the Scriptures do *not* teach that ' *doctrinal* purity' is to be preferred to a ' peaceful spirit.' However pure a man's doctrine may be, if he has not the peaceful spirit he is none of Christ's. But the common view of this passage is not chargeable with any such absurdity. It supposes only that there may be circumstances in which the spirit of peace, *though possessed*, cannot be exercised, except in meek submission to wrong for conscience sake; never can it turn traitor to truth, or make any compromise with error. The ' first' of the apostle does not indicate even preference of the pure *spirit* to the peaceful spirit, but only the *order* in which they are to be exercised. There must be no attempts to reach peace by overleaping purity. The maxim that a pure heart ought not to sacrifice truth on any consideration whatever, never gave rise to persecution: it has made many martyrs, but never one persecutor; it has pined in the dungeon, but never immured any there; it has burned amid the flames, but never lighted the faggot; it has ascended scaffolds, but never erected them; it has preserved and bequeathed civil and religious liberty, but never assaulted them; it is a divine principle—the principle by which Christianity became strong, and will ultimately command the homage of the world. There is another principle, with which this has no brotherhood, that denies the right of private judgment, and enforces uniformity by the sword: its progeny are inquisitors, and Lauds and Sharpes; and let it have the credit of its own offspring.]

¶ *Then peaceable.* The effect of true religion—the wisdom which is from above—will be to dispose a man to live in peace with all others. See Notes on

Rom. xiv. 19. Heb. xii. 14. ¶ *Gentle.* Mild, inoffensive, clement. The word here used (ἐπιικὴς) is rendered *moderation* in Phil. iv. 5 ; *patient* in 1 Tim. iii. 3 ; and *gentle* in Titus iii. 2 ; James iii. 17, and 1 Pet. ii. 18. It does not occur elsewhere in the New Testament. Every one has a clear idea of the virtue of *gentleness*—gentleness of spirit, of deportment, and of manners; and every one can see that that is the appropriate spirit of religion. Comp. Notes on 2 Cor. x. 1. It is from this word that we have derived the word *gentleman;* and the effect of true religion is to make every one, in the proper and best sense of the term, a *gentleman.* How can a man have evidence that he is a true Christian, who is not such? The highest title which can be given to a man is, that he is a *Christian gentleman.* ¶ And *easy to be entreated.* The word here used does not elsewhere occur in the New Testament. It means *easily persuaded, compliant.* Of course, this refers only to cases where it is right and proper to be easily persuaded and complying. It cannot refer to things which are in themselves wrong. The sense is, that he who is under the influence of the wisdom which is from above, is not a stiff, stern, obstinate, unyielding man. He does not take a position, and then hold it whether right or wrong; he is not a man on whom no arguments or persuasions can have any influence. He is not one who cannot be affected by any appeals which may be made to him on the grounds of patriotism, justice, or benevolence; but is one who is ready to yield when truth requires him to do it, and who is willing to sacrifice his own convenience for the good of others. See this illustrated in the case of the apostle Paul, in 1 Cor. ix. 20–22. Comp. Notes on that passage. ¶ *Full of mercy.* Merciful ; disposed to show compassion to others. This is one of the results of the wisdom that is from above, for it makes us like God, the ' Father of mercies.' See Notes on Matt. v. 7. ¶ And *good fruits.* The fruits of good living ; just, benevolent, and kind actions. Notes, Phil. i. 11; 2 Cor. ix. 10. Comp. James ii. 14–26. ¶ *Without partiality.* Marg. ' or *wrangling.*' The word here used (ἀδιάκριτος)

18 And the fruit ^a of righteous- ness is sown in peace of them that
  _{a He.12.11.} make peace.

---

occurs nowhere else in the New Testa- ment. It means, properly, *not to be distinguished.* Here it may mean either of the following things : (*a*) not open to distinction or doubt; that is, unambiguous, so that there shall be no doubt about its origin or nature; (*b*) making no distinction, that is, in the treatment of others, or *impartial* to- wards them; or (*c*) without strife, from διακρίνω, to contend. The second mean- ing here suggested seems best to accord with the sense of the passage ; and ac- cording to this the idea is, that the wis- dom which is from above, or true reli- gion, makes us impartial in our treat- ment of others : that is, we are not influenced by a regard to dress, rank, or station, but we are disposed to do equal justice to all, according to their moral worth, and to show kindness to all, according to their wants. See ch. ii. 1–4. ¶ *And without hypocrisy.* What it professes to be ; sincere. There is no disguise or mask assumed. What the man pretends to be, he is. This is everywhere the nature of true religion. It has nothing of its own of which to be ashamed, and which needs to be con- cealed ; its office is not to hide or conceal any thing that is wrong. It neither *is* a mask, nor does it *need* a mask. If such is the nature of the 'wisdom which is from above,' who is there that should be ashamed of it? Who is there that should not desire that its blessed in- fluence should spread around the world?

18. *And the fruit of righteousness.* That which the righteousness here re- ferred to produces, or that which is the effect of true religion. The meaning is, that righteousness or true religion produces certain results on the life, like the effects of seed sown in good ground. Righteousness or true religion as certainly produces such effects, as seed that is sown produces a harvest. ¶ *Is sown in peace.* Is scattered over the world in a peaceful manner. That is, it is not done amidst contentions, and brawls, and strifes. The farmer sows his seed in peace. The fields are not

sown amidst the tumults of a mob, or the excitements of a battle or a camp. Nothing is more calm, peaceful, quiet, and composed, than the farmer, as he walks with measured tread over his fields, scattering his seed. So it is in sowing the 'seed of the kingdom,' in preparing for the great harvest of righteousness in the world. It is done by men of peace; it is done in peaceful scenes, and with a peaceful spirit ; it is not in the tumult of war, or amidst the hoarse brawling of a mob. In a pure and holy life ; in the peaceful scenes of the sanctuary and the Sabbath; by noiseless and unobtrusive labourers, and the seed is scattered over the world, and the result is seen in an abundant harvest in producing peace and order. ¶ *Of them that make peace.* By those who desire to produce peace, or who are of a peace- ful temper and disposition. They are engaged everywhere in scattering these blessed seeds of peace, contentment, and order; and the result shall be a glorious harvest for themselves and for mankind —a harvest rich and abundant on earth and in heaven. The whole effect, there- fore, of religion, is to produce peace. It is all peace—peace in its origin and in its results; in the heart of the individual, and in society; on earth, and in heaven. The idea with which the apostle com- menced this chapter seems to have been that such persons only should be ad- mitted to the office of public teachers. From that, the mind naturally turned to the effect of religion in general ; and he states that in the ministry and out of it ; in the heart of the individual and on society at large; here and hereafter, the effect of religion is to produce peace. Its nature is peaceful as it exists in the heart, and as it is developed in the world ; and wherever and however it is mani- fested, it is like seed sown, not amid the storms of war and the contentions of battle, but in the fields of quiet hus- bandry, producing in rich abundance a harvest of peace. In its origin, and in all its results, it is productive only of contentment, sincerity, goodness, and peace. Happy he who has this religion

CHAPTER IV.

FROM whence *come* wars and [1] fightings among you? *come*

they not hence, *even* of your [2] lusts that war *a* in your members?

1 Or, *brawlings*.   2 Or, *pleasures*.   *a* 1 Pe.2.11.

in his heart; happy he who with liberal hand scatters its blessings broadcast over the world!

CHAPTER IV.

ANALYSIS OF THE CHAPTER.

IN the previous chapter (vs. 13–18) the apostle had contrasted the wisdom which is from above with that which is from beneath. The former is peaceable, pure, and gentle, leading to universal kindness and order ; the latter earthly, sensual, and devilish. The points suggested in this chapter grow directly out of the remarks made there, and are designed to show the effect of the 'wisdom which descendeth not from above,' as evinced in the spirit of this world, and thus by contrast to show the value of true wisdom, or of the spirit of religion. Accordingly, the apostle illustrates the effects of the wisdom of this world, or the spirit of this world, by showing what it produces, or what they do who are under its influence. We are not to suppose that the persons to whom the apostle addressed this epistle were actually *guilty* of the things here referred to themselves, but such things had an existence in the world, and it gave more life and spirit to the discussion to represent them as existing 'among them.' In illustrating the subject, he refers to the following things as resulting from the spirit that is opposite to the wisdom which is from above, viz.: (1.) Wars and fightings, which are to be traced solely to the lusts of men, (vs. 1, 2); (2.) The neglect of prayer, showing the reason why they did not have the things which were necessary, (ver. 2); (3.) The fact that *when* they prayed they did not obtain what they needed, because they prayed with improper motives, in order to have the means of gratifying their sensual desires, (ver. 3); (4.) The desire of the friendship of the world as one of the fruits of being under the influence of the wisdom which is not from above, (ver. 4); (5.) *Envy*, as another of these fruits, ver. 5. In view of these things, and of the danger to which they were exposed of acting under their influence,

the apostle proceeds to give them some solemn cautions and admonitions. He tells them that God resists all who are proud, but gives grace to all who are humble, (ver. 6); he counsels them to submit to God, (ver. 7), to resist the devil, (ver. 7), to draw nigh to God, (ver. 8), to cleanse their hands and their hearts, (ver. 8), to be afflicted and mourn over their sins, and to become serious and devout, (ver. 9), and to humble themselves before God that he might lift them up (ver. 10); he commands them not to speak evil one of another, since by so doing they in fact set themselves up to be judges, and in the circumstances became judges of the law as well as of their brethren, vs. 11, 12. He then rebukes the confident spirit which lays its plans for the future with no just view of the frailty and uncertainty of human life, and shows them that all their plans for the future should be formed with a distinct recognition of their dependence on God for success, and even for the continuance of life, vs. 13–16. The chapter closes with an affirmation that to him that knows how to do good and does it not, to him it is sin, (ver. 17), implying that all he had said in the chapter might indeed be obvious, and that they would be ready to admit that these things were true, and that if they knew this, and did not do right, they must be regarded as guilty.

1. *From whence* come *wars and fightings among you?*   Marg. *brawlings.* The reference is to strifes and contentions of all kinds ; and the question, then, as it is now, was an important one, what was their source or origin? The answer is given in the succeeding part of the verse. Some have supposed that the apostle refers here to the contests and seditions existing among the Jews, which afterwards broke out in rebellion against the Roman authority, and which led to the overthrow of the Jewish nation. But the more probable reference is to domestic broils, and to the strifes of sects and parties ; to the disputes which were carried on among the Jewish people, and which perhaps

2 Ye lust, and have not: ye ¹ kill, and desire to have, and cannot

obtain: ye fight and war, yet ye have not, because ye ask not.

¹ Or, *envy.*

led to scenes of violence, and to popular outbreaks among themselves. When the apostle says 'among *you*,' it is not necessary to suppose that he refers to those who were members of the Christian church as actually engaged in these strifes, though he was writing to such; but he speaks of them as a part of the Jewish people, and refers to the contentions which prevailed among them *as a people*—contentions in which those who were Christian converts were in great danger of participating, by being drawn into their controversies, and partaking of the spirit of strife which existed among their countrymen. It is known that such a spirit of contention prevailed among the Jews at that time in an eminent degree, and it was well to put those among them who professed to be Christians on their guard against such a spirit, by stating the causes of *all* wars and contentions. The solution which the apostle has given of the causes of the strifes prevailing then, will apply substantially to all the wars which have ever existed on the earth. ¶ Come they *not hence, even of your lusts?* Is not this the true source of all war and contention? The word rendered *lusts* is in the margin rendered *pleasures.* This is the usual meaning of the word (ἡδονὴ); but it is commonly applied to the pleasures of sense, and thence denotes *desire, appetite, lust.* It may be applied to any desire of sensual gratification, and then to the indulgence of any corrupt propensity of the mind. The lust or desire of rapine, of plunder, of ambition, of fame, of a more extended dominion, would be properly embraced in the meaning of the word. The word would equally comprehend the spirit which leads to a brawl in the street, and that which prompted to the conquests of Alexander, Cæsar, or Napoleon. All this is the same spirit evinced on a larger or smaller scale. ¶ *That war in your members.* The word *member* (μέλος) denotes, properly, a limb or member of the body; but it is used in the New Testament to denote the members of the body collectively; that is,

the body itself as the seat of the desires and passions, Rom. vi. 13, 19; vii. 5, 23; Col. iii. 5. The word *war* here refers to the conflict between those passions which have their seat in the flesh, and the better principles of the mind and conscience, producing a state of agitation and conflict. See Notes on Rom. vii. 23. Comp. Gal. v. 17. Those corrupt passions which have their seat in the flesh, the apostle says are the causes of war. Most of the wars which have occurred in the world can be traced to what the apostle here calls *lusts.* The desire of booty, the love of conquest, the ambition for extended rule, the gratification of revenge, these and similar causes have led to all the wars that have desolated the earth. Justice, equity, the fear of God, the spirit of true religion, never originated any war, but the corrupt passions of men have made the earth one great battle-field. If true religion existed among all men, there would be no more war. War always supposes that wrong has been done on one side or the other, and that one party or the other, or both, is indisposed to do right. The spirit of justice, equity, and truth, which the religion of Christ would implant in the human heart, would put an end to war *for ever.*

2. *Ye lust, and have not.* That is, you wish to have something which you do not now possess, and to which you have no just claim, and this prompts to the effort to obtain it by force. You desire extension of territory, fame, booty, the means of luxurious indulgence, or of magnificence and grandeur, and this leads to contest and bloodshed. These are the causes of wars on the large scale among nations, and of the contentions and strifes of individuals. The general reason is, that others have that which we have not, and which we desire to have; and not content with endeavouring to obtain it, if we can, in a peaceful and honest manner, and not willing to content ourselves without its possession, we resolve to secure it by force. Socrates is reported by Plato to have said on the day of his death,

'nothing else but the body and its desires cause wars, seditions, and contests of every kind; for all wars arise through the possession of wealth.' Phædo of Plato, by Taylor, London, 1793, p. 158. The system of wars in general, therefore, has been a system of *great robberies*, no more honest or honourable than the purposes of the foot-pad, and more dignified only because it involves greater skill and talent. It has been said that 'to kill one man makes a murderer, to kill many makes a hero.' So it may be said, that to steal a horse, or to rob a house, makes a man a thief or burglar; to fire a dwelling subjects him to the punishment of arson; but to plunder kingdoms and provinces, and to cause cities, towns, and hamlets to be wrapped in flames, makes an illustrious conqueror, and gives a title to what is deemed a bright page in history. The one enrols the name among felons, and consigns the perpetrator to the dungeon or the gibbet; the other, accompanied with no more justice, and with the same spirit, sends the name down to future times as immortal. Yet in the two the all-discerning eye of God may see no difference except in the magnitude of the crime, and in the extent of the injury which has been inflicted. In his way, and according to the measure of his ability, the felon who ends his life in a dungeon, or on the gibbet, is as worthy of grateful and honoured remembrance as the conqueror triumphing in the spoils of desolated empires. ¶ *Ye kill.* Marg. or *envy.*' The marginal reading '*envy*' has been introduced from some doubt as to the correct reading of the text, whether it should be φονεύτε, ye kill, or φθονεῖτε, ye envy. The latter reading has been adopted by Erasmus, Schmidius, Luther, Beza, and some others, though merely from conjecture. There is no authority from the manuscripts for the change. The correct reading undoubtedly is, *ye kill.* This expression is probably to be taken in the sense of *having a murderous disposition,* or *fostering a brutal and murderous spirit.* t is not exactly that they killed or committed murder previous to 'desiring to have,' but that they had such a covetous desire of the possessions of others as to produce a murderous and

bloody temper. The spirit of *murder* was at the bottom of the whole; or there was such a desire of the possessions of others as to lead to the commission of this crime. Of what aggressive wars which have ever existed is not this true? ¶ *Desire to have.* That is, what is in the possession of others. ¶ *And cannot obtain.* By any fair and honest means; by purchase or negociation: and this leads to bloody conquest. All wars might have been avoided if men had been content with what they had, or could rightfully obtain, and had not desired to have what was in the possession of others, which they could not obtain by honest and honourable means. Every war might have been avoided by fair and honourable negociation. ¶ *Ye fight and war, yet ye have not, because ye ask not.* Notwithstanding you engage in contentions and strifes, you do not obtain what you seek after. If you sought that from God which you truly need. you would obtain it, for he would bestow upon you all that is really necessary. But you seek it by contention and strife, and you have no security of obtaining it. He who seeks to gain anything by war seeks it in an unjust manner, and cannot depend on the Divine help and blessing. The true way of obtaining anything which we really need is to seek it from God by prayer, and then to make use of just and fair means of obtaining it, by industry and honesty, and by a due regard for the rights of others. Thus sought, we shall obtain it if it would be for our good; if it is withheld, it will be because it is best for us that it should not be ours. In all the wars which have been waged on the earth, whether for the settlement of disputed questions, for the adjustment of boundaries, for the vindication of violated rights, or for the permanent extension of empire, how rare has it been that the object which prompted to the war has been secured! The course of events has shown that, indisposed as men are to do justice, there is much more probability of obtaining the object by patient negotiation than there is by going to war.

3. *Ye ask, and receive not.* That is, some of you ask, or you ask on some occasions. Though seeking in general

3 Ye ask, and receive not, because ye ask amiss, that ye may consume it upon your [1] lusts.

4 Ye adulterers and adulteresses,

Or, *pleasures.*

what you desire by strife, and without regard to the rights of others, yet you sometimes pray. It is not uncommon for men who go to war to pray, or to procure the services of a chaplain to pray for them. It sometimes happens that the covetous and the quarrelsome; that those who live to wrong others, and who are fond of litigation, pray. Such men may be professors of religion. They keep up a form of worship in their families. They pray for success in their worldly engagements, though those engagements are all based on covetousness. Instead of seeking property that they may glorify God, and do good; that they may relieve the poor and distressed; that they may be the patrons of learning, philanthropy, and religion, they do it that they may live in splendour, and be able to pamper their lusts. It is not indeed *very* common that persons with such ends and aims of life pray, but they sometimes do it; for, alas! there are many professors of religion who have no higher aims than these, and not a few such professors feel that consistency demands that they should observe some form of prayer. If such persons do not receive what they ask for, if they are not prospered in their plans, they should not set it down as evidence that God does not hear prayer, but as evidence that their prayers are offered for improper objects, or with improper motives. ¶ *Because ye ask amiss.* Ye do it with a view to self-indulgence and carnal gratification. ¶ *That you may consume it upon your lusts.* Marg., *pleasures.* This is the same word which is used in ver. 1, and rendered *lusts.* The reference is to sensual gratifications, and the word would include all that comes under the name of sensual *pleasure,* or carnal appetite. It was not that they might have a decent and comfortable living, which would not be improper to desire, but that they might have the means of luxurious dress and living; perhaps the means of gross sensual gratifications. Prayers offered that we may have the

know ye not that the friendship [a] of the world is enmity with God? whosoever therefore will be a friend of the world, is the enemy of God.

a 1 John 2.15.

means of sensuality and voluptuousness, we have no reason to suppose God will answer, for he has not promised to hear such prayers; and it becomes every one who prays for worldly prosperity, and for success in business, to examine his motives with the closest scrutiny. Nowhere is deception more likely to creep in than into such prayers; nowhere are we more likely to be mistaken in regard to our real motives, than when we go before God and ask for success in our worldly employments.

4. *Ye adulterers and adulteresses.* These words are frequently used to denote those who are faithless towards God, and are frequently applied to those who forsake God for idols, Hos. iii. 1; Isa. lvii. 3, 7; Ezek. xvi., xxiii. It is not necessary to suppose that the apostle meant that those to whom he wrote were literally guilty of the sins here referred to; but he rather refers to those who were unfaithful to their covenant with God by neglecting their duty to him, and yielding themselves to the indulgence of their own lusts and passions. The idea is, 'You have in effect broken your marriage covenant with God by loving the world more than him; and, by the indulgence of your carnal inclinations, you have violated those obligations to self-mortification and self-denial to which you were bound by your religious engagements.' To convince them of the evil of this, the apostle shows them what was the true nature of that friendship of the world which they sought. It may be remarked here, that no terms could have been found which would have shown more decidedly the nature of the sin of forgetting the covenant vows of religion for the pleasures of the world, than those which the apostle uses here. It is a deeper crime to be unfaithful to God than to any created being; and it will yet be seen that even the violation of the marriage contract, great as is the sin, is a slight offence compared with unfaithfulness toward God. ¶ *Know ye not that the friend-*

ship of the world. Comp. 1 John ii. 15. The term *world* here is to be understood not of the physical world as God made it, for we could not well speak of the *'friendship'* of that, but of the *community*, or *people*, called *'the world,'* in contradistinction from the people of God. Comp. John xii. 31 ; 1 Cor. i. 20 ; iii. 19 ; Gal. iv. 3 ; Col. ii. 8. The *'friendship* of the world' (φιλία τοῦ κόσμου) is the *love* of that world ; of the maxims which govern it, the principles which reign there, the ends that are sought, the amusements and gratifications which characterize it as distinguished from the church of God. It consists in setting our hearts on those things ; in conforming to them ; in making them the object of our pursuit with the same spirit with which they are sought by those who make no pretensions to religion. See Notes, Rom. xii. 2. ¶ *Is enmity with God.* Is in fact hostility against God, since that world is arrayed against him. It neither obeys his laws, submits to his claims, nor seeks to honour him. To love that world is, therefore, to be arrayed against God ; and the spirit which would lead us to this is, in fact, a spirit of hostility to God. ¶ *Whosoever therefore will be a friend of the world.* ' *Whoever* ' he may be, whether in the church or out of it. The fact of being a member of the church makes no difference in this respect, for it is as easy to be a friend of the world in the church as out of it. The phrase ' whosoever *will* ' (βουληθῇ) implies *purpose, intention, design.* It supposes that the *heart* is set on it ; or that there is a deliberate purpose to seek the friendship of the world. It refers to that strong desire which often exists, even among professing Christians, to secure the friendship of the world ; to copy its fashions and vanities ; to enjoy its pleasures ; and to share its pastimes and its friendships. Wherever there is a manifested purpose to find our chosen friends and associates there rather than among Christians ; wherever there is a greater desire to enjoy the smiles and approbation of the world than there is to enjoy the approbation of God and the blessings of a good conscience ; and wherever there is more conscious pain because we have failed

to win the applause of the world, or have offended its votaries, and have sunk ourselves in its estimation, than there is because we have neglected our duty to our Saviour, and have lost the enjoyment of religion, there is the clearest proof that the heart *wills* or *desires* to be the ' friend of the world.' ¶ *Is the enemy of God.* This is a most solemn declaration, and one of fearful import in its bearing on many who are members of the church. It settles the point that any one, no matter what his professions, who is characteristically a friend of the world, cannot be a true Christian. In regard to the meaning of this important verse, then, it may be remarked, (1.) that there *is* a sense in which the love of this world, or of the physical universe, is not wrong. That kind of love for it as the work of God, which perceives the evidence of his wisdom and goodness and power in the various objects of beauty, usefulness, and grandeur, spread around us, is not evil. The world as such—the physical structure of the earth, of the mountains, forests flowers, seas, lakes, and vales—is full of illustrations of the Divine character, and it cannot be wrong to contemplate those things with interest, or with warm affection toward their Creator. (2.) When that world, however, becomes our portion ; when we study it only as a matter of science, without ' looking through nature up to nature's God ;' when we seek the wealth which it has to confer, or endeavour to appropriate as our supreme portion its lands, its minerals, its fruits ; when we are satisfied with what it yields, and when in the possession or pursuit of these things, our thoughts never rise to God ; and when we partake of the spirit which rules in the hearts of those who avowedly seek this world as their portion, though we profess religion, then the love of the world becomes evil, and comes in direct conflict with the spirit of true religion. (3.) The statement in this verse is, therefore, one of most fearful import for many professors of religion. There are many in the church who, so far as human judgment can go, are characteristically *lovers of the world.* This is shown (*a*) by their conformity to it in all in which the world is distinguished

5 Do ye think that the Scripture

1 Or, *enviously.*   *a* Ec.4.4.

saith in vain, The spirit that dwelleth in us lusteth [1]to envy? *a*

from the church as such; (*b*) in their
seeking the friendship of the world, or
their finding their friends there rather
than among Christians; (*c*) in preferring
the amusements of the world to the
scenes where spiritually-minded Christians find their chief happiness; (*d*) in
pursuing the same pleasures that the
people of the world do, with the same expense, the same extravagance, the same
luxury; (*e*) in making their worldly interests the great object of living, and
everything else subordinate to that.
This spirit exists in all cases where no
worldly interest is sacrificed for religion;
where everything that religion peculiarly requires is sacrificed for the world.
If this be so, then there are many professing Christians who are the 'enemies
of God.' See Notes on Phil. iii. 18.
They have never known what is true
friendship for him, and by their lives
they show that they can be ranked only
among his foes. It becomes every professing Christian, therefore, to examine
himself with the deepest earnestness to
determine whether he is characteristically a friend of the world or of God;
whether he is living for this life only,
or is animated by the high and pure
principles of those who are the friends
of God. The great Searcher of hearts
cannot be deceived, and soon our appropriate place will be assigned us, and our
final Judge will determine to which
class of the two great divisions of the
human family we belong—to those who
are the friends of the world, or to those
who are the friends of God.

5. *Do ye think that the Scripture
saith in vain.* Few passages of the
New Testament have given expositors
more perplexity than this. The difficulty has arisen from the fact that no
such passage as that which seems here
to be quoted is found in the Old Testament; and to meet this difficulty, expositors have resorted to various conjectures and solutions. Some have supposed that the passage is spurious, and
that it was at first a gloss in the margin,
placed there by some transcriber, and
was then introduced into the text; some

that the apostle quotes from an apocryphal book; some, that he quotes the
general spirit of the Old Testament
rather than any particular place; some
regard it not as a quotation, but read
the two members separately, supplying
what is necessary to complete the sense,
thus : ' Do you think that the Scripture
speaks in vain, or without a good reason,
when it condemns such a worldly temper?
No; that you cannot suppose. Do you
imagine that the Spirit of God, which
dwelleth in us Christians, leads to covetousness, pride, envy? No. On the contrary, to such as follow his guidance
and direction, he gives more abundant
grace and favour.' This is the solution
proposed by Benson, and adopted by
Bloomfield. But this solution is by no
means satisfactory. Two things are
clear in regard to the passage: (1.) that
James meant to adduce something that
was *said* somewhere, or which could be
regarded as *a quotation*, or as *authority*
in the case, for he uses the formula by
which such quotations are made; and,
(2.) that he meant to refer, not to an
apocryphal book, but to the inspired
and canonical Scriptures, for he uses a
term (ἡ γραφὴ—*the Scripture*) which is
everywhere employed to denote the Old
Testament, and which is nowhere applied to an apocryphal book, Matt. xxi.
42; xxii. 29; xxvi. 54, 56; John ii. 22;
v. 39; vii. 38, 42; x. 35, *et al.* The
word is used more than fifty times in
the New Testament, and is never applied
to any books but those which were regarded by the Jews as inspired, and
which constitute now the Old Testament, except in 2 Pet. iii. 16, where it
refers to the writings of Paul. The
difficulty in the case arises from the
fact that no such passage as the one
here quoted is found in so many words
in the Old Testament, nor any of which
it can fairly be regarded as a quotation.
The only solution of the difficulty which
seems to me to be at all satisfactory, is
to suppose that the apostle, in the remark made here in the form of a quotation, refers to the Old Testament, but
that he had not his eye on any parti-

cular passage, and did not mean to quote the *words* literally, but meant to refer to what was the current teaching or general spirit of the Old Testament; or that he meant to say that this *sentiment* was found there, and designed himself to embody the sentiment in words, and to put it into a condensed form. His eye was on *envy* as at the bottom of many of the contentions and strifes existing on earth, (chap. iii. 16,) and of the spirit of the world which prevailed everywhere, (chap. iv. 4;) and he refers to the *general teaching* of the Old Testament that the soul is by nature inclined to envy; or that this has a deep lodgement in the heart of man. That truth which was uttered everywhere in the Scriptures, was not taught 'in vain.' The abundant facts which existed showing its developement and operation in contentions, and wars, and a worldly spirit, proved that it was deeply imbedded in the human soul. This general truth, that man is prone to envy, or that there is much in our nature which inclines us to it, is abundantly taught in the Old Testament. Eccl. iv. 4, 'I considered all travail, and every right work, that for this a man is envied of his neighbour.' Job v. 2, 'Wrath killeth, and envy slayeth the silly one.' Prov. xiv. 30, 'Envy is the rottenness of the bones.' Prov. xxvii. 4, 'Who is able to stand before envy?' For particular *instances* of this, and the effects, see Gen. xxvi. 14; xxx. 1; xxxvii. 11; Psal. cvi. 16; lxxiii. 3. These passages prove that there is a strong propensity in human nature to envy, and it was in accordance with the design of the apostle to show this. The effects of envy to which he himself referred evinced the same thing, and demonstrated that the utterance given to this sentiment in the Old Testament was not 'in vain,' or was not false, for the records in the Old Testament on the subject found a strong confirmation in the wars and strifes and worldliness of which he was speaking. ¶ *Saith in vain.* 'Says falsely;' that is, the testimony thus borne is true. The apostle means that what was said in the Old Testament on the subject found abundant confirmation in the facts which were continually occurring, and espe-

cially in those to which he was adverting. ¶ *The spirit that dwelleth in us.* Many have supposed that the word *spirit* here refers to the Holy Spirit, or the Christian spirit; but in adopting this interpretation they are obliged to render the passage, 'the spirit that dwells in us lusteth *against* envy,' or tends to check and suppress it. But this interpretation is forced and unnatural, and one which the Greek will not well bear. The more obvious interpretation is to refer it to our spirit or disposition as we are by nature, and it is equivalent to saying that we are naturally prone to envy. ¶ *Lusteth to envy.* Strongly tends to envy. The margin is 'enviously,' but the sense is the same. The idea is, that there is in man a strong inclination to look with dissatisfaction on the superior happiness and prosperity of others; to desire to make what they possess our own; or at any rate to deprive them of it by detraction, by fraud, or by robbery. It is this feeling which leads to calumny, to contentions, to wars, and to that strong worldly ambition which makes us anxious to surpass all others, and which is so hostile to the humble and contented spirit of religion. He who could trace all wars and contentions and worldly plans to their source—all the schemes and purposes of even professed Christians, that do so much to mar their religion and to make them worldly-minded, to their real origin—would be surprised to find how much is to be attributed to envy. We are pained that others are more prosperous than we are; we desire to possess what others have, though we have no right to it; and this leads to the various guilty methods which are pursued to lessen their enjoyment of it, or to obtain it ourselves, or to show that they do not possess as much as they are commonly supposed to. This purpose will be accomplished if we can obtain more than they have; or if we can diminish what they actually possess; or if by any statements to which we can give currency in society, the general impression shall be that they do *not* possess as much wealth, domestic peace, happiness, or honour, as is commonly supposed—for thus the spirit of envy in our bosoms will be gratified.

6 But he giveth more grace:
Wherefore he saith, ^a God resisteth
a Prov.29.23.

the proud, but giveth grace unto
the humble.

---

6. *But he giveth more grace.* The
reference here is undoubtedly to God.
Some have regarded this clause as a
continuation of the quotation in the previous verse, but it is rather to be considered as a declaration of the apostle
himself. The writer had just spoken
of envy, and of the crimes which grew
out of it. He thought of the wars and
commotions of the earth, and of the
various lusts which reigned among men.
In the contemplation of these things, it
seems suddenly to have occurred to him
that *all* were not under the influence
of these things; that there were cases
where men were restrained, and where
a spirit opposite to these things prevailed. Another passage of Scripture
struck his mind, containing the truth
that there was a class of men to whom
God gave grace to restrain these passions, and to subdue these carnal propensities. They were the humble, in
contradistinction to the proud; and
he states the fact that 'God giveth
more grace;' that is, that in some instances he confers more grace than in
the cases referred to; to some he gives
more grace to overcome their evil passions, and to subdue their corrupt inclinations, than he does to others. The
meaning may be thus expressed:—' It
is true that the natural spirit in man is
one that tends to envy, and thus leads
to all the sad consequences of envy.
But there are instances in which higher
grace or favour is conferred; in which
these feelings are subdued, and these
consequences are prevented. They are
not indeed to be found among the
proud, whom God always resists; but
they are to be found among the meek
and the humble. Wherefore submit
yourselves to his arrangements; resist
the devil; draw nigh to God; purify
yourselves, and weep over your past
offences, and you shall find that the
Lord will lift you up, and bestow his
favour upon you,' ver. 10. ¶ *Wherefore
he saith.* The reference here is to
Prov. iii. 34, 'Surely he scorneth the
scorners; but he giveth grace unto the
lowly.' The quotation is made exactly

from the Septuagint, which, though not
entirely literal, expresses the sense of
the Hebrew without essential inaccu-
racy. This passage is also quoted in
1 Pet. v. 5. ¶ *God resisteth the proud.*
The *proud* are those who have an inor-
dinate self-esteem; who have a high
and unreasonable conceit of their own
excellence or importance. This may
extend to any thing; to beauty, or
strength, or attainments, or family, or
country, or equipage, or rank, or even
religion. A man may be proud of any
thing that belongs to him, or which can
in any way be construed as a part of
himself, or as pertaining to him. This
does not, of course, apply to a *correct*
estimate of ourselves, or to the mere
knowledge that we may excel others.
One may *know* that he has more
strength, or higher attainments in learning or in the mechanic arts, or greater
wealth than others, and yet have properly no *pride* in the case. He has
only a *correct* estimate of himself, and
he attaches no undue importance to
himself on account of it. His heart is
not lifted up; he claims no undue deference to himself; he concedes to all
others what is their due; and he is
humble before God, feeling that all that
he has, and is, is nothing in his sight.
He is willing to occupy his appropriate
place in the sight of God and men, and
to be esteemed just as he is. Pride goes
beyond this, and gives to a man a degree of self-estimation which is not war-
ranted by any thing that he possesses.
God looks at things as they are; and
hence he abhors and humbles this arrogant claim, Lev. xxvi. 19; Job xxxiii.
17; Ps. lix. 12; Prov. viii. 13; xvi.
18; xxix. 13; Isa. xxiii. 9; xxviii. 1;
Dan. iv. 37; Zech. x. 11. This resistance of pride he shows not only in the
explicit declarations of his word, but in
the arrangements of his providence and
grace. (1.) In his providence, in the
reverses and disappointments which
occur; in the necessity of abandoning
the splendid mansion which we had
built, or in disappointing us in some favourite plan by which our pride was to

7 Submit yourselves therefore to God. Resist *a* the devil, and he will flee from you.

8 Draw *b* nigh to God, and he will draw nigh to you. Cleanse *c your* hands, *ye* sinners ; and purify *your* hearts, *ye* double-minded.

a 1 Pe.5.9.   *b* 2 Ch.15.2.   *c* Is.1.16.

be nurtured and gratified. (2.) In sickness, taking away the beauty and strength on which we had so much valued ourselves, and bring us to the sad condition of a sick bed. (3.) In the grave, bringing us down to corruption and worms. Why should one be proud who will soon become so offensive to his best friends that they will gladly hide him in the grave? (4.) In the plan of salvation he opposes our pride. Not a feature of that plan is fitted to foster pride, but all is adapted to make us humble. (*a*) The *necessity* for the plan—that we are guilty and helpless sinners ; (*b*) the selection of a Saviour —one who was so poor, and who was so much despised by the world, and who was put to death on a cross ; (*c*) our entire dependence on him for salvation, with the assurance that we have no merit of our own, and that salvation is all of grace ; (*d*) the fact that we are brought to embrace it only by the agency of the Holy Spirit, and that if we were left to ourselves we should never have one right thought or holy desire—all this is fitted to humble us, and to bring us low before God. God has done nothing to foster the self-estimation of the human heart ; but how much has he done to 'stain the pride of all glory!' See Notes on Isa. xxiii. 9. ¶ *But giveth grace unto the humble.* The meaning is, that he shows them *favour ;* he bestows upon them the grace needful to secure their salvation. This he does (1,) because they feel their need of his favour ; (2,) because they will welcome his teaching and value his friendship ; (3,) because all the arrangements of his grace are adapted only to such a state of mind. You cannot *teach* one who is so wise that he already supposes he knows enough ; you cannot bestow grace on one who has no sense of the need of it. The arrangements of salvation are adapted only to an humble heart.

7. *Submit yourselves therefore to God.* That is, in his arrangements for obtaining his favour. Yield to what he has

judged necessary for your welfare in the life that is, and your salvation in the life to come. The duty here enjoined is that of entire acquiescence in the arrangements of God, whether in his providence or grace. All these are for our good, and submission to them is required by the spirit of true humility. The object of the command here, and in the succeeding injunctions to particular duties, is to show them how they might obtain the grace which God is willing to bestow, and how they might overcome the evils against which the apostle had been endeavouring to guard them. The true method of doing this is by submitting ourselves *in all things* to God. ¶ *Resist the devil, and he will flee from you.* While you yield to God in all things, you are to yield to the devil in none. You are to resist and oppose him in whatever way he may approach you, whether by allurements, by flattering promises, by the fascinations of the world, by temptation, or by threats. See 1 Pet. v. 9. Satan makes his way, and secures his triumphs, rather by art, cunning, deception, and threatenings, than by true courage; and when opposed manfully, he flies. The true way of meeting him is by direct resistance, rather than by argument; by steadfastly *refusing* to yield in the slightest degree, rather than by a belief that we can either convince him that he is wrong, or can return to virtue when we have gone a certain length in complying with his demands. No one is safe who yields in the least to the suggestions of the tempter; there is no one who is *not* safe if he does not yield. A man, for example, is always safe from intemperance if he *resists* all allurements to indulgence in strong drink, and never yields in the slightest degree ; no one is certainly safe if he drinks even moderately.

8. *Draw nigh to God, and he will draw nigh to you.* Comp. 2 Chron. xv. 2. This declaration contains a great and important principle in religion. If we wish the favour of God, we must

9 Be afflicted, and mourn, and weep: let your laughter be turned to mourning, and *your* joy to heaviness.

come to him; nor can we hope for his mercy, unless we approach him and ask him for it. We cannot come *literally* any nearer to God than we always are, for he is always round about us; but we may come nearer in a spiritual sense. We may address him directly in prayer; we may approach him by meditation on his character; we may draw near to him in the ordinances of religion. We can never hope for his favour while we prefer to remain at a distance from him; none who in fact draw near to him will find him unwilling to bestow on them the blessings which they need. ¶ *Cleanse your hands, ye sinners.* There may possibly be an allusion here to Isa. i. 15, 16: 'Your hands are full of blood; wash you, make you clean; put away the evil of your doings from before mine eyes; cease to do evil.' The *heart* is the seat of motives and intentions—that by which we devise anything; the *hands*, the instruments by which we execute our purposes. The hands here are represented as defiled by blood, or by acts of iniquity. To *wash* or cleanse the hands was, therefore, emblematic of putting away transgression, Mat. xxvii. 24. Comp. Deut. xxi. 6; Psa. xxvi. 6. The heathen and the Jews were accustomed to wash their hands before they engaged in public worship. The particular idea here is, that in order to obtain the favour of God, it is necessary to put away our sins; to approach him with a desire to be pure and holy. The mere washing of the hands, in itself, could not recommend us to his favour; but that of which the washing of the hands would be an emblem, would be acceptable in his sight. It may be inferred from what is said here that no one can hope for the favour of God who does not abandon his transgressions. The *design* of the apostle is, evidently, to state one of the conditions on which we can make an acceptable approach to God. It is indispensable that we come with a purpose and desire to wash ourselves from all iniquity, to put away from us all our transgressions. So David said, 'I will wash my hands in innocency; so will I compass thine altar. O Lord,' Psa. xxvi. 6.

['To obtain the favour of God, it is necessary to put away our sins '—is somewhat unguarded phraseology. If the favour of God were not obtained but on this condition, none ever would obtain it. The passage is a strong injunction to holiness and singleness of heart: it does not say, however, that BY these we obtain acceptance with God. Of his favour, holiness is the fruit, the effect, and not the cause. The sinner must not think of getting quit of his sins *to prepare* him for going to God by Jesus; but he must *first* go to Jesus to prepare for laying aside his sins. Yet in every approach to God, it is true there must be a 'desire' to be free from sin; and this doubtless is the view of the commentary; indeed it is so expressed, though some words are objectionable.]

¶ *And purify* your *hearts*. That is, do not rest satisfied with a mere external reformation; with putting away your outward transgressions. There must be a deeper work than that; a work which shall reach to the heart, and which shall purify the affections. This agrees with all the requisitions of the Bible, and is in accordance with what must be the nature of religion. If the heart is wrong, nothing can be right. If, while we seek an external reformation, we still give indulgence to the secret corruptions of the heart, it is clear that we can have no true religion. ¶ Ye *double-minded.* See Notes on chap. i. 8. The apostle here seems to have had his eye on those who were vacillating in their purposes; whose hearts were not decidedly fixed, but who were halting between good and evil. The *heart* was not right in such persons. It was not settled and determined in favour of religion, but vibrated between that and the world. The proper business of such persons, therefore, was to cleanse the heart from disturbing influences, that it might settle down in unwavering attachment to that which is good.

9. *Be afflicted, and mourn, and weep.* That is, evidently, on account of your sins. The sins to which the apostle refers are those which he had specified in the previous part of the chapter, and which he had spoken of as so evil in their nature, and so dangerous in their tendency. The word rendered 'be afflicted' means, properly, to endure

10 Humble *a* yourselves in the sight of the Lord, and he shall lift you up.

11 Speak *b* not evil one of another, brethren. He that speaketh

a Mat.23.12.　　　*b* Ep.4.31; 1 Pe.2.1.

toil or hardship; then to endure affliction or distress; and here means, that they were *to afflict themselves*—that is, they were to feel distressed and sad on account of their transgressions. Comp. Ezra viii. 21. The other words in this clause are those which are expressive of deep grief or sorrow. The language here used shows that the apostle supposed that it was possible that those who had done wrong should voluntarily feel sorrow for it, and that, therefore, it was proper to call upon them to do it.

[All who feel true sorrow for sin, do so *voluntarily*; but it is not intended by this assertion to insinuate that repentance is not the work of the Spirit. He operates on men without destroying their freedom, or doing violence to their will: 'in the day of his power they are willing.' Nor is it improper to call on men to do that for which they require the Spirit's aid. That aid is not withheld in the hour of need; and everywhere the Bible commands sinners to believe and repent.]

¶ *Let your laughter be turned to mourning.* It would seem that the persons referred to, instead of suitable sorrow and humiliation on account of sin, gave themselves to joyousness, mirth, and revelry. See a similar instance in Isa. xxii. 12, 13. It is often the case, that those for whom the deep sorrows of repentance would be peculiarly appropriate, give themselves to mirth and vanity. The apostle here says that such mirth did not become them. Sorrow, deep and unfeigned, was appropriate on account of their sins, and the sound of laughter and of revelry should be changed to notes of lamentation. To how many of the assemblies of the vain, the gay, and the dissipated, might the exhortation in this passage with propriety be now addressed! ¶ *Your joy to heaviness.* The word here rendered *heaviness* occurs nowhere else in the New Testament. It means *dejection, sorrow.* It is not gloom, melancholy, or moroseness, but it is sorrow on

evil of *his* brother, and judgeth his brother, speaketh evil of the law, and judgeth the law : but if thou judge the law, thou art not a doer of the law, but a judge.

account of sin. God has so made us that we should feel sorrow when we are conscious that we have done wrong, and it is appropriate that we should do so. 10. *Humble yourselves in the sight of the Lord.* Comp. Matt. xxiii. 12. See Notes on ver. 6. That is, be willing to take your appropriate place in the dust on account of your transgressions. This is to be ' in the sight of the Lord,' or before him. Our sins have been committed against him ; and their principal aggravation, whoever may have been wronged by them, and great as is their criminality in other respects, arises from that consideration. Psa. li. 4, ' Against thee, thee only, have I sinned, and done this evil in thy sight.' Luke xv. 18, ' I will arise and go to my father, and will say to him, Father, I have sinned *against heaven,* and before thee.' As the Being against whom we have sinned is the only one who can pardon, it is proper that we should humble ourselves before him with penitent confession. ¶ *And he shall lift you up.* He will exalt you from the condition of a broken-hearted penitent to that of a forgiven child ; will wipe away your tears, remove the sadness of your heart, fill you with joy, and clothe you with the garments of salvation. This declaration is in accordance with all the promises in the Bible, and with all the facts which occur on the earth, that God is willing to show mercy to the humble and contrite, and to receive those who are truly penitent into his favour. Comp. Luke xv. 22.

11. *Speak not evil one of another, brethren.* It is not known to whom the apostle here particularly refers, nor is it necessary to know. It is probable that among those whom he addressed there were some who were less circumspect in regard to speaking of others than they should be, and perhaps this evil prevailed. There are few communities where such an injunction would not be

proper at any time, and few churches where some might not be found to whom the exhortation would be appropriate. Comp. Notes on Eph. iv. 31 ; 1 Pet. ii. 1. The evil here referred to is that of *talking against* others—against their actions, their motives, their manner of living, their families, &c. Few things are more common in the world; nothing is more decidedly against the true spirit of religion. ¶ *He that speaketh evil of* his *brother.* Referring here probably to a Christian brother, or to a fellow Christian. The word *may* however be used in a larger sense to denote any one—a brother of the human race. Religion forbids both, and would restrain us from *all* evil speaking against any human being. ¶ *And judgeth his brother.* His motives, or his conduct. See Notes on Matt. vii. 1. ¶ *Speaketh evil of the law, and judgeth the law.* Instead of manifesting the feelings of a brother, he sets himself up as judge, and not only a judge of his brother, but a judge of *the law.* The *law* here referred to is probably the law of Christ, or the rule which all Christians profess to obey. It is that which James elsewhere calls the 'law of liberty,' (Notes, chap. i. 25;) the law which released men from the servitude of the Jewish rites, and gave them liberty to worship God without the restraint and bondage (Acts xv. 10; Gal. iv. 21–31) implied in that ancient system of worship ; and the law by which it was contemplated that they should be free from sin. It is not absolutely certain to what the apostle refers here, but it would seem probable that it is to some course of conduct which one portion of the church felt they were at liberty to follow, but which another portion regarded as wrong, and for which they censured them. The explanation which will best suit the expressions here used, is that which supposes that it refers to some difference of opinion which existed among Christians, especially among those of Jewish origin, about the binding nature of the Jewish laws, in regard to circumcision, to holy days, to ceremonial observances, to the distinctions of meats, &c. A part regarded the law on these subjects as still binding, another portion supposed that the obligation in regard to these matters had

ceased by the introduction of the gospel. Those who regarded the obligation of the Mosaic law as still binding, would of course *judge* their brethren, and regard them as guilty of a disregard of the law of God by their conduct. We know that differences of opinion on these points gave rise to contentions, and to the formation of parties in the church, and that it required all the wisdom of Paul and of the other apostles to hush the contending elements to peace. Comp. Notes on Col. ii. 16–18. To some such source of contention the apostle doubtless refers here ; and the meaning probably is, that they who held the opinion that all the Jewish ceremonial laws were still binding on Christians, and who judged and condemned their brethren who did not [observe them], by such a course judged and condemned ' the law of liberty' under which they acted—the law of Christianity that had abolished the ceremonial observances, and released men from their obligation. The *judgment* which they passed, therefore, was not only on their brethren, but was on that law of Christianity which had given greater liberty of conscience, and which was intended to abolish the obligation of the Jewish ritual. The same thing now occurs when we judge others for a course which their consciences approve, because they do not deem it necessary to comply with all the rules which *we* think to be binding. Not a few of the harsh judgments which one class of religionists pronounce on others, are in fact judgments on *the laws of Christ.* We set up our own standards, or our own interpretations, and then we judge others for not complying with them, when in fact they may be acting only as the law of Christianity, properly understood, would allow them to do. They who set up a claim to a right to judge the conduct of others, should be certain that they understand the nature of religion themselves. It may be *presumed,* unless there is evidence to the contrary, that others are as conscientious as we are ; and it may commonly be supposed that they who differ from us have some *reason* for what they do, and *may be* desirous of glorifying their Lord and Master, and *that they may possibly be*

12 There is one Lawgiver, who *a* is able to save and to destroy: who art thou that judgest another? 13 Go to now, ye that say, To-

a Mat.10.28.

day or to-morrow we will go into such a city, and continue there a year, and buy and sell, and get gain:

---

right. It is commonly not safe to judge hastily of a man who has turned his attention to a particular subject, or to suppose that he has no reasons to allege for his opinions or conduct. ¶ *But if thou judge the law, thou art not a doer of the law, but a judge.* It is implied here that it is the simple duty of every Christian to *obey* the law. He is not to assume the office of a judge about its propriety or fitness; but he is to do what he supposes the law to require of him, and is to allow others to do the same. Our business in religion is not to make laws, or to declare what they should have been, or to amend those that are made; it is simply to *obey* those which are appointed, and to allow others to do the same, as they understand them. It would be well for all individual Christians, and Christian denominations, to learn this, and to imbibe the spirit of charity to which it would prompt.

12. *There is one lawgiver.* There is but one who has a right to give law. The reference here is undoubtedly to the Lord Jesus Christ, the great Legislator of the church. *This,* too, is a most important and vital principle, though one that has been most imperfectly understood and acted on. The tendency everywhere has been to enact *other* laws than those appointed by Christ —the laws of synods and councils—and to claim that Christians are bound to observe them, and should be punished if they do not. But it is a fundamental principle in Christianity that no laws are binding on the conscience, but those which Christ has ordained; and that all attempts to make other laws pertaining to religion binding on the conscience is a usurpation of his prerogatives. The church is safe while it adheres to this as a settled principle; it is not safe when it submits to any legislation in religious matters as binding the conscience. ¶ *Who is able to save and to destroy.* Comp. Matt. x. 28. The idea

here would seem to be, that he is able to save those whom you condemn, and to destroy you who pronounce a judgment on them. Or, in general, it may mean that he is intrusted with all power, and is abundantly able to administer his government; to restrain where it is necessary to restrain; to save where it is proper to save; to punish where it is just to punish. The whole matter pertaining to *judgment,* therefore, may be safely left in his hands; and, as he is abundantly qualified for it, we should not usurp his prerogatives. ¶ *Who art thou that judgest another?* 'Who art thou, a weak and frail and erring mortal, thyself accountable to that Judge, that thou shouldest interfere, and pronounce judgment on another, especially when he is doing only what that Judge permits him to do?' See this sentiment explained at length in the Notes on Rom. xiv. 4. Comp. Notes, Rom. ii. 1, and Matt. vii. 1. There is nothing more decidedly condemned in the Scriptures than the habit of pronouncing a judgment on the motives and conduct of others. There is nothing in which we are more liable to err, or to indulge in wrong feelings; and there is nothing which God claims more for himself as his peculiar prerogative.

13. *Go to now.* The apostle here introduces a new subject, and refers to another fault which was doubtless prevalent among them, as it is everywhere, that of a presumptuous confidence respecting the future, or of forming plans stretching into the future, without any proper sense of the uncertainty of life, and of our absolute dependence on God. The phrase 'go to now,' (ἄγε νῦν,) is a phrase designed to arrest attention, as if there were something that demanded their notice, and especially, as in this case, with the implied thought that that to which the attention is called is wrong. See ch. v. 1. Comp. Gen. xi. 7; Isa. i. 18. ¶ *Ye that say.* You that form your plans in this manner or that speak

14 Whereas, ye know not what *shall be* on the morrow: For what *is* your life? It [1] is even a vapour, *a* that appeareth for a little time, and then vanisheth away.

1 *For it is.*   *a* Job 7.7.

thus confidently of what you will do in the future. The word *say* here probably refers to what was in their thoughts, rather than to what was openly expressed. ¶ *To-day or to-morrow we will go into such a city.* That is, they say this without any proper sense of the uncertainty of life, and of their absolute dependence on God. ¶ *And continue there a year.* Fixing a definite time; designating the exact period during which they would remain, and when they would leave, without any reference to the will of God. The apostle undoubtedly means to refer here to this as a mere *specimen* of what he would reprove. It cannot be supposed that he refers to this single case alone as wrong. All plans are wrong that are formed in the same spirit. ' The practice to which the apostle alludes,' says the editor of the Pictorial Bible, ' is very common in the East to this day, among a very respectable and intelligent class of merchants. They convey the products of one place to some distant city, where they remain until they have disposed of their own goods and have purchased others suitable for another distant market; and thus the operation is repeated, until, after a number of years, the trader is enabled to return prosperously to his home. Or again, a shopkeeper or a merchant takes only the first step in this process—conveying to a distant town, where the best purchases of his own line are to be made, such goods as are likely to realise a profit, and returning, without any farther stop, with a stock for his own concern. These operations are seldom very rapid, as the adventurer likes to wait opportunities for making advantageous bargains; and sometimes opens a shop in the place to which he comes, to sell by retail the goods which he has bought.' The practice is common in India. See Roberts' Oriental Illustrations. ¶ *And buy and sell, and get gain.* It is not improbable that there is an allusion here to the commercial habits of the Jews at the time

when the apostle wrote. Many of them were engaged in foreign traffic, and for this purpose made long journeys to distant trading cities, as Alexandria, Antioch, Ephesus, Corinth, etc.—*Bloomfield.*

14. *Whereas, ye know not what* shall be *on the morrow.* They formed their plans as if they knew; the apostle says it could not be known. They had no means of ascertaining what would occur; whether they would live or die; whether they would be prospered, or would be overwhelmed with adversity. Of the *truth* of the remark made by the apostle here, no one can doubt; but it is amazing how men act as if it were false. We have no power of penetrating the future so as to be able to determine what will occur in a single day or a single hour, and yet we are almost habitually forming our plans as if we saw with certainty all that is to happen. The classic writings abound with beautiful expressions respecting the uncertainty of the future, and the folly of forming our plans as if it were known to us. Many of those passages, some of them almost precisely in the words of James, may be seen in Grotius and Priceus, *in loc.* Such passages occur in Anacreon, Euripides, Menander, Seneca, Horace, and others, suggesting an obvious but much-neglected thought, that the future is to us all unknown. Man cannot penetrate it ; and his plans of life should be formed in view of the possibility that his life may be cut off and all his plans fail, and consequently in constant preparation for a higher world. ¶ *For what is your life?* All your plans must depend of course on the continuance of your life; but what a frail and uncertain thing is that ! How transitory and evanescent as a basis on which to build *any* plans for the future ! Who can calculate on the permanence of a vapour ? Who can build any solid hopes on a mist ? ¶ *It is even a vapour.* Marg., *For it is.* The margin is the more correct rendering. The previous question had turned the attention to

15 For that ye *ought* to say, If the Lord will, we shall live, and do this, or that.

16 But now ye rejoice in your

a Lu.12.47.

boastings: all such rejoicing is evil.

17 Therefore *a* to him that knoweth to do good, and doeth *it* not, to him it is sin.

---

life as something peculiarly frail, and as of such a nature that no calculation could be based on its permanence. This expression gives a *reason* for that, to wit, that it is a mere vapour. The word *vapour* (ἀτμὶς,) means a mist, an exhalation, a smoke; such a vapour as we see ascending from a stream, or as lies on the mountain side on the morning, or as floats for a little time in the air, but which is dissipated by the rising sun, leaving not a trace behind. The comparison of life with a vapour is common, and is as beautiful as it is just. Job says,

O remember that my life is wind;
Mine eyes shall no more see good.
Job. vii. 7.

So the Psalmist,

For he remembered that they were but flesh,
A wind that passeth away and that cometh not again.
Ps. lxviii. 39.

Comp. 1 Chron. xxix. 15 ; Job xiv. 10, 11. ¶ *And then vanisheth away.* Wholly disappears. Like the dissipated vapour, it is entirely gone. There is no remnant, no outline, *nothing* that reminds us that it ever was. So of life. Soon it disappears altogether. The works of art that man has made, the house that he has built, or the book that he has written, remain for a little time, but *the life* has gone. There is nothing of it remaining—any more than there is of the vapour which in the morning climbed silently up the mountain side. The animating principle has vanished for ever. On such a frail and evanescent thing, who can build any substantial hopes ?

15. *For that ye* ought *to say.* Instead of what you *do* say, ' we will go into such a city,' you *ought* rather to recognise your absolute dependence on God, and feel that life and success are subject to his will. The meaning is not that we ought always to be *saying* that in so many words, for this might become a mere ostentatious *form*, offensive by constant unmeaning repetition ; but

we are, in the proper way, to recognise our dependence on him, and to form all our plans with reference to his will. ¶ *If the Lord will*, etc. This is proper, because we are wholly dependent on him for life, and as dependent on him for success. He alone can keep us, and he only can make our plans prosperous. In a thousand ways he can thwart our best-laid schemes, for all things are under his control. We need not travel far in life to see how completely all that we have is in the hands of God, or to learn how easily he can frustrate us if he pleases. There is nothing on which the success of our plans depends over which we have absolute control; there is nothing, therefore, on which we can base the assurance of success but his favour.

16. *But now ye rejoice in your boastings.* That is, probably, in your boastings of what you can do; your reliance on your own skill and sagacity. You form your plans for the future as if with consummate wisdom, and are confident of success. You do not anticipate a failure; you do not see how plans so skilfully formed *can* fail. You form them as if you were certain that you would live; as if secure from the numberless casualties which may defeat your schemes. ¶ *All such rejoicing is evil.* It is founded on a wrong view of yourselves and of what may occur. It shows a spirit forgetful of our dependence on God; forgetful of the uncertainty of life ; forgetful of the many ways by which the best-laid plans may be defeated. We should never boast of any wisdom or skill in regard to the future. A day, an hour may defeat our best-concerted plans, and show us that we have not the slightest power to control coming events.

17. *Therefore to him that knoweth to do good, and doeth* it *not, to him it is sin.* That is, he is guilty of sin if he does not do it. Cotton Mather adopted it as a principle of action, ' that the ability to do good in any case imposes

an obligation to do it.' The proposition in the verse before us is of a general character, but probably the apostle meant that it should refer to the point specified in the previous verses—the forming of plans respecting the future. The particular meaning then would be, 'that he who knows what sort of views he should take in regard to the future, and how he should form his plans in view of the uncertainty of life, and still does *not* do it, but goes on recklessly, forming his plans boastingly and confident of success, is guilty of sin against God.' Still, the proposition will admit of a more general application. It is universally true that if a man knows what is right, and does not do it, he is guilty of sin. If he understands what his duty is; if he has the means of doing good to others; if by his name, his influence, his wealth, he can promote a good cause; if he can, consistently with other duties, relieve the distressed, the poor, the prisoner, the oppressed; if he can send the gospel to other lands, or can wipe away the tear of the mourner; if he has talents by which he can lift a voice that shall be heard in favour of temperance, chastity, liberty, and religion, he is under obligations to do it: and if, by indolence, or avarice, or selfishness, or the dread of the loss of popularity, he does not do it, he is guilty of sin before God. No man can be released from the obligation to do good in this world to the extent of his ability; no one should desire to be. The highest privilege conferred on a mortal, besides that of securing the salvation of his own soul, is that of doing good to others—of alleviating sorrow, instructing ignorance, raising up the bowed down, comforting those that mourn, delivering the wronged and the oppressed, supplying the wants of the needy, guiding inquirers into the way of truth, and sending liberty, knowledge, and salvation around the world. If a man does *not* do this when he has the means, he sins against his own soul, against humanity, and against his Maker; if he does it cheerfully and to the extent of his means, it likens him more than anything else to God.

CHAPTER V.

ANALYSIS OF THE CHAPTER.

THE subjects which are introduced in this chapter are the following :—

I. An address to rich men, and a severe condemnation of the manner in which they lived, vers. 1–6. There have been various opinions in regard to the persons here referred to. (1.) Some have supposed that the address is to unbelieving Jews, and that the punishment which the apostle threatens was that which was about to be brought on the nation by the Roman armies. But, as Benson well observes, it can hardly be presumed that the apostle supposed that his letter would be read by the Jews, and it is not probable, therefore, that he would in this manner directly address them. (2.) Another opinion has been, that this, like the rest of the epistle, is addressed to professed Christians who had been Jews, and that the design is to reprove faults which prevailed among them. It is not supposed indeed, by those who hold this opinion, that *all* of those who were rich among them were guilty of the sins here adverted to, nor even that they were very prevalent among them. The rebuke would be proper if the sins here referred to existed at all, and were practised by any who bore the Christian name. As to any improbability that professed Christians would be guilty of these faults, it might be remarked that the period has been rare in the church, if it has occurred at all, in which all that is here said of ' rich men ' would not be applicable to *some* members of the church. Certainly it is applicable in all those countries where slavery prevails; in countries where religion is allied to the state; in all places where the mass are poor, and the few are rich. It would be difficult now to find any extended church on earth in relation to which the denunciation here would not be applicable to some of its members. But still it can hardly be supposed that men were tolerated in the church, in the times of the apostles, who were guilty of the oppressions and wrongs here referred to, or who lived in the manner here specified. It is true, indeed, that such men have been, and are still found,

CHAPTER V.

G O to now, *ye* rich *ᵃ*men, weep and howl for your miseries that shall come upon *you.*

2 Your riches *ᵇ* are corrupted, and your garments are moth-eaten.*ᶜ*

a Pr.11.28; Lu.6.24. *b* Jer.17.11. *c* Job 13.28.

in the Christian church; but we should not, without the clearest proof, suppose that such cases existed in the times of the apostles. (3.) The correct opinion therefore seems to be, that the design of the apostle in this chapter was to encourage and strengthen poor and oppressed Christians; to impart consolation to those who, under the exactions of rich men, were suffering wrong. In doing this, nothing would be more natural than for him first to declare his views in regard to those who were guilty of these wrongs, and who made use of the power which wealth gave to injure those in the humble walks of life. This he does in the form of an address to rich men—not perhaps expecting that *they* would see what he had written, but with a design to set before those to whom he wrote, and for whose benefit the statement is made, in a vivid manner, the nature of the wrongs under which they were suffering, and the nature of the punishment which must come upon those who oppressed them. Nothing would tend more effectually to reconcile those to whom he wrote to their own lot, or do more to encourage them to bear their trials with patience. At the same time, nothing would do more to keep them from envying the lot of the rich, or desiring the wealth which was connected with such a mode of life.

II. The apostle exhorts those who were suffering under these wrongs to exercise patience, vers. 7–11. He encourages them with the hope that the Lord would come; he refers them to the example of the farmer, who waits long for the fruit of the earth; he cautions them against indulging in hard feelings and thoughts against others more prospered than they were; he refers them, as examples of patience, to the prophets, to the case of Job, and to the Lord Jesus himself.

III. He adverts to a fault among them on the subject of *swearing*, ver. 12. This subject is introduced here apparently because they were in danger,

through impatience, of expressing themselves in a severe manner, and even of uttering imprecations on those who oppressed them. To guard against this, he exhorts them to control their temper, and to confine themselves in their conversation to a simple affirmative or denial.

IV. He refers to the case of those who were sick and afflicted among them, and directs them what to do, vers. 14–18. The duty of those who were sick was to employ prayer—as the duty of those who were in health and prosperity was praise. The afflicted were to pray; the sick were to call for the elders of the church, who were to pray over them, and to anoint them with the oil in the name of the Lord, not as 'extreme unction,' or *with a view to their dying,* but *with a view to their living.* To encourage them thus to call in the aid of praying men, he refers them to an illustrious instance of the power of prayer in the case of Elijah.

V. In the close of the chapter and of the epistle, the apostle adverts to the possibility that some among them might err from the truth, and urges the duty of endeavouring to convert such, vers. 19, 20. To encourage them to do this, he states the important consequences which would follow where such an effort would be successful. He who should do this, would have the satisfaction of saving a soul from death, and would hide from the universe a multitude of sins, which otherwise, in the case of the erring brother, could not but have been exposed in the great day of judgment.

1. *Go to now.* Notes on chap. iv. 13. ¶ Ye *rich men.* Not *all* rich men, but only that class of them who are specified as unjust and oppressive. There is no sin in merely being rich; where sin exists peculiarly among the rich, it arises from the manner in which wealth is acquired, the spirit which it tends to engender in the heart, and the way in which it is used. Comp. Notes on Luke vi. 24; 1 Tim. vi. 9. ¶ *Weep and*

3 Your gold and silver is cankered; and the rust of them shall be a witness against you, and shall

eat your flesh as it were fire. Ye have heaped *a* treasure together for the last days.

a Rom.2.5.

howl. Gr., ' Weep howling.' This would be expressive of very deep distress. The language is intensive in a high degree, showing that the calamities which were coming upon them were not only such as would produce tears, but tears accompanied with loud lamentations. In the East, it is customary to give expression to deep sorrow by loud outcries. Comp. Isa. xiii. 6; xiv. 31; xv. 2; xvi. 7; Jer. iv. 8; xlvii. 2; Joel i. 5. ¶ *For your miseries that shall come upon you.* Many expositors, as Benson, Whitby, Macknight, and others, suppose that this refers to the approaching destruction of Jerusalem by the Romans, and to the miseries which would be brought in the siege upon the Jewish people, in which the *rich* would be the peculiar objects of cupidity and vengeance. They refer to passages in Josephus, which describe particularly the sufferings to which the rich were exposed; the searching of their houses by the zealots, and the heavy calamities which came upon them and their families. But there is no reason to suppose that the apostle referred particularly to those events. The poor as well as the rich suffered in that siege, and there were no such special judgments then brought upon the rich as to show that they were the marked objects of the Divine displeasure. It is much more natural to suppose that the apostle means to say that such men as he here refers to exposed themselves always to the wrath of God, and that they had great reason to weep in the anticipation of his vengeance. The sentiments here expressed by the apostle are not applicable merely to the Jews of his time. If there is any class of men which has special reason to dread the wrath of God at all times, it is just the class of men here referred to. 2. *Your riches are corrupted.* The word here rendered *corrupted* (σήπω) does not occur elsewhere in the New Testament. It means, to cause to rot, to corrupt. to destroy. The reference

here is to their hoarded treasures; and the idea is, that they had accumulated more than they needed for their own use; and that, instead of distributing them to do good to others, or employing them in any useful way, they kept them until they rotted or spoiled. It is to be remembered, that a considerable part of the treasures which a man in the East would lay up, consisted of perishable materials, as garments, grain, oil, etc. Such articles of property were often stored up, expecting that they would furnish a supply for many years, in case of the prevalence of famine or wars. Comp. Luke xii. 18, 19. A suitable provision for the time to come cannot be forbidden; but the reference here is to cases in which great quantities had been laid up, perhaps while the poor were suffering, and which were kept until they became worthless. ¶ *Your garments are moth-eaten.* The same idea substantially is expressed here in another form. As the fashions in the East did not change as they do with us, wealth consisted much in the garments that were laid up for show or for future use. See Notes on Matt. vi. 19. Q. Curtius says that when Alexander the Great was going to take Persepolis, the riches of all Asia were gathered there together, which consisted not only of a great abundance of gold and silver, but also of garments, Lib. vi. c. 5. Horace tells us that when Lucullus the Roman was asked if he could lend a hundred garments for the theatre, he replied that he had five thousand in his house, of which they were welcome to take part or all. Of course, such property would be liable to be moth-eaten; and the idea here is, that they had amassed a great amount of this kind of property which was useless to them, and which they kept until it became destroyed. 3. *Your gold and silver is cankered.* That is, that you have heaped together, by injustice and fraud, a large amount, and have kept it from those to whom it

4 Behold, the hire *a* of the labourers who have reaped down your fields, which is of you kept back by

a Jer.22.13; Mal.3.5.

fraud, crieth: and the cries of them which have reaped are entered *b* into the ears of the Lord of sabaoth.

b Ex.22.27.

is due, (ver. 4,) until it has become corroded. The word rendered *is cankered*, (*κατίωται*,) does not occur elsewhere in the New Testament. It properly means, *to cause to rust; to rust out, (Passow;) to be corroded with rust, (Robinson;)* to be spotted with rust. It is true that gold and silver do not properly *rust*, or become *oxidized*, and that they will not be corroded like iron and steel; but by being kept long in a damp place they will contract a dark colour, resembling rust in appearance. This seems to be the idea in the mind of the apostle. He speaks of gold and silver as they *appear* after having been long laid up without use; and undoubtedly the *word* which he uses here is one which would to an ancient have expressed that idea, as well as the mere literal idea of the *rusting* or *oxidizing* of metals. There is no reason to suppose that the word was then used in the strict chemical sense of *rusting*, for there is no reason to suppose that the nature of oxidization was then fully understood. ¶ *And the rust of them.* Another word is used here—*ἰὸς.* This properly denotes something sent out or emitted, (from *ἵημι*,) and is applied to a missile weapon, as an arrow; to poison, as emitted from the tooth of a serpent; and to *rust*, as it seems to be emitted from metals. The word refers to the dark discoloration which appears on gold and silver, when they have remained long without use. ¶ *Shall be a witness against you.* That is, the rust or discoloration shall bear testimony against you that the money is not used as it should be, either in paying those to whom it is due, or in doing good to others. Among the ancients, the gold and silver which any óne possessed was laid up in some secret and safe place. Comp. Notes on Isa. xlv. 3. There were no banks then in which money might be deposited; there were few ways of investing money so as to produce regular interest; there were no corporations to employ money in joint operations; and it was not very common to invest money in the purchase of real

estate, and stocks and mortgages were little known. ¶ *And shall eat your flesh as it were fire.* This cannot be taken literally. It must mean that the effect would be *as if* it should corrode or consume their very flesh; that is, the fact of their laying up treasures would be followed by painful consequences. The thought is very striking, and the language in which it is conveyed is singularly bold and energetic. The effect of thus heaping up treasure will be as corroding as fire in the flesh. The reference is to the punishment which God would bring on them for their avarice and injustice—effects that will come on all now for the same offences. ¶ *Ye have heaped treasure together for the last days.* The day of judgment; the closing scenes of this world. You have been heaping up treasure; but it will be treasure of a different kind from what you have supposed. It is treasure not laid up for ostentation, or luxury, or use in future life, but treasure the true worth of which will be seen at the judgment-day. So Paul speaks of 'treasuring up wrath against the day of wrath, and revelation of the righteous judgment of God,' Rom. ii. 5. There are many who suppose they are accumulating property that may be of use to them, or that may secure them the reputation of possessing great wealth, who are in fact accumulating a most fearful treasure against the day of final retribution. Every man who is rich should examine himself closely to see whether there is anything in the manner in which he has gained his property, or in which he now holds it, that will expose him to the wrath of God in the last day. That on which he so much prides himself may yet bring down on him the vengeance of heaven; and in the day of judgment he may curse his own madness and folly in wasting his probation in efforts to amass property.

4. *Behold, the hire of the labourers who have reaped down your fields.* In the previous verses the form of the sin which the apostle specified was that

they had *hoarded* their property. He now states another form of their guilt, that, while doing this, they had withheld what was due from the very labourers who had cultivated their fields, and to whose labour they were indebted for what they had. The phrase 'who have reaped down your fields,' is used to denote labour in general. This particular thing is specified, perhaps, because the reaping of the harvest seems to be more immediately connected with the accumulation of property. What is said here, however, will apply to all kinds of labour. It may be remarked, also, that the sin condemned here is one that may exist not only in reference to those who are hired to cultivate a farm, but to *all* in our employ—to day-labourers, to mechanics, to seamen, etc. It will apply, in an eminent degree, to those who hold others in slavery, and who live by their unrequited toils. The very essence of slavery is, that the slave shall produce by his labour so much *more* than he receives for his own maintenance as to support the master and his family in indolence. The slave is to do the work which the master would otherwise be obliged to do; the advantage of the system is supposed to be that the master is not under a necessity of labouring at all. The amount which the slave receives is not *presumed* to oe what is a fair equivalent for what he does, or what a freeman could be hired for; but so much *less* than his labour is fairly worth, as to be a source of so much *gain* to the master. If slaves were fairly compensated for their labour; if they received what was understood to be a just *price* for what they do, or what they would be willing to bargain for if they were free, the system would at once come to an end. No owner of a slave would keep him if he did not suppose that out of his unrequited toil he might make money, or might be relieved himself from the necessity of labour. He who hires a freeman to reap down his fields pays what the freeman regards as a fair equivalent for what he does; he who employs a slave does *not* give what the slave would regard as an equivalent, and expects that what he gives will be so much *less* than an equivalent, that he may be free alike from the ne-

cessity of labour and of paying him what he has fairly earned. The very *essence* of slavery, therefore, is fraud; and there is nothing to which the remarks of the apostle here are more applicable than to that unjust and oppressive system. ¶ *Which is of you kept back by fraud.* The Greek word here used (ἀποστερέω) is rendered *defraud,* in Mark x. 10; 1 Cor. vi. 7, 8; vii. 5; and *destitute,* in 1 Tim. vi. 5. It occurs nowhere else, except in the passage before us. It means to deprive of, with the notion that that to which it is applied was *due* to one, or that he had a *claim* on it. The *fraud* referred to in keeping it back, may be anything by which the payment is withheld, or the claim evaded—whether it be mere neglect to pay it; or some advantage taken in making the bargain; or some evasion of the law; or mere vexatious delay; or such superior power that he to whom it is due cannot enforce the payment; or such a system that he to whom it is fairly due is supposed in the laws to have no rights, and to be incapable of suing or being sued. Any one of these things would come under the denomination of *fraud.* ¶ *Crieth.* That is, cries out to God for punishment. The voice of this wrong goes up to heaven. ¶ *And the cries of them which have reaped are entered into the ears of the Lord of sabaoth.* That is, he hears them, and he will attend to their cry. Comp. Exod. xxii. 27. They are oppressed and wronged; they have none to regard their cry on earth, and to redress their wrongs, and they go and appeal to that God who *will* regard their cry, and avenge them. On the phrase 'Lord of sabaoth,' or *Lord of hosts,* for so the word *sabaoth* means, see Notes on Isa. i. 9, and Rom. ix. 29. Perhaps by the use of the word here it is implied that the God to whom they cry—the mighty Ruler of all worlds—is *able* to vindicate them. It may be added, that the cry of the oppressed and the wronged is going up constantly from all parts of the earth, and is always heard by God. In his own time he will come forth to vindicate the oppressed, and to punish the oppressor. It may be added, also, that if what is here said were regarded as it should be by all

5 Ye have lived in pleasure *a on the earth, and been wanton; ye have nourished your hearts, as in a day of slaughter.

a Lu.16.19,25.

men, slavery, as well as other systems of wrong, would soon come to an end. If everywhere the workman was fairly paid for his earnings; if the poor slave who cultivates the fields of the rich were properly compensated for his toil; if he received what a freeman would contract to do the work for; if there was no *fraud* in withholding what he earns, the system would soon cease in the earth. Slavery could not live a day if this were done. Now there is no such compensation; but the cry of oppressed millions will continue to go up to heaven, and the period must come when the system shall cease. Either the master must be brought to such a sense of right that he will be disposed to do justice, and let the oppressed go free; or God will so impoverish the lands where the system prevails as to make all men see that the system is unprofitable and ruinous as compared with free labour; or the oppressed will somehow become so acquainted with their own strength and their rights that they shall arise and assert their freedom; or under the prevalence of true religion better views will prevail, and oppressors, turned to God, shall relax the yoke of bondage; or God will so bring heavy judgments in his holy providence on the oppresssors, that the system of slavery will everywhere come to an end on the earth. Nothing is more certain than that the whole system is condemned by the passage of Scripture before us; that it is contrary to the genuine spirit of Christianity, and that the prevalence of true religion would bring it to an end. Probably *all* slaveholders feel that to place the Bible in the hands of slaves, and to instruct them to read it, would be inconsistent with the perpetuity of the system. Yet a system which cannot survive the most full and free circulation of the sacred Scriptures, *must* be founded in wrong.

5. *Ye have lived in pleasure on the earth.* One of the things to which the rich are peculiarly addicted. Their wealth is supposed to be of value, because it furnishes them the means of doing it. Comp. Luke xii. 19; xvi. 19.

The word translated 'lived in pleasure, (τρυφάω) occurs only here in the New Testament. It means, to live delicately, luxuriously, at ease. There is not in the word essentially the idea or *vicious* indulgence, but that which characterizes those who live for enjoyment. They lived in ease and affluence on the avails of the labours of others; they indulged in what gratified the taste, and pleased the ear and the eye, while those who contributed the means of this were groaning under oppression. A life of mere indolence and ease, of delicacy and luxury, is nowhere countenanced in the Bible; and even where unconnected with oppression and wrong to others, such a mode of living is regarded as inconsistent with the purpose for which God made man, and placed him on the earth. See Luke xii. 19, 20. Every man has high and solemn duties to perform, and there is enough to be done on earth to give employment to every human being, and to fill up every hour in a profitable and useful way. ¶ *And been wanton.* This word now probably conveys to most minds a sense which is not in the original. Our English word is now commonly used in the sense of *lewd, lustful, lascivious.* It was, however, formerly used in the sense of *sportive, joyous, gay,* and was applied to anything that was variable or fickle. The Greek word used here (σπαταλάω) means, to live luxuriously or voluptuously. Comp. Notes on 1 Tim. v. 6, where the word is explained. It does not refer necessarily to gross criminal pleasures, though the kind of living here referred to often leads to such indulgences. There is a close connection between what the apostle says here, and what he refers to in the previous verses—the oppression of others, and the withholding of what is due to those who labour. Such acts of oppression and wrong are commonly resorted to in order to obtain the means of luxurious living, and the gratification of sensual pleasures. In all countries where slavery exists, the things here referred to are found in close connection. The fraud and wrong by which the re-

6 Ye have condemned *and* killed
a Mat.5.39.

ward of hard toil is withheld from the
slave is connected with indolence and
sensual indulgence on the part of the
master. ¶ *Ye have nourished your
hearts.* Or, yourselves—the word *hearts*
here being equivalent to *themselves.*
The meaning is, that they appeared to
have been *fattening* themselves, like
stall-fed beasts, for the day of slaughter.
As cattle are carefully fed, and are fattened *with a view* to their being slaugh-
tered, so they seemed to have been fattened for the slaughter that was to
come on them—the day of vengeance.
Thus many now live. They do no work;
they contribute nothing to the good of
society; they are mere consumers—
fruges, consumere nati; and, like stall-
fed cattle, they seem to live only with
reference to the day of slaughter, and
to the recompense which awaits them
after death. ¶ *As in a day of slaughter.*
There has been much variety in the
interpretation of this expression. Robinson (*Lex.*) renders it, 'like beasts in
the day of slaughter, without care or
forethought.' Rosenmüller (*Morgenland*) supposes that it means, *as in a
festival;* referring, as he thinks, to the
custom among the ancients of having a
feast when a part of the animal was
consumed in sacrifice, and the rest was
eaten by the worshippers. So Benson.
On such occasions, indulgence was given
to appetite almost without limit; and
the idea then would be, that they had
given themselves up to a life of pampered
luxury. But probably the more correct
idea is, that they had fattened themselves as for the day of destruction; that
is, as animals are fattened for slaughter.
They lived only to eat and drink, and
to enjoy life. But, by such a course,
they were as certainly preparing for
perdition, as cattle were prepared to be
killed by being stall-fed.
6. *Ye have condemned* and *killed the
just.* τὸν δίκαιον—*the just one,* or *the
just man*—for the word used is in the
singular number. This may either refer
to the condemnation and crucifixion of
Christ—meaning that their conduct towards his people had been similar to the
treatment of the Saviour, and was in

the just; *and* he doth not resist
a you.

fact a condemnation and crucifixion of
him afresh; or, that by their rejection
of him in order to live in sin, they in
fact condemned him and his religion; or,
that they had condemned and killed *the
just man*—meaning that they had persecuted those who were Christians; or,
that by their harsh treatment of others
in withholding what was due to them,
they had deprived them of the means of
subsistence, and had, as it were, killed
the righteous. Probably the true meaning is, that it was one of their characteristics that they had been guilty of
wrong towards good men. Whether it
refers, however, to any particular act of
violence, or to such a course as would
wear out their lives by a system of oppression, injustice, and fraud, cannot
now be determined. ¶ And *he doth not
resist you.* Some have supposed that
this refers to God, meaning that *he* did
not oppose them; that is, that he bore
with them patiently while they did it.
Others suppose that it should be read as
a question—'and doth he not resist you?'
meaning that God would oppose them,
and punish them for their acts of oppression and wrong. But probably the true
reference is to the 'just man' whom
they condemned and killed; meaning
that they were so powerful that all
attempts to resist them would be vain,
and that the injured and oppressed could
do nothing but submit patiently to their
acts of injustice and violence. The sense
may be either that they could not oppose
them—the rich men being so powerful,
and they who were oppressed so feeble;
or that they bore their wrongs with
meekness, and did not attempt it. The
sins, therefore, condemned in these verses (1–6), and for which it is said the
Divine vengeance would come upon those
referred to, are these four: (1,) that of
hoarding up money when it was unnecessary for their real support and comfort, and when they might do so much
good with it, (comp. Matt. vi. 19;) (2,)
that of keeping back the wages which
was due to those who cultivated their
fields; that is, keeping back what would
be a fair compensation for their toil—
applicable alike to hired men and to

7 ¹ Be patient therefore, brethren, unto the coming of the Lord. Behold, the husbandman waiteth for

1 Or, Be long patient ; or, Suffer with long patience.

slaves; (3,) that of giving themselves up to a life of ease, luxury, and sensual indulgence; and, (4,) that of wronging and oppressing good and just men—men, perhaps in humble life, who were unable to vindicate their rights, and who had none to undertake their cause; men who were too feeble to offer successful resistance, or who were restrained by their principles from attempting it. It is needless to say that there are multitudes of such persons now on the earth, and that they have the same reason to dread the Divine vengeance which the same class had in the time of the apostle James.

7. *Be patient therefore, brethren.* That is, under such wrongs as the apostle had described in the previous verses. Those whom he addressed were doubtless suffering under those oppressions, and his object was to induce them to bear their wrongs without murmuring and without resistance. One of the methods of doing this was by showing *them*, in an address to their rich oppressors, that those who injured and wronged them would be suitably punished at the day of judgment, or that their cause was in the hands of God; and another method of doing it was by the direct inculcation of the duty of patience. Comp. Notes on Matt. v. 38–41, 43–45. The margin here is, *be long patient,* or *suffer with long patience.* The sense of the Greek is, ' be long-suffering, or let not your patience be exhausted. Your courage, vigour, and forbearance is not to be *short-lived,* but is to be *enduring.* Let it continue as long as there is need of it, even to the coming of the Lord. Then you will be released from sufferings.' ¶ *Unto the coming of the Lord.* The coming of the Lord Jesus—either to remove you by death, or to destroy the city of Jerusalem and bring to an end the Jewish institutions, or to judge the world and receive his people to himself. The ' coming of the Lord ' in any way was an event which Christians were taught to expect, and which would be

the precious fruit of the earth, and hath long patience for it, until he receive the early *ᵃ* and latter rain.

a De.11.14.

connected with their deliverance from troubles. As the *time* of his appearing was not revealed, it was not improper to refer to that as an event that might *possibly* be near; and as the removal of Christians by death is denoted by the phrase ' the coming of the Lord '—that is, his coming to each one of us—it was not improper to speak of death in that view. On the general subject of the expectations entertained among the early Christians of the second advent of the Saviour, see Notes on 1 Cor. xv. 51; 2 Thess. ii. 2, 3. ¶ *Behold, the husbandman waiteth for the precious fruit of the earth.* The farmer waits patiently for the grain to grow. It requires time to mature the crop, and he does not become impatient. The idea seems to be, that we should wait for things to develope themselves in their proper season, and should not be impatient before that season arrives. In due time we may expect the harvest to be ripened. We cannot hasten it. We cannot control the rain, the sun, the season; and the farmer therefore patiently waits until in the regular course of events he has a harvest. So we cannot control and hasten the events which are in God's own keeping; and we should patiently wait for the developments of his will, and the arrangements of his providence, by which we may obtain what we desire. ¶ *And hath long patience for it.* That is, his patience is not exhausted. It extends through the whole time in which, by the Divine arrangements, he may expect a harvest. ¶ *Until he receive the early and latter rain.* In the climate of Palestine there are two rainy seasons, on which the harvest essentially depends—the autumnal and the spring rains—called here and elsewhere in the Scriptures *the early and the latter rains.* See Deut. xi. 14; Job xxix. 23; Jer. v. 24. The autumnal or early rains of Scripture, usually commence in the latter half of October or the beginning of November; not suddenly, but by degrees, which gives opportunity for the

8 Be ye also patient; stablish your hearts: for *a* the coming of the Lord draweth nigh.

a Re.22.20.

husbandman to sow his fields of wheat and barley. The rains come mostly from the west or south-west, continuing for two or three days at a time, and falling especially during the nights. The wind then chops round to the north or east, and several days of fine weather succeed. During the months of November and December the rains continue to fall heavily; afterwards they return only at longer intervals, and are less heavy; but at no period during the winter do they entirely cease to occur. Snow often falls in Jerusalem, in January and February, to the depth of a foot or more, but it does not last long. Rain continues to fall more or less through the month of March, but it is rare after that period. At the present time there are not any particular periods of rain, or successions of showers, which might be regarded as distinct rainy seasons. The whole period from October to March now constitutes only one continued rainy season, without any regularly intervening time of prolonged fair weather. Unless, therefore, there has been some change in the climate since the times of the New Testament, the early and the latter rains for which the husbandman waited with longing, seem rather to have implied the first showers of autumn, which revived the parched and thirsty earth, and prepared it for the seed; and the latter showers of spring, which continued to refresh and forward the ripening crops and the vernal products of the fields. In ordinary seasons, from the cessation of the showers in spring until their commencement in October or November, rain never falls,and the sky is usually serene.—*Robinson's Biblical Researches*, vol. ii.,pp. 96–100.

8. *Be ye also patient.* As the farmer is. In due time, as he expects the return of the rain, so you may anticipate deliverance from your trials. ¶ *Stablish your hearts.* Let your purposes and your faith be firm and unwavering. Do not become weary and fretful; but bear with constancy all that is laid upon you, until the time of your deliverance shall come ¶ *For the coming of the Lord draweth nigh.* Comp. Rev. xxii. 10, 12, 20; Notes, 1 Cor. xv. 51. It is clear, I think, from this place, that the apostle expected that that which *he* understood by 'the coming of the Lord' was soon to occur; for it was to be that by which *they* would obtain deliverance from the trials which they then endured. See ver. 7. Whether it means that he was soon to come to judgment, or to bring to an end the Jewish policy and to set up his kingdom on the earth, or that they would soon be removed by death, cannot be determined from the mere use of the language. The most natural interpretation of the passage, and one which will accord well with the time when the epistle was written, is, that the predicted time of the destruction of Jerusalem (Matt. xxiv.) was at hand; that there were already indications that that would soon occur; and that there was a prevalent expectation among Christians that that event would be a release from many trials of persecution, and would be followed by the setting up of the Redeemer's kingdom. Perhaps many expected that the judgment would occur at that time, and that the Saviour would set up a personal reign on the earth. But the expectation of others might have been merely—what is indeed all that is necessarily implied in the predictions on the subject—that there would be after that a rapid and extensive spread of the principles of the Christian religion in the world. The destruction of Jerusalem and of the temple would contribute to that by bringing to an end the whole system of Jewish types and sacrifices; by convincing Christians that there was not to be one central rallying-point, thus destroying their lingering prejudices in favour of the Jewish mode of worship; and by scattering them abroad through the world to propagate the new religion. The epistle was written, it is supposed, some ten or twelve years before the destruction of Jerusalem, (Intro., § 3,) and it is not improbable that there were already some indications of that approaching event.

9 ¹ Grudge not one against another, brethren, lest ye be condemned : behold, the Judge standeth ᵃ before the door.

10 Take, my brethren, the prophets, who have spoken in the name of the Lord, for an example of suffering affliction, ᵇ and of patience.

11 Behold, we count them ᶜ happy which endure. Ye have heard of the patience ᵈ of Job, and have seen the end ᵉ of the Lord ; that the Lord is very pitiful, and of tender mercy.

1 Or *Groan*; or, *grieve.* ᵃ Re.3.20. ᵇ He.11.35-38. ᶜ Ps.94.12; Mat.5.10. ᵈ Job 1.21,&c. ᵉ Job 42.10,&c.

9. *Grudge not one against another.* Marg., '*groan, grieve.*' The Greek word (στινάζω) means, *to sigh, to groan,* as of persons in distress, (Rom. viii. 23 ;) and then to sigh or groan through impatience, fretfulness, ill-humour; and hence *to murmur, to find fault, to complain.* The exact idea here is, not that of *grudging* in the sense of dissatisfaction with what others possess, or of being envious; it is that of being fretful and impatient—or, to use a common word which more exactly expresses the sense that of *grumbling.* This may arise from many causes; either because others have advantages which we have not, and we are discontented and unhappy, as if it were *wrong* in them to have such enjoyments; or because we, without reason, suppose they intend to slight and neglect us; or because we are ready to take offence at any little thing, and to 'pick a quarrel' with them. There are some persons who are always *grumbling.* They have a sour, dissatisfied, discontented temper; they see no excellence in other persons; they are displeased that others are more prospered, honoured, and beloved than they are themselves; they are always complaining of what others do, not because they are injured, but because others seem to them to be weak and foolish; they seem to feel that it becomes them to complain if everything is not done precisely as in their estimation it should be. It is needless to say that this spirit —the offspring of pride—will make any man lead a wretched life ; and equally needless to say that it is wholly contrary to the spirit of the gospel. Comp. Luke iii. 14; Phil. iv. 11 ; 1 Tim. vi. 8; Heb. xiii. 5. ¶ *Lest ye be condemned.* That is, for *judging* others with this spirit—for this spirit is in fact *judging* them. Comp. Notes on Matt. vii. 1. ¶ *Behold, the judge standeth*

before the door. The Lord Jesus, who is soon to come to judge the world. See ver. 8. He is, as it were, even now approaching the door—so near that he can hear all that you say.

10. *Take, my brethren, the prophets.* That is, in your trials and persecutions. To encourage them to the exercise of patience, he points them to the example of those who had trod the same thorny path before them. The prophets were in general a much persecuted race of men; and the argument on which the apostle relies from their example is this :—(1,) that if the prophets were persecuted and tried, it may be expected that other good men will be; (2,) that they showed such patience in their trials as to be a model for us. ¶ *An example of suffering affliction.* That is, they showed us how evils are to be borne.

11. *Behold, we count them happy which endure.* The word rendered ' we count them happy' (μακαρίζομεν,) occurs only here and in Luke i. 48, where it is rendered ' *shall call* me *blessed.*' The word μακάριος (*blessed,* or *happy,*) however, occurs often. See Matt. v. 3-11; xi. 6 ; xiii. 6, *et sæpe.* The sense here is, we speak of their patience with commendation. They have done what they ought to do, and their name is honoured and blessed. ¶ *Ye have heard of the patience of Job.* As one of the most illustrious instances of patient sufferers. See Job i. 21. The book of Job was written, among other reasons, to show that true religion would *bear* any form of trial to which it could be subjected. See Job i. 9-11 ; ii. 5, 6. ¶ *And have seen the end of the Lord.* That is, the end or design which the Lord had in the trials of Job, or the result to which he brought the case at last—to wit, that he showed himself to be very merciful to the poor sufferer ; that he met him with the expressions of his approbation

12 But above all things, my brethren, swear *a* not, neither by heaven, neither by the earth, neither

a Mat.5.34,&c.

by any other oath : but let your yea
be yea, and *your* nay, nay ; lest ye
fall into condemnation.

13 Is any among you afflicted?

---

for the manner in which he bore his
trials ; and that he doubled his former
possessions, and restored him to more
than his former happiness and honour.
See Job xlii. Augustine, Luther, Wetstein, and others, understand this as referring to the death of the Lord Jesus,
and as meaning that they had seen the
manner in which he suffered death, as
an example for us. But, though this
might strike many as the true interpretation, yet the objections to it are insuperable. (1.) It does not accord with
the proper meaning of the word *end*,
(τέλος). That word is in no instance
applied to *death*, nor does it properly
express death. It properly denotes an
end, term, termination, completion ;
and is used in the following senses :—
(*a*) to denote the end, the termination,
or the *last* of anything, Mark iii. 26 ;
1 Cor. xv. 24 ; Luke xxi. 9 ; Heb. vii.
3 ; (*b*) an event, issue, or result, Matt.
xxvi. 58 ; Rom. vi. 21 ; 2 Cor. xi. 18 ;
(*c*) the final purpose, that to which all
the parts tend, and in which they terminate, 1 Tim. i. 5 ; (*d*) tax, custom,
or tribute — what is paid for public
ends or purposes, Matt. xvii. 25 ; Rom.
xiii. 7. (2) This interpretation, referring it to the death of the Saviour,
would not accord with the remark of
the apostle in the close of the verse,
' that the Lord is very merciful.' That
is, what he says was ' *seen*,' or this was
what was particularly illustrated in the
case referred to. Yet this was not *particularly* seen in the death of the Lord
Jesus. He was indeed most patient and
submissive in his death, and it is true
that he showed mercy to the penitent
malefactor ; but this was not the particular and most prominent trait which
he evinced in his death. Besides, if it
had been, that would not have been the
thing to which the apostle would have
referred here. His object was to recommend *patience under trials ;* and this he
does by showing (*a*) that Job was an
eminent instance of it, and (*b*) that the

result was such as to encourage us to
be patient. The *end* or the *result* of
the Divine dealings in his case was,
that the Lord was ' very pitiful and of
tender mercy ;' and we may hope that it
will be so in our case, and should therefore be encouraged to be patient under
our trials. ¶ *That the Lord is very
pitiful.* As he showed deep compassion
in the case of Job, we have equal reason to suppose that he will in our own.
12. *But above all things.* That is
be especially careful on this point ;
whatever else is done, let not this be.
The manner in which James speaks of
the practice referred to here, shows that
he regarded it as a sin of a very heinous nature ; one that was by all means
to be avoided by those whom he addressed. The habit of swearing by various things was a very common one
among the Jews, and it was important
to guard those who from among them
had been converted to Christianity on
that subject. ¶ *Swear not.* See this
command illustrated in the Notes on
Matt. v. 33, 34. Nearly the same
things are mentioned here, as objects
by which they were accustomed to
swear, which are referred to by the
Saviour. ¶ *But let your yea be yea.*
Let there be a simple affirmation, unaccompanied by any oath or appeal
to God or to any of his works. A man
who makes that his common method of
speech is the man who will be believed.
See Notes on Matt. v. 37. ¶ *Lest you
fall into condemnation.* That is, for
profaning the name of God. ' The Lord
will not hold him guiltless that taketh
his name in vain,' Exod. xx. 7.
13. *Is any among you afflicted ?* By
sickness, bereavement, disappointment,
persecutions, loss of health or property.
The word used here refers to suffering
evil of any kind, (κακοπαθεῖ.) ¶ *Let
him pray.* That is, prayer is appropriate to trial. The mind naturally resorts
to it, and in every way it is proper.
God only can remove the source of sorrow ; he can grant unto us ' a happy

let *a* him pray. Is any merry? let him sing psalms.

14 Is any sick *c* among you? let

a 2 Ch.33.12; Jonah 2.2,&c.   *b* Ep.5.19.   *c* Mar.16.18.

him call for the elders of the church; and let them pray over him, anointing him with oil in the name of the Lord:

---

issue out of all our afflictions;' he can make them the means of sanctifying the soul. Comp. 2 Chron. xxxiii. 12; Ps. xxxiv. 4; cvii. 6, 13, 28. It matters not what is the form of the trial, it is a privilege which all have to go to God in prayer. And it is an inestimable privilege. Health fails, friends die, property is lost, disappointments come upon us, danger threatens, death approaches—and to whom shall we go but to God? He ever lives. He never fails us or disappoints us if we trust in him, and his ear is ever open to our cries. This would be a sad world indeed, if it were not for the privilege of prayer. The last resource of millions who suffer—for millions suffer every day—would be taken away, if men were denied the access to the throne of grace. As it is, there is no one so poor that he may not pray; no one so disconsolate and forsaken that he may not find in God a friend; no one so broken-hearted that he is not able to bind up his spirit. One of the *designs* of affliction is to lead us to the throne of grace; and it is a happy result of trials if we are led by our trials to seek God in prayer. ¶ *Is any merry?* The word *merry* now conveys an idea which is not properly found in the original word here. It refers now, in common usage, to light and noisy pleasure; to that which is jovial; to that which is attended with laughter, or which causes laughter, as a *merry* jest. In the Scriptures, however, the word properly denotes *cheerful, pleasant, agreeable*, and is applied to a state of mind free from trouble—the opposite of affliction—happy, Prov. xv. 13, 15; xvii. 22; Isa. xxiv. 7; Luke xv. 23, 24, 29, 32. The Greek word used here (*εὐθυμεῖ*) means, literally, *to have the mind well*, (*εὖ* and *θυμός*;) that is, to have it happy, or free from trouble; to be cheerful. ¶ *Let him sing psalms.* That is, if any one is happy; if he is in health, and is prospered; if he has his friends around him, and there is nothing to produce

anxiety; if he has the free exercise of conscience and enjoys religion, it is proper to express that in notes of praise. Comp. Eph. v. 19, 20. On the meaning of the word here rendered 'sing psalms,' see Notes, Eph. v. 19, where it is rendered *making melody.* It does not mean to sing *psalms* in contradistinction from singing *hymns*, but the reference is to any songs of praise. Praise is appropriate to such a state of mind. The heart naturally gives utterance to its emotions in songs of thanksgiving. The sentiment in this verse is well expressed in the beautiful stanza,

In every joy that crowns my days,
In every pain I bear,
My heart shall find delight in praise,
Or seek relief in prayer.

Mrs. Williams.

14. *Is any sick among you?* In the previous verse the reference was to affliction in general, and the duty there urged was one that was applicable to all forms of trial. The subject of sickness, however, is so important, since it so often occurs, that a specific direction was desirable. That direction is to call in the aid of others to lead our thoughts, and to aid us in our devotions, because one who is sick is less able to direct his own reflections and to pray for himself than he is in other forms of trial. Nothing is said here respecting the *degree* of sickness, whether it is that which would be fatal if these means were used or not; but the direction pertains to any kind of illness. ¶ *Let him call for the elders of the church.* Gr. *presbyters.* See Notes on Acts xv. 2; xi. 30. It cannot be supposed that this refers to the *apostles*, for it could not be that they would be always accessible; besides, instructions like this were designed to have a permanent character, and to be applicable to the church at all times and in all places. The reference, therefore, is doubtless to the ordinary religious teachers of the congregation; the officers of the church intrusted with its spiritual interests. The spirit of the command would embrace those

who are pastors, and any others to whom the spiritual interests of the congregation are confided—ruling elders, deacons, etc. If the allusion is to the ordinary officers of the church, it is evident that the cure to be hoped for (ver. 15) was not *miraculous*, but was that to be expected in the use of appropriate means accompanied by prayer. It may be added, as worthy of note, that the apostle says they should '*call*' for the elders of the church; that is, they should *send* for them. They should not *wait* for them to hear of their sickness, as they might happen to, but they should cause them to be informed of it, and give them an opportunity of visiting them and praying with them. Nothing is more common than for persons—even members of the church—to be sick a long time, and to *presume* that their pastor must know all about it; and then they wonder that he does not come to see them, and think hard of him because he does not. A pastor cannot be supposed to know everything; nor can it be presumed that he knows when persons are sick, any more than he can know anything else, unless he is apprized of it; and many hard thoughts, and many suspicions of neglect would be avoided, if, when persons are sick, they would in some way inform their pastor of it. It should always be presumed of a minister of the gospel that he is ready to visit the sick. But how can he go unless he is in some way apprized of the illness of those who need his counsel and his prayers? The sick *send* for their family physician; why should they *presume* that their pastor will know of their illness any more than that their physician will? ¶ *And let them pray over him.* With him, and for him. A man who is sick is often little capable of praying himself; and it is a privilege to have some one to lead his thoughts in devotion. Besides, the prayer of a good man may be of avail in restoring him to health, ver. 15. Prayer is always one important means of obtaining the Divine favour, and there is no place where it is more appropriate than by the bed-side of sickness. That relief from pain may be granted; that the mind may be calm and submissive; that the medicines employed may be blessed to

a restoration to health; that past sins may be forgiven; that he who is sick may be sanctified by his trials; that he may be restored to health, or prepared for his 'last change'—all these are subjects of prayer which we feel to be appropriate in such a case, and every sick man should avail himself of the aid of those who 'have an interest at the throne of grace,' that they may be obtained. ¶ *Anointing him with oil.* Oil, or unguents of various kinds, were much used among the ancients, both in health and in sickness. The oil which was commonly employed was olive oil. See Notes on Isa. i. 6; Luke x. 34. The custom of anointing the sick with oil still prevails in the East, for it is believed to have medicinal or healing properties. Niebuhr (Beschrieb. von Arabien, s. 131) says, 'The southern Arabians believe that to anoint with oil strengthens the body, and secures it against the oppressive heat of the sun, as they go nearly naked. They believe that the oil closes the pores of the skin, and thus prevents the effect of the excessive heat by which the body is so much weakened; perhaps also they regard it as contributing to beauty, by giving the skin a glossy appearance. I myself frequently have observed that the sailors in the ships from Dsjidda and Loheia, as well as the common Arabs in Tehama, anointed their bodies with oil, in order to guard themselves against the heat. The Jews in Mocha assured Mr. Forskal, that the Mohammedans as well as the Jews, in Sana, when they were sick, were accustomed to anoint the body with oil.' *Rosenmüller, Morgenland*, in loc. ¶ *In the name of the Lord.* By the authority or direction of the Lord; or as an act in accordance with his will, and that will meet with his approbation. When we do anything that tends to promote virtue, to alleviate misery, to instruct ignorance, to save life, or to prepare others for heaven, it is right to feel that we are doing it in the name of the Lord Comp., for such uses of the phrase 'in the name of the Lord,' and 'in my name,' Matt. x. 22; xviii. 5, 20; xix. 29; xxiv. 9; Mark. ix. 41; xiii. 13; Luke xxi. 12, 17; Rev. ii. 3; Col. iii. 17. There is no reason to think that the phrase is

15 And the prayer of faith shall save the sick, and the Lord shall raise him up ; and if *a* he have com- | mitted sins, they shall be forgiven him.

a Is.33.4.

used here to denote any *peculiar* religious rite or 'sacrament.' It was to be done in the name of the Lord, as any other good deed is.

15. *And the prayer of faith.* The prayer offered in faith, or in the exercise of confidence in God. It is not said that the particular form of the faith exercised shall be that the sick man will certainly recover; but there is to be unwavering confidence in God, a belief that he will do what is best, and a cheerful committing of the cause into his hands. We express our earnest wish, and leave the case with him. The prayer of faith is to accompany the use of means, for all means would be ineffectual without the blessing of God. ¶ *Shall save the sick, and the Lord shall raise him up.* This must be understood, as such promises are everywhere, with this restriction, that they will be restored to health if it shall be the will of God; if he shall deem it for the best. It cannot be taken in the absolute and unconditional sense, for then, if these means were used, the sick person would always recover, no matter how often he might be sick, and he need never die. The design is to encourage them to the use of these means with a strong hope that it would be effectual. It may fairly be inferred from this statement, (1,) that there would be cases in large numbers where these means would be attended with this happy result; and, (2,) that there was so much encouragement to do it that it would be proper in any case of sickness so make use of these means. It may be added, that no one can demonstrate that this promise has not been in numerous instances fulfilled. There *are* instances, not a few, where recovery from sickness *seems* to be in direct answer to prayer, and no one can *prove* that it is not so. Compare the case of Hezekiah, in Isa. xxxviii. 1–5. ¶ *And if he have committed sins, they shall be forgiven him.* Perhaps there may be a particular allusion here to sins which may have brought on the sickness as a punishment. In that case the removal of the

disease in answer to prayer would be an evidence that the sin was pardoned. Comp. Matt. ix. 2. But the promise may be understood in a more general sense as denoting that such sickness would be the means of bringing the sins of the past life to remembrance, especially if the one who was sick had been unfaithful to his Christian vows ; and that the sickness in connection with the prayers offered would bring him to true repentance, and would recover him from his wanderings. On backsliding and erring Christians sickness often has this effect ; and the subsequent life is so devoted and consistent as to show that the past unfaithfulness of him who has been afflicted is forgiven.

This passage (vers. 14, 15) is important, not only for the counsel which it gives to the sick, but because it has been employed by the Roman Catholic communion as almost the only portion of the Bible referred to to sustain one of the peculiar rites of their religion—that of 'extreme unction'—a 'sacrament,' as they suppose, to be administered to those who are dying. It is of importance, therefore, to inquire more particularly into its meaning. There can be but three views taken of the passage : I. That it refers to a *miraculous* healing by the apostles, or by other early ministers of religion who were endowed with the power of healing diseases in this manner. This is the interpretation of Doddridge, Macknight, Benson, and others. But to this view the objections seem to me to be insuperable. (*a*) Nothing of this kind is said by the apostle, and this is not necessary to be supposed in order to a fair interpretation of the passage. (*b*) The reference, as already observed, is clearly not to the *apostles*, but to the ordinary officers of the church —for such a reference would be naturally understood by the word *presbyters;* and to suppose that this refers to miracles, would be to suppose that this was a common endowment of the ordinary ministers of religion. But there was no promise of this, and there is no evidence that they possessed it. In regard to the *extent* of the promise, 'they shall lay hands on the sick, and they shall recover,' see Notes on Mark xvi. 17, 18. (c) If this referred to the power of working miracles, and if the promise was absolute, then death would not have occurred at all among the early disciples. It would have been easy to secure a restoration to health in any instance where a minister of religion was at hand. II. It is supposed by the Roman Catholics to give sanction to the practice of 'extreme unction,' and to prove that this was practised in the primitive church. But the objections to this are still more obvious. (a) It was not to be performed at death, or in the immediate prospect of death, but in sickness at any time. There is no hint that it was to be only when the patient was past all hope of recovery, or in view of the fact that he was to die. But 'extreme unction,' from its very nature, is to be practised only where the patient is past all hope of recovery. (b) It was not with a view to his *death*, but to his *living*, that it was to be practised at all. It was not that he might be prepared *to die*, but that he might be restored *to health*—' and the prayer of faith shall save the sick, *and the Lord shall raise him up.*' But 'extreme unction' can be with no such reference, and no such hope. It is *only* with the expectation that the patient is about to die; and if there were any expectation that he would be raised up even by *this* ordinance, it could not be administered as '*extreme* unction.' (c) The ordinance practised as 'extreme unction' is a rite wholly unauthorized in the Scriptures, unless it be by this passage. There are instances indeed of persons being embalmed *after* death. It was a fact also that the Saviour said of Mary, when she poured ointment on his body, that she ' did it *for his burial*,' or with reference to his burial, (Notes, Matt. xxvi. 12;) but the Saviour did not say that it was with reference *to his death*, or was designed in any way to prepare him to die, nor is there any instance in the Bible in which such a rite is mentioned. The ceremony of extreme unction has its foundation in two things: first, in superstition, in the desire of

something that shall operate as a charm, or that shall possess physical efficiency in calming the apprehensions of a troubled conscience, and in preparing the guilty to die; and, second, in the fact that it gives immense power to the priesthood. Nothing is better adapted to impart such power than a prevalent belief that a minister of religion holds in his hands the ability to alleviate the pangs of the dying, and to furnish a sure passport to a world of bliss. There is deep philosophy in that which has led to the belief of this doctrine—for the dying look around for consolation and support, and they grasp at anything which will promise ease to a troubled conscience, and the hope of heaven. The *gospel* has made arrangements to meet this state of mind in a better way —in the evidence which the guilty may have that by repentance and faith their sins are blotted out through the blood of the cross. III. The remaining supposition, therefore, and, as it seems to me, the true one, is, that the anointing with oil was, in accordance with a common custom, regarded as medicinal, and that a blessing was to be invoked on this as a means of restoration to health. Besides what has been already said, the following suggestions may be made in addition: (a) This was, as we have seen, a common usage in the East, and is to this day. (b) This interpretation meets all that is demanded to a fair understanding of what is said by the apostle. (c) Everything thus directed is rational and proper. It is proper to call in the ministers of religion in time of sickness, and to ask their counsels and their prayers. It is proper to make use of the ordinary means of restoration to health. It was proper then, as it is now, to do this ' in the name of the Lord;' that is, believing that it is in accordance with his benevolent arrangements, and making use of means which he has appointed. And it was proper then, as it is now, having made use of those means, to implore the Divine blessing on them, and to feel that their efficacy depends wholly on him. Thus used, there was ground of *hope* and of *faith* in regard to the recovery of the sufferer; and no one can show that in thousands of instances in the apostles'

16 Confess *your* faults one to another, and pray one for another, that ye may be healed. The effec-

tual fervent prayer of a righteous man availeth much.[b]

a Ac.19.18.   b Ps.145.19

day, and since, the prayer of faith, accompanying the proper use of means, may not have raised up those who were on the borders of the grave, and who *but* for these means would have died.

16. *Confess* your *faults one to another.* This seems primarily to refer to those who were *sick*, since it is added, ' *that ye may be healed.*' The fair interpretation is, that it might be supposed that such *confession* would contribute to a restoration to health. The case supposed all along here (see ver. 15) is, that the sickness referred to had been brought upon the patient for his sins, apparently as a punishment for some particular transgressions. Comp. Notes on 1 Cor. xi. 30. In such a case, it is said that if those who were sick would make confession of their sins, it would, in connection with prayer, be an important means of restoration to health. The duty inculcated, and which is equally binding on all now, is, that if we are sick, and are conscious that we have injured any persons, to make confession to them. This indeed is a duty at all times, but in health it is often neglected, and there is a special propriety that such confession should be made when we are sick. The particular *reason* for doing it which is here specified is, that it would contribute to a restoration to health—' that ye may be healed.' In the case specified, this might be supposed to contribute to a restoration to health from one of two causes: (1.) If the sickness had been brought upon them as a *special* act of Divine visitation for sin, it might be hoped that when the confession was made the hand of God would be withdrawn; or (2) in any case, if the mind was troubled by the recollection of guilt, it might be hoped that the calmness and peace resulting from confession would be favourable to a restoration to health. The former case would of course be more applicable to the times of the apostles; the latter would pertain to all times. Disease is often greatly aggravated by the trouble of mind which arises from conscious guilt; and, in such a case,

nothing will contribute more directly to recovery than the restoration of peace to the soul agitated by guilt and by the dread of a judgment to come. This may be secured by *confession*—confession made first to God, and then to those who are wronged. It may be added, that this is a duty to which we are prompted by the very nature of our feelings when we are sick, and by the fact that no one is willing to die with guilt on his conscience; without having done everything that he can to be at peace with all the world. This passage is one on which Roman Catholics rely to demonstrate the propriety of ' *auricular confession,*' or confession made to a priest with a view to an absolution of sin. The doctrine which is held on that point is, that it is a duty to confess to a priest, at certain seasons, *all* our sins, secret and open, of which we have been guilty; all our improper thoughts, desires, words, and actions; and that the priest has power to declare on such confession that the sins are forgiven. But never was any text *less* pertinent to prove a doctrine than this passage to demonstrate that. For, (1,) the confession here enjoined is not to be made by a person in health, that he may obtain salvation, but by a sick person, that he may be healed. (2.) As *mutual* confession is here enjoined, a priest would be as much bound to confess to the people as the people as to a priest. (3.) No mention is made of a *priest* at all, or even of a minister of religion, as the one to whom the confession is to be made. (4.) The confession referred to is for ' faults ' with reference to ' one another,' that is, where one has injured another; and nothing is said of confessing faults to those whom we have not injured at all. (5.) There is no mention here of *absolution*, either by a priest or any other person. (6.) If anything is meant by *absolution* that is scriptural, it may as well be pronounced by one person as another; by a layman as a clergyman. All that it *can* mean is, that God *promises* pardon to those who are truly penitent, and this **fact** may as well be stated by one person as another. No priest, no man whatever, is empowered to say to another either that he *is* truly penitent, or to *forgive* sin. 'Who can forgive sins but God only?' None but he whose law has been violated, or who has been wronged, can pardon an offence. No third person can forgive a sin which a man has committed against a neighbour; no one but a parent can pardon the offences of which his own children have been guilty towards him; and who can put himself in the place of God, and presume to pardon the sins which his creatures have committed against him? (7.) The practice of 'auricular confession' is 'evil, and only evil, and that continually.' Nothing gives so much power to a priesthood as the supposition that they have the power of absolution. Nothing serves so much to pollute the soul as to keep impure thoughts before the mind long enough to make the confession, and to *state* them in words. Nothing gives a man so much power over a female as to have it supposed that it is required by religion, and appertains to the sacred office, that all that passes in the mind should be disclosed to him. The thought which but for the necessity of confession would have vanished at once; the image which would have departed as soon as it came before the mind, but for the necessity of retaining it to make confession —these are the things over which a man would seek to have control, and to which he would desire to have access, if he wished to accomplish purposes of villany. *The very thing which a seducer would desire would be the power of knowing all the thoughts of his intended victim; and if the thoughts which pass through the soul could be known, virtue would be safe nowhere.* Nothing probably under the name of religion has ever done more to corrupt the morals of a community than the practice of auricular confession. ¶ *And pray one for another.* One for the other; mutually. Those who have done injury, and those who are injured, should pray for each other. The apostle does not seem here, as in vers. 14, 15, to refer particularly to the prayers of the ministers of religion, or the elders of the church, but refers to it as a duty appertaining to all Christians.

¶ *That ye may be healed.* Not with reference to death, and therefore not relating to 'extreme unction,' but in order that the sick may be restored again to health. This is said in connection with the duty of *confession*, as well as *prayer;* and it seems to be implied that both might contribute to a restoration to health. Of the way in which *prayer* would do' this, there can be no doubt; for all healing comes from God, and it is reasonable to suppose that this might be bestowed in answer to prayer. Of the way in which *confession* might do this, see the remarks already made. We should be deciding without evidence if we should say that sickness never comes now as a particular judgment for some forms of sin, and that it might not be removed if the suffering offender would make full confession to God, or to him whom he has wronged, and should resolve to offend no more. Perhaps this is, oftener than we suppose, one of the methods which God takes to bring his offending and backsliding children back to himself, or to warn and reclaim the guilty. When, after being laid on a bed of pain, his children are led to reflect on their violated vows and their unfaithfulness, and resolve to sin no more, they are raised up again to health, and made eminently useful to the church. So calamity, by disease or in other forms, often comes upon the vicious and the abandoned. They are led to reflection and to repentance. They resolve to reform, and the natural effects of their sinful course are arrested, and they become examples of virtue and usefulness in the world.

¶ *The effectual fervent prayer.* The word *effectual* is not the most happy translation here, since it seems to do little more than to state a truism—that a prayer which is *effectual* is availing— that is, that it is effectual. The Greek word (ἐνεργουμένη) would be better rendered by the word *energetic*, which indeed is derived from it. The word properly refers to that which has power; which in its own nature is fitted to produce an effect. It is not so much that it actually *does* produce an effect, as that it is *fitted* to do it. This is the kind of prayer referred to here. It is not listless, indifferent, cold, lifeless. as

17 Elias was a man subject to like passions as we are, and he ^aprayed ¹ earnestly that it might

not rain ; and it rained not on the earth by the space of three years and six months.

a 1 Ki.17.1.   1 in prayer.

if there were no vitality in it, or power, but that which is adapted to be efficient —earnest, sincere, hearty, persevering. There is but a single word in the original to answer to the translation *effectual fervent.* Macknight and Doddridge suppose that the reference is to a kind of prayer ' *inwrought* by the Spirit,' or the ' *inwrought* prayer ;' but the whole force of the original is expressed by the word *energetic,* or *earnest.* ¶ *Of a righteous man.* The quality on which the success of the prayer depends is not the talent, learning, rank, wealth, or *office* of the man who prays, but the fact that he is a ' righteous man,' that is, a good man ; and this may be found in the ranks of the poor, as certainly as the rich ; among laymen, as well as among the ministers of religion ; among slaves, as well as among their masters. ¶*Availeth much. ἰσχύει.* Is strong ; has efficacy ; prevails. The idea of *strength* or *power* is that which enters into the word ; strength that overcomes resistance and secures the object. Comp. Matt. vii. 28 ; Acts xix. 16 ; Rev. xii. 8. It has been said that ' prayer moves the arm that moves the world ;' and if there is anything that can prevail with God, it is prayer—humble, fervent, earnest *petitioning.* We have no power to control him ; we cannot dictate or prescribe to him ; we cannot resist him in the execution of his purposes ; but we may ASK him for what we desire, and he has graciously said that such asking may effect much for our own good and the good of our fellow-men. Nothing has been more clearly demonstrated in the history of the world than that *prayer* is effectual in obtaining blessings from God, and in accomplishing great and valuable purposes. It has indeed no intrinsic power ; but God has graciously purposed that his favour shall be granted to those who call upon him, and that what no mere human power can effect should be produced by *his* power in answer to prayer.

17. *Elias.* The common way of

writing the word *Elijah* in the New Testament, Matt. xi. 14 ; xvi. 14 ; xvii. 3, etc. ¶ *Was a man subject to like passions as we are.* This does not mean that Elijah was *passionate* in the sense in which that word is now commonly used ; that is, that he was excitable or irritable, or that he was the victim of the same corrupt passions and propensities to which other men are subject ; but that he was *like affected;* that he was capable of suffering the same things, or being affected in the same manner. In other words, he was a mere man, subject to the same weaknesses and infirmities as other men. Comp. Notes on Acts xiv. 15. The apostle is illustrating the efficacy of prayer. In doing this, he refers to an undoubted case where prayer *had* such efficacy. But to this it might be objected that Elijah was a distinguished prophet, and that it was reasonable to suppose that *his* prayer would be heard. It might be said that his example could not be adduced to prove that the prayers of those who were not favoured with such advantages would be heard ; and especially that it could not be argued from his case that the prayers of the ignorant, and of the weak, and of children and of servants, would be answered. To meet this, the apostle says that he was a mere man, with the same natural propensities and infirmities as other men, and that therefore his case is one which should encourage all to pray. It was an instance of the efficacy of *prayer,* and not an illustration of the power of a prophet. ¶ *And he prayed earnestly.* Greek, ' He *prayed with prayer* '—a Hebraism, to denote that he prayed earnestly. Comp. Luke xxii. 15. This manner of speaking is common in Hebrew. Comp. 1 Sam. xxvi. 25 ; Psa. cxviii. 18 ; Lam. i. 2. The reference here is undoubtedly to 1 Kings xvii. 1. In that place, however, it is not said that Elijah *prayed,* but that he said, ' As the Lord God of Israel liveth, before whom I stand, there shall not be

18 And he prayed again, *a* and the heaven gave rain, and the earth brought forth her fruit.

19 Brethren, if any of you do err

from the truth, and one *b* convert him,

20 Let him know, that he which

dew nor rain these three years, but according to my word.' Either James interprets this as a prayer, because it could be accomplished only *by* prayer, or he states what had been handed down by tradition as the way in which the miracle was effected. There can be no reasonable doubt that prayer was employed in the case, for even the miracles of the Saviour were accomplished in connexion with prayer, John xi. 41, 42. ¶ *That it might not rain.* Not to gratify any private resentment of his, but as a punishment on the land for the idolatry which prevailed in the time of Ahab. Famine was one of the principal methods by which God punished his people for their sins. ¶ *And it rained not on the earth.* On the land of Palestine, for so the word *earth* is frequently understood in the Bible. See Notes on Luke ii. 1. There is no reason to suppose that the famine extended beyond the country that was subject to Ahab. ¶ *By the space.* For the time. ¶ *Of three years and six months.* See this explained in the Notes on Luke iv. 25. Comp. Lightfoot, Horæ Hebraicæ, on Luke iv. 25.

18. *And he prayed again.* The allusion here seems to be to 1 Kings xviii. 42, 45, though it is not expressly said there that he *prayed.* Perhaps it might be fairly gathered from the narrative that he *did* pray, or at least that would be the presumption, for he put himself into a natural attitude of prayer. ' He cast himself down upon the earth, and put his face between his knees,' 1 Kings xviii. 42. In such circumstances, it is to be fairly presumed that such a man *would* pray; but it is remarkable that it is not expressly mentioned, and quite as remarkable that James should have made his argument turn on a thing which is *not* expressly mentioned, but which seems to have been a matter of *inference.* It seems probable to me, therefore, that there was some tradition on which he relied, or that it was a common interpretation of the passage in 1 Kings, that Elijah prayed earnestly,

and that this was generally believed by those to whom the apostle wrote. Of the *fact* that Elijah was a man of prayer, no one could doubt; and in these circumstances the tradition and common belief were sufficient to justify the argument which is employed here. ¶ *And the heaven gave rain.* The clouds gave rain. ' The heaven was black with clouds and wind, and there was a great rain,' 1 Kings xviii. 45. ¶ *And the earth brought forth her fruit.* The famine ceased, and the land again became productive. The case referred to here was indeed a miracle, but it was a case of *the power of prayer*, and therefore to the point. If God would work a miracle in answer to prayer, it is reasonable to presume that he will bestow upon us the blessings which we need in the same way.

19. *Brethren, if any of you do err from the truth.* Either doctrinally and speculatively, by embracing error; or practically, by falling into sinful practices. Either of these may be called ' erring from the truth,' because they are contrary to what the truth teaches and requires. What is here said does not appear to have any connexion with what precedes, but the apostle seems to have supposed that such a case *might* occur; and, in the conclusion of the epistle, he called their attention to the importance of endeavouring to save an erring brother, if such an instance should happen. The exhortation would be proper in addressing a letter to any church, or in publicly addressing any congregation. ¶ *And one convert him.* This does not mean *convert him as a sinner,* or *regenerate him,* but turn him from the error of his way; bring him back from his wanderings; re-establish him in the truth, and in the practice of virtue and religion. So far as the word used here is concerned, (ἐπιστρέψῃ,) he who had erred from the truth, and who was to be converted, may have been a true Christian before. The word means simply *to turn,* sc., from his way of error. See Notes on Luke xxii. 32.

20. *Let him know.* Let him who

converteth the sinner from the error of his way shall save a soul from

death, and shall hide *a* a multitude of sins.

a Pr.10.12; 1 Pe.4.8.

converts the other know for his encouragement. ¶ *That he which converteth the sinner from the error of his way.* Any sinner; any one who has done wrong. This is a general principle, applicable to this case and to all others of the same kind. It is a universal truth that he who turns a sinner from a wicked path does a work which is acceptable to God, and which will in some way receive tokens of his approbation. Comp. Deut. xii. 3. No work which man can perform is more acceptable to God; none will be followed with higher rewards. In the language which is used here by the apostle, it is evidently intended not to deny that success in converting a sinner, or in reclaiming one from the error of his ways, is to be traced to the grace of God; but the apostle here refers only to the Divine feeling towards the individual who shall attempt it, and the rewards which he may hope to receive. The reward bestowed, the good intended and done, would be the same as if the individual were able to do the work himself. God approves and loves his aims and efforts, though the success is ultimately to be traced to himself. ¶ *Shall save a soul from death.* It has been doubted whether this refers to his own soul, or to the soul of him who is converted. Several manuscripts, and the Vulgate, Syriac, Arabic, and Coptic versions, here read, ' *his soul.*' The most natural interpretation of the passage is to refer it to the soul of the one converted, rather than of him who converts him. This accords better with the uniform teaching of the New Testament, since it is nowhere else taught that the method of saving *our* souls is by converting others; and this interpretation will meet all that the scope of the passage demands. The object of the apostle is to present a *motive* for endeavouring to convert one who has wandered away; and assuredly a sufficient motive for that is furnished in the fact, that by this means an immortal soul would be saved from eternal ruin. The word *death* here must refer to eternal death, or to future punish-

ment. There is no other *death* which the soul is in danger of dying. The body dies and moulders away, but the soul is immortal. The apostle cannot mean that he would save the soul from *annihilation*, for it is in no danger of that. This passage proves, then, that there is a death which the soul may die; that there is a condition which may properly be called death as a consequence of sin; and that the soul will suffer that unless it is converted. ¶ *And shall hide a multitude of sins.* Shall cover them over so that they shall not be seen; that is, they shall not be punished. This must mean either the sins which he has committed who is thus converted and saved, or the sins of him who converts him. Whichever is the meaning, a strong *motive* is presented for endeavouring to save a sinner from the error of his ways. It is not easy to determine which is the true sense. Expositors have been about equally divided respecting the meaning. Doddridge adopts substantially *both* interpretations, paraphrasing it, ' not only procuring the pardon of those committed by the convert, but also engaging God to look with greater indulgence on his own character, and to be less ready to mark severely what he has done amiss.' The Jews regarded it as a meritorious act to turn a sinner from the error of his ways, and it is *possible* that James may have had some of their maxims in his eye. Comp. Clarke, *in loc.* Though it may not be possible to determine with certainty whether the apostle here refers to the sins of him who converts another, or of him who is converted, yet it seems to me that the reference is probably to the latter, for the following reasons: (1.) Such an interpretation will meet all that is fairly implied in the language. (2.) This interpretation will furnish a strong motive for what the apostle expects us to do. The motive presented is, according to this, that *sin* will not be punished. But this is always a good motive for putting forth efforts in the cause of religion, and quite as powerful when drawn from our doing good to others as when applied to ourselves. (3.) This is a *safe* interpretation; the other is attended with danger. According to this, the effort would be one of pure benevolence, and there would be no danger of depending on what we do as a ground of acceptance with God. The other interpretation would seem to teach that our sins might be forgiven on some other ground than that of the atonement—by virtue of some act of our own. And (4) there might be danger, if it be supposed that this refers to the fact that *our* sins are to be covered up by this act, of supposing that by endeavouring to convert others *we* may live in sin with impunity; that however we live, we shall be safe if we lead others to repentance and salvation. If the motive be the simple desire to hide the sins of others—to procure their pardon —to save a soul from death, without any supposition that *by* that we are making an atonement for our own sins —it is a good one, a safe one. But if the idea is that by this act we are making some atonement for our own offences, and that we may thus work out a righteousness of our own, the idea is one that is every way dangerous to the great doctrine of justification by faith, and is contrary to the whole teaching of the Bible. For these rea-

sons it seems to me that the true interpretation is, that the passage refers to the sins of others, not our own; and that the simple motive here presented is, that in this way we may save a fellow-sinner from being punished for his sins. It may be added, in the conclusion of the Notes on this epistle, that this motive is one which is sufficient to stimulate us to great and constant efforts to save others. Sin is the source of all the evil in the universe: and the great object which a benevolent heart ought to have, should be that its desolating effects may be stayed; that the sinner may be pardoned; and that the guilty soul may be saved from its consequences in the future world. This is the design of God in the plan of redemption; this was the object of the Saviour in giving himself to die; this is the purpose of the Holy Spirit in renewing and sanctifying the soul; and this is the great end of all those acts of Divine Providence by which the sinner is warned and turned to God. When we come to die, as we shall soon, it will give us more pleasure to be able to recollect that we have been the means of saving one soul from death, than to have enjoyed all the pleasures which sense can furnish, or to have gained all the honour and wealth which the world can give.

THE

FIRST EPISTLE GENERAL OF PETER

INTRODUCTION

THE first epistle of Peter has never been doubted to be the production of the apostle of that name. While there were doubts respecting the genuineness of the second epistle, (see Intro. to that epistle, § 1,) the unvarying testimony of history, and the uniform belief of the church, ascribe this epistle to him. Indeed, there is no ancient writing whatever of which there is more certainty in regard to the authorship.

The history of Peter is so fully detailed in the New Testament, that it is not necessary to go into any extended statement of his biography in order to an exposition of his epistles. No particular light would be reflected on them from the details of his life; and in order, therefore, to their exposition, it is not necessary to have any farther information of him than what is contained in the New Testament itself. Those who may wish to obtain all the knowledge of his life which can now be had, may find ample details in Lardner, vol. vi. pp. 203–254, ed. London, 1829; Koppe, Proleg.; and Bacon's Lives of the Apostles, pp. 43–286. There are some questions, however, which it is important to consider in order to an intelligent understanding of his epistles.

§ 1. The persons to whom the first Epistle was addressed.

THIS epistle purports to have been addressed 'to the strangers scattered throughout Pontus, Galatia, Cappadocia, Asia, and Bithynia.' All these were provinces of Asia Minor; and there is no difficulty, therefore, in regard to the *places* where those to whom the epistle was written resided. The only question is, who they were who are thus designated as 'strangers scattered abroad,' or *strangers of the dispersion,* (παρεπιδήμοις διασπορᾶς.) Comp. Notes on chap. i. 1. In regard to this, various opinions have been held.

(1.) That they were native-born Jews, who had been converted to the Christian faith. Of this opinion were Eusebius, Jerome, Grotius, Beza, Mill, Cave, and others. The principal argument for this opinion is the appellation given to them, (chap. i. 1,) 'strangers scattered abroad,' and what is said in chap. ii. 9; iii. 6, which it is supposed is language which would be applied only to those of Hebrew extraction.

(2.) A second opinion has been that the persons to whom it was sent were all of Gentile origin. Of this opinion were Procopius, Cassiodorus, and more recently Wetstein. This belief is founded chiefly on such passages as the following: chap. i. 18; ii. 10; iv. 3—which are supposed to show that they who were thus addressed were formerly idolaters.

(3.) A third opinion has been that they were Gentiles by birth, but had been Jewish proselytes, or 'proselytes of the gate,' and had then been converted to Christianity. This sentiment was defended by Michaelis, chiefly on the ground that the phrase in chap. i. 1, 'strangers of the dispersion,' when followed by the name of a heathen country or people, in the genitive case, denotes the Jews whó were dispersed there, and yet that there is evidence in the epistle that they were not native-born Jews.

(4.) A fourth opinion has been that the persons referred to were not Jews in general, but those of the ten tribes who had wandered from Babylon and the adjacent regions into Asia Minor. This opinion is mentioned by Michaelis as having been entertained by some persons, but no reasons are assigned for it.

(5.) A fifth opinion has been that the persons referred to were Christians, converted from both Jews and Gentiles, with no particular reference to their extraction; that there were those among them who had been converted from the Jews, and those who had been Gentiles, and that the apostle addresses them *as* Christians, though employing language such as the Jews had been accustomed to, when speaking of those of their own nation who were scattered abroad. This is the opinion of Lardner, Estius, Whitby, Wolfius, and Doddridge.

That this last opinion is the correct one, seems to me to be clear from the epistle itself. Nothing can be plainer than that the apostle, while in the main he addresses Christians as such, whether they had been Jews or heathen, yet occasionally makes such allusions, and uses such language, as to show that he had his eye, at one time, on some who had been Jews, and again on some who had been pagans. This is clear, I think, from the following considerations:

(1.) The address of the epistle is general, not directed particularly either to the Jews or to the Gentiles. Thus in chap. v. 14, he says, ' Peace be with you all that are in Christ Jesus.' From this it would seem that the epistle was addressed to *all* true Christians in the region designated in chap. i. 1. But no one can doubt that there were Christians there who had been Jews, and also those who had been Gentiles. The same thing is apparent from the second epistle; for it is certain, from 2 Pet. iii. 2, that the second epistle was addressed to the same persons as the first. But the address in the second epistle is to Christians residing in Asia Minor, without particular reference to their origin. Thus in chap. i. 1, ' To them that have obtained like precious faith with us through the righteousness of God and our Saviour Jesus Christ.' The same thing is apparent also from the address of the first epistle : ' To the elect strangers scattered throughout Pontus,' etc.; that is, ' to the strangers of the dispersion who are chosen, or who are true Christians, scattered abroad.' The term 'elect' is one which would apply to all who were Christians ; and the phrase, ' the strangers of the dispersion,' is that which one who had been educated as a Hebrew would be likely to apply to those whom he regarded as the people of God dwelling out of Palestine. The Jews were accustomed to use this expression to denote their own people who were dispersed among the Gentiles ; and nothing would be more natural than that one who had been educated as a Hebrew, and then converted to Christianity, as Peter had been, should apply this phrase indiscriminately to Christians living out of Palestine. See the Notes on the passage. These considerations make it clear that in writing this epistle he had reference to Christians *as such*, and meant that *all* who were Christians in the parts of Asia Minor which he mentions, (chap. i. 1,) should regard the epistle as addressed to them.

(2.) Yet there are some allusions in the epistle which look as if a part of them at least had been Jews before their conversion, or such as a Jew would better understand than a Gentile would. Indeed, nothing is more probable than that there were Jewish converts in that region. We know that there were many Jews in Asia Minor ; and, from the Acts of the Apostles, it is morally certain that not a few of them had been converted to the Christian faith under the labours of Paul. Of the allusions of the kind referred to in the epistle, the following may be taken as specimens: ' But ye are a chosen generation, a royal priesthood, an holy nation, a peculiar people,' chap. ii. 9. This is such language as was commonly used by the Jews when addressing their own countrymen as the people of God ; and would seem to imply that to some of those at least to whom the epistle was addressed, it was language which would be familiar. See also chap. iii. 6. It should be said, however, that these passages are not *positive* proof that any among them were Hebrews. While it is true that it is such language as would be naturally employed in addressing those who were, and while it supposes an acquaintance among them with the Old Testament, it is also true that it is such language as one who had himself been educated as an Hebrew would not unnaturally employ when addressing any whom he regarded as the people of God.

(3.) The passages in the epistle which imply that many of those to whom it was addressed had been Gentiles or idolaters, are still more clear. Such passages are the following: 'As obedient children, not fashioning yourselves according to your former lusts in your ignorance,' chap. i. 14. 'This,' says Dr. Lardner, 'might be very pertinently said to men converted from Gentilism to Christianity; but no such thing is ever said by the apostles concerning the Jewish people who had been favoured with the Divine revelation, and had the knowledge of the true God.' So in chap. ii. 9, Peter speaks of them as 'having been called out of darkness into marvellous light.' The word 'darkness' is one which would be naturally applied to those who had been heathens, but would not be likely to be applied to those who had had the knowledge of God as revealed in the Jewish Scriptures. So in chap. ii. 10, it is expressly said of them, 'which in time past was not a people, but are now the people of God'—language which would not be applied to those who had been Jews. So also chap. iv. 3, 'For the time past of our life may suffice us to have wrought the will of the Gentiles, when we walked in lasciviousness, lusts, excess of wine, revellings, banquetings, and abominable idolatries.' Though the apostle here uses the word '*us*,' grouping himself with them, yet it cannot be supposed that he means to charge himself with these things. It is a mild and gentle way of speech, adopted not to give offence, and is such language as a minister of the gospel would now use, who felt that he was himself a sinner, in addressing a church made up of many individuals. Though it might be true that *he* had not been guilty of the particular offences which he specifies, yet in speaking in the name of the church, he would use the term *we*, and use it honestly and correctly. It would be *true* that the church had been formerly guilty of these things; and this would be a much more mild, proper, and effective method of address, than to say *you*. But the passages adduced here prove conclusively that some of those whom Peter addresses in the epistle had been formerly idolaters, and had been addicted to the sins which idolaters are accustomed to commit.

These considerations make it clear that the epistle was addressed to those Christians in general who were scattered throughout the various provinces of Asia Minor which are specified in chap. i, 1, whether they had been Jews or Gentiles. It is probable that the great body of them had been converted from the heathen, though there were doubtless Jewish converts intermingled with them; and Peter uses such language as would be natural for one who had been a Jew himself in addressing those whom he now regarded as the chosen of God.

§ II.—*The time and place of writing the epistle.*

On this point also there has been no little diversity of opinion. The only designation of the *place* where it was written which occurs in the epistle is in chap. v. 13 : 'The church that is at Babylon, elected together with you, saluteth you.' From this it is clear that it was written at *Babylon*, but still there has been no little difference of opinion as to what place is meant here by Babylon. Some have supposed that it refers to the well-known place of that name on the Euphrates; others to a Babylon situated in Lower Egypt; others to Jerusalem or Rome, represented as Babylon. The claims of each of these places it is proper to examine. The order in which this is done is not material.

(1.) The opinion that the ' Babylon' mentioned in the epistle refers to a place of that name in Egypt, not far from Cairo. This opinion was held by Pearson and Le Clerc, and by most of the *Coptic* interpreters, who have endeavoured to vindicate the honour of their own country, Egypt, as a place where one of the books of Scripture was composed. See Koppe, Proleg. 12. That there *was* such a place in Egypt, there can be no doubt. It was a small town to the northeast of Cairo, where there was a strong castle in the time of Strabo, (i. 17, p. 807,) in which, under Tiberius, there were quartered three Roman legions, designed to keep the Egyptians in order. But there is little reason to suppose that there were many Jews there, or that a church was early collected there. The Jews would have been little likely to resort to a place which was merely a Roman garrison, nor would the apostles have been likely to go early to such a place to preach the gospel. Comp. Basnage, Ant. 36, num. xxvii. As Lardner well remarks, if Peter had written an epistle from Egypt, it would have been likely to have been from Alexandria. Besides, there is not, for the first four centuries, any notice of a church at Babylon in Egypt; a fact which can hardly be accounted for, if it had been supposed that one of the sacred books had been composed there.—Lardner, vol. vi. 265. It may be added, also, that as there was another place of that name on the Euphrates, a place much better known, and which would be naturally supposed to be the one referred to, it is probable that if the epistle had been composed at the Babylon in Egypt, there would have been something said clearly to distinguish it. If the epistle was written at the Babylon on the Euphrates, so well known was that place that no one would be likely to understand that the Babylon in Egypt was the place referred to; on the other supposition, however, nothing would be more likely than that a mistake should occur.

(2.) Others have supposed that Jerusalem is intended, and that the name was given to it on account of its wickedness, and because it resembled Babylon. This was the opinion of Capellus, Spanheim, Hardouin, and some others. But the objections to this are obvious: (*a*) There is no evidence that the name *Babylon* was ever given to Jerusalem, or *so* given to it as to make it commonly understood that that was the place intended when the term was employed. If not so, its use would be likely to lead those to whom the epistle was addressed into a mistake. (*b*) There is every reason to suppose that an apostle in writing a letter, if he mentioned the place at all where it was written, would mention the *real* name. So Paul uniformly does. (*c*) The name Babylon is not one which an apostle would be likely to give to Jerusalem; certainly not as the name by which it was to be familiarly known. (*d*) If the epistle had been written there, there is no conceivable reason why the name of the place should not have been mentioned.

(3.) Others have supposed that *Rome* is intended by the name Babylon. This was the opinion of many of the Fathers, and also of Bede, Valesius, Grotius, Cave, Whitby, and Lardner. The principal reasons for this are, that such is the testimony of Papias, Eusebius, and Jerome; and that at that time Babylon on the Euphrates was destroyed. See Lardner. But the objections to this opinion seem to me to be insuperable. (*a*) There is no evidence that at that early period the name Babylon was given to Rome, nor were there any existing reasons why it should be. The name is generally supposed to have been applied to it by John, in the book of Revelation, (chap. xvi. 19; xvii. 5; xviii. 10, 21;) but this was probably long after this epistle was written, and for reasons which did not exist in the time of Peter. There is no evidence that it was given familiarly to it in the time of Peter, or even at all until after his death. Certain it is, that it was not given so familiarly to it that when the name *Babylon* was mentioned it would be generally understood that Rome was intended. But the only reason which Peter could have had for mentioning the name Babylon at all, was to convey some definite and certain information to those to whom he wrote. (*b*) As has been already observed, the apostles, when they sent an epistle to the churches, and mentioned a place as the one where the epistle was written, were accustomed to mention the real place. (c) It would be hardly consistent with the dignity of an apostle, or any grave writer, to make use of what would be regarded as a *nickname*, when suggesting the name of a place where he then was. (d) If Rome had been meant, it would have been hardly respectful to *the church* there which sent the salutation—' The church that is at Babylon, elected together with you '—to have given it this name. Peter mentions the church with respect and kindness; and yet it would have been scarcely regarded as kind to mention it as a ' Church *in Babylon*,' if he used the term Babylon, as he must have done on such a supposition, to denote a place of eminent depravity. (e) The testimony of the Fathers on this subject does not demonstrate that Rome was the place intended. So far as appears from the extracts relied on by Lardner, they do not give this as *historical testimony*, but as their own interpretation; and, from anything that appears, we are as well qualified to interpret the word as they were. (f) In regard to the objection that Babylon was at that time destroyed, it may be remarked that this is true so far as the original splendour of the city was concerned, but still there may have been a sufficient population there to have constituted a church. The destruction of Babylon was gradual. It had not become an utter desert in the time of the apostles. In the first century of the Christian era a part of it was inhabited, though the greater portion of its former site was a waste. See Notes on Isa. xiii. 19. Comp. Diod. Sic., ii. 27. All that time, there is no improbability in supposing that a Christian church may have existed there. It should be added here, however, that on the supposition that the word Babylon refers to Rome, rests nearly all the evidence which the Roman Catholics can adduce that the apostle Peter was ever at Rome at all. There is nothing else in the New Testament that furnishes the slightest proof that he ever was there. The only passage on which Bellarmine relies to show that Peter was at Rome, is the very passage now under consideration. ' That Peter was one time at Rome,' he says, ' we show first from the testimony of Peter himself, who thus speaks at the end of his first epistle: " The church that is at Babylon, elected together with you, saluteth you." ' He does not pretend to cite any other evidence from Scripture than this; nor does any other writer.

(4.) There remains the fourth opinion, that the well-known Babylon on the Euphrates was the place where the epistle was written. This was the opinion of Erasmus, Drusius, Lightfoot, Bengel, Wetstein, Basnage, Beausobre, and others. That this is the correct opinion seems to me to be clear from the following considerations: (a) It is the most natural and obvious interpretation. It is that which would occur to the great mass of the readers of the New Testament now, and is that which would have been naturally adopted by those to whom the epistle was sent. The word *Babylon*, without something to give it a different application, would have been understood anywhere to denote the well-known place on the Euphrates. (b) There is, as has been observed already, no improbability that there was a Christian church there, but there are several circumstances which render it probable that this would be the case: 1st. Babylon had been an important place; and its history was such, and its relation to the Jews such, as to make it probable that the attention of the apostles would be turned to it. 2nd. The apostles, according to all the traditions which we have respecting them, travelled extensively in the East, and nothing would be more natural than that they should visit Babylon. 3rd. There were many Jews of the captivity remaining in that region, and it would be in the highest degree probable that they would seek to carry the gospel to their own countrymen there. See Koppe, Proleg., pp. 16–18. Jos. Ant., b. xv., chap. ii., § 2; chap. iii., § 1. Philo. De Virtut., p. 587.

These considerations make it clear that the place where the epistle was written was Babylon on the Euphrates, the place so celebrated in ancient sacred and profane history. If this be the correct view, then this is a fact of much interest, as showing that even in apostolic times there was a true church in a place once so distinguished for splendour and wickedness, and so memorable for its acts in oppressing the ancient people of God.   Our information respecting this church, however, ceases here.   We know not by whom it was founded ; we know not who were its pastors; nor do we know how long it survived.   As Babylon, however, continued rapidly to decline, so that in the second century nothing remained but the walls, (comp. Notes on Isa. xiii. 19,) there is no reason to suppose that the church long existed there.   Soon the ancient city became a heap of ruins; and excepting that now and then a Christian traveller or missionary has visited it, it is not known that a prayer has been offered there from generation to generation, or that amidst the desolations there has been a single worshipper of the true God.   See this subject examined at length in Bacon's Lives of the Apostles, pp. 258—263.

In regard to the *time* when this first epistle was written, nothing certainly can be determined.   There are no marks of time in the epistle itself, and there are no certain data from which we can determine when it was composed.   Lardner supposes that it was in the year 63, or 64, or at the latest 65; Michaelis, that it was about the year 60.   If it was written at Babylon, it was probably some time between the year 58 and 61.   The time is not material, and it is impossible now to determine it.

§ 3. *The characteristics of the first Epistle of Peter.*

(1.) THE epistles of Peter are distinguished for great tenderness of manner, and for bringing forward prominently the most consolatory parts of the gospel. He wrote to those who were in affliction; he was himself an old man, (2 Pet. i. 14;) he expected soon to be with his Saviour ; he had nearly done with the conflicts and toils of life; and it was natural that he should direct his eye onward, and should dwell on those things in the gospel which were adapted to support and comfort the soul.   There is, therefore, scarcely any part of the New Testament where the ripe and mellow Christian will find more that is adapted to his matured feelings, or to which he will more naturally turn.

(2.) There is great compactness and terseness of thought in his epistles.   They seem to be composed of a succession of *texts*, each one fitted to constitute the subject of a discourse.   There is more that a pastor would like to preach on in a course of expository lectures, and less that he would be disposed to pass over as not so well adapted to the purposes of public instruction, than in almost any other part of the New Testament.   There is almost nothing that is local or of temporary interest; there are no discussions about points pertaining to Jewish customs such as we meet with in Paul; there is little that pertains particularly to one age of the world or country.   Almost all that he has written is of universal applicability to Christians, and may be read with as much interest and profit now by *us* as by the people to whom his epistles were addressed.

(3.) There is evidence in the epistles of Peter that the author was well acquainted with the writings of the apostle Paul.   See this point illustrated at length in Eichhorn, Einleitung in das Neue Tes. viii. 606—618, § 284, and Michaelis, Intro., vol. iv. p. 323, seq.   Peter himself speaks of his acquaintance with the epistles of Paul, and ranks them with the inspired writings.   2 Pet. iii. 15, 16, 'Even as our beloved brother Paul also, according to the wisdom given unto him, hath written unto you; as also in all his epistles, speaking in them of these things; in which are some things hard to be understood, which they that are unlearned and unstable wrest, as they do also the other Scriptures, unto their own destruction.'   Indeed, to any one who will attentively compare the epistles of Peter with those of Paul, it will be apparent that he was acquainted with the writings of the Apostle of the Gentiles, and had become so familiar with the modes of expression which he employed, that he naturally fell into it.   There is that kind of coincidence which would be expected when one was accustomed to read what another had written, and when he had great respect for him, but not that when there was a purpose to *borrow* or *copy* from him. This will be apparent by a reference to a few parallel passages:—

PAUL.	PETER.
Eph. i. 3. Blessed be the God and Father of our Lord Jesus Christ. See also 2 Cor. i. 3.	1 Pet. i. 3. Blessed be the God and Father of our Lord Christ Jesus.
Col. iii. 8. But now ye also put off all these ; anger, wrath, malice, blasphemy, filthy communication out of your mouth.	1 Pet. ii. 1. Wherefore laying aside all malice, and all guile, and all hypocrisies, and envies, and all evil speakings.
Eph. v. 22. Wives, submit yourselves to your own husbands as unto the Lord.	1 Pet. iii. 1. Likewise ye wives, be in subjection to your own husbands.
Eph. v. 21. Submitting yourselves one to another in the fear of God.	1 Pet. v. 5. Yea, all of you be subject one to another.
1 Thess. v. 6. Let us watch and be sober.	1 Pet. v. 8. Be sober: be vigilant. [In the Greek the same words, though the order is reversed.]
1 Cor. xvi. 20. Greet ye one another with an holy kiss. 2 Cor. xiii. 12; Rom. xvi. 16; 1 Thess. v. 26.	1 Pet. v. 14. Greet ye one another with a kiss of love, (ἐν φιλήματι ἀγάπης.)
Rom. viii. 18. The glory that shall be revealed unto us.	1 Pet. v. 1. The glory that shall be revealed.
Rom. iv. 24. If we believe on him that raised up Jesus our Lord from the dead.	1 Pet. i. 21. Who by him do believe in God, that raised him up from the dead.
Rom. xiii. 1, 3, 4. Let every soul be subject unto the higher powers. For there is no power but of God ; the powers that be are ordained of God....Do that which is good, and thou shalt have praise of the same....For he is a minister of God, a revenger to execute wrath upon him that doeth evil.	1 Pet. ii. 13, 14. Submit yourselves to every ordinance of man for the Lord's sake ; whether it be to the king, as supreme ; or unto governors, as unto them that are sent by him for the punishment of evil doers, and for the praise of them that do well.

See also the following passages:

Rom. xii. 6, 7. 1 Peter iv. 10.
1 Tim. ii. 9. 1 Peter iii. 3.
1 Tim. v. 5. 1 Peter iii. 5.

These coincidences are not such as would occur between two authors when one had no acquaintance with the writings of the other; and they thus demonstrate, what may be implied in 2 Pet. iii. 15, that Peter was familiar with the epistles of Paul. This also would seem to imply that the epistles of Paul were in general circulation.

(4.) 'In the structure of his periods,' says Michaelis, 'St. Peter has this peculiarity, that he is fond of beginning a sentence in such a manner that it shall refer to a principal word in the preceding. The consequence of this structure is, that the sentences, instead of being rounded, according to the manner of the Greeks, are drawn out to a great length ; and in many places where we should expect that a sentence would be closed, a new clause is attached, and another again to this, so that before the whole period comes to an end, it contains parts which, at the commencement of the period, do not appear to have been designed for it.' This manner of writing is also found often in the epistles of Paul.

The canonical authority of this epistle has never been disputed. For a view of the contents of it, see the analysis prefixed to the several chapters.

FIRST EPISTLE GENERAL OF PETER

CHAPTER I.

PETER, an apostle of Jesus Christ, to the strangers scat-tered *a* throughout Pontus, Galatia, Cappadocia, Asia, and Bithynia,

a Ac.8.4.

CHAPTER I.

ANALYSIS OF THE CHAPTER.

This epistle was evidently addressed to those who were passing through severe trials, and probably to those who were, at that time, enduring persecution, chap. i. 6, 7; iii. 14; vi. 1, 12–19. The main object of this chapter is to comfort them in their trials; to suggest such considerations as would enable them to bear them with the right spirit, and to show the sustaining, elevating, and purifying power of the gospel. In doing this, the apostle adverts to the following considerations:—

(1.) He reminds them that they were the elect of God; that they had been chosen according to his foreknowledge, by the sanctifying agency of the Holy Ghost, and in order that they might be obedient, vers. 1, 2.

(2.) He reminds them of the lively hope to which they had been begotten, and of the inheritance that was reserved for them in heaven. That inheritance was incorruptible, and undefiled, and glorious; it would be certainly theirs, for they would be kept by the power of God unto it, though now they were subjected to severe trials, vers. 3–6.

(3.) Even now they could rejoice in hope of that inheritance, (ver. 6 ;) their trial was of great importance to them-selves in order to test the genuineness of their piety, (ver. 7;) and in the midst of all their sufferings they could rejoice in the love of their unseen Saviour, (ver. 8;) and they would certainly obtain the great object for which they had believed—the salvation of their souls, ver. 9. By these considerations the

apostle would reconcile them to their sufferings; for they would thus show the genuineness and value of Christian piety, and would be admitted at last to higher honour.

(4.) The apostle proceeds, in order further to reconcile them to their suf-ferings, to say that the nature of the salvation which they would receive had been an object of earnest inquiry by the prophets. They had searched diligently to know precisely what the Spirit by which they were inspired meant by the revelations given to them, and they had understood that they ministered to the welfare of those who should come after them, vers. 10–12. Those who thus suffered ought, therefore, to rejoice in a salvation which had been revealed to them in this manner; and in the fact that they had knowledge which had not been vouchsafed even to the prophets; and under these circumstances they ought to be willing to bear the trials which had been brought upon them by. a religion so communicated to them.

(5.) In view of these things, the apos-tle (vers. 13–17) exhorts them to be faithful and persevering to the end. In anticipation of what was to be revealed to them at the final day, they should be sober and obedient; and as he who had called them into his kingdom was holy, so it became them to be holy also.

(6.) This consideration is enforced (vers. 18–21) by a reference to the price that was paid for their redemption. They should remember that they had been redeemed, not with silver and gold, but with the precious blood of Christ. He had been appointed from eternity to be their Redeemer; he had been mani-

fested in those times for them ; he had
been raised from the dead for them, and
their faith and hope were through him.
For these reasons they ought to be
steadfast in their attachment to him.
(7.) The apostle enjoins on them the
especial duty of brotherly love, vers. 22,
23. They had purified their hearts by
obeying the truth, and as they were all
one family, they should love one another
fervently. Thus they would show to
their enemies and persecutors the transforming nature of their religion, and furnish an impressive proof of its reality.
(8.) To confirm all these views, the
apostle reminds them that all flesh must
soon die. The glory of man would fade
away. Nothing would abide but the
word of the Lord. They themselves
would soon die, and be released from
their troubles, and they should be willing, therefore, to bear trials for a little
time. The great and the rich, and those
apparently more favoured in this life,
would soon disappear, and all the splendour of their condition would vanish;
and they should not envy them, or repine at their own more humble and
painful lot, vers. 24, 25. The keenest
sufferings here are brief, and the highest
honours and splendours of life here soon
vanish away; and our main solicitude
should be for the eternal inheritance.
Having the prospect of that, and building on the sure word of God, which
abides for ever, we need not shrink from
the trials appointed to us here below.

1. *Peter, an apostle of Jesus Christ.*
On the word *apostle*, see Notes on Rom.
i. 1; 1 Cor. ix. 1, seq. ¶ *To the
strangers.* In the Greek, the word
'elect' (see ver. 2) occurs here : ἐκλεκτοῖς
παρεπιδήμοις, 'to the elect strangers.'
He here addresses them as elect ; in the
following verse he shows them in what
way they were elected. See the Notes
there. The word rendered *strangers*
occurs only in three places in the New
Testament ; Heb. xi. 13, and 1 Pet. ii.
11, where it is rendered *pilgrims*, and
in the place before us. See Notes on
Heb. xi. 13. The word means, literally,
a *by-resident*, a sojourner among a people not one's own.—*Robinson.* There
has been much diversity of opinion as
to the persons here referred to : some
supposing that the epistle was written

to those who had been Jews, who were
now converted, and who were known by
the common appellation among their
countrymen as 'the scattered abroad,'
or the 'dispersion ;' that is, those who
were strangers or sojourners away from
their native land ; others, that the reference is to those who were called,
among the Jews, 'proselytes of the
gate,' or those who were admitted to
certain external privileges among the
Jews, (see Notes on Matt. xxiii. 15;)
and others, that the allusion is to Christians as such, without reference to their
origin, and who are spoken of as strangers
and pilgrims. That the apostle did not
write merely to those who had been
Jews, is clear from chap. iv. 3, 4, (comp.
Intro. § 1;) and it seems probable that
he means here *Christians as such*, without reference to their origin, who were
scattered through the various provinces
of Asia Minor. Yet it seems also probable that he did not use the term as
denoting that they were 'strangers and
pilgrims on the earth,' or with reference
to the fact that the earth was not their
home, as the word is used in Heb. xi.
13; but that he used the term as a Jew
would naturally use it, accustomed, as
he was, to employ it as denoting his
own countrymen dwelling in distant
lands. He would regard them still as
the people of God, though dispersed
abroad; as those who were away from
what was properly the home of their
fathers. So Peter addresses these Christians as the people of God, now scattered abroad; as similar in their condition to the Jews who had been dispersed
among the Gentiles. Comp. the Intro.
§ 1. It is not necessarily implied that
these persons were strangers to Peter,
or that he had never seen them ; though
this was not improbably the fact in regard to most of them. ¶ *Scattered.*
Greek, *of the dispersion*, (διασπορᾶς;) a
term which a Jew would be likely to
use who spoke of his countrymen dwelling among the heathen. See Notes on
John vii. 35, and James i. 1, where the
same Greek word is found. It does not
elsewhere occur in the New Testament.
Here, however, it is applied to Christians as dispersed or scattered abroad.
¶ *Throughout Pontus*, &c. These were
provinces of Asia Minor. Their position

2 Elect [a] according to the fore-knowledge [b] of God the Father, through sanctification [c] of the Spirit, unto [d] obedience and sprink-ling [e] of the blood of Jesus Christ Grace unto you, and peace, be multiplied. [f]

a Ep.1.4.   *b* Rom.8.29.   *c* 2 Th.2.13.
d Ro.16.26.   *e* Heb.12.24.   *f* Jude 2.

may be seen in the map prefixed to the Acts of the Apostles. On the situation of Pontus, see Notes on Acts ii. 9. ¶ *Galatia.* On the situation of this province, and its history, see Intro. to the Notes on Galatians, § 1. ¶ *Cappadocia.* See Notes, Acts ii. 9. ¶ *Asia.* Meaning a province of Asia Minor, of which Ephesus was the capital. Notes, Acts ii. 9. ¶ *And Bithynia.* See Notes on Acts xvi. 7.

2. *Elect.* That is, chosen. The meaning here is, that they were *in fact* chosen. The word does not refer to the *purpose to choose,* but to the fact that they were chosen or selected by God as his people. It is a word commonly applied to the people of God as being *chosen* out of the world, and called to be his. The use of the word does not determine whether God had a previous eternal purpose to choose them or not. That must be determined by something else than the mere use of the term. This word has reference to the *act* of selecting them, without throwing any light on the question why it was done. See Matt. xxiv. 22, 24, 31; Mark xiii. 20; Luke xviii. 7; Rom. viii. 33; Col. iii. 12. Comp. Notes on John xv. 16. The meaning is, that God had, on some account, a preference for them above others as his people, and had chosen them from the midst of others to be heirs of salvation. The word should be properly understood as applied to the *act* of choosing them, not to the *purpose* to choose them; the *fact* of his selecting them to be his, not the *doctrine* that he would choose them; and is a word, therefore, which should be freely and gratefully used by all Christians, for it is a word in frequent use in the Bible, and there is nothing for which men should be more grateful than the fact that God has chosen them to salvation. *Elsewhere* we learn that the purpose to choose them was eternal, and that the reason of it was his own good pleasure. See Notes on Eph. i. 4, 5. We are here also informed that it was in accordance with 'the foreknowledge of God the Father.'

¶ *According to the foreknowledge of God the Father.* The Father is regarded, in the Scriptures, as the Author of the plan of salvation, and as having chosen his people to life, and given them to his Son to redeem and save, John vi. 37, 65; xvii. 2, 6, 11. It is affirmed here that the fact that they were elect was in some sense in accordance with the 'foreknowledge of God.' On the meaning of the phrase, see Notes on Rom. viii. 29. The passage does not affirm that *the thing* which God 'foreknew,' and which was the reason of their being chosen, was, that they would of themselves be disposed to embrace the offer of salvation. The foreknowledge referred to might have been of many other things as constituting the reason which operated in the case ; and it is not proper to *assume* that it could have been of this alone. It *may* mean that God foreknew all the events which would ever occur, and that he saw reasons why they should be selected rather than others; or that he foreknew all that could be made to bear on their salvation; or that he foreknew all that he would himself do to secure their salvation; or that he foreknew them as having been designated by his own eternal counsels; or that he foreknew all that could be accomplished by their instrumentality; or that he saw that they would believe; but it should not be assumed that the word means necessarily any one of these things. The simple fact here affirmed, which no one can deny, is, that there was *foreknowledge* in the case on the part of God. It was not the result of ignorance or of blind chance that they were selected. But if *foreknown,* must it not be *certain ?* How could a thing which is foreknown be contingent or doubtful? The essential idea here is, that the original *choice* was on the part of God, and not on *their* part, and that this choice was founded on what he before knew to be best. He undoubtedly saw good and sufficient *reasons* why the

3 Blessed *a be* the God and Father of our Lord Jesus Christ, which

according to his ¹ abundant *b* mercy

choice should fall on them. I do not know that the reasons why he did it are revealed, or that they could be fully comprehended by us if they were. I am quite certain that it is *not* stated that it is because they would be more disposed of themselves to embrace the Saviour than others; for the Scriptures abundantly teach, what every regenerated person feels to be true, that the fact that we are disposed to embrace the Saviour is to be traced to a Divine influence on our hearts, and not to ourselves. See John vi. 65; Rom. ix. 16; Titus iii. 5; Psa. cx. 2, 3. ¶ *Through sanctification of the Spirit.* The Holy Spirit, the third person of the Trinity. The Greek is, '*by* (ἐν) sanctification of the Spirit;' that is, it was by this influence or agency. The election that was purposed by the Father was carried into effect by the agency of the Spirit in making them holy. The word rendered *sanctification* (ἁλιασμός) is not used here in its usual and technical sense to denote *the progressive holiness of believers,* but in its more primitive and usual sense of *holiness.* Comp. Notes, 1 Cor. i. 30. It means here *the being made holy;* and the idea is, that we become in fact the chosen or elect of God by a work of the Spirit on our hearts making us holy; that is, renewing us in the Divine image. We are chosen by the Father, but it is necessary that the heart should be renewed and made holy by a work of grace, in order that we may actually *become* his chosen people. Though we are sinners, he proposes to save us; but we are not saved *in* our sins, nor can we regard ourselves as the children of God until we have evidence that we are born again. The purpose of God to save us found us unholy, and we become in fact his friends by being renewed in the temper of our mind. A man has reason to think that he is one of the elect of God, just so far as he has evidence that he has been renewed by the Holy Spirit, and so far as he has holiness of heart and life, AND NO FARTHER. ¶ *Unto obedience and sprinkling of the blood of Jesus Christ.* This expresses the *design*

for which they had been chosen by the Father, and renewed by the Spirit. It was that they might obey God, and lead holy lives. On the phrase 'unto obedience,' see Notes on Rom. i. 5. The phrase 'unto sprinkling of the blood of Jesus Christ,' means to cleansing from sin, or to holiness, since it was by the sprinkling of that blood that they were to be made holy. See it explained in the Notes on Heb. ix. 18–23; xii. 24. ¶ *Grace unto you, and peace, be multiplied.* Notes, Rom. i. 7. The phrase 'be multiplied' means, 'may it abound,' or 'may it be conferred abundantly on you.' From this verse we may learn that they who are chosen should be holy. Just in proportion as they have evidence that God has chosen them at all, they have evidence that he has chosen them to be holy; and, in fact, all the evidence which any man *can* have that he is among the elect, is that he *is* practically a holy man, and desires to become more and more so. No man can penetrate the secret counsels of the Almighty. No one can go up to heaven, and inspect the book of life to see if his name be there. No one should *presume* that his name is there without evidence. No one should depend on dreams, or raptures, or visions, as proof that his name is there. No one should expect a new revelation declaring to him that he is among the elect. All the proof which any man *can* have that he is among the chosen of God, is to be found in the evidences of personal piety; and any man who is willing to be a true Christian may have all that evidence in his own case. If any one, then, wishes to settle the question whether he is among the elect or not, the way is plain. Let him become a true Christian, and the whole matter is determined, for that is all the proof which any one has that *he* is chosen to salvation. Till a man is *willing* to do that, he should not complain of the doctrine of election. If he is not *willing* to become a Christian and to be saved, assuredly he should not complain that those who are think that they have evidence that they are the chosen of God.

hath begotten us again *a* unto a lively hope by the resurrection *b* of Jesus Christ from the dead,

4 To an inheritance *c* incorrup-

tible, and undefiled, and that fadeth *d* not away, reserved *e* in heaven for *1* you,

a Jn.3.3,5.　　b 1 Co.15.20.　　c He.9.15.
d 1 Pet.5.4.　　e Col.1.5.　　1 Or, us.

3. *Blessed be the God and Father of our Lord Jesus Christ.* See Notes on 2 Cor. i. 3. ¶ *Which according to his abundant mercy.* Marg., as in the Greek, *much.* The idea is, that there was great mercy shown them in the fact that they were renewed. They had no claim to the favour, and the favour was great. Men are not begotten to the hope of heaven because they have any claim on God, or because it would not be right for him to withhold the favour. See Notes on Eph. ii. 4. ¶ *Hath begotten us again.* The meaning is, that as God is the Author of our life in a natural sense, so he is the Author of our second life by regeneration. The Saviour said, (John iii. 3,) that 'except a man be born again,' or begotten again, (*γεννηθῇ ἄνωθεν*,) 'he cannot see the kingdom of God.' Peter here affirms that that change *had* occurred in regard to himself and those whom he was addressing. The *word* used here as a compound (*ἀναγεννάω*) does not elsewhere occur in the New Testament, though it corresponds entirely with the words used by the Saviour in John iii. 3, 5, 7. Perhaps the phrase 'begotten again' would be better in each instance where the word occurs, the sense being rather that of being *begotten again*, than of being *born again.* ¶ *Unto a lively hope.* The word *lively* we now use commonly in the sense of *active, animated, quick;* the word here used, however, means *living,* in contradistinction from that which is *dead.* The hope which they had, had living power. It was not cold, inoperative, dead. It was not a mere form—or a mere speculation—or a mere sentiment; it was that which was vital to their welfare, and which was active and powerful. On the nature of *hope,* see Notes, Rom. 8, 24. Comp. Eph. ii. 12. ¶ *By the resurrection of Jesus Christ from the dead.* The resurrection of the Lord Jesus is the foundation of our hope. It was a confirmation of what he declared as truth when he lived; it was a proof of the doctrine of

the immortality of the soul; it was a pledge that all who are united to him will be raised up. See Notes on 1 Cor. xv. 1–20; 2 Tim. i. 10; 1 Thes. iv. 14. On this verse we may remark, that the fact that Christians are *chosen* to salvation should be a subject of gratitude and praise. Every man should rejoice that *any* of the race may be saved, and the world should be thankful for every new instance of Divine favour in granting to any one a hope of eternal life. Especially should this be a source of joy to true Christians. Well do they know that if God had not chosen them to salvation, they would have remained as thoughtless as others; if he had had no purpose of mercy towards them, they would never have been saved. Assuredly, if there is *anything* for which a man should be grateful, it is that God has so loved him as to give him the hope of eternal life; and if he has had *an eternal purpose* to do this, our gratitude should be proportionably increased.

4. *To an inheritance.* Through the resurrection of the Lord Jesus we now cherish the hope of that future inheritance in heaven. On the word *inheritance,* see Notes on Acts xx. 32; Eph. i. 11, 14, 18; Col. i. 12. Christians are regarded as the adopted children of God, and heaven is spoken of as their *inheritance*—as what their Father will bestow on them as the proof of his love. ¶ *Incorruptible.* It will not fade away and vanish, as that which we inherit in this world does. See the word explained in the Notes on 1 Cor. ix. 25. The meaning here is, that the inheritance will be imperishable, or will endure for ever. Here, to whatever we may be heirs, we must soon part with the inheritance; there it will be eternal. ¶ *And undefiled.* See Notes, Heb. vii. 26; xiii. 4; James i. 27. The word does not elsewhere occur in the New Testament. As applied to an *inheritance,* it means that it will be *pure.* It will not have been obtained by dishonesty, nor will it be held by

5 Who are kept *a* by the power
of God through faith *b* unto salva-

a Jude 1,24.　　　b Ep.2.8.

tion, ready to be revealed in the
last time.

fraud; it will not be such as will corrupt
the soul, or tempt to extravagance,
sensuality, and lust, as a rich inheritance often does here; it will be such that
its eternal enjoyment will never tend in
any manner to defile the heart. 'How
many estates,' says Benson, 'have been
got by fraudulent and unjust methods;
by poisoning, or in some other way mur-
dering the right heir; by cheating of
helpless orphans; by ruining the fatherless and widows; by oppressing their
neighbours, or grinding the faces of the
poor, and taking their garments or vine-
yards from them! But this future inheritance of the saints is stained by none
of these vices; it is neither got nor detained by any of these methods; nor
shall persons polluted with vice have
any share in it.' Here no one can be
heir to an inheritance of gold or houses
without danger of soon sinking into indolence, effeminacy, or vice; there the
inheritance may be enjoyed for ever,
and the soul continually advance in
knowledge, holiness, and the active service of God. ¶ *And that fadeth not
away.* Gr. ἀμάραντον. This word occurs nowhere else in the New Testament,
though the word ἀμαράντινος (*amaran-
tine*) occurs in chap. v. 4, applied to a
crown or garland. The word is properly
applied to that which does not fade or
wither, in contradistinction from a flower
that fades. It may then denote anything that is enduring, and is applied to
the future inheritance of the saints to
describe its perpetuity *in all its bril-
liance and splendour*, in contrast with
the fading nature of all that is earthly.
The idea here, therefore, is not precisely
the same as is expressed by the word
'incorruptible.' Both words indeed denote *perpetuity*, but that refers to perpetuity in contrast with *decay;* this
denotes perpetuity in the sense that
everything there *will be kept in its
original brightness and beauty.* The
crown of glory, though worn for millions
of ages, will not be dimmed; the golden
streets will lose none of their lustre; the
flowers that bloom on the banks of the
river of life will always be as rich in

colour, and as fragant, as when we first
beheld them. ¶ *Reserved in heaven for
you.* Marg., *us.* The difference in the
text and the margin arises from the
various readings in MSS. The common
reading is 'for *you.*' The sense is not
materially affected. The idea is, that
it is an inheritance appointed for us,
and kept by one who can make it sure
to us, and who will certainly bestow it
upon us. Comp. Notes on Matt. xxv.
34; John xiv. 2; Col. i. 5.

5. *Who are kept by the power of God.*
That is, 'kept' or preserved in the faith
and hope of the gospel; who are preserved from apostacy, or so kept that
you will finally obtain salvation. The
word which is here used, and rendered
kept, (φρουρέω—*phroureo*,) is rendered
in 2 Cor. xi. 32, *kept with a garrison;*
in Gal. iii. 23, and here, *kept;* in Phil.
iv. 7, *shall keep.* It does not elsewhere
occur in the New Testament. It means
to keep, as in a garrison or fortress; or
as with a military watch. The idea is,
that there was a faithful guardianship
exercised over them to save them from
danger, as a castle or garrison is watched
to guard it against the approach of an
enemy. The meaning is, that they were
weak in themselves, and were surrounded
by temptations; and that the only reason
why they were preserved was, that God
exerted his power to keep them. The
only reason which any Christians have
to suppose they will ever reach heaven,
is the fact that God keeps them by his
own power. Comp. Notes, Phil. i. 6;
2 Tim. i. 12; iv. 18. If it were left to
the will of man; to the strength of his
own resolutions; to his power to meet
temptations, and to any probability that
he would of himself continue to walk in
the path of life, there would be no certainty that any one would be saved.
¶ *Through faith.* That is, he does not
keep us by the mere exertion of *power*,
but he excites *faith* in our hearts, and
makes that the *means* of keeping us.
As long as we have faith in God, and in
his promises, we are safe. When that
fails, we are weak; and if it should fail
altogether, we could not be saved. Comp.

6 Wherein ye greatly rejoice, though now for a season, if need *be, ye are in heaviness through manifold temptations:

a He.12.7-11.

Notes, Eph. ii. 8. ¶ *Unto salvation.* Not preserved for a little period, and then suffered to fall away, but *so* kept as to be saved. We may remark here that Peter, as well as Paul, believed in the doctrine of the perseverance of the saints. If he did not, how could he have addressed these Christians in this manner, and said that they were 'kept by the power of God *unto salvation?'* What evidence could he have had that they would obtain salvation, unless he believed in the general truth that it was the purpose of God to keep *all* who were truly converted? ¶ *Ready to be revealed in the last time.* That is, when the world shall close. Then it shall be made manifest to assembled worlds that such an inheritance was 'reserved' for you, and that you were 'kept' in order to inherit it. Comp. Matt. xxv. 34. This verse, then, teaches that the doctrine that the saints will *persevere* and be saved, is true. They are '*kept* by the power of God to salvation;' and as God has *all* power, and guards them with reference to this end, it cannot be but that they will be saved. It may be added (*a*) that it is very *desirable* that the doctrine should be true. Man is so weak and feeble, so liable to fall, and so exposed to temptation, that it is in itself every way a thing to be wished that his salvation should be in some safer hands than his own. (*b*) If it is *desirable* that it should be true, it is fair to infer that it *is* true, for God has made all the arrangements for the salvation of his people which are really desirable and proper. (*c*) The only *security* for the salvation of any one is founded on that doctrine. If it were left entirely to the hands of men, even the best of men, what assurance could there be that any one could be saved? Did not Adam fall? Did not holy angels fall? Have not some of the best of men fallen into sin? And who has such a strength of holiness that he could certainly confide in it to make his own salvation sure? Any man must know little of himself, and of the human heart, who supposes that he has such a strength of virtue that he would never

fall away if left to himself. But if this be so, then his only hope of salvation is in the fact that God intends to 'keep his people by his own power through faith unto salvation.'

6. *Wherein ye greatly rejoice.* In which hope of salvation. The idea is, that the prospect which they had of the future inheritance was to them a source of the highest joy, even in the midst of their many sufferings and trials. On the *general* grounds for rejoicing, see Notes, Rom. v. 1, 2; Phil. iii. 1; iv. 4; 1 Thess. v. 16. See also the Notes on ver. 8 of this chapter. The *particular* meaning here is, that the hope which they had of their future inheritance enabled them to rejoice *even in the midst of persecutions and trials.* It not only *sustained* them, but it made them *happy.* That must be a valuable religion which will make men *happy* in the midst of persecutions and heavy calamities. ¶ *Though now for a season.* A short period—ὀλίγον. It would be in fact only for a brief period, even if it should continue through the whole of life. Comp. Notes, 2 Cor. iv. 17: ' Our light affliction which is *but for a moment.'* It is possible, however, that Peter supposed that the trials which they then experienced would soon pass over. They may have been suffering persecutions which he hoped would not long continue. ¶ *If need be.* This phrase seems to have been thrown in here to intimate that there was a necessity for their afflictions, or that there was 'need' that they should pass through these trials. There was some good to be accomplished by them, which made it desirable and proper that they should be thus afflicted. The sense is, 'since there is need;' though the apostle expresses it more delicately by suggesting the possibility that there *might* be need of it, instead of saying absolutely that there *was* need. It is the kind of language which we would use in respect to one who was greatly afflicted, by suggesting to him, in the most tender manner, that there *might* be things in his character which God designed to correct

7 That the trial of *a* your faith, being much more precious than of gold that perisheth, though it be

a Ja.1.3,12.   *b* 1 Co.3.13.

tried with *b* fire, might be found unto praise and *c* honour and glory at the appearing *d* of Jesus Christ:

c Ro.2.7,10.   *d* Re·1.7.

by trials, instead of saying roughly and bluntly that such *was* undoubtedly the fact. We would not say to such a person, 'you certainly *needed* this affliction to lead you to amend your life;' but, 'it *may be* that there is something in your character which makes it desirable, or that God intends that some good results shall come from it which will show that it is wisely ordered.' ¶ *Ye are in heaviness*. Gr., ' Ye are sorrowing,' (λυπηθέντες;) you are sad, or grieved, Matt. xiv. 9; xvii. 23. ¶ *Through manifold temptations*. Through many kinds of *trials*, for so the word rendered *temptation* (πειρασμός) means, James i. 2, 12. Notes, Matt. iv. 1; vi. 13. The meaning here is, that they now endured many things which were fitted to *try* or *test* their faith. These might have consisted of poverty, persecution, sickness, or the efforts of others to lead them to renounce their religion, and to go back to their former state of unbelief. Any one or all of these would *try* them, and would show whether their religion was genuine. On the various ways which God has of trying his people, comp. Notes, Isa. xxviii. 23–29.

7. *That the trial of your faith*. The putting of your religion to the test, and showing what is its real nature. Comp. James i. 3, 12. ¶ *Being much more precious than of gold*. This does not mean that their *faith* was much more precious than gold, but that *the testing of it*, (δοκίμιον.) the process of *showing* whether it was or was not genuine, was a much more important and valuable process than that of testing gold in the fire. More important results were to be arrived at by it, and it was more desirable that it should be done. ¶ *That perisheth*. Not that gold perishes by the process of being tried in the fire, for this is not the fact, and the connexion does not demand this interpretation. The idea is, that gold, however valuable it is, is a *perishable* thing. It is not an enduring, imperishable, indestructible thing, like religion. It may not perish in the fire, but it will in some way, for

it will not endure for ever. ¶ *Though it be tried with fire*. This refers to the *gold*. See the Greek. The meaning is, that gold, though it will bear the action of fire, is yet a destructible thing, and will not endure for ever. It is more desirable to *test* religion than it is gold, because it is more valuable. It pertains to that which is eternal and indestructible, and it is therefore of more importance to show its true quality, and to free it from every improper mixture. ¶ *Might be found unto praise*. That is, might be found to be genuine, and such as to meet the praise or commendation of the final judge. ¶ *And honour*. That honour might be done to it before assembled worlds. ¶ *And glory*. That it might be rewarded with that glory which will be then conferred on all who have shown, in the various trials of life, that they had true religion. ¶ *At the appearing of Jesus Christ*. To judge the world. Comp. Matt. xxv. 31; Acts i. 11; 1 Thess. iv. 16; 2 Thess. ii. 8; 1 Tim. vi. 14; 2 Tim. iv. 1, 8; Tit. ii. 13. From these two verses (6 and 7) we may learn: I. That it is desirable that the faith of Christians should be *tried*. (*a*) It is desirable to know whether that which appears to be religion is *genuine*, as it is desirable to know whether that which appears to be gold is genuine. To gold we apply the action of intense heat, that we may know whether it is what it appears to be; and as religion is of more value than gold, so it is more desirable that it should be subjected to the proper tests, that its nature may be ascertained. There is much which *appears* to be gold, which is of no value, as there is much which *appears* to be religion, which is of no value. The one is worth no more than the other, unless it is genuine. (*b*) It is desirable in order to show its true *value*. It is of great importance to know what that which is claimed to be gold is *worth* for the purposes to which gold is usually applied; and so it is in regard to religion. Religion claims to be of more value to man

8 Whom having not *a* seen, ye | love; in whom, though now ye see

a 1 Jn.4.20.

than anything else. It asserts its power to do that for the intellect and the heart which nothing else can do; to impart consolation in the various trials of life which nothing else can impart; and to give a support which nothing else can on the bed of death. It is very desirable, therefore, that in these various situations it should show its power; that is, that its friends should be *in* these various conditions, in order that they may illustrate the true value of religion. (*c*) It is desirable that true religion should be separated from all *alloy*. There is often much alloy in gold, and it is desirable that it should be separated from it, in order that it may be pure. So it is in religion. It is often combined with much that is unholy and impure; much that dims its lustre and mars its beauty; much that prevents its producing the effect which it would otherwise produce. Gold is, indeed, often *better*, for some purposes, for having some alloy mixed with it; but not so with religion. It is never better for having a little pride, or vanity, or selfishness, or meanness, or worldliness, or sensuality mingled with it; and that which will remove these things from our religion will be a favour to us. II. God takes various methods of trying his people, with a design to test the value of their piety, and to separate it from all impure mixtures. (1.) He tries his people by *prosperity*—often as decisive a test of piety as can be applied to it. There is much pretended piety, which will bear adversity, but which will not bear prosperity. The piety of a man is decisively tested by popularity; by the flatteries of the world; by a sudden increase of property; and in such circumstances it is often conclusively shown that there is no true religion in the soul. (2.) He tries his people in adversity. He lays his hand on them heavily, to show (*a*) whether they will *bear up* under their trials, and persevere in his service; (*b*) to show whether their religion will keep them from murmuring or complaining; (*c*) to show whether it is adapted to comfort and sustain the soul. (3.) He tries his people *by sudden transition*

from one to the other. We get accustomed to a uniform course of life, whether it be joy or sorrow; and the religion which is adapted to a uniform course may be little fitted to transitions from one condition of life to another. In *prosperity* we may have shown that we were grateful, and benevolent, and disposed to serve God; but our religion will be subjected to a new test, if we are suddenly reduced to poverty. In sickness and poverty, we learn to be patient and resigned, and perhaps even happy. But the religion which we then cultivated may be little adapted to a sudden transition to prosperity; and in such a transition, there would be a new trial of our faith. That piety which shone so much on a bed of sickness, might be little fitted to shine in circumstances of sudden prosperity. The human frame may become accustomed either to the intense cold of the polar regions, or to the burning heats of the equator; but in neither case might it bear a transition from one to the other. It is such a *transition* that is a more decisive test of its powers of endurance than either intense heat or cold, if steadily prolonged. III. Religion will *bear* any trial which may be applied to it, as gold will bear the action of fire. IV. Religion is *imperishable* in its nature. Even the most fine gold will perish. Time will corrode it, or it will be worn away by use, or it will be destroyed at the universal conflagration; but time and use will not wear out religion, and it will live on through the fires that will consume everything else. V. Christians should be *willing* to pass trough trials. (*a*) They will purify their religion, as the fire will remove dross from gold. (*b*) They will make it shine more brightly, as gold does when it comes out of the furnace. (*c*) They will disclose more fully its value. (*d*) They will furnish an evidence that we shall be saved; for that religion which will bear the tests that God applies to it in the present life, will bear the test of the final trial.

8. *Whom having not seen, ye love.* This epistle was addressed to those

him not, yet believing, ye rejoice | with joy *a* unspeakable and full of
a Jn.16.22. | glory :

who were 'strangers scattered abroad,' (Notes, ver. 1,) and it is evident that they had not personally seen the Lord Jesus. Yet they had heard of his character, his preaching, his sacrifice for sin, and his resurrection and ascension, and they had learned to love him. (1.) It is possible to love one whom we have not seen. Thus we may love God, whom no 'eye hath seen,' (comp. 1 John iv. 20 ;) and thus we may love a benefactor, from whom we have received important benefits, whom we have never beheld. (2.) We may love the *character* of one whom we have never seen, and from whom we may never have received any particular favours. We may love his uprightness, his patriotism, his benignity, as represented to us. We might love him the more if we should become personally acquainted with him, and if we should receive important favours from him ; but it is possible to feel a sense of strong admiration for such a character in itself. (3.) That may be a very *pure* love which we have for one whom we have never seen. It may be based on simple excellence of character ; and in such a case there is the least chance for any intermingling of selfishness, or any improper emotion of any kind. (4.) We may love a friend as *really* and as *strongly* when he is absent, as when he is with us. The wide ocean that rolls between us and a child, does not diminish the ardour of our affection for him ; and the Christian friend that has gone to heaven, we may love no less than when he sat with us at the fireside. (5.) Millions, and hundreds of millions, have been led to love the Saviour, who have never seen him. They have seen —not with the bodily eye, but with the eye of faith—the inimitable beauty of his character, and have been brought to love him with an ardour of affection which they never had for any other one. (6.) There is every reason why we *should* love him. (*a*) His character is infinitely lovely. (*b*) He has done more for us than any other one who ever lived among men. He died for us, to redeem our souls. He rose, and brought life and immortality to light. He ever lives to

intercede for us in heaven. He is employed in preparing mansions of rest for us in the skies, and he will come and take us to himself, that we may be with him for ever. Such a Saviour *ought* to be loved, *is* loved, and *will* be loved. The strongest attachments which have ever existed on earth have been for this unseen Saviour. There has been a love for him stronger than that for a father, or mother, or wife, or sister, or home, or country. It has been so strong, that thousands have been willing, on account of it, to bear the torture of the rack or the stake. It has been so strong, that thousands of youth of the finest minds, and the most flattering prospects of distinction, have been willing to leave the comforts of a civilized land, and to go among the benighted heathen, to tell them the story of a Saviour's life and death. It has been so strong, that unnumbered multitudes have longed, more than they have for all other things, that they might see him, and be with him, and abide with him for ever and ever. Comp. Notes, Phil. i. 23. ¶ *In whom, though now ye see* him *not, yet believing.* He is now in heaven, and to mortal eyes now invisible, like his Father. *Faith* in him is the source and fountain of our joy. It makes invisible things real, and enables us to feel and act, in view of them, with the same degree of certainty *as if* we saw them. Indeed, the conviction to the mind of a true believer that there *is* a Saviour, is as certain and as strong as if he saw him ; and the same may be said of his conviction of the existence of heaven, and of eternal realities. If it should be said that faith may deceive us, we may reply, (1,) May not our bodily senses also deceive us ? Does the *eye* never deceive ? Are there no optical illusions ? Does the *ear* never deceive ? Are there no sounds which are mistaken ? Do the *taste* and the *smell* never deceive ? Are we never mistaken in the report which they bring to us ? And does the sense of *feeling* never deceive ? Are we never mistaken in the size, the hardness, the figure of objects which we handle ? But, (2,) for all the practical purposes of life, the senses are

9 Receiving the end of your faith, | *even* the salvation of *your* souls.

---

correct guides, and do not in general lead us astray. So, (3,) there are objects of faith about which we are never deceived, and where we do act and must act with the same confidence as if we had personally seen them. Are we deceived about the existence of London, or Paris, or Canton, though we may never have seen either? May not a merchant embark with perfect propriety in a commercial enterprise, on the supposition that there *is* such a place as London or Canton, though he has never seen them? Would he not be reputed mad, if he should *refuse* to do it on this ground? And so, may not a man, in believing that there is a heaven, and in forming his plans for it, though he has not yet seen it, act as rationally and as wisely as he who forms his plans on the supposition that there is such a place as Canton? ¶ *Ye rejoice.* Ye *do rejoice;* not merely ye *ought to rejoice.* It may be said of Christians that they *do in fact* rejoice; they *are* happy. The people of the world often suppose that religion makes its professors sad and melancholy. That there are those who have not great comfort in their religion, no one can doubt; but this arises from several causes entirely independent of their religion. Some have melancholy temperaments, and are not happy in anything. Some have little evidence that they are Christians, and their sadness arises not from religion, but from the want of it. But that true religion *does* make its possessors happy, any one may easily satisfy himself by asking any number of sincere Christians, of any denomination, whom he may meet. With one accord they will say to him that they have a happiness which they never found before; that however much they may have possessed of the wealth, the honours, and the pleasures of the world —and they who are now Christians have not all of them been strangers to these things—they never knew solid and substantial peace till they found it in religion. And why should they not be believed? The world would believe them in other things; why will they not when they declare that religion does not

make them gloomy, but happy? ¶ *With joy unspeakable.* A very strong expression, and yet verified in thousands of cases among young converts, and among those in the maturer days of piety. There are thousands who can say that their happiness when they first had evidence that their sins were forgiven, that the burden of guilt was rolled away, and that they were the children of God, was unspeakable. They had no words to express it, it was so full and so new.

> "Tongue can never express
> The sweet comfort and peace
> Of a soul in its earliest love."

And so there have been thousands of mature Christians who can adopt the same language, and who could find no words to express the peace and joy which they have found in the love of Christ, and the hope of heaven. And why are not all Christians enabled to say constantly that they 'rejoice with joy unspeakable?' Is it not a privilege which they might possess? Is there anything in the nature of religion which forbids it? Why should *not* one be filled with constant joy who has the hope of dwelling in a world of glory for ever? Comp. John xiv. 27; xvi. 22. ¶ *And full of glory.* (1.) Of anticipated glory—of the prospect of enjoying the glory of heaven. (2.) Of present glory—with a joy *even now* which is of the same nature as that in heaven; a happiness the same in kind, though not in degree, as that which will be ours in a brighter world. The saints on earth partake of the same *kind* of joy which they will have in heaven; for the happiness of heaven will be but an expansion, a prolongation, and a purifying of that which they have here. Comp. Notes on Eph. i. 14.

9. *Receiving the end of your faith,* even *the salvation of* your *souls.* The *result* or *object* of your faith; that is, what your faith is designed and adapted to secure. Comp. Notes on Rom. x. 4. The word rendered *receiving* is used here as indicating that they would surely obtain that. They even now had such peace and joy in believing, that it furnished undoubted evidence that they

10 Of which salvation the prophets have enquired *a* and searched diligently, who prophesied of the grace that should come unto you:
11 Searching what, or what man-

a Da.9.3.

ner of time the Spirit *b* of Christ which was in them did signify, when it testified before-hand the sufferings of Christ, and the glory that should follow:

b 2 Pe.1.21.

would be saved; and such that it might be said that even now they *were* saved. The condition of one who is a true Christian here is so secure that it may even now be called *salvation.*
10. *Of which salvation.* Of the certainty that this system of religion, securing the salvation of the soul, would be revealed. The *object* of this reference to the prophets seems to be to lead them to value the religion which they professed more highly, and to encourage them to bear their trials with patience. They were in a condition, in many respects, far superior to that of the prophets. They had the full light of the gospel. The prophets saw it only at a distance and but dimly, and were obliged to search anxiously that they might understand the nature of that system of which they were appointed to furnish the comparatively obscure prophetic intimations. ¶ *The prophets.* This language would imply that this had been a common and prevalent wish of the prophets. ¶ *Have enquired.* This word is *intensive.* It means that they sought out, or scrutinized with care the revelations made to them, that they might understand exactly what was implied in that which they were appointed to record in respect to the salvation which was to be made known through the Messiah. See the following places where the same word is used which occurs here: Luke xi. 50, 51; Acts xv. 17; Rom. iii. 11; Heb. xi. 6; xii. 17. ¶ *And searched diligently—ἐξηρεύνάω.* Comp. Dan. ix. 2, 3. The word here used means *to search out, to trace out, to explore.* It is not elsewhere used in the New Testament, though one of the words from which this is compounded (ἐρευνάω) occurs. See John v. 39, (Notes;) vii. 52; Rom. viii. 27; 1 Cor. ii. 10; Rev. ii. 23. The idea is, that they perceived that in their communications there were some great and glorious truths which they did not fully comprehend, and that they dili-

gently employed their natural faculties to understand that which they were appointed to impart to succeeding generations. They thus became students and interpreters for themselves of their own predictions. They were not only *prophets*, but *men.* They had souls to be saved in the same way as others. They had hearts to be sanctified by the truth; and it was needful, in order to this, that truth should be applied to their own hearts in the same way as to others. The mere fact that they were the channels or organs for imparting truth to others would not save them, any more than the fact that a man now preaches truth to others will save himself, or than the fact that a sutler delivers bread to an army will nourish and support his own body. ¶ *Who prophesied of the grace* that should come *unto you.* Of the favour that should be shown to you in the gospel. Though the predictions which they uttered appeared to the men of their own times, and perhaps to themselves, obscure, yet they were in fact *prophecies* of what was to come, and of the favours which, under another dispensation, would be bestowed upon the people of God. The apostle does not mean to say that they prophesied particularly of those persons to whom he was then writing, but that their prophecies were *in fact* for their benefit, for the things which they predicted had actually terminated on them. The benefit was as real as though the predictions had been solely on their account.
11. *Searching what.* That is, examining their own predictions with care, to ascertain what they meant. They studied them as we do the predictions which others have made; and though the prophets were the medium through which the truth was made known, yet their own predictions became a subject of careful investigation to themselves. The expression here used in the origi-

nal, rendered 'what,' (εἰς τίνα,) literally, 'unto what,' may mean, so far as the Greek is concerned, either 'what time,' or 'what people,' or 'what person;' that is, with reference to what person the prophecies were really uttered. The latter, it seems to me, is the correct interpretation, meaning that they inquired in regard to him, who he would be, what would be his character, and what would be the nature of the work which he would perform. There can be no doubt that they understood that their predictions related to the Messiah ; but still it is not improper to suppose that it was with them an interesting inquiry what sort of a person he would be, and what would be the nature of the work which he would perform. This interpretation of the phrase εἰς τίνα, (unto what or whom,) it should be observed, however, is not that which is commonly given of the passage. Bloomfield, Rosenmüller, Doddridge, Whitby, Benson, and Grotius suppose it to refer to time, meaning that they inquired at what time, or when these things would occur. Macknight thinks it refers to people, (λαον,) meaning that they diligently inquired what people would put him to death. But the most obvious interpretation is that which I have suggested above, meaning that they made particular inquiry to whom their prophecies related—what was his rank and character, and what was to be the nature of his work. What would be a more natural inquiry for them than this? What would be more important? And how interesting is the thought that when Isaiah, for example, had given utterance to the sublime predictions which we now have of the Messiah, in his prophecies, he sat himself down with the spirit of a little child, to learn by prayer and study, what was fully implied in the amazing words which the Spirit had taught him to record! How much of mystery might seem still to hang around the subject! And how intent would such a mind be to know what was the full import of those words! ¶ Or what manner of time. This phrase, in Greek, (ποῖον καιρὸν,) would properly relate, not to the exact time when these things would occur, but to the character or condition of the age when they would take place;

perhaps referring to the state of the world at that period, the preparation to receive the gospel, and the probable manner in which the great message would be received. Perhaps, however, the inquiry in their minds pertained to the time when the predictions would be fulfilled, as well as to the condition of the world when the event takes place. The meaning of the Greek phrase would not exclude this latter sense. There are not unfrequent indications of time in the prophets, (comp. Dan. ix. 24, seq. ;) and these indications were of so clear a character, that when the Saviour actually appeared there was a general expectation that the event would then occur. See Notes on Matt. ii. 2. ¶ The Spirit of Christ which was in them. This does not prove that they knew that this was the Spirit of Christ, but is only a declaration of Peter that it was actually so. It is not probable that the prophets distinctly understood that the Spirit of inspiration, by which they were led to foretell future events, was peculiarly the Spirit of Christ. They understood that they were inspired; but there is no intimation, with which I am acquainted, in their writings, that they regarded themselves as inspired by the Messiah. It was not improper, however, for Peter to say that the Spirit by which they were influenced was in fact the Spirit of Christ, so called because that Spirit which suggested these future events to them was given as the great Medium of all revealed truth to the world. Comp. Heb. i. 3; John i. 9; xiv. 16, 26; xvi. 7; Isa. xlix. 6. It is clear from this passage, (1,) that Christ must have had an existence before his incarnation ; and, (2,) that he must have understood then what would occur to him when he should become incarnate ; that is, it must have been arranged or determined beforehand. ¶ Did signify. Meant to intimate or manifest to them, (ἰδήλου ;) or what was implied in the communications made to them. ¶ When it testified beforehand the sufferings of Christ. As Isaiah, chap. liii ; Daniel, chap. ix. 25–27. They saw clearly that the Messiah was to suffer; and doubtless this was the common doctrine of the prophets, and the common expectation of the pious part of the Jewish nation. Yet it is not necessary

12 Unto whom it was revealed, that not *a* unto themselves, but unto us they did minister the things, which are now reported unto you by them that have preached the

gospel unto you with the Holy Ghost *b* sent down from heaven; which things the angels *c* desire to look into.

a He.2.39,40.   *b* Ac.2.4; 2 Co.1.22.   *c* Ep.3.10.

to suppose that they had clear apprehensions of his sufferings, or were able to reconcile all that was said on that subject with what was said of his glory and his triumphs. There was much about those sufferings which *they* wished to learn, as there is much still which *we* desire to know. We have no reason to suppose that there were any views of the sufferings of the Messiah communicated to the prophets except what we now have in the Old Testament; and to see the force of what Peter says, we ought to imagine what would be *our* views of him if all that we have known of Christ as *history* were obliterated, and we had only the knowledge which we could derive from the Old Testament. As has been already intimated, it is probable that they studied their own predictions, just as *we* would study them if we had not the advantage of applying to them the *facts* which have actually occurred. ¶ *And the glory that should follow.* That is, they saw that there *would be* glory which would be the result of his sufferings, but they did not clearly see what it would be. They had some knowledge that he would be raised from the dead, (Psa. xvi. 8–11; Comp. Acts ii. 25–28;) they knew that he would ' see of the travail of his soul, and would be satisfied,' (Isa. liii. 11;) they had some large views of the effects of the gospel on the nations of the earth, Isa. xi; xxv. 7, 8; lx; lxvi. But there were many things respecting his glorification which it cannot be supposed they clearly understood; and it is reasonable to presume that they made the comparatively few and obscure intimations in their own writings in relation to this, the subject of profound and prayerful inquiry.

12. *Unto whom it was revealed.* They were not permitted to know fully the import of the predictions which they were made the instruments of communicating to mankind, but they understood that they were intended for the

benefit of future ages. ¶ *That not unto themselves.* We are not to suppose that they derived *no* benefit from their own predictions; for, as far as they understood the truth, it was as much adapted to sanctify and comfort them as it is us now: but the meaning is, that their messages had reference mainly to future times, and that the full benefit of them would be experienced only in distant ages. Comp. Heb. xi. 39, 40. ¶ *Unto us they did minister the things, which are now reported unto you.* Not unto us *by name*, but their ministrations had reference to the times of the Messiah; and those to whom Peter wrote, in common with all Christians, were those who were to enjoy the fruits of the communications which they made. The word *reported* means *announced*, or *made known*. ¶ *By them that have preached the gospel unto you.* The apostles, who have made known unto you, in their true sense, the things which the prophets predicted, the import of which they themselves were so desirous of understanding. ¶ *With the Holy Ghost sent down from heaven.* Accompanied by the influences of the Holy Ghost bearing those truths to the heart, and confirming them to the soul. It was the same Spirit which inspired the prophets which conveyed those truths to the souls of the early Christians, and which discloses them to true believers in every age. Comp. John xvi. 13, 14; Acts ii. 4; x. 44, 45. The *object* of Peter by thus referring to the prophets, and to the interest which they took in the things which those to whom he wrote now enjoyed, seems to have been, to impress on them a deep sense of the value of the gospel, and of the great privileges which they enjoyed. They were reaping the benefit of all the labours of the prophets. They were permitted to see truth clearly, which the prophets themselves saw only obscurely. They were, in many respects, more favoured than even those holy men had been. It was for them that the prophets had spoken the word of the Lord ; for them and their salvation that a long line of the most holy men that the world ever saw, had lived, and toiled, and suffered ; and while they themselves had not been allowed to understand the full import of their own predictions, the most humble believer was permitted to see what the most distinguished prophet never saw. See Matt. xiii. 17. ¶ *Which things the angels desire to look into.* The object of this reference to the angels is the same as that to the prophets. It is to impress on Christians a sense of the value of that gospel which they had received, and to show them the greatness of their privileges in being made partakers of it. It had excited the deepest interest among the most holy men on earth, and even among the inhabitants of the skies. They were enjoying the full revelation of what even the angels had desired more fully to understand, and to comprehend which they had employed their great powers of investigation. The *things* which are here referred to, (*εἰς ἃ—unto which,*) are those which the prophets were so desirous to understand—the great truths respecting the sufferings of Christ, the glory which would follow, and the nature and effects of the gospel. In all the events pertaining to the redemption of a world they felt a deep interest. The word which is rendered ' to look,' (*παρα-κύψαι,*) is rendered *stooping down,* and *stooped down,* in Luke xxiv. 12 ; John xx. 5, 11; *looketh,* in James i. 25; and *look,* in the place before us. It does not elsewhere occur in the New Testament. It properly means, to stoop down near by anything ; to bend forward near, in order to look at anything more closely.—*Robinson, Lex.* It would denote that state where one, who was before at so great a distance that he could not clearly see an object, should draw nearer, stooping down in order that he might observe it more distinctly. It is possible, as Grotius supposes, that there may be an allusion here to the posture of the cherubim over the mercy-seat, represented as looking down with an intense gaze, as if to behold what was in the ark. But it is not necessary to suppose that this is the allusion, nor is it absolutely certain that that was the

posture of the cherubim. See Notes on Heb. ix. 5. All that is necessarily implied in the language is, that the angels had an intense desire to look into these things; that they contemplated them with interest and fixed attention, like one who comes near to an object, and looks narrowly upon it. In illustration of this sentiment, we may make the following suggestions : I. The angels, doubtless, desire to look into *all* the manifestations of the character of God, wherever those manifestations are made. (1.) It is not unreasonable to suppose that, to a great degree, they acquire the knowledge of God as all other creatures do. They are not omniscient, and cannot be supposed to comprehend at a glance all his doings. (2.) They doubtless employ their faculties, substantially as we do, in the investigation of truth; that is, from things known they seek to learn those that are even unknown. (3.) It is not unreasonable to suppose that there are many things in relation to the Divine character and plans, which they do not yet understand. They know, undoubtedly, much more than we do; but there are plans and purposes of God which are yet made known to none of his creatures. No one can doubt that these plans and purposes must be the object of the attentive study of all holy created minds. (4.) They doubtless feel a great interest in the welfare of other beings—of their fellow-creatures, wherever they are. There is in the universe one great brotherhood, embracing all the creatures of God. (5.) They cannot but feel a deep interest in man—a fallen creature, tempted, suffering, dying, and exposed to eternal death. This they have shown in every period of the world's history. Notes on Heb. i. 14. II. It is probable, that in each one of the worlds which God has made, there is some peculiar manifestation of his glory and character; something which is not to be found at all in any other world, or, if found, not in so great perfection; and that the angels would feel a deep interest in all these manifestations, and would desire to look into them. (1.) This is probable from the nature of the case, and from the variety which we see in the form, size, movements, and glory of the heavenly orbs. There is no reason to suppose, that on *any one* of those worlds *all* the glory of the Divine character would be manifest, which he intends to make known to the universe. (2.) This is probable from what *we* can now see of the worlds which he has made. We know as yet comparatively little of the heavenly bodies, and of the manifestations of the Deity there; and yet, as far as we *can* see, there must be far more striking exhibitions of the power, and wisdom, and glory of God, in many or most of those worlds that roll above us, than there are on our earth. On the body of the sun—on the planets Jupiter and Saturn, so vast in comparison with the earth—there must be far more impressive exhibitions of the glory of the Creator, than there is on our little planet. Saturn, for example, is 82,000 miles in diameter, 1100 times as large as our earth; it moves at the rate of 22,000 miles an hour; it is encircled by two magnificent rings, 5000 miles apart, the innermost of which is 21,000 miles from the body of the planet, and 22,000 miles in breadth, forming a vast illuminated *arch* over the planet above the brightness of our moon, and giving a most beautiful appearance to the heavens there. It is also, doubtless, true of *all* the worlds which God has made, that in each one of them there may be some peculiar manifestation of the glory of the Deity. (3.) The universe, therefore, seems fitted up to give eternal employment to *mind* in contemplating it; and, in the worlds which God has made, there is enough to employ the study of his creatures *for ever*. On our own world, the most diligent and pious student of the works of God might spend many thousand years, and then leave much, very much, which he did not comprehend; and it may yet be the eternal employment of holy minds to range from world to world, and in each new world to find much to study and to admire; much that shall proclaim the wisdom, power, love, and goodness of God, which had not elsewhere been seen. (4.) Our world, therefore, though small, a mere speck in creation, may have something to manifest the glory of the Creator which may not exist in any other. It cannot

be its magnitude; for, in that respect, it is among the smallest which God has made. It may not be the height and the majesty of our mountains, or the length and beauty of our rivers, or the fragrance of our flowers, or the clearness of our sky; for, in these respects, there may be much more to admire in other worlds: it is the exhibition of the character of God in the work of redemption; the illustration of the way in which a sinner may be forgiven; the manifestation of the Deity as incarnate, assuming permanently a union with one of his own creatures. This, so far as we know, is seen in no other part of the universe; *and this is honour enough for one world*. To see this, the angels may be attracted down to earth. When they come, they come not to contemplate our works of art, our painting and our sculpture, or to read our books of science or poetry: they come to gather around the cross, to minister to the Saviour, to attend on his steps while living, and to watch over his body when dead; to witness his resurrection and ascension, and to bless, with their offices of kindness, those whom he died to redeem, Heb. i. 4. III. What, then, is there in our world which we may suppose would attract their attention? What is there which they would not see in other worlds? I answer, that the manifestation of the Divine character in the plan of redemption, is that which would peculiarly attract their attention here, and lead them from heaven down to earth. (1.) The mystery of the incarnation of the Son of God would be to them an object of the deepest interest. This, so far as we know, or have reason to suppose, has occurred nowhere else. There is no evidence that in any other world God has taken upon himself the form of one of his own creatures dwelling there, and stooped to live and act like one of them; to mingle with them; to share their feelings; and to submit to toil, and want, and sacrifice, for their welfare. (2.) The *fact* that the guilty *could* be pardoned would attract their attention, for (a) it is elsewhere unknown, no inhabitant of heaven having the need of pardon, and no offer of pardon having been made to a rebel angel. (*b*) There are great and diffi-cult questions about the whole subject of forgiveness, which an angel could easily *see*, but which he could not so easily *solve*. How could it be done consistently with the justice and truth of God? How could he forgive, and yet maintain the honour of his own law, and the stability of his own throne? There is no more difficult subject in a human administration than that of *pardon;* and there is none which so much perplexes those who are intrusted with executive power. (3.) The *way* in which pardon has been shown to the guilty here would excite their deep attention. It has been in a manner entirely consistent with justice and truth; showing, through the great sacri-fice made on the cross, that the attri-butes of justice and mercy may both be exercised: that, while God may pardon to any extent, he does it in no instance at the expense of justice and truth. This blending of the attributes of the Almighty in beautiful harmony; this manifesting of mercy to the guilty and the lost; this raising up a fallen and rebellious race to the favour and friend-ship of God; and this opening before a dying creature the hope of immortality, was what could be seen by the angels nowhere else: and hence it is no wonder that they hasten with such interest to our world, to learn the mysteries of redeeming love. Every step in the pro-cess of recovering a sinner must be new to them, for it is unseen elsewhere; and the whole work, the atonement, the pardon and renovation of the sinner, the conflict of the child of God with his spiritual foes, the supports of religion in the time of sickness and temptation, the bed of death, the sleep in the tomb, the separate flight of the soul to its final abode, the resurrection of the body, and the solemn scenes of the judgment, all must open new fields of thought to an angelic mind, and attract the heavenly inhabitants to our world, to learn here what they cannot learn in their own abodes, however otherwise bright, where sin, and suffering, and death, and re-demption are unknown. In view of these truths we may add: (1.) The work of redemption is worthy of the study of the profoundest minds. Higher talent

than *any* earthly talent has been em-ployed in studying it; for, to the most exalted intellects of heaven, it has been a theme of the deepest interest. No mind on earth is too exalted to be en-gaged in this study; no intellect here is so profound that it would not find in this study a range of inquiry worthy of itself. (2.) This is a study that is peculiarly appropriate to man. The angels have no other interest in it than that which arises from a desire to know God, and from a benevolent regard for the welfare of others; *we* have a personal interest in it of the highest kind. It pertains primarily to us. The plan was formed for us. Our eternal all depends upon it. The angels would be safe and happy if they did *not* fully understand it ; if *we* do not understand it, we are lost for ever. It has claims to *their* attention as a wonderful exhibition of the character and purposes of God, and as they are interested in the welfare of *others;* it claims *our* attention because our eternal welfare depends on our accepting the offer of mercy made through a Saviour's blood. (3.) How amazing, then, how wonderful, is the indifference of man to this great and glorious work! How wonderful, that neither as a matter of speculation, nor of personal concern, he can be induced 'to look into these things!' How wonderful that all other subjects engross his attention, and excite inquiry; but that for *this* he feels no concern, and that here he finds nothing to interest him! It is not unreasonable to suppose, that amidst all the other topics of wonder in this plan as seen by angels, this is not the least—that man by nature takes no interest in it ; that in so stupendous a work, performed in his own world, he feels no concern; that he is unmoved when he is told that even God became incarnate, and appeared on the earth where he himself dwells ; and that, busy and interested as he is in other things, often of a most trifling nature, he has *no* concern for that on which is suspended his own eternal hap-piness. If heaven was held in mute astonishment when the Son of God left the courts of glory to be poor, to be persecuted, to bleed, and to die, not less must be the astonishment than when, from those lofty heights, the angelic

13 Wherefore gird *a* up the loins of your mind, be sober, *b* and hope *1* to the end *c* for the grace that is to be brought unto you at the revelation of Jesus Christ;

14 As obedient children, not fa-

shioning *d* yourselves according to the former lusts in your ignorance:

15 But as he which hath called you is holy, so be ye holy in all manner of conversation;

a Lu.12.35.　　　b Lu.21.34.　　　1 *perfectly.*
c He.10.35.　　　　　　　d Ro.12.2.

hosts look down upon a race unconcerned amidst wonders such as those of the incarnation and the atonement!

13. *Wherefore gird up the loins of your mind.* The allusion here is to the manner in which the Orientals were accustomed to dress. They wear loose, flowing robes, so that, when they wish to run, or to fight, or to apply themselves to any business, they are obliged to bind their garments close around them. See Notes on Matt. v. 38–41. The meaning here is, that they were to have their minds in constant preparation to discharge the duties, or to endure the trials of life—like those who were prepared for labour, for a race, or for a conflict. ¶ *Be sober.* See Notes on 1 Tim. iii. 2; Titus i. 8; ii. 2. ¶ *And hope to the end.* Marg., *perfectly.* The translation in the text is the most correct. It means, that they were not to become faint or weary in their trials. They were not to abandon the hopes of the gospel, but were to cherish those hopes to the end of life, whatever opposition they might meet with, and however much might be done by others to induce them to apostatize. Comp. Notes on Heb. x. 35, 36. ¶ *For the grace that is to be brought unto you.* For the *favour* that shall then be bestowed upon you; to wit, salvation. The word *brought* here means, that this great favour which they hoped for would be borne to them by the Saviour on his return from heaven. ¶ *At the revelation of Jesus Christ.* When the Lord Jesus shall be revealed from heaven in his glory; that is, when he comes to judge the world. See Notes, 2 Thess. i. 7.

14. *As obedient children.* That is, conduct yourselves as becomes the children of God, by obeying his commands; by submitting to his will; and by manifesting unwavering confidence in him as your Father, at all times. ¶ *Not fashioning yourselves.* Not forming or modelling your life. Comp. Notes, Rom.

xii. 2. The idea is, that they were to have *some* model or example, in accordance with which they were to frame their lives, but that they were *not* to make their own former principles and conduct the model. The Christian is to be as different from what he was before his conversion as he is from his fellow-men. He is to be governed by new laws, to aim at new objects, and to mould his life in accordance with new principles. Before conversion, he was (*a*) supremely selfish; (*b*) he lived for personal gratification; (*c*) he gave free indulgence to his appetites and passions, restrained only by a respect for the decencies of life, and by a reference to his own health, property, or reputation, without regard to the will of God; (*d*) he conformed himself to the customs and opinions around him, rather than to the requirements of his Maker; (*e*) he lived for worldly aggrandizements, his supreme object being wealth or fame; or (*f*) in many cases, those who are now Christians, gave indulgence to every passion which they wished to gratify, regardless of reputation, health, property, or salvation. Now they are to be governed by a different rule, and their own former standard of morals and of opinions is no longer their guide, but the will of God. ¶ *According to the former lusts in your ignorance.* When you were ignorant of the requirements of the gospel, and gave yourselves up to the unrestrained indulgence of your passions.

15. *But as he which hath called you is holy.* On the word *called,* see Notes on Eph. iv. 1. The meaning here is, that the model or example in accordance with which they were to frame their lives, should be the character of that God who had called them into his kingdom. They were to be like him. Comp. Notes, Matt. v. 48. ¶ *So be ye holy in all manner of conversation.* In all your conduct. On the word *conversation,*

16 Because it is written, *a* Be ye holy; for I am holy.

17 And if ye call on the Father, who without respect of persons judgeth according to every man's work, pass the time of your sojourning *here* in fear: *b*

18 Forasmuch as ye know that ye were not redeemed with corruptible things, *as* silver and gold, from your vain conversation *received* by tradition from your fathers;

a Le.11.44.　　　*b* Phi.2.12.

---

see Notes on Phil. i. 27. The meaning is, that since God is holy, and we profess to be his followers, we ought also to be holy.

16. *Because it is written, Be ye holy; for I am holy.* Lev. xi. 44. This command was addressed at first to the Israelites, but it is with equal propriety addressed to Christians, as the professed people of God. The foundation of the command is, that they professed to be his people, and that *as* his people they ought to be like their God. Comp. Micah iv. 5. It is a great truth, that men everywhere will imitate the God whom they worship. They will form their character in accordance with his. They will regard what he does as right. They will attempt to rise no higher in virtue than the God whom they adore, and they will practise freely what he is supposed to do or approve. Hence, by knowing what are the characteristics of the gods which are worshipped by any people, we may form a correct estimate of the character of the people themselves; and hence, as the God who is the object of the Christian's worship is perfectly holy, the character of his worshippers *should* also be holy. And hence, also, we may see that the tendency of true religion is to *make* men pure. As the worship of the impure gods of the heathen moulds the character of the worshippers into their image, so the worship of Jehovah moulds the character of his professed friends into his image, and they become like him.

17. *And if ye call on the Father.* That is, if you are true Christians, or truly pious—piety being represented in the Scriptures as calling on God, or as the worship of God. Comp. Acts ix. 11; Gen. iv. 26; 1 Kings xviii. 24; Psa. cxvi. 17; 2 Kings v. 11; 1 Chron. xvi. 8; Joel ii. 32; Rom. x. 13; Zeph. iii. 9; 1 Cor. i. 2; Acts ii. 21. The word 'Father' here is used evidently

not to denote the Father in contradistinction to the Son, but as referring to God as the Father of the universe. See ver. 14—' As obedient *children.*' God is often spoken of as the Father of the intelligent beings whom he has made. Christians worship him *as* a Father— as one having all the feelings of a kind and tender parent towards them. Comp. Psa. ciii. 13, seq. ¶ *Who without respect of persons.* Impartiality. Who is not influenced in his treatment of men by a regard to rank, wealth, beauty, or any external distinction. See Notes on Acts x. 34, and Rom. ii. 11. ¶ *Judgeth according to every man's work.* He judges each one according to his character; or to what *he has done,* Rev. xxii. 12. Notes, 2 Cor. v. 10. The meaning is, 'You worship a God who will judge every man according to his real character, and you should therefore lead such lives as he can approve.' ¶ *Pass the time of your sojourning.* 'Of your temporary residence on earth. This is not your permanent home, but you are strangers and sojourners.' See Notes on Heb. xi. 13. ¶ *In fear.* Notes, Phil. ii. 12; Heb. xii. 28. With true reverence or veneration for God and his law. Religion is often represented as the reverent fear of God, Deut. vi. 2, 13, 24; Prov. i. 7; iii. 13; xiv. 26, 27, *et sæpe al.*

18. *Forasmuch as ye know.* This is an argument for a holy life, derived from the fact that they were redeemed, and from the manner in which their redemption had been effected. There is no more effectual way to induce true Christians to consecrate themselves entirely to God, than to refer them to the fact that they are not their own, but have been purchased by the blood of Christ. ¶ *That ye were not redeemed.* On the word rendered *redeemed,* (λυτρόω —*lutroo,*) see Notes, Titus ii. 14. The word occurs in the New Testament only

19 But with the precious blood | of Christ, as of a lamb *a* without

a Jn.1.29,36; Re.7.14.

blemish and without spot:

in Luke xxiv. 21; Titus ii. 14, and in this place. The noun (λύτρον—*lutron*) is found in Matt. xx. 28; Mark x. 45, rendered *ransom*. For the meaning of the similar word, (ἀπολύτρωσις—*apolutrosis*,) see Notes on Rom. iii. 24. This word occurs in Luke xxi. 28; Rom. iii. 24; viii. 23; 1 Cor. i. 30; Eph. i. 7, 14; iv. 30; Col. i. 14; Heb. ix. 15, in all which places it is rendered *redemption;* and in Heb. xi. 35, where it is rendered *deliverance*. The word here means that they were rescued from sin and death by the blood of Christ, as *the valuable consideration* on account of which it was done; that is, the blood, or the life of Christ offered as a sacrifice, effected the same purpose in regard to justice and to the maintenance of the principles of moral government, which the punishment of the sinner himself would have done. It was that which God was pleased to accept in the place of the punishment of the sinner, as answering the same great ends in his administration. The principles of his truth and justice could as certainly be maintained in this way as by the punishment of the guilty themselves. If so, then there was no obstacle to their salvation; and they might, on repentance, be consistently pardoned and taken to heaven. ¶ *With corruptible things*, as *silver and gold*. On the word *corruptible*, as applicable to gold, see Notes on ver. 7. Silver and gold usually constitute the price or the valuable consideration paid for the redemption of captives. It is clear that the obligation of one who is redeemed, to love his benefactor, is in proportion to the price which is paid for his ransom. The idea here is, that a price far more valuable than any amount of silver or gold had been paid for the redemption of the people of God, and that they were under proportionate obligation to devote themselves to his service. They were redeemed by the life of the Son of God offered in their behalf; and between the value of that life and silver and gold there could be no comparison. ¶ *From your vain conversation*. Your vain *conduct*, or *manner of*

life. Notes on ver. 15. The word *vain* applied to conduct, (ματαίας,) means properly *empty, fruitless*. It is a word often applied to the worship of idols, as being *nothing, worthless, unable to help*, (Acts xiv. 15; 1 Kings xvi. 13; 2 Kings xvii. 15; Jer. ii. 5, 8, 19,) and is probably used in a similar sense in this place. The apostle refers to their former worship of idols, and to all the abominations connected with that service, as being vain and unprofitable; as the worship of nothing real, (comp. 1 Cor. viii. 4, 'We know that an idol is *nothing* in the world;') and as resulting in a course of life that answered none of the proper ends of living. From that they had been redeemed by the blood of Christ. ¶ Received *by tradition from your fathers*. The mode of worship which had been handed down from father to son. The worship of idols depends on no better reason than that it is that which has been practised in ancient times; and it is kept up now in all lands, in a great degree, only by the fact that it has had the sanction of the venerated men of other generations.

19. *But with the precious blood of Christ*. On the use of the word *blood*, and the reason why the efficacy of the atonement is said to be in the *blood*, see Notes on Rom. iii. 25. The word *precious* (τίμιος) is a word which would be applied to that which is worth much; which is costly. Comp. for the use of the noun (τιμή) in this sense, Matt. xxvii. 6, ' The *price* of blood;' Acts iv. 34; v. 2, 3; vii. 16. See also for the use of the adjective, (τίμιος,) Rev. xvii. 4, 'gold and *precious* stones.' Rev. xviii. 12, 'vessels of most *precious* wood.' Rev. xxi. 11, ' a stone most *precious*.' The meaning here is, that the blood of Christ had a *value* above silver and gold; it was *worth* more, to wit, (1,) in itself — being a more valuable thing — and (2,) in effecting our redemption. It accomplished what silver and gold could not do. The universe had nothing more valuable to offer, of which we can conceive, than the blood of the Son of God. ¶ *As of a*

20 Who verily was foreordained before ᵃ the foundation of the world, but was manifest in these last times for you,

21 Who by him do believe in God,

a Re.13.8.

that raised him up from the dead, and ᵇ gave him glory; that your faith and hope might be in God.

22 Seeing ye have purified your souls in obeying the truth ᶜ through

b Mat.28.18; Phi.2.9.   *c* Jn.17.17,19.

---

lamb. That is, of Christ regarded *as* a lamb offered for sacrifice. Notes on John i. 29. ¶ *Without blemish and without spot.* Such a lamb only was allowed to be offered in sacrifice, Lev. xxii. 20–24; Mal. i. 8. This was re-quired, (1,) because it was *proper* that man should offer that which was re-garded as perfect in its kind; and, (2,) because only that would be a proper symbol of the great sacrifice which was to be made by the Son of God. The idea was thus kept up from age to age that he, of whom all these victims were the emblems, would be perfectly pure. 20. *Who verily was foreordained before the foundation of the world.* That is, it was foreordained, or predetermined, that he should be the great atoning Sacrifice for sin. On the meaning of the word *foreordained,* (προγινώσκω,) see Rom. viii. 29. The word is ren-dered *which knew,* Acts xxvi. 5; *fore-knew* and *foreknow,* Rom. viii. 29; xi. 2; *foreordained,* 1 Pet. i. 20; and *know before,* 2 Pet. ii. 17. It does not elsewhere occur in the New Testament. The sense is, that the plan was formed, and the arrangements made for the atonement, before the world was created. ¶ *Before the foundation of the world.* That is, from eternity. It was before man was formed; before the earth was made; before any of the material uni-verse was brought into being; before the angels were created. Comp. Notes on Matt. xxv. 34; John xvii. 24; Eph. i. 4. ¶ *But was manifest.* Was revealed. Notes on 1 Tim. iii. 16. ¶ *In these last times.* In this, the last dispensa-tion of things on the earth. Notes on Heb. i. 2. ¶ *For you.* For your benefit or advantage. See Notes on ver. 12. It follows from what is said in this verse, (1,) that the atonement was not an *after-thought* on the part of God. It entered into his plan when he made the world, and was revolved in his pur-poses from eternity. (2.) It was not a

device to supply a *defect* in the system; that is, it was not adopted because the system did not work well, or because God had been disappointed. It was arranged *before* man was created, and when none but God could know whether he would stand or fall. (3.) The crea-tion of the earth must have had some reference to this plan of redemption, and that plan must have been regarded as in itself so glorious, and so desirable, that it was deemed best to bring the world into existence that the plan might be developed, though it would involve the certainty that the race would fall, and that many would perish. It was, on the whole, more wise and benevo-lent that the race should be created with a certainty that they would apos-tatize, than it would be that the race should *not* be created, and the plan of salvation be unknown to distant worlds. See Notes on ver. 12. 21. *Who by him do believe in God.* Faith is sometimes represented parti-cularly as exercised in God, and some-times in Christ. It is always a charac-teristic of true religion that a man has faith in God. Comp. Notes on Mark xi. 22. ¶ *That raised him up from the dead.* Notes on Acts ii. 24; iii. 15, 26; iv. 10; v. 30; xiii. 30; Rom. iv. 24; vi. 4; 1 Cor. xv. 15. ¶ *And gave him glory.* By exalting him at his own right hand in heaven, Phil. ii. 9; 1 Tim. iii. 16; Eph. i. 20, 21. ¶ *That your faith and hope might be in God.* That is, by raising up the Lord Jesus, and exalting him to heaven, he has laid the foundation of confidence in his promises, and of the hope of eternal life. Comp. Notes on ver. 3. Comp. 1 Cor. xv.; Col. i. 27; 1 Thess. i. 3; 1 Tim. i. 1. 22. *Seeing ye have purified your souls.* Greek, ' Having purified your souls.' The apostles were never afraid of referring to human agency as having an important part in saving the soul

the Spirit unto unfeigned love *ᵃ* of

a 1 Jn.3.14,18.

the brethren, *see that ye* love one another with a pure heart fervently:

Comp. 1 Cor. iv. 15. No one is made pure without personal intention or effort — any more than one becomes accomplished or learned without personal exertion. One of the leading effects of the agency of the Holy Spirit is to excite us to *make* efforts for our own salvation; and there is no true piety which is not the fair result of culture, as really as the learning of a Porson or a Parr, or the harvest of the farmer. The amount of effort which we make ' in purifying our souls ' is usually also the *measure* of our attainments in religion. No one can expect to have any true piety *beyond* the amount of effort which he makes to be conformed to God, any more than one can expect wealth, or fame, or learning, without exertion. ¶ *In obeying the truth.* That is, your yielding to the requirements of truth, and to its fair influence on your minds, has been the means of your becoming pure. The *truth* here referred to is, undoubtedly, that which is revealed in the gospel— the great system of truth respecting the redemption of the world. ¶ *Through the Spirit.* By the agency of the Holy Spirit. It is his office to apply truth to the mind; and however precious the truth may be, and however adapted to secure certain results on the soul, it will never produce those effects without the influences of the Holy Spirit. Comp. Titus iii. 5, 6. Notes on John iii. 5. ¶ *Unto unfeigned love of the brethren.* The effect of the influence of the Holy Spirit in applying truth has been to produce sincere love to all who are true Christians. Comp. Notes on John xiii. 34; 1 Thess. iv. 9. See also 1 John iii. 14-18. ¶ See that ye *love one another with a pure heart fervently.* Comp. Notes on Heb. xiii. 1; John xiii. 34, 35; Eph. v. 2. The phrase ' with a pure heart fervently,' means (1) that it should be *genuine* love, proceeding from a heart in which there is no guile or hypocrisy; and (2) that it should be *intense* affection, (ἐκτενῶς;) not cold and formal, but ardent and strong. If there is any reason why we should love true Christians at all, there is the

same reason why our attachment to them should be intense. This verse establishes the following points : (1.) That *truth* was at the foundation of their piety. They had none of which this was not the proper basis; and in which the foundation was not as broad as the superstructure. There is no religion in the world which is not the fair developement of truth; which the truth is not fitted to produce. (2.) They became Christians as the result of *obeying* the truth; or by yielding to its fair influence on the soul. Their own minds complied with its claims; their own hearts yielded : there was the exercise of their own volitions. This expresses a doctrine of great importance. (*a*) There is always the exercise of the powers of the mind in true religion ; always a yielding to truth ; always a voluntary reception of it into the soul. (*b*) Religion is always of the nature of *obedience*. It consists in yielding to what is true and right; in laying aside the feelings of opposition, and in allowing the mind to follow where truth and duty lead. (*c*) This would always take place when the truth is presented to the mind, if there were no voluntary resistance. If all men were ready to *yield* to the truth, they would become Christians. The only reason why all men do not love and serve God, is that they refuse to yield to what they know to be true and right. (3.) The agency by which this was accomplished was that of the Holy Ghost. Truth is adapted in itself to a certain end or result, as seed is adapted to produce a harvest. But it will no more of itself produce its appropriate effects on the soul, than seed will produce a harvest without rains, and dews, and suns. In *all* cases, therefore, the proper effect of truth on the soul is to be traced to the influence of the Holy Spirit, as the germination of the seed in the earth is to the foreign cause that acts on it. No man was ever converted by the mere effect of truth without the agency of the Holy Ghost, any more than seed germinates when laid on a hard rock. (4.) The *effect* of this influence of the Holy Spirit in applying

23 Being born ^a again, not of corruptible seed, but of incorruptible, by the word ^b of God, which liveth and abideth for ever. 24 ¹ For ^c all flesh *is* as grass,

and all the glory of man as the flower of grass. The grass withereth, and the flower thereof falleth away; *a* Jn.1.13.　*b* Ja.1.18.　1 Or, *for that.*　*c* Is.40.6-8.

the truth is to produce love to all who are Christians. Love to Christian brethren springs up in the soul of every one who is truly converted: and this love is just as certain evidence that the seed of truth has germinated in the soul, as the green and delicate blade that peeps up through the earth is evidence that the seed sown has been quickened into life. Comp. Notes on 1 Thess. iv. 9; 1 John iii. 14. We may learn hence, (*a*) that *truth* is of inestimable value. It is as valuable as religion itself, for all the religion in the world is the result of it. (*b*) Error and falsehood are mischievous and evil in the same degree. There is no true religion which is the fair result of error ; and all the pretended religion that is sustained by error is worthless. (*c*) If a system of religion, or a religious measure or doctrine, cannot be defended by *truth*, it should be at once abandoned. Comp. Notes on Job xiii. 7. (*d*) We should avoid the places where error is taught. Prov. xix. 27, ' Cease, my son, to hear the instruction that causeth to err from the words of knowledge.' (*e*) We should place ourselves under the teachings of truth, for there is truth enough in the world to occupy all our time and attention ; and it is only *by* truth that our minds can be benefited.

23. *Being born again.* See Notes on John iii. 3. ¶ *Not of corruptible seed.* ' Not by virtue of any descent from human parents.'—*Doddridge.* The result of such a birth, or of being *begotten* in this way—for so the word rendered *born again* more properly signifies—is only corruption and decay. We are begotten only to die. There is no permanent, enduring life produced by that. It is in this sense that this is spoken of as ' *corruptible* seed,' because it results in decay and death. The word here rendered *seed—σπορά*—occurs nowhere else in the New Testament. ¶ *But of incorruptible.* By *truth*, communicating a living principle to the soul which

can never decay. Comp. 1 John iii. 9 : ' His seed remaineth in him ; and he cannot sin, because he is born of God.' ¶ *By the word of God.* See Note on James i. 18: ' Of his own will begat he us with the word of truth, that we should be a kind of first-fruits of his creatures.' Comp. Notes on John i. 13. It is the uniform doctrine of the Scriptures that Divine *truth* is made the instrument of quickening the soul into spiritual life. ¶ *Which liveth and abideth for ever.* This expression may either refer to God, as living for ever, or to the *word* of God, as being for ever true. Critics are about equally divided in the interpretation. The Greek will bear either construction. Most of the recent critics incline to the latter opinion—that it refers to the word of God, or to his doctrine. So Rosenmüller, Doddridge, Bloomfield, Wolf, Macknight, Clarke. It seems to me, however, that the more natural construction of the Greek is to refer it to God, as ever-living or enduring ; and this interpretation agrees well with the connection. The idea then is, that as God is ever-living, that which is produced directly by him in the human soul, by the instrumentality of truth, may be expected also to endure for ever. It will not be like the offspring of human parents, themselves mortal, liable to early and certain decay, but may be expected to be as enduring as its ever-living Creator.

24. *For all flesh is as grass.* That is, all human beings, all men. The connection here is this : The apostle, in the previous verse, had been contrasting that which is begotten by man with that which is begotten by God, in reference to its *permanency.* The former was corruptible and decaying ; the latter abiding. The latter was produced by God, who lives for ever ; the former by the agency of man, who is himself corruptible and dying. It was not unnatural, then, to dwell upon the feeble, frail, decaying nature of *man,*

25 But the word of the Lord endureth for ever. And this *a* is

a Ja.1.1,14; 2 Pe.1.19.

the word which by the gospel is preached unto you.

in contrast with God ; and the apostle, therefore, says that ' *all* flesh, every human being, is like grass. There is no stability in anything that man does or produces. He himself resembles grass that soon fades and withers; but God and his word endure for ever the same.' The comparison of a human being with grass, or with flowers, is very beautiful, and is quite common in the Scriptures. The comparison turns on the fact, that the grass or the flower, however green or beautiful it may be, soon loses its freshness ; is withered ; is cut down, and dies. Thus in Psalm ciii. 15, 16 :—

" As for man, his days are as grass ;
As a flower of the field, so he flourisheth ;
For the wind passeth over it and it is gone,
And the place thereof shall know it no more."

So in Isaiah xl. 6–8; a passage which is evidently referred to by Peter in this place :—

" The voice said, Cry.
And he said, What shall I cry ?
All flesh is grass,
And all the goodliness thereof is as the flower of the field.
The grass withereth,
The flower fadeth,
When the wind of Jehovah bloweth upon it :
Surely the people is grass,
The grass withereth,
The flower fadeth,
But the word of our God shall stand for ever."

See also James i. 10, 11. This sentiment is beautifully imitated by the great dramatist in the speech of Wolsey :—

" This is the state of man ; to-day he puts forth
The tender leaves of hope, to-morrow blossoms,
And bears his blushing honours thick upon him.
The third day comes a frost, a killing frost,
And—when he thinks, good easy man, full surely
His greatness is a ripening—nips his root,
And then he falls."

Comp. Notes on Isa. xl. 6–8. ¶ *And all the glory of man.* All that man prides himself on—his wealth, rank, talents, beauty, learning, splendour of equipage or apparel. ¶ *As the flower of grass.* The word rendered '*grass*,' (χόρτος,) properly denotes herbage ; that which furnishes food for animals— pasture, hay. Probably the prophet

Isaiah, from whom this passage is taken, referred rather to the appearance of a meadow or a field, with mingled grass and flowers, constituting a beautiful landscape, than to mere grass. In such a field, the grass soon withers with heat, and with the approach of winter ; and the flowers soon fade and fall. ¶ *The grass withereth, and the flower thereof falleth away.* This is repeated, as is common in the Hebrew writings, for the sake of emphasis, or strong confirmation.

25. *But the word of the Lord.* In Isaiah (xl. 8,) ' the word of our God.' The sense is not materially varied. ¶ *Endureth for ever.* Is unmoved, fixed, permanent. Amidst all the revolutions on earth, the fading glories of natural objects, and the wasting strength of man, his truth remains unaffected. Its beauty never fades ; its power is never enfeebled. The gospel system is as lovely now as it was when it was first revealed to man, and it has as much power to save as it had when first applied to a human heart. We see the grass wither at the coming on of autumn ; we see the flower of the field decay ; we see man, though confident in his strength, and rejoicing in the vigour of his frame, cut down in an instant ; we see cities decline, and kingdoms lose their power : but the word of God is the same now that it was at first, and, amidst all the changes which may ever occur on the earth, that will remain the same. ¶ *And this is the word which by the gospel is preached unto you.* That is, this gospel is the ' word ' which was referred to by Isaiah in the passage which has been quoted. In view, then, of the affecting truth stated in the close of this chapter, (vers. 24, 25,) let us learn habitually to reflect on our feebleness and frailty. ' We all do fade as a leaf,' Isa. lxiv. 6. Our glory is like the flower of the field. Our beauty fades, and our strength disappears, as easily as the beauty and vigour of the flower that grows up in the morning, and that in the evening is cut down, Ps. xc. 6. The rose that blossoms on the cheek of youth

CHAPTER II.

WHEREFORE laying aside ᵃall malice, and all guile, and hypocrisies, and envies, and all evil speakings,

a Ep.4.22,31.

may wither as soon as any other rose ; the brightness of the eye may become dim, as readily as the beauty of a field covered with flowers ; the darkness of death may come over the brow of manliness and intelligence, as readily as night settles down on the landscape ; and our robes of adorning may be laid aside, as soon as beauty fades in a meadow full of flowers before the scythe of the mower. There is not an object of natural beauty on which we pride ourselves that will not decay ; and soon all our pride and pomp will be laid low in the tomb. It is sad to look on a beautiful lily, a rose, a magnolia, and to think how soon all that beauty will disappear. It is more sad to look on a rosy cheek, a bright eye, a lovely form, an expressive brow, an open, serene, intelligent countenance, and to think how soon all that beauty and brilliancy will fade away. But amidst these changes which beauty undergoes, and the desolations which disease and death spread over the world, it is cheering to think that all is not so. There is that which does not change, which never loses its beauty. 'The word of the Lord' abides. His cheering promises, his assurances that there is a brighter and better world, remain amidst all these changes the same. The traits which are drawn on the character by the religion of Christ, more lovely by far than the most delicate colouring of the lily, remain for ever. There they abide, augmenting in loveliness, when the rose fades from the cheek; when the brilliancy departs from the eye ; when the body moulders away in the sepulchre. The beauty of religion is the only permanent beauty in the earth ; and he that has that need not regret that that which in this mortal frame charms the eye shall fade away like the flower of the field.

CHAPTER II.

ANALYSIS OF THE CHAPTER.

THIS chapter may be divided into three parts :—

I. An exhortation to those whom the apostle addressed, to lay aside all malice, and all guile, and to receive the simple and plain instructions of the word of God with the earnestness with which babes desire their appropriate food, vers. 1–3. Religion *reproduces* the traits of character of children in those whom it influences, and they ought to regard themselves as new-born babes, and seek that kind of spiritual nutriment which is adapted to their condition as such.

II. The privileges which they had obtained by becoming Christians, while so many others had stumbled at the very truths by which they had been saved, vers. 4–10. (*a*) They had come to the Saviour, as the living stone on which the whole spiritual temple was founded, though others had rejected him ; they had become a holy priesthood ; they had been admitted to the privilege of offering true sacrifices, acceptable to God, vers. 4, 5. (*b*) To them Christ was precious as the chief corner-stone, on which all their hopes rested, and on which the edifice that was to be reared was safe, though that foundation of the Christian hope had been rejected and disallowed by others, vers. 6–8. (*c*) They were now a chosen people, an holy nation, appointed to show forth on earth the praises of God, though formerly they were not regarded as the people of God, and were not within the range of the methods by which he was accustomed to show mercy, vers. 9, 10.

III. Various duties growing out of these privileges, and out of the various relations which they sustained in life, vers. 11–25. (*a*) The duty of living as strangers and pilgrims ; of abstaining from all those fleshly lusts which war against the soul; and of leading lives of entire honesty in relation to the Gentiles, by whom they were surrounded, vers. 11, 12. (*b*) The duty of submitting to civil rulers, vers. 13–17. (*c*) The duty of servants to submit to their masters, though their condition was a hard one in life, and they were often called to suffer wrongfully, vers. 18–20.

2 As new-born babes, *a* desire the sincere milk *b* of the word, that ye may grow thereby:

a Mat.18.3.   b 1 Co.3.2.

(d) This duty was enforced on servants, and on all, from the example of Christ, who was more wronged than any others can be, and who yet bore all his sufferings with entire patience, leaving us an example that we should follow in his steps, ver. 21–25.

1. *Wherefore laying aside.* On the word rendered *laying aside,* see Rom. xiii. 12; Eph. iv. 22, 25; Col. iii. 8. The allusion is to putting off clothes; and the meaning is, that we are to cast off these things entirely; that is, we are no longer to practise them. The word *wherefore* (οὖν) refers to the reasonings in the first chapter. In view of the considerations stated there, we should renounce all evil. ¶ *All malice.* All evil, (κακίαν.) The word *malice* we commonly apply now to a particular kind of evil, denoting extreme enmity of heart, ill-will, a disposition to injure others without cause, from mere personal gratification, or from a spirit of revenge. —*Webster.* The Greek word, however, includes evil of all kinds. See Notes on Rom. i. 29. Comp. Acts viii. 22, where it is rendered *wickedness,* and 1 Cor. v. 8; xiv. 20; Eph. iv. 31; Col. iii. 8; Titus iii. 3. ¶ *And all guile.* Deceit of all kinds. Notes on Rom. i. 29; 2 Cor. xii. 16; 1 Thess. ii. 3. ¶ *And hypocrisies.* Notes on 1 Tim. iv. 2 ; Matt. xxiii. 28; Gal. ii. 13, on the word rendered *dissimulation.* The word means, feigning to be what we are not; assuming a false appearance of religion ; cloaking a wicked purpose under the appearance of piety. ¶ *And envies.* Hatred of others on account of some excellency which they have, or something which they possess which we do not. See Notes on Rom. i. 29. ¶ *And all evil speaking.* Greek, speaking against others. This word (καταλαλιὰ) occurs only here and in 2 Cor. xii. 20, where it is rendered *backbitings.* It would include all unkind or slanderous speaking against others. This is by no means an uncommon fault in the world, and it is one of the designs of religion to guard against it. Religion teaches us to lay aside whatever guile, insincerity, and false appearances we may have acquired, and to put on the simple honesty and openness of children. We all acquire more or less of guile and insincerity in the course of life. We learn to conceal our sentiments and feelings, and almost unconsciously come to appear different from what we really are. It is not so with children. In the child, every emotion of the bosom appears as it is. *Nature there works well and beautifully.* Every emotion is expressed ; every feeling of the heart is developed ; and in the cheeks, the open eye, the joyous or sad countenance, we know all that there is in the bosom, as certainly as we know all that there is in the rose by its colour and its fragrance. Now, it is one of the purposes of religion to bring us back to this state, and to *strip off* all the subterfuges which we may have acquired in life; and he in whom this effect is not accomplished has never been converted. A man that is characteristically deceitful, cunning, and crafty, cannot be a Christian. ‘Except ye be converted, and become as little children, ye shall not enter into the kingdom of heaven,’ Matt. xviii. 3.

2. *As new-born babes.* The phrase here used would properly denote those which were just born, and hence Christians who had just begun the spiritual life. See the word explained in the Notes on 2 Tim. iii. 15. It is not uncommon, in the Scriptures, to compare Christians with little children. See Notes, Matt. xviii. 3, for the reasons of this comparison. Comp. Notes, 1 Cor. iii. 2; Heb. v. 12, 14. ¶ *Desire the sincere milk of the word.* The *pure* milk of the word. On the meaning of the word *sincere,* see Notes, Eph. vi. 24. The Greek word here (ἄδολον) means, properly, that which is without guile or falsehood ; then unadulterated, pure, genuine. The Greek adjective rendered ' of the word,' (λογικὸν,) means properly *rational,* pertaining to reason, or mind; and, in the connection here with milk, means that which is adapted to sustain the soul. Comp. Notes, Rom. xii. 1. There is no doubt that there is allusion to the gospel in its purest and most simple form, as adapted to be the nutriment of the new-born soul. Probably

3 If so be ye have tasted *a* that the Lord is gracious.

4 To whom coming, *as unto a*

a Ps.34.8.

living stone, disallowed *b* indeed of men, but chosen of God, *and* precious,

b Ps.118.22.

there are two ideas here ; one, that the proper aliment of piety is simple truth; the other, that the truths which they were to desire were the more elementary truths of the gospel, such as would be adapted to those who were babes in knowledge. ¶ *That ye may grow thereby.* As babes grow on their proper nutriment. Piety in the heart is susceptible of growth, and is made to grow by its proper aliment, as a plant or a child is, and will grow in proportion as it has the proper kind of nutriment. From this verse we may see, (1,) the reason of the injunction of the Saviour to Peter, to ' feed his lambs,' John xxi. 15; 1 Pet. ii. 1, 2. Young Christians strongly resemble children, babes; and they need watchful care, and kind attention, and appropriate aliment, as much as new-born infants do. Piety receives its form much from its commencement; and the character of the whole Christian life will be determined in a great degree by the views entertained at first, and the kind of instruction which is given to those who are just entering on their Christian course. We may also see, (2,) that it furnishes evidence of conversion, if we have a love for the simple and pure truths of the gospel. It is evidence that we have spiritual life, as really as the desire of appropriate nourishment is evidence that an infant has natural life. The new-born soul loves the truth. It is nourished by it. It perishes without it. The gospel is just what it wants; and without that it could not live. We may also learn from this verse, (3,) that the truths of the gospel which are best adapted to that state, are those which are simple and plain. Comp. Heb. v. 12–14. It is not philosophy that is needed then; it is not the profound and difficult doctrines of the gospel; it is those elementary truths which lie at the coundation of all religion, and which can be comprehended by children. Religion makes every one docile and humble as a child; and whatever may be the age at which one is converted, or whatever attainments he may have made in

science, he relishes the same truths which are loved by the youngest and most unlettered child that is brought into the kingdom of God.

3. *If so be ye have tasted that the Lord is gracious.* Or rather, as Doddridge renders it, ' *Since you have tasted* that the Lord is gracious.' The apostle did not mean to express any doubt on the subject, but to state that, since they had had an experimental acquaintance with the grace of God, they should desire to increase more and more in the knowledge and love of him. On the use of the word *taste,* see Notes on Heb. vi. 4.

4. *To whom coming.* To the Lord Jesus, for so the word ' Lord ' is to be understood in ver. 3. Comp. Notes on Acts i. 24. The idea here is, that *they* had come to him for salvation, while the great mass of men rejected him. Others ' disallowed ' him, and turned away from him, but they had seen that he was the one chosen or appointed of God, and had come to him in order to be saved. Salvation is often represented as *coming* to Christ. See Matt. xi. 28. ¶ As unto *a living stone.* The allusion in this passage is to Isa. xxviii. 16, ' Behold, I lay in Zion for a foundation a stone, a tried stone, a precious corner-stone, a sure foundation: he that believeth shall not make haste.' See Notes on that passage. There may be also possibly an allusion to Psa. cxviii. 22, ' The stone which the builders disallowed, is become the head-stone of the corner.' The reference is to Christ as the foundation on which the church is reared. He occupied the same place in regard to the church which a foundation-stone does to the edifice that is reared upon it. Comp. Matt. vii. 24, 25. See Notes on Rom. ix. 33, and Eph. ii. 20–22. The phrase ' *living stone* ' is however unusual, and is not found, I think, except in this place. There seems to be an incongruity in it, in attributing *life* to a stone, yet the meaning is not difficult to be understood. The purpose was not to speak of a temple, like that at

5 Ye also, as lively stones, ¹ are built up a spiritual house, ª an holy priesthood, ᵇ to offer up spiritual

ᶜ sacrifices, acceptable to God by Jesus Christ.

1 Or, *be ye.*   a He.3.6.   b Is.61.6; Re.1.6.   c Mal.1.11.

Jerusalem, made up of gold and costly stones; but of a temple made up of *living* materials—of redeemed men—in which God now resides. In speaking of that, it was natural to refer to the foundation on which the whole rested, and to speak of that as corresponding to the whole edifice. It was all a *living temple*—a temple composed of living materials—from the foundation to the top. Compare the expression in John iv. 10, 'He would have given thee *living water;*' that is, water which would have imparted life to the soul. So Christ imparts life to the whole spiritual temple that is reared on him as a foundation. ¶ *Disallowed indeed of men.* Rejected by them, first by the Jews, in causing him to be put to death; and then by all men when he is offered to them as their Saviour. See Notes, Isa. liii. 3. Psa. cxviii. 22 : 'Which the builders refused.' Comp. Notes, Matt. xxi. 42; Acts iv. 11. ¶ *But chosen of God.* Selected by him as the suitable foundation on which to rear his church. ¶ And *precious.* Valuable. The universe had nothing more valuable on which to rear the spiritual temple.

5. *Ye also, as lively stones.* Gr., '*living* stones.' The word should have been so rendered. The word *lively* with us now has a different meaning from *living,* and denotes *active, quick, sprightly.* The Greek word is the same as that used in the previous verse, and rendered *living.* The meaning is, that the materials of which the temple here referred to was composed, were *living* materials throughout. The foundation is a living foundation, and all the superstructure is composed of living materials. The purpose of the apostle here is to compare the church to a beautiful temple—such as the temple in Jerusalem, and to show that it is complete in all its parts, as that was. It has within itself what corresponds with everything that was valuable in that. It is a beautiful structure like that; and as in that there was a priesthood, and there were real and acceptable sacrifices offered, so it is in

the Christian church. The Jews prided themselves much on their temple. It was a most costly and splendid edifice. It was the place where God was worshipped, and where he was supposed to dwell. It had an imposing service, and there was acceptable worship rendered there. As a new dispensation was introduced; as the tendency of the Christian system was to draw off the worshippers from that temple, and to teach them that God could be worshipped as acceptably elsewhere as at Jerusalem, (John iv. 21–23;) as Christianity did not inculcate the necessity of rearing splendid temples for the worship of God; and as in fact the temple at Jerusalem was about to be destroyed for ever, it was important to show that in the Christian church there might be found all that was truly beautiful and valuable in the temple at Jerusalem; that it had what corresponded to what *was* in fact most precious there, and that there was still a most magnificent and beautiful temple on the earth. Hence the sacred writers labour to show that all was found in the church that had made the temple at Jerusalem so glorious, and that the great design contemplated by the erection of that splendid edifice—the maintenance of the worship of God—was now accomplished in a more glorious manner than even in the services of that house. For there was a temple, made up of living materials, which was still the peculiar dwelling-place of God on the earth. In that temple there was a holy priesthood—for every Christian was a priest. In that temple there were sacrifices offered, as acceptable to God as in the former—for they were spiritual sacrifices, offered continually. These thoughts were often dwelt upon by the apostle Paul, and are here illustrated by Peter, evidently with the same design, to impart consolation to those who had never been permitted to worship at the temple in Jerusalem, and to comfort those Jews, now converted to Christianity, who saw that that splendid and glorious edifice was about to be destroyed. The peculiar abode of God on the earth was now removed from that temple to the Christian church. The *first* aspect in which this is illustrated here is, that the temple of God was made up of ' living stones ;' that is, that the materials were not inanimate stones, but cnduod with life, and so much more valuable than those employed in the temple at Jerusalem, as the soul is more precious than any materials of stone. There were living beings which composed that temple, constituting a more beautiful structure, and a more appropriate dwelling-place for God, than any edifice could be made of stone, however costly or valuable. ¶ *A spiritual house.* A spiritual temple, not made of perishable materials, like that at Jerusalem ; net composed of *matter*, as that was, but made up of redeemed souls—a temple more appropriate to be the residence of one who is a pure spirit. Comp. Notes on Eph. ii. 19–22, and 1 Cor. vi. 19, 20. ¶ *An holy priesthood.* In the temple at Jerusalem, the priesthood appointed to minister there, and to offer sacrifices, constituted an essential part of the arrangement. It was important, therefore, to show that this was not overlooked in the spiritual temple that God was raising. Accordingly, the apostle says that this is amply provided for, by constituting *the whole body of Christians* to be in fact a priesthood. Every one is engaged in offering acceptable sacrifice to God. The business is not intrusted to a particular class to be known *as* priests; there is not a particular portion to whom the name is to be peculiarly given ; but *every* Christian is in fact a priest, and is engaged in offering an acceptable sacrifice to God. See Rom. i. 6: 'And hath made us kings and priests unto God.' The Great High Priest in this service is the Lord Jesus Christ, (see the Epistle to the Hebrews, *passim ;*) but besides him there is no one who sustains this office, except as it is borne by all the Christian members. There are *ministers, elders, pastors, evangelists* in the church ; but there is no one who is *a priest*, except in the general sense that *all* are priests —for the great sacrifice has been offered, and there is no expiation now to be made. The narne *priest*, therefore,

should never be conferred on a minister of the gospel. It is never so given in the New Testament, and there was a *reason* why it should not be. The proper idea of a *priest* is one who offers sacrifice ; but the ministers of the New Testament have no sacrifices to offer—the one great and perfect oblation for the sins of the world having been made by the Redeemer on the cross. To him, and him alone, under the New Testament dispensation, should the name *priest* be given, as it is uniformly in the New Testament, except in the general sense in which it is given to all Christians. In the Roman Catholic communion it is *consistent* to give the name priest to a minister of the gospel, but it is *wrong* to do it. It is *consistent*, because they claim that a true *sacrifice* of the body and blood of Christ is offered in the mass. It is *wrong*, because that doctrine is wholly contrary to the New Testament, and is derogatory to the one perfect oblation which has been once made for the sins of the world, and in conferring on a class of men a degree of importance and of power to which they have no claim, and which is so liable to abuse. But in a *Protestant* church it is *neither* consistent *nor* right to give the name to a minister of religion. The only sense in which the term can now be used in the Christian church is a sense in which it is applicable to *all* Christians alike—that they ' offer the sacrifice of prayer and praise.' ¶ *To offer up spiritual sacrifices.* Not bloody offerings, the blood of lambs and bullocks, but those which are the offerings of the heart—the sacrifices of prayer and praise. As there is a *priest*, there is also involved the notion of a *sacrifice ;* but that which is offered is such as all Christians offer to God, proceeding from the heart, and breathed forth from the lips, and in a holy life. It is called *sacrifice*, not because it makes an expiation for sin, but because it is of the nature of *worship.* Comp. Notes on Heb. xiii. 15; x. 14. ¶ *Acceptable to God by Jesus Christ.* Comp. Notes on Rom. xii. 1. Through the merits of the great sacrifice made by the Redeemer on the cross. Our prayers and praises are in themselves so imperfect, and proceed from such polluted lips and

6 Wherefore also it is contained in the scripture, *Behold I lay in Sion a chief corner-stone, elect, precious: and he that believeth on him shall not be confounded.

7 Unto you therefore which be-

lieve *he is* [1] precious: but unto them which be disobedient, the stone [b] which the builders disallowed, the same is made the head of the corner,

a Is.28.16.　　1 Or, *an honour.*　　b Mat. 21.42.

hearts, that they can be acceptable only through him as our intercessor before the throne of God. Comp. Notes on Heb. ix. 24, 25; x. 19–22.

6. *Wherefore also it is contained in the scripture.* Isa. xxviii. 16. The quotation is substantially as it is found in the Septuagint. ¶ *Behold, I lay in Sion.* See Notes, Isa. xxviii. 16, and Rom. ix. 33. ¶ *A chief corner-stone.* The principal stone on which the corner of the edifice rests. A stone is selected for this which is large and solid, and, usually, one which is squared, and wrought with care; and as such a stone is commonly laid with solemn ceremonies, so, perhaps, in allusion to this, it is here said by God that *he would lay* this stone at the foundation. The solemnities attending this were those which accompanied the great work of the Redeemer. See the word explained in the Notes on Eph. ii. 20. ¶ *Elect.* Chosen of God, or selected for this purpose, ver. 4. ¶ *And he that believeth on him shall not be confounded.* Shall not be ashamed. The Hebrew is, 'shall not make haste.' See it explained in the Notes on Rom. ix. 33.

7. *Unto you therefore which believe.* Christians are often called simply *believers,* because faith in the Saviour is one of the prominent characteristics by which they are distinguished from their fellow-men. It sufficiently describes *any* man, to say that he is a *believer* in the Lord Jesus. ¶ *He is precious.* Marg., *an honour.* That is, according to the margin, it is an honour to believe on him, and should be so regarded. This is true, but it is very doubtful whether this is the idea of Peter. The Greek is ἡ τιμή; literally, ' esteem, honour, respect, reverence;' then 'value or price.' The noun is probably used in the place of the adjective, in the sense of honourable, valued, precious; and it is not incorrectly rendered in the text, ' he is precious.' The *connection* demands this

interpretation. The apostle was not showing that it was *an honour* to believe on Christ, but was stating the estimate which was put on him by those who believe, as contrasted with the view taken of him by the world. The truth which is taught is, that while the Lord Jesus is rejected by the great mass of men, he is regarded by all Christians as of inestimable value. I. Of the *fact* there can be no doubt. *Somehow,* Christians perceive a value in him which is seen in nothing else. This is evinced (*a*) in their *avowed* estimate of him as their best friend; (*b*) in their being willing so far to honour him as to commit to him the keeping of their souls, resting the whole question of their salvation on him alone; (*c*) in their readiness to keep his commands, and to serve him, while the mass of men disobey him; and (*d*) in their being willing to die for him. II. The *reasons* why he is so precious to them are such as these : (1.) They are brought into a condition where they can appreciate his worth. To see the value of food, we must be hungry; of clothing, we must be exposed to the winter's blast ; of home, we must be wanderers without a dwelling-place; of medicine, we must be sick; of competence, we must be poor. So, to see the value of the Saviour, we must see that we are poor, helpless, dying sinners; that the soul is of inestimable worth; that we have no merit of our own ; and that unless some one interpose, we must perish. Every one who becomes a true Christian is brought to this condition; and in this state he can appreciate the worth of the Saviour. In this respect the condition of Christians is unlike that of the rest of mankind—for they are in no better state to appreciate the worth of the Saviour, than the man in health is to appreciate the value of the healing art, or than he who has never had a want unsupplied, the kindness of one who comes to us with an abundant

8 And a stone of stumbling, and a rock of offence, *even to them* which stumble at the word, being disobe-

dient: whereunto *a* also they were appointed.

a Jude 4.

supply of food. (2.) The Lord Jesus is *in fact* of more value to them than any other benefactor. We have had benefactors who have done us good, but none who have done us *such* good as he has. We have had parents, teachers, kind friends, who have provided for us, taught us, relieved us ; but all that they have done for us is slight, compared with what *he* has done. The fruit of their kindness, for the most part, pertains to the present world ; and they have not laid down their lives for us. What *he* has done pertains to our welfare to all eternity; it is the fruit of the sacrifice of his own life. How precious should the name and memory of one be who has laid down his own life to save us ! (3.) We owe all our hopes of heaven to him ; and in proportion to the value of such a hope, he is precious to us. We have *no* hope of salvation but in him. Take that away—blot out the name and the work of the Redeemer—and we see no way in which we could be saved ; we have no prospect of being saved. As our hope of heaven, therefore, is valuable to us ; as it supports us in trial ; as it comforts us in the hour of death, *so* is the Saviour precious : and the estimate which we form of him is in proportion to the value of such a hope. (4.) There is an intrinsic value and excellency in the character of Christ, apart from his relation to us, which makes him precious to those who can appreciate his worth. In his character, abstractedly considered, there was more to attract, to interest, to love, than in that of any other one who ever lived in our world. There was more purity, more benevolence, more that was great in trying circumstances, more that was generous and self-denying, more that resembled God, than in any other one who ever appeared on earth. In the moral firmament, the character of Christ sustains a pre-eminence above all others who have lived, as great as the glory of the sun is superior to the feeble lights, though so numerous, which glimmer at midnight. With such views of him, it is not to be wondered at that, however he may be

estimated by the world, 'to them who believe, he is PRECIOUS.' ¶ *But unto them which be disobedient.* Literally, *unwilling to be persuaded,* (ἀπειθής ;) that is, those who refused to believe ; who were obstinate or contumacious, Luke i. 17; Rom. i. 30. The meaning is, that to them he is made a stone against which they impinge, and ruin themselves. Notes, ver. 8. ¶ *The stone which the builders disallowed.* Which they rejected, or refused to make a corner-stone. The allusion here, by the word 'builders,' is primarily to the Jews, represented as raising a temple of salvation, or building with reference t · eternal life. They refused to lay this stone, which God had appointed, as the foundation of their hopes, but preferred some other foundation. See this passage explained in the Notes on Matt. xxi. 42; Acts iv. 11; and Rom. ix. 33. ¶ *The same is made the head of the corner.* That is, though it is rejected by the mass of men, yet God has in fact made it the corner-stone on which the whole spiritual temple rests, Acts iv. 11, 12. However men may regard it, there is, in fact, no other hope of heaven than that which is founded on the Lord Jesus. If men are not saved by him, he becomes to them a stone of stumbling, and a rock of offence.

8. *And a stone of stumbling.* A stone over which they stumble, or against which they impinge. The idea seems to be that of a corner-stone which projects from the building, against which they dash themselves, and by which they are made to fall. See Notes on Matt. xxi. 44. The rejection of the Saviour becomes the means of their ruin. They refuse to build on him, and it is *as if* one should run against a solid projecting corner-stone of a house, that would certainly be the means of their destruction. Comp. Notes, Luke i. 34. An idea similar to this occurs in Matt. xxi. 44: ' Whosoever shall fall on this stone shall be broken.' The meaning is, that if this foundation-stone is not the means of their salvation, it will be of their ruin. It is not a matter of indifference

whether they believe on him or not—whether they accept or reject him. They cannot reject him without the most fearful consequences to their souls. ¶ *And a rock of offence.* This expresses substantially the same idea as the phrase ' stone of stumbling.' The word rendered ' *offence,*' (*σκάνδαλον,*) means properly ' a *trap-stick*—a crooked stick on which the bait is fastened, which the animal strikes against, and so springs the trap,' (*Robinson, Lex.;*) then a trap, gin, snare; and then anything which one strikes or stumbles against; a stumbling-block. It then denotes that which is the cause or occasion of ruin. This language would be strictly applicable to the Jews, who rejected the Saviour on account of his humble birth, and whose rejection of him was made the occasion of the destruction of their temple, city, and nation. But it is also applicable to *all* who reject him, from whatever cause; for their rejection of him will be followed with ruin to their souls. It is a crime for which God will judge them as certainly as he did the Jews who disowned him and crucified him, for the offence is substantially the same. What might have been, therefore, the means of their salvation, is made the cause of their deeper condemnation. ¶ Even to them *which stumble at the word.* To *all* who do this. That is, they take the same kind of offence at the gospel which the Jews did at the Saviour himself. It is substantially the same thing, and the consequences must be the same. How does the conduct of the man who rejects the Saviour now, differ from that of him who rejected him when he was on the earth? ¶ *Being disobedient.* Ver. 7. The *reason* why they reject him is, that they are not disposed to obey. They are solemnly commanded to believe the gospel; and a refusal to do it, therefore, is as really an act of *disobedience* as to break any other command of God. ¶ *Whereunto they were appointed.* (*εἰς ὃ καὶ ἐτέθησαν.*) The word ' *whereunto*' means *unto which.* But unto what? It cannot be supposed that it means that they were ' appointed ' to believe on him and be saved by him; for (1) this would involve all the difficulty which is *ever* felt in the doctrine

of decrees or election; for it would then mean that he had eternally designated them to be saved, which is the doctrine of predestination; and (2) *if* this were the true interpretation, the consequence would follow that God had been foiled in his plan—for the reference here is to those who would *not* be saved, that is, to those who ' stumble at that stumbling-stone,' and are destroyed. Calvin supposes that it means, ' unto which rejection and destruction they were designated in the purpose of God.' So Bloomfield renders it, ' Unto which (disbelief) they were destined,' (*Crit. Digest;*) meaning, as he supposes, that ' into this stumbling and disobedience they were *permitted* by God to fall.' Doddridge interprets it, ' To which also they were appointed by the righteous sentence of God, long before, even as early as in his first purpose and decree he ordained his Son to be the great foundation of his church.' Rosenmüller gives substantially the same interpretation. Clemens Romanus says it means that ' they were appointed, not that they should *sin,* but that, sinning, they should be *punished.*' See Wetstein. So Macknight, · To which *punishment* they were appointed.' Whitby gives the same interpretation of it, that because they were disobedient, (referring, as he supposes, to the Jews who rejected the Messiah,) ' they were appointed, for the punishment of that disobedience, to fall and perish.' Dr. Clark supposes that it means that *they were prophesied of* that they should thus fall; or that, long before, it was predicted that they should thus stumble and fall. In reference to the meaning of this difficult passage, it is proper to observe that there is in the Greek verb necessarily the idea of *designation, appointment, purpose.* There was some agency or intention by which they were put in that condition; some act of *placing* or *appointing,* (the word *τίθημι* meaning *to set, put, lay, lay down, appoint, constitute,*) by which this result was brought about. The fair sense, therefore, and one from which we cannot escape, is, that this did not happen by chance or accident, but that there was a Divine arrangement, appointment, or plan on the part of God in re-

9 But ye *are* a chosen generation, a royal priesthood, an holy nation, a ¹peculiar ªpeople; that ye should

1 Or, *purchased.*　　　a De.4.20.

shew forth the ²praises of him who hath called you out of darkness ᵇ into his marvellous light:

2 Or, *virtues.*　　　b Ac.26.18.

ference to this result, and that the result was in conformity with that. So it is said in Jude 4, of a similar class of men, ' For there are certain men crept in unawares, who were before of old ordained to this condemnation.' The facts were these: (1.) That God appointed his Son to be the corner-stone of his church. (2.) That there was a portion of the world which, from some cause, would embrace him and be saved. (3.) That there was another portion who, it was certain, would *not* embrace him. (4.) That it was known that the appointment of the Lord Jesus as a Saviour would be the occasion of their rejecting him, and of their deeper and more aggravated condemnation. (5.) That the arrangement was nevertheless made, with the understanding that all this *would* be so, and because it was best on the whole that it *should* be so, even *though* this consequence would follow. That is, it was better that the arrangement should be made for the salvation of men even with this result, that a part would sink into deeper condemnation, than that *no* arrangement should be made to save any. The primary and originating arrangement, therefore, did not contemplate *them* or their destruction, but was made with reference to others, and notwithstanding they would reject him, and would fall. The expression *whereunto* (*εἰς ὅ*) refers to this plan, as involving, under the circumstances, the result which actually followed. Their stumbling and falling was not a matter of chance, or a result which was not contemplated, but entered into the original arrangement; and the *whole*, therefore, might be said to be in accordance with a wise plan and purpose. And, (6.) it might be said in this sense, and in this connection, that those who would reject him were appointed to this stumbling and falling. It was what was foreseen; what entered into the general arrangement; what was involved in the purpose to save any. It was not a matter that was unforeseen, that the consequence of giving a

Saviour would result in the condemnation of those who should crucify and reject him; but *the whole thing*, as it actually occurred, entered into the Divine arrangement. It may be added, that as, in the facts in the case, nothing wrong has been done by God, and no one has been deprived of any rights, or punished more than he deserves, it was not wrong in him to make the arrangement. It was better that the arrangement should be made as it is, even with this consequence, than that none at all should be made for human salvation. Comp. Notes on Rom. ix. 15–18; John xii. 39, 40. This is just a statement, in accordance with what everywhere occurs in the Bible, that all things enter into the eternal plans of God; that nothing happens by chance; that there is nothing that was not foreseen; and that the plan is such as, on the whole, God saw to be best and wise, and therefore adopted it. If there is nothing unjust and wrong in the actual *developement* of the plan, there was nothing in forming it. At the same time, no man who disbelieves and rejects the gospel should take refuge in this as an excuse. He was ' appointed ' to it no otherwise than as it actually occurs; and as they know that they are voluntary in rejecting him, they cannot lay the blame of this on the purposes of God. They are not *forced* or *compelled* to do it; but it was seen that this consequence would follow, and the plan was laid to send the Saviour notwithstanding.

9. *But ye* are *a chosen generation.* In contradistinction from those who, by their disobedience, had rejected the Saviour as the foundation of hope. The people of God are often represented as his *chosen* or *elected* people. See Notes on chap. i. 2. ¶ *A royal priesthood.* See Notes on ver. 5. The meaning of this is, probably, that they ' at once bore the dignity of kings, and the sanctity of priests.'—*Doddridge.* Comp. Rev. i. 6: ' And hath made us kings and priests unto God.' See also Isa. lxi. 6: ' But ye shall be named priests

of the Lord; men shall call ye ministers of our God.' It may be, however, that the word *royal* is used only to denote the dignity of the priestly office which they sustained, or that they constituted, as it were, an entire nation or kingdom of priests. They were a kingdom over which he presided, and they were all priests; so that it might be said they were a kingdom of priests—a kingdom in which all the subjects were engaged in offering sacrifice to God. The expression appears to be taken from Exod. xix. 6—' And ye shall be unto me a kingdom of priests'—and is such language as one who had been educated as a Jew would be likely to employ to set forth the dignity of those whom he regarded as the people of God. ¶ *An holy nation*. This is also taken from Exod. xix. 6. The Hebrews were regarded as a nation consecrated to God; and now that they were cast off or rejected for their disobedience, the same language was properly applied to the people whom God had chosen in their place—the Christian church. ¶ *A peculiar people.* Comp. Notes on Titus ii. 14. The margin here is *purchased*. The word *peculiar*, in its common acceptation now, would mean that they were distinguished from others, or were singular. The reading in the margin would mean that they had been bought or redeemed. Both these things are so, but neither of them expresses the exact sense of the original. The Greek (λαὸς εἰς περι-ποίησιν) means, ' a people for a possession;' that is, as pertaining to God. They are a people which he has secured as a possession, or as his own; a people, therefore, which belong to him, and to no other. In this sense they are *peculiar* as being his; and, being such, it may be inferred that they *should be* peculiar in the sense of being unlike others in their manner of life. But that idea is not necessarily in the text. There seems to be here also an allusion to Exod. xix. 5: ' Ye shall be a peculiar treasure with me (Sept. λαὸς περιούσιος) above all people.' ¶ *That ye should shew forth the praises of him*. Marg., *virtues*. The Greek word (ἀρετὴ) means properly *good quality, excellence* of any kind. It means here the excellences of God—his goodness, his wondrous deeds,

or those things which make it proper to praise him. This shows one great object for which they were redeemed. It was that they might proclaim the glory of God, and keep up the remembrance of his wondrous deeds in the earth. This is to be done (*a*) by proper ascriptions of praise to him in public, family, and social worship; (*b*) by being always the avowed friends of God, ready ever to vindicate his government and ways; (*c*) by endeavouring to make known his excellences to all those who are ignorant of him; and (*d*) by such a life as shall constantly proclaim his praise—as the sun, the moon, the stars, the hills, the streams, the flowers do, showing what God *does*. The consistent life of a devoted Christian is a constant setting forth of the praise of God, showing to all that the God who has made him such is worthy to be loved. ¶ *Who hath called you out of darkness into his marvellous light*. On the word *called*, see Notes on Eph. iv. 1. *Darkness* is the emblem of ignorance, sin, and misery, and refers here to their condition before their conversion; *light* is the emblem of the opposite, and is a beautiful representation of the state of those who are brought to the knowledge of the gospel. See Notes on Acts xxvi. 18. The word *marvellous* means *wonderful*; and the idea is, that the light of the gospel was such as was unusual, or not to be found elsewhere, as that excites wonder or surprise which we are not accustomed to see. The primary reference here is, undoubtedly, to those who had been heathens, and to the great change which had been produced by their having been brought to the knowledge of the truth as revealed in the gospel; and, in regard to this, no one can doubt that the one state deserved to be characterized as darkness, and the other as light. The contrast was as great as that between midnight and noonday. But what is here said is substantially correct of all who are converted, and is often as strikingly true of those who have been brought up in Christian lands, as of those who have lived among the heathen. The change in conversion is often so great and so rapid, the views and feelings are so different before and after conversion, that it seems like a sudden transition

10 Which ^a in time past *were* not a people, but *are* now the people of God: which had not obtained mercy, but now have obtained mercy.

a Ro.9.25.　　　　　*b* Ps.119.19.

11 Dearly beloved, I beseech *you* as strangers ^b and pilgrims, abstain from ^c fleshly lusts, which war ^d against the soul;

c Ga 5.16-21.　　　　　*d* Ro.8.13; Ja.4.1.

---

from midnight to noon. In *all* cases, also, of true conversion, though the change may not be so striking, or apparently so sudden, there *is* a change of which this may be regarded as substantially an accurate description. In many cases the convert can adopt this language in all its fulness, as descriptive of his own conversion; in *all* cases of genuine conversion it is true that each one can say that he has been called from a state in which his mind was dark to one in which it is comparatively clear.

10. *Which in time past* were *not a people.* That is, who formerly were not regarded as the people of God. There is an *allusion* here to the passage in Hosea ii. 23, ' And I will have mercy upon her that had not obtained mercy; and I will say to them which were not my people, Thou art my people; and they shall say, Thou art my God.' It is, however, a *mere* allusion, such as one makes who uses the language of another to express his ideas, without meaning to say that both refer to the same subject. In Hosea, the passage refers evidently to the reception of one portion of the Israelites into favour after their rejection; in Peter, it refers mainly to those who had been Gentiles, and who had never been recognised as the people of God. The language of the prophet would exactly express his idea, and he therefore uses it without intending to say that this was its original application. See it explained in the Notes on Rom. ix. 25. Comp. Notes on Eph. ii. 11, 12. ¶ *Which had not obtained mercy.* That is, who had been living unpardoned, having no knowledge of the way by which sinners might be forgiven, and no evidence that your sins were forgiven. They were then in the condition of the whole heathen world, and they had not then been acquainted with the glorious method by which God forgives iniquity.

11. *Dearly beloved, I beseech* you *as strangers and pilgrims.* On the

word rendered *strangers,* (παροίκους,) see Notes on Eph. ii. 19, where it is rendered *foreigners.* It means, properly, one dwelling near, neighbouring; then a by-dweller, a sojourner, one without the rights of citizenship, as distinguished from a citizen; and it means here that Christians are not properly citizens of this world, but that their citizenship is in heaven, and that they are here mere sojourners. Comp. Notes on Phil. iii. 20, 'For our conversation [*citizenship*] is in heaven.' On the word rendered *pilgrims,* (παρεπιδήμους,) see Notes on chap. i. 1; Heb. xi. 13. A *pilgrim,* properly, is one who travels to a distance from his own country to visit a holy place, or to pay his devotion to some holy object; then a traveller, a wanderer. The meaning here is, that Christians have no permanent home on earth; their citizenship is not here; they are mere sojourners, and they are passing on to their eternal home in the heavens. They should, therefore, act as become such persons; as sojourners and travellers do. They should not (*a*) regard the earth as their home. (*b*) They should not seek to acquire permanent possessions *here,* as if they were to remain here, but should act as travellers do, who merely seek a temporary lodging, without expecting permanently to reside in a place. (*c*) They should not allow any such attachments to be formed, or arrangements to be made, as to impede their journey to their final home, as pilgrims seek only a temporary lodging, and steadily pursue their journey. (*d*) Even while engaged here in the necessary callings of life—their studies, their farming, their merchandise—their thoughts and affections should be on other things. One in a strange land thinks much of his country and home; a pilgrim, much of the land to which he goes; and even while his time and attention may be necessarily occupied by the arrangements needful for the journey, his thoughts and affections will be

12 Having your conversation honest among the Gentiles: that, ¹ whereas they speak against you as evil doers, they may by *your* good works, ᵃ which they shall behold, glorify God in the day of visitation.

far away. (*e*) We should not *encumber* ourselves with much of this world's goods. Many professed Christians get so many worldly things around them, that it is impossible for them to make a journey to heaven. They burden themselves as no traveller would, and they make no progress. A traveller takes along as few things as possible; and a staff is often all that a pilgrim has. We make the most rapid progress in our journey to our final home when we are least encumbered with the things of this world. ¶ *Abstain from fleshly lusts.* Such desires and passions as the carnal appetites prompt to. See Notes on Gal. v. 19–21. A sojourner in a land, or a pilgrim, does not give himself up to the indulgence of sensual appetites, or to the soft pleasures of the soul. All these would hinder his progress, and turn him off from his great design. Comp. Rom. xiii. 4; Gal. v. 24; 2 Tim. ii. 22; Titus ii. 12; 1 Pet. i. 14. ¶ *Which war against the soul.* Comp. Notes on Rom. viii. 12, 13. The meaning is, that indulgence in these things makes war against the nobler faculties of the soul; against the conscience, the understanding, the memory, the judgment, the exercise of a pure imagination. Comp. Notes on Gal. v. 17. There is not a faculty of the mind, however brilliant in itself, which will not be ultimately ruined by indulgence in the carnal propensities of our nature. The effect of intemperance on the noble faculties of the soul is well known; and alas, there are too many instances in which the light of genius, in those endowed with splendid gifts, at the bar, in the pulpit, and in the senate, is extinguished by it, to need a particular description. But there is one vice preeminently, which prevails all over the heathen world, (Comp. Notes on Rom. i. 27–29,) and extensively in Christian lands, which more than all others, blunts the moral sense, pollutes the memory, defiles the imagination, hardens the heart, and sends a withering influence through all the faculties of the soul.

'The soul grows clotted by contagion,
Embodies, and embrutes, till she quite lose
The divine property of her first being.'

Of this passion, Burns beautifully and truly said—

' But oh! *it hardens a° within,*
And petrifies the feeling.'

From all these passions the Christian pilgrim is to abstain.

12. *Having your conversation honest.* Your conduct. Notes, Phil. i. 27. That is, lead upright and consistent lives. Comp. Notes on Phil. iv. 8. ¶ *Among the Gentiles.* The heathen by whom you are surrounded, and who will certainly observe your conduct. Notes on 1 Thess. iv. 12, 'That ye may walk honestly towards them that are without.' Comp. Rom. xiii. 13. ¶ *That, whereas they speak against you as evil doers.* Marg., *wherein.* Gr. ἐν ᾧ—*in what;* either referring to *time,* and meaning that *at the very time* when they speak against you in this manner they may be silenced by seeing your upright lives; or meaning *in respect to which*—that is, that in respect to the very matters for which they reproach you they may see by your meek and upright conduct that there is really no ground for reproach. Wetstein adopts the former, but the question which is meant is not very important. Bloomfield supposes it to mean *inasmuch, whereas.* The sentiment is a correct one, whichever interpretation is adopted. It should be true that at the very time when the enemies of religion reproach us, they should see that we are actuated by Christian principles, and that in the very matter for which we are reproached we are conscientious and honest. ¶ *They may, by your good works, which they shall behold.* Gr., 'which they shall closely or narrowly inspect.' The meaning is, that upon a close and narrow examination, they may see that you are actuated by upright principles, and ultimately be

13 Submit yourselves *a* to every
ordinance of man for the Lord's
a Mat.22.21; Ro.13.1-7.

sake: whether it be to the king, as
supreme;

disposed to do you justice. It is to be remembered that the heathen were very little acquainted with the nature of Christianity; and it is known that in the early ages they charged on Christians the most abominable vices, and even accused them of practices at which human nature revolts. The meaning of Peter is, that while they charged these things on Christians, whether from ignorance or malice, they ought so to live as that a more full acquaintance with them, and a closer inspection of their conduct, would disarm their prejudices, and show that their charges were entirely unfounded. The truth taught here is, *that our conduct as Christians should be such as to bear the strictest scrutiny; such that the closest examination will lead our enemies to the conviction that we are upright and honest.* This *may* be done by every Christian; this his religion solemnly requires him to do. ¶ *Glorify God.* Honour God; that is, that they may be convinced by your conduct of the pure and holy nature of that religion which he has revealed, and be led also to love and worship him. See Notes, Matt. v. 16. ¶ *In the day of visitation.* Many different opinions have been entertained of the meaning of this phrase, some referring it to the day of judgment; some to times of persecution; some to the destruction of Jerusalem; and some to the time when the gospel was preached among the Gentiles, as a period when God visited them with mercy. The word visitation (ἐπισκοπή,) means the act of visiting or being visited for any purpose, usually with the notion of inspecting conduct, of inflicting punishment, or of conferring favours. Comp. Matt. xxv. 36, 43; Luke i. 68, 78; vii. 16; xix. 44. In the sense of visiting for the purpose of punishing, the word is often used in the Septuagint for the Heb. פָּקַד (*pakad*,) though there is no instance in which the word is, so used in the New Testament, unless it be in the verse before us. The 'visitation' here referred to is undoubtedly that of God; and the reference is to some time when he would

make a 'visitation' to men for some purpose, and when the fact that the Gentiles had narrowly inspected the conduct of Christians would lead them to honour him. The only question is, to *what* visitation of that kind the apostle referred. The prevailing use of the word in the New Testament would seem to lead us to suppose that the 'visitation' referred to was designed to confer favours rather than to inflict punishment, and indeed the word seems to have somewhat of a *technical* character, and to have been familiarly used by Christians to denote God's coming to men to bless them; to pour out his Spirit upon them; to revive religion. This seems to me to be its meaning here; and, if so, the sense is, that when God appeared among men to accompany the preaching of the gospel with saving power, the result of the observed conduct of Christians would be to lead those around them to honour him by giving up their hearts to him; that is, their consistent lives would be the means of the revival and extension of true religion. *And is it not always so?* Is not the pure and holy walk of Christians an occasion of his bending his footsteps down to earth to bless dying sinners, and to scatter spiritual blessings with a liberal hand? Comp. Notes, 1 Cor. xiv. 24, 25.

13. *Submit yourselves to every ordinance of man.* Gr., 'to every *creation* of man,' (ἀνθρωπίνῃ κτίσει.) The meaning is, to every institution or appointment of man; to wit, of those who are in authority, or who are appointed to administer government. The laws, institutes, and appointments of such a government may be spoken of as the *creation* of man; that is, as what man makes. Of course, what is here said must be understood with the limitation everywhere implied, that what is ordained by those in authority is not contrary to the law of God. See Notes on Acts iv. 19. On the general duty here enjoined of subjection to civil authority, see Notes on Rom. xiii. 1-7. ¶ *For the Lord's sake.* Because he has required

14 Or unto governors, as unto them that are sent by him for the punishment of evil doers, and for the praise of them that do well.

15 For so is the will of God, that *a* with well doing ye may put to silence the ignorance of foolish men:

a Tit.2.8.

it, and has intrusted this power to civil rulers. Notes, Rom. xiii. 5. Comp. Notes, Eph. vi. 7. ¶ *Whether it be to the king.* It has been commonly supposed that there is reference here to the Roman emperor, who might be called *king*, because in him the supreme power resided. The common title of the Roman sovereign was, as used by the Greek writers, ἀυτοκράτωρ, and among the Romans themselves, *imperator,* (*emperor;*) but the title *king* was also given to the sovereign. John xix. 15, ' We have no *king* but Cesar.' Acts xvii. 7, 'And these all do contrary to the decrees of Cesar, saying that there is another king, one Jesus.' Peter undoubtedly had particular reference to the Roman emperors, but he uses a general term, which would be applicable to all in whom the supreme power resided, and the injunction here would require submission to such authority, by whatever name it might be called. The meaning is, that we are to be subject to that authority whether exercised by the sovereign in person, or by those who are appointed by him. ¶ *As supreme.* Not supreme in the sense of being superior to God, or not being subject to him, but in the sense of being over all subordinate officers.

14. *Or unto governors.* Subordinate officers, appointed by the chief magistrate, over provinces. Perhaps Roman proconsuls are here particularly intended. ¶ *As unto them that are sent by him.* By the king, or the Roman emperor. They represent the supreme power. ¶ *For the punishment of evil doers.* One of the leading ends of government. ' The Roman governors had the power of life and death in such conquered provinces as those mentioned in chap. i. 1.'—*Doddridge.* Ulpian, the celebrated Roman lawyer, who flourished two hundred years after Christ, thus describes the power of the governors of the Roman provinces: ' It is the duty of a good and vigilant president to see to it that his province be

peaceable and quiet. And that he ought to make diligent search after sacrilegious persons, robbers, man-stealers, and thieves, and to punish every one according to their guilt.' Again, ' They who govern whole provinces, have the power of sending to the mines.' And again, ' The presidents of provinces have the highest authority, next to the emperor.' Peter has described the office of the Roman governors in language nearly resembling that of Ulpian. See Lardner's Credibility, (Works, i. 77, edit. 8vo., Lond. 1829.) ¶ *And for the praise of them that do well.* Praise here stands opposed to *punishment,* and means commendation, applause, reward. That is, it is a part of their business to reward in a suitable manner those who are upright and virtuous as citizens. This would be by protecting their persons and property; by defending their rights, and, perhaps, by admitting those to share the honours and emoluments of office who showed that they were worthy to be trusted. It is as important a part of the functions of magistracy to protect the innocent, as it is to punish the wicked.

15. *For so is the will of God.* That is, it is in accordance with the Divine will that in this way you should put them to silence. ¶ *That with well doing.* By a life of uprightness and benevolence. ¶ *Ye may put to silence the ignorance of foolish men.* See Notes on Titus ii. 8. The reference here is to men who brought charges against Christians, by accusing them of being inimical to the government, or insubordinate, or guilty of crimes. Such charges, it is well known, were often brought against them by their enemies in the early ages of Christianity. Peter says they were brought by *foolish* men, perhaps using the word *foolish* in the sense of evil-disposed, or wicked, as it is often used in the Bible. Yet, though there might be malice at the bottom, the charges were really based on *ignorance.* They were not thoroughly

16 As free, *a* and not ¹ using *your* liberty for a cloke of maliciousness,

a Ga.5.1,13.　　　1 *having.*　　　but as the servants of God.

---

acquainted with the principles of the Christian religion; and the way to meet those charges was to act in every way as became good citizens, and so as ' to live them down.' One of the best ways of meeting the accusations of our enemies is to lead a life of strict integrity. It is not easy for the wicked to reply to this argument. 16. *As free.* That is, they were to consider themselves as freemen, as having a right to liberty. The Jews boasted much of their freedom, and regarded it as a birthright privilege that they were free, John viii. 33. They never willingly acknowledged their subjection to any other power, but claimed it as an elementary idea of their civil constitution that God only was their Sovereign. They were indeed conquered by the Romans, and paid tribute, but they did it because they were compelled to do it, and it was even a question much debated among them whether they should do it or not, Matt. xxii. 17. Josephus has often referred to the fact that the Jews rebelled against the Romans under the plea that they were a *free people,* and that they were subject only to God. This idea of essential freedom the Jews had when they became Christians, and every thing in Christianity tended to inspire them with the love of liberty. They who were converted to the Christian faith, whether from among the Jews or the Gentiles, were made to feel that they were the children of God; that his law was the supreme rule of their lives; that in the ultimate resort they were subject to him alone; that they were redeemed, and that, therefore, the yoke of bondage could not be properly imposed on them; that God ' had made of one blood all nations of men, for to dwell on all the face of the earth,' (Acts xvii. 26;) and that, therefore, they were on a level before him. The meaning here is, that they were not to consider themselves as slaves, or to act as slaves. In their subjection to civil authority they were not to forget that they were freemen in the highest sense, and that

liberty was an invaluable blessing. They had been made free by the Son of God, John viii. 32, 36. They were free from sin and condemnation. They acknowledged Christ as their supreme Head, and the whole spirit and tendency of his religion prompted to the exercise of freedom. They were not to submit to the chains of slavery; not to allow their consciences to be bound, or their essential liberty to be interfered with; nor in their subjection to the civil magistrate were they ever to regard themselves otherwise than as freemen. As a matter of fact, Christianity has always been the friend and promoter of liberty. Its influence emancipated the slaves throughout the Roman empire; and all the civil freedom which we enjoy, and which there is in the world, can be traced to the influence of the Christian religion. To spread the gospel in its purity everywhere would be to break every yoke of oppression and bondage, and to make men everywhere free. It is the essential right of every man who is a Christian to be a *freeman* —to be free to worship God; to read the Bible; to enjoy the avails of his own labour; to train up his children in the way in which he shall deem best; to form his own plans of life, and to pursue his own ends, provided only that he does not interfere with the equal rights of others—and every system which prevents this, whether it be that of civil government, of ecclesiastical law, or of domestic slavery, is contrary to the religion of the Saviour. ¶ *And not using* your *liberty for a cloke of maliciousness.* Marg., as in Greek, *having.* Not making your freedom a mere pretext under which to practise all kinds of evil. The word rendered *maliciousness—κακία—*means more than our word *maliciousness* does; for it denotes *evil* of any kind, or all kinds. The word *maliciousness* refers rather to enmity of heart, ill-will, an intention to injure. The apostle has reference to an abuse of freedom, which has often occurred. The pretence of those who have acted in this manner has been,

17 ¹ Honour all *men.*ᵃ Love ᵇ the
1 Or, *esteem.*   a Ro.12.10; Phi.2.3.
b Jn.13.35.   c Ps.111.10.   d Pr.24.21.

brotherhood. Fear ᶜ God. Honour
the king.ᵈ

that the freedom of the gospel implied deliverance from all kinds of restraint; that they were under *no* yoke, and bound by no laws; that, being the children of God, they had a right to all kinds of enjoyment and indulgence; that even the moral law ceased to bind them, and that they had a right to make the most of liberty in all respects. Hence they have given themselves up to all sorts of sensual indulgence, claiming exemption from the restraints of morality as well as of civil law, and sinking into the deepest abyss of vice. Not a few have done this who have professed to be Christians; and, occasionally, a fanatical sect now appears who make the freedom which they say Christianity confers, a pretext for indulgence in the most base and degrading vices. The apostles saw this tendency in human nature, and in nothing are they more careful than to guard against this abuse. ¶ *But as the servants of God.* Not free from all restraint; not at liberty to indulge in all things, but bound to serve God in the faithful obedience of his laws. Thus bound to obey and serve him, they could not be at liberty to indulge in those things which would be in violation of his laws, and which would dishonour him. See this sentiment explained in the Notes on 1 Cor. vii. 22; ix. 21.

17. *Honour all* men. That is, show them the respect which is due to them according to their personal worth, and to the rank and office which they sustain. Notes, Rom. xiii. 7. ¶ *Love the brotherhood.* The whole fraternity of Christians, regarded as a band of brothers. The word here used occurs only in this place and in chap. v. 9, where it is rendered *brethren.* The *idea* expressed here occurs often in the New Testament. See Notes, John xiii. 34, 35. ¶ *Fear God.* A duty everywhere enjoined in the Bible, as one of the first duties of religion. Comp. Lev. xxv. 17; Psa. xxiii. 18; xxiv. 7; xxv. 14; Prov. i. 7; iii. 13; ix. 10; xxiii. 17; Notes, Rom. iii. 18; 2 Cor. vii. 1. The word *fear,* when used to express our duty to

God, means that we are to reverence and honour him. Religion, in one aspect, is described as the fear of God; in another, as the love of God; in another, as submission to his will, &c. A holy veneration or fear is always an elementary principle of religion. It is the fear, not so much of punishment as of his disapprobation; not so much the dread of suffering as the dread of doing wrong. ¶ *Honour the king.* Referring here primarily to the Roman sovereign, but implying that we are always to respect those who have the rule over us. See Notes, Rom. xiii. 1–7. The doctrine taught in these verses (13–17) is, that we are faithfully to perform all the relative duties of life. There are duties which we owe to ourselves, which are of importance in their place, and which we are by no means at liberty to neglect. But we also owe duties to our fellow-men, to our Christian brethren, and to those who have the rule over us; and religion, while it is honoured by our faithful performance of our duty to ourselves, is more *openly* honoured by our performance of our duties to those to whom we sustain important relations in life. Many of the duties which we owe to ourselves are, from the nature of the case, hidden from public observation. All that pertains to the examination of the heart; to our private devotions; to the subjugation of our evil passions; to our individual communion with God, must be concealed from public view. Not so, however, with those duties which pertain to others. In respect to them, we are open to public view. The eye of the world is upon us. The judgment of the world in regard to us is made up from their observation of the manner in which we perform them. If religion fails there, they judge that it fails altogether; and however devout we may be in private, if it is not seen by the world that our religion leads to the faithful performance of the duties which we owe in the various relations of life, it will be regarded as of little value.

18. *Servants,* be *subject to* your mas-

18 Servants, *a be* subject to *your* masters with all fear ; not only to the good and gentle, but also to the froward.

19 For this *is* [1] thank-worthy, if a man for conscience toward God endure grief, suffering wrongfully.

a Ep.6.5,&c.　　　1 Or, *thank*, Lu.6.32.

ters. On the duty here enjoined, see Notes, Eph. vi. 5–9. The Greek word here used (οἰκέται) is not the same which is employed in Ephesians, (δοῦλοι.) The word here means properly *domestics*—those employed about a house, or living in the same house—from οἶκος, *house.* These persons might have been slaves, or might not. The word would apply to them, whether they were hired, or whether they were owned as slaves. The word should not and cannot be employed to *prove* that slavery existed in the churches to which Peter wrote, and still less to prove that he approved of slavery, or regarded it as a good institution. The exhortation here would be, and still is, strictly applicable to any persons employed as domestics, though they had voluntarily hired themselves out to be such. It would be incumbent on them, while they remained in that condition, to perform with fidelity their duties as Christians, and to bear with Christian meekness all the wrongs which they might suffer from those in whose service they were. Those who are hired, and who are under a necessity of ' going out to service ' for a living, are not always free from hard usage, for there are trials incident to that condition of life which cannot be always avoided. It might be better, in many cases, to bear much than to attempt a change of situation, even though they were entirely at liberty to do so. It must be admitted, however, that the exhortation here will have more force if it is supposed that the reference is to slaves, and there can be no doubt that many of this class were early converted to the Christian faith. The word here rendered *masters* (δεσπόταις) is not the same which is used in Eph. vi. 5, (κυρίοις.) Neither of these words necessarily implies that those who were under them were *slaves.* The word here used is applicable to the head of a family, *whatever* may be the condition of those under him. It is frequently applied to God, and to Christ; and it cannot be maintained that those

to whom God sustains the relation of δεσπότης, or *master*, are *slaves.* See Luke ii. 29 ; Acts iv. 24; 2 Tim. ii. 21; 2 Pet. ii. 1; Jude 4; Rev. vi. 10. The word, indeed, is one that *might* be applied to those who were owners of slaves. If that be the meaning here, it is not said, however, that those to whom it is applied were Christians. It is rather implied that they were pursuing such a course as was inconsistent with real piety. Those who were under them are represented as suffering grievous wrongs. ¶ *With all fear.* That is, with all proper reverence and respect. Notes, Eph. vi. 5. ¶ *Not only to the good and gentle, but also to the froward.* The word rendered *froward* (σκολιοῖς) means properly *crooked, bent;* then perverse, wicked, unjust, peevish. Any one who is a servant or domestic is liable to be employed in the service of such a master; but while the relation continues, the servant should perform *his* duty with fidelity, whatever may be the character of the master. *Slaves* are certainly liable to this; and even those who voluntarily engage as servants to others, cannot always be sure that they will have kind employers. Though the *terms* used here do not necessarily imply that those to whom the apostle gave this direction were *slaves*, yet it may be presumed that they probably were, since slavery abounded throughout the Roman empire ; but the directions will apply to *all* who are engaged in the service of others, and are therefore of permanent value. Slavery will, sooner or later, under the influence of the gospel, wholly cease in the world, and instructions addressed to masters and slaves will have no permanent value; but it will always be true that there will be those employed as domestics, and it is the duty of all who are thus engaged to evince true fidelity and a Christian spirit themselves, whatever may be the character of their employers.

19. *For this* is *thank-worthy.* Marg., *thank.* Gr., ' This is *grace*,' (χάρις).

20 For what glory *is it*, if, when ye be buffeted for your faults, ye shall take it patiently? but if, when

a Mat.5.10-12.

ye do well, and suffer *for it*, ye takε it patiently, this *ᵃis* ¹acceptable with God.

1 Or, *thank,* Lu.6.32.

Doddridge renders the expression, 'This is *graceful* indeed.' Various interpretations of this expression have been proposed; but the meaning evidently is, that *it is acceptable to God,* (see ver. 20, 'this is acceptable to God'—χάρις παρὰ Θεῷ;) that is, this will be regarded by him with *favour.* It does not mean that it was worthy of *thanks,* or that God would *thank* them for doing it, (comp. Luke xvii. 9, 10;) but that such conduct would meet with his approbation. ¶ *If a man for conscience toward God.* If, in the conscientious discharge of his duty, or if, in the endurance of this wrong, he regards himself as serving God. That is, if he feels that God, by his providence, has placed him in the circumstances in which he is, and that it is a duty which he owes to him to bear every trial incident to that condition with a submissive spirit. If he does this, he will evince the true nature of religion, and will be graciously accepted of God. ¶ *Endure grief.* That is, endure that which is fitted to *produce grief,* or that which is wrong. ¶ *Suffering wrongfully.* Suffering injury, or where there is *injustice,* (πάσχων ἀδίκως.) This, though a general remark, has particular reference to *servants,* and to their duty in the relation which they sustain to their masters. In view of what is here said, we may remark, (1.) that if this has reference to *slaves,* as has been usually supposed, it proves that they are very *liable* to be abused; that they have little or no security against being wronged; and that it was a special and very desirable characteristic of those who were *in* that condition, to be able to bear *wrong* with a proper spirit. It is impossible so to modify slavery that this shall not be the case; for the whole system is one of oppression, and there can be nothing that shall effectually secure the slave from being ill-treated. (2.) It would follow from this passage, if this refers to slavery, that that is a very hard and undesirable condition of life; for that is a very undesirable condition where the principal virtue, which

they who are in it are required to exercise, is *patience under wrongs.* Such a condition cannot be in accordance with the gospel, and cannot be designed by God to be *permanent.* The relation ot parent and child is never thus represented. It is never. said or implied in the Scriptures that the principal virtue to which children are exhorted is *patience under wrongs;* nor, in addressing them, is it ever supposed that the most prominent thing in their condition is, that they would need the exercise of such patience. (3.) It is acceptable to God, if we bear wrong with a proper spirit, from whatever quarter it may come. Our proper business in life is, to do the will of God; to evince the right spirit, however others may treat us; and to show, even under excessive wrong, the sustaining power and the excellence of true religion. Each one who is oppressed and wronged, therefore, has an eminent opportunity to show a spirit which will honour the gospel; and the slave and the martyr may do more to honour the gospel than if they were both permitted to enjoy liberty and life undisturbed.

20. *For what glory* is it. What honour or credit would it be. ¶ *If, when ye be buffeted for your faults.* That is, if you are punished when you deserve it. The word *buffet* (κολαφίζω) means, to strike with the fist; and then to strike in any way; to maltreat, Matt. xxvi. 67; Mark xiv. 65; 1 Cor. iv. 11; 2 Cor. xii. 7. Perhaps there may be a reference here to the manner in which servants were commonly treated, or the kind of punishment to which they were exposed. They would be likely to be *struck* in sudden anger, either by the hand, or by anything that was accessible. The word rendered 'for your faults,' is *sinning,* (ἁμαρτάνοντες.) That is, 'if being guilty of an offence, or having done wrong.' The idea is, that if they were *justly* punished, and should take it patiently, there would be no credit or honour in it. ¶ *Ye shall take it patiently.* ' If, even then, you evince an uncomplaining

21 For even hereunto *were ye called: because Christ also suffered 1 for us, leaving us an example, that ye should follow *his steps:

22 Who *did no sin, neither was guile found in his mouth:

a Mat.16.24; 1 Th.3.3,4.　　1 Some read, *for you.*
b 1 Jn.3.16; Re.12.11.　　　　*c* Is.53.9.

spirit, and bear it with the utmost calmness and patience, it would be regarded as comparatively no virtue, and as entitling you to no honour. The feeling of all who saw it would be that you *deserved* it, and there would be nothing to excite their sympathy or compassion. The patience evinced might indeed be as great as in the other case, but there would be the feeling that you *deserved* all that you received, and the spirit evinced in that case could not be regarded as entitled to any particular praise. If your masters are inflicting on you only what you deserve, it would be in the highest degree shameful for you to rise up against them, and resist them, for it would be only adding to the wrong which you had already done.' The expression here is, doubtless, to be understood *comparatively.* The meaning is not that absolutely there would be no more credit due to one who should bear his punishment patiently when he had done wrong, than if he had met it with resistance and murmuring; but that there is *very little* credit in that compared with the patience which an innocent person evinces, who, from regard to the will of God, and by control over all the natural feelings of resentment, meekly endures wrong. This expresses the common feeling of our nature. We attribute no particular credit to one who submits to a just punishment even with a calm temper. We feel that it would be wrong in the highest degree for him to do otherwise. So it is when calamities are brought on a man on account of his sins. If it is *seen* to be the fruit of intemperance or crime, we do not feel that there is any great virtue exhibited if he bears it with a calm temper. But if he is overwhelmed with calamity when it seems to have no particular connection with his sins, or to be a punishment for any particular fault; if he suffers at the hand of man, where there is manifest injustice done him, and yet evinces a calm, submissive, and meek temper, we feel that in such cases

there is eminent virtue. ¶ *This* is *acceptable with God.* Marg., as in ver. 19, *thank.* It is that which is agreeable to him, or with which he is pleased. 21. *For even hereunto were ye called.* Such a spirit is required by the very nature of your Christian vocation; you were called into the church in order that you might evince it. See Notes, 1 Thess. iii. 3. ¶ *Because Christ also suffered for us.* Marg., 'some read, *for you.*' The latest editions of the Greek Testament adopt the reading ' for *you.*' The sense, however, is not essentially varied. The object is, to hold up the example of Christ to those who were called to suffer, and to say to them that they should bear their trials in the same spirit that he evinced in his. See Notes, Phil. iii. 10. ¶ *Leaving us an example.* The apostle does not say that this was the *only* object for which Christ suffered, but that it was *an* object, and an important one. The word rendered *example* (ὑπογραμμὸν) occurs nowhere else in the New Testament. It means properly a *writing copy,* such as is set for children ; or an outline or sketch for a painter to fill up ; and then, in general, an example, a pattern for imitation. ¶ *That ye should follow his steps.* That we should *follow* him, *as if* we trod exactly along behind him, and should place our feet precisely where his were. The meaning is, that there should be the closest imitation or resemblance. The *things* in which we are to imitate him are specified in the following verses. 22. *Who did no sin.* Who was in all respects perfectly holy. There is an allusion here to Isa. liii. 9 ; and the sense is, that he was entirely innocent, and that he suffered without having committed any crime. In this connection the meaning is, that *we* are to be careful that, if we suffer, it should be without committing any crime. We should so live, as the Saviour did, as not to *deserve* to be punished, and thus only shall we entirely follow his example. It

23 Who, when he was reviled, reviled not again ; when he suffered, he threatened not ; but committed

¹ *himself* to him that judgeth ᵃ righteously:

1 Or, *his cause*.   a Lu.23.46.

is as much our duty to live so as not to *deserve* the reproaches of others, as it is to bear them with patience when we are called to suffer them. The first thing in regard to hard treatment from others, is so to live that there shall be no just occasion for it; the next is, if reproaches come upon us when we have not deserved them, to bear them as the Saviour did. If he suffered unjustly, we should esteem it to be no strange thing that we should ; if he bore the injuries done him with meekness, we should learn that it is *possible* for us to do it also ; and should learn also that we have not the spirit of his religion unless we actually do it. On the expression here used, comp. Notes, Isa. liii. 9 ; Heb. vii. 26. ¶ *Neither was guile found in his mouth.* There was no deceit, hypocrisy, or insincerity. He was in all respects what he professed to be, and he imposed on no one by any false and unfounded claim. All this has reference to the time when the Saviour was put to death; and the sense is, that though he was condemned as an impostor, yet that the charge was wholly unfounded. As in his whole life before he was perfectly sincere, so he was eminently on that solemn occasion.

23. *Who, when he was reviled, reviled not again.* He did not use harsh and opprobrious words in return for those which he received. (1.) He *was* reviled. He was accused of being a seditious man ; spoken of as a deceiver; charged with being in league with Beelzebub, the 'prince of the devils' and condemned as a blasphemer against God. This was done (*a*) by the great and the influential of the land ; (*b*) in the most public manner ; (*c*) with a design to alienate his friends from him ; (*d*) with most cutting and severe sarcasm and irony ; and (*e*) in reference to everything that would most affect a man of delicate and tender sensibility. (2.) He did not revile those who had reproached him. He asked that justice might be done. He demanded that if he had spoken evil, they should bear witness of the evil; but beyond that he

did not go. He used no harsh language. He showed no anger. He called for no revenge. He prayed that they might be forgiven. He calmly stood and bore it all, for he came to endure all kinds of suffering in order that he might set us an example, and make an atonement for our sins. ¶ *When he suffered, he threatened not.* That is, when he suffered injustice from others, in his trial and in his death, he did not threaten punishment. He did not call down the wrath of heaven. He did not even *predict* that they would be punished ; he expressed no wish that they should be. ¶ *But committed* himself *to him that judgeth righteously.* Marg., *his cause.* The sense is much the same. The meaning is, that he committed his cause, his name, his interests, *the whole case*, to God. The meaning of the phrase ' that judgeth righteously ' here is, that God would do him exact justice. Though wronged by men, he felt assured that *he* would do right. He would rescue his name from these reproaches ; he would give him the honour in the world which he deserved ; and he would bring upon those who had wronged him all that was necessary in order to show his disapprobation of what they had done, and all that would be necessary to give the highest support to the cause of virtue. Comp. Luke xxiii. 46. This is the example which is set before us when we are wronged. The whole example embraces these points : (1.) We should see to it that we ourselves are *guiltless* in the matter for which we are reproached or accused. Before we fancy that we are suffering as Christ did, we should be sure that our lives are such as not to deserve reproach. We cannot indeed hope to be as pure in all things as he was ; but we may so live that if we *are* reproached and reviled we may be certain that it is not for any wrong that we have done to others, or that we do not deserve it from our fellow-men. (2.) When we are reproached and reviled, we should feel that we were called to this by our profession ; that it was one of the things which we were taught to

24 Who his own self bare ^a our sins in his own body ¹ on the tree, that we, being dead to sins, should

live ^b unto righteousness : by whose ^c stripes ye were healed.

a Is.53.4,&c.   1 Or, to.   b Ro.6.11.   c Is.53.5,6.

expect when we became Christians; that it is what the prophets and apostles endured, and what the Master himself suffered in an eminent degree ; and that if we meet with the scorn of the great, the gay, the rich, the powerful, it is no more than the Saviour did, and no more than we have been taught to expect will be our portion. It may be well, too, to remember our unworthiness ; and to reflect, that though we have done no wrong to the individual who reviles us, yet that we are sinners, and that such reproaches may not be a useless admonisher of our being guilty before God. So David felt when reproached by Shimei : ' So let him curse, because the Lord hath said unto him, Curse David. Who shall then say, Wherefore hast thou done so ?' 2 Sam. xvi. 10.   (3.) When this occurs, we should calmly and confidently commit our cause to God.   Our name, our character, our influence, our reputation, while living and after we are dead, we should leave entirely with him. We should not seek nor desire revenge. We should not call down the wrath of God on our persecutors and slanderers. We should calmly feel that God will give us the measure of reputation which we ought to have in the world, and that he will suffer no ultimate injustice to be done us. ' Commit thy way unto the Lord ; trust also in him, and he shall bring it to pass ; and he shall bring forth thy righteousness as the light, and thy judgment as the noon-day,' Ps. xxxvii. 5, 6. The Latin Vulgate has here, ' But he committed himself to him who judged him unjustly,' judicanti se injusté; that is, to Pontius Pilate, meaning that he left himself in his hands, though he knew that the sentence was unjust. But there is no authority for this in the Greek, and this is one of the instances in which that version departs from the original.

24. *Who his own self.* See Notes, Heb. i. 3, on the phrase ' when he had *by himself* purged our sins.' The meaning is, that he did it in his own proper person ; he did not make expiation by

offering a bloody victim, but was himself the sacrifice. ¶ *Bare our sins.* There is an allusion here undoubtedly to Is. liii. 4, 12. See the meaning of the phrase ' to bear sins' fully considered in the Notes on those places. As this cannot mean that Christ so took upon himself the sins of men as to become himself a sinner, it must mean that he put himself in the place of sinners, and bore that which those sins deserved ; that is, that he endured in his own person that which, if it had been inflicted on the sinner himself, would have been a proper expression of the Divine displeasure against sin, or would have been a proper punishment for sin.   See Notes, 2 Cor. v. 21.   He was treated *as if* he had been a sinner, in order that we might be treated *as if* we had not sinned ; that is, as if we were righteous.   There is no other way in which we can conceive that one bears the sins of another. They cannot be *literally* transferred to another ; and all that can be meant is, that he should take the consequences on himself, and suffer *as if* he had committed the transgressions himself.

[See also the Supplementary Notes on 2 Cor. v. 21 ; Rom. iv. v.; and Gal. iii. 13, in which the subject of imputation is discussed at large.]

¶ *In his own body.* This alludes undoubtedly to his sufferings. The sufferings which he endured on the cross were such *as if* he had been guilty ; that is, he was treated as *he would have been* if he had been a sinner. He was treated as a malefactor ; crucified as those most guilty were; endured the same kind of bodily pain that the guilty do who are punished for their own sins ; and passed through mental sorrows strongly resembling—as much so as the case admitted of—what the guilty themselves experience when they are left to distressing anguish of mind, and are abandoned by God. The sufferings of the Saviour were in all respects made as nearly *like* the sufferings of the most guilty, as the sufferings of a perfectly innocent being could be. ¶ *On the tree.* Marg., ' *to* the tree.'

25 For ye were as sheep going astray;*a* but are now returned unto

the Shepherd *b*and Bishop of your souls.

a Ps.119.176.

b Eze.34.23; Jn.10.11-16.

Gr., ἐπὶ τὸ ξύλον. The meaning is rather, as in the text, that while himself *on* the cross, he bore the sorrows which our sins deserved. It does not mean that he conveyed our sorrows there, but that *while* there he suffered under the intolerable burden, and was by that burden crushed in death. The phrase ' on the tree,' literally ' on the *wood*,' means the cross. The same Greek word is used in Acts v. 30 ; x. 39 ; xiii. 29 ; Gal. iii. 13, as applicable to the cross, in all of which places it is rendered *tree*. ¶ *That we, being dead to sins*. In virtue of his having thus been suspended on a cross ; that is, his being put to death as an atoning sacrifice was *the means* by which we become dead to sin, and live to God. The phrase ' being dead to sins ' is, in the original, ταῖς ἁμαρτίαις ἀπογενόμενοι— literally, ' *to be absent from sins*.' The Greek word was probably used (by an euphemism) to denote *to die*, that is, *to be absent from the world*. This is a milder and less repulsive word than to say *to die*. It is not elsewhere used in the New Testament. The meaning is, that we being *effectually separated* from sin—that is, being so that it no longer influences us—should live unto God. We are to be, in regard to sin, *as if* we were dead ; and it is to have no more influence over us than if we were in our graves. See Notes, Rom. vi. 2–7. The *means* by which this is brought about is the death of Christ, (Notes, Rom. vi. 8 ;) for as he died literally on the cross on account of our sins, the effect has been to lead us to see the evil of transgression, and to lead new and holy lives. ¶ *Should live unto righteousness*. Though dead in respect to sin, yet we have real life in another respect. We are made alive unto God, to righteousness, to true holiness. Notes, Rom. vi. 11 ; Gal. ii. 20. ¶ *By whose stripes*. This is taken from Isa. liii. 5. See it explained in the Notes on that verse. The word rendered *stripes* (μώλωπι) means, properly, the livid and swollen mark of a blow ; the mark designated by us when we use the expres-

sion ' black and blue.' It is not properly a bloody wound, but that made by pinching, beating, scourging. The idea seems to be that the Saviour was scourged or whipped ; and that the effect on us is the same in producing spiritual healing, or in recovering us from our faults, *as if* we had been scourged ourselves. By faith we see the bruises inflicted on him, the black and blue spots made by beating ; we remember that they were on account of *our* sins, and not for his ; and the effect in reclaiming us is the same as if they had been inflicted on us. ¶ *Ye were healed*. Sin is often spoken of as a disease, and redemption from it as a restoration from a deadly malady. See this explained in the Notes on Is. liii. 5.

25. *For ye were as sheep going astray*. Here also is an allusion to Isa. liii. 6, ' All we like sheep have gone astray.' See Notes on that verse. The figure is plain. We were like a flock without a shepherd. We had wandered far away from the true fold, and were following our own paths. We were without a protector, and were exposed to every kind of danger. This aptly and forcibly expresses the condition of the whole race before God recovers men by the plan of salvation. A flock thus wandering without a shepherd, conductor, or guide, is in a most pitiable condition ; and so was man in his wanderings before he was sought out and brought back to the true fold by the Great Shepherd. ¶ *But are now returned unto the Shepherd and Bishop of your souls*. To Christ, who thus came to seek and save those who were lost. He is often called a *Shepherd*. See Notes, John x. 1–16. The word rendered *bishop*, (ἐπίσκοπος,) means *overseer*. It may be applied to one who *inspects* or *oversees* anything, as public works, or the execution of treaties ; to any one who is an inspector of wares offered for sale ; or, in general, to any one who is a superintendent. It is applied in the New Testament to. those who are appointed to *watch over* the interests of the church, and especially to the officers of the church. Here it

is applied to the Lord Jesus as the great Guardian and Superintendent of his church; and the title of universal Bishop belongs to him alone.

REMARKS.

In the conclusion of this chapter we may remark:—

(1.) That there is something very beautiful in the expression '*Bishop of souls.*' It implies that the soul is the peculiar care of the Saviour; that it is the object of his special interest; and that it is of great value—so great that it is that which mainly deserves regard. He is the Bishop *of the soul* in a sense quite distinct from any care which he manifests for the *body. That* too, in the proper way, is the object of his care; but that has no importance compared with the soul. *Our* care is principally employed in respect to the body; the care of the Redeemer has especial reference to the soul.

(2.) It follows that the welfare of the soul may be committed to him with confidence. It is the object of his special guardianship, and he will not be unfaithful to the trust reposed in him. There is nothing more *safe* than the human soul is when it is committed in faith to the keeping of the Son of God. Comp. 2 Tim. i. 12.

(3.) As, therefore, he has shown his regard for us in seeking us when we were wandering and lost; as he came on the kind and benevolent errand to find us and bring us back to himself, let us show our gratitude to him by resolving to wander no more. As we regard our own safety and happiness, let us commit ourselves to him as our great Shepherd, to follow where he leads us, and to be ever under his pastoral inspection. We had all wandered away. We had gone where there was no happiness and no protector. We had no one to provide for us, to care for us, to pity us. We were exposed to certain ruin. In that state he pitied us, sought us out, brought us back. If we had remained where we were, or had gone farther in our wanderings, we should have gone certainly to destruction. He has sought us out; he has led us back; he has taken us under his own protection and guidance; and we shall be safe as long as we follow where he leads, and no longer. To him then, a Shepherd who never forsakes his flock, let us at all times commit ourselves, following where he leads, feeling that under him our great interests are secure.

(4.) We may learn from this chapter, indeed, as we may from every other part of the New Testament, that in doing this we may be called to suffer. We may be reproached and reviled as the great Shepherd himself was. We may become the objects of public scorn on account of our devoted attachment to him. We may suffer in name, in feeling, in property, in our business, by our honest attachment to the principles of his gospel. Many who are his followers may be in circumstances of poverty or oppression. They may be held in bondage; they may be deprived of their rights; they may feel that their lot in life is a hard one, and that the world seems to have conspired against them to do them wrong; but let us in all these circumstances look to Him 'who made himself of no reputation, and took upon him the form of a servant, and became obedient unto death, even the death of the cross,' (Phil. ii. 7, 8;) and let us remember that it is 'enough for the disciple that he be as his master, and the servant as his lord,' Matt. x. 25. In view of the example of our Master, and of all the promises of support in the Bible, let us bear with patience all the trials of life, whether arising from poverty, an humble condition, or the reproaches of a wicked world. Our trials will soon be ended; and soon, under the direction of the 'Shepherd and Bishop of souls,' we shall be brought to a world where trials and sorrows are unknown.

(5.) In our trials here, let it be our main object so to live that our sufferings shall not be on account of our own faults. See vers. 19–22. Our Saviour so lived. He was persecuted, reviled, mocked, condemned to die. But it was for no fault of his. In all his varied and prolonged sufferings, he had the ever-abiding consciousness that he was innocent; he had the firm conviction that it would yet be seen and confessed by all the world that he was 'holy, harmless, undefiled,' ver. 23. His were not the sufferings produced by a guilty con-

CHAPTER III.

LIKEWISE, ye wives, *a be* in subjection to your own husbands; that, if any obey not the

word, they also may without the word be won by the conversation of the wives;

science, or by the recollection that he had wronged any one. So, if we must suffer, let our trials come upon us. Be it our first aim to have a conscience void of offence, to wrong no one, to give no occasion for reproaches and revilings, to do our duty faithfully to God and to men. Then, if trials come, we shall feel that we suffer as our Master did; and then we may, as he did, commit our cause 'to him that judgeth righteously,' assured that in due time 'he will bring forth our righteousness as the light, and our judgment as the noon-day,' Psa. xxxvii. 6.

CHAPTER III.

ANALYSIS OF THE CHAPTER.

THIS chapter embraces the following subjects:—

I. The duty of wives, vers. 1-6. Particularly (a) that their conduct should be such as would be adapted to lead their unbelieving husbands to embrace a religion whose happy influence was seen in the pure conduct of their wives, vers. 1, 2. (b) In reference to dress and ornaments, that they should not seek that which was external, but rather that which was of the heart, vers. 3, 4. (c) For an illustration of the manner in which these duties should be performed, the apostle refers them to the holy example of the wife of Abraham, as one which Christian females should imitate, vers. 5, 6.

II. The duty of husbands, ver. 7. It was their duty to render all proper honour to their wives, and to live with them as fellow-heirs of salvation, that their prayers might not be hindered; implying, (1,) that in the most important respects they were on an equality; (2,) that they *would* pray together, or that there *would be* family prayer; and, (3,) that it was the duty of husband and wife so to live together that their prayers might ascend from united hearts, and that it would be consistent for God to answer them.

III. The general duty of unity and

of kindness, vers. 8-14. They were (a) to be of one mind; to have compassion; to love as brethren, ver. 8. (b) They were never to render evil for evil, or railing for railing, ver. 9. (c) They were to remember the promises of length of days, and of honour, made to those who were pure in their conversation, and who were the friends of peace, vers. 9, 10. (d) They were to remember that the eyes of the Lord were always on the righteous; that they who were good were under his protection, ver. 12; and that if, while they maintained this character, they were called to suffer, they should count it rather an honour than a hardship, vers. 13, 14.

IV. The duty of being ready always to give to every man a reason for the hope they entertained; and, if they were called to suffer persecution and trial in the service of God, of being able still to show good reasons why they professed to be Christians, and of so living that those who wronged them should see that their religion was more than a name, and was founded in such truth as to command the assent even of their persecutors, vers. 15-17.

V. In their persecutions and trials they were to remember the example of Christ, *his* trials, *his* patience, and *his* triumphs, vers. 18-22. Particularly (a) the apostle refers them to the fact that he had suffered, though he was innocent, and that he was put to death though he had done no wrong, ver. 18. (b) He refers them to the *patience* and *forbearance* of Christ in a former age, an age of great and abounding wickedness, when in the person of his representative and ambassador Noah, he suffered much and long from the opposition of the guilty and perverse men who were finally destroyed, and who are now held in prison, showing us how *patient* we ought to be when offended by others in our attempts to do them good, vers. 19, 20. (c) He refers to the fact that notwithstanding all the opposition which Noah met with in bearing a message, as

2 While they behold your chaste | conversation *coupled* with fear.

an ambassador of the Lord, to a wicked generation, he and his family were saved, ver. 21. The *design* of this allusion evidently is to show us, that if we are patient and forbearing in the trials which we meet with in the world, we shall be saved also. Noah, says the apostle, was saved by water. We, too, says he, are saved in a similar manner by water. In his salvation, and in ours, *water* is employed as the means of salvation: in *his* case by bearing up the ark, in *ours* by becoming the emblem of the washing away of sins. (*d*) The apostle refers to the fact that Christ has ascended to heaven, and has been exalted over angels, and principalities, and powers; thus showing that having borne all his trials with patience he ultimately triumphed, and that in like manner we, if we are patient, shall triumph also, ver. 22. He came off a conqueror, and was exalted to the highest honours of heaven; and so, if faithful, we may hope to come off conquerors also, and be exalted to the honours of heaven as he was. The whole argument here is drawn from the example of Christ, first, in his patience and forbearance with the whole world, and then when he was personally on the earth; from the fact, that in the case of that messenger whom he sent to the ungodly race before the flood, and in his own case when personally on earth, there was ultimate triumph after all that they met with from ungodly men; and thus, if we endure opposition and trials in the same way, we may hope also to triumph in heaven with our exalted Saviour.

1. *Likewise, ye wives,* be *in subjection to your own husbands.* On the duty here. enjoined, see Notes, 1 Cor. xi. 3–9, and Eph. v. 22. ¶ *That, if any obey not the word.* The word of God; the gospel. That is, if any wives have husbands who are not true Christians. This would be likely to occur when the gospel was first preached, as it does now, by the fact that wives might be converted, though their husbands were not. It cannot be inferred from this, that after they themselves had become Christians they had married unbelieving husbands. The term '*word*' here refers

particularly to the gospel *as preached;* and the idea is, that if they were regardless of that gospel when preached—if they would not attend on preaching, or if they were unaffected by it, or if they openly rejected it, there might be hope still that they would be converted by the Christian influence of a wife at home. In such cases, a duty of special importance devolves on the wife. ¶ *They also may without the word be won.* In some other way than by preaching. This does not mean that they would be converted independently of the influence of *truth*—for truth is always the instrument of conversion, (James i. 18; John xvii. 17;) but that it was to be by another influence than *preaching.* ¶ *By the conversation of the wives.* By the conduct or *deportment* of their wives. See Notes, Phil. i. 27. The word *conversation,* in the Scriptures, is never confined, as it is now with us, to *oral discourse,* but denotes conduct in general. It *includes* indeed 'conversation' as the word is now used, but it embraces also much more—including everything that we *do.* The meaning here is, that the habitual deportment of the wife was to be such as to show the reality and power of religion; to show that it had such influence on her temper, her words, her whole deportment, as to demonstrate that it was from God.

2. *While they behold your chaste conversation.* Your pure conduct. The word *chaste* here (ἁγνὴν) refers to purity of conduct in all respects, and not merely to chastity properly so called. It includes that, but it also embraces much more. The conduct of the wife is to be in all respects *pure;* and this is to be the grand instrumentality in the conversion of her husband. A wife may be strictly *chaste,* and yet there may be many other things in her conduct and temper which would mar the beauty of her piety, and prevent any happy influence on the mind of her husband. ¶ Coupled *with fear.* The word *fear,* in this place, may refer either to the fear of God, or to a proper respect and reverence for their husbands, Eph. v. 33. The trait of character which is referred to is that of proper

3 Whose adorning, *a* let it not be that outward *adorning* of plaiting

a 1 Ti.2.9,10.

the hair, and of wearing of gold, or of putting on of apparel;

---

respect and reverence in all the relations which she sustained, as opposed to a trifling and frivolous mind. Leighton suggests that the word *fear* here relates particularly to the other duty enjoined —that of chaste conversation—'fearing the least stain of chastity, or the very appearance of anything not suiting with it. It is a delicate, timorous grace, afraid of the least air, or shadow of anything that hath but a resemblance of wronging it, in carriage, or speech, or apparel.'

3. *Whose adorning.* Whose ornament. The apostle refers here to a propensity which exists in the heart of woman to seek that which would be esteemed ornamental, or that which will *appear well* in the sight of others, and commend us to them. The desire of this is laid deep in human nature, and therefore, when properly regulated, is not wrong. The only question is, what is the true and appropriate ornament? What should be primarily sought as the right kind of adorning? The apostle does not condemn true ornament, nor does he condemn the desire to appear in such a way as to secure the esteem of others. God does not condemn real ornament. The universe is full of it. The colours of the clouds and of the rainbow; the varied hues of flowers; the plumage of birds, and the covering of many of the animals of the forest; the green grass; the variety of hill and dale; the beauty of the human complexion, the ruddy cheek, and the sparkling eye, are all of the nature of *ornament.* They are something *superadded* to what would be merely useful, *to make them appear well.* Few or none of these things are absolutely necessary to the things to which they are attached; for the eye could see without the various tints of beauty that are drawn upon it, and the lips and the cheeks could perform their functions without their beautiful tints, and the vegetable world could exist without the variegated colours that are painted on it; but God *meant* that this should be a beautiful world; that it

should *appear well;* that there should be something more than mere utility. The true notion of ornament or adorning is that which will make any person or thing *appear well,* or *beautiful,* to others; and the apostle does not prohibit that which would have this effect in the wife. The grand thing which she was to seek, was not that which is merely external, but that which is internal, and which God regards as of so great value. ¶ *Let it not be that outward* adorning. Let not this be the main or principal thing; let not her heart be set on this. The apostle does not say that she should wholly neglect her personal appearance, for she has no more right to be offensive to her husband by neglecting her personal appearance, than by a finical attention to it. Religion promotes neatness, and cleanliness, and a proper attention to our external appearance according to our circumstances in life, as certainly as it does to the internal virtue of the soul. On this whole passage, see Notes, 1 Tim. ii. 9, 10. ¶ *Of plaiting the hair.* See Notes, 1 Tim. ii. 9; Comp. Notes, Isa. iii. 24. Great attention is paid to this in the East, and it is to this that the apostle here refers. 'The women in the eastern countries,' says Dr. Shaw, (Travels, p. 294,) 'affect to have their hair hang down to the ground, which they collect into one lock, upon the hinder part of the head, binding and plaiting it about with ribbons. Above this, or on the top of their heads, persons of better fashion wear flexible plates of gold or silver, variously cut through, and engraved in imitation of lace.' We are not to suppose that a mere braiding or plaiting of the hair is improper, for there may be no more simple or convenient way of disposing of it. But the allusion here is to the excessive care which then prevailed, and especially to their setting the heart on such ornaments rather than on the adorning which is internal. It may not be easy to fix the exact limit of propriety about the method of arranging the hair, or about any other ornament;

4 But *let it be* the hidden man of the heart, *a* in that which is not corruptible, *even the ornament* of a

but those whose *hearts* are right, generally have little difficulty on the subject. Every ornament of the body, however beautiful, is soon to be laid aside; the adorning of the soul will endure for ever. ¶ *And of wearing of gold.* The gold here particularly referred to is probably that which was interwoven in the hair, and which was a common female ornament in ancient times. Thus Virgil says, *crines nodantur in aurum.* And again, *crinem implicat auro.* See Homer, Il., B. 872; Herod. i. 82; and Thucyd. i. 6. The wearing of gold in the hair, however, was more common among women of loose morals than among virtuous females.—Pollux iv. 153. It cannot be supposed that *all* wearing of gold about the person is wrong, for there is nothing evil in gold itself, and there may be some articles connected with apparel made of gold that may in no manner draw off the affections from higher things, and may do nothing to endanger piety. The meaning is, that such ornaments should not be sought; that Christians should be in no way distinguished for them; that they should not engross the time and attention; that Christians should so dress as to show that their minds are occupied with nobler objects, and that in their apparel they should be models of neatness, economy, and plainness. If it should be said that this expression teaches that it is wrong to wear gold *at all*, it may be replied that on the same principle it would follow that the next clause teaches that it is wrong *to put on apparel at all.* There is really no difficulty in such expressions. We are to dress decently, and in the manner that will attract least attention, and we are to show that *our hearts* are interested supremely in more important things than in outward adorning. ¶ *Or of putting on of apparel.* That is, this is not to be the ornament which we principally seek, or for which we are distinguished. We are to desire a richer and more permanent adorning—that of the heart.

meek *b* and quiet spirit, which is in the sight of God of great price.

a Ps.45.13; Ro.2.29.   b Ps.25.9; 149.4; Mat.5.5.

4. *But* let it be *the hidden man of the heart.* This expression is substantially the same as that of Paul in Rom. vii. 22, 'the inward man.' See Notes on that place. The word *'hidden'* here means that which is concealed; that which is not made apparent by the dress, or by ornament. It lies within, pertaining to the affections of the soul. ¶ *In that which is not corruptible.* Properly, 'in the incorruptible ornament of a meek and quiet spirit.' This is said to be incorruptible in contradistinction to gold and apparel. They will decay; but the internal ornament is ever enduring. The sense is, that whatever pertains to outward decoration, however beautiful and costly, is fading; but that which pertains to the soul is enduring. As the soul is immortal, so all that tends to adorn that will be immortal too; as the body is mortal, so all with which it can be invested is decaying, and will soon be destroyed. ¶ The ornament *of a meek and quiet spirit.* Of a calm temper; a contented mind; a heart free from passion, pride, envy, and irritability; a soul not subject to the agitations and vexations of those who live for fashion, and who seek to be distinguished for external adorning. The connection here shows that the apostle refers to this, not only as that which would be of great price in the sight of God, but as that which would tend to secure the affection of their husbands, and win them to embrace the true religion, (see vers. 1, 2;) and, in order to this, he recommends them, instead of seeking external ornaments, to seek those of the mind and of the heart, as more agreeable to their husbands; as better adapted to win their hearts to religion; as that which would be most permanently proved. In regard to this point we may observe, (1.) that there are, undoubtedly, *some* husbands who are pleased with excessive ornaments in their wives, and who take a pleasure in seeing them decorated with gold, and pearls, and costly array. (2.) That *all* are pleased and gratified with a suitable attention to personal appear-

ance on the part of their wives. It is as much the duty of a wife to be cleanly in her person, and neat in her habits, in the presence of her husband, as in the presence of strangers; and no wife can hope to secure the permanent affection of her husband who is not attentive to her personal appearance in her own family; especially if, while careless of her personal appearance in the presence of her husband, she makes it a point to appear gaily dressed before others. Yet (3.) the decoration of the body is not all, nor is it the principal thing which a husband desires. He desires primarily in his wife the more permanent adorning which pertains to the heart. Let it be remembered, (a) that a large part of the ornaments on which females value themselves are *lost* to a great extent on the other sex. Many a man cannot tell the difference between diamonds and cut-glass, or paste in the form of diamonds; and few are such connoisseurs in the matter of female ornaments as to appreciate at all the difference in the quality or colour of silks, and shawls, and laces, which might appear so important to a female eye. The fact is, that those personal ornaments which to females appear of so much value, are much less regarded and prized by men than they often suppose. It is a rare thing that a man is so thoroughly skilled in the knowledge of the distinctions that pertain to fashions, as to appreciate that on which the heart of a female often so much prides itself; and it is no great credit to him if he *can* do this. His time usually, unless he is a draper or a jeweller, might have been much better employed than in making those acquisitions which are needful to qualify him to appreciate and admire the peculiarities of gay female apparel. (b) But a man has a real interest in what constitutes the ornaments of the heart. His happiness, in his intercourse with his wife, depends on these. He knows what is denoted by a kind temper; by gentle words; by a placid brow; by a modest and patient spirit; by a heart that is calm in trouble, and that is affectionate and pure; by freedom from irritability, fretfulness, and impatience; *and he can fully appreciate the value of these things.* No professional skill is necessary to qua-

lify him to see their worth; and no acquired tact in discrimination is requisite to enable him to estimate them according to their full value. A wife, therefore, if she would permanently please her husband, should seek the adorning of the soul rather than the body; the ornament of the heart rather than gold and jewels. The one can never be a substitute for the other; and whatever outward decorations she may have, unless she have a gentleness of spirit, a calmness of temper, a benevolence and purity of soul, and a cultivation of mind that her husband can love, she cannot calculate on his permanent affection. ¶ *Which is in the sight of God of great price.* Of great value; that being of great value for which a large price is paid. He has shown his sense of its value (a) by commending it so often in his word; (b) by making religion to consist so much in it, rather than in high intellectual endowments, learning, skill in the arts, and valour; and (c) by the character of his Son, the Lord Jesus, in whom this was so prominent a characteristic. Sentiments not unlike what is here stated by the apostle, occur not unfrequently in heathen classic writers. There are some remarkable passages in Plutarch, strongly resembling it:—'An ornament, as Crates said, is that which adorns. The proper ornament of a woman is that which becomes her best. This is neither gold, nor pearls, nor scarlet, but those things which are an evident proof of gravity, regularity, and modesty.'— *Conjugalio Præcept.*, c. xxvi. The wife of Phocion, a celebrated Athenian general, receiving a visit from a lady who was elegantly adorned with gold and jewels, and her hair with pearls, took occasion to call the attention of her guest to the elegance and costliness of her dress. ' My ornament,' said the wife of Phocion, ' is my husband, now for the twentieth year general of the Athenians.'--*Plutarch's Life of Phocion.* 'The Sicilian tyrant sent to the daughters of Lysander garments and tissues of great value, but Lysander refused them, saying, " These ornaments will rather put my daughters out of countenance than adorn them." '—*Plutarch.* So in the fragments of Naumachius, as quoted by Benson, there is a precept

5 For after this manner, in the old time, the holy women also, who trusted in God, adorned themselves, being in subjection unto their own husbands:

6 Even as Sara obeyed Abraham, calling him lord: [a]whose [1] daughters ye are, as long as ye do well, and are not afraid with any amazement.

a Ge.18.12.   1 *children.*

much like this of Peter: ' Be not too fond of gold, neither wear purple hyacinth about your neck, or the green jasper, of which foolish persons are proud. Do not covet such vain ornaments, neither view yourself too often in the glass, nor twist your hair into a multitude of curls,' &c.

5. *For after this manner, in the old time.* The allusion here is particularly to the times of the patriarchs, and the object of the apostle is to state another reason why they should seek that kind of ornament which he had been commending. The reason is, that this characterised the pious and honoured females of ancient times—those females who had been most commended of God, and who were most worthy to be remembered on earth. ¶ *Who trusted in God.* Greek, ' Who *hoped* in God ;' that is, who were truly pious. They were characterised by simple trust or hope in God, rather than by a fondness for external adorning. ¶ *Adorned themselves.* To wit, with a meek and quiet spirit, manifested particularly by the respect evinced for their husbands. ¶ *Being in subjection unto their own husbands.* This was evidently a characteristic of the early periods of the world ; and piety was understood to consist much in proper respect for others, according to the relations sustained towards them.

6. *Even as Sara obeyed Abraham.* Sarah was one of the most distinguished of the wives of the patriarchs, and her case is referred to as furnishing one of the best illustrations of the duty to which the apostle refers. Nothing is said, in the brief records of her life, of any passion for outward adorning ; much is said of her kindness to her husband, and her respect for him. Comp. Gen. xii. 5 ; xviii. 6. ¶ *Calling him Lord.* See Gen. xviii. 12. It was probably inferred from this instance, by the apostle, and not without reason, that Sarah habitually used this respectful appellation,

acknowledging by it that he was her superior, and that he had a right to rule in his own house. The word *lord* has the elementary idea of *ruling,* and this is the sense here—that she acknowledged that he had a right to direct the affairs of his household, and that it was her duty to be in subjection to him as the head of the family. In what respects this is a duty, may be seen by consulting the Notes on Eph. v. 22. Among the Romans, it was quite common for wives to use the appellation *lord,* (*dominus*), when speaking of their husbands. The same custom also prevailed among the Greeks. See Grotius, *in loc.* This passage does not prove that the term *lord* should be the particular appellation by which Christian wives should address their husbands now, but it proves that there should be the same respect and deference which was implied by its use in patriarchal times. The welfare of society, and the happiness of individuals, are not diminished by showing proper respect for all classes of persons in the various relations of life. ¶ *Whose daughters ye are.* That is, you will be worthy to be regarded as her daughters, if you manifest the same spirit that she did. The margin here, as the Greek, is *children.* The sense is, that if they demeaned themselves correctly in the relation of wives, it would be proper to look upon her as their mother, and to feel that they were not unworthy to be regarded as her daughters. ¶ *As long as ye do well.* In respect to the particular matter under consideration. ¶ *And are not afraid with any amazement.* This passage has been variously understood. Some have supposed that this is suggested as an argument to persuade them to *do well,* from the consideration that by so doing they would be preserved from those alarms and terrors which a contest with superior power might bring with it, and which would prove as injurious to their peace as to their character. Rosenmüller explains

7 Likewise, ye husbands, *a* dwell with *them* according to knowledge, giving honour unto the wife, as

a Col.3.19.

unto the weaker vessel, and as being heirs together of the grace of life; that your prayers be not hindered.

---

it, 'If ye do well, terrified by no threats of unbelieving husbands, if they should undertake to compel you to deny the Christian faith.' Doddridge supposes that it means that they were to preserve their peace and fortitude in any time of danger, so as not to act out of character, through amazement or danger. Calvin, Benson, and Bloomfield understand it of that firmness and intrepidity of character which would be necessary to support their religious independence, when united with heathen husbands; meaning that they were not to be deterred from doing their duty by any threats or terrors, either of their unbelieving husbands, or of their enemies and persecutors. Dr. Clarke supposes that it means that if they did well, they would live under no dread of being detected in improprieties of life, or being found out in their *infidelities* to their husbands, as those must always be who are unfaithful to their marriage vows. The word rendered *amazement* ($\pi\tau\acute{o}\eta\sigma\iota\varsigma$) does not elsewhere occur in the New Testament. It means *terror*, *trepidation*, *fear;* and the literal translation of the Greek is, 'not fearing any fear.' It seems to me that the following may express the sense of the passage : (1.) There is undoubtedly an allusion to the character of Sarah, and the object of the apostle is to induce them to follow her example. (2.) The thing in Sarah which he would exhort them to imitate, was her pure and upright life, her faithful discharge of her duties as a woman fearing God. This she did constantly wherever she was, regardless of consequences. Among friends and strangers, at home and abroad, she was distinguished for *doing well*. Such was her character, such her fidelity to her husband and her God, such her firm integrity and benevolence, that she at all times lived to do good, and would have done it, unawed by terror, undeterred by threats. To whatever trial her piety was exposed, it bore the trial; and such was her strength of virtue, that it was certain her integrity would be

firm by whatever consequences she might have been threatened for her adherence to her principles. (3.) They were to imitate her in this, and were thus to show that they were worthy to be regarded as her daughters. They were to do well ; to be faithful to their husbands ; to be firm in their principles ; to adhere steadfastly to what was true and good, whatever trials they might pass through, however much they might be threatened with persecution, or however any might attempt to deter them from the performance of their duty. Thus, by a life of Christian fidelity, unawed by fear from any quarter, they would show that they were imbued with the same principles of unbending virtue which characterised the wife of the father of the faithful, and that they were not unworthy to be regarded as her daughters.

7. *Likewise, ye husbands*. On the general duty of husbands, see Notes, Eph. v. 25, seq. ¶ *Dwell with* them. That is, 'Let your manner of living with them be that which is immediately specified.' ¶ *According to knowledge*. In accordance with an intelligent view of the nature of the relation; or, as becomes those who have been instructed in the duties of this relation according to the gospel. The meaning evidently is, that they should seek to obtain just views of what Christianity enjoins in regard to this relation, and that they should allow those intelligent views to control them in all their intercourse with their wives. ¶ *Giving honour unto the wife*. It was an important advance made in society when the Christian religion gave such a direction as this, for everywhere among the heathen, and under all false systems of religion, woman has been regarded as worthy of little honour or respect. She has been considered as a slave, or as a mere instrument to gratify the passions of man. It is one of the elementary doctrines of Christianity, however, that woman is to be treated with respect; and one of the first and most marked effects of religion

on society is to elevate the wife to a condition in which she will be worthy of esteem. The particular reasons for the honour which husbands are directed to show to their wives, here specified, are two : she is to be treated with special kindness as being more feeble than man, and as having a claim therefore to delicate attention ; and she is to be honoured as the equal heir of the grace of life. Doddridge, Clarke, and some others, suppose that the word *honour* here refers to maintenance or support ; and that the command is, that the husband is to provide for his wife so that she may not want. But it seems to me that the word is to be understood here in its more usual signification, and that it inculcates a higher duty than that of merely providing for the temporal wants of the wife, and strikes at a deeper evil than a mere neglect of meeting her temporal necessities. The *reasons* assigned for doing this seem to imply it. ¶ *As unto the weaker vessel.* It is not uncommon in the Scriptures to compare the body to a *vessel*, (Comp. Notes, 1 Thess. iv. 4,) and thence the comparison is extended to the whole person. This is done either because the body is frail and feeble, like an earthen vessel easily broken ; or because it is that in which the soul is lodged ; or because, in accordance with a frequent use of the word, (see below,) the body is the *instrument* by which the soul accomplishes its purposes, or is the *helper* of the soul. Comp. Acts ix. 15; Rom. ix. 22, 23; 2 Cor. iv. 7. In the later Hebrew usage it was common to apply the term *vessel* (Heb. כְּלִי, Gr. σκεύος) to a wife, as is done here. See Schoettgen, Hor. Heb. p. 827. Expressions similar to this, in regard to the comparative *feebleness* of woman, occur frequently in the classic writers. See Wetstein *in loc.* The *reasons* why the term *vessel* was given to a wife, are not very apparent. A not unfrequent sense of the word used here (σκεύος) in the Greek classics was that of an instrument ; a helper ; one who was employed by another to accomplish anything, or to aid him, (Passow,) and it seems probable that this was the reason why the term was given to the wife. Comp. Gen. ii. 18. The reason here assigned for the honour that was to be shown to

the wife is, that she is 'the *weaker* vessel.' By this it is not necessarily meant that she is of feebler capacity, or inferior mental endowments, but that she is more tender and delicate ; more subject to infirmities and weaknesses ; less capable of enduring fatigue and toil ; less adapted to the rough and stormy scenes of life. As such, she should be regarded and treated with special kindness and attention. This is a reason, the force of which all can see and appreciate. So we feel toward a sister ; so we feel toward a beloved child, if he is of feeble frame and delicate constitution ; and so every man should feel in relation to his wife. She may have mental endowments equal to his own ; she may have moral qualities in every way superior to his ; but the God of nature has made her with a more delicate frame, a more fragile structure, and with a body subject to many infirmities to which the more hardy frame of man is a stranger. ¶ *And as being heirs together of the grace of life.* The grace that is connected with eternal life ; that is, as fellow-Christians. They were equal heirs of the everlasting inheritance, called in the Scripture '*life*;' and the same ' grace ' connected with that inheritance had been conferred on both. This passage contains a very important truth in regard to the female sex. Under every other system of religion but the Christian system, woman has been regarded as in every way inferior to man. Christianity teaches that, in respect to her higher interests, the interests of religion, *she is every way his equal.* She is entitled to all the hopes and promises which religion imparts. She is redeemed as he is. She is addressed in the same language of tender invitation. She has the same privileges and comforts which religion imparts here, and she will be elevated to the same rank and privileges in heaven. This single truth would raise the female sex everywhere from degradation, and check at once half the social evils of the race. Make her the equal of man in the hope of heaven, and at once she rises to her appropriate place. Home is made what it should be, a place of intelligence and pure friendship ; and a world of suffering and sadness smiles under the benefactions of Christian woman. ¶ *That your prayers be not hindered.* It is fairly implied here, (1.) that it was supposed there would be united or family prayer. The apostle is speaking of 'dwelling with the wife,' and of the right manner of treating her; and it is plainly supposed that united prayer would be one thing that would characterise their living together. He does not direct that there *should* be prayer. He seems to take it for granted that there *would be;* and it may be remarked, that where there is true religion in right exercise, there is prayer as a matter of course. The head of a family does not ask whether he *must* establish family worship; he does it as one of the spontaneous fruits of religion—as a thing concerning which no formal command is necessary. Prayer in the family, as everywhere else, is a privilege; and the true question to be asked on the subject is not whether a man *must,* but whether he *may* pray. (2.) It is implied that there might be such a way of living as effectually to hinder prayer; that is, to prevent its being offered aright, and to prevent any answer. This might occur in many ways. If the husband treated the wife unkindly; if he did not show her proper respect and affection; if there were bickerings, and jealousies, and contentions between them, there could be no hope that acceptable prayer would be offered. A spirit of strife; irritability and unevenness of temper; harsh looks and unkind words; a disposition easily to take offence, and an unwillingness to forgive, all these prevent a 'return of prayers.' Acceptable prayer never can be offered in the tempest of passion, and there can be no doubt that such prayer is often 'hindered' by the inequalities of temper, and the bickerings and strifes that exist in families. Yet how desirable is it that husband and wife should so live together that their prayers may not be hindered! How desirable for their own peace and happiness in that relation; how desirable for the welfare of children! In view of the exposition in this verse we may remark, (*a*) that Christianity has done much to elevate the female sex. It has taught that woman is an heir of the grace of life as well as man; that, while she is inferior in bodily vigour, she is

his equal in the most important respect; that she is a fellow-traveller with him to a higher world; and that in every way she is entitled to all the blessings which redemption confers, as much as he is. This single truth has done more than all other things combined to elevate the female sex, and is all that is needful to raise her from her degradation all over the world. (*b*) They, therefore, who desire the elevation of the female sex, who see woman ignorant and degraded in the dark parts of the earth, should be the friends of all well-directed efforts to send the gospel to heathen lands. Every husband who has a pure and intelligent wife, and every father who has an accomplished daughter, and every brother who has a virtuous sister, should seek to spread the gospel abroad. To that gospel only he owes it that he *has* such a wife, daughter, sister; and that gospel, which has given to him such an intelligent female friend, would elevate woman everywhere to the same condition. The obligation which he owes to religion in this respect can be discharged in no better way than by aiding in diffusing that gospel which would make the wife, the daughter, the sister, everywhere what she is in his own dwelling. (*c*) Especially is this the duty of the Christian female. She owes her elevation in society to Christianity, and what Christianity has made her, it would make the sunken and debased of her own sex all over the earth; and how can she better show her gratitude than by aiding in any and every way in making that same gospel known in the dark parts of the world? (*d*) Christianity makes a happy home. Let the principles reign in any family which are here enjoined by the apostle, and that family will be one of intelligence, contentment, and peace. There is a simple and easy way of being happy in the family relation. *It is to allow the spirit of Christ and his gospel to reign there.* That done, though there be poverty, and disappointment, and sickness, and cares, and losses, yet there will be peace within, for there will be mutual love, and the cheerful hope of a brighter world. Where that is wanting, no outward splendour, no costly furniture or viands, no gilded equipage, no

8 Finally, *be ye* all of one mind, *having compassion one of another; [1]love *b* as brethren, *be* pitiful, *be* courteous:

9 Not rendering *c* evil for evil, or

railing for railing; but contrariwise blessing; knowing that ye are thereunto called, that ye should inherit a blessing.

a Ro.12.16.	1 Or, *loving to the.*	*b* 1 Jn.3.18.
c Mat.5.44.; Ep.4.32.

long train of servants, no wine, or music, or dances, can secure happiness in a dwelling. With all these things there may be the most corroding passions; in the mansion where these things are, pale disease, disappointment, and death may come, and there shall be nothing to console and support.

8. *Finally.* As the last direction, or as general counsel in reference to your conduct in all the relations of life. The apostle had specified most of the important relations which Christians sustain, (chap. ii. 13–25; iii. 1–7;) and he now gives a general direction in regard to their conduct in all those relations. ¶ *Be ye all of one mind.* See Notes, Rom. xii. 16. The word here used (*ὁμόφρων*) does not elsewhere occur in the New Testament. It means, *of the same mind; like-minded;* and the object is to secure harmony in their views and feelings. ¶ *Having compassion one of another. Sympathizing,* (*συμπαθεῖς;*) entering into one another's feelings, and evincing a regard for each other's welfare. Notes, Rom. xii. 15. Comp. 1 Cor. xii. 26; John xi. 35. The Greek word here used does not elsewhere occur in the New Testament. It describes that state of mind which exists when we enter into the feelings of others *as if* they were our own, as the different parts of the body are affected by that which affects one. Notes, 1 Cor. xii. 26. ¶ *Love as brethren.* Marg., *loving to the;* i. e., the brethren. The Greek word (*φιλάδελφος*) does not elsewhere occur in the New Testament. It means *loving one's brethren;* that is, loving each other as Christian brethren.—*Rob. Lex.* Thus it enforces the duty so often enjoined in the New Testament, that of love to Christians as brethren of the same family. Notes, Rom. xii. 10. Comp. Heb. xiii. 1; John xiii. 34. ¶ Be *pitiful.* The word here used (*εὔσπλαγχνος*) occurs nowhere else in the New Testament, except in Eph. iv. 32, where it is rendered *tender-hearted.* See Notes on

that verse. ¶ Be *courteous.* This word also (*φιλόφρων*) occurs nowhere else in the New Testament. It means *friendly-minded, kind, courteous.* Later editions of the New Testament, instead of this, read (*ταπεινόφρονες*) of a lowly or humble mind. See Hahn. The sense is not materially varied. In the one word, the idea of *friendliness* is the one that prevails; in the other, that of *humility.* Christianity requires both of these virtues, and either word enforces an important injunction. The *authority* is in favour of the latter reading; and though Christianity requires that we should be courteous and gentlemanly in our treatment of others, *this* text can hardly be relied on as a proof-text of that point.

9. *Not rendering evil for evil.* See Notes, Matt. v. 39, 44; Rom. xii. 17. ¶ *Or railing for railing.* See Notes, 1 Tim. vi. 4. Comp. Mark xv. 29; Luke xxiii. 39. ¶ *But contrariwise blessing.* In a spirit contrary to this. See Notes, Matt. v. 44. ¶ *Knowing that ye are thereunto called, that ye should inherit a blessing.* 'Knowing that you were called to be Christians in order that you should obtain a blessing infinite and eternal in the heavens. Expecting such a blessing yourselves, you should be ready to scatter blessings on all others. You should be ready to bear all their reproaches, and even to wish them well. The hope of eternal life should make your minds calm; and the prospect that *you* are to be so exalted in heaven should fill your hearts with benignity and love.' There is nothing which is better fitted to cause our hearts to overflow with benignity, to make us ready to forgive all others when they injure us, than the hope of salvation. Cherishing such a hope ourselves, we cannot but wish that all others may share it, and this will lead us to wish for them every blessing. A man who has a hope of heaven should abound in every virtue, and show that he is a sincere well-wisher of the race. Why

10 For he *a* that will love life, and see good days, let him refrain his | tongue from evil, and his lips that they speak no guile:

a Ps.34,12,&c.

should one who expects soon to be in heaven harbour malice in his bosom? Why should he wish to injure a fellow-worm? How can he?

10. *For he that will love life.* Gr., 'He willing, (*θέλων*,) or that *wills* to love life.' It implies that there is some positive desire to live; some active wish that life should be prolonged. This whole passage (vers. 10–12) is taken, with some slight variations, from Psalm xxxiv. 12–16. In the Psalm this expression is, 'What man is he that desireth life, and loveth many days, that he may see good?' The sense is substantially the same. It is implied here that it is right to love life, and to desire many days. The desire of this is referred to by the psalmist and by the apostle, without any expression of disapprobation, and the way is shown by which length of days may be secured. Life is a blessing; a precious gift of God. We are taught so to regard it by the instinctive feelings of our nature; for we are so made as to love it, and to dread its extinction. Though we should be prepared to resign it when God commands, yet there are important reasons why we should desire to live. Among them are the following: (1.) Because, as already intimated, life, as such, is to be regarded as a blessing. We instinctively shrink back from death, as one of the greatest evils; we shudder at the thought of annihilation. It is not wrong to love that, in proper degree, which, by our very nature, we are prompted to love; and we are but acting out one of the universal laws which our Creator has impressed on us, when, with proper submission to his will, we seek to lengthen out our days as far as possible. (2.) That we may see the works of God, and survey the wonders of his hand on earth. The world is full of wonders, evincing the wisdom and goodness of the Deity; and the longest life, nay, many such lives as are allotted to us here, could be well employed in studying his works and ways. (3.) That we may make preparation for eternity. Man *may*, indeed, make pre-

paration in a very brief period; but the longest life is not too much to examine and settle the question whether we have a well-founded hope of heaven. If man had nothing else to do, the longest life could be well employed in inquiries that grow out of the question whether we are fitted for the world to come. In the possibility, too, of being deceived, and in view of the awful consequences that will result from deception, it is desirable that length of days should be given us that we may bring the subject to the severest test, and so determine it, that we may go sure to the changeless world. (4.) That we may do good to others. We *may*, indeed, do good in another world; but there are ways of doing good which are probably confined to this. What good we may do hereafter to the inhabitants of distant worlds, or what ministrations, in company with angels, or without them, we may exercise towards the friends of God on earth after we leave it, we do not know; but there are certain things which we are morally certain we shall *not* be permitted to do in the future world. We shall not (*a*) personally labour for the salvation of sinners, by conversation and other direct efforts; (*b*) we shall not illustrate the influence of religion by example in sustaining us in trials, subduing and controlling our passions, and making us dead to the world; (*c*) we shall not be permitted to pray for our impenitent friends and kindred, as we may now; (*d*) we shall not have the opportunity of contributing of our substance for the spread of the gospel, or of going personally to preach the gospel to the perishing; (*e*) we shall not be employed in instructing the ignorant, in advocating the cause of the oppressed and the wronged, in seeking to remove the fetters from the slave, in dispensing mercy to the insane, or in visiting the prisoner in his lonely cell; (*f*) we shall not have it in our power to address a kind word to an impenitent child, or seek to guide him in paths of truth, purity, and salvation. What we can do personally and directly for

11 Let him eschew evil, and do good ; let him seek peace, and ensue it.

12 For the eyes of the Lord are over the righteous, and his ears are open unto their prayers : but the face of the Lord is [1] against them that do evil.

[1] upon.

---

the salvation of others is to be done in this world ; and, considering how much there is to be done, and how useful life may be on the earth, it is an object which we should desire, that our days may be lengthened out, and should use all proper means that it may be done. While we should ever be ready and willing to depart when God calls us to go ; while we should not wish to linger on these mortal shores beyond the time when we may be useful to others, yet, as long as he permits us to live, we should regard life as a blessing, and should pray that, if it be his will, we may not be cut down in the midst of our way.

"Love not thy life, nor hate; but what thou livest
Live well; how long, or short, permit to heaven."
                              Paradise Lost.

¶ *And see good days.* In the Psalm (xxxiv. 12) this is, ' and loveth many days, that he may see good.' The quotation by Peter throughout the passage is taken from the Septuagint, excepting that there is a change of the person from the second to the third : in the psalm, e. g., ' refrain thy tongue from evil,' &c.; in the quotation, ' let him refrain his tongue from evil,' &c. 'Good days' are prosperous days ; happy days ; days of usefulness ; days in which we may be respected and loved. ¶ *Let him refrain his tongue from evil.* The general meaning of all that is said here is, ' let him lead an upright and pious life ; doing evil to no one, but seeking the good of all men.' To refrain the tongue from evil, is to avoid all slander, falsehood, obscenity, and profaneness, and to abstain from uttering erroneous and false opinions. Comp. James i. 26; iii. 2. ¶ *And his lips that they speak no guile.* No deceit ; nothing that will lead others astray. The words should be an exact representation of the truth. Rosenmüller quotes a passage from the Hebrew book *Musar*, which may be not an inappropriate illustration of this : ' A certain Assyrian

wandering through the city, cried and said, " Who will receive the elixir of life ?" The daughter of Rabbi Jodus heard him, and went and told her father. " Call him in," said he. When he came in, Rabbi Jannei said to him, " What is that elixir of life which thou art selling ?" He said to him, " Is it not written, What man is he that desireth life, and loveth days that he may see good ? Keep thy tongue from evil, and thy lips that they speak no guile. Lo, this is the elixir of life which is in the mouth of a man !" '

11. *Let him eschew evil.* Let him avoid all evil. Comp. Job i. 1. ¶ *And do good.* In any and every way ; by endeavouring to promote the happiness of all. Comp. Notes, Gal. vi. 10. ¶ *Let him seek peace, and ensue it.* Follow it ; that is, practise it. See Notes, Matt. v. 9 ; Rom. xii. 18. The meaning is, that a peaceful spirit will contribute to length of days. (1.) A peaceful spirit—a calm, serene, and equal temper of mind—is favourable to health, avoiding those corroding and distracting passions which do so much to wear out the physical energies of the frame ; and (2.) such a spirit will preserve us from those contentions and strifes to which so many owe their death. Let any one reflect on the numbers that are killed in duels, in battles, and in brawls, and he will have no difficulty in seeing how a peaceful spirit will contribute to length of days.

12. *For the eyes of the Lord are over the righteous.* That is, he is their Protector. His eyes are indeed on all men, but the language here is that which describes continual guardianship and care. ¶ *And his ears are open unto their prayers.* He *hears* their prayers. As he is a hearer of prayer, they are at liberty to go to him at all times, and to pour out their desires before him. This passage is taken from Psa. xxxiv. 15, and it is designed to show the reason why a life of piety will contribute to

13 And who ^a is he that will harm
a Pr.16.7; Ro.8.28.
you, if ye be followers of that which
is good?

length of days. ¶ *But the face of the Lord is against them that do evil.* Marg., *upon.* The sense of the passage, however, is *against.* The Lord sets his face against them: an expression denoting disapprobation, and a determination to punish them. His face is not mild and benignant towards them, as it is towards the righteous. The general sentiment in these verses (10-12) is, that while length of days is desirable, it is to be secured by virtue and religion, or that virtue and religion will contribute to it. This is not to be understood as affirming that *all* who are righteous will enjoy long life, for we know that the righteous are often cut down in the midst of their way; and that in fire, and flood, and war, and the pestilence, the righteous and the wicked often perish together. But still there is a sense in which it is true that a life of virtue and religion will contribute to length of days, and that the law is so general as *to be a basis of calculation* in reference to the future. I. Religion and virtue contribute to those things which are favourable to length of days, which are conducive to health and to a vigorous constitution. Among those things are the following: (*a*) a calm, peaceful, and contented mind—avoiding the wear and tear of the raging passions of lusts, avarice, and ambition; (*b*) temperance in eating and drinking—always favourable to length of days; (*c*) industry—one of the essential means, as a general rule, of promoting long life; (*d*) prudence and economy—avoiding the extravagancies by which many shorten their days; and (*e*) a conscientious and careful regard of life itself. Religion makes men feel that life is a blessing, and that it should not be thrown away. Just in proportion as a man is under the influence of religion, does he regard life as of importance, and does he become careful in preserving it. Strange and paradoxical as it may seem, the want of religion often makes men reckless of life, and ready to throw it away for any trifling cause. Religion shows a man what great issues depend on life, and makes him, therefore, desirous of living to

secure his own salvation and the salvation of all others. II. Multitudes lose their lives who would have preserved them if they had been under the influence of religion. To see this, we have only to reflect (*a*) on the millions who are cut off in war as the result of ambition, and the want of religion; (*b*) on the countless hosts cut down in middle life, or in youth, by intemperance, who would have been saved by religion; (*c*) on the numbers who are the victims of raging passions, and who are cut off by the diseases which gluttony and licentiousness engender; (*d*) on the multitude who fall in duels, all of whom would have been saved by religion; (*e*) on the numbers who, as the result of disappointment in business or in love, close their own lives, who would have been enabled to bear up under their troubles if they had had religion; and (*f*) on the numbers who are cut off from the earth as the punishment of their crimes, all of whom would have continued to live if they had had true religion. III. God protects the righteous. He does it by saving them from those vices by which the lives of so many are shortened; and often, we have no reason to doubt, in answer to their prayers, when, but for those prayers, they would have fallen into crimes that would have consigned them to an early grave, or encountered dangers from which they would have had no means of escape. No one can doubt that *in fact* those who are truly religious are saved from the sins which consign millions to the tomb; nor is there any less reason to doubt that a protecting shield is often thrown before the children of God when in danger. Comp. Psa. xci.

13. *And who is he that will harm you, if ye be followers of that which is good?* This question is meant to imply, that as a general thing they need apprehend no evil if they lead an upright and benevolent life. The idea is, that God would in general protect them, though the next verse shows that the apostle did not mean to teach that there would be absolute security, for it is implied there that they *might* be called to suffer

14 But and if ye suffer for righteousness' sake, happy *are ye:* and
be *a* not afraid of their terror, neither
be troubled;
15 But sanctify the Lord God in

a Is.8.12,13; 51.12. b Ps.119.46.

your hearts; and *be* ready *b* always
to *give* an answer to every man that
asketh you a reason of the hope
that is in you with meekness and
1 fear:

1 Or, *reverence.*

for righteousness' sake. While it is true
that the Saviour was persecuted by
wicked men, though his life was wholly
spent in doing good; while it is true
that the apostles were put to death,
though following his example; and while
it is true that good men have often suffered persecution, though labouring only
to do good, still it is true as a general
thing that a life of integrity and benevolence conduces to safety, even in a
wicked world. Men who are upright
and pure; who live to do good to others;
who are characteristically benevolent;
and who are imitators of God—are those
who usually pass life in most tranquillity
and security, and are often safe when
nothing else would give security but
confidence in their integrity. A man
of a holy and pure life may, under the
protection of God, rely on that character
to carry him safely through the world,
and to bring him at last to an honoured
grave. Or should he be calumniated
when living, and his sun set under a
cloud, still his name will be vindicated,
and justice will ultimately be done to
him when he is dead. The world ultimately judges right respecting character,
and renders 'honour to whom honour is
due.' Comp. Psa. xxxvii. 3–6.
    14. *But and if ye suffer for righteous-
ness' sake.* Implying that though, in
general, a holy character would constitute safety, yet that there was a possibility that they might suffer persecution.
Comp. Notes, Matt. v. 10; 2 Tim. iii.
12. ¶ *Happy* are ye. Perhaps alluding
to what the Saviour says in Matt. v. 10:
'Blessed are they which are persecuted
for righteousness' sake.' On the meaning of the word *happy* or *blessed,* see
Notes on Matt. v. 3. The meaning
here is, not that they would find positive
enjoyment *in* persecution on account of
righteousness, but that they were to
regard it as *a blessed condition;* that is,
as a condition that might be favourable
to salvation; and they were not there-

fore, on the whole, to regard it as an
evil. ¶ *And be not afraid of their terror.*
Of anything which they can do to cause
terror. There is evidently an allusion
here to Isa. viii. 12, 13: 'Neither fear
ye their fear, nor be afraid. Sanctify
the Lord of hosts himself; and let him
be your fear, and let him be your dread.'
See Notes on that passage. Comp. Isa.
li. 12; Matt. x. 28. ¶ *Neither be troubled.*
With apprehension of danger. Comp.
Notes, John xiv. 1. If we are true
Christians, we have really no reason to
be alarmed in view of anything that can
happen to us. God is our protector, and
he is abundantly able to vanquish all
our foes; to uphold us in all our trials;
to conduct us through the valley of
death, and to bring us to heaven. 'All
things are yours; whether Paul, or
Apollos, or Cephas, or the world, *or life,*
or *death,* or things present, or things to
come,' 1 Cor. iii. 21, 22.
    15. *But sanctify the Lord God in
your hearts.* In Isaiah (viii. 13) this
is, 'sanctify the Lord of hosts himself;'
that is, in that connection, regard him
as your Protector, and be afraid of him,
and not of what man can do. The
sense in the passage before us is, 'In
your hearts, or in the affections of the
soul, regard the Lord God as holy, and
act towards him with that confidence
which a proper respect for one so great
and so holy demands. In the midst of
dangers, be not intimidated; dread not
what man can do, but evince proper reliance on a holy God, and flee to him
with the confidence which is due to one
so glorious.' This contains, however, a
more general direction, applicable to
Christians at all times. It is, that in
our hearts we are to esteem God as a
holy being, and in all our deportment
to act towards him as such. The *object*
of Peter in quoting the passage from
Isaiah, was to lull the fears of those
whom he addressed, and preserve them
from any alarms in view of the perse-

cutions to which they might be exposed; the trials which would be brought upon them by men. Thus, in entire accordance with the sentiment as employed by Isaiah, he says, 'Be not afraid of their terror, neither be troubled ; but sanctify the Lord God in your hearts.' That is, 'in order to keep the mind calm in trials, sanctify the Lord in your hearts ; regard him as your holy God and Saviour ; make him your refuge. This will allay all your fears, and secure you from all that you dread.' The sentiment of the passage then is, that *the sanctifying of the Lord God in our hearts, or proper confidence in him as a holy and righteous God, will deliver us from fear.* As this is a very important sentiment for Christians, it may be proper, in order to a just exposition of the passage, to dwell a moment on it. I. What is meant by our sanctifying the Lord God ? It cannot mean to *make* him holy, for he *is* perfectly holy, whatever may be our estimate of him ; and our views of him evidently can make no change in his character. The meaning therefore must be, that we should regard him as holy in our estimate of him, or in the feelings which we have towards him. This may include the following things : (1.) To *esteem* or *regard* him as a holy being, in contradistinction from all those feelings which rise up in the heart against him—the feelings of complaining and murmuring under his dispensations, as if he were severe and harsh ; the feelings of dissatisfaction with his government, as if it were partial and unequal ; the feelings of rebellion, as if his claims were unfounded or unjust. (2.) To desire that he *may be regarded by others* as holy, in accordance with the petition in the Lord's prayer, (Matt. vi. 9,) ' hallowed be thy name ;' that is, ' let thy name be *esteemed to be holy* everywhere ;' a feeling in opposition to that which is regardless of the honour which he may receive in the world. When we esteem a friend, we desire that all due respect should be shown him by others ; we wish that all who know him should have the same views that we have ; we are sensitive to his honour, just in proportion as we love him. (3.) To *act towards him as holy;* that is, to

obey his laws, and acquiesce in all his requirements, as if they were just and good. This implies, (*a*) that we are to speak of him as holy, in opposition to the language of disrespect and irreverence so common among mankind ; (*b*) that we are to flee to him in trouble, in contradistinction from withholding our hearts from him, and flying to other sources of consolation and support. II. What is it to do this in the heart ? ' Sanctify the Lord God *in your hearts ;'* that is, in contradistinction from a mere external service. This may imply the following things : (1.) In contradistinction from a mere intellectual assent to the proposition that he is holy. Many admit the doctrine that God is holy into their creeds, who never suffer the sentiment to find its way to the heart. All is right on this subject in the articles of their faith ; all in their hearts may be murmuring and complaining. In their creeds he is spoken of as just and good ; in their hearts they regard him as partial and unjust, as severe and stern, as unamiable and cruel. (2.) In contradistinction from a mere outward form of devotion. In our prayers, and in our hymns, we, of course, ' ascribe holiness to our Maker.' But how much of this is the mere language of form ! How little does the heart accompany it ! And even in the most solemn and sublime ascriptions of praise, how often are the feelings of the heart entirely at variance with what is expressed by the lips ! What would more justly offend us, than for a professed friend to approach us with the language of friendship, when every feeling of his heart belied his expressions, and we knew that his honeyed words were false and hollow ! III. Such a sanctifying of the Lord in our hearts will save us from fear. We dread danger, we dread sickness, we dread death, we dread the eternal world. We are alarmed when our affairs are tending to bankruptcy ; we are alarmed when a friend is sick and ready to die; we are alarmed if our country is invaded by a foe, and the enemy already approaches our dwelling. The sentiment in the passage before us is, that if we sanctify the Lord God with proper affections, we shall be delivered from these alarms, and the mind will be calm. (1.) The fear of the Lord, as Leighton (*in loc.*) expresses it, 'as greatest, overtops and nullifies all lesser fears : the heart possessed with this fear hath no room for the other.' It is an absorbing emotion ; making everything else comparatively of no importance. If we fear God, wo have nothing else to fear. The highest emotion which there can be in the soul is the fear of God ; and when that exists, the soul will be calm amidst all that might tend otherwise to disturb it. ' What time I am afraid,' says David, ' I will trust in thee,' Psa. lvi. 3. ' We are not careful,' said Daniel and his friends, ' to answer thee, O king. Our God can deliver us; but if not, we will not worship the image,' Dan. iii. 16. (2.) If we sanctify the Lord God in our hearts, there will be a belief that he will do all things *well*, and the mind will be calm. However dark his dispensations may be, we shall be assured that everything is ordered aright. In a storm at sea, a child may be calm when he feels that his father is at the helm, and assures him that there is no danger. In a battle, the mind of a soldier may be calm, if he has confidence in his commander, and he assures him that all is safe. So in anything, if we have the assurance that the *best* thing is done that can be, that the issues will all be right, the mind will be calm. But in this respect the highest confidence that can exist, is that which is reposed in God. (3.) There will be the assurance that all is *safe*. ' Though I walk,' says David, ' through the valley of the shadow of death, I will fear no evil, for thou art with me,' Psa. xxiii. 4. ' The Lord is my light and my salvation ; whom shall I fear ? The Lord is the strength of my life ; of whom shall I be afraid ?' Psa. xxvii. 1. ' God is our refuge and strength, a very present help in trouble : therefore will not we fear, though the earth be removed, and though the mountains be carried into the midst of the sea ; though the waters thereof roar and be troubled, though the mountains shake with the swelling thereof,' Psa. xlvi. 1–3. Let us ever then regard the Lord as holy, just, and good. Let us flee to him in all the trials of the present life, and in the hour of death

repose on his arm. Every other source of trust will fail; and whatever else may be our reliance, when the hour of anguish approaches, that reliance will fail, and that which we dreaded will overwhelm us. Nor riches, nor honours, nor earthly friends, can save us from those alarms, or be a security for our souls when ' the rains descend, and the floods come, and the winds blow ' upon us. ¶ *And* be *ready always*. That is, (*a*) be always *able* to do it ; have such reasons for the hope that is in you that they *can* be stated ; or, have good and substantial reasons ; and (*b*) be *willing* to state those reasons on all proper occasions. No man ought to entertain opinions for which a good reason cannot be given ; and every man ought to be willing to state the grounds of his hope on all proper occasions. A Christian should have such intelligent views of the truth of his religion, and such constant evidence in his own heart and life that he is a child of God, as to be able at any time to satisfy a candid inquirer that the Bible is a revelation from heaven, and that it is proper for him to cherish a hope of salvation. ¶ *To* give *an answer*. Greek, An apology, (ἀπολογίαν.) This word formerly did not mean, as the word *apology* does now, an *excuse* for anything that is done as if it were wrong, but a *defence* of anything. We apply the word now to denote something written or said in extenuation of what appears to others to be wrong, or what might be construed as wrong—as when we make an apology to others for not fulfilling an engagement, or for some conduct which might be construed as designed neglect. The word originally, however, referred rather to that which was thought not to be *true*, than that which might be construed as *wrong;* and the defence or ' apology ' which Christians were to make of their religion, was not on the supposition that others would regard it as *wrong*, but in order to show them that it was *true*. The word here used is rendered *defence*, Acts xxii. 1; Phil. i. 7, 17; *answer*, Acts xxv. 16; 1 Cor. ix. 3; 2 Tim. iv. 16; 1 Pet. iii. 15; and *clearing of yourselves* in 2 Cor. vii. 11. We are not to hold ourselves ready to make an apology for our religion as if it were a *wrong* thing to be a Christian; but we are always to be ready to give reasons for regarding it as *true.* ¶ *To every man that asketh you.* Any one has a right respectfully to ask another on what grounds he regards his religion as true; for every man has a common interest in religion, and in knowing what is the truth on the subject. If *any* man, therefore, asks us candidly and respectfully by what reasons we have been led to embrace the gospel, and on what grounds we regard it as true, we are under obligation to state those grounds in the best manner that we are able. We should regard it not as an impertinent intrusion into our private affairs, but as an opportunity of doing good to others, and to honour the Master whom we serve. Nay, we should hold ourselves in readiness to state the grounds of our faith and hope, whatever may be the motive of the inquirer, and in whatever manner the request may be made. Those who were persecuted for their religion, were under obligation to make as good a defence of it as they could, and to state to their persecutors the 'reason' of the hope which they entertained. And so now, if a man attacks our religion; if he ridicules us for being Christians; if he tauntingly asks us what reason we have for believing the truth of the Bible, it is better to tell him in a kind manner, and to meet his taunt with a kind and strong argument, than to become angry, or to turn away with contempt. The best way to disarm him, is to show him that by embracing religion we are not fools in understanding; and, by a kind temper, to convince him that the influence of religion over us when we are *abused* and *insulted,* is a 'reason' why we should love our religion, and why *he* should too. ¶ *A reason of the hope that is in you.* Gr., 'an account,' (λόγον.) That is, you are to state on what ground you cherish that hope. This refers to the *whole ground* of our hope, and includes evidently two things : (1.) The reason why we regard Christianity as true, or as furnishing a ground of hope for men ; and, (2.) the reason which we have ourselves for cherishing a hope of heaven, or the experimental and practical views which we have of religion,

which constitute a just ground of hope. It is not improbable that the former of these was more directly in the eye of the apostle than the latter, though both seem to be implied in the direction to state the reasons which ought to satisfy others that it is proper for us to cherish the hope of heaven. The *first* part of this duty—that we are to state the reasons why we regard the system of religion which we have embraced as true —implies, that we should be acquainted with the *evidences* of the truth of Christianity, and be able to state them to others. Christianity is founded on *evidence;* and though it cannot be supposed that every Christian will be able to understand *all* that is involved in what are called the *evidences* of Christianity, or to meet all the objections of the enemies of the gospel; yet every man who becomes a Christian should have such intelligent views of religion, and of the evidences of the truth of the Bible, that he can show to others that the religion which he has embraced has claims to their attention, or that it is not a mere matter of education, of tradition, or of feeling. It should also be an object with every Christian to increase his acquaintance with the evidences of the truth of religion, not only for his own stability and comfort in the faith, but that he may be able to defend religion if attacked, or to guide others if they are desirous of knowing what is truth. The *second* part of this duty, that we state the reasons which we have for cherishing the hope of heaven as a personal matter, implies (*a*) that there *should be,* in fact, a well-founded hope of heaven ; that is, that we have evidence that we are true Christians, since it is impossible to give a '*reason*' of the hope that is in us unless there are reasons for it; (*b*) that we be able to state in a clear and intelligent manner what constitutes evidence of piety, or what should be reasonably regarded as such; and (*c*) that we be ever *ready* to state these reasons. A Christian should always be willing to converse about his religion. He should have such a deep conviction of its truth, of its importance, and of his personal interest in it ; he should have a hope so firm, so cheering, so sustaining, that he

16 Having a good conscience; that, whereas they speak evil of you, as of evil doers, they may be ashamed that falsely accuse your good conversation in Christ.

will be always prepared to converse on the prospect of heaven, and to endeavour to lead others to walk in the path to life. ¶ *With meekness*. With modesty; without any spirit of ostentation; with gentleness of manner. This seems to be added on the supposition that they sometimes might be rudely assailed; that the questions might be proposed in a spirit of cavil; that it might be done in a taunting or insulting manner. Even though this should be done, they were not to fall into a passion, to manifest resentment, or to retort in an angry and revengeful manner; but, in a calm and gentle spirit, they were to state the *reasons* of their faith and hope, and leave the matter there. ¶ *And fear.* Marg., *reverence.* The sense seems to be, 'in the fear of God; with a serious and reverent spirit; as in the presence of Him who sees and hears all things.' It evidently does not mean with the fear or dread of those who propose the question, but with that serious and reverent frame of mind which is produced by a deep impression of the importance of the subject, and a conscious sense of the presence of God. It follows, from the injunction of the apostle here, (1,) that every professing Christian should have clear and intelligent views of his own personal interest in religion, or such evidences of piety that they *can* be stated to others, and that they *can* be made satisfactory to other minds; (2,) that every Christian, however humble his rank, or however unlettered he may be, may become a valuable defender of the truth of Christianity; (3,) that we should esteem it a privilege to bear our testimony to the truth and value of religion, and to stand up as the advocates of truth in the world. Though we may be rudely assailed, it is an honour to speak in defence of religion; though we are persecuted and reviled, it is a privilege to be permitted in any way to show our fellow-men that there is such a thing as true religion, and that man *may* cherish the hope of heaven.

16. *Having a good conscience.* That is, a conscience that does not accuse you of having done wrong. Whatever may be the accusations of your enemies, so live that you may be at all times conscious of uprightness. Whatever you suffer, see that you do not suffer the pangs inflicted by a guilty conscience, the anguish of remorse. On the meaning of the word *conscience*, see Notes on Rom. ii. 15. The word properly means the judgment of the mind respecting right and wrong; or the judgment which the mind passes on the immorality of its own actions, when it instantly approves or condemns them. There is always a feeling of *obligation* connected with operations of conscience, which precedes, attends, and follows our actions. 'Conscience is first occupied in ascertaining our duty, before we proceed to action; then in judging of our actions when performed.' A 'good conscience' implies two things: (1.) That it be properly enlightened to know what is right and wrong, or that it be not under the dominion of ignorance, superstition, or fanaticism, prompting us to do what would be a violation of the Divine law; and (2.) that its dictates be always obeyed. Without the first of these—clear views of that which is right and wrong—conscience becomes an unsafe guide; for it merely prompts us to do what we esteem to be right, and if our views of what is right and wrong are erroneous, we may be prompted to do what may be a direct violation of the law of God. Paul thought he '*ought*' to do many things contrary to the name of Jesus of Nazareth, (Acts xxvi. 9;) the Saviour said, respecting his disciples, that the time would come when whosoever should kill them would think that they were doing God service, (John xvi. 2;) and Solomon says, 'There is a way which seemeth right unto a man, but the end thereof are the ways of death,' (Prov. xiv. 12; xvi. 25.) Under an unenlightened and misguided conscience, with the plea and pretext of religion, the most atrocious crimes have been committed; and no man should infer

17 For *it is* better, if the will of God be so, that ye suffer for well doing than for evil doing.

18 For Christ *a* also hath once suffered for sins, the just *b* for the unjust, that he might bring us to

a 1 Pe.2.21.   b 2 Co.5.21.

that he is certainly doing *right,* because he follows the promptings of conscience. No man, indeed, should act *against* the dictates of his conscience; but there may have been a previous *wrong* in not using proper means to ascertain what *is* right. Conscience is not revelation, nor does it answer the purpose of a revelation. It communicates no new truth to the soul, and is a safe guide only so far as the mind has been properly enlightened to see what *is* truth and duty. Its office is *to prompt us to the performance of duty,* not *to determine what is right.* The other thing requisite that we may have a good conscience is, that its decisions *should be obeyed.* Conscience is appointed to be the 'vicegerent' of God in inflicting punishment, if his commands are not obeyed. It pronounces a sentence on our own conduct. Its penalty is remorse; and that penalty will be demanded if its promptings be not regarded. It is an admirable device, as a part of the moral government of God, urging man to the performance of duty, and, in case of disobedience, making the mind its own executioner. There is no penalty that will more certainly be inflicted, sooner or later, than that incurred by a guilty conscience. It needs no witnesses; no process for arresting the offender; no array of judges and executioners; no stripes, imprisonment, or bonds. Its inflictions will follow the offender into the most secluded retreat; overtake him in his most rapid flight; find him out in northern snows, or on the sands of the equator; go into the most splendid palaces, and seek out the victim when he is safe from all the vengeance that man can inflict; pursue him into the dark valley of the shadow of death, or arrest him as a fugitive in distant worlds. No one, therefore, can over-estimate the importance of having a good conscience. A true Christian should aim, by incessant study and prayer, to know what is right, *and then always do it,* no matter what may be the consequences. ¶ *That, whereas they speak evil of you.* They

who are your enemies and persecutors. Christians are not to hope that men will always speak well of them, Matt. v. 11; Luke vi. 26. ¶ *As of evil doers.* Notes, chap. ii. 12. ¶ *They may be ashamed.* They may see that they have misunderstood your conduct, and regret that they have treated you as they have. We should expect, if we are faithful and true, that even our enemies will yet appreciate our motives, and do us justice. Comp. Psa. xxxvii. 5, 6. ¶ *That falsely accuse your good conversation in Christ.* Your good conduct as Christians. They may accuse you of insincerity, hypocrisy, dishonesty; of being enemies of the state, or of monstrous crimes; but the time will come when they will see their error, and do you justice. See Notes on chap. ii. 12.

17. *For* it is *better, if the will of God be so.* That is, if God sees it to be necessary for your good that you should suffer, it is better that you should suffer for doing well than for crime. God often sees it to be necessary that his people should suffer. There are effects to be accomplished by affliction which can be secured in no other way; and some of the happiest results on the soul of a Christian, some of the brightest traits of character, are the effect of trials. But it should be *our* care that our sufferings should not be brought upon us for our own crimes or follies. No man can promote his own highest good by doing wrong, and then enduring the penalty which his sin incurs; and no one should *do* wrong with any expectation that it may be overruled for his own good. If we are to suffer, let it be by the direct hand of God, and not by any fault of our own. If we suffer then, we shall have the testimony of our own conscience in our favour, and the feeling that we may go to God for support. If we suffer for our own faults, in addition to the outward pain of body, we shall endure the severest pangs which man can suffer—those which the guilty mind inflicts on itself.

18. *For Christ also hath once suffered*

God, being put to death *a*in the | flesh, but quickened by the Spirit:

a Ro.4.25.

---

for sins. Comp. Notes on chap. ii. 21. The *design* of the apostle in this reference to the sufferings of Christ, is evidently to remind them that he suffered as an innocent being, and not for any wrong-doing, and to encourage and comfort them in their sufferings by his example. The reference to his sufferings leads him (vers. 18–22) into a statement of the various ways in which Christ suffered, and of his ultimate triumph. By his example in his sufferings, and by his final triumph, the apostle would encourage those whom he addressed to bear with patience the sorrows to which their religion exposed them. He assumes that all suffering for adhering to the gospel is the result of well-doing; and for an encouragement in their trials, he refers them to the example of Christ, the highest instance that ever was, or ever will be, both of well-doing, and of suffering on account of it. The expression, 'hath *once* suffered,' in the New Testament, means *once for all;* once, in the sense that it is not to occur again. Comp. Heb. vii. 27. The particular point here, however, is not that he *once* suffered ; it is that he *had* in fact suffered, and that in doing it he had left an example for them to follow. ¶ *The just for the unjust.* The one who was just, (δίκαιος,) on account of, or in the place of, those who were unjust, (ὑπὲρ ἀδίκων;) or one who was righteous, on account of those who were wicked. Comp. Notes, Rom. v. 6; 2 Cor. v. 21; Heb. ix. 28. The idea on which the apostle would particularly fix their attention was, that he was *just* or *innocent.* Thus he was an example to those who suffered for well-doing. ¶ *That he might bring us to God.* That his death might be the means of reconciling sinners to God. Comp. Notes on John iii. 14; xii. 32. It is through that death that mercy is proclaimed to the guilty; it is by that alone that God can be reconciled to men ; and the fact that the Son of God loved men, and gave himself a sacrifice for them, enduring such bitter sorrows, is the most powerful appeal which can be made to mankind to induce them to return to God. There is no

appeal which can be made to us more powerful than one drawn from the fact that another *suffers* on our account. We could resist the *argument* which a father, a mother, or a sister would use to reclaim us from a course of sin ; but if we perceive that our conduct involves them in suffering, that fact has a power over us which no mere argument could have. ¶ *Being put to death in the flesh.* As a man ; in his human nature. Comp. Notes, Rom. i. 3, 4. There is evidently a contrast here between ' the flesh ' in which it is said he was ' put to death,' and ' the Spirit ' by which it is said he was ' quickened.' The words '*in the flesh*' are clearly designed to denote something that was *peculiar* in his death ; for it is a departure from the usual method of speaking of *death.* How singular would it be to say of Isaiah, Paul, or Peter, that they were put to death *in the flesh!* How obvious would it be to ask, In what other way are men usually put to death? What was there peculiar in their case, which would distinguish their death from the death of others? The use of this phrase would suggest the thought at once, that though, in regard to that which is properly expressed by the phrase, '*the flesh,*' they died, yet that there was something else in respect to which they did not die. Thus, if it were said of a man that he was deprived of his rights *as a father,* it would be implied that in other respects he was not deprived of his rights ; and this would be especially true if it were added that he continued to enjoy his rights as a neighbour, or as holding an office under the government. The only proper inquiry, then, in this place is, What is fairly implied in the phrase, *the flesh?* Does it mean simply *his body,* as distinguished from his human soul? or does it refer to him *as a man,* as distinguished from some higher nature, over which death had no power ? Now, that the latter is the meaning seems to me to be apparent, for these reasons : (1.) It is the usual way of denoting the human nature of the Lord Jesus, or of saying that he became incarnate, or was a man, to speak of his being in the flesh. See Rom. i. 2: 'Made of the seed of David according to the flesh.' John i. 14: 'And the Word was made flesh.' 1 Tim. iii. 16: 'God was manifest in the flesh.' 1 John iv. 2: 'Every spirit that confesseth that Jesus Christ is come in the flesh, is of God.' 2 John 7: 'Who confess not that Jesus Christ is come in the flesh.' (2.) So far as appears, the effect of death on the human *soul* of the Redeemer was the same as in the case of the soul of any other person; in other words, the effect of *death* in his case was not confined to the mere body or the flesh. Death, with him, was what death is in any other case—the separation of the soul and body, with all the attendant pain of such dissolution. It is not true that his *'flesh,'* as such, died without the ordinary accompaniments of death on the soul, so that it could be said that the one died, and the other was kept alive. The purposes of the atonement required that he should meet death in the usual form; that the great laws which operate everywhere else in regard to dissolution, should exist in his case; nor is there in the Scriptures any intimation that there was, in this respect, anything peculiar in his case. If his soul had been exempt from whatever there is involved in death in relation to the spirit, it is unaccountable that there is no hint on this point in the sacred narrative. But if this be so, then the expression 'in the flesh' refers to him as a man, and means, that so far as his human nature was concerned, he died. In another important respect, he did *not* die. On the meaning of the word *flesh* in the New Testament, see Notes on Rom. i. 3. ¶ *But quickened.* Made alive—ζωοποιηθείς. This does not mean *kept alive,* but *made alive;* recalled to life; reanimated. The word is never used in the sense of *maintained alive,* or *preserved alive.* Compare the following places, which are the only ones in which it occurs in the New Testament: John v. 21, *twice;* vi. 63; Rom. iv. 17; viii. 11; 1 Cor. xv. 36, 45; 1 Tim. vi. 13; 1 Pet. iii. 18; in all which it is rendered *quickened, quicken, quickeneth;* 1 Cor. xv. 22, *be made alive;* 2 Cor. iii. 6, *giveth life;* and Gal. iii. 21, *have given life.* 'Once the word

refers to God, as he who giveth life to all creatures, 1 Tim. vi. 13; three times it refers to the life-giving power of the Holy Ghost, or of the doctrines of the gospel, John vi. 63; 2 Cor. iii. 6; Gal. iii. 21; seven times it is used with direct reference to the raising of the dead, John v. 21; Rom. iv. 17; viii. 11; 1 Cor. xv. 22, 36, 45; 1 Pet. iii. 18.' See Biblical Repos., April, 1845, p. 269. See also *Passow,* and *Robinson, Lex.* The sense, then, cannot be that, in reference to his soul or spirit, he was *preserved* alive when his body died, but that there was some agency or power *restoring* him to life, or reanimating him after he was dead. ¶ *By the Spirit.* According to the common reading in the Greek, this is τῷ Πνεύματι—with the article *the*—'*the* Spirit.' Hahn, Tittman, and Griesbach omit the article, and then the reading is, 'quickened in spirit;' and thus the reading corresponds with the former expression, 'in flesh' (σαρκὶ,) where the article also is wanting. The word *spirit,* so far as the mere use of the word is concerned, might refer to his own soul, to his Divine nature, or to the Holy Spirit. It is evident (1.) that it does not refer to his own soul, for, (a) as we have seen, the reference in the former clause is to his human nature, including all that pertained to him as a man, body and soul; (b) there was no power in his own spirit, regarded as that appertaining to his human nature, to raise him up from the dead, any more than there is such a power in any other human soul. That power does not belong to a human soul in any of its relations or conditions. (2.) It seems equally clear that this does not refer to the Holy Spirit, or the Third Person of the Trinity, for it may be doubted whether the work of raising the dead is anywhere ascribed to that Spirit. His peculiar province is to enlighten, awaken, convict, convert, and sanctify the soul; to apply the work of redemption to the hearts of men, and to lead them to God. This influence is *moral,* not *physical;* an influence accompanying *the truth,* not the exertion of mere physical *power.* (3.) It remains, then, that the reference is to his own Divine nature—a nature by which he was restored to life after he was

19 By which also he went and | preached unto the spirits in prison; [a]

a Is.42.7.

crucified; to the Son of God, regarded as the Second Person of the Trinity. This appears, not only from the facts above stated, but also (a) from the connection. It is stated that it was in or by this spirit that he went and preached in the days of Noah. But it was not his spirit as a man that did this, for his human soul had then no existence. Yet it seems that he did this personally or directly, and not by the influences of the Holy Spirit, for it is said that ' *he* went and preached.' The reference, therefore, cannot be to the Holy Ghost, and the fair conclusion is that it refers to his Divine nature. (*b*) This accords with what the apostle Paul says, (Rom. i. 3, 4,) ' which was made of the seed of David according to the flesh,'—that is, in respect to his human nature,— ' and declared to be the Son of God with power, according to the Spirit of holiness,'—that is, in respect to his Divine nature,—' by the resurrection from the dead.' See Notes on that passage. (*c*) It accords with what the Saviour himself says, John x. 17, 18 : ' I lay down my life, that I might take it again. No man taketh it from me, but I lay it down of myself. I have power to lay it down, and I have power to take it again.' This must refer to his Divine nature, for it is impossible to conceive that a human soul should have the power of restoring its former tenement, the body, to life. See Notes on the passage. The conclusion, then, to which we have come is, that the passage means, that as a man, a human being, he was put to death ; in respect to a higher nature, or by a higher nature, here denominated *Spirit*, (Πνεῦμα,) he was restored to life. As a man, he died ; as the incarnate Son of God, the Messiah, he was made alive again by the power of his own Divine Spirit, and exalted to heaven. Comp. Robinson's Lex. on the word Πνεῦμα, C.

19. *By which.* Evidently by the *Spirit* referred to in the previous verse —ἐν ᾧ—the Divine nature of the Son of God; that by which he was ' quickened ' again, after he had been put to death; the Son of God regarded as a Divine Being, or in that same nature which afterwards became incarnate, and whose agency was employed in quickening the man Christ Jesus, who had been put to death. The meaning is, that the same ' Spirit' which was efficacious in restoring him to life, after he was put to death, was that by which he preached to the spirits in prison. ¶ *He went.* To wit, in the days of Noah. No particular stress should be laid on the phrase ' he went.' The literal sense is, ' he, *having gone*, preached,' &c.— πορευθεὶς. It is well known that such expressions are often redundant in Greek writers, as in others. So these things they *spake; saying*'—for they said. ' And he, *speaking*, *said ;*' that is, he said. So Eph. ii. 17, ' And came and preached peace,' &c. Matt. ix. 13, ' But *go* and learn what that meaneth,' &c. So God is often represented as *coming*, as *descending*, &c., when he brings a message to mankind. Thus Gen. xi. 5, ' The Lord *came down* to see the city and the tower.' Exod. xix. 20, ' The Lord *came down* upon Mount Sinai.' Numb. xi. 25, ' The Lord *came down* in a cloud.' 2 Sam. xxii. 10, ' He bowed the heavens and came down.' The idea, however, would be conveyed by this language that he did this *personally*, or by *himself*, and not merely by employing the agency of another. It would then be implied here, that though the instrumentality of Noah was employed, yet that it was done not by the Holy Spirit, but by him who afterwards became incarnate. On the supposition, therefore, that this whole passage refers to his preaching to the antediluvians in the time of Noah, and not to the ' spirits' *after* they were confined in prison, this is language which the apostle would have properly and probably used. If that supposition meets the full force of the language, then no *argument* can be based on it in proof that he went to preach to them *after* their death, and while his body was lying in the grave. ¶ *And preached.* The word used here (ἐκήρυξεν) is of a *general* character, meaning to make a proclamation of any kind, as a crier does,

or to deliver a message, and does not necessarily imply that it was the gospel which was preached, nor does it determine anything in regard to the nature of the message. It is not affirmed that he preached *the gospel*, for if that specific idea had been expressed it would have been rather by another word—*εὐαγγελίζω*. The word here used would be appropriate to such a message as Noah brought to his contemporaries, or to *any* communication which God made to men. See Matt. iii. 1; iv. 17; Mark i. 35; v. 20; vii. 36. It is implied in the expression, as already remarked, that he did this himself; that it was the Son of God who subsequently became incarnate, and not the Holy Spirit, that did this; though the language is consistent with the supposition that he did it by the instrumentality of another, to wit, Noah. *Qui facit per alium, facit per se.* God really proclaims a message to mankind when he does it by the instrumentality of the prophets, or apostles, or other ministers of religion; and all that is necessarily implied in this language would be met by the supposition that Christ delivered a message to the antediluvian race by the agency of Noah. No *argument*, therefore, can be derived from this language to prove that Christ went and *personally* preached to those who were confined in hades or in prison. ¶ *Unto the spirits in prison.* That is, clearly, to the spirits *now* in prison, for this is the fair meaning of the passage. The obvious sense is, that Peter supposed there were 'spirits in prison' at the time when he wrote, and that to those same spirits the Son of God had at some time 'preached,' or had made some proclamation respecting the will of God. As this is the only passage in the New Testament on which the Romish doctrine of purgatory is supposed to rest, it is important to ascertain the fair meaning of the language here employed. There are three obvious inquiries in ascertaining its signification. Who are referred to by *spirits?* What is meant by *in prison?* Was the message brought to them while in the prison, or at some previous period? I. Who are referred to by *spirits?* The specification in the next verse determines this. They were

those 'who were sometimes disobedient, when once the long-suffering of God waited in the days of Noah.' No others are specified; and if it should be maintained that this means that he went down to hell, or to sheol, and preached to those who are confined there, it could be inferred from this passage only that he preached to that portion of the lost spirits confined there which belonged to the particular generation in which Noah lived. *Why* he should do this; or *how* there should be such a separation made in hades that it could be done; or what was the nature of the message which he delivered to that portion, are questions which it is impossible for any man who holds to the opinion that Christ went down to hell after his death *to preach,* to answer. But if it means that he preached to those who lived in the days of Noah, while they were yet alive, the question will be asked why are they called 'spirits?' Were they *spirits* then, or were they men like others? To this the answer is easy. Peter speaks of them as they were when he wrote; not as they *had been,* or were at the time when the message was preached to them. The idea is, that to those spirits who were then in prison who had formerly lived in the days of Noah, the message had been in fact delivered. It was not necessary to speak of them precisely as they were at the *time* when it was delivered, but only in such a way as to *identify* them. We should use similar language now. If we saw a company of men in prison who had seen better days—a multitude now drunken, and debased, and poor, and riotous—it would not be improper to say that 'the prospect of wealth and honour was once held out *to this ragged and wretched multitude.* All that is needful is to *identify* them as the same persons who once had this prospect. In regard to the inquiry, then, who these 'spirits' were, there can be no difference of opinion. *They were that wicked race which lived in the days of Noah.* There is no allusion in this passage to any other; there is no intimation that to any others of those 'in prison' the message here referred to had been delivered. II. What is meant by *prison* here? Purgatory, or the *limbus* patrum, say the Romanists—a place in which departed souls are supposed to be confined, and in which their final destiny may still be effected by the purifying fires which they endure, by the prayers of the living, or by a message in some way conveyed to their gloomy abodes—in which such sins may be expiated as do not deserve eternal damnation. The Syriac here is '*in sheol*,' referring to the abodes of the dead, or the place in which departed spirits are supposed to dwell. The word rendered *prison*, (φυλακῇ,) means properly *watch, guard*—the act of keeping watch, or the guard itself; then watchpost, or station; then a place where any one is watched or guarded, as a prison; then a watch in the sense of a division of the night, as the morning watch. It is used in the New Testament, with reference to the future world, only in the following places: 1 Pet. iii. 19, 'Preached unto the spirits *in prison*;' and Rev. xx. 7, 'Satan shall be loosed out of his *prison*.' An *idea* similar to the one here expressed may be found in 2 Pet. ii. 4, though the word *prison* does not there occur: 'God spared not the angels that sinned, but cast them down to hell, and delivered them into chains of darkness, to be reserved unto judgment;' and in Jude 6, 'And the angels which kept not their first estate, but left their own habitation, he hath reserved in everlasting chains, under darkness, unto the judgment of the great day.' The allusion, in the passage before us, is undoubtedly to confinement or imprisonment in the invisible world; and perhaps to those who are reserved there with reference to some future arrangement—for this idea enters commonly into the use of the word prison. There is, however, no specification of the *place* where this is; no intimation that it is *purgatory*—a place where the departed are supposed to undergo purification; no intimation that their condition can be affected by anything that we can do; no intimation that those particularly referred to differ in any sense from the others who are confined in that world; no hint that they can be released by any prayers or sacrifices of ours. This passage, therefore, cannot be adduced to support the Roman Catholic doctrine of purgatory, for (1,) the essential ideas which enter into the doctrine of purgatory are not to be found in the word here used; (2,) there is no evidence in the fair interpretation of the passage that any message is borne to them while *in* prison; (3,) there is not the slightest hint that they can be released by any prayers or offerings of those who dwell on the earth. The simple idea is that of persons *confined* as in a prison; and the passage will prove only that in the time when the apostle wrote there *were* those who were thus confined. III. Was the message brought to them while *in* prison, or at some previous period? The Romanists say that it was while *in* prison; that Christ, after he was put to death in the body, was still kept alive in his spirit, and went and proclaimed his gospel to those who were in prison. So Bloomfield maintains, (*in loc.*,) and so Œcumenius and Cyril, as quoted by Bloomfield. But against this view there are plain objections drawn from the language of Peter himself. (1.) As we have seen, the fair interpretation of the passage 'quickened by the Spirit,' is not that he was *kept alive as to his human soul*, but that he, after being dead, was *made alive* by his own Divine energy. (2.) If the meaning be that he went and preached *after* his death, it seems difficult to know why the reference is to those only who 'had been disobedient in the days of Noah.' Why were *they* alone selected for this message? Are they separate from others? Were they the only ones in purgatory who could be beneficially affected by his preaching? On the other method of interpretation, we can suggest a reason why they were particularly specified. But how can we on this? (3.) The language employed does not demand this interpretation. Its full meaning is met by the interpretation that Christ once preached to the spirits then in prison, to wit, in the days of Noah; that is, that he caused a Divine message to be borne to them. Thus it would be proper to say that 'Whitefield came to America, and preached to the souls in perdition;' or to go among the graves of the first settlers of New Haven, and say, 'Davenport came from England to preach to the dead men around us.' (4.) This interpretation accords

20 Which sometime were disobedient, when once *a* the long suffering
of God waited in the days of Noah,

a Ge.vi.,&c.

with the design of the apostle in inculcating the duty of patience and forbearance in trials; in encouraging those
whom he addressed to be patient in
their persecutions. See the analysis of
the chapter. With this object in view,
there was entire propriety in directing
them to the long-suffering and forbearance evinced by the Saviour, through
Noah. *He* was opposed, reviled, disbelieved, and, we may suppose, persecuted.
It was to the purpose to direct them to
the fact that he was saved as the result
of his steadfastness to Him who had
commanded him to preach to that ungodly generation. But what pertinency
would there have been in saying that
Christ went down to hell, and delivered
some sort of a message there, we know
not what, to those who are confined there?
20. *Which sometime were disobedient.* Which were *once*, or *formerly*,
(ποτε,) disobedient or rebellious. The
language here does not imply that they
had *ceased* to be disobedient, or that
they had become obedient at the time
when the apostle wrote; but the object
is to direct the attention to a former
race of men characterized by disobedience, and to show the patience evinced
under their provocations, in endeavouring to do them good. To say that men
were formerly rebellious, or rebellious in
a specified age, is no evidence that they
are otherwise now. The meaning here
is, that they did not obey the command
of God when he called them to repentance by the preaching of Noah. Comp.
2 Pet. ii. 5, where Noah is called 'a
preacher of righteousness.' ¶ *When
once the long suffering of God waited
in the days of Noah.* God waited on
that guilty race a hundred and twenty
years, (Gen. vi. 3,) a period sufficiently
protracted to evince his long-suffering
toward one generation. It is not improbable that during that whole period
Noah was, in various ways, preaching
to that wicked generation. Comp. Notes
on Heb. xi. 7. ¶ *While the ark was a
preparing.* It is probable that preparations were made for building the ark

while the ark was a preparing,
wherein few, that is, eight souls,
were saved by water.

during a considerable portion of that
time. St. Peter's, at Rome, was a
much longer time in building; and it is
to be remembered that in the age of the
world when Noah lived, and with the
imperfect knowledge of the arts of naval
architecture which must have prevailed,
it was a much more serious undertaking to construct an ark that would
hold such a variety and such a number
of animals as that was designed to,
and that would float safely for more
than a year in an universal flood, than
it was to construct such a fabric as
St. Peter's, in the days when that
edifice was reared. ¶ *Wherein few,
that is, eight souls.* Eight *persons*—
Noah and his wife, his three sons and
their wives, Gen. vii. 7. The allusion
to their being saved here seems to be to
encourage those whom Peter addressed
to perseverance and fidelity, in the
midst of all the opposition which they
might experience. Noah was not disheartened. Sustained by the Spirit of
Christ—the presence of the Son of God
—he continued to preach. He did not
abandon his purpose, and the result
was that he was saved. True, they
were few in number who were saved;
the great mass continued to be wicked;
but this very fact should be an encouragement to us—that though the
great mass of any one generation may
be wicked, God can protect and save
the few who are faithful. ¶ *By water.*
They were borne up by the waters, and
were thus preserved. The thought on
which the apostle makes his remarks
turn, and which leads him in the next
verse to the suggestions about baptism,
is, that *water* was employed in their
preservation, or that they owed their
safety, in an important sense, to that
element. In like manner we owe *our*
salvation, in an important sense, to
water; or, there is an important agency
which it is made to perform in our salvation. The apostle does not say that it
was in the same way, or that the one was
a type *designed* to represent the other,
or even that the efficacy of water was

21 The like figure whereunto, *even* baptism, *a* doth also now save us, (not the putting away of the

a Ep.5.26.

in both cases the same; but he says, that as Noah owed *his* salvation to water, so there is an important sense in which water is employed in *ours*. There is in *certain respects*—he does not say in *all* respects—a resemblance between the agency of water in the salvation of Noah, and the agency of water in our salvation. In both cases water is employed, though it may not be that it is in the same manner, or with precisely the same efficacy.

21. *The like figure whereunto*, even *baptism, doth also now save us.* There are some various readings here in the Greek text, but the sense is not essentially varied. Some have proposed to read (ᾧ) *to which* instead of (ὅ) *which*, so as to make the sense 'the antitype *to which* baptism now also saves us.' The antecedent to the relative, whichever word is used, is clearly not *the ark*, but *water;* and the idea is, that as Noah was saved by water, so there is a sense in which water is made instrumental in our salvation. The mention of *water* in the case of Noah, in connection with *his* being saved, by an obvious association suggested to the mind of the apostle the use of *water* in our salvation, and hence led him to make the remark about the connection of baptism with our salvation. The Greek word here rendered *figure—ἀντίτυπον—antitype* means properly, *resisting a blow* or *impression*, (from ἀντί and τύπος;) that is, *hard, solid*. In the New Testament, however, it is used in a different sense; and (ἀντί) *anti*, in composition, implies resemblance, correspondence; and hence the word means, *formed after a type* or *model; like; corresponding; that which corresponds to a type.—Rob. Lex.* The word occurs only in this place and Heb. ix. 24, rendered *figures*. The meaning here is, that *baptism corresponded to*, or *had a resemblance to*, the water by which Noah was saved; or that there was a use of water in the one case which corresponded in some respects to the water that was used in the other; to wit, *in effecting salvation*.

filth of the flesh, but the answer of a good conscience *b* toward God,) by the resurrection of Jesus Christ:

b Ac.8.37; Ro.10.10.

The apostle does not say that it corresponded *in all respects;* in respect, e. g., to quantity, or to the manner of the application, or to the efficacy; but there is a sense in which water performs an important part in our salvation, as it did in his. ¶ *Baptism.* Not the *mere* application of water, for that idea the apostle expressly disclaims, when he says that it involves not ' putting away the filth of the flesh, but the answer of a good conscience toward God.' The sense is, that baptism, including all that is properly meant by baptism as a religious rite—that is, baptism administered in connection with true repentance, and true faith in the Lord Jesus, and when it is properly a symbol of the putting away of sin, and of the renewing influences of the Holy Spirit, and an act of unreserved dedication to God —now saves us. On the meaning of the word *baptism*, see Notes on Matt. iii. 6. ¶ *Doth also now save us.* The water saved Noah and his family from perishing in the flood ; to wit, by bearing up the ark. Baptism, in the proper sense of the term, as above explained, where the water used is a symbol, in like manner now saves us ; that is, the water is an emblem of that purifying by which we are saved. It may be said to save us, not as the meritorious cause, but as the indispensable condition of salvation. No man can be saved without that renewed and purified heart of which baptism is the appropriate symbol, and when it would be *proper* to administer that ordinance. The apostle cannot have meant that water saves us *in the same way* in which it saved Noah, for that cannot be true. It is neither the same in quantity, nor is it applied in the same way, nor is it efficacious in the same manner. It is indeed connected with our salvation in its own proper way, as an emblem of that purifying of the heart by which we are saved. Thus it corresponds with the salvation of Noah by water, and is the (ἀντίτυπον) *antitype* of that. Nor does it mean that the salvation of Noah by water was *designed* to be a type of Christian baptism. There is not the least evidence of that; and it should not be affirmed without proof. The apostle saw a *resemblance* in some respects between the one and the other; such a resemblance that the one naturally suggested the other to his mind, and the resemblance was so important as to make it the proper ground of remark.

[But if Noah's preservation in the ark, be the type of that salvation of which baptism is the emblem, who shall say it was not so designed of God? Must we indeed regard the resemblance between Noah's deliverance and ours, as a happy coincidence merely? But the author is wont to deny typical design in very clear cases; and in avoiding one extreme seems to have gone into another. Some will have types everywhere; and, therefore, others will allow them nowhere. See Supp. Note, Heb. vii. 1; M'Knight's Essay, viii. Sect. v., on the laws of typical interpretation, with his commentary *in loco.*]

The points of resemblance in the two cases seem to have been these: (1.) There was *salvation* in both; Noah was saved from death, and we from hell. (2.) *Water* is employed in both cases— in the case of Noah to uphold the ark; in ours to be a symbol of our purification. (3.) The water in both cases is *connected with* salvation: in the case of Noah by sustaining the ark; in ours by being a symbol of salvation, of purity, of cleansing, of that by which we may be brought to God. The meaning of this part of the verse, therefore, may be thus expressed: 'Noah and his family were saved by water, the antitype to which (to wit, that which in important respects corresponds to that) baptism (not the putting away of the filth of the flesh, or the mere application of material water, but that purifying of the heart of which it is the appropriate emblem) now saves us.' ¶ *Not the putting away of the filth of the flesh.* Not a mere external washing, however solemnly done. No outward ablution or purifying saves us, but that which pertains to the conscience. This important clause is thrown in to guard the statement from the abuse to which it would otherwise be liable, the supposition that baptism has of itself a purifying and saving power. To guard against this, the apostle expressly declares that he means much more than

a mere outward application of water. ¶ *But the answer of a good conscience toward God.* The word here rendered *answer* (ἐπερώτημα) means properly a *question, an inquiry.* It is 'spoken of a *question* put to a convert at baptism, or rather of the whole process of question and answer; that is, by implication, *examination, profession.*' — Robinson, Lex. It is designed to mark the spiritual character of the baptismal rite in contrast with a mere external purification, and evidently refers to something that occurred *at* baptism; some question, inquiry, or examination, that took place then; and it would seem to imply, (1,) that when baptism was performed, there was some question or inquiry in regard to the belief of the candidate; (2,) that an answer was expected, implying that there was a good conscience; that is, that the candidate had an enlightened conscience, and was sincere in his profession; and, (3,) that the real efficacy of baptism, or its power in saving, was not in the mere external rite, but in the state of the heart, indicated by the question and answer, of which that was the emblem. On the meaning of the phrase ' a good conscience,' see Notes on ver. 16 of this chapter. Compare on this verse Neander, Geschich der Pflanz. u. Leit. der chr, Kirche, i. p. 203, seq., in Bibl. Reposi. iv. 272, seq. It is in the highest degree probable that questions would be proposed to candidates for baptism respecting their belief, and we have an instance of this fact undoubtedly in the case before us. How extensive such examinations would be, what points would be embraced, how much reference there was to personal experience, we have, of course, no certain means of ascertaining. We may suppose, however, that the examination pertained to what constituted the essential features of the Christian religion, as distinguished from other systems, and to the cordial belief of that system by the candidate. ¶ *By the resurrection of Jesus Christ.* That is, we are saved in this manner through the resurrection of Jesus Christ. The whole efficiency in the case is derived from that. If he had not been raised from the dead, baptism would have been vain, and there would have been no power to save

22 Who is gone into heaven, and is on the right hand of God: angels

^a and authorities and powers being made subject unto him.

a Ep.1.21.

us. See this illustrated at length in the Notes on Rom. vi. 4, 5. The points, therefore, which are established in regard to baptism by this important passage are these : (1.) That Christian baptism is not a mere *external* rite ; a mere outward ablution ; a mere application of water to the body. It is not contemplated that it shall be an empty form, and its essence does not consist in a mere ' putting away of the filth of the flesh.' There is a work to be done in respect to the *conscience* which cannot be reached by the application of water. (2.) That there was an examination among the early Christians when a candidate was about to be baptized, and of course such an examination is proper now. Whatever was the ground of the examination, it related to that which existed *before* the baptism was administered. It was not expected that it should be accomplished *by* the baptism. There is, therefore, implied evidence here that there was no reliance placed on that ordinance to *produce* that which constituted the ' answer of a good conscience ; ' in other words, that it was not supposed to have an efficacy to produce that of itself, and was not a converting or regenerating ordinance. (3.) The ' answer ' which was returned in the inquiry, was to be such as indicated a good conscience ; that is, as Bloomfield expresses it, (New Test. *in loc.,*) ' that which enables us to return such an answer as springs from a good conscience towards God, which can be no other than the inward change and renovation wrought by the Spirit.' It was supposed, therefore, that there would be an internal work of grace ; that there would be much more than an outward rite in the whole transaction. The application of water is, in fact, but an emblem or symbol of that grace in the heart, and is to be administered as denoting that. It does not *convey* grace to the soul by any physical efficacy of the water. It is a symbol of the purifying influences of religion, and is made a means of grace in the same way as obedience to any other of the commands

of God. (4.) There is no efficacy in the mere application of water in any form, or with any ceremonies of religion, to put away sin. It is the ' good conscience,' the renovated heart, the purified soul, of which baptism is the emblem, that furnishes evidence of the Divine acceptance and favour. Comp. Heb. ix. 9, 10. There must be a deep internal work on the soul of man, in order that he may be acceptable to God ; and when that is wanting, no external rite is of any avail. Yet, (5,) it does not follow from this that baptism is of no importance. The argument of the apostle here is, that it *is* of great importance. Noah was saved by water ; and so baptism has an important connection with our salvation. As water bore up the ark, and was the means of saving Noah, so baptism by water is the emblem of our salvation ; and when administered in connection with a ' good conscience,' that is, with a renovated heart, it is as certainly connected with our salvation as the sustaining waters of the flood were with the salvation of Noah. No man can prove from the Bible that baptism has no important connection with salvation ; and no man can prove that by neglecting it he will be as likely to obtain the Divine favour as he would by observing it. It is a means of exhibiting great and important truths in an impressive manner to the soul ; it is a means of leading the soul to an entire dedication to a God of purity ; it is a means through which God manifests himself to the soul, and through which he imparts grace, as he does in all other acts of obedience to his commandments.

22. *Who is gone into heaven.* Notes, Acts i. 9. ¶ *And is on the right hand of God.* Notes, Mark xvi. 19. ¶ *Angels and authorities and powers being made subject unto him.* See Notes, Eph. i. 20, 21. The reason why the apostle here adverts to the fact that the Lord Jesus is raised up to the right hand of God, and is so honoured in heaven, seems to have been to encourage those to whom he wrote to persevere in the service of God, though they were persecuted. The

Lord Jesus was in like manner persecuted. He was reviled, and rejected,
and put to death. Yet he ultimately
triumphed. He was raised from the
dead, and was exalted to the highest
place of honour in the universe. Even
so they, if they did not faint, might
hope to come off in the end triumphant.
As Noah, who had been faithful and
steadfast when surrounded by a scoffing
world, was at last preserved by his faith
from ruin, and as the Redeemer, though
persecuted and put to death, was at last
exalted to the right hand of God, so
would it be with them if they bore their
trials patiently, and did not faint or fail
in the persecutions which they endured.

In view of the exposition in vers. 1
and 2, we may remark, (1,) that it is
our duty to seek the conversion and
salvation of our impenitent relatives and
friends. All Christians have relatives
and friends who are impenitent ; it is a
rare thing that some of the members of
their own families are not so. In most
families, even Christian families, there
is a husband or a wife, a father or a
mother, a son or daughter, a brother or
sister, who is not converted. To all
such, they who are Christians owe important duties, and there is none *more*
important than that of seeking their
conversion. That this *is* a duty is
clearly implied in this passage in reference to a wife, and for the same reason
it is a duty in reference to all other
persons. It may be further apparent
from these considerations : (*a*) It is an
important part of the business of *all*
Christians to seek the salvation of
others. This is clearly the duty of
ministers of the gospel; but it is no less
the duty of all who profess to be followers of the Saviour, and to take him
as their example and guide. Comp.
James v. 19, 20. (*b*) It is a duty peculiarly devolving on those who have relatives who are unconverted, on account
of the *advantages* which they have for
doing it. They are with them constantly; they have their confidence and
affection ; they can feel more for them
than any one else can ; and if *they* are
not concerned for their salvation, they
cannot hope that any others will be.
(*c*) It is not wholly an improper motive
to seek their salvation from the happi-

ness which it would confer on those who
are already Christians. It is not improper that a wife should be stimulated
to desire the conversion of her husband
from the increased enjoyment which she
would have if her partner in life were
united with her in the same hope of
heaven, and from the pleasure which it
would give to enjoy the privilege of
religious worship in the family, and the
aid which would be furnished in training
up her children in the Lord. A Christian wife and mother has important
duties to perform towards her children ;
it is not improper that in performing
those duties she should earnestly desire
the co-operation of her partner in life.

(2.) Those who have impenitent husbands and friends should be *encouraged*
in seeking their conversion. It is plainly
implied (vers. 1, 2) that it was not to
be regarded as a *hopeless* thing, but that
in all cases they were to regard it as
possible that unbelieving husbands *might*
be brought to the knowledge of the truth.
If this is true of *husbands*, it is no less
true of other friends. We should never
despair of the conversion of a friend as
long as life lasts, however far he may
be from the path of virtue and piety.
The grounds of encouragement are such
as these : (*a*) You have an *influence* over
them which no other one has ; and that
influence may be regarded as *capital*,
which will give you great advantages in
seeking their conversion. (*b*) You have
access to them at times when their minds
are most open to serious impressions.
Every man has times when he may be
approached on the subject of religion;
when he is pensive and serious ; when
he is disappointed and sad ; when the
affairs of this world do not go well with
him, and his thoughts are drawn along
to a better. There are times in the life
of every man when he is ready to open
his mind to a friend on the subject of
religion, and when he would be glad of
a word of friendly counsel and encouragement. It is much to have access to
a man at such times. (*c*) If all the
facts were known which have occurred,
there would be no lack of encouragement
to labour for the conversion of impenitent relatives and friends. Many a
husband owes his salvation to the persevering solicitude and prayers of a wife;

many a son will enter heaven because a mother never ceased to pray for his salvation, even when to human view there seemed no hope of it.

(3.) We may learn (vers. 1, 2) what are the principal *means* by which we are to hope to secure the conversion and salvation of impenitent friends. It is to be mainly by a pure life; by a holy walk; by a consistent example. *Conversation*, properly so called, is not to be regarded as excluded from those means, but the main dependence is to be on a holy life. This is to be so, because (*a*) most persons form their notions of religion from what they see in the lives of its professed friends. It is not so much what they hear in the pulpit, for they regard preaching as a mere professional business, by which a man gets a living; not so much by books in defence and explanation of religion, for they seldom or never read them; not by what religion enabled the martyrs to do, for they may have scarcely heard the names of even the most illustrious of the martyrs; but by what they see in the walk and conversation of those who profess to be Christians, especially of those who are their near relations. The husband is forming his views of religion constantly from what he sees on the brow and in the eye of his professedly Christian wife; the brother from what he sees in his sister; the child from what he sees in the parent. (*b*) Those who profess to be Christians have an opportunity of showing the power of religion in a way which is superior to any abstract argument. It controls their temper; it makes them kind and gentle; it sustains them in trial; it prompts them to deeds of benevolence; it disposes them to be contented, to be forgiving, to be patient in the reverses of life. Every one may thus be always doing something to make an impression favourable to religion on the minds of others. Yet it is *also* true that much may be done, and should be done for the conversion of others, by *conversation* properly so called, or by direct address and appeal. There is nothing, however, which requires to be managed with more prudence than conversation with those who are not Christians, or direct efforts to lead them to attend to the subject of religion. In regard to this it may be observed, (*a*,) that it does no good to be *always* talking with them. Such a course only produces disgust. (*b*) It does no good to talk to them at unseasonable and improper times. If they are specially engaged in their business, and would not like to be interrupted—if they are in company with others, or even with their family —it does little good to attempt a conversation with them. It is 'the word that is *fitly* spoken that is like apples of gold in pictures of silver,' Prov. xxv. 11. (*c*) It does no good to *scold* them on the subject of religion, with a view to make them Christians. In such a case you show a spirit the very reverse of that religion which you are professedly endeavouring to persuade them to embrace. (*d*) All conversation with impenitent sinners should be kind, and tender, and respectful. It should be addressed to them when they will be disposed to listen; usually when they are alone; and especially when from trials or other causes they may be in such a state of mind that they will be willing to listen. It may be added, that impenitent sinners are much more frequently in such a state of mind than most Christians suppose, and that they often wonder that their Christian friends do *not* speak to them about the salvation of the soul.

From the exposition given of the important verses 18–21, we may derive the following inferences:—

(1.) The pre-existence of Christ. If he preached to the antediluvians in the time of Noah, he must have had an existence at that time.

(2.) His divinity. If he was 'quickened' or restored to life by his own exalted nature, he must be Divine; for there is no more inalienable attribute of the Deity than the power of raising the dead.

(3.) If Christ preached to the heathen world in the time of Noah, for the same reason it may be regarded as true that *all* the messages which are brought to men, calling them to repentance, in any age or country, are through him. Thus it was Christ who spake by the prophets and by the apostles; and thus he speaks now by his ministers.

(4.) If this interpretation is well-founded, it takes away one of the

CHAPTER IV.

FORASMUCH then as Christ hath suffered for us in the flesh, arm yourselves likewise with the same mind : *a* for he *b* that hath suffered in the flesh hath ceased from sin ;

a Phi.2.5.   *b* Ro.6.2,7

strongest supports of the doctrine of purgatory. There is no *stronger* passage of the Bible in support of this doctrine than the one before us ; and if *this* does not countenance it, it may be safely affirmed that it has not a shadow of proof in the sacred Scriptures.

(5.) It follows that there is no hope or prospect that the gospel will be preached to those who are lost. This is the *only* passage in the Bible that could be supposed to teach any such doctrine ; and if the interpretation above proposed be correct, this furnishes no ground of belief that if a man dies impenitent he will ever be favoured with another offer of mercy. This interpretation also accords with all the other representations in the Bible. ' As the tree falleth, so it lies.' ' He that is holy, let him be holy still ; and he that is filthy, let him be filthy still.' All the representations in the Bible lead us to suppose that the eternal destiny of the soul after death is fixed, and that the only change which can ever occur in the future state is that which will be produced by DEVELOPEMENT : the developement of the principles of piety in heaven ; the developement of the principles of evil in hell.

(6.) It follows, that if there is not a place of *purgatory* in the future world, there is a place of *punishment*. If the word *prison*, in the passage before us, does not mean purgatory, and does not refer to a detention with a prospect or possibility of release, it must refer to detention of another kind, and for another purpose, and that can be only with reference ' to the judgment of the great day,' 2 Pet. ii. 14 ; Jude 6. From that gloomy prison there is no evidence that any have been, or will be, released.

(7.) Men should embrace the gospel at once. Now it is offered to them ; in the future world it will not be. But even if it could be proved that the gospel would be offered to them in the future world, it would be better to embrace it now. Why should men go down to that

world to suffer long before they become reconciled to God ? Why choose to taste the sorrows of hell before they embrace the offers of mercy ? Why go to that world of woe at all ? Are men so in love with suffering and danger that they esteem it wise to go down to that dark prison-house, with the intention or the hope that the gospel may be offered to them there, and that when there they may be disposed to embrace it ? Even if it could be shown, therefore, that they *might* again hear the voice of mercy and salvation, how much wiser would it be to hearken to the voice now, and become reconciled to God here, and never experience in any way the pangs of the second death ! But of any such offer of mercy in the world of despair, the Bible contains no intimation ; and he who goes to the eternal world unreconciled to God, perishes for ever. The moment when he crosses the line between time and eternity, he goes for ever beyond the boundaries of hope.

CHAPTER IV.

ANALYSIS OF THE CHAPTER.

THIS chapter relates principally to the manner in which those to whom the apostle wrote ought to bear their trials, and to the encouragements to a holy life, notwithstanding their persecutions. He had commenced the subject in the preceding chapter, and had referred them particularly to the example of the Saviour. His great solicitude was, that if they suffered, it should not be for crime, and that their enemies should not be able to bring any well-founded accusation against them He would have them pure and harmless, patient and submissive ; faithful in the performance of their duties, and confidently looking forward to the time when they should be delivered. He exhorts them, therefore, to the following things : (*a*) To arm themselves with the same mind that was in Christ ; to consider that the past time of their lives was enough for them to have wrought

2 That he *a* no longer should live the rest of *his* time in the flesh to the lusts of men, but to the will of God.

3 For the time *b* past of *our* life

a 2 Co.5.15.

the will of the flesh, and that now it was their duty to be separate from the wicked world, in whatever light the world might regard their conduct—remembering that they who calumniated them must soon give account to God, vers. 1–6. (*b*) He reminds them that the end of all things was at hand, and that it became them to be sober, and watch unto prayer, ver. 7. (*c*) He exhorts them to the exercise of mutual love and hospitality—virtues eminently useful in a time of persecution and afflictions, vers. 8, 9. (*d*) He exhorts them to a performance of every duty with seriousness of manner, and fidelity —whether it were in preaching, or in dispensing alms to the poor and needy, vers. 10, 11. (*e*) He tells them not to think it strange that they were called to pass through fiery trials, nor to suppose that any unusual thing had happened to *them;* reminds them that they only partook of Christ's sufferings, and that it was to be regarded as a favour if any one suffered as a Christian; and presses upon them the thought that they ought to be careful that none of them suffered for crime, vers. 12–16. (*f*) He reminds them that the righteous would be saved with difficulty, and that the wicked would certainly be destroyed; and exhorts them, therefore, to commit the keeping of their souls to a faithful Creator, vers. 18, 19.

1. *Forasmuch then as Christ hath suffered for us in the flesh.* Since he as a man has died for us. Notes, chap. iii. 18. The design was to set the suffering Redeemer before them as an example in their trials. ¶ *Arm yourselves likewise with the same mind.* That is, evidently, the same mind that he evinced —a readiness to suffer in the cause of religion, a readiness to die as he had done. This readiness to suffer and die, the apostle speaks of as *armour,* and having this is represented as being armed. Armour is put on for offensive or defensive purposes in war; and the

may suffice us to have wrought the will of the Gentiles, when we walked in lasciviousness, lusts, excess of wine, revellings, banquetings, and abominable idolatries ;

b 1 Co.6.11; Tit.3.3.

idea of the apostle here is, that that state of mind when we are *ready* to meet with persecution and trial, and when we are ready to die, will answer the purpose of armour in engaging in the conflicts and strifes which pertain to us as Christians, and especially in meeting with persecutions and trials. We are to put on the same fortitude which the Lord Jesus had, and this will be the best defence against our foes, and the best security of victory. ¶ *For he that hath suffered in the flesh hath ceased from sin.* Comp. Notes, Rom. vi. 7. To 'suffer in the flesh' is *to die.* The expression here has a proverbial aspect, and seems to have meant something like this : ' when a man is dead, he will sin no more ;' referring of course to the present life. So if a Christian becomes *dead* in a moral sense—dead to this world, dead by being crucified with Christ (see Notes, Gal. ii. 20)—he may be expected to cease from sin. The reasoning is based on the idea that there is such a union between Christ and the believer that his death on the cross *secured* the death of the believer to the world. Comp. 2 Tim. ii. 11 ; Col. ii. 20; iii. 3.

2. *That he no longer should live.* That is, he has become, through the death of Christ, dead to the world and to the former things which influenced him, *in order* that he should hereafter live not to the lusts of the flesh. See Notes, 2 Cor. v. 15. ¶ *The rest of* his *time in the flesh.* The remainder of the time that he is to continue in the flesh; that is, that he is to live on the earth. ¶ *To the lusts of men.* Such lusts as men commonly live for and indulge in. Some of these are enumerated in the following verse. ¶ *But to the will of God.* In such a manner as God commands. The object of redemption is to rescue us from being swayed by wicked lusts, and to bring us to be conformed wholly to the will of God.

3. *For the time past of* our *life may suffice us.* ' We have spent sufficient

time in indulging ourselves, and following our wicked propensities, and we should hereafter live in a different manner.' This does not mean that it was ever *proper* thus to live, but that, as we would say, 'we have had *enough* of these things ; we have tried them ; there is no reason why we should indulge in them any more.' An expression quite similar to this occurs in Horace—Lusisti satis, edisti satis, atque bibisti. Tempus abire tibi est, &c.—Epis. ii. 213. ¶ *To have wrought the will of the Gentiles.* This does not mean to be subservient to their will, but to have done what they willed to do ; that is, to live as they did. That the Gentiles or heathen lived in the manner immediately specified, see demonstrated in the Notes on Rom. i. 21-32. ¶ *When we walked in lasciviousness.* When we *lived* in the indulgence of corrupt passions—the word *walk* being often used in the Scriptures to denote the manner of life. On the word *lasciviousness*, see Notes on Rom. xiii. 13. The apostle says *we*, not as meaning that *he* himself had been addicted to these vices, but as speaking of those who were Christians in general. It is common to say that *we* lived so and so, when speaking of a collection of persons, without meaning that each one was guilty of *all* the practices enumerated. See Notes on 1 Thess. iv. 17, for a similar use of the word *we*. The use of the word *we* in this place would show that the apostle did not mean to set himself up as better than they were, but was willing to be identified with them. ¶ *Lusts.* The indulgence of unlawful desires. Notes, Rom. i. 24. ¶ *Excess of wine.* The word here used (οἰνοφλυγία) occurs nowhere else in the New Testament. It properly means *overflowing of wine*, (οἶνος, wine, and φλύω, to overflow ;) then wine-drinking ; drunkenness. That this was a common vice need not be proved. Multitudes of those who became Christians had been drunkards, for intemperance abounded in all the heathen world. Comp. 1 Cor. vi. 9-11 It should not be inferred here from the English translation, ' *excess* of wine,' that wine is improper only when used to excess, or that the moderate use of wine is proper. Whatever may be true on that point, nothing can be de-

termined in regard to it from the use of this word. The apostle had his eye on one thing—on such a use of wine as they had indulged in before their conversion. About the impropriety of that, there could be no doubt. Whether *any* use of wine, by Christians or other persons, was lawful, was another question. It should be added, moreover, that the phrase ' *excess* of wine ' does not precisely convey the meaning of the original. The word *excess* would naturally imply something more than was needful ; or something beyond the proper limit or measure ; but no such idea is in the original word. That refers merely to the *abundance* of wine, without any reference to the inquiry whether there was *more* than was proper or not. Tindal renders it, somewhat better, *drunkenness*. So Luther, *Trunkenheit.* ¶ *Revellings.* Rendered *rioting* in Rom. xiii. 13. See Notes on that verse. The Greek word (κῶμος) occcurs only here, and in Rom. xiii. 13, and Gal. v. 21. It means *feasting, revel;* ' a carousing or merry-making after supper, the guests often sallying into the streets, and going through the city with torches, music, and songs in honour of Bacchus,' &c. — *Robinson, Lex.* The word would apply to all such noisy and boisterous processions now—scenes wholly inappropriate to the Christian. ¶ *Banquetings.* The word here used (πότος) occurs nowhere else in the New Testament. It means properly *drinking ; an act of drinking; then a drinking bout; drinking together.* The thing forbidden by it is *an assembling together for the purpose of drinking.* There is nothing in this word referring to *eating*, or to *banqueting*, as the term is now commonly employed. The idea in the passage is, that it is improper for Christians to meet together for the purpose of drinking—as wine, toasts, &c. The prohibition would apply to all those assemblages where this is understood to be the main object. It would forbid, therefore, an attendance on all those celebrations in which drinking toasts is understood to be an essential part of the festivities, and all those where hilarity and joyfulness are sought to be produced by the intoxicating bowl. Such are not proper places for Chris-

4 Wherein they think it strange that ye run not with *them* to the same excess of riot, speaking evil *a* of *you:*

a Ac.13.45.

tians. ¶ *And abominable idolatries.* Literally, *unlawful idolatries;* that is, unlawful to the Jews, or forbidden by their laws. Then the expression is used in the sense of *wicked, impious,* since what is unlawful is impious and wrong. That the vices here referred to were practised by the heathen world is well known. See Notes on Rom. i. 26–31. That many who became Christians were guilty of them before their conversion is clear from this passage. The fact that *they* were thus converted shows the power of the gospel, and also that we should not despair in regard to those who are indulging in these vices now. They seem indeed almost to be hopeless, but we should remember that many who became Christians when the gospel was first preached, as well as since, were of this character. If *they* were reclaimed; if those who had been addicted to the gross and debasing vices referred to here, were brought into the kingdom of God, we should believe that those who are living in the same manner now may also be recovered. From the statement made in this verse, that 'the time past of our lives may *suffice* to have wrought the will of the Gentiles,' we may remark that the same may be said by all Christians of themselves ; the same thing is true of all who are living in sin. (1.) It is true of all who are Christians, and they feel it, that they lived *long enough* in sin. (*a*) They made a fair trial— many of them with ample opportunities; with abundant wealth ; with all that the fashionable world can furnish ; with all that can be derived from low and gross indulgences. Many who are now Christians had opportunities of living in splendour and ease; many moved in gay and brilliant circles ; many occupied stations of influence, or had brilliant prospects of distinction ; many gave indulgence to gross propensities ; many were the companions of the vile and the abandoned. Those who are *now* Christians, take the church at large, have had ample opportunity of making the fullest trial of what sin and the world can furnish. (*b*) They *all* feel that the past

is enough for this manner of living. It is 'sufficient' to satisfy them that the world cannot furnish what the soul demands. They need a better portion ; and they can now see that there is no reason why they should desire to continue the experiment in regard to what the world can furnish. On that unwise and wicked experiment they have expended time enough ; and satisfied with that, they desire to return to it no more. (2.) The same thing is true of the wicked —of all who are living for the world. The time past *should* be regarded as sufficient to make an experiment in sinful indulgences ; for (*a*) the experiment has been made by millions before them, and has always failed ; and they can hope to find in sin only what has always been found—disappointment, mortification, and despair. (*b*) *They* have made a sufficient experiment. They have never found in those indulgences what they flattered themselves they would find, and they have seen enough to satisfy them that what the immortal soul needs can never be obtained there. (*c*) They have spent sufficient *time* in this hopeless experiment. Life is short. Man has no time to waste. He may soon die—and at whatever period of life any one may be who is living in sin, we may say to him that he has already wasted *enough* of life ; he has thrown away *enough* of probation in a fruitless attempt to find happiness where it can never be found. For any purpose whatever for which any one could ever suppose it to be desirable to live in sin, the past should suffice. But why should it ever be deemed desirable at all? The fruits of sin are always disappointment, tears, death, despair.

4. *Wherein they think it strange.* In respect to which vices, they who were once your partners and accomplices now think it strange that you no longer unite with them. They do not understand the reasons why you have left them. They regard you as abandoning a course of life which has much to attract and to make life merry, for a severe and gloomy superstition. This is a true account of

the feelings which the people of the world have when their companions and friends leave them and become Christians. It is to them a strange and unaccountable thing, that they give up the pleasures of the world for a course of life which to them seems to promise anything but happiness. Even the kindred of the Saviour regarded him as 'beside himself,' (Mark iii. 21,) and Festus supposed that Paul was mad, Acts xxvi. 24. There is almost nothing which the people of the world so little comprehend as the reasons which influence those with ample means of worldly enjoyment to leave the circles of gaiety and vanity, and to give themselves to the serious employments of religion. The epithets of fool, enthusiast, fanatic, are terms which frequently occur to the heart to denote this, if they are not always allowed to escape from the lips. The *reasons* why they esteem this so strange, are something like the following : (1.) They do not appreciate the *motives* which influence those who leave them. They feel that it is proper to enjoy the world, and to make life cheerful, and they do not understand what it is to act under a deep sense of responsibility to God, and with reference to eternity. They live for themselves. They seek happiness as the end and aim of life. They have never been accustomed to direct the mind onward to another world, and to the account which they must soon render at the bar of God. Unaccustomed to act from any higher motives than those which pertain to the present world, they cannot appreciate the conduct of those who begin to live and act for eternity. (2.) They do not yet see the guilt and folly of sinful pleasures. They are not convinced of the deep sinfulness of the human soul, and they think it strange that others should abandon a course of life which seems to them so innocent. They do not see why those who have been so long accustomed to these indulgences should have changed their opinions, and why they now regard those things as sinful which they once considered to be harmless. (3.) They do not see the force of the argument for religion. Not having the views of the unspeakable importance of religious truth and duty which Christians now

have, they wonder that they should break off from the course of life which they formerly pursued, and separate from the mass of their fellow-men. Hence they sometimes regard the conduct of Christians as amiable weakness ; sometimes as superstition ; sometimes as sheer folly ; sometimes as madness ; and sometimes as sourness and misanthropy. In all respects they esteem it *strange*.

"Lions and beasts of savage name
Put on the nature of the lamb,
While the wide world esteems it strange,
Gaze, and admire, and hate the change."

¶ *That ye run not with* them. There may be an allusion here to the well-known orgies of Bacchus, in which his votaries *ran* as if excited by the furies, and were urged on as if transported with madness. See Ovid, Metam. iii. 529, thus translated by Addison :

"For now, through prostrate Greece, young Bacchus rode,
Whilst howling matrons celebrate the god ;
All ranks and sexes to his *orgies* ran,
To mingle in the pomp and fill the train."

The language, however, will well describe revels of any sort, and at any period of the world. ¶ *To the same excess of riot.* The word rendered *excess* (ἀνάχυσις) means, properly, a *pouring out, an affusion;* and the idea here is, that all the sources and forms of riot and disorder were *poured out together.* There was no withholding, no restraint. The most unlimited indulgence was given to the passions. This was the case in the disorder referred to among the ancients, as it is the case now in scenes of midnight revelry. On the meaning of the word *riot*, see Notes on Eph. v. 18; Tit. i. 6. ¶ *Speaking evil of* you. Gr., *blaspheming.* Notes, Matt. ix. 3. The meaning here is, that they used harsh and reproachful epithets of those who would not unite with them in their revelry. They called them fools, fanatics, hypocrites, &c. The idea is not that they blasphemed God, or that they charged Christians with crime, but that they used language fitted to injure the feelings, the character, the reputation of those who would no longer unite with them in the ways of vice and folly. 5. *Who shall give account.* That is, they shall not do this with impunity. They are guilty in this of a great wrong

5 Who shall give account to him that is ready to judge the quick and the dead.

6 For, for this cause was the gos-

a Mat.24.9.

pel preached also to them that are dead, that they might be judged *a* according to men in the flesh, but live *b* according to God in the spirit.

b Re.14.13.

and they must answer for it to God. ¶ *That is ready to judge.* That is, 'who is prepared to judge'—τῷ ἑτοίμως ἔχοντι. See the phrase used in Acts xxi. 13: 'I am *ready* not to be bound only, but also to die at Jerusalem.' 2 Cor. xii. 14: 'The third time I am *ready* to come to you.' Compare the word *ready*—ἕτοιμός—in Matt. xxii. 4, 8; xxiv. 44; xxv. 10; Luke xii. 40; xxii. 33; 1 Pet. i. 5. The meaning is, not that he was *about* to do it, or that the day of judgment was near at hand —whatever the apostle may have supposed to be true on that point—but that he was *prepared* for it; all the arrangements were made with reference to it; there was nothing to hinder it. ¶ *To judge the quick and the dead.* The *living* and the dead; that is, those who shall be alive when he comes, and those in their graves. This is a common phrase to denote all who shall be brought before the bar of God for judgment. See Notes, Acts x. 42; 1 Thess. iv. 16, 17; 2 Tim. iv. 1. The meaning in this connection seems to be, that they should bear their trials and the opposition which they would meet with patiently, not feeling that they were forgotten, nor attempting to avenge themselves; for the Lord would vindicate them when he should come to judgment, and call those who had injured them to an account for all the wrongs which they had done to the children of God.

6. *For, for this cause.* The expression, 'For, for this cause,' refers to an *end* to be reached, or an *object* to be gained, or a *reason* why anything referred to is done. The end or reason why the thing referred to here, to wit, that 'the gospel was preached to the dead,' was done, is stated in the subsequent part of the verse to have been 'that they might be judged,' &c. It was with reference to this, or in order that this might be, that the gospel was preached to them. ¶ *Was the gospel preached also to them that are dead.* Many, as Doddridge, Whitby, and others,

understand this of those who are *spiritually dead*, that is, the Gentiles, and suppose that the object for which this was done was that 'they might be brought to such a state of life as their carnal neighbours would look upon as a kind of condemnation and death.'— *Doddridge*. Others have supposed that it refers to those who had suffered martyrdom in the cause of Christianity; others, that it refers to the sinners of the old world, (*Saurin*,) expressing a hope that some of them might be saved; and others, that it means that the Saviour went down and preached to those who are dead, in accordance with one of the interpretations given of chap. iii. 19. It seems to me that the most natural and obvious interpretation is to refer it to those who were *then* dead, to whom the gospel had been preached when living, and who had become true Christians. This is the interpretation proposed by Wetstein, Rosenmüller, Bloomfield, and others. In support of this it may be said, (1.) that this is the natural and obvious meaning of the word *dead*, which should be understood literally, unless there is some good reason in the connection for departing from the common meaning of the word. (2.) The apostle had just used the word in that sense in the previous verse. (3.) This will suit the connection, and accord with the design of the apostle. He was addressing those who were suffering persecution. It was natural, in such a connection, to refer to those who had died in the faith, and to show, for their encouragement, that though they had been put to death, yet they still lived to God. He therefore says, that the design in publishing the gospel to them was, that though they might be judged by men in the usual manner, and put to death, yet that in respect to their higher and nobler nature, *the spirit*, they might live unto God. It was not uncommon nor unnatural for the apostles, in writing to those who were suffering persecution, to refer to those who had been removed

7 But the end *a* of all things is at
a Ja.5.8,9.   *b* Lu.21.36.

hand : be ye therefore sober, and
watch *b* unto prayer.

by death, and to make their condition and example an argument for fidelity and perseverance. Compare 1 Thess. iv. 13; Rev. xiv. 13. ¶ *That they might be judged according to men in the flesh.* That is, *so far as men are concerned,* (κατὰ ἀνθρώπους,) or in respect to the treatment which they received from men in the flesh, they were judged and condemned ; in respect to God, and the treatment which they received from him, (κατὰ Θεὸν,) they would live in spirit. Men judged them severely, and put them to death for their religion ; God gave them life, and saved them. By the one they were condemned in the flesh—so far as pain, and sorrow, and death could be inflicted on the body; by the other they were made to live in spirit—to be his, to live with him. The word *judged* here, I suppose, therefore, to refer to a sentence passed on them for their religion, consigning them to death for it. There is a *particle* in the original—μὶν, *indeed*—which has not been retained in the common translation, but which is quite important to the sense : 'that they might *indeed* be judged in the flesh, but live,' &c. The direct object or design of preaching the gospel to them was not that they might be condemned and put to death by man, but this was *indeed* or *in fact* one of the results in the way to a higher object. ¶ *But live according to God.* In respect to God, or so far as he was concerned. By *him* they would not be condemned. By *him* they would be made to live—to have the true life. The gospel was preached to them *in order* that so far as God was concerned, so far as their relation to him was concerned, so far as he would deal with them, they might *live.* The word *live* here seems to refer to the *whole life* that was the consequence of their being brought under the power of the gospel ; (*a*) that they might have *spiritual* life imparted to them ; (*b*) that they might live a life of holiness in this world ; (*c*) that they might live hereafter in the world to come. In one respect, and so far as men were concerned, their embracing the gospel was

followed by *death ;* in another respect, and so far as God was concerned, it was followed by *life.* The value and permanence of the latter, as contrasted with the former, seems to have been the thought in the mind of the apostle in encouraging those to whom he wrote to exercise patience in their trials, and to show fidelity in the service of their Master. ¶ *In the spirit.* In their souls, as contrasted with their body. In respect to that—to the flesh—they were put to death ; in respect to their souls—their higher natures—they were made truly to live. The argument, then, in this verse is, that in the trials which we endure on account of religion, we should remember the example of those who have suffered for it, and should remember why the gospel was preached to them. It was in a subordinate sense, indeed, that they might glorify God by a martyr's death ; but in a higher sense, that in this world and the next they might truly live. The flesh might suffer in consequence of their embracing the gospel that was preached to them, but the soul would live. Animated by their example, we should be willing to suffer in the flesh, if we may for ever live with God.

7. *But the end of all things is at hand.* This declaration is also evidently designed to support and encourage them in their trials, and to excite them to lead a holy life, by the assurance that the end of all things was drawing nigh. The phrase, ' the end of all things,' would naturally refer to the end of the world ; the winding up of human affairs. It is not absolutely certain, however, that the apostle used it here in this sense. It might mean that *so far as they were concerned,* or *in respect to them,* the end of all things drew near. Death is to each one the end of all things here below ; the end of his plans and of his interest in all that pertains to sublunary affairs. Even *if* the phrase did originally and properly refer to the end of the world, it is probable that it would soon come to denote the end of life in relation to the affairs of each individual ; since, if it was be-

lieved that the end of the world was near, it must consequently be believed that the termination of the earthly career of each one also drew near to a close. It is possible that the latter signification may have come ultimately to predominate, and that Peter may have used it in this sense without referring to the other. Comp. Notes on 2 Pet. iii. 8–14, for his views on this subject. See also Notes on Rom. xiii. 11, 12. The word rendered 'is at hand,' (ἤγγικε,) may refer either to proximity of place or *time*, and it always denotes that the place or the time referred to was not far off. In the former sense, as referring to nearness of *place*, see Matt. xxi. 1; Mark xi. 1; Luke vii. 12; xv. 25; xviii. 35, 40; xix. 29, 37, 41; xxiv. 15; Acts ix. 3; x. 9; xxi. 33; in the latter sense, as referring to *time* as being near, see Matt. iii. 2; iv. 17; x. 7; xxi. 34; xxvi. 45; Mark i. 15; Luke xxi. 20, 28; Acts vii. 17; Rom. xiii. 12; Heb. x. 25; 1 Pet. iv. 7. The idea as applied to *time*, or to *an approaching event*, is undoubtedly that it is *close by; it is not far off; it will soon occur*. If this refers to the end of the world, it would mean that it was soon to occur; if to death, that this was an event which could not be far distant—perhaps an event that was to be hastened by their trials. The fact that it is such language as we now naturally address to men, saying that in respect to them 'the end of all things is at hand,' shows that it cannot be demonstrated that Peter did not use it in the same sense, and consequently that it cannot be proved that he meant to teach that the end of the world was then soon to occur. ¶ *Be ye therefore sober.* Serious; thoughtful; considerate. Let a fact of so much importance make a solemn impression on your mind, and preserve you from frivolity, levity, and vanity. See the word explained in the Notes on 1 Tim. iii. 2. ¶ *And watch unto prayer.* Be looking out for the end of all things in such a manner as to lead you to embrace all proper opportunities for prayer. Comp. Notes on Matt. xxvi. 39, 41. The word rendered *watch*, means to be sober, temperate, abstinent, especially in respect to wine; then watchful, circumspect. The important truth, then, taught by

this passage is, that *the near approach of the end of all things should make us serious and prayerful*. I. The *end* may be regarded as approaching. This is true (1) of all things; of the winding up of the affairs of this world. It is constantly drawing nearer and nearer, and no one can tell how soon it will occur. The period is wisely hidden from the knowledge of all men, (see Matt. xxiv. 36; Acts i. 7,) among other reasons, in order that we may be always ready. No man can certainly at what time it will come; no man can demonstrate that it *may not* come at any moment. Everywhere in the Scriptures it is represented that it will come at an unexpected hour, as a thief in the night, and when the mass of men shall be slumbering in false security, Matt. xxiv. 37–39, 42, 43; 1 Thess. v. 2; Luke xxi. 34. (2.) It is near in relation to each one of us. The day of our death *cannot be* far distant; it *may be* very near. The very next thing that we may have to do, may be to lie down and die. II. It is proper that such a nearness of the end of all things should lead us to be serious, and to pray. (1.) *To be serious;* for (*a*) the end of all things, in regard to us, is a most important event. It closes our probation. It fixes our character. It seals up our destiny. It makes all ever onward in character and doom unchangeable. (*b*) We are so made as to be serious in view of such events. God has so constituted the mind, that when we lose property, health, or friends; when we look into a grave, or are beset with dangers; when we are in the room of the dying or the dead, we are serious and thoughtful. It is unnatural *not* to be so. Levity and frivolity on such occasions are as contrary to all the finer and better feelings of our nature as they are to the precepts of the Bible. (*c*) There are *advantages* in seriousness of mind. It enables us to take better views of things, Eccl. vii. 2, 3. A calm, sober, sedate mind is the best for a contemplation of truth, and for looking at things as they are. (2.) *To be watchful unto prayer.* (*a*) Men naturally pray when they suppose that the end of all things is coming. An earthquake induces them to pray. An eclipse, or any other supposed prodigy,

8 And above all things have fervent charity among yourselves: for *a* charity ¹ shall cover the multitude of sins.

9 Use hospitality *b* one to another, without grudging.

a 1 Co.13.7.　　　1 Or. *will*.　　　*b* He.13.2,16.

leads men to pray if they suppose the end of the world is drawing near. A shipwreck, or any other sudden danger, leads them to pray, Ps. cvii. 28. So men often pray in sickness who have never prayed in days of health. (*b*) It is *proper* to do it. Death is an important event, and in anticipation of such an event we should pray. Who can help us then but God? Who can conduct us through the dark valley but he? Who can save us amidst the wrecks and ruins of the universe but he? Who can dissipate our fears, and make us calm amidst the convulsions of dissolving nature, but God? As that event, therefore, may come upon us at any hour, it should lead us to constant prayer; and the more so because, *when* it comes, we may be in no state of mind to pray. The posture in which we should feel that it would be most appropriate that the messenger of death should find us, would be that of prayer.

8. *And above all things.* More than all things else. ¶ *Have fervent charity among yourselves.* Warm, ardent *love* towards each other. On the nature of *charity*, see Notes on 1 Cor. xiii. 1. The word rendered *fervent*, means properly *extended;* then intent, earnest, fervent. ¶ *For charity shall cover the multitude of sins.* Love to another shall so cover or hide a great many imperfections in him, that you will not notice them. This passage is quoted from Prov. x. 12 : 'Love covereth all sins.' For the *truth* of it we have only to appeal to the experience of every one. (*a*) True love to another makes us kind to his imperfections, charitable towards his faults, and often blind even to the existence of faults. We *would not* see the imperfections of those whom we love; and our attachment for what we esteem their real excellencies, makes us insensible to their errors. (*b*) If we love them we are ready to cover over their faults, even those which we may see in them. Of love the Christian poet says—

'Tis gentle, delicate, and kind,
To faults compassionate or blind.

The passage before us is not the same in signification as that in James v. 20, 'He which converteth the sinner from the error of his way shall save a soul from death, and shall hide a multitude of sins.' See Notes on that passage. That passage means, that by the *conversion* of another the sins of him who is converted shall be covered over, or not brought to judgment for condemnation; that is, they shall be covered over so far as *God* is concerned :—this passage means that, under the influence of love, the sins of another shall be covered over so far as *we* are concerned; that is, they shall be unobserved or forgiven. The language here used does not mean, as the Romanists maintain, that 'charity shall procure us pardon for a multitude of sins ;' for, besides that such a doctrine is contrary to the uniform teachings of the Scriptures elsewhere, it is a departure from the obvious meaning of the passage. The *subject* on which the apostle is treating is the advantage of *love* in our conduct towards others, and this he enforces by saying that it will make us kind to their imperfections, and lead us to overlook their faults. It is nowhere taught in the Scriptures that our 'charity' to others will be an *atonement* or *expiation* for our own offences. If it could be so, the atonement made by Christ would have been unnecessary. Love, however, is of inestimable value in the treatment of others; and imperfect as we are, and liable to go astray, we all have occasion to cast ourselves on the charity of our brethren, and to avail ourselves much and often of that 'love which covers over a multitude of sins.'

9. *Use hospitality one to another.* On the duty of hospitality, see Notes on Rom. xii. 13; Heb. xiii. 2. ¶ *Without grudging.* Greek, 'without murmurs ;' that is, without complaining of the hardship of doing it; of the time, and expense, and trouble required in doing

10 As every man hath received *a* the gift, *even so* minister the same one to another, as good stewards *b* of the manifold grace of God.

11 If any man speak, *let him speak* as the oracles of God; if any

man minister, *let him do it* as of the ability which God giveth: that God in all *c* things may be glorified through Jesus Christ, to *d* whom be praise and dominion for ever and ever. Amen.

a Ro.12.6-8.   *b* Lu.12.42.   *c* 1 Co.10.31.   *d* Re.1.6.

it. The idea of *grudging*, in the common sense of that word—that is, of doing it *unwillingly*, or regretting the expense, and considering it as ill-bestowed, or as not producing an equivalent of any kind—is not exactly the idea here. It is that we are to do it without murmuring or complaining. It greatly enhances the value of hospitality, that it be done on our part with entire cheerfulness. One of the duties involved in it is to make a guest happy; and this can be done in no other way than by showing him that he is welcome. 10. *As every man hath received the gift.* The word rendered *the gift,* (χάρισμα,) in the Greek, without the article, means endowment of any kind, but especially that conferred by the Holy Spirit. Here it seems to refer to every kind of endowment by which we can do good to others; especially every kind of qualification furnished by religion by which we can help others. It does not refer here particularly to the ministry of the word—though it is applicable to that, and includes that—but to all the gifts and graces by which we can contribute to the welfare of others. All this is regarded as a gift, or *charisma*, of God. It is not owing to ourselves, but is to be traced to him. See the word explained in the Notes on 1 Tim. iv. 14. ¶ *Even so minister the same one to another.* In anything by which you can benefit another. Regard what you have and they have not as a *gift* bestowed upon you by God for the common good, and be ready to impart it as the wants of others require. The word *minister* here (διακονοῦντες) would refer to any kind of ministering, whether by counsel, by advice, by the supply of the wants of the poor, or by preaching. It has here no reference to any one of these exclusively; but means, that in whatever God has favoured us more than others, we should be ready to *minister*

to their wants. See 2 Tim. i. 18; 2 Cor. iii. 3; viii. 19, 20. ¶ *As good stewards.* Regarding yourselves as the mere *stewards* of God; that is, as appointed by him to do this work for him, and intrusted by him with what is needful to benefit others. *He* intends to do them good, but he means to do it through your instrumentality, and has intrusted to you as a steward what he designed to confer on them. This is the true idea, in respect to any special endowments of talent, property, or grace, which we may have received from God. Comp. Notes on 1 Cor. iv. 1, 2; Luke xvi. 1, 2, 8. ¶ *Of the manifold grace of God.* The grace or favour of God evinced in many ways, or by a variety of gifts. His favours are not confined to one single thing; as, for example, to talent for doing good by preaching; but are extended to a great many things by which we may do good to others—influence, property, reputation, wisdom, experience. All these are to be regarded as his gifts; all to be employed in doing good to others as we have opportunity. 11. *If any man speak.* As a preacher, referring here particularly to the office of the ministry. ¶ Let him speak *as the oracles of God.* As the oracles of God speak; to wit, in accordance with the truth which God has revealed, and with an impressive sense of the responsibility of delivering a message from him. The word rendered *oracles* (λόγια) means, properly, something *spoken* or *uttered;* then anything uttered by God —a Divine communication—a revelation. See Notes, Rom. iii. 2; Heb. v. 12. See the general duty here inculcated illustrated at length in the Notes on Rom. xii. 6-8. The passage here has a strong resemblance to the one in Romans. ¶ *If any man minister.* διακονεῖ. This may refer either, so far as the *word* is concerned, to the office

12 Beloved, think it not strange concerning the fiery *a* trial which is to try you, as though some strange thing happened unto you:

13 But rejoice, *b* inasmuch as ye are partakers of Christ's sufferings; that, when *c* his glory shall be re-

vealed, ye may be glad also with exceeding joy.

14 If *d* ye be reproached for the name of Christ, happy *are ye ;* for the spirit of glory and of God resteth upon you: on their part he is evil spoken of, but on your part he is glorified.

a 1 Co.3.13.   *b* Ja.1.2.   *c* 2 Ti.2.12.   *d* Mat.5.11.

---

of a deacon, or to *any* service which one renders to another. See ver. 10. The word commonly refers to service in general; to attendance on another, or to aid rendered to another; to the distribution of alms, &c. It seems probable that the word here does not refer to the office of a *deacon* as such, because the peculiarity of that office was to take charge of the poor of the church, and of the funds provided for them, (see Acts vi. 2, 3;) but the apostle here says that they to whom he referred should 'minister as of the *ability which God giveth,*' which seems to imply that it was rather to distribute what was their *own,* than what was committed to them by the church. The word may refer to any aid which we render to others in the church, as distributing alms, attending on the sick, &c. Comp. Notes, Rom. xii. 7, 8. ¶ *As of the ability which God giveth.* In regard to property, talent, strength, influence, &c. This is the limit of all obligation. No one is bound to go *beyond* his ability; every one is required to *come up* to it. Comp. Mark xiv. 8; Luke xvii. 10. ¶ *That God in all things may be glorified.* That he may be honoured; to wit, by our doing all the good we can to others, and thus showing the power of his religion. See Notes, 1 Cor. x. 31. ¶ *Through Jesus Christ.* That is, as the medium through whom all those holy influences come by which God is honoured. ¶ *To whom.* That is, to God; for he is the main subject of the sentence. The apostle says that in all things he is to be glorified by us, and then adds in this doxology that he is *worthy* to be thus honoured. Comp. Rev. i. 6; Notes, 2 Tim. iv. 18. Many, however, suppose that the reference here is to the Son of God. That it would be true of him, and appropriate, see Notes, Rom. ix. 5.

12. *Beloved, think it not strange.* Do

not consider it as anything which you had no reason to expect; as anything which may not happen to others also. ¶ *Concerning the fiery trial which is to try you.* Referring, doubtless, to some severe persecution which was then impending. We have not the means of determining precisely what this was. The word rendered *fiery trial* (πυρώσει) occurs only here and in Rev. xviii. 9, 18; in both of which latter places it is rendered *burning.* It means, properly, *a being on fire, burning, conflagration ;* and then any severe trial. It cannot be demonstrated from this word that they were literally to suffer by *fire,* but it is clear that some heavy calamity was before them. ¶ *As though some strange thing happened unto you.* Something unusual ; something which did not occur to others.

13. *But rejoice, inasmuch as ye are partakers of Christ's sufferings.* That is, sufferings of the same kind that he endured, and inflicted for the same reasons. Comp. Col. i. 24; James i. 2; Notes, Matt. v. 12. The meaning here is, that they were to regard it as a matter of rejoicing that they were identified with Christ, even in suffering. See this sentiment illustrated at length in the Notes on Phil. iii. 10. ¶ *That, when his glory shall be revealed.* At the day of judgment. See Notes, Matt. xxvi. 30. ¶ *Ye may be glad also with exceeding joy.* Being admitted to the rewards which he will then confer on his people. Comp. 1 Thess. ii. 19. Every good man will have joy when, immediately at death, he is received into the presence of his Saviour ; but his joy will be complete only when, in the presence of assembled worlds, he shall hear the sentence which shall confirm him in happiness for ever.

14. *If ye be reproached for the name of Christ, happy* are ye. That is, in

15 But let none of you suffer as a murderer, or *as* a thief, or *as* an evil doer, or as a busy-body in other men's matters.

16 Yet if *any man suffer* as a Christian, let him not be ashamed ; but let him glorify God on this behalf.

his cause, or on his account. See Notes, Matt. v. 11. The sense of the word *happy* here is the same as *blessed* in Matt. v. 3–5, &c. It means that they were to regard their condition or lot as a blessed one; not that they would find personal and positive enjoyment on being reproached and vilified. It would be a blessed condition, because it would be like that of their Saviour; would show that they were his friends ; would be accompanied with rich spiritual influences in the present world; and would be followed by the rewards of heaven. ¶ *For the spirit of glory and of God resteth upon you.* The glorious and Divine Spirit. There is no doubt that there is reference here to the Holy Spirit ; and the meaning is, that they might expect that that Spirit would rest upon them, or abide with them, if they were persecuted for the cause of Christ. There may be some allusion here, in the language, to the fact that the Spirit of God descended and abode on the Saviour at his baptism, (John i. 33;) and, in like manner, they might hope to have the same Spirit resting on them. The essential idea is, that, if they were called to suffer in the cause of the Redeemer, they would not be left or forsaken. They might hope that God would impart his Spirit to them in proportion to their sufferings in behalf of religion, and that they would have augmented joy and peace. This is doubtless the case with those who suffer persecution, and this is the secret reason why they are so sustained in their trials. Their persecutions are made the reason of a much more copious effusion of the Spirit on their souls. The same principle applies, doubtless, to all the forms of trial which the children of God pass through ; and in sickness, bereavement, loss of property, disappointment in their worldly plans, and death itself, they may hope that larger measures of the Spirit's influences will rest upon them. Hence it is often gain to the believer to suffer. ¶ *On their part.* So far as they are

concerned ; or by them. ¶ *He is evil spoken of.* That is, the Holy Spirit. They only *blaspheme* him, (Greek ;) they reproach his sacred influences by their treatment of you and your religion. ¶ *But on your part he is glorified.* By your manner of speaking of him, and by the honour done to him in the patience evinced in your trials, and in your purity of life.

15. *But let none of you suffer as a murderer.* If you must be called to suffer, see that it be not for crime. Comp. Notes, chap. iii. 14, 17. They were to be careful that their sufferings were brought upon them only in consequence of their religion, and not because any crime could be laid to their charge. If even such charges were brought against them, there should be no pretext furnished for them by their lives. ¶ *As an evil doer.* As a wicked man ; or as guilty of injustice and wrong towards others. ¶ *Or as a busy-body in other men's matters.* The Greek word here used (ἀλλοτριοεπίσκοπος) occurs nowhere else in the New Testament. It means, properly, an inspector of strange things, or of the things of others. Professor Robinson (*Lex.*) supposes that the word *may* refer to one who is ' a director of heathenism ;' but the more obvious signification, and the one commonly adopted, is that which occurs in our translation —*one who busies himself with what does not concern him;* that is, one who pries into the affairs of another ; who attempts to control or direct them as if they were his own. In respect to the vice here condemned, see Notes, Phil. ii. 4. Comp. 2 Thess. iii. 11, and 1 Tim. v. 13.

16. *Yet if* any man suffer *as a Christian.* Because he is a Christian ; if he is persecuted on account of his religion. This was often done, and they had reason to expect that it might occur in their own case. Comp. Notes, chap. iii. 17. On the import of the word *Christian,* and the reasons why the name was given to the disciples of the Lord Jesus, see Notes, Acts xi. 26. ¶ *Let him not be*

17 For the time *is come* that judgment must begin ᵃ at the house of

a Is.10.12; Je.49.12; Eze.9.6.

God: and if *it* first *begin* at us, what
shall the end *be* of them that obey
not the gospel of God ?

ashamed. (1.) Ashamed of religion so
as to refuse to suffer on account of it.
(2.) Ashamed that he *is* despised and
maltreated. He is to regard his religion
as every way honourable, and all that
fairly results from it in time and eternity as in every respect desirable. He
is not to be ashamed to be called a
Christian ; he is not to be ashamed of
the doctrines taught by his religion ; he
is not to be ashamed of the Saviour
whom he professes to love ; he is not to
be ashamed of the society and fellowship
of those who are true Christians, poor
and despised though they may be ; he
is not to be ashamed to perform any of
the duties demanded by his religion ; he
is not to be ashamed to have his name
cast out, and himself subjected to reproach and scorn. A man should be
ashamed only of that which is wrong.
He should glory in that which is right,
whatever may be the consequences to
himself. Christians now, though not
subjected to open persecution, are frequently reproached by the world on account of their religion ; and though the
rack may not be employed, and the fires
of martyrdom are not enkindled, yet it
is often true that one who is a believer
is called to ' suffer as a Christian.' He
may be reviled and despised. His views
may be regarded as bigoted, narrow,
severe. Opprobrious epithets, on account
of his opinions, may be applied to him.
His former friends and companions may
leave him because he has become a
Christian. A wicked father, or a gay
and worldly mother, may oppose a child,
or a husband may revile a wife, on account of their religion. In all these
cases, the same spirit essentially is required which was enjoined on the early
Christian martyrs. We are never to be
ashamed of our religion, whatever results may follow from our attachment
to it. Comp. Notes, Rom. i. 16. ¶ *But
let him glorify God on this behalf.* Let
him praise God that he is deemed not
unworthy to suffer in such a cause. It
is a matter of thankfulness (1.) that
they may have *this* evidence that they

are true Christians ; (2,) that they may
desire the advantages which may result
from suffering as Christ did, and in his
cause. See Notes, Acts v. 41, where
the sentiment here expressed is fully
illustrated. Comp. Notes, Phil. iii. 10 ;
Col. i. 24.
　17. *For the time* is come. That is,
this is now to be expected. There is
reason to think that this trial will now
occur, and there is a propriety that it
should be made. Probably the apostle
referred to some indications then apparent that this was about to take place.
¶ *That judgment must begin.* The
word *judgment* here (κρίμα) seems to
mean *the severe trial which would determine character.* It refers to such
calamities as would settle the question whether there was any religion, or
would test the value of that which was
professed. It was to '*begin*' at the house
of God, or be applied to the church first,
in order that the nature and worth of
religion might be seen. The reference
is, doubtless, to some fearful calamity
which would primarily fall on the ' house
of God ;' that is, to some form of persecution which was to be let loose upon
the church. ¶ *At the house of God.*
Benson, Bloomfield, and many others,
suppose that this refers to the *Jews,*
and to the calamities that were to come
around the temple and the holy city
about to be destroyed. But the more
obvious reference is to *Christians,* spoken
of as the *house* or *family* of God. There
is probably in the language here an allusion to Ezek. ix. 6 : ' Slay utterly old
and young, both maids, and little children, and women ; *and begin at my
sanctuary.*' Comp. Jer. xxv. 29. But
the language used here by the apostle
does not denote literally the temple, or
the Jews, but those who were in his
time regarded as the people of God—
Christians—the church. So the phrase
(בֵּית יְהֹוָה) *house of Jehovah* is used to
denote the family or people of God,
Numb. xii. 7; Hos. viii. 1. Comp. also
1 Tim. iii. 15, and the Note on that
verse. The sense here is, therefore, that

18 And if *a* the righteous scarcely be saved, where shall the ungodly and the sinner appear?

a Je.25.29; Lu.23.31.

the series of calamities referred to were to commence with the church, or were to come first upon the people of God. Schoettgen here aptly quotes a passage from the writings of the Rabbins : 'Punishments never come into the world unless the wicked are in it; but they do not begin unless they commence first with the righteous.' ¶ *And if it first begin at us, what shall the end be of them that obey not the gospel of God ?* If God brings such trials upon us who have obeyed his gospel, what have we not reason to suppose he will bring upon those who are yet in their sins? And if we are selected first as the objects of this visitation, if there is that in us which requires such a method of dealing, what are we to suppose will occur in the end with those who make no pretensions to religion, but are yet living in open transgression? The sentiment is, that if God deals thus strictly with his people ; if there is that in them which makes the visitations of his judgment proper on them, there is a certainty that they who are not his people, but who live in iniquity, will in the end be overwhelmed with the tokens of severer wrath. Their punishment hereafter will be certain ; and who can tell what will be the measure of its severity? Every wicked man, when he sees the trials which God brings upon his own people, should tremble under the apprehension of the deeper calamity which will hereafter come upon himself. We may remark, (1.) that the judgments which God brings upon his own people make it certain that the wicked will be punished. If he does not spare his own people, why should he spare others? (2.) The punishment of the wicked is merely delayed. It *begins* at the house of God. Christians are tried, and are recalled from their wanderings, and are prepared by discipline for the heavenly world. The punishment of the wicked is often delayed to a future world, and in this life they have almost uninterrupted prosperity, but in the end it will be certain. See Psa. lxxiii. 1–19. The punishment will come *in the end.* It

cannot be evaded. Sooner or later justice requires that the wicked should be visited with the expressions of Divine displeasure on account of sin, and in the future world there will be ample time for the infliction of all the punishment which they deserve.

18. *And if the righteous scarcely be saved.* If they are saved *with difficulty.* The word here used (μόλις) occurs in the following places : Acts xiv. 18, '*scarce* restrained they the people;' xxvii. 7, '*and scarce* were come over against Cnidus;' ver. 8, '*and hardly* passing it;' ver. 16, 'we had much work to come by the boat'—literally, we were able *with difficulty* to get the boat; Rom. v. 7, '*scarcely* for a righteous man will one die ;' and in the passage before us. The word implies that there is some difficulty, or obstruction, so that the thing came very near not to happen, or so that there was much risk about it. Compare Luke xiii. 31. The apostle in this passage seems to have had his eye on a verse in Proverbs, (xi. 31,) and he has merely expanded and illustrated it : 'Behold, the righteous shall be recompensed in the earth : much more the wicked and the sinner.' By the question which he employs, he *admits* that the righteous are saved with difficulty, or that there are perils which jeopard their salvation, and which are of such a kind as to make it very near not to happen. They *would* indeed be saved, but it would be in such a manner as to show that the circumstances were such as to render it, to human appearances, doubtful and problematical. This peril may have arisen from many circumstances : (*a*) The difficulty of forming a plan of salvation, involving a degree of wisdom wholly beyond that of man, and of such a character that beforehand it would have been problematical and doubtful whether it could be. There was but one way in which it could be done. But what human wisdom could have devised that, or thought of it? There was but one being who could save. But who would have supposed that the Son of God would have been willing to become a man, and

19 Wherefore, let them that suffer according to the will of God, commit *a* the keeping of their souls *to him* in well-doing, as unto a faithful Creator.

to die on a cross to do it? If *he* had been unwilling to come and die, the righteous could not have been saved. (*b*) The difficulty of bringing those who are saved to a willingness to accept of salvation. All were disposed alike to reject it; and there were many obstacles in the human heart, arising from pride, and selfishness, and unbelief, and the love of sin, which must be overcome before any would accept of the offer of mercy. There was but one agent who could overcome these things, and induce any of the race to embrace the gospel—the Holy Spirit. But who could have anticipated that the Spirit of God would have undertaken to renew and sanctify the polluted human heart? Yet, if *he* had failed, there could have been no salvation for any. (*c*) The difficulty of keeping them from falling away amidst the temptations and allurements of the world. Often it seems to be wholly doubtful whether those who have been converted *will be* kept to eternal life. They have so little religion; they yield so readily to temptation; they conform so much to the world; they have so little strength to bear up under trials, that it seems as if there was no power to preserve them and bring them to heaven. They are saved when they seemed *almost* ready to yield everything. (*d*) The difficulty of rescuing them from the power of the great enemy of souls. The adversary has vast power, and he *means*, if he can, to destroy those who are the children of God. Often they are in most imminent danger, and it seems to be a question of doubtful issue whether they will not be entirely overcome, and perish. It is no small matter to rescue a soul from the dominion of Satan, and to bring it to heaven, so that it shall be eternally safe. Through the internal struggles and the outward conflicts of life, it seems often a matter of doubt whether with all their effort they will be saved; and when they *are* saved, they will feel that they have been rescued from thousands of dangers, and that there has been many a time when they have stood on the very verge of ruin, and when, to human appearances, it was scarcely possible that they could be saved. ¶ *Where shall the ungodly and the sinner appear?* What hope is there of their salvation? The meaning is, that they would certainly perish; and the doctrine in the passage is, that the fact that the righteous are saved with so much difficulty is proof that the wicked will not be saved at all. This follows, because (*a*) there is the same difficulty in their salvation which there was in the salvation of those who became righteous; the same difficulty arising from the love of sin, the hardness of the heart, and the arts and power of the adversary. (*b*) No one can be saved without effort, and in fact the righteous are saved only by constant and strenuous effort on their part. But the wicked make no effort for their own salvation. They make use of no means for it; they put forth no exertions to obtain it; they do not make it a part of their plan of life. How, then, can they be saved? But *where* will they appear? I answer, (*a*) they will appear *somewhere*. They will not cease to exist when they pass away from this world. Not one of them will be annihilated; and though they vanish from the earth, and will be seen here no more, yet they will make their appearance in some other part of the universe. (*b*) They will appear at the judgment-seat, as all others will, to receive their sentence according to the deeds done in the body. It follows from this, (1.) that the wicked will certainly be destroyed. If the righteous are *scarcely* saved, how can *they* be? (2.) That there will be a state of future punishment, for this refers to what is to occur in the future world. (3.) That the punishment of the wicked will be eternal, for it is the opposite of what is meant by *saved*. The time will never come when it will be said that they are *saved!* But if so, their punishment must be eternal!

19. *Wherefore, let them that suffer according to the will of God.* That is,

CHAPTER V.

THE elders which are among you I exhort, who am also an elder, and a witness of the sufferings of Christ, and also a partaker of the glory *a* that shall be revealed :

a Ro.8.17,18.

who endure the kind of sufferings that he, by his Providence, shall appoint. Comp. chap. iii. 17; iv. 15, 16. ¶ *Commit the keeping of their souls* to him. Since there is so much danger ; since there is no one else that can keep them ; and since he is a Being so faithful, let them commit all their interests to him. Comp. Psa. xxxvii. 5. The word *souls* here ($\psi\nu\chi\grave{\alpha}s$) is equivalent to *themselves*. They were to leave everything in his hand, faithfully performing every duty, and not being anxious for the result. ¶ *In well doing.* Constantly doing good, or seeking to perform every duty in a proper manner. *Their* business was always to do right ; the result was to be left with God. A man who is engaged always in well-doing, may safely commit all his interest to God. ¶ *As unto a faithful Creator.* God may be trusted, or confided in, in all his attributes, and in all the relations which he sustains as Creator, Redeemer, Moral Governor, and Judge. In these, and in all other respects, we may come before him with confidence, and put unwavering trust in him. As *Creator* particularly ; as one who has brought us, and all creatures and things into being, we may be sure that he will be 'faithful' to the design which he had in view. From that design he will never depart until it is fully accomplished. He abandons no purpose which he has formed, and we may be assured that he will faithfully pursue it to the end. As *our* Creator we may come to him, and look to him for his protection and care. He made us. He had a design in our creation. He so endowed us that we might live for ever, and so that we might honour and enjoy him. He did not create us that we *might be* miserable ; nor does he wish that we *should be*. He formed us in such a way that, if we choose, we may be eternally happy. In that path in which he has appointed us to go, if we pursue it, we may be sure of his aid and protection. If we really aim to accomplish the purposes for which we were

made, we may be certain that he will show himself to be a '*faithful* Creator ;' one in whom we may always confide. And even though we have wandered from him, and have long forgotten why we were made, and have loved and served the creature more than the Creator, we may be sure, if we will return to him, that he will not forget the design for which he originally made us. *As* our Creator we may still confide in him. Redeemed by the blood of his Son, and renewed by his Spirit after the image of Him who created us, we may still go to him as our Creator, and may pray that even yet the high and noble ends for which we were made may be accomplished in us. Doing this, we shall find him as true to that purpose as though we had never sinned.

CHAPTER V.

ANALYSIS OF THE CHAPTER.

THIS chapter embraces the following subjects : I. An exhortation to the elders of the churches to be faithful to the flocks committed to their charge, vers. 1-4. II. An exhortation to the younger members of the church to evince all proper submission to those who were older ; to occupy the station in which they were placed with a becoming spirit, casting all their care on God, vers. 5-7. III. An exhortation to be sober and vigilant, in view of the dangers which beset them, and the arts and power of their great adversary, the devil, and especially to bear with patience the trials to which they were subjected, in common with their Christian brethren elsewhere, vers. 8-11. IV. Salutations, vers. 12-14.

1. *The elders which are among you I exhort.* The word *elder* means, properly, one who is old ; but it is frequently used in the New Testament as applicable to the officers of the church ; probably because aged persons were at first commonly appointed to these offices. See Notes on Acts xi. 30; xiv. 23; xv. 2. There is evidently an allusion here to the fact that such persons were selected

2 Feed *a* the flock of God ¹ which
is among you, taking the oversight
thereof, not by constraint, but will-

ingly ; *b* not for filthy lucre, *c* but
of a ready mind;

a Jn.21.15-17; Ac.20.28.   1 Or, *as much as in you is.*
b 1Co.9.17.   c 1 Ti.3.3,8.

on account of their *age*, because in the
following verses (4, seq.) the apostle
addresses particularly *the younger*. It is
worthy of remark, that he here refers
only to one class of ministers. He does
not speak of three 'orders,' of 'bishops,
priests, and deacons;' and the evidence
from the passage here is quite strong
that there *were* no such orders in the
churches of Asia Minor, to which this
epistle was directed. It is also worthy
of remark, that the word *'exhort'* is
here used. The language which Peter
uses is not that of stern and arbitrary
command ; it is that of kind and mild
Christian exhortation. Comp. Notes
on Philemon, 8, 9. ¶ *Who am also
an elder.* Gr., 'a fellow-presbyter,'
(συμπρεσβύτερος.) This word occurs nowhere else in the New Testament. It
means that he was a co-presbyter with
them ; and he makes this one of the
grounds of his exhortation to them. He
does not put it on the ground of his
apostolical authority; or urge it because
he was the 'vicegerent of Christ ;' or
because he was the head of the church;
or because he had any pre-eminence
over others in any way. Would he
have used this language if he had been
the 'head of the church' on earth ?
Would he if he supposed that the distinction between apostles and other
ministers was to be perpetuated? Would
he if he believed that there were to be
distinct orders of clergy ? The whole
drift of this passage is adverse to such a
supposition. ¶ *And a witness of the
sufferings of Christ.* Peter was indeed
a witness of the sufferings of Christ
when on his trial, and doubtless also
when he was scourged and mocked, and
when he was crucified. After his denial
of his Lord, he wept bitterly, and evidently then followed him to the place
where he was crucified, and, in company
with others, observed with painful solicitude the last agonies of his Saviour.
It is not, so far as I know, expressly
said in the Gospels that *Peter* was present at the crucifixion of the Saviour ;
but it is said (Luke xxiii. 49) that 'all

his acquaintance, and the women that
followed him from Galilee, stood afar
off, beholding these things,' and nothing
is more probable than that Peter was
among them. His warm attachment to
his Master, and his recent bitter repentance for having denied him, would
lead him to follow him to the place of
his death ; for after the painful act of
denying him he would not be likely to
expose himself to the charge of neglect,
or of any want of love again. His own
solemn declaration here makes it certain
that he was present. He alludes to it
now, evidently because it qualified him
to exhort those whom he addressed. It
would be natural to regard with peculiar
respect one who had actually seen the
Saviour in his last agony, and nothing
would be more impressive than an exhortation falling from the lips of such a
man. A son would be likely to listen
with great respect to *any* suggestions
which should be made by one who had
seen his father or mother die. The
impression which Peter had of that
scene he would desire to have transferred
to those whom he addressed, that by a
lively view of the sufferings of their
Saviour they might be excited to fidelity
in his cause. ¶ *And a partaker of the
glory that shall be revealed.* Another
reason to make his exhortation impressive and solemn. He felt that he was
an heir of life. He was about to partake of the glories of heaven. Looking
forward, as they did also, to the blessed
world before him and them, he had a
right to exhort them to the faithful performance of duty. Any one, who is
himself an heir of salvation, may appropriately exhort his fellow-Christians
to fidelity in the sevice of their common
Lord.
  2. *Feed the flock of God.* Discharge
the duties of a shepherd towards the
flock. On the word *feed*, see Notes on
John xxi. 15. It is a word which Peter
would be likely to remember, from the
solemn manner in which the injunction
to perform the duty was laid on him by
the Saviour. The direction means to

3 Neither as ¹ being lords over
1 Or, *overruling.*   *a* 1 Ti.4.12.

God's heritage, but being ensamples *a* to the flock.

take such an oversight of the church as a shepherd is accustomed to take of his flock. See Notes on John x. 1–16. ¶ *Which is among you.* Marg., *as much as in you is.* The translation in the text is the more correct. It means the churches which were among them, or over which they were called to preside. ¶ *Taking the oversight* thereof —ἐπισκοποῦντες. The fair translation of this word is, *discharging the episcopal office;* and the word implies all that is ever implied by the word *bishop* in the New Testament. This idea should have been expressed in the translation. The meaning is not merely *to take the oversight*—for that might be done in a subordinate sense by any one in office ; but it is to take such an oversight as is implied in the episcopate, or by the word *bishop.* The words *episcopate, episcopal,* and *episcopacy,* are merely the Greek word used here and its correlatives transferred to our language. The sense is that of overseeing; taking the oversight of ; looking after, as of a flock ; and the word has originally no reference to what is now spoken of as peculiarly the *episcopal* office. It is a word strictly applicable to *any* minister of religion, or officer of a church. In the passage before us this duty was to be performed by those who, in ver. 1, are called *presbyters,* or *elders;* and this is one of the numerous passages in the New Testament which prove that all that is properly implied in the performance of the episcopal functions pertained to those who were called *presbyters,* or *elders.* If so, there was no higher grade of ministers to which the peculiar duties of the episcopate were to be intrusted; that is, there was no class of officers corresponding to those who are now called *bishops.* Comp. Notes, Acts xx. 28. ¶ *Not by constraint, but willingly.* Not as if you felt that a heavy yoke was imposed on you, or a burden from which you would gladly be discharged. Go cheerfully to your duty as a work which you love, and act like a freeman in it, and not as a slave. Arduous as are the labours of the ministry, yet there is no work on earth in which a man can and

should labour more cheerfully. ¶ *Not for filthy lucre.* Shameful or dishonourable gain. Notes, 1 Tim. iii. 3. ¶ *But of a ready mind.* Cheerfully, promptly. We are to labour in this work, not under the influence of the desire of gain, but from the promptings of love. There is all the difference conceivable between one who does a thing because he is *paid* for it, and one who does it from *love*—between, for example, the manner in which one attends on us when we are sick who *loves* us, and one who is merely *hired* to do it. Such a difference is there in the spirit with which one who is actuated by mercenary motives, and one whose heart is in the work, will engage in the ministry. 3. *Neither as being lords.* Marg., *overruling.* The word here used (κατα-κυριεύω) is rendered *exercise dominion over,* in Matt. xx. 25 ; *exercise lordship over,* in Mark x. 42 ; and *overcame,* in Acts xix. 16. It does not elsewhere occur in the New Testament. It refers properly to that kind of jurisdiction which civil rulers or magistrates exercise. This is an exercise of *authority,* as contradistinguished from the influence of reason, persuasion, and example. The latter pertains to the ministers of religion ; the former is forbidden to them. Their dominion is not to be that of temporal lordship; it is to be that of love and truth. This command would prohibit all assumption of temporal power by the ministers of religion, and all conferring of titles of nobility on those who are preachers of the gospel. It needs scarcely to be said that it has been very little regarded in the church. ¶ *Over* God's *heritage*—τῶν κλήρων. Vulgate, *in cleris*—over the clergy. The Greek word here (κλῆρος—*kleros*) is that from which the word *clergy* has been derived; and some have interpreted it here as referring to the *clergy,* that is, to priests and deacons who are under the authority of a bishop. Such an interpretation, however, would hardly be adopted now. The word means properly, (*a,*) a *lot, die,* anything used in determining chances; (*b*) a *part* or *portion,* such as is assigned by lot ; hence (*c*) an *office* to which one

4 And when the chief ^a Shepherd shall appear, ye shall receive a crown ^b of glory that fadeth not away.

5 Likewise, ye younger, submit

a He.13.20.　　　　*b* 2 Ti.4.8.

yourselves unto the elder: yea, all ^c of you be subject one to another, and be clothed with humility: for God ^d resisteth the proud, and giveth grace to the humble.

c Ep.5.21.　　　　*d* Ja.4.6.

is designated or appointed, by lot or otherwise; and (*d*) in general any possession or heritage, Acts xxvi. 18; Col. i. 12. The meaning here is, 'not lording it over the possessions or the heritage of God.' The reference is, undoubtedly, to the church, as that which is peculiarly his property; his own in the world. Whitby and others suppose that it refers to the possessions or property of the church; Doddridge explains it—'not assuming dominion over those who fall to your lot,' supposing it to mean that they were not to domineer over the particular congregations committed by Providence to their care. But the other interpretation is most in accordance with the usual meaning of the word. ¶ *But being ensamples to the flock.* Examples. See Notes, 1 Tim. iv. 12. Peter has drawn here with great beauty, the appropriate character of the ministers of the gospel, and described the spirit with which they should be actuated in the discharge of the duties of their office. But how different it is from the character of many who have claimed to be ministers of religion; and especially how different from that corrupt communion which professes in a special manner to recognise Peter as the head, and the vicegerent of Christ. It is well remarked by Benson on this passage, that 'the church of Rome could not well have acted more directly contrary to this injunction of St. Peter's if she had studied to disobey it, and to form herself upon a rule that should be the reverse of this.'

4. *And when the chief Shepherd shall appear.* The prince of the pastors—the Lord Jesus Christ. 'Peter, in the passage above, ranks himself with the *elders;* here he ranks Christ himself with the *pastors*.'—*Benson.* See Notes, chap. ii. 25. Comp. Heb. xiii. 20. ¶ *Ye shall receive a crown of glory.* A glorious crown or diadem. Comp. Notes, 2 Tim. iv. 8. ¶ *That fadeth not away.* This is essentially the same word, though somewhat different in form, which occurs

in chap. i. 4. See Notes on that verse. The word occurs nowhere else in the New Testament. Comp. Notes, 1 Cor. ix. 25.

5. *Likewise, ye younger.* All younger persons of either sex. ¶ *Submit yourselves unto the elder.* That is, with the respect due to their age, and to the offices which they sustain. There is here, probably, a particular reference to those who sustained the *office* of elders or teachers, as the same word is used here which occurs in ver. 1. As there was an allusion in that verse, by the use of the word, to *age,* so there is in this verse to the fact that they sustained an *office* in the church. The general duty, however, is here implied, as it is everywhere in the Bible, that all suitable respect is to be shown to the aged. Comp. Lev. xix. 32; 1 Tim. v. 1; Acts xxiii. 4; 2 Pet. ii. 9. ¶ *Yea, all* of you *be subject one to another.* In your proper ranks and relations. You are not to attempt to lord it over one another, but are to treat each other with deference and respect. See Notes, Eph. v. 21; Phil. ii. 3. ¶ *And be clothed with humility.* The word here rendered *be clothed* (ἐγκομβόομαι) occurs nowhere else in the New Testament. It is derived from κόμβος—a strip, string, or loop to fasten a garment; and then the word refers to a garment that was fastened with strings. The word ἐγκόμβωμα (*egkomboma*) refers particularly to a long white apron, or outer garment, that was commonly worn by slaves. See *Rob. Lex.; Passow, Lex.* There is, therefore, peculiar force in the use of this word here, as denoting an humble mind. They were to be willing to take any place, and to perform any office, however humble, in order to serve and benefit others. They were not to assume a style and dignity of state and authority, as if they would lord it over others, or as if they were better than others; but they were to be willing to occupy any station, however humble, by which they might honour God. It is known

6 Humble *a* yourselves therefore under the mighty hand of God, that he may exalt you in due time:

7 Casting *b* all your care upon him; for he careth for you.

a Is.57.15.   b Ps.55.22.

that not a few of the early Christians actually sold themselves as slaves, in order that they might preach the gospel to those who were in bondage. The sense here is, they were to put on humility as a garment bound fast to them, as a servant bound fast to him the apron that was significant of his station. Comp. Col. iii. 13. It is not unusual in the Scriptures, as well as in other writings, to compare the virtues with articles of apparel; as that with which we are clothed, or in which we are seen by others. Comp. Isa. xi. 5; lix. 17. ¶ *For God resisteth the proud,* &c. This passage is quoted from the Greek translation in Prov. iii. 34. See it explained in the Notes on James iv. 6, where it is also quoted.

6. *Humble yourselves therefore.* Be willing to take a low place—a place such as becomes you. Do not arrogate to yourselves what does not belong to you; do not evince pride and haughtiness in your manner; do not exalt yourselves above others. See Notes, Luke xiv. 7 –11. Comp. Prov. xv. 33; xviii. 12; xxii. 4; Mic. vi. 8; Phil. ii. 8. ¶ *Under the mighty hand of God.* This refers probably to the calamities which he had brought upon them, or was about to bring upon them; represented here, as often elsewhere, as the infliction of *his hand*—the hand being that by which we accomplish anything. When that hand was upon them they were not to be lifted up with pride and with a spirit of rebellion, but were to take a lowly place before him, and submit to him with a calm mind, believing that he would exalt them in due time. There is no situation in which one will be more likely to feel humility than in scenes of affliction. ¶ *That he may exalt you in due time.* When he shall see it to be a proper time. (1.) They might be assured that this would be done at some time. He would not always leave them in this low and depressed condition. He would take off his heavy hand, and raise them up from their state of sadness and suffering. (2.) This would be in due time; that is, in the proper time, in the

best time. (*a*) It might be in the present life. (*b*) It would certainly be in the world to come. There they would be exalted to honours which will be more than an equivalent for all the persecution, poverty, and contempt which are suffered in this world. He may well afford to be humble here who is to be exalted to a throne in heaven.

7. *Casting all your care upon him.* Comp. Psa. lv. 22, from whence this passage was probably taken. ' Cast thy burden upon the Lord, and he shall sustain thee; he shall never suffer the righteous to be moved.' Compare, for a similar sentiment, Matt. vi. 25–30. The meaning is, that we are to commit our whole cause to him. If we suffer heavy trials; if we lose our friends, health, or property; if we have arduous and responsible duties to perform; if we feel that we have no strength, and are in danger of being *crushed* by what is laid upon us, we may go and cast all upon the Lord; that is, we may look to him for grace and strength, and feel assured that he will enable us to sustain all that is laid upon us. The *relief* in the case will be as real, and as full of consolation, as if he took the burden and bore it himself. He will enable us to bear with ease what we supposed we could never have done; and the burden which he lays upon us will be light, Matt. xi. 30. Comp. Notes, Phil. iv. 6, 7. ¶ *For he careth for you.* Notes, Matt. x. 29–31. He is not like the gods worshipped by many of the heathen, who were supposed to be so exalted, and so distant, that they did not interest themselves in human affairs; but He condescends to regard the wants of the meanest of his creatures. It is one of the glorious attributes of the true God, that he *can* and *will* thus notice the wants of the mean as well as the mighty; and one of the richest of all consolations when we are afflicted, and are despised by the world, is the thought that we are not forgotten by our heavenly Father. He who remembers the falling sparrow, and who hears the young ravens when they cry, will not be unmindful of us.

8 Be sober, be vigilant; because
your adversary the devil, as *a* a roaring lion, walketh about, seeking
whom he may devour:

a Re.12.12.

9 Whom resist, *b* steadfast in the
faith, knowing that the same afflictions are accomplished in your
brethren that are in the world.

b Ja.4.7.

' Yet *the* LORD *thinketh on me*,' was the
consolation of David, when he felt that
he was 'poor and needy,' Psa. xl. 17.
' When my father and my mother forsake me, then the Lord will take me up,'
Psa. xxvii. 10. Comp. Isa. xlix. 15.
What more can one wish than to be
permitted to feel that the great and
merciful Jehovah *thinks* on him? What
are we—what have we done, that should
be worthy of such condescension? Remember, poor, despised, afflicted child of
God, that you will never *be* forgotten.
Friends on earth, the great, the gay, the
noble, the rich, may forget you; God
never will. Remember that you will
never be entirely neglected. Father,
mother, neighbour, friend, those whom
you have loved, and those to whom you
have done good, may neglect you, but
God never will. You may become poor,
and they may pass by you; you may
lose your office, and flatterers may no
longer throng your path; your beauty
may fade, and your admirers may leave
you; you may grow old, and be infirm,
and appear to be useless in the world,
and no one may seem to care for you;
but it is not thus with the God whom
you serve. When he loves, he always
loves; if he regarded you with favour
when you were rich, he will not forget
you when you are poor; he who watched
over you with a parent's care in the
bloom of youth, will not cast you off
when you are 'old and grey-headed,'
Psa. lxxi. 18. If we are what we should
be, we shall never be without a friend
as long as there is a God.

8. *Be sober.* While you cast your
cares upon God, and have no anxiety
on that score, let your solicitude be
directed to another point. Do not doubt
that he is able and willing to support and
befriend you, but be watchful against
your foes. See the word used here fully
explained in the Notes on 1 Thess. v. 6.
¶ *Be vigilant.* This word (γρηγορέω) is
everywhere else in the New Testament
rendered *watch.* See Matt. xxiv. 42,
43; xxv. 13; xxvi. 38, 40, 41. It means

that we should exercise careful circumspection, as one does when he is in danger. In reference to the matter here
referred to, it means that we are to be
on our guard against the wiles and the
power of the evil one. ¶ *Your adversary the devil.* Your enemy; he who is
opposed to you. Satan opposes man in
his best interests. He resists his efforts
to do good; his purposes to return to
God; his attempts to secure his own
salvation. There is no more appropriate
appellation that can be given to him
than to say that he resists all our efforts
to obey God and to secure the salvation
of our own souls. ¶ *As a roaring lion.*
Comp. Rev. xii. 12. Sometimes Satan
is represented as transforming himself
into an angel of light, (see Notes, 2 Cor.
xi. 14;) and sometimes, as here, as a
roaring lion: denoting the efforts which
he makes to alarm and overpower us.
The lion here is not the *crouching* lion
—the lion stealthfully creeping towards
his foe—but it is the raging monarch
of the woods, who by his terrible roar
would intimidate all so that they might
become an easy prey. The *particular*
thing referred to here, doubtless, is
persecution, resembling in its terrors a
roaring lion. When error comes in;
when seductive arts abound; when the
world allures and charms the representation of the character of the foe is not
of the roaring lion, but of the silent influence of an enemy that has clothed
himself in the garb of an angel of light,
2 Cor. xi. 14. ¶ *Walketh about, seeking
whom he may devour.* 'Naturalists have
observed that a lion roars when he is
roused with hunger, for then he is most
fierce, and most eagerly seeks his prey.
See Judg. xiv. 5; Psa. xxii. 13; Jer. ii.
15; Ezek. xxii. 25; Hos. xi. 10; Zeph.
iii. 3; Zech. xi. 3.'—*Benson.*

9. *Whom resist.* See Notes, James
iv. 7. You are in no instance to yield
to him, but are in all forms to stand up
and oppose him. Feeble in yourselves,
you are to confide in the arm of God.
No matter in what form of terror he

approaches, you are to fight manfully the fight of faith. Comp. Notes, Eph. vi. 10–17. ¶ *Steadfast in the faith.* Confiding in God. You are to rely on him alone, and the means of successful resistance are to be found in the resources of faith. See Notes, Eph. vi. 16. ¶ *Knowing that the same afflictions are accomplished in your brethren that are in the world.* Comp. for a similar sentiment, 1 Cor. x. 13. The meaning is, that you should be encouraged to endure your trials by the fact that your fellow-Christians suffer the same things. This consideration might furnish consolation to them in their trials in the following ways: (1.) They would feel that they were suffering only the common lot of Christians. There was no evidence that God was peculiarly angry with them, or that he had in a peculiar manner forsaken them. (2.) The fact that others were enabled to bear their trials should be an argument to prove to them that they would also be able. If they looked abroad, and saw that others were sustained, and were brought off triumphant, they might be assured that this would be the case with them. (3.) There would be the support derived from the fact that they were not *alone* in suffering. We can bear pain more easily if we feel that we are not alone—that it is the common lot—that we are in circumstances where we may have sympathy from others. This remark may be of great practical value to *us* in view of persecutions, trials, and death. The consideration suggested here by Peter to sustain those whom he addressed, in the trials of persecution, may be applied now to sustain and comfort *us* in every form of apprehended or real calamity. We are all liable to suffering. We are exposed to sickness, bereavement, death. We often feel as if we could not bear up under the sufferings that may be before us, and especially do we dread *the great trial*—DEATH. It may furnish us some support and consolation to remember, (1.) that this is the common lot of men. There is nothing peculiar in our case. It proves nothing as to the question whether we are accepted of God, and are beloved by him, that we suffer; for those whom he has loved most have

been often among the greatest sufferers. We often think that *our* sufferings are peculiar; that there have been none like them. Yet, if we knew all, we should find that thousands—and among them the most wise, and pure, and good— have endured sufferings of the same *kind* as ours, and perhaps far more intense in *degree.* (2.) Others have been conveyed triumphantly through their trials. We have reason to hope and to believe that we shall also, for (*a*) our trials have been no greater than theirs have been; and (*b*) their natural strength was no greater than ours. Many of them were timid, and shrinking, and trembling, and felt that they had no strength, and that they should fail under the trial. (3.) The grace which sustained them can sustain us. The hand of God is not shortened that it cannot save; his ear is not heavy that it cannot hear. His power is as great, and his grace is as fresh, as it was when the first sufferer was supported by him; and that Divine strength which supported David and Job in their afflictions, and the apostles and martyrs in theirs, is just as powerful as it was when they applied to God to be upheld in their sorrows. (4.) We are especially fearful of death—fearful that our faith will fail, and that we shall be left to die without support or consolation. Yet let us remember that death is the common lot of man. Let us remember *who* have died — tender females ; children; the timid and the fearful ; those, in immense multitudes, who had no more strength by nature than we have. Let us think of our own kindred who have died. A wife has died, and shall a husband be afraid to die? A child, and shall a father? A sister, and shall a brother? It does much to take away the dread of death, to remember that a mother has gone through the dark valley; that that gloomy vale has been trod by delicate, and timid, and beloved sisters. Shall *I* be afraid to go where they have gone? Shall I apprehend that I shall find no grace that is able to sustain me where they have found it? Must the valley of the shadow of death be dark and gloomy to me, when they found it to be illuminated with the opening light of heaven?

10 But the God of all grace, who hath called us unto his eternal glory by Christ Jesus, after that ye have suffered a while, *a* make you perfect, *b* stablish, *c* strengthen, *d* settle *e* you.

a 2 Co.4.16.   *b* He.13.21.   *c* 2 Thess.3.3.
d Zec.10.6,12.   *e* Ps.138.7,8.

11 To him *be* glory *f* and dominion for ever and ever.   Amen.

12 By Silvanus, *g* a faithful brother unto you, as I suppose, I have written briefly, exhorting, and testifying that this is the true grace of God wherein ye *h* stand.

f 1 Pe.4.11.   *g* 2 Co.1.19.   *h* 1 Co.15.1.

Above all, it takes away the fear of death when I remember that my Saviour has experienced all the horrors which can ever be in death; that he has slept in the tomb, and made it a hallowed resting-place.

10. *But the God of all grace.* The God who imparts all needful grace. It was proper in their anticipated trials to direct them to God, and to breathe forth in their behalf an earnest and affectionate prayer that they might be supported. A prayer of this kind by an apostle would also be to them a sort of pledge or assurance that the needed grace would be granted them. ¶ *Who hath called us unto his eternal glory.* And who means, therefore, that we shall be saved. As he has called us to his glory, we need not apprehend that he will leave or forsake us. On the meaning of the word *called,* see Notes, Eph. iv. 1. ¶ *After that ye have suffered a while.* After you have suffered as long as he shall appoint. The Greek is, 'having suffered *a little,*' and may refer either to *time* or *degree.* In both respects the declaration concerning afflictions is true. They are *short,* compared with eternity; they are *light,* compared with the exceeding and eternal weight of glory. See Notes, 2 Cor. iv. 16–18. ¶ *Make you perfect.* By means of your trials. The tendency of affliction is to make us perfect. ¶ *Stablish.* The Greek word means *to set fast; to fix firmly; to render immovable,* Luke xvi. 26; ix. 51; xxii. 32; Rom. i. 11; xvi. 25; 1 Thess. iii. 2, 13, *et al.* ¶ *Strengthen.* Give you strength to bear all this. ¶ *Settle you.* Literally, *found you,* or establish you on a firm foundation—θεμελιώσει. The allusion is to a house which is so firmly fixed on a foundation that it will not be moved by winds or floods. Comp. Notes, Matt. vii. 24. seq.

11. *To him* be *glory,* &c. See Notes, chap. iv. 11.

12. *By Silvanus.* Or *Silas.* See Notes, 2 Cor. i. 19; 1 Thess. i. 1. He was the intimate friend and companion of Paul, and had laboured much with him in the regions where the churches were situated to which this epistle was addressed. In what manner he became acquainted with Peter, or why he was now with him in Babylon, is unknown. ¶ *A faithful brother unto you, as I suppose.* The expression 'as I suppose' —ὡς λογίζομαι—does not imply that there was any doubt on the mind of the apostle, but indicates rather a firm persuasion that what he said was true. Thus, Rom. viii. 18, 'For I *reckon* (λογίζομαι) that the sufferings of this present time are not worthy to be compared,' &c. That is, I am fully persuaded of it; I have no doubt of it. Peter evidently had *no doubt* on this point, but he probably could not speak from any personal knowledge. He had not been with them when Silas was, and perhaps not at all; for they may have been 'strangers' to him personally —for the word 'strangers,' in chap. i. 1, *may* imply that he had no personal acquaintance with them. Silas, however, had been much with them, (comp. Acts xv. 17–31,) and Peter had no doubt that he had shown himself to be 'a faithful brother' to them. An epistle conveyed by his hands could not but be welcome. It should be observed, however, that the expression 'I suppose' has been differently interpreted by some. Wetstein understands it as meaning, 'Not that he supposed Silvanus to be a faithful brother, for who, says he, could doubt that? but that he had written as he understood matters, having carefully considered the subject, and as he regarded things to be true;' and refers for illustration to Rom. viii. 18; Phil. iv.

13 The *church that is* at Babylon, elected together with *you*, saluteth you; and *so doth* Marcus my son.

14 Greet *a* ye one another with a

kiss of charity. Peace *b be* with you all that are in Christ Jesus. Amen.

a Ro.16.16.　　　　　*b* Ep.6.23.

8; Heb. xi. 9. Grotius understands it as meaning, 'If I remember right ;' and supposes that the idea is, that he shows his affection for them by saying that this was not the first time that he had written to them, but that he had written before briefly, and sent the letter, as well as he could remember, by Silvanus. But there is no evidence that he had written to them before, and the common interpretation is undoubtedly to be preferred. ¶ *Exhorting*. No small part of the epistle is taken up with exhortations. ¶ *And testifying*. Bearing witness. The main design of the office of the apostles was to bear witness to the truth, (Notes, 1 Cor. ix. 1;) and Peter in this epistle discharged that part of the functions of his office towards the scattered Christians of Asia Minor. ¶ *That this is the true grace of God wherein ye stand*. That the religion in which you stand, or which you now hold, is that which is identified with the grace or favour of God. Christianity, not Judaism, or Paganism, was the true religion. To show this, and bear continual witness to it, was the leading design of the apostolic office.

13. *The church that is at Babylon, elected together with* you. It will be seen at once that much of this is supplied by our translators ; the words ' church that is ' not being in the original. The Greek is, ἡ ἐν Βαβυλῶνι συνεκλεκτὴ ; and might refer to a church, or to a female. Wall, Mill, and some others, suppose that the reference is to

a Christian woman, perhaps the wife of Peter himself. Comp. 2 John 1. But the Arabic, Syriac, and Vulgate, as well as the English versions, supply the word *church*. This interpretation seems to be confirmed by the word rendered *elected together with*—συνεκλεκτὴ. This word would be properly used in reference to one *individual* if writing to another *individual*, but would *hardly* be appropriate as applied to an individual addressing *a church*. It could not readily be supposed, moreover, that any one female in Babylon could have such a prominence, or be so well known, that nothing more would be necessary to designate her than merely to say, ' the elect female.' On the word Babylon here, and the place denoted by it, see the Intro., § 2. ¶ *And so doth Marcus my son*. Probably John Mark. See Notes, Acts xii. 12; xv. 37. Why he was now with Peter is unknown. If this was the Mark referred to, then the word *son* is a title of affection, and is used by Peter with reference to his own superior age. It is possible, however, that some other Mark may be referred to, in whose conversion Peter had been instrumental.

14. *Greet ye one another with a kiss of charity*. A kiss of *love ;* a common method of affectionate salutation in the times of the apostles. See Notes, Rom. xvi. 16. ¶ *Peace be with you all that are in Christ Jesus*. That are true Christians. Notes, Eph. vi. 23; Phil. iv. 7.

SECOND EPISTLE GENERAL OF PETER

INTRODUCTION

§ 1. *Genuineness and authenticity of the Epistle.*

It is well known that at an early period of the Christian history there were doubts respecting the canonical authority of the Second Epistle of Peter. The sole ground of the doubt was, whether Peter was the author of it. Eusebius, in the chapter of his ecclesiastical history where he speaks of the New Testament in general, reckons it among the αντιλεγομενα, (*antilegomena*,) or those books which were not universally admitted to be genuine; literally, '*those which were spoken against*,' b. iii. chap. 25. This does not imply that even he, however, disbelieved its genuineness, but merely that it was numbered among those about which there had not been always entire certainty. Jerome says, 'Peter wrote two epistles, called Catholic; the second of which is denied by many to be his, because of the difference of style from the former.' Origen, before him, had also said, 'Peter, on whom the church is built, has left one epistle [universally] acknowledged. Let it be granted that he also wrote a second. For it is doubted of.' See Lardner, vol. vi., p. 255, Ed. Lond. 1829. Both the epistles of Peter, however, were received as genuine in the fourth and following centuries by all Christians, except the Syrians. The first epistle was never doubted to have been the production of Peter. In regard to the second, as remarked above, it was doubted by some. The principal ground of the doubt, if not the entire ground, was the difference of style between the two, especially in the second chapter, and the fact that the old Syriac translator, though he admitted the Epistle of James, which was also reckoned among the 'doubtful' epistles, did not translate the Second Epistle of Peter. That version was made, probably, at the close of the first century, or in the second; and it is said that it is to be presumed that if this epistle had been then in existence, and had been regarded as genuine, it would also have been translated by him.

It is of importance, therefore, to state briefly the evidence of the genuineness and authenticity of this epistle. In doing this, it is proper to regard the *first* epistle as undoubtedly genuine and canonical, for that was never called in question. That being admitted, the genuineness of this epistle may be argued on the following grounds : (1.) It does not appear to have been *rejected* by any one. It was merely *doubted* whether it was genuine. How far even this *doubt* extended is not mentioned. It is referred to only by Jerome, Origen, and Eusebius, though there is not the least evidence that even *they* had any doubts of its genuineness. They merely state that there were some persons who had doubts on the subject, from the difference of style between this and the former epistle. This fact, indeed, as Wall has remarked, (Critical Notes on the New Testament, pp. 358, 359,) will serve at least to show the care which was evinced in admitting books to be canonical, proving that they were not received without the utmost caution, and that if the slightest doubt existed in the case of any one, it was honestly expressed. (2.) Even all doubt on the subject disappeared as early as the third and

fourth centuries, and the epistle was received as being unquestionably the production of Peter. The effect of the examination in the case was to remove all
suspicion, and it has never since been doubted that the epistle was written by
Peter; at least, no doubt has arisen, except from the fact stated by Jerome and
Origen, that it was not universally admitted to be genuine. (3.) This epistle
purports to have been written by the author of the former, and has all the internal marks of genuineness which could exist. (*a*) It bears the inscription of the
name of the same apostle: ' Simon Peter, a servant and an apostle of Jesus
Christ,' chap. i. 1. (*b*) There is an allusion in chap. i. 14, which Peter only
could appropriately make, and which an impostor, or forger of an epistle, would
hardly have thought of introducing: ' Knowing that shortly I must put off this
my tabernacle, even as our Lord Jesus Christ hath showed me.' Here, there is
an evident reference to the Saviour's prediction of the death of Peter, recorded
in John xxi. 18, 19. It is conceivable, indeed, that an adroit forger of an epistle
might have introduced such a circumstance; but the supposition that it is genuine is much more natural. It is such an allusion as Peter would naturally
make ; it would have required much skill and tact in another to have introduced
it so as not to be easily detected, even if it had occurred to him to personate
Peter at all. Would not a forger of an epistle have been likely to mention particularly what *kind* of death was predicted by the Saviour, and not to have made
a mere allusion ? (*c*) In chap. i. 16–18, there is another allusion of a similar
kind. The writer claims to have been one of the ' eye-witnesses of the majesty '
of the Lord Jesus when he was transfigured in the holy mount. It was natural
for Peter to refer to this, for he was with him ; and he has mentioned it just as
one would be likely to do who had actually been with him, and who was writing
from personal recollection. A forger of the epistle would have been likely to be
more particular, and would have described the scene more minutely, and the place
where it occurred, and would have dwelt more on the nature of the evidence furnished there of the Divine mission of the Saviour. (*d*) In chap. iii. 1, it is stated
that this is a second epistle written to the same persons, as a former one had
been ; and that the writer aimed at substantially the same object in both. Here
the plain reference is to the first epistle of Peter, which has always been acknowledged to be genuine. It may be said that one who forged the epistle might have
made this allusion. This is true, but it may be doubtful whether he *would* do
it. It would have increased the liability to detection, for it would not be easy to
imitate the manner, and to carry out the views of the apostle. (4.) To these
considerations it may be added, that there is clear internal evidence of another
kind to show that it was written by Peter. This evidence, too long to be introduced here, may be seen in Michaelis' Introduction, iv. 349–356. The sum of
this internal evidence is, that it would not have been practicable for a writer of
the first or second century to have imitated Peter so as to have escaped detection ; and that, in general, it is not difficult to detect the books that were forged
in imitation of, and in the name of, the apostles.

As to the alleged objection in regard to the difference of the style in the second
chapter, see Michaelis, iv. 352–356. Why it was not inserted in the old Syriac
version is not known. It is probable that the author of that version was exceedingly cautious, and did not admit any books about which *he* had any doubt. The
fact that this was doubted by some, and that these doubts were not removed from
his mind, as in the case of the epistle of James, was a good reason for his not
inserting it, though it by no means proves that it is not genuine. It came, however, to be acknowledged afterwards by the Syrians as genuine and canonical
Ephrem the Syrian, a writer of the fourth century, not only quotes several passages of it, but expressly ascribes it to Peter. Thus, in the second volume of his
Greek works, p. 387, he says, ' The blessed Peter, also, the Coryphæus of the
apostles, cries, concerning that day, saying, The day of the Lord cometh as a thief
in the night, in which the heavens being on fire shall be dissolved, and the elements shall melt with fervent heat.' This is literally quoted (in the Greek) from

2 Pet. iii. 12. See Michaelis, as above, p. 348. And Asseman, in his catalogue of the Vatican Manuscripts, gives an account of a Syriac book of Lessons, to be read, in which is one taken from this epistle. See Michaelis.

These considerations remove all reasonable doubt as to the propriety of admitting this epistle into the canon, as the production of Peter.

§ 2. *The time when the Epistle was written.*

In regard to the *time* when this epistle was written, nothing can be determined with absolute certainty. All that appears on that subject from the epistle itself, is, that at the time of writing it the author was expecting soon to die. Chap. i. 14, ' Knowing that shortly I must put off this my tabernacle, even as our Lord Jesus Christ hath showed me.' What evidence he had that he was soon to die he has not informed us; nor is it known even what he meant precisely by the word *shortly*. The Greek word (ταχινή) is indeed one that would imply that the event was expected not to be far off ; but a man would not unnaturally use it who felt that he was growing old, even though he should in fact live several years afterwards. The Saviour (John xxi. 18) did not state to Peter *when* his death would occur, except that it would be when he should be ' *old ;*' and the probability is, that the fact that he was growing *old* was the only intimation that he had that he was soon to die. Ecclesiastical history informs us that he died at Rome, A. D. 66, in the 12th year of the reign of Nero. See Calmet, *Art.* Peter. Comp. Notes, John xxi. 18, 19. Lardner supposes, from chap. i. 13–15 of this epistle, that this was written not long after the first, as he then says that he ' would not be *negligent* to put them in remembrance of these things.' The two epistles he supposes were written in the year 63 or 64, or at the latest 65. Michaelis supposes it was in the year 64; Calmet that it was in the year of Christ 68, or according to the Vulgar Era, A. D. 65. Probably the year 64 or 65 would not be far from the real date of this epistle. If so, it was, according to Calmet, one year only before the martyrdom of Peter, (A. D. 66,) and six years before the destruction of Jerusalem by Titus, A. D. 71.

§ 3. *The persons to whom this Epistle was written, and the place where.*

On this subject there is no room for doubt. In chap. iii. 1, the writer says, ' this second epistle, beloved, I now write unto you; in both which I stir up your pure minds by way of remembrance.' This epistle was written, therefore, to the same persons as the former. On the question to whom that was addressed, see the Introduction to that epistle, § 1. The epistles were addressed to persons who resided in Asia Minor, and in both they are regarded as in the midst of trials. No certain intimation of the *place* where this epistle was written is given in the epistle itself. It is probable that it was at the same place as the former, as, if it had not been, we may presume that there would have been some reference to the fact that he had changed his residence, or some local allusion which would have enabled us to determine the fact. If he wrote this epistle from Babylon, as he did the former one, (see Intro. to that epistle, § 2,) it is not known why he was so soon removed to Rome, and became a martyr there. Indeed, everything respecting the last days of this apostle is involved in great uncertainty. See the article *Peter* in Calmet's Dictionary. See these questions examined also in Bacon's Lives of the Apostles, pp. 258–279.

§ 4.—*The occasion on which the Epistle was written.*

The first epistle was written in view of the trials which those to whom it was addressed were then enduring, and the persecutions which they had reason to anticipate, chap. i. 6, 7; iv. 12–19; v. 8–11. The main object of that epistle was to comfort them in their trials, and to encourage them to bear them with a Christian spirit, imitating the example of the Lord Jesus. This epistle appears to have been written, not so much in view of persecutions and bodily sufferings, real or prospective, as in view of the fact that there were teachers of error among them, the tendency of whose doctrine was to turn them away from the gospel. To those teachers of error, and to the dangers to which they were exposed on that account, there is no allusion in the first epistle, and it would seem not to be improbable that Peter had been informed that there were such teachers among them after he had written and despatched that. Or, if he was not thus *informed* of it, it seems to have occurred to him that this was a point of great importance which had not been noticed in the former epistle, and that an effort should be made by apostolic influence and authority to arrest the progress of error, to counteract the influence of the false teachers, and to confirm the Christians of Asia Minor in the belief of the truth. A large part of the epistle, therefore, is occupied in characterising the teachers of error, in showing that they would certainly be destroyed, and in stating the true doctrine in opposition to what they held. It is evident that Peter supposed that the danger to which Christians in Asia Minor were exposed from these errors, was not less than that to which they were exposed from persecution, and that it was of as much importance to guard them from those errors as it was to sustain them in their trials.

The characteristics of the teachers referred to in this epistle, and the doctrines which they taught, were the following :—

(1.) One of the prominent errors was a denial of the Lord that bought them, chap. ii. 1. On the nature of this error, see Notes on that verse.

(2.) They gave indulgence to carnal appetites, and were sensual, corrupt, beastly, lewd, vers. 10, 12, 13, 14, 19. Comp. Jude 4, 8, 16. It is remarkable that so many professed *reformers* have been men who have been sensual and lewd—men who have taken advantage of their character as professed religious teachers, and as *reformers*, to corrupt and betray others. Such reformers often begin with pure intentions, but a constant familiarity with a certain class of vices tends to corrupt the mind, and to awaken in the soul passions which would otherwise have slept ; and they fall into the same vices which they attempt to reform. It should be said, however, that many professed reformers are corrupt at heart, and only make use of their pretended zeal in the cause of reformation to give them the opportunity to indulge their base propensities.

(3.) They were disorderly in their views, and '*radical*' in their movements. The tendency of their doctrines was to unsettle the foundations of order and government ; to take away all restraint from the indulgence of carnal propensities, and to break up the very foundations of good order in society, chap. ii. 10–12. They 'walked after the flesh in the lust of uncleanness;' they 'despised government' or authority ; they were 'presumptuous and self-willed;' they 'were not afraid to speak evil of dignities;' they were like 'natural brute beasts;' they 'spoke evil of the subjects which they did not understand.' It is by no means an uncommon thing for professed reformers to become anti-government men, or to suppose that all the restraints of law stand in their way, and that they must be removed in order to success. They fix the mind on *one* thing to be accomplished. That thing magnifies itself until it fills all the field of vision. Everything which *seems* to oppose their efforts, or to uphold the evil which they seek to remove, they regard as an evil itself ; and as the laws and the government of a country often seem to sustain the evil, they become opposed to the government itself, and denounce it as an evil. Instead of endeavouring to enlighten the public mind, and to modify the laws by a course of patient effort, they array themselves against them, and seek to overturn them. For the same reason, also, they suppose that *the church* upholds the evil, and become the deadly foe of all church organizations.

(4.) They were seductive and artful, and adopted a course of teaching that was fitted to beguile the weak, and especially to produce licentiousness of living, chap. ii. 14. They were characterised by 'adulterous' desires; and they practised their arts particularly on the 'unstable,' those who were easily led away by any new and plausible doctrine that went to unsettle the foundations of rigid morality.

(5.) They adopted a pompous mode of teaching, distinguished for sound rather than for sense, and proclaimed themselves to be the special friends of liberal views, and of a liberal Christianity, chap. ii. 17–19. They were like 'wells without water;' 'clouds that were carried about with a tempest;' they spake 'great swelling words of vanity,' and they promised 'liberty' to those who would embrace their views, or freedom from the restraints of bigotry and of a narrow and gloomy religion. This appeal is usually made by the advocates of error.

(6.) They had been professed Christians, and had formerly embraced the more strict views on morals and religion which were held by Christians in general, chap. ii. 20–22. From this, however, they had departed, and had fallen into practices quite as abominable as those of which they had been guilty before their pretended conversion.

(7.) They denied the doctrines which the apostles had stated respecting the end of the world. The *argument* on which they based this denial was the fact that all things continued unchanged as they had been from the beginning, and that it might be inferred from that that the world would be stable, chap. iii. 3, 4. They saw no change in the laws of nature; they saw no indications that the world was drawing to a close, and they *inferred* that laws so stable and settled as those were which existed in nature would continue to operate, and that the changes predicted by the apostles were impossible.

A large part of the epistle is occupied in meeting these errors, and in so portraying the characters of their advocates as to show what degree of reliance was to be placed on their preaching. For a particular view of the manner in which these errors are met, see the analyses to chapters ii. iii.

This epistle is characterised by the same earnest and tender manner as the first, and by a peculiarly 'solemn grandeur of imagery and diction.' The apostle in the last two chapters had to meet great and dangerous errors, and the style of rebuke was appropriate to the occasion. He felt that he himself was soon to die, and, in the prospect of death, his own mind was peculiarly impressed with the solemnity and importance of coming events. He believed that the errors which were broached tended to sap the very foundations of the Christian faith and of good morals, and his whole soul is roused to meet and counteract them. The occasion required that he should state in a solemn manner what *was* the truth in regard to the second advent of the Lord Jesus; what great changes *were* to occur; what the Christian *might* look for hereafter; and his soul kindles with the sublime theme, and he describes in glowing imagery, and in impassioned language, the end of all things, and exhorts them to live as became those who were looking forward to so important events. The practical effect of the whole epistle is to make the mind intensely solemn, and to put it into a position of waiting for the coming of the Lord. On the similarity between this epistle (chap. ii.) and the epistle of Jude, see Introduction to Jude.

THE

SECOND EPISTLE GENERAL OF PETER

CHAPTER I.

SIMON [1] Peter, a servant and an apostle of Jesus Christ, to them that have obtained like *a* precious

CHAPTER I.

ANALYSIS OF THE CHAPTER.

THIS chapter comprises the following subjects :—

I. The usual salutations, vers. 1, 2.

II. A statement that all the mercies which they enjoyed pertaining to life and godliness, had been conferred by the power of God, and that he had given them exceeding great and precious promises, vers. 3, 4. It was mainly with reference to these ' promises ' that the epistle was written, for they had been assailed by the advocates of error, (chaps. ii. iii.,) and it was important that Christians should see that they *had* the promise of a future life. Comp. chap. iii. 5–14.

III. An exhortation to abound in Christian virtues ; to go on making constant attainments in knowledge, and temperance, and patience, and godliness, and brotherly kindness, and charity, vers. 5–9.

IV. An exhortation to endeavour to make their calling and election sure, that so an entrance might be ministered unto them abundantly into the kingdom of the Redeemer, vers. 10, 11.

V. The apostle says that he will endeavour to keep these things before their minds, vers. 12–15. He knew well that they were then established in the truth, (ver. 12,) but he evidently felt that they were in danger of being shaken in the faith by the seductive influence of error, and he says therefore, (vers. 13,) that it was proper, as long as he remained on earth, to endeavour to excite in their minds a lively remembrance of the truths which they had believed ;

faith with us through the righteousness of [2] God and our Saviour Jesus Christ:

1 Or, *Symeon.*   a Ep.4.5.   2 *our God and Saviour.*

that the opportunity for his doing this must soon cease, as the period was approaching when he must be removed to eternity, in accordance with the prediction of the Saviour, (ver. 14,) but that he would endeavour to make so permanent a record of his views on these important subjects that they might always have them in remembrance, ver. 15.

VI. A solemn statement that the doctrines which had been taught them, and which they had embraced, were not cunningly-devised fables, but were true, vers. 16–21. In support of this the apostle appeals to the following things :—

(*a*) The testimony to the fact that Jesus was the Son of God, which Peter had himself heard given on the mount of transfiguration, vers. 17, 18.

(*b*) Prophecy. These truths, on which he expected them to rely, had been the subject of distinct prediction, and they should be held, whatever were the plausible arguments of the false teachers, vers. 19, 20.

The general object, therefore, of this chapter is to affirm the truth of the great facts of religion, on which their hopes were based, and thus to prepare the way to combat the errors by which these truths were assailed. He first assures them that the doctrines which they held were true, and then, in chaps. ii. and iii., meets the errors by which they were assailed.

1. *Simon Peter.* Marg., *Symeon.* The name is written either *Simon* or *Simeon*—Σίμων or Συμεών. Either word properly means *hearing*; and perhaps, like other names, was at first significant. The first epistle (chap. i. 1) begins simply, ' Peter, an apostle,' &c. The name

2 Grace and peace *a* be multiplied unto you through the knowledge of God, and of Jesus our Lord.

3 According as his divine power hath given unto us all *b* things that

pertain unto life and godliness, through the knowledge of him that hath called us [1] to glory and virtue : *c*

a Da.4.1; 6.25.　　b Ps.84.11; 1 Ti.4.8.
1 Or, *by*.　　　c 2 Ti.1.9.

Simon, however, was, his proper name —*Peter*, or *Cephas*, having been added to it by the Saviour, John i. 42. Comp. Matt. xvi. 18. ¶ *A servant and an apostle of Jesus Christ.* In the first epistle the word *apostle* only is used. Paul, however, uses the word *servant* as applicable to himself in Rom. i. 1, and to himself and Timothy in the commencement of the epistle to the Philippians, chap. i. 1. See Notes, Rom. i. 1. ¶ *To them that have obtained like precious faith with us.* With us who are of Jewish origin. This epistle was evidently written to the same persons as the former, (Intro., § 3,) and that was intended to embrace many who were of Gentile origin. Notes, 1 Pet. i. 1. The apostle addresses them all now, whatever was their origin, as heirs of the common faith, and as in all respects brethren. ¶ *Through the righteousness of God.* Through the method of justification which God has adopted. See this fully explained in the Notes on Rom. i. 17.

[The original is ἐν δικαιοσυνη, IN the righteousness, &c., which makes the righteousness the *object* of faith. We cannot but regard the author's rendering of the famous phrase here used by Peter, and by Paul, Rom. i. 17; iii. 21, as singularly unhappy. That Archbishop Newcome used it and the Socinian version adopted it, would not make us reject it; but when the apostles state *specially* the GROUND of justification, why should they be made to speak *indefinitely* of its general 'plan,' or method. The rendering of Stuart, viz., 'justification of God,' is not more successful; it confounds the *thing itself* with the *ground* of it. Why not prefer the apostle's own words to any change or periphrasis? See Supplementary Note, Rom. i. 17.]

¶ *God and our Saviour Jesus Christ.* Marg., *our God and Saviour.* The Greek will undoubtedly *bear* the construction given in the margin ; and if this be the true rendering, it furnishes an argument for the divinity of the Lord Jesus Christ. Bishop Middleton, Slade, Valpy, Bloomfield, and others, contend that this is the true and proper render-

ing. It is doubted, however, by Wetstein, Grotius, and others. Erasmus supposes that it may be taken in either sense. The construction, though certainly not a violation of the laws of the Greek language, is not so free from all doubt as to make it proper to use the passage as a proof-text in an argument for the divinity of the Saviour. It is easier to prove the doctrine from other texts that are plain, than to show that this *must* be the meaning here.

2. *Grace and peace be multiplied unto you through the knowledge of God, and of Jesus our Lord.* That is, grace and peace *abound* to us, or may be expected to be conferred on us abundantly, if we have a true knowledge of God and of the Saviour. Such a knowledge constitutes true religion : for in that we find *grace*—the grace that pardons and sanctifies ; and *peace*—peace of conscience, reconciliation with God, and calmness in the trials of life. See Notes, John xvii. 3.

3. *According as his divine power hath given unto us.* All the effects of the gospel on the human heart are, in the Scriptures, traced to the *power* of God. See Notes, Rom. i. 16. There are no moral means which have ever been used that have such *power* as the gospel ; none through which God has done so much in changing the character and affecting the destiny of man. ¶ *All things that* pertain *unto life and godliness.* The reference here in the word *life* is undoubtedly to the life of religion ; the life of the soul imparted by the gospel. The word *godliness* is synonymous with piety. The phrase ' according as ' (ὡς) seems to be connected with the sentence in ver. 5, ' Forasmuch as he has conferred on us these privileges and promises connected with life and godliness, we are bound, in order to obtain all that is implied in these things, to give all diligence to add to our faith, knowledge,' &c. ¶ *Through the knowledge of him.* By a proper acquaintance

4 Whereby are given unto us exceeding great and precious promises;[a] that by these ye might be

a 2 Co.7.1.

partakers [b] of the divine nature, having escaped [c] the corruption that is in the world through lust.

b He.12.10.   *c* 2 Pe.2.18,20.

with him, or by the right kind of knowledge of him. Notes, John xvii. 3. ¶ *That hath called us to glory and virtue.* Margin, *by.* Greek, '*through* glory,' &c. Doddridge supposes that it means that he has done this ' by the strengthening virtue and energy of his spirit.' Rosenmüller renders it, ' *by* glorious benignity.' Dr. Robinson (*Lex.*) renders it, ' through a glorious display of his efficiency.' The *objection* which any one feels to this rendering arises solely from the word *virtue*, from the fact that we are not accustomed to apply that word to God. But the original word (ἀρετή) is not as limited in its signification as the English word is, but is rather a word which denotes a good quality or excellence of any kind. In the ancient classics it is used to denote manliness, vigour, courage, valour, fortitude; and the word would rather denote *energy* or *power* of some kind, than what we commonly understand by virtue, and would be, therefore, properly applied to the *energy* or *efficiency* which God has displayed in the work of our salvation. Indeed, when applied to moral excellence at all, as it is in ver. 5, of this chapter, and often elsewhere, it is perhaps with a reference to the *energy, boldness, vigour*, or *courage* which is evinced in overcoming our evil propensities, and resisting allurements and temptations. According to this interpretation, the passage teaches that it is *by a glorious Divine efficiency* that we are called into the kingdom of God.

4. *Whereby.* Δι ὦν. 'Through which' —in the plural number, referring either to the *glory* and *virtue* in the previous verse, and meaning that it was by that glorious Divine efficiency that these promises were given; or, to all the things mentioned in the previous verse, meaning that it was through those arrangements, and in order to their completion, that these great and glorious promises were made. The promises given are in connection with the plan of securing ' life and godliness,' and are a part of the gracious arrangements for that ob-

ject. ¶ *Exceeding great and precious promises.* A *promise* is an assurance on the part of another of some good for which we are dependent on him. It implies, (1,) that the thing is in his power; (2,) that he may bestow it or not, as he pleases; (3,) that we cannot infer from any process of reasoning that it is his purpose to bestow it on us; (4,) that it is a favour which we can obtain *only* from him, and not by any independent effort of our own. The promises here referred to are those which pertain to salvation. Peter had in his eye probably all that then had been revealed which contemplated the salvation of the people of God. They are called ' exceeding great and precious,' because of their value in supporting and comforting the soul, and of the honour and felicity which they unfold to us. The promises referred to are doubtless those which are made in connection with the plan of salvation revealed in the gospel, for there are no *other* promises made to man. They refer to the pardon of sin; strength, comfort, and support in trial; a glorious resurrection; and a happy immortality. If we look at the greatness and glory of the objects, we shall see that the promises are in fact exceedingly precious; or if we look at their influence in supporting and elevating the soul, we shall have as distinct a view of their value. The promise goes beyond our reasoning powers; enters a field which we could not otherwise penetrate—the distant future; and relates to what we could not otherwise obtain. All that we need in trial, is the simple *promise* of God that he will sustain us; all that we need in the hour of death, is the assurance of our God that we shall be happy for ever. What would this world be without a *promise?* How impossible to penetrate the future! How dark that which is to come would be! How bereft we should be of consolation! The past has gone, and its departed joys and hopes can never be recalled to cheer us again; the present may be an hour of pain, and sadness, and disappointment, and gloom, with perhaps not a ray of comfort; the future only opens fields of happiness to our vision, and everything there depends on the will of God, and all that we can know of it is from his promises. Cut off from these, we have no way either of obtaining the blessings which we desire, or of ascertaining that they can be ours. For the promises of God, therefore, we should be in the highest degree grateful, and in the trials of life we should cling to them with unwavering confidence as the only things which can be an anchor to the soul. ¶ *That by these.* Greek, '*through* these.' That is, these constitute the basis of your hopes of becoming partakers of the divine nature. Comp. Notes on 2 Cor. vii. 1. ¶ *Partakers of the divine nature.* This is a very important and a difficult phrase. An expression somewhat similar occurs in Ileb. xii. 10: 'That we might be partakers of his holiness.' See Notes on that verse. In regard to the language here used, it may be observed, (1,) that it is directly contrary to all the notions of *Pantheism*—or the belief that all things are *now* God, or a part of God—for it is said that the object of the promise is, that we '*may become* partakers of the divine nature,' not that we are now. (2.) It cannot be taken in so literal a sense as to mean that we can ever partake of the divine *essence*, or that we shall be *absorbed* into the divine nature so as to lose our individuality. This idea is held by the Budhists; and the perfection of being is supposed by them to consist in such absorption, or in losing their own individuality, and their ideas of happiness are graduated by the approximation which may be made to that state. But this cannot be the meaning here, because (a) it is in the nature of the case impossible. There must be for ever an essential difference between a created and an uncreated mind. (b) This would argue that the Divine Mind is not perfect. If this absorption was necessary to the completeness of the character and happiness of the Divine Being, then he was imperfect before; if before perfect, he would *not* be after the absorption of an infinite number of finite and imperfect minds. (c) In all

the representations of heaven in the Bible, the idea of *individuality* is one that is prominent. *Individuals* are represented everywhere as worshippers there, and there is no intimation that the separate existence of the redeemed is to be absorbed and lost in the essence of the Deity. Whatever is to be the condition of man hereafter, he is to have a separate and individual existence, and the *number* of intelligent beings is never to be diminished either by annihilation, or by their being united to any other spirit so that they shall become *one*. The reference then, in this place, must be to the *moral* nature of God; and the meaning is, that they who are renewed become participants of the same *moral* nature; that is, of the same views, feelings, thoughts, purposes, principles of action. Their nature as they are born, is sinful, and prone to evil, (Eph. ii. 3;) their nature as they are born again, becomes like that of God. They are made *like* God; and this resemblance will increase more and more for ever, until in a much higher sense than can be true in this world, they may be said to have become '*partakers* of the divine nature.' Let us remark, then, (a) that man only, of all the dwellers on the earth, is capable of rising to this condition. The nature of all the other orders of creatures here below is incapable of any such transformation that it can be said that they become '*partakers* of the divine nature.' (b) It is impossible now to estimate the degree of approximation to which man may yet rise towards God, or the exalted sense in which the term may yet be applicable to him; but the prospect before the believer in this respect is most glorious. Two or three circumstances may be referred to here as mere *hints* of what we may yet be : (1.) Let any one reflect on the amazing advances made by himself since the period of infancy. But a few, very few years ago, he knew *nothing*. He was in his cradle, a poor, helpless infant. He knew not the use of eyes, or ears, or hands, or feet. He knew not the name or use of anything, not even the name of father or mother. He could neither walk, nor talk, nor creep. He knew not even that a candle would burn him if he put his finger there. He

5 And beside this, giving all dili- | gence, add to your faith virtue; [a]
a Phi.4.8.　　　　　　*b* Phi.1.9. | and to virtue knowledge; [b]

knew not how to grasp or hold a rattle, or what was its sound, or whence that sound or any other sound came. Let him think what he is at twenty, or forty, in comparison with this; and then, if his improvement in every similar number of years hereafter *should* be equal to this, who can tell the height to which he will rise? (2.) We are here limited in our own powers of learning about God through his works. We become acquainted with him *through* his works —by means of *the senses.* But by the appointment of this method of becoming acquainted with the external world, the design seems to have been to accomplish a double work quite contradictory—one to help us, and the other to hinder us. One is to give us the means of communicating with the external world—by the sight, the hearing, the smell, the touch, the taste; the other is to shut us *out* from the external world, except by these. The body is a *casement*, an enclosure, a prison in which the soul is incarcerated, from which we can *look out* on the universe only through these organs. But suppose, as may be the case in a future state, there shall be *no* such enclosure, and that the whole soul may look directly on the works of God—on spiritual existences, on God himself— who can then calculate the height to which man may attain in becoming a 'partaker of the divine nature?' (3.) We shall have an *eternity* before us to grow in knowledge, and in holiness, and in conformity to God. Here, we attempt to climb the hill of knowledge, and having gone a few steps—while the top is still lost in the clouds—we lie down and die. We look at a few things ; become acquainted with a few elementary principles ; make a little progress in virtue, and then all our studies and efforts are suspended, and 'we fly away.' In the future world we shall have an *eternity* before us to make progress in knowledge, and virtue, and holiness, uninterrupted ; and who can tell in what exalted sense it may yet be true that we shall be ' partakers of the divine nature,' or what attainments we may yet make ? ¶ *Having escaped the cor-*

ruption that is in the world through lust. The world is full of corruption. It is the design of the Christian plan of redemption to deliver us from that, and to make us holy; and the means by which we are to be made like God, is by rescuing us from its dominion. 5. *And beside this.* Καὶ αὐτὸ τοῦτο. Something here is necessary to be understood in order to complete the sense. The *reference* is to ver. 3 ; and the connection is, ' since (ver. 3) God has given us these exalted privileges and hopes, *in respect to this*, (κατὰ or διὰ being understood,) or as a *consequence* fairly flowing from this, we ought to give all diligence that we may make good use of these advantages, and secure as high attainments as we possibly can. We should add one virtue to another, that we may reach the highest possible elevation in holiness.' ¶ *Giving all diligence.* Greek, ' Bringing in all zeal or effort.' The meaning is, that we ought to make this a distinct and definite object, and to apply ourselves to it as a thing to be accomplished. ¶ *Add to your faith virtue.* It is not meant in this verse and the following that we are to endeavour particularly to add these things one to another *in the order* in which they are specified, or that we are to seek first to have faith, and then to add to *that* virtue, and then to add knowledge to virtue rather than to faith, &c. The *order* in which this is to be done, the *relation* which one of these things may have to another, is not the point aimed at ; nor are we to suppose that any other order of the words would not have answered the purpose of the apostle as well, or that any one of the virtues specified would not sustain as direct a relation to any other, as the one which he has specified. The design of the apostle is to say, in an emphatic manner, that we are to strive to possess and exhibit all these virtues ; in other words, we are not to content ourselves with a single grace, but are to cultivate *all* the virtues, and to endeavour to make our piety complete in all the relations which we sustain. The essential idea in the passage before us seems to be, that in our

6 And to knowledge temperance; *a* and to temperance patience; *b* and to patience godliness; *c*

7 And to godliness brotherly kindness; *d* and to brotherly kindness charity. *e*

8 For if these things be in you, and abound, they make *you that ye shall* neither *be* ¹ barren nor unfruitful *f* in the knowledge of our Lord Jesus Christ.

a 1 Co.9.25.　　b Ja.1.4.　　c 1 Ti.4.7.
d Jn.13.34,35.　e 1 Co.13.1-3.　1 *idle.*　f Jn.15.2-6.

religion we are not to be satisfied with one virtue, or one class of virtues, but that there is to be (1,) a diligent CULTIVATION of our virtues, since the graces of religion are as susceptible of cultivation as any other virtues; (2,) that there is to be PROGRESS made from one virtue to another, seeking to reach the highest possible point in our religion; and, (3,) that there is to be an ACCUMULATION of virtues and graces—or we are not to be satisfied with one class, or with the attainments which we can make in one class. We are to endeavour to *add on* one after another until we have become possessed of all. Faith, perhaps, is mentioned first, because that is the foundation of all Christian virtues; and the other virtues are required to be added to that, because, from the place which faith occupies in the plan of justification, many might be in danger of supposing that if they had that they had all that was necessary. Comp. James ii. 14, seq. In the Greek word rendered ' *add,*' (ἐπιχορηγήσατε,) there is an allusion to a *chorus-leader* among the Greeks, and the sense is well expressed by Doddridge: ' Be careful to accompany that belief with all the lovely train of attendant graces.' Or, in other words, ' let faith lead on as at the head of the choir or the graces, and let all the others follow in their order.' The word here rendered *virtue* is the same which is used in ver. 3; and there is included in it, probably, the same general idea which was noticed there. All the things which the apostle specifies, unless *knowledge* be an exception, are *virtues* in the sense in which that word is commonly used; and it can hardly be supposed that the apostle here meant to use a *general* term which would include all of the others. The probability is, therefore, that by the word here he has reference to the common meaning of the Greek word, as referring to manliness, courage,

vigour, energy; and the sense is, that he wished them to evince whatever firmness or courage might be necessary in maintaining the principles of their religion, and in enduring the trials to which their faith might be subjected. True *virtue* is not a tame and passive thing. It requires great energy and boldness, for its very essence is firmness, manliness, and independence. ¶ *And to virtue knowledge.* The knowledge of God and of the way of salvation through the Redeemer, ver. 3. Comp. chap. iii. 8. It is the duty of every Christian to make the highest possible attainments in *knowledge*.

6. *And to knowledge temperance.* On the meaning of the word *temperance*, see Notes on Acts xxiv. 25, and 1 Cor. ix. 25. The word here refers to the mastery over all our evil inclinations and appetites. We are to allow none of them to obtain control over us. See Notes on 1 Cor. vi. 12. This would include, of course, abstinence from intoxicating drinks; but it would also embrace *all* evil passions and propensities. Everything is to be confined within proper limits, and to no propensity of our nature are we to give indulgence beyond the limits which the law of God allows. ¶ *And to temperance patience.* Notes on James i. 4. ¶ *And to patience godliness.* True piety. Notes on ver. 3. Comp. 1 Tim. ii. 2; iii. 16; iv. 7, 8; vi. 3, 5, 6, 11.

7. *And to godliness brotherly kindness.* Love to Christians as such. See Notes on John xiii. 34; Heb. xiii. 1. ¶ *And to brotherly kindness charity.* Love to all mankind. There is to be a peculiar affection for Christians as of the same family; there is to be a true and warm love, however, for all the race. See Notes on 1 Cor. xiii.

8. *For if these things be in you, and abound.* If they are in you in rich abundance; if you are eminent for these

9 But he that lacketh these things is blind,[a] and cannot see afar off, and hath forgotten that he was purged from his old sins.

10 Wherefore the rather, bre-thren, give diligence [b] to make your calling and election sure : for [c] if ye do these things, ve shall never fall :

a 1 Jn.2.9-11.   b 2 Pe.3.17.   c 1 Jn.3.19; Re.22.14.

things. ¶ *They make* you that ye shall *neither* be *barren nor unfruitful.* They will show that you are not barren or unfruitful. The word rendered *barren,* is, in the margin, *idle.* The word *idle* more accurately expresses the sense of the original. The meaning is, that if they evinced these things, it would show (1) that they were diligent in cultivating the Christian graces, and (2) that it was not a vain thing to attempt to grow in knowledge and virtue. Their efforts would be followed by such happy results as to be an encouragement to exertion. In nothing is there, in fact, more encouragement than in the attempt to become eminent in piety. On no other efforts does God smile more propitiously than on the attempt to secure the salvation of the soul and to do good. A small part of the exertions which men put forth to become rich, or learned, or celebrated for oratory or heroism, would secure the salvation of the soul. In the former, also, men often fail ; in the latter, never.

9. *But he that lacketh these things is blind.* He has no clear views of the nature and the requirements of religion. ¶ *And cannot see afar off.* The word used here, which does not occur elsewhere in the New Testament, (μυωπάζω,) means to shut the eyes ; i. e., to contract the eyelids, to blink, to twinkle, as one who cannot see clearly, and hence to be *near-sighted.* The meaning here is, that he is like one who has an indistinct vision ; one who can see only the objects that are near him, but who has no correct apprehension of objects that are more remote. He sees but a little way into the true nature and design of the gospel. He does not take those large and clear views which would enable him to comprehend the whole system at a glance. ¶ *And hath forgotten that he was purged from his old sins.* He does not remember the obligation which grows out of the fact that a system has been devised to purify the heart, and that he

has been so far brought under the power of that system as to have his sins forgiven. If he had any just view of that, he would see that he was under obligation to ~make as high attainments as possible, and to cultivate to the utmost extent the Christian graces.

10. *Wherefore the rather, brethren, give diligence.* Ver. 5. ' In view of these things, give the greater diligence to secure your salvation.' The considerations on which Peter based this appeal seem to have been the fact that such promises are made to us, and such hopes held out before us ; the degree of uncertainty thrown over the whole matter of our personal salvation by low attainments in the divine life, and the dreadful condemnation which will ensue if in the end it shall be found that we are destitute of all real piety. The general thought is, that religion is of sufficient importance to claim our highest diligence, and to arouse us to the most earnest efforts to obtain the assurance of salvation. ¶ *To make your calling and election sure.* On the meaning of the word *calling,* see Notes on Eph. iv. 1. On the meaning of the word *election,* see Notes on Rom. ix. 11; 1 Thess. i. 4. Comp. Eph. i. 5. The word rendered election here, (ἐκλογή,) occurs only in this place and in Acts ix. 15; Rom. ix. 11; xi. 5, 7, 28; 1 Thess. i. 4; though corresponding words from the same root denoting *the elect, to elect, to choose,* frequently occur. The word here used means *election,* referring to the act of God, by which those who are saved are *chosen* to eternal life. As the word *calling* must refer to the act of God, so the word *election* must ; for it is God who both *calls* and *chooses* those who shall be saved. The word in the Scriptures usually refers to the actual *choosing* of those who shall be saved; that is, referring to the time when they, in fact, *become* the children of God, rather than to the *purpose* of God that it shall be done; but still there must have been an

eternal purpose, for God makes no choice which he did not always intend to make. The word *sure*, means firm, steadfast, secure, (βιβαίαν.) Here the reference must be to *themselves;* that is, they were so to act as to make it certain to themselves that they had been chosen, and were truly called into the kingdom of God. It cannot refer to God, for no act of theirs could make it more certain on his part, if they had been actually chosen to eternal life. Still, God everywhere treats men as moral agents ; and what may be absolutely certain in his mind from the mere purpose that it *shall* be so, is to be made certain to us only by evidence, and in the free exercise of our own powers. The meaning here is, that they were to obtain such evidences of personal piety as to put the question whether they were *called* and *chosen*, so far as their own minds were concerned, to rest ; or so as to have undoubted evidence on this point. The Syriac, the Vulgate, and some Greek manuscripts, insert here the expression 'by your good works ;' that is, they were to make their calling sure *by* their good works, or by holy living. This clause, as Calvin remarks, is not authorized by the best authority, but it does not materially affect the sense. It was undoubtedly by their ' good works ' in the sense of holy living, or of lives consecrated to the service of God, that they were to obtain the evidence that they were true Christians; that is, that they had been really called into the kingdom of God, for there is nothing else on which we can depend for such evidence. God has given no assurance to us by name that he intends to save us. We can rely on no voice, or vision, or new revelation, to prove that it is so. No internal feeling of itself, no raptures, no animal excitement, no confident persuasion in our own minds that we are elected, can be proof in the case ; and the only certain *evidence* on which we can rely is that which is found in a life of sincere piety. In view of the important statement of Peter in this verse, then, we may remark, (1.) that he believed in the doctrine of election, for he uses language which obviously implies this, or such as they are accustomed to use who believe the doctrine. (2.) The fact that God has chosen

those who shall be saved, does not make our own efforts unnecessary to make that salvation sure to us. It can be made sure to our own minds only by our own exertions; by obtaining evidence that we are in fact the children of God. There can be no evidence that salvation will be ours, unless there is a holy life ; that is, unless there is true religion. Whatever may be the secret purpose of God in regard to us, the only evidence that we have that we shall be saved is to be found in the fact that we are sincere Christians, and are honestly endeavouring to do his will. (3.) It is possible to make our calling and election sure ; that is, to have such evidence on the subject that the mind shall be calm, and that there will be no danger of deception. If we can determine the point that we are *in fact* true Christians, that settles the matter—for then the unfailing promise of God meets us that we shall be saved. In making our salvation sure to our own minds, if we are in fact true Christians, we have not to go into an argument to prove that we have sufficient strength to resist temptation, or that we shall be able in any way to keep ourselves. All that matter is settled by the promise of God, that if we are Christians we shall be kept *by him* to salvation. The only question that is to be settled is, whether we are in fact true Christians, and all beyond that may be regarded as determined immutably. But assuredly it is possible for a man to determine the question whether he is or is not a true Christian. (4.) If it *can* be done, it *should* be. Nothing is more important for us to do than this ; and to this great inquiry we should apply our minds with unfaltering diligence, until by the grace of God we can say that there are no lingering doubts in regard to our final salvation. ¶ *For if ye do these things.* The things referred to in the previous verses. If you use all diligence to make as high attainments as possible in piety, and *it* you practise the virtues demanded by religion, vers. 5–7. ¶ *Ye shall never fall.* You shall never fall into perdition. That is, you shall certainly be saved. 11. *For so an entrance.* In this manner you shall be admitted into the kingdom of God. ¶ *Shall be ministered*

11 For so an entrance shall be ministered unto you abundantly into the everlasting kingdom of our Lord and Saviour Jesus Christ.

12 Wherefore I will not be negligent to put you always in remem-

brance of these things, though ye know *them*, and be established in the present truth.

13 Yea, I think it meet, as long as I am in this tabernacle, to stir *

a 2 Pe.3.1.

---

unto you. The same Greek word is here used which occurs in ver. 5, and which is there rendered *add.* See Notes on that verse. There was not improbably in the mind of the apostle a recollection of that word; and the sense may be, that 'if they would lead on the virtues and graces referred to in their beautiful order, those graces would attend them in a radiant train to the mansions of immortal glory and blessedness.' See Doddridge *in loc.* ¶ *Abundantly.* Gr., *richly.* That is, the most ample entrance would be furnished; there would be no doubt about their admission there. The gates of glory would be thrown wide open, and they, adorned with all the bright train of graces, would be admitted there. ¶ *Into the everlasting kingdom,* &c. Heaven. It is here called *everlasting,* not because the Lord Jesus shall preside over it as the Mediator, (comp. Notes, 1 Cor. xv. 24,) but because, in the form which shall be established when 'he shall have given it up to the Father,' it will endure for ever. The empire of God which the Redeemer shall set up over the souls of his people shall endure to all eternity. The object of the plan of redemption was to secure their allegiance to God, and that will never terminate.

12. *Wherefore I will not be negligent.* That is, in view of the importance of these things. ¶ *To put you always in remembrance.* To give you the means of having them always in remembrance; to wit, by his writings. ¶ *Though ye know* them. It was of importance for Peter, as it is for ministers of the gospel now, to bring known truths to remembrance. Men are liable to forget them, and they do not exert the influence over them which they ought. It is the office of the ministry not only to impart to a people truths which they did not know before, but a large part of their work is to bring to recollection well-known truths, and to seek that they may exert

a proper influence on the life. Amidst the cares, the business, the amusements, and the temptations of the world, even true Christians are prone to forget them; and the ministers of the gospel render them an essential service, even if they should do nothing more than remind them of truths which are well understood, and which they have known before. A pastor, in order to be useful, need not always aim at originality, or deem it necessary always to present truths which have never been heard of before. He renders an essential service to mankind who *reminds* them of what they know but are prone to forget, and who endeavours to impress plain and familiar truths on the heart and conscience, for these truths are most important for man. ¶ *And be established in the present truth.* That is, the truth which is with you, or which you have received.—*Rob. Lex.* on the word τάρμμι. The apostle did not doubt that they were now confirmed in the truth as far as it had been made known to them, but he felt that amidst their trials, and especially as they were liable to be drawn away by false teachers, there was need of reminding them of the grounds on which the truths which they had embraced rested, and of adding his own testimony to confirm their Divine origin. Though we may be very firm in our belief of the truth, yet there is a propriety that the grounds of our faith should be stated to us frequently, that they may be always in our remembrance. The mere fact that at present we are firm in the belief of the truth, is no certain evidence that we shall always continue to be; nor because we are thus firm should we deem it improper for our religious teachers to state the grounds on which our faith rests, or to guard us against the arts of those who would attempt to subvert our faith.

13. *Yea, I think it meet.* I think it becomes me as an apostle. It is my

you up, by putting *you* in remembrance;

14 Knowing that shortly I must put off *this* my tabernacle, even as

a Jn.21,18,19.

our Lord Jesus Christ hath shewed me.[a]

15 Moreover, I will endeavour that ye may be able after my decease to have these things always in remembrance.

---

appropriate duty; a duty which is felt the more as the close of life draws near. ¶ *As long as I am in this tabernacle.* As long as I live; as long as I am in the body. The body is called a tabernacle, or *tent,* as that in which the soul resides for a little time. See Notes, 2 Cor. v. 1. ¶ *To stir you up, by putting* you *in remembrance.* To excite or arouse you to a diligent performance of your duties; to keep up in your minds a lively sense of Divine things. Religion becomes more important to a man's mind always as he draws near the close of life, and feels that he is soon to enter the eternal world.

14. *Knowing that shortly I must put off* this *my tabernacle.* That I must die. This he knew, probably, because he was growing old, and was reaching the outer period of human life. It does not appear that he had any express revelation on the point. ¶ *Even as our Lord Jesus Christ hath shewed me.* See Notes, John xxi. 18, 19. This does not mean that he had any new revelation on the subject, showing him that he was soon to die, as many of the ancients supposed; but the idea is, that the time drew near when he was to die *in the manner* in which the Saviour had told him that he would. He had said (John xxi. 18) that this would occur when he should be 'old,' and as he was now becoming old, he felt that the predicted event was drawing near. Many years had now elapsed since this remarkable prophecy was uttered. It would seem that Peter had never doubted the truth of it, and during all that time he had had before him the distinct assurance that he must die by violence; by having 'his hands stretched forth;' and by being conveyed by force to some place of death to which he would not of himself go, (John xxi. 18;) but, though the prospect of such a death must have been painful, he never turned away from it; never sought to abandon his Master's cause;

and never doubted that it would be so. This is one of the few instances that have occurred in the world, where a man knew distinctly, long beforehand, what would be the manner of his own death, and where he could have it constantly in his eye. *We* cannot foresee this in regard to ourselves, but we may learn to feel that death is not far distant, and may accustom ourselves to think upon it in whatever manner it may come upon us, as Peter did, and endeavour to prepare for it. Peter would naturally seek to prepare himself for death in the particular form in which he knew it would occur to him; we should prepare for it in whatever way it may occur to us. The subject of crucifixion would be one of peculiar interest to him; to us death itself should be the subject of peculiar interest—the manner is to be left to God. Whatever may be the signs of its approach, whether sickness or grey hairs, we should meditate much upon an event so solemn to us; and as these indications thicken we should be more diligent, as Peter was, in doing the work that God has given us to do. Our days, like the fabled Sybil's leaves, become more valuable as they are diminished in number; and as the 'inevitable hour' draws nearer to us, we should labour more diligently in our Master's cause, gird our loins more closely, and trim our lamps. Peter thought of the cross, for it was such a death that he was led to anticipate. Let us think of the bed of languishing on which we may die, or of the blow that may strike us suddenly down in the midst of our way, calling us without a moment's warning into the presence of our Judge.

15. *Moreover, I will endeavour.* I will leave such a permanent record of my views on these subjects that you may not forget them. He meant not only to declare his sentiments orally, but to record them that they might be

perused when he was dead. He had such a firm conviction of the truth and value of the sentiments which he held, that he would use all the means in his power that the church and the world should not forget them. ¶ *After my decease.* My *exode,* (ἔξοδον;) my journey out; my departure ; my exit from life. This is not the usual word to denote death, but is rather a word denoting that he was going on a journey *out* of this world. He did not expect to cease to be, but he expected to go on his travels to a distant abode. This idea runs through all this beautiful description of the feelings of Peter as he contemplated death. Hence he speaks of taking down the 'tabernacle' or *tent,* the temporary abode of the soul, that his spirit might be removed to another place, (ver. 13 ;) and hence he speaks of an *exode* from the present life—a journey to another world. This is the true notion of death ; and if so, two things follow from it : (1,) we should make preparation for it, as we do for a journey, and the more in proportion to the distance that we are to travel, and the time that we are to be absent ; and (2,) when the preparation is made, we should not be unwilling to enter on the journey, as we are not now when we are prepared to leave our homes to visit some remote part of our own country, or a distant land. ¶ *To have these things always in remembrance.* By his writings. We may learn from this, (1.) that when a Christian grows old, and draws near to death, his sense of the value of Divine truth by no means diminishes. As he approaches the eternal world ; as from its borders he surveys the past, and looks on to what is to come ; as he remembers what benefit the truths of religion have conferred on him in life, and sees what a miserable being he would now be if he had no such hope as the gospel inspires ; as he looks on the whole influence of those truths on his family and friends, on his country and the world, their value rises before him with a magnitude which he never saw before, and he desires most earnestly that they should be seen and embraced by all. A man on the borders of eternity is likely to have a very deep sense of the value of the Christian religion ; and is he not then in favourable circumstances

to estimate this matter aright? Let any one place himself in imagination in the situation of one who is on the borders of the eternal world, as all in fact soon will be, and can he have any doubt about the value of religious truth? (2.) We may learn from what Peter says here, that it is the *duty* of those who are drawing near to the eternal world, and who are the friends of religion, to do all they can that the truths of Christianity 'may be always had in remembrance.' Every man's experience of the value of religion, and the results of his examination and observation, should be regarded as the property of the world, and should not be lost. As he is about to die, he should seek, by all the means in his power, that those truths should be perpetuated and propagated. This duty may be discharged by some in counsels offered to the young, as they are about to enter on life, giving them the results of their own experience, observation, and reflections on the subject of religion ; by some, by an example so consistent that it cannot be soon forgotten—a legacy to friends and to the world of much more value than accumulated silver and gold ; by some, by solemn warnings or exhortations on the bed of death ; in other cases, by a recorded experience of the conviction and value of religion, and a written defence of its truth, and illustration of its nature—for every man who can write a good book owes it to the church and the world to do it ; by others, in leaving the means of publishing and spreading good books in the world. He does a good service to his own age, and to future ages, who records the results of his observations and his reflections in favour of the truth in a book that shall be readable ; and though the book itself may be ultimately forgotten, it may have saved some persons from ruin, and may have accomplished its part in keeping up the knowledge of the truth in his own generation. Peter, as a minister of the gospel, felt himself bound to do this, and no men have so good an opportunity of doing this now as ministers of the gospel ; no men have more ready access to the press ; no men have so much certainty that they will have the public attention, if they will write anything worth reading ; no men, commonly, in a

16 For we have not followed cunningly devised fables, *a* when we made known unto you the power

a 2 Co.4.2.

and coming of our Lord Jesus Christ, but were eye-witnesses *b* of his majesty.

b Mat.17.1-5; Jn.1.14.

community are better educated, or are more accustomed to write ; no men, by their profession, seem to be so much called to address their fellow-men in any way in favour of the truth ; and it is matter of great marvel that men who have such opportunities, and who seem especially called to the work, do not do more of this kind of service in the cause of religion. Themselves soon to die, how can they help desiring that they may leave *something* that shall bear an honourable, though humble, testimony to truths which they so much prize, and which they are appointed to defend ? A tract may live long after the author is in the grave ; and who can calculate the results which have followed the efforts of Baxter and Edwards to keep up in the world the remembrance of the truths which they deemed of so much value ? This little epistle of Peter has shed light on the path of men now for eighteen hundred years, and will continue to do it until the second coming of the Saviour.

16. *For we have not followed cunningly devised fables.* That is, fictions or stories invented by artful men, and resting on no solid foundation. The doctrines which they held about the coming of the Saviour were not, like many of the opinions of the Greeks, defended by weak and sophistical reasoning, but were based on solid evidence—evidence furnished by the personal observation of competent witnesses. It is true of the gospel, in general, that it is not founded on cunningly devised fables ; but the particular point referred to here is the promised coming of the Saviour. The evidence of that fact Peter proposes now to adduce. ¶ *When we made known unto you.* Probably Peter here refers particularly to statements respecting the coming of the Saviour in his first epistle, (chap. i. 5, 13 ; iv. 13 ;) but this was a common topic in the preaching, and in the epistles, of the apostles. It may, therefore, have referred to statements made to them at some time in his preaching, as well as to what he said in his former epistle. The apostles laid

great stress on the second coming of the Saviour, and often dwelt upon it. Comp. 1 Thess. iv. 16 ; Notes, Acts i. 11. ¶ *The power and coming.* These two words refer to the same thing ; and the meaning is, his *powerful coming*, or his *coming in power.* The advent of the Saviour is commonly represented as connected with the exhibition of power. Matt. xxiv. 30, ‘Coming in the clouds of heaven, with power.’ See Notes on that verse. Comp. Luke xxii. 69 ; Mark iii. 9. The *power* evinced will be by raising the dead ; summoning the world to judgment ; determining the destiny of men, &c. When the coming of the Saviour, therefore, was referred to by the apostles in their preaching, it was probably always in connection with the declaration that it would be accompanied by exhibitions of great power and glory—as it undoubtedly will be. The fact that the Lord Jesus would thus return, it is clear, had been denied by some among those to whom this epistle was addressed, and it was important to state the evidence on which it was to be believed. The *grounds* on which they denied it (chap. iii. 4) were, that there were no appearances of his approach ; that the promise had not been fulfilled ; that all things continued as they had been ; and that the affairs of the world moved on as they always had done. To meet and counteract this error—an error which so prevailed that many were in danger of ‘falling from their own steadfastness,’ (chap. iii. 17,)—Peter states the proof on which he believed in the coming of the Saviour. ¶ *But were eye-witnesses of his majesty.* On the mount of transfiguration, Matt. xvii. 1—5. See Notes on that passage. That transfiguration was witnessed only by Peter, James, and John. But it may be asked, how the facts there witnessed demonstrate the point under consideration—that the Lord Jesus will come with power ? To this it may be replied, (1,) that these apostles had there such a view of the Saviour in his glory as to convince them beyond doubt

17 For he received from God the Father honour and glory, when there came such a voice to him from the excellent glory, This is my beloved Son, in whom I am well pleased.

18 And this voice which came

a Ps.119.105; Pr.6.23.   *b* Re.2.28; 22.16.

from heaven we heard, when we were with him in the holy mount.

19 We have also a more sure word of prophecy; whereunto ye do well that ye take heed, as unto a light *a* that shineth in a dark place, until the day dawn, and the day-star *b* arise in your hearts:

---

that he was the Messiah. (2.) That there was a direct attestation given to that fact by a voice from heaven, declaring that he was the beloved Son of God. (3.) That that transfiguration was understood to have an important reference to the coming of the Saviour in his kingdom and his glory, and was designed to be a representation of the manner in which he would then appear. This is referred to distinctly by each one of the three evangelists who have mentioned the transfiguration. Matt. xvi. 28, 'There be some standing here which shall not taste of death till they see the Son of man coming in his kingdom;' Mark ix. 1, 2; Luke ix. 27, 28. The transfiguration which occurred soon after these words were spoken was *designed* to show them what he would be in his glory, and to furnish to them a demonstration which they could never forget, that he would yet set up his kingdom in the world. (4.) They had in fact such a view of him as he would be in his kingdom, that they could entertain no doubt on the point; and the fact, as it impressed their own minds, they made known to others. The evidence as it lay in Peter's mind was, that that transfiguration was *designed* to furnish proof to them that the Messiah would certainly appear in glory, and to give them a view of him as coming to reign which would never fade from their memory. As that had not yet been accomplished, he maintained that the evidence was clear that it must occur at some future time. As the transfiguration was *with reference* to his coming in his kingdom, it was proper for Peter to use it with that reference, or as bearing on that point.

17. *For he received from God the Father honour and glory.* He was honoured by God in being thus addressed. ¶ *When there came such a voice*

to him from the excellent glory. The magnificent splendour; the bright cloud which overshadowed them, Matt. xvii 5. ¶ *This is my beloved Son, in whom I am well pleased.* See Notes, Matt. xvii. 5 ; iii. 17. This demonstrated that he was the Messiah. Those who heard that voice could not doubt this ; they never did afterwards doubt.

18. *And this voice which came from heaven we heard.* To wit, Peter, and James, and John. ¶ *When we were with him in the holy mount.* Called *holy* on account of the extraordinary manifestation of the Redeemer's glory there. It is not certainly known what mountain this was, but it has commonly been supposed to be Mount Tabor. See Notes, Matt. xvii. 1.

19. *We have also a more sure word of prophecy.* That is, a prophecy pertaining to the coming of the Lord Jesus; for that is the point under discussion. There has been considerable diversity of opinion in regard to the meaning of this passage. Some have supposed that the apostle, when he says, 'a *more sure* word,' did not intend to make any comparison between the miracle of the transfiguration and prophecy, but that he meant to say merely that the word of prophecy was *very* sure, and could certainly be relied on. Others have supposed that the meaning is, that the prophecies which foretold his coming into the world having been confirmed by the fact of his advent, are rendered more sure and undoubted than when they were uttered, and may now be confidently appealed to. So Rosenmüller, Benson, Macknight, Clarke, Wetstein, and Grotius. Luther renders it, 'we have a firm prophetic word;' omitting the comparison. A literal translation of the passage would be, 'and we have the prophetic word more firm.' If a comparison is intended, it may be either

that the prophecy was more sure than the *fables* referred to in ver. 16; or than the miracle of the transfiguration; or than the word which was heard in the holy mount ; or than the prophecies even in the time when they were first spoken. If such a comparison was designed, the most obvious of these interpretations would be, that the prophecy was more certain proof than was furnished in the mount of transfiguration. But it seems probable that no *comparison* was intended, and that the thing on which Peter intended to fix the eye was not that the prophecy was a *better* evidence respecting the advent of the Messiah than other evidences, but that it was a *strong* proof which demanded their particular attention, as being of a firm and decided character. There can be no doubt that the apostle refers here to what is contained in the Old Testament ; for, in ver. 21, he speaks of the prophecy as that which was spoken 'in old time, by men that were moved by the Holy Ghost.' The *point* to which the prophecies related, and to which Peter referred, was the great doctrine respecting the coming of the Messiah, embracing perhaps all that pertained to his work, or all that he designed to do by his advent. They had had one illustrious proof respecting his advent as a glorious Saviour by his transfiguration on the mount ; and the apostle here says that the prophecies abounded with truths on these points, and that they ought to give earnest heed to the disclosures which they made, and to compare them diligently with facts as they occurred, that they might be confirmed more and more in the truth. If, however, as the more obvious sense of this passage *seems* to be, and as many suppose to be the correct interpretation, (see Doddridge, *in loc.*, and Professor Stuart, on the canon of the Old Test., p. 329,) it means that the prophecy was more sure, more steadfast, more to be depended on than even what the three disciples had seen and heard in the mount of transfiguration, this may be regarded as true in the following respects: (1.) The prophecies are *numerous*, and by their number they furnish a stronger proof than could be afforded by a single manifestation, however clear and glorious. (2.) They were *recorded*, and might be the subject of careful comparison with the events as they occurred. (3.) They were written long beforehand, and it could not be urged that the testimony which the prophets bore was owing to any illusion on their minds, or to any agreement among the different writers to impose on the world. Though Peter regarded the testimony which he and James and John bore to the glory of the Saviour, from what they saw on the holy mount, as strong and clear confirmation that he was the Son of God, yet he could not but be aware that it might be suggested by a caviller that they might have *agreed* to impose on others, or that they might have been dazzled and deceived by some natural phenomenon occurring there. Comp. Kuinoel on Matt. xvii. 1, seq. (4.) Even supposing that there was a miracle in the case, the evidence of the prophecies, embracing many points in the same general subject, and extending through a long series of years, would be more satisfactory than any single miracle whatever. See Doddridge, *in loc.* The general meaning is, that the fact that he had come as the Messiah was disclosed in the mount by such a manifestation of his glory, and of what he would be, that they who saw it could not doubt it; the same thing the apostle says was more fully shown also in the prophecies, and these prophecies demanded their close and prolonged attention. ¶ *Whereunto ye do well that ye take heed.* They are worthy of your study, of your close and careful investigation. There is perhaps no study more worthy of the attention of Christians than that of the prophecies. ¶ *As unto a light that shineth in a dark place.* That is, the prophecies resemble a candle, lamp, or torch, in a dark room, or in an obscure road at night. They make objects distinct which were before unseen; they enable us to behold many things which would be otherwise invisible. The object of the apostle in this representation seems to have been, to state that the prophecies do not give a *perfect* light, or that they do not remove *all* obscurity, but that they shed some light on objects which would otherwise be *entirely* dark, and that the light which they furnished

20 Knowing this first, that no | prophecy of the scripture is of any private interpretation.

was so valuable that we ought by all means to endeavour to avail ourselves of it. Until the day shall dawn, and we shall see objects by the clear light of the sun, they are to be our guide. A lamp is of great value in a dark night, though it may not disclose objects so clearly as the light of the sun. But it may be a safe and sure guide ; and a man who has to travel in dark and dangerous places, does 'well' to 'take heed' to his lamp. ¶ *Until the day dawn.* Until you have the clearer light which shall result from the dawning of the day. The reference here is to the morning light as compared with a lamp ; and the meaning is, that we should attend to the light furnished by the prophecies until the truth shall be rendered more distinct by the events as they shall actually be disclosed—until the brighter light which shall be shed on all things by the glory of the second advent of the Saviour, and the clearing up of what is now obscure in the splendours of the heavenly world. The point of comparison is between the necessary obscurity of prophecy, and the clearness of events when they actually occur—a difference like that which is observable in the objects around us when seen by the shining of the lamp and by the light of the sun. The apostle directs the mind onward to a period when all shall be clear—to that glorious time when the Saviour shall return to receive his people to himself in that heaven where all shall be light. Comp. Rev. xxi. 23—25; xxii. 5. Meantime we should avail ourselves of all the light which we have, and should apply ourselves diligently to the study of the prophecies of the Old Testament which are still unfulfilled, and of those in the New Testament which direct the mind onward to brighter and more glorious scenes than this world has yet witnessed. In our darkness they are a cheering lamp to guide our feet, till that illustrious day shall dawn. Comp. Notes, 1 Cor. xiii. 9, 10. ¶ *And the day-star.* The morning star —the bright star that at certain periods of the year leads on the day, and which

is a pledge that the morning is about to dawn. Comp. Rev. ii. 28; xxii. 16. ¶ *Arise in your hearts.* *On* your hearts; that is, sheds its beams on your hearts. Till you see the indications of that approaching day in which all is light. The period referred to here by the approaching day that is to diffuse this light, is when the Saviour shall return in the full revelation of his glory—the splendour of his kingdom. Then all will be clear. Till that time, we should search the prophetic records, and strengthen our faith, and comfort our hearts, by the predictions of the future glory of his reign. Whether this refers, as some suppose, to his reign on earth, either personally or by the principles of his religion universally prevailing, or, as others suppose, to the brighter revelations of heaven when he shall come to receive his people to himself, it is equally clear that a brighter time than any that has yet occurred is to dawn on our race, and equally true that we should regard the prophecies, as we do the morning star, as the cheering harbinger of day.

20. *Knowing this first.* Bearing this steadily in mind as a primary and most important truth. ¶ *That no prophecy of the Scripture.* No prophecy contained in the inspired records. The word *scripture* here shows that the apostle referred particularly to the prophecies recorded in the Old Testament. The remark which he makes about prophecy is general, though it is designed to bear on a particular class of the prophecies. ¶ *Is of any private interpretation.* The expression here used (ἰδίας ἐπιλύσεως) has given rise to as great a diversity of interpretation, and to as much discussion, as perhaps any phrase in the New Testament; and to the present time there is no general agreement among expositors as to its meaning. It would be foreign to the design of these Notes, and would be of little utility, to enumerate the different interpretations which have been given of the passage, or to examine them in detail. It will be sufficient to remark, preparatory to endeavouring to ascertain the true sense

of the passage, that some have held that it teaches that no prophecy can be interpreted of itself, but can be understood only by comparing it with the event; others, that it teaches that the prophets did not themselves understand what they wrote, but were mere passive organs under the dictation of the Holy Spirit to communicate to future times what they could not themselves explain; others, that it teaches that 'no prophecy is of self-interpretation,' (*Horsley;*) others, that it teaches that the prophecies, besides having a literal signification, have also a hidden and mystical sense which cannot be learned from the prophecies themselves, but is to be perceived by a peculiar power of insight imparted by the Holy Ghost, enabling men to understand their recondite mysteries. It would be easy to show that some of these opinions are absurd, and that none of them are sustained by the fair interpretation of the language used, and by the drift of the passage. The more correct interpretation, as it seems to me, is that which supposes that the apostle teaches that the truths which the prophets communicated were not originated by themselves; were not of their own suggestion or invention; were not their own opinions, but were of higher origin, and were imparted by God; and according to this the passage may be explained, 'knowing this as a point of first importance when you approach the prophecies, or always bearing this in mind, that it is a great principle in regard to the prophets, that what they communicated *was not of their own disclosure;* that is, was not revealed or originated by them.' That this is the correct interpretation will be apparent from the following considerations: (1.) It accords with the *design* of the apostle, which is to produce an impressive sense of the importance and value of the prophecies, and to lead those to whom he wrote to study them with diligence. This could be secured in no way so well as by assuring them that the writings which he wished them to study did not contain truths originated by the human mind, but that they were of higher origin. (2.) This interpretation accords with what is said in the following verse, and is the only one of all those proposed that is

consistent with that, or in connection with which that verse will have any force. In that verse (21,) a *reason* is given for what is said here: '*For* (γὰρ) the prophecy came not in old time *by the will of man,*' &c. But this can be a good reason for what is said here only on the supposition that the apostle meant to say that what they communicated was not originated by themselves; that it was of a higher than human origin; that the prophets spake 'as they were moved by the Holy Ghost.' This fact was a good reason why they should show profound respect for the prophecies, and study them with attention. But how could the fact that *they were moved by the Holy Ghost* be a reason for studying them, if the meaning here is that the prophets could not understand their own language, or that the prophecy could be understood only by the event, or that the prophecy had a double meaning, &c.? If the prophecies were of Divine origin, then *that* was a good reason why they should be approached with reverence, and should be profoundly studied. (3.) This interpretation accords as well, to say the least, with the fair meaning of the language employed, as either of the other opinions proposed. The word rendered *interpretation* (ἐπί-λυσις) occurs nowhere else in the New Testament. It properly means *solution,* (Rob. Lex.,) *disclosure,* (Prof. Stuart on the Old Testament, p. 328,) *making free (Passow,)* with the notion that what is thus released or loosed was before bound, entangled, obscure. The verb from which this word is derived (ἐπιλύω) means, *to let loose upon,* as dogs upon a hare, (Xen. Mem. 7,8; *ib* 9,10;) to loose or open letters; to loosen a band; to loose or disclose a riddle or a dark saying, and then to enlighten, illustrate, &c.—*Passow.* It is twice used in the New Testament. Mark iv. 34, 'He *ex-pounded* all things to his disciples; Acts xix. 39, 'It shall be *determined* in a lawful assembly.' The verb would be applicable to loosing anything which is bound or confined, and thence to the explanation of a mysterious doctrine or a parable, or to a disclosure of what was before unknown. The word, according to this, in the place before us, would mean the disclosure of what was before

21 For the prophecy came not [1] in *a* old time by the will of man : but holy men of God spake *as they were* moved by *b* the Holy Ghost.

[1] Or, *at any.*   *a* Lu.1.70.   *b* 2 Ti.3.16.

bound, or retained, or unknown ; either what had never been communicated at all, or what had been communicated obscurely ; and the idea is, ' no prophecy recorded in the Scripture is of, or comes from, any exposition or disclosure of the will and purposes of God by the prophets themselves.' It is not a thing of their own, or a private matter originating with themselves, but it is to be traced to a higher source. If this be the true interpretation, then it follows that the prophecies are to be regarded as of higher than any human origin ; and then, also, it follows that this passage should not be used to prove that the prophets did not understand the nature of their own communications, or that they were mere unconscious and passive instruments in the hand of God to make known his will. Whatever may be the truth on those points, this passage proves nothing in regard to them, any more than the fact that a minister of religion now declares truth which he did not originate, but which is to be traced to God as its author, proves that he does not understand what he himself says. It follows, also, that this passage cannot be adduced by the Papists to prove that the people at large should not have free access to the word of God, and should not be allowed to interpret it for themselves. It makes no affirmation on that point, and does not even contain any *principle* of which such a use can be made ; for, (1.) whatever it means, it is confined to *prophecy ;* it does not embrace the whole Bible. (2.) Whatever it means, it merely states a *fact ;* it does not enjoin a *duty.* It states, as a fact, that there was *something* about the prophecies which was not of private solution, but it does not state that it is the duty of the church to *prevent* any private explanation or opinion even of the prophecies. (3.) It says nothing about *the church* as empowered to give a public or authorized interpretation of the prophecies. There is not a hint, or an intimation of any kind, that the church is intrusted with any such power what-

ever. There never was any greater perversion of a passage of Scripture than to suppose that this teaches that any class of men is not to have free access to the Bible. The effect of the passage, properly interpreted, should be to lead us to study the Bible with profound reverence, as having a higher than any human origin, not to turn away from it as if it were unintelligible, or to lead us to suppose that it can be interpreted only by one class of men. The fact that it discloses truths which the human mind could not of itself have originated, is a good reason for studying it with diligence and with prayer—not for supposing that it is unlawful for us to attempt to understand it ; a good reason for reverence and veneration for it—not for sanctified neglect.

21. *For the prophecy came not in old time.* Marg., ' or, *at any.*' The Greek word (ποτὶ) will bear either construction. It would be true in either sense, but the reference is particularly to the recorded prophecies in the Old Testament. What was true of them, however, is true of all prophecy, that it is not by the will of man. The word *prophecy* here is without the article, meaning prophecy in general—all that is prophetic in the Old Testament ; or, in a more general sense still, all that the prophets taught, whether relating to future events or not. ¶ *By the will of man.* It was not of human origin ; not discovered by the human mind. The word *will,* here seems to be used in the sense of *prompting* or *suggestion ;* men did not speak by their own suggestion, but as truth was brought to them by God. ¶ *But holy men of God.* Pious men commissioned by God, or employed by him as his messengers to mankind. ¶ *Spake as they were moved by the Holy Ghost.* Comp. 2 Tim. iii. 16. The Greek phrase here (ὑπὸ Πνεύματος ἁγίου φερόμενοι) means *borne along, moved, influenced* by the Holy Ghost. The idea is, that in what they spake they were *carried along* by an influence from above. They moved in the case

CHAPTER II.

BUT there *a* were false prophets also among the people even as there shall be false teachers among you, *b* who privily shall bring in damnable heresies, even denying the Lord that bought them, and bring upon themselves swift destruction.

a De.13.1,&c.   b Mat.24.5,24; Ac.20.29,30; 1 Ti.4.1.

only as they were moved ; they spake only as the influence of the Holy Ghost was upon them. They were no more self-moved than a vessel at sea is that is impelled by the wind ; and as the progress made by the vessel is to be measured by the impulse bearing upon it, so the statements made by the prophets are to be traced to the impulse which bore upon their minds. They were not, indeed, in all respects like such a vessel, but only in regard to the fact that all they said as prophets was to be traced to the foreign influence that bore upon their minds. There could not be, therefore, a more decided declaration than this in proof that the prophets were inspired. If the authority of Peter is admitted, his positive and explicit assertion settles the question. If this be so, also, then the point with reference to which he makes this observation is abundantly confirmed, that the prophecies demand our earnest attention, and that we should give all the heed to them which we would to a light or lamp when travelling in a dangerous way, and in a dark night. In a still more general sense, the remark here made may also be applied to the whole of the Scriptures. We are in a dark world. We see few things clearly ; and all around us, on a thousand questions, there is the obscurity of midnight. By nature there is nothing to cast light on those questions, and we are perplexed, bewildered, embarrassed. The Bible is given to us to shed light on our way. It is the *only* light which we have respecting the future, and though it does not give *all* the information which we might desire in regard to what is to come, yet it gives us sufficient light to guide us to heaven. It teaches us what it is necessary to know about God, about our duty, and about the way of salvation, in order to conduct us safely ; and no one who has committed himself to its direction, has been suffered to wander finally away from the paths of salva-

tion. It is, therefore, a duty to attend to the instructions which the Bible imparts, and to commit ourselves to its holy guidance in our journey to a better world : for soon, if we are faithful to its teachings, the light of eternity will dawn upon us, and there, amidst its cloudless splendour, we shall see as we are seen, and know as we are known ; then we shall ' need no candle, neither light of the sun ; for the Lord God shall give us light, and we shall reign for ever and ever.' Comp. Rev. xxi. 22–24 ; xxii. 5.

CHAPTER II.

ANALYSIS OF THE CHAPTER.

THE general subject of this chapter is stated in the first verse, and it embraces these points : (1,) that it might be expected that there would be false teachers among Christians, as there were false prophets in ancient times ; (2,) that they would introduce destructive errors, leading many astray ; and, (3,) that they would be certainly punished. The design of the chapter is to illustrate and defend these points.

I. That there would be such false teachers the apostle expressly states in ver. 1 ; and incidentally in that verse, and elsewhere in the chapter, he notices some of their characteristics, or some of the doctrines which they would hold. (*a*) They would deny the Lord that bought them, ver. 1. See Notes on that verse. (*b*) They would be influenced by covetousness, and their object in their attempting to seduce others from the faith, and to induce them to become followers of themselves, would be to make money, ver. 3. (*c*) They would be corrupt, beastly, and licentious in their conduct ; and it would be one design of their teaching to show that the indulgence of gross passions was not inconsistent with religion ; ver. 10, ' that walk after the flesh, in the lust of uncleanness ;' ver. 12, ' as natural brute beasts ;' ' shall perish in their own corruption ;' ver. 14, 'having eyes full of adultery, and that cannot cease from sin ;' ver. 22, ' the dog has returned to his own vomit again.' (d) They would be proud, arrogant, and self-willed; men who would despise all proper government, and who would be thoroughly 'radical' in their views ; ver. 10, 'and despise government; presumptuous are they and self-willed, they are not afraid to speak evil of dignities ;' ver. 18, ' they speak great swelling words of vanity.' (e) They were persons who had been formerly of corrupt lives, but who had become professing Christians. This is implied in vers. 20–22. They are spoken of as having ' escaped the pollutions of the world, through the knowledge of the Lord and Saviour Jesus Christ ;' as ' having known the ways of righteousness,' but as having turned again to their former corrupt practices and lusts ; ' it has happened to them according to the true proverb,' &c. There were various classes of persons in primitive times, coming under the general appellation of the term Gnostic, to whom this description would apply, and it is probable that they had begun to broach their doctrines in the times of the apostles. Among those persons were the Ebionites, Corinthians, Nicolaitanes, &c.

II. These false teachers would obtain followers, and their teachings would be likely to allure many. This is intimated more than once in the chapter : ver. 2, ' and many shall follow their pernicious ways ;' ver. 3, ' and through covetousness shall they with feigned words make merchandise of you ;' ver. 14, ' beguiling unstable souls.' Comp. ver. 18.

III. They would certainly be punished. A large part of the chapter is taken up in proving this point, and especially in showing from the examples of others who had erred in a similar manner, that they could not escape destruction. In doing this, the apostle refers to the following facts and illustrations : (1.) The case of the angels that sinned, and that were cast down to hell, ver. 4. If God brought such dreadful punishment on those who were once before his throne, wicked men could have no hope of escape. (2.) The case of the wicked in the time of Noah, who were

cut off by the flood, ver. 5. (3.) The case of Sodom and Gomorrah, ver. 6. (4.) The character of the persons referred to was such that they could have no hope of escape. (a) They were corrupt, sensual, presumptuous, and self-willed, and were even worse than the rebel angels had been—men that seemed to be made to be taken and destroyed, vers. 10–12. (b) They were spots and blemishes, sensual and adulterers, emulating the example of Balaam, who was rebuked by even a dumb ass for his iniquity, vers. 13–16. (c) They allured others to sin under the specious promise of liberty, while they were themselves the slaves of debased appetites, and gross and sensual passions, vers. 17–19. From the entire description in this chapter, it is clear that the persons referred to, though once professors of religion, had become eminently abandoned and corrupt. It may not, indeed, be easy to identify them with any particular sect or class then existing and now known in history, though not a few of the sects in the early Christian church bore a strong resemblance to this description ; but there have been those in every age who have strongly resembled these persons ; and this chapter, therefore, possesses great value as containing important warnings against the arts of false teachers, and the danger of being seduced by them from the truth. Compare Introduction to the Epistle of Jude, § 3, 4.

1. But there were false prophets also among the people. In the previous chapter, (vers. 19–21,) Peter had appealed to the prophecies as containing unanswerable proofs of the truth of the Christian religion. He says, however, that he did not mean to say that all who claimed to be prophets were true messengers of God. There were many who pretended to be such, who only led the people astray. It is unnecessary to say, that such men have abounded in all ages where there have been true prophets. ¶ Even as there shall be false teachers among you. The fact that false teachers would arise in the church is often adverted to in the New Testament. Compare Matt. xxiv. 5. 24 ; Acts xx. 29, 30. ¶ Who privily That is, in a secret manner, or under

plausible arts and pretences. They would not at first make an open avowal of their doctrines, but would, in fact, while their teachings *seemed* to be in accordance with truth, covertly maintain opinions which would sap the very foundations of religion. The Greek word here used, and which is rendered ' who privily shall bring in,' (παρεισάγω,) means properly *to lead in by the side of others ; to lead in along with others.* Nothing could better express the usual way in which error is introduced. It is *by the side*, or *along with*, other doctrines which are true ; that is, while the mind is turned mainly to other subjects, and is off its guard, gently and silently to lay down some principle, which, being admitted, would lead to the error, or from which the error would follow as a natural consequence. Those who inculcate error rarely do it openly. If they would at once boldly ' deny the Lord that bought them,' it would be easy to meet them, and the mass of professed Christians would be in no danger of embracing the error. But when principles are laid down which may lead to that ; when doubts on remote points are suggested which may involve it ; or when a long train of reasoning is pursued which may secretly tend to it ; there is much more probability that the mind will be corrupted from the truth. ¶ *Damnable heresies.* αἱρέσεις ἀπωλείας. ' Heresies of destruction ;' that is, heresies that will be followed by destruction. The Greek word which is rendered *damnable*, is the same which in the close of the verse is rendered *destruction.* It is so rendered also in Matt. vii. 13 ; Rom. ix. 22 ; Phil. iii. 19 ; 2 Pet. iii. 16—in all of which places it refers to the future loss of the soul. The same word also is rendered *perdition* in John xvii. 12 ; Phil. i. 28 ; 1 Tim. vi. 9 ; Heb. x. 39 ; 2 Pet. iii. 7 ; Rev. xvii. 8, 11—in all which places it has the same reference. On the meaning of the word rendered ' *heresies*,' see Notes on Acts xxiv. 14 ; 1 Cor. xi. 19. The idea of *sect* or *party* is that which is conveyed by this word, rather than doctrinal errors ; but it is evident that in this case the formation of the sect or party, as is the fact in most cases, would be founded on error of doctrine.

The thing which these false teachers would attempt would be divisions, alienations, or parties, in the church, but these would be based on the erroneous doctrines which they would promulgate. What would be the particular doctrine in this case is immediately specified, to wit, that they 'would deny the Lord that bought them.' The idea then is, that these false teachers would form sects or parties in the church, of a destructive or ruinous nature, founded on a denial of the Lord that bought them. Such a formation of sects would be ruinous to piety, to good morals, and to the soul. The authors of these sects, holding the views which they did, and influenced by the motives which they would be, and practising the morals which they would practise, as growing out of their principles, would bring upon themselves swift and certain destruction. It is not possible now to determine to what particular class of errorists the apostle had reference here, but it is generally supposed that it was to some form of the Gnostic belief. There were many early sects of so-called *heretics* to whom what he here says would be applicable. ¶ *Even denying the Lord that bought them.* This must mean that they held doctrines which were *in fact* a denial of the Lord, or the tendency of which would be a denial of the Lord, for it cannot be supposed that, while they professed to be Christians, they would openly and avowedly deny him. To 'deny the Lord' may be either to deny his existence, his claims, or his attributes ; it is to withhold from him, in our belief and profession, anything which is essential to a proper conception of him. The particular thing, however, which is mentioned here as entering into that self-denial, is something connected with the fact that he had ' *bought*' them. It was such a denial of the Lord *as having bought them*, as to be in fact a renunciation of the peculiarity of the Christian religion. There has been much difference of opinion as to the meaning of the word *Lord* in this place —whether it refers to God the Father, or to the Lord Jesus Christ. The Greek word is Δεσπότης — *despotes.* Many expositors have maintained that it refers to the Father, and that when it is said that he had *bought* them, it means in a general sense that he was the Author of the plan of redemption, and had *caused* them to be purchased or redeemed. Michaelis supposes that the Gnostics are referred to as denying the Father by asserting that he was not the Creator of the universe, maintaining that it was created by an inferior being.—Intro. to New Testament, iv. 360. Whitby, Benson, Slade, and many others, maintain that this refers to the Father as having originated the plan by which men are redeemed; and the same opinion is held, of necessity, by those who deny the doctrine of general atonement. The only *arguments* to show that it refers to God the Father would be, (1,) that the word used here (Δισπότης) is not the usual term (κύριος) by which the Lord Jesus is designated in the New Testament; and (2,) that the admission that it refers to the Lord Jesus would lead inevitably to the conclusion that some will perish for whom Christ died. That it *does*, however, refer to the Lord Jesus, seems to me to be plain from the following considerations : (1.) It is the obvious interpretation; that which would be given by the great mass of Christians, and about which there could never have been any hesitancy if it had not been supposed that it would lead to the doctrine of general atonement. As to the alleged fact that the word used (*Despotes*) is not that which is commonly applied to the Lord Jesus, that may be admitted to be true, but still the word here may be understood as applied to him. It properly means a *master* as opposed to a servant; then it is used as denoting supreme authority, and is thus applied to God, and may be in that sense to the Lord Jesus Christ, as head over all things, or as having supreme authority over the church. It occurs in the New Testament only in the following places: 1 Tim. vi. 1, 2 ; Titus ii. 9 ; 1 Pet. ii. 18, where it is rendered *masters;* Luke ii. 29; Acts iv. 24 ; Rev. vi. 10, where it is rendered *Lord*, and is applied to God ; and in Jude 4, and in the passage before us, in both which places it is rendered *Lord*, and is probably to be regarded as applied to the Lord Jesus. There is nothing in the proper signification of the

word which would forbid this. (2.) The phrase is one that is properly applicable to the Lord Jesus as having *bought* us with his blood. The Greek word is ἀγοράζω—a word which means properly *to market, to buy, to purchase,* and then to redeem, or acquire for one's self by a price paid, or by a ransom. It is rendered *buy* or *bought* in the following places in the New Testament : Matt. xiii. 44, 46; xiv. 15; xxi. 12; xxv. 9, 10; xxvii. 7; Mark.vi. 36, 37; xi. 15; xv. 46; xvi. 1; Luke ix. 13; xiv. 18, 19; xvii. 28; xix. 45; xxii. 36; John iv. 8; vi. 5; xiii. 29; 1 Cor. vii. 30; Rev. iii. 18; xiii. 17; xviii. 11,—in all which places it is applicable to ordinary transactions of *buying.* In the following places it is also rendered *bought*, as applicable to the redeemed, as being bought or purchased by the Lord Jesus : 1 Cor. vi. 20; vii. 23, 'Ye are *bought* with a price;' and in the following places it is rendered *redeemed*, Rev. v. 9 ; xiv. 3, 4. It does not elsewhere occur in the New Testament. It is true that in a large sense this word might be applied to the Father as having caused his people to be redeemed, or as being the Author of the plan of redemption; but it is also true that the word is more properly applicable to the Lord Jesus, and that, when used with reference to redemption, it is uniformly given to him in the New Testament. Compare the passages referred to above. It is strictly and properly true only of the Son of God that he has '*bought*' us. The Father indeed is represented as making the arrangement, as giving his Son to die, and as the great Source of all the blessings secured by redemption ; but the *purchase* was actually made by the Son of God by his sacrifice on the cross. Whatever there was of the nature of a *price* was paid by him; and whatever obligations may grow out of the fact that we are purchased or ransomed are due particularly to him ; 2 Cor. v. 15. These considerations seem to me to make it clear that Peter referred here to the Lord Jesus Christ, and that he meant to say that the false teachers mentioned held doctrines which were in fact a *denial* of that Saviour. He does not specify particularly what constituted

2 And many shall follow their
1 pernicious ways; by reason of

1 Or, *lascivious*, as some copies read.

such a denial; but it is plain that any
doctrine which represented him, his
person, or his work, as essentially
different from what was the truth, would
amount to such a denial. If he was
Divine, and that fact was denied, making
him wholly a different being; if he
actually made an expiatory sacrifice by
his death, and that fact was denied,
and he was held to be a mere religious
teacher, changing essentially the character of the work which he came to
perform; if he, in some proper sense,
'bought' them with his blood, and that
fact was denied in such a way that according to their views it was not strictly
proper to speak of him as having *bought*
them at all, which would be the case if
he were a mere prophet or religious
teacher, then it is clear that such a representation would be in fact a denial
of his true nature and work. That some
of these views entered into their *denial*
of him is clear, for it was with reference
to the fact that he had 'bought' them,
or redeemed them, that they denied him.
¶ *And bring upon themselves swift destruction.* The *destruction* here referred
to can be only that which will occur in
the future world, for there can be no
evidence that Peter meant to say that
this would destroy their health, their
property, or their lives. The Greek
word (ἀπώλειαν) is the same which is
used in the former part of the verse, in
the phrase '*damnable heresies.*' See
Notes. In regard, then, to this important passage, we may remark, (1.) that
the apostle evidently believed that some
would perish for whom Christ died. (2.)
If this be so, then the same truth may
be expressed by saying that he died for
others besides those who will be saved;
that is, that the atonement was not
confined merely to the elect. This one
passage, therefore, demonstrates the doctrine of general atonement. This conclusion would be drawn from it by the
great mass of readers, and it may be
presumed, therefore, that this is the
fair interpretation of the passage.

[See the Supplementary Notes on 2 Cor. v. 14;
Heb. ii. 9 for a general view of the question re-

whom the way of truth shall be evil
spoken of.

garding the extent of the atonement. On this
text Scott has well observed: ' Doubtless Christ
intended to redeem those, and those only, who
he foresaw would *eventually* be saved by faith
in him; yet his ransom was of infinite sufficiency,
and men are continually addressed according to
their profession.' Christ has indeed laid down
such a price as that all the human family may
claim and find salvation in him. An unhappy
ambiguity of terms has made this controversy
very much a war of words. When the author
here says, 'Christ died for others besides those
who will be saved,' he does not use the words
in the common sense of an actual *design* on the
part of Christ to save all. The reader will see,
by consulting the Notes above referred to, how
much disputing might be saved by a careful definition of terms.]
(3.) It follows that men may destroy
themselves by a denial of the great and
vital *doctrines* of religion. It cannot be
a harmless thing, then, to hold erroneous
opinions; nor can men be safe who deny
the fundamental doctrines of Christianity. It is truth, not error, that saves
the soul; and an erroneous opinion on
any subject may be as dangerous to a
man's ultimate peace, happiness, and
prosperity, as a wrong course of life.
How many men have been ruined in
their worldly prospects, their health,
and their lives, by holding false sentiments on the subject of morals, or in
regard to medical treatment! Who
would regard it as a harmless thing if a
son should deny in respect to his father
that he was a man of truth, probity,
and honesty, or should attribute to him
a character which does not belong to
him—a character just the reverse of
truth? Can the same thing be innocent
in regard to God our Saviour? (4.) Men
bring destruction '*on themselves.*' No
one *compels* them to deny the Lord that
bought them; no one *forces* them to
embrace any dangerous error. If men
perish, they perish by their own fault,
for (*a*) ample provision was made for
their salvation as well as for others, (*b*)
they were freely invited to be saved;
(*c*) it was, in itself, just as easy for
them to embrace the truth as it was for
others; and (*d*) it was as easy to embrace the truth as to embrace error.

2. *And many shall follow their per-*

3 And through covetousness shall they with feigned words make merchandise of you : whose judgment

a now of a long time lingereth not, and their damnation slumbereth not.

a Jude 4-7.

nicious ways. Marg., *lascivious.* A large number of manuscripts and versions read *lascivious* here—ἀσελγείαις—instead of *pernicious*—ἀπωλείαις, (see Wetstein ,) and this reading is adopted in the editions of the Greek Testament by Tittman, Griesbach, and Hahn, and it seems probable that this is the correct reading. This will agree well with the account elsewhere given of these teachers, that their doctrines tended to licentiousness, vers. 10, 14, 18, 19. It is a very remarkable circumstance, that those who have denied the essential doctrines of the gospel have been so frequently licentious in their own conduct, and have inculcated opinions which tended to licentiousness. Many of the forms of religious error have somehow had a connection with this vice. Men who are corrupt at heart often seek to obtain for their corruptions the sanction of religion. ¶ *By reason of whom the way of truth shall be evil spoken of.* (1.) Because they were professors of religion, and religion would seem to be held responsible for their conduct ; and, (2.) because they were professed teachers of religion, and, by many, would be understood as expounding the true doctrines of the gospel.

3. *And through covetousness.* This shows what *one* of the things was by which they were influenced—a thing which, like licentiousness, usually exerts a powerful influence over the teachers of error. The religious principle is the strongest that is implanted in the human bosom ; and men who can obtain a livelihood in no other way, or who are too unprincipled or too indolent to labour for an honest living, often turn public teachers of religion, and adopt the kind of doctrines that will be likely to give them the greatest power over the purses of others. True religion, indeed, requires of its friends to devote all that they have to the service of God and to the promotion of his cause ; but it is very easy to pervert this requirement, so that the teacher of error shall take advantage of it for his own aggrandizement. ¶ *Shall they with feigned words.* Gr. formed,

fashioned ; then those which are *formed* for the occasion—feigned, false, deceitful. The idea is, that the doctrines which they would defend were not maintained by solid and substantial arguments, but that they would make use of plausible reasoning *made up* for the occasion. ¶ *Make merchandise of you.* Treat you not as rational beings but as a bale of goods, or any other article of traffic. That is, they would endeavour to make money out of them, and regard them only as fitted to promote that object. ¶ *Whose judgment.* Whose condemnation. ¶ *Now of a long time lingereth not.* Greek, 'of old ; long since.' The idea seems to be, that justice had been long attentive to their movements, and was on its way to their destruction. It was not a new thing—that is, there was no new principle involved in their destruction ; but it was a principle which had always been in operation, and which would certainly be applicable to them, and of a long time justice had been impatient to do the work which it was accustomed to do. What had occurred to the angels that sinned, (ver. 4,) to the old world, (ver. 5,) and to Sodom and Gomorrah, (ver 6,) would occur to them ; and the same justice which had overthrown them might be regarded as on its way to effect their destruction. Comp. Notes, Isa. xviii. 4. ¶ *And their damnation slumbereth not.* Their condemnation, (Notes, 1 Cor. xi. 29,) yet here referring to future punishment. 'Mr. Blackwell observes, that this is a most beautiful figure, representing the vengeance that shall destroy such incorrigible sinners as an angel of judgment pursuing them on the wing, continually approaching nearer and nearer, and in the mean time keeping a watchful eye upon them, that he may at length discharge an unerring blow.'—*Doddridge.* It is not uncommon to speak of 'sleepless justice ;' and the idea here is, that however justice may have *seemed* to slumber or to linger, it was not really so, but that it had on them an ever-watchful eye, and was on its way to do that which was right in regard to them.

4 For if God spared not the angels that sinned, but cast *them* down to hell, and delivered *them* into chains

of darkness. to be reserved unto judgment;

5 And spared not the old world,

A sinner should never forget that there is an eye of unslumbering vigilance always upon him, and that everything that he does is witnessed by one who will yet render exact justice to all men. No man, however careful to conceal his sins, or however bold in transgression, or however unconcerned he may seem to be, can hope that justice will always linger, or destruction always slumber.

4. *For if God spared not the angels that sinned.* The apostle now proceeds to the *proof* of the proposition that these persons would be punished. It is to be remembered that they had been, or were even then, professing Christians, though they had really, if not in form, apostatized from the faith, (vers. 20–22;) and a part of the proofs, therefore, are derived from the cases of those who had apostatized from the service of God. He appeals, therefore, to the case of the angels that had revolted. Neither their former rank, their dignity, nor their holiness, saved them from being thrust down to hell; and if God punished them so severely, then false teachers could not hope to escape. The apostle, by the *angels* here, refers undoubtedly to a revolt in heaven—an event referred to in Jude 6, and everywhere implied in the Scriptures. *When* that occurred, however—*why* they revolted, or what was the number of the apostates—we have not the slightest information, and on these points conjecture would be useless. In the supposition that it occurred, there is no improbability; for there is nothing more absurd in the belief that angels have revolted than that men have; and if there are evil angels, as there is no more reason to doubt than that there are evil men, it is morally certain that they must have fallen at some period from a state of holiness, for it cannot be believed that God *made* them wicked. ¶ *But cast* them *down to hell.* Gr., ταρταρώσας—'thrusting them down to Tartarus.' The word here used occurs nowhere else in the New Testament, though it is common in the classical writers. It is a verb formed from Τάρ-ταρος (*Tartarus,*) which in Greek my-

thology was the lower part, or abyss of hades where the shades of the wicked were supposed to be imprisoned and tormented, and answered to the Jewish word Γέεννα—*Gehenna.* It was regarded, commonly, as beneath the earth; as entered through the grave; as dark, dismal, gloomy; and as a place of punishment. Comp. Notes, Job x. 21, 22, and Matt. v. 22. The word here is one that properly refers to a place of punishment, since the whole argument relates to that, and since it cannot be pretended that the 'angels that sinned' were removed to a place of happiness on account of their transgression. It must also refer to punishment in some other world than this, for there is no evidence that *this* world is made a place of punishment for fallen angels. ¶ *And delivered* them *into chains of darkness.* 'Where darkness lies like chains upon them.'—*Rob. Lex.* The meaning seems to be, that they are confined in that dark prison-house *as if* by chains. We are not to suppose that spirits are literally bound; but it was common to bind or fetter prisoners who were in dungeons, and the representation here is taken from that fact. This representation that the mass of fallen angels are confined in *Tartarus,* or in hell, is not inconsistent with the representations which elsewhere occur that their leader is permitted to roam the earth, and that even many of those spirits are allowed to tempt men. It may be still true that the mass are confined within the limits of their dark abode; and it may even be true also that Satan and those who are permitted to roam the earth are under bondage, and are permitted to range only within certain bounds, and that they are so secured that they will be brought to trial at the last day. ¶ *To be reserved unto judgment:* Jude 6, 'to the judgment of the great day.' They will then, with the revolted inhabitants of this world, be brought to trial for their crimes. That the fallen angels will be punished *after* the judgment is apparent from Rev. xx. 10. The argument in this verse is, that if God punished the angels who revolted but saved Noah ^a the eighth *person*, a preacher of righteousness, bringing in the flood upon the world of the ungodly;

6 And turning the cities of ^b Sodom and Gomorrha into ashes, con-

a Ge.7.1,&c.   b Ge.19.24,25.

demned *them* with an overthrow, making ^c *them* an ensample unto those that after should live ungodly;

7 And delivered just Lot, ^d vexed with the filthy conversation of the wicked;

c De.29.23.   d Ge.19.16.

---

from him, it is a fair inference that he will punish wicked men, though they were once professors of religion.

5. *And spared not the old world.* The world before the flood. The argument here is, that he cut off that wicked race, and thus showed that he would punish the guilty. By that awful act of sweeping away the inhabitants of a world, he showed that men could not sin with impunity, and that the incorrigibly wicked must perish. ¶ *But saved Noah the eighth* person. This reference to Noah, like the reference to Lot in ver. 7, seems to have been thrown in in the progress of the argument as an incidental remark, to show that the righteous, however few in number, would be saved when the wicked were cut off. The phrase 'Noah the eighth,' means Noah, one of eight; that is, Noah and seven others. This idiom is found, says Dr. Bloomfield, in the best writers—from Herodotus and Thucydides downwards. See examples in Wetstein. The meaning in this place then is, that eight persons, and eight only of that race, were saved; thus showing, that while the wicked would be punished, however numerous they might be, the righteous, however few, would be saved. ¶ *A preacher of righteousness.* In Gen. vi. 9, it is said of Noah that he was 'a just man and perfect in his generations, and Noah walked with God;' and it may be presumed that during his long life he was faithful in reproving the wickedness of his age, and warned the world of the judgment that was preparing for it. Compare Notes, Heb. xi. 7. ¶ *Bringing in the flood upon the world of the ungodly.* Upon all the world besides that pious family. The argument here is, that if God would cut off a wicked race in this manner, the principle is settled that the wicked will not escape.

6. *And turning the cities of Sodom and Gomorrha into ashes.* Gen. xix.

24, 25. This is a third example to demonstrate that God will punish the wicked. Comp. Notes, Jude 7. The word rendered 'turning into ashes,' (τεφρώσας.) occurs nowhere else in the New Testament. It is from τέφρα, *(ashes,)* and means to reduce to ashes, and then to consume or destroy. ¶ *Condemned* them *with an overthrow.* By the fact of their being overthrown, he showed that they were to be condemned, or that he disapproved their conduct. Their calamity came expressly on account of their enormous sins; as it is frequently the case now that the awful judgments that come upon the licentious and the intemperate, are as plain a proof of the Divine disapprobation as were the calamities that came upon Sodom and Gomorrah. ¶ *Making* them *an ensample, &c.* That is, they were a demonstration that God disapproved of the crimes for which they were punished, and would disapprove of the same crimes in every age and in every land. The punishment of one wicked man or people always becomes a warning to all others.

7. *And delivered just Lot.* Gen. xix. 16. This case is incidentally referred to, to show that God makes a distinction between the righteous and the wicked; and that while the latter will be destroyed, the former will be saved. See ver. 9. Lot is called *just*, because he preserved himself uncontaminated amidst the surrounding wickedness. As long as he lived in Sodom he maintained the character of an upright and holy man. ¶ *Vexed with the filthy conversation of the wicked.* By the corrupt and licentious conduct of the wicked around him. On the word *conversation*, see Notes, Phil. i. 27. The original phrase, which is rendered *filthy*, has reference to licentiousness. The corruption of Sodom was open and shameless; and as Lot was compelled to see much of it, his

8 (For that righteous man dwelling among them, in seeing and hearing, vexed *his* righteous soul from

day to day with *their* unlawful deeds;)

9 The Lord knoweth how to ᵃ de-
ᵃ Ps.34.15-18.

---

heart was pained. The word here rendered *vexed*, means that he was wearied or burdened. The crimes of those around him he found it hard to bear with. 8. *For that righteous man dwelling among them.* The Latin Vulgate renders this, ' For in seeing and hearing he was just;' meaning that he maintained his uprightness, or that he did not become contaminated by the vices of Sodom. Many expositors have supposed that this is the correct rendering; but the most natural and the most common explanation is that which is found in our version. According to that, the meaning is, that compelled as he was, while living among them, to see and to hear what was going on, his soul was constantly troubled. ¶ *In seeing and hearing.* Seeing their open acts of depravity, and hearing their vile conversation. The effect which this had on the mind of Lot is not mentioned in Genesis, but nothing is more probable than the statement here made by Peter. Whether this statement was founded on tradition, or whether it is a suggestion of inspiration to the mind of Peter, cannot be determined. The words rendered *seeing* and *hearing* may refer to the *act* of seeing, or to the *object* seen. Wetstein and Robinson suppose that they refer here to the latter, and that the sense is, that he was troubled by what he saw and heard. The meaning is not materially different. Those who live among the wicked are compelled to see and hear much that pains their hearts, and it is well if they do not become indifferent to it, or contaminated by it. *Vexed* his *righteous soul from day to day with* their *unlawful deeds.* Tortured or tormented his soul—ἰβασάνιζιν. Comp. Matt. viii. 6, 29; Luke viii. 28; Rev. ix. 5; xi. 10; xiv. 10; xx. 10, where the same word is rendered *tormented.* The use of this word would seem to imply that there was something *active* on the part of Lot which produced this distress on account of their conduct. He was not merely troubled as if his soul were passively

acted on, but there were strong mental exercises of a positive kind, arising perhaps from anxious solicitude how he might prevent their evil conduct, or from painful reflections on the consequences of their deeds to themselves, or from earnest pleadings in their behalf before God, or from reproofs and warnings of the wicked. At all events, the language is such as would seem to indicate that he was not a mere passive observer of their conduct. This, it would seem, was ' from day to day;' that is, it was constant. There were doubtless reasons why Lot should remain among such a people, and why, when he might so easily have done it, he did not remove to another place. Perhaps it was one purpose of his remaining to endeavour to do them good, as it is often the duty of good men now to reside among the wicked for the same purpose. Lot is supposed to have resided in Sodom—then probably the most corrupt place on the earth—for sixteen years; and we have in that fact an instructive demonstration that a good man *may* maintain the life of religion in his soul when surrounded by the wicked, and an illustration of the effects which the conduct of the wicked will have on a man of true piety when he is compelled to witness it constantly. We may learn from the record made of Lot what those effects will be, and what is evidence that one *is* truly pious who lives among the wicked. (1.) He will not be *contaminated* with their wickedness, or will not conform to their evil customs. (2.) He will not become *indifferent* to it, but his heart will be more and more affected by their depravity. Comp. Psa. cxix. 136; Luke xix. 41; Acts xvii. 16. (3.) He will have not only constant, but growing solicitude in regard to it—solicitude that will be felt every day: ' He vexed his soul *from day to day.*' It will not only be at intervals that his mind will be affected by their conduct, but it will be an habitual and constant thing. True piety is not fitful, periodical, and spasmodic; it is constant and steady. It

liver the godly out of temptations, and to reserve *a* the unjust unto the day of judgment to be punished: 10 But chiefly them *b* that walk after the flesh in the lust of unclean-

ness, and despise ¹ government: presumptuous *are they*, self-willed ; they are not afraid to speak evil of dignities. *c*

a Jude 14,15.   *b* He.13.4.   1 Or, *dominion.*
                  c Jude 8,10.

is not a *jet* that occasionally bursts out ; it is a fountain always flowing. (4.) He will seek to do them good. We may suppose that this was the case with Lot ; we are certain that it is a characteristic of true religion to seek to do good to all, however wicked they may be. (5.) He will secure their confidence. He will practise no improper arts to do this, but it will be one of the usual results of a life of integrity, that a good man will secure the confidence of even the wicked. It does not appear that Lot lost that confidence, and the whole narrative in Genesis leads us to suppose that even the inhabitants of Sodom regarded him as a good man. The wicked may *hate* a good man because he is good; but if a man lives as he should, they will regard him as upright, and they will give him the credit of it when he dies, if they should withhold it while he lives.

9. *The Lord knoweth,* &c. That is, the cases referred to show that God is able to deliver his people when tempted, and understands the best way in which it should be done. He sees a way to do it when we cannot, though it is often a way which we should not have thought of. He can send an angel to take his tempted people by the hand; he can interpose and destroy the power of the tempter; he can raise up earthly friends; he can deliver his people completely and for ever from temptation, by their removal to heaven. ¶ *And to reserve the unjust.* As he does the rebel angels, ver. 4. The case of the angels shows that God can keep wicked men, as if under bonds, reserved for their final trial at his bar. Though they seem to go at large, yet they are under his control, and are kept by him with reference to their ultimate arraignment.

10. *But chiefly.* That is, it may be presumed that the principles just laid down would be applicable in an eminent degree to such persons as he proceeds to designate. ¶ *That walk after the flesh.* That live for the indulgence of their

carnal appetites.   Notes, Rom. viii. 1. ¶ *In the lust of uncleanness.* In polluted pleasures. Comp. Notes, ver. 2. ¶ *And despise government.* Marg., *dominion.* That is, they regard all government in the state, the church, and the family, as an evil. Advocates for unbridled freedom of all sorts ; declaimers on liberty and on the evils of oppression ; defenders of what they regard as the rights of injured man, and yet secretly themselves lusting for the exercise of the very power which they would deny to others—they make no just distinctions about what constitutes true freedom, and in their zeal array themselves against government in all forms. No topic of declamation would be more popular than this, and from none would they hope to secure more followers ; for if they could succeed in removing all respect for the just restraints of law, the way would be open for the accomplishment of their own purposes, in setting up a dominion over the minds of others. It is a common result of such views, that men of this description become impatient of the government of God himself, and seek to throw off *all* authority, and to live in the unrestrained indulgence of their vicious propensities. ¶ *Presumptuous are they.* Τολμηταὶ—daring, bold, audacious, presumptuous men. ¶ *Self-willed—αὐθάδεις.* See Notes, Titus i. 7. ¶ *They are not afraid to speak evil of dignities.* The word rendered *dignities* here, (δόξας,) means properly honour, glory, splendour ; then that which is fitted to inspire respect ; that which is dignified or exalted. It is applied here to men of exalted rank ; and the meaning is, that they did not regard rank, or station, or office—thus violating the plainest rules of propriety and of religion. See Notes, Acts xxiii. 4, 5. Jude, between whose language and that of Peter in this chapter there is a remarkable resemblance, has expressed this more fully. He says, (ver.

11 Whereas angels, which are greater in power and might, bring not railing accusation ¹against them before the Lord.

12 But these, as natural brute

1 Some read, *against themselves.*

ᵃ beasts, made to be taken and destroyed, speak evil of the things that they understand not; and shall utterly perish in their own corruption ;

a Je.12.3.

8,) 'These filthy dreamers defile the flesh, despise dominion, and speak evil of dignities.' It is one of the effects of religion to produce respect for superiors; but when men are self-willed, and when they purpose to give indulgence to corrupt propensities, it is natural for them to dislike all government. Accordingly, it is by no means an unfrequent effect of certain forms of error to lead men to speak disrespectfully of those in authority, and to attempt to throw off all the restraints of law. It is a very certain indication that men hold wrong opinions when they show disrespect to those in authority, and despise the restraints of law.

11. *Whereas angels.* The object, by the reference to angels here, is to show that they, even when manifesting the greatest zeal in a righteous cause, and even when opposing others, did not make use of reproachful terms, or of harsh and violent language. It is not known precisely to what Peter alludes here, nor on what the statement here is based. There can be little doubt, however, as Benson has remarked, that, from the strong resemblance between what Peter says and what Jude says, (Jude 9, 10,) there is allusion to the same thing, and probably both referred to some common tradition among the Jews respecting the contention of the archangel Michael with the devil about the body of Moses. See Notes, Jude 9. As the statement in Jude is the most full, it is proper to explain the passage before us by a reference to that; and we may suppose that, though Peter uses the plural term, and speaks of *angels,* yet that he really had the case of Michael in his eye, and meant to refer to that as an example of what the angels do. Whatever may have been the origin of this tradition, no one can doubt that what is here said of the angels accords with probability, and no one can prove that it is not true. ¶ *Which are greater in power and*

might. And who might, therefore, if it were in any case proper, speak freely of things of an exalted rank and dignity. It would be more becoming for them than for men. On this difficult passage, see Notes on Jude 9. ¶ *Bring not railing accusation.* They simply say, ' The Lord rebuke thee,' Jude 9. Comp. Zech. iii. 2. The Greek here is, ' bring not blasphemous or reproachful judgment, or condemnation'—βλάσφη-μον κρίσιν. They abhor all scurrility and violence of language ; they simply state matters as they are. No one can doubt that this accords with what we should expect of the angels; and that if they had occasion to speak of those who were opposers, it would be in a calm and serious manner, not seeking to overwhelm them by reproaches. ¶ *Against them.* Margin, *against themselves.* So the Vulgate. The more correct reading is *against them ;* that is, against those who might be regarded as their adversaries, (Jude 9,) or those of their own rank who had done wrong—the fallen angels. ¶ *Before the Lord.* When standing before the Lord ; or when represented as reporting the conduct of evil spirits. Comp. Zech. iii. 1, 2. This phrase, however, is wanting in many manuscripts. See Wetstein.

12. *But these, as natural brute beasts.* These persons, who resemble so much irrational animals which are made to be taken and destroyed. The *point* of the comparison is, that they are like fierce and savage beasts that exercise no control over their appetites, and that *seem* to be made only to be destroyed. These persons, by their fierce and ungovernable passions, appear to be made only for destruction, and rush blindly on to it. The word rendered *natural,* (which, however, is wanting in several manuscripts,) means *as they are by nature,* following the bent of their natural appetites and passions. The idea is, that they exercised no more restraint over their passions than beasts

13 And shall receive the reward of unrighteousness, *as* they *a* that count it pleasure to riot in the day-

a Phi.3.19; Jude 12,&c.

time. Spots *they are* and blemishes, sporting themselves with their own deceivings, while they feast with you;

---

do over their propensities. They were entirely under the dominion of their natural appetites, and did not allow their reason or conscience to exert any constraint. The word rendered *brute*, means without reason; irrational. Man *has* reason, and should allow it to control his passions; the brutes have no rational nature, and it is to be expected that they will act out their propensities without restraint. Man, as an animal, has many passions and appetites resembling those of the brute creation, but he is also endowed with a higher nature, which is designed to regulate and control his inferior propensities, and to keep them in subordination to the requirements of law. If a man sinks himself to the level of brutes, he must expect to be treated like brutes; and as wild and savage animals—lions, and panthers, and wolves, and bears—are regarded as dangerous, and as ' made to be taken and destroyed,' so the same destiny must come upon men who make themselves like them. ¶ *Made to be taken and destroyed.* They are not only useless to society, but destructive; and men feel that it is right to destroy them. We are not to suppose that this teaches that the only object which *God* had in view in making wild animals was that they *might be* destroyed; but that *men* so regard them. ¶ *Speak evil of the things that they understand not.* Of objects whose worth and value they cannot appreciate. This is no uncommon thing among men, especially in regard to the works and ways of God. ¶ *And shall utterly perish in their own corruption.* Their views will be the means of their ruin; and they render them fit for it, just as much as the fierce passions of the wild animals do.

13. *And shall receive the reward of unrighteousness.* The appropriate recompense of their wickedness in the future world. Such men do not always receive the due recompense of their deeds in the present life; and as it is a great and immutable principle that all will be

treated, under the government of God, as they deserve, or that justice will be rendered to every rational being, it follows that there must be punishment in the future state. ¶ As *they that count it pleasure to riot in the day-time.* As men peculiarly wicked, shameless, and abandoned; for only such revel in open day. Comp. Notes, Acts ii. 15; 1 Thess. v. 7. ¶ *Spots* they are *and blemishes.* That is, they are like a dark spot on a pure garment, or like a deformity on an otherwise beautiful person. They are a scandal and disgrace to the Christian profession. ¶ *Sporting themselves.* The Greek word here means to live delicately or luxuriously; to revel. The idea is not exactly that of *sporting,* or playing, or amusing themselves; but it is that they take advantage of their views to live in riot and luxury. Under the garb of the Christian profession, they give indulgence to the most corrupt passions. ¶ *With their own deceivings.* Jude, in the parallel place, (ver. 12,) has, ' These are spots in your feasts of charity, when they feast with you.' Several versions, and a few manuscripts also, here read *feasts* instead of *deceivings,* (ἀγάπαις for ἀπάταις.) The common reading, however, is undoubtedly the correct one, (see Wetstein, *in loc.;*) and the meaning is, that they took advantage of their false views to turn even the sacred feasts of charity, or perhaps the Lord's Supper itself, into an occasion of sensual indulgence. Comp. Notes, 1 Cor. xi. 20–22. The difference between these persons, and those in the church at Corinth, seems to have been that these did it of design, and for the purpose of leading others into sin; those who were in the church at Corinth erred through ignorance. ¶ *While they feast with you.* συνευωχούμενοι. This word means to feast several together; to feast with any one; and the reference seems to be to some festival which was celebrated by Christians, where men and women were assembled together, (ver. 14,) and where they could convert the festival into a

14 Having eyes full of [1] adultery, and that cannot cease from sin ; beguiling unstable souls : an heart they have exercised with covetous practices ; cursed children ;

1 an adulteress.

15 Which have forsaken the right way, and are gone astray, following the way of Balaam [a] the son of Bosor, who loved the wages of unrighteousness ;

a Nu.22 5,&c.

scene of riot and disorder. If the Lord's Supper was celebrated by them as it was at Corinth, that would furnish such an occasion ; or if it was preceded by a 'feast of charity,' (Notes, Jude 12,) that would furnish such an occasion. It would seem to be probable that a festival of some kind was connected with the observance of the Lord's Supper, (Notes, 1 Cor. xi. 21,) and that this was converted by these persons into a scene of riot and disorder. 14. *Having eyes full of adultery.* Marg., as in the Greek, *an adulteress;* that is, gazing with desire after such persons. The word *full* is designed to denote that the corrupt passion referred to had wholly seized and occupied their minds. The eye was, as it were, full of this passion ; it saw nothing else but some occasion for its indulgence ; it expressed nothing else but the desire. The reference here is to the sacred festival mentioned in the previous verse ; and the meaning is, that they celebrated that festival with licentious feelings, giving free indulgence to their corrupt desires by gazing on the females who were assembled with them. In the passion here referred to, the *eye* is usually the first offender, the inlet to corrupt desires, and the medium by which they are expressed. Comp. Notes, Matt. v. 28. The wanton glance is a principal occasion of exciting the sin ; and there is much often in dress, and mien, and gesture, to charm the eye and to deepen the debasing passion. ¶ *And that cannot cease from sin.* They cannot look on the females who may be present without sinning. Comp. Matt. v. 28. There are many men in whom the presence of the most virtuous woman only excites impure and corrupt desires. The expression here does not mean that they have no natural ability to cease from sin, or that they are impelled to it by any physical necessity, but only that they are so corrupt and unprincipled that they certainly will sin always.

¶ *Beguiling unstable souls.* Those who are not strong in Christian principle, or who are naturally fluctuating and irresolute. The word rendered *beguiling* means to bait, to entrap, and would be applicable to the methods practised in hunting. Here it means that it was one of their arts to place specious allurements before those who were known not to have settled principles or firmness, in order to allure them to sin. Comp. 2 Tim. iii. 6. ¶ *An heart they have exercised with covetous practices.* Skilled in the arts which covetous men adopt in order to cheat others out of their property. A leading purpose which influenced these men was to obtain money. One of the most certain ways for dishonest men to do this is to make use of the religious principle ; to corrupt and control the conscience ; to make others believe that they are eminently holy, or that they are the special favourites of heaven ; and when they can do this, they have the purses of others at command. For the religious principle is the most powerful of all principles ; and he who can control that, can control all that a man possesses. The idea here is, that these persons had made this their study, and had learned the ways in which men could be induced to part with their money under religious pretences. We should always be on our guard when professedly religious teachers propose to have much to do with money matters While we should always be ready to aid every good cause, yet we should remember that unprincipled and indolent men often assume the mask of religion that they may practise their arts on the credulity of others, and that their real aim is to obtain their property, not to save their souls. ¶ *Cursed children.* This is a Hebraism, meaning literally, 'children of the curse;' that is, persons devoted to the curse, or who will certainly be destroyed.

15. *Which have forsaken the right way.* The straight path of honesty and

16 But was rebuked for his iniquity : the dumb ass, speaking with

man's voice, forbad the madness
of the prophet.

integrity. Religion is often represented as a straight path, and to do wrong
is to go out of that path in a crooked
way. ¶ *Following the way of Balaam
the son of Bosor.* See Numb. xxii. 5,
seq. In the Book of Numbers, Balaam
is called the son of *Beor.* Perhaps the
name Beor was corrupted into Bosor; or,
as Rosenmüller suggests, the father of
Balaam may have had two names.
Schleusner (*Lex.*) supposes that it was
changed by the Greeks because it was
more easily pronounced. The Seventy,
however, read it Βεὼς — *Beor.* The
meaning here is, that they *imitated*
Balaam. The particular point to which
Peter refers in which they imitated him,
seems to have been the love of gain, or
covetousness. Possibly, however, he
might have designed to refer to a more
general resemblance, for *in fact* they
imitated him in the following things:
(1,) in being professed religious teachers,
or the servants of God; (2,) in their
covetousness; (3,) in inducing others to
sin, referring to the same kind of sins
in both cases. Balaam counselled the
Moabites to entice the children of Israel
to illicit connection with their women,
thus introducing licentiousness into the
camp of the Hebrews, (Numb. xxxi. 16 ;
comp. Numb. xxv. 1–9 ;) and in like
manner these teachers led others into
licentiousness, thus corrupting the
church. ¶ *Who loved the wages of
unrighteousness.* Who was supremely
influenced by the love of gain, and was
capable of being employed, for a price,
in a wicked design ; thus prostituting
his high office, as a professed prophet of
the Most High, to base and ignoble
ends. That Balaam, though he professed to be influenced by a supreme
regard to the will of God, (Numb. xxii.
18, 38,) was really influenced by the
desire of reward, and was willing to
prostitute his great office to secure such
a reward, there can be no doubt. (1.)
The elders of Moab and of Midian came
to Balaam with ' the rewards of divina-
tion in their hand,' (Numb. xxii. 7,) and
with promises from Balak of promoting
him to great honour, if he would curse
the children of Israel, Numb. xxii. 17.

(2.) Balaam was disposed to go with
them, and was restrained from going at
once only by a direct and solemn prohibition from the Lord, Numb. xxii. 11.
(3.) Notwithstanding this solemn prohibition, and notwithstanding he said to
the ambassadors from Balak that he
would do only as God directed, though
Balak should give him his house full of
silver and gold, (Numb. xxii. 18,) yet
he did not regard the matter as settled,
but proposed to them that they should
wait another night, with the hope that
the Lord would give a more favourable
direction in reference to their request,
thus showing that his *heart* was in the
service which they required, and that
his inclination was to avail himself of
their offer, Numb. xxii. 19. (4.) When
he *did* obtain permission to go, it was
only to say that which the Lord should
direct him to say, (Numb. xxii. 20 ;)
but he went with a ' perverse ' heart,
with a secret wish to comply with the
desire of Balak, and with a knowledge
that he was doing wrong, (Numb. xxii.
34,) and was restrained from uttering
the curse which Balak desired only by
an influence from above which he could
not control. Balaam was undoubtedly
a wicked man, and was constrained by
a power from on high to utter sentiments which God *meant* should be
uttered, but which Balaam would never
have expressed of his own accord.
16. *But was rebuked for his iniquity.*
The object of Peter in this seems to be
to show that God employed the very
extraordinary means of causing the ass
on which he rode to speak, because his
iniquity was so monstrous. The guilt
of thus debasing his high office, and
going forth to curse the people of God—
a people who had done him no wrong,
and given no occasion for his malediction—was so extraordinary, that means
as extraordinary were proper to express
it. If God employed means so extraordinary to rebuke *his* depravity, it was
to be expected that in some appropriate
way he would express his sense of the
wickedness of those who resembled him.
¶ *The dumb ass, speaking with man's
voice.* Numb. xxii. 28. God seems to

17 These are wells without water, | tempest ; to whom the mist of dark-
clouds *a* that are carried with a | ness is reserved for ever.

a Ep.4.14.

---

have designed that both Balaam and Balak should be convinced that the children of Israel were his people ; and so important was it that this conviction should rest fully on the minds of the nations through whom they passed, that he would not suffer even a pretended prophet to make use of his influence to curse them. He designed that all that influence should be in favour of the cause of truth, thus furnishing a striking instance of the use which he often makes of wicked men. To convince Balaam of the error of his course, and to make him sensible that God was an observer of his conduct, and to induce him to utter only what he should direct, nothing would be better fitted than this miracle. The very animal on which he rode, dumb and naturally stupid, was made to utter a reproof ; a reproof as directly from heaven as though the stones had cried out beneath his feet, or the trees of the wood had uttered the language of remonstrance. As to the nature of the miracle here referred to, it may be remarked, (1,) that it was as easy for God to perform this miracle as any other ; and (2,) that it was a miracle that would be as likely to be effectual, and to answer the purpose, as any other. No man can show that it could *not* have occurred ; and the occasion was one in which some decided rebuke, in language beyond that of conscience, was necessary. ¶ *Forbade the madness of the prophet.* That is, the mad or perverse design of the prophet. The word here rendered *madness* means, properly, being aside from a right mind. It is not found elsewhere in the New Testament. It is used here to denote that Balaam was engaged in an enterprise which indicated a headstrong disposition ; an acting contrary to reason and sober sense. He was so under the influence of avarice and ambition that his sober sense was blinded, and he acted like a madman. He knew indeed what was right, and had professed a purpose to do what was right, but he did not allow that to control him ; but, for the sake of gain, went against his own sober conviction,

and against what he knew to be the will of God. He was so mad or infatuated that he allowed neither reason, nor conscience, nor the will of God, to control him.

17. *These are wells without water.* Jude (12, 13) employs several other epithets to describe the same class of persons. The language employed both by Peter and Jude is singularly terse, pointed, and emphatic. Nothing to an oriental mind would be more expressive than to say of professed religious teachers, that they were ‘ wells without water.’ It was always a sad disappointment to a traveller in the hot sands of the desert to come to a well where it was expected that water might be found, and to find it dry. It only aggravated the trials of the thirsty and weary traveller. Such were these religious teachers. In a world, not unaptly compared, in regard to its real comforts, to the wastes and sands of the desert, they would only grievously disappoint the expectations of all those who were seeking for the refreshing influences of the truths of the gospel. There are many such teachers in the world. ¶ *Clouds that are carried with a tempest.* Clouds that are driven about by the wind, and that send down no rain upon the earth. They promise rain, only to be followed by disappointment. Substantially the same idea is conveyed by this as by the previous phrase. ‘ The Arabs compare persons who put on the appearance of virtue, when yet they are destitute of all goodness, to a light cloud which makes a show of rain, and afterwards vanishes.’—*Benson.* The sense is this : The cloud, as it rises, promises rain. The expectation of the farmer is excited that the thirsty earth is to be refreshed with needful showers. Instead of this, however, the wind ‘ gets into ’ the cloud ; it is driven about, and no rain falls, or it ends in a destructive tornado which sweeps everything before it. So of these religious teachers. Instruction in regard to the way of salvation was expected from them ; but, instead of that, they disappointed the expectations of those who were desirous of

18 For when they speak [a] great swelling *words* of vanity, they allure through the lusts of the flesh, *through*

a Ps.73.8.

much wantonness, those that were clean[1] escaped from them who live in error.

1 Or, *for a little while*, as some read.

knowing the way of life, and their doctrines only tended to destroy. ¶ *To whom the mist of darkness is reserved for ever.* The word rendered *mist* here, (ζόφος,) means properly muskiness, thick gloom, darkness, (see ver. 4;) and the phrase 'mist of darkness' is designed to denote *intense* darkness, or the thickest darkness. It refers undoubtedly to the place of future punishment, which is often represented as a place of intense darkness. See Notes, Matt. viii. 12. When it is said that this is *reserved* for them, it means that it is *prepared* for them, or is kept in a state of readiness to receive them. It is like a jail or penitentiary which is built in anticipation that there will be criminals, and with the expectation that there will be use for it. So God has constructed the great prison-house of the universe, the world where the wicked are to dwell, with the knowledge that there would be occasion for it ; and so he keeps it from age to age that it may be ready to receive the wicked when the sentence of condemnation shall be passed upon them. Comp. Matt. xxv. 41. The word *for ever* is a word which denotes properly eternity, (εἰς αἰῶνα,) and is such a word as could *not* have been used if it had been meant that they would not suffer for ever. Comp. Notes, Matt. xxv. 46.

18. *For when they speak great swelling words of vanity.* When they make pretensions to wisdom and learning, or seem to attach great importance to what they say, and urge it in a pompous and positive manner. Truth is simple, and delights in simple statements. It expects to make its way by its own intrinsic force, and is willing to pass for what it is worth. Error is noisy and declamatory, and hopes to succeed by substituting sound for sense, and by such tones and arts as shall induce men to believe that what is said is true, when it is known by the speaker to be false. ¶ *They allure through the lusts of the flesh.* The same word is used here which in ver. 14 is rendered *beguiling*, and in James i. 14, *enticed.* It does not else-

where occur in the New Testament. It means that they make use of deceitful arts to allure, ensnare, or beguile others. The *means* which it is here said they employed, were *the lusts of the flesh;* that is, they promised unlimited indulgence to the carnal appetites, or taught such doctrines that their followers would feel themselves free to give unrestrained liberty to such propensities. This has been quite a common method in the world, of inducing men to embrace false doctrines. ¶ Through much *wantonness.* See Notes, 2 Tim. iii. 6. The meaning here is, that they made use of every variety of lascivious arts to beguile others under religious pretences. This has been often done in the world ; for religion has been abused to give seducers access to the confidence of the innocent, only that they might betray and ruin them. It is *right* that for all such the ' mist of darkness should be reserved for ever;' and if there were *not* a place of punishment prepared for such men, there would be defect in the moral administration of the universe. ¶ *Those that were clean escaped from them who live in error.* Marg., *for a little while.* The difference between the margin and the text here arises from a difference of reading in the Greek. Most of the later editions of the Greek Testament coincide with the reading in the margin, (ὀλίγως,) meaning *little, but a little, scarcely.* This accords better with the scope of the passage ; and, according to this, it means that they had *almost escaped* from the snares and influences of those who live in error and sin. They had begun to think of their ways ; they had broken off many of their evil habits ; and there was hope that they would be entirely reformed, and would become decided Christians, but they were allured again to the sins in which they had so long indulged. This seems to me to accord with the design of the passage, and it certainly accords with what frequently occurs, that those who are addicted to habits of vice become apparently in-

19 While they promise them liberty, they themselves are the servants of corruption: for *a* of whom a man is overcome, of the same is he brought in bondage

20 For if after they have escaped

a Jn.8.34; Ro.6.16.

the pollutions of the world, through the knowledge of the Lord and Saviour Jesus Christ, they are again *b* entangled therein and overcome, the latter end is worse with them than the beginning.

b Lu.11.26; Heb.6.4,&c.; 10.26,27.

---

terested in religion, and abandon many of their evil practices, but are again allured by the seductive influences of sin, and relapse into their former habits. In the case referred to here it was by professedly religious teachers—and is this never done now? Are there none, for example, who have been addicted to habits of intemperance, who had been almost reformed, but who are led back again by the influence of religious teachers? Not directly and openly, indeed, would they lead them into habits of intemperance. But, when their reformation is begun, its success and its completion depend on total abstinence from all that intoxicates. In this condition, nothing more is necessary to secure their entire reformation and safety than mere abstinence; and nothing more may be necessary to lead them into their former practices than the example of others who indulge in moderate drinking, or than the doctrine inculcated by a religious teacher that such moderate drinking is not contrary to the spirit of the Bible.

19. *While they promise them liberty.* True religion always promises and produces liberty, (see Notes, John viii. 36;) but the particular liberty which these persons seem to have promised, was freedom from what they regarded as needless restraint, or from strict and narrow views of religion. ¶ *They themselves are the servants of corruption.* They are the slaves of gross and corrupt passions, themselves utter strangers to freedom, and bound in the chains of servitude. These passions and appetites have obtained the entire mastery over them, and brought them into the severest bondage. This is often the case with those who deride the restraints of serious piety. They are themselves the slaves of appetite, or of the rules of fashionable life, or of the laws of honour, or of vicious indulgences. ' He

is a freeman whom the truth makes free, and all are slaves besides.' Comp. Notes, 2 Cor. iii. 17. ¶ *For of whom a man is overcome,* &c. Or rather ' by *what* (*ᾧ*) any one is overcome;' that is, *whatever* gets the mastery of him, whether it be avarice, or sensuality, or pride, or any form of error. See Notes, Rom. vi. 16, where this sentiment is explained.

20. *For if after they have escaped the pollutions of the world.* This does not necessarily mean that they had been true Christians, and had fallen from grace. Men may outwardly reform, and escape from the open corruptions which prevail around them, or which they had themselves practised, and still have no true grace at heart. ¶ *Through the knowledge of the Lord and Saviour Jesus Christ.* Neither does *this* imply that they were true Christians, or that they had ever had any saving knowledge of the Redeemer. There is a knowledge of the doctrines and duties of religion which may lead sinners to abandon their outward vices, which has no connection with saving grace. They may profess religion, and may *know* enough of religion to understand that it requires them to abandon their vicious habits, and still never be true Christians. ¶ *They are again entangled therein and overcome.* The word rendered *entangled,* (ἐμπλέκω,) from which is derived our word *implicate,* means to braid in, to interweave; then to involve in, to entangle. It means here that they become implicated in those vices like an animal that is entangled in a net. ¶ *The latter end is worse with them than the beginning.* This is usually the case. Apostates become worse than they were before their professed conversion. Reformed drunkards, if they go back to their ' cups' again, become more abandoned than ever. Thus it is with those who

21 For it had been better *a for them not to have known the way of *b righteousness, than, after they have known *it*, to turn from the holy commandment delivered unto them.

a Mat.11.23,24; Lu.12.47,48.

22 But it is happened unto them according to the true proverb, *c The dog *is turned to his own vomit again ; and the sow that was washed, to her wallowing in the mire.

b Pr.12.28.　　c Pr.26.11.

have been addicted to any habits of vice, and who profess to become religious, and then fall away. The *reasons of this may be, (1,) that they are willing now to show to others that they are no longer under the restraints by which they had professedly bound themselves ; (2,) that God gives them up to indulgence with fewer restraints than formerly ; and (3,) their old companions in sin may be at special pains to court their society, and to lead them into temptation, in order to obtain a triumph over virtue and religion.

21. *For it had been better for them, &c. Comp. Notes on Matt. xxvi. 24. It would have been better for them, for (1) then they would not have dishonoured the cause of religion as they have now done ; (2) they would not have sunk so deep in profligacy as they now have ; and (3) they would not have incurred so aggravated a condemnation in the world of woe. If men are resolved on being wicked, they had better never pretend to be good. If they are to be cast off at last, it had better not be as apostates from the cause of virtue and religion.

22. *But it is happened unto them according to the true proverb. The *meaning of the proverbs here quoted is, that they have returned to their former vile manner of life. Under all the appearances of reformation, still their evil nature remained, as really as that of the dog or the swine, and that nature finally prevailed. There was no thorough internal change, any more than there is in the swine when it is washed, or in the dog. This passage, therefore, would seem to demonstrate that there never had been any real change of heart, and of course there had been no falling away from true religion. It should not, therefore, be quoted to prove that true Christians may fall from grace and perish. The dog and the swine had never been anything else than the dog and the swine, and these persons had never been

anything else than sinners. ¶ *The dog is *turned to his own vomit again. That is, to eat it up. The passage would seem to imply, that whatever pains should be taken to change the habits of the dog, he would return to them again. The quotation here is from Prov. xxvi. 11 : 'As a dog returneth to his vomit, so a fool returneth to his folly.' A similar proverb is found in the Rabbinical writers. Of the truth of the disgusting *fact here affirmed of the dog, there can be no doubt. Phaedrus (Fab. 27.) states a fact still more offensive respecting its habits. In the view of the Orientals, the dog was reckoned among the most vile and disgusting of all animals. Comp. Deut. xxiii. 18 ; 1 Sam. xvii. 43; 2 Sam. iii. 8 ; ix. 8 ; xvi. 9; Matt. vii. 6; Phil. iii. 2. See also Horace, II. Epis. 1, 26 :—

Vixisset canis immundus, vel amica luto sus.

On the use of this proverb, see Wetstein, *in loc. ¶ *And the sow that was washed, &c. This proverb is not found in the Old Testament, but it was common in the Rabbinical writings, and is found in the Greek classics. See Wetstein, *in loc. Its meaning is plain, and of the truth of what is affirmed no one can have any doubt. No matter how clean the swine is made by washing, this would not prevent it, in the slightest degree, from rolling in filth again. It will act out its real nature. So it is with the sinner. No external reformation will certainly prevent his returning to his former habits ; and when he *does return, we can only say that he is acting according to his real nature—a nature which has never been changed, any more than the nature of the dog or the swine. On the *characteristics of the persons referred to in this chapter, (vers. 9–19,) see the Introduction, § 3.

This passage is often quoted to prove 'the possibility of falling from grace, and from a very high degree of it too.' But it is one of the last passages in the

CHAPTER III.

THIS second epistle, beloved, I now write unto you; in *both*

which I stir up your pure minds by way of remembrance:

2 That *a* ye may be mindful of

<small>a Jude 17,18.</small>

Bible that should be adduced to prove that doctrine. The true point of this passage is to show that the persons referred to never *were* changed; that whatever external reformation might have occurred, their nature remained the same; and that when they apostatized from their outward profession, they merely acted out their nature, and showed that in fact there had been *no* real change. This passage will prove—what there are abundant facts to confirm—that persons may reform externally, and then return again to their former corrupt habits; it can never be made to prove that one *true* Christian will fall away and perish. It will also prove that we should rely on no mere external reformation, no outward cleansing, as certain evidence of piety. Thousands who have been externally reformed have ultimately shown that they had no religion, and there is nothing in mere outward reformation that can fit us for heaven. God looks upon the heart; and it is only the religion that has its seat there, that can secure our final salvation.

CHAPTER III.

ANALYSIS OF THE CHAPTER.

THE principal design of this chapter is to demonstrate, in opposition to the objections of scoffers, that the Lord Jesus will return again to this world; that the world will be destroyed by fire, and that there will be a new heaven and a new earth; and to show what effect this should have on the minds of Christians. The chapter, without any very exact arrangement by the author, essentially consists of two parts.

I. The argument of the objectors to the doctrine that the Lord Jesus will return to the world, and that it will be destroyed, vers. 1–4. In doing this, the apostle (vers. 1, 2) calls their attention to the importance of attending diligently to the things which had been spoken by the prophets, and to the commands of the apostles, reminding them that it was to be expected that in the last days there would be scoffers who

would deride the doctrines of religion, and who would maintain that there was no evidence that what had been predicted would be fulfilled, ver. 3. He then (ver. 4) adverts to the *argument* on which they professed to rely, that there were no signs or indications that those events were to take place; that there were no natural causes in operation which could lead to such results; and that the fact of the stability of the earth since the time of the creation, demonstrated that the predicted destruction of the world could not occur.

II. The argument of Peter, in reply to this objection; a strong affirmation of the truth of the doctrine that the Lord Jesus will return; that the earth and all which it contains will be burned up; that there will be a new heaven and a new earth; and the effect which the prospect of the coming of the Lord Jesus, and of the destruction of the world by fire, should have on the minds of Christians, vers. 5–18.

(1.) The arguments of Peter, in reply to the objection from the long-continued stability of the earth, are the following: (*a*) He refers to the destruction of the old world by the flood—a fact against which the same objections could have been urged, beforehand, which are urged against the predicted destruction of the world by fire, vers. 5–7. With just as much plausibility it might have been urged then that the earth had stood for thousands of years, and that there were no natural causes at work to produce that change. It might have been asked where the immense amount of water necessary to drown a world could come from; and perhaps it might have been argued that God was too *good* to destroy a world by a flood. Every objection which could be urged to the destruction of the world by fire, could have been urged to its destruction by water; and as, in fact, those objections, as the event showed, would have had no real force, so they should be regarded as having no real force now. (*b*) No argument against this predicted event can be

the words which were spoken before by *a* the holy prophets, and of the

a 1 Ti.4.1; 2 Ti.3.1.

commandment of us the apostles of the Lord and Saviour:

derived from the fact that hundreds and thousands of years are suffered to elapse before the fulfilment of the predictions, vers. 8, 9. What seems long to men is not long to God. A thousand years with him, in reference to this point, are as one day. He does not measure time as men do. They soon die; and if they cannot execute their purpose in a brief period, they cannot at all. But this cannot apply to God. He has infinite ages in which to execute his purposes, and therefore no argument can be derived from the fact that his purposes are long delayed, to prove that he will not execute them at all. (*c*) Peter says (ver. 15, seq.) that the delay which was observed in executing the plans of God should not be interpreted as a proof that they would *never* be accomplished, but as an evidence of his long-suffering and patience; and, in illustration of this, he refers to the writings of Paul, in which he says that the same sentiments were advanced. There were indeed, he says, in those writings, some things which were hard to be understood; but on this point they were plain.

(2.) A strong affirmation of the truth of the doctrine, vers. 9, 10, 13. He declares that these events will certainly occur, and that they should be expected to take place suddenly, and without any preintimations of their approach—as the thief comes at night without announcing his coming.

(3.) The practical suggestions which Peter intersperses in the argument illustrative of the effect which these considerations should have on the mind, are among the most important parts of the chapter : (1.) We should be holy, devout, and serious, ver. 11. (2.) We should look forward with deep interest to the new heavens and earth which are to succeed the present, ver. 12. (3.) We should be diligent and watchful, that we may be found on the return of the Saviour 'without spot and blameless,' ver. 14. (4.) We should be cautious that we be not seduced and led away by the errors which deny these great doctrines, (ver. 17;) and (5) we

should grow in grace, and in the knowledge of the Lord Jesus Christ, ver. 18.

1. *This second epistle, beloved, 1 now write unto you.* This expression proves that he had written a former epistle, and that it was addressed to the same persons as this. Comp. Intro., § 3. ¶ *In* both *which I stir up your pure minds, &c.* That is, the main object of both epistles is the same—to call to your remembrance important truths which you have before heard, but which you are in danger of forgetting, or from which you are in danger of being turned away by prevailing errors. Comp. Notes, chap. i. 12–15. The word rendered *pure* (εἰλικρινής) occurs only here and in Phil. i. 10, where it is rendered *sincere.* The word properly refers to *that which may be judged of in sunshine ;* then it means *clear, manifest ;* and then *sincere, pure*—as that in which there is no obscurity. The idea here perhaps is, that their minds were open, frank, candid, sincere, rather than that they were *pure.* The apostle regarded them as *disposed* to see the truth, and yet as liable to be led astray by the plausible errors of others. Such minds need to have truths often brought fresh to their remembrance, though they are truths with which they had before been familiar.

2. *That ye may be mindful of the words.* Of the doctrines ; the truths ; the prophetic statements. Jude (ver. 18) says that it had been foretold by the apostles, that in the last days there would be scoffers. Peter refers to the instructions of the apostles and prophets in general, though evidently designing that his remarks should bear particularly on the fact that there would be scoffers. ¶ *Which were spoken before by the holy prophets.* The predictions of the prophets before the advent of the Saviour, respecting his character and work. Peter had before appealed to them, (chap. i. 19–21,) as furnishing important evidence in regard to the truth of the Christian religion, and valuable instruction in reference to its nature. See Notes on that passage.

3 Knowing this first, that there shall come in the last days scoffers, walking[a] after their own lusts, 4 And saying, Where [b]is the

a Is.5.19.

promise of his coming? for since the fathers fell asleep, all things continue as *they were* from the beginning of the creation.

b Je.17.15; Eze.12.22-27; Mat.24.48.

Many of the most important doctrines respecting the kingdom of the Messiah are stated as clearly in the Old Testament as in the New, (comp. Isa. liii.,) and the prophecies therefore deserve to be studied as an important part of Divine revelation. It should be added here, however, that when Peter wrote there was this special reason why he referred to the prophets, that the canon of the New Testament was not then completed, and he could not make his appeal to that. To some parts of the writings of Paul he could and did appeal, (vers. 15, 16,) but probably a very small part of what is now the New Testament was known to those to whom this epistle was addressed. ¶ *And of the commandment of us the apostles of the Lord and Saviour.* As being equally entitled with the prophets to state and enforce the doctrines and duties of religion. It may be observed, that no man would have used this language who did not regard himself and his fellow-apostles as inspired, and as on a level with the prophets. 3. *Knowing this first.* As among the first and most important things to be attended to—as one of the predictions which demand your special regard. Jude (ver. 18) says that the fact that there would be 'mockers in the last time,' had been particularly foretold by them. It is probable that Peter refers to the same thing, and we may suppose that this was so well understood by all the apostles that they made it a common subject of preaching. ¶ *That there shall come in the last days.* In the last dispensation; in the period during which the affairs of the world shall be wound up. The apostle does not say that that was the last time in the sense that the world was about to come to an end; nor is it implied that the period called 'the last day' might not be a very long period, longer in fact than either of the previous periods of the world. He says that during that pe-

riod it had been predicted there would arise those whom he here calls *scoffers.* On the meaning of the phrase ' in the last days,' as used in the Scriptures, see Notes, Acts ii. 17; Heb. i. 2; Isa. ii. 2. ¶ *Scoffers.* In Jude (ver. 18) the same Greek word is rendered *mockers.* The word means those who deride, reproach, ridicule. There is usually in the word the idea of contempt or malignity towards an object. Here the sense seems to be that they would treat with derision or contempt the predictions respecting the advent of the Saviour, and the end of the world. It would appear probable that there was a particular or definite class of men referred to ; a class who would hold peculiar opinions, and who would urge plausible objections against the fulfilment of the predictions respecting the end of the world, and the second coming of the Saviour—for those are the points to which Peter particularly refers. It scarcely required inspiration to foresee that there would be *scoffers* in the general sense of the term—for they have so abounded in every age, that no one would hazard much in saying that they would be found at any particular time ; but the eye of the apostle is evidently on a particular class of men, the special form of whose reproaches would be the ridicule of the doctrines that the Lord Jesus would return ; that there would be a day of judgment ; that the world would be consumed by fire, &c. Archbishop Tillotson explains this of the Carpocratians, a large sect of the Gnostics, who denied the resurrection of the dead, and the future judgment. ¶ *Walking after their own lusts.* Living in the free indulgence of their sensual appetites   See Notes, chap. ii. 10, 12, 14, 18, 19.

4. *And saying, Where is the promise of his coming?* That is, either, Where is the *fulfilment* of that promise ; or, Where are the *indications* or *signs* that he will come? They evidently meant

5 For this they willingly are ignorant of, that *a* by the word of God the heavens were of old, and

the earth [1] standing out of the water *b* and in the water;

to imply that the promise had utterly failed; that there was not the slightest evidence that it would be accomplished; that they who had believed this were entirely deluded. It is possible that some of the early Christians, even in the time of the apostles, had undertaken to fix the time when these events would occur, as many have done since; and that as *that* time had passed by, they inferred that the prediction had utterly failed. But whether this were so or not, it was easy to allege that the predictions respecting the second coming of the Saviour *seemed* to imply that the end of the world was near, and that there were no indications that they would be fulfilled. The laws of nature were uniform, as they had always been, and the alleged promises had failed. ¶ *For since the fathers fell asleep.* Since they *died*—death being often, in the Scriptures, as elsewhere, represented as sleep. Notes, John xi. 11; 1 Cor. xi. 30. This reference to the ' fathers,' by such scoffers, was probably designed to be ironical and contemptuous. Perhaps the meaning may be thus expressed: ' Those old men, the prophets, indeed foretold this event. They were much concerned and troubled about it; and their predictions alarmed others, and filled their bosoms with dread. They looked out for the signs of the end of the world, and expected that that day was drawing near. But those good men have died. They lived to old age, and then died as others; and since they have departed, the affairs of the world have gone on very much as they did before. The earth is suffered to have rest, and the laws of nature operate in the same way that they always did.' It seems not improbable that the immediate reference in the word *fathers* is not to the prophets of former times, but to aged and pious men of the times of the apostles, who had dwelt much on this subject, and who had made it a subject of conversation and of preaching. Those old men, said the scoffing objector, have died like others; and, notwithstanding their confident predic-

tions, things now move on as they did from the beginning. ¶ *All things continue as* they were *from the beginning of the creation.* That is, the laws of nature are fixed and settled. The *argument* here—for it was doubtless designed to be an argument—is based on the stability of the laws of nature, and the uniformity of the course of events. Thus far all these predictions had failed. Things continued to go on as they had always done. The sun rose and set; the tides ebbed and flowed; the seasons followed each other in the usual order; one generation succeeded another, as had always been the case; and there was every indication that those laws would continue to operate as they had always done. This argument for the stability of the earth, and against the prospect of the fulfilment of the predictions of the Bible, would have more force with many minds now than it had then, for eighteen hundred years more have rolled away, and the laws of nature remain the same. Meantime, the expectations of those who have believed that the world was coming to an end have been disappointed; the time set for this by many interpreters of Scripture has passed by; men have looked out in vain for the coming of the Saviour, and sublunary affairs move on as they always have done. Still there are no indications of the coming of the Saviour; and perhaps it would be said that the farther men search, by the aid of science, into the laws of nature, the more they become impressed with their stability, and the more firmly they are convinced of the improbability that the world will be destroyed in the manner in which it is predicted in the Scriptures that it will be. The specious and plausible objection arising from this source, the apostle proposes to meet in the following verses.

5. *For this they willingly are ignorant of.* Λανθάνει γὰρ αὐτοὺς τοῦτο θέλοντας. There is some considerable variety in the translation of this passage. In our common version the Greek word (θέλον-

ται) is rendered as if it were an adverb, or as if it referred to their *ignorance* in regard to the event; meaning, that while they might have known this fact, they took no pains to do it, or that they preferred to have its recollection far from their minds. So Beza and Luther render it. Others, however, take it as referring to what follows, meaning, 'being so minded; being of that opinion; or affirming.' So Bloomfield, Robinson, (*Lex.*,) Mede, Rosenmüller, &c. According to this interpretation the sense is, 'They who thus *will* or think; that is, they who hold the opinion that all things will continue to remain as they were, are ignorant of this fact that things have *not* always thus remained; that there has been a destruction of the world once by water.' The Greek seems rather to demand this interpretation; and then the sense of the passage will be, 'It is concealed or hidden from those who hold this opinion, that the earth has been once destroyed.' It is implied, whichever interpretation is adopted, that the *will* was concerned in it; that they were influenced by that rather than by sober judgment and by reason; and whether the word refers to their *ignorance*, or to their *holding that opinion*, there was obstinacy and perverseness about it. The *will* has usually more to do in the denial and rejection of the doctrines of the Bible than the *understanding* has. The argument which the apostle appeals to in reply to this objection is a simple one. The adversaries of the doctrine affirmed that the laws of nature had always remained the same, and they affirmed that they always would. The apostle denies the fact which they assumed, in the sense in which they affirmed it, and maintains that those laws have *not* been so stable and uniform that the world has never been destroyed by an overwhelming visitation from God. It has been destroyed by a flood; it may be again by fire. There was the same improbability that the event would occur, so far as the argument from the stability of the laws of nature is concerned, in the one case that there is in the other, and consequently the objection is of no force. ¶ *That by the word of God.* By the *command* of God. 'He *spake*, and it

was done.' Comp. Gen. i. 6, 9; Psa. xxxiii. 9. The idea here is, that everything depends on his word or will. As the heavens and the earth were originally *made* by his command, so by the same command they can be destroyed. ¶ *The heavens were of old.* The heavens were formerly made, Gen. i. 1. The word *heaven* in the Scriptures sometimes refers to the atmosphere, sometimes to the starry worlds as they appear above us, and sometimes to the exalted place where God dwells. Here it is used, doubtless, in the popular signification, as denoting the heavens as they *appear*, embracing the sun, moon, and stars. ¶ *And the earth standing out of the water and in the water.* Marg., consisting. Gr., συνιστῶσα. The Greek word, when used in an intransitive sense, means *to stand with*, or *together;* then tropically, *to place together*, to constitute, place, bring into existence.—*Robinson.* The idea which our translators seem to have had is, that, in the formation of the earth, a part was out of the water, and a part under the water; and that the former, or the inhabited portion, became entirely submerged, and that thus the inhabitants perished. This was not, however, probably the idea of Peter. He doubtless has reference to the account given in Gen. i. of the creation of the earth, in which *water* performed so important a part. The thought in his mind seems to have been, that *water* entered materially into the formation of the earth, and that in its very origin there existed the means by which it was afterwards destroyed. The word which is rendered '*standing*' should rather be rendered *consisting of*, or *constituted of;* and the meaning is, that the creation of the earth was the result of the Divine agency acting on the mass of elements which in Genesis is called *waters*, Gen. i. 2, 6, 7, 9. There was at first a vast fluid, an immense unformed collection of materials, called *waters*, and from that the earth arose. The point of time, therefore, in which Peter looks at the earth here, is not when the mountains, and continents, and islands, seem to be standing partly out of the water and partly in the water, but when there was a vast mass of materials called *waters* from which the

6 Whereby the world that then was, being overflowed with water, ^aperished:

7 But the heavens and the earth which are now, by the same word are kept in store, reserved unto fire ^b against the day of judgment and perdition of ungodly men.

a Ge.7.11.   b Ps.50.3; Zep.3.8; 2 Thess.1.8.

earth was formed. The phrase *'out of the water'* (ἰξ ὕδατος) refers to the *origin* of the earth. It was formed *from*, or *out of*, that mass. The phrase *'in the water'* (δι' ὕδατος) more properly means *through* or *by*. It does not mean that the earth stood *in* the water in the sense that it was partly submerged; but it means not only that the earth arose *from* that mass that is called *water* in Gen. i., but that that mass called *water* was in fact the grand material out of which the earth was formed. It was *through* or *by means of* that vast mass of mingled elements that the earth was made as it was. Everything arose out of that chaotic mass; through that, or by means of that, all things were formed, and from the fact that the earth was thus formed out of the water, or that water entered so essentially into its formation, there existed causes which ultimately resulted in the deluge.

6. *Whereby.* Δι' ὧν. Through which, or by means of which. The pronoun here is in the plural number, and there has been much difference of opinion as to what it refers. Some suppose that it refers to the heavens mentioned in the preceding verse, and to the fact that the windows of heaven were opened in the deluge, (*Doddridge;*) others that the Greek phrase is taken in the sense of (διὸ) *whence.* Wetstein supposes that it refers to the 'heavens and the earth.' But the most obvious reference, though the plural number is used, and the word *water* in the antecedent is in the singular, is to *water.* The fact seems to be that the apostle had the *waters* mentioned in Genesis prominently in his eye, and meant to describe the effect produced *by* those waters. He has also twice, in the same sentence, referred to *water*—*'out of the water* and in the *water.'* It is evidently to these *waters* mentioned in Genesis, out of which the world was originally made, that he refers here. The world was formed from that fluid mass; by these waters which ex-

isted when the earth was made, and out of which it arose, it was destroyed. The antecedent to the word in the plural number is rather that which was in the mind of the writer, or that of which he was thinking, than the *word* which he had used. ¶ *The world that then was,* &c. Including all its inhabitants. Rosenmüller supposes that the reference here is to some universal catastrophe which occurred before the deluge in the time of Noah, and indeed before the earth was fitted up in its present form, as described by Moses in Gen. i. It is rendered more than probable, by the researches of geologists in modern times, that such changes have occurred; but there is no evidence that Peter was acquainted with them, and his purpose did not require that he should refer to them. All that his argument demanded was the fact that the world had been once destroyed, and that therefore there was no improbability in believing that it would be again. They who maintained that the prediction that the earth would be destroyed was improbable, affirmed that there were no signs of such an event; that the laws of nature were stable and uniform; and that as those laws had been so long and so uniformly unbroken, it was absurd to believe that such an event could occur. To meet this, all that was necessary was to show that, in a case where the same objections substantially might be urged, it had actually occurred that the world had been destroyed. There was, in itself considered, as much improbability in believing that the world could be destroyed by water as that it would be destroyed by fire, and consequently the objection had no real force. Notwithstanding the apparent stability of the laws of nature, the world had been once destroyed; and there is, therefore, no improbability that it may be again. On the objections which *might* have been plausibly urged against the flood, see Notes on Heb. xi. 7.

7. *But the heavens and the earth which are now.* As they now exist. There is no difficulty here respecting what is meant by the word *earth*, but it is not so easy to determine precisely how much is included in the word *heavens*. It cannot be supposed to mean *heaven* as the place where God dwells ; nor is it necessary to suppose that Peter understood by the word all that would now be implied in it, as used by a modern astronomer. The word is doubtless employed in a popular signification, referring to the *heavens as they appear to the eye;* and the idea is, that the conflagration would not only destroy the earth, but would change the heavens as they now appear to us. If, in fact, the earth with its atmosphere should be subjected to an universal conflagration, all that is properly implied in what is here said by Peter would occur. ¶ *By the same word.* Dependent solely on the will of God. He has only to give command, and all will be destroyed. The laws of nature have no stability independent of his will, and at his pleasure all things could be reduced to nothing, as easily as they were made. A single word, a breath of command, from one Being, a Being over whom we have no control, would spread universal desolation through the heavens and the earth. Notwithstanding the laws of nature, as they are called, and the precision, uniformity, and power with which they operate, the dependence of the universe on the Creator is as entire as though there were no such laws, and as though all were conducted by the mere will of the Most High, irrespective of such laws. In fact, those laws have no efficiency of their own, but are a mere statement of the way in which God produces the changes which occur, the methods by which He operates who 'works all in all.' At any moment he could suspend them ; that is, he could cease to act, or withdraw his efficiency, and the universe would cease to be. ¶ *Are kept in store.* Gr., '*Are treasured up.*' The allusion in the Greek word is to anything that is treasured up, or reserved for future use. The apostle does not say that this is the *only* purpose for which the heavens and the earth are preserved, but that this is one object, or

this is *one* aspect in which the subject may be viewed. They are like treasure reserved for future use. ¶ *Reserved unto fire.* Reserved or kept to be burned up. See Notes on ver. 10. The first mode of destroying the world was by water, the next will be by fire. That the world would at some period be destroyed by fire was a common opinion among the ancient philosophers, especially the Greek Stoics. What was the foundation of that opinion, or whence it was derived, it is impossible now to determine ; but it is remarkable that it should have accorded so entirely with the statements of the New Testament. The authorities in proof that this opinion was entertained may be seen in Wetstein, *in loc.* See Seneca, N. Q. iii. 28 ; Cic. N. D. ii. 46 ; Simplicius in Arist. de Cœlo i. 9 ; Eusebius, P. xv. 18. It is quite remarkable that there have been among the heathen in ancient and modern times so many opinions that accord with the statements of revelation —opinions, many of them, which could not have been founded on any investigations of science among them, and which must, therefore, have been either the result of conjecture, or handed down by tradition. Whatever may have been their origin, the fact that such opinions prevailed and were believed, may be allowed to have some weight in showing that the statements in the Bible are not improbable. ¶ *Against the day of judgment and perdition of ungodly men.* The world was destroyed by a flood on account of the wickedness of its inhabitants. It would seem from this passage that it will be destroyed by fire with reference to the same cause ; at least, that its destruction by fire will involve the perdition of wicked men. It cannot be inferred from this passage that the world will be *as* wicked at the general conflagration as it was in the time of Noah ; but the idea in the mind of Peter seems to have been, that in the destruction of the world by fire the perdition of the wicked will be involved, or will at that time occur. It also seems to be implied that the fire will accomplish an important agency in that destruction, as the water did on the old world. It is not said, in the passage before us, whether those to be destroyed will be

8 But, beloved, be not ignorant of this one thing, that one day *is* with the Lord as a thousand years, and a *ᵃ* thousand years as one day. 9 The Lord is not slack *ᵇ* con-

ᵃ Ps.90.4.   *ᵇ* Ha.2.3.

cerning his promise, as some men count slackness; but is long-suffering *ᶜ* to us-ward, not willing *ᵈ* that any should perish, but that all should *ᵉ* come to repentance.

ᶜ Ps.86.15; Is.30.18.   *ᵈ* Eze.33.11.   *ᵉ* 1 Ti.2.4.

---

living at that time, or will be raised up from the dead, nor have we any means of determining what was the idea of Peter on that point. All that the passage essentially teaches is, that the world is reserved now with reference to such a consummation by fire; that is, that there are elements kept in store that may be enkindled into an universal conflagration, and that such a conflagration will be attended with the destruction of the wicked.

8. *But, beloved, be not ignorant of this one thing, that one day* is *with the Lord as a thousand years.* This (vers. 8, 9) is the second consideration by which the apostle meets the objection of scoffers against the doctrine of the second coming of the Saviour. The objection was, that much time, and perhaps the time which had been supposed to be set for his coming, had passed away, and still all things remained as they were. The reply of the apostle is, that no argument could be drawn from this, for that which may seem to be a long time to us is a brief period with God. In the infinity of his own duration there is abundant time to accomplish his designs, and it can make no difference with him whether they are accomplished in one day or extended to a thousand years. Man has but a short time to live, and if he does not accomplish his purposes in a very brief period, he never will. But it is not so with God. He always lives ; and we cannot therefore infer, because the execution of his purposes seems to be delayed, that they are abandoned. With Him who always lives it will be as easy to accomplish them at a far distant period as now. If it is his pleasure to accomplish them in a single day, he can do it; if he chooses that the execution shall be deferred to a thousand years, or that a thousand years shall be consumed in executing them, he has power to carry them onward through what seems to us to be so vast a duration. The

wicked, therefore, cannot infer that they will escape because their punishment is delayed; nor should the righteous fear that the Divine promises will fail because ages pass away before they are accomplished. The expression here used, that 'one day is with the Lord as a thousand years,' &c., is common in the Rabbinical writings. See Wetstein *in loc.* A similar thought occurs in Psa. xc. 4 : 'For a thousand years in thy sight are but as yesterday when it is past, and as a watch in the night.'

9. *The Lord is not slack concerning his promise.* That is, it should not be inferred because his promise seems to be long delayed that therefore it will fail. When *men,* after a considerable lapse of time, fail to fulfil their engagements, we infer that it is because they have changed their plans, or because they have forgotten their promises, or because they have no ability to perform them, or because there is a want of principle which makes them regardless of their obligations. But no such inference can be drawn from the apparent delay of the fulfilment of the Divine purposes. Whatever may be the reasons why they seem to be deferred, we may be sure that it is from no such causes as these. ¶ *As some men count slackness.* It is probable that the apostle here had his eye on some professing Christians who had become disheartened and impatient, and who, from the delay in regard to the coming of the Lord Jesus, and from the representations of those who denied the truth of the Christian religion, arguing from that delay that it was false, began to fear that his promised coming would indeed never occur. To such he says that it should not be inferred from his delay that he would not return, but that the delay should be regarded as an evidence of his desire that men should have space for repentance, and an opportunity to secure their salvation. See

Notes on ver. 15. ¶ *But is long-suffering to us-ward.* Toward us. The delay should be regarded as a proof of his forbearance, and of his desire that men should be saved. Every sinner should consider the fact that he is not cut down in his sins, not as a proof that God will not punish the wicked, but as a demonstration that he is now forbearing, and is willing that he should have an ample opportunity to obtain eternal life. No man should infer that God will not execute his threatenings, unless he can look into the most distant parts of a coming eternity, and demonstrate that there is no suffering appointed for the sinner there ; any man who sins, and who is spared even for a moment, should regard the respite as a proof that God is merciful and forbearing now. ¶ *Not willing that any should perish.* That is, he does not *desire* it or *wish* it. His nature is benevolent, and he sincerely desires the eternal happiness of all, and his patience towards sinners *proves* that he is willing that they should be saved. If he were not willing, it would be easy for him to cut them off, and exclude them from hope at once. This passage, however, should not be adduced to prove (1) that sinners never *will* in fact perish ; for (*a*) the passage does not refer to what God will do as the final Judge of mankind, but to what are his feelings and desires now towards men. (*b*) One may have a sincere desire that others should not perish, and yet it may be that, in entire consistency with that, they will perish. A parent has a sincere *wish* that his children should not be punished, and yet he himself may be under a moral necessity to punish them. A lawgiver may have a sincere wish that no one should ever break the laws, or be punished, and yet he himself may build a prison, and construct a gallows, and cause the law to be executed in a most rigorous manner. A judge on the bench may have a sincere desire that no man should be executed, and that every one arraigned before him should be found to be innocent, and yet even he, in entire accordance with that wish, and with a most benevolent heart, even with tears in his eyes, may pronounce the sentence of the law. (*c*) It cannot be inferred that all that the heart of

infinite benevolence would desire will be accomplished by his mere *will.* It is evidently as much in accordance with the benevolence of God that no man should be miserable in this world, as it is that no one should suffer in the next, since the difficulty is not in the question *where* one shall suffer, but in the fact itself that *any* should suffer ; and it is just as much in accordance with his nature that all should be happy *here*, as that they should be happy hereafter. And yet no man can maintain that the fact that God is benevolent proves that no one will suffer here. As little will that fact prove that none will suffer in the world to come. (2.) The passage should not be adduced to prove that God has no *purpose*, and has formed no *plan*, in regard to the destruction of the wicked ; for (*a*) the word here used has reference rather to his disposition, or to his nature, than to any act or plan. (*b*) There is a sense, as is admitted by all, in which he does will the destruction of the wicked—to wit, if they do not repent—that is, if they deserve it. (*c*) Such an act is as inconsistent with his general benevolence as an eternal purpose in the matter, since his eternal purpose can only have been to do what he actually does ; and if it be consistent with a sincere desire that sinners should be saved to *do* this, then it is consistent to *determine* beforehand to do it—for to determine beforehand to do what is in fact right, cannot but be a lovely trait in the character of any one. (3.) The passage then proves (*a*) that God has a sincere *desire* that men should be saved ; (*b*) that any purpose in regard to the destruction of sinners is not founded on mere will, or is not arbitrary ; (*c*) that it would be agreeable to the nature of God, and to his arrangements in the plan of salvation, if all men should come to repentance, and accept the offers of mercy ; (*d*) that if any come to him truly penitent, and desirous to be saved, they will not be cast off ; (*e*) that, since it is in accordance with his nature that he should desire that all men may be saved, it may be presumed that he has made an arrangement by which it is possible that they should be ; and (*f*) that, since this is his desire, it is proper for the ministers of religion to

10 But the day of the Lord will come as a thief *a* in the night; in the which the heavens *b* shall pass away with a great noise, and the

elements shall melt with fervent heat: the earth also, and the works that are therein, shall be burned up.

a Mat.24.42,43; Re.16.15.
b Ps.102.26; Is.51.6; Re.20.11.

offer salvation to every human being. Comp. Ezek. xxxiii. 11. 10. *But the day of the Lord.* The day of the Lord Jesus. That is, the day in which he will be manifested. It is called *his* day, because he will then be the grand and prominent object as the Judge of all. Comp. Luke xvii. 27. ¶ *Will come as a thief in the night.* Unexpectedly; suddenly. See Notes, 1 Thess. v. 2. ¶ *In the which the heavens shall pass away with a great noise.* That is, what seems to *us* to be the heavens. It cannot mean that the holy abode where God dwells will pass away; nor need we suppose that this declaration extends to the starry worlds and systems as disclosed by the modern astronomy. The word is doubtless used in a popular sense—that is, as things appear to us; and the *fair* interpretation of the passage would demand only such a change as would occur by the destruction of this world by fire. If a conflagration should take place, embracing the earth and its surrounding atmosphere, all the phenomena would occur which are here described; and, if this would be so, then this is all that can be proved to be meant by the passage. Such a destruction of the elements could not occur without 'a great noise.' ¶ *And the elements shall melt with fervent heat.* Gr., 'the elements being burned, or burning, (καυσούμενα,) shall be dissolved.' The idea is, that the *cause* of their being ' dissolved' shall be fire; or that there will be a conflagration extending to what are here called the ' elements,' that shall produce the effects here described by the word ' dissolved.' There has been much difference of opinion in regard to the meaning of the word here rendered *elements*, (στοιχεῖα.) The word occurs in the New Testament only in the following places: Gal. iv. 3, 9; 2 Pet. iii. 10, 12, in which it is rendered *elements;* Col. ii. 8, 20, in which it is rendered *rudiments;* and in Heb. v. 12, where it is rendered *principles.* For the general meaning of the word,

see Notes, Gal. iv. 3. The word denotes the *rudiments* of anything; the minute parts or portions of which anything is composed, or which constitutes the simple portions out of which anything grows, or of which it is compounded. Here it would properly denote the component parts of the material world; or those which enter into its composition, and of which it is made up. It is not to be supposed that the apostle used the term with the same exact signification with which a chemist would use it now, but in accordance with the popular use of the term in his day. In all ages, and in all languages, some such word, with more or less of scientific accuracy, has been employed to denote the primary materials out of which others were formed, just as, in most languages, there have been characters or letters to denote the elementary sounds of which language is composed. The ancients in general supposed that the elements out of which all things were formed were four—air, earth, fire, and water. Modern science has entirely overturned this theory, and has shown that these, so far from being simple elements, are themselves compounds; but the tendency of modern science is still to show that the elements of all things are in fact few in number. The word, as here used by Peter, would refer to the elements of things as then understood in a popular sense; it would now not be an improper word to be applied to the few elements of which all things are composed, as disclosed by modern chemistry. In either case the use of the word would be correct. Whether applied to the one or the other, science has shown that all are capable of combustion. Water, in its component parts, is inflammable in a high degree; and even the diamond has been shown to be combustible. The idea contained in the word ' dissolved,' is, properly, only the change which *heat* produces. Heat changes the *forms* of things; dissolves them into their elements; dissipates those which were solid by driving them off into gases, and produces new compounds, but it *annihilates* nothing. It could not be demonstrated from this phrase that the world would be annihilated by fire; it could be proved only that it will undergo important changes. So far as the action of fire is concerned, the *form* of the earth may pass away, and its aspect be changed; but unless the direct power which created it interposes to annihilate it, the *matter* which now composes it will still be in existence. ¶ *The earth also, and the works that are therein, shall be burned up.* That is, whether they are the works of God or man—the whole vegetable and animal creation, and all the towers, the towns, the palaces, the productions of genius, the paintings, the statuary, the books, which man has made.

" The cloud-capp'd towers, the gorgeous palaces,
The solemn temples, the great globe itself,
And all that it inherits, shall *dissolve*,
And, like the baseless fabric of a vision,
Leave not one wreck behind."

The word rendered 'burned up,' like the word just before used and rendered *fervent heat*—a word of the same origin, but here *intensive*—means that they will undergo such a change as fire will produce ; not, necessarily, that the matter composing them will be annihilated. If the matter composing the earth is ever to be destroyed entirely, it must be by the immediate power of God, for only He who created can destroy. There is not the least evidence that a particle of matter originally made has been *annihilated* since the world began ; and there are no fires so intense, no chemical powers so mighty, as to cause a particle of matter to cease wholly to be. So far as the power of man is concerned, and so far as one portion of matter can prey on another, matter is as imperishable as mind, and neither can be destroyed unless *God* destroys it. Whether it is his purpose to *annihilate* any portion of the matter which he has made, does not appear from his word ; but it is clear that he intends that the universe shall undergo important *changes*. As to the possibility or probability of such a destruction by fire as is here predicted, no one can have any doubt who is acquainted with the disclosures of modern science in regard to the internal struc-

ture of the earth. Even the ancient philosophers, from some cause, supposed that the earth would yet be destroyed by fire, (Notes, ver. 7;) and modern science has made it probable that the interior of the earth is a melted and intensely heated mass of burning materials; that the habitable world is but a comparatively thin crust or shell over those internal fires ; that earthquakes are caused by the vapours engendered by that heated mass when water comes in contact with it ; and that volcanoes are but openings and vent-holes through which those internal flames make their way to the surface. Whether these fires will everywhere make their way to the surface, and produce an universal conflagration, perhaps could not be determined by science ; but no one can doubt that the simple command of God would be all that is necessary to pour those burning floods over the earth, as he once caused the waters to roll over every mountain and through every valley. As to the question whether it is probable that such a change produced by fire, and bringing the present order of things to a close, will occur, it may be remarked farther, that there is reason to believe that such changes are in fact taking place in other worlds. 'During the last two or three centuries, upwards of thirteen fixed stars have disappeared. One of them, situated in the northern hemisphere, presented a peculiar brilliancy, and was so bright as to be seen by the naked eye at mid-day. It seemed to be on fire, appearing at first of a dazzling white, then of a reddish yellow, and lastly of an ashy pale colour. La Place supposes that it was burned up, as it has never been seen since. The conflagration was visible about sixteen months.' The well-known astronomer, Von Littrow, in the section of his work on 'New and Missing Stars,' (entitled Die Wunder der Himmels oder Gemeinfassliche Darstellung der Weltsystems, Stuttgard, 1843, § 227,) observes : ' Great as may be the revolutions which take place on the surface of those fixed stars, which are subject to this alternation of light, what entirely different changes may those others have experienced, which in regions of the firmament where no star had ever been be-

11 *Seeing* then *that* all these things shall be dissolved, what manner *of persons* ought ye to be in *all* holy conversation and godliness;
12 Looking for *a* and *1* hasting

a Tit.2.13.   1 Or, *hasting the coming.*

unto the coming of the day of God, wherein the heavens, being on fire, shall be dissolved, and the elements shall melt *b* with fervent heat?
13 Nevertheless we, according to

b Is.34.4, Mic.1.4.

fore, appeared to blaze up in clear flames, and then to disappear, perhaps for ever.' He then gives a brief history of those stars which have excited the particular attention of astronomers. ' In the year 1572, on the 11th of November,' says he, ' Tycho, on passing from his chemical laboratory to the observatory, through the court of his house, observed in the constellation Cassiopeia, at a place where before he had only seen very small stars, a new star of uncommon magnitude. It was so bright that it surpassed even Jupiter and Venus in splendour, and was visible even in the day-time. During the whole time in which it was visible, Tycho could observe no parallax or change of position. At the end of the year, however, it gradually diminished; and at length, in March 1574, sixteen months after its discovery, entirely disappeared, since which all traces of it have been lost. When it first appeared, its light was of a dazzling white colour; in January 1573, two months after its reviving, it became yellowish; in a few months it assumed a reddish hue, like Mars or Aldebaran; and in the beginning of the year 1574, two or three months before its total disappearance, it glimmered only with a gray or lead-coloured light, similar to that of Saturn.' See Bibliotheca Sacra, iii., p. 181. If such things occur in other worlds, there is nothing improbable or absurd in the supposition that they may yet occur on the earth.

11. *Seeing then* that *all these things shall be dissolved.* Since this is an undoubted truth. ¶ *What manner of persons ought ye to be in* all *holy conversation and godliness.* In holy conduct and piety. That is, this fact ought to be allowed to exert a deep and abiding influence on us, to induce us to lead holy lives. We should feel that there is nothing permanent on the earth; that this is not our abiding home; and that our great interests are in another world. We should be serious, humble,

and prayerful; and should make it our great object to be prepared for the solemn scenes through which we are soon to pass. An habitual contemplation of the truth, that all that we see is soon to pass away, would produce a most salutary effect on the mind. It would make us serious. It would repress ambition. It would lead us not to desire to accumulate what must so soon be destroyed. It would prompt us to lay up our treasures in heaven. It would cause us to ask with deep earnestness whether we are prepared for these amazing scenes, should they suddenly burst upon us.

12. *Looking for.* Not knowing *when* this may occur, the mind should be in that state which constitutes *expectation;* that is, a belief that it will occur, and a condition of mind in which we would not be taken by surprise should it happen at any moment. See Notes, Titus ii. 13. ¶ *And hasting unto the coming.* Marg., as in Greek, ' *hasting the coming.*' The Greek word rendered *hasting,* (σπινδω,) means to urge on, to hasten; and then to hasten after anything, to await with eager desire. This is evidently the sense here.— *Weistein* and *Robinson.* The state of mind which is indicated by the word is that when we are anxiously desirous that anything should occur, and when we would hasten or accelerate it if we could. The true Christian does not dread the coming of that day. He looks forward to it as the period of his redemption, and would welcome, at any time, the return of his Lord and Saviour. While he is willing to wait as long as it shall please God for the advent of his Redeemer, yet to him the brightest prospect in the future is that hour when he shall come to take him to himself. ¶ *The coming of the day of God.* Called ' the day of God,' because God will then be manifested in his power and glory.

13. *Nevertheless we, according to his promise.* The allusion here seems to

his promise, look for new *a* heavens
a Re.21.1,27.

and a new earth, wherein dwelleth righteousness.

---

be, beyond a doubt, to two passages in Isaiah, in which a promise of this kind is found. Isa. lxv. 17: 'For, behold, I create new heavens, and a new earth: and the former shall not be remembered, nor come into mind.' Isa. lxvi. 22 : 'For as the new heavens and the new earth, which I will make, shall remain before me, saith the Lord,' &c. Comp. Rev. xxi. 1, where John says he had a vision of the new heaven and the new earth which was promised : 'And I saw a new heaven and a new earth; for the first heaven and the first earth were passed away, and there was no more sea.' See Notes, Isa. lxv. 17. ¶ *Look for new heavens and a new earth.* It may not be easy to answer many of the questions which might be asked respecting the 'new heaven and earth' here mentioned. One of those which are most naturally asked is, whether the apostle meant to say that this earth, after being purified by fire, would be fitted up again for the abode of the redeemed ; but this question it is impossible to answer with certainty. The following remarks may perhaps embrace all that is known, or that can be shown to be probable, on the meaning of the passage before us. I. The 'new heavens and the new earth' referred to will be such as will exist *after* the world shall have been destroyed by fire ; that is, *after* the general judgment. There is not a word expressed, and not a hint given, of any 'new heaven and earth' *previous* to this, in which the Saviour will reign personally over his saints, in such a renovated world, through a long millennial period. The *order* of events stated by Peter, is (*a*) that the heavens and earth which are now, are 'kept in store, reserved unto fire *against the day of judgment*, and perdition of ungodly men,' ver. 7; (*b*) that the day of the Lord will come suddenly and unexpectedly, ver. 10 ; that *then* the heavens and earth will pass away with a great noise, the elements will melt, and the earth with all its works be burned up, ver. 10; and (*c*) that *after* this (ver. 13) we are to expect the 'new heavens and

new earth.' Nothing is said of a personal reign of Christ ; nothing of the resurrection of the saints to dwell with him on the earth ; nothing of the world's being fitted up for their abode *previous* to the final judgment. If Peter had any knowledge of such events, and believed that they would occur, it is remarkable that he did not even allude to them here. The passage before us is one of the very few places in the New Testament where allusion is made to the manner in which the affairs of the world will be closed ; and it cannot be explained why, if he looked for such a glorious personal reign of the Saviour, the subject should have been passed over in total silence. II. The word 'new,' applied to the heavens and the earth that are to succeed the present, might express one of the following three things —that is, either of these things would correspond with all that is fairly implied in that word : (*a*) If a new world was literally created out of nothing after this world is destroyed ; for that would be in the strictest sense *new.* That such an event is possible no one can doubt, though it is not revealed. (*b*) If an inhabitant of the earth should dwell after death on any other of the worlds now existing, it would be to him a 'new' abode, and everything would appear new. Let him, for instance, be removed to the planet *Saturn,* with its wonderful ring, and its seven moons, and the whole aspect of the heavens, and of the world on which he would then dwell, would be *new* to him. The same thing would occur if he were to dwell on any other of the heavenly bodies, or if he were to pass from world to world. See this illustrated at length in the works of Thomas Dick, LL.D.—'Celestial Scenery,' &c. Comp. Notes, 1 Pet. i. 12. (*c*) *If* the earth should be renovated, and fitted up for the abode of man *after* the universal conflagration, it would then be a new abode. III. This world, thus renovated, may be from time to time the temporary abode of the redeemed, after the final judgment. No one can prove that this may not be, though there is no evidence that it will be their permanent and eternal abode, or that even all the redeemed will at any one time find a home on this globe, for no one can suppose that the earth is spacious enough to furnish a dwelling-place for all the unnumbered millions that are to be saved. But that the earth *may* again be revisited from time to time by the redeemed ; that in a purified and renovated form it may be *one* of the 'many mansions' which are to be fitted up for them, (John xiv. 2,) may not appear wholly improbable from the following suggestions : (1.) It seems to have been a law of the earth that in its progress it should be *prepared* at one period for the dwelling-place of a higher order of beings at another period. Thus, according to the disclosures of geology, it existed perhaps for countless ages before it was fitted to be an abode for man ; and that it was occupied by the monsters of an inferior order of existence, who have now passed away to make room for a nobler race. Who can tell but the present order ot things may pass away to make place for the manifestations of a more exalted mode of being ? (2.) There is no certain evidence that any world has been *annihilated*, though some have disappeared from human view. Indeed, as observed above, (Notes, ver. 10,) there is no proof that a single particle of matter ever has been annihilated, or ever will be. It may change its form, but it may still exist. (3.) It seems also to accord most with probability, that, though the earth may undergo important changes by flood or fire, it will not be annihilated. It seems difficult to suppose that, as a world, it will be wholly displaced from the system of which it is now a part, or that the system itself will disappear. The earth, as one of the worlds of God, has occupied too important a position in the history of the universe to make it to be easily believed that the place where the Son of God became incarnate and died, shall be utterly swept away. It would, certainly, accord more with all the *feelings* which we can have on such a subject, to suppose that a world once so beautiful when it came from the hand of its Maker, should be restored to

primitive loveliness ; that a world which seems to have been *made* primarily (see Notes, 1 Pet. i. 12) with a view to illustrate the glory of God in redemption, should be preserved in some appropriate form to be the theatre of the exhibition of the developement of that plan in far distant ages to come. (4.) To the redeemed, it would be most interesting again to visit the spot where the great work of their redemption was accomplished ; where the Son of God became incarnate and made atonement for sin ; and where there would be so many interesting recollections and associations, even after the purification by fire, connected with the infancy of their existence, and their preparation for eternity. Piety would at least *wish* that the world where Gethsemane and Calvary are should never be blotted out from the universe. But (5.) if, after their resurrection and reception into heaven, the redeemed shall ever revisit a world so full of interesting recollections and associations, where they began their being, where their Redeemer lived and died, where they were renewed and sanctified, and where their bodies once rested in the grave, there is no reason to suppose that this will be their permanent and unchanging abode. It may be mere speculation, but it seems to accord best with the goodness of God, and with the manner in which the universe is made, to suppose that every portion of it may be visited, and become successively the abode of the redeemed ; that they may pass from world to world, and survey the wonders and the works of God as they are displayed in different worlds. The universe, so vast, seems to have been fitted up for such a purpose, and nothing else that we can conceive of will be so adapted to give employment without weariness to the minds that God has made, in the interminable duration before them. IV. The new heavens and earth will be *holy*. They will be the abode of righteousness for ever. (*a*) This fact is clearly revealed in the verse before us ; 'wherein dwelleth righteousness.' It is also the correct statement of the Scriptures, Rev. xxi. 27; 1 Cor. vi. 9, 10; Heb. xii. 14. (*b*) This will be in strong contrast with what has occurred

14 Wherefore, beloved, seeing that ye look for such things, be diligent ^athat ye may be found of him in peace, without spot, and blameless.

<hr>

a 1 Co. 15.58; 1 Th. 5.23.

15 And account *that* the long-suffering of our Lord *is* salvation; ^beven as our beloved brother Paul also, according to the wisdom given unto him, hath written unto you;

<hr>

b Ro. 2.4.

on earth. The history of this world has been almost entirely a history of *sin* —of its nature, developements, results. There have been no perfectly holy beings on the earth, except the Saviour, and the angels who have occasionally visited it. There has been no perfectly holy place—city, village, hamlet; no perfectly holy community. But the future world, in strong contrast with this, will be perfectly pure, and will be a fair illustration of what religion in its perfect form will do. (*c*) It is for this that the Christian desires to dwell in that world, and waits for the coming of his Saviour. It is not primarily that he may be happy, desirable as that is, but that he may be in a world where he himself will be perfectly pure, and where all around him will be pure; where every being that he meets shall be 'holy as God is holy,' and every place on which his eye rests, or his foot treads, shall be uncontaminated by sin. To the eye of faith and hope, how blessed is the prospect of such a world!

14. *Wherefore, beloved, seeing that ye look for such things, be diligent.* That is, in securing your salvation. The effect of such hopes and prospects should be to lead us to an earnest inquiry whether we are prepared to dwell in a holy world, and to make us diligent in performing the duties, and patient in bearing the trials of life. He who has such hopes set before him, should seek earnestly that he may be enabled truly to avail himself of them, and should make their attainment the great object of his life. He who is so soon to come to an end of all weary toil, should be willing to labour diligently and faithfully while life lasts. He who is so soon to be relieved from all temptation and trial, should be willing to bear a little longer the sorrows of the present world. What are all these compared with the glory that awaits us? Comp. Notes, 1 Cor. xv. 58; Rom. viii. 18, seq.; 2 Cor. iv. 16-18. ¶ *That ye may be*

found of him in peace. Found by him when he returns in such a state as to secure your eternal peace. ¶ *Without spot, and blameless.* See Notes, Eph. v. 27. It should be an object of earnest effort with us to have the last stain of sin and pollution removed from our souls. A deep feeling that we are soon to stand in the presence of a holy God, our final Judge, cannot but have a happy influence in making us pure.

15. *And account that the long-suffering of our Lord is salvation.* Regard his delay in coming to judge the world, not as an evidence that he never will come, but as a proof of his desire that we should be saved. Many had drawn a different inference from the fact that the Saviour did not return, and had supposed that it was a proof that he would never come, and that his promises had failed. Peter says that that conclusion was not authorized, but that we should rather regard it as an evidence of his mercy, and of his desire that we should be saved. This conclusion is as proper now as it was then. Wicked men should not infer, because God does not cut them down, that therefore they never will be punished, or that God is not faithful to his threatenings. They should rather regard it as a proof that he is willing to save them; for (1) he might justly cut them off for their sins; (2) the only reason of which we have knowledge why he spares the wicked is to give them space for repentance; and (3) as long as life is prolonged a sinner has the opportunity to repent, and may turn to God. We may therefore, in our own case, look on all the delays of God to punish—on all his patience and forbearance towards us, notwithstanding our sins and provocations—on the numberless tokens of his kindness scattered along our way, as evidence that he is not willing that we should perish. What an accumulated argument in any case would this afford of the willingness of God to save! Let any man look on

16 As also in all *his* epistles, *a* speaking in them of these things; in which are some things hard to be understood, which they that are

unlearned and unstable wrest, as *they do* also the other scriptures, unto their own destruction.

a Ro.8.19; 1 Co.15.24; 1 Th.iv.,v.; 2 Th.1.5–10.

his own sins, his pride, and selfishness, and sensuality; let him contemplate the fact that he has sinned through many years, and against many mercies; let him endeavour to estimate the number and magnitude of his offences, and upon God's patience in bearing with him while these have been committed, and who can overrate the force of such an argument in proof that God is slow to anger, and is willing to save? Comp. Notes, Rom. ii. 4. ¶ *Even as our beloved brother Paul also.* From this reference to Paul the following things are clear: (1) that Peter was acquainted with his writings; (2) that he presumed that those to whom he wrote were also acquainted with them; (3) that Peter regarded Paul as a 'beloved brother,' notwithstanding the solemn rebuke which Paul had had occasion to administer to him, Gal. ii. 2, seq.; (4) that he regarded him as authority in inculcating the doctrines and duties of religion; and (5) that he regarded him as an inspired man, and his writings as a part of Divine truth. See Notes, ver. 16. That Peter has shown in his epistles that he was acquainted with the writings of Paul, has been abundantly proved by Eichhorn, (Einleitung in das N. Tes. viii. 606, seq.,) and will be apparent by a comparison of the following passages: Eph. i. 3, with 1 Pet. iii. 1; Col. iii. 8, with 1 Pet. ii. 1; Eph. v. 22, with 1 Pet. iii. 1; Eph. v. 21, with 1 Pet. v. 5; 1 Thess. v. 6, with 1 Pet. v. 8; 1 Cor. xvi. 20, with 1 Pet. v. 14; Rom. viii. 18, with 1 Pet. v. 1; Rom. iv. 24, with 1 Pet. i. 21; Rom. xiii. 1, 3, 4, with 1 Pet. ii. 13, 14; 1 Tim. ii. 9, with 1 Pet. iii. 3; 1 Tim. v. 5, with 1 Pet. iii. 5. The writings of the apostles were doubtless extensively circulated; and one apostle, though himself inspired, could not but feel a deep interest in the writings of another. There would be cases also, as in the instance before us, in which one would wish to confirm his own sentiments by the acknowledged wisdom, experience,

and authority of another. ¶ *According to the wisdom given unto him.* Peter evidently did not mean to disparage that wisdom, or to express a doubt that Paul was endowed with wisdom; he meant undoubtedly that, in regard to Paul, the same thing was true which he would have affirmed of himself or of any other man, that whatever wisdom he had was to be traced to a higher than human origin. This would at the same time tend to secure more respect for the opinion of Paul than if he had said it was his own, and would keep up in the minds of those to whom he wrote a sense of the truth that *all* wisdom is from above. In reference to ourselves, to our friends, to our teachers, and to all men, it is proper to bear in remembrance the fact that *all* true wisdom is from the 'Father of lights.' Comp. Notes, James i. 5, 17. ¶ *Hath written unto you.* It is not necessary to suppose that Paul had written any epistles addressed specifically, and by name, to the persons to whom Peter wrote. It is rather to be supposed that the persons to whom Peter wrote (1 Pet. i. 1) lived in the regions to which some of Paul's epistles were addressed, and that they might be regarded as addressed to them. The epistles to the Galatians, Ephesians, and Colossians were of this description, all addressed to churches in Asia Minor, and all, therefore, having reference to the same people to whom Peter addressed his epistles. 16. *As also in all his epistles.* Not only in those which he addressed to the churches in Asia Minor, but in his epistles generally. It is to be presumed that they might have had an acquaintance with some of the other epistles of Paul, as well as those sent to the churches in their immediate vicinity. ¶ *Speaking in them of these things.* The things which Peter had dwelt upon in his two epistles. The great doctrines of the cross; of the depravity of man; of the Divine purposes; of the new birth; of the consummation of all things;

of the return of the Saviour to judge the world, and to receive his people to himself; the duty of a serious, devout, and prayerful life, and of being prepared for the heavenly world. These things are constantly dwelt upon by Paul, and to his authority in these respects Peter might appeal with the utmost confidence. ¶ *In which.* The common reading in this passage is ἐν οἷς, and according to this the reference is to the *subjects* treated of—'in which *things*'—referring to what he had just spoken of —'speaking of these *things.*' This reading is found in the common editions of the New Testament, and is supported by far the greater number of MSS., and by most commentators and critics. It is found in Griesbach, Tittman, and Hahn, and has every evidence of being the genuine reading. Another reading, however, (ἐν αἷς,) is found in some valuable MSS., and is supported by the Syriac and Arabic versions, and adopted by Mill, (Proleg. 1484,) and by Beza. According to this, the reference is to the *epistles* themselves—as would seem to be implied in our common version. The true construction, so far as the evidence goes, is to refer it not directly to the *epistles,* but to the *things* of which Peter says Paul wrote; that is, not to the style and language of Paul, but to the great truths and doctrines which he taught. Those doctrines were indeed contained in his epistles, but still, according to the fair construction of the passage before us, Peter should not be understood as accusing Paul of obscurity of *style.* He refers not to the difficulty of understanding what Paul *meant,* but to the difficulty of comprehending the great *truths* which he taught. This is, generally, the greatest difficulty in regard to the statements of Paul. The difficulty is not that the meaning of the writer is not plain, but it is either (*a*) that the mind is overpowered by the grandeur of the thought, and the incomprehensible nature of the theme, or (*b*) that the truth is so unpalatable, and the mind is so prejudiced against it, that we are *unwilling* to receive it. Many a man knows well enough what Paul means, and would receive his doctrines without hesitation if the heart was not opposed to it; and in this state

of mind Paul is charged with obscurity, when the real difficulty lies only in the *heart* of him who makes the complaint. If this be the true interpretation of this passage, then it should not be adduced to prove that Paul is an obscure writer, whatever may be true on that point. There *are,* undoubtedly, obscure things in his writings, as there are in all other ancient compositions, but this passage should not be adduced to prove that he had not the faculty of making himself understood. An honest heart, a willingness to receive the truth, is one of the best qualifications for understanding the writings of Paul; and when this exists, no one will fail to find truth that may be comprehended, and that will be eminently adapted to sanctify and save the soul. ¶ *Are some things hard to be understood.* Things pertaining to high and difficult subjects, and which are not easy to be comprehended. Peter does not call in question the truth of what Paul had written; he does not intimate that he himself would differ from him His language is rather that which a man would use who regarded the writings to which he referred as true, and what he says here is an honourable testimony to the authority of Paul. It may be added, (1,) that Peter does not say that *all* the doctrines of the Bible, or even *all* the doctrines of Paul, are hard to be understood, or that nothing is plain. (2.) He says nothing about withholding the Bible, or even the writings of Paul, from the mass of Christians, on the ground of the difficulty of understanding the Scriptures; nor does he intimate that that was the design of the Author of the Bible. (3.) It is perfectly manifest, from this very passage, that the writings of Paul were in fact in the hands of the people, else how could they wrest and pervert them? (4.) Peter says nothing about an infallible interpreter of any kind, nor does he intimate that either he or his 'successors' were authorized to interpret them for the church. (5.) With what propriety can the *pretended* successor of Peter—the pope—undertake to expound those difficult doctrines in the writings of Paul, when even Peter himself did not undertake it, and when he did not profess to be able to comprehend them?

Is the pope more skilled in the knowledge of divine things than the apostle Peter? Is he better qualified to interpret the sacred writings than an inspired apostle was? (6.) Those portions of the writings of Paul, for anything that appears to the contrary, are just as 'hard to be understood' now, as they were before the 'infallible' church undertook to explain them. The world is little indebted to any claims of infallibility in explaining the meaning of the oracles of God. It remains yet to be seen that any portion of the Bible has been made clearer by *any* mere authoritative explanation. And (7.) it should be added, that without any such exposition, the humble inquirer after truth may find enough in the Bible to guide his feet in the paths of salvation. No one ever approached the sacred Scriptures with a teachable heart, who did not find them '*able* to make him wise unto salvation.' Comp. Notes on 2 Tim. iii. 15. ¶ *Which they that are unlearned.* The evil here adverted to is that which arises in cases where those without competent knowledge undertake to become expounders of the word of God. It is not said that it is not proper for them to attempt to become instructed by the aid of the sacred writings, but the danger is, that without proper views of interpretation, of language, and of ancient customs, they might be in danger of perverting and abusing certain portions of the writings of Paul. Intelligence among the people is everywhere in the Bible presumed to be proper in understanding the sacred Scriptures; and ignorance may produce the same effects in interpreting the Bible which it will produce in interpreting other writings. Every good thing is liable to abuse; but the proper way to correct this evil, and to remove this danger, is not to *keep* the people in ignorance, or to appoint some one to be an infallible interpreter; it is to remove the ignorance itself by enlightening the people, and rendering them better qualified to understand the sacred oracles. The way to remove error is not to perpetuate ignorance; it is to enlighten the mind, so that it may be qualified to appreciate the truth. ¶ *And unstable.* Who have no settled principles and views. The evil here

adverted to is that which arises where those undertake to interpret the Bible who have no established principles. They regard nothing as settled. They have no landmarks set up to guide their inquiries. They have no stability in their character, and of course nothing can be regarded as settled in their methods of interpreting the Bible. They are under the control of feeling and emotion, and are liable to embrace one opinion to-day, and another directly opposite to-morrow. But the way to prevent *this* evil is not by attempting to give to a community an authoritative interpretation of the Bible; it is to diffuse abroad just principles, that men may obtain from the Bible an intelligent view of what it means. ¶ *Wrest.* Pervert—στρεβλοῦσιν. The word here used occurs nowhere else in the New Testament. It is derived from a word meaning a windlass, winch, instrument of torture, (στρεβλή,) and means to roll or wind on a windlass; then to wrench, or turn away, as by the force of a windlass; and then to wrest or pervert. It implies a turning out of the way by the application of force. Here the meaning is, that they apply those portions of the Bible to a purpose for which they were never intended. It is doubtless true that this may occur. Men may abuse and pervert anything that is good. But the way to prevent this is not to set up a pretended infallible interpreter. With all the perversities arising from ignorance in the interpretation of the Bible; in all the crude, and weak, and fanciful expositions which could be found among those who have interpreted the Scriptures for themselves—and they are many—if they were all collected together, there would not be found so many adapted to corrupt and ruin the soul, as have come from the interpretations attempted to be palmed upon the world by the one church that claims to be the infallible expounder of the word of God. ¶ *As* they do *also the other scriptures.* This is an unequivocal declaration of Peter that he regarded the writings of Paul as a part of the holy Scriptures, and of course that he considered him as inspired. The word 'Scriptures,' as used by a Jew, had a technical signification—meaning the in-

17 Ye therefore, beloved, seeing ye know *these things* before, beware lest ye also, being led away with the error of the wicked, fall from your own steadfastness.

a Col.1.10.

18 But grow *a* in grace, and *in* the knowledge of our Lord and Saviour Jesus Christ. To him *b be* glory, both now and for ever Amen.

b 2 Ti.4.18.

spired writings, and was the common word which was applied to the sacred writings of the Old Testament. As Peter uses this language, it implies that he regarded the writings of Paul as on a level with the Old Testament; and as far as the testimony of one apostle can go to confirm the claim of another to inspiration, it proves that the writings of Paul are entitled to a place in the sacred canon. It should be remarked, also, that Peter evidently speaks here of the *common estimate* in which the writings of Paul were held. He addresses those to whom he wrote, not in such a way as to declare to them that the writings of Paul were to be regarded as a part of the inspired volume, but as if this were already known, and were an admitted point. ¶ *Unto their own destruction.* By embracing false doctrines. Error destroys the soul; and it is very possible for a man so to read the Bible as only to confirm himself in error. He may find passages which, by a perverted interpretation, shall seem to sustain his own views; and, instead of embracing the truth, may live always under delusion, and perish at last. It is not to be inferred that every man who reads the Bible, or even every one who undertakes to be its public expounder, will certainly be saved.

17. *Seeing that ye know* these things *before.* Being aware of this danger, and knowing that such results may follow. Men should read the Bible with the feeling that it is *possible* that they may fall into error, and be deceived at last. This apprehension will do much to make them diligent, and candid, and prayerful, in studying the word of God. ‖ *With the error of the wicked.* Wicked men. Such as he had referred to in chap. ii., who became public teachers of religion. ¶ *Fall from your own steadfastness.* Your firm adherence to the truth. The particular danger here referred to is not that of falling from grace, or from true religion, but from

the firm and settled principles of religious truth into error.

18. *But grow in grace.* Comp. Col. i. 10. Religion in general is often represented as *grace*, since every part of it is the result of grace, or of unmerited favour; and to 'grow in grace' is to increase in that which constitutes true religion. Religion is as susceptible of cultivation and of growth as any other virtue of the soul. It is feeble in its beginnings, like the grain of mustard seed, or like the germ or blade of the plant, and it increases as it is cultivated. There is no piety in the world which is not the result of cultivation, and which cannot be measured by the degree of care and attention bestowed upon it. No one becomes eminently pious, any more than one becomes eminently learned or rich, who does not intend to ; and ordinarily men in religion are what they design to be. They have about as much religion as they wish, and possess about the character which they intend to possess. When men reach extraordinary elevations in religion, like Baxter, Payson, and Edwards, they have gained only what they *meant* to gain ; and the gay and worldly professors of religion, who have little comfort and peace, have in fact the characters which they designed to have. If these things are so, then we may see the propriety of the injunction ' to grow in grace ;' and then too we may see the reason why so feeble attainments are made in piety by the great mass of those who profess religion. ¶ *And* in *the knowledge of our Lord and Saviour Jesus Christ.* See Notes, John xvii. 3. Comp. Notes on Col. i. 10. To know the Lord Jesus Christ—to possess just views of his person, character, and work —is the sum and essence of the Christian religion; and with this injunction, therefore, the apostle appropriately closes this epistle. He who has a saving knowledge of Christ, has in fact all that is essential to his welfare in the

life that is, and in that which is to come; he who has not this knowledge, though he may be distinguished in the learning of the schools, and may be profoundly skilled in the sciences, has in reality no knowledge that will avail him in the great matters pertaining to his eternal welfare. ¶ *To him be glory, &c.* Comp. Notes, Rom. xvi. 27; 2 Tim. iv.

18. With the desire that honour and glory should be rendered to the Redeemer, all the aspirations of true Christians appropriately close. There is no wish more deeply cherished in their hearts than this; there is nothing that will enter more into their worship in heaven. Compare Rev. i. 5, 6; v. 12, 13.

THE

FIRST EPISTLE GENERAL OF JOHN

INTRODUCTION

§ 1. *The authenticity of the Epistle.*

LITTLE need be said respecting the authenticity of this epistle, or the evidence that it was written by the apostle John. There are, in general, two sources of evidence in regard to ancient writings: the external evidence, or that which may be derived from the testimony of other writers; and the evidence which may be derived from some marks of the authorship in the writing itself, which is called the internal evidence. Both of these are remarkably clear in regard to this epistle.

(1.) The external evidence. (*a*) It is quoted or referred to by the early Christian writers as the undoubted production of the apostle John. It is referred to by Polycarp in the beginning of the second century; it is quoted by Papias, and also by Irenæus. Origen says, 'John, beside the Gospel and Revelation, has left us an epistle of a few lines. Grant also a second, and a third; for all do not allow these to be genuine.' See Lardner, vi. 275, and Lücke, Einlei. i. Dionysius of Alexandria admitted the genuineness of John's first epistle; so also did Cyprian. All the three epistles were received by Athanasius, by Cyril of Jerusalem, and by Epiphanius. Eusebius says, 'Beside his Gospel, his first epistle is universally acknowledged by those of the present time, and by the ancients; but the other two are contradicted.' (*b*) It is found in the old Syriac version, probably made in the first century, though the second and third epistles are not there. (*c*) The genuineness of the first epistle was never extensively called in question, and it was never reckoned among the doubtful or disputed epistles. (*d*) It was rejected or doubted only by those who rejected his Gospel, and for the same reasons. Some small sects of those who were called 'heretics,' rejected *all* the writings of John, because they conflicted with their peculiar views; but this was confined to a small number of persons, and never affected the general belief of the church. See Lücke, Einlei. 9, seq.

(2.) There is strong internal evidence that the same person wrote this epistle who was the author of the Gospel which bears the same name. The resemblance in the mode of expression, and in the topics referred to, are numerous, and at the same time are not such as would be made by one who was *attempting* to imitate the language of another. The allusions of this kind, moreover, are to what is *peculiar* in the Gospel of John, and not to what is common to that Gospel and the other three. There is nothing in the epistle which would particularly remind us of the Gospel of Matthew, or Mark, or Luke; but it is impossible to read it and not be reminded constantly of the Gospel by John. Among those passages and expressions the following may be referred to:

EPISTLE.		GOSPEL.
Chapter i. 1	compared with	Chapter i. 1, 4, 14.
ii. 5		xiv. 23.
ii. 6		xv. 4.
ii. 8; iii. 11		xiii. 34.
ii. 8, 10		i. 5, 9; xi. 10
ii. 13, 14		xvii. 3.
iii. 1		i. 12.
iii. 2		xvii. 24.
iii. 8		viii. 44.
iii. 13		xv. 20.
iv. 9		iii. 16.
iv. 12		i. 18.
v. 13		xx. 31.
v. 14		xiv. 14.
v. 20		xvii. 2.

This language in the epistle, as will be easily seen by a comparison, is such as the real author of the Gospel by John would be likely to use if he wrote an epistle. The passages referred to are in his style ; they show that the mind of the author of both was turned to the same points, and those not such points as might be found in all writers, but such as indicated a peculiar mode of thinking. They are not such expressions as Matthew, or Mark, or Luke, or Paul would have used in an epistle, but just such as we should expect from the writer of the Gospel of John. It must be clear to any one that either the author of the Gospel was also the author of this epistle, or that the author of the epistle *meant* to imitate the author of the Gospel, and to leave the impression that the apostle John was the author. But there are several things which make it clear that this is not a forgery. (*a*) The passages where the resemblance is found are not exact quotations, and are not such as a man would make if he *designed* to imitate another. They are rather such as the same man would use if he were writing twice on the same subject, and should express himself the second time without intending to copy what he had said the first. (*b*) If it had been an intentional fraud or forgery, there would have been some allusion to the name or authority of the author ; or, in other words, the author of the epistle would have endeavoured to sustain himself by some distinct reference to the apostle, or to his authority, or to his well-known characteristics as a teller of truth. See John xix. 35; xxi. 24. Compare 3 John 12. But nothing of the kind occurs in this epistle. It is written without disclosing the name of the author, or the place where he lived, or the persons to whom it was addressed, and 'with no allusions to the Gospel, except such as show that the author thought in the same manner, and had the same things in his eye, and was intent on the same object. It is, throughout, the style and manner of one who felt that his method of expressing himself was so well understood, that he did not need even to mention his own name; as if, without anything further, it would be apparent from the very epistle itself who had written it, and what right he had to speak. But this would be a device too refined for forgery. It bears all the marks of sincerity and truth.

§ 2. *The time and place of writing the Epistle.*

Almost nothing is known of the time and place of writing the epistle, and nearly all that is said on this point is mere conjecture. Some recent critics have supposed that it was in fact a part of the Gospel, though in some way it afterwards became detached from it; others, that it was sent *as an epistle* at the same time with the Gospel, and to the same persons. Some have supposed that it was written before the destruction of Jerusalem, and some long after, when John was very aged; and these last suppose that they find evidences of the very advanced age of the author in the epistle itself, in such characteristics as commonly mark the conversation and writings of an old man. An examination of these opinions may be found in Lücke, Einlei. Kap. 2; and in Hug, Introduction, p. 456, seq., p. 732, seq.

There are *very few* marks of time in the epistle, and none that can determine the time of writing it with any degree of certainty. Nor is it of much importance that we should be able to determine it. The truths which it contains are, in the main, as applicable to one age as to another, though it cannot be denied (see § 3) that the author had some prevailing forms of error in his eye. The only marks of time in the epistle by which we can form any conjecture as to the period when it was written are the following: (1.) It was in what the author calls *the last time*, (ἐσχάτη ὥρα,) ch. ii. 18. From this expression it might perhaps be inferred by some that it was just before the destruction of Jerusalem, or that the writer supposed that the end of the world was near. But nothing can be certainly determined from this expression in regard to the exact period when the epistle was written. This phrase, as used in the Scriptures, denotes no more than, the last dispensation or economy of things, the dispensation under which the affairs of the world would be wound up, though that period might be in fact much longer than any one that had preceded it. See Notes on Isa. ii. 2; Acts ii. 17; Heb. i. 2. The object of the writer of this epistle, in the passage referred to, (chap. ii. 18,) is merely to show that the closing dispensation of the world had actually come; that is, that there were certain things which it was known would mark that dispensation, which actually existed then, and by which it could be known that they were living under the last or closing period of the world. (2.) It is quite evident that the epistle was composed *after* the Gospel by John was published. Of this no one can have any doubt who will compare the two together, or even the parallel passages referred to above, § 1. The Gospel is manifestly the original; and it was evidently presumed by the writer of the epistle that the Gospel was in the hands of those to whom he wrote. The statements there made are much more full; the circumstances in which many of the peculiar doctrines adverted to were first advanced are detailed; and the writer of the epistle clearly supposed that all that was necessary in order to an understanding of these doctrines was to state them in the briefest manner, and almost by mere allusion. On this point Lücke well remarks, 'the more brief and condensed expression of the same sentiment by the same author, especially in regard to peculiarities of idea and language, is always the later one; the more extended statement, the unfolding of the idea, is an evidence of an earlier composition,' Einlei. p. 21. Yet while this is clear, it determines little or nothing about the time when the epistle was written, for it is a matter of great uncertainty when the Gospel itself was composed. Wetstein supposes that it was soon after the ascension of the Saviour; Dr. Lardner that it was about the year 68; and Mill and Le Clerc that it was about the year 97. In this uncertainty, therefore, nothing can be determined absolutely from this circumstance in regard to the time of writing the epistle. (3.) The only other note of time on which any reliance has been placed is the supposed fact that there were indications in the epistle itself of the *great age* of the author, or evidences that he was an old man, and that consequently it was written near the close of the life of John. There *is* some evidence in the epistle that it was written when the author was an old man, though none that he was in his *dotage*, as Eichhorn and some others have maintained. The evidence that he was even an old man is not positive, but there is a certain air and manner in the epistle, in its repetitions, and its want of exact order, and especially in the style in which he addresses those to whom he wrote, as *little children*—τικνία—(chap. ii. 1, 12, 28; iii. 7,

18; iv. 4; v. 21)—which would seem to be appropriate only to an aged man. Comp. Lücke, Einlei. pp. 23, 25, and Stuart in Hug's Introduction, pp. 732, 733. As little is known about the *place* where the epistle was written as about the *time*. There are no local references in it; no allusions to persons or opinions which can help us to determine where it was written. As John spent the latter part of his life, however, in Ephesus and its vicinity, there is no impropriety in supposing that it was written there. Nothing, in the interpretation of the epistle, depends on our being able to ascertain the place of its composition. Hug supposes that it was written in Patmos, and was sent as a letter accompanying his Gospel, to the church at Ephesus.—Intro. § 69. Lücke supposes that it was a circular epistle addressed to the churches in Asia Minor, and sent from Ephesus. —Einlei. p. 27.

To *whom* the epistle was written is also unknown. It bears no inscription, as many of the other epistles of the New Testament do, and as even the second and third of John do, and there is no reference to any particular class of persons by which it can be determined for whom it was designed. Nor is it known why the name of the author was not attached to it, or why the persons for whom it was designed were not designated. All that can be determined on this subject from the epistle itself is the following : (1.) It seems to have been addressed to no particular church, but rather to have been of a circular character, designed for the churches in a region of country where certain dangerous opinions prevailed. (2.) The author presumed that it would be known who wrote it, either by the style, or by the sentiments, or by its resemblance to his other writings, or by the messenger who bore it, so that it was unnecessary to affix his name to it. (3.) It appears to have been so composed as to be adapted to *any* people where those errors prevailed ; and hence it was thought better to give it a *general* direction, that all might feel themselves to be addressed, than to designate any particular place or church. There is, indeed, an ancient tradition that it was written to the *Parthians*. Since the time of Augustine this has been the uniform opinion in the Latin church. Venerable Bede remarks, that 'many of the ecclesiastical writers, among whom is St. Athanasius, testify that the first epistle of John was written to the Parthians.' Various conjectures have been made as to the origin of this opinion, and of the title which the epistle bears in the Latin MSS., (*ad Parthos*,) but none of them are satisfactory. No such title is found in the epistle itself, nor is there any intimation in it to whom it was directed. Those who are disposed to examine the conjectures which have been made in regard to the origin of the title may consult Lücke, Enlei. p. 28, seq. No reason can be assigned why it should have been sent to the Parthians, nor is there any sufficient evidence to suppose that it was.

§ 3. *The object of the Epistle.*

It is evident from the epistle itself that there were some prevailing errors among those to whom it was written, and that one design of the writer was to counteract those errors. Yet very various opinions have been entertained in regard to the nature of the errors that were opposed, and the persons whom the writer had in his eye. Loeffler supposes that *Jews* and *Judaizers* are the persons opposed ; Semler, Tittman, Knapp, and Lange suppose that they were *Judaizing Christians*, and especially *Ebionites*, or apostate Christians ; Michaelis, Kleuker, Paulus, and others, suppose that the *Gnostics* are referred to ; others, as Schmidt, Lücke, Vitringa, Bertholdt, Prof. Stuart, suppose that the *Docetæ* was the sect that was principally opposed.

It is impossible now to determine with accuracy to whom particularly the writer referred, nor could it be well done without a more accurate knowledge than we now have of the peculiarities of the errors which prevailed in the time of the author, and among the people to whom he wrote. All that we can learn on the subject that is certain, is to be derived from the epistle itself; and there the intimations are few, but they are so clear that we may obtain some knowledge to guide us.

(1.) The persons referred to had been professing Christians, and were now apostates from the faith. This is clear from ch. ii. 19, ' They went out from us, but they were not of us,' &c. They had been members of the church, but they had now become teachers of error.

(2.) They were probably of the sect of the *Docetœ;* or if that sect had not then formally sprung up, and was not organized, they held the opinions which they afterwards embraced. This sect was a branch of the great Gnostic family; and the peculiarity of the opinion which they held was that Christ was only in appearance and seemingly, but not in reality, a man; that though he seemed to converse, to eat, to suffer, and to die, yet this was merely an *appearance* assumed by the Son of God for important purposes in regard to man. He had, according to this view, no *real humanity;* but though the Son of God had actually appeared in the world, yet all this was only an assumed form for the purpose of a manifestation to men. The opinions of the *Docetes* are thus represented by Gibbon : ' They denied the truth and authenticity of the Gospels, as far as they relate the conception of Mary, the birth of Christ, and the thirty years which preceded the first exercise of his ministry. He first appeared on the banks of the Jordan in the form of perfect manhood; but it was a form only, and not a substance ; a human figure created by the hand of Omnipotence to imitate the faculties and actions of a man, and to impose a perpetual illusion on the senses of his friends and enemies. Articulate sounds vibrated on the ears of his disciples ; but the image which was impressed on their optic nerve, eluded the more stubborn evidence of the touch, and they enjoyed the spiritual, but not the corporeal presence of the Son of God. The rage of the Jews was idly wasted against an impassive phantom, and the mystic scenes of the passion and death, the resurrection and ascension of Christ, were represented on the theatre of Jerusalem for the benefit of mankind.'—Decl. and Fall, vol. iii. p. 245, Ed. New York, 1829. Comp. vol, i. 440.

That these views began to prevail in the latter part of the first century there can be no reason to doubt ; and there can be as little doubt that the author of this epistle had this doctrine in his eye, and that he deemed it to be of special importance in this epistle, as he had done in his Gospel, to show that the Son of God had actually *come in the flesh;* that he was truly and properly a man ; that he lived and died in reality, and not in appearance only. Hence the allusion to these views in such passages as the following: ' That which was from the beginning, which we have heard, which we have seen with our eyes, which we have looked upon, and *our hands have handled,* of the Word of life—that which we have seen and heard declare we unto you,' chap. i. 1, 3. ' Many false prophets are gone out into the world. Hereby know we the Spirit of God: Every spirit that confesseth that Jesus Christ *is come in the flesh* is of God ;. and every spirit that confesseth not that Jesus Christ is come in the flesh is not of God ; and this is that spirit of antichrist, whereof ye have heard that it should come,' chap. iv. 1–3. Comp. vers. 9, 14, 15; v. 1, 6, 10–12. John had written his Gospel to show that Jesus was the Christ, (chap. xx. 31;) he had furnished ample proof that he was Divine, or was equal with the Father, (chap. i. 1–14,) and also that he was truly a man, (chap. xv. 25–28;) but still it seemed proper to furnish a more unequivocal statement that he had actually appeared *in the flesh,* not in appearance only but in reality, and this purpose evidently was a leading design of this epistle.

The main scope of the epistle the author has himself stated in chap. v. 13 : ' These things have I written unto you that believe on the name of the Son of God ; that ye may know that ye have eternal life, and that ye may believe on the name of the Son of God ;' that is, that you may have just views of him, and exercise an intelligent faith.

In connection with this general design, and keeping in view the errors to which they to whom the epistle was written were exposed, there are two leading trains of thought, though often intermingled, in the epistle. (*a*) The author treats of the doctrine that Jesus is the Christ, and (*b*) the importance of *love* as an evidence of being united to him, or of being true Christians. Both these things are characteristic of John ; they agree with the design for which he wrote his gospel, and they were in accordance with his peculiarity of mind as 'the *beloved* disciple,' the disciple whose heart was full of love, and who made religion consist much in that.

The main characteristics of this epistle are these : (1.) It is full of love. The writer dwells on it; places it in a variety of attitudes; enforces the duty of loving one another by a great variety of considerations, and shows that it is essential to the very nature of religion. (2.) The epistle abounds with statements on the evidences of piety, or the characteristics of true religion. The author seems to have felt that those to whom he wrote were in danger of embracing false notions of religion, and of being seduced by the abettors of error. He is therefore careful to lay down the characteristics of real piety, and to show in what it essentially consists. A large part of the epistle is occupied with this, and there is perhaps no portion of the New Testament which one could study to more advantage who is desirous of ascertaining whether he himself is a true Christian. An anxious inquirer, a man who wishes to know what true religion is, could be directed to no portion of the New Testament where he would more readily find the instruction that he needs, than to this portion of the writings of the aged and experienced disciple whom Jesus loved. A true Christian can find nowhere else a more clear statement of the nature of his religion, and of the evidences of real piety, than in this epistle.

FIRST EPISTLE GENERAL OF JOHN.

CHAPTER I.

THAT which was from the *a* beginning, which we have heard, which we have seen *b* with our eyes, which we have looked upon, and our hands have *c* handled, of the Word of life;

a Jn.1.1,&c.   *b* 2 Pe.1.16.   *c* Lu.24.39.

CHAPTER I.

ANALYSIS OF THE CHAPTER.

THIS short chapter embraces the following subjects : I. A strong affirmation that the Son of God, or the ' Life,' had appeared in the flesh, vers. 1—3. The evidence of this, the writer says, was that he had seen him, heard him, handled him ; that is, he had had all the evidence which could be furnished by the senses. His declaration on this point he repeats, by putting the statement into a variety of forms, for he seems to regard it as essential to true religion. II. He says that he wrote to them, in order that they might have fellowship with him in the belief of this truth, and might partake of the joy which flows from the doctrine that the Son of God has actually come in the flesh, vers. 3, 4. III. He states that the sum and substance of the whole message which he had to bring to them was, that God is light, and that if we profess to have fellowship with him we must walk in the light, vers. 5—10. (*a*) In God is no darkness, no impurity, no sin, ver. 5. (*b*) If we are in darkness, if we are ignorant and sinful, it proves that we cannot have any fellowship with him, ver. 6. (*c*) If we walk in the light as he is in the light, if we partake of his character and spirit, then we shall have fellowship one with another, and we may believe that the blood of Christ will cleanse us from all sin, ver. 7. (*d*) Yet we are to guard ourselves from one point of danger, we are not to allow ourselves to feel that we have *no* sin. We are to bear with us the constant recollection that we are

sinners, and are to permit that fact to produce its proper impression on our minds, vers. 8, 10. (*e*) Yet we are not to be desponding though we do feel this, but are to remember, that if we will truly confess our sins he will be found faithful to his promises, and just to the general arrangements of grace, by which our sins may be forgiven, ver. 9.

1. *That which was from the beginning.* There can be no doubt that the reference here is to the Lord Jesus Christ, or the ' Word' that was made flesh. See Notes, John i. 1. This is such language as John would use respecting him, and indeed the phrase ' the beginning,' as applicable to the Lord Jesus, is peculiar to John in the writings of the New Testament : and the language here may be regarded as one proof that this epistle was written by him, for it is just such an expression as *he* would use, but not such as one would be likely to adopt who should attempt to palm off his own writings as those of John. One who should have attempted that would have been likely to introduce the name *John* in the beginning of the epistle, or in some way to have claimed his authority. The apostle, in speaking of ' that *which* was from the beginning,' uses a word in the neuter gender instead of the masculine, (*δ*.) It is not to be supposed, I think, that he meant to apply this term *directly* to the Son of God, for if he had he would have used the masculine pronoun ; but though he had the Son of God in view, and meant to make a strong affirmation respecting him, yet the particular thing here referred to was *whatever* there was respecting that

incarnate Saviour that furnished testimony to any of the senses, or that pertained to his character and doctrine, he had borne witness to. He was looking rather at the *evidence* that he was incarnate; the *proofs* that he was manifested; and he says that those proofs had been subjected to the trial of the senses, and he had borne witness to them, and now did it again. This is what is referred to, it seems to me, by the phrase 'that which,' (*ὅ*.) The sense may be this: 'Whatever there was respecting the Word of life, or him who is the living Word, the incarnate Son of God, from the very beginning, from the time when he was first manifested in the flesh; whatever there was respecting his exalted nature, his dignity, his character, that could be subjected to the testimony of the senses, to be the object of sight, or hearing, or touch, *that* I was permitted to see, and that I declare to you respecting him.' John claims to be a competent witness in reference to everything which occurred as a *manifestation* of what the Son of God was. If this be the correct interpretation, then the phrase 'from the beginning' (*ἀπ' ἀρχῆς*) does not here refer to his eternity, or his being *in* the beginning of all things, as the phrase '*in* the beginning' (*ἐν ἀρχῇ*) does in John i. 1; but rather means from the very commencement of his *manifestation* as the Son of God, the very first indications on earth of what he was as the Messiah. When the writer says (ver. 3) that he 'declares' this to them, it seems to me that he has not reference merely to what he *would* say in this epistle, for he does not go extensively into it here, but that he supposes that they had his Gospel in their possession, and that he also means to refer to that, or presumes that they were familiar with the testimony which he had borne *in* that Gospel respecting the evidence that the 'Word became flesh.' Many have indeed supposed that this epistle accompanied the Gospel when it was published, and was either a part of it that became subsequently detached from it, or was a letter that accompanied it. See *Hug*, Intro. P. II. § 68. There is, it seems to me, no certain evidence of that; but no one can doubt

that he supposed that those to whom he wrote had access to that Gospel, and that he refers here to the testimony which he had borne in that respecting the incarnate Word. ¶ *Which we have heard.* John was with the Saviour through the whole of his ministry, and he has recorded more that the Saviour *said* than either of the other evangelists. It is on what he *said* of himself that he grounds much of the evidence that he was the Son of God. ¶ *Which we have seen with our eyes.* That is, pertaining to his person, and to what he did. 'I have seen *him*; seen what he was as a man; how he appeared on earth; and I have seen whatever there was in his works to indicate his character and origin.' John professes here to have seen enough in this respect to furnish evidence that he was the Son of God. It is not hearsay on which he relies, but he had the testimony of his own eyes in the case. Comp. Notes, 2 Pet. i. 16. ¶ *Which we have looked upon.* The word here used seems designed to be more emphatic or intensive than the one before occurring. He had just said that he had 'seen him with his eyes,' but he evidently designs to include an idea in this word which would imply something more than *mere* beholding or seeing. The additional idea which is couched in this word seems to be that of *desire* or *pleasure*; that is, that he had looked on him with desire, or satisfaction, or with the pleasure with which one beholds a beloved object. Comp. Matt. xi. 7; Luke vii. 24; John i. 14; x. 45. See *Rob. Lex.* There was an intense and earnest gaze, as when we behold one whom we have desired to see, or when one goes out purposely to look on an object. The evidences of the incarnation of the Son of God had been subjected to such an intense and earnest gaze. ¶ *And our hands have handled.* That is, the evidence that he was *a man* was subjected to the sense of *touch*. It was not merely that he had been seen by the eye, for then it might be pretended that this was a mere *appearance* assumed without reality; or that what occurred might have been a mere optical illusion; but the evidence that he appeared in the flesh was subjected to more senses than one; to the fact that

2 (For the life was manifested, and we have seen *it*, and bear witness, and shew unto you that eternal

his voice was heard; that he was seen with the eyes; that the most intense scrutiny had been employed; and, lastly, that he had been actually *touched* and *handled*, showing that it could not have been a mere *appearance*, an assumed form, but that it was a reality. This kind of proof that the Son of God had appeared *in the flesh*, or that he was truly and properly *a man*, is repeatedly referred to in the New Testament. Luke xxiv. 39: 'Behold my hands and my feet, that it is I myself: handle me and see; for a spirit hath not flesh and bones as ye see me have.' Comp. John xx. 25–27. There is evident allusion here to the opinion which early prevailed, which was held by the *Docetes*, that the Son of God did not truly and really become a man, but that there was only an *appearance* assumed, or that he *seemed* to be a man. See the Intro., § 3. It was evidently with reference to this opinion, which began early to prevail, that the apostle dwells on this point, and repeats the idea so much, and shows by a reference to all the senses which could take any cognizance in the case, that he was truly and properly a man. The amount of it is, that we have the same evidence that he was properly a man which we can have in the case of any other human being; the evidence on which we constantly act, and in which we cannot believe that our senses deceive us. ¶ *Of the Word of life.* Respecting, or pertaining to, the Word of life. 'That is, whatever there was pertaining to the Word of life, which was manifested from the beginning in his speech and actions, of which the senses could take cognizance, and which would furnish the evidence that he was truly incarnate, that we have declared unto you.' The phrase 'the Word of life,' means the Word in which life resided, or which was the source and fountain of life. See Notes, John i. 1, 3. The reference is undoubtedly to the Lord Jesus Christ.

2. *For the life was manifested.* Was made manifest or visible unto us. He who was the life was made known to men by the incarnation. He appeared

life, *a* which was with the Father, and was manifested unto us;)

a Jn.17.3.

among men so that they could see him and hear him. Though originally with God, and dwelling with him, (John i. 1, 2,) yet he came forth and appeared among men. Comp. Notes, Rom. i. 3; 1 Tim. iii. 16. He is the great source of all life, and he appeared on the earth, and we had an opportunity of seeing and knowing what he was. ¶ *And we have seen it.* This repetition, or turning over the thought, is designed to express the idea with emphasis, and is much in the manner of John. See John i. 1–3. He is particularly desirous of impressing on them the thought that he had been a personal *witness* of what the Saviour was, having had every opportunity of knowing it from long and familiar intercourse with him. ¶ *And bear witness.* We testify in regard to it. John was satisfied that his own character was known to be such that credit would be given to what he said. He felt that he was known to be a man of truth, and hence he never doubts that faith would be put in all his statements. See John xix. 35; xxi. 24; Rev. i. 2; 3 John 12. ¶ *And shew unto you that eternal life.* That is, we declare unto you what that life was—what was the nature and rank of him who was the life, and how he appeared when on earth. He here attributes *eternity* to the Son of God— implying that he had always been with the Father. ¶ *Which was with the Father.* Always before the manifestation on the earth. See John i. 1. 'The word was with God.' This passage demonstrates the pre-existence of the Son of God, and proves that he was eternal. Before he was manifested on earth he had an existence to which the word *life* could be applied, and that was *eternal*. He is the Author of eternal life to us. ¶ *And was manifested unto us.* In the flesh; as a man. He who was the *life* appeared unto men. The idea of John evidently is, (1,) that the Being here referred to was for ever with God; (2,) that it was proper before the incarnation that the word *life* should be given to him as descriptive of his nature; (3,) that there was a manifestation of

3 That which we have seen and heard declare we unto you, that ye also may have fellowship with us :

and truly our fellowship *is* with the Father, and with his Son Jesus Christ.

a Jn.17.21.

him who was thus called *life*, on earth; that he appeared among men; that he had a real existence here, and not a merely *assumed* appearance; and (4,) that the true characteristics of this incarnate Being could be borne testimony to by those who had seen him, and who had been long with him. This second verse should be regarded as a parenthesis. 3. *That which we have seen and heard declare we unto you.* We *announce* it, or make it known unto you—referring either to what he purposes to say in this epistle, or more probably embracing *all* that he had written respecting him, and supposing that his Gospel was in their hands. He means to call their attention to *all* the testimony which he had borne on the subject, in order to counteract the errors which began to prevail. ¶ *That ye may have fellowship with us.* With us the apostles ; with us who actually saw him, and conversed with him. That is, he wished that they might have the same belief, and the same hope, and the same joy which he himself had, arising from the fact that the Son of God had become incarnate, and had appeared among men. To 'have fellowship,' means to have anything *in common* with others ; to partake of it ; to share it with them, (see Notes, Acts ii. 42;) and the idea here is, that the apostle wished that they might *share* with him all the peace and happiness which resulted from the fact that the Son of God had appeared in human form in behalf of men. The *object* of the apostle in what he wrote was, that they might have the same views of the Saviour which he had, and partake of the same hope and joy. This is the true notion of *fellowship* in religion. ¶ *And truly our fellowship is with the Father.* With God the Father. That is, there was something *in common* with him and God; something of which he and God partook together, or which they shared. This cannot, of course, mean that his *nature* was the same as that of God, or that in *all things* he shared with God, or that in *anything* he was *equal* with God; but

it means that he partook, in some respects, of the feelings, the views, the aims, the joys which God has. There was a union in feeling, and affection, and desire, and plan, and this was to him a source of joy. He had an attachment to the same things, loved the same truth, desired the same objects, and was engaged in the same work ; and the *consciousness* of this, and the *joy* which attended it, was what was meant by *fellowship*. Comp. Notes on 1 Cor. x. 16; 2 Cor. xii. 14. The fellowship which Christians have with God relates to the following points : (1.) Attachment to the same truths, and the same objects; love for the same principles, and the same beings. (2.) The same *kind* of happiness, though not in the same *degree*. The happiness of God is found in holiness, truth, purity, justice, mercy, benevolence. The happiness of the Christian is of the same kind that God has ; the same kind that angels have ; the same kind that he will himself have in heaven—for the joy of heaven is only that which the Christian has now, expanded to the utmost capacity of the soul, and freed from all that now interferes with it, and prolonged to eternity. (3.) Employment, or co-operation with God. There *is* a sphere in which God works alone, and in which we can have no co-operation, no fellowship with him. In the work of creation; in upholding all things; in the government of the universe ; in the transmission of light from world to world; in the return of the seasons, the rising and setting of the sun, the storms, the tides, the flight of the comet, we can have no joint agency, no co-operation with him. There God works alone. But there is also a large sphere in which he admits us graciously to a co-operation with him, and in which, unless *we* work, his agency will not be put forth. This is seen when the farmer sows his grain ; when the surgeon binds up a wound ; when we take the medicine which God has appointed as a means of restoration to health. So in the moral world. In

4 And these things write we unto you, that *your joy may be full.

5 This then is the message which

a Jn.15.11.

we have heard of him, and declare unto you, that God is light, *b* and in him is no darkness at all.

b Jn.1.4,9; 1 Ti.6.16.

our efforts to save our own souls and the souls of others, God graciously works with us; and unless *we* work, the object is not accomplished. This co-operation is referred to in such passages as these: 'We are labourers together (*συνεργοί*) with God,' 1 Cor. iii. 9. 'The Lord working *with them*,' Mark xvi. 20. 'We then as workers together with him,' 2 Cor. vi. 1. 'That we might be fellow-helpers to the truth,' 3 John 8. In all such cases, while the *efficiency* is of God —alike in exciting us to effort, and in crowning the effort with success—it is still true that if *our* efforts were not put forth, the work would not be done. In this department God would not work by himself alone ; he would not secure the result by miracle. (4.) We have fellow-ship with God by direct communion with him, in prayer, in meditation, and in the ordinances of religion. Of this all true Christians are sensible, and this constitutes no small part of their pecu-liar joy. The nature of this, and the happiness resulting from it, is much of the same nature as the communion of friend with friend—of one mind with another kindred mind—that to which we owe no small part of our happiness in this world. (5.) The Christian will have fellowship with his God and Sa-viour in the triumphs of the latter day, when the scenes of the judgment shall occur, and when the Redeemer shall appear, that he may be admired and adored by assembled worlds. Comp. Notes, 2 Thess. i. 10. See also Matt. xix. 28; Rev. iii. 21. ¶ *And with his Son Jesus Christ.* That is, in like manner there is much which we have *in common* with the Saviour—in character, in feeling, in desire, in spirit, in plan. There is a *union* with him in these things—and the consciousness of this gives peace and joy.

[There is a *real* union between Christ and his people, which lies at the foundation of this fellow-ship. Without *this* union there can be no com-munion. But a 'union with Christ in these things, *i. e.*, in character and feeling, &c,' is nothing more than the union which subsists

between any chief and his followers; and why the apostle Paul, or others after him, should reckon this a great mystery, is not easily com-prehended. Eph. v. 32; Col. i. 27. For a full view of the subject, see the Author's Notes, with the Supplementary Note, Rom. viii. 10.]

4. *And these things write we unto you.* These things respecting him who was manifested in the flesh, and respect-ing the results which flow from that. ¶ *That your joy may be full.* This is almost the same language which the Saviour used when addressing his dis-ciples as he was about to leave them, (John xv. 11;) and there can be little doubt that John had that declaration in remembrance when he uttered this re-mark. See Notes on that passage. The sense here is, that full and clear views of the Lord Jesus, and the fellowship with him and with each other, which would follow from that, would be a source of happiness. Their joy would be complete if they had that ; for their real happiness was to be found in their Saviour. The best editions of the Greek Testament now read ' *your* joy,' instead of the common reading ' *our* joy.'

5. *This then is the message which we have heard of him.* This is the sub-stance of the announcement (*ἐπαγγελία*) which we have received of him, or which he made to us. The *message* here refers to what he communicated as the sum of the revelation which he made to man. The phrase ' of him ' (*ἀπ' αὐτοῦ*) does not mean *respecting him,* or *about him,* but *from him;* that is, this is what we received from his preaching ; from all that he said. The peculiarity, the sub-stance of all that he said, may be summed up in the declaration that God is light, and in the consequences which follow from this doctrine. He came as the messenger of Him who is *light;* he came to inculcate and defend the truths which flow from that central doctrine, in regard to sin, to the danger and duty of man, to the way of recovery, and to the rules by which men ought to live. ¶ *That God is light.* Light, in the Scriptures, is the emblem of purity, truth, know-

6 If we say that we have fellowship with him, and walk in darkness, we lie, and do not the truth:

ledge, prosperity, and happiness—as darkness is of the opposite. John here says that ' God is *light'—φῶς*—not *the* light, or *a* light, but *light itself;* that is, he is himself all light, and is the source and fountain of light in all worlds. He is perfectly pure, without any admixture of sin. He has all knowledge, with no admixture of ignorance on any subject. He is infinitely happy, with nothing to make him miserable. He is infinitely true, never stating or countenancing error ; he is blessed in all his ways, never knowing the darkness of disappointment and adversity. Comp. Notes on James i. 17; John i. 4, 5; 1 Tim. vi. 16. ¶ *And in him is no darkness at all.* This language is much in the manner of John, not only affirming that a thing is so, but guarding it so that no mistake could possibly be made as to what he meant. Comp. John i. 1–3. The expression **here** is designed to affirm that God is absolutely perfect ; that there is nothing in him which is in any way imperfect, or which would dim or mar the pure splendour of his character, not even as much as the smallest spot would on the sun. The language is probably designed to guard the mind from an error to which it is prone, that of charging God with being the Author of the sin and misery which exist on the earth; and the apostle seems to design to teach that whatever was the source of sin and misery, it was not in any sense to be charged on God. This doctrine that God is a pure light, John lays down as the substance of all that he had to teach ; of all that he had learned from him who was made flesh. It is, in fact, the fountain of all just views of truth on the subject of religion, and all proper views of religion take their origin from this.

6. *If we say that we have fellowship with him.* If we reckon ourselves among his friends, or, in other words, if we profess to be like him : for a profession of religion involves the idea of having *fellowship* with God, (comp. Notes on ver. 3,) and he who professes that should be like him. ¶ *And walk in darkness.* Live in sin and error. To ' walk in **darkness** ' now commonly denotes to be in doubt about our religious state, in contradistinction from living in the enjoyment of religion. That is not, however, probably the whole idea here. The leading thought is, that if we live in sin, it is a proof that our profession of religion is false. Desirable as it is to have the comforts of religion, yet it is not always true that they who do not are not true Christians, nor is it true by any means that they intend to deceive the world. ¶ *We lie.* We are false professors ; we are deceived if we think that we can have fellowship with God, and yet live in the practice of sin. As God is pure, so must we be, if we would be his friends. This does not mean necessarily that they *meant* to deceive, but that there was an irreconcilable contradiction between a life of sin and fellowship with God. ¶ *And do not the truth.* Do not act truly. The profession is a false one. Comp. Notes on John iii. 22. To *do the truth* is to act in accordance with truth; and the expression here means that such an one could not be a Christian. And yet how many there are who are living in known sin who profess to be Christians! How many whose minds are dark on the whole subject of religion, who have never known anything of the real peace and joy which it imparts, who nevertheless entertain the belief that they are the friends of God, and are going to heaven ! They trust in a name, in forms, in conformity to external rites, and have never known anything of the internal peace and purity which religion imparts, and in fact have never had any true fellowship with that God who is light, and in whom there is no darkness at all. Religion is light; religion is peace, purity, joy ; and though there are cases where for a time a true Christian may be left to darkness, and have no spiritual joy, and be in doubt about his salvation, yet still it is a great truth, that unless we know by personal experience what it is to walk habitually in the light, to have the comforts of religion, and to experience in our own souls the influences which make the heart pure, and which bring us into conformity to the God who

7 But if we walk *a* in the light, as he is in the light, we have fellowship one with another, and the blood *b* of Jesus Christ his Son cleanseth us from all sin.

8 If we say that we have no sin, *c* we deceive ourselves, and the truth is not in us.

a Jn.12.35.   *b* Ep.1.7; He.9.14; 1 Pe.1.19; Re.1.5.
c 1 Ki.8.46; Job 25.4; Ec.7.20; Ja.3.2.

---

is light, we can have no true religion. All else is but a name, which will not avail us on the final day.

7. *But if we walk in the light.* Comp. Notes on ver. 5. Walking in the light may include the three following things: (1.) Leading lives of holiness and purity; that is, the Christian must be characteristically a holy man, a light in the world, by his example. (2.) Walking in the truth; that is, embracing the truth in opposition to all error of heathenism and infidelity, and having clear, spiritual views of truth, such as the unrenewed never have. See 2 Cor. iv. 6; 1 Cor. ii. 9–15; Eph. i. 18. (3.) Enjoying the comforts of religion; that is, having the joy which religion is fitted to impart, and which it does impart to its true friends, Psa. xciv. 19; Isa. lvii. 8; 2 Cor. i. 3; xiii. 11. Comp. Notes on John xii. 35. ¶ *As he is in the light.* In the same kind of light that he has. The measure of light which we may have is not the same in *degree,* but it is of the same *kind.* The true Christian in his character and feelings resembles God. ¶ *We have fellowship one with another.* As we all partake of his feelings and views, we shall resemble each other. Loving the same God, embracing the same views of religion, and living for the same ends, we shall of course have much that is *common* to us all, and thus shall have fellowship with each other. ¶ *And the blood of Jesus Christ his Son cleanseth us from all sin.* See the sentiment here expressed fully explained in the Notes on Heb. ix. 14. When it is said that his blood cleanses us from *all* sin, the expression must mean one of two things—either that it is through that blood that all past sin is forgiven, or that that blood will ultimately purify us from all transgression, and make us perfectly holy. The general meaning is plain, that in regard to any and every sin of which we may be conscious, there is efficacy in that blood to remove it, and to make us wholly pure.

There is no stain made by sin so deep that the blood of Christ cannot take it entirely away from the soul. The *connection* here, or the reason why this is introduced here, seems to be this: The apostle is stating the substance of the message which he had received, ver. 5. The first or leading part of it was, that God is light, and in him is no darkness, and that his religion requires that all his friends should resemble him by their walking in the light. Another, and a material part of the same message was, that provision was made in his religion for cleansing the soul from sin, and making it like God. No system of religion intended for man could be adapted to his condition which did not contain this provision, and this *did* contain it in the most full and ample manner. Of course, however, it is meant that that blood cleanses from all sin only on the conditions on which its efficacy can be made available to man—by repentance for the past, and by a cordial reception of the Saviour through faith.

8. *If we say that we have no sin.* It is not improbable that the apostle here makes allusion to some error which was then beginning to prevail in the church. Some have supposed that the allusion is to the sect of the Nicolaitanes, and to the views which they maintained, particularly that nothing was forbidden to the children of God under the gospel, and that in the freedom conferred on Christians they were at liberty to do what they pleased, Rev. ii. 6, 15. It is not certain, however, that the allusion is to them, and it is not necessary to suppose that there is reference to *any* particular sect that existed at that time. The object of the apostle is to show that it is implied in the very nature of the gospel that we are sinners, and that if, on any pretence, we denied that fact, we utterly deceived ourselves. In all ages there have been those who have attempted, on some pretence, to justify their conduct; who have felt that they

9 If we confess *a* our sins, he is faithful and just to forgive us *our*

a Job 33.27,28; Ps.32.5; Pr.28.13.

did not need a Saviour; who have maintained that they had a right to do what they pleased; or who, on pretence of being perfectly sanctified, have held that they live without the commission of sin. To meet these, and all similar cases, the apostle affirms that it is a great elementary truth, which on no pretence is to be denied, that we are all sinners. We are at all times, and in all circumstances, to admit the painful and humiliating truth that we are transgressors of the law of God, and that we need, even in our best services, the cleansing of the blood of Jesus Christ. The fair interpretation of the declaration here will apply not only to those who maintain that they have not been guilty of sin in the past, but also to those who profess to have become perfectly sanctified, and to live without sin. In any and every way, if we say that we have no sin, we deceive ourselves. Compare Notes on James iii. 2. ¶ *We deceive ourselves.* We have wrong views about our character. This does not mean that the self-deception is wilful, but that it in fact exists. No man knows himself who supposes that in all respects he is perfectly pure. ¶ *And the truth is not in us.* On this subject. A man who should maintain that he had never committed sin, could have no just views of the truth in regard to himself, and would show that he was in utter error. In like manner, according to the obvious interpretation of this passage, he who maintains that he is wholly sanctified, and lives without any sin, shows that he is deceived in regard to himself, and that the truth, in this respect, is not in him. He may hold the truth on other subjects, but he does not on this. The very nature of the Christian religion supposes that we feel ourselves to be sinners, and that we should be ever ready to acknowledge it. A man who claims that he is absolutely perfect, that he is holy as God is holy, must know little of his own heart. Who, after all his reasoning on the subject, would dare to go out under the open heaven, at midnight, and lift up

sins, and to cleanse *b* us from all unrighteousness.

b Ps.51.2; 1 Co.6.11.

his hands and his eyes towards the stars, and say that he had no sin to confess—that he was as pure as the God that made those stars?

9. *If we confess our sins.* Pardon in the Scriptures, always supposes that there is confession, and there is no promise that it will be imparted unless a full acknowledgment has been made. Compare Psa. li.; xxxii.; Luke xv. 18, seq.; vii. 41, seq.; Prov. xxviii. 13. ¶ *He is faithful.* To his promises. He will do what he has assured us he will do in remitting them. ¶ *And just to forgive us* our *sins.* The word *just* here cannot be used in a strict and proper sense, since the forgiveness of sins is never an act of *justice*, but is an act of *mercy.* If it were an act of justice it could be demanded or enforced, and that is the same as to say that it is not forgiveness, for in that case there could have been no sin to be pardoned. But the word *just* is often used in a larger sense, as denoting upright, equitable, acting properly in the circumstances of the case, &c. Comp. Notes on Matt. i. 19. Here the word may be used in one of the following senses: (1.) Either as referring to his general excellence of character, or his disposition to do what is proper; that is, he is one who will act in every way as becomes God; or, (2,) that he will be just in the sense that he will be true to his promises; or that, since he has *promised* to pardon sinners, he will be found faithfully to adhere to those engagements; or perhaps, (3,) that he will be just to his Son in the covenant of redemption, since, now that an atonement has been made by him, and a way has been opened through his sufferings by which God can consistently pardon, and with a view and an understanding that he might and would pardon, it would be an act of injustice to *him* if he did not pardon those who believe on him. Viewed in either aspect, we may have the fullest assurance that God is ready to pardon us if we exercise true repentance and faith. No one can come to God without finding him ready to do

10 If we say that we have not sinned, we make him a liar, and his word is not in us.

all that is appropriate for a God to do in pardoning transgressors; no one who will not, in fact, receive forgiveness if he repents, and believes, and makes confession; no one who will not find that God is just to his Son in the covenant of redemption, in pardoning and saving all who put their trust in the merits of his sacrifice. ¶ *And to cleanse us from all unrighteousness.* By forgiving all that is past, treating us as if we were righteous, and ultimately by removing all the stains of guilt from the soul.

10. *If we say that we have not sinned.* In times that are past. Some perhaps might be disposed to say this; and as the apostle is careful to guard every point, he here states that if a man should take the ground that his past life had been wholly upright, it would prove that he had no true religion. The statement here respecting the *past* seems to prove that when, in ver. 8, he refers to the present—' if we say we *have* no sin'—he meant to say that if a man should claim to be perfect, or to be wholly sanctified, it would demonstrate that he deceived himself; and the two statements go to prove that neither in reference to the past nor the present can any one lay claim to perfection. ¶ *We make him a liar.* Because he has everywhere affirmed the depravity of all the race. Compare Notes on Rom. i. ii. iii. On no point have his declarations been more positive and uniform than on the fact of the universal sinfulness of man. Comp. Gen. vi. 11, 12; Job xiv. 4; xv. 16; Psa. xiv. 1, 2, 3; li. 5; lviii. 3; Rom. iii. 9–20; Gal. iii. 21. ¶ *And his word is not in us.* His truth; that is, we have no true religion. The whole system of Christianity is based on the fact that man is a fallen being, and needs a Saviour; and unless a man admits that, of course he cannot be a Christian.

REMARKS.

(1.) The importance of the doctrine of the incarnation of the Son of God, vers. 1, 2. On that doctrine the apostle lays great stress; begins his epistle with it; presents it in a great variety of forms; dwells upon it as if he would not have it forgotten or misunderstood. It *has* all the importance which he attached to it, for (*a*) it is the most wonderful of all the events of which we have any knowledge; (*b*) it is the most deeply connected with our welfare.

(2.) The intense interest which true piety always takes in this doctrine, vers. 1, 2. The feelings of John on the subject are substantially the feelings of all true Christians. The world passes it by in unbelief, or as if it were of no importance; but no true Christian can look at the fact that the Son of God became incarnate but with the deepest emotion.

(3.) It is an object of ardent desire with true Christians that all others should share their joys, vers. 3, 4. There is nothing selfish, or narrow, or exclusive in true religion; but every sincere Christian who is happy desires that all others should be happy too.

(4.) Wherever there is true fellowship with God, there is with all true Christians, vers. 3, 4. There is but one church, one family of God; and as all true Christians have fellowship with God, they must have with each other.

(5.) Wherever there is true fellowship with Christians, there is with God himself, vers. 3, 4. If we love his people, share their joys, labour with them in promoting his cause, and love the things which they love, we shall show that we love him. There is but one God, and one church; and if all the members love each other, they will love their common God and Saviour. An evidence, therefore, that we love Christians, becomes an evidence that we love God.

(6.) It is a great privilege to be a Christian, vers. 3, 4. If we are Christians, we are associated with (*a*) God the Father; (*b*) with his Son Jesus Christ; (*c*) with all his redeemed on earth and in heaven; (*d*) with all holy angels. There is one bond of fellowship that unites all together; and what a privilege it is to be united in the eternal bonds of friendship with all the holy minds in the universe!

(7.) If God is *light*, (ver. 5,) then all that occurs is reconcilable with the idea that he is worthy of confidence. What he does may *seem* to be dark to us, but we may be assured that it is all light with him. A cloud may come between us and the sun, but beyond the cloud the sun shines with undimmed splendour, and soon the cloud itself will pass away. At midnight it is dark to us, but it is not because the sun is shorn of his beams, or is extinguished. He will rise again upon our hemisphere in the fulness of his glory, and all the darkness of the cloud and of midnight is reconcilable with the idea that the sun is a bright orb, and that in him is no darkness at all. So with God. We may be under a cloud of sorrow and of trouble, but above that the glory of God shines with splendour, and soon that cloud will pass away, and reveal him in the fulness of his beauty and truth.

(8.) We should, therefore, at all times exercise a cheerful confidence in God, ver. 5. Who supposes that the sun is never again to shine when the cloud passes over it, or when the shades of midnight have settled down upon the world? We confide in that sun that it will shine again when the cloud has passed off, and when the shades of night have been driven away. So let us confide in God, for with more absolute certainty we shall yet see him to be light, and shall come to a world where there is no cloud.

(9.) We may look cheerfully onward to heaven, ver. 5. There all is light. There we shall see God as he is. Well may we then bear with our darkness a little longer, for soon we shall be ushered into a world where there is no need of the sun or the stars; where there is no darkness, no night.

(10.) Religion is elevating in its nature, vers. 6, 7. It brings us from a world of darkness to a world of light. It scatters the rays of light on a thousand dark subjects, and gives promise that all that is now obscure will yet become clear as noonday. Wherever there is true religion, the mind emerges more and more into light; the scales of ignorance and error pass away.

(11.) There is no sin so great that it may not be removed by the blood of the atonement, ver. 7, *last clause.* This blood has shown its efficacy in the pardon of all the great sinners who have applied to it, and its efficacy is as great now as it was when it was applied to the first sinner that was saved. No one, therefore, however great his sins, need hesitate about applying to the blood of the cross, or fear that his sins are so great that they cannot be taken away.

(12.) The Christian will yet be made wholly pure, ver. 7, *last clause.* It is of the nature of that blood which the Redeemer shed that it ultimately cleanses the soul entirely from sin. The prospect before the true Christian that he will become perfectly holy is absolute; and whatever else may befall him, he is sure that he will yet be holy as God is holy.

(13.) There is no use in attempting to conceal our offences, ver. 8. They are known, all known, to one Being, and they will at some future period all be disclosed. We cannot hope to evade punishment by hiding them; we cannot hope for impunity because we suppose they may be passed over *as if* unobserved. No man can escape on the presumption either that his sins are unknown, or that they are unworthy of notice.

(14.) It is manly to make confession when we have sinned, vers. 9, 10. All *meanness* was in doing the wrong, not in confessing it; what we should be ashamed of is that we are guilty, not that confession is to be made. When a wrong has been done, there is no nobleness in trying to conceal it; and as there is no nobleness in such an attempt, so there could be no safety.

(15.) Peace of mind, when wrong has been done, can be found only in confession, vers. 9, 10. That is what nature prompts to when we have done wrong, if we would find peace, and that the religion of grace demands. When a man has done wrong, the least that he can do is to make confession; and when that is done and the wrong is pardoned, all is done that *can* be to restore peace to the soul.

(16.) The *ease* of salvation, ver. 9. What more easy terms of salvation could we desire than an acknowledgment of

CHAPTER II.

M Y little children, these things write I unto you, that ye sin

our sins? No painful sacrifice is demanded; no penance, pilgrimage, or voluntary scourging; all that is required is that there should be an acknowledgment of sin at the foot of the cross, and if this is done with a true heart the offender will be saved. If a man is not *willing* to do this, why should he be saved? How can he be?

CHAPTER II.

ANALYSIS OF THE CHAPTER.

THE *subjects* which are introduced into this chapter are the following : I. A statement of the apostle that the great object which he had in writing to them was that they should not sin ; and yet if they sinned, and were conscious that they were guilty before God, they should not despair, for they had an Advocate with the Father who had made propitiation for the sins of the world, vers. 1, 2. This is properly a continuation of what he had said in the close of the previous chapter, and should not have been separated from that. II. The evidence that we know God, or that we are his true friends, is to be found in the fact that we keep his commandments, vers. 3–6. III. The apostle says that what he had been saying was no new commandment, but was what they had always heard concerning the nature of the gospel ; but though in this respect the law of love which he meant particularly to enforce was no new commandment, none which they had not heard before, yet in another respect it *was* a new commandment, for it was one which in its peculiarity was originated by the Saviour, and which he meant to make the characteristic of his religion, vers. 7–11. A large part of the epistle is taken up in explaining and enforcing this commandment requiring love to the brethren. IV. The apostle specifies (vers. 12–14) various reasons why he had written to them—reasons derived from the peculiar character of different classes among them — little children, fathers, young men. V. Each of these classes he solemnly commands not to love

not. And if any man sin, we have an advocate *a* with the Father, Jesus Christ the righteous :

a Ro.8.34; He.7.25.

the world, or the things that are in the world, for that which constitutes the peculiarity of the ' world ' as such is not of the Father, and all ' that there is in the world is soon to pass away,' vers. 15 –17. VI. He calls their attention to the fact that the closing dispensation of the world had come, vers. 18–20. The evidence of this was, that antichrist had appeared. VII. He calls their attention to the characteristics of the antichrist. The essential thing would be that antichrist would deny that Jesus was the Christ, involving a practical denial of both the Father and the Son. Persons of this character were abroad, and they were in great danger of being seduced by their arts from the way of truth and duty, vers. 21–26. VIII. The apostle, in the close of the chapter, (vers. 27–29,) expresses the belief that they would not be seduced, but that they had an anointing from above which would keep them from the arts of those who would lead them astray. He earnestly exhorts them to abide in God the Saviour, that when he should appear they might have confidence and not be ashamed at his coming.

1. *My little children.* Τεκνία μοῦ. This is such language as an aged apostle would be likely to use when addressing a church, and its use in this epistle may be regarded as one evidence that John had reached an advanced period of life when he wrote the epistle. ¶ *These things write I unto you.* To wit, the things stated in chap. i. ¶ *That ye sin not.* To keep you from sin, or to induce you to lead a holy life. ¶ *And if any man sin.* As all are liable, with hearts as corrupt as ours, and amidst the temptations of a world like this, to do. This, of course, does not imply that it is *proper* or *right* to sin, or that Christians should have no concern about it; but the meaning is, that all are liable to sin, and when we are conscious of sin the mind should not yield to despondency and despair. It *might* be supposed, perhaps, that if one sinned after baptism, or after being converted, there could be

no forgiveness. The apostle designs to guard against any such supposition, and to show that the atonement made by the Redeemer had respect to all kinds of sin, and that under the deepest consciousness of guilt and of personal unworthiness, we may feel that we have an advocate on high. ¶ *We have an advocate with the Father.* God only can forgive sin; and though we have no claim on him, yet there is one with him who can plead our cause, and on whom we can rely to manage our interests there. The word rendered *advocate* (παράκλητος —*paraclete*) is elsewhere applied to the Holy Spirit, and is in every other place where it occurs in the New Testament rendered *comforter*, John xiv. 16, 26; xv. 26; xvi. 7. On the meaning of the word, see Notes on John xiv. 16. As used with reference to the Holy Spirit (John xiv. 16, *et al.*) it is employed in the more general sense of *helper*, or *aid;* and the particular manner in which the Holy Spirit aids us, may be seen stated in the Notes on John xiv. 16. As usual here with reference to the Lord Jesus, it is employed in the more limited sense of the word *advocate*, as the word is frequently used in the Greek writers to denote an advocate in court; that is, one whom we *call to our aid;* or *to stand by us*, to defend our suit. Where it is applied to the Lord Jesus, the language is evidently figurative, since there can be no *literal* pleading for us in heaven; but it is expressive of the great truth that he has undertaken our cause with God, and that he performs for us all that we expect of an advocate and counsellor. It is not to be supposed, however, that he manages our cause in the same way, or on the same principles on which an advocate in a human tribunal does. An advocate in court is employed to *defend* his client. He does not begin by admitting his guilt, or in any way basing his plea on the conceded fact that he *is* guilty; his proper business is to show that he is *not* guilty, or, if he be proved to be so, to see that no injustice shall be done him. The proper business of an advocate in a human court, therefore, embraces two things: (1.) To show that his client is not guilty in the form and manner charged on him.

This he may do in one of two ways, either, (*a*) by showing that he did not do the act charged on him, as when he is charged with murder, and can prove an *alibi*, or show that he was not present at the time the murder was committed; or (*b*) by proving that he had a *right* to do the deed—as, if he is charged with murder, he may admit the fact of the killing, but may show that it was in self-defence. (2.) In case his client is convicted, his office is to see that no injustice is done to him in the sentence; to stand by him still; to avail himself of all that the law allows in his favour, or to state any circumstance of age, or sex, or former service, or bodily health, which would in any way mitigate the sentence. The advocacy of the Lord Jesus in our behalf, however, is wholly different from this, though the same general object is pursued and sought, the good of those for whom he becomes an advocate. The nature of his advocacy may be stated in the following particulars: (1.) He admits the guilt of those for whom he becomes the advocate, to the full extent charged on them by the law of God, and by their own consciences. He does not attempt to hide or conceal it. He makes no apology for it. He neither attempts to deny *the fact*, nor to show that they had *a right* to do as they have done. He could not do this, for it would not be true; and any plea before the throne of God which should be based on a denial of our guilt would be fatal to our cause. (2.) As our advocate, he undertakes to be security that no wrong shall be done to the universe if we are *not* punished as we deserve; that is, if we are pardoned, and treated *as if* we had not sinned. This he does by pleading what he has done in behalf of men; that is, by the plea that his sufferings and death in behalf of sinners have done as much to honour the law, and to maintain the truth and justice of God, and to prevent the extension of apostasy, as if the offenders themselves had suffered the full penalty of the law. If sinners are punished in hell, there will be some object to be accomplished by it; and the simple account of the atonement by Christ is, that his death will secure all the good results to the uni-

2 And he is the propitiation *a* for our sins: and not for ours only,

a Ro.3.25.

but also for *the sins of* the whole world.

---

verse which would be secured by the punishment of the offender himself. It has done as much to maintain the honour of the law, and to impress the universe with the truth that sin cannot be committed with impunity. If all the good results can be secured by substituted sufferings which there would be by the punishment of the offender himself, then it is clear that the guilty may be acquitted and saved. Why should they not be? The Saviour, as our advocate, undertakes to be security that this shall be. (3.) As our advocate, he becomes a *surety* for our good behaviour; gives a pledge to justice that we will obey the laws of God, and that he will keep us in the paths of obedience and truth; that, *if* pardoned, we will not continue to rebel. This pledge or surety can be given in no human court of justice. No man, advocate or friend, can give security when one is pardoned who has been convicted of stealing a horse, that he will not steal a horse again; when one who has been guilty of murder is pardoned, that he will never be guilty of it again; when one who has been guilty of forgery is pardoned, that he will not be guilty of it again. If he *could* do this, the subject of pardon would be attended with much fewer difficulties than it is now. But the Lord Jesus becomes such a pledge or surety for us, (Heb. vii. 22,) and hence he becomes such an advocate with the Father as we need. ¶ *Jesus Christ the righteous.* One who is eminently righteous himself, and who possesses the means of rendering others righteous. It is an appropriate feeling when we come before God in his name, that we come pleading the merits of one who is eminently righteous, and on account of whose righteousness we may be justified and saved.

2. *And he is the propitiation for our sins.* The word rendered *propitiation* (ἱλασμός) occurs nowhere else in the New Testament, except in chap. iv. 10 of this epistle; though words of the same derivation, and having the same essential meaning, frequently occur.

The corresponding word ἱλαστήριον (*hilasterion*) occurs in Rom. iii. 25, rendered *propitiation*—'whom God hath set forth to be a *propitiation* through faith in his blood;' and in Heb. ix. 5, rendered *mercy-seat*—'shadowing the *mercy-seat.*' The verb ἱλάσκομαι (*hilaskomai*) occurs also in Luke xviii. 3— ' God *be merciful* to me a sinner;' and Heb. ii. 17—' to *make reconciliation* for the sins of the people.' For the idea expressed by these words, see Notes on Rom. iii. 25. The proper meaning of the word is that of reconciling, appeasing, turning away anger, rendering propitious or favourable. The idea is, that there is anger or wrath, or that something has been done to offend, and that it is needful to turn away that wrath, or to appease. This may be done by a sacrifice, by songs, by services rendered, or by bloody offerings. So the word is often used in Homer.— *Passow.* We have similar words in common use, as when we say of one that he has been offended, and that something must be done to appease him, or to turn away his wrath. This is commonly done with us by making restitution; or by an acknowledgment; or by yielding the point in controversy; or by an expression of regret; or by different conduct in time to come. But this idea must not be applied too literally to God; nor should it be explained away. The essential thoughts in regard to him, as implied in this word, are, (1,) that his will has been disregarded, and his law violated, and that he has reason to be offended with us; (2,) that in that condition he cannot, consistently with his perfections, and the good of the universe, treat us as if we had not done it; (3,) that it is proper that, in some way, he should show his displeasure at our conduct, either by punishing us, or by something that shall answer the same purpose; and, (4,) that the means of propitiation come in here, and accomplish this end, and make it proper that he should treat us as if we had not sinned; that is, he is reconciled, or appeased, and his anger is turned away. This is done, it is supposed, by the death of the Lord Jesus, accomplishing, in most important respects, what would be accomplished by the punishment of the offender himself. In regard to this, in order to a proper understanding of what is accomplished, it is necessary to observe two things—what is *not* done, and what *is*. I. There are certain things which do *not* enter into the idea of propitiation. They are such as these: (*a*) That it does not change the fact that the wrong was done. That is a fact which cannot be denied, and he who undertakes to make a propitiation for sin does not deny it. (*b*) It does not change God ; it does not make him a different being from what he was before ; it does not *buy him over* to a willingness to show mercy; it does not change an inexorable being to one who is compassionate and kind. (*c*) The offering that is made to secure reconciliation does not necessarily produce reconciliation in fact. It prepares the way for it on the part of God, but whether they for whom it is made will be disposed to accept it is another question. When two men are alienated from each other, you may go to B and say to him that all obstacles to reconciliation on the part of A are removed, and that he is disposed to be at peace, but whether B will be willing to be at peace is quite another matter. The mere fact that his adversary is disposed to be at peace, determines nothing in regard to his disposition in the matter. So in regard to the controversy between man and God. It may be true that all obstacles to reconciliation on the part of God are taken away, and still it may be quite a separate question whether man will be willing to lay aside his opposition, and embrace the terms of mercy. In itself considered, one does not necessarily determine the other, or throw any light on it. II. The amount, then, in regard to the propitiation made for sin is, that it removes all obstacles to reconciliation on the part of God; it does whatever is necessary to be done to maintain the honour of his law, his justice, and his truth ; it makes it consistent for him to offer pardon— that is, it removes whatever there was that made it necessary to inflict punish-

ment, and thus, so far as the word can be applied to God, it appeases him, or turns away his anger, or renders him propitious. This it does, not in respect to producing any *change* in God, but in respect to the fact that it removes whatever there was in the nature of the case that prevented the free and full offer of pardon. The idea of the apostle in the passage before us is, that when we sin we may be assured that this has been done, and that pardon may now be freely extended to us. ¶ *And not for our's only.* Not only for the sins of us who are Christians, for the apostle was writing to such. The idea which he intends to convey seems to be, that when we come before God we should take the most liberal and large views of the atonement ; we should feel that the most ample provision has been made for our pardon, and that in no respect is there any limit as to the sufficiency of that work to remove *all* sin. It is sufficient for us; sufficient for all the world. ¶ *But also for* the sins of *the whole world.* The phrase ' *the sins of* ' is not in the original, but is not improperly supplied, for the connection demands it. This is one of the expressions occurring in the New Testament which demonstrate that the atonement was made for all men, and which cannot be reconciled with any other opinion. If he had died only for a part of the race, this language *could not* have been used. The phrase, ' the whole world,' is one which naturally embraces all men ; is such as would be used if it be supposed that the apostle *meant* to teach that Christ died for all men ; and is such as cannot be explained on any other supposition. If he died only for the elect, it is not true that he is the ' propitiation for the sins of the whole world' in any proper sense, nor would it be possible then to assign a sense in which it could be true. This passage, interpreted in its plain and obvious meaning, teaches the following things : (1.) That the atonement in its own nature is *adapted* to all men, or that it is as much fitted to one individual, or one class, as another ; (2,) that it is *sufficient* in merit for all ; that is, that if any more should be saved than actually will be, there would be no need of any additional suffering in order to save

3 And hereby we do know that
we know him, if we keep *a* his commandments.

4 He that saith, I know him,
and keepeth not his commandments,
is a liar, and the truth is not in
him.

a Lu.6.46; Jn.14.15,23.

5 But whoso keepeth his word,
in him verily is the love of God
perfected: hereby know we that we
are in him.

6 He that saith, he abideth *b* in
him, ought himself also so to walk,
c even as he walked.

b Jn.15.4,5.　　　　*c* Jn.13.15.

---

them; (3,) that it has no *special* adaptedness to one person or class more than
another; that is, that in its own nature
it did not render the salvation of one
more easy than that of another. It so
magnified the law, so honoured God, so
fully expressed the Divine sense of the
evil of sin in respect to all men, that the
offer of salvation might be made as
freely to one as to another, and that any
and all might take shelter under it and
be safe. Whether, however, God might
not, for wise reasons, resolve that its
benefits should be applied to a part only,
is another question, and one which does
not affect the inquiry about the intrinsic
nature of the atonement. On the
evidence that the atonement was made
for all, see Notes on 2 Cor. v. 14, and
Heb. ii. 9.

[See also the Supplementary Notes on these
passages, for a general review of the argument
regarding the extent of atonement.]

3. *And hereby we do know that we
know him.* To wit, by that which follows, we have evidence that we are truly
acquainted with him, and with the requirements of his religion; that is, that
we are truly his friends. The word *him,*
in this verse, seems to refer to the Saviour. On the meaning of the word
know, see Notes, John xvii. 3. The
apostle had stated in the previous part
of this epistle some of the leading points
revealed by the Christian religion, and
he here enters on the consideration of
the nature of the evidence required to
show that we are personally interested
in it, or that we are true Christians.
A large part of the epistle is occupied
with this subject. The first, the grand
evidence—that without which all others
would be vain—he says is, that we keep
his commandments. ¶ *If we keep his
commandments.* See Notes, John xiv.
15. Comp. John xiv. 23, 24; xv. 10, 14.

4. *He that saith, I know him.* He

who professes to be acquainted with the
Saviour, or who professes to be a Christian. ¶ *And keepeth not his commandments.* What he has appointed to be
observed by his people; that is, he who
does not *obey* him. ¶ *Is a liar.* Makes
a false profession; professes to have that
which he really has not. Such a profession is a falsehood, because there can
be no true religion where one does not
obey the law of God.

5. *But whoso keepeth his word.* That
is, what he has spoken or commanded.
The term *word* here will include all that
he has made known to us as his will in
regard to our conduct. ¶ *In him verily
is the love of God perfected.* He professes to have the love of God in his
heart, and that love receives its *completion* or *filling up* by obedience to the
will of God. That obedience is the
proper carrying out, or the exponent of
the love which exists in the heart. Love
to the Saviour would be defective without that, for it is never complete without obedience. If this be the true interpretation, then the passage does not
make any affirmation about sinless *perfection,* but it only affirms that if true
love exists in the heart, it will be carried
out in the life; or that love and obedience are parts of the same thing; that
one will be manifested by the other;
and that where obedience exists, it is
the completion or perfecting of love.
Besides, the apostle does not say that
either the love or the obedience would
be in themselves absolutely perfect; but
he says that one cannot fully develope
itself without the other. ¶ *Hereby know
we that we are in him.* That is, by
having in fact such love as shall insure
obedience. To be *in* him, is to be
united to him; to be his friends. Comp.
Notes, John vi. 56; Rom. xiii. 14.

6. *He that saith, he abideth in him.*
Gr., *remains* in him; that is, abides or

7 Brethren, I write no new commandment unto you, but an old commandment, which ye had from the beginning. The old command-

ment is the word which ye have heard from the beginning.

8 Again, a new *a* commandment

remains in the belief of his doctrines, and in the comfort and practice of religion. The expression is one of those which refer to the intimate union between Christ and his people. A great variety of phrase is employed to denote that. For the meaning of this word in John, see Notes, chap. iii. 6. ¶ *Ought himself also so to walk, even as he walked.* Ought to live and act as he did. If he is *one* with him, or professes to be united to him, he ought to imitate him in all things. Comp. John xiii. 15. See also Notes, chap. i. 6.

7. *Brethren, I write no new commandment unto you.* That is, what I am now enjoining is not new. It is the same doctrine which you have always heard. There has been much difference of opinion as to what is referred to by the word *commandment*, whether it is the injunction in the previous verse to live as Christ lived, or whether it is what he refers to in the following verses, the duty of brotherly love. Perhaps neither of these is exactly the idea of the apostle, but he may mean in this verse to put in a *general* disclaimer against the charge that what he enjoined was *new*. In respect to *all* that he taught, the views of truth which he held, the duties which he enjoined, the course of life which he would prescribe as proper for a Christian to live, he meant to say that it was not at all *new ;* it was nothing which he had originated himself, but it was in fact the same system of doctrines which they had always received since they became Christians. He might have been induced to say this because he apprehended that some of those whom he had in his eye, whose doctrines he meant to oppose, might say that this was all new; that it was not the nature of religion as it had been commonly understood, and as it was laid down by the Saviour. In a somewhat different sense, indeed, he admits (ver. 8) that there *was* a 'new' commandment which it was proper to enjoin—for he did not forget that the Saviour himself called that '*new ;*' and

though that commandment had also been all along inculcated under the gospel, yet there was a sense in which it was proper to call *that* new, for it had been so called by the Saviour. But in respect to *all* the doctrines which he maintained, and in respect to *all* the duties which he enjoined, he said that they were not new in the sense that he had originated them, or that they had not been enjoined from the beginning. Perhaps, also, the apostle here may have some allusion to false teachers who were in fact scattering new doctrines among the people, things before unheard of, and attractive by their novelty; and he may mean to say that *he* made no pretensions to any such novelty, but was content to repeat the old and familiar truths which they had always received. Thus, if *he* was charged with broaching new opinions, he denies it fully ; if *they* were advancing new opinions, and were even 'making capital' out of them, he says that he attempted no such thing, but was content with the old and established opinions which they had always received. ¶ *But an old commandment.* Old, in the sense that it has always been inculcated; that religion has always enjoined it. ¶ *Which ye had from the beginning.* Which you have always received ever since you heard anything about the gospel. It was preached when the gospel was first preached; it has always been promulgated when that has been promulgated; it is what you first heard when you were made acquainted with the gospel. Compare Notes, chap. i. 1. ¶ *The old commandment is the word which ye have heard from the beginning.* Is the *doctrine;* or is what was enjoined. John is often in the habit of putting a truth in a new form or aspect in order to make it emphatic, and to prevent the possibility of misapprehension. See John i. 1, 2. The sense here is, All that I am saying to you is in fact an old commandment, or one which you have always had. There is nothing new in what I am enjoining on you.'

8. *Again, a new commandment I*

I write unto you ; which thing is true in him and in you, because the darkness *a* is past, and the true light now shineth.

9 He that saith he is in the light,

a Ro.13.12.

and hateth his brother, is in darkness *b* even until now.

10 He that loveth his brother abideth in the light, and there is none 1 occasion of stumbling in him.

b 2 Pe.1.9.   1 *scandal.*

write unto you. ' And yet, that which I write to you, and particularly enjoin on you, deserves in another sense to be called a new commandment, though it has been also inculcated from the beginning, for it was called *new* by the Saviour himself.' Or the meaning may be, ' In addition to the general precepts which I have referred to, I do now call your attention to *the new* commandment of the Saviour, that which he himself called new.' There can be no doubt here that John refers to the commandment to 'love one another,' (see vers. 9–11,) and that it is here called *new*, not in the sense that *John* inculcated it as a novel doctrine, but in the sense that the Saviour called it such. For the reasons why it was so called by him, see Notes, John xiii. 34. ¶ *Which thing is true in him.* In the Lord Jesus. That is, which commandment or law of love was illustrated in him, or was manifested by him in his intercourse with his disciples. That which was most prominent in him was this very love which he enjoined on all his followers. ¶ *And in you.* Among you. That is, you have manifested it in your intercourse with each other. It is not new in the sense that you have never heard of it, and have never evinced it, but in the sense only that he called it new. ¶ *Because the darkness is past, and the true light now shineth.* The ancient systems of error, under which men hated each other, have passed away, and you are brought into the light of the true religion. Once you were in darkness, like others; now the light of the pure gospel shines around you, and that requires, as its distinguishing characteristic, *love.* Religion is often represented as *light;* and Christ spoke of himself, and was spoken of, as the light of the world. See Notes, John i. 4, 5. Comp. John viii. 12; xii. 35, 36, 46 ; Isa. ix. 2.

9. *He that saith he is in the light.* That he has true religion, or is a Christian. See chap. i. 7. ¶ *And hateth his*

brother. The word *brother* seems here to refer to those who professed the same religion. The word is indeed sometimes used in a larger sense, but the reference here appears to be to that which is properly brotherly love among Christians. Comp. Lücke, *in loc.* ¶ *Is in darkness even until now.* That is, he cannot have true religion unless he has love to the brethren. The command to love one another was one of the most solemn and earnest which Christ ever enjoined, (John xv. 17;) he made it the peculiar badge of discipleship, or that by which his followers were to be everywhere known, (John xiii. 35;) and it is, therefore, impossible to have any true religion without love to those who are sincerely and truly his followers. If a man has not that, he is in deep darkness, whatever else he may have, on the whole subject of religion. Comp. Notes, 1 Thess. iv. 9.

10. *He that loveth his brother abideth in the light.* Has true religion, and enjoys it. ¶ *And there is none occasion of stumbling in him.* Marg., *scandal.* Greek, ' and there is no stumbling ' [or scandal—σκάνδαλον—in him.] The word here used, means anything against which one strikes or stumbles ; and then a stumbling-block, an impediment, or anything which occasions a fall. Then it is used in a moral or spiritual sense, as denoting that which is the occasion of falling into sin. See Notes, Matt. v. 29, and Rom. xiv. 13. Here it refers to an individual in respect to his treatment of others, and means that there is nothing, so far as he is concerned, to lead him into sin.—*Rob. Lex.* If he has love to the brethren, he has true religion ; and there is, so far as the influence of this shall extend, nothing that will be the occasion of his falling into sin in his conduct towards them, for ' love worketh no ill to his neighbour,' Rom. xiii. 10. His course will be just, and upright, and benevolent. He will have no envy towards them in their

11 But he that hateth his brother is in darkness, and walketh
a in darkness, and knoweth not
whither he goeth, because that
darkness hath blinded his eyes.

12 I write unto you, little children, because your sins are forgiven you for his *b* name's sake.

a Pr.4.15; Jn.12.35.
b Ps.25.11; Lu.24.47; Ac.10.43.

prosperity, and will not be disposed to
detract from their reputation in adversity; he will have no feelings of exulta-
tion when they fall, and will not be
disposed to take advantage of their mis-
fortunes; and, loving them as brethren,
he will be in no respect under temptation to do them wrong. In the bosom
of one who loves his brother, the baleful
passions of envy, malice, hatred, and
uncharitableness, can have no place.
At the same time, this love of the brethren would have an important effect on
his whole Christian life and walk, for
there are few things that will have more
influence on a man's character in keeping him from doing wrong, than the
love of the good and the pure. He who
truly loves good men, will not be likely
in any respect to go astray from the
paths of virtue.
11. *But he that hateth his brother.*
The word here used would, in this connection, include both the mere absence
of love, and positive hatred. It is designed to include the whole of that state
of mind where there is not love for the
brethren. ¶ *Is in darkness.* Ver. 9.
¶ *And walketh in darkness.* He is like
one who walks in the dark, and who
sees no object distinctly. See Notes, John
xii. 35. ¶ *And knoweth not whither he
goeth.* Like one in the dark. He
wanders about not knowing what direction he shall take, or where the course
which he is on will lead. The general
meaning is, that he is ignorant of the
whole nature of religion; or, in other
words, love to the brethren is a central
virtue in religion, and when a man has
not that, his mind is entirely clouded on
the whole subject, and he shows that he
knows nothing of its nature. There is
no virtue that is designed to be made
more prominent in Christianity; and
there is none that will throw its influence
farther over a man's life.
12. *I write unto you, little children.*
There has been much difference of opinion among commentators in regard to

this verse and the three following verses,
on account of their apparent tautology.
Even Doddridge supposes that considerable error has here crept into the text,
and that a portion of these verses should
be omitted in order to avoid the repetition. But there is no authority for
omitting any portion of the text, and
the passage is very much in accordance
with the general style of the apostle
John. The author of this epistle was
evidently accustomed to express his
thoughts in a great variety of ways,
having even the appearance of tautology,
that the exact idea might be before his
readers, and that his meaning might not
be misapprehended. In order to show
that the truths which he was uttering
in this epistle pertained to all, and to
secure the interest of all in them, he
addresses himself to different classes,
and says that there were reasons existing
in regard to each class why he wrote to
them. In the expressions 'I write,'
and 'I have written,' he refers to what
is found in the epistle itself, and the
statements in these verses are designed
to be *reasons* why he brought these
truths before their minds. The word
here rendered *little children* (τεκνία) is
different from that used in ver. 13. and
rendered there *little children*, (παιδία ;)
but there can be little doubt that the
same class of persons is intended. Some
have indeed supposed that by the term
little children here, as in ver. 1, the
apostle means to address all believers—
speaking to them as a father; but it
seems more appropriate to suppose that
he means in these verses to divide the
body of Christians whom he addressed
into three classes—children, young men,
and the aged, and to state particular
reasons why he wrote to each. If the
term (τεκνία) *little children* here means
the same as the term (παιδία) *little children* in ver. 13, then he addresses each
of these classes *twice* in these two verses,
giving each time somewhat varied reasons why he addressed them. That, by

the term 'little children' here, he means children literally, seems to me to be clear, (1,) because this is the usual meaning of the word, and should be understood to be the meaning here, unless there is something in the connection to show that it is used in a metaphorical sense; (2,) because it seems necessary to understand the other expressions, 'young men,' and 'fathers,' in a literal sense, as denoting those more advanced in life; (3,) because this would be quite in character for the apostle John. He had recorded, and would doubtless remember the solemn injunction of the Saviour to Peter, (John xxi. 15,) to 'feed his lambs,' and the aged apostle could not but feel that what was worthy of so solemn an injunction from the Lord, was worthy of his attention and care as an apostle; and (4,) because in that case, each class, fathers, young men, and children, would be twice addressed in these two verses; whereas if we understood this of Christians in general, then fathers and young men would be twice addressed, and children but once. If this be so, it may be remarked, (1,) that there were probably quite young children in the church in the time of the apostle John, for the word would naturally convey that idea. (2,) The *exact* age cannot be indeed determined, but two things are clear: (*a*) one is, that they were undoubtedly under twenty years of age, since they were younger than the '*young men*'— νεανίσκοι—a word usually applied to those who were in the vigour of life, from about the period of twenty up to forty years, (Notes, ver. 13,) and this word would embrace all who were younger than that class; and (*b*) the other is, that the word itself would convey the idea that they were in quite early life, as the word *children*—a fair translation of it—does not war with us. It is not possible to determine, from the use of this word, *precisely* of what age the class here referred to was, but the word would imply that they were in quite early life. No rule is laid down in the New Testament as to the age in which children may be admitted to the communion. The whole subject is left to the wise discretion of the church, and is safely left there. Cases must vary so much

that no rule could be laid down; and little or no evil has arisen from leaving the point undetermined in the Scriptures. It may be doubted, however, whether the church has not been rather in danger of erring by having it deferred too late, than by admitting children too early. (3.) Such children, if worthy the attention of an aged apostle, should receive the particular notice of pastors now. Comp. Notes, John xxi. 15. There are reasons in all cases now, as there were then, why this part of a congregation should receive the special attention of a minister of religion. The hopes of a church are in them. Their minds are susceptible to impression. The character of the piety in the next age will depend on their views of religion. All that there is of value in the church and the world will soon pass into their hands. The houses, farms, factories; the pulpits, and the chairs of professors in colleges; the seats of senators and the benches of judges; the great offices of state, and all the offices in the church; the interests of learning, and of benevolence and liberty, are all soon to be under their control. Everything valuable in this world will soon depend on their conduct and character; and who, therefore, can over-estimate the importance of training them up in just views of religion. As John *wrote* to this class, should not pastors *preach* to them? ¶ *Because*—ὅτι. This particle may be rendered *for*, or *because*; and the meaning may be either that the fact that their sins were forgiven was a *reason* for writing to them, since it would be proper, on that ground, to exhort them to a holy life; or that he wrote to them because it was a privilege to address them as those who were forgiven, for he felt that, in speaking to *them*, he could address them as such. It seems to me that it is to be taken as a *causal* particle, and that the apostle, in the various specifications which he makes, designs to assign particular *reasons* why he wrote to each class, enjoining on them the duties of a holy life. Comp. ver. 21. ¶ *Your sins are forgiven you.* That is, this is a *reason* why he wrote to them, and enjoined these things on them. The meaning seems to be, that the fact that our past sins are blotted

13 I write unto you, fathers, because ye have known him *a* *that is* from the beginning. I write unto you, young men, because ye have

overcome the wicked one. I write unto you, little children, because ye have known the Father. *b*

a 1 Jn.1.1.　　　　　　*b* Jn.14.7,9,

out furnishes a strong *reason* why we should be holy. That reason is founded on the goodness of God in doing it, and on the obligation under which we are brought by the fact that God has had mercy on us. This is a consideration which children will feel as well as others ; for there is nothing which will tend more to make a child obedient hereafter, than the fact that a parent freely forgives the past. ¶ *For his name's sake.* On account of the name of Christ ; that is, in virtue of what he has done for us. In ver. 13, he states another reason why he wrote to this same class—"because they had known the Father."

13. *I write unto you, fathers.* As there were special reasons for writing to children, so there were also for writing to those who were more mature in life. The class here addressed would embrace all those who were in advance of the *νεανίσκοι*, or *young men*, and would properly include those who were at the head of families. ¶ *Because ye have known him* that is *from the beginning.* That is, the Lord Jesus Christ. Notes, chap. i. 1. The argument is, that they had been long acquainted with the principles of his religion, and understood well its doctrines and duties. It cannot be certainly inferred from this that they had had a *personal* acquaintance with the Lord Jesus : yet that this might have been is not impossible, for John had himself personally known him, and there may have been some among those to whom he wrote who had also seen and known him. If this were so, it would give additional impressiveness to the reason assigned here for writing to them, and for reminding them of the principles of that religion which they had learned from his own lips and example. But perhaps all that is necessarily implied in this passage is, that they had had long opportunity of becoming acquainted with the religion of the Son of God, and that having understood that thoroughly, it was proper to address them as aged and established Christians,

and to call on them to maintain the true doctrines of the gospel, against the specious but dangerous errors which then prevailed. ¶ *I write unto you, young men.* *νεανίσκοι.* This word would properly embrace those who were in the vigour of life, midway between children and old men. It is uniformly rendered *young men* in the New Testament: Matt. xix. 20, 22 ; Mark xiv. 51; xvi. 5 ; Luke vii. 14 ; Acts ii. 17 ; v. 10 ; and in the passages before us. It does not elsewhere occur. It is commonly understood as embracing those in the prime and vigour of manhood up to the period of about forty years.—*Robinson.* ¶ *Because ye have overcome the wicked one.* That is, because you have vigour, (see the next verse,) and that vigour you have shown by overcoming the assaults of the wicked one—the devil. You have triumphed over the passions which prevail in early life ; you have combated the allurements of vice, ambition, covetousness, and sensuality; and you have shown that there is a strength of character and of piety on which reliance can be placed in promoting religion. It is proper, therefore, to exhort you not to disgrace the victory which you have already gained, but to employ your vigour of character in maintaining the cause of the Saviour. The thing to which John appeals here is the energy of those at this period of life, and it is proper at all times to make this the ground of appeal in addressing a church. It is right to call on those who are in the prime of life, and who are endowed with energy of character, to employ their talents in the service of the Lord Jesus, and to stand up as the open advocates of truth. Thus the apostle calls on the three great classes into which a community or a church may be considered as divided : *youth,* because their sins were already forgiven, and, though young, they had actually entered on a career of virtue and religion, a career which by all means they ought to be exhorted to pursue; *fathers,* or

14 I have written unto you, fathers, because ye have known him *that is* from the beginning. I have written unto you, young men, be-

aged men, because they had had long experience in religion, and had a thorough acquaintance with the doctrines and duties of the gospel, and they might be expected to stand steadfastly as examples to others; and *young men*, those who were in the vigour and prime of life, because they had shown that they had power to resist evil, and were endowed with strength, and it was proper to call on them to exert their vigour in the sacred cause of religion. ¶ *I write unto you, little children.* Many MSS. read here, *I have written—ἔγραψα*—instead of *I write—γράφω.* This reading is found in both the ancient Syriac versions, and in the Coptic; it was followed by Origen, Cyril, Photius, and Œcumenius; and it is adopted by Grotius, Mill, and Hahn, and is probably the true reading. The connection seems to demand this. In vers. 12, 13, the apostle uses the word *γράφω—I write—*in relation to children, fathers, and young men; in the passage before us, and in the next verse, he again addresses children, fathers, and young men, and in relation to the two latter, he says *ἔγραψα—I have written.* The connection, therefore, seems to demand that the same word should be employed here also. Some persons have supposed that the whole passage is spurious, but of that there is no evidence; and, as we have elsewhere seen, it is not uncommon for John to repeat a sentiment, and to place it in a variety of lights, in order that he might make it certain that he was not misapprehended. Some have supposed, also, that the expression ' I *have* written,' refers to some former epistle which is now lost, or to the Gospel by the same author, which had been sent to them, (*Hug.*) and that he means here to remind them that he had written to them on some former occasion, inculcating the same sentiments which he now expressed. But there is no evidence of this, and this supposition is not necessary in order to a correct understanding of the passage. In the former expression, ' *I write*,' the state of mind would be that of one who

cause ye are strong, [a] and the word of God abideth [b] in you, and ye have overcome [c] the wicked one.

[a] Ep.6.10.   [b] Jn.15.7.   [c] Re.2.7,&c.

fixed his attention on what he was *then* doing, and the particular reason *why* he did it—and the apostle states these reasons in vers. 12, 13. Yet it would not be unnatural for him immediately to throw his mind into the past, and to state the reasons why he had resolved to write to them at all, and then to look at what he had purposed to say as already done, and to state the reasons why that was done. Thus one who sat down to write a letter to a friend might appropriately state in any part of the letter the reasons which had induced him to write at all to him on the subject. If he fixed his attention on the fact that he was *actually* writing, and on the reasons why he wrote, he would express himself in the present tense—*I write ;* if on the previous purpose, or the reasons which induced him to write at all, he would use the past tense—*I have written* for such and such reasons. So John seems here, in order to make what he says emphatic, to refer to two states of his own mind : the one when he *resolved* to write, and the reasons which occurred to him then ; and the other when he was *actually* writing, and the reasons which occurred to him then. The reasons are indeed substantially the same, but they are contemplated from different points of view, and that fact shows that what he did was done with deliberation, and from a deep sense of duty. ¶ *Because ye have known the Father.* In verse 12, the reason assigned for writing to this class is, that their sins were forgiven. The reason assigned here is, that in early life they had become acquainted with God as a Father. He desires that they would show themselves dutiful and faithful children in this relation which they sustained to him. Even children may learn to regard God as their Father, and may have towards him all the affectionate interest which grows out of this relation.

14. *I have written unto you, fathers, because*, &c. The reason assigned here for writing to fathers is the same which is given in the previous verse. It would

15 Love *a* not the world, neither *b* any man love the world, the love the things *that are* in the world. If of the Father is not in him.

a Ro.12.2.   *b* Mat.6.24; Ga.1.10; Ja.4.4.

seem that, in respect to them, the apostle regarded this as a sufficient reason for writing to them, and only meant to enforce it by repeating it. The fact that they had through many years been acquainted with the doctrines and duties of the true religion, seemed to him a sufficient reason for writing to them, and for exhorting them to a steadfast adherence to those principles and duties. ¶ *I have written unto you, young men, because ye are strong,* &c. The two additional circumstances which he here mentions as reasons for writing to young men are, that they are strong, and that the word of God abides in them. The first of these reasons is, that they were strong; that is, that they were qualified for active and useful service in the cause of the Redeemer. Children were yet too young and feeble to appeal to them by this motive, and the powers of the aged were exhausted; but those who were in the vigour of life might be called upon for active service in the cause of the Lord Jesus. The same appeal may be made now to the same class; and the fact that they *are* thus vigorous is a proper ground of exhortation, for the church needs their active services, and they are bound to devote their powers to the cause of truth. The other additional ground of appeal is, that the word of God abode in them; that is, that those of this class to whom he wrote had showed, perhaps in time of temptation, that they adhered firmly to the principles of religion. They had not flinched from an open defence of the truths of religion when assailed; they had not been seduced by the plausible arts of the advocates of error, but they had had strength to overcome the wicked one. The reason here for appealing to this class is, that in fact they *had* showed that they could be relied on, and it was proper to depend on them to advocate the great principles of Christianity.

15. *Love not the world.* The term *world* seems to be used in the Scriptures in three senses: (1.) As denoting the physical universe; the world as it appears to the eve; the world considered

as the work of God, as a material creation. (2.) The world as applied to the *people* that reside in it—' the world of mankind.' (3.) As the dwellers on the earth are by nature without religion, and act under a set of maxims, aims, and principles that have reference only to this life, the term comes to be used with reference to that community; that is, to the objects which *they* peculiarly seek, and the principles by which they are actuated. Considered with reference to the first sense of the word, it is not improper to love the world as the work of God, and as illustrating his perfections; for we may suppose that God loves his own works, and it is not wrong that we should find pleasure in their contemplation. Considered with reference to the second sense of the word, it is not wrong to love the *people* of the world with a love of benevolence, and to have attachment to our kindred and friends who constitute a part of it, though they are not Christians. It is only with reference to the word as used in the third sense that the command here can be understood to be applicable, or that the love of the world is forbidden; with reference to the objects sought, the maxims that prevail, the principles that reign in that community that lives for this world as contradistinguished from the world to come. The meaning is, that we are not to fix our affections on worldly objects—on what the world can furnish—as our portion, with the spirit with which they do who live only for this world, regardless of the life to come. We are not to make this world the object of our chief affection; we are not to be influenced by the maxims and feelings which prevail among those who do. Comp. Notes, Rom. xii. 2, and James iv. 4. See also Matt. xvi. 26; Luke ix. 25; 1 Cor. i. 20; iii. 19; Gal. iv. 3; Col. ii. 8. ¶ *Neither the things that are in the world.* Referred to in the next verse as ' the lust of the flesh, the lust of the eyes, and the pride of life.' This explanation shows what John meant by ' the things that are in the world.' He does not say that we are in

16 For all that *is* in the world, the lust of the flesh, *ᵃ* and the lust of the *ᵇ* eyes, and the pride *ᶜ* of life, is not of the Father, but is of the world.

17 And *ᵈ* the world passeth away, and the lust thereof : but he that doeth the will of God abideth for ever.

ᵃ 2Pe.2.10.   *ᵇ* Ps.119.37.   *ᶜ* Ps.73.6.
ᵈ Ps.39.6; 1 Co.7.31.

---

no sense to love *anything* that is in the material world ; that we are to feel no interest in flowers, and streams, and forests, and fountains ; that we are to have no admiration for what God has done as the Creator of all things ; that we are to cherish no love for any of the inhabitants of the world, our friends and kindred ; or that we are to pursue none of the objects of this life in making provision for our families ; but that we are *not* to love the things which are sought merely to pamper the appetite, to please the eye, or to promote pride in living. These are the objects sought by the people of the world ; these are not the objects to be sought by the Christian. ¶ *If any man love the world, &c.* If, in this sense, a man loves the world, it shows that he has no true religion ; that is, if characteristically he loves the world as his portion, and lives for that ; if it is the ruling principle of his life to gain and enjoy that, it shows that his heart has never been renewed, and that he has no part with the children of God. See Notes, James iv. 4; Matt. vi. 24.

16. *For all that* is *in the world.* That is, all that really constitutes the world, or that enters into the aims and purposes of those who live for this life. All that that community lives for may be comprised under the following things. ¶ *The lust of the flesh.* The word *lust* is used here in the general sense of *desire,* or that which is the object of desire —not in the narrow sense in which it is now commonly used to denote libidinous passion. See Notes, James i. 14. The phrase, ' the lust *of the flesh,*' here denotes that which pampers the appetites, or all that is connected with the indulgence of the mere animal propensities. A large part of the world lives for little more than this. This is the lowest form of worldly indulgence ; those which are immediately specified being of a higher order, though still merely worldly. ¶ *And the lust of the eyes.* That which is designed merely to gratify the sight.

This would include, of course, costly raiment, jewels, gorgeous furniture, splendid palaces, pleasure-grounds, &c. The object is to refer to the gay vanities of this world, the thing on which the eye delights to rest where there is no higher object of life. It does not, of course, mean that the eye is never to be gratified, or that we can find as much pleasure in an ugly as in a handsome object, or that it is sinful to find pleasure in beholding objects of real beauty—for the world, as formed by its Creator, is full of such things, and he could not but have intended that pleasure should enter the soul through the eye, or that the beauties which he has shed so lavishly over his works should contribute to the happiness of his creatures ; but the apostle refers to this when it is the great and leading object of life—when it is sought without any connection with religion or reference to the world to come. ¶ *And the pride of life.* The word here used means, properly, ostentation or boasting, and then arrogance or pride. —*Robinson.* It refers to whatever there is that tends to promote pride, or that is an index of pride, such as the ostentatious display of dress, equipage, furniture, &c. ¶ *Is not of the Father.* Does not proceed from God, or meet with his approbation. It is not of the nature of true religion to seek these things, nor can their pursuit be reconciled with the existence of real piety in the heart. The sincere Christian has nobler ends ; and he who has not any higher ends, and whose conduct and feelings can all be accounted for by a desire for these things, cannot be a true Christian. ¶ *But is of the world.* Is originated solely by the objects and purposes of this life, where religion and the life to come are excluded.

17. *And the world passeth away.* Everything properly constituting this world where religion is excluded. The reference here does not seem to be so much to the material world, as to the

18 Little children, it is the last
ª time: and as ye have heard ᵇ that
antichrist shall come, even now are

there many antichrists; whereby we
know that it is the last time.

a He.1.2.   *b* Mat.24.24; 1 Ti.4.1.

scenes of show and vanity which make
up the world. These things are passing
away like the shifting scenes of the
stage. See Notes, 1 Cor. vii. 31. ¶ *And
the lust thereof.* All that is here so
much the object of desire. These
things are like a pageant, which only
amuses the eye for a moment, and then
disappears for ever. ¶ *But he that
doeth the will of God abideth for ever.*
This cannot mean that he will never
die ; but it means that he has built his
happiness on a basis which is secure,
and which can never pass away. Comp.
Notes, Matt. vii. 24–27.

18. *Little children.* See ver. 1. ¶ *It
is the last time.* The closing period
or dispensation ; that dispensation in
which the affairs of the world are ultimately to be wound up. The apostle
does not, however, say that the end of
the world would soon occur, nor does he
intimate how long this dispensation
would be. That period might continue
through many ages or centuries, and
still be the last dispensation, or that in
which the affairs of the world would be
finally closed. See Notes, Isa. ii. 2 ;
Acts ii. 17 ; Heb. i. 2. Some have
supposed that the ' last time' here refers to the destruction of Jerusalem,
and the end of the Jewish economy;
but the more natural interpretation is
to refer it to the last dispensation of
the world, and to suppose that the
apostle meant to say that there were
clear evidences that that period had
arrived. ¶ *And as ye have heard that
antichrist shall come.* The word *antichrist* occurs in the New Testament
only in these epistles of John, 1 John ii.
18, 22 ; iv. 3 ; 2 John 7. The proper
meaning of *anti* (ἀντί) in composition
is, (1,) *over-against,* as ἀντιτάττειν ;
(2,) *contrary to,* as ἀντιλέγειν ; (3,) re-
ciprocity, as ἀνταποδίδωμι ; (4,) *substi-
tution,* as ἀντιβασιλεύς ; (5,) the place of
the king, or ἀνθύπατος—*proconsul.* The
word *antichrist,* therefore, might denote
any one who either was or claimed to
be in the place of Christ, or one who,
for any cause, was in opposition to him.
The word, further, would apply to one

opposed to him, on whatever ground
the opposition might be; whether it
were open and avowed, or whether it
were only *in fact,* as resulting from
certain claims which were adverse to
his, or which were inconsistent with
his. A *vice-functionary,* or an *opposing functionary,* would be the idea
which the word would naturally suggest.
If the word stood alone, and there were
nothing said further to explain its
meaning, we should think, when the
word *antichrist* was used, either of one
who claimed to be the Christ, and who
thus was a rival ; or of one who stood
in opposition to him on some other
ground. That which constituted the
characteristics of antichrist, according
to John, who only has used the word,
he has himself stated. Ver. 22, ' Who
is a liar, but he that denieth that Jesus
is the Christ? He is antichrist, that
denieth the Father and the Son.' Chap.
iv. 3, ' And every spirit that confesseth
not that Jesus Christ is come in the
flesh, is not of God ; and this is that
spirit of antichrist.' 2 John 7, ' For
many deceivers are entered into the
world, who confess not that Jesus Christ
is come in the flesh. This is a deceiver
and an antichrist.' From this it is
clear, that John understood by the word
all those that denied that Jesus is the
Messiah, or that the Messiah has come
in the flesh. If they held that Jesus
was a deceiver, and that he was not the
Christ, or if they maintained that,
though Christ had come, he had not
come in the flesh, that is, with a proper
human nature, this showed that such
persons had the spirit of antichrist.
They arrayed themselves against him,
and held doctrines which were in fact
in entire opposition to the Son of God.
It would appear then that John does
not use the word in the sense which it
would bear as denoting one who set up
a rival claim, or who came in the place
of Christ, but in the sense of those who
were opposed to him by denying essential doctrines in regard to his person
and advent. It is not certainly known
to what persons he refers, but it would

seem not improbable to Jewish adversaries, (see Suicer's Thesaur. s. voc.,) or to some forms of the Gnostic belief. See Notes, chap. iv. 2. The doctrine respecting antichrist, as stated in the New Testament, may be summed up in the following particulars: (1.) That there would be those, perhaps in considerable numbers, who would openly claim to be the Christ, or the true Messiah, Matt. xxiv. 5, 24. (2.) That there would be a spirit, which would manifest itself early in the church, that would strongly tend to some great apostasy under some one head or leader, or to a concentration on an individual, or a succession of individuals, who would have eminently the spirit of antichrist, though for a time the developement of that spirit would be hindered or restrained. See Notes, 2 Thess. ii. 1-7. (3.) That this would be ultimately concentrated on a single leader—' the man of sin ' —and embodied under some great apostasy, at the head of which would be that ' man of sin,' 2 Thess. ii. 3, 4, 8, 9, 10. It is to this that *Paul* particularly refers, or this is the view which he took of this apostacy, and it is this which *he* particularly describes. (4.) That, in the mean time, and before the elements of the great apostasy should be concentrated and embodied, there might not be a few who would partake of the same general spirit, and who would be equally opposed to Christ in their doctrines and aims; that is, who would embody in themselves the essential spirit of antichrist, and by whose appearing it might be known that the last dispensation had come. It is to these that *John* refers, and these he found in his own age. *Paul* fixed the eye on future times, when the spirit of antichrist should be embodied under a distinct and mighty organization; *John* on his own time, and found then essentially what it had been predicted would occur in the church. He here says that they had been taught to expect that antichrist would come under the last dispensation; and it is implied that it could be ascertained that it was the last time, from the fact that the predicted opposer of Christ had come. The reference is probably to the language of the Saviour, that before the end should be, and as a sign

that it was coming, many would arise claiming to be Christ, and, of course, practically denying that he was the Christ. Matt. xxiv. 5, ' Many shall come in my name, saying, *I am Christ*; and shall deceive many.' Ver. 24, ' And there shall arise false Christs, and false prophets; and they shall show great signs and wonders, insomuch that, if it were possible, they shall deceive the very elect.' This prediction it is probable the apostles had referred to wherever they had preached, so that there was a general expectation that one or more persons would appear claiming to be the Christ, or maintaining such opinions as to be inconsistent with the true doctrine that Jesus was the Messiah. Such persons, John says, had then in fact appeared, by which it could be known that they were living under the closing dispensations of the world referred to by the Saviour. Comp. Notes, 2 Thess. ii. 2-5. ¶ *Even now are there many antichrists.* There are many who have the characteristics which it was predicted that antichrist would have; that is, as explained above, there are many who deny that Jesus is the Messiah, or who deny that he has come in the flesh. If they maintained that Jesus was an impostor and not the true Messiah, or if, though they admitted that the Messiah had come, they affirmed, as the *Docetæ* did, (Note on chap. iv. 2,) that he had come in *appearance* only, and not really come in the flesh, this was the spirit of antichrist. John says that there were many such persons in fact in his time. It would seem from this that John did not refer to a single individual, or to a succession of individuals who should come previous to the winding up of the affairs of the world, as Paul did, (2 Thess. ii. 2, seq.,) but that he understood that there might be many at the same time who would evince the spirit of antichrist. Both he and Paul, however, refer to the expectation that before the coming of the Saviour to judge the world there would be prominent adversaries of the Christian religion, and that the end would not come until such adversaries appeared. Paul goes more into detail, and describes the characteristics of the great apostasy more at length, (2 Thess. ii. 2, seq.; 1

19 They went out from us, but they were not of us: for *a* if they had been of us, they would *no doubt* have continued with us: but *they* *went out*, that they might be made manifest *b* that they were not all of us.

a 2 Ti.2.19. *b* 2 Ti.3.9,

Tim. iv. 1, seq.; 2 Tim. iii. 1, seq.;) John says, not that the appearing of these persons indicated that the end of the world was near, but that they had such characteristics as to show that they were living in the last dispensation. Paul so describes them as to show that the end of the world was not to be immediately expected, (Notes, 2 Thess. ii. 1, seq.;) John, without referring to that point, says that there were enough of that character then to prove that the last dispensation had come, though he does not say how long it would continue. ¶ *Whereby we know it is the last time.* They have the characteristics which it was predicted many would have before the end of the world should come. The evidence that it was 'the last time,' or the closing dispensation of the world, derived from the appearing of these persons, consists simply in the fact that it was predicted that such persons would appear under the Christian, or the last dispensation, Matt. xxiv. 5, 24–27. Their appearance was to precede the coming of the Saviour, though it is not said *how long* it would precede that; but at any time the appearing of such persons would be an evidence that it was the closing dispensation of the world, for the Saviour, in his predictions respecting them, had said that they would appear before he should return to judgment. It cannot now be determined precisely to what classes of persons there is reference here, because we know too little of the religious state of the times to which the apostle refers. No one can prove, however, that there were *not* persons at that time who so fully corresponded to the predictions of the Saviour as to be a complete fulfilment of what he said, and to demonstrate that the last age had truly come. It would seem probable that there may have been reference to some Jewish adversaries, who denied that Jesus was the Messiah, (*Rob. Lex.*,) or to some persons who had already broached the doctrine of the *Docetæ*, that though Jesus was the Mes-

siah, yet that he was a man in appearance only, and had not really come in the flesh. Classes of persons of each description abounded in the early ages of the church. 19. *They went out from us.* From the church. That is, they had once been professors of the religion of the Saviour, though their apostasy showed that they never had any true piety. John refers to the fact that they had once been in the church, perhaps to remind those to whom he wrote that they knew them well, and could readily appreciate their character. It was a humiliating statement that those who showed themselves to be so utterly opposed to religion had once been members of the Christian church; but this is a statement which we are often compelled to make. ¶ *But they were not of us.* That is, they did not really belong to us, or were not true Christians. See Notes, Matt. vii. 23. This passage proves that these persons, whatever their pretensions and professions may have been, were never sincere Christians. The same remark may be made of all who apostatize from the faith, and become teachers of error. They never were truly converted; never belonged really to the spiritual church of Christ. ¶ *For if they had been of us.* If they had been sincere and true Christians. ¶ *They would* no doubt *have continued with us.* The words '*no doubt*' are supplied by our translators, but the affirmation is equally strong without them : 'they would have remained with us.' This affirms, without any ambiguity or qualification, that if they had been true Christians they *would* have remained in the church ; that is, they would not have apostatized. There could not be a more positive affirmation than that which is implied here, that those who are true Christians will continue to be such ; or that the saints will not fall away from grace. John affirms it of these persons, that if they had been true Christians they would never have departed from the church. He makes the declaration so general that it may be regarded as a universal truth, that if *any* are truly 'of us,' that is, if they are true Christians, they will continue in the church, or will never fall away. The statement is so made also as to teach that if any *do* fall away from the church, the fact is full proof that they never had any religion, for if they had had they would have remained steadfast in the church. ¶ *But* they went out, *that they might be made manifest that they were not all of us.* It was suffered or permitted in the providence of God that this should occur, *in order* that it might be seen and known that they were not true Christians, or in order that their real character might be developed. It was desirable that this should be done, (*a*,) in order that the church might be purified from their influence—comp. Notes, John xv. 2 ; (*b*) in order that it might not be responsible for their conduct, or reproached on account of it ; (*c*) in order that their real character might be developed, and they might themselves see that they were not true Christians ; (*d*) in order that, being seen and known as apostates, their opinions and conduct might have less influence than if they were connected with the church ; (*e*) in order that they might themselves understand their own true character, and no longer live under the delusive opinion that they were Christians and were safe, but that, seeing themselves in their true light, they might be brought to repentance. For there is only a most slender prospect that any who are deceived *in* the church will ever be brought to true repentance there ; and slight as is the hope that one who apostatizes will be, such an event is much more probable than it would be if he remained in the church. Men are more likely to be converted when their character is known and understood, than they are when playing a game of deception, or are themselves deceived. What is here affirmed of these persons often occurs now ; and those who have no true religion are often suffered to apostatize from their profession for the same purposes. It is better that they should

cease to have any connection with the church than that they should remain in it ; and God often suffers them to fall away even from the profession of religion, in order that they may not do injury as professing Christians. This very important passage, then, teaches the following things : (1.) That when men apostatize from the profession of religion, and embrace fatal error, or live in sin, it proves that they never had any true piety. (2.) The fact that such persons fall away cannot be adduced to prove that Christians ever fall from grace, for it demonstrates nothing on that point, but proves only that these persons never had any real piety. They may have had much that seemed to be religion ; they may have been zealous, and apparently devoted to God, and may even have had much comfort and peace in what they took to be piety ; they may have been eminently 'gifted' in prayer, or may have even been successful preachers of the gospel, but all this does not prove that they ever had any piety, nor does the fact that such persons apostatize from their profession throw any light on a question quite foreign to this—whether true Christians ever fall from grace. Comp. Matt. vii. 22, 23. (3.) The passage before us proves that if any are true Christians they will remain in the church, or will certainly persevere and be saved. They may indeed backslide grievously ; they may wander far away, and pain the hearts of their brethren, and give occasion to the enemies of religion to speak reproachfully ; but the apostle says, 'if they had been of us, they would have continued with us.' (4.) One of the best evidences of true piety is found in the fact of continuing with the church. I do not mean nominally and formally, but really and spiritually, having the heart with the church ; loving its peace and promoting its welfare ; identifying ourselves with real Christians, and showing that we are ready to co-operate with those who love the Lord Jesus and its cause. (5.) The main reason why professing Christians are suffered to apostatize is to show that they had no true religion. It is desirable that they should see it themselves ; desirable that others should

20 But ye have an unction *a* from the Holy One, and ye know *b* all things.

see it also. It is better that it should be known that they had no true religion than that they should remain in the church to be a burden on its movements, and a reproach to the cause. By being allowed thus to separate themselves from the church, they *may* be brought to remember their violated vows, and the church will be free from the reproach of having those in its bosom who are a dishonour to the Christian name. We are not to wonder, then, if persons apostatize who have been professors of true religion; and we are not to suppose that the greatest injury is done to the cause when they do it. A *greater* injury by far is done when such persons remain in the church.

20. *But ye have an unction from the Holy One.* The apostle in this verse evidently intends to say that he had no apprehension in regard to those to whom he wrote that *they* would thus apostatize, and bring dishonour on their religion. They had been so anointed by the Holy Spirit that they understood the true nature of religion, and it might be confidently expected that they would persevere. The word *unction* or *anointing* (χρίσμα) means, properly, ' something rubbed in or ointed ;' oil for anointing, *ointment ;* then it means an anointing. The allusion is to the anointing of kings and priests, or their inauguration or coronation, (1 Sam. x. 1; xvi. 13; Exod. xxviii. 41; xl. 15; comp. Notes on Matt. i. 1;) and the idea seems to have been that the oil thus used was emblematic of the gifts and graces of the Holy Spirit as qualifying them for the discharge of the duties of their office. Christians, in the New Testament, are described as ' kings and priests,' (Rev. i. 6; v. 10,) and as a ' royal priesthood,' (Notes, 1 Pet. ii. 5, 9;) and hence they are represented as *anointed*, or as endowed with those graces of the Spirit, of which anointing was the emblem. The phrase ' the Holy One' refers here, doubtless, to the Holy Spirit, that Spirit whose influences are imparted to the people of God, to enlighten, to sanctify, and to comfort them in their trials. The particular reference here is to the influences of that Spirit as giving them clear and just views of the nature of religion, and thus securing them from error and apostasy. ¶ *And ye know all things.* That is, all things which it is essential that you should know on the subject of religion. See Notes, John xvi. 13; 1 Cor. ii. 15. The meaning cannot be that they knew all things pertaining to history, to science, to literature, and to the arts; but that, under the influences of the Holy Spirit, they had been made so thoroughly acquainted with the truths and duties of the Christian religion, that they might be regarded as safe from the danger of fatal error. The same may be said of all true Christians now, that they are so taught by the Spirit of God, that they have a practical acquaintance with what religion is, and with what it requires, and are secure from falling into fatal error. In regard to the general meaning of this verse, then, it may be observed : I. That it does *not* mean any one of the following things : (1.) That Christians are literally instructed by the Holy Spirit in *all* things, or that they literally understand all subjects. The teaching, whatever it may be, refers only to religion. (2.) It is not meant that any new faculties of mind are conferred on them, or any increased intellectual endowments, by their religion. It is not a fact that Christians, as such, are superior in mental endowments to others ; nor that by their religion they have any mental traits which they had not before their conversion. Paul, Peter, and John had essentially the same mental characteristics after their conversion which they had before ; and the same is true of all Christians. (3.) It is not meant that any new truth is revealed to the mind by the Holy Spirit. All the truth that is brought before the mind of the Christian is to be found in the word of God, and *revelation*, as such, was completed when the Bible was finished. (4.) It is not meant that anything is perceived by Christians which they had not the natural faculty for

21 I have not written unto you because ye know not the truth, but because ye know it, and that no lie is of the truth.

perceiving before their conversion, or which other men have not also the natural faculty for perceiving. The difficulty with men is not a defect of natural faculties, it is in the blindness of the heart. II. The statement here made by John *does* imply, it is supposed, the following things: (1.) That the minds of Christians are so enlightened that they have a new perception of the truth. They see it in a light in which they did not before. They see it *as* truth. They see its beauty, its force, its adaptedness to their condition and wants. They understand the subject of religion better than they once did, and better than others do. What was once dark appears now plain; what once had no beauty to their minds now appears beautiful; what was once repellant is now attractive. (2.) They see this *to be* true; that is, they see it in such a light that they cannot doubt that it *is* true. They have such views of the doctrines of religion, that they have no doubt that they are true, and are willing on the belief of their truth to lay down their lives, and stake their eternal interests. (3.) Their knowledge of truth is enlarged. They become acquainted with *more* truths than they would have known if they had not been under the teaching of the Holy Spirit. Their range of thought is greater; their vision more extended, as well as more clear. III. The *evidence* that this is so is found in the following things : (1.) The express statements of Scripture. See 1 Cor. ii. 14, 15, and the Notes on that passage. Comp. John xvi. 13, 14. (2.) It is a matter of fact that it is so. (*a*) Men by nature do not perceive any beauty in the truths of religion. They are distasteful to them, or they are repulsive and offensive. ' The doctrine of the cross is to the Jew a stumbling-block, and to the Greek foolishness.' They may see indeed the force of an argument, but they do not see the beauty of the way of salvation. (*b*) When they are converted they do. These things appear to them to be changed, and they see them in a new light, and perceive a beauty in them which they never did

before. (*c*) There is often a surprising *developement* of religious knowledge when persons are converted. They seem to understand the way of salvation, and the whole subject of religion, in a manner and to an extent which cannot be accounted for, except on the supposition of a teaching from above. (*d*) This is manifest also in the knowledge which persons otherwise ignorant exhibit on the subject of religion. With few advantages for education, and with no remarkable talents, they show an acquaintance with the truth, a knowledge of religion, an ability to defend the doctrines of Christianity, and to instruct others in the way of salvation, which could have been derived only from some source superior to themselves. Comp John vii. 15; Acts iv. 13. (*e*) The same thing is shown by their *adherence to truth* in the midst of persecution, and simply because they perceive that for which they die to be the truth. And is there anything incredible in this? May not the mind see what truth is? How do we judge of an axiom in mathematics, or of a proposition that is demonstrated, but by the fact that the mind *perceives* it to be true, and cannot doubt it? And may it not be so in regard to religious truth—especially when that truth is seen to accord with what we know of ourselves, our lost condition as sinners, and our need of a Saviour, and when we see that the truths revealed in the Scriptures are exactly adapted to our wants?

[See also the Supplementary Note under 1 Cor. ii. 14.]

21. *I have not written unto you because ye know not the truth.* You are not to regard my writing to you in this earnest manner as any evidence that I do not suppose you to be acquainted with religion and its duties. Some, perhaps, might have been disposed to put this construction on what he had said, but he assures them that that was not the reason why he had thus addressed them. The very fact that they *did* understand the subject of religion, he says, was rather the reason why he

22 Who is a liar, but he that *denieth that Jesus is the Christ?

a 1 Jn.4.3.

He is antichrist, that denieth the Father and the Son.

wrote to them. ¶ *But because ye know it.* This was the ground of his hope that his appeal would be effectual. If they had never known what religion was, if they were ignorant of its nature and its claims, he would have had much less hope of being able to guard them against error, and of securing their steady walk in the path of piety. We may always make a strong and confident appeal to those who really understand what the nature of religion is, and what are the evidences of its truth. ¶ *And that no lie is of the truth.* No form of error, however plausible it may appear, however ingeniously it may be defended, and however much it may seem to be favourable to human virtue and happiness, can be founded in truth. What the apostle says here has somewhat the aspect of a truism, but it contains a real truth of vital importance, and one which should have great influence in determining our minds in regard to any proposed opinion or doctrine. Error often appears plausible. It seems to be adapted to relieve the mind of many difficulties which perplex and embarrass it on the subject of religion. It seems to be adapted to promote religion. It seems to make those who embrace it happy, and for a time they apparently enjoy religion. But John says that however plausible all this may be, however much it may seem to prove that the doctrines thus embraced are of God, it is a great and vital maxim that *no* error can have its foundation in truth, and, of course, that it must be worthless. The grand question is, *what is truth;* and when that is determined, we can easily settle the inquiries which come up about the various doctrines that are abroad in the world. Mere plausible appearances, or temporary good results that may grow out of a doctrine, do not prove that it is based on truth ; for whatever those results may be, it is impossible that any error, however plausible, should have its origin in the truth.

22. *Who is a liar.* That is, who is false ; who maintains an erroneous doctrine ; who is an impostor, if he is not ?

The object of the apostle is to specify one of the prevailing forms of error, and to show that, however plausible the arguments might be by which it was defended, it was impossible that it should be true. Their own knowledge of the nature of religion must convince them at once that this opinion was false. ¶ *That denieth that Jesus is the Christ.* It would seem that the apostle referred to a class who admitted that Jesus lived, but who denied that he was the true Messiah. On what grounds they did this is unknown ; but to maintain this was, of course, the same as to maintain that he was an impostor. The ground taken may have been that he had not the characteristics ascribed to the Messiah in the prophets ; or that he did not furnish evidence that he was sent from God ; or that he was an enthusiast. Or perhaps some peculiar form of error may be referred to, like that which is said to have been held by Corinthus, who in his doctrine separated Jesus from Christ, maintaining them to be two distinct persons.—*Doddridge.* ¶ *He is antichrist.* Notes, ver. 18. He has all the characteristics and attributes of antichrist ; or, a doctrine which practically involves the denial of both the Father and the Son, must be that of antichrist. ¶ *That denieth the Father and the Son.* That denies the peculiar truths pertaining to God the Father, and to the Son of God. The charge here is not that they entertained incorrect views of God *as such*—as almighty, eternal, most wise, and good ; but that they denied the doctrines which religion taught respecting God *as* Father and Son. Their opinions tended to a denial of what was revealed respecting God as a Father—not in the general sense of being the *Father* of the universe, but in the particular sense of his relation to the Son. It cannot be supposed that they denied the existence and perfections of God as such, nor that they denied that God is a *Father* in the relation which he sustains to the universe ; but the meaning must be that what they held went to a practical

23 Whosoever *a* denieth the Son, the same hath not the Father: [*but*] *he that acknowledgeth the Son, hath the Father also.*
24 Let *b* that therefore abide in you, which ye have heard from the beginning. If that which ye have

heard from the beginning shall remain in you, ye also shall continue in the Son, and in the Father.
25 And this is the promise that he hath promised us, *even eternal* *c* life.

a Jn.15.23.   *b* 2 Jn.6.   *c* Jn.17.3.

denial of that which is peculiar to the true God, considered as sustaining the relation of a Father to his Son Jesus Christ. Correct views of the Father could not be held without correct views of the Son ; correct views of the Son could not be held without correct views of the Father. The doctrines respecting the Father and the Son were so connected that one could not be held without holding the other, and one could not be denied without denying the other. Compare Notes, Matt. xi. 27 ; John v. 23. No man can have just views of God the Father who has not right apprehensions of the Son. As a matter of fact in the world, men have right apprehensions of God only when they have correct views of the character of the Lord Jesus Christ.
23. *Whosoever denieth the Son, the same hath not the Father.* That is, has no just views of the Father, and has no evidence of his friendship. It is only by the Son of God that the Father is made known to men, (Matt. xi. 27 ; Heb. i. 2, 3,) and it is only through him that we can become reconciled to God, and obtain evidence of his favour. Notes on John v. 23. ¶ *But he that acknowledges the Son, hath the Father also.* This passage, in the common version of the New Testament, is printed in Italics, as if it were not in the original, but was supplied by the translators. It is true that it is not found in all the MSS. and versions ; but it is found in a large number of MSS., and in the Vulgate, the Syriac, the Æthiopic, the Coptic, the Armenian, and the Arabic versions, and in the critical editions of Griesbach, Tittmann, and Hahn. It is probable, therefore, that it should be regarded as a genuine portion of the sacred text. It is much in the style of John, and though not necessary to complete the sense, yet it well suits the connection. As it was true that if one denied the Son of God

he could have no pretensions to any proper acquaintance with the Father, so it seemed to follow that if any one had any proper knowledge of the Son of God, and made a suitable confession of him, he had evidence that he was acquainted with the Father. Compare John xvii. 3 ; Rom. x. 9. Though, therefore, this passage was wanting in many of the MSS. consulted by the translators of the Bible, and though in printing it in the manner in which they have they showed the great caution with which they acted in admitting anything doubtful into their translation, yet the passage should be restored to the text, and be regarded as a genuine portion of the word of God. The great truth can never be too clearly stated, or too often inculcated, that it is only by a knowledge of the Lord Jesus Christ that we can have any true acquaintance with God, and that all who have just views of the Saviour are in fact acquainted with the true God, and are heirs of eternal life.
24. *Let that therefore abide in you.* Adhere steadfastly to it ; let the truth obtain a permanent lodgement in the soul. In view of its great importance, and its influence on your happiness here and hereafter, let it never depart from you. ¶ *Which ye have heard from the beginning.* That is, the same doctrines which you have always been taught respecting the Son of God and the way of salvation. Notes, ver. 7. ¶ *Ye also shall continue in the Son, and in the Father.* Truly united to the Son and to the Father ; or having evidence of the favour and friendship of the Son and the Father.
25. *And this is the promise that he hath promised us, even eternal life.* This is evidently added to encourage them in adhering to the truths which they had embraced respecting the Son of God. In maintaining these truths they had the promise of eternal life ; in

26 These *things* have I written unto you concerning them that seduce you.

27 But the anointing which ye have received of him abideth in you, and ye need not that any man teach you: but as the same anointing teacheth *a* you of all things, and is truth, and is no lie, and even as it hath taught you, ye shall abide in [1] him.

28 And now, little children, abide in him; that, when he shall appear,

a Jn.14.26.   1 Or, *it.*

---

departing from them they had none, for the *promise* of heaven in our world is made only to those who embrace one class of doctrines or opinions. No one can show that any *promise* of heaven is made to the mere possessor of beauty, or wealth, or talent; to the accomplished or the gay; to those who are distinguished for science, or skill in the arts; to rank, or birth, or blood; to courage or strength. Whatever expectation of heaven any one may entertain on account of any of these things, must be traced to something else than a *promise*, for there is none in the Bible to that effect. The *promise* of heaven to men is limited to those who repent of their sins, who believe in the Lord Jesus Christ, and who lead a holy life; and if any one will base his hope of heaven *on a promise*, it must be limited to these things. And yet what well-founded hope of heaven *can* there be, except that which is based *on a promise?* How does any one know that he can be saved, unless he has some assurance from God that it may and shall be so? Is not heaven his home? How does any one know that he may dwell there, without some assurance from him that he may? Is not the crown of life his gift? How can any one know that he will possess it, unless he has some promise from him? However men may reason, or conjecture, or hope, the only *promise* of eternal life is found in the Bible; and the fact that we have such a promise should surely be a sufficient inducement to us to hold fast the truth. On the promise of life in the gospel, see John xvii. 2; Rom. ii. 6, 7; Mark xvi. 16; Matt. xxv. 46.

26. *These* things *have I written unto you concerning them that seduce you.* Respecting their character, and in order to guard you against their arts. The word *seduce* means to lead astray; and it here refers to those who would seduce them *from the truth,* or lead them into

dangerous error. The apostle does not mean that they had actually seduced them, for he states in the following verse that they were yet safe; but he refers to the fact that there was danger that they might be led into error.

27. *But the anointing which ye have received of him.* See Notes on ver. 20. ¶ *Abideth in you.* The meaning is, that the influence on your heart and life, which results from the fact that you are anointed of God, permanently abides with you, and will keep you from dangerous error. The apostle evidently meant to say that he felt assured that they would not be seduced from the truth, and that his confidence in regard to this was placed in the fact that they had been truly anointed unto God as kings and priests. Thus understood, what he here says is equivalent to the expression of a firm conviction that those who are true Christians will not fall away. Comp. Notes on vers. 19, 20. ¶ *And ye need not that any man teach you.* That is, what are the things essential to true religion. See Notes on ver. 20. ¶ *But as the same anointing teacheth you of all things.* This cannot mean that the mere act of *anointing*, if that had been performed in their case, would *teach* them; but it refers to what John includes in what he calls the anointing—that is, in the solemn consecrating to the duties of religion under the influences of the Holy Spirit. ¶ *And is truth, and is no lie.* Leads to truth, and not to error. No man was ever led into error by those influences which result from the fact that he has been consecrated to the service of God. ¶ *Ye shall abide in him.* Marg., ' or *it.*' The Greek will bear either construction. The connection, however, seems to demand that it should be understood as referring to *him* —that is, to the Saviour.

28. *And now, little children.* Notes,

we may have confidence, and not be ashamed before him at his coming. 29 If ye know that he is righ-

teous, [1] ye know that *a* every one that doeth righteousness is born of him.

1 Or, *know ye.*

a Je.13. 23; Mat.7.16-18.

ver. 1. ¶ *Abide in him ; that, when he shall appear.* In the end of the world, to receive his people to himself. Notes, John xiv. 2, 3. ¶ *We may have confidence.* Greek, *boldness*—παῤῥησίαν. This word is commonly used to denote openness, plainness, or boldness in speaking, Mark viii. 32; John vii. 4, 13, 26; Acts ii. 29; iv. 13, 29; 2 Cor. iii. 12; vii. 4. Here it means the kind of boldness, or calm assurance, which arises from evidence of piety, and of preparation for heaven. It means that they would not be overwhelmed and confounded at the coming of the Saviour, by its being then found that all their hopes were fallacious. ¶ *And not be ashamed before him at his coming.* By having all our hopes taken away; by being held up to the universe as guilty and condemned. We feel ashamed when our hopes are disappointed; when it is shown that we have a character different from what we professed to have; when our pretensions to goodness are stripped off, and the heart is made bare. Many will thus be ashamed in the last day, (Matt. vii. 21–23;) but it is one of the promises made to those who truly believe on the Saviour, that they shall never be ashamed or confounded. See Notes on 1 Pet. ii. 6. Comp. Isa. xlv. 17; Rom. v. 5; 1 Pet. iv. 16; Mark viii. 38.

29. *If ye know that he is righteous.* This is not said as if there could be any doubt on the subject, but merely to call their attention to it as a well-known truth, and to state what followed from it. Every one who has any true acquaintance with God, must have the fullest conviction that he is a righteous Being. But, if this be so, John says, then it must follow that only those who are truly righteous can regard themselves as begotten of him. ¶ *Ye know.* Marg., *know ye.* The Greek will bear either construction, and either would make good sense. Assuming that God is righteous, it would be proper to state, as in the text, that it followed from this that they must know that only those who are righteous can be regarded as

begotten of him; or, assuming this to be true, it was proper to exhort them *to be* righteous, as in the margin. Whichever interpretation is adopted, the great truth is taught, that only those who are truly righteous can regard themselves as the children of God. ¶ *That every one that doeth righteousness is born of him.* Or rather, is *begotten* of him; is truly a child of God. This truth is everywhere taught in the Bible, and is worthy of being often repeated. No one who is not, in the proper sense of the term, a righteous man, can have any well-founded pretensions to being regarded as a child of God. If this be so, then it is not difficult to determine whether we are the children of God. (1.) If we are unjust, false, dishonest, we cannot be his children. (2.) If we are indulging in any known sin, we cannot be. (3.) If we are not truly righteous, all visions and rapture, all zeal and ardour, though in the cause of religion, all that we may pride ourselves on in being fervent in prayer, or eloquent in preaching, is vain. (4.) If we *are* righteous, in the true and proper sense, doing that which is *right* toward God and toward men, to ourselves, to our families, to our neighbours, to the world at large, to the Saviour who died for us, then we are true Christians; and then, no matter how soon he may appear, or how solemn and overwhelming the scenes that shall close the world, we shall not be ashamed or confounded, for we shall hail him as our Saviour, and rejoice that the time has come that we may go and dwell with him for ever.

CHAPTER III.

ANALYSIS OF THE CHAPTER.

THIS chapter embraces the following subjects :—

I. The fact that Christians are now the sons of God, vers. 1–3. (1.) We are the sons of God, and this will explain the reason why the world does not appreciate our character, or understand the reasons of our conduct, ver. 1. (2.) The consequences of sustaining that re-

CHAPTER III.

BEHOLD, what manner of love ^a the Father hath bestowed upon us, that we should be called

the sons ^b of God! therefore the world ^c knoweth us not, because it knew him not.

a Ep.2.4,5.   b Jn.1.12; Re.21.7.   c Jn.17.25.

lation to God, or of being regarded as his sons. (a) We shall be like him when he appears, ver. 2. (b) We shall purify ourselves under the influence of this hope, ver. 3.

II. The fact that he who is an adopted child of God does not commit sin, vers. 4–10. (1.) All sin is the transgression of the law, ver. 4; (2.) Christ was manifested to take away our sins, ver. 5; (3.) he that commits sin is of the devil, ver. 8; and, (4.) as a matter of fact, he who is of God does *not* commit sin, vers. 7, 9, 10.

III. True religion will be manifested by love to the Christian brotherhood, vers. 10–18. (1.) As a man who is not righteous cannot be a true Christian, neither can he who does not love his brother, ver. 10. (2.) It is the solemn command of the Saviour that his followers should love one another, vers. 11. (3.) The importance of this is seen by the opposite conduct of Cain, ver. 12. (4.) Love to the brethren furnishes the most certain evidence that we have passed from death unto life. ver. 14. (5.) A man who hates another is in fact a murderer, and, of course, cannot be a true child of God, ver. 15. (6.) We should be stimulated to the love of the brethren by the example of the Saviour, who laid down his life for us, ver. 16. (7.) If we see a brother in want, and have the means of aiding him, and do not do it, we cannot have the love of God dwelling in us, vers. 17, 18.

IV. We may have evidence that we love God by the consciousness of our feelings towards him, as well as by outward acts towards his friends, vers. 19–21.

V. If we keep his commandments our prayers will be answered, vers. 22, 23. (1.) There is an assurance that we shall receive what we need if we ask it, and keep his commandments, ver. 22. (2.) The particular commandments on which the efficacy of prayer so much depends, are (a) that we believe on the name of the Saviour, and (b) that we love the Christian brotherhood, ver. 23.

VI. We may know that we abide in God by the spirit which he has given us, as well as by keeping his commandments, ver. 24.

This chapter, therefore, is occupied mainly with stating what are the evidences of true piety; and, in order to determine this question, there is perhaps no part of the Bible that may be studied with more profit than this portion of the writings of John.

1. *Behold, what manner of love.* What love, in *kind* and in *degree.* In *kind* the most tender and the most ennobling, in adopting us into his family, and in permitting us to address him as our Father; in *degree* the most exalted, since there is no higher love that can be shown than in adopting a poor and friendless orphan, and giving him a parent and a home. Even God could bestow upon us no more valuable token of affection than that we should be adopted into his family, and permitted to regard him as our Father. When we remember how insignificant we are as creatures, and how ungrateful, rebellious, and vile we have been as sinners, we may well be amazed at the love which would adopt us into the holy family of God, so that we may be regarded and treated as the children of the Most High. A prince could manifest no higher love for a wandering, ragged, vicious orphan boy, found in the streets, than by adopting him into his own family, and admitting him to the same privileges and honours as his own sons; and yet this would be a trifle compared with the honour which God has bestowed on us. ¶ *The Father hath bestowed upon us.* God, regarded as a Father, or as at the head of the universe considered as one family. ¶ *That we should be called the sons of God.* That is, that we should be the sons of God—the word *called* being often used in the sense of *to be.* On the nature and privileges of adoption, see Notes, Rom. viii. 15–17, and 2 Cor. vi. 18, and practical remarks on that chapter, 19 20 ¶ *Therefore the*

2 Beloved, now are we the sons *a* of God; and it doth not yet appear what we shall be: but we know that, when he shall appear, we shall be

a Ro.8.14,18.   *b* 1 Co.15.49; Phi.3.21; 2 Pe.1.4.
c Job 19.26; Ps.17.15; Mat.5.8: 1 Co.13.12.

like him; *b* for we shall see *c* him as he is.

3 And every man that hath this hope in him purifieth himself, even as he is pure.

world knoweth us not. Does not understand our principles; the reasons of our conduct; the sources of our comforts and joys. The people of the world regard us as fanatics or enthusiasts; as foolish in abandoning the pleasures and pursuits which they engage in; as renouncing certain happiness for that which is uncertain; as cherishing false and delusive hopes in regard to the future, and as practising needless austerities, with nothing to compensate for the pleasures which are abandoned. There is nothing which the gay, the ambitious, and the selfish *less* understand than they do the elements which go into the Christian's character, and the nature and source of the Christian's joys. ¶ *Because it knew him not.* Did not know the Lord Jesus Christ. That is, the world had no right views of the real character of the Lord Jesus when he was on the earth. They mistook him for an enthusiast or an impostor; and it is no wonder that, having wholly mistaken his character, they should mistake ours. On the fact that the world did not know him, see Notes, 1 Cor. ii. 8; Acts iii. 17. Comp. John xvii. 25. On the fact that Christians may be expected to be regarded and treated as their Saviour was, see Notes on John xv. 18–20. Comp. Matt. x. 24, 25.

2. *Beloved, now are we the sons of God.* We now in fact sustain this rank and dignity, and on that we may reflect with pleasure and gratitude. It is in itself an exalted honour, and may be contemplated as such, whatever may be true in regard to what is to come. In the dignity and the privileges which we now enjoy, we may find a grateful subject of reflection, and a cause of thankfulness, even if we should look to nothing beyond, or when we contemplate the fact by itself. ¶ *And it doth not yet appear what we shall be.* It is not fully revealed what we shall be hereafter; what will be the full result of being regarded as the children of

God. There are, indeed, certain things which may be inferred as following from this. There is enough to animate us with hope, and to sustain us in the trials of life. There is *one* thing which is clear, that we shall be like the Son of God; but what is fully involved in this is not made known. Perhaps (1) it could not be so revealed that we could understand it, for that state may be so unlike the present that no words would fully convey the conception to our minds. Perhaps (2) it may be necessary to our condition here, as on probation, that no more light should be furnished in regard to the future than to stimulate us to make efforts to reach a world where all is light. For an illustration of the sentiment expressed here by the apostle, comp. Notes on 2 Pet. i. 4. ¶ *But we know that, when he shall appear, we shall be like him.* It is revealed to us that we shall be made like Christ; that is, in the bodies with which we shall be raised up, in character, in happiness, in glory. Comp. Notes, Phil. iii. 21; 2 Cor. iii. 18. This is enough to satisfy the Christian in his prospects for the future world. To be like Christ is the object of his supreme aim. For that he lives, and all his aspirations in regard to the coming world may be summed up in this—that he wishes to be like the glorified Son of God, and to share his honours and his joys. See Notes, Phil. iii. 10. ¶ *For we shall see him as he is.* It is clearly implied here that there will be an influence in beholding the Saviour as he is, which will tend to make us like him, or to transform us into his likeness. See the nature of this influence explained in the Notes on 2 Cor. iii. 18. ¶ *And every man that hath this hope in him.* This hope of seeing the Saviour, and of being made like him; that is, every true Christian. On the nature and influence of hope, see Notes on Rom. viii. 24, 25. ¶ *Purifieth him-*

4　Whosoever　committeth　sin　| transgresseth also the law: for sin is the transgression of the law.

self. Makes himself holy. That is, under the influence of this hope of being like the Saviour, he puts forth those efforts in struggling against sin, and in overcoming his evil propensities, which are necessary to make him pure. The apostle would not deny that for the success of these efforts we are dependent on Divine aid ; but he brings into view, as is often done in the sacred writings, the agency of man himself as essentially connected with success. Comp. Phil. ii. 12. The particular thought here is, that the hope of being like Christ, and of being permitted to dwell with him, will lead a man to earnest efforts to become holy, and will be actually followed by such a result. ¶ *Even as he is pure.* The same *kind* of purity here, the same *degree* hereafter. That is, the tendency of such a hope is to make him holy now, though he may be imperfect ; the effect will be to make him *perfectly* holy in the world to come. It cannot be shown from this passage that the apostle meant to teach that any one actually becomes as pure in the present life as the Saviour is, that is, becomes perfectly holy ; for all that is fairly implied in it is, that those who have this hope in them *aim* at the same purity, and will *ultimately* obtain it. But the apostle does not say that it is attained in this world. If the passage *did* teach this, it would teach it respecting *every one* who has this hope, and then the doctrine would be that no one can be a Christian who does not become absolutely perfect on earth ; that is, not that some Christians *may* become perfect here, but that all actually *do*. But none, it is presumed, will hold this to be a true doctrine. A true Christian does not, indeed, habitually and wilfully sin ; but no one can pretend that all Christians attain to a state of sinless perfection on earth, or are, in fact, *as* pure as the Saviour was. But unless the passage proves that *every* Christian becomes absolutely perfect in the present life, it does not prove that in fact *any* do. It proves (1) that the tendency, or the fair influence of this hope, is to make the Christian pure ; (2)

that all who cherish it will, in fact, *aim* to become as holy as the Saviour was ; and (3) that this object will, at some future period, be accomplished. There is a world where all who are redeemed shall be perfectly holy.

4. *Whosoever committeth sin transgresseth also the law.* The law of God given to man as a rule of life. The object of the apostle here is to excite them to holiness, and to deter them from committing sin, perhaps in view of the fact stated in ver. 3, that every one who has the hope of heaven will aim to be holy like the Saviour. To confirm this, he shows them that, as a matter of fact, those who are born of God *do* lead lives of obedience, (vers. 5—10 ;) and this he introduces by showing what is the nature of sin, in the verse before us. The considerations by which he would deter them from indulging in sin are the following : (*a*) all sin is a violation of the law of God, ver. 4 ; (*b*) the very object of the coming of Christ was to deliver men from sin, ver. 5 ; (*c*) those who are true Christians do not habitually sin, ver. 6 ; (*d*) those who sin cannot be true Christians, but are of the devil, ver. 8 ; and (*e*) he who is born of God has a germ or principle of true piety in him, and cannot sin, ver. 9. It seems evident that the apostle is here combating an opinion which then existed that men might sin, and yet be true Christians, (ver. 7 ;) and he apprehended that there was danger that this opinion would become prevalent. On what *ground* this opinion was held is unknown. Perhaps it was held that all that was necessary to constitute religion was to embrace the doctrines of Christianity, or to be orthodox in the faith ; perhaps that it was not expected that men would become holy in this life, and therefore they might indulge in acts of sin ; perhaps that Christ came to modify and relax the law, and that the *freedom* which he procured for them was freedom to indulge in whatever men chose ; perhaps that, since Christians were heirs of all things, they had a right to enjoy all things ; perhaps that the passions of

men were so strong that they could not be restrained, and that therefore it was not wrong to give indulgence to the propensities with which our Creator has formed us. All these opinions have been held under various forms of Antinomianism, and it is not at all improbable that some or all of them prevailed in the time of John. The argument which he urges would be applicable to any of them. The consideration which he here states is, that all sin is a transgression of law, and that he who commits it, under whatever pretence, is to be held as a transgressor of the law. The literal rendering of this passage is, ‘He who doeth sin (ἁμαρτίαν) doeth also transgression’—ἀνομίαν. Sin is the generic term embracing all that would be wrong. The word transgression (ἀνομία) is a specific term, showing where the wrong lay, to wit, in violating the law. ¶ *For sin is the transgression of the law.* That is, all sin involves this as a consequence that it is a violation of the law. The object of the apostle is not so much to define sin, as to deter from its commission by stating what is its essential nature—though he has in fact given the best definition of it that could be given. The essential idea is, that God has given a law to men to regulate their conduct, and that whatever is a departure from that law in any way is held to be sin. The law measures our duty, and measures therefore the degree of guilt when it is not obeyed. The law determines what is right in all cases, and, of course, what is wrong when it is not complied with. The law is the expression of what is the will of God as to what we shall do; and when that is not done, there is sin. The law determines what we shall love or not love; when our passions and appetites shall be bounded and restrained, and to what extent they may be indulged; what shall be our motives and aims in living; how we shall act toward God and toward men; and whenever, in any of these respects, its requirements are not complied with, there is sin. This will include everything in relation to which the law is given, and will embrace what we *omit* to do when the law has commanded a thing to be done, as well as a

positive act of transgression where the law has forbidden a thing. This idea is properly found in the original word rendered *transgression of the law—* ἀνομία. This word occurs in the New Testament only in the following places: Matt. vii. 23; xiii. 41; xxiii. 28; xxiv. 12; Rom. iv. 7; vi. 19; 2 Thess. ii. 7; Titus ii. 14; Heb. i. 9; viii. 12; x. 17, in all which places it is rendered *iniquity* and *iniquities;* in 2 Cor. vi. 14, where it is rendered *unrighteousness;* and in the verse before us twice. It properly means *lawlessness,* in the sense that the requirements of the law are not conformed to, or complied with; that is, either by not obeying it, or by positively violating it. When a parent commands a child to do a thing, and he does not do it, he is as really guilty of violating the law as when he does a thing which is positively forbidden. This important verse, therefore, may be considered in two aspects—as a definition of the nature of sin, and as an argument against indulgence in it, or against committing it. I. As a definition of the nature of sin. It teaches (*a*) that there is a rule of law by which the conduct of mankind is to be regulated and governed, and to which it is to be conformed. (*b*) That there is sin in all cases where that law is not complied with; and that all who do *not* comply with it are guilty before God. (*c*) That the particular thing which determines the guilt of sin, and which measures it, is that it is a departure from law, and consequently that there is no sin where there is no departure from law. The essential thing is, that the law has not been respected and obeyed, and sin derives its character and aggravation from that fact. No one can reasonably doubt as to the *accuracy* of this definition of sin. It is founded on the fact (*a*) that God has an absolute right to prescribe what we may and may not do; (*b*) that it is to be presumed that what he prescribes will be in accordance with what is right; and (*c*) that nothing else in fact constitutes sin. Sin can consist in nothing else. It does not consist of a particular height of stature, or a particular complexion; of a feeble intellect, or an intellect *made* feeble, as the

5 And ye know ^a that he was manifested to take away our sins; and in him is no sin.

result of any former apostasy; of any constitutional propensity, or any disposition founded in our nature as creatures. For none of these things do our consciences condemn us; and however we may lament them, we have no consciousness of wrong.

[In these remarks the author has in view the doctrine of original sin, or imputed sin, which he thinks as absurd as sin of stature or complexion. His views will be found at large in the Notes on Rom. v. throughout, and by comparing these with the Supplementary Notes on the same place, the reader will be able to form his own opinion. There does not seem to be anything affecting the point in this passage.]

II. As an argument against the commission of sin. This argument may be considered as consisting of two things—the wrong that is done by the violation of law, and the exposure to the penalty. (1.) The wrong itself. This wrong, as an argument to deter from sin, arises mainly from two things : (a) because sin is a violation of the will of God, and it is in itself wrong to disregard that will ; and (b) because it is to be presumed that when God has given law there is a good reason why he has done it. (2.) The fact that the law has a penalty is an argument for not violating the law. All law has a penalty ; that is, there is some suffering, disadvantage, forfeit of privileges, &c., which the violation of law draws in its train, and which is to be regarded as an expression of the sense which the lawgiver entertains of the value of his law, and of the evil of disobeying it. Many of these penalties of the violation of the Divine law are seen in this life, and all will be certain to occur sooner or later, in this world or in the world to come. With such views of the law and of sin—of his obligations, and of the evils of disobedience—a Christian should not, and will not, deliberately and habitually violate the law of God.

5. *And ye know that he was manifested.* The Lord Jesus, the Son of God. ' You know that he became incarnate, or appeared among men, for the very purpose of putting an end to

sin,' Matt. i. 21. Comp. Notes, 1 Tim. iii. 16. This is the *second* argument in this paragraph, (vers. 4–10,) by which the apostle would deter us from sin. The argument is a clear one, and is perhaps the strongest that can be made to bear on the mind of a true Christian —that the Lord Jesus saw sin to be so great an evil, that he came into our world, and gave himself to the bitter sorrows of death on the cross, to redeem us from it. ¶ *To take away our sins.* The essential argument here is, that the whole work of Christ was designed to deliver us from the dominion of sin, not to furnish us the means of indulgence in it ; and that, therefore, we should be deterred from it by all that Christ has done and suffered for us. He perverts the whole design of the coming of the Saviour who supposes that his work was in any degree designed to procure for his followers the indulgences of sin, or who so interprets the methods of his grace as to suppose that it is now lawful for him to indulge his guilty passions. The argument essentially is this : (1.) That we profess to be the followers of Christ, and should carry out his ends and views in coming into the world ; (2,) that the great and leading purpose of his coming was to set us free from the bondage of transgression; (3,) that in doing this he gave himself up to a life of poverty, and shame, and sorrow, and to a most bitter death on the cross ; and, (4,) that we should not indulge in that from which he came to deliver us, and which cost him so much toil and such a death. How could we indulge in that which has brought heavy calamity on the head of a father, or which has pierced a sister's heart with many sorrows ? Still more, how 'can we be so ungrateful and hardhearted as to indulge in that which crushed our Redeemer in death ? ¶ *And in him is no sin.* An additional consideration to show that we should be holy. As he was perfectly pure and spotless, so should all his followers aim to be; and none can truly pretend to be his who do not desire and design to become like him. On the

6 Whosoever abideth in him sin- | neth not: whosoever *sinneth, hath

a 3 Jn.11. | not seen him, neither known him.

---

personal holiness of the Lord Jesus, see Notes on Heb. vii. 26, and 1 Pet. ii. 23. 6. *Whosoever abideth in him.* See chap. ii. 6. The word here employed (μίνων) properly means to remain, to continue, to abide. It is used of persons remaining or dwelling in a place, in the sense of abiding there permanently, or lodging there, and this is the common meaning of the word, Matt. x. 11; xxvi. 38; Mark vi. 10; Luke i.56, *et sæpe.* In the writings of John, however, it is quite a favourite word to denote the *relation* which one sustains to another, in the sense of being united to him, or remaining with him in affection and love; being with him in heart and mind and will, as one makes his home in a dwelling. The sense seems to be that we have some sort of relation to him similar to that which we have to our home; that is, some fixed and permanent attachment to him. We live in him; we remain steadfast in our attachment to him, as we do to our own home. For the use of the word in John, in whose writings it so frequently occurs, see John v. 38; vi. 56; xiv. 10, 17; xv. 4–7, 9; 1 John iii. 6, 10, 14, 17, 27, 28; iii. 6, 24; iv. 12, 13, 15, 16. In the passage before us, as in his writings generally, it refers to one who lives the life of a Christian, as if he were always with Christ, and abode with him. It refers to the Christian considered as adhering steadfastly to the Saviour, and not as following him with transitory feelings, emotions, and raptures.

[See the Supplementary Note, Rom. viii. 10. We abide in Christ by union with him. The phrase expresses the *continuance* of the union; of which see in the Note as above. Scott explains, ' whoever abides in Christ *as one with him* and as maintaining communion with him.']

It does not of itself necessarily mean that he will always do this; that is, it does not *prove* the doctrine of the perseverance of the saints, but it refers to the adherence to the Saviour as a *continuous* state of mind, or as having permanency; meaning that there is a life of continued faith in him. It is of a person thus attached to the Saviour that

the apostle makes the important declaration in the passage before us, that he does not sin. This is the *third* argument to show that the child of God should be pure ; and the substance of the argument is, that *as a matter of fact* the child of God is not a sinner. ¶ *Sinneth not.* There has been much difference of opinion in regard to this expression, and the similar declaration in ver. 9. Not a few have maintained that it teaches the 'doctrine of perfection,' or that Christians may live entirely without sin ; and some have held that the apostle meant to teach that this is always the characteristic of the true Christian. Against the interpretation, however, which supposes that it teaches that the Christian is absolutely perfect, and lives wholly without sin, there are three insuperable objections : (1.) If it teaches that doctrine at all, it teaches that *all* Christians are perfect; '*whosoever* abideth in him,' '*whosoever* is born of God,' ' he *cannot* sin,' ver. 9. (2.) This is not true, and cannot be held to be true by those who have any just views of what the children of God have been and are. Who can maintain that Abraham, or Isaac, or Jacob ; that Moses, David, or Job; that Peter, John, or Paul, were absolutely perfect, and were never, after their regeneration, guilty of an act of sin ? Certainly they never affirmed it of themselves, nor does the sacred record attribute to them any such perfection. And who can affirm this of *all* who give evidence of true piety in the world ? Who can of themselves ? Are we to come to the painful conclusion that all who are not absolutely perfect in thought, word, and deed, are destitute of any religion, and are to be set down as hypocrites or self-deceivers ? And yet, unless this passage proves that *all* who have been born again are absolutely perfect, it will not prove it of any one, for the affirmation is not made of a part, or of what any favoured individual may be, but of what every one is in fact who is born of God. (3.) This interpretation is not necessary to a fair exposition of the passage. The language used is such

7 Little children, let no man deceive you: he [a] that doeth righ-

a Eze.18.5-9; Ro.2.13.

teousness is righteous, even as he is righteous.

as would be employed by any writer if he designed to say of one that he is not characteristically a sinner; that he is a good man; that he does not commit habitual and wilful transgression. Such language is common throughout the Bible, when it is said of one man that he is a saint, and of another that he is a sinner; of one that he is righteous, and of another that he is wicked; of one that he obeys the law of God, and of another that he does not. John expresses it strongly, but he affirms no more in fact than is affirmed elsewhere. The passage teaches, indeed, most important truths in regard to the true Christian; and the fair and proper meaning may be summed up in the following particulars : (*a*) He who is born again does not sin *habitually*, or is not *habitually* a sinner. If he does wrong, it is when he is overtaken by temptation, and the act is against the habitual inclination and purpose of his soul. If a man sins habitually, it proves that he has never been renewed. (*b*) That he who is born again does not do wrong *deliberately* and of *design*. He means to do right. He is not wilfully and deliberately a sinner. If a man deliberately and intentionally does wrong, he shows that he is not actuated by the spirit of religion. It is true that when one does wrong, or commits sin, there is a momentary assent of the will; but it is under the influence of passion, or excitement, or temptation, or provocation, and not as the result of a deliberate plan or purpose of the soul. A man who deliberately and intentionally does a wrong thing, shows that he is not a true Christian; and if this were all that is understood by *perfection*, then there would be many who are perfect, for there are many, very many Christians, who cannot recollect an instance for many years in which they have intentionally and deliberately done a wrong thing. Yet these very Christians see much corruption in their own hearts over which to mourn, and against which they earnestly strive; in comparing themselves with the perfect law of God, and

with the perfect example of the Saviour, they see much in which they come short. (*c*) He who is born again will not sin *finally*, or will not fall away. 'His seed remaineth in him,' ver. 9. See Notes on that verse. There is a principle of grace by which he will ultimately be restrained and recovered. This, it seems to me, is fairly implied in the language used by John; for if a man might be a Christian, and yet wholly fall away and perish, how could it be said with any truth that such a man 'sinneth not;' how that 'he doth not commit sin;' how that 'his seed' remaineth in him, and he cannot sin?' Just the contrary would be true if this were so. ¶ *Whosoever sinneth.* That is, as explained above, habitually, deliberately, characteristically, and finally. —*Doddridge.* 'Who habitually and avowedly sinneth.' ¶ *Hath not seen him, nor known him.* Has had no just views of the Saviour, or of the nature of true religion. In other words, cannot be a true Christian.

7. *Little children.* Notes on chap. ii. 1. ¶ *Let no man deceive you.* That is, in the matter under consideration; to wit, by persuading you that a man may live in sinful practices, and yet be a true child of God. From this it is clear that the apostle supposed there were some who would attempt to do this, and it was to counteract their arts that he made these positive statements in regard to the nature of true religion. ¶ *He that doeth righteousness is righteous.* This is laid down as a great and undeniable principle in religion— a maxim which none could dispute, and as important as it is plain. And it is worthy of all the emphasis which the apostle lays on it. The man who does righteousness, or leads an upright life, is a righteous man, and no other one is. No matter how any one may claim that he is justified by faith; no matter how he may conform to the external duties and rites of religion; no matter how zealous he may be for orthodoxy, or for the order of the church; no matter what visions and raptures he may have,

8 He *a* that committeth sin is of the devil; for the devil sinneth from the beginning. For this purpose the Son of God was manifested, that *b* he might destroy the works of the devil.

9 Whosoever *c* is born of God doth not commit sin; for his seed *d* remaineth in him: and he cannot sin, because he is born of God.

a Jn.8.44.   *b* He.2.14.   *c* 1Jn.5.18.
d 1Pe.1.23.

or of what peace and joy in his soul he may boast; no matter how little he may fear death, or hope for heaven— unless he is in fact a righteous man, in the proper sense of the term, he cannot be a child of God. Compare Matt. vii. 16—23. If he is, in the proper sense of the word, a man who keeps the law of God, and leads a holy life, he is righteous, for that is religion. Such a man, however, will always feel that his claim to be regarded as a righteous man is not to be traced to what he is in himself, but to what he owes to the grace of God. ¶ *Even as he is righteous.* See notes on ver. 3. Not necessarily in this world to the same *degree*, but with the same *kind* of righteousness. Hereafter he will become wholly free from all sin, like his God and Saviour, ver. 2. 8. *He that committeth sin.* Habitually, wilfully, characteristically. ¶ *Is of the devil.* This cannot mean that no one who commits *any* sin, or who is not absolutely perfect, can be a Christian, for this would cut off the great mass, even according to the belief of those who hold that the Christian may be perfectly holy, from all claim to the Christian character. But what the apostle here says is true in two senses: (1.) That all who commit sin, even true believers, so far as they are imperfect, in this respect resemble Satan, and are under his influence, since sin, just so far as it exists at all, makes us resemble him. (2.) All who habitually and characteristically sin are of the devil. This latter was evidently the principal idea in the mind of the apostle. His *object* here is to show that those who sinned, in the sense in which it would seem some maintained that the children of God might sin, could have no real evidence of piety, but really belonged to Satan. ¶ *For the devil sinneth from the beginning.* The beginning of the world; or from the first account we have of him. It does not

mean that he sinned from the beginning of his existence, for he was made holy like the other angels. Notes, Jude 6. The meaning is, that he introduced sin into the universe, and that he has continued to practise it ever since. The word *sinneth* here implies *continued* and *habitual* sin. He did not commit one act of sin and then reform; but he has continued, and still continues, his course of sin. This may confirm what has been already said about the kind of sin that John refers to. He speaks of sinning habitually, continuously, wilfully; and any one who does this shows that he is under the influence of him whose characteristic it has been and is to sin. ¶ *For this purpose the Son of God was manifested.* Became incarnate, and appeared among men, ver. 5. Comp. Notes on 1 Tim. iii. 16. ¶ *That he might destroy the works of the devil.* All his plans of wickedness, and his control over the hearts of men. Compare notes on Matt. viii. 39; Mark i. 24; Heb. ii. 14. The *argument* here is, that as the Son of God came to destroy all the works of the devil, he cannot be his true follower who lives in sin.

9. *Whosoever is born of God doth not commit sin.* This passage must either mean that they who are born of God, that is, who are true Christians, do not sin habitually and characteristically, or that every one who is a true Christian is absolutely perfect, and never commits any sin. If it can be used as referring to the doctrine of absolute perfection at all, it proves, not that Christians *may* be perfect, or that a *portion* of them are, but that *all* are. But who can maintain this? Who can believe that John meant to affirm this? Nothing can be clearer than that the passage has *not* this meaning, and that John did not teach a doctrine so contrary to the current strain of the Scriptures, and to fact; and if he did not teach this,

10 In this the children of God are | manifest, and the children of the

then in this whole passage he refers to those who are habitually and characteristically righteous. ¶ *For his seed remaineth in him.* There is much obscurity in this expression, though the general sense is clear, which is, that there is something abiding in the heart of the true Christian which the apostle here calls *seed*, which will prevent his sinning. The word '*his*' in this phrase, '*his* seed,' may refer either to the individual himself—in the sense that this can now be properly called *his*, inasmuch as it is a part of himself, or a principle abiding in him ; or it may refer to God—in the sense that what is here called 'seed' is *his*, that is, he has implanted it, or it is a germ of Divine origin. Robinson (*Lex.*) understands it in the latter sense, and so also do Macknight, Doddridge, Lücke, and others, and this is probably the true interpretation. The word *seed* (σπέρμα) means properly seed sown, as of grain, plants, trees ; then anything that resembles it, anything which germinates, or which springs up, or is produced. It is applied in the New Testament to the word of God, or the gospel, as that which produces effects in the heart and life similar to what seed that is sown does. Comp. Matt. xiii. 26, 37, 38. Augustin, Clemens, (*Alex.*,) Grotius, Rosenmüller, Benson, and Bloomfield, suppose that this is the signification of the word here. The proper idea, according to this, is that the seed referred to is truth, which God has implanted or sown in the heart, from which it may be expected that the fruits of righteousness will grow. But that which abides in the heart of a Christian is not the naked word of God ; the mere gospel, or mere truth ; it is rather that word as made vital and efficacious by the influences of his Spirit ; the germ of the Divine life ; the principles of true piety in the soul. Comp. the words of Virgil : —Igneus est illi vigor et cœlestis origo semini. The exact idea here, as it seems to me, is not that the 'seed' refers to *the word of God*, as Augustin and others suppose, or to *the Spirit of God*, but to the germ of piety which has been produced in the heart *by* the word and

Spirit of God, and which may be regarded as having been implanted there by God himself, and which may be expected to produce holiness in the life. There is, probably, as Lücke supposes, an allusion in the word to the fact that we are *begotten* (ὁ γεγεννημένος) of God. The word *remaineth*—μένει, comp. Notes on ver. 6—is a favourite expression of John. The expression here used by John, thus explained, would seem to imply two things : (1,) that the germ or seed of religion implanted in the soul abides there as a constant, vital principle, so that he who is born of God cannot become habitually a sinner ; and, (2,) that it will so continue to live there that he will not fall away and perish. The idea is clearly that the germ or principle of piety so permanently abides in the soul, that he who is renewed never can become again characteristically a sinner. ¶ *And he cannot sin.* Not merely he will not, but he cannot ; that is, in the sense referred to. This cannot mean that one who is renewed has not physical ability to do wrong, for every moral agent has ; nor can it mean that no one who is a true Christian never does, in fact, do wrong in thought, word, or deed, for no one could seriously maintain that : but it must mean that there is somehow a certainty as absolute *as if* it were physically impossible, that those who are born of God will not be characteristically and habitually sinners ; that they will not sin in such a sense as to lose all true religion and be numbered with transgressors ; that they will not fall away and perish. Unless this passage teaches that no one who is renewed ever *can* sin in any sense ; or that every one who becomes a Christian is, and must be, absolutely and always perfect, no words could more clearly prove that true Christians will never fall from grace and perish. How can what the apostle here says be true, if a real Christian can fall away and become again a sinner ? ¶ *Because he is born of God.* Or begotten of God. God has given him, by the new birth, real, spiritual life, and that life can never become extinct.

10. *In this the children of God are manifest, &c.* That is, this furnishes a

devil: whosoever doeth not righteousness, is not of God, neither he that loveth not his brother.

11 For this is the [1]message that ye heard from the beginning, that *a* we should love one another.

12 Not as Cain, *b* who was of that

wicked one, and slew his brother. And wherefore slew he him? Because his own works were evil, and his brother's righteous.

13 Marvel not, my brethren, if the world *c* hate you.

1 Or, *commandment.*   *a* Jn.15.12.   *b* Ge.4.4-8.
                         c Jn.15.18,19.

---

test of their true character. The test is found in doing righteousness, and in the love of the brethren. The former he had illustrated; the latter he now proceeds to illustrate. The general idea is, that if a man is not truly a righteous man, and does not love the brethren, he cannot be a child of God. Perhaps by the phrase '*in this*,' using a pronoun in the singular number, he means to intimate that an important part of righteousness consists in brotherly love. ¶ *Whosoever doeth not righteousness, is not of God.* In ver. 7, he had said that 'he that doeth righteousness *is* of God.' If that is true, then what he here affirms must be true also, that a man who does *not* righteousness is not of God. The general idea is the same, that no one can be a true Christian who is not in fact a righteous man. ¶ *Neither he that loveth not his brother.* The illustration of this point continues to ver.18. The general sense is, that brotherly love is essential to the Christian character, and that he who does not possess it cannot be a Christian. On the nature and importance of brotherly love as an evidence of piety, see Notes on John xiii. 34, 35.

11. *For this is the message.* Marg., *commandment.* In the received text, this is ἀγγελία—*a message brought;* in several mss., and in later editions, it is ἐπαγγελία — *annunciation, announcement;* an order given, or a commandment, Acts xxiii. 21. It is not very material which reading is followed. The word *command* or *rule* would express the sense with sufficient clearness. The reference is to the law given by the Saviour as a permanent direction to his disciples. ¶ *That ye heard from the beginning, that we should love one another.* See Notes, John xiii. 34, 35; 1 John ii. 7.

12. *Not as Cain.* Not manifesting

the spirit which Cain did. His was a most remarkable and striking instance of a want of love to a brother, and the case was well adapted to illustrate the propriety of the duty which the apostle is enjoining. See Gen. iv. 4–8. ¶ *Who was of that wicked one.* Of the devil; that is, he was under his influence, and acted from his instigation. ¶ *And wherefore slew he him? Because his own works were evil, and his brother's righteous.* He acted under the influence of envy. He was dissatisfied that his own offering was not accepted, and that his brother's was. The apostle seems desirous to guard those to whom he wrote against the indulgence of *any* feelings that were the opposite of love; from anything like envy toward more highly favoured brethren, by showing to what this would lead if fairly acted out, as in the case of Cain. A large part of the crimes of the earth have been caused, as in the murder of Abel, by the want of brotherly love. Nothing but love would be necessary to put an end to the crimes, and consequently to a large part of the misery, of the world.

13. *Marvel not.* Do not think it so unusual, or so little to be expected, as to excite astonishment. ¶ *If the world hate you.* The emphasis here is to be placed on the word *you.* The apostle had just adverted to the fact that Cain hated Abel, his brother, without cause, and he says that they were not to deem it strange if the world hated *them* in like manner. The Saviour (John xv. 17, 18) introduced these subjects in the same connection. In enjoining the duty of brotherly love on his disciples, he adverts to the fact that they must expect to be hated by the world, and tells them to remember that the world hated him before it hated them. The object of all this was to show more clearly the necessity of strong and tender mutual affec-

14 We know that we have passed from death unto life, because we love the brethren. He *a* that loveth not *his* brother abideth in death.

15 Whosoever *b* hateth his brother is a murderer: and ye know that

a 1 Jn.2.9,11.   *b* Mat.5.21,22.

no murderer hath eternal life abiding in him.

16 Hereby *c* perceive we the love of God, because he laid down his life for us: and we ought to lay down our lives for the brethren.

c Jn.15.13; Ro.5.8.

tion among Christians, since they could hope for none from the world. See Notes, John xv. 18, 19.

14. *We know that we have passed from death unto life.* From spiritual death (Notes, Eph. ii. 1) to spiritual life, that is, that we are true Christians. ¶ *Because we love the brethren.* The sentiment here is, that it is an infallible evidence of true piety if we love the followers of Christ as such. See this sentiment illustrated in the Notes on John xiii. 35. But how easy it would seem to be to apply such a test of piety as this! Who cannot judge accurately of his own feelings, and determine whether he loves a Christian because he bears the name and image of the Saviour—loves him the more just in proportion as he bears that image? Who cannot, if he chooses, look beyond the narrow bounds of his own sect, and determine whether he is pleased with the true Christian character wherever it may be found, and whether he would prefer to find his friends among those who bear the name and the image of the Son of God, than among the people of the world? The Saviour meant that his followers should be known by this badge of discipleship all over the world, John xiii. 34, 35. John says, in carrying out the sentiment, that Christians, by this test, may know *among themselves* whether they have any true religion. ¶ *He that loveth not* his *brother abideth in death.* He remains dead in sins; that is, he has never been converted. Comp. Notes, ver. 6. As love to the Christian brotherhood is essential to true piety, it follows that he who has not that remains unconverted, or is in a state of spiritual death. He is by nature dead in sin, and unless he has evidence that he is brought out of that state, he *remains* or *abides* in it.

15. *Whosoever hateth his brother is a murderer,* &c. That is, he has the

spirit of a murderer; he has that which, if it were acted out, would lead him to commit murder, as it did Cain. The private malice, the secret grudge, the envy which is cherished in the heart, is murderous in its tendency, and were it not for the outward restraints of human laws, and the dread of punishment, it would often lead to the act of murder. The apostle does not say that he who hates his brother, though he does not in fact commit murder, is guilty to the same degree as if he had actually done it; but he evidently means to say that the spirit which would lead to murder is there, and that God will hold him responsible for it. Nothing is wanting but the removal of outward restraints to lead to the commission of the open deed, and God judges men as he sees them to be *in their hearts.* What a fearful declaration, then, is this! How many real murderers there are on the earth besides those who are detected and punished, and besides those open violators of the laws of God and man who go at large! And who is there that should not feel humbled and penitent in view of his own heart, and grateful for that sovereign mercy which has restrained him from open acts of guilt? —for who is there who has not at some period of his life, and perhaps often, indulged in feelings of hatred, and envy, and malice towards others, which, if acted out, would have led to the commission of the awful crime of taking human life? Any man may well shudder at the remembrance of the secret sins of his own heart, and at the thought of what he *would* have been but for the restraining grace of God. And how wonderful is that grace which, in the case of the true Christian, not only restrains and checks, but which effectually subdues all these feelings, and implants in their place the principles of love!

16. *Hereby perceive we the love of*

God. The words ' *of God* ' are not in the original, and should not have been introduced into the translation, though they are found in the Latin Vulgate, and in the Genevan versions, and in one manuscript. They would naturally convey the idea that *God* laid down his life for us; or that God himself, in his Divine nature, suffered. But this idea is not expressed in this passage as it is in the original, and of course no argument can be derived from it either to prove that Christ is God, or that the Divine nature is capable of suffering. The original is much more expressive and emphatic than it is with this addition : ' By this we know love ;' that is, we know what true love is ; we see a most affecting and striking illustration of its nature. *Love itself*—its real nature, its power, its sacrifices, its influences—was seen in its highest form, when the Son of God gave himself to die on a cross. For an illustration of the sentiment, see Notes on John iii. 16, and xv. 13. ¶ *Because he laid down his life for us.* There can be no doubt that the Saviour is here referred to, though his name is not mentioned particularly. There are several instances in the New Testament where he is mentioned under the general appellation ' *he*,' as one who was well known, and about whom the writers were accustomed to speak. ¶ *And we ought to lay down* our *lives for the brethren.* For the good of our fellow-Christians, if it be necessary. That is, circumstances may occur where it would be proper to do it, and we ought always to be ready to do it. The spirit which led the Saviour to sacrifice his life for the good of the church, should lead us to do the same thing for our brethren if circumstances should require it. That this is a correct principle no one can doubt; for (1) the Saviour did it, and we are bound to imitate his example, and to possess his spirit ; (2) the prophets, apostles, and martyrs did it, laying down their lives in the cause of truth, and for the good of the church and the world ; and (3) it has always been held that it is right and proper, in certain circumstances, for a man to lay down his life for the good of others. So we speak of the patriot who sacrifices his life for the good of his country;

so we feel in the case of a shipwreck, that it may be the duty of a captain to sacrifice his life for the good of his passengers and crew ; so in case of a pestilential disease, a physician should not regard his own life, if he may save others ; and so we always hold the man up to honour who is willing to jeopard his own life on noble principles of self-denial for the good of his fellow-men. In what cases this should occur the apostle does not state ; but the general principle would seem to be, that it is to be done when a greater good would result from our self-sacrifice than from carefully guarding our own lives. Thus, in the case of a patriot, his death, in the circumstances, might' be of greater value to his country than his life would be ; or, his exposing himself to death would be a greater service to his country, than if that should not be done. Thus the Saviour laid down his life for the good of mankind ; thus the apostles exposed their lives to constant peril in extending the principles of religion; and thus the martyrs surrendered their lives in the cause of the church and of truth. In like manner we ought to be ready to hazard our lives, and even to lay them down, if in that way we may promote the cause of truth, and the salvation of sinners, or serve our Christian brethren. In what way this injunction was understood by the primitive Christians, may be perceived from what the world is reported to have said of them, ' Behold, how they love one another ; they are ready to die for one another.' —Tertull. Apol. c. 39. So Eusebius (Eccl. His. vii. 22) says of Christians, that ' in a time of plague they visited one another, and not only hazarded their lives, but actually lost them in their zeal to preserve the lives of others.' We are not indeed to throw away our lives; we are not to expose them in a rash, reckless, imprudent manner ; but when, in the discharge of duty, we are placed in a situation where life is exposed to danger, we are not to shrink from the duty, or to run away from it. Perhaps the following would embrace the principal instances of the duty here enjoined by the apostle: (1.) We ought to have such love for the church that we should be *willing* to die for it, as

17 But *a* whoso hath this world's good, and seeth his brother have need, and shutteth up his bowels *of compassion* from him, how *b* dwelleth the love of God in him?

18 My little children, let *c* us not

love in word, neither in tongue; but in deed and in truth.

19 And hereby *d* we know that we are of the truth, and shall ¹ assure our hearts before him.

a De.15.7.   *b* 1 Jn.4.20.   *c* Eze.33.31; Ro.12.9;
Ja.2.15,16; 1 Pe.1.22.   *d* Jn.13.35.   1 Or, *persuade.*

patriot is willing to die for his country. (2.) We ought to have such love for Christians as to be willing to jeopard our lives to aid them—as in case of a pestilence or plague, or when they are in danger by fire, or flood, or foes. (3.) We ought to have such love for the truth as to be willing to sacrifice our lives rather than deny it. (4.) We ought to have such love for the cause of our Master as to be willing to cross oceans, and snows, and sands; to visit distant and barbarous regions, though at imminent risk of our lives, and though with the prospect that we shall never see our country again. (5.) We ought to have such love for the church that we shall engage heartily and constantly in services of labour and self-sacrifice on its account, until, our work being done, exhausted nature shall sink to rest in the grave. In one word, we should regard ourselves as devoted to the service of the Redeemer, living or dying to be found engaged in his cause. If a case should actually occur where the question would arise whether a man would abandon his Christian brother or die, he ought not to hesitate; in all cases he should regard his life as consecrated to the cause of Sion and its friends. Once, in the times of primitive piety, there was much of this spirit in the world; how little, it is to be feared, does it prevail now!

17. *But whoso hath this world's good.* Has property—called 'this world's good,' or a good pertaining to this world, because it is of value to us only as it meets our wants this side of the grave; and perhaps also because it is sought supremely by the men of the world. The general meaning of this verse, in connection with the previous verse, is, that if we ought to be willing to lay down our lives for others, we ought to be willing to make those comparatively smaller sacrifices which are necessary to relieve them in their dis-

tresses; and that if we are unwilling to do this, we can have no evidence that the love of God dwells in us. ¶ *And seeth his brother have need.* Need of food, of raiment, of shelter; or sick, and poor, and unable to provide for his own wants and those of his family. ¶ *And shutteth up his bowels* of compassion *from him.* The bowels, or *upper viscera*, embracing the heart, and the region of the chest generally, are in the Scriptures represented as the seat of mercy, piety, and compassion, because when the mind feels compassion it is that part which is affected. Comp. Notes, Isa. xvi. 11. ¶ *How dwelleth the love of God in him?* How can a man love God who does not love those who bear his image? See Notes, chap. iv. 20. On the general sentiment here, see Notes on James ii. 14—16. The meaning is plain, that we cannot have evidence of piety unless we are ready to do good to others, especially to our Christian brethren. See Notes, Matt. xxv. 45; Gal. vi. 10.

18. *My little children, let us not love in word, neither in tongue.* By mere profession; by merely *saying* that we love each other. See 1 Pet. i. 22. ¶ *But in deed and in truth.* In such acts as shall show that our professed love is sincere and real. Let us do the deed of love, whether anything is said about it or not. See Notes on Matt. vi. 3.

19. *And hereby.* Gr., *by this;* that is, by the fact that we have true love to others, and that we manifest it by a readiness to make sacrifices to do them good. ¶ *We know that we are of the truth.* That we are not deceived in what we profess to be; that is, that we are true Christians. To be of the truth stands opposed to cherishing false and delusive hopes. ¶ *And shall assure our hearts before him.* Before God, or before the Saviour. In the margin, as in the Greek, the word rendered *shall assure*, is *persuade.* The Greek word

20 For if our heart condemn us, God is greater than our heart, and knoweth all things.

a Job 27.6; Ps.101.2.

21 Beloved, if our heart *a* condemn us not, *then* have we confidence *b* toward God.

b He.10.22.

is used as meaning to *persuade*, e. g., to the reception and belief of truth; then to persuade any one who has unkind or prejudiced feelings towards us, or to bring over to kind feelings, *to conciliate*, and thus to pacify or quiet. The meaning here seems to be, that we shall in this way allay the doubts and trouble of our minds, and produce a state of quiet and peace, to wit, by the evidence that we are of the truth. Our consciences are often restless and troubled in view of past guilt; but, in thus furnishing the evidence of true piety by love to others, we shall pacify an accusing mind, and conciliate our own hearts, and persuade or convince ourselves that we are truly the children of God. See Rob. Lex. sub voce πείθω, I. *b.* In other words, though a man's heart may condemn him as guilty, and though he knows that God sees and condemns the sins of his past life, yet the agitations and alarms of his mind may be calmed down and soothed by evidence that he is a child of God, and that he will not be finally condemned. A true Christian does not attempt to conceal the fact that there is much for which his own heart and conscience might justly accuse him; but he finds, notwithstanding all this, evidence that he is a child of God, and he is persuaded that all will be well.

20. *For if our heart condemn us.* We cannot hope for peace from any expectation that our own hearts will never accuse us, or that we ourselves can approve of all that we have done. The reference here is not so much to our past lives, as to our present conduct and deportment. The object is to induce Christians so to live that their hearts will not condemn them for any secret sins, while the outward deportment may be unsullied. The general sentiment is, that if they should so live that their own hearts would condemn them for present insincerity and hypocrisy, they could have no hope of peace, for God knows all that is in the heart. In view of the past—when the heart accuses us of what we *have* done—we may find

peace by such evidences of piety as shall allay the troubles of an agitated soul, (ver. 9,) but we cannot have such peace if our hearts condemn us for the indulgence of secret sins, now that we profess to be Christians. If our hearts condemn us for present insincerity, and for secret sins, we can never 'persuade' or soothe them by any external act of piety. In view of the consciousness of past guilt, we may find peace; we can find none if there is a present purpose to indulge in sin. ¶ *God is greater than our heart, and knoweth all things.* We cannot hope to find peace by hiding anything from his view, or by any supposition that he is not acquainted with the sins for which our consciences trouble us. He knows all the sins of which we are conscious, and sees all their guilt and aggravation as clearly as we do. He knows more than this. He knows all the sins which we have forgotten; all those acts which we endeavour to persuade ourselves are not sinful, but which are evil in his sight; and all those aggravations attending our sins which it is impossible for us fully and distinctly to conceive. He is more disposed to condemn sin than we are; he looks on it with less allowance than we do. We cannot hope, then, for a calm mind in any supposition that God does not see our sins as clearly as we do, or in any hope that he will look on them with more favour and indulgence. Peace cannot be found in the indulgence of sin in the hope that God will not perceive or regard it, for we can sooner deceive ourselves than we can him; and while therefore, (ver. 19,) in reference to the past, we can only 'persuade' our hearts, or soothe their agitated feelings by evidence that we are of the truth now, and that our sins are forgiven; in reference to the present and the future, the heart can be kept calm only by such a course of life that our own hearts and our God shall approve the manner in which we live.

21. *Beloved, if our heart condemn us not.* If we so live as to have an ap-

22 And whatsoever *a* we ask, we receive of him, because we keep his commandments, and do those things that are pleasing in his sight.

23 And this *b* is his commandment, That we should believe on the name of his Son Jesus Christ,

a Ps.145.18,19; Pr.15.29; Mar.11.24.
b De.18.15-19; Jn.14.1.

and love one another, as he gave us commandment.

24 And he *c* that keepeth his commandments dwelleth in him, and he in him. And hereby *d* we know that he abideth in us, by the Spirit which he hath given us.

c Jn.14.23; 15.10.   *d* Ro.8.9,14.

proving conscience—that is, if we indulge in no secret sin ; if we discharge faithfully every known duty ; if we submit without murmuring to all the allotments of Divine Providence. ¶ Then *have we confidence toward God.* Comp. Notes, ver. 19; chap. i. 28; Acts xxiv. 16. The apostle evidently does not mean that we have confidence towards God on the ground of what we do, as if it were meritorious, or as if it constituted a claim to his favour ; but that we may so live as to have evidence of personal piety, and that we may look forward with a confident hope that we shall be accepted of him in the great day. The word here rendered *confidence*—παῤῥησίαν—means properly *boldness ;* usually boldness or openness in speaking our sentiments. See Notes, chap. ii. 28. The confidence or boldness which we have towards our Maker is founded solely on the evidence that he will graciously accept us as pardoned sinners; not in the belief that we deserve his favour.

22. *And whatsoever we ask, we receive of him.* If we are truly his children, and ask in a proper manner. See Notes, Matt. vii. 7. Comp. Mark xi. 24; Luke xi. 9; xviii. 1, seq.; John xiv. 13; xv. 7; 1 John v. 14. The declaration here made must be understood with these limitations : (1,) that we ask in a proper manner, James iv. 3; and, (2,) that the thing asked shall be such as will be consistent for God to give; that is, such as he shall see to be best for us, 1 John v. 14. See Notes on this latter passage. ¶ *Because we keep his commandments.* Not that this is the meritorious ground of our being heard, but that it furnishes evidence that we are his children, and he hears his children as such. ¶ *And do those things that are pleasing in his sight.* As a parent is disposed to bestow favours on obedient,

affectionate, and dutiful children, so God is on those who please him by their obedience and submission to his will. We can have no hope that he will hear us unless we do so live as to please him. 23. *And this is his commandment.* His commandment, by way of eminence; the leading, principal thing which he enjoins on us ; the commandment which lies at the foundation of all true obedience. ¶ *That we should believe on the name of his Son Jesus Christ.* See Notes, Mark xvi. 16. Comp. John xvi. 1; Acts xvi. 31. ¶ *And love one another,* &c. This follows from the other, and hence they are mentioned as together constituting his commandment. Notes, John xiii. 35. 24. *And he that keepeth his commandments,* &c. See Notes, John xiv. 23. ¶ *And hereby we know that he abideth in us.* That is, this is another certain evidence that we are true Christians. The Saviour had promised (John xiv. 23) that he would come and take up his abode with his people. John says that we have proof that he does this by the Spirit which he has given us. That is, the Holy Spirit is imparted to his people to enlighten their minds ; to elevate their affections ; to sustain them in times of trial ; to quicken them in the performance of duty ; and to imbue them with the temper and spirit of the Lord Jesus. When these effects exist, we may be certain that the Spirit of God is with us ; for these are the 'fruits' of that Spirit, or these are the effects which he produces in the lives of men. Comp. Notes, Gal. v. 22, 23. On the evidence of piety here referred to, see Notes on Rom. viii. 9, 14, 16. No man can be a true Christian in whom that Spirit does not constantly dwell, or to whom he is not 'given.' And yet no one can determine that the Spirit dwells in him, except by the *effects* produced

CHAPTER IV.

BELOVED, believe ^a not every spirit, but try ^b the spirits

<small>a Je.29.8; Mat.24.4.   b 1 Th.5.21; Re.2.2.</small>

in his heart and life. In the following chapter, the apostle pursues the subject suggested here, and shows that we should examine ourselves closely, to see whether the ' Spirit' to which we trust, as furnishing evidence of piety, is truly the Spirit of God, or is a spirit of delusion.

CHAPTER IV.

ANALYSIS OF THE CHAPTER.

THERE are two principal subjects discussed in this chapter:—

I. The method by which we may determine that we have the Spirit of God, vers. 1—6. The apostle had said (chap. iii. 24) that it could be determined that God dwells in them by the Spirit which he has given them; but as it is probable that the teachers of error, the persons whom John regarded as 'antichrist,' (chap. ii. 18, 19,) would lay claim to the same thing, it was important to know how it could be ascertained that the Spirit of God had been really given to them, or how it could be determined that the spirit that was in them was not the spirit of antichrist, the very thing against which he would guard them. In doing this, he (1) cautions them against trusting to every kind of spirit, or supposing that every spirit which animated even the professed friends of religion was the Spirit of God, ver. 1; and (2) he shows them how it might be determined that they had really the Spirit of God, or what would be the effect of the influences of the Spirit on the mind. This evidence consisted of the following things: (a) they had the Spirit of God who confessed that Jesus Christ had come in the flesh, ver. 2; (b) they who denied that, had not the Spirit of God, and the denial of this was the real spirit of antichrist, ver. 3; (c) they who had the Spirit of God had not the spirit of this world, vers. 4, 5; and (d) they who had the Spirit of God would hear those who were his apostles, or who were sent by him, ver. 6.

II. The duty, power, and influence of love, vers. 7—21. This is a favourite

whether they are of God: because ^c many false prophets are gone out into the world.

<small>c 2 Pe.2.8.</small>

subject with John, and he here considers it at length, as a subject that was essential in determining the evidences of piety. The duty and value of love are enforced by the following considerations: (1.) Love has its origin in God, and every one who has true love is born of God, vers. 7, 8. (2.) God has shown his great love to us by having given his Son to die for us; and as he has so loved us, we ought also to love one another, vers. 9—11. (3.) If we love one another, it furnishes the best evidence that God dwells in us, vers. 12—15. (4.) God is love, and if we have true love we dwell in him, and he dwells in us, ver. 16. (5.) Love will furnish us great advantage in the day of judgment, by giving us confidence when we come before him, ver. 17. (6.) Love will cast out all fear, and will make our minds calm in view of the events which are to come, ver. 18. (7.) The very fact that he has first manifested his love to us should lead us to the exercise of love, ver. 19. (8.) A man cannot truly love God and yet hate his brother, ver. 20; and (9) it is the solemn command of God that he who loves God should love his brother also.

1. *Beloved, believe not every spirit.* Do not confide implicitly in every one who professes to be under the influences of the Holy Spirit. Comp. Matt. xxiv. 4, 5. The true and the false teachers of religion alike claimed to be under the influence of the Spirit of God, and it was of importance that all such pretensions should be examined. It was not to be admitted because any one claimed to have been sent from God that therefore he was sent. Every such claim should be subjected to the proper proof before it was conceded. All pretensions to divine inspiration, or to being authorised teachers of religion, were to be examined by the proper tests, because there were many false and delusive teachers who set up such claims in the world. ¶ *But try the spirits whether they are of God.* There were those in the early Christian church who had the

2 Hereby know ye the Spirit of God: Every *spirit that confesseth | that Jesus Christ is come in the flesh, is of God:

a 1 Co.12.3.

gift of 'discerning spirits,' (see Notes, 1 Cor. xii. 10,) but it is not certain that the apostle refers here to any such supernatural power. It is more probable, as he addresses this command to Christians in general, that he refers to the ability of doing this by a comparison of the doctrines which they professed to hold with what was revealed, and by the fruits of their doctrines in their lives. If they taught what God had taught in his word, and if their lives corresponded with his requirements, and if their doctrines agreed with what had been inculcated by those who were admitted to be true apostles, (ver. 6,) they were to receive them as what they professed to be. If not, they were to reject them, and hold them to be impostors. It may be remarked, that it is just as proper and as important now to examine the claims of all who profess to be teachers of religion, as it was then. In a matter so momentous as religion, and where there is so much at stake, it is important that *all* pretensions of this kind should be subjected to a rigid examination. No man should be received as a religious teacher without the clearest evidence that he has come in accordance with the will of God, nor unless he inculcates the very truth which God has revealed. See Notes on Isa. viii. 20, and Acts xvii. 11. ¶ *Because many false prophets are gone out into the world.* The word *prophet* is often used in the New Testament to denote religious instructors or preachers. See Notes, Rom. xii. 6. Compare Notes, 2 Pet. ii. 1. Such false teachers evidently abounded in the times here referred to. See Notes, chap. ii. 18. The meaning is, that many had gone out into the world pretending to be true teachers of religion, but who inculcated most dangerous doctrines; and it was their duty to be on their guard against them, for they had the very spirit of antichrist, ver. 3.

2. *Hereby.* Gr., 'By this;' that is, by the test which is immediately specified. ¶ *Know ye the Spirit of God.* You may discern who are actuated by the Spirit of God. ¶ *Every spirit.*

Every one professing to be under the influence of the Spirit of God. The apostle uses the word *spirit* here with reference to the person who made the claim, on the supposition that every ono professing to be a religious teacher was animated by some spirit or foreign influence, good or bad. If the Spirit of God influenced them, they would confess that Jesus Christ had come in the flesh ; if some other spirit, the spirit of error and deceit, they would deny this. ¶ *That confesseth.* That is, that makes a proper acknowledgment of this ; that inculcates this doctrine, and that gives it a due place and prominence in his instructions. It cannot be supposed that a mere statement of this in words would show that they were of God in the sense that they were true Christians ; but the sense is, that if this constituted one of the doctrines which they held and taught, it would show that they were advocates of truth, and not apostles of error. If they did not do this, (ver. 3,) it would be decisive in regard to their character and claims. ¶ *That Jesus Christ is come in the flesh.* Benson and some others propose to render this, 'That Jesus, who came in the flesh, is the Christ.' But this is liable to serious objections. (1.) It is not the obvious interpretation. (2.) It is unusual to say that '*Jesus* had come in the flesh,' though the expression 'the Son of God has come in the flesh,' or 'God was manifested in the flesh,' would be in accordance with the usage of the New Testament. (3.) This would not, probably, meet the real point in the case. The thing denied does not appear to have been that Jesus was the Messiah, for their pretending to be Christian teachers at all implied that they admitted this ; but that the Son of God was *really a man,* or that he actually assumed human nature in permanent union with the Divine. The point of the remark made by the apostle is, that the acknowledgment was to be that Christ assumed human nature; that he was really a man as he appeared to be : or that there was a real incar-

3 And every spirit that confesseth not that Jesus Christ is come in the flesh, is not of God : and this is that *spirit* of antichrist, whereof

ye have heard that it should come; and even now already is it in the world.

4 Ye are of God, little children,

nation, in opposition to the opinion that he came in *appearance* only, or that he merely *seemed* to be a man, and to suffer and die. That this opinion was held by many, see the Intro. § III. 2. It is quite probable that the apostle here refers to such sentiments as those which were held by the *Docetæ;* and that he meant to teach that it was indispensable to proper evidence that any one came from God, that he should maintain that Jesus was truly *a man,* or that there was a real *incarnation* of the Son of God. John always regarded this as a very important point, and often refers to it, John xix. 34, 35 ; xx. 25—27; 1 John v. 6. It is as important to be held now as it was then, for the fact that there was a real incarnation is essential to all just views of the atonement. If he was *not* truly a man, if he did not literally shed his blood on the cross, of course all that was done was in appearance only, and the whole system of redemption as revealed was merely a splendid illusion. There is little danger that this opinion will be held now, for those who depart from the doctrine laid down in the New Testament in regard to the person and work of Christ, are more disposed to embrace the opinion that he was a mere man ; but still it is important that the truth that he was truly incarnate should be held up constantly before the mind, for in no other way can we obtain just views of the atonement. ¶ *Is of God.* This does not necessarily mean that every one who confessed this was personally a true Christian, for it is clear that a doctrine might be acknowledged to be true, and yet that the heart might not be changed ; nor does it mean that the acknowledgment of this truth was *all* which it was essential to be believed in order that one might be recognised as a Christian ; but it means that it was *essential* that this truth should be admitted by every one who truly came from God. They who taught this held a truth which he had revealed, and which was essential to be held : and they thus showed that they

did not belong to those to whom the name 'antichrist' could be properly given. Still, whether they held this doctrine in such a sense, and in such connection with other doctrines, as to show that they were sincere Christians, was quite another question, for it is plain that a man may hold and teach the true doctrines of religion, and yet have no evidence that he is a child of God.

3. *And every spirit that confesseth not,* &c. That is, this doctrine is *essential* to the Christian system ; and he who does not hold it cannot be regarded either as a Christian, or recognised as a Christian teacher. If he was not a man, then all that occurred in his life, in Gethsemane, and on the cross, was in *appearance* only, and was assumed only to delude the senses. There were no real sufferings ; there was no shedding of blood ; there was no death on the cross ; and, of course, there was no atonement. A mere show, an appearance assumed, a vision, could not make atonement for sin ; and a denial, therefore, of the doctrine that the Son of God had come in the flesh, was in fact a denial of the doctrine of expiation for sin. The Latin Vulgate here reads *qui solvit Jesum,* 'who dissolves or divides Jesus ;' and Socrates (H. E. vii. 32) says that in the old copies of the New Testament it is written ὃ λίει τὸν Ἰησοῦν, 'who dissolves or divides Jesus ;' that is, who *separates* his true nature or person, or who supposes that there were *two* Christs, one in appearance, and one in reality. This reading was early found in some MSS., and is referred to by many of the Fathers, (see Wetstein,) but it has no real authority, and was evidently introduced, perhaps at first from a marginal note, to oppose the prevailing errors of the times. The common reading, ' who confesseth not,' is found in all the Gr. MSS., in the Syriac versions, in the Arabic ; and, as Lücke says, the other reading is manifestly of Latin origin. The common reading in the text is that which is sustained by

and have overcome *a* them: because greater is he that is in you, than he that is in the world.

5 They are of the world: *b* therefore speak they of the world, and the world heareth them.

6 We are of God: he that knoweth God, heareth us; he that is not of God, heareth not us. Hereby *c* know we the spirit of truth, and the spirit of error.

a Ro.8.37.　　　*b* Jn.3.31.　　　*c* Is.8.20.

authority, and is entirely in accordance with the manner of John. ¶ *And this is that* spirit *of antichrist.* This is one of the things which characterize antichrist. John here refers not to an *individual* who should be known as antichrist, but to a class of persons. This does not, however, forbid the idea that there might be some one individual, or a succession of persons in the church, to whom the name might be applied by way of eminence. See Notes, chap. ii. 18. Comp. Notes, 2 Thess. ii. 3, seq. ¶ *Whereof ye have heard that it should come.* See Notes, chap. ii. 18.

4. *Ye are of God.* You are of his family; you have embraced his truth, and imbibed his Spirit. ¶ *Little children.* Notes, chap. ii. 1. ¶ *And have overcome them.* Have triumphed over their arts and temptations; their endeavours to draw you into error and sin. The word '*them*' in this place seems to refer to the false prophets or teachers who collectively constituted antichrist. The meaning is, that they had frustrated or thwarted all their attempts to turn them away from the truth. ¶ *Because greater is he that is in you, than he that is in the world.* God, who dwells in your hearts, and by whose strength and grace alone you have been enabled to achieve this victory, is more mighty than Satan, who rules in the hearts of the people of this world, and whose seductive arts are seen in the efforts of these false teachers. The apostle meant to say that it was by no power of their own that they achieved this victory, but it was to be traced solely to the fact that God dwelt among them, and had preserved them by his grace. What was true then is true now. He who dwells in the hearts of Christians by his Spirit, is infinitely more mighty than Satan, 'the ruler of the darkness of this world;' and victory, therefore, over all his arts and temptations may be sure. In his conflicts with

sin, temptation, and error, the Christian should never despair, for his God will insure him the victory.

5. *They are of the world.* This was one of the marks by which those who had the spirit of antichrist might be known. They belonged not to the church of God, but to the world. They had its spirit ; they acted on its principles ; they lived for it. Comp. Notes, chap. ii. 15. ¶ *Therefore speak they of the world.* Comp. Notes, chap. iii. 31. This may mean either that their conversation pertained to the things of this world, or that they were wholly influenced by the love of the world, and not by the Spirit of God, in the doctrines which they taught. The general sense is, that they had no higher ends and aims than they have who are influenced only by worldly plans and expectations. It is not difficult to distinguish, even among professed Christians and Christian teachers, those who are heavenly in their conversation from those who are influenced solely by the spirit of the world. 'Out of the abundance of the heart the mouth speaketh,' and the general turn of a man's conversation will show what 'spirit is within him.' ¶ *And the world heareth them.* The people of the world—the gay, the rich, the proud, the ambitious, the sensual—receive their instructions, and recognize them as teachers and guides, for their views accord with their own. See Notes, John xv. 19. A professedly religious teacher may always determine much about himself by knowing what class of people are pleased with him. A professed Christian of any station in life may determine much about his evidences of piety, by asking himself what kind of persons desire his friendship, and wish him for a companion.

6. *We are of God.* John here, doubtless, refers to himself, and to those who taught the same doctrines which he did. He takes it for granted that those to whom he wrote would admit this, and

7 Beloved, let us love ᵃ one another: for love is of God; and

ᵃ 1 Jn.3.11,23.

every one that loveth, is born of God, and knoweth God.

argues from it as an indisputable truth. He had given them such evidence of this, as to establish his character and claims beyond a doubt; and he often refers to the fact that he was what he claimed to be, as a point which was so well established that no one would call it in question. See John xix. 35; xxi. 24; 3 John 12. Paul, also, not unfrequently refers to the same thing respecting himself; to the fact—a fact which no one would presume to call in question, and which might be regarded as the basis of an argument—that he and his fellow-apostles were what they claimed to be. See 1 Cor. xv. 14, 15; 1 Thess. ii. 1—11. Might not, and ought not, all Christians, and all Christian ministers, so to live that the same thing might be assumed in regard to them in their intercourse with their fellow-men; that their characters for integrity and purity might be so clear that no one would be disposed to call them in question? There are such men in the church and in the ministry now; why might not all be such? ¶ *He that knoweth God, heareth us.* Every one that has a true acquaintance with the character of God will receive our doctrine. John might assume this, for it was not doubted, he presumed, that he was an apostle and a good man; and if this were admitted, it would follow that those who feared and loved God would receive what he taught. ¶ *Hereby.* By this; to wit, by the manner in which they receive the doctrines which we have taught. ¶ *Know we the spirit of truth, and the spirit of error.* We can distinguish those who embrace the truth from those who do not. Whatever pretensions they might set up for piety, it was clear that if they did not embrace the doctrines taught by the true apostles of God, they could not be regarded as his friends; that is, as true Christians. It may be added that the same test is applicable now. They who do not receive the plain doctrines laid down in the word of God, whatever pretensions they may make to piety, or whatever zeal they may evince in the cause which they have espoused, can have no well-founded

claims to the name Christian. One of the clearest evidences of true piety is a readiness to receive all that God has taught. Comp. Matt. xviii. 1–3; Mark x. 15; James i. 19–21.

7. *Beloved, let us love one another.* This verse introduces a new topic, the consideration of which occupies the remainder of the chapter. See the Analysis. The subject is one on which John dwells more than on any other—that of love. His own character peculiarly inclined him to the exercise of love; and the remarkable affection which the Lord Jesus had shown for him, seems to have had the effect to give this grace a peculiar prominence in his views of what constituted true religion. Compare John xiii. 23. On the duty here enjoined, see Notes on John xiii. 34, 35, and 1 John iii. 11, 23. ¶ *For love is of God.* (1.) All true love has its origin in God. (2.) Real love shows that we have his Spirit, and that we belong to him. (3.) It assimilates us to God, or makes us more and more like him. What is here said by the apostle is based on the truth of what he elsewhere affirms, (ver. 8,) that God is love. Hatred, envy, wrath, malice, all have their source in something else than God. He neither originates them, commends them, nor approves them. ¶ *And every one that loveth, is born of God.* Is a regenerated man. That is, every one who has true love to Christians as such, or true brotherly love, is a true Christian. This cannot mean that every one that loves his wife and children, his classmate, his partner in business, or his friend—his house, or his farms, or his horses, or his hounds, is a child of God; it must be understood as referring to the point under discussion. A man may have a great deal of natural affection towards his kindred; a great deal of benevolence in his character towards the poor and needy, and still he may have none of the love to which John refers. He may have no real love to God, to the Saviour, or to the children of God as such; and it would be absurd for such a one to argue because he loves his wife and children

8 He that loveth not, knoweth not God ; for God is love. [a]

9 In this [b] was manifested the love of God toward us, because that God sent his only begotten Son

into the world, that [c] we might live through him.

10 Herein is love, not that we loved God, but that he loved us, and sent his Son to be the propitiation [d] for our sins.

[a] ver.16; 2Co.13.11.　[b] Jn.3.16.　[c] Jn.6.51.　[d] 1Jn.2.2.

---

that *therefore* he loves God, or is born again.

8. *He that loveth not, knoweth not God.* Has no true acquaintance with God ; has no just views of him, and no right feelings towards him. The reason for this is implied in what is immediately stated, that ' God is love,' and of course if they have no love reigning in their hearts, they cannot pretend to be like him. ¶ *For God is love.* He is not merely benevolent, he is benevolence itself. Compare Notes, 2 Cor. xiii. 11. Never was a more important declaration made than this ; never was more meaning crowded into a few words than in this short sentence—*God is love.* In the darkness of this world of sin—in all the sorrows that come now upon the race, and that will come upon the wicked hereafter—we have the assurance that a God of infinite benevolence rules over all ; and though we may not be able to reconcile all that occurs with this declaration, or see how the things which he has permitted to take place are consistent with it, yet in the exercise of faith on his own declarations we may find consolation in *believing* that it is so, and may look forward to a period when all his universe shall *see* it to be so. In the midst of all that occurs on the earth of sadness, sin, and sorrow, there are abundant evidences that God is love. In the original structure of things before sin entered, when all was pronounced ' good ;' in the things designed to promote happiness, where the only thing contemplated is happiness, and where it would have been as easy to have caused pain ; in the preservation of a guilty race, and in granting that race the opportunity of another trial ; in the ceaseless provision which God is making in his providence for the wants of unnumbered millions of his creatures ; in the arrangements made to alleviate sorrow, and to put an end to it ; in the gift of a Saviour more than all, and in the

offer of eternal life on terms simple and easy to be complied with—in all these things, which are the *mere* expressions of love, not *one* of which would have been found under the government of a malignant being, we see illustrations of the sublime and glorious sentiment before us, that ' God is love.' Even in this world of confusion, disorder, and darkness, we have evidence sufficient to prove that he is benevolent, but the full glory and meaning of that truth will be seen only in heaven. Meantime let us hold on to the truth that he is love. Let us believe that he sincerely desires our good, and that what seems dark to us may be designed for our welfare ; and amidst all the sorrows and disappointments of the present life, let us feel that our interests and our destiny are in the hands of the God of love.

9. *In this was manifested the love of God.* That is, in an eminent manner, or this was a most signal proof of it. The apostle does not mean to say that it has been manifested in no other way, but that this was so prominent an instance of his love, that all the other manifestations of it seemed absorbed and lost in this. ¶ *Because that God sent his only begotten Son,* &c. See Notes on John iii. 16. ¶ *That we might live through him.* He died that we might have eternal life through the merits of his sacrifice. The *measure* of that love, then, which was manifested in the gift of a Saviour, is to be found, (1,) in the worth of the soul; (2,) in its exposure to eternal death ; (3,) in the greatness of the gift ; (4,) in the greatness of his sorrows for us ; and, (5,) in the immortal blessedness and joy to which he will raise us. Who can estimate all this ? All these things will magnify themselves as we draw near to eternity ; and *in* that eternity to which we go, whether saved or lost, we shall have an ever-expanding view of the wonderful love of God.

11 Beloved, if ^a God so loved us, we ought also to love one another.

12 No ^b man hath seen God at

a Mat.18.33; Jn.15.12,13.　　　*b* 1Ti.6.16.

any time. If we love one another, God dwelleth in us, and his love is perfected ^c in us.

c 1 Co.13.13.

10. *Herein is love.* In this great gift is the highest expression of love, as if it had done all that it can do. ¶ *Not that we loved God.* Not that we were in such a state that we might suppose he would make such a sacrifice for us, but just the opposite. If we had loved and obeyed him, we might have had reason to believe that he would be willing to show his love to us in a corresponding manner. But we were alienated from him. We had even no desire for his friendship and favour. In *this* state he showed the greatness of his love for us by giving his Son to die for his enemies. See Notes on Rom. v. 7, 8. ¶ *But that he loved us.* Not that he approved our character, but that he desired our welfare. He loved us not with the love of complacency, but with the love of benevolence. ¶ *And sent his Son to be the propitiation for our sins.* On the meaning of the word *propitiation*, see Notes on Rom. iii. 25. Comp. Notes, 1 John ii. 2.

11. *Beloved, if God so loved us, we ought also to love one another.* (1.) Because he is so much exalted above us, and if he has loved those who were so inferior and so unworthy, we ought to love those who are on a level with us ; (2,) because it is only in this way that we can show that we have his Spirit ; and, (3,) because it is the nature of love to seek the happiness of all. There are much stronger reasons why we should love one another than there were why God should love us; and unless we do this, we can have no evidence that we are his children.

12. *No man hath seen God at any time.* See Notes, John i. 18, where the same declaration occurs. The statement seems to be made here in order to introduce a remark to show in what way we may know that we have any true knowledge of God. The idea is, ‘ He has never indeed been seen by mortal eyes. We are not, then, to expect to become acquainted with what he is in that way. But there is a method by which we may be assured that we have

a true knowledge of him, and that is, by evidence that we love one another, and by the presence of his Spirit in our hearts. We cannot become acquainted with him by sight, but we may by love.’ ¶ *If we love one another, God dwelleth in us.* Though we cannot see him, yet there is a way by which we may be assured that he is near us, and that he even dwells in us. That way is by the exercise of love. Comp. Notes, John xiv. 23, 24. ¶ *And his love is perfected in us.* Is carried out to completion. That is, our love for each other is the proper exponent of love to him reigning in our hearts. The idea here is not that we are absolutely perfect, or even that our love is perfect, whatever may be true on those points, but that this love to others is the proper carrying out of our love towards him ; that is, without this our love to him would not have accomplished what it was adapted and designed to do. Unless it produced this effect, it would be defective or incomplete. Comp. ver. 17. The general sense is this : ‘ We claim to have the love of God in our hearts, or that we are influenced and controlled by love. But however high and exalted that may seem to be as exercised toward God, it would be defective; it would not exert a fair influence over us, unless it led us to love our Christian brethren. It would be like the love which we might profess to have for a father, if it did not lead us to love our brothers and sisters. True love will diffuse itself over all who come within its range, and will thus become complete and entire.’ This passage, therefore, cannot be adduced to demonstrate the doctrine of sinless perfection, or to prove that Christians are ever absolutely perfect in this life. It proves only that love to God is not complete, or fully developed, unless it leads those who profess to have it to love each other. See Notes on Job i. 1. On the meaning of the Greek word here used, (τελειόω,) see Notes on Phil. iii. 12. Comp. Notes, Heb. ii. 10.

13. *Hereby know we that we dwell in*

13 Hereby *a* know we that we dwell in him, and he in us, because he hath given us of his Spirit.

14 And we have seen, and do testify, that the Father sent the Son *to be* the Saviour of the world.

15 Whosoever *b* shall confess that

a Jn.14.20; 1Jn.3.24.

Jesus is the Son of God, God dwelleth in him, and he in God.

16 And we have known and believed the love that God hath to us. God *e* is love ; and he that dwelleth in love dwelleth in God, and God in him.

b Ro.10.9.   *c* ver.8.

him. Here is another, or an additional evidence of it. ¶ *Because he hath given us of his Spirit.* He has imparted the influences of that Spirit to our souls, producing 'love, joy, peace, long-suffering, gentleness, goodness, faith,' &c., Gal. v. 22, 23. It was one of the promises which the Lord Jesus made to his disciples that he would send the Holy Spirit to be with them after he should be withdrawn from them, (John xiv. 16, 17, 26; xv. 26; xvi. 7,) and one of the clearest evidences which we can have that we are the children of God, is derived from the influences of that Spirit on our hearts. See this sentiment illustrated in the Notes on Rom. viii. 16.

14. *And we have seen.* Notes on chap. i. 1. ¶ *And do testify.* Notes on chap. i. 3. That is, we who are apostles bear witness to you of this great truth, that God has sent his Son to be a Saviour. Comp. Notes, John xx. 31. The reason why this is referred to here is not quite apparent, but the train of thought in this passage would seem to be this : The writer is discoursing of the love of God, and of its manifestation in the gift of the Saviour, and of the proper influence which it should have on us. Struck with the greatness and importance of the subject, his mind adverts to the *evidence* on which what he was saying rested—the evidence that the Father had *really* thus manifested his love. That evidence he repeats, that he had actually *seen* him who had been sent, and had the clearest demonstration that what he deemed so important had really occurred.

15. *Whosoever shall confess that Jesus is the Son of God.* In the true sense, and from the heart. This will *always* prove that a man is a Christian. But the passage cannot mean that if he merely says so in words, or if he does it insincerely, or without any proper

sense of the truth, it will prove that he is a Christian. On the meaning of the sentiment here expressed, see Notes on ver. 2. Comp. Notes, Rom. x. 10.

16. *And we have known and believed,* &c. We all have assurance that God has loved us, and the fullest belief in the great fact of redemption by which he has manifested his love to us. ¶ *God is love.* Notes on ver. 8. It is not uncommon for John to repeat an important truth. He delights to dwell on such a truth as that which is here expressed ; and who should not ? What truth is there on which the mind can dwell with more pleasure ; what is there that is better fitted to win the heart to holiness ; what that will do more to sustain the soul in the sorrows and trials of this life ? In our trials ; in the darkness which is around us; in the perplexities which meet and embarrass us in regard to the Divine administration ; in all that seems to us incomprehensible in this world, and in the prospect of the next, let us learn to repeat this declaration of the favoured disciple, ' *God is love.*' What trials may we not bear, if we feel assured of that ! What dark cloud that seems to hang over our way, and to involve all things in gloom, will not be bright, if from the depths of our souls we can always say, ' *God is love !* ' ¶ *And he that dwelleth in love,* &c. Religion is all love. God is love ; he has loved us ; we are to love him ; we are to love one another ; we are to love the whole world. Heaven is filled with love, and there is nothing else there. The earth is filled with love just as far as religion prevails, and would be entirely if it should prevail everywhere. Love would remove all the corrupt passions, the crimes, the jealousies, the wars on the earth, and would diffuse around the globe the bliss of heaven. If a man, therefore, is actuated by this, he has

17 Herein is [1] our love made perfect, that we may have boldness in the day of judgment: because as he is, so are we in this world.

18 There is no fear in love; but perfect love casteth out fear; because fear hath torment. He that feareth, is not made perfect in love.

19 We love him, because he [a] first loved us.

1 *love with us.*

a Jn.15.16.

---

the spirit of the heavenly world reigning in his soul, and lives in an atmosphere of love.

17. *Herein is our love made perfect.* Marg., *love with us.* The margin accords with the Greek—μεθ' ἡμῶν. The meaning is, ' the love that is within us, or in us, is made perfect.' The expression is unusual; but the general idea is, that *love* is rendered complete or entire in the manner in which the apostle specifies. In this way love becomes what it should be, and will prepare us to appear with confidence before the judgment-seat. Comp. Notes on ver. 12. ¶ *That we may have boldness in the day of judgment.* By the influence of love in delivering us from the fear of the wrath to come, ver. 18. The idea is, that he who has true love to God will have nothing to fear in the day of judgment, and may even approach the awful tribunal where he is to receive the sentence which shall determine his everlasting destiny without alarm. ¶ *Because as he is, so are we in this world.* That is, we have the same traits of character which the Saviour had, and, resembling him, we need not be alarmed at the prospect of meeting him.

18. *There is no fear in love.* Love is not an affection which produces fear. In the love which we have for a parent, a child, a friend, there is no fear. If a man had perfect love to God, he would have no fear of anything—for what would he have to dread? He would have no fear of death, for he would have nothing to dread beyond the grave. It is guilt that makes men fear what is to come ; but he whose sins are pardoned, and whose heart is filled with the love of God, has nothing to dread in this world or the world to come. The angels in heaven, who have always loved God and one another, have no fear, for they have nothing to dread in the future; the redeemed in heaven, rescued from all danger, and filled with the love of God, have nothing to dread; and as far as

that same loves operates on earth, it delivers the soul now from all apprehension of what is to come. ¶ *But perfect love casteth out fear.* That is, love that is complete, or that is allowed to exert its proper influence on the soul. As far as it exists, its tendency is to deliver the mind from alarms. If it should exist in any soul in an absolutely perfect state, that soul would be entirely free from all dread in regard to the future. ¶ *Because fear hath torment.* It is a painful and distressing emotion. Thus men suffer from the fear of poverty, of losses, of bereavement, of sickness, of death, and of future woe. From all these distressing apprehensions, that love of God which furnishes an evidence of true piety delivers us. ¶ *He that feareth, is not made perfect in love.* He about whose mind there lingers the apprehension of future wrath, shows that love in his soul has not accomplished its full work. Perhaps it never will on any soul until we reach the heavenly world, though there are many minds so full of love to God, as to be prevailingly delivered from fear.

19. *We love him, because he first loved us.* This passage is susceptible of two explanations ; either (1) that the fact that he first loved us is the *ground* or *reason* why we love him, or (2) that as a matter of fact we have been brought to love him in consequence of the love which he has manifested towards us, though the real ground of our love may be the excellency of his own character. If the former be the meaning, and if that were the *only* ground of love, then it would be mere selfishness, (comp. Matt. v. 46, 47;) and it cannot be believed that John meant to teach that that is the *only* reason of our love to God. It is true, indeed, that that is *a* proper ground of love, or that we are bound to love God in proportion to the benefits which we have received from his hand; but still genuine love to God is something which cannot be explained by

20 If a man say, I love God, and
hateth his brother, he is a liar : for
he that loveth not his brother whom
he hath seen, how *can he love
God whom he hath not seen?
21 And this commandment have
we from him, That *he who loveth
God love his brother also.

CHAPTER V.

WHOSOEVER *believeth that
Jesus is the Christ, is born
of God : and every one that loveth
him that begat, loveth him also
that is begotten of him.

a 1Jn.3.17.　　*b* Jn.13.34.　　*c* Jn.1.12,13.

the mere fact that we have received
favours from him. The true, the original ground of love to God, is *the excellence of his own character,* apart from
the question whether we are to be benefited or not. There is that in the Divine
nature which a holy being will love,
apart from the benefits which he is to
receive, and from any thought even of
his own destiny. It seems to me, therefore, that John must have meant here,
in accordance with the second interpretation suggested above, that *the fact
that we love God is to be traced to the
means which he has used to bring us to
himself, but without saying that this
is the sole or even the main *reason* why
we love him. It was his love manifested
to us by sending his Son to redeem us
which will explain *the fact* that we now
love him; but still the real ground or
reason why we love him is the infinite
excellence of his own character. It
should be added here, that many suppose
that the Greek words rendered ' we
love ' (ἡμεῖς ἀγαπῶμεν) are not in the
indicative, but in the subjunctive; and
that this is an exhortation—' let us love
him, because he first loved us.' So the
Syriac, the Arabic, and the Vulgate
read it; and so it is understood by Benson, Grotius, and Bloomfield. The main
idea would not be essentially different;
and it is a proper ground of exhortation
to love God because he has loved us,
though the highest ground is, because
his character is infinitely worthy of love.
　20. *If a man say, I love God, and
hateth his brother.* His Christian
brother ; or, in a larger sense, any man.
The sense is, that no man, whatever
may be his professions and pretensions,
can have any true love to God, unless
he love his brethren. ¶ *He is a liar.*
Comp. Notes, chap. i. 6. It is not
necessary, in order to a proper interpretation of this passage, to suppose that

he *intentionally* deceives. The sense is,
that this must be a false profession.
¶ *For he that loveth not his brother whom
he hath seen, &c.* It is more reasonable
to expect that we should love one whom
we have seen and known personally,
than that we should love one whom we
have not seen. The apostle is arguing
from human nature as it is, and every
one feels that we are more likely to love
one with whom we are familiar than one
who is a stranger. If a professed Christian, therefore, does not love one whom
he sees and knows, how can he love that God
whose image he bears, whom he has not
seen? Comp. Notes on chap. iii. 17.
　21. *And this commandment have we
from him.* That is, the command to
love a brother is as obligatory as that
to love God. If one is obeyed, the other
ought to be also ; if a man feels that one
is binding on him, he should feel that
the other is also ; and he can never have
evidence that he is a true Christian,
unless he manifests love to his brethren
as well as love to God. See Notes on
James ii. 10. ¶ *That he who loveth God
love his brother also.* See Notes, John
xiii. 34, 35. Comp. John xv. 12, 17.

CHAPTER V.

ANALYSIS OF THE CHAPTER.

THIS chapter embraces the following
subjects : I. A continuance of the discussion about *love,* vers. 1—3. These
verses should have been attached to the
previous chapter. II. The victory which
is achieved over the world by those who
are born of God. The grand instrumentality by which this is done, is by the
belief that Jesus is the Son of God, vers.
4, 5. III. The evidence that Jesus *is*
the Son of God ; or the means by which
that truth is so believed as to secure a
victory over the world, vers. 6—12. In
this part of the chapter the apostle goes

2 By this we know that we love the children of God, when we love God, and keep his commandments.

fully into the nature of this evidence, or the ways in which the Christian becomes so thoroughly convinced of it as to give to faith this power. He refers to these sources of evidence : (a) The witness of the Spirit, ver. 6. (b) The record borne in heaven, ver. 7—if that verse be genuine. (c) The evidence borne on earth, by the Spirit, the water, and the blood —all bearing witness to that one truth. (d) The credit which is due to the testimony of God, or which the soul pays to it, ver. 8. (e) The fact that he who believes on the Son of God has the witness in himself, ver. 10. (f) The amount of the record, that God has given to us eternal life through his Son, vers. 11, 12. IV. The reason why all this was written by the apostle, ver. 13. It was that they might know that they had eternal life, and might believe on the name of the Saviour. V. The effect of this in leading us to the throne of grace, with the assurance that God will hear us, and will grant our requests, vers. 14, 15. VI. The power of prayer, and the duty of praying for those who have sinned. The encouragement to this is, that there are many sins which are not unto death, and that we may hope that God will be merciful to those who have not committed the unpardonable offence, vers. 16, 17. VII. A summary of all that the apostle had said to them, or of the points of which they were sure in the matter of salvation, vers. 18–20. They knew that those who are born of God do not sin ; that the wicked one cannot permanently injure them ; that they were of God, while all the world lay in wickedness ; that the Son of God had come, and that they were truly united to that Saviour who is the true God, and who is eternal life. VIII. An exhortation to keep themselves from all idolatry, ver. 21.

1. *Whosoever believeth that Jesus is the Christ.* Is the Messiah ; the anointed of God. On the meaning of the word *Christ*, see Notes on Matt. i. 1. Of course it is meant here that the proposition, that ' Jesus is the Christ,' should be believed or received in the true and proper sense, in order to fur-

nish evidence that any one is born of God. Comp. Notes on chap. iv. 3. It cannot be supposed that a mere intellectual acknowledgment of the proposition that Jesus is the Messiah is all that is meant, for that is not the proper meaning of the word *believe* in the Scriptures. That word, in its just sense, implies that the truth which is believed should make its fair and legitimate impression on the mind, or that we should feel and act *as if* it were true. See Notes, Mark xvi. 16. If, in the proper sense of the phrase, a man does believe that Jesus *is* the *Christ*, receiving him as he is revealed as the Anointed of God, and a Saviour, it is undoubtedly true that that constitutes him a Christian, for that is what is required of a man in order that he may be saved. See Notes, Acts viii. 37. ¶ *Is born of God.* Or rather, ' is begotten of God.' See Notes, John iii. 3 ¶ *And every one that loveth him that begat.* That loves that God who has thus begotten those whom he has received as his children, and to whom he sustains the endearing relation of Father. ¶ *Loveth him also that is begotten of him.* That is, he will love all the true children of God ; all Christians. See Notes on chap. iv. 20. The general idea is, that as all Christians are the children of the same Father ; as they constitute one family ; as they all bear the same image ; as they share his favour alike ; as they are under the same obligation of gratitude to him, and are bound to promote the same common cause, and are to dwell together in the same home for ever, they should therefore love one another. As all the children in a family love their common father, so it should be in the great family of which God is the Head.

2. *By this we know that we love the children of God, &c.* This is repeating the same truth in another form. ' As it is universally true that if we love him who has begotten us, we shall also love his children, or our Christian brethren, so it is true also that if we love his children it will follow that we love him.' In other places, the apostle

3 For this is the love of God, that ^a we keep his commandments: and his commandments are not ^b grievous.

a Jn.14.15,21.　　　b Ps.119.45; Mat.11.30.

4 For whatsoever is born of God overcometh ^c the world : and this is the victory that overcometh the world, *even* our faith.

c 1Co.15.57.

says that we may know that we love God if we love those who bear his image, chap. iii. 14. He here says, that there is another way of determining what we are. We may have undoubted evidence that we love *God*, and from that, as the basis of an argument, we may infer that we have true love to his children. Of the fact that we may have evidence that we love God, apart from that which we derive from our love to his children, there can be no doubt. We may be conscious of it; we may find pleasure in meditating on his perfections ; we may feel sure that we are moved to obey him by true attachment to him, as a child may in reference to a father. But, it may be asked, how can it be inferred from this that we truly love his children? Is it not more easy to ascertain this of itself than it is to determine whether we love God? Comp. chap. iv. 20. To this it may be answered, that we may love Christians from many motives : we may love them as personal friends ; we may love them because they belong to our church, or sect, or party; we may love them because they are naturally amiable : but the apostle says here, that when we are conscious that an attachment *does* exist towards Christians, we may ascertain that it is genuine, or that it does not proceed from any improper motive, by the fact that we love God. We shall then love him *as* his children, whatever *other* grounds of affection there may be towards them. ¶ *And keep his commandments*. See Notes, John xiv. 15.

3. *For this is the love of God, that we keep his commandments*. This constitutes true love ; this furnishes the evidence of it. ¶ *And his commandments are not grievous*. Greek, *heavy*— βαρεῖαι ; that is, difficult to be borne as a burden. See Matt. xi. 30. The meaning is, that his laws are not unreasonable ; the duties which he requires are not beyond our ability ; his government is not oppressive. It is

easy to obey God when the heart is right ; and those who endeavour in sincerity to keep his commandments do not complain that they are hard. All complaints of this kind come from those who are not disposed to keep his commandments. *They*, indeed, object that his laws are unreasonable ; that they impose improper restraints ; that they are not easily complied with ; and that the Divine government is one of severity and injustice. But no such complaints come from true Christians. They find *his* service easier than the service of sin, and the laws of God more mild and easy to be complied with than were those of fashion and honour, which they once endeavoured to obey. The service of God is freedom ; the service of the world is bondage. No man ever yet heard a true Christian say that the laws of God, requiring him to lead a holy life, were stern and 'grievous.' But who has not felt this in regard to the inexorable laws of sin ? What votary of the world would not say this if he spoke his real sentiments ? Comp. Notes, John viii. 32.

4. *For whatsoever is born of God overcometh the world*. The world, in its maxims, and precepts, and customs, does not rule him, but he is a freeman. The idea is, that there is a conflict between religion and the world, and that in the heart of every true Christian religion secures the victory, or triumphs. In John xvi. 33, the Saviour says, ' Be of good cheer ; I have overcome the world.' See Notes on that verse. He obtained a complete triumph over him ' who rules the darkness of the world,' and laid the foundation for a victory by his people over all vice, error, and sin. John makes this affirmation of *all* who are born of God. ' *Whatsoever*,' or, as the Greek is, ' Everything which is begotten of God,' (πᾶν τὸ γεγεννημένον ;) meaning to affirm, undoubtedly, that *in every instance* where one is truly regenerated, there is this victory over the world. See Notes, James iv. 4 ; 1 John

5 Who is he that overcometh the world, but he that believeth that Jesus is the Son of God?

6 This is he that came *a* by water and blood, *even* Jesus Christ; not

a Jn.19.34.

ii. 15, 16. It is one of the settled maxims of religion, that every man who is a true Christian gains a victory over the world; and consequently a maxim *as* settled, that where the spirit of the world reigns supremely in the heart, there is no true religion. But, if this be a true principle, how many professed Christians are there who are strangers to all claims of piety—for how many are there who are wholly governed by the spirit of this world! ¶ *And this is the victory.* This is the source or means of the victory which is thus achieved. ¶ Even *our faith.* Faith in the Lord Jesus Christ, ver. 5. He overcame the world, (John xvi. 33,) and it is by that faith which makes us one with him, and that imbues us with his Spirit, that we are able to do it also.

5. *Who is he, &c.* Where is there one who can pretend to have obtained a victory over the world, except he who believes in the Saviour? All else are worldly, and are governed by worldly aims and principles. It is true that a man may gain a victory over *one* worldly passion; he may subdue some one evil propensity; he may abandon the gay circle, may break away from habits of profaneness, may leave the company of the unprincipled and polluted; but still, unless he has faith in the Son of God, the spirit of the world will reign supreme in his soul in some form. The appeal which John so confidently made in his time may be as confidently made now. *We* may ask, as *he* did, where is there one who shows that he has obtained a complete victory over the world, except the true Christian? Where is there one whose end and aim is not the present life? Where is there one who shows that all his purposes in regard to this world are made subordinate to the world to come? There are those now, as there were then, who break away from one form of sin, and from one circle of sinful companions; there are those who change the ardent passions of youth for the soberness of middle or advanced life;

there are those who see the folly of profaneness, and of gaiety, and intemperance; there are those who are disappointed in some scheme of ambition, and who withdraw from political conflicts; there are those who are satiated with pageantry, and who, oppressed with the cares of state, as Diocletian and Charles V. were, retire from public life; and there are those whose hearts are crushed and broken by losses, and by the death, or what is worse than death, by the ingratitude of their children, and who cease to cherish the fond hope that their family will be honoured, and their name perpetuated in those whom they tenderly loved—but still there is no victory over the world. Their deep dejection, their sadness, their brokenness of spirit, their lamentations, and their want of cheerfulness, all show that the spirit of the world still reigns in their hearts. If the calamities which have come upon them could be withdrawn; if the days of prosperity could be restored, they would show as much of the spirit of the world as ever they did, and would pursue its follies and its vanities as greedily as they had done before. Not many years or months elapse before the worldly mother who has followed one daughter to the grave, will introduce another into the gay world with all the brilliancy which fashion prescribes; not long will a worldly father mourn over the death of a son before, in the whirl of business and the exciting scenes of ambition, he will show that his heart is as much wedded to the world as it ever was. If such sorrows and disappointments conduct to the Saviour, as they sometimes do; if they lead the troubled mind to seek peace in his blood, and support in the hope of heaven, then a real victory is obtained over the world; and then, when the hand of affliction is withdrawn, it is seen that there has been a work of grace in the soul that has effectually changed all its feelings, and secured a triumph that shall be eternal.

6. *This is he.* This Son of God re-

by water only, but by water and blood. And it is the Spirit *a* that

a Jn.14.17.

beareth witness, because the Spirit is truth.

ferred to in the previous verse. The object of the apostle in this verse, in connection with verse 8, is to state the nature of the evidence that Jesus is the Son of God. He refers to three well-known things on which he probably had insisted much in his preaching—the water, and the blood, and the Spirit. These, he says, furnished evidence on the very point which he was illustrating, by showing that that Jesus on whom they believed was the Son of God. 'This,' says he, ' is the same one, the very person, to whom the well-known and important testimony is borne; to him, and him alone, these undisputed things appertain, and not to any other who should claim to be the Messiah ; and they all agree on the same one point,' ver. 8. ¶ *That came.* ὁ ἰλθὼν. This does not mean that when he came into the world he was accompanied in some way by water and blood; but the idea is, that the water and the blood were clearly manifest during his appearing on earth, or that they were remarkable testimonials in some way to his character and work. An ambassador might be said to *come* with credentials; a warrior might be said to *come* with the spoils of victory; a prince might be said to *come* with the insignia of royalty ; a prophet *comes* with signs and wonders; and the Lord Jesus might also be said to have come with power to raise the dead, and to heal disease, and to cast out devils; but John here fixes the attention on a fact so impressive and remarkable in his view as to be worthy of special remark, that he *came* by water and blood. ¶ *By water.* There have been many opinions in regard to the meaning of this phrase. See Pool's Synopsis. Compare also Lücke, *in loc.* A mere reference to some of these opinions may aid in ascertaining the true interpretation. (1.) Clement of Alexandria supposes that by *water* regeneration and faith were denoted, and by *blood* the public acknowledgment of that. (2.) Some, and among them Wetstein, have held that the words are used to denote the fact

that the Lord Jesus was truly a man, in contradistinction from the doctrine of the *Docetæ;* and that the apostle means to say that he had all the properties of a human being—a spirit, or soul, blood, and the watery humours of the body. (3.) Grotius supposes that by his coming 'by water,' there is reference to his pure life, as water is the emblem of purity; and he refers to Ezek. xxxvi. 25 ; Isa. i. 16 ; Jer. iv. 14. As a sign of that purity, he says that John baptized him, John i. 28. A sufficient objection to this view is, that as in the corresponding word *blood* there is undoubted reference to blood literally, it cannot be supposed that the word *water* in the same connection would be used figuratively. Moreover, as Lücke (p. 287) has remarked, water, though a *symbol* of purity, is never used to denote *purity itself,* and therefore cannot here refer to the pure life of Jesus. (4.) Many expositors suppose that the reference is to the baptism of Jesus, and that by his 'coming by water and blood,' as by the latter there is undoubted reference to his death, so by the former there is reference to his baptism, or to his entrance on his public work. Of this opinion were Tertullian, Œcumenius, Theophylact, among the fathers, and Capellus, Heumann, Stroth, Lange, Ziegler, A. Clarke, Bengel, Rosenmüller, Macknight, and others, among the moderns. A leading argument for this opinion, as alleged, has been that it was then that the Spirit bare witness to him, (Matt. iii. 16,) and that this is what John here refers to when he says, ' It is the Spirit that beareth witness,' &c. To this view, Lücke urges substantially the following objections : (*a*) That if it refers to baptism, the phrase would much more appropriately express the fact that Jesus came baptizing others, if that were so, than that he was baptized himself. The phrase would be strictly applicable to John the Baptist, who came baptizing, and whose ministry was distinguished for that, (Matt. iii. 1 ;) and if Jesus had baptized in the same manner, or if this had been a prominent characteristic of his ministry, it would be applicable to him. Comp. John iv. 2. But if it means that he was *baptized*, and that he came in that way 'by water,' it was equally true of all the apostles who were baptized, and of all others, and there was nothing *so* remarkable in the fact that he was baptized as to justify the prominence given to the phrase in this place. (*b*) If reference be had here, as is supposed in this view of the passage, to the 'witness' that was borne to the Lord Jesus on the occasion of his baptism, then the reference should have been not to the '*water*' as the witness, but to the 'voice that came from heaven,' (Matt. iii. 17,) for it was that which was the witness in the case. Though this occurred at the *time* of the baptism, yet it was quite an independent thing, and was important enough to have been referred to. See Lücke, *Com. in loc.* These objections, however, are not insuperable. Though Jesus did not come baptizing others himself, (John iv. 2,) and though the phrase would have expressed that if he had, yet, as Christian baptism began with him; as this was the first act in his entrance on public life; as it was by this that he was set apart to his work; and as he designed that this should be always the initiatory rite of his religion, there was no impropriety in saying that his 'coming,' or his advent in this world, was at the beginning characterized by water, and at the close by blood. Moreover, though the 'witness' at his baptism was really borne by a voice from heaven, yet his baptism was the prominent thing; and if we take the baptism to denote *all* that in fact occurred when he was baptized, all the objections made by Lücke here vanish. (5.) Some, by the 'water' here, have understood the ordinance of baptism as it is appointed by the Saviour to be administered to his people, meaning that the ordinance was instituted by him. So Beza, Calvin, Piscator, Calovius, Wolf, Beausobre, Knapp, Lücke, and others understand it. According to this the meaning would be, that he appointed baptism by water as a symbol of the cleansing of the heart, and shed his blood to effect the ransom of man, and that thus it might be said that he 'came

by water and blood;' to wit, by these two things as effecting the salvation of men. But it seems improbable that the apostle should have grouped these things together in this way. For (*a*) the 'blood' is that which he shed; which pertained to him personally; which he poured out for the redemption of man ; and it is clear that, whatever is meant by the phrase '*he came*,' his coming by 'water' is to be understood in some sense similar to his coming by 'blood ;' and it seems incredible that the apostle should have joined a mere *ordinance* of religion in this way with the shedding of his blood, and placed them in this manner on an equality. (*b*) It cannot be supposed that John meant to attach so much importance to baptism as would be implied by this. The shedding of his blood was essential to the redemption of men ; can it be supposed that the apostle meant to teach that baptism by water is equally necessary ? (*c*) If this be understood of baptism, there is no natural connection between that and the 'blood' referred to ; nothing by which the one would suggest the other ; no reason why they should be united. If he had said that he 'came' by the appointment of two ordinances for the edification of the church, 'baptism and *the supper*,' however singular such a statement might be in some respects, yet there would be a connection, a reason why they should be suggested together. But why should baptism and the blood shed by the Saviour on the cross be grouped together as designating the principal things which characterized his coming into the world? (6.) There remains, then, but one other interpretation ; to wit, that he refers to the 'water and the blood' which flowed from the side of the Saviour when he was pierced by the spear of the Roman soldier. John had himself laid great stress on this occurrence, and on the fact that he had himself witnessed it, (see Notes on John xix. 34, 35;) and as, in these epistles, he is accustomed to allude to more full statements made in his Gospel, it would seem most natural to refer the phrase to that event as furnishing a clear and undoubted proof of the death of the Saviour. This would be the obvious interpretation, and would be

7 For there are three that bear record in heaven, the Father, ^athe

Word, ^band the Holy Ghost: ^cand these three are one.

entirely clear, if John did not immediately speak of the 'water' and the 'blood' as *separate* witnesses, each as bearing witness to an important point, *as* separate as the 'Spirit' and the 'water,' or the 'Spirit' and the 'blood;' whereas, if he refers to the mingled water and blood flowing from his side, they both witness only the same fact, to wit, his death. There was no *special* significancy in the water, no distinct testifying to anything different from the flowing of the blood; but together they bore witness to the *one* fact that he actually died. But here he seems to suppose that there is some special significancy in each. ' Not by water *only*, but by water *and* blood.' ' There are *three* that bear witness, the Spirit, *and* the water, *and* the blood, and these three agree in one.' These considerations seem to me to make it probable, on the whole, that the fourth opinion, above referred to, and that which has been commonly held in the Christian church, is correct, and that by the 'water' the *baptism* of the Saviour is intended; his baptism as an emblem of his own purity; as significant of the nature of his religion; as a rite which was to be observed in his church at all times. That furnished an important attestation to the fact that he was the Messiah, (comp. Notes on Matt. iii. 15,) for it was by that that he entered on his public work, and it was then that a remarkable testimony was borne to his being the Son of God. He himself ' *came* ' thus by water as an emblem of purity ; and the water used in his church in all ages in baptism, together with the ' blood' and the ' Spirit,' bears public testimony to the pure nature of his religion. It is *possible* that the mention of the ' water' in his baptism suggested to John also the water which flowed from the side of the Saviour at his death, intermingled with blood ; and that though the primary thought in his mind was the fact that Jesus was baptized, and that an important attestation was then given to his Messiahship, yet he *may* have instantly adverted to the fact that *water* per-

formed so important a part, and was so important a symbol through all his work; water at his introduction to his work, as an ordinance in his church, as symbolical of the nature of his religion, and even at his death, as a public attestation, in connection with flowing blood, to the fact that he truly *died*, in reality, and not, as the *Docetæ* pretended, in appearance only, thus completing the work of the Messiah, and making an atonement for the sins of the world. Comp. Notes, John xix. 34, 35. ¶ *And blood.* Referring, doubtless, to the shedding of his blood on the cross. He ' *came* ' by that ; that is, he was manifested by that to men, or that was one of the forms in which he appeared to men, or by which his coming into the world was characterized. The apostle means to say that the blood shed at his death furnished an important evidence or ' witness ' of what he was. In what way this was done, see Notes on ver. 8. ¶ *Not by water only, but by water and blood.* John the Baptist came ' by water only;' that is, he came to baptize the people, and to prepare them for the coming of the Messiah. Jesus was distinguished from him in the fact that his ministry was characterized by the shedding of blood, or the shedding of his blood constituted one of the peculiarities of his work. ¶ *And it is the Spirit.* Evidently the Holy Spirit. ¶ *That beareth witness.* That is, he is the *great* witness in the matter, confirming all others. He bears witness to the soul that Jesus came ' by water and blood,' for that would not be received by us without his agency. In what way he does this, see Notes on ver. 8. ¶ *Because the Spirit is truth.* Is so eminently *true* that he may be called *truth itself*, as God is so eminently benevolent that he may be called *love itself.* See Notes on chap. iv. 8.

7. *For there are three that bear record in heaven, &c.* There are three that *witness*, or that *bear witness*—the same Greek word which, in ver. 8, is rendered *bear witness*—μαρτυροῦντες. There is no passage of the New Testa-

ment which has given rise to so much discussion in regard to its genuineness as this. The supposed importance of the verse in its bearing on the doctrine of the Trinity has contributed to this, and has given to the discussion a degree of consequence which has pertained to the examination of the genuineness of no other passage of the New Testament. On the one hand, the clear testimony which it seems to bear to the doctrine of the Trinity, has made that portion of the Christian church which holds the doctrine reluctant in the highest degree to abandon it; and on the other hand, the same clearness of the testimony to that doctrine, has made those who deny it not less reluctant to admit the genuineness of the passage. It is not consistent with the design of these Notes to go into a full investigation of a question of this sort. And all that can be done is to state, in a brief way, the *results* which have been reached, in an examination of the question. Those who are disposed to pursue the investigation further, can find all that is to be said in the works referred to at the bottom of the page.* The portion of the passage, in vers. 7. 8, whose genuineness is disputed, is included in brackets in the following quotation, as it stands in the common editions of the New Testament: ' For there are three that bear record [in heaven, the Father, the Word, and the Holy Ghost: and these three are one. And there are three that bear witness on earth,] the Spirit, and the water, and the blood; and these three agree in one.' If the disputed passage, therefore, be omitted as spurious, the whole passage will read, ' For there are three that bear record, the Spirit, and the water, and the blood; and these three agree in one.' The reasons which seem to me to prove that the passage included in brackets is spurious, and should not be regarded as a part of the inspired

writings, are briefly the following : I. It is wanting in all the earlier Greek manuscripts, for it is found in *no* Greek ms. written before the sixteenth century. Indeed, it is found in only two Greek manuscripts of any age—one the Codex Montfortianus, or Britannicus, written in the beginning of the sixteenth century, and the other the Codex Ravianus, which is a mere transcript of the text, taken partly from the third edition of Stephen's New Testament, and partly from the Complutensian Polyglott. But it is incredible that a genuine passage of the New Testament should be wanting in *all* the early Greek manuscripts. II. It is wanting in the earliest versions, and, indeed, in a large part of the versions of the New Testament which have been made in all former times. It is wanting in both the Syriac versions— one of which was made probably in the first century; in the Coptic, Armenian, Sclavonic, Ethiopic, and Arabic. III. It is never quoted by the Greek fathers in their controversies on the doctrine of the Trinity—a passage which would be so much in point, and which could not have failed to be quoted if it were genuine ; and it is not referred to by the Latin fathers until the time of Vigilius, at the end of the fifth century. If the passage were believed to be genuine—nay, if it were known at all to be in existence, and to have any probability in its favour—it is incredible that in all the controversies which occurred in regard to the Divine nature, and in all the efforts to define the doctrine of the Trinity, this passage should never have been referred to. But it never was; for it must be plain to any one who examines the subject with an unbiassed mind, that the passages which are relied on to prove that it was quoted by Athanasius, Cyprian, Augustin, &c., (Wetstein, II., p. 725,) are not taken from this place, and are not such as they would have made if they had been acquainted with this passage, and had designed to quote it. IV. The argument against the passage from the external proof is confirmed by internal evidence, which makes it morally certain that it cannot be genuine. (a) The connection does not demand it. It does not contribute to advance what the

---

* Mill. New Test., pp. 379-386; Wetstein, II. 721-727; Father Simon, Crit Hist. New Test.; Michaelis, Intro. New Test., iv. 412 seq.; Semler, Histor. und Krit. Sammlungen über die sogenannten Beweistellen der Dogmatik. Erstes Stuck über, 1 John v. 7; Griesbach, Diatribe in locum, 1 John v. 7, 8, second edit., New Test., vol. II., appendix 1; and Lucke's Commentary *in loc.*

apostle is saying, but breaks the thread of his argument entirely. He is speaking of certain things which bear 'witness' to the fact that Jesus is the Messiah; certain things which were well known to those to whom he was writing—the Spirit, and the water, and the blood. How does it contribute to strengthen the force of this to say that *in heaven* there are 'three that bear witness'—three not before referred to, and having no connection with the matter under consideration? (*b*) The *language* is not such as John would use. He does, indeed, elsewhere use the term *Logos*, or *Word*—ὁ Λόγος, (John i. 1, 14; 1 John i. 1,) but it is never in this form, 'The Father, and the Word;' that is, the terms '*Father*' and '*Word*' are never used by him, or by any of the other sacred writers, as correlative. The word *Son*—ὁ Υἱός—is the term which is correlative to the *Father* in every other place as used by John, as well as by the other sacred writers. See 1 John i. 3; ii. 22—24; iv. 14; 2 John iii. 9; and the Gospel of John, *passim*. Besides, the correlative of the term *Logos*, or *Word*, with John, is not *Father*, but *God*. See John i. 1. Comp. Rev. xix. 13. (*c*) Without this passage, the sense of the argument is clear and appropriate. There are three, says John, which bear witness that Jesus is the Messiah. These are referred to in ver. 6; and in immediate connection with this, in the argument, (ver. 8,) it is affirmed that their testimony goes to one point, and is harmonious. To say that there are *other* witnesses elsewhere, to say that they are one, contributes nothing to illustrate the nature of the testimony of these three—the water, and the blood, and the Spirit; and the internal sense of the passage, therefore, furnishes as little evidence of its genuineness as the external proof. V. It is easy to imagine how the passage found a place in the New Testament. It was at first written, perhaps, in the margin of some Latin manuscript, as expressing the belief of the writer of what was true in heaven, as well as on earth, and with no more intention to deceive than we have when we make a marginal note in a book. Some transcriber copied it **into** the body of the text, perhaps with

a sincere belief that it was a genuine passage, omitted by accident; and then it became too important a passage in the argument for the Trinity, ever to be displaced but by the most clear critical evidence. It was rendered into Greek, and inserted in one Greek manuscript of the 16th century, while it was wanting in all the earlier manuscripts. VI. The passage is now omitted in the best editions of the Greek Testament, and regarded as spurious by the ablest critics. See Griesbach and Hahn. On the whole, therefore, the evidence seems to me to be clear that this passage is not a genuine portion of the inspired writings, and should not be appealed to in proof of the doctrine of the Trinity. One or two remarks may be made, in addition, in regard to its use. (1.) Even on the supposition that it *is* genuine, as Bengel believed it was, and as he believed that some Greek manuscript *would* yet be found which would contain it;* yet it is not wise to adduce it as a proof-text. It would be much easier to prove the doctrine of the Trinity from other texts, than to demonstrate the genuineness of this. (2.) It is not *necessary* as a proof-text. The doctrine which it contains can be abundantly established from other parts of the New Testament, by passages about which there can be no doubt. (3.) The removal of this text does nothing to weaken the evidence for the doctrine of the Trinity, or to modify that doctrine. As it was never used to shape the early belief of the Christian world on the subject, so its rejection, and its removal from the New Testament, will do nothing to modify that doctrine. The doctrine was embraced, and held, and successfully defended without it, and it can and will be so still.

8. *And there are three that bear witness in earth.* This is a part of the text, which, if the reasoning above is correct, is to be omitted. The genuine passage reads, (ver. 7,) ' For there are three that bear record, [or witness—

---

* Et tamen etiam atque etiam sperare licet, si non autographum Joanneum, at alios vetustissimos codices Græcos, qui hanc periocham habeant, in occultis providentiæ divinæ forulis adhuc latentes suo tempore productum iri.

8 And there are three that bear witness in earth, the Spirit,^a and

a Jn.15.26; Ac.2.2-4; 2 Co.1.22.

the water,^b and the blood:^c and these three agree in one.

b 1Pe.3.21.   *c* He.13.12.

μαρτυροῦντις,] the Spirit, and the water, and the blood.' There is no reference to the fact that it is done '*in earth.*' The phrase was introduced to correspond with what was said in the interpolated passage, that there are three that bear record '*in heaven.*' ¶ *The Spirit.* Evidently the Holy Spirit. The assertion here is, that that Spirit bears witness to the fact that Jesus is the Son of God, ver. 5. The testimony of the Holy Ghost to this fact is contained in the following things: (1.) He did it at the baptism of Jesus. Notes, Matt. iii. 16, 17. (2.) Christ was eminently *endowed* with the influences of the Holy Spirit; as it was predicted that the Messiah would be, and as it was appropriate he should be, Isa. xi. 2; lxi. 1. Compare Luke iv. 18; Notes, John iii. 34. (3.) The Holy Spirit bore witness to his Messiahship, after his ascension, by descending, according to his promise, on his apostles, and by accompanying the message which they delivered with saving power to thousands in Jerusalem, Acts ii. (4.) He still bears the same testimony on every revival of religion, and in the conversion of every individual who becomes a Christian, convincing them that Jesus is the Son of God. Comp. John xvi. 14, 15. (5.) He does it in the hearts of all true Christians, for ' no man can say that Jesus is Lord but by the Holy Ghost,' 1 Cor. xii. 3. See Notes on that passage. The Spirit of God has thus always borne witness to the fact that Jesus is the Christ, and he will continue to do it to the end of time, convincing yet countless millions that he was sent from God to redeem and save lost men. ¶ *And the water.* See Notes, ver. 6. That is, the baptism of Jesus, and the scenes which occurred when he was baptized, furnished evidence that he was the Messiah. This was done in these ways: (1.) It was proper that the Messiah should be baptized when he entered on his work, and perhaps it was expected; and the fact that he was baptized showed that he had *in fact* entered on his work as

Redeemer. See Notes, Matt. iii. 15. (2.) An undoubted attestation was then furnished to the fact that he was 'the Son of God,' by the descent of the Holy Spirit in the form of a dove, and by the voice that addressed him from heaven, Matt. iii. 16, 17. (3.) His baptism with water was an emblem of the purity of his own character, and of the nature of his religion. (4.) Perhaps it may be implied here, also, that water used in baptism now bears witness to the same thing, (*a*,) as it is the ordinance appointed by the Saviour; (*b*) as it keeps up his religion in the world; (*c*) as it is a public symbol of the purity of his religion; (*d*) and as, in every case where it is administered, it is connected with the public expression of a belief that Jesus is the Son of God. ¶ *And the blood.* There is undoubted allusion here to the blood shed on the cross; and the meaning is, that that blood bore witness also to the fact that he was the Son of God. This it did in the following respects: (1.) The shedding of the blood showed that he was truly dead—that his work was complete—that he died in *reality*, and not in *appearance* only. See Notes, John xix. 34, 35. (2.) The remarkable circumstances that attended the shedding of this blood—the darkened sun, the earthquake, the rending of the veil of the temple—showed in a manner that convinced even the Roman centurion that he was the Son of God. See Notes, Matt. xxvii. 54. (3.) The fact that an *atonement* was thus made for sin was an important ' witness ' for the Saviour, showing that he had done that which the Son of God only could do, by disclosing a way by which the sinner may be pardoned, and the polluted soul be made pure. (4.) Perhaps, also, there *may* be here an allusion to the Lord's Supper, as designed to set forth the shedding of this blood; and the apostle may mean to have it implied that the representation of the shedding of the blood in this ordinance is intended to keep up the conviction that Jesus is the Son of God. If so, then the general

9 If we receive the witness of men, the witness of God is greater: for this is the witness of God, which he hath testified of his Son.

10 He that believeth on the Son of God hath the witness *a* in himself : he that believeth not God hath made him a liar ; because he believeth not the record that God gave of his Son.

a Ro.8.16.

sense is, that that blood—however set before the eyes and the hearts of men—on the cross, or by the representation of its shedding in the Lord's Supper—is a witness in the world to the truth that Jesus is the Son of God, and to the nature of his religion. Comp. Notes, 1 Cor. xi. 26. ¶ *And these three agree in one.* εἰς τὸ ἓν εἰσι. They agree in one thing; they bear on one and the same point, to wit, the fact that Jesus is the Son of God. All are appointed by God as witnesses of this fact ; and all harmonize in the testimony which is borne. The apostle does not say that there are no other witnesses to the same thing ; nor does he even say that these are the most important or decisive which have been furnished ; but he says that these *are* important witnesses, and are entirely harmonious in their testimony.

9. *If we receive the witness of men.* As we are accustomed to do, and as we must do, in courts of justice, and in the ordinary daily transactions of life. We are constantly acting on the belief that what others say is true ; that what the members of our families, and our neighbours say, is true ; that what is reported by travellers is true ; that what we read in books, and what is sworn to in courts of justice, is true. We could not get along a single day if we did not act on this belief ; nor are we accustomed to call it in question, unless we have reason to suspect that it is false. The mind is so made that it must credit the testimony borne by others; and if this should cease even for a single day, the affairs of the world would come to a pause. ¶ *The witness of God is greater.* Is more worthy of belief ; as God is more true, and wise, and good than men. Men may be deceived, and may undesignedly bear witness to that which is not true —God never can be ; men may, for sinister and base purposes, intend to deceive—God never can ; men may act from partial observation, from rumours unworthy of credence—God never can ;

men may desire to excite admiration by the marvellous—God never can ; men have deceived—God never has ; and though, from these causes, there are many instances where we are not certain that the testimony borne by men is true, yet we are always certain that that which is borne by God is not false. The only question on which the mind ever hesitates is, whether we actually *have* his testimony, or certainly *know* what he bears witness to ; when that is ascertained, the human mind is so made that it *cannot* believe that God would deliberately deceive a world. See Notes, Heb. vi. 18. Comp. Titus i. 2. ¶ *For this is the witness of God,* &c. The testimony above referred to—that borne by the Spirit, and the water, and the blood. Who that saw his baptism, and heard the voice from heaven, (Matt. iii. 16, 17,) could doubt that he was the Son of God ? Who that saw his death on the cross, and that witnessed the amazing scenes which occurred there, could fail to join with the Roman centurion in saying that this was the Son of God ? Who that has felt the influences of the Eternal Spirit on his heart, ever doubted that Jesus was the Son of God? Comp. Notes, 1 Cor. xii. 3. Any one of these is sufficient to convince the soul of this ; all combined bear on the same point, and confirm it from age to age.

10. *He that believeth on the Son of God hath the witness in himself.* The evidence that Jesus is the Son of God. Comp. Notes, Rom. viii. 16. This cannot refer to any distinct and immediate revelation of that fact, that Jesus is the Christ, to the soul of the individual, and is not to be understood as independent of the external evidence of that truth, or as superseding the necessity of that evidence ; but the 'witness' here referred to is the fruit of *all* the evidence, external and internal, on the heart, producing this result ; that is, there is the deepest conviction of the truth that Jesus is the Son of God. There is the evi-

11 And this is the record, that God hath given to us eternal life, and this life *a* is in his Son.

12 He *b* that hath the Son, hath life ; *and* he that hath not the Son of God, hath not life.

a Jn.1.4.   *b* Jn.5.24.

13 These things have I written unto you that believe on the name of the Son of God ; that ye *c* may know that ye have eternal life, and that ye may believe on the name of the Son of God.

c Jn.20.31.

---

dence derived from the fact that the soul has found peace by believing on him ; from the fact that the troubles and anxieties of the mind on account of sin have been removed by faith in Christ ; from the new views of God and heaven which have resulted from faith in the Lord Jesus ; from the effect of this in disarming death of its terrors ; and from the whole influence of the gospel on the intellect and the affections—on the heart and the life. These things constitute a mass of evidence for the truth of the Christian religion, whose force the believer cannot resist, and make the sincere Christian ready to sacrifice anything rather than his religion ; ready to go to the stake rather than to renounce his Saviour. Comp. Notes, 1 Pet. iii. 15. ¶ *He that believeth not God hath made him a liar.* Comp. Notes, chap. i. 10. ¶ *Because he believeth not the record,* &c. The idea is, that in various ways—at his baptism, at his death, by the influences of the Holy Spirit, by the miracles of Jesus, &c.—God had become a *witness* that the Lord Jesus was sent by him as a Saviour, and that to doubt or deny this partook of the same character as doubting or denying any other testimony ; that is, it was practically charging him who bore the testimony with falsehood.

11. *And this is the record.* This is the *sum,* or the *amount,* of the testimony (μαρτυρία) which God has given respecting him. ¶ *That God hath given to us eternal life.* Has provided, through the Saviour, the means of obtaining eternal life. See Notes, John v. 24 ; xvii. 2, 3. ¶ *And this life is in his Son.* Is treasured up in him, or is to be obtained through him. See Notes, John i. 4 ; xi. 25 ; xiv. 6 ; Col. iii. 3.

12. *He that hath the Son, hath life.* See Notes, John v. 24. John evidently designs to refer to that passage in the verse before us, and to state a principle

laid down by the Saviour himself. This is the sense of all the important testimony that had ever been borne by God on the subject of salvation, that he who believes in the Lord Jesus already *has* the elements of eternal life in his soul, and will certainly obtain salvation. Comp. Notes, John xvii. 3. ¶ And *he that hath not the Son of God, hath not life.* He that does not believe on him will not attain to eternal life. See Notes, John iii. 36 ; Mark xvi. 16.

13. *These things have I written unto you.* The things in this epistle respecting the testimony borne to the Lord Jesus. ¶ *That believe on the name of the Son of God.* To believe on his *name,* is to believe on himself—the word *name* often being used to denote the *person.* See Notes, Matt. xxviii. 19. ¶ *That ye may know that ye have eternal life.* That you may see the evidence that eternal life has been provided, and that you may be able, by self-examination, to determine whether you possess it. Comp. Notes, John xx. 31. ¶ *And that ye may believe,* &c. That you may *continue* to believe, or may *persevere* in believing. He was assured that they actually *did* believe on him then ; but he was desirous of so setting before them the nature of religion, that they would *continue* to exercise faith in him. It is often one of the most important duties of ministers of the gospel, to present to real Christians such views of the nature, the claims, the evidences, and the hopes of religion, as shall be adapted to secure their perseverance in the faith. In the human heart, even when converted, there is such a proneness to unbelief ; the religious affections so easily become cold ; there are so many cares pertaining to the world that are fitted to distract the mind ; there are so many allurements of sin to draw the affections away from the Saviour ; that there is need of being constantly reminded of the nature of re-

14 And this is the confidence that we have ¹in him, that, if we

1 *concerning.*

ask any thing according to his will, he heareth us:

---

ligion, in order that the heart may not be wholly estranged from the Saviour. No small part of preaching, therefore, must consist of the re-statement of arguments with which the mind has been before fully convinced; of motives whose force has been once felt and acknowledged; and of the grounds of hope and peace and joy which have already, on former occasions, diffused comfort through the soul. It is not less important to *keep* the soul, than it is to *convert* it; to save it from coldness, and deadness, and formality, than it was to impart to it the elements of spiritual life at first. It may be as important to trim a vine, if one would have grapes, as it is to set it out; to keep a garden from being overrun with weeds in the summer, as it was to plant it in the spring.

14. *And this is the confidence that we have in him.* Marg., *concerning.* Greek, 'towards him,' or in respect to him— πρὸς αὐτὸν. The confidence referred to here is that which relates to the answer to prayer. The apostle does not say that this is the *only* thing in respect to which there is to be confidence in him, but that it is one which is worthy of special consideration. The sense is, that one of the effects of believing on the Lord Jesus (ver. 13) is, that we have the assurance that our prayers will be answered. On the word *confidence*, see Notes on chap. iii. 21; iv. 17. ¶ *That, if we ask any thing according to his will, he heareth us.* This is the proper limitation in all prayer. God has not promised to grant anything that shall be contrary to his will, and it could not be right that he should do it. We ought not to wish to receive anything that should be contrary to what he judges to be best. No man could hope for good who should esteem his own wishes to be a better guide than the will of God; and it is one of the most desirable of all arrangements that the promise of any blessing to be obtained by prayer should be limited and bounded by the will of God. The limitation here, 'according to his will,' probably implies the following things: (1.) In accordance

with what he has *declared* that he is willing to grant. Here the range is large, for there are many things which we know to be in accordance with his will, if they are sought in a proper manner—as the forgiveness of sins, the sanctification of the soul, (1 Thess. iv. 3,) comfort in trial, the needful supply of our wants, grace that we may do our duty, wisdom to direct and guide us, (James i. 5,) deliverance from the evils which beset us, the influences of his Spirit to promote the cause of religion in the world, and our final salvation. Here is a range of subjects of petition that may gratify the largest wishes of prayer. (2.) The expression, 'according to his will,' must limit the answer to his will to what *he* sees to be best for us. Of that we are not always good judges. We never perceive it as clearly as our Maker does, and in many things we might be wholly mistaken. Certainly we ought not to desire to be permitted to ask anything which *God* would judge not to be for our good. (3.) The expression must limit the petition to what it will be *consistent* for God to bestow upon us. We cannot expect that he will work a miracle in answer to our prayers; we cannot ask him to bestow blessings in violation of any of the laws which he has ordained, or in any other way than that which he has appointed. It is better that the particular blessing should be withheld from us, than that the laws which he has appointed should be disregarded. It is better that an idle man should *not* have a harvest, though he should pray for it, than that God should violate the laws by which he has determined to bestow such favours as a reward of industry, and work a special miracle in answer to a lazy man's prayers. (4.) The expression, 'according to his will,' must limit the promise to what will be *for the good of the whole.* God presides over the universe : and though in him there is an infinite fulness, and he regards the wants of every individual throughout his immense empire, yet the interests of the whole, as well as of the individual, are to be consulted and re-

15 And if we know *a* that he hear us, whatsoever we ask, we know that we have the petitions that we desired of him.

16 If any man see his brother sin a sin *which is* not unto death,

he shall ask, and he shall give him life for them that sin not unto death. There is a sin unto death : *b* I do not say *c* that he shall pray for it.

a Pr.15.29; Jer.29.12,13.   *b* Mat.12,31,32.   *c* Jer.7.16.

garded. In a family, it is conceivable that a child might ask for some favour whose bestowment would interfere materially with the rights of others, or be inconsistent with the good of the whole, and in such a case a just father would of course withhold it. With these necessary limitations the range of the promise in prayer is ample; and, with these limitations, it is true beyond a question that he does hear and answer prayer.

15. *And if we know that he hear us.* That is, if we are assured of this as a true doctrine, then, even though we may not *see* immediately that the prayer is answered, we may have the utmost confidence that it is not disregarded, and that it will be answered in the way best adapted to promote our good. The specific thing that we asked may not indeed be granted, (comp. Luke xxii. 42 ; 2 Cor. xii. 8, 9,) but the prayer will not be disregarded, and the thing which is most for our good will be bestowed upon us. The *argument* here is derived from the faithfulness of God ; from the assurance which we feel that when he has promised to hear us, there will be, sooner or later, a *real* answer to the prayer. ¶ *We know that we have the petitions,* &c. That is, evidently, we know that we *shall* have them, or that the prayer will be answered. It cannot mean that we already have the precise thing for which we prayed, or that will be a real answer to the prayer, for (*a*) the prayer may relate to something future, as protection on a journey, or a harvest, or restoration to health, or the safe return of a son from a voyage at sea, or the salvation of our souls—all of which are *future,* and which cannot be expected to be granted at once; and (*b*) the answer to prayer is sometimes delayed, though ultimately granted. There may be reasons why the answer should be deferred, and the promise is not that it shall be immediate. The *delay* may arise from such causes as these : (1.)

To try our faith, and see whether the blessing is earnestly desired. (2.) Perhaps it could not be at once answered without a miracle. (3.) It might not be consistent with the Divine arrangements respecting others to grant it to us at once. (4.) Our own condition may not be such that it would be best to answer it at once. We may need further trial, further chastisement, before the affliction, for example, shall be removed ; and the answer to the prayer may be delayed for months or years. Yet, in the meantime, we may have the firmest assurance that the prayer *is* heard, and that it *will be* answered in the way and at the period when God shall see it to be best.

16. *If a man see his brother sin a sin,* &c. From the general assurance that God hears prayer, the apostle turns to a particular case in which it may be benevolently and effectually employed, in rescuing a brother from death. There has been great diversity of opinion in regard to the meaning of this passage, and the views of expositors of the New Testament are by no means settled as to its true sense. It does not comport with the design of these Notes to examine the opinions which have been held in detail. A bare reference, however, to some of them will show the difficulty of determining with certainty what the passage means, and the impropriety of any very great confidence in one's own judgment in the case. Among these opinions are the following. Some have supposed that the sin against the Holy Ghost is intended ; some that the phrase denotes any great and enormous sin, as murder, idolatry, adultery ; some that it denotes some sin that was punishable by death by the laws of Moses ; some that it denotes a sin that subjected the offender to excommunication from the synagogue or the church ; some that it refers to sins which brought fatal disease upon the offender, as in the case

of those who abused the Lord's Supper at Corinth, (see Notes on 1 Cor. xi. 30;) some that it refers to crimes committed against the laws, for which the offender was sentenced to death, meaning that when the charge alleged was false, and the condemnation unjust, they ought to pray for the one who was condemned to death, and that he would be spared; but that when the offence was one which had been really committed, and the offender deserved to die, they ought not to pray for him, or, in other words, that by 'the sin unto death,' offences against the civil law are referred to, which the magistrate had no power to pardon, and the punishment of which he could not commute; and by the 'sin not unto death,' offences are referred to which might be pardoned, and when the punishment might be commuted; some that it refers to sins *before* and *after* baptism, the former of which might be pardoned, but the latter of which might not be; and some, and perhaps this is the common opinion among the Roman Catholics, that it refers to sins that might or might not be pardoned *after* death, thus referring to the doctrine of purgatory. These various opinions may be seen stated more at length in Rosenmüller, Lücke, Pool, (*Synopsis*,) and Clarke, *in loc.* To go into an examination of all these opinions would require a volume by itself, and all that can be done here is to furnish what seems to me to be the fair exposition of the passage. The word *brother* may refer either to a member of the church, whether of the particular church to which one was attached or to another, or it may be used in the larger sense which is common as denoting a fellow-man, a member of the great family of mankind. There is nothing in the word which necessarily limits it to one in the church; there is nothing in the connection, or in the reason assigned, why what is said should be limited to such an one. The *duty* here enjoined would be the same whether the person referred to was in the church or not; for it is our duty to pray for those who sin, and to seek the salvation of those whom we see to be going astray, and to be in danger of ruin, wherever they are, or whoever they may be. At the same time, the correct interpretation

of the passage does not depend on determining whether the word *brother* refers to one who is a professed Christian or not.

¶ *A sin which is not unto death.* The great question in the interpretation of the whole passage is, what is meant by the 'sin unto death.' The Greek (*ἁμαρτία πρὸς θάνατον*) would mean properly a sin which *tends* to death; which would *terminate* in death; of which death was the penalty, or would be the result, unless it were arrested; a sin which, if it had its own course, would terminate thus, as we should speak of a disease 'unto death.' Comp. Notes, John xi. 4. The word *death* is used in three significations in the New Testament, and as employed here might, so far as the *word* is concerned, be applied in any one of those senses. It is used to denote (*a*) literally the death of the body; (*b*) spiritual death, or death 'in trespasses and sin,' Eph. ii. 1; (*c*) the 'second death,' death in the world of woe and despair. If the sin here mentioned refers to *temporal* death, it means such a sin that temporal death *must* inevitably follow, either by the *disease* which it has produced, or by a judicial sentence where there was no hope of pardon or of a commutation of the punishment; if it refers to death in the future world, the second death, then it means such a sin as is unpardonable. That this last *is* the reference here seems to me to be probable, if not clear, from the following considerations: (1.) There *is* such a sin referred to in the New Testament, a sin for which there is forgiveness 'neither in this life nor the life to come.' See Notes, Matt. xii. 31, 32. Comp. Mark iii. 29. If there *is* such a sin, there is no impropriety in supposing that John would refer to it here. (2.) This is the *obvious* interpretation. It is that which would occur to the mass of the readers of the New Testament, and which it is presumed they do adopt; and this, in general, is one of the best means of ascertaining the sense of a passage in the Bible. (3.) The other significations attached to the word *death*, would be quite inappropriate here. (*a*) It cannot mean 'unto *spiritual death*,' that is, to a continuance in sin, for how could that be known? and if such a case occurred, why would it be improper to pray for it? Besides, the phrase 'a sin unto spiritual death,' or 'unto continuance in sin,' is one that is unmeaning. (*b*) It cannot be shown to refer to a disease that should be unto death, miraculously inflicted on account of sin, because, if such cases occurred, they were very rare, and even if a disease came upon a man miraculously in consequence of sin, it could not be certainly known whether it was, or was not, unto death. All who were visited in this way did not certainly die. Comp. 1 Cor. v. 4, 5, with 2 Cor. ii. 6, 7. See also 1 Cor. xi. 30. (*c*) It cannot be shown that it refers to the case of those who were condemned by the civil magistrate to death, and for whom there was no hope of reprieve or pardon, for it is not certain that there were such cases; and if there were, and the person condemned were innocent, there was every reason to pray that *God* would interpose and save them, even when there was no hope from man; and if they were guilty, and deserved to die, there was no reason why they should not pray that the sin might be forgiven, and that they might be prepared to die, unless it were a case where the sin was unpardonable. It seems probable, therefore, to me, that the reference here is to the sin against the Holy Ghost, and that John means here to illustrate the duty and the power of prayer, by showing that for *any sin short of that*, however aggravated, it was their duty to pray that a brother might be forgiven. Though it might not be easy to determine what *was* the unpardonable sin, and John does not say that those to whom he wrote could determine that with certainty, yet there were many sins which were manifestly *not* of that aggravated character, and for those sins it was proper to pray. There was clearly but *one* sin that was unpardonable — 'there is *a* sin unto death;' there might be many which were not of this description, and in relation to them there was ample scope for the exercise of the prayer of faith. The same thing is true now. It is not easy to define the unpardonable sin, and it is impossible for us to determine in any case with absolute certainty that a man

has committed it. But there are multitudes of sins which men commit, which on no proper interpretation of the passages respecting the sin which 'hath never forgiveness,' can come under the description of that sin, and for which it is proper, therefore, to pray that they may be pardoned. We know of cases enough where sin *may* be forgiven; and, without allowing the mind to be disturbed about the question respecting the unpardonable sin, it is our duty to bear such cases on our hearts before God, and to plead with him that our erring brethren may be saved. ¶ *He shall ask.* That is, he shall pray that the offender may be brought to true repentance, and may be saved. ¶ *And he shall give him life for them that sin not unto death.* That is, *God* shall give life, and he shall be saved from the eternal death to which he was exposed. This, it is said, would be given to 'him' who offers the prayer; that is, his prayer would be the means of saving the offending brother. What a motive is this to prayer! How faithful and constant should we be in pleading for our fellow-sinners, that we may be instrumental in saving their souls! What joy will await those in heaven who shall see there many who were rescued from ruin in answer to their prayers! Comp. Notes, James v. 15, 19, 20. ¶ *There is a sin unto death.* A sin which is of such a character that it throws the offender beyond the reach of mercy, and which is not to be pardoned. See Mark iii. 28, 29. The apostle does not here say what that sin is; nor how they might know what it is; nor even that in any case they could determine that it had been committed. He merely says that there *is* such a sin, and that he does not design that his remark about the efficacy of prayer should be understood as extending to that. ¶ *I do not say that he shall pray for it.* 'I do not intend that my remark shall be extended to *all* sin, or mean to affirm that all possible forms of guilt are the proper subjects of prayer, for I am aware that there is one sin which is an exception, and my remark is not to be applied to that.' He does not say that this sin was of common occurrence: or that they could know when it had been committed; or even that a case could ever occur in

17 All unrighteousness *a* is sin :
and there *b* is a sin not unto death.
18 We know that whosoever is
born of God sinneth not; but he

that is begotten of God keepeth
himself, *c* and that wicked one
toucheth him not.

a 1 Jn.3.4.   *b* Ro.5.20,21.   *c* Ja.1.27.

which they could determine that; he
merely says that in respect to that sin
he did *not* say that prayer should be
offered. It is indeed implied in a most
delicate way that it would not be proper
to pray for the forgiveness of such a sin,
but he does not say that a case would
ever happen in which they would *know*
certainly that the sin had been committed. There were instances in the
times of the prophets in which the sin
of the people became so universal and
so aggravated, that they were forbidden
to pray for them. Isa. xiv. 11, ' Then
said the Lord unto me, Pray not for this
people for their good ;' xv. 1, ' Then said
the Lord unto me, Though Moses and
Samuel stood before me, yet my mind
could not be toward this people; cast
them out of my sight, and let them go
forth.' Comp. Notes, Isa. i. 15. But these
were cases in which the prophets were
directly instructed by God not to pray
for a people. We have no such instruction; and it may be said now with truth,
that as we can never be certain respecting any one that he has committed the
unpardonable sin, there is no one for
whom we may not with propriety pray.
There may be those who are so far gone
in sin that there may seem to be little,
or almost no ground of hope. They may
have cast off all the restraints of religion, of morality, of decency; they may
disregard all the counsels of parents and
friends ; they may be sceptical, sensual,
profane; they may be the companions of
infidels and of mockers; they may have
forsaken the sanctuary, and learned to
despise the sabbath; they may have been
professors of religion, and now may have
renounced the faith of the gospel altogether, but still, while there is life it is
our duty to pray for them, ' if peradven-
ture God will give them repentance to
the acknowledging of the truth,' 2 Tim.
ii. 25. ' *All things* are possible with
God ;' and he has reclaimed offenders
more hardened, probably, than any that
we have known, and has demonstrated
that there is no form of depravity which
he has not the power to subdue. Let

us remember the cases of Manasseh, of
Saul of Tarsus, of Augustine, of Bunyan,
of Newton, of tens of thousands who have
been reclaimed from the vilest forms of
iniquity, and then let us never despair
of the conversion of any, in answer to
prayer, who may have gone astray, as
long as they are in this world of probation and of hope. Let no parent despair
who has an abandoned son ; let no wife
cease to pray who has a dissipated husband. How many a prodigal son has
come back to fill with happiness an aged
parent's heart! How many a dissipated
husband has been reformed to give joy
again to the wife of his youth, and to
make a paradise again of his miserable
home !

17. *All unrighteousness is sin, &c.*
This seems to be thrown in to guard
what he had just said, and there is *one*
great and enormous sin, a sin which
could not be forgiven. But he says also
that there are many other forms and
degrees of sin, sin for which prayer may
be made. Everything, he says, which
is *unrighteous* — ἀδικία — everything
which does not conform to the holy law
of God, and which is not *right* in the
view of that law, is to be regarded as
sin ; but we are not to suppose that *all*
sin of that kind is of such a character
that it cannot possibly be forgiven.
There are many who commit sin who
we may hope will be recovered, and for
them it is proper to pray. Deeply
affected as we may be in view of the
fact that there is a sin which can never
be pardoned, and much as we may pity
one who has been guilty of such a sin,
yet we should not hastily conclude in
any case that it has been committed,
and should bear constantly in mind that
while there is one such sin, there are
multitudes that may be pardoned, and
that for them it is our duty unceasingly
to pray.

18. *We know that whosoever is born
of God sinneth not.* Is not habitually
and characteristically a sinner ; does
not ultimately and finally sin and perish;
cannot, therefore, commit the unpar-

19 *And* we know that we are of God, and the whole world lieth in wickedness.

20 And we know that the Son of God is come, and hath given us an understanding, *a* that we may know him that is true: and we are in *a* Lu.24.45.

---

donable sin. Though he may fall into sin, and grieve his brethren, yet we are never to cease to pray for a true Christian ; we are never to feel that he has committed the sin which has never forgiveness, and that he has thrown himself beyond the reach of our prayers. This passage, in its connection, is a full proof that a true Christian *will* never commit the unpardonable sin, and, therefore, is a proof that he will never fall from grace. Comp. Notes, Heb. vi. 4–8 ; x. 26. On the *meaning* of the assertion here made, that ' whosoever is born of God sinneth not,' see Notes on chap. iii. 6–9. ¶ *Keepeth himself.* It is not said that he does it by his own strength, but he will put forth his best efforts to keep himself from sin, and by Divine assistance he will be able to accomplish it. Comp. Notes on chap. iii. 3 ; Jude 21. ¶ *And that wicked one toucheth him not.* The great enemy of all good is repelled in his assaults, and he is kept from falling into his snares. The word *toucheth* (ἅπτεται) is used here in the sense of harm or *injure*.

19. And *we know that we are of God.* We who are Christians. The apostle supposed that true Christians might have so clear evidence on that subject as to leave no doubt on their own minds that they were the children of God. Comp. chap. iii. 14 ; 2 Tim. i. 12. ¶ *And the whole world.* The term *world* here evidently means not the *material* world, but the *people* that dwell on the earth, including all idolaters, and all sinners of every grade and kind. ¶ *Lieth in wickedness.* ' In the wicked one,' or under the power of the wicked one— ἐν τῷ πονηρῷ. It is true that the word πονηρῷ may be used here in the neuter gender, as our translators have rendered it, meaning ' in that which is evil,' or in ' wickedness ;' but it may be in the masculine gender, meaning ' the wicked one;' and then the sense would be that the whole world is under his control or dominion. That this is the meaning of the apostle seems to be clear, because

(1) the corresponding phrase, (ver. 20,) ἐν τῷ ἀληθινῷ, ' in him that is true,' is evidently to be construed in the masculine, referring to God the Saviour, and meaning ' him that is true,' and not that we are ' in truth.' (2.) It makes better sense to say that the world lies under the control of the wicked one, than to say that it lies ' in wickedness.' (3.) This accords better with the other representations in the Bible, and the usuage of the word elsewhere. Comp. 1 John ii. 13, ' Ye have overcome the *wicked* one ;' ver. 14, ' ye have overcome the *wicked* one ;' iii. 12, ' who was of that *wicked* one.' See also Notes, 2 Cor. iv. 4, on the expression ' the god of this world ;' John xii. 31, where he is called ' the prince of this world ;' and Eph. ii. 2, where he is called ' the prince of the power of the air.' In all these passages it is supposed that Satan has control over the world, especially the heathen world. Comp. Eph. vi. 12 ; 1 Cor. x. 20. In regard to the *fact* that the heathen world was pervaded by wickedness, see Notes on Rom. i. 21–32. (4.) It may be added, that this interpretation is adopted by the most eminent critics and commentators. It is that of Calvin, Beza, Benson, Macknight, Bloomfield, Piscator, Lücke, &c. The word *lieth* here (κεῖται) means, properly, to lie ; to be laid ; to recline ; to be situated, &c. It seems here to refer to the *passive* and *torpid* state of a wicked world under the dominion of the prince of evil, as acquiescing in his reign ; making no resistance ; not even struggling to be free. It *lies* thus as a beast that is subdued, a body that is dead, or anything that is wholly passive, quiet, and inert. There is no energy ; no effort to throw off the reign ; no resistance ; no struggling. The dominion is complete, and body and soul, individuals and nations, are entirely subject to his will. This striking expression will not unaptly now describe the condition of the heathen world, or of sinners in general. There would seem to be no government under which men are so little restive, and against which

him that is true, *even* in his Son | Jesus Christ. This ⸱ is the true

a Is.9.6.

God, and eternal life.

they have so little disposition to rebel, as that of Satan. Comp. 2 Tim. ii. 26. **20. And we know that the Son of God is come.** We know this by the evidence that John had referred to in this epistle, chap. i. 1–4; v. 6–8. ¶ *And hath given us an understanding.* Not an 'understanding' considered as a faculty of the mind, for religion gives us no new faculties; but he has so instructed us that we do understand the great truths referred to. Comp. Notes, Luke xxiv. 45. All the correct *knowledge* which we have of God and his government, is to be traced directly or indirectly to the great Prophet whom God has sent into the world, John i. 4, 18; viii. 12; ix. 5; Heb. i. 1–3; Matt. xi. 27. ¶ *That we may know him that is true.* That is, the true God. See Notes, John xvii. 3. ¶ *And we are in him that is true.* That is, we are united to him; we belong to him; we are his friends. This idea is often expressed in the Scriptures by being '*in* him.' It denotes a most intimate union, *as if* we were one with him—or were a *part* of him—as the branch is *in* the vine, John xv. 4, 6. The Greek construction is the same as that applied to 'the wicked one,' ver. 19, (ἐν τῷ ἀληθινῷ.) ¶ *This is the true God.** There has been much difference of opinion in regard to this important passage; whether it refers to the Lord Jesus Christ, the immediate antecedent, or to a more remote antecedent—referring to God, as such. The question is of importance in its bearing on the doctrine of the divinity of the Saviour; for if it refers to him, it furnishes an unequivocal declaration that he is Divine. The question is, whether John *meant* that it should be referred to him? Without going into an extended ex-

amination of the passage, the following considerations seem to me to make it morally certain that by the phrase 'this is the true God,' &c., he did refer to the Lord Jesus Christ. (1.) The grammatical construction favours it. Christ is the immediate antecedent of the pronoun *this—οὗτος.* This would be regarded as the obvious and certain construction so far as the grammar is concerned, unless there were something in the thing affirmed which led us to seek some more remote and less obvious antecedent. No doubt would have been ever entertained on this point, if it had not been for the reluctance to admit that the Lord Jesus *is* the true God. If the assertion had been that '*this* is the true Messiah;' or that '*this* is the Son of God;' or that '*this* is he who was born of the Virgin Mary,' there would have been no difficulty in the construction. I admit that this argument is not absolutely decisive; for cases do occur where a pronoun refers, not to the immediate antecedent, but to one more remote; but cases of that kind depend on the ground of necessity, and can be applied only when it would be a clear violation of the sense of the author to refer it to the immediate antecedent. (2.) This construction seems to be demanded by the adjunct which John has assigned to the phrase 'the true God'—'ETERNAL LIFE.' This is an expression which John would be likely to apply to the Lord Jesus, considered as *life*, and *the source of life*, and not to God as such. 'How familiar is this language with John, as applied to Christ! "In him (i. e. Christ) was LIFE, and the LIFE was the light of men—giving LIFE to the world—the bread of LIFE—my words are spirit and LIFE—I am the way, and the truth, and the LIFE. This LIFE (Christ) was manifested, and we have *seen it*, and do testify to you, and declare the ETERNAL LIFE which was with the Father, and was manifested to us," 1 John i. 2.'—Prof. Stuart's Letters to Dr. Channing, p. 83. There is no instance in the writings of John, in which the appellation LIFE, and *eternal* LIFE is bestowed upon the Father, to designate him as the author of spiritual

* Many MSS. here insert the word *God*—'the true *God*'—τὸν ἀληθινὸν Θεόν. This is also found in the Vulgate, Coptic, Æthiopic, and Arabic versions, and in the Complutensian edition of the New Testament. The reading, however, is not so well sustained as to be adopted by Griesbach, Tittman, or Hahn. That it *may* be a genuine reading is indeed possible, but the evidence is against it. Lücke supposes that it is genuine, and endeavours to account for the manner in which it was omitted in the MSS.— *Commentary,* p. 349.

21 Little children, keep your- | selves from idols.ᵃ Amen.

and eternal life; and as this occurs so frequently in John's writings as applied to Christ, the laws of exegesis require that both the phrase 'the true God,' and 'eternal life,' should be applied to him. (3.) If it refers to God as such, or to the word 'true'—τὸν ἀληθινόν [Θεὸν] it would be mere tautology, or a mere truism. The rendering would then be, 'That we may know the true God, and we are in the true God: this *is* the true God, and eternal life.' Can we believe that an inspired man would affirm gravely, and with so much solemnity, and as if it were a truth of so much magnitude, that the true God *is* the true God? (4.) This interpretation accords with what we are sure John *would* affirm respecting the Lord Jesus Christ. Can there be any doubt that he who said, 'In the beginning was the Word, and the Word was with God, and the Word was God;' that he who said, 'all things were made by him, and without him was not anything made that was made;' that he who recorded the declaration of the Saviour, 'I and my Father are one,' and the declaration of Thomas, 'my Lord and my God,' would apply to him the appellation *the true God!* (5.) If John did *not* mean to affirm this, he has made use of an expression which was liable to be misunderstood, and which, as facts have shown, would be misconstrued by the great portion of those who might read what he had written; and, moreover, an expression that would lead to the *very* sin against which he endeavours to guard in the next verse —the sin of substituting a creature in the place of God, and rendering to another the honour due to him. The language which he uses is just such as, according to its natural interpretation, would lead men to worship one as the true God who is *not* the true God, unless the Lord Jesus be Divine. For these reasons, it seems to me that the fair interpretation of this passage demands that it should be understood as referring to the Lord Jesus Christ. If so, it is a direct assertion of his divinity, for there could be no higher proof of it than to affirm that he is the true God.

¶ *And eternal life.* Having 'life in himself,' (John v. 26,) and the source and fountain of life to the soul. No more frequent appellation, perhaps, is given to the Saviour by John, than that he is life, and the source of life. Comp. John i. 4; v. 26, 40; x. 10; vi. 33, 35, 48, 51, 53, 63; xi. 25; xiv. 6; xx. 31; 1 John i. 1, 2; v. 12.

21. *Little children.* This is a favourite mode of address with John, (see Notes on chap. ii. 1,) and it was proper to use it in giving his parting counsel; embracing, in fact, all that he had to say —that they should keep themselves from idols, and suffer nothing to alienate their affections from the true God. His great object had been to lead them to the knowledge and love of God, and all his counsels would be practically followed, if, amidst the temptations of idolatry, and the allurements of sin, nothing were allowed to estrange their hearts from him. ¶ *Keep yourselves from idols.* From worshipping them; from all that would imply communion with them or their devotees. Compare Notes, 1 Cor. x. 14. The word rendered *idols* here (εἰδώλων) means, properly, an image, spectre, shade—as of the dead; then any image or figure which would represent anything, particularly anything invisible; and hence anything designed to represent God, and that was set up with a view to be acknowledged as representing him, or to bring him, or his perfections, more vividly before the mind. The word is applicable to idol-gods— heathen deities, 1 Cor. viii. 4, 7; x. 19; Rom. ii. 22; 2 Cor. vi. 16; 1 Thess. i. 9; but it would, also, be applicable to any *image* designed to represent the true God, and through or by which the true God was to be adored. The essential things in the word seem to be, (*a*,) an image or representation of the Deity, and (*b*) the making of that an object of adoration instead of the true God. Since one of these things would be likely to lead to the other, both are forbidden in the prohibitions of idolatry, Exod. xx. 4, 5. This would forbid all attempts to represent God by paintings or statuary; all idol-worship, or worship of heathen

gods ; all images and pictures that would be substituted in the place of God as objects of devotion, or that might transfer the homage from God to the image ; and all giving of those affections to other beings or objects which are due to God. Why the apostle closed this epistle with this injunction he has not stated, and it may not be easy to determine. It may have been for such reasons as these : (1.) Those to whom he wrote were surrounded by idolaters, and there was danger that they might fall into the prevailing sin, or in some way so act as to be understood to lend their sanction to idolatry. (2.) In a world full of alluring objects, there was danger then, as there is at all times, that the affections should be fixed on other objects than the supreme God, and that what is due to him should be withheld. It may be added, in the conclusion of the exposition of this epistle, that the same caution is as needful for us as it was for those to whom John wrote. We are not in danger, indeed, of bowing down to idols, or of engaging in the grosser forms of idol-worship. But we may be in no less danger than they to whom John wrote were, of substituting other things in our affections in the place of the true God, and of devoting to them the time and the affection which are due to him. Our children it is possible to love with such an attachment as shall effectually exclude the true God from the heart. The world—its wealth, and pleasures, and honours—we may love with a degree of attachment such as

even an idolater would hardly shew to his idol-gods ; and all the time which he would take in performing his devotions in an idol-temple, we may devote with equal fervour to the service of the world. There is practical idolatry all over the world ; in nominally Christian lands as well as among the heathen ; in families that acknowledge no God but wealth and fashion ; in the hearts of multitudes of individuals who would scorn the thought of worshipping at a pagan altar ; and it is even to be found in the heart of many a one who professes to be acquainted with the true God, and to be an heir of heaven. God should have the supreme place in our affections. The love of everything else should be held in strict subordination to the love of him. He should reign in our hearts ; be acknowledged in our closets, our families, and in the place of public worship ; be submitted to at all times as having a right to command and control us ; be obeyed in all the expressions of his will, by his word, by his providence, and by his Spirit ; be so loved that we shall be willing to part without a murmur with the dearest object of affection when he takes it from us ; and so that, with joy and triumph, we shall welcome his messenger, the angel of death, when he shall come to summon us into his presence. To all who may read these illustrations of the epistle of the ‘beloved disciple,’ may God grant this inestimable blessing and honour. Amen.

INTRODUCTION

TO THE

SECOND AND THIRD EPISTLES OF JOHN.

§ 1. *The authenticity of the second and third Epistles of John.*

THE authenticity of these two epistles was doubted by many in the early Christian church, and it was not before a considerable time had elapsed that their canonical authority was fully admitted. The first of the three epistles was always received as the undoubted production of the apostle John ; but, though not positively and absolutely rejected, there were many doubts entertained in regard to the authorship of the second and third. Their exceeding brevity, and the fact that they were addressed to individuals, and seemed not designed for general circulation, made them less frequently referred to by the early Christian writers, and renders it more difficult to establish their genuineness.

The *evidence* of their genuineness is of two kinds—external and internal. Though, from their brevity, the proof on these points must be less full and clear than it is in regard to the first epistle; yet it is such as to satisfy the mind, on the whole, that they are the production of the apostle John, and are entitled to a place in the canon of Scripture.

(1.) *External evidence.* The evidence of this kind, either for or against the authenticity of these epistles, is found in the following testimonies respecting them in the writings of the Fathers, and the following facts in regard to their admission into the canon.

(*a*) In the church and school at Alexandria they were both well known, and were received as a part of the sacred writings. Clement of Alexandria, and Alexander, bishop of Alexandria, quote them, or refer to them, as the writings of the apostle John.—Lardner's works, vi. 275 ; Lücke, p. 329. Origen, the successor of Clement, says, ' John left behind him an epistle of very few *stichoi;* perhaps also a second and third, though some do not consider these genuine. Both these together, however, contain only an hundred *stichoi.*' Dionysius of Alexandria shows that he was acquainted with all of them, but calls the two last φερόμεναι—writings alleged to be genuine. For the import of this word, as used by Dionysius, see Lücke's Com., pp. 330, 331.

(*b*) These epistles were known and received in the western churches in the second and third centuries. Of this fact, an important witness is found in Irenæus, who, on account of the place where he resided during his youth, and the school in which he was educated, deserves especial regard as a witness respecting the works of John.—*Hug.* He was born at Smyrna, and lived not long after the times of the apostles. He was a disciple of Polycarp, who was acquainted. with the apostle John ; and having passed his early years in Asia Minor, must, in the circumstances in which he was placed, have been familiar with the writings of John, and have known well what writings were attributed to him. He quotes the second epistle, (ver. 11,) and with express reference to John as the author, under the name of ' John, the disciple of our Lord.' In another place, also, he refers to this epistle. After quoting from the first epistle, he continues, ' And

John, the disciple of Jesus, in the epistle before mentioned, commanded that they (the heretics) should be shunned, saying,' &c. He then quotes, word for word, the seventh and eighth verses of the epistle.

(c) The African church, in the third century, regarded the second epistle, at least, as the production of John. At a synod in Carthage, under Cyprian, Aurelius, the bishop of Chullabi, in giving his vote on the question of baptizing heretics, quotes the tenth verse of the second epistle as authority, saying, ' John, in his epistle, declares,' &c.

(d) There is some doubt in regard to the Syrian church, whether these epistles were at first received as genuine or not. The manuscripts of the Peshito, or old Syriac version, at least since the sixth century, do not contain the epistle of Jude, the second epistle of Peter, or the second and third of John. Yet Ephrem the Syrian, in the fourth century, quotes the epistle of Jude, the second epistle of Peter, and the second of John, as genuine and canonical. As this father in the Syrian church was not acquainted with the Greek language, (*Lücke*,) it is clear that he must have read these epistles in a translation, and as would seem most probable in some Syriac version. The probability would seem to be, as these epistles are not in the oldest Syriac version, that there was some doubt about their authenticity when that version was made, but that before the time of Ephrem they had come to be regarded as genuine, and were translated by some other persons. Their use in the time of Ephrem would at least show that they were then regarded as genuine. They may have been, indeed, at some period attached to the ancient version, but at a later period, as they did not originally belong to that version, they may have been separated from it.—*Lücke, in loc.* At all events, it is clear that at an early period in the Syrian church they were regarded as genuine.

(e) Though there were doubts among many of the Fathers respecting the genuineness of these epistles, yet they were admitted in several councils of the church to be genuine. In the eighty-fifth of the apostolic canons, (so called ;) in the sixtieth canon of the synod of Laodicea ; the council at Hippo, (A.D. 393,) and the third council of Carthage, (A.D. 397,) they were reckoned as undoubtedly pertaining to the inspired canon of Scripture.

(f) All doubts on the subject of the genuineness of these epistles were, however, subsequently removed in the view of Christian writers, and in the middle ages they were universally received as the writings of the apostle John. Some of the Reformers again had doubts of their genuineness. Erasmus quoted the sentiment of Jerome, that it was not the *apostle* John who wrote these epistles, but a *presbyter* of the same name ; and Calvin seems to have entertained some doubt of their genuineness, for he has omitted them in his commentaries ; but these doubts have also disappeared, and the conviction has again become general, and indeed almost universal, that they are to be ranked among the genuine writings of the apostle John.

It may be added here, that the doubts which have been entertained on the subject, and the investigations to which they have given rise, show the care which has been evinced in forming the canon of the New Testament, and demonstrate that the Christian world has not been *disposed* to receive books as of sacred authority without evidence of their genuineness.

(2.) There is strong *internal* evidence that they are genuine. This is found in their style, sentiment, and manner. It is true that one who was familiar with the writings of the apostle John *might* compose two short epistles like these, that should be mistaken for the real productions of the apostle. There are, even in these brief epistles, not a few passages which seem to be a mere repetition of what John has elsewhere said. But there are some things in regard to the internal evidence that they are the writings of the apostle John, and were not designedly forged, which deserve a more particular notice. They are such as these :—

(a) As already said, the style, sentiment, and manner are such as are appropriate to John. There is nothing in the epistles which we might not suppose he would write ; there is much that accords with what he has written ; there is much in the style which would not be likely to be found in the writings of another man ; and there is nothing in the sentiments which would lead us to suppose that the manner of the apostle John had been *assumed*, for the purpose of palming upon the world productions which were not his. Resemblances between these epistles will strike every reader, and it is unnecessary to specify them. The following passages, however, are so decidedly in the manner of John, that it may be presumed that they were either written by him, or by one who designed to copy from him : second epistle, vers. 5–7, 9 ; third epistle, vers. 11, 12.

(*b*) The fact that the *name* of the writer is not affixed to the epistles is much in the manner of John. Paul, in every case except in the epistle to the Hebrews, affixed his name to his epistles ; Peter, James, and Jude did the same thing. John, however, has never done it in any of his writings, except the Apocalypse. He seems to have supposed that there was something about his style and manner which would commend his writings as genuine ; or that in some other way they would be so well understood to be his, that it was not necessary to specify it. Yet the omission of his name, or of something that would lay claim to his authority as an apostle, would not be likely to occur if these epistles were fabricated with a design of palming them upon the world as his. The artifice would be too refined, and would be too likely to defeat itself, to be adopted by one who should form such a plan.

(*c*) The apparently severe and harsh remarks made in the epistle in regard to heretics, may be adverted to as an evidence that these epistles are the genuine writings of John the apostle. Thus, in the second epistle, ver. 10, he says, ' If there come any unto you, and bring not this doctrine, receive him not into your house, neither bid him God speed.' So in the third epistle, ver. 10 : ' If I come, I will remember his deeds which he doeth, prating against us with malicious words,' &c. It has been made an objection to the genuineness of these epistles, that this is not in the spirit of the mild and amiable ' disciple whom Jesus loved ;' that it breathes a temper of uncharitableness and severity which could not have existed in him at any time, and especially when, as an old man, he is said to have preached nothing but ' love one another.' But two circumstances will show that this, so far from being an objection, is rather a proof of their genuineness. One is, that in fact these expressions accord with what we *know* to have been the character of John. They are *not* inappropriate to one who was named by the Master himself, ' Boanerges—a son of thunder,' (Mark iii. 17 ;) or to one who was disposed to call down fire from heaven on the Samaritan who would not receive the Lord Jesus, (Luke ix. 54 ;) or to one who, when he saw another casting out devils in the name of Jesus, took upon himself the authority to forbid him, (Mark ix. 38.) The truth is, that there was a remarkable mixture of *gentleness* and *severity* in the character of John ; and though the former was the most prominent, and may be supposed to have increased as he grew old, yet the other also often manifested itself. There was that in the character of John, which, under some circumstances, and under other teaching than that of the Lord Jesus, *might* have been developed in the form of great exclusiveness, bigotry, and sternness—perhaps in the form of open persecution. Under the teaching of the Saviour, and through his example, his milder and better nature prevailed, and so decidedly acquired the ascendency, that we almost never think of the harsher traits of his character. The other circumstance is, that it would never have occurred to one who should have attempted to forge an epistle in the name of John, to have *introduced* a passage of this kind. The artifice would have been too little likely to have accomplished the end, to have occurred to the mind, or to have been adopted. The public character of John was so amiable ; he was so uniformly spoken of as the ' disciple whom Jesus loved ;' gentleness and kindness seemed to be such pervading traits in his nature, that no one would have thought of introducing sentiments which *seemed* to be at variance with these traits, even though, on a close analysis, it could be made out that they were *not* contrary to his natural character.

(*d*) Perhaps, also, the appellation which the writer gives himself in these two epistles, (*ὁ πρεσβύτερος*—*the elder*,) may be regarded as some evidence that they are the writings of the apostle John ; that is, it is more probable that he would use this appellation than that any other writer would. It has, indeed, been made a ground of objection that the use of this term proves that they are *not* the productions of John. See Lücke, p. 340. But, as we have seen, John was not accustomed to prefix his own name to his writings ; and if these epistles were written by him when he was at Ephesus, nothing is more probable than that he should use this term. It can hardly be regarded as an appellation pertaining to *office*, for as there were many *elders* or *presbyters* in the church, (Acts xx. 17,) the use of the term ' *the* elder ' would not be sufficiently distinctive to designate the writer. It may be presumed, therefore, to have a particular respect to age ; and, under the circumstances supposed, it would apply to no one with so much propriety as to the apostle John—one who would be well known as *the* aged and venerable disciple of the Saviour. Compare, however, Lücke (pp. 340–343) on the use of this word.

§ 2. *Of the person to whom John addressed his second Epistle.*

This epistle purports to be addressed, as it is in our translation, to ' the elect lady '—*ἐκλεκτῇ κυρίᾳ*. There has been great diversity of opinion in regard to the person here referred to, and there are questions respecting it which it is impossible to determine with absolute certainty. The different opinions which have been entertained are the following : (*a*) Some have supposed that a Christian matron is referred to, a friend of John, whose name was either *Ἐκλεκτή* (*Eclecte*,) or *Κυρία*, (*Cyria*.) Œcumenius and Theophylact supposed that the proper name of the female referred to was *Eclecte ;* others have adopted the other opinion, that the name was *Cyria*. (*b*) Others among the ancients, and particularly Clement, supposed that the *church* was denoted by this name, under the delicate image of an elect lady ; either some particular church to whom the epistle was sent, or to the church at large. This opinion has been held by some of the modern writers also. (*c*) Others have supposed, as is implied in our common version, that it was addressed to some Christian matron, whose name is not mentioned, but who was well known to John, and perhaps to many others, for her piety, and her acts of kindness to Christians. The reason why her name was suppressed, it has been supposed, was that if it had been mentioned it might have exposed her to trouble in some way, perhaps to persecution. (*d*) Recently, Knauer (Studien und Kritik., 1833, Heft 2. s. 452, ff.) has endeavoured to show that it was addressed to the Virgin Mary, who is supposed then to have resided in Galilee. The improbability of this opinion is shown by Lücke, pp. 352, 353.

These questions are not very important to be determined, even if they could be with accuracy ; and at this period of time, and with the few data which we have for forming a correct judgment on the subject, it is not possible to settle them with entire certainty. The probable truth in regard to this point, and all which it seems now possible to ascertain with any degree of certainty, may be expressed in the following specifications :

(1.) The letter was addressed to an individual, and not to a church. If it had been to a particular church, it would have been specified, for this is the uniform mode in the New Testament. If it were addressed to the church at large, it is in the highest degree improbable that John should have departed from the style of address in his first epistle ; improbable in every way that he should have adopted another style so mystical and unusual in a plain prose composition. It is only in poetry, in prophecy, in compositions where figurative language abounds, that the church is represented as a female at all ; and it is wholly improbable that John, at the outset of a brief epistle, should have adopted this appellation. The fact that it was addressed to an individual female is further apparent from the mention of her children : vers. 1, 4, ' Unto the elect lady and *her children ;*' ' I found of *thy children* walking in truth.' This is not such language as one would use in ..ddressing a church.

(2.) It is probable that the *name* of this lady was designed to be specified, and that it was *Cyria,* (Κυρία.) This, indeed, is not absolutely certain ; but the Greek will readily bear this, and it accords best with apostolic usage to suppose that the name of the person to whom the letter was addressed would be designated. This occurs in the third epistle of John, the epistles of Paul to Philemon, to Timothy, and to Titus, and, so far as appears, there is no reason why it should not have been done in the case before us. The Syriac and Arabic translators so understand it, for both have retained the name *Cyria.* It may do something to confirm this view, to remark that the name *Cyria* was not uncommon, in subsequent times, at least, among Christian females. See Corp. Inscript. Gruter, p. 1127, Num. xi. Φένισπος καὶ ἡ γυνὴ αὐτοῦ Κυρία. Comp. Lex. Hagiologic. Lips. 1719, p. 448, where two female martyrs of that name are mentioned. See also other instances referred to by Lücke, Com. p. 351. If these views are correct, then the true rendering of the passage would be, ' The presbyter unto the elect Cyria.'

(3.) Of this pious female, however, nothing more is known than what is mentioned in this epistle. From that we learn that John was warmly attached to her, (ver. 5 ;) that she was a mother, and that her children were pious, (vers. 1, 4 ;) and that she was of a hospitable character, and would be likely to entertain those who came professedly as religious teachers, vers. 10, 11. Where or when she lived, or when she died, we have no information whatever. At the time of writing this epistle, John had strong hopes that he would be permitted to come soon and see her, but whether he ever did so, we are not informed, ver. 12.

§. 3. *The canonical authority of the second and third Epistles of John.*

The canonical authority of these epistles depends on the following things :

(1.) On the evidence that they are the writings of the apostle John. In proportion as that evidence is clear, their canonical authority is of course established.

(2.) Though brief, and though addressed to individuals, they are admitted into the canon of Scripture with the same propriety as the epistles to Timothy, to Titus, and to Philemon, for those were addressed also to individuals.

(3.) Like those epistles, also, these contain things of general interest to the church. There is nothing in either that is inconsistent with what John has elsewhere written, or that conflicts with any other part of the New Testament; there is much in them that is in the manner of John, and that breathes his spirit; there is enough in them to tell us of the way of salvation.

Of the time when these epistles were written, and the place where, nothing is known, and conjecture would be useless, as there are no marks of time or place in either, and there is no historical statement that gives the information. It has been the common opinion that they were written at Ephesus, and when John was old. The appellation which he gives of himself, ' *the elder,*' accords with this supposition, though it does not make it absolutely certain.

SECOND EPISTLE OF JOHN

THE elder unto the elect lady and her children, whom I love | in the truth; and not I only, but also all they that have known the truth;

ANALYSIS OF THE SECOND EPISTLE.

THE points embraced in this epistle are these : A salutation to the female to whom it is addressed, and an expression of warm attachment to her family, vers. 1–3. An expression of joy and gratitude that he had been permitted to learn that her children had embraced the truth, and were walking in it, ver. 4. An exhortation to live in the exercise of mutual love, in obedience to the great commandment of the Saviour, vers. 5, 6. The fact that many deceivers had gone out into the world, and an exhortation to be on their guard against their arts, vers. 7, 8. A test by which they might bo known, and their true character ascertained, ver. 9. An exhortation to show them no countenance whatever ; not to treat them in any such way, even in the rites of hospitality, as to give occasion to the charge that she was friendly to their doctrines, vers. 10, 11. A statement that, as he hoped to see her soon, he would not write more to her, ver. 12. And the salutation of the children of some one who is spoken of as her elect sister, ver. 13.

1. *The elder.* See the Intro., § 1, (2, *d.*) ¶ *Unto the elect lady.* The elect or chosen Cyria. See Intro., § 2. He addresses her as one chosen of God to salvation, in the use of a term often applied to Christians in the New Testament. ¶ *And her children.* The word here rendered *children* (τέκνα) would include in itself both sons and daughters, but as the apostle immediately uses a masculine pronoun, οὖς it would seem more probable that sons only were intended. At all events, the use of such a pronoun proves that

some at least of her children were sons. Of their number and character we have no information, except that (Notes on ver. 4) a part of them were Christians. ¶ *Whom I love in the truth.* See Notes, 1 John iii. 18. The meaning here is, that he *truly* or *sincerely* loved them. The introduction of the article *the* here, which is not in the original, (ἐν αληθία) somewhat obscures the sense, as if the meaning were that he loved them so far as they embraced the truth. The meaning however is, that he was sincerely attached to them. The word 'whom' here, (οὖς,) embraces both the mother and her children, though the pronoun is in the masculine gender, in accordance with the usage of the Greek language. No mention is made of her husband, and it may thence be inferred that she was a widow. Had he been living, though he might not have been a Christian, it is to be presumed that some allusion would have been made to him as well as to the children, especially as there is reason to believe that only a part of her children were pious. See Notes, ver. 4. ¶ *And not I only, but also all they that have known the truth.* That is, all those Christians who had had an opportunity of knowing them, were sincerely attached to them. It would seem, from a subsequent part of the epistle, (ver. 10,) that this female was of a hospitable character, and was accustomed to entertain at her house the professed friends of religion, especially religious teachers, and it is probable that she was the more extensively known from this fact. The commendation of the apostle here shows that it is *possible* that a family shall be extensively known as one of order, peace, and

2 For the truth's sake, which dwelleth in us, and shall be with us for ever.

3 Grace be with you, mercy, *and* peace, from God the Father, and from the Lord Jesus Christ, the

Son of the Father, in truth and love.

4 I rejoiced greatly that I found of thy children walking in truth, as we have received a commandment from the Father.

---

religion, so that all who know it or hear of it shall regard it with interest, respect, and love.

2. *For the truth's sake.* They love this family *because* they love the truth, and see it so cordially embraced and so happily exemplified. They who love the gospel itself will rejoice in all the effects which it produces in society, on individuals, families, neighbourhoods, and their hearts will be drawn with warm affection to the places where its influence is most fully seen. ¶ *Which dwelleth in us.* In us who are Christians; that is, the truths of the gospel which we have embraced. Truth may be said to have taken up a permanent abode in the hearts of all who love religion. ¶ *And shall be with us for ever.* Its abode with us is not for a night or a day; not for a month or a year; not for the few years that make up mortal life; it is not a passing stranger that finds a lodging like the weary traveller for a night, and in the morning is gone to be seen no more; it has come to us to make our hearts its permanent home, and it is to be with us in all worlds, and while ceaseless ages shall roll away.

3. *Grace be unto you,* &c. See Notes Rom. i. 7. This salutation does not differ from those commonly employed by the sacred writers, except in the emphasis which is placed on the fact that the Lord Jesus Christ is ' the Son of the Father.' This is much in the style of John, in all of whose writings he dwells much on the fact that the Lord Jesus is the Son of God, and on the importance of recognising that fact in order to the possession of true religion. Comp. 1 John ii. 22, 23; iv. 15; v. 1, 2, 10–12, 20. ¶ *In truth and love.* This phrase is not to be connected with the expression ' the Son of the Father,' as if it meant that he was his Son ' in truth and love,' but is rather to be connected with the ' grace, mercy, and peace' referred to, as a prayer that they

might be manifested to this family in promoting truth and love.

4. *I rejoiced greatly that 1 found,* &c. That I learned this fact respecting some of thy children. The apostle does not say *how* he had learned this. It may have been that he had become personally acquainted with them when they were away from their home, or that he had learned it from others. The word used (εὕρηκα) would apply to either method. Grotius supposed that some of the sons had come on business to Ephesus, and that John had become acquainted with them there. ¶ *Of thy children walking in truth.* That is, true Christians; living in accordance with the truth, for this constitutes the essence of religion. The expression used here, ' of thy children,' (ἐκ τῶν τέκνων,) means *some* of thy children; implying that he knew of a part of them who were true Christians. This is clear from the Greek construction, because (*a*) if he had meant to say that he had found them *all* to be of this description, the sentiment would have been directly expressed, ' *thy* children;' but as it is, some word is necessary to be understood to complete the sense; and (*b*) the same thing is demanded by the fact that the participle used (*walking*—περιπατοῦντας) is in the accusative case. If he had referred to them all, the participle would have been in the genitive, agreeing with the word *children*, (τῶν περιπατούντων.)—*Lücke.* Whether the apostle means to say that only a part of them had in fact embraced the gospel, or that he had only known that a part of them had done it, though the others might have done it without his knowledge, is not quite clear, though the former supposition appears to be the correct one, for if they had all become Christians it is to be presumed that he would have been informed of it. The probability seems to be that a part of her children only were truly pious, though there is no evidence that the

5 And now I beseech thee, lady, not as though I wrote a new commandment unto thee, but that which we had from the beginning, that we love *a* one another.

6 And this is love, *b* that we walk after his commandments. This is the commandment, That, as ye have

beard from the beginning, ye should walk in it.

7 For many *c* deceivers are entered into the world, who confess not that Jesus Christ is come in the flesh. This is a deceiver and an antichrist.

a 1 Jn.3.23.　　*b* Jn.14.15,21.　　*c* 1 Jn.4.1.

others were otherwise than correct in their moral conduct. If there had been improper conduct in any of her other children, John was too courteous, and too delicate in his feelings, to allude to so disagreeable a circumstance. But ' if that pious lady,' to use the language of Benson, ' had some wicked children, her lot was not peculiar. Her consolation was that she had some who were truly good. John commended those who were good, in order to excite them in the most agreeable manner to persevere.' ¶ *As we have received a commandment from the Father.* That is, as he has commanded us to live ; in accordance with the truth which he has revealed. The *Father*, in the Scripture, is everywhere represented as the source of law.

5. *And now I beseech thee, lady.* Dr. ' And now I entreat thee, *Cyria* ' (*κυρία.*) See Intro. § 2. If this was her proper name, there is no impropriety in supposing that he would address her in this familiar style. John was probably then a very old man ; the female to whom the epistle was addressed was doubtless much younger. ¶ *Not as though I wrote a new commandment unto thee.* John presumed that the command to love one another was understood as far as the gospel was known ; and he might well presume it, for true Christianity never prevails anywhere without prompting to the observance of this law. See Notes, 1 Thess. iv. 9. ¶ *But that which we had from the beginning.* From the time when the gospel was first made known to us. See Notes, 1 John ii. 7 ; iii. 11. ¶ *That we love one another.* That is, that there be among the disciples of Christ mutual love ; or that in all circumstances and relations they should love one another, John xv. 12, 17. This general command, addressed to all the disciples of the Saviour, John doubtless

means to say was as applicable to him and to the pious female to whom he wrote as to any others, and ought to be exercised by them towards all true Christians ; and he exhorts her, as he did all Christians, to exercise it. It was a command on which, in his old age, he loved to dwell ; and he had little more to say to her than this, to exhort her to obey this injunction of the Saviour.

6. *And this is love, that we walk after his commandments.* This is the proper expression or evidence of love to God. See Notes, John xiv. 15, 21. ¶ *This is the commandment.* That is, this is his great and peculiar commandment ; the one by which his disciples are to be peculiarly characterized, and by which they are to be distinguished in the world. See Notes, John xiii. 34.

7. *For.* Ὅτι. This word *for* is not here to be regarded as connected with the previous verse, and as giving a reason why there should be the exercise of mutual love, but is rather to be understood as connected with the following verse, (8,) and as giving a reason for the caution there expressed : ' Because it is a truth that many deceivers have appeared, or since it has occurred that many such are abroad, look to yourselves lest you be betrayed and ruined.' The fact that there were many such deceivers was a good reason for being constantly on their guard, lest they should be so far drawn away as not to receive a full reward. ¶ *Many deceivers are entered into the world.* Are abroad in the world, or have appeared among men. Several MSS. read here, ' *have gone out* into the world,' (ἐξῆλθον,) instead of ' have entered into,' (εἰσῆλθον.) The common reading is the correct one, and the other was originated, probably, from the unusual form of the expression, ' have come into the world,' as if they had come from another abode. That, however, is not

8 Look *a* to yourselves, that we *b* lose not those things which we have[1] wrought, but that we receive a full reward.

a Mar.13.9.   *b* Phi.3.16; Re.3.11.

[1] Or, *gained.* Some copies read, *which ye have gained, but that ye.*

necessarily implied, the language being such as would be properly used to denote the idea that there were such deceivers in the world. ¶ *Who confess not that Jesus Christ is come in the flesh.* Who maintain that he assumed the *appearance* only of a man, and was not really incarnate. See Notes, 1 John iv. 2, 3. ¶ *This is a deceiver.* Every one who maintains this is to be regarded as a deceiver. ¶ *And an antichrist.* See Notes, 1 John ii. 18 ; iv. 3.

8. *Look to yourselves.* This seems to be addressed to the lady to whom he wrote, and to her children. The idea is, that they should be particularly on their guard, and that their first care should be to secure their own hearts, so that they should not be exposed to the dangerous attacks of error. When error abounds in the world, our first duty is not to attack it and make war upon it ; it is to look to the citadel of our own souls, and see that all is well guarded there. When an enemy invades a land, the first thing will not be to go out against him, regardless of our own strength, or of the security of our own fortresses, but it will be to see that our forts are well manned, and that we are secure *there* from his assaults. If that is so, we may then go forth with confidence to meet him on the open field. In relation to an error that is in the world, the first thing for a Christian to do is to take care of his own heart. ¶ *That which we lose not those things which we have wrought.* Marg., ' Or, *gained.* Some copies read, *which ye have gained, but that ye.*' The reading here referred to in the margin is found in several MSS. and also in the Vulgate, Syriac, and Æthiopic versions. It is not, however, adopted in the late critical editions of the New Testament, and the common reading is probably genuine. The sense is not materially varied, and the common reading is not unnatural. John was exhorting the family to whom this epistle was written to take good heed to themselves while so many artful errorists were around them, lest they

should be drawn away from the truth, and lose a part of the full reward which they might hope to receive in heaven. In doing this, nothing was more natural than that he, as a Christian friend, should group himself with them, and speak of himself as having the same need of caution, and express the feeling that he ought to strive also to obtain the full reward, thus showing that he was not disposed to address an exhortation to them which he was not willing to regard as applicable to himself. The *truth* which is taught here is one of interest to all Christians—that it is possible for even genuine Christians, by suffering themselves to be led into error, or by failure in duty, to lose a part of the reward which they might have obtained. The crown which they will wear in heaven will be less bright than that which they might have worn, and the throne which they will occupy will be less elevated. The rewards of heaven will be in accordance with the services rendered to the Redeemer ; and it would not be right that they who turn aside, or falter in their course, should have the same exalted honours which they might have received if they had devoted themselves to God with ever-increasing fidelity. It is painful to think how many there are who begin the Christian career with burning zeal, as if they would strike for the highest rewards in heaven, but who soon waver in their course, and fall into some paralysing error, until at last they receive, perhaps, not half the reward which they might have obtained. ¶ *But that we receive a full reward.* Such as will be granted to a life uniformly consistent and faithful ; all that God has to bestow on his people when *most* faithful and true. But who can estimate the '*full* reward' of heaven, the unspeakable glory of those who make it the grand business of their lives to obtain all they can of its bliss. And who is there that does not feel that he *ought* to strive for a crown in which not one gem shall be wanting that *might* have sparkled there for ever ?

9 Whosoever transgresseth, and abideth not in *a* the doctrine of Christ, hath not God. He that abideth in the doctrine of Christ, he hath both the Father and the Son.

10 If *b* there come any unto you, and bring not this doctrine, receive him not into *your* house, neither bid him God speed:

a Jn.15.6.   *b* Ga.1.8,9.

9. *Whosoever transgresseth, and abideth not in the doctrine of Christ, hath not God.* In the doctrine which Christ taught, or the true doctrine respecting him. The language is somewhat ambiguous, like the phrase 'the love of Christ,' which may mean either his love to us, or our love to him. Comp. John xv. 9. It is difficult to determine here which is the true sense—whether it means the doctrine or precepts which he taught, or the true doctrine respecting him. Macknight understands by it the doctrine *taught* by Christ and his apostles. It would seem most probable that this is the sense of the passage, but then it would include, of course, all that Christ taught respecting himself, as well as his other instructions. The essential idea is, that the truth must be held respecting the precepts, the character, and the work of the Saviour. Probably the immediate allusion here is to those to whom John so frequently referred as 'antichrist,' who denied that Jesus had come in the flesh, ver. 7. At the same time, however, he makes the remark general, that if any one did not hold the true doctrine respecting the Saviour, he had no real knowledge of God. See John i. 18; v. 23; xv. 23; xvii. 3; 1 John ii. 23. ¶ *Hath not God.* Has no true knowledge of God. The truth taught here is, that it is essential to piety to hold the true doctrine respecting Christ. ¶ *He that abideth in the doctrine of Christ.* In the true doctrine respecting Christ, or in the doctrine which he taught. ¶ *He hath both the Father and the Son.* There is such an intimate union between the Father and the Son, that he who has just views of the one has also of the other. Comp. Notes on John xiv. 7, 9, 10, 11, and 1 John ii. 23.
10. *If there come any unto you.* Any professed teacher of religion. There can be no doubt that she to whom this epistle was written was accustomed to entertain such teachers. ¶ *And bring not this*

doctrine. This doctrine which Christ taught, or the true doctrine respecting him and his religion. ¶ *Receive him not into* your *house.* This cannot mean that *no* acts of kindness, in any circumstances, were to be shown to such persons; but that there was to be nothing done which could be fairly construed as encouraging or countenancing them *as religious teachers.* The true rule would seem to be, in regard to such persons, that, so far as we have intercourse with them as neighbours, or strangers, we are to be honest, true, kind, and just, but we are to do *nothing* that will countenance them *as* religious teachers. We are not to attend on their instruction, (Prov. xix. 27;) we are not to receive them into our houses, or to entertain them as religious teachers; we are not to commend them to others, or to give them any reason to use our names or influence in propagating error. It would not be difficult to practise this rule, and yet to show to others all the kindness, and all the attention in circumstances of want, which religion demands. A man who is truly consistent is never suspected of countenancing error, even when he is distinguished for liberality, and is ready, like the good Samaritan, to pour in oil and wine in the wounds of *any* waylaid traveller. The command not to 'receive such an one into the house,' in such circumstances as those referred to by John, would be probably understood literally, as he doubtless designed that it should be. To do that, to meet such persons with a friendly greeting, would be construed as countenancing their doctrine, and as commending them to others; and hence it was forbidden that they should be entertained as such. This treatment would not be demanded where no such interpretation could be put on receiving a friend or relative who held different and even erroneous views, or in showing kindness to a stranger who differed from us, but it *would* apply to the receiving

11 For he that biddeth him God speed, is partaker *a* of his evil deeds.

12 Having many things to write unto you, I would not *write* with

a 1 Ti.5.22.

paper and ink: but I trust to come unto you, and speak [1] face to face, that [2] our joy *b* may be full.

13 The children of thy elect sister greet thee. Amen.

1 *mouth to mouth.*   2 Or, *your.*   *b* 1 Jn.1.4.

and entertaining *a professed teacher of religion, as such;* and the rule is as applicable now as it was then. ¶ *Neither bid him God speed.* Καὶ χαίρειν αὐτῷ μὴ λέγετε—'and do not say to him, *hail,* or *joy.*' Do not wish him joy; do not hail, or salute him. The word used expresses the common form of salutation, as when we wish one health, success, prosperity, Matt. xxvi. 49 ; Acts xv. 23 ; xxiii. 26 ; James i. 1. It would be understood as expressing a wish for success in the enterprise in which they were embarked; and though we should love all men, and desire their welfare, and sincerely seek their happiness, yet we can properly wish no one success in a career of sin and error.

11. *For he that biddeth him God speed, is partaker of his evil deeds.* Shows that he countenances and approves of the doctrine which is taught. Comp. Notes, 1 Tim. v. 22.

12. *Having many things to write unto you.* That I would wish to say. This language is such as would be used by one who was hurried, or who was in feeble health, or who hoped soon to see the person written to. In such a case only the points would be selected which were of most immediate and pressing importance, and the remainder would be reserved for a more free personal interview. ¶ *I would not* write *with paper.* The word *paper* here conveys an idea which is not strictly correct. *Paper,* as that term is now understood, was not invented until long after this period. The material designated by the word used by John (χάρτης) was the Egyptian papyrus, and the particular thing denoted was a leaf made out of that plant. The sheets were made from membranes of the plant closely pressed together. This plant was found also in Syria and Babylon, but it was produced in greater abundance in Egypt, and that was the plant which was commonly used. It was so comparatively cheap, that it in a great measure superseded the earlier

materials for writing—plates of lead, or stone, or the skins of animals. It is probable that the books of the New Testament were written on this species of paper. Comp. Hug, Intro. chap. iii., § 11. *And ink.* The ink which was commonly employed in writing was made of soot and water, with a mixture of some species of gum to give it consistency and durability.—*Lücke.* The instrument or *pen* was made of a reed. ¶ *But I trust to come unto you, and speak face to face.* Marg., as in Greek, *mouth to mouth.* The phrase is a common one, to denote conversation with any one, especially free and confidential conversation. Comp. Numb. xii. 8 ; Jer. xxxii. 4. ¶ *That our joy may be full.* Marg., *your.* The marginal reading has arisen from a variation in the Greek copies. The word *our* is best sustained, and accords best with the connection. John would be likely to express the hope that *he* would find pleasure from such an interview. See Notes, 1 John i. 4. Comp. Rom. i. 11, 12.

13. *The children of thy elect sister greet thee.* Of this ' elect sister ' nothing more is known. It would seem probable, from the fact that she is not mentioned as sending her salutations, that she was either dead, or that she was absent. John mentions her, however, as a Christian—as one of the elect or chosen of God.

REMARKS ON THIS EPISTLE.

In view of the exposition of this epistle we may make the following remarks :—

(1.) It is desirable for a family to have a character for piety so consistent and well understood that all who know it shall perceive it and love it, ver. 1. In the case of this lady and her household, it would seem that, as far as they were known, they were known as a well-ordered Christian household. Such a family John said he loved ; and he said that it was loved by all who had any knowledge of them. What is more lovely to the view than such a household? What is better fitted to make an impression on the world favourable to religion?

(2.) It is a matter of great rejoicing when *any* part of a family become truly religious, ver. 4. We should rejoice with our friends, and should render unfeigned thanks to God, if *any* of their children are converted, and walk in the truth. No greater blessing can descend on a family than the early conversion of children; and as angels rejoice over one sinner that is converted, we should rejoice when the children of our friends are brought to a knowledge of the truth, and devote themselves to God in early life.

(3.) It is our duty to be on our guard against the arts of the teachers of error, ver. 7. They abound in every age. They are often learned, eloquent, and profound. They study and understand the arts of persuasion. They adapt their instructions to the capacity of those whom they would lead astray. They flatter their vanity; accommodate themselves to their peculiar views and tastes; court their society, and seek to share their friendship. They often appear to be eminently meek, and serious, and devout, and prayerful, for they know that no others can succeed who profess to inculcate the principles of religion. There are few arts more profound than that of leading men into error; few that are studied more, or with greater success. Every Christian, therefore, should be on his guard against such arts; and while he should on all subjects be open to conviction, and be ready to yield his own opinions when convinced that they are wrong, yet he should yield to *truth*, not to men; to *argument*, not to the influence of the *personal character* of the professed religious teacher.

(4.) We may see that it is *possible* for us to lose a portion of the reward which we *might* enjoy in heaven, ver. 8. The rewards of heaven will be apportioned to our character, and to our services in the cause of religion in this life, and they who 'sow sparingly shall reap also sparingly.' Christians often begin their course with great zeal, and

as if they were determined to reap the highest rewards of the heavenly world. If they should persevere in the course which they have commenced, they would indeed shine as the stars in the firmament. But, alas! their zeal soon dies away. They relax their efforts, and lose their watchfulness. They engage in some pursuit that absorbs their time, and interferes with their habits of devotion. They connive at error and sin; begin to love the comforts of this life; seek the honours or the riches of this world; and though they may be saved at last, yet they lose half their reward. It should be a fixed purpose with all Christians, and especially with such as are just entering on the Christian life, to wear in heaven a crown as bright and studded with as many jewels *as can possibly be obtained.*

(5.) We may learn from this epistle how to regard and treat the teachers of error, ver. 10. *We are not to do anything that can be fairly construed as countenancing their doctrines.* This simple rule would guide us to a course that is right. We are to have minds open to conviction. We are to love the truth, and be ever ready to follow it. We are not to be prejudiced against anything. We are to treat all men with kindness; to be true, and just, and faithful in our intercourse with all; to be hospitable, and ever ready to do good to *all* who are needy, whatever their name, colour, rank, or opinions. We are not to cut the ties which bind us to our friends and kindred, though they embrace opinions which we deem erroneous or dangerous; but we are in no way to become the patrons of error, or to leave the impression that we are indifferent as to what is believed. The friends of truth and piety we should receive cordially to our dwellings, and should account ourselves honoured by their presence, (Ps. ci. 6, 7;) strangers we should not forget to entertain, for thereby we may entertain angels unawares, (Heb. xiii. 2;) but the open advocate of what we regard as dangerous error, we are *not* to receive in any such sense or way as to have our treatment of him fairly construed as patronising his errors, or commending him as a teacher to the favourable regards of our fellow-men. Neither by our influence, our names, our money, our personal friendship, are we to give him increased facilities for spreading pernicious error through the world. As men, as fellow-sufferers, as citizens, as neighbours, as the friends of temperance, of the prisoner, of the widow, the orphan, and the slave, and as the patrons of learning, we may be united in promoting objects dear to our hearts, but *as religious teachers* we are to show them no countenance, not so much as would be implied in the common form of salutation wishing them success. In all this there is no breach of charity, and no want of true love, for we are to love the truth more than we are the persons of men.

To the man himself we should be ever ready to do good. Him we should never injure in any way, in his person, property, or feelings. We should never attempt to deprive him of the right of cherishing his own opinions, and of spreading them in his own way, answerable, not to us, but to God. We should impose no pains or penalties on him for the opinions which he holds. But we should do nothing to give him increased power to propagate them, and should never place ourselves by any alliance of friendship, family, or business, in such a position that we shall not be perfectly free to maintain our own sentiments, and to oppose what we deem to be error, whoever may advocate it.

THIRD EPISTLE. OF JOHN

THE elder unto the well-beloved Gaius, whom I love ¹ in the truth.

1 Or, *truly*.

2 Beloved, I ² wish above all things that thou mayest prosper

2 Or, *pray*.

ANALYSIS OF THE EPISTLE.

THIS brief epistle, written to a Christian whose name was Gaius, of whom nothing more is known, (comp. Notes on ver. 1,) and in respect to which the time and place of writing it are equally unknown, embraces the following subjects: I. The address, with an expression of tender attachment, and an earnest wish for his welfare and happiness, vers. 1, 2. II. A commendation of his character and doings, as the writer had learned it from some brethren who had visited him particularly; (*a*) for his attachment to the truth, and (*b*) for his kindness shown to the members of his own church, and to strangers who had gone forth to some work of charity, vers. 3-8. III. The writer then adverts to the fact that he had written on this subject to the church, commending these strangers to their attention, but that Diotrephes would not acknowledge his authority, or receive those whom he introduced to them. This conduct, he said, demanded rebuke; and he says that when he himself came, he would take proper measures to assert his own authority, and show to him and to the church the duty of receiving Christian brethren commended to them from abroad, vers. 9, 10. IV. He exhorts Gaius to persevere in that which was good—in a life of love and kindness, in an imitation of the benevolent God, ver. 11. V. Of another person—Demetrius—who, it would seem, had been associated with Gaius in the honourable course which he had pursued, in opposition to what the church had done, he also speaks in terms of commendation,

and says that the same honourable testimony had been borne of him which had been of Gaius, ver. 12. VI. As in the second epistle, he says, in the close, that there were many things which he would be glad to say to him, but there were reasons why they should not be set down 'with ink and pen,' but he hoped soon to confer with him freely on those subjects face to face, and the epistle is closed by kind salutations, vers. 13, 14.

The *occasion* on which the epistle was written is no farther known than appears from the epistle itself. From this, the following facts are all that can now be ascertained: (1.) That Gaius was a Christian man, and evidently a member of the church, but of what church is unknown. (2.) That there were certain persons known to the writer of the epistle, and who either lived where he did, or who had been commended to him by others, who proposed to travel to the place where Gaius lived. Their particular *object* is not known, further than that it is said (ver. 7) that they 'went for his name's sake;' that is, in the cause of religion. It further appears that they had resolved not to be dependent on the heathen for their support, but wished the favour and friendship of the church—perhaps designing to preach to the heathen, and yet apprehending that if they desired their maintenance from them, it would be charged on them that they were mercenary in their ends. (3.) In these circumstances, and with this view, the author of this epistle wrote to the church, commending these brethren to their kind and fraternal regards. (4.)

and be in health, even as thy soul prospereth.

This recommendation, so far as appears, would have been successful, had it not been for one man, Diotrephes, who had so much influence, and who made such violent opposition, that the church refused to receive them, and they became dependent on private charity. The *ground* of the opposition of Diotrephes is not fully stated, but it seems to have arisen from two sources: (*a*) a desire to rule in the church; and (*b*) a particular opposition to the writer of this epistle, and a denial of any obligation to recognise his instructions or commendations as binding. The idea seems to have been that the church was entirely independent, and might receive or reject any whom it pleased, though they were commended to them by an apostle. (5.) In these circumstances, Gaius, as an individual, and against the action of the church, received and hospitably entertained these strangers, and aided them in the prosecution of their work. In this office of hospitality another member of the church, Demetrius, also shared; and to commend them for this work, particularly Gaius, at whose house probably they were entertained, is the design of this epistle. (6.) After having returned to the writer of this epistle, who had formerly commended them to the church, and having borne honourable testimony to the hospitality of Gaius, it would seem that they resolved to repeat their journey for the same purpose, and that the writer of the epistle commended them now to the renewed hospitality of Gaius. On this occasion, probably, they bore this epistle to him. See Notes on vers. 6, 7. Of Diotrephes nothing more is known than is here specified. Erasmus and Bede supposed that he was the author of a new sect; but of this there is no evidence, and if he had been, it is probable that John would have cautioned Gaius against his influence. Many have supposed that he was a bishop or pastor in the church where he resided; but there is no evidence of this, and as John wrote to ' *the church*,' commending the strangers to *them*, this would seem to be hardly probable. Comp. Rev. ii. 1, 8, 12, 18; iii. 1, 7, 14. Others have sup-

posed that he was a deacon, and had charge of the funds of the church, and that he refused to furnish to these strangers the aid out of the public treasury which they needed, and that by so doing he hindered them in the prosecution of their object. But all this is mere conjecture, and it is now impossible to ascertain what office he held, if he held any. That he was a man of influence is apparent; that he was proud, ambitious, and desirous of ruling, is equally clear; and that he prevailed on the church *not* to receive the strangers commended to them by the apostle is equally manifest. Of the rank and standing of Demetrius nothing more is known. Benson supposes that he was the bearer of this letter, and that he had gone with the brethren referred to to preach to the Gentiles. But it seems more probable that he was a member of the church to which Gaius belonged, and that he had concurred with him in rendering aid to the strangers who had been rejected by the influence of Diotrephes. If he had gone *with* these strangers, and had carried this letter, it would have been noticed, and it would have been in accordance with the apostolic custom, that he should have been commended to the favourable attentions of Gaius. In regard to the authenticity and the canonical authority of this epistle, see the Introduction at the beginning of the second epistle.

1. *The elder.* See Notes on the Second Epistle, ver. 1. ¶ *Unto the well-beloved Gaius.* Three persons of this name are elsewhere mentioned in the New Testament—Gaius, whom Paul in Rom. xvi. 23 calls ' his host,' and whom he says (1 Cor. i. 15) he baptized, residing at Corinth, (see Notes, Rom. xvi. 23;) Gaius of Macedonia, one of Paul's companions in travel, who was arrested by an excited mob at Ephesus, (Acts xix. 29;) and Gaius of Derbe, who went with Paul and Timothy into Asia, Acts xx. 4. Whether either of these persons is referred to here, cannot with certainty be determined. If it were any of them it was probably the last mentioned—Gaius of Derbe. There is no objection to the supposition that he was the one

3 For I rejoiced greatly when the brethren came and testified of the truth that is in thee, even as thou walkest ^a in the truth.

unless it be from the fact that this epistle was probably written many years after the transaction mentioned in Acts xx. 4, and the probability that Gaius might not have lived so long. The name was not an uncommon one, and it cannot be determined now who he was, or where he lived. Whether he had any office in the church is unknown, but he seems to have been a man of wealth and influence. The word translated 'well-beloved,' means simply *beloved*. It shows that he was a personal friend of the writer of this epistle. ¶ *Whom I love in the truth.* Marg., ' or truly.' See Notes on the Second Epistle, ver. 1.

2. *Beloved, I wish above all things.* Marg., *pray.* The word used here commonly means in the New Testament to pray; but it is also employed to express a strong and earnest desire for anything, Acts xxvii. 29; Rom. ix. 3; 2 Cor. xiii. 9. This is probably all that is implied here. The phrase rendered 'above all things'—περὶ πάντων—would be more correctly rendered here 'concerning, or in respect to all things;' and the idea is, that John wished earnestly that *in all respects* he might have the same kind of prosperity which his soul had. The common translation ' *above all things* ' would seem to mean that John valued health and outward prosperity more than he did anything else; that he wished that more than his usefulness or salvation. This cannot be the meaning, and is not demanded by the proper interpretation of the original. See this shown by Lücke, *in loc.* The sense is, ' In every respect, I wish that it may go as well with you as it does with your soul; that in your worldly prosperity, your comfort, and your bodily health, you may be as prosperous as you are in your religion.' This is the reverse of the wish which we are commonly constrained to express for our friends; for such is usually the comparative want of prosperity and advancement in their spiritual interests, that it is an expression of benevolence to desire that they might prosper in that respect

as much as they do in others. ¶ *That thou mayest prosper.* εὐοδοῦσθαι. This word occurs in the New Testament only in the following places: Rom. i. 10, rendered *have a prosperous journey* ; 1 Cor. xvi. 2, rendered *hath prospered* ; and in the passage before us. It means, properly, *to lead in a good way ; to prosper one's journey;* and then to make prosperous ; to give success to; to be prospered. It would apply here to any plan or purpose entertained. It would include success in business, happiness in domestic relations, or prosperity in any of the engagements and transactions in which a Christian might lawfully engage. It shows that it is right to wish that our friends may have success in the works of their hands and their plans of life. ¶ *And be in health.* To enjoy bodily health. It is not necessary to suppose, in order to a correct interpretation of this, that Gaius was at that time suffering from bodily indisposition, though perhaps it is most natural to suppose that, as John makes the wish for his health so prominent. But it is common, in all circumstances, to wish for the health and prosperity of our friends; and it is as proper as it is common, if we do not give that a degree of prominence above the welfare of the soul. ¶ *Even as thy soul prospereth.* John had learned, it would seem, from the ' brethren ' who had come to him, (ver. 3,) that Gaius was living as became a Christian; that he was advancing in the knowledge of the truth, and was exemplary in the duties of the Christian life; and he prays that in all other respects he might be prospered as much as he was in that. It is not *very* common that a man is more prospered in his spiritual interests than he is in his other interests, or that we can, in our wishes for the welfare of our friends, make the prosperity of the soul, and the practice and enjoyment of religion, the standard of our wishes in regard to other things. It argues a high state of piety when we can, as the expression of our highest desire for the welfare of our friends, express the hope that they may be in

4 I have no greater joy *a* than to hear that my children walk in truth.

5 Beloved, thou doest faithfully

b whatsoever thou doest to the brethren, and to strangers:

a Pr.23.24.   *b* 1 Pe.4.10.

all respects as much prospered as they are in their spiritual concerns.

3. *For I rejoiced greatly when the brethren came.* Who these were is not certainly known. They may have been members of the same church with Gaius, who, for some reason, had visited the writer of this epistle ; or they may have been the ' brethren ' who had gone from him with a letter of commendation to the church, (ver. 9,) and had been rejected by the church through the influence of Diotrephes, and who, after having been hospitably entertained by Gaius, had again returned to the writer of this epistle. In that case, they would of course bear honourable testimony to the kindness which they had received from Gaius, and to his Christian character. ¶ *And testified of the truth that is in thee.* That you adhere steadfastly to the truth, notwithstanding the fact that errors abound, and that there are many false teachers in the world. ¶ *Even as thou walkest in the truth.* Livest in accordance with the truth. The writer had made the same remark of the children of Cyria, to whom the second epistle was directed. See Notes on ver. 4 of that epistle.

4. *I have no greater joy than to hear that my children walk in truth.* That they adhere steadfastly to the truth, and that they live in accordance with it. This is such language as would be used by an aged apostle when speaking of those who had been converted by his instrumentality, and who looked up to him as a father ; and we may, therefore, infer that Gaius had been converted under the ministry of John, and that he was probably a much younger man than he was. John, the aged apostle, says that he had no higher happiness than to learn, respecting those who regarded him as their spiritual father, that they were steadfast in their adherence to the doctrines of religion. The same thing may be said now (*a*) of all the ministers of the gospel, that their highest comfort is found in the fact that those to whom they minister, whether still under their

care or removed from them, persevere in a steadfast attachment to the true doctrines of religion, and live accordingly ; and (*b*) of all Christian parents respecting their own children. The highest joy that a Christian parent can have is to know that his children, whether at home or abroad, adhere to the truths of religion, and live in accordance with the requirements of the gospel of Christ. If a child wished to confer the highest possible happiness on his parents when with them, it would be by becoming a decided Christian ; if, when abroad, in foreign lands or his own, he wished to convey intelligence to them that would most thrill their hearts with joy, it would be to announce to them that he had given his heart to God. There is no joy in a family like that when children are converted ; there is no news that comes from abroad that diffuses so much happiness through the domestic circle as the intelligence that a child is truly converted to the Saviour. There is nothing that would give more peace to the dying pillow of the Christian parent, than to be able to leave the world with the assurance that his children would always walk in truth.

5. *Beloved, thou doest faithfully.* In the previous verses the writer had commended Gaius for his attachment to truth, and his general correctness in his Christian life. He now speaks more particularly of his acts of generous hospitality, and says that he had fully, in that respect, done his duty as a Christian. ¶ *Whatsoever thou doest.* In all your intercourse with them, and in all your conduct towards them. The particular thing which led to this remark was his hospitality ; but the testimony respecting his general conduct had been such as to justify this commendation. ¶ *To the brethren.* Probably to Christians who were well known to him—perhaps referring to Christians in his own church. ¶ *And to strangers.* Such as had gone to the church of which he was a member with a letter of commendation from John.

6 Which have borne witness of thy charity before the church: whom if thou bring forward *a* on their journey [1] after a godly sort, thou shalt do well:

7 Because that for his name's

sake they went forth, taking *b* nothing of the Gentiles.

8 We therefore ought to receive *c* such, that we might be fellow-helpers to the truth.

a Ac.15.3.　　1 *worthy of God.*　　*b* 1 Co.9.15,18.
　　　　　　　c Mat.10.40.

Compare Notes on Rom. xii. 13, and Heb. xiii. 2.

6. *Which have borne witness of thy charity before the church.* It would seem that they had returned to John, and borne honourable testimony to the love manifested to them by Gaius. Before *what* church they had borne this testimony is unknown. Perhaps it was the church in Ephesus. ¶ *Whom if thou bring forward on their journey.* οὓς προπέμψας. ' Whom bringing forward, or having brought forward.' The word refers to aid rendered them in their journey, in facilitating their travels, either by personally accompanying them, by furnishing them the means of prosecuting their journey, or by hospitably entertaining them. Probably Gaius aided them in every way in which it was practicable. It has been made a question whether this refers to the fact that he *had* thus aided them in some visit which they had made to the church where Gaius was, or to a visit which they purposed to make. The Greek would seem to favour the latter construction, and yet it would appear from the epistle, that the ' brethren and strangers' actually had been with him : that they had been rejected by the church through the influence of Diotrephes, and had been thrown upon the hospitality of Gaius, and that they had returned, and had borne honourable testimony to his hospitality. These views can be reconciled by supposing, as Lücke does, that having been once on their travels, and having shared the hospitality of Gaius, they were purposing to visit that region again, and that John, praising him for his former hospitality, commends them again to him, stating the reason (vers. 9, 10) why he did not, in accordance with the usual custom, recommend them to the care of the church. They had now gone out (ver. 7) on the same errand on which they had formerly gone, and

they had now equal claims to the hospitality of the friends of religion. ¶ *After a godly sort.* Margin, as in Greek, *worthy of God.* The meaning is, As becomes those who serve God ; or as becomes those who are professors of his religion. ¶ *Thou shalt do well.* You will do that which religion requires in these circumstances.

7. *Because that for his name's sake.* The word ' *his* ' here refers to God ; and the idea is, that they had undertaken this journey not on their own account, but in the cause of religion. ¶ *They went forth.* Or, *they have gone forth*—ἐξῆλθον—referring to the journey which they had then undertaken ; not to the former one. ¶ *Taking nothing of the Gentiles.* The term *Gentile* embraced all who were not *Jews*, and it is evident that these persons went forth particularly to labour among the heathen. When they went, they resolved, it seems, to receive no part of their support from them, but to depend on the aid of their Christian brethren, and hence they were at first commended to the church of which Gaius and Diotrephes were members, and on this second excursion were commended particularly to Gaius. *Why* they resolved to take nothing of the Gentiles is not stated, but it was doubtless from prudential considerations, lest it should hinder their success among them, and expose them to the charge of being actuated by a mercenary spirit. There were circumstances in the early propagation of Christianity which made it proper, in order to avoid this reproach, to preach the gospel ' without charge,' though the doctrine is everywhere laid down in the Bible that it is the *duty* of those to whom it is preached to contribute to its maintenance, and that it is the *right* of those who preach to expect and receive a support. On this subject, see Notes on 1 Cor. ix., particularly vers. 15, 18.

9 I wrote unto the church: but Diotrephes, who loveth to have the pre-eminence ^a among them, receiveth us not.

<small>a Mat.23.4-8; 1 Ti.6.3,4</small>

8. *We therefore ought to receive such.* All of us ought hospitably to entertain and aid such persons. The work in which they are engaged is one of pure benevolence. They have no selfish aims and ends in it. They do not even look for the supplies of their wants among the people to whom they go to minister; and we ought, therefore, to aid them in their work, and to contribute to their support. The apostle doubtless meant to urge this duty particularly on Gaius; but in order to show that he recognised the obligation himself, he uses the term 'we,' and speaks of it as a duty binding on all Christians. ¶ *That we might be fellow-helpers to the truth.* All Christians cannot go forth to preach the gospel, but all may contribute something to the support of those who do; and in this case they would have a joint participation in the work of spreading the truth. The same reasoning which was applicable to that case, is also applicable now in regard to the duty of supporting those who go forth to preach the gospel to the destitute.

9. *I wrote unto the church.* That is, on the former occasion when they went forth. At that time, John naturally commended them to the kind attentions of the church, not doubting but that aid would be rendered them in prosecuting their benevolent work among the Gentiles. The epistle which was written on that occasion is now lost, and its contents cannot now be ascertained. It was, probably, however, a letter of mere commendation, perhaps stating the object which these brethren had in view, and soliciting the aid of the church. The Latin Vulgate renders this, *scripsissem forsan ecclesiœ,* ' *I would have written,* perhaps, to the church, but Diotrephes,' &c. Macknight also renders this, ' I would have written,' supposing the sense to be, that John would have commended them to the whole church rather than to a private member, if he had not been aware of the influence and opposition of Diotrephes. The Syriac version also adopts the same rendering. Several manuscripts also,

of later date, introduced a particle, (ἂν,) by which the same rendering would be demanded in the Greek, though that reading is not sustained by good authority. Against this mode of rendering the passage, the reasons seem to me to be clear. (1.) As already remarked, the reading in the Greek which would require it is not sustained by good authority. (2.) The fair and obvious interpretation of the Greek word used by the apostle, (ἔγραψα,) without that particle, is, *I wrote*—implying that it had been already done. (3.) It is more probable that John had written to the church on some former occasion, and that his recommendation had been rejected by the influence of Diotrephes, than that he would be deterred by the apprehension that his recommendation *would be* rejected. It seems to me, therefore, that the fair interpretation of this passage is, that these brethren had gone forth on some former occasion, commended by John to the church, and had been rejected by the influence of Diotrephes, and that now he commends them to Gaius, by whom they had been formerly entertained, and asks him to renew his hospitality to them. ¶ *But Diotrephes, who loveth to have the pre-eminence among them, receiveth us not.* Does not admit our authority, or would not comply with any such recommendation. The idea is, that he rejected his interference in the matter, and was not disposed to acknowledge him in any way. Of Diotrephes, nothing more is known than is here specified. Compare the analysis of the epistle. Whether he were an officer in the church—a pastor, a ruling elder, a deacon, a vestry-man, a warden, or a private individual—we have no means of ascertaining. The presumption, from the phrase 'who *loveth* to have the pre-eminence,' would rather seem to be that he was an aspiring man, arrogating rights which he had not, and assuming authority to which he was not entitled by virtue of any office. Still he might have held an office, and might have arrogated authority, as many have done, beyond

10 Wherefore, if I come, I will remember his deeds which he doeth, prating *a* against us with malicious words: and not content therewith,

a Pr.10.8,10.

what properly belonged to it. The single word rendered 'who loveth to have the pre-eminence,' (φιλοπρωτεύων,) occurs nowhere else in the New Testament. It means simply, *who loves to be first*— meaning that he loved to be at the head of all things, to rule, to lord it over others. It is clearly supposed here, that the church would have complied with the request of the writer if it had not been for this man. What were the *alleged* grounds for the course which he constrained the church to take, we are not informed; the *real* ground, the apostle says, was his desire to rule. There may have been at the bottom of it some secret dislike of John, or some private grudge; but the *alleged* ground may have been, that the church was independent, and that it should reject all foreign interference; or that the church was unable to support those men; or that the work in which they were engaged was one of doubtful propriety. Whatever was the *cause*, the case furnishes an illustration of the bad influence of one ambitious and arrogant man in a church. It is often in the power of one such man to bring a whole church under his control, and effectually to embarrass all its movements, and to prevent all the good which it would otherwise accomplish. When it is said, 'but Diotrephes *receiveth* us not,' the reference is doubtless to John, and the meaning is, either that he did not acknowledge him as an apostle, or that he did not recognize his right to interfere in the affairs of the church, or that he did not regard his recommendation of these brethren. The first of these suppositions is hardly probable; but, though he may have admitted that he was an apostle, there were perhaps some reasons operating in this particular case why he prevailed on the church to reject those who had been thus commended to their hospitality.

10. *Wherefore, if I come.* He was evidently expecting soon to make a visit to Gaius, and to the church. ver 14.

neither doth he himself receive the brethren, and forbiddeth them that would, and casteth *them* out *b* of the church.

b Is.66.5.

¶ *I will remember his deeds which he doeth.* That is, he would punish his arrogance and presumption; would take measures that he should be dealt with in a proper manner. There is no evidence whatever that this is said in a vindictive or revengeful spirit, or that the writer spoke of it merely as a personal matter. From anything that can be shown to the contrary, if it had been a private and personal affair merely, the matter might have been dropped, and never referred to again. But what had been done was public. It pertained to the authority of the apostle, the duty of the church, and the character of the brethren who had been commended to them. If the letter was written, as is supposed by the aged John, and his authority had been utterly rejected by the influence of this one man, then it was proper that that authority should be asserted. If it was the duty of the church to have received these men, who had been thus recommended to them, and it had been prevented from doing what it would otherwise have done, by the influence of one man, then it was proper that the influence of that man should be restrained, and that the church should see that he was not to control it. If the feelings and the character of these brethren had been injured by being rudely thrust out of the church, and held up as unworthy of public confidence, then it was proper that their character should be vindicated, and that the author of the wrong should be dealt with in a suitable manner. No one can show that this was not all that the apostle proposed to do, or that any feelings of private vindictiveness entered into his purpose to 'remember' what Diotrephes had done; and the existence of any such feelings should not be charged on the apostle without proof. There is no more reason to suppose this in his case than there was in the case of Paul, in administering discipline in the church of Corinth, (1 Cor. v. 3–5,) or than there is in any instance of administering dis-

11 Beloved, follow *a* not that which is evil, but that which is good. He *b* that doeth good is of God: but he that doeth evil hath not seen God.

a Ps.37.2?.

12 Demetrius hath good report of all *men*, and of the truth itself: yea, and we *also* bear record; and ye know that our record is true.

b 1 Jn.3.6-9.

cipline now. ¶ *Prating against us.* The word *prate*, (φλυαρίω,) occurring nowhere else in the New Testament, means to 'overflow with talk,' (Gr. φλύω, Lat. *fluo*, flow;) to talk much without weight, or to little purpose; to be loquacious; to trifle; or, to use an expression common among us, and which accords well with the Greek, *to run on* in talk, without connection or sense. The word does not properly imply that there was malignity or ill-feeling in what was said, but that the talk was of an idle, foolish, and unprofitable character. As John here, however, specifies that there *was* a bad spirit in the manner in which Diotrephes expressed himself, the real thing which is implied in the use of the word here is, that there were *much* talk of that kind; that he was addicted to this habit of *running on* against the apostle; and that he was thus constantly undermining his influence, and injuring his character. ¶ *With malicious words.* Gr., '*evil* words;' words that were fitted to do injury. ¶ *And not content therewith.* Not satisfied with venting his private feelings in talk. Some persons seem to be satisfied with merely talking against others, and take no other measures to injure them; but Diotrephes was not. He himself rejected the brethren, and persuaded the church to do the same thing. Bad as evil talking is, and troublesome as a man may be who is always 'prating' about matters that do not go according to his mind, yet it would be comparatively well if things always ended with that, and if the loquacious and the dissatisfied never took measures openly to wrong others. ¶ *Neither doth he himself receive the brethren.* Does not himself treat them as Christian brethren, or with the hospitality which is due to them. He had not done it on the former visit, and John evidently supposed that the same thing would occur again. ¶ *And forbiddeth them that would.* From this it is clear that there were those in the church who were disposed to receive them in a proper

manner; and from anything that appears, the church, as such, would have been inclined to do it, if it had not been for the influence of this one man. ¶ *And* casteth them *out of the church.* Comp. Luke vi. 22. It has been made a question whether the reference here is to the members of the church who were disposed to receive these brethren, or to the brethren themselves. Lücke, Macknight, and some others, suppose that it refers to those in the church who were willing to receive them, and whom Diotrephes had excommunicated on that account. Heumann, Carpzoviius, Rosenmüller, Bloomfield, and others, suppose that it refers to these strangers, and that the meaning is, that Diotrephes would not receive them into the society of Christians, and thus compelled them to go to another place. That this latter is the correct interpretation seems to me to be evident, for it was of the treatment which they had received that the apostle was speaking.

11. *Beloved, follow not that which is evil, but that which is good.* There can be no doubt that in this exhortation the writer had Diotrephes particularly in his eye, and that he means to exhort Gaius not to imitate his example. He was a man of influence in the church, and though Gaius had shown that he was disposed to act in an independent manner, yet it was not improper to exhort him not to be influenced by the example of any one who did wrong. John wished to excite him to acts of liberal and generous hospitality. ¶ *He that doeth good is of God.* He shows that he resembles God, for God continually does good. See the sentiment explained in the Notes on 1 John iii. 7. ¶ *He that doeth evil hath not seen God.* See Notes, 1 John iii. 8–10

12. *Demetrius hath good report of all* men. Little is known of Demetrius. Lücke supposes that he resided near the place where the author of this epistle lived, and was connected with the church there, and was probably the bearer of

13 I had many things to write, but I will not with ink and pen write unto thee:

14 But I trust I shall shortly see

thee, and we shall speak [1] face to face. Peace *be* to thee. *Our* friends salute thee. Greet the friends by name.

[1] *mouth to mouth.*

---

this epistle. It is impossible to determine with certainty on this point, but there is one circumstance which seems to make it probable that he was a member of the same church with Gaius, and had united with him in showing Christian hospitality to these strangers. It is the use of the phrase ' hath good report of all,' implying that some *testimony* was borne to his character beyond what the writer personally knew. It is possible, indeed, that the writer would have used this term respecting him if he lived in the same place with himself, as expressing the fact that he bore a good character, but it is a phrase which would be more appropriately used if we suppose that he was a member of the same church with Gaius, and that John means to say than an honourable testimony was borne of his character by all those brethren, and by all others as far as he knew. ¶ *And of the truth itself.* Not only by men, who might possibly be deceived in the estimate of character, but by *fact.* It was not merely a reputation founded on what *appeared* in his conduct, but in truth and reality. His deportment, his life, his deeds of benevolence, all concurred with the testimony which was borne by men to the excellency of his character. There is, perhaps, particular reference here to his kind and hospitable treatment of those brethren. ¶ *Yea, and we* also *bear record.* John himself had personally known him. He had evidently visited the place where he resided on some former occasion, and could now add his own testimony, which no one would call in question, to ·his excellent character. ¶ *And ye know that our record is true.* This is in the manner of John, who always spoke of himself as having such a character for truth that no one who knew him would call it in question. Every Christian *should* have such a character; every man *might* if he would. Comp. Notes, John xix. 35; xxi. 24.

13. *I had many things to write, &c.* This epistle closes, as the second does,

with a statement that he had many things to say, but that he preferred waiting till he should see him rather than put them on paper. Perhaps there were some things which he wished to say which he would not like to have exposed to the possibility of being seen by the public eye. ¶ *But I will not with ink and pen, &c.* Notes on the Second Epistle, ver. 12.

14. *But I trust I shall shortly see thee, &c.* Notes on the Second Epistle, ver. 12. ¶ Our *friends salute thee.* That is, your friends and mine. This would seem rather to refer to private friends of John and Gaius than to Christians as such. They had, doubtless, their warm personal friends in both places. ¶ *Greet the friends by name.* That is, each one individually. He remembered them as individuals, but did not deem it proper to specify them.

PRACTICAL REMARKS ON THE EPISTLE.

(1.) It is proper to desire for our friends all temporal good ; to wish their happiness in every respect, ver. 2. The welfare of the soul is indeed the great object, and the first desire in regard to a friend should be that his salvation may be secured ; but in connection with that we may properly wish them health of body, and success in their lawful undertakings. It is not common that in their spiritual interests they are so much more prosperous than they are in other respects, that we can make *that* the standard of our wishes in regard to them, but it sometimes does occur, as in the case of Gaius. In such cases we may indeed rejoice with a friend, and feel that all will be well with him. But in how few cases, even among professed Christians, can we with propriety make the prosperity of the soul the standard by which to measure the happiness which we desire for them in other respects ! Doddridge says, ' What a curse would this bring upon many to wish that they might prosper even as their souls prospered !' Of how much property would they at once be deprived; how embarrassed would be their affairs; how pale, and wan, and sickly would they be, if they should be in all respects as they are in their spiritual interests!

(2.) It is an unspeakable pleasure to a Christian to learn that his friends are living and acting as becomes sincere Christians; that they love what is true, and abound in the duties of hospitality, charity, and benevolence, vers. 3–6. When a friend learns this of a distant friend; when a pastor learns this of his people from whom he may be for a time separated; when those who have been instrumental in converting others learn this of their spiritual children; when a parent learns it of a son or daughter separated from him; when a teacher learns it of those who were formerly under his care, there is no joy that goes more directly to the heart than this— nothing that fills the soul with more true thankfulness and peace.

(3.) It is the duty and the privilege of those who love the cause of religion to go and preach the gospel to those who are destitute, expecting to receive nothing from them, and doing it as a work of pure benevolence, ver. 7. The missionary spirit existed early in the Christian church, and indeed may be regarded as the *prevailing* spirit in those times. It has always been the prevailing spirit when religion has flourished in the church. At such times there have been many who were willing to leave their own quiet homes, and the religious privileges connected with a well-organized church, and to break away from the ties which bind to country and kindred, and to go among a distant people to publish salvation. In this cause, and with this spirit, the apostles spent their lives. In this cause, the 'brethren' referred to by John went forth to labour. In this cause, thousands have laboured in former times, and to the fact that they were *willing* to do it is to be traced all the happy influence of religion in the world. Our own religious privileges now we owe to the fact that in former times there were those who were willing to ' go forth taking nothing of the Gentiles,' devoting themselves, without hope of reward or

fame, to the business of making known the name of the Saviour in what were then the dark places of the earth. The same principle is acted on now in Christian missions, and with the same propriety; and as *we* in Christian lands owe the blessings which we enjoy to the fact that in former times there were those who were willing thus to go forth, so it will be true that the richest blessings which are to descend on India, and Africa, and the islands of the sea, will be traced in future times to the fact that there are in *our* age those who are willing to follow the example of the apostles in going forth to do good to a dying world.

(4.) It is our duty to contribute to the support of those who thus go among the heathen, and to aid them in every way in which we can promote the object which they have in view. So John felt it to be the duty of the church in regard to those who went forth in his time; and so, when the church, under the influence of Diotrephes, had refused to do it, he commended Gaius for performing that duty, vers. 6, 8. Now, as then, from the nature of the case, missionaries to the heathen must go 'taking nothing' of those among whom they labour, and expecting that, for a long time at least, they will do nothing for their support. They go as strangers. They go to those who do not believe the truth of the gospel; who are attached to their own superstitions; who contribute largely to the support of their own temples, and altars, and priesthood; who are, as yet, incapable of appreciating the value of a purer religion; who have no desire for it, and who are disposed to reject it. In many cases, the heathen to whom the missionary goes are miserably poor, and it is only this religion, which as yet they are not disposed to receive, that can elevate them to habits of industry, and furnish them with the means of supporting religious teachers from abroad. Under these circumstances, no duty is more obvious than that of contributing to the support of those who go to such places as Christian missionaries. If the churches value the gospel enough to *send* their brethren among the heathen to propagate it, they should value it enough to minister to their wants when there ; if they regard it as the duty of any of their number to leave their comfortable homes in a Christian land in order to preach to the heathen, they should feel that those who go make far greater sacrifices than those who contribute to their support. *They* give up all ; *we* give only the small sum, not diminishing our own comforts, which is needful to sustain them.

(5.) For the same reason it is our duty to contribute to the support of missionaries in the destitute places of our own land, ver. 8. They often go among a people who are as destitute, and who will as little appreciate the gospel, and who are as much prejudiced against it, and who are as poor, as the heathen. They are as likely to be charged with being actuated by mercenary motives, if they ask for support, as missionaries among the heathen are. They often go among people as little able and disposed to build churches and school-houses as the heathen are. Nothing is more obvious, therefore, than that those who have the gospel, and who have learned to prize and value it in some measure as it should be, should contribute to the support of those who go to convey its blessings to others, until those to whom they go shall so learn to prize it as to be able and willing to maintain it. That, under a faithful ministry, and with the Divine blessing, will not be long ; for the gospel *always*, when it secures a hold in a community, makes men feel that it confers infinitely more blessings than it takes away, and that, even in a pecuniary point of view, it contributes more by far than it takes. What community is more prospered, or is more rich in all that promotes the temporal welfare of man, than that where the gospel has the most decided influence ?

(6.) We may see from this epistle that churches *ought* to be united in promoting the cause of religion, vers. 8, 9. They should regard it as a common cause in which one has as much concern as another, and where each should feel it a privilege to co-operate with his brethren. One church, in proportion to its ability, has as much interest in the spread of Christianity as another, and should feel that it has much responsi-

bility in doing it. Between different churches there should be that measure of confidence and love that they will deem it a privilege to aid each other in the common cause, and that one shall be ready to further the benevolent designs undertaken by another. In every Christian land, and among the people of every Christian denomination, missionaries of the gospel should find friends who will be willing to co-operate with them in advancing the common cause, and who, though they may bear a different name, and may speak a different language, should cheerfully lend their aid in spreading the common Christianity.

(7.) We may see, from this epistle, the evil of having *one* troublesome man in the church, ver. 10. Such a man, by his talents, his address, his superior learning, his wealth, or by his arrogance, pride, and self-confidence, may control a church, and effectually hinder its promoting the work of religion. The church referred to by the apostle would have done its duty well enough, if it had not been for one ambitious and worldly man. No one can properly estimate the evil which one such man can do, nor the calamity which comes upon a church when such a man places himself at its head. As a man of wealth, of talents, and of learning, may do great good, if his heart is right, so may a man similarly endowed do proportionate evil if his heart is wicked. Yet how often has the spirit which actuated Diotrephes prevailed in the church ! There is nothing that confers so much *power* on men as the control in religious matters ; and hence, in all ages, proud and ambitious men have sought dominion over the conscience, and have sought to bring the sentiments of men on religion to subjection to their will.

(8.) There may be circumstances where it is proper—where it is a duty —to receive those who have been cast out of the church, ver. 8. The decisions of a church, under some proud and ambitious partisan leader, are often eminently unjust and harsh. The most modest, humble, devoted, and zealous men, under a charge of heresy, or of some slight aberration from the formulas of doctrine, may be cast out as unworthy to be recognized as ministers of the gospel, or even as unworthy to have a place at the table of the Lord. Some of the best men on earth have been thus disowned by the church; and it is no *certain* evidence against a man when he is denounced as a heretic, or disowned as a member, by those who bear the Christian name. If *we* are satisfied that a man is a Christian, we should receive him as such, however he may be regarded by others; nor should we hesitate to help him forward in his Christian course, or in any way to assist him to do good.

(9.) Finally, let us learn from the examples commended in this brief epistle, to do good. Let us follow the example of Gaius—the hospitable Christian; the large-hearted philanthropist; the friend of the stranger; the helper of those who were engaged in the cause of the Lord —a man who opened his heart and his house to welcome them when driven out and disowned by others. Let us imitate Demetrius, in obtaining a good report of those who know us; in so living that, if the aged apostle John were still on earth, we might be worthy of his commendation, and more than all, of the approbation of that gracious Saviour before whom these good men have long since gone, and in whose presence we also must soon appear.

THE

GENERAL EPISTLE OF JUDE

INTRODUCTION

§ 1. *The author of this Epistle.*

LITTLE is known of the author of this brief epistle. He styles himself (ver. 1) 'the servant of Jesus Christ, and brother of James;' but there has been some difference of opinion as to what *James* is meant. He does not call himself an *apostle*, but supposes that the terms which he uses would sufficiently identify him, and would be a sufficient reason for his addressing his brethren in the manner in which he does in this epistle. There were two of the name of *James* among the apostles, (Luke vi. 14, 15 ;) and it has been made a question of which of them he was the brother. There were also two of the name of Judas, or Jude ; but there is no difficulty in determining which of them was the author of this epistle, for the other had the surname of Iscariot, and was the traitor. In the catalogue of the apostles given by Matthew, (chap. x. 3,) the tenth place is given to an apostle who is there called 'Lebbeus,' whose surname was 'Thaddeus ;' and as this name does not occur in the list given by Luke, (chap. vi. 15,) and as the tenth place in tho catalogue is occupied by 'Simon, called Zelotes,' and as he afterwards mentions 'Judas the brother of James,' it is supposed that Lebbeus and Judas were the same persons. It was not uncommon for persons to have two or more names. Comp. Robinson's Harmony of the Gospels, § 40 ; Bacon's Lives of Apostles, p. 447 ; and Michaelis, iv., 365.

The title which he assumes, 'brother of James,' was evidently chosen because the James referred to was well-known, and because the fact that he was his brother would be a sufficient designation of himself, and of his right to address Christians in this manner. The name of the elder James, who was slain by Herod, (Acts xii. 2,) can hardly be supposed to be referred to, as he had been dead some time when this epistle is supposed to have been written ; and as that James was the brother of John, who was then living, it would have been much more natural for him to have mentioned that he was the brother of that beloved disciple. The other James—'James the Less,' or 'James the Just'—was still living ; was a prominent man in Jerusalem ; and was, besides, known as 'the brother of the Lord Jesus ;' and the fact of relationship to that James would sufficiently designate the writer. There can be little doubt, therefore, that this is the James here intended. In regard to his character and influence, see Intro. to the Epistle of James, § 1. If the author of this epistle was the brother of *that* James, it was sufficient to refer to that fact, without mentioning that he was an apostle, in order to give to his epistle authority, and to settle its canonical character.

Of Jude little is known. His name is found in the list of the apostles, but, besides that, it is but once mentioned in the Gospels. The only thing that is preserved of him in the Evangelists, is a question which he put to the Saviour, on the eve of his crucifixion. The Saviour had said, in his parting address to his disciples, 'He that hath my commandments, and keepeth them, he it is that loveth me ; and he that loveth me shall be loved of my Father ; and I will love him, and will manifest myself unto him.' In regard to the meaning of this remark, Judas is said to have asked the following question : ' Lord, how is it that thou wilt manifest thyself unto us, and not unto the world ?' John xiv. 21, 22. To this question the Saviour gave him a kind and satisfactory answer, and that is the last that is said of him in the Gospels.

Of his subsequent life we know little. In Acts xv. 22, he is mentioned as surnamed ' Barsabas,' and as being sent with Paul and Barnabas and Silas to Antioch. Paulinus says that he preached in Lybia, and that his body remained there. Jerome affirms, that after the ascension he was sent to Edessa, to king Abgarus ; and the modern Greeks say that he preached in that city, and throughout Mesopotamia, and in Judea, Samaria, Idumea, Syria, and principally in Armenia and Persia.—*Calmet's Dict.* Nothing certainly can be known in reference to the field of his labours, or to the place and circumstances of his death. On the question whether the Thaddeus who first preached the gospel in Syria was the same person as Jude, see Michaelis, Intro. iv., 367–371.

§ 2. The authenticity of the Epistle.

If this epistle was written by the apostle Jude, the brother of James and of our Lord, there can be no doubt of its canonical authority, and its claim to a place in the New Testament. It is true that he does not call himself an apostle, but simply mentions himself as ' a servant of Jesus Christ, and a brother of James.' By this appellation, however, he has practically made it known that he was one of the apostles, for all who had a catalogue of the apostles would know ' that Judas, the brother of James,' was one of them. At the same time, as the relation of James to our Lord was well understood, (Gal. i. 19,) his authority would be recognized as soon as he was known to be the author of the epistle. It may be asked, indeed, if he was an apostle, why he did not call himself such ; and why he did not seek to give authority and currency to his epistle, by adverting to the fact that he was the ' Lord's brother.' To the first of these questions, it may be replied, that to have called himself ' Judas, the apostle,' would not have designated him so certainly, as to call himself ' the brother of James ;' and besides, the naked title, ' Judas, the apostle,' was one which he might not choose to see applied to himself. After the act of the traitor, and the reproach which he had brought upon that name, it is probable that he would prefer to designate himself by some other appellation than one which had such associations connected with it. It may be added, also, that in several of his epistles Paul himself does not make use of the name of the apostle, Phil. i. 1 ; 1 Thess. i. 1 ; 2 Thess. i. 1 ; Philemon 1. To the second question, it may be replied, that *modesty* may have kept him from applying to himself the title, the ' Lord's brother.' Even James never uses it of himself ; and we only know that he sustained this relation from an incidental remark of the apostle Paul, Gal. i. 19. Great honour would be attached to that relationship, and it is possible that the reason why it was not referred to by James and Jude was an apprehension that it might produce jealousy, as if they claimed some special pre-eminence over their brethren.

For the evidence of the canonical authority of this epistle, the reader is referred to Lardner, vol. vi., pp. 304–313, and to Michaelis, Intro. vol. iv., p. 374, seq. Michaelis, chiefly on the internal evidence, supposes that it is not an inspired production. There were indeed, at first, doubts about its being inspired, as there were respecting the epistle of James, and the second epistle of Peter, but those doubts were ultimately removed, and it was received as a canonical epistle. Clemens of Alexandria cites the epistle under Jude's name, as the production of a prophetic mind. Origen calls it a production full of heavenly grace. Eusebius says that his predecessors were divided in opinion respecting it, and that it was not ranked among the universally acknowledged writings. It was not universally received among the Syrians, and is not found in the Peschito, the oldest Syriac version of the Scriptures. In the time of Jerome, however, it came to be ranked among the other sacred Scriptures as of Divine authority.—Hug, Intro., § 180.

The principal ground of doubt in regard to the canonical authority of the epistle, arose from the supposed fact that the author has quoted two apocryphal writings, vers. 9, 14. The consideration of this objection will be more appropriate in the Notes on those verses, for it obviously depends much on the true interpretation of these passages. I shall, therefore, reserve what I have to say on that point to the exposition of those verses. Those who are disposed to examine it at length, may consult Hug, Intro., § 183 ; Lardner, vi. 309–314, and Michaelis, Intro., iv., 378, seq.

§ 3. *The question when the Epistle was written, to whom, and its design.*

Nothing can be determined with entire certainty in regard to the persons to whom this epistle was written. Witsius supposed that it was addressed to Christians everywhere ; Hammond, that it was addressed to Jewish Christians alone, who were scattered abroad, and that its design was to secure them against the errors of the Gnostics ; Benson, that it was directed to Jewish believers, especially to those of the western dispersion ; Lardner, that it was written to all, without distinction, who had embraced the gospel. The principal argument for supposing that it was addressed to Jewish converts is, that the apostle refers mainly for proof to Hebrew writings, but this might be sufficiently accounted for by the fact that the writer himself was of Jewish origin.

The only way of determining anything on this point is from the epistle itself. The inscription is, ' To them that are sanctified by God the Father, and preserved in Jesus Christ, and called,' ver. 1. From this it would appear evident that he had no *particular* classes of Christians in his eye, whether of Jewish or Gentile origin, but that he designed the epistle for the general use of all who had embraced the Christian religion. The errors which he combats in the epistle were evidently wide-spread, and were of such a nature that it was proper to warn all Christians against them. They might, it is true, be more prevalent in some quarters than in others, but still they were so common that Christians everywhere should be put on their guard against them.

The *design* for which Jude wrote the epistle he has himself stated, ver. 3. It was with reference to the ' common salvation '—the doctrines pertaining to salvation which were held by *all* Christians, and to show them the reasons for ' contending earnestly for the faith once delivered to the saints.' That faith was assailed. There were teachers of error abroad. They were insinuating and artful men—men who had crept in unawares, and who, while they professed to hold the Christian doctrine, were really undermining its faith, and spreading corruption through the church. The *purpose*, therefore, of the epistle is to put those to whom it was written on their guard against the corrupt teachings of these men, and to encourage them to stand up manfully for the great principles of Christian truth.

Who these errorists were, it is not easy now to determine. The leading charge against them, both by Jude and Peter, (2 Peter ii. 1,) is, that they denied our Lord, (ver. 4 ;) and yet it is said that they were numbered among Christians, and were found in their assemblies, 2 Peter ii. 13 ; Jude, ver. 12. By this denial, however, we are not to suppose that they literally and professedly denied that Jesus was the Christ, but that they held *doctrines* which amounted to a denial of him in fact. Comp. Notes, 2 Pet. ii. 1. For the general characteristics of these teachers, see Intro. to 2 Pet. § 4.

At this distance of time, and with our imperfect knowledge of the characteristics of the early erroneous sects in the church, it is difficult to determine precisely who they were. It has been a common opinion, that reference is had by Peter and Jude to the sect of the Nicolaitanes; and this opinion, Hug remarks, is ' neither improbable nor incompatible with the expressions of the two apostles, so far as we have any certain knowledge concerning this sect.' ' The statements of the ancients, in regard to their profligacy and their detestable course of life, are so consonant with each other and with the charges of the apostles, that the two epistles may be pertinently considered as referring to them.'—Intro., § 182.

It is not possible to ascertain with certainty the time when the epistle was written. There are no marks of time in it by which that can be known, nor is there any account among the early Christian writers which determines this. Benson supposes that it was written before the destruction of Jerusalem, a few weeks or months after the second epistle of Peter; Mill, that it was written about A. D. 90; Dodwell and Cave, that it was written *after* the destruction of Jerusalem, in the year 71 or 72; L'Enfant and Beausobre, that it was between the year 70 and 75; Witsius and Estius, that it was in the apostle's old age; Lardner, that it was about the year 65 or 66; Michaelis, that it was before the destruction of Jerusalem; and Macknight, that it was in the latter part of the apostolic age, and not long before the death of Jude. All this, it is manifest, is mostly conjecture. There are only *two* things, it seems to me, in the epistle, which can be regarded as *any* indication of the time. One is the striking resemblance to the second epistle of Peter, referring clearly to the same kind of errors, and warning those whom he addressed against the arts of the same kind of teachers, thus showing that it was written at about the same time as that epistle; and the other is, that it seems to have been written *before* the destruction of Jerusalem, for, as Michaelis has well remarked, ' As the author has mentioned (vers. 5–8) several well-known instances of Divine justice in punishing sinners, he would probably, if Jerusalem had been already destroyed, not have neglected to add to his other examples this most remarkable instance of Divine vengeance, especially as Christ had himself foretold it.'—Intro. iv. 372. As there is reason to suppose that the second epistle of Peter was written about A.D. 64 or 65, we shall not, probably, err in supposing that this was written not far from that time.

§ IV. *The resemblance between this Epistle and the second chapter of the second Epistle of Peter.*

One of the most remarkable things respecting this epistle, is its resemblance to the second chapter of the second epistle of Peter—a similarity so striking as to make it quite certain that one of these writers had seen the epistle of the other, and copied from it; or rather, perhaps, adopted the language of the other as expressing his own views. It is evident, that substantially the same class of teachers is referred to by both; that they held the same errors, and were guilty of the same corrupt and dangerous practices; and that the two apostles, in describing them, made use of the same expressions, and employed the same arguments against them. They refer to the same facts in history, and to the same arguments from tradition; and if either of them quoted an apocryphal book, both have done it. On the resemblance, compare the following places:—Jude 8, with 2 Pet. ii. 10; Jude 10, with 2 Pet. ii. 12; Jude 16, with 2 Pet. ii. 18; Jude 4, with 2 Pet. i. 2, 3; Jude 7, with 2 Pet. ii. 6; Jude 9, with 2 Pet. ii. 11. The similarity between the two is so striking, both in the general structure of the argument and in the particular expressions, that it cannot have been accidental. It is not such a resemblance as would be likely to occur in two authors, if they had been writing in a wholly independent manner. In regard to this resemblance, there is but one of three ways in which it can be accounted for: either that the Holy Spirit inspired both of them to say the same thing, without the one having any knowledge of what the other said; or that they both copied from a common document, which is now lost; or that one copied from the other.

As to the first of these solutions, that the Holy Spirit inspired them both to say the same thing, it may be observed that no one can deny that this is *possible*, but is by no means probable. No other instance of the kind occurs in the Bible, and the supposition would not be in accordance with what seems to have been a law in inspiration, that the sacred writers were allowed to express themselves according to the bent of their own genius. See Notes, 1 Cor. xiv. 32.

As to the second of these suppositions, that they both copied from a common document, which is now lost, it may be observed, that this is wholly without evidence. That such a thing was *possible*, there can be no doubt, but the supposition should not be adopted without necessity. If there had been such an original inspired document, it would probably have been preserved ; or there would have been, in one or both of those who copied from it, some such allusion to it that it would have been possible to verify the supposition.

The remaining way of accounting for the resemblance, therefore, is to suppose that one of them had seen the epistle of the other, and adopted the same line of argument, and many of the same expressions. This will account for all the facts in the case, and can be supposed to be true without doing violence to any just view of their inspiration. A question still arises, however, whether Peter or Jude is the original writer from which the other has copied. This question it is impossible to determine with certainty, and it is of little importance. If the common opinion which is stated above be correct, that Peter wrote his epistle *first*, of course that determines the matter. But that is not absolutely certain, nor is there any method by which it can be determined. Hug adopts the other opinion, and supposes that Jude was the original writer. His reasons for this opinion are substantially these : (1.) That there is little probability that Jude, in so brief an epistle as his, consisting of only twenty-five verses, would have made use of foreign aid. (2.) That the style and phraseology of Jude is simple, unlaboured, and without ornament ; while that of Peter is artificial, and wears the appearance of embellishment and amplification ; that the simple language of Jude seems to have been moulded by Peter into a more elegant form, and is embellished with participles, and even with rhetorical flourishes. (3.) That there is allusion in both epistles (2 Pet. ii. 11; Jude 9) to a controversy between angels and fallen spirits ; but that it is so alluded to by Peter, that it would not be understood without the more full statement of Jude ; and that Peter evidently supposed that the letter of Jude was in the hands of those to whom he wrote, and that thus the allusion would be at once understood. It could not be supposed that every reader would be acquainted with the fact alluded to by Peter ; it was not stated in the sacred books of the Jews, and it seems probable that there must have been some book to which they had access, where the information was more full. Jude, however, as the original writer, stated it more at length, and having done this, a bare allusion to it by Peter was all that was necessary. Jude states the matter definitely, and expressly mentions the dispute of Michael with the devil about the body of Moses. But the language of Peter is so general and indefinite, that we could not know what he meant unless we had Jude in our possession. See Hug's Intro., § 176. It must be admitted that these considerations have much weight, though they are not absolutely conclusive. It should be added, that whichever supposition is adopted, the fact that one has expressed substantially the same sentiments as the other, and in nearly the same language, is no reason for rejecting either, any more than the coincidence between the Gospels is a reason for concluding that only one of them can be an inspired document. There might have been good reasons why the same warnings and counsels should have proceeded from two inspired men.

GENERAL EPISTLE OF JUDE.

JUDE, *a* the servant of Jesus Christ, and brother of James, to them that are *b* sanctified by God the Father, and preserved *c* in Jesus Christ, *and* called: *d*

a Lu.6.16. b Ac.20.32. c 1 Pe.1.5. d Ro.8.30.

ANALYSIS OF THE EPISTLE.

(1.) THE inscription and salutation, vers. 1, 2. (2.) A statement of the reasons why the epistle was written, vers. 3, 4. The author felt it to be necessary to write to them, because certain plausible errorists had crept in among them, and there was danger that their faith would be subverted. (3.) A reference to past facts, showing that men who embraced error, and who followed corrupt and licentious practices, would be punished, vers. 5–7. He refers particularly to the unbelieving Hebrews whom God had delivered out of Egypt; to the apostate angels; and to the corrupt inhabitants of Sodom and Gomorrah. The object in this is to warn them from following the examples of those who would certainly lead them to destruction. (4.) He describes particularly the characteristics of these persons, agreeing substantially in the description with the statement of Peter, vers. 8–16. For these characteristics, comp. Intro. to 2 Peter, § 4. In general, they were corrupt, sensual, lewd, proud, arrogant, disorganizing, covetous, murmurers, complainers, wordy, windy, spots in their feasts of love. They had been and were professors of religion; they were professed reformers; they made great pretensions to uncommon knowledge of religious things. In the course of this description, the apostle contrasts their spirit with that of the archangel Michael, (ver. 9,) and declares that it was with reference to such a class of men that Enoch long ago uttered a solemn prophecy, vers. 14, 15. (5.) He calls to their remembrance the fact that

it had been predicted that there would be such mockers in the last periods of the world; and that the faith of true Christians, therefore, was not to be shaken, but rather confirmed by the fact of their appearance, vers. 17–19. (6.) In view of these facts and dangers, the apostle addresses to them two exhortations: (*a*) to adhere steadfastly to the truths which they had embraced, vers. 20, 21; and (*b*) to endeavour to recall and save those who were led astray—carefully guarding themselves from the same contamination while they sought to save others, vers. 22, 23. (7.) The epistle closes with an appropriate ascription of praise to him who was able to keep them from falling, and to present them faultless before his throne, vers. 24, 25.

1. *Jude, the servant of Jesus Christ.* If the view taken in the Introduction to the epistle is correct, Jude sustained a near relation to the Lord Jesus, being, as James was, 'the Lord's brother,' Gal. i. 19. The reasons why he did not advert to this fact here, as an appellation which would serve to designate him, and as showing his authority to address others in the manner in which he proposed to do in this epistle, probably were, (1,) that the right to do this did not rest on his mere *relationship* to the Lord Jesus, but on the fact that he had called certain persons to be his apostles, and had authorized them to do it; and, (2,) that a reference to this relationship, as a ground of authority, might have created jealousies among the apostles themselves. We may *learn* from the fact that Jude merely calls himself 'the *servant* of the Lord Jesus,' that is, a Christian, (*a*), that this is a distinction

2 Mercy unto you, and peace, and love, be multiplied.

3 Beloved, when I gave all diligence to write unto you of the common salvation, *a* it was needful for

me to write unto you, and exhort *you* that ye should earnestly contend *b* for the faith which was once delivered unto the saints.

a Tit.1.4.　　　　　*b* Ga.2.5.

---

more to be desired than would be a mere natural relationship to the Saviour, and consequently (*b*) that it is a higher honour than *any* distinction arising from birth or family. Comp. Matt. xii. 46–50. ¶ *And brother of James.* See Intro., § 1. ¶ *To them that are sanctified by God the Father.* To those who are *holy*, or who are *saints.* Comp. Notes, Rom. i. 7; Phil. i. 1. Though this title is general, it can hardly be doubted that he had some *particular* saints in his view, to wit, those who were exposed to the dangers to which he refers in the epistle. See Intro., § 3. As the epistle was probably *sent* to Christians residing in a certain place, it was not necessary to designate them more particularly, though it was often done. The Syriac version adds here, ‘ To the *Gentiles* who are called, beloved of God the Father,’ &c. ¶ *And preserved in Jesus Christ.* See Notes, 1 Pet. i. 5. The meaning is, that they owed their preservation wholly to him ; and if they were brought to everlasting life, it would be only by him. What the apostle here says of those to whom he wrote, is true of all Christians. They would all fall away and perish if it were not for the grace of God keeping them. ¶ And *called.* Called to be saints. See Notes, Rom. i. 7; Eph. iv. 1.

2. *Mercy unto you, and peace, and love, be multiplied.* This is not quite the form of salutation used by the other apostles, but it is one equally expressive of an earnest desire for their welfare. These things are mentioned as the choicest blessings which could be conferred on them : *mercy*—in the pardon of all their sins and acceptance with God ; *peace*—with God, with their fellow-men, in their own consciences, and in the prospect of death ; and *love*—to God, to the brethren, to all the world. What blessings are there which these do not include ?

3. *Beloved.* An expression of strong affection used by the apostles when ad-

dressing their brethren, Rom. i. 7; 1 Cor. iv. 14 ; x. 14; xv. 58; 2 Cor. vii. 1; xii. 19; Phil. ii. 12; iv. 1; and often elsewhere. ¶ *When I gave all diligence.* When I applied my mind earnestly ; implying that he had reflected on the subject, and thought particularly what it would be desirable to write to them. The state of mind referred to is that of one who was purposing to write a letter, and who thought over carefully what it would be proper to say. The mental process which led to writing the epistle seems to have been this : (*a*) For some reasons—mainly from his strong affection for them—he purposed to write to them. (*b*) The general subject on which he designed to write was, of course, something pertaining to the common salvation—for he and they were Christians. (*c*) On reflecting what particular thing pertaining to this common salvation it was best for him to write on, he felt that, in view of their peculiar dangers, it ought to be an exhortation to contend earnestly for the faith once delivered to them. Macknight renders this less correctly, ‘ Making all haste to write to you,’ &c. But the idea is rather that he set himself diligently and earnestly to write to them of the great matter in which they had a common interest. ¶ *To write unto you of the common salvation.* The salvation common to Jews and Gentiles, and to all who bore the Christian name. The meaning is, that he did not think of writing on any subject pertaining to a particular class or party, but on some subject in which all who were Christians had a common interest. There are great matters of religion held in common by all Christians, and it is important for religious teachers to address their fellow Christians on those common topics. After all, they are more important than the things which we may hold as peculiar to our own party or sect, and should be more frequently dwelt upon. ¶ *It was needful*

4 For there are certain men crept in unawares, *a* who *b* were before of old ordained to this condemnation; ungodly men, turning *c* the grace of our God into lasciviousness, and denying the only Lord God, and our Lord Jesus Christ.

a 2 Pe.2.1.   *b* Ro.9.22.   *c* Ti.1.15,16.

---

for me to write to you. ' I reflected on the general subject, prompted by my affectionate regard to write to you of things pertaining to religion in general, and, on looking at the matter, I found there was a particular topic or aspect of the subject on which it was *necessary* to address you. I saw the danger in which you were from false teachers, and felt it not only necessary that I should write to you, but that I should make *this* the particular subject of my counsels.' ¶ *And exhort* you. ' That I should make my letter in fact an exhortation on a particular topic.' ¶ *That ye should earnestly contend.* Comp. Gal. ii. 5. The word here rendered *earnestly contend* — ἐπαγωνίζεσθαι — is one of those words used by the sacred writers which have allusion to the Grecian games. Comp. Notes, 1 Cor. ix. 24, seq. This word does not elsewhere occur in the New Testament. It means *to contend upon*—i. e. *for* or *about* anything ; and would be applicable to the earnest effort put forth in those games to obtain the prize. The reference here, of course, is only to contention by argument, by reasoning, by holding fast the principles of religion, and maintaining them against all opposers. It would not justify ' contention ' by arms, by violence, or by persecution ; for (*a*) that is contrary to the spirit of true religion, and to the requirements of the gospel elsewhere revealed ; (*b*) it is not demanded by the proper meaning of the word, all that that fairly implies being the effort to maintain truth by argument and by a steady life ; (*c*) it is not the most effectual way to keep up truth in the world to attempt to do it by force and arms. ¶ *For the faith.* The system of religion revealed in the gospel. It is called *faith*, because that is the cardinal virtue *in* the system, and because all depends on that. The rule here will require that we should contend in this manner for all *truth*. ¶ *Once delivered unto the saints.* The word here used (ἅπαξ) may mean either

once for *all*, in the sense that it was then complete, and would not be repeated ; or *formerly*, to wit, by the author of the system. Doddridge, Estius, and Beza, understand it in the former way ; Macknight and others in the latter ; Benson improperly supposes that it means *fully* or *perfectly*. Perhaps the more usual sense of the word would be, that it was done *once* in the sense that it is not to be done again, and therefore in the sense that it was then complete, and that nothing was to be added to it. There is indeed the idea that it was *formerly* done, but with this additional thought, that it was then complete. Compare, for this use of the Greek word rendered *once*, Heb. ix. 26 —28 ; x. 2 ; 1 Pet. iii. 18. The *delivering* of this faith to the saints here referred to is evidently that made by revelation, or the system of truth which *God* has made known in his word. Everything which He has revealed, we are to defend as true. We are to surrender no part of it whatever, for every part of that system is of value to mankind. By a careful study of the Bible we are to ascertain what that system *is*, and then in all places, at all times, in all circumstances, and at every sacrifice, we are to maintain it.

4. *For there are certain men crept in unawares.* The apostle now gives a *reason* for thus defending the truth, to wit, that there were artful and wicked men who had crept into the church, pretending to be religious teachers, but whose doctrines tended to sap the very foundations of truth. The apostle Peter, describing these same persons, says, ' who *privily* shall bring in damnable heresies.' See Notes, 2 Pet. ii. 1. Substantially the same idea is expressed here by saying that they ' had crept in *unawares;*' that is, they had come in by *stealth;* they had not come by a bold and open avowal of their real sentiments. They professed to teach the Christian religion, when in fact they denied some of its fundamental doc-

trines; they professed to be holy, when in fact they were living most scandalous lives. In all ages there have been men who were willing to do this for base purposes. ¶ *Who were before of old ordained to this condemnation.* That is, to the condemnation (*χρίμα*) which he proceeds to specify. The statements in the subsequent part of the epistle show that by the word used here he refers to the wrath that shall come upon the ungodly in the future world. See vers. 5–7, 15. The meaning clearly is, that the punishment which befell the unbelieving Israelites, (ver. 5;) the rebel angels, (ver. 6;) the inhabitants of Sodom, (ver. 7;) and of which Enoch prophesied, (ver. 15,) awaited those persons. The phrase *of old—πάλαι*—means *long ago,* implying that a considerable time had elapsed, though without determining how much. It is used in the New Testament only in the following places: Matt. xi. 21, 'they would have repented *long ago;*' Mark xv. 44, ' whether he had been *any while* dead;' Luke x. 13, 'they had *a great while ago* repented;' Heb. i. 1, ' spake *in time past* unto the fathers;' 2 Pet. i. 9, 'purged from his *old* sins;' and in the passage before us. So far as this word is concerned, the reference here may have been to *any* former remote period, whether in the time of the prophets, of Enoch, or in eternity. It does not *necessarily* imply that it was *eternal,* though it *might* apply to that, if the thing referred to was, from other sources, certainly known to have been from eternity. It may be doubted, however, whether, if the thing referred to had occurred from eternity, this would have been the word used to express it, (comp. Eph. i. 4;) and it is certain that it cannot be *proved* from the use of this word (*πάλαι*) that the 'ordination to condemnation' was eternal. Whatever may be referred to by that word ' ordaining to condemnation, *this* word will not prove that it was an eternal ordination. All that is *fairly* implied in it will be met by the supposition that it occurred in *any* remote period, say in the time of the prophets. The word here rendered '*before ordained*'—*προγεγραμμένοι,* from *προγράφω*—occurs in the New Testament only here and in the following places : Rom. xv. 4, twice,

' Whatsoever things *were written aforetime, were written* for our learning;' Gal. iii. 1, ' Jesus Christ *hath been evidently set forth ;*' and Eph. iii. 3. ' As *I wrote afore* in few words.' Comp. Notes, Gal. iii. 1. In these places there is evidently no idea implied of *ordaining,* or *pre-ordaining,* in the sense in which those words are now commonly understood. To that word there is usually attached the idea of designating or appointing as by an arbitrary decree ; but no such meaning enters into the word here used. The Greek word properly means, *to write before ;* then *to have written before ;* and then, with reference to time future, *to post up beforehand in writing ; to announce by posting up on a written tablet,* as of some ordinance, law, or requirement ; as descriptive of what will be, or what should be. Comp. Rob. Lexicon. Burder (in Rosenmüller's Morgenland, *in loc.*) remarks that ' the names of those who were to be tried were usually posted up in a public place, as was also their sentence after their condemnation, and that this was denoted by the same Greek word which the apostle uses here. Elsner,' says he, ' remarks that the Greek authors use the word as applicable to those who, among the Romans, were said to be *proscribed;* that is, those whose names were posted up in a public place, whereby they were appointed to death, and in reference to whom a reward was offered to any one who would kill them.' The idea here clearly is that of some such designation beforehand as *would occur* if the persons had been publicly *posted* as appointed to death. Their *names,* indeed, were not mentioned, but there was such a description of them, or of their character, that it was clear who were meant. In regard to the question what the apostle *means* by such a designation or appointment beforehand, it is clear that he does not refer in this place to any arbitrary or eternal decree, but to such a designation as was made by the facts to which he immediately refers—that is, to the Divine prediction that there would be such persons, (vers. 14, 15, 18;) and to the consideration that in the case of the unbelieving Israelites, the rebel angels, and the inhabitants of

5 I will therefore put you in re-membrance, though ye once knew this, how that the Lord, *a* having

a 1 Co.10.5-12.

saved the people out of the land of Egypt, afterward destroyed *b* them that believed not.

b Nu.14.29,37; He.3.16-19.

Sodom, there was as clear a proof that such persons would be punished as if their names had been posted up. All these instances bore on just such cases as these, and in these facts they might read their sentence as clearly as if their names had been written on the face of the sky. This interpretation seems to me to embrace all that the words *fairly* imply, and all that the exigence of the case demands ; and if this be correct, then two things follow : (1,) that this passage should not be adduced to prove that God has from all eternity, by an arbitrary decree, ordained a certain portion of the race to destruction, what-ever may be true on that point ; and, (2,) that *all* abandoned sinners now may see, in the facts which have occurred in the treatment of the wicked in past times, just as certain evidence of their destruction, if they do not repent, as if their names were written in letters of light, and if it were announced to the universe that they would be damned. ¶ *Ungodly men.* Men without piety or true religion, whatever may be their pretensions. ¶ *Turning the grace of our God into lasciviousness.* Abusing the doctrines of grace so as to give in-dulgence to corrupt and carnal pro-pensities. That is, probably, they gave this form to their teaching, as Anti-nomians have often done, that by the gospel they were released from the ob-ligations of the law, and might give in-dulgence to their sinful passions in order that grace might abound. Antinomian-ism began early in the world, and has always had a wide prevalence. The liability of the doctrines of grace to be thus abused was foreseen by Paul, and against such abuse he earnestly sought to guard the Christians of his time, Rom. vi. 1, seq. ¶ *And denying the only Lord God, and our Saviour Jesus Christ.* See Notes, 2 Pet. ii. 1. That is, the doctrines which they held were in fact a denial of the only true God, and of the Redeemer of men. It can-not be supposed that they openly and formally did this, for then they could

have made no pretensions to the name Christian, or even to religion of any kind ; but the meaning must be, that *in fact* the doctrines which they held amounted to a denial of the true God, and of the Saviour in his proper nature and work. Some have proposed to read this, ' denying the only Lord God, *even* (*και*) our Lord Jesus Christ ;' but the Greek does not demand this construc-tion even if it would admit it, and it is most in accordance with Scripture usage to retain the common translation. It may be added, also, that the common translation expresses all that the exi-gence of the passage requires. Their doctrines and practice tended as really to the denial of the true God as they did to the denial of the Lord Jesus. Peter in his second epistle, (ch. ii. 1,) has adverted only to *one* aspect of their doctrine—that it denied the Saviour ; Jude adds, if the common reading be correct, that it tended also to a denial of the true God. The word *God* (Θεόν) is wanting in many manuscripts, and in the Vulgate and Coptic versions, and Mill, Hammond, and Bengel sup-pose it should be omitted. It is also wanting in the editions of Tittman, Griesbach, and Hahn. The amount of *authority* seems to be against it. The word rendered *Lord,* in the phrase ' Lord God,' is (Δεσπότης,) *despotes,* and means here *Sovereign,* or *Ruler,* but it is a word which may be appropriately ap-plied to the Lord Jesus Christ. It is the same word which is used in the parallel passage in 2 Pet. ii. 1. See it explained in the Notes on that verse. If the word ' God ' is to be omitted in this place, the passage would be wholly applicable, beyond question, to the Lord Jesus, and would mean, ' denying our only Sovereign and Lord, Jesus Christ.' It is perhaps impossible now to deter-mine with certainty the true reading of the text ; nor is it *very* material. Which-ever of the readings is correct ; whether the word (Θεόν) *God* is to be retained or not, the sentiment expressed would be true, that their doctrines amounted to a

6 And the angels *a*which kept not their ¹first estate, but left their own habitation, he hath reserved in

a Jn.8.44.   1 principality.

everlasting chains, *b* under darkness, unto the judgment *c* of the great day.

b 2 Pe.2.4.   c Re.20.10.

practical denial of the only true God; and equally so that they were a denial of the only Sovereign and Lord of the true Christian.

5. *I will therefore put you in remembrance.* ' To show you what must be the doom of such men, I will call certain facts to your recollection, with which you are familiar, respecting the Divine treatment of the wicked in times past.' ¶ *Though ye once knew this.* That is, you were formerly made acquainted with these things, though they may not be now fresh in your recollection. On the different significations affixed to the word *once* in this place, see Bloomfield, *Crit. Digest, in loc.* The thing which seems to have been in the mind of the apostle was an intention to call to their recollection, as bearing on the case before him, facts with which they had formerly been familiar, and about which there was no doubt. It was the thing which we often endeavour to do in argument —to *remind* a person of some fact which he once knew very well, and which bears directly on the case. ¶ *How that the Lord, having saved the people out of the land of Egypt.* Comp. Notes, 1 Cor. x. 5-12. The bearing of this fact on the case, before the mind of Jude, seems to have been this—that, as those who had been delivered from Egypt were afterward destroyed for their unbelief, or as the mere fact of their being rescued did not prevent destruction from coming on them, so the fact that these persons *seemed* to be delivered from sin, and had become professed followers of God, would not prevent their being destroyed if they led wicked lives. It might rather be inferred from the example of the Israelites that they would be. ¶ *Afterward.* τὸ δεύτερον—*the second;* that is, the second thing in order, or again. The expression is unusual in this sense, but the apostle seems to have fixed his mind on this event as a *second* great and important fact in regard to them. The *first* was that they were delivered; the second, that they were destroyed. ¶ *Destroyed them that believed not.*

That is, *on account* of their unbelief. They were not permitted to enter the promised land, but were cut off in the wilderness. See the Notes on Heb. iii. 16-19.

6. *And the angels which kept not their first estate.* A second case denoting that the wicked would be punished. Comp. Notes, 2 Pet. ii. 4. The word rendered *estate* (ἀρχὴν) is, in the margin, *principality.* The word properly means, *beginning, commencement;* ·and then that which surpasses others, which is *first, &c.,* in point of rank and honour; or pre-eminence, priority, precedence, princedom. Here it refers to the rank and dignity which the angels had in heaven. That rank or pre-eminence they did not keep, but fell from it. On the word used here, comp. Eph. i. 2; iii. 10; Col. ii. 10, as applied to angels; 1 Cor. xv. 24; Eph. vi. 12; Col. ii. 15, as applied to demons. ¶ *But left their own habitation.* To wit, according to the common interpretation, in heaven. The word rendered *habitation* (οἰκητήριον) occurs nowhere else in the New Testament. It means here that heaven was their native abode or dwelling-place. They left it by sin ; but the expression here would seem possibly to mean that they became *dissatisfied* with their abode, and voluntarily preferred to change it for another. If they did become thus dissatisfied, the cause is wholly unknown, and conjecture is useless. Some of the later Jews supposed that they relinquished heaven out of love for the daughters of men.—*Robinson.* ¶ *He hath reserved in everlasting chains.* See Notes, 2 Pet. ii. 4. Peter says, ' chains of darkness;' that is, the darkness encompasses them *as* chains. Jude says that those chains are ' everlasting,' (δεσμοῖς ἀϊδίοις.) Comp. Rom. i. 20, 'his *eternal* power and Godhead.' The word does not elsewhere occur. It is an appropriate word to denote that which is eternal ; and no one can doubt that if a Greek *wished* to express that idea, this would be a proper word to use. The sense is, that that deep darkness always

7 Even as Sodom *ᵃ* and Gomorrha, and the cities about them, in like manner giving themselves over to fornication, and going after ¹ strange

flesh, are set forth for an example, suffering the vengeance of eternal fire.

endures; there is no intermission; no light; it will exist for ever. This passage in itself does not prove that the punishment of the rebel angels will be eternal, but merely that they are kept in a dark prison in which there is no light, and which is to exist for ever, with reference to the final trial. The punishment of the rebel angels *after* the judgment is represented as an everlasting fire, which has been prepared for them and their followers, Matt. xxv. 41. 7. *Even as Sodom and Gomorrha.* Notes, 2 Pet. ii. 6. ¶ *And the cities about them.* Admah and Zeboim, Gen. xiv. 2; Deut. xxix. 23; Hosea xi. 8. There may have been other towns, also, that perished at the same time, but these are particularly mentioned. They seem to have partaken of the same general characteristics, as neighbouring towns and cities generally do. ¶ *In like manner.* 'In a manner like to these,' (τὸν ὅμοιον τούτοις τρόπον.) The Greek word *these,* is in the plural number. There has been much diversity in interpreting this clause. Some refer it to the angels, as if it meant that the cities of Sodom and Gomorrah committed sin in a way similar to the angels; some suppose that it refers to the wicked teachers about whom Jude was discoursing, meaning that Sodom and Gomorrah committed the same kind of sins which they did; some that the meaning is, that 'the cities round about Sodom and Gomorrah' sinned in the same way as those cities; and some that they were punished in the same manner, and were set forth like them as an example. I see no evidence that it refers to the angels; and if it did, it would not prove, as some have supposed, that their sin was of the same kind as that of Sodom, since there might have been a resemblance in *some* respects, though not in all. I see no reason to believe, as Macknight holds, that it refers to *false teachers,* since that would be to suppose that the inhabitants of Sodom copied their example long *before* the example was set. It seems to me, therefore,

that the reference is to the cities round about Sodom; and that the sense is, that they committed iniquity in the same manner as the inhabitants of Sodom did, and were set forth in the same way as an example. ¶ *Going after strange flesh.* Marg., *other.* The reference seems to be to the peculiar sin which, from the name Sodom, has been called *sodomy.* Comp. Rom. i. 27. The meaning of the phrase *going after* is, that they were greatly addicted to this vice. The word *strange,* or *other,* refers to that which is contrary to nature. Doddridge, however, explains it, 'going after strange and detestable gratifications of their pampered and indulged flesh.' ¶ *Are set forth for an example.* They furnish a warning against all such conduct, and a demonstration that punishment shall come upon the ungodly. The condemnation of any sinner, or of any class of sinners, always furnishes such a warning. See Notes, 2 Pet. ii. 6. ¶ *Suffering the vengeance of eternal fire.* The word rendered *suffering* (ὑπέχουσαι) means, properly, *holding under*—as, for example, the hand; then to hold towards any one, as the ear—to give attention; then it is used as denoting to hold a discourse towards or with any one, or to hold satisfaction to any one, to make atonement; and then as *undergoing, paying,* or *suffering punishment,* when united, as it is here, with the word δίκην, (*punishment,* or *vengeance.*) See *Rob. Lex.* Here it expresses the idea of undergoing punishment. The word properly agrees in the construction with *cities,* (πόλεις,) referring to Sodom and Gomorrah, and the cities around them; but the things affirmed relate to the *inhabitants* of those cities. The word *vengeance* means punishment; that is, such vengeance as the Lord takes on the guilty; not vengeance for the gratification of private and personal feeling, but like that which a magistrate appoints for the maintenance of the laws; such as justice demands. The phrase 'eternal fire' is one that is often used to denote future punishment—as ex-

8 Likewise also these *filthy* dreamers defile *ª* the flesh, despise dominion, and speak evil of dignities.

9 Yet Michael *ᵇ* the archangel, when contending with the devil he disputed about the body of Moses, *ᶜ* durst *ᵈ* not bring against him a railing accusation, but said, The Lord *ᵉ* rebuke thee.

a 2 Pe.2.10,11.　　　*b* Da.12.1.　　　*c* De.34.6.
d Ex.22.28.　　　　　*e* Ze.3.2.

pressing the severity and intensity of the suffering. See Notes, Matt. xxv. 41. As here used, it cannot mean that the fires which consumed Sodom and Gomorrah were literally eternal, or were kept always burning, for that was not true. The expression seems to denote, in this connection, two things : (1.) That the destruction of the cities of the plain, with their inhabitants, was as entire and perpetual *as if* the fires had been always burning—the consumption was absolute and enduring—the sinners were wholly cut off, and the cities for ever rendered desolate ; and (2) that, in its nature and duration, this was a striking emblem of the destruction which will come upon the ungodly. I do not see that the apostle here means to affirm that those particular sinners who dwelt in Sodom would be punished for ever, for his expressions do not directly affirm that, and his argument does not demand it ; but still the *image* in his mind, in the destruction of those cities, was clearly that of the utter desolation and ruin of which this was the emblem ; of the perpetual destruction of the wicked, like that of the cities of the plain. If this had not been the case, there was no reason why he should have used the word *eternal*—meaning here *perpetual* —since, if in his mind there was no image of future punishment, all that the argument would have demanded was the simple statement that they were cut off by fire. The passage, then, cannot be used to prove that the particular dwellers in Sodom will be punished for ever —whatever may be the truth on that point ; but that there *is* a place of eternal punishment, of which that was a striking emblem. The meaning is, that the case was one which furnished a demonstration of the fact that God will punish sin ; that this was an example of the punishment which God sometimes inflicts on sinners in this world, and a type of that eternal punishment which will be inflicted in the next.

8. *Likewise also.* In the same way do these persons defile the flesh, or resemble the inhabitants of Sodom ; that is, they practise the same kind of vices. What the apostle says is, that their character resembled that of the inhabitants of Sodom ; the example which he adduces of the punishment which was brought on those sinners, leaves it to be clearly inferred that the persons of whom he was speaking would be punished in a similar manner. ¶ *These* filthy *dreamers.* The word *filthy* has been supplied by our translators, but there is no good reason why it should have been introduced. The Greek word (ἐνυπνιάζω) means to dream ; and is applied to these persons as holding doctrines and opinions which sustained the same relation to truth which dreams do to good sense. Their doctrines were the fruits of mere imagination, foolish vagaries and fancies. The word occurs nowhere else in the New Testament, except in Acts ii. 17. where it is applied to visions in dreams, ¶ *Defile the flesh.* Pollute themselves ; give indulgence to corrupt passions and appetites. See Notes, 2 Pet. ii. 10. ¶ *Despise dominion.* The same Greek word is used here which occurs in 2 Pet. ii. 10. See Notes on that verse. ¶ *And speak evil of dignities.* See Notes on 2 Pet. ii. 10.

9. *Yet Michael the archangel,* &c. This verse has given more perplexity to expositors than any other part of the epistle ; and in fact the difficulties in regard to it have been so great that some have been led to regard the epistle as spurious. The difficulty has arisen from these two circumstances : (1.) Ignorance of the origin of what is said here of Michael the archangel, nothing of this kind being found in the Old Testament ; and (2.) the improbability of the story itself, which looks like a mere Jewish fable. Peter in his second epistle, chap. ii. 2, made a *general* reference to angels as not bringing railing accusations against others before the

Lord; but Jude refers to a particular case—the case of Michael when contending about the body of Moses. The methods proposed of reconciling the passage with the proper ideas of inspiration have been various, though perhaps no one of them relieves it of all difficulty. It would be inconsistent with the design of these Notes to go into an extended examination of this passage. Those who wish to see a full investigation of it may consult Michaelis' Introduction to the New Testament, vol. iv. pp. 378–393; Lardner, vol. vi. p. 312, seq.; Hug, Intro. § 183; Benson, *in loc.;* Rosenmüller's Morgenland, iii. pp. 196, 197; and Wetstein, *in loc.* The principal methods of relieving the difficulty have been the following: I. Some have supposed that the reference is to the passage in Zechariah, chap. iii. 1, seq. 'And he showed me Joshua the high priest standing before the angel of the Lord, and Satan standing at his right hand to resist him. And the Lord said unto Satan, The Lord rebuke thee, O Satan,' &c. The opinion that Jude refers to this passage was held by Lardner. But the objections to this are very obvious: (1.) There is no similarity between the two, except the expression, 'the Lord rebuke thee.' (2.) The name Michael does not occur at all in the passage in Zechariah. (3.) There is no mention made of the 'body of Moses' there, and no allusion to it whatever. (4.) There is no intimation that there was any such contention about his body. There is a mere mention that Satan resisted the angel of the Lord, as seen in the vision, but no intimation that the controversy had *any* reference to Moses in any way. (5.) The reason of the resistance which Satan offered to the angel in the vision as seen by Zechariah *is* stated. It was in regard to the consecration of Joshua to the office of high priest implying a return of prosperity to Jerusalem, and the restoration of the worship of God there in its purity; see Zech. iii. 2. To this Satan was of course opposed, and the vision represents him as resisting the angel in his purpose thus to set him apart to that office. These reasons seem to me to make it clear that Jude did not refer to the passage in Zechariah, nor is there any other place in the Old

Testament to which it can be supposed he had reference. II. Hug supposes that the reference here, as well as that in ver. 14, to the prophecy of Enoch, is derived from some apocryphal books existing in the time of Jude; and that though those books contained mere fables, the apostle appealed to them, not as conceding what was said to be true, but in order to refute and rebuke those against whom he wrote, out of books which they admitted to be of authority. Intro. § 183. Arguments and confutations, he says, drawn from the sacred Scriptures, would have been of no avail in reasoning with them, for these they evaded, (2 Pet. iii. 16,) and there were no surer means of influencing them than those writings which they themselves valued as the sources of their peculiar views. According to this, the apostle did not mean to vouch for the *truth* of the story, but merely to make use of it in argument. The objection to this is, that the apostle does in fact seem to refer to the contest between Michael and the devil as true. He speaks of it in the same way in which he would have done if he had spoken of the death of Moses, or of his smiting the rock, or of his leading the children of Israel across the Red Sea, or of any other fact in history. If he regarded it as a mere fable, though it would have been honest and consistent with all proper views of inspiration for him to have said to those against whom he argued, that on their own principles such and such things were true, yet it would not be honest to speak of it as a fact which *he* admitted to be true. Besides, it should be remembered that he is not arguing with *them,* in which case it might be admissible to reason in this way, but was making statements to others *about* them, and showing that they manifested a spirit entirely different from that which the angels evinced even when contending in a just cause against the prince of all evil. III. It has been supposed that the apostle quotes an apocryphal book existing in his time, containing this account, and that he means to admit that the account is true. Origen mentions such a book, called 'the Assumption of Moses,' (Αναληψις του Μωσεως,) as extant in his time, containing this very account of the contest between Michael and the devil about the body of Moses. That was a Jewish Greek book, and Origen supposed that this was the source of the account here. That book is now lost. There is still extant a book in Hebrew, called פטירת משה—'the Death of Moses,' which some have supposed to be the book referred to by Origen. That book contains many fabulous stories about the death of Moses, and is evidently the work of some Jew drawing wholly upon his imagination. An account of it may be seen in Michaelis, Intro. iv. p. 381, seq. There is no reason to suppose that this is the same book referred to by Origen under the name of 'the Assump-tion of Moses;' and there is a moral certainty that an inspired writer could not have quoted it as of authority. Fur-ther, there can be no reasonable doubt that such a book as Origen refers to, under the title of 'the Assumption of Moses,' was extant in *his* time, but that does not prove by any means that it was extant in the time of Jude, or that he quoted it. There is, indeed, no posi-tive proof that it was *not* extant in the time of Jude, but there is none that it was, and all the facts in the case will be met by the supposition that it was written afterwards, and that the tradi-tion on the subject here referred to by Jude was incorporated into it. IV. The remaining supposition is, that Jude here refers to a prevalent *tradition* among the Jews, and that he has adopted it as containing an important truth, and one which bore on the subject under discus-sion. In support of this, it may be ob-served, (a) that it is well known that there were many traditions of this nature among the Jews. See Notes, Matt. xv. 2. (b) That though many of these tradi-tions were puerile and false, yet there is no reason to doubt that some of them might have been founded in truth. (c) That an inspired writer might select those which were true, for the illustra-tion of his subject, with as much pro-priety as he might select what was written; since if what was thus handed down by tradition was *true*, it was as proper to use it as to use a fact made known in any other way. (d) That in fact such traditions *were* adopted by the inspired writers when they would

serve to illustrate a subject which they were discussing. Thus Paul refers to the tradition about Jannes and Jambres as true history. See Notes, 2 Tim. iii. 8. (e) If, therefore, what is here said was *true*, there was no impropriety in its being referred to by Jude as an illustra-tion of his subject. The only material question then is, whether it is *true*. And who can prove that it is not? What evidence is there that it is not? How is it possible to demonstrate that it is not? There are many allusions in the Bible to angels; there is express mention of such an angel as Michael, (Dan. xii. 1;) there is frequent mention of the devil; and there are numerous affirmations that both bad and good angels are employed in important transactions on the earth. Who can prove that such spirits never meet, never come in conflict, never en-counter each other in executing their purposes? Good men meet bad men, and why is it any more absurd to sup-pose that good angels may encounter bad ones? It should be remembered, further, that there is no need of sup-posing that the subject of the dispute was about burying the body of Moses; or that Michael sought to bury it, and the devil endeavoured to prevent it— the one in order that it might not be worshipped by the Israelites, and the other that it might be. This indeed became incorporated into the tradition in the apocryphal books which were afterwards written; but Jude says not one word of this, and is in no way responsible for it. All that he says is, that there was a contention or dispute (διακρινόμενος διελέγετο) respecting *his body*. But when it was, or what was the occasion, or how it was conducted, he does *not* state, and we have no right to ascribe to him sentiments which he has not expressed. If ever such a con-troversy of any kind existed respecting that body, it is all that Jude affirms, and is all for which he should be held responsible. The sum of the matter, then, it seems to me is, that Jude has, as Paul did on another occasion, adopted a tradition which was prevalent in his time; that there is nothing necessarily absurd or impossible in the fact affirmed by the tradition, and that no one can possibly demonstrate that it is not true.

10 But these speak evil of those things which they know not: but what they know naturally, as brute beasts, in those things they corrupt themselves.

11 Woe unto them! for they have

¶ *The archangel.* The word *archangel* occurs only in one other place in the Scriptures. See Notes, 1 Thess. iv. 16. It means *ruling* or *chief* angel—the chief among the hosts of heaven. It is nowhere else applied to Michael, though his name is several times mentioned, Dan. x. 13, 21; xii. 1; Rev. xii. 7. ¶ *When contending.* This word (διακρινόμενος) refers here to a contention or strife with words—*a disputation.* Nothing farther is necessarily implied, for it is so used in this sense in the New Testament, Acts xi. 2, 12, (*Greek.*) ¶ *He disputed.* διελέγετο. *This* word also would denote merely a controversy or contention of words, Mark ix. 34; Acts xvii. 2, 17; xviii. 4, 19; xxiv. 12. ¶ *About the body of Moses.* The nature of this controversy is wholly unknown, and conjecture is useless. It is *not* said, however, that there was a strife which should get the body, or a contention about burying it, or any physical contention about it whatever. That there *may* have been, no one indeed can disprove; but all that the apostle says would be met by a supposition that there was *any* debate of any kind respecting that body, in which Michael, though provoked by the opposition of the worst being in the universe, still restrained himself from any outbreaking of passion, and used only the language of mild but firm rebuke. ¶ *Durst not.* οὐκ ἐτόλμησε—' Did not dare.' It is not said that he did not dare to do it because he feared Satan; but all that the word implies is met by supposing that he did not dare to do it because he feared the Lord, or because in any circumstances it would be wrong. ¶ *A railing accusation.* The Greek word is *blasphemy.* The meaning is, he did not indulge in the language of mere reproach : and it is implied here that such language would be wrong anywhere. If it would be right to bring a railing accusation against any one, it would be against the devil. ¶ *But said, The Lord rebuke thee.* The word here used (ἐπιτιμάω) means, properly, to put honour upon; and then to adjudge or confirm. Then it came to be used in the sense of commanding or *restraining*—as, e. g., the winds and waves, Matt. viii. 26; Mark iv. 39. Then it is used in the sense of *admonishing strongly ;* of enjoining upon one, *with the idea of censure,* Matt. xviii. 18; Mark i. 25; Luke iv. 35, 41. This is the idea here —the expression of a wish that *the Lord* would take the matter of the dispute to himself, and that he would properly restrain and control Satan, with the implied idea that his conduct was wrong. The *language* is the same as that recorded in Zech. iii. 2, as used by 'the angel' respecting Satan. But, as before observed, there is no reason to suppose that the apostle referred to that. The fact, however, that the angel is said to have used the language on that occasion may be allowed to give confirmation to what is said here, since it shows that it is the language which angelic beings naturally employ.

10. *But these speak evil of those things which they know not.* These false and corrupt teachers employ reproachful language of those things which lie wholly beyond the reach of their vision. Notes, 2 Pet. ii. 12. ¶ *But what they know naturally.* As mere men ; as animals; that is, in things pertaining to their physical nature, or in which they are on a level with the brute creation. The reference is to the natural instincts, the impulses of appetite, and passion, and sensual pleasure. The idea of the apostle seems to be, that their knowledge was confined to those things. They did not rise above them to the intelligent contemplation of those higher things, against which they used only the language of reproach. There are multitudes of such men in the world. Towards high and holy objects they use only the language of reproach. They do not understand them, but they can rail at them. Their knowledge is confined to the subjects of sensual indulgence, and all their intelligence in that respect is employed only to corrupt and destroy themselves. ¶ *As*

gone in the way of Cain, ^a and ran greedily after the error of Balaam ^b for reward, and perished in the gainsaying of Core. ^c

12 These are spots ^d in your feasts of charity, when they feast with you,

a Ge.4.5.   *b* Nu.22.7,21.   *c* Nu.16.1,&c.

feeding *themselves without fear: clouds *f* they are without water, carried *g* about of winds; trees whose fruit *h* withereth, without fruit, twice dead, *i* plucked *j* up by the roots;

d 2 Pe.2.13.   *e* Phi.3.19.   *f* Pr.25.14.   *g* Ep.4.14.
h Jn.15.4-6.   *i* He.6.4-6.   *j* Mat.15.13.

---

brute beasts. Animals without intelligence. Notes, 2 Pet. ii. 12. ¶ *In those things they corrupt themselves.* They live only for sensual indulgence, and sink deeper and deeper in sensual gratifications.
11. *Woe unto them!* See Matt. xi. 21. ¶ *For they have gone in the way of Cain.* Gen. iv. 5–12. That is, they have evinced disobedience and rebellion as he did ; they have shown that they are proud, corrupt, and wicked. The apostle does not specify the points in which they had imitated the example of Cain, but it was probably in such things as these—pride, haughtiness, the hatred of religion, restlessness under the restraints of virtue, envy that others were more favoured, and a spirit of hatred of the brethren (comp. 1 John iii. 15) which would lead to murder. ¶ *And ran greedily after the error of Balaam for reward.* The word rendered *ran greedily*—ἐξεχύθησαν, from ἐκχέω—means to pour out ; and then, when spoken of persons, that they are *poured out*, or that they *rush tumultuously* on an object, that is, that they give themselves up to anything. The idea here is, that all restraint was relaxed, and that they rushed on tumultuously to any course of life that promised gain. See Notes, 2 Pet. ii. 15. ¶ *And perished.* They perish, or they will perish. The result is so certain, that the apostle speaks of it as if it were already done. The thought seems to have lain in his mind in this manner : he thinks of them as having the same character as Korah, and then at once thinks of them as destroyed in the same manner, or as if it were already done. They are *identified* with him in their character and doom. The word rendered *perish* (ἀπόλλυμι) is often used to denote future punishment, Matt. x. 28, 39 ; xviii. 14 ; Mark i. 24 ; Luke xiii. 3, 5 ; John iii. 15, 16 · x. 28 ; 2 Thess.

ii. 10 ; 2 Pet. iii. 9. ¶ *In the gainsaying of Core.* Of Korah, Numb. xvi. 1 –30. The word *gainsaying* here means properly contradiction, or speaking against ; then controversy, question, strife ; then contumely, reproach, or rebellion. The idea here seems to be, that they were guilty of insubordination ; of possessing a restless and dissatisfied spirit ; of a desire to rule, &c.
12. *These are spots.* See Notes, 2 Pet. ii. 13. The word used by Peter, however, is not exactly the same as that used here. Peter uses the word σπῖλοι — *spiloi* ; Jude, σπιλάδες — *spilades*. The word used by Jude means, properly, *a rock* by or in the sea ; a cliff, &c. It may either be a rock *by* the sea, against which vessels may be wrecked, or a hidden rock *in* the sea, on which they may be stranded at an unexpected moment. See Hesychius and Pollux, as quoted by Wetstein, *in loc.* The idea here seems to be, not that they were *spots* and *blemishes* in their sacred feasts, but that they were like hidden rocks to the mariner. As those rocks were the cause of shipwreck, so these false teachers caused others to make shipwreck of their faith. They were as dangerous in the church as hidden rocks are in the ocean. ¶ *In your feasts of charity.* Your feasts of love. The reference is probably to the Lord's Supper, called a feast or festival of love, because (1,) it revealed the love of Christ to the world ; (2,) because it was the means of strengthening the mutual love of the disciples : a festival which love originated, and where love reigned. It has been supposed by many, that the reference here is to festivals which were subsequently called *Agapæ*, and which are now known as *love-feasts*—meaning a festival immediately *preceding* the celebration of the Lord's Supper. But there are strong objections to the supposition that there is reference here to such a

festival. (1.) There is no evidence, unless it be found in this passage, that such celebrations had the sanction of the apostles. They are nowhere else mentioned in the New Testament, or alluded to, unless it is in 1 Cor. xi. 17–34, an instance which is mentioned only to reprove it, and to show that such appendages to the Lord's Supper were wholly unauthorized by the original institution, and were liable to gross abuse. (2.) The supposition that they existed, and that they are referred to here, is not necessary in order to a proper explanation of this passage. All that it fairly means will be met by the supposition that the reference is to the Lord's Supper. *That* was in every sense a festival of love or charity. The words will appropriately apply to that, and there is no necessity of supposing anything else in order to meet their full signification. (3.) There can be no doubt that such a custom early existed in the Christian church, and extensively prevailed; but it can readily be accounted for without supposing that it had the sanction of the apostles, or that it existed in their time. (*a*) Festivals prevailed among the Jews, and it would not be unnatural to introduce them into the Christian church. (*b*) The custom prevailed among the heathen of having a 'feast upon a sacrifice,' or in connection with a sacrifice; and as the Lord's Supper commemorated the great sacrifice for sin, it was not unnatural, in imitation of the heathen, to append a feast or festival to that ordinance, either before or after its celebration. (*c*) This very passage in Jude, with perhaps some others in the New Testament, (comp. 1 Cor. xi. 25; Acts ii. 46; vi. 2,) might be so construed as to seem to lend countenance to the custom. For these reasons it seems clear to me that the passage before us does not refer to *love-feasts*; and, therefore, that they are not authorized in the New Testament. See, however, Coleman's Antiquities of the Christian church, chap. xvi., § 13. ¶ *When they feast with you.* Showing that they were professors of religion. Notes on 2 Pet. ii. 13. ¶ *Feeding themselves without fear.* That is, without any proper reverence or respect for the ordinance; attending on the Lord's Supper as if it

were an ordinary feast, and making it an occasion of riot and gluttony. See 1 Cor. xi. 20–22. ¶ *Clouds* they are, &c. Notes, 2 Pet. ii. 17. Comp. Eph. iv. 14. ¶ *Trees whose fruit withereth.* The idea here is substantially the same as that expressed by Peter, when he says that they were 'wells without water;' and by him and Jude, when they say that they are like clouds driven about by the winds, that shed down no refreshing rain upon the earth. Such wells and clouds only disappoint expectations. So a tree that should promise fruit, but whose fruit should always wither, would be useless. The word rendered *withereth* ($\phi\theta\iota\nu o\pi\omega\rho\iota\nu\grave{\alpha}$) occurs nowhere else in the New Testament. It means, properly, *autumnal;* and the expression here denotes *trees of autumn*, that is, trees stripped of leaves and verdure; trees on which there is no fruit. —*Robinson's Lex.* The sense, in the use of this word, therefore, is not exactly that which is expressed in our translation, that the fruit has *withered*, but rather that they are like the trees of autumn, which are stripped and bare So the Vulgate, *arbores autumnales.* The idea of their being without fruit is expressed in the next word. The *image* which seems to have been before the mind of Jude in this expression, is that of the naked trees of autumn as contrasted with the bloom of spring and the dense foliage of summer. ¶ *Without fruit.* That is, they produce no fruit. Either they are wholly barren, like the barren fig-tree, or the fruit which was set never ripens, but falls off. They are, therefore, useless as religious instructors—as much so as a tree is which produces no fruit. ¶ *Twice dead.* That is, either meaning that they are seen to be dead in two successive seasons, showing that there is no hope that they will revive and be valuable; or, using the word *twice* to denote emphasis, meaning that they are absolutely or altogether dead. Perhaps the idea is, that successive summers and winters have passed over them, and that no signs of life appear. ¶ *Plucked up by the roots.* The wind blows them down, or they are removed by the husbandman as only cumbering the ground. They are not cut down—leaving a

13 Raging waves *a* of the sea, foaming out their own shame; wandering *b* stars, to whom is reserved the blackness of darkness for ever.

a Is.57.20.   *b* Re.8.10,11.

14 And Enoch also, the seventh from Adam, prophesied of these, saying, Behold, the Lord *c* cometh with ten thousand of his saints,

c Ze.14.5.

stump that might sprout again —but they are extirpated root and branch; that is, they are wholly worthless. There is a regular ascent in this climax. First, the apostle sees a tree apparently of autumn, stripped and leafless; then he sees it to be a tree that bears no fruit; then he sees it to be a tree over which successive winters and summers pass and no signs of life appear; then as wholly extirpated. So he says it is with these men. They produce no fruits of holiness; months and years show that there is no vitality in them; they are fit only to be extirpated and cast away. Alas! how many professors of religion are there, and how many religious teachers, who answer to this description!

13. *Raging waves of the sea.* Comp. 2 Pet. ii. 18. They are like the wild and restless waves of the ocean. The image here seems to be, that they were noisy and bold in their professions, and were as wild and ungovernable in their passions as the billows of the sea. ¶ *Foaming out their own shame.* The waves are lashed into foam, and break and dash on the shore. They seem to produce nothing *but* foam, and to proclaim their own shame, that after all their wild roaring and agitation they should effect no more. So with these noisy and vaunting teachers. What they impart is as unsubstantial and valueless as the foam of the ocean waves, and the result is in fact a proclamation of their own shame. Men with so loud professions *should* produce much more. ¶ *Wandering stars.* The word rendered *wandering* (πλανῆται) is that from which we have derived the word *planet.* It properly means one who wanders about; a wanderer; and was given by the ancients to planets because they seemed to wander about the heavens, now forward and now backward among the other stars, without any fixed law. —Pliny, Nat. Hist. ii. 6. Cicero, however, who saw that they were governed by certain established laws, says that the

name seemed to be given to them without reason.—De Nat. Deo. ii. 20. So far as the *words* used are concerned, the reference may be either to the planets, properly so called, or to comets, or to *ignes fatui*, or meteors. The proper idea is that of stars that have no regular motions, or that do not move in fixed and regular orbits. The laws of the planetary motions were not then understood, and their movements seemed to be irregular and capricious; and hence, if the reference is to them, they might be regarded as not an unapt illustration of these teachers. The sense seems to be, that the aid which we derive from the stars, as in navigation, is in the fact that they are regular in their places and movements, and thus the mariner can determine his position. If they had no regular places and movements, they would be useless to the seaman. So with false religious teachers. No dependence can be placed on them. It is not uncommon to compare a religious teacher to a star, Rev. i. 16; ii. 1. Comp. Rev. xxii. 16. ¶ *To whom is reserved the blackness of darkness for ever.* Not to the stars, but to the teachers. The language here is the same as in 2 Pet. ii. 17. See Notes on that verse.

14. *And Enoch also, the seventh from Adam.* The seventh in the direct line of descent from Adam. The line of descent is Adam, Seth, Enos, Cainan, Mahaleel, Jared, Enoch; see Gen. v. 3, seq. On the character of Enoch, see Notes on Heb. xi. 5. ¶ *Prophesied of these.* Uttered prophecies applicable to these men, or respecting just such men as these. It is not necessarily meant that he had these men specifically in his eye; but all that is fairly implied is, that his predictions were descriptive of them. There is no mention made in the writings of Moses of the fact that Enoch was a prophet; but nothing is more probable in itself, and there is no absurdity in supposing that a true prophecy, though unrecord-

15 To execute judgment upon all; *a* and to convince all that are ungodly among them of all their ungodly deeds which they have un-

godly committed, and of all their hard *speeches* *b* which ungodly sinners have spoken against him.

a Re.20.13.   *b* Ps.73.9.

ed, might be handed down by tradition. See Notes, 2 Tim. iii. 8 ; Jude 9. The source from which Jude derived this passage respecting the prophecy of Enoch is unknown. Amidst the multitude of traditions, however, handed down by the Jews from a remote antiquity, though many of them were false, and many of a trifling character, it is reasonable to presume that some of them were true and were of importance. No man can *prove* that the one before us is not of that character ; no one can show that an inspired writer might not be led to make the selection of a true prophecy from a mass of traditions ; and as the prophecy before us is one that would be every way worthy of a prophet, and worthy to be preserved, its quotation furnishes no argument against the inspiration of Jude. There is no clear evidence that he quoted it from any *book* extant in his time. There is, indeed, now an apocryphal writing called 'the Book of Enoch,' containing a prediction strongly resembling this, but there is no certain proof that it existed so early as the time of Jude, nor, if it did, is it absolutely certain that he quoted from it. Both Jude and the author of that book may have quoted a common tradition of their time, for there can be no doubt that the passage referred to was handed down by tradition. The passage as found in 'the Book of Enoch' is in these words : ' Behold he comes with ten thousand of his saints, to execute judgment upon them, and destroy the wicked, and reprove all the carnal, for everything which the sinful and ungodly have done and committed against him,' chap. ii. Bib. Repository, vol. xv. p. 86. If the Book of Enoch was written after the time of Jude, it is natural to suppose that the prophecy referred to by him, and handed down by tradition, would be inserted in it. This book was discovered in an Æthiopic version, and was published with a translation by Dr. Laurence of Oxford, in 1821, and republished in 1832. A full account of it

and its contents may be seen in an article by Prof. Stuart in the Bib. Repository for January 1840, pp. 86–137. ¶ *The Lord cometh.* That is, the Lord will come. See Notes, 1 Cor. xvi. 22. It would seem from this to have been an early doctrine that the Lord would *descend* to the earth for judgment. ¶ *With ten thousand of his saints.* Or, *of his holy ones.* The word *saints* we now apply commonly to *redeemed* saints, or to Christians. The original word is, however, applicable to all who are *holy*, angels as well as men. The common representation in the Scriptures is, that he would come attended by the angels. (Matt. xxv. 31,) and there is doubtless allusion here to such beings. It is a common representation in the Old Testament also that God, when he manifests himself, is accompanied by great numbers of heavenly beings. See Psa. lxviii. 17 ; Deut. xxxiii. 2.

15. *To execute judgment upon all.* That is, he shall come to judge all the dwellers upon the earth, good and bad. ¶ *And to convince all.* The word *convince* we now use commonly in a somewhat limited sense, as meaning *to satisfy* a man's own mind either of the truth of some proposition, or of the fact that he has done wrong, as being in this latter sense synonymous with the word *convict.* This *conviction* is commonly produced by argument or truth, and is not necessarily followed by any sentence of disapprobation, or by any judicial condemnation. But this is clearly not the sense in which the word is used here. The purpose of the coming of the Lord will not be to *convince* men in that sense, though it is undoubtedly true that the wicked will see that their lives have been wrong ; but it will be to pronounce a sentence on them as the result of the evidence of their guilt. The Greek word which is here used occurs nowhere else in the New Testament. ¶ *All that are ungodly among them.* All that are not pious ; all that have no religion. ¶ *Of all their ungodly deeds, &c.* Of their

16 These are murmurers, complainers, walking after their own lusts; and their mouth speaketh great swelling *words*, having men's persons in admiration because of advantage.

17 But, beloved, remember ye the words which were spoken before of the apostles of our Lord Jesus Christ;

18 How that they told you *ª* there

a 1 Ti.4.1.

---

wicked actions and words. This is the common doctrine of the Bible, that all the wicked actions and words of men will be called into judgment. In regard to this passage, thus quoted from an ancient prophecy, we may remark, (1.) that the *style* bears the marks of its being a quotation, or of its being preserved by Jude in the language in which it had been handed down by tradition. It is not the style of Jude. It is not so terse, pointed, energetic. (2.) It has every probable mark of its having been actually delivered by Enoch. The age in which he lived was corrupt. The world was ripening for the deluge. He was himself a good man, and, as would seem perhaps, almost the only good man of his generation. Nothing would be more natural than that he should be reproached by hard words and speeches, and nothing more natural than that he should have pointed the men of his own age to the future judgment. (3.) The doctrine of the final judgment, if this was uttered by Enoch, was an early doctrine in the world. It was held even in the first generations of the race. It was one of those great truths early communicated to man to restrain him from sin, and to lead him to prepare for the great events which are to occur on the earth. The same doctrine has been transmitted from age to age, and is now one of the most important and the most affecting that refers to the final destiny of men.

16. *These are murmurers.* The word here used does not elsewhere occur, though the word *murmur* is frequent, Matt. xx. 11; Luke v. 30; John vi. 41, 43, 61; vii. 32; 1 Cor. x. 10. Comp. John vii. 12; Acts vi. 1; Phil. ii. 14; 1 Pet. iv. 9. The sense is that of repining or complaining under the allotments of Providence, or finding fault with God's plans, and purposes, and doings. ¶ *Complainers.* Literally, finding fault with one's own lot (*μεμψίμοιροι.*) The *word*

does not elsewhere occur in the New Testament; the *thing* often occurs in this world. Nothing is more common than for men to complain of their lot : to think that it is hard; to compare theirs with that of others, and to blame God for not having made their circumstances different. The poor complain that they are not rich like others ; the sick that they are not well; the enslaved that they are not free; the bereaved that they are deprived of friends; the ugly that they are not beautiful ; those in humble life that their lot was not cast among the great and the gay. The virtue that is opposed to this is *contentment*—a virtue of inestimable value. See Notes, Phil. iv. 11. ¶ *Walking after their own lusts.* Giving unlimited indulgence to their appetites and passions. See Notes, 2 Pet. iii. 3. ¶ *And their mouth speaketh great swelling* words. Notes on 2 Pet. ii. 18. ¶ *Having men's persons in admiration.* Showing great respect to certain persons, particularly the rich and the great. The idea is, that they were not *just* in the esteem which they had for others, oɪ that they did not appreciate them according to their real worth, but paid special attention to one class in order to promote their selfish ends. ¶ *Because of advantage.* Because they hoped to derive some benefit to themselves.

17, 18. *But, beloved, remember ye,* &c. There is a striking similarity between these two verses and 2 Pet. iii. 1–3. It occurs in the same connection, following the description of the false and dangerous teachers against whom the apostle would guard them, and couched almost in the same words. See it explained in Notes on the similar passage in Peter. When Jude (ver. 17) entreats them to remember the words which were spoken by *the apostles*, it is not necessarily to be inferred that he was not himself an apostle, for he is speaking of what was past, and there might

should be mockers in the last time, who should walk after their own ungodly lusts.

19 These be they who separate *a* themselves, sensual, having not the Spirit.

20 But ye, beloved, building *b* up

a He.10.25.   b Col.2.7.   c Ep.6.18.
d Jn.15.2,10.   e Tit.2.13.

have been a special reason why he should refer to something that they would distinctly remember which had been spoken by the *other* apostles on this point. Or it might be that he meant also to include himself among them, and to speak of the apostles collectively, without particularly specifying himself. ¶ *Mockers.* The word rendered *mockers* here is the same which in the parallel place in 2 Pet. iii. 3 is rendered *scoffers.* Peter has stated more fully what was the particular subject on which they scoffed, and has shown that there was no occasion for it, 2 Pet. iii. 4, seq.

19. *These be they who separate themselves.* That is, from their brethren, and from the work of benevolence and truth. Comp. Rom. xvi. 17; Judg. v. 16, 23. ¶ *Sensual.* Under the influence of gross passions and appetites. ¶ *Having not the spirit.* The Holy Spirit, or the spirit of true religion.

20. *But ye, beloved, building up yourselves on your most holy faith.* Comp. Notes on ver. 3. On the word *building,* see Notes on 1 Cor. iii. 9, 10; Eph. ii. 20. It is said here that they were to 'build up *themselves;*' that is, they were to act as moral and responsible agents in this, or were to put forth their own proper exertions to do it. Dependent, as we are, and as all persons with correct views will feel themselves to be, yet it is proper to endeavour to do the work of religion as if we had ample power of ourselves. See Notes, Phil. ii. 12. The phrase 'most holy faith' here refers to the system of religion which was founded on faith; and the meaning is, that they should seek to establish themselves most firmly in the belief of the doctrines, and in the practice of the duties of that system of religion. ¶ *Praying in the Holy Ghost.* See Notes. Eph. vi. 18.

yourselves on your most holy faith, praying *c* in the Holy Ghost,

21 Keep yourselves *d* in the love of God, looking *e* for the mercy of our Lord Jesus Christ unto eternal life.

22 And of some have compassion, making a difference :

21. *Keep yourselves in the love of God.* Still adverting to their own agency. On the duty here enjoined, see Notes on John xv. 9. The phrase 'the love of God' *may* mean either God's love to us, or our love to him. The latter appears, however, to be the sense here, because it is not a subject which could be enjoined, that we should keep up *God's love to us.* That is a point over which we can have no control, except so far as it may be the result of our obedience ; but we *may* be commanded to love him, and to *keep* ourselves in that love. ¶ *Looking for the mercy of our Lord Jesus Christ.* Particularly when he shall come to receive his people to himself. See Notes, Tit. ii. 13 ; 2 Pet. iii. 12; 2 Tim. iv. 8.

22. *And of some have compassion.* This cannot be intended to teach that they were not to have compassion for all men, or to regard the salvation of all with solicitude, but that they were to have special and peculiar compassion for a certain class of persons, or were to approach them with feelings appropriate to their condition. The idea is, that the peculiar feeling to be manifest towards a certain class of persons in seeking their salvation was tender affection and kindness. They were to approach them in the gentlest manner, appealing to them by such words as *love* would prompt. Others were to be approached in a different manner, indicated by the phrase, 'save with fear.' The class here referred to, to whom *pity* (ἐλεεῖτε) was to be shown, and in whose conversion and salvation tender compassion was to be employed, appear to have been the timid, the gentle, the unwary; those who had not yet fallen into dangerous errors, but who might be exposed to them ; those, for there are such, who would be more likely to be influenced by kind words and a gentle manner

23 And others save with fear, pulling *a them* out of the fire; hating even the garment *b* spotted by the flesh.

24 Now unto him *c* that is able

to keep *d* you from falling, and to present *e* you faultless before the presence of his glory with exceeding joy,

a Ze.3.2-5.　　*b* Re.3,4,18.　　*c* Ro.16.25-27.
d 2 Ti.4.18.　　　　　　　*e* Col.1.22.

than by denunciation. The direction then amounts to this, that while we are to seek to save all, we are to adapt ourselves wisely to the character and circumstances of those whom we seek to save. See Notes, 1 Cor. ix. 19–22. ¶ *Making a difference.* Making a distinction between them, not in regard to your *desires* for their salvation, or your *efforts* to save them, but to the *manner* in which it is done. To be able to do this is one of the highest qualifications to be sought by one who endeavours to save souls, and is indispensable for a good minister of the gospel. The young, the tender, the delicate, the refined, need a different kind of treatment from the rough, the uncultivated, the hardened. This wisdom was shown by the Saviour in all his preaching; it was eminent in the preaching of Paul. 23. *And others.* Another class; those who were of such a character, or in such circumstances, that a more bold, earnest, and determined manner would be better adapted to them. ¶ *Save with fear.* That is, by appeals adapted to produce fear. The idea seems to be that the arguments on which they relied were to be drawn from the dangers of the persons referred to, or from the dread of future wrath. It is undoubtedly true, that while there is a class of persons who can be won to embrace religion by mild and gentle persuasion, there is another class who can be aroused only by the terrors of the law. Every method is to be employed, in its proper place, that we ' by all means may save some.' ¶ *Pulling* them *out of the fire.* As you would snatch persons out of the fire; or as you would seize on a person that was walking into a volcano. Then, a man would not use the mild and gentle language of persuasion, but by word and gesture show that he was deeply in earnest. ¶ *Hating even the garment spotted by the flesh.* The allusion here is not quite certain, though the idea

which the apostle meant to convey is not difficult to be understood. By ' tho garment spotted by the flesh ' there *may be* an allusion to a garment worn by one who had had the plague, or some offensive disease which might be communicated to others by touching even the clothing which they had worn. Or there may be an allusion to the ceremonial law of Moses, by which all those who came in contact with dead bodies were regarded as unclean, Lev. xxi. 11, Numb. vi. 6; ix. 6; xix. 11. Or there may be an allusion to the case mentioned in Lev. xv. 4, 10, 17; or perhaps to a case of leprosy. In all such instances, there would be the idea that the thing referred to by which the garment had been spotted was polluting, contagious, or loathsome, and that it was proper not even to touch such a garment, or to come in contact with it in any way. To something of this kind the apostle compares the sins of the persons here referred to. While the utmost effort was to be made to save them, they were in no way to partake of their sins; their conduct was to be regarded as loathsome and contagious; and those who attempted to save them were to take every precaution to preserve their own purity. There is much wisdom in this counsel. While we endeavour to save the *sinner,* we cannot too deeply loathe his *sins;* and in approaching some classes of sinners there is need of as much care to avoid being defiled by them, as there would be to escape the plague if we had any transaction with one who had it. Not a few have been deeply corrupted in their attempts to reform the polluted. There never could be, for example, too much circumspection and prayer for personal safety from pollution, in attempting to reform licentious and abandoned females.

24. *Now unto him that is able to keep you from falling.* This ascription to one who was able to keep them from falling is made in view of the facts ad-

25 To ^a the only wise God our | dominion and power, both now and
Saviour, *be* glory and majesty, | ever. Amen.

a 1 Tim.1.17.

---

verted to in the epistle—the dangers of
being led away by the arts and the example of these teachers of error. Comp.
ver. 3. On the ascription itself, comp.
Notes on Rom. xvi. 25–27. The phrase
'to keep from falling' means here to preserve from falling into sin, from yielding
to temptation, and dishonouring their
religion. The word used (ἀπταιστους)
occurs nowhere else in the New Testament. It means properly, *not stumbling*
as of a horse; then *without falling
into sin, blameless*. It is God only who,
amidst the temptations of the world, can
keep us from falling ; but, blessed be his
name, he can do it, and if we trust in
him he will. ¶ *And to present* you
faultless. The word here rendered *faultless* is the same which is rendered *un-
blamable* in Col. i. 22. See the sentiment here expressed explained in the
Notes on that passage. ¶ *Before the
presence of his glory*. In his own glorious presence ; before himself encompassed with glory in heaven. The saints
are to be presented there as redeemed
and sanctified, and as made worthy by
grace to dwell there for ever. ¶ *With
exceeding joy*. With the abounding joy
that they are redeemed ; that they are
rescued from sorrow, sin, and death, and
that heaven is to be their eternal home.
Who now can form an adequate idea of
the happiness of that hour ?
25. *To the only wise God*. See Notes,
Rom. xvi. 27; 1 Tim. i. 17. ¶ *Our
Saviour*. The word *Saviour* may be
appropriately applied to God as such,
because he is the great Author of salvation, though it is commonly applied to

the Lord Jesus Christ. That it *may*
have been designed that it should be
applied here to the Lord Jesus no one
can certainly deny, nor can it be demonstrated that it was; and in these
circumstances, as all that is fairly implied in the language may be applied to
God as such, it is most natural to give
the phrase that interpretation. ¶ Be
glory and majesty. Notes, 1 Tim. i. 17;
Rom. xvi. 17. ¶ *Dominion and power*,
&c. See Matt. vi. 13. It is common in
the Scriptures to ascribe power, dominion, and glory to God, expressing the
feeling that all that is great and good
belongs to him, and the desire of the
heart that he may reign in heaven and
on earth. Comp. Rev. iv. 11; xix. 1.
With the expression of such a desire it
was not inappropriate that this epistle
should be closed—and it is not inappropriate that this volume should be closed
with the utterance of the same wish.
In all our affections and aspirations,
may God be supreme ; in all the sin and
woe which prevail here below, may we
look forward with strong desire to the
time when his dominion shall be set up
over all the earth ; in all our own sins
and sorrows, be it ours to look onward
to the time when in a purer and happier
world his reign may be set up over our
own souls, and when we may cast every
crown at his feet and say, ' Thou art
worthy, O Lord, to receive glory, and
honour, and power : for thou hast created
all things, and for thy pleasure they are
and were created.—Alleluia; Salvation,
and glory, and honour, and power, unto
the Lord our God,' Rev. iv. 11 : xix. 1.